# Solved Programming In

## FOR

***(All Indian Universities, Engineering and Technical Colleges and Institutions, IIT's And IT Organizations)***

**Rachhpal Singh**
Head,
PG Deptt of Computer Sc. & Applications,
Khalsa College,
Amritsar.

**Ikvinderpal Singh**
Lecturer,
PG Deptt of Computer Sc. & Applicatio
Khalsa. College,
Amritsar.

# SOLVED PROGRAMMING IN C++

RACHHPAL SINGH AND IKVINDERPAL SINGH

*Published by* ***KHANNA BOOK PUBLISHING CO. (P) LTD.***
*Regd. Office : 1694-95 Nai Sarak, Delhi - 110 006*
*Ph : 011-23256658, 23283211, Fax : 011-23256658*
*Email contact@khannaedu.com*
*Website : www.khannaedu.com*



ISBN : 978-93-80016-18-4



*Laser Typesetted by :*
**Stride Computers (Delhi)**

*Printed in India*
**M.K. Press**

# Preface

This book is intended for beginners, intermediate level, and all those who want to learn or expand their knowledge in C++ programming. A systematic approach has been followed from the beginning of this book to the end.

About 2200 solved programs have been provided in this book to help students master the programming language. Few day–to-day problems have also been solved. This book teaches you not only developing application programs but also familiarizes with system-level programming.

Each and every program given in the book is perfectly working. We expect that the learners should try their level best to learn the programs by executing them. We also believe that expertise in programming is achieved by practice and experience. Hence, by writing more and more programs and a thorough study of programming concepts will enable the learner to become an expert.

If you study in a right spirit you will become an expert in C++ programming.

**Best of luck!**

**RACHHPAL SINGH**
**rachhpal_kca@yahoo.co.in**

**IKVINDERPAL SINGH**
**ips_sikand@yahoo.com**

# DEDICATION

No project could ever get in progress much less accomplished, without help from a lot of fantastic people. We would like to express gratitude to our reverential parents. We are grateful to Almighty God who has given us strength to take and complete this project.

*To my mother Smt. Surinder Kaur and father S. Diwan Singh, biggest embrace and warm thanks to my wife Dr. Satwinderjeet Kaur, Reader, Deptt. of Botanical & Environmental Sciences, GNDU, Amritsar and to my buddies.*

***RACHHPAL SINGH***

To my mother Smt. Sharanjeet Kaur and father S. Jasjit Singh, biggest embrace and warm thanks to my grandmother Narinderjeet Kaur, to my sisters and to my dear students who have encorged me to complete this project.

***IKVINDERPAL SINGH***

// Acknowledgements

We express our deep gratitude to Dr. Karanjit Singh Kahlon, Professor and Head, Department of Computer Science & Engineering, G.N.D.U., Dr. Hardeep Singh, Professor, Department of Computer Science & Engineering, G.N.D.U., Dr. Gurvinder Singh, Reader, DCSE, GNDU, Amritsar, Prof. Amardeep Gupta, Head, Computer Sc, DAV College, Amritsar, Prof. Nishey Behal, Head, DAV College for Boys, Jalandhar city , Mr. Inderpal Singh, Mr. Baljinder Singh, Mr. Avtar Singh Riar, Mr. Lovedeep Singh, Mr. Sukhwant Singh and our colleagues for their valuable co-operation and guidance. We are grateful to the entire team of *Khanna Book Publishing Co. (P) Ltd.* for their encouragement and motivation during this project.

**RACHHPAL SINGH** **IKVINDERPAL SINGH**

# *Special Thanks*

Our special thanks go to Dr. Daljit Singh, Principal, Khalsa College, Amritsar for their valuable guidance and timely support during the compilation of this book.

**RACHHPAL SINGH** **IKVINDERPAL SINGH**

# SOLVED PROGRAMMING IN C++

## CONTENTS

# CHAPTER 1

# INTRODUCTION TO C++

## SIMPLE C++ PROGRAMS:

**Problem 1. Write a simple C++ program.**

***Program:***

```
#include<iostream.h>
#include<conio.h>
void main()
{
cout << "I like programming";
getch();
}
```

**OUTPUT:**

I like programming

**Problem 2.Write a C++ program to display Hello: output String.**

***Program:***

```
#include <iostream.h>
#include<conio.h>
void main()
{
cout<<"Hello";
getch();
}
```

**OUTPUT:**

Hello

**Problem 3. Write a C++ program to display Hello and your name.**

***Program:***

```
#include <iostream.h>
#include<conio.h>
void main()
{
cout<<"HELLO, RACHHPAL AND IKVINDER!";
getch();
}
```

**OUTPUT:**

HELLO, RACHHPAL AND IKVINDER!

**Problem 4. Write a C++ program to calculating with integer constants.**

***Program:***

```
#include<iostream.h>
#include<conio.h>
void main()
{
cout << 1 + 2     << endl;
cout << 1 - 5     << endl;
cout << 1 - 2     << endl;
cout << 1 * 2     << endl;
cout << 1/3       << endl;
cout << 1  3      << endl;
cout << 1  -3     << endl;
cout << -1  3     << endl;
cout << -1  -3    << endl;
cout << 1 + 2/1 - 5        << endl;
cout << (1 + 2)/(1 - 5)    << endl;
cout << 1 + 2/(1 - 5)      << endl;
cout << (1 + 2)/1 - 5      << endl;
cout << 4*5/3 + 7/3        << endl;
getch();
}
```

**OUTPUT:**

```
3
-4
-1
2
0
1
1
-1
-1
-2
0
1
-2
4
```

**Problem 5. Write a C++ program for working with integer variables.**

***Program:***

```
#include<iostream.h>
#include<conio.h>
void main()
{
int a = 10;
```

```
int b = 3;
cout << a/b;
cout << a % b;
getch();
}
```

**OUTPUT:**

31

**Problem 6. Write a C++ program using the assignment operator.**

***Program :***

```
#include<iostream.h>
#include<conio.h>
void main()
{
int a = 10;
int b = 6;
int c = 3;
int d = 4;
int f = (a + b)/(c + d);
cout << f ;
getch();
}
```

**OUTPUT:**

2

## MAIN() FUNCTION:

**Problem 7. Write a C++ program main function.**

***Program:***

```
#include <iostream.h>
#include<conio.h>
void main()
{
cout<<"This is a short C++ program.";
getch();
}
```

**OUTPUT:**

This is a short C++ program.

**Problem 8. Write a C++ program to call a function in main.**

***Program:***

```
#include<iostream.h>
#include<conio.h>
void DemonstrationFunction()
{
cout << "In Demonstration Function\n";
}
void main()
{
cout << "In main\n" ;
DemonstrationFunction();
cout << "Back in main\n";
getch();
}
```

**OUTPUT:**

In main
In Demonstration Function
Back in main

## CONST:

**Problem 9. Write a C++ program to find the area and circumference of the circle.**

***Program:***

```
#include <iostream.h>
#include<conio.h>
void main()
{
int r;
float cir, area;
const int PI=3.1427;
cout<<ENTER THE RADIUS OF THE CIRCLE:
";
cin>>r;
cir = 2*PI*r;
area=PI*r*r;
cout<<"\n THE CIRCUMFERENCE OF CIRCLE
IS= "<< cir;
cout<<"\n THE AREA OF CIRCLE IS="<< area;
getche();
}
```

**OUTPUT:**

ENTER THE RADIUS OF THE CIRCLE: 5
THE CIRCUMFERENCE OF CIRCLE IS=
31.427
THE AREA OF CIRCLE IS= 78.5675

**Problem 10. Write a C++ program to compute the circumference and volume of a sphere.**

***Program:***

```
#include <iostream.h>
#include<conio.h>
void main()
{
int r;
float cir, vol;
const int PI=3.1427;
```

```
cout<<"\n ENTER THE RADIUS OF THE
SPHERE:;
cin>>r;
cir=4*PI*r*r;
vol=4/3*PI*r*r*r;
cout<<"\n CIRCUMFERENCE OF SPHERE
IS="<< cir;
cout<<"\n THE VOLUME OF SPHERE IS="<<
vol;
getche();
}
```

**OUTPUT:**

```
ENTER THE RADIUS OF THE SPHERE: 5
CIRCUMFERENCE OF SPHERE IS=314.27
THE VOLUME OF SPHERE IS= 523.78331
```

**Problem 11. Write a C++ program const function in all c++ programs: main() function**

***Program:***

```
#include <iostream.h>
#include<stdio.h>
#include<conio.h>
void main()
{
puts("program");
getch();
}
```

**OUTPUT:**

```
program
```

## VARIABLES:

**Problem 12. Write a C++ program to assign value to a variable.**

***Program:***

```
#include<iostream.h>
#include<conio.h>
void main()
{
int length; // this declares a variable
length = 7; // this assigns 7 to length
cout << "The length is ";
cout << length; // This displays 7
getch();
}
```

**OUTPUT:**

```
The length is 7
```

**Problem 13. Write a C++ program demonstrate the use of variables.**

***Program:***

```
#include <iostream.h>
#include<conio.h>
void main()
{
int variable;
int variable_2;
int variable_3;
clrscr();
variable = 3 * 5;
variable_2 = 2 * variable;
variable_3 = 3 * variable;
getch();
}
```

**Problem 14. Write a C++ program for For and cin.**

***Program:***

```
#include <iostream.h>
#include<conio.h>
void main()
{
int number = 0;
int count = 5;
long sum = 0L;
float average = 0.0f;
int i = 0;
clrscr();
for(i = 1; i <= count; i ++)
{
cout<<"Enter grade: ";
cin>>number;
sum += number;
}
average = (float)sum/count;
cout<<"Average of the five numbers entered is:
"<< average;
getch();
}
```

**OUTPUT:**

```
Enter grade: 34
Enter grade: 65
Enter grade: 23
Enter grade: 76
Enter grade: 45
Average of the five numbers entered is: 48.599998
```

**Problem 15. Write a C++ program to finding the size of a type.**

*Program:*

```
#include <iostream.h>
#include<conio.h>
void main()
{
cout<<"\n  char occupy"<< sizeof(char)<<"bytes";
cout<<"\n short occupy"<< sizeof(short)<<" bytes";
cout<<"\n int occupy "<< sizeof(int)<<"bytes";
cout<<"\n long occupy "<<sizeof(long) <<"bytes";
cout<<"\n float occupy "<<sizeof(float)<<" bytes";
cout<<"\n double occupy
"<<sizeof(double)<<"bytes";
cout<<"\n long double occupy"<< sizeof(long
double)<<" bytes";
getch();
}
```

**OUTPUT:**

```
char occupy 1 bytes
short occupy 2 bytes
int occupy 2 bytes
long occupy 4 bytes
float occupy 4 bytes
double occupy 8 bytes
long double occupy 10 bytes
```

**Problem 16. Write a C++ program for dynamic initialization.**

*Program:*

```
#include<iostream.h>
#include<conio.h>
void main()
{
double radius = 4.0, height = 5.0;
// dynamically initializ volume
double volume = 3.1416 * radius * radius * height;
cout << "Volume is " << volume;
getch();
}
```

**OUTPUT:**

```
Volume is 251.328
```

**Problem 17. Write a C++ program for scoping example.**

*Program:*

```
#include<iostream.h>
#include<conio.h>
void useLocal( void );
void useStaticLocal( void );
void useGlobal( void );
int x = 1;
void main()
{
int x = 5;
cout << x << endl;
{
int x = 7;
cout << "local x in main's inner scope is " << x <<
endl;
}
cout << x << endl;
useLocal();
useStaticLocal();
useGlobal();
useLocal();
useStaticLocal();
useGlobal();
cout << x << endl;
getch();
}
void useLocal( void )
{
int x = 25;
cout << "local x is " << x << " on entering
useLocal" << endl;
x = x + 20;
cout << "local x is " << x << " on exiting
useLocal" << endl;
}
void useStaticLocal( void )
{
static int x = 50;
cout << "local static x is " << x << " on entering
useStaticLocal"<< endl;
x = x + 20;
cout << "local static x is " << x << " on exiting
useStaticLocal"<< endl;
}

void useGlobal( void )
{
cout << "global x is " << x << " on entering
useGlobal" << endl;
x = x + 20;
cout << "global x is " << x << " on exiting
useGlobal" << endl;
}
```

**OUTPUT:**

```
5
local x in main's inner scope is 7
5
local x is 25 on entering useLocal
local x is 45 on exiting useLocal
```

local static x is 50 on entering useStaticLocal
local static x is 70 on exiting useStaticLocal
global x is 1 on entering useGlobal
global x is 21 on exiting useGlobal
local x is 25 on entering useLocal
local x is 45 on exiting useLocal
local static x is 70 on entering useStaticLocal
local static x is 90 on exiting useStaticLocal
global x is 21 on entering useGlobal
global x is 41 on exiting useGlobal
5

**Problem 18. Write a C++ program to define and use Global variables.**

***Program:***

```
#include <iostream.h>
#include<conio.h>
int count = 0;
void test1(void);
void test2(void);
void main()
{
int count = 0;
for( ; count < 5; count++)
{
test1();
test2();
getch();
}
}
void test1(void)
{
cout<<"\ntest1   count = "<< ++count;
}
void test2(void)
{
static int count;
cout<<"\ntest2   count =   " ++count;
}
```

**OUTPUT:**

test1 count=1
test2 count=1
test1 count=2
test2 count=2
test1 count=3
test2 count=3
test1 count=4
test2 count=4
test1 count=5
test2 count=5

**Problem 19. Write a C++ program for variable scope: in and out a block.**

***Program:***

```
#include <iostream.h>
#include<conio.h>
void main()
{
int c = 0;
do
{
int c = 0;
++c ;
cout<<"\n c  = "<< c ;
}
while( ++c  <= 3 );
cout<<"\n c = "<< c<<endl;
getch();
}
```

**OUTPUT:**

c=1
c=1
c=1
c=1
c=4

**Problem 20. Write a C++ program to define block inside a function.**

***Program:***

```
#include <iostream.h>
#include<conio.h>
void main()
{
int  i = 10;
{
int i = 0;
for( i=0;i<2;i++)
{
cout<<"i = "<<i<<endl;
}
}
cout<<"i = "<<i<<"\n";
getch();
}
```

**OUTPUT:**

i=0
i=1
i=10

**Problem 21. Write a C++ program to define variable in a block.**

***Program:***

```
#include <iostream.h>
#include<conio.h>
void main()
{
int k = 10;
int i = 100;
{
int i;
for(i = 0; i < 2; i++ ) {
cout<<"i = "<<i<<endl;
}
}
cout<<"i = "<<i<<endl;
getch();
}
```

**OUTPUT:**

i=0
i=1
i=100

**Problem 22. Write a C++ program to define and use global variable and function.**

***Program:***

```
#include <iostream.h>
#include<conio.h>
int i =0;   //Global variable
void f1(void)
{
int k; // local variable for f1.
i = 50;
}
void main()
{
int j; // local variable in main
f1();
i =0;
cout<<" i in main "<<i<<endl;
f1();
cout<<" i after call "<<i<<endl;
getch();
}
```

**OUTPUT:**

i in main 0
i after call 50

**Problem 23. Write a C++ program to define local variable for a function.**

***Program:***

```
#include <iostream.h>
#include<conio.h>
int i =0;   //Global variable
void f(void);
void main()
{
int i ;   // local variable for main
i =0;
cout<<"value of i in main "<<i<<endl;
f();
cout<<"value of i after call"<<i<<endl;
getch();
}
void f(void)
{
int i=0; //local variable for f
i = 50;
}
```

**OUTPUT:**

value of i in main 0
value of i after call 0

**Problem 24. Write a C++ program working with global variable.**

***Program:***

```
#include <iostream.h>
#include<conio.h>
int sample;
void main()
{
cout<<sample;
getch();
}
```

**OUTPUT:**

0356

**Problem 25. Write a C++ program for free-standing block statement.**

***Program:***

```
#include <iostream.h>
#include<conio.h>
void main()
{
int i;
{
i = 1;
cout<<i;
}
getch();
}
```

**OUTPUT:**

1

**Problem 26. Write a C++ program for variable scope: inside a function.**

***Program:***

```
#include <iostream.h>
#include<conio.h>
void main()
{
int x;
x = 10;
if(x == 10) {
int x;
x = 99;
clrscr();
cout<<"Inner x:"<< x<<endl;;
}
cout<<"Outer x: "<< x<<endl;
getch();
}
```

**OUTPUT:**

```
Inner x:99
Outer x:10
```

**Problem 27. Write a C++ program use global vars.**

***Program:***

```
#include <iostream.h>
#include<conio.h>
int first = 10, last = 20;
void main()
{
extern int first, last;
cout<<first << last;
getch();
}
```

**OUTPUT:**

```
10 20
```

**Problem 28. Write a C++ program use global variable in function.**

***Program:***

```
#include <iostream.h>
#include<conio.h>
int max;
void f(void)
{
int i;
for(i=0; i<max; i++)
cout<<i;
}
void main()
{
max = 10;
f();
getch();
}
```

**OUTPUT:**

```
0 1 2 3 4 5 6 7 8 9
```

**Problem 29. Write a C++ program assign value to global variable.**

***Program:***

```
#include <iostream.h>
#include<conio.h>
int count;
void main()
{
extern int count;
count = 10;
cout<< count;
getch();
}
```

**OUTPUT:**

```
10
```

**Problem 30. Write a C++ program using the unary scope resolution operator.**

***Program:***

```
#include<conio.h>
#include<iostream.h>
int n = 7;
void main()
{
double n = 10.5;
cout << "Local double value of n = " << n
<< "\nGlobal int value of n = " << ::n << endl;
getch();
}
```

**OUTPUT:**

```
Local double value of n = 10.5
Global int value of n = 7
```

**Problem 31. Write a C++ program to find maximum and minimum values for data types.**

***Program:***

```
#include<conio.h>
#include<limits.h>
#include<iostream.h>
void main()
{
cout << "The range for type short is from "
<< numeric_limits<short>::min()<< " to "
<< numeric_limits<short>::max();
```

```
cout << "The range for type int is from "
<< numeric_limits<int>::min()
<< " to "<< numeric_limits<int>::max();
cout << "The range for type long is from "
<< numeric_limits<long>::min()
<< " to "
<< numeric_limits<long>::max();
cout << "The range for type float is from "
<< numeric_limits<float>::min()
<< " to "
<< numeric_limits<float>::max();
cout << "The range for type double is from "
<< numeric_limits<double>::min()
<< " to "
<< numeric_limits<double>::max();
cout << "The range for type long double is from "
<< numeric_limits<long double>::min()
<< " to "
<< numeric_limits<long double>::max();
cout << endl;
getch();
}
```

**OUTPUT:**

The range for type short is from -32768 to 32767The range for type int is from -
2147483648 to 2147483647The range for type long is from -2147483648 to 214748364
7The range for type float is from 1.17549e-038 to 3.40282e+038The range for type
double is from 2.22507e-308 to 1.79769e+308The range for type long double is from 0 to 1.#INF

**Problem 32. Write a C++ program to comparing data values.**

***Program:***

```
#include<iostream.h>
#include<conio.h>
void main()
{
char first = 10;
char second = 20;
cout << "The value of the expression first < second
is: "
<< (first < second)<< endl;
<< "The value of the expression first == second is: "
<< (first == second)<< endl;
getch();
}
```

**OUTPUT:**

The value of the expression first < second is: 1
The value of the expression first == second is: 0

## VARIABLE SIZE:

**Problem 33. Write a C++ program to find variable size: int, short, long, char, float and double.**

***Program:***

```
#include<iostream.h>
#include<conio.h>
void main()
{
cout << "The size of an int is:\t\t";
cout << sizeof(int) << " bytes.\n";
cout << "The size of a short int is:\t";
cout << sizeof(short) << " bytes.\n";
cout << "The size of a long int is:\t";
cout << sizeof(long) << " bytes.\n";
cout << "The size of a char is:\t\t";
cout << sizeof(char) << " bytes.\n";
cout << "The size of a float is:\t\t";
cout << sizeof(float) << " bytes.\n";
cout << "The size of a double is:\t";
cout << sizeof(double) << " bytes.\n";
getch();
}
```

**OUTPUT:**

```
The size of an int is:        4 bytes.
The size of a short int is:   2 bytes.
The size of a long int is:    4 bytes.
The size of a char is:        1 bytes.
The size of a float is:       4 bytes.
The size of a double is:      8 bytes.
```

## GLOBAL VARIABLE:

**Problem 34. Write a C++ program use a global variable.**

***Program:***

```
#include<iostream.h>
#include<conio.h>
void func1();
void func2();
int count; // This is a global variable.
void main()
{
int i; // This is a local variable
for(i=0; i<10; i++)
{
count = i * 2;
func1();
```

```
}
getch();
}
void func1()
{
cout << "count: " << count; // access global count
cout << '\n';
func2();
}
void func2()
{
int count;
for(count=0; count<3; count++)
cout << '.';
}
```

**OUTPUT:**

count: 0
...count: 2
...count: 4
...count: 6
...count: 8
...count: 10
...count: 12
...count: 14
...count: 16
...count: 18
...

**Problem 35. Write a C++ program for global class variable.**

***Program:***

```
#include<iostream.h>
#include<conio.h>
class test
{
int i;
public:
test()
{
i=25;
for(int ctr=0; ctr<10;ctr++)
{
cout<<"Counting at"<<ctr<<"\n";
}
}
~test(){};
};
test anObject;
void main()
{
getch();
}
```

**OUTPUT:**

Counting at0
Counting at1
Counting at2
Counting at3
Counting at4
Counting at5
Counting at6
Counting at7
Counting at8
Counting at9

## BLOCK SCOPE VARIABLE:

**Problem 36. Write a C++ program for variable block scope.**

***Program:***

```
#include<iostream.h>
#include<conio.h>
void main()
{
int count1 = 10;
int count3 = 50;
cout << endl << "Value of outer count1 = " <<
count1;
{
int count1 = 20;
int count2 = 30;
cout << endl << "Value of inner count1 = " <<
count1;
count1 += 3;
count3 += count2;
}
cout << endl
<< "Value of outer count1 = " << count1
<< endl
<< "Value of outer count3 = " << count3;
cout << endl;
getch();
}
```

**OUTPUT:**

Value of outer count1 = 10
Value of inner count1 = 20
Value of outer count1 = 10
Value of outer count3 = 80

**Problem 37. Write a C++ program for variables can be local to a block.**

***Program:***

```
#include<iostream.h>
#include<conio.h>
void main()
{
int x = 19; // x is known to all code.
if(x == 19)
{
int y = 20;
cout << "x + y is " << x + y << "\n";
}
// y not known here.
getch();
}
```

**OUTPUT:**

```
x + y is 39
```

**Problem 38. Write a C++ program for inner block variable scope.**

***Program:***

```
#include<conio.h>
#include<iostream.h>
void main()
{
int i;
int j;
i = 10;
j = 100;
if(j > 0)
{
int i; // this i is separate from outer i
i = j / 2;
cout << "inner i: " << i << '\n';
}
cout << "outer i: " << i << '\n';
getch();
}
```

**OUTPUT:**

```
inner i: 50
outer i: 10
```

**Problem 39. Write a C++ program for names in inner scopes can hide names in outer scopes.**

***Program:***

```
#include<iostream.h>
#include<conio.h>
void main()
{
for (int i = 0; i< 10; ++i)
{
int x = 2;
if (x < i)
{
double x = 3.4;
cout << x;
}
cout << x;
}
//std::cout << x;     // Error: no x declared in this
scope
getch();
}
```

**OUTPUT:**

```
2223.423.423.423.423.423.423.42
```

**Problem 40. Write a C++ program using the scope resolution operator: '::'.**

***Program:***

```
#include<iostream.h>
#include<conio.h>
int count1 = 100;
void main()
{
int count1 = 10;
int count3 = 50;
cout << endl << "Value of outer count1 = " <<
count1;
cout << endl << "Value of global count1 = " <<
::count1;
{
int count1 = 20;
int count2 = 30;
cout << endl << "Value of inner count1 = " <<
count1;
cout << endl << "Value of global count1 = " <<
::count1;
count3 += count2;
}
cout << endl
<< "Value of outer count1 = " << count1
<< endl
<< "Value of outer count3 = " << count3;
cout << endl;
getch();
}
```

**OUTPUT:**

```
Value of outer count1 = 10
Value of global count1 = 100
Value of inner count1 = 20
Value of global count1 = 100
Value of outer count1 = 10
Value of outer count3 = 80
```

**Problem 41. Write a C++ program to view global and block scope.**

***Program:***

```
#include<iostream.h>
#include<conio.h>
int n=0; //Global
void main()
{
int n = 1;
{
int n = 2 ;
{
int n = 3;
cout << "In inner  n=" <<n<<endl;
cout << "Global    n=" << ::n <<endl;
}
cout << "In outter n=" <<n<<endl;
cout << "Global    n=" <<::n<<endl;
}
cout << "In main() n=" << n<<endl;
getch() ;
}
```

**OUTPUT:**

```
In inner  n=3
Global    n=0
In outter n=2
Global    n=0
In main() n=1
```

**Problem 42. Write a C++ program using the scope resolution operator (2).**

***Program:***

```
#include<iostream.h>
#include<conio.h>
namespace n
{
struct counter
{
static int n;
};
double n = 2.8;
}
int n::counter::n = 7;
void main()
{
int counter = 0;
int n = 10;
cout << n::counter::n;
cout << n::n;
cout << x.n;
cout << n;
cout << counter;
getch();
}
```

**OUTPUT:**

```
Value of outer count1 = 10
Value of global count1 = 100
Value of inner count1 = 20
Value of global count1 = 100
Value of outer count1 = 10
Value of outer count3 = 80
```

# EXPRESSION:

**Problem 43. Write a C++ program using function in an expression.**

***Program:***

```
#include <iostream.h>
#include<conio.h>
double box(double length, double width, double
height); // use double data
void main()
{
double sum;
sum = box(10.1, 11.2, 3.3) + box(5.5, 6.6, 7.7) +
box(4.0, 5.0, 8.0);
cout << "The sum of the volumes is " << sum <<
"\n";
cout << "The average volume is " << sum / 3.0 <<
"\n";
getch();
}
// This version of box uses double data.
double box(double length, double width, double
height)
{
return length * width * height ;
}
```

**OUTPUT:**

```
The sum of the volumes is 812.806
The average volume is 270.935
```

**Problem 44. Write a C++ program using a properly initialized constant variable.**

***Program:***

```
#include<iostream.h>
#include<conio.h>
void main()
{
const int x = 7;
cout << x << endl;
```

```
getch();
}
```

**OUTPUT:**

7

**Problem 45. Write a C++ program to demonstrating the const type qualifier.**

***Program:***

```
#include<iostream.h>
#include<conio.h>
void f( const int [] );
void main()
{
int a[] = { 10, 20, 30 };
f( a );
cout << a[ 0 ] <<' ' << a[ 1 ] <<' '
<< a[ 2 ] << '\n';
getch();
}
void f( const int b[] )
{
cout << b[ 0 ];
}
```

**OUTPUT:**

1010 20 30

## ENDL:

**Problem 46. Write a C++ program to state working of endl.**

***Program:***

```
#include <iostream.h>
#include<conio.h>
void main()
{
clrscr();
cout<<"America"
<<endl
<<"Africa"
<<endl
<<"Asia";
getch();
}
```

**OUTPUT:**

America
Africa
Asia

**Problem 47. Write a C++ program to add 5 numbers.**

***Program:***

```
#include <iostream.h>
void main()
{
int a=1,b,sum=0,num;
cout<<"Enter the 5 digit no";
cin>>num;
while(a!=0)
{
a=num/10;
b=num%10;
sum=sum+b;
num=a;
}
cout<<"sum is "<<sum;
getch();
}
```

**OUTPUT:**

Enter the 5 digit no 12345
sum is 15

## NAMESPACE:

**Problem 48. Write a C++ program for a namespace.**

***Program:***

```
namespace MyNameSpace
{
int start;
int end;
class counter
{
int count;
public:
counter(int n)
{
count = n;
}
void reset(int n)
{
count = n;
} };
}
```

**Problem 49. Write a C++ program using a namespace.**

***Program:***

```
#include<iostream.h>
#include<conio.h>
namespace MyNameSpace
{
int start;
int end;
class counter
{
int count;
public:
counter(int n)
{
if(n <= start) count = n;
else count = start;
}
void reset(int n)
{
if(n <= start) count = n;
}
int run()
{
if(count > end) return count--;
else return end;
}
};
}
 void main()
{
MyNameSpace::start = 100;
MyNameSpace::end = 0;
MyNameSpace::counter ob1(10);
int i;
do
{
i = ob1.run();
cout << i << " ";
} while(i > MyNameSpace::end);
cout << endl;
MyNameSpace::counter ob2(20);
do {
i = ob2.run();
cout << i << " ";
}while(i > MyNameSpace::end);
cout << endl;
ob2.reset(100);
MyNameSpace::end = 90;
do
{
i = ob2.run();
cout << i << " ";
} while(i > MyNameSpace::end);
getch();
}
```

**OUTPUT:**

```
10 9 8 7 6 5 4 3 2 1 0
20 19 18 17 16 15 14 13 12 11 10 9 8 7 6 5 4 3 2 1
0
100 99 98 97 96 95 94 93 92 91 90
```

**Problem 50. Write a C++ program for a nested namespace.**

***Program:***

```
#include<iostream.h>
#include<conio.h>
namespace MyNamespace1
{
int i;
namespace MyNamespace2
{                                    // a nested
namespace
int j;
}
}
void main()
{
MyNamespace1::i = 19;
MyNamespace1::MyNamespace2::j = 10; // this is
right
cout << MyNamespace1::i << " "<<
MyNamespace1::MyNamespace2::j << "\n";
// use MyNamespace1
using namespace MyNamespace1;
cout << i * MyNamespace2::j;
getch();
}
```

**OUTPUT:**

```
19 10
190
```

**Problem 51. Write a C++ program to reuse namespace.**

***Program:***

```
#include<iostream.h>
#include<conio.h>
namespace MyNamespace
{
int i;
}
namespace MyNamespace
{
int j;
}
```

```
void main()
{
MyNamespace::i = MyNamespace::j = 10;
// refer to MyNamespace specifically
cout << MyNamespace::i * MyNamespace::j <<
"\n";
// use MyNamespace namespace
using namespace MyNamespace;
cout << i * j;
getch();
}
```

**OUTPUT:**

```
100
100
```

**Problem 52. Write a C++ program for reference variables in namespaces.**

***Program:***

```
#include<iostream.h>
#include<conio.h>
namespace first
{
int var = 5;
}
namespace second
{
double var = 3.1416;
}
void main ()
{
cout << first::var << endl;
cout << second::var << endl;
getch();
}
```

**OUTPUT:**

```
5
3.1416
```

**Problem 53. Write a C++ program using namespace in program block.**

***Program:***

```
#include<iostream.h>
#include<conio.h>
namespace first
{
int var = 5;
}
namespace second
{
double var = 3.1416;
}
void main ()
{
{
using namespace first;
cout << var << endl;
}
{
using namespace second;
cout << var << endl;
}
getch();
}
```

**OUTPUT:**

```
5
3.1416
```

**Problem 54. Write a C++ program for reference global variable, variable in the nested namespace.**

***Program:***

```
#include<iostream.h>
#include<conio.h>
int integer1 = 98;
namespace
{
double doubleInUnnamed = 88.22;
}
namespace Example
{
const double PI = 3.14159;
void printValues();
int integer1 = 100;
namespace Inner
{
int integer1 = 99;
}
}
void main()
{
cout << "doubleInUnnamed = " <<
doubleInUnnamed;
cout << "\n(global) integer1 = " << integer1;
cout << Example::integer1 << "\nIinteger1 = "
<< Example::Inner::integer1 << endl;
getch();
}
```

**OUTPUT:**

```
doubleInUnnamed = 88.22
(global) integer1 = 98100
Iinteger1 = 99
```

**Problem 55. Write a C++ program using namespace to organize functions.**

***Program:***

```
#include<iostream.h>
#include<conio.h>
void f(int i)
{
cout << "int: " << i << '\n';
}
namespace MyNamespace
{
void f(double d)
{
cout << "double: " << showpoint << d << '\n';
}
void call_f()
{
// finds MyNamespace::f(double) first.
f(3);
}
}
void main()
{
MyNamespace::call_f();
using MyNamespace::f;
using ::f;
f(4);
getch();
}
```

**OUTPUT:**

double: 3.00000
int: 4

**Problem 56. Write a C++ program function in a namespace reference variables in the same namespace.**

***Program:***

```
#include<iostream.h>
#include<conio.h>
int integer1 = 98;
namespace Example
{
const double PI = 3.14159;
void printValues();
namespace Inner
{
enum Years { FISCAL1 = 1990, FISCAL2, a };
}
}
namespace
{
double doubleInUnnamed = 88.22;
}
void main()
{
Example::printValues();
getch();
}
void Example::printValues()
{
cout << integer1 << "\n(global) integer1 = " <<
integer1
<< "\nIinteger1 = " << Inner::a << endl;
}
```

**OUTPUT:**

98
(global) integer1 = 98
Iinteger1 = 1992

**Problem 57. Write a C++ program how using namespace std.**

***Program:***

```
#include<iostream.h>
#include<conio.h>
void main()
{
// Print hello world on the screen
std::cout << "Hello World";
getch();
}
```

**OUTPUT:**

Hello World"

**Problem 58. Write a C++ program using function defined in a namespace.**

***Program:***

```
#include<iostream.h>
#include<conio.h>
#include <stdlib.h>
namespace MyLib {
double readAndProcessSum (istream&);
}
void main()
{
using namespace std;
double sum;
try
{
sum = MyLib::readAndProcessSum(cin);
}
catch (const ios::failure& error)
{
```

```
cerr << "I/O exception: " << error.what() << endl;
return EXIT_FAILURE;
}
catch (const exception& error)
{
cerr << "standard exception: " << error.what() <<
endl;
return EXIT_FAILURE;
}
catch (...)
{
cerr << "unknown exception" << endl;
return EXIT_FAILURE;
}
// print sum
cout << "sum: " << sum << endl;
getch();
}
namespace MyLib
{
double readAndProcessSum (std::istream& strm)
{
double value, sum;
sum = 0;
while (strm >> value)
{
sum += value;
}
if (!strm.eof())
{
throw std::ios::failure
 ("input error in readAndProcessSum()");
}
// return sum
return sum;
}
}
```

**OUTPUT:**

a
I/O exception: input error in readAndProcessSum()

**Problem 59. Write a C++ program using unnamed namespaces.**

***Program:***

```
#include<iostream.h>
#include<conio.h>
namespace
{
int i = 10;
}
namespace
{
int j;          // same unnamed namespace
namespace X
{
int i = 20;
}
namespace Y = X;
int f() { return i; }
}
void main()
{
cout << f() << '\n';
cout << Y::i << '\n';
cout << f() << '\n';
}
```

**OUTPUT:**

10
20
10

**Problem 60. Write a C++ program using namespace aliases.**

***Program:***

```
#include <iostream.h>
#include<conio.h>
namespace original
{
int f();
}
namespace ns = original;
int ns::f() { return 42; }
using ns::f;
int g() { return f(); }
void main()
{
cout << ns::f() << '\n';
cout << original::f() << '\n';
cout << g() << '\n';
getch();
}
```

**OUTPUT:**

42
42
42

**Problem 61. Write a C++ program using the *using* directive.**

***Program:***

```
#include<iostream.h>
#include<conio.h>
namespace A
```

```
{
int x = 1;
}
namespace B {
int y = 2;
}
namespace C {
int z = 3;
using namespace B;
}
namespace D {
int z = 4;
using namespace B;
int y = 5;
}
void main()
{
int x = 60;
using namespace A;
using namespace C;
cout << x << '\n';
cout << y << '\n';
cout << C::y << '\n';
cout << D::y << '\n';
getch();
}
```

**OUTPUT:**

60
2
2
5

## GLOBAL NAMESPACE:

**Problem 62. Write a C++ program using explicit std:: qualification.**

***Program:***

```
#include<iostream.h>
#include<conio.h>
using namespace std;
void main()
{
int val;
std::cout << "Enter a number: ";
std::cin >> val;
std::cout << "This is your number: ";
std::cout << std::hex << val;
getch();
}
```

**OUTPUT:**

Enter a number: 1
This is your number: 1

**Problem 63. Write a C++ program bring only a few names into the global namespace.**

***Program:***

```
#include<iostream.h>
#include<conio.h>
void main()
{
int val;
cout << "Enter a number: ";
cin >> val;
cout << "This is your number: ";
cout << hex << val;
getch();
}
```

**OUTPUT:**

Enter a number: 1
This is your number: 1

## COMMENTS:

**Problem 64. Write a C++ program for C-style and C++ style comments.**

***Program:***

```
#include<iostream.h>
#include<conio.h>
void main()
{
cout << "Hello World!\n";
// this c++-style comment ends at the end of the
line
cout << "That comment ended!";
getch();
}
```

**OUTPUT:**

Hello World!
That comment ended!

## STATIC:

**Problem 65. Write a C++ program using a static long variable.**

***Program:***

```
#include<iomanip.h>
#include<iostream.h>
#include<conio.h>
long next();
void main()
```

```
{
for(int i = 0 ; i < 30 ; i++)
{
cout << setw(12) << next ();
}
cout << endl;
getch();
}
long next ()
{
static long last = 0;
last = last + 1;
return last;
}
```

**OUTPUT:**

```
1       2       3       4       5       6  7
8       9       10      11      12      13      14
15      16      17      18      19      20
21      22      23      24      25      26  27
28      29      30
```

**Problem 66. Write a C++ program using static variable to compute a running average of numbers entered by the user.**

***Program:***

```
#include<iostream.h>
#include<conio.h>
int f(int i);
void main()
{
int num;
do {
cout << "Enter numbers (-1 to quit): ";
cin >> num;
if(num != -1)
cout << "average is: " << f(num) << "\n";
} while(num > -1);
getch();
}
int f(int i)
{
static int sum = 0, count = 0;
sum = sum + i;
count++;
return sum / count;
}
```

**OUTPUT:**

```
Enter numbers (-1 to quit): 1
average is: 1
Enter numbers (-1 to quit): 2
average is: 1
Enter numbers (-1 to quit): 3
average is: 2
Enter numbers (-1 to quit): 2
average is: 2
Enter numbers (-1 to quit): 1
average is: 1
Enter numbers (-1 to quit): 2
average is: 1
Enter numbers (-1 to quit): 3
average is: 2
Enter numbers (-1 to quit): -1
```

**Problem 67. Write a C++ program to initialize static member field outside the class declaration.**

***Program:***

```
#include<iostream.h>
#include<conio.h>
class Box
{
public:
Box()
{
cout << "Default constructor called" << endl;
++objectCount;
length = width = height = 1.0;
}
Box(double lvalue, double wvalue, double hvalue)
:length(lvalue), width(wvalue),height(hvalue)
{
cout << "Box constructor called" << endl;
++objectCount;
}
double volume() const
{
return length * width * height;
}
int getObjectCount() const {return objectCount;}
private:
static int objectCount;
double length;
double width;
double height;
};
int Box::objectCount = 0;
void main()
{
cout << endl;
Box firstBox(17.0, 11.0, 5.0);
cout << "Object count is " <<
firstBox.getObjectCount() << endl;
```

```
Box boxes[5];
cout << "Object count is " <<
firstBox.getObjectCount() << endl;
cout << "Volume of first box = "
<< firstBox.volume()
<< endl;
const int count = sizeof boxes/sizeof boxes[0];
cout <<"The boxes array has " << count << "
elements."
<< endl;
cout <<"Each element occupies " << sizeof boxes[0]
<< " bytes."
<< endl;
for(int i = 0 ; i < count ; i++)
cout << "Volume of boxes[" << i << "] = "
<< boxes[i].volume()
<< endl;
getch();
}
```

**OUTPUT:**

```
Box constructor called
Object count is 1
Default constructor called
Default constructor called
Default constructor called
Default constructor called
Default constructor called
Object count is 6
Volume of first box = 935
The boxes array has 5 elements.
Each element occupies 24 bytes.
Volume of boxes[0] = 1
Volume of boxes[1] = 1
Volume of boxes[2] = 1
Volume of boxes[3] = 1
Volume of boxes[4] = 1
```

## USING:

**Problem 68. Write a C++ program using the *using* keyword.**

***Program:***

```
#include<iostream.h>
#include<conio.h>
using namespace std;
void main()
{
using std::cout;
using std::endl;
cout << "Here is 5: " << 5 << "\n";
cout << 8+5 << endl;
getch();
}
```

**OUTPUT:**

```
Here is 5: 5
13
```

**Problem 69. Write a C++ program using namespace std.**

***Program:***

```
#include<iostream.h>
#include<conio.h>
void main()
{
using namespace std;
cout << "a new line ";
cout <<  endl;
getch();
}
```

**OUTPUT:**

```
a new line
```

## MUTABLE:

**Problem 70. Write a C++ program to demonstrate mutable.**

***Program:***

```
#include<iostream.h>
#include<conio.h>
class MyClass
{
mutable int i;
int j;
public:
int geti() const
{
return i; // ok
}
void seti(int x) const
{
i = x; // now, OK.
}
};
void main()
{
MyClass ob;
ob.seti(1900);
cout << ob.geti();
getch();
}
```

**OUTPUT:**

1900

**Problem 71. Write a C++ program to demonstrating storage-class specifier mutable.**

***Program:***

```
#include<iostream.h>
#include<conio.h>
class MyClass
{
public:
MyClass( int v )
{
value = v;
}
int getValue() const
{
return value++;
}
private:
mutable int value;
};
void main()
{
const MyClass test( 99 );
cout << "Initial value: " << test.getValue();
cout << "\nModified value: " << test.getValue() <<
endl;
getch();
}
```

**OUTPUT:**

Initial value: 99
Modified value: 100

## EXTERN:

**Problem 72. Write a C++ program to link as a C function.**

***Program:***

```
#include<iostream.h>
#include<conio.h>
extern "C" void myCfunc();
void main()
{
myCfunc();
getch();
}
// This will link as a C function.
void myCfunc()
{
cout << "This links as a C function.\n";
}
```

**OUTPUT:**

This links as a C function.

**Problem 73. Write a C++ program A for loop inside main function.**

***Program:***

```
#include <iostream.h>
#include<conio.h>
void main()
{
int x;
for(x = 1; x <= 10; x++)
cout<< x;
getch();
}
```

**OUTPUT:**

1 2 3 4 5 6 7 8 9 10

# CHAPTER 2

# ALL DATA TYPES

## INT:

**Problem 1. Write a C++ program to define an int variable.**

***Program:***

```
#include<iostream.h>
#include<conio.h>
void main()
{
int length; // this declares a variable
length = 7; // this assigns 7 to length
cout << "The length is ";
cout << length; // This displays 7
getch();
}
```

**OUTPUT:**

The length is 7"

**Problem 2. Write a C++ program to define and assign int variables.**

***Program:***

```
#include<iostream.h>
#include<conio.h>
void main()
{
int a=0, b=0, x=0, y=35;
cout << "a: " << a << " b: " << b;
cout << " x: " << x << " y: " << y << endl;
a = 9;
b = 7;
y = x = a+b;
cout << "a: " << a << " b: " << b;
cout << " x: " << x << " y: " << y <<endl;
getch();
}
```

**OUTPUT:**

a: 0 b: 0 x: 0 y: 35
a: 9 b: 7 x: 16 y: 16

**Problem 3. Write a C++ program using arithmetic operator to get the product of two integers.**

***Program:***

```
#include<iostream.h>
#include<conio.h>
void main()
{
int length;
int width;
int area;
length = 7;
width = 5;
area = length * width; // compute area
cout << "The area is ";
cout << area;
getch();
}
```

**OUTPUT:**

The area is 35"

**Problem 4. Write a C++ program for performing calculation in cout.**

***Program:***

```
#include<iostream.h>
#include<conio.h>
void main()
{
int length;
int width;
length = 7;
width = 5;
cout << "The area is ";
cout << length * width;
getch();
}
```

**OUTPUT:**

The area is 35

**Problem 5. Write a C++ program to convert gallons to liters.**

***Program:***

```
#include<iostream.h>
#include<conio.h>
void main()
{
int gallons, liters;
```

```
cout << "Enter number of gallons: ";
cin >> gallons;    // this inputs from the user
liters = gallons * 4; // convert to liters
cout << "Liters: " << liters;
getch();
}
```

**OUTPUT:**

Enter number of gallons: 12
Liters: 48

**Problem 6. Write a C++ program to calculate the product of three integers.**

***Program:***

```
#include<iostream.h>
#include<conio.h>
void main()
{
int x;
int y;
int z;
int result;
cout << "Enter three integers: ";
cin >> x >> y >> z; // read three integers from user
result = x * y * z;
cout << "The product is " << result << endl;
getch();
}
```

**OUTPUT:**

Enter three integers: 1 2
3
The product is 6

**Problem 7. Write a C++ program to comparing integers using if statements, relational operators and equality operators.**

***Program:***

```
#include<iostream.h>
#include<conio.h>
void main()
{
int number1;
int number2;
cout << "Enter two integers to compare: ";
cin >> number1 >> number2;
if ( number1 == number2 )
cout << number1 << " == " << number2 << endl;
if ( number1 != number2 )
cout << number1 << " != " << number2 << endl;
if ( number1 < number2 )
cout << number1 << " < " << number2 << endl;
if ( number1 > number2 )
cout << number1 << " > " << number2 << endl;
if ( number1 <= number2 )
cout << number1 << " <= " << number2 << endl;
if ( number1 >= number2 )
cout << number1 << " >= " << number2 << endl;
getch();
}
```

**OUTPUT:**

Enter two integers to compare: 4
3
4 != 3
4 > 3
4 >= 3

**Problem 8. Write a C++ program to perform bit operation on integers: AND, OR, XOR.**

***Program:***

```
#include <iostream.h>
#include<conio.h>
void main()
{
int num1, num2,iand,ior,ixor;
num1 = 1;
num2 = 2;
iand = num1 & num2;
ior = num1 | num2;
ixor = num1 ^ num2;
cout << num1 << " AND " << num2 << " is " <<
iand << endl;
cout << num1 << " OR " << num2 << " is " << ior
<< endl;
cout << num1 << " XOR " << num2 << " is " <<
ixor << endl;
getch();
}
```

**OUTPUT:**

1 AND 2 is 0
1 OR 2 is 3
1 XOR 2 is 3

**Problem 9. Write a C++ program to calculate the value of product and quotient.**

***Program:***

```
#include<iostream.h>
#include<conio.h>
void main()
{
int x = 5;
int product = 5;
int quotient = 5;
product *= x++;
```

```
cout << product << endl;
cout << x << endl << endl;
x = 5;
quotient /= ++x;
cout << quotient << endl;
cout << x << endl;
getch();
}
```

**OUTPUT:**

```
25
6
0
6
```

## INT READ:

**Problem 10. Write a C++ program to read integer from console using cin.**

***Program:***

```
#include<iostream.h>
#include<conio.h>
void main()
{
int length;
int width;
cout << "Enter the length: ";
cin >> length; // input the length
cout << "Enter the width: ";
cin >> width; // input the width
cout << "The area is ";
cout << length * width;
getch();
}
```

**OUTPUT:**

```
Enter the length: 12
Enter the width: 12
The area is 144"
```

## INT POINTER:

**Problem 11. Write a C++ program for int pointers.**

***Program:***

```
#include<iostream.h>
#include<conio.h>
void main()
{
int intValue;          // a variable
int * intPointer = 0;  // a pointer
intValue = 5;
intPointer = &intValue;    // assign address of intValue to intPointer
cout << "intValue: " << intValue << "\n";
cout << "*intPointer: " << *intPointer << "\n\n";
cout << "*intPointer = 7\n";
*intPointer = 7;       // sets intValue to 7
cout << "*intPointer: " << *intPointer << "\n";
cout << "intValue: " << intValue << "\n\n";
cout << "intValue = 9\n";
intValue = 9;
cout << "intValue: " << intValue << "\n";
cout << "*intPointer: " << *intPointer << "\n";
getch();
}
```

**OUTPUT:**

```
intValue: 5
*intPointer: 5
*intPointer = 7
*intPointer: 7
intValue: 7
intValue = 9
intValue: 9
*intPointer: 9
```

**Problem 12. Write a C++ program to get address of an int variable.**

***Program:***

```
#include<iostream.h>
#include<conio.h>
void main()
{
int total;
int *ptr;
int val;
total = 3200; // assign 3,200 to total
ptr = &total; // get address of total
val = *ptr;  // get value at that addres
cout << "Total is: " << val << '\n';
getch();
}
```

**OUTPUT:**

```
Total is: 3200
```

**Problem 13. Write a C++ program to perform calculation based on pointer.**

***Program:***

```
#include<iostream.h>
#include<conio.h>
void main()
{
int *p, num;
```

```
p = &num;
*p = 100;
cout << num << ' ';
(*p)++;
cout << num << ' ';
(*p)--;
cout << num << '\n';
getch();
}
```

**OUTPUT:**

100 101 100

## INT ARRAY:

**Problem 14. Write a C++ program to declare int array.**

***Program:***

```
#include<iostream.h>
#include<conio.h>
void main()
{
int sample[10]; // this reserves 10 integer elements
int t;
// load the array
for(t=0; t<10; ++t) sample[t] = t;
// display the array
for(t=0; t<10; ++t)
cout << "This is sample[" << t << "]: " << sample[t]
<< "\n";
getch();
}
```

**OUTPUT:**

This is sample[0]: 0
This is sample[1]: 1
This is sample[2]: 2
This is sample[3]: 3
This is sample[4]: 4
This is sample[5]: 5
This is sample[6]: 6
This is sample[7]: 7
This is sample[8]: 8
This is sample[9]: 9

**Problem 15. Write a C++ program to compute the average of a set of values.**

***Program:***

```
#include<iostream.h>
#include<conio.h>
void main()
{
int i, avg, min_val, max_val;
int nums[10];
nums[0] = 13;
nums[1] = 18;
nums[2] = 75;
nums[3] = 120;
nums[4] = 1321;
nums[5] = 56;
nums[6] = 13124;
nums[7] = 12123;
nums[8] = -19312;
nums[9] = 88123;
// compute the average
avg = 0;
for(i=0; i<10; i++)
avg += nums[i];
avg /= 10;
cout << "Average is " << avg << '\n';
getch();
}
```

**OUTPUT:**

Average is 9566

**Problem 16. Write a C++ program to find the minimum and maximum of a set of values.**

***Program:***

```
#include<iostream.h>
#include<conio.h>
void main()
{
int i, avg, min_val, max_val;
int nums[10];
nums[0] = 13;
nums[1] = 18;
nums[2] = 75;
nums[3] = 120;
nums[4] = 1321;
nums[5] = 56;
nums[6] = 13124;
nums[7] = 12123;
nums[8] = -19312;
nums[9] = 88123;
// find minimum and maximum values
min_val = max_val = nums[0];
for(i=1; i<10; i++)
{
if(nums[i] < min_val) min_val = nums[i];
if(nums[i] > max_val) max_val = nums[i];
}
cout << "Minimum value: " << min_val << '\n';
cout << "Maximum value: " << max_val << '\n';
```

```
getch();
}
```

**OUTPUT:**

Minimum value: -19312
Maximum value: 88123

## BOOL:

**Problem 17. Write a C++ program for bool values.**

***Program:***

```
#include<iostream.h>
#include<conio.h>
void main()
{
bool b;
b = false;
cout << "b is " << b << "\n";
b = true;
cout << "b is " << b << "\n";
if(b) cout << "This is executed.\n";
b = false;
if(b) cout << "This is not executed.\n";
getch();
}
```

**OUTPUT:**

b is 0
b is 1
This is executed.
10 > 9 is 1

**Problem 18. Write a C++ program how bool value can control the if statement.**

***Program:***

```
#include<iostream.h>
#include<conio.h>
void main()
{
bool b;
b = false;
cout << "b is " << b << "\n";
b = true;
cout << "b is " << b << "\n";
if(b) cout << "This is executed.\n";
b = false;
if(b) cout << "This is not executed.\n";
getch();
}
```

**OUTPUT:**

b is 0
b is 1
This is executed.

**Problem 19. Write a C++ program to check outcome of a relational operator is a true/false value.**

***Program:***

```
#include<iostream.h>
#include<conio.h>
void main()
{
bool b;
b = false;
cout << "b is " << b << "\n";
b = true;
cout << "b is " << b << "\n";
getch();
}
```

**OUTPUT:**

b is 0
b is 1
10 > 9 is 1

**Problem 20. Write a C++ program for variable size of bool**

***Program:***

```
#include<iostream.h>
#include<conio.h>
void main()
{
cout << "The size of a bool is:"     << sizeof(bool)
<< " bytes.\n";
getch();
}
```

**OUTPUT:**

The size of a bool is:1 bytes.

**Problem 21. Write a C++ program for logical && Operator.**

***Program:***

```
#include<iostream.h>
#include<conio.h>
void main(void)
{
int age;
char choice;
bool citizen;
cout << "Enter your age: ";
cin >> age;
cout << "Are you a citizen (Y/N): ";
cin >> choice;
```

```
if (choice == 'Y')
citizen = true;
else
citizen = false;
if (age >= 18 && citizen == true)
cout << "You are eligible to vote";
else
cout << "You are not eligible to vote";
getch();
}
```

**Problem 22. Write a C++ program for !(Exclamation mark) Operator.**

***Program:***

```
#include<iostream.h>
#include<conio.h>
void main(void)
{
int age;
cout << "Enter your age: ";
cin >> age;
if (!(age > 12 && age < 65))
cout << "Admission is free";
else
cout << "You have to pay";
getch();
}
```

**Problem 23. Write a C++ program for Logical operators.**

***Program:***

```
#include<iostream.h>
#include<conio.h>
void main()
{
// create truth table for && (logical AND) operator
cout << boolalpha << "Logical AND (&&)"
<< "\nfalse && false: " << ( false && false )
<< "\nfalse && true: " << ( false && true )
<< "\ntrue && false: " << ( true && false )
<< "\ntrue && true: " << ( true && true ) << "\n\n";
// create truth table for || (logical OR) operator
cout << "Logical OR (||)"
<< "\nfalse || false: " << ( false || false )
<< "\nfalse || true: " << ( false || true )
<< "\ntrue || false: " << ( true || false )
<< "\ntrue || true: " << ( true || true ) << "\n\n";
// create truth table for ! (logical negation) operator
cout << "Logical NOT (!)"
<< "\n!false: " << ( !false )
<< "\n!true: " << ( !true ) << endl;
getch();
}
```

**OUTPUT:**

```
Logical AND (&&)
false && false: false
false && true: false
true && false: false
true && true: true
Logical OR (||)
false || false: false
false || true: true
true || false: true
true || true: true
Logical NOT (!)
!false: true
!true: false
```

## DOUBLE:

**Problem 24. Write a C++ program to convert feet to meters using doubles.**

***Program:***

```
#include<iostream.h>
#include<conio.h>
void main()
{
double f; // holds the length in feet
double m; // holds the conversion to meters
cout << "Enter the length in feet: ";
cin >> f; // read the number of feet
m = f / 3.28; // convert to meters
cout << f << " feet is " << m << " meters.";
getch();
}
```

**OUTPUT:**

```
Enter the length in feet: 12
12 feet is 3.65854 meters."
```

**Problem 25. Write a C++ program to analyze differences between int and double during 'divide'.**

***Program:***

```
#include<iostream.h>
#include<conio.h>
void  main()
{
int ivar;
double dvar;
ivar = 100;
dvar = 100.0;
```

```
cout << "Original value of ivar: " << ivar << "\n";
cout << "Original value of dvar: " << dvar << "\n";
cout << "\n";
ivar = ivar / 3;
dvar = dvar / 3.0;
cout << "ivar after division: " << ivar << "\n";
cout << "dvar after division: " << dvar << "\n";
getch();
}
```

**OUTPUT:**

Original value of ivar: 100
Original value of dvar: 100
ivar after division: 33
dvar after division: 33.3333

**Problem 26. Write a C++ program using the Pythagorean theorem to find find the length of the hypotenuse.**

***Program:***

```
#include<iostream.h>
#include<conio.h>
#include <math.h>
void main()
{
double x, y, z;
x = 5;
y = 4;
z = sqrt(x*x + y*y);
cout << "Hypotenuse is " << z;
getch();
}
```

**OUTPUT:**

Hypotenuse is 6.40312"

**Problem 27. Write a C++ program to perform calculation by double variables.**

***Program:***

```
#include<iostream.h>
#include<conio.h>
void main()
{
double distance;
double lightspeed;
double delay;
double delay_in_min;
distance = 34000000.0; // 34,000,000 miles
lightspeed = 186000.0; // 186,000 per second
delay = distance / lightspeed;
cout << "Time delay when talking to Mars: " <<
delay << " seconds.\n";
delay_in_min = delay / 60.0;
cout << "This is " << delay_in_min << "
minutes.";
getch();
}
```

**OUTPUT:**

Time delay when talking to Mars: 182.796 seconds.
This is 3.04659 minutes."

**Problem 28. Write a C++ program to compute the regular payments for a loan.**

***Program:***

```
#include<iostream.h>
#include<conio.h>
#include <math.h>
void main()
{
double Principal = 11.11;
double IntRate = 0.075;
double PayPerYear = 12.0;
double NumYears = 25;
double Payment;
double numer, denom;
double b, e;
numer = IntRate * Principal / PayPerYear;
e = -(PayPerYear * NumYears);
b = (IntRate / PayPerYear) + 1;
denom = 1 - pow(b, e);
Payment = numer / denom;
cout << "Payment is " << Payment;
getch();
}
```

**OUTPUT:**

Payment is 0.0821019"

**Problem 29. Write a C++ program to show square roots of 1 to 99.**

***Program:***

```
#include<iostream.h>
#include<conio.h>
#include<math.h>
void main()
{
int num;
double sq_root;
for(num=1; num < 100; num++)
{
sq_root = sqrt((double) num);
cout << num << " " << sq_root << '\n';
}
getch();
```

}

**OUTPUT:**

```
1 1
2 1.41421
3 1.73205
4 2
5 2.23607
6 2.44949
7 2.64575
8 2.82843
9 3
10 3.16228
11 3.31662
12 3.4641
13 3.60555
14 3.74166
15 3.87298
16 4
17 4.12311
18 4.24264
19 4.3589
20 4.47214
21 4.58258
22 4.69042
23 4.79583
24 4.89898
25 5
26 5.09902
27 5.19615
28 5.2915
29 5.38516
30 5.47723
31 5.56776
32 5.65685
33 5.74456
34 5.83095
35 5.91608
36 6
37 6.08276
38 6.16441
39 6.245
40 6.32456
41 6.40312
42 6.48074
43 6.55744
44 6.63325
45 6.7082
46 6.78233
47 6.85565
48 6.9282
49 7
50 7.07107
51 7.14143
52 7.2111
53 7.28011
54 7.34847
55 7.4162
56 7.48331
57 7.54983
58 7.61577
59 7.68115
60 7.74597
61 7.81025
62 7.87401
63 7.93725
64 8
65 8.06226
66 8.12404
67 8.18535
68 8.24621
69 8.30662
70 8.3666
71 8.42615
72 8.48528
73 8.544
74 8.60233
75 8.66025
76 8.7178
77 8.77496
78 8.83176
79 8.88819
80 8.94427
81 9
82 9.05539
83 9.11043
84 9.16515
85 9.21954
86 9.27362
87 9.32738
88 9.38083
89 9.43398
90 9.48683
91 9.53939
92 9.59166
93 9.64365
94 9.69536
95 9.74679
96 9.79796
97 9.84886
98 9.89949
99 9.94987
```

**Problem 30. Write a C++ program to compare double base on precision.**

***Program:***

```
#include<math.h>
#include<iostream.h>
#include<conio.h>
bool doubleEquals(double left, double right, double
epsilon)
{
return (fabs(left - right) < epsilon);
}
bool doubleLess(double left, double right, double
epsilon, bool orequal = false)
{
if (fabs(left - right) < epsilon)
{
return (orequal);
}
return (left < right);
}
bool doubleGreater(double left, double right, double
epsilon, bool orequal = false)
{
if (fabs(left - right) < epsilon)
{
return (orequal);
}
return (left > right);
}
void main( )
{
double first = 0.33333333;
double second = 1.0 / 3.0;
cout << first << endl;
cout << second << endl;
cout << boolalpha << (first == second) << endl;
cout << doubleEquals(first, second, .0001) << endl;
cout << doubleLess(first, second, .0001) << endl;
cout << doubleGreater(first, second, .0001) << endl;
cout << doubleLess(first, second, .0001, true) <<
endl;
cout << doubleGreater(first, second, .0001, true) <<
endl;
getch();
}
```

**OUTPUT:**

```
0.333333
0.333333
false
true
false
false
true
true
```

## FLOAT:

**Problem 31. Write a C++ program for float point constant number.**

***Program:***

```
#include<math.h>
#include<iostream.h>
#include<conio.h>
const float PI = 3.1415926;
inline float Area(const float r);
void main()
{
float radius = 2.9;
cout << "The Area is " << Area(radius) << "\n";
}
float Area(const float r)
{
return PI * r * r;
}
```

**OUTPUT:**

The Area is 26.4208

**Problem 32. Write a C++ program for float number array.**

***Program:***

```
#include<math.h>
#include<iostream.h>
#include<conio.h>
float data[5]; // data to average and total
float total;  // the total of the data items
float average; // average of the items
void main()
{
data[0] = 34.0;
data[1] = 27.0;
data[2] = 46.5;
data[3] = 82.0;
data[4] = 22.0;
total = data[0] + data[1] + data[2] + data[3] +
data[4];
average = total / 5.0;
cout << "Total " << total << " Average " <<
average << '\n';
getch();
}
```

**OUTPUT:**

Total 211.5 Average 42.3

**Problem 33. Write a C++ program to read float point numbers from keyboard and save them to a float array.**

***Program:***

```
#include<iostream.h>
#include<conio.h>
void main()
{
float temp[5];
cout << "float number \n";
cin >> temp[0];
cout << "float number \n";
cin >> temp[1];
cout << "float number \n";
cin >> temp[2];
cout << "float number \n";
cin >> temp[3];
cout << "float number \n";
cin >> temp[4];
cout << temp[0] << ", " << temp[1] << ", "<<
temp[2] <<     ", "<< temp[3] << ", ";
cout << temp[4] << endl;
getch();
}
```

**OUTPUT:**

```
float number
123.123
float number
..123.123
float number
float number
123.123.
float number
123.123, 0.123, 0.123, 123.123, 7.93782e+033
```

**Problem 34. Write a C++ program to define function whose parameter and return value are both float.**

***Program:***

```
#include<iostream.h>
#include<conio.h>
float cube_number(float num);
void main()
{
float number;
float number3;
cout << "Please enter a number \n";
cin >> number;
number3 = cube_number(number);
cout << number << " cubed is " << number3;
return 1;
}
float cube_number(float num)
{
float answer;
answer = num * num * num;
return answer;
}
```

**OUTPUT:**

```
Please enter a number
123
123 cubed is 1.86087e+006"
```

## FLOAT READ:

**Problem 35. Write a C++ program to read float number from console.**

***Program:***

```
#include<iostream.h>
#include<conio.h>
float Convert(float);
void main()
{
float TempFer;
float TempCel;
cout << "Please enter the temperature in
Fahrenheit: ";
cin >> TempFer;
TempCel = Convert(TempFer);
cout << "\nHere's the temperature in Celsius: ";
cout << TempCel << endl;
getch();
}
float Convert(float TempFer)
{
float TempCel;
TempCel = ((TempFer - 32) * 5) / 9;
return TempCel;
}
```

**OUTPUT:**

```
Please enter the temperature in Fahrenheit: 12
Here's the temperature in Celsius: -11.1111
```

## LONG:

**Problem 36. Write a C++ program for pointer to long value.**

***Program:***

```
#include<iostream.h>
```

```
#include<conio.h>
void main()
{
long number = 50L;
long* pnumber;
pnumber = &number;
cout << endl
    << "The value stored in the variable number is "
    << *pnumber<< endl;
getch();
}
```

**OUTPUT:**

The value stored in the variable number is 50

**Problem 37. Write a C++ program using long as function parameter and return type.**

***Program:***

```
#include<iostream.h>
#include<conio.h>
long Exp(long x,long n);
void main()
{
long  a,b,c;
cout << "Enter 2 integers:";
cin >> a >> b ;
c = Exp(a,b);
cout << "\nResult is:" << c << endl;
getch();
}
long Exp(long x,long n)
{
long res=1;
for (int i=1;i<=n;i++)
res = res*x;
return res;
}
```

**OUTPUT:**

Enter 2 integers:1 2
Result is:1

**Problem 38 . Write a C++ program to cast int to long.**

***Program:***

```
#include<iostream.h>
#include<conio.h>
void main()
{
int n = 123;
for(int i=n;i<=n+9;i++)
{
cout<<i;
cout<<" "<<long(i)*i<<" "<<long(i)*i*i;
cout<<endl;
}
getch();
}
```

**OUTPUT:**

```
123 15129 1860867
124 15376 1906624
125 15625 1953125
126 15876 2000376
127 16129 2048383
128 16384 2097152
129 16641 2146689
130 16900 2197000
131 17161 2248091
132 17424 2299968
```

**Problem 39. Write a C++ program for OUTPUT pointer value using cout.**

***Program:***

```
#include<iostream.h>
#include<conio.h>
void main()
{
long* pnumber;
long number1 = 55L;
long number2 = 99L;
pnumber = &number1;
*pnumber += 11;
cout << endl<< "number1 = "   << number1
<< "   &number1 = " << pnumber<< endl;
pnumber = &number2;
number1 = *pnumber * 10;
cout << "number1 = "     << number1
<< "   pnumber = "  << pnumber
<< "   *pnumber = " << *pnumber<< endl;
getch();
}
```

**OUTPUT:**

number1 = 66   &number1 = 0x22ff70
number1 = 990  pnumber = 0x22ff6c  *pnumber = 99

## BINARY BIT:

**Problem 40. Write a C++ program to printing an unsigned integer in bits.**

***Program:***

```
#include<iostream.h>
#include<conio.h>
#include <iomanip.h>
```

```
void main()
{
unsigned value = 123;
const int SHIFT = 8 * sizeof( unsigned ) - 1;
const unsigned MASK = 1 << SHIFT;
for ( int i = 1; i <= SHIFT + 1; i++ )
{
cout << ( value & MASK ? '1' : '0' );
value <<= 1;
if ( i  8 == 0 )
cout << ' ';
}
cout << endl;
getch();
}
```

**OUTPUT:**

00000000 00000000 00000000 01111011

**Problem 41. Write a C++ program to display the bits within a byte.**

***Program:***

```
#include<iostream.h>
#include<conio.h>
void show_binary(unsigned int u);
void main()
{
show_binary(89);
getch();
}
void show_binary(unsigned int u)
{
int t;
for(t=128; t>0; t = t/2)
if(u & t) cout << "1 ";
else cout << "0 ";
cout << "\n";
}
```

**OUTPUT:**

0 1 0 1 1 0 0 1

**Problem 42. Write a C++ program for Bitwise operators: Complement, AND, OR.**

***Program:***

```
#include<iomanip.h>
#include<iostream.h>
#include<conio.h>
void main()
{
unsigned long red = 0XFF0000UL;     // Color red
unsigned long white = 0XFFFFFFUL;    // Color
white - RGB all maximum
cout << hex;                    // Set hexadecimal
OUTPUT format
cout << setfill('0');              // Set fill character for
OUTPUT
cout << "\nTry out bitwise AND and OR
operators.";
cout << "\nInitial value  red         = " << setw(8) <<
red;
cout << "\nComplement    ~red        = " <<
setw(8) << ~red;
cout << "\nInitial value  white       = " << setw(8)
<< white;
cout << "\nComplement    ~white      = " <<
setw(8) << ~white;
cout << "\n Bitwise AND   red & white = " <<
setw(8) << (red & white);
cout << "\n Bitwise OR    red | white = " <<
setw(8) << (red | white);
getch();
}
```

**OUTPUT:**

```
Try out bitwise AND and OR operators.
Initial value  red        = 00ff0000
Complement    ~red        = ff00ffff
Initial value  white      = 00ffffff
Complement    ~white      = ff000000
Bitwise AND   red & white = 00ff0000
Bitwise OR    red | white = 00ffffff
```

**Problem 43. Write a C++ program for Bitwise operator: ^.**

***Program:***

```
#include<iomanip.h>
#include<iostream.h>
#include<conio.h>
void main()
{
unsigned long red = 0XFF0000UL;     // Color red
unsigned long white = 0XFFFFFFUL;    // Color
white - RGB all maximum
cout << hex;                    // Set hexadecimal
OUTPUT format
cout << setfill('0');              // Set fill character for
OUTPUT
unsigned long mask = red ^ white;
cout << "\n       mask = red  white = " << setw(8)
<< mask;
cout << "\n              mask  red = " << setw(8) <<
(mask ^ red);
cout << "\n            mask  white = " << setw(8) <<
(mask ^ white);
```

```
getch();
}
```

**OUTPUT:**

```
mask = red ^ white = 0000ffff
mask ^ red = 00ffffff
mask ^ white = 00ff0000
```

**Problem 44. Write a C++ program using masks to select or set a particular flag bit.**

***Program:***

```
#include <iomanip.h>
#include <iostream.h>
#include<conio.h>
void main()
{
unsigned long flags = 0xFF;          // Flags variable
unsigned long bit1mask = 0x1;        // Selects bit 1
unsigned long bit6mask = 0x20;       // Selects bit 6
unsigned long bit20mask = 0x80000;   // Selects bit
20
cout << "\nSelect bit 1 from flags    : " << setw(8)
<< (flags & bit1mask);
cout << "\nSelect bit 6 from flags    : " << setw(8)
<< (flags & bit6mask);
cout << "\nSwitch off bit 6 in flags  : " << setw(8)
<< (flags &= ~bit6mask);
cout << "\nSwitch on bit 20 in flags  : " << setw(8)
<< (flags |= bit20mask);
cout << endl;
getch();
}
```

**OUTPUT:**

```
Select bit 1 from flags    :       1
Select bit 6 from flags    :      32
Switch off bit 6 in flags  :     223
Switch on bit 20 in flags  :  524511
```

## SHIFT:

**Problem 45. Write a C++ program for Shift left.**

***Program:***

```
#include <iostream.h>
#include<conio.h>
void show_binary(unsigned int u);
void  main()
{
int i=1, t;
for(t=0; t < 8; t++)
{
show_binary(i);
i = i << 1 ;
}
getch;
}
// Display the bits within a byte.
void show_binary(unsigned int u)
{
int t;
for(t=128; t>0; t=t/2)
if(u & t) cout << "1 ";
else cout << "0 ";
cout << "\n";
}
```

**OUTPUT:**

```
0 0 0 0 0 0 0 1
0 0 0 0 0 0 1 0
0 0 0 0 0 1 0 0
0 0 0 0 1 0 0 0
0 0 0 1 0 0 0 0
0 0 1 0 0 0 0 0
0 1 0 0 0 0 0 0
1 0 0 0 0 0 0 0
```

**Problem 46. Write a C++ program for Shift right.**

***Program:***

```
#include <iostream.h>
#include<conio.h>
void show_binary(unsigned int u);
void  main()
{
int i=1, t;
for(t=0; t < 8; t++)
{
i = i >> 1;
show_binary(i);
}
getch();
}
// Display the bits within a byte.
void show_binary(unsigned int u)
{
int t;
for(t=128; t>0; t=t/2)
if(u & t) cout << "1 ";
else cout << "0 ";
cout << "\n";
}
```

**OUTPUT:**

```
0 0 0 0 0 0 0 0
0 0 0 0 0 0 0 0
0 0 0 0 0 0 0 0
```

```
0 0 0 0 0 0 0 0
0 0 0 0 0 0 0 0
0 0 0 0 0 0 0 0
0 0 0 0 0 0 0 0
0 0 0 0 0 0 0 0
```

**Problem 47. Write a C++ program for left rotate functions for byte values.**

***Program:***

```
#include <iostream.h>
#include<conio.h>
unsigned char lrotate(unsigned char val, int n);
void show_binary(unsigned int u);
void main()
{
char ch = 'A';
cout << "Original value in binary:\n";
show_binary(ch);
cout << "Rotating left 8 times:\n";
for(int i=0; i < 8; i++)
{
ch = lrotate(ch, 1);
show_binary(ch);
}
getch();
}
unsigned char lrotate(unsigned char val, int n)
{
unsigned int t;
t = val;
for(int i=0; i < n; i++) {
t = t << 1;
/* If a bit shifts out, it will be in bit 8
    of the integer t. If this is the case,
    put that bit on the right side. */
if(t & 256)
t = t | 1; // put a 1 on the right end
}
 return t; // return the lower 8 bits.
}
// Display the bits within a byte.
void show_binary(unsigned int u)
{
int t;
for(t=128; t>0; t = t/2)
if(u & t) cout << "1 ";
else cout << "0 ";
cout << "\n";
}
```

**OUTPUT:**

```
Original value in binary:
0 1 0 0 0 0 0 1
Rotating left 8 times:
1 0 0 0 0 0 1 0
0 0 0 0 0 1 0 1
0 0 0 0 1 0 1 0
0 0 0 1 0 1 0 0
0 0 1 0 1 0 0 0
0 1 0 1 0 0 0 0
1 0 1 0 0 0 0 0
0 1 0 0 0 0 0 1
```

**Problem 48. Write a C++ program to right rotate functions for byte values.**

***Program:***

```
#include <iostream.h>
#include<conio.h>
unsigned char rrotate(unsigned char val, int n);
void show_binary(unsigned int u);
void main()
{
char ch = 'T';
cout << "Original value in binary:\n";
show_binary(ch);
cout << "Rotating right 8 times:\n";
for(int i=0; i < 8; i++)
{
ch = rrotate(ch, 1);
show_binary(ch);
}
getch();
}
// Right-rotate a byte n places.
unsigned char rrotate(unsigned char val, int n)
{
unsigned int t;
t = val;
// First, move the value 8 bits higher.
t = t << 8;
for(int i=0; i < n; i++)
{
t = t >> 1;
/* If a bit shifts out, it will be in bit 7
    of the integer t. If this is the case,
    put that bit on the left side. */
if(t & 128)
t = t | 32768; // put a 1 on left end
}
/* Finally, move the result back to the
    lower 8 bits of t. */
t = t >> 8;
return t;
```

```
}
// Display the bits within a byte.
void show_binary(unsigned int u)
{
int t;
for(t=128; t>0; t = t/2)
if(u & t)
cout << "1 ";
else
cout << "0 ";
cout << "\n";
}
```

**OUTPUT:**

Original value in binary:
0 1 0 1 0 1 0 0
Rotating right 8 times:
0 0 1 0 1 0 1 0
0 0 0 1 0 1 0 1
1 0 0 0 1 0 1 0
0 1 0 0 0 1 0 1
1 0 1 0 0 0 1 0
0 1 0 1 0 0 0 1
1 0 1 0 1 0 0 0
0 1 0 1 0 1 0 0

**Problem 49. Write a C++ program to demonstrate bitwise left shift.**

***Program:***

```
#include <iostream.h>
#include<conio.h>
#include <iomanip.h>
void displayBits( unsigned ); // prototype
void main()
{
unsigned number1 = 960;
cout << "The result of left shifting\n";
displayBits( number1 );
cout << "8 bit positions using the left-shift operator
is\n";
displayBits( number1 << 8 );
getch();
}
void displayBits( unsigned value )
{
const int SHIFT = 8 * sizeof( unsigned ) - 1;
const unsigned MASK = 1 << SHIFT;
cout << setw( 10 ) << value << " = ";
for ( unsigned i = 1; i <= SHIFT + 1; i++ )
{
cout << ( value & MASK ? '1' : '0' );
value <<= 1;
if ( i - 8 == 0 )
cout << ' ';
}
cout << endl;
}
```

**OUTPUT:**

The result of left shifting
960 = 00000000 00000000 00000011 11000000
8 bit positions using the left-shift operator is
245760 = 00000000 00000011 11000000 00000000

**Problem 50. Write a C++ program to demonstrate bitwise right shift.**

***Program:***

```
#include <iostream.h>
#include<conio.h>
#include <iomanip.h>
void displayBits( unsigned ); // prototype
void main()
{
unsigned number1 = 960;
cout << "\nThe result of right shifting\n";
displayBits( number1 );
cout << "8 bit positions using the right-shift
operator is\n";
displayBits( number1 >> 8 );
getch();
}
void displayBits( unsigned value )
{
const int SHIFT = 8 * sizeof( unsigned ) - 1;
const unsigned MASK = 1 << SHIFT;
cout << setw( 10 ) << value << " = ";
for ( unsigned i = 1; i <= SHIFT + 1; i++ )
{
cout << ( value & MASK ? '1' : '0' );
value <<= 1;
if ( i - 8 == 0 )
cout << ' ';
}
cout << endl;
}
```

**OUTPUT:**

The result of right shifting
960 = 00000000 00000000 00000011 11000000
8 bit positions using the right-shift operator is
3 = 00000000 00000000 00000000 00000011

## HEXADECIMAL:

**Problem 51. Write a C++ program to show the base in hexadecimal.**

***Program:***

```
#include <iomanip.h>
#include <string.h>
#include <sstream.h>
#include <iostream.h>
#include<conio.h>
void main( )
{
stringstream ss;
ss << showbase << hex << 16; // Show the base in
hexadecimal
cout << ss.str( ) << endl;
getch();
}
```

**OUTPUT:**

0x10

**Problem 52. Write a C++ program to convert hex number to integer.**

***Program:***

```
#include <iostream.h>
#include<conio.h>
#include <string.h>
#include <stdlib.h>
long hex2int(const string& hexStr);
void main( )
{
string str1 = "0x12AB";
cout << hex2int(str1) << endl;
string str2 = "12AB";
cout << hex2int(str2) << endl;
}
long hex2int(const string& hexStr)
{
char *offset;
if (hexStr.length( ) > 2)
{
if (hexStr[0] == '0' && hexStr[1] == 'x')
{
return strtol(hexStr.c_str( ), &offset, 0);
}
else
{
cout << "hex must start with 0x";
getch();
}}}
```

**OUTPUT:**

4779
hex must start with 0x0

## UNSIGNED INT:

**Problem 53. Write a C++ program to analyze difference between signed and unsigned integers.**

***Program:***

```
#include <iostream.h>
#include<conio.h>
void main()
{
short int i;          // a signed short integer
short unsigned int j; // an unsigned short integer
j = 60000;
i = j;
cout << i << " " << j;
getch();
}
```

**OUTPUT;**

-5536 60000

## UNSIGNED LONG:

**Problem 54. Write a C++ program for unsigned long.**

***Program:***

```
#include <iostream.h>
#include<conio.h>
void main()
{
int n = 123;
unsigned long factor=1;
for(int i=n;i>1;i--)
factor=factor*i;
cout<<n<<"!="<<factor<<endl;
getch();
}
```

**OUTPUT:**

123!=0

## UNSIGNED SHORT:

**Problem 55. Write a C++ program to create an unsigned short and initialize with result of multiplying two unsigned short variables.**

***Program:***

```
#include <iostream.h>
#include<conio.h>
```

```
void main()
{
unsigned short int Width = 5, Length;
Length = 10;
unsigned short int Area = Width * Length;
cout << "Width: " << Width << "\n";
cout << "Length: " << Length <<endl;
cout << "Area: " << Area << endl;
getch();
}
```

**OUTPUT:**

```
Width: 5
Length: 10
Area: 50
```

**Problem 56. Write a C++ program for unsigned short int: overflow.**

***Program:***

```
#include <iostream.h>
#include<conio.h>
void main()
{
unsigned short int smallNumber;
smallNumber = 65535;
cout << "small number:" << smallNumber << endl;
smallNumber++;
cout << "small number:" << smallNumber << endl;
smallNumber++;
cout << "small number:" << smallNumber <<endl;
short int smallNumber1;
smallNumber1 = 32767;
cout << "small number:" << smallNumber1 << endl;
smallNumber1++;
cout << "small number:" << smallNumber1 <<endl;
smallNumber1++;
cout << "small number:" << smallNumber1 << endl;
getch();
}
```

**OUTPUT:**

```
small number:65535
small number:0
small number:1
small number:32767
small number:-32768
small number:-32767
```

## CHAR:

**Problem 57. Write a C++ program for char and unsigned char.**

***Program:***

```
#include <iostream.h>
#include<conio.h>
void main()
{
int n1 = 100,n2;
short int s1 = 2,s2;
char c1 = 'A',c2;
unsigned char u1 = 'U',u2;
n2 = s1;
s2 = n1 + c1;
c2 = u1;
u2 = n1;
cout << n1 << " " << n2 ;
cout << s1 << " " << s2 ;
cout << c1 << " " << c2 ;
cout << (int)c1 << " " << int(c2);
cout << u1 << " " ;
cout << (int)u1 << " " << (int)u2;
getch();
}
```

**OUTPUT:**

```
100 22 165A U65 85U 85 100"
```

**Problem 58. Write a C++ program to write Charset To File.**

***Program:***

```
#include <iostream.h>
#include<conio.h>
#include <string.h>
#include <fstream.h>
#include <iomanip.h>
#include <stdlib.h>
// forward declarations
void writeCharsetToFile (const string& filename);
void OUTPUTFile (const string& filename);
void main ()
{
writeCharsetToFile("charset.out");
OUTPUTFile("charset.out");
}
void writeCharsetToFile (const string& filename)
{
// open OUTPUT file
ofstream file(filename.c_str());
// file opened?
if (! file)
{
// NO, abort program
cerr << "can't open OUTPUT file \"" << filename
<< "\""
<< endl;
```

```
exit(EXIT_FAILURE);
}
// write character set
for (int i=32; i<256; i++)
{
file << "value: " << setw(3) << i << "  "
<< "char:  " << static_cast<char>(i) << endl;
}
}  // closes file automatically
void OUTPUTFile (const string& filename)
{
// open input file
ifstream file(filename.c_str());
// file opened?
if (! file)
{
// NO, abort program
cerr << "can't open input file \"" << filename << "\""
<< endl;
exit(EXIT_FAILURE);
}
// copy file contents to cout
char c;
while (file.get(c))
{
cout.put(c);
}
}  // closes file automatically
```

**OUTPUT:**

```
value:  32   char:
value:  33   char:  !
value:  34   char:  "
value:  35   char:  #
value:  36   char:  $
value:  37   char:  %
value:  38   char:  &
value:  39   char:  '
value:  40   char:  (
value:  41   char:  )
value:  42   char:  *
value:  43   char:  +
value:  44   char:  ,
value:  45   char:  -
value:  46   char:  .
value:  47   char:  /
value:  48   char:  0
value:  49   char:  1
value:  50   char:  2
value:  51   char:  3
value:  52   char:  4
value:  53   char:  5
value:  54   char:  6
value:  55   char:  7
value:  56   char:  8
value:  57   char:  9
value:  58   char:  :
value:  59   char:  ;
value:  60   char:  <
value:  61   char:  =
value:  62   char:  >
value:  63   char:  ?
value:  64   char:  @
value:  65   char:  A
value:  66   char:  B
value:  67   char:  C
value:  68   char:  D
value:  69   char:  E
value:  70   char:  F
value:  71   char:  G
value:  72   char:  H
value:  73   char:  I
value:  74   char:  J
value:  75   char:  K
value:  76   char:  L
value:  77   char:  M
value:  78   char:  N
value:  79   char:  O
value:  80   char:  P
value:  81   char:  Q
value:  82   char:  R
value:  83   char:  S
value:  84   char:  T
value:  85   char:  U
value:  86   char:  V
value:  87   char:  W
value:  88   char:  X
value:  89   char:  Y
value:  90   char:  Z
value:  91   char:  [
value:  92   char:  \
value:  93   char:  ]
value:  94   char:  ^
value:  95   char:  _
value:  96   char:  `
value:  97   char:  a
value:  98   char:  b
value:  99   char:  c
value: 100   char:  d
value: 101   char:  e
value: 102   char:  f
value: 103   char:  g
value: 104   char:  h
```

value: 105 char: i
value: 106 char: j
value: 107 char: k
value: 108 char: l
value: 109 char: m
value: 110 char: n
value: 111 char: o
value: 112 char: p
value: 113 char: q
value: 114 char: r
value: 115 char: s
value: 116 char: t
value: 117 char: u
value: 118 char: v
value: 119 char: w
value: 120 char: x
value: 121 char: y
value: 122 char: z
value: 123 char: {
value: 124 char: |
value: 125 char: }
value: 126 char: ~
........................
........................
value: 255 char: ?

**Problem 59. Write a C++ program Using a nested if with char type.**

***Program:***

```
#include <iostream.h>
#include<conio.h>
void main()
{
char letter = 'S';
if(letter >= 'A')
{
if(letter <= 'Z')
{
cout << "You entered an uppercase letter."
<< endl;
return0;
}
}
if(letter >= 'a')
if(letter <= 'z')
{
cout << "You entered a lowercase letter."
<< endl ;
return 0;
}
getch();
}
```

**OUTPUT:**

You entered an uppercase letter.

## CHAR ARRAY:

**Problem 60. Write a C++ program for char array buffers.**

***Program:***

```
#include <iostream.h>
#include<conio.h>
void main()
{
char buffer[80];
cout << "Enter the string: ";
cin >> buffer;
cout << "Here's the buffer:  " << buffer <<
std::endl;
getch();
}
```

**OUTPUT:**

Enter the string: string
Here's the buffer: string

**Problem 61. Write a C++ program treating character arrays as strings.**

***Program:***

```
#include <iostream.h>
#include<conio.h>
void main()
{
char string1[ 20 ];
char string2[] = "string literal";
cout << "Enter the string: ";
cin >> string1;
cout << "string1 is: " << string1 << "\nstring2 is: "
<< string2;
for ( int i = 0; string1[ i ] != '\0'; i++ )
cout << string1[ i ] << ' ';
cin >> string1;
cout << "\nstring1 is: " << string1 << endl;
getch();
}
```

**OUTPUT:**

Enter the string: string
string1 is: string
string2 is: string literals t r i n g
string
string1 is: string

**Problem 62. Write a C++ program using cin.get() to read a string based on char array.**

***Program:***

```
#include <iostream.h>
#include<conio.h>
void main()
{
char buffer[80];
cout << "Enter the string: ";
cin.get(buffer, 79);      // get up to 79 or newline
cout << "Here's the buffer:  " << buffer << std::endl;
getch();
}
```

**OUTPUT:**

```
Enter the string: string
Here's the buffer:  string
```

**Problem 63. Write a C++ program to reverse case using array indexing.**

***Program:***

```
#include <iostream.h>
#include<conio.h>
#include <ctype.h>
void main()
{
int i;
char str[80] = "This Is A Test";
cout << "Original string: " << str << "\n";
for(i = 0; str[i]; i++)
{
if(isupper(str[i]))
str[i] = tolower(str[i]);
else if(islower(str[i]))
str[i] = toupper(str[i]);
}
cout << "Inverted-case string: " << str;
getch();
}
```

**OUTPUT:**

```
Original string: This Is A Test
Inverted-case string: tHIS iS a tEST
```

**Problem 64. Write a C++ program to reverse a string in place.**

***Program:***

```
#include <iostream.h>
#include<conio.h>
#include <string.h>
void main()
{
str[] = "this is a test";
char *start, *end;
int len;
char t;
cout << "Original: " << str << "\n";
len = strlen(str);
start = str;
end = &str[len-1];
while(start < end)
{
// swap chars
t = *start;
*start = *end;
*end = t;
// advance pointers
start++;
end--;
}
cout << "Reversed: " << str << "\n";
getch();
}
```

**OUTPUT:**

```
Original: this is a test
Reversed: tset a si siht
```

**Problem 65. Write a C++ program to copying a string using array notation.**

***Program:***

```
#include <iostream.h>
#include<conio.h>
void copy1( char *, const char * );
void main()
{
char string1[ 10 ];
char *string2 = "Hello";
copy1( string1, string2 );
cout << "string1 = " << string1 << endl;
getch();
}
void copy1( char * s1, const char * s2 )
{
for ( int i = 0; ( s1[ i ] = s2[ i ] ) != '\0'; i++ );
}
```

**OUTPUT:**

```
string1 = Hello
```

**Problem 66. Write a C++ program to copying a string using pointer notation.**

***Program:***

```
#include <iostream.h>
#include<conio.h>
void copy( char *, const char * );
```

```
void main()
{
char string1[ 10 ];
char string2[] = "Good Bye";
copy( string1, string2 );
cout << "string1 = " << string2 << endl;
getch();
}
void copy( char *s1, const char *s2 )
{
for ( ; ( *s1 = *s2 ) != '\0'; s1++, s2++ );
}
```

**OUTPUT:**

string1 = Good Bye

**Problem 67. Write a C++ program to initializing char pointers with strings.**

***Program:***

```
#include <iostream.h>
#include<conio.h>
void main()
{
const char* pstar1 = "AAA";
const char* pstar2 = "BBBB";
const char* pstar3 = "CCCCC";
const char* pstar4 = "DDDDDD";
const char* pstar5 = "EEEEEEE";
const char* pstar6 = "FFFFFFFF";
const char* pstr  = "GGGGGGGGG";
cout << pstar1;
cout << pstar2;
cout << pstar3;
cout << pstar4;
cout << pstar5;
cout << pstar6;
getch();
}
```

**OUTPUT:**

AAABBBBCCCCCDDDDDDEEEEEEEFFFFFFFF

**Problem 68. Write a C++ program using an array of pointers to char.**

***Program:***

```
#include <iostream.h>
#include<conio.h>
void main()
{
const char* pstars[] =
{"A","BB","CCC","DDDD","EEEEE","FFFFFF"};
cout << pstars[2];
cout << endl;
getch();
}
```

**OUTPUT:**

CCC

## CHAR POINTER:

**Problem 69. Write a C++ program to reverse string case using pointer arithmetic.**

***Program:***

```
#include <iostream.h>
#include<conio.h>
#include <ctype.h>
void main()
{
char *p;
char str[80] = "This Is A Test";
cout << "Original string: " << str << "\n";
p = str; // assign p the address of the start of the
array
while(*p)
{
if(isupper(*p))
*p = tolower(*p);
else if(islower(*p))
*p = toupper(*p);
p++;
}
cout << "Inverted-case string: " << str;
getch();
}
```

**OUTPUT:**

Original string: This Is A Test
Inverted-case string: tHIS iS a tEST

**Problem 70. Write a C++ program for printing the address stored in a char * variable.**

***Program:***

```
#include <iostream.h>
#include<conio.h>
void main()
{
char *word = "again";
cout << "Value of word is: " << word << endl
<< "Value of static_cast< void * >( word ) is: "
<< static_cast< void * >( word ) << endl;
getch();
}
```

**OUTPUT:**

Value of word is: again

Value of static_cast< void * >( word ) is: 0x43e000

**Problem 71. Write a C++ program to display value of char *, then display value of char static_cast to void *.**

***Program:***

```
#include <iostream.h>
#include<conio.h>
void main()
{
char *word = "again";
cout << "Value of word is: " << word << endl
     << "Value of static_cast< void * >( word ) is: "
     << static_cast< void * >( word ) << endl;
getch();
}
```

**OUTPUT:**

Value of word is: again
Value of static_cast< void * >( word ) is: 0x43e000

**Problem 72. Write a C++ program to converting lowercase letters to uppercase letters using a pointer.**

***Program:***

```
#include <iostream.h>
#include<conio.h>
#include <ctype.h>
void f( char * );
void main()
{
char phrase[] = "characters";
f( phrase );
cout << phrase << endl;
getch();
}
void f( char *sPtr )
{
while ( *sPtr != '\0' )
{
*sPtr = toupper( *sPtr );
sPtr++;
}}
```

## CHARACTERS:

**Problem 73. Write a C++ program for printing a string one character at a time using a pointer.**

***Program:***

```
#include <iostream.h>
#include<conio.h>
void f( const char * );
void main()
{
const char phrase[] = "a string";
f( phrase );
getch();
}
void f( const char *sPtr )
{
for ( ; *sPtr != '\0'; sPtr++ )
cout << *sPtr;
}
```

**OUTPUT:**

a string

## CHAR FUNCTIONS:

**Problem 74. Write a C++ program using functions isdigit().**

***Program:***

```
#include <iostream.h>
#include<conio.h>
#include <ctype.h>
void main()
{
cout << "According to isdigit:\n"
<< ( isdigit( '8' ) ? "8 is a" : "8 is not a" ) << "
digit\n"
<< ( isdigit( '#' ) ? "# is a" : "# is not a" ) << "
digit\n";
getch();
}
```

**OUTPUT:**

According to isdigit:
8 is a digit
# is not a digit

**Problem 75. Write a C++ program using functions isalpha().**

***Program:***

```
#include <iostream.h>
#include<conio.h>
#include <ctype.h>
void main()
{
cout << "\nAccording to isalpha:\n"
<< ( isalpha( 'A' ) ? "A is a" : "A is not a" ) << "
letter\n"
<< ( isalpha( 'b' ) ? "b is a" : "b is not a" ) << "
letter\n"
```

```
<< ( isalpha( '&' ) ? "& is a" : "& is not a" ) << "
letter\n"
<< ( isalpha( '4' ) ? "4 is a" : "4 is not a" ) << "
letter\n";
getch();
}
```

**OUTPUT:**

According to isalpha:
A is a letter
b is a letter
& is not a letter
4 is not a letter

**Problem 76. Write a C++ program using functions isalnum().**

***Program:***

```
#include <iostream.h>
#include<conio.h>
#include <ctype.h>
void main()
{
cout << "\nAccording to isalnum:\n"
<< ( isalnum( 'A' ) ? "A is a" : "A is not a" )
<< " digit or a letter\n"
<< ( isalnum( '8' ) ? "8 is a" : "8 is not a" )
<< " digit or a letter\n"
<< ( isalnum( '#' ) ? "# is a" : "# is not a" )
<< " digit or a letter\n";
getch();
}
```

**OUTPUT:**

According to isalnum:
A is a digit or a letter
8 is a digit or a letter
# is not a digit or a letter

**Problem 77. Write a C++ program using functions isxdigit().**

***Program:***

```
#include <iostream.h>
#include<conio.h>
#include <ctype.h>
void main()
{
cout << "\nAccording to isxdigit:\n"
<< ( isxdigit( 'F' ) ? "F is a" : "F is not a" )
<< " hexadecimal digit\n"
<< ( isxdigit( 'J' ) ? "J is a" : "J is not a" )
<< " hexadecimal digit\n"
<< ( isxdigit( '7' ) ? "7 is a" : "7 is not a" )
<< " hexadecimal digit\n"
<< ( isxdigit( '$' ) ? "$ is a" : "$ is not a" )
<< " hexadecimal digit\n"
<< ( isxdigit( 'f' ) ? "f is a" : "f is not a" )
<< " hexadecimal digit" << endl;
getch();
}
```

**OUTPUT:**

According to isxdigit:
F is a hexadecimal digit
J is not a hexadecimal digit
7 is a hexadecimal digit
$ is not a hexadecimal digit
f is a hexadecimal digit

**Problem 78. Write a C++ program using function islower().**

***Program:***

```
#include <iostream.h>
#include<conio.h>
#include <ctype.h>
void main()
{
cout << "According to islower:\n"
<< ( islower( 'p' ) ? "p is a" : "p is not a" )
<< " lowercase letter\n"
<< ( islower( 'P' ) ? "P is a" : "P is not a" )
<< " lowercase letter\n"
<< ( islower( '5' ) ? "5 is a" : "5 is not a" )
<< " lowercase letter\n"
<< ( islower( '!' ) ? "! is a" : "! is not a" )
<< " lowercase letter\n";
getch();
}
```

**OUTPUT:**

According to islower:
p is a lowercase letter
P is not a lowercase letter
5 is not a lowercase letter
! is not a lowercase letter

**Problem 79. Write a C++ program using function isupper().**

***Program:***

```
#include <iostream.h>
#include<conio.h>
#include <ctype.h>
void main()
{
cout << "\nAccording to isupper:\n"
<< ( isupper( 'D' ) ? "D is an" : "D is not an" )
<< " uppercase letter\n"
```

```
<< ( isupper( 'd' ) ? "d is an" : "d is not an" )
<< " uppercase letter\n"
<< ( isupper( '8' ) ? "8 is an" : "8 is not an" )
<< " uppercase letter\n"
<< ( isupper('$') ? "$ is an" : "$ is not an" )
<< " uppercase letter\n";
getch();
}
```

**OUTPUT:**

According to isupper:
D is an uppercase letter
d is not an uppercase letter
8 is not an uppercase letter
$ is not an uppercase letter

**Problem 80. Write a C++ program both for toupper() and tolower().**

***Program:***

```
#include <iostream.h>
#include<conio.h>
#include <ctype.h>
void  main()
{
cout << "\nu converted to uppercase is "
<< static_cast< char >( toupper( 'u' ) )
<< "\n7 converted to uppercase is "
<< static_cast< char >( toupper( '7' ) )
<< "\n$ converted to uppercase is "
<< static_cast< char >( toupper( '$' ) )
<< "\nL converted to lowercase is "
<< static_cast< char >( tolower( 'L' ) ) << endl;
getch();
}
```

**OUTPUT:**

u converted to uppercase is U
7 converted to uppercase is 7
$ converted to uppercase is $
L converted to lowercase is l

**Problem 81. Write a C++ program using function isspace().**

***Program:***

```
#include <iostream.h>
#include<conio.h>
#include <ctype.h>
void  main()
{
cout << "According to isspace:\nNewline "
<< ( isspace( '\n' ) ? "is a" : "is not a" )
<< " whitespace character\nHorizontal tab "
<< ( isspace( '\t' ) ? "is a" : "is not a" )
<< " whitespace character\n"
<< ( isspace( ' is a" : " is not a" )
<< " whitespace character\n";
getch();
}
```

**OUTPUT:**

According to isspace:
Newline is a whitespace character
Horizontal tab is a whitespace character
% is not a whitespace character

**Problem 82. Write a C++ program using function iscntrl().**

***Program:***

```
#include <iostream.h>
#include<conio.h>
#include <ctype.h>
void main()
{
cout << "\nAccording to iscntrl:\nNewline "
<< ( iscntrl( '\n' ) ? "is a" : "is not a" )
<< " control character\n"
<< ( iscntrl( '$' ) ? "$ is a" : "$ is not a" )
<< " control character\n";
getch();
}
```

**OUTPUT:**

According to iscntrl:
Newline is a control character
$ is not a control character

**Problem 83. Write a C++ program using function ispunct().**

***Program:***

```
#include <iostream.h>
#include<conio.h>
#include <ctype.h>
void  main()
{
cout << "\nAccording to ispunct:\n"
<< ( ispunct( ';' ) ? "; is a" : "; is not a" )
<< " punctuation character\n"
<< ( ispunct( 'Y' ) ? "Y is a" : "Y is not a" )
<< " punctuation character\n"
<< ( ispunct('#') ? "# is a" : "# is not a" )
<< " punctuation character\n";
getch();
}
```

**OUTPUT:**

According to ispunct:
; is a punctuation character

Y is not a punctuation character
# is a punctuation character

**Problem 84. Write a C++ program using function isprint().**

***Program:***

```
#include <iostream.h>
#include<conio.h>
#include <ctype.h>
void main()
{
cout << "\nAccording to isprint:\n"
<< ( isprint( '$' ) ? "$ is a" : "$ is not a" )
<< " printing character\nAlert "
<< ( isprint( '\a' ) ? "is a" : "is not a" )
<< " printing character\nSpace "
<< ( isprint( ' ' ) ? "is a" : "is not a" )
<< " printing character\n";
getch();
}
```

**OUTPUT:**

According to isprint:
$ is a printing character
Alert is not a printing character
Space is a printing character

**Problem 85. Write a C++ program using function isgraph().**

***Program:***

```
#include <iostream.h>
#include<conio.h>
#include <ctype.h>
void main()
{
cout << "\nAccording to isgraph:\n"
<< ( isgraph( 'Q' ) ? "Q is a" : "Q is not a" )
<< " printing character other than a space\nSpace "
<< ( isgraph(' ') ? "is a" : "is not a" )
<< " printing character other than a space" << endl;
getch();
}
```

**OUTPUT:**

According to isgraph:
Q is a printing character other than a space
Space is not a printing character other than a space

## STRING CREATE:

**Problem 86. Write a C++ program to create a string base on the start and end of another string.**

***Program:***

```
#include <string.h>
#include <algorithm.h>
#include <iostream.h>
#include<conio.h>
#include <ctype.h>
void main()
{
const string hello("Hello, how are you?");
string s(hello.begin(),hello.end());
// iterate through all of the characters
string::iterator pos;
for (pos = s.begin(); pos != s.end(); ++pos)
{
cout << *pos;
}
cout << endl;
getch();
}
```

**OUTPUT:**

Hello, how are you?

## STRING FUNCTION:

**Problem 87. Write a C++ program using strcpy().**

***Program:***

```
#include <iostream.h>
#include<conio.h>
#include <string.h>
void main()
{
char String1[] = "test";
char String2[80];
strcpy(String2,String1);
cout << "String1: " << String1 << endl;
cout << "String2: " << String2 <<endl;
getch();
}
```

**OUTPUT:**

String1: test
String2: test

**Problem 88. Write a C++ program using strncpy().**

***Program:***

```
#include <iostream.h>
#include<conio.h>
#include <string.h>
void main()
```

```
{
const int MaxLength = 80;
char String1[] = "test";
char String2[MaxLength+1];
strncpy(String2,String1,MaxLength);
String2[strlen(String1)] = '\0'; // add a null to the end
cout << "String1: " << String1 << endl;
cout << "String2: " << String2 << endl;
getch();
}
```

**OUTPUT:**

String1: test
String2: test

**Problem 89. Write a C++ program using strcpy, strlen, strcmp, strcat.**

***Program:***

```
#include <iostream.h>
#include<conio.h>
#include <string.h>
#include <stdio.h>
void main()
{
char s1[80], s2[80];
strcpy(s1, "C++");
strcpy(s2, " is power programming.");
cout << "lengths: " << strlen(s1);
cout << ' ' << strlen(s2) << '\n';
if(!strcmp(s1, s2))
cout << "The strings are equal\n";
else cout << "not equal\n";
strcat(s1, s2);
cout << s1 << '\n';
strcpy(s2, s1);
cout << s1 << " and " << s2 << "\n";
if(!strcmp(s1, s2))
cout << "s1 and s2 are now the same.\n";
getch();
}
```

**OUTPUT:**

lengths: 3 22
not equal
C++ is power programming.
C++ is power programming. and C++ is power programming.
s1 and s2 are now the same.

**Problem 90. Write a C++ program to convert a string to uppercase.**

***Program:***

```
#include <iostream.h>
#include<conio.h>
#include <string.h>
#include <ctype.h>
void main()
{
char str[80];
int i;
strcpy(str, "this is a test");
for(i=0; str[i]; i++) str[i] = toupper(str[i]);
cout << str;
getch();
}
```

**OUTPUT:**

THIS IS A TEST

**Problem 91. Write a C++ program using strcat and strncat.**

***Program:***

```
#include <iostream.h>
#include<conio.h>
#include <string.h>
void main()
{
char s1[ 20 ] = "123456";
char s2[] = "abcdefghi";
char s3[ 40 ] = "";
strcat( s1, s2 );
cout << s1 << "\ns2 = " << s2;
strncat( s3, s1, 6 ); // places '\0' after last character
cout << s1 << "\ns3 = " << s3;
strcat( s3, s1 );
cout << s1 << "\ns3 = " << s3 << endl;
getch();
}
```

**OUTPUT:**

123456abcdefghi
s2 = abcdefghi123456abcdefghi
s3 = 123456123456abcdefghi
s3 = 123456123456abcdefghi

**Problem 92. Write a C++ program using strcmp and strncmp.**

***Program:***

```
#include <iostream.h>
#include<conio.h>
#include <string.h>
#include <iomanip.h>
void main()
{
char *s1 = "abc";
char *s2 = "abC";
```

```
char *s3 = "Abc";
cout << "s1 = " << s1 << "\ns2 = " << s2 << "\ns3 =
" << s3
<< "\n\nstrcmp(s1, s2) = " << strcmp( s1, s2 )
<< "\nstrcmp(s1, s3) = " << strcmp( s1, s3 )
<< "\nstrcmp(s3, s1) = " << strcmp( s3, s1 );
cout << "\n\nstrncmp(s1, s3, 6) = "
<< strncmp( s1, s3, 2 ) << "\nstrncmp(s1, s3, 7) = "
<< strncmp( s1, s3, 2 ) << "\nstrncmp(s3, s1, 7) = "
<< strncmp( s3, s1, 5 ) << endl;
getch();
}
```

**OUTPUT:**

```
s1 = abc
s2 = abC
s3 = Abc
strcmp(s1, s2) = 1
strcmp(s1, s3) = 1
strcmp(s3, s1) = -1
strncmp(s1, s3, 6) = 1
strncmp(s1, s3, 7) = 1
strncmp(s3, s1, 7) = -1
```

**Problem 93. Write a C++ program using strtok.**

***Program:***

```
#include <iostream.h>
#include<conio.h>
#include <string.h>
void main()
{
char sentence[] = "a c d e f g e a c d e y gb ";
char *tokenPtr;
tokenPtr = strtok( sentence, " " );
while ( tokenPtr != NULL )
{
cout << tokenPtr << '\n';
tokenPtr = strtok( NULL, " " );
}
getch();
}
```

**OUTPUT:**

```
a
c
d
e
f
g
e
a
c
d
e
y
gb
```

**Problem 94. Write a C++ program using strlen.**

***Program:***

```
#include <iostream.h>
#include<conio.h>
#include <string.h>
void main()
{
char *string1 = "asdfasdfasdfasdf";
char *string2 = "    f    ";
char *string3 = "       ";
cout << "The length of \"" << string1 << "\" is " <<
strlen( string1 )
<< "\nThe length of \"" << string2 << "\" is " <<
strlen( string2 )
<< "\nThe length of \"" << string3 << "\" is " <<
strlen( string3 )
<< endl;
getch();
}
```

**OUTPUT:**

```
The length of "asdfasdfasdfasdf" is 16
The length of "    f    " is 10
The length of "       " is 7
```

# STRING READ:

**Problem 95. Write a C++ program using cin to read a string from the keyboard.**

***Program:***

```
#include <iostream.h>
#include<conio.h>
#include <string.h>
void main()
{
char str[80];
cout << "Enter a string: ";
cin >> str; // read string from keyboard
cout << "Here is your string: ";
cout << str;
getch();
}
```

**OUTPUT:**

```
Enter a string: Prof. Rachhpal Singh
Here is your string: Prof. Rachhpal Singh
```

**Problem 96. Write a C++ program using gets() to read a string from the keyboard.**

***Program:***

```
#include <iostream.h>
#include<conio.h>
#include <string.h>
#include <stdio.h>
void main()
{
char str[80];
cout << "Enter a string: ";
gets(str); // read a string using gets()
cout << "Here is your string: ";
cout << str;
getch();
}
```

**OUTPUT:**

Enter a string: Ikvinderpal Singh
Here is your string: Ikvinderpal Singh

## COMPLEX NUMBERS:

**Problem 97. Write a C++ program to create complex numbers based on double value.**

***Program:***

```
#include <iostream.h>
#include<conio.h>
#include <string.h>
#include <complex.h>
void main()
{
complex<double> cmpx1(1, 0);
complex<double> cmpx2(1, 1);
cout << cmpx1 << " " << cmpx2 << endl;
getch();
}
```

**OUTPUT:**

(1,0) (1,1)

**Problem 98. Write a C++ program to Plus two complex numbers together.**

***Program:***

```
#include <iostream.h>
#include<conio.h>
#include <complex.h>
void main()
{
complex<double> cmpx1(1, 0);
complex<double> cmpx2(1, 1);
cout << cmpx1 << " " << cmpx2 << endl;
complex<double> cmpx3 = cmpx1 + cmpx2;
cout << cmpx3 << endl;
getch();
}
```

**OUTPUT:**

(1,0) (1,1)
(2,1)

**Problem 99. Write a C++ program for Complex + integer.**

***Program:***

```
#include <iostream.h>
#include<conio.h>
#include <complex.h>
void main()
{
complex<double> cmpx1(1, 0);
complex<double> cmpx2(1, 1);
cout << cmpx1 << " " << cmpx2 << endl;
cmpx1 += 10;
cmpx2 += 10;
cout << cmpx1 << " " << cmpx2 << endl;
getch();
}
```

**OUTPUT:**

(1,0) (1,1)
(11,0) (11,1)

**Problem 100. Write a C++ program using polar to create complex number.**

***Program:***

```
#include <iostream.h>
#include<conio.h>
#include <complex.h>
void main( )
{
double rho = 3.0; // magnitude
double theta = 3.141592 / 2; // angle
complex<double> coord = polar(rho, theta);
cout << "rho = " << abs(coord) << ", theta = " <<
arg(coord) << endl;
coord += polar(4.0, 0.0);
cout << "rho = " << abs(coord) << ", theta = " <<
arg(coord) << endl;
getch();
}
```

**OUTPUT:**

rho = 3, theta = 1.5708
rho = 5, theta = 0.643501

**Problem 101. Write a C++ program Complex number: magnitude, squared magnitude and phase angle.**

***Program:***

```
#include <iostream.h>
#include<conio.h>
#include <complex.h>
void main()
{
/* complex number with real and imaginary parts
* - real part: 4.0
* - imaginary part: 3.0
*/
complex<double> c1(4.0,3.0);
cout << "c1: " << c1 << endl;
/* create complex number from polar coordinates
* - magnitude: 5.0
* - phase angle: 0.75
*/
complex<float> c2(polar(5.0,0.75));
// print complex numbers as polar coordinates
cout << "c1: magnitude: " << abs(c1)
<< " (squared magnitude: " << norm(c1) << ") "
<<    " phase angle: " << arg(c1) << endl;
cout << "c2: magnitude: " << abs(c2)
<< " (squared magnitude: " << norm(c2) << ") "
<<    " phase angle: " << arg(c2) << endl;
getch();
}
```

**OUTPUT:**

```
c1: (4,3)
c1: magnitude: 5 (squared magnitude: 25)  phase
angle: 0.643501
c2: magnitude: 5 (squared magnitude: 25)  phase
angle: 0.75
```

**Problem 102. Write a C++ program complex conjugates.**

***Program:***

```
#include <iostream.h>
#include<conio.h>
#include <complex.h>
void main()
{
/* complex number with real and imaginary parts
* - real part: 4.0
* - imaginary part: 3.0
*/
complex<double> c1(4.0,3.0);
cout << "c1: " << c1 << endl;
/* create complex number from polar coordinates
* - magnitude: 5.0
* - phase angle: 0.75
*/
complex<float> c2(polar(5.0,0.75));
// print complex conjugates
cout << "c1 conjugated:  " << conj(c1) << endl;
cout << "c2 conjugated:  " << conj(c2) << endl;
getch();
}
```

**OUTPUT:**

```
c1: (4,3)
c1 conjugated:  (4,-3)
c2 conjugated:  (3.65844,-3.40819)
```

**Problem 103. Write a C++ program for complex number + float number.**

***Program:***

```
#include <iostream.h>
#include<conio.h>
#include <complex.h>
void main()
{
/* complex number with real and imaginary parts
* - real part: 4.0
* - imaginary part: 3.0
*/
complex<double> c1(4.0,3.0);
cout << "c1: " << c1 << endl;
/* create complex number from polar coordinates
* - magnitude: 5.0
* - phase angle: 0.75
*/
complex<float> c2(polar(5.0,0.75));
// print result of a computation
cout << "4.4 + c1 * 1.8: " << 4.4 + c1 * 1.8 <<
endl;
getch();
}
```

**OUTPUT:**

```
c1: (4,3)
4.4 + c1 * 1.8: (11.6,5.4)
```

**Problem 104. Write a C++ program to print sum of two complex numbers.**

***Program:***

```
#include <iostream.h>
#include<conio.h>
#include <complex.h>
void main()
{
/* complex number with real and imaginary parts
```

```
* - real part: 4.0
* - imaginary part: 3.0
*/
complex<double> c1(4.0,3.0);
cout << "c1: " << c1 << endl;
/* create complex number from polar coordinates
* - magnitude: 5.0
* - phase angle: 0.75
*/
complex<float> c2(polar(5.0,0.75));
/* print sum of c1 and c2:
* - note: different types
*/
cout << "c1 + c2:        "
<< c1 + complex<double>(c2.real(),c2.imag()) <<
endl;
getch();
}
```

**OUTPUT:**

```
c1: (4,3)
c1 + c2:      (7.65844,6.40819)
```

**Problem 105. Write a C++ program to compute an Impedance with Complex Numbers.**

***Program:***

```
#include <iostream.h>
#include<conio.h>
#include <complex.h>
#include <iomanip.h>
#include <math.h>
complex<double> parallel_RLC_impedance( double
frequency, double resistance, double inductance,
double capacitance );
void main( )
{
const double R = 1000.0;
const double L = 0.2;
const double C = 10.0e-9;
double frequency;
frequency = 1.0 / sqrt( L * C );
complex<double> impedance =
parallel_RLC_impedance( frequency, R, L, C );
cout << impedance << "   Magnitude = " << abs(
impedance ) << "   Phase = " << arg( impedance )
<< endl;
impedance = parallel_RLC_impedance( frequency /
10, R, L, C );
cout << impedance << "   Magnitude = " << abs(
impedance ) << "   Phase = " << arg( impedance )
<< endl;
impedance = parallel_RLC_impedance( frequency
* 10, R, L, C );
cout << impedance << "   Magnitude = " << abs(
impedance ) << "   Phase = " << arg( impedance )
<< endl;
getch();
}
Inline complex<double>
parallel_RLC_impedance( double
frequency,double resistance, double inductance,
double capacitance )
{
complex<double> impedance_inverse( 1.0 /
resistance,frequency * capacitance - 1.0 / (
frequency * inductance ) );
return 1.0 / impedance_inverse;
}
```

**Problem 106. Write a C++ program for << and >> operators are overloaded relative to complex numbers.**

***Program:***

```
#include <iostream.h>
#include<conio.h>
#include <complex.h>
void main(void)
{
complex<double> num(10, 1);
cout << num;
getch();
}
```

**Problem 107. Write a C++ program to add square root of two complex numbers and print the result.**

***Program:***

```
#include <iostream.h>
#include<conio.h>
#include <complex.h>
void main()
{
/* complex number with real and imaginary parts
* - real part: 4.0
* - imaginary part: 3.0
*/
complex<double> c1(4.0,3.0);
cout << "c1: " << c1 << endl;
/* create complex number from polar coordinates
* - magnitude: 5.0
* - phase angle: 0.75
*/
```

```
complex<float> c2(polar(5.0,0.75));
// add square root of c1 to c1 and print the result
cout << "c1 += sqrt(c1): " << (c1 += sqrt(c1)) <<
endl;
getch();
}
```

**OUTPUT:**

```
c1: (4,3)
c1 += sqrt(c1): (6.12132,3.70711)
```

## ENUM:

**Problem 108. Write a C++ program to define and OUTPUT an enumeration.**

***Program:***

```
#include <iostream.h>
#include<conio.h>
enum Language { English, French, German, Italian,
Spanish };
void main()
{
cout << "\nPossible languages are:\n"
<< English << ". English\n"
<< French << ". French\n"
<< German << ". German\n"
<< Italian << ". Italian\n"
<< Spanish << ". Spanish\n";
getch();
}
```

**OUTPUT:**

```
Possible languages are:
0. English
1. French
2. German
3. Italian
4. Spanish
```

**Problem 109. Write a C++ program for demonstration of Enumerated Constants.**

***Program:***

```
#include <iostream.h>
#include<conio.h>
void main()
{
enum Days { Sunday, Monday,
Tuesday,Wednesday, Thursday, Friday, Saturday };
Days today;
today = Monday;
if (today == Sunday || today == Saturday)
cout << " love the weekends!\n";
else
cout << "\nBack to work.\n";
getch();
}
```

**Problem 110. Write a C++ program to Demonstrate an enumeration.**

***Program:***

```
#include <iostream.h>
#include<conio.h>
enum Letter { A, B, C, D, E };
char name[][20] = {
 "Automobile",
 "Bank",
 "Cat",
 "Day",
 "eagle"
};
void main()
{
Letter how;
how = A;
cout << name[how] << '\n';
how = C;
cout << name[how] << '\n';
how = D;
cout << name[how] << '\n';
getch();
}
```

**OUTPUT:**

```
Automobile
Cat
Day
```

**Problem 111. Write a C++ program for an enumeration variable.**

***Program:***

```
#include <iostream.h>
#include<conio.h>
enum Language { English, French, German,
Italian, Spanish };
void main()
{
Language tongue = German;
cout << "\n Current language is " << tongue;
getch();
}
```

**OUTPUT:**

```
Current language is 2
```

**Problem 112. Write a C++ program for an enumeration static_cast.**

***Program:***

```
#include <iostream.h>
#include<conio.h>
enum Language { English, French, German, Italian,
Spanish };
void main()
{
Language tongue = German;
tongue = static_cast<Language>(tongue + 1);
cout << "\n Current language is now " << tongue
<< endl;
getch();
}
```

**OUTPUT:**

Current language is now 3

**Problem 113. Write a C++ program to return enum from a function.**

***Program:***

```
#include <iostream.h>
#include<conio.h>
enum ERR_CODE { SUCCESS, ERROR };
ERR_CODE f(int, int&, int&);
void main()
{
int number = 2, squared, cubed;
ERR_CODE result;
result = f(number, squared, cubed);
if (result == SUCCESS)
{
;
}
else
cout << "Error encountered!!\n";
getch();
}
ERR_CODE f(int n, int &rSquared, int &rCubed)
{
return ERROR;   // simple error code
}
```

**OUTPUT:**

Error encountered!!

**Problem 114. Write a C++ program using consts and enums in Arrays.**

***Program:***

```
#include <iostream.h>
#include<conio.h>
void main()
{
enum WeekDays { Sun, Mon, Tue,Wed, Thu, Fri,
Sat, DaysInWeek };
int ArrayWeek[DaysInWeek] = { 10, 20, 30, 40,
50, 60, 70 };
cout << "The value at Tuesday is: " <<
ArrayWeek[Tue];
getch();
}
```

**Problem 115. Write a C++ program to compare enum elements.**

***Program:***

```
#include <iostream.h>
#include<conio.h>
enum color{
RED=1,
GREEN=6,
BLUE=9
};
void main()
{
enum color v1=RED,v2;
cout<<"RED="<<RED<<endl;
cout<<"GREEN="<<GREEN<<endl;
cout<<"BLUE="<<BLUE<<endl;
cout<<"v1="<<v1<<endl;
v2=GREEN;
cout<<"(v1<v2)="<<(v1<v2)<<endl;
getch();
}
```

**OUTPUT:**

RED=1
GREEN=6
BLUE=9
v1=1
(v1<v2)=v1

## REGISTER VARIABLES:

**Problem 116. Write a C++ program to demonstrate register variables.**

***Program:***

```
#include <iostream.h>
#include<conio.h>
int f(int nums[], int n);
void main()
{
int vals[] = { 1, 2, 3, 4, 5 };
int result;
```

```
result = f(vals, 5);
cout << "Summation is " << result << "\n";
getch();
}
int f(int nums[], int n)
{
register int i;
register int sum = 0;
for(i = 0; i < n; i++)
sum = sum + nums[i];
return sum;
}
```

**OUTPUT:**

Summation is 15

## COVERT FROM STRING:

**Problem 117. Write a C++ program using atof().**

***Program:***

```
#include <iostream.h>
#include<conio.h>
#include <stdlib.h>
void main()
{
double d = atof( "99.0" );
cout << d / 2.0 << endl;
getch();
}
```

**OUTPUT:**

49.5

**Problem 118. Write a C++ program using atoi().**

***Program:***

```
#include <iostream.h>
#include<conio.h>
#include <stdlib.h>
void main()
{
int i = atoi( "2593" );
cout << i - 593 << endl;
getch();
}
```

**OUTPUT:**

2000

**Problem 119. Write a C++ program using atoll().**

***Program:***

```
#include <iostream.h>
#include<conio.h>
#include <stdlib.h>
void main()
{
long x = atol( "1000000" );
cout << x / 2 << endl;
getch();
}
```

**OUTPUT:**

500000

**Problem 120. Write a C++ program using strtod().**

***Program:***

```
#include <iostream.h>
#include<conio.h>
#include <stdlib.h>
void main()
{
double d;
const char *string1 = "51.2 are admitted";
char *stringPtr;
d = strtod( string1, &stringPtr );
cout << d << endl;
getch();
}
```

**OUTPUT:**

51.2

**Problem 121. Write a C++ program using strtol().**

***Program:***

```
#include <iostream.h>
#include<conio.h>
#include <stdlib.h>
void main()
{
long x;
const char *string1 = "-1234567abc";
char *remainderPtr;
x = strtol( string1, &remainderPtr, 0 );
cout << x << " " << remainderPtr << " " << x +
567 << endl;
getch();
}
```

**OUTPUT:**

-1234567 abc -1234000

**Problem 122. Write a C++ program using strtoul().**

***Program:***

```
#include <iostream.h>
#include<conio.h>
```

```
#include <stdlib.h>
void main()
{
unsigned long x;
const char *string1 = "1234567abc";
char *remainderPtr;
x = strtoul( string1, &remainderPtr, 0 );
cout << x << "  "<< x - 567 << endl;
getch();
}
```

**OUTPUT:**

1234567 1234000

## CAST:

**Problem 123. Write a C++ program to perform casting to float.**

***Program:***

```
#include <iostream.h>
#include<conio.h>
#include <stdlib.h>
void main()
{
int i;
for(i=1; i <= 10; ++i )
cout << i << "/ 2 is: " << (float) i / 2 << '\n';
getch();
}
```

**OUTPUT:**

```
1/ 2 is: 0.5
2/ 2 is: 1
3/ 2 is: 1.5
4/ 2 is: 2
5/ 2 is: 2.5
6/ 2 is: 3
7/ 2 is: 3.5
8/ 2 is: 4
9/ 2 is: 4.5
10/ 2 is: 5
```

**Problem 124. Write a C++ program for ambiguous function call when data type casting from int to char and unsigned char.**

***Program:***

```
#include <iostream.h>
#include<conio.h>
char myfunc(unsigned char ch);
char myfunc(char ch);
void main()
{
cout << myfunc('c'); // this calls myfunc(char)
//cout << myfunc(88) << " "; // ambiguous
getch();
}
char myfunc(unsigned char ch)
{
return ch-1;
}
char myfunc(char ch)
{
return ch+1;
}
```

**OUTPUT:**

d

**Problem 125. Write a C++ program for ambiguous function call when data type casting from int to double and float.**

***Program:***

```
#include <iostream.h>
#include<conio.h>
float myfunc(float i);
double myfunc(double i);
void main()
{
cout << myfunc(10.1) << " "; // unambiguous, calls
myfunc(double)
//cout << myfunc(10); // ambiguous
getch();
}
float myfunc(float i)
{
return i;
}
double myfunc(double i)
{
return -i;
}
```

**OUTPUT:**

-10.1

**Problem 126. Write a C++ program using Explicit Casts.**

***Program:***

```
#include <iostream.h>
#include<conio.h>
void main()
{
const long a = 3;
const long b = 12;
double c = 234.0;
```

```
long d = 0;
long f = 0;
long g = 0;
d = static_cast<long>(c);
f = static_cast<long>((c - d) * a);
g = static_cast<long>(c * a * b) b;
cout << c << " \n "
<< d << " \n "
<< f << " \n "
<< g << " \n ";
cout << endl;
getch();
}
```

**OUTPUT:**

```
234
234
0
0
```

## CONST_CAST:

**Problem 127. Write a C++ program for const_cast int value.**

***Program:***

```
#include <iostream.h>
#include<conio.h>
void sqrval(const int *val)
{
int *p;
// cast away const-ness.
p = const_cast<int *> (val);
*p = *val * *val; // now, modify object through v
}
void main()
{
int x = 10;
cout << "x before call: " << x << endl;
sqrval(&x);
cout << "x after call: " << x << endl;
getch();
}
```

**OUTPUT:**

```
x before call: 10
x after call: 100
```

**Problem 128. Write a C++ program for const_cast char type.**

***Program:***

```
#include <iostream.h>
#include<conio.h>
#include <string.h>
#include <ctype.h>
const char *maximum( const char *first, const char
*second )
{
return ( strcmp( first, second ) >= 0 ? first : second
);
}
void main()
{
char s1[] = "h";
char s2[] = "g";
char *maxPtr = const_cast< char * >( maximum(
s1, s2 ) );
cout << "The larger string is: " << maxPtr << endl;
getch();
}
```

**OUTPUT:**

```
The larger string is: h
```

**Problem 129. Write a C++ program using const_cast on a const reference.**

***Program:***

```
#include <iostream.h>
#include<conio.h>
void sqrval(const int &val)
{
const_cast<int &> (val) = val * val;
}
void main()
{
int x = 10;
cout << "x before call: " << x << endl;
sqrval(x);
cout << "x after call: " << x << endl;
getch();
}
```

**OUTPUT:**

```
x before call: 10
x after call: 100
```

## REFERENCE:

**Problem 130. Write a C++ program to creating and using References.**

***Program:***

```
#include <iostream.h>
#include<conio.h>
void main()
{
```

```
int intValue;
int &intReference = intValue;
intValue = 5;
cout << "intValue: " << intValue << endl;
cout << "intReference: " << intReference <<endl;
intReference = 7;
cout << "intValue: " << intValue << endl;
cout << "intReference: " << intReference <<endl;
getch();
}
```

**OUTPUT:**

```
intValue: 5
intReference: 5
intValue: 7
intReference: 7
```

**Problem 131. Write a C++ program using References operator &.**

***Program:***

```
#include <iostream.h>
#include<conio.h>
void main()
{
int intValue;
int &intReference = intValue;
intValue = 5;
cout << "intValue: " << intValue << endl;
cout << "intReference: " << intReference << endl;
cout << "&intValue: " << &intValue<< endl;
cout << "&intReference: " << &intReference
<<endl;
getch();
}
```

**OUTPUT:**

```
intValue: 5
intReference: 5
&intValue: 0x22ff74
&intReference: 0x22ff74
```

**Problem 132. Write a C++ program for references must be initialized.**

***Program:***

```
#include <iostream.h>
#include<conio.h>
void main()
{
int x = 321;
int &y = x;
cout << "x = " << x << "    y = " << y << endl;
y = 123;
cout << "x = " << x << "    y = " << y << endl;
getch();
}
```

**OUTPUT:**

```
x = 321    y = 321
x = 123    y = 123
```

**Problem 133. Write a C++ program to change reference value.**

***Program:***

```
#include <iostream.h>
#include<conio.h>
void main()
{
int a[] = {1,3,5,7,9};
int i=2 ;
int &r = a[i];
cout <<r<<endl;
r=99;
cout <<a[i]<<endl;
getch();
}
```

**OUTPUT:**

```
5
99
```

**Problem 134. Write a C++ program to reassigning a reference.**

***Program:***

```
#include <iostream.h>
#include<conio.h>
void main()
{
int intValue;
int &intReference = intValue;
intValue = 5;
cout << "intValue:\t" << intValue << endl;
cout << "intReference:\t" << intReference << endl;
cout << "&intValue:\t" << &intValue << endl;
cout << "&intReference:\t" << &intReference <<
endl;
int intTwo = 8;
intReference = intTwo; // not what you think!
cout << "\nintValue:\t" << intValue << endl;
cout << "intTwo:\t" << intTwo << endl;
cout << "intReference:\t" << intReference << endl;
cout << "&intValue:\t" << &intValue << endl;
cout << "&intTwo:\t" << &intTwo << endl;
cout << "&intReference:\t" << &intReference <<
endl;
getch();
}
```

**OUTPUT:**

```
intValue:      5
intReference:  5
&intValue:     0x22ff74
&intReference: 0x22ff74
intValue:      8
intTwo: 8
intReference:  8
&intValue:     0x22ff74
&intTwo:       0x22ff6c
&intReference: 0x22ff74
```

**Problem 135. Write a C++ program to returning a reference.**

***Program:***

```
#include <iostream.h>
#include<conio.h>
double &f();
double val = 100.0;
void main()
{
double x;
cout << f() << '\n';
x = f();         // assign value of val to x
cout << x << '\n';
getch();
}
double &f()
{
return val; // return reference to val
}
```

**OUTPUT:**

```
100
100
```

**Problem 136. Write a C++ program to assign value to a reference-return.**

***Program:***

```
#include <iostream.h>
#include<conio.h>
double &f();
double val = 100.0;
void main()
{
double x;
f() = 99.1;
cout << f() << '\n';
getch();
}
double &f()
{
return val; // return reference to val
}
```

**OUTPUT:**

```
99.1
```

**Problem 137. Write a C++ program to return a reference to an array element.**

***Program:***

```
#include <iostream.h>
#include<conio.h>
double &f(int i); // return a reference
double vals[] = { 1.1, 2.2, 3.3, 4.4, 5.5 };
void main()
{
int i;
cout << "Here are the original values: ";
for(i=0; i < 5; i++)
cout << vals[i] << ' ';
f(1) = 8.23;   // change 2nd element
f(3) = -8.8;   // change 4th element
cout << "\nHere are the changed values: \n";
for(i=0; i < 5; i++)
cout << vals[i] << ' ';
getch();
}
double &f(int i)
{
return vals[i]; // return a reference to the ith element
}
```

**OUTPUT:**

```
Here are the original values: 1.1 2.2 3.3 4.4 5.5
Here are the changed values:
1.1 8.23 3.3 -8.8 5.5
```

**Problem 138. Write a C++ program using an independent reference.**

***Program:***

```
#include <iostream.h>
#include<conio.h>
void main()
{
int j, k;
int &i = j;   // independent reference
j = 10;
cout << j << " " << i; // OUTPUTs 10 10
k = 121;
i = k;      // copies k's value into j, not k's address
cout << "\n" << j;  // OUTPUTs 121
getch();
}
```

**OUTPUT:**
10 10
121

**Problem 139. Write a C++ program for class to counted reference semantics.**

***Program:***

```
#include <iostream.h>
#include<conio.h>
#include <list.h>
#include <deque.h>
#include <algorithm.h>
template <class T>
class CountedPtr
{
private:
T* ptr;       // pointer to the value
long* count;  // shared number of owners
public:
// initialize pointer with existing pointer
// - requires that the pointer p is a return value of
new
explicit CountedPtr (T* p=0): ptr(p), count(new
long(1))
{   }
// copy pointer (one more owner)
CountedPtr (const CountedPtr<T>& p) throw():
ptr(p.ptr), count(p.count)
{
++*count;
}
// destructor (delete value if this was the last owner)
~CountedPtr () throw()
{
dispose();
}
// assignment (unshare old and share new value)
CountedPtr<T>& operator= (const CountedPtr<T>&
p) throw()
{
if (this != &p)
{
dispose();
ptr = p.ptr;
count = p.count;
++*count;
}
return *this;
}
// access the value to which the pointer refers
T& operator*() const throw()
{
return *ptr;
}
T* operator->() const throw()
{
return ptr;
}
private:
void dispose()
{
if (--*count == 0)
{
delete count;
delete ptr;
}
}
};
void printCountedPtr (CountedPtr<int> elem)
{
cout << *elem << ' ';
}
void  main()
{
// array of integers (to share in different containers)
static int values[] = { 3, 5, 9, 1, 6, 4 };
// two different collections
typedef CountedPtr<int> IntPtr;
deque<IntPtr> coll1;
list<IntPtr> coll2;
for (int i=0; i<sizeof(values)/sizeof(values[0]);
++i) {
IntPtr ptr(new int(values[i]));
coll1.push_back(ptr);
coll2.push_front(ptr);
}
// print contents of both collections
for_each (coll1.begin(),
coll1.end(),printCountedPtr);
cout << endl;
for_each (coll2.begin(),
coll2.end(),printCountedPtr);
cout << endl << endl;
*coll1[2] *= *coll1[2];
(**coll1.begin()) *= -1;
(**coll2.begin()) = 0;
// print contents of both collections again
for_each (coll1.begin(),
coll1.end(),printCountedPtr);
cout << endl;
for_each (coll2.begin(),
coll2.end(),printCountedPtr);
```

```
cout << endl;
getch();
}
```

**OUTPUT:**

```
3 5 9 1 6 4
4 6 1 9 5 3
-3 5 81 1 6 0
0 6 1 81 5 -3
```

**Problem 140. Write a C++ program to use reference to swap value.**

***Program:***

```
#include <iostream.h>
#include<conio.h>
void Swap(int& x,int& y);
void main(void)
{
int n1 = 1, n2 = 2;
Swap(n1,n2);
cout << n1 << " " << n2 << endl;
getch();
}
void Swap(int& x,int& y)
{
int t = x;     x = y;  y = t;
}
```

**OUTPUT:**

```
2 1
```

**Problem 141. Write a C++ program to use reference as a return type.**

***Program:***

```
#include <iostream.h>
#include<conio.h>
int& Fn(int * p,int i);
void main()
{
const int S=4;
int a[S] = {1,3,5,-1};
for (int j = 0; j<S; j++)
{
Fn(a,j) += 1;
cout << Fn(a,j) << endl;
}
getch();
}
int& Fn(int * p,int i)
{
return p[i];
}
```

**OUTPUT:**

```
2
4
6
0
```

## TIME:

**Problem 142. Write a C++ program to displays the current date and time.**

***Program:***

```
#include <iostream.h>
#include<conio.h>
#include <time.h>
void main()
{
time_t currentTime;
time( &currentTime );
cout << asctime( localtime( &currentTime ) );
getch();
}
```

**OUTPUT:**

```
Sun Apr 29 10:56:45 2007
```

**Problem 143. Write a C++ program to show standard time and date string.**

***Program:***

```
#include <iostream.h>
#include<conio.h>
#include <time.h>
void main()
{
char str[64];
// Get the current system time.
time_t t = time(NULL);
// Show standard time and date string.
strftime(str, 64, "%c", localtime(&t));
cout << "Standard format: " << str << endl;
getch();
}
```

**Problem 144. Write a C++ program to show a custom time and date string.**

***Program:***

```
#include <iostream.h>
#include<conio.h>
#include <time.h>
void main()
{
char str[64];
// Get the current system time.
```

```
time_t t = time(NULL);
// Show a custom time and date string.
strftime(str, 64, "%A, %B %d %Y %I:%M %p",
localtime(&t));
cout << "Custom format: " << str << endl;
getch();
}
```

**Problem 145. Write a C++ program for %c specifies the standard time and date pattern.**

***Program:***

```
#include <iostream.h>
#include<conio.h>
#include <locale.h>
#include <string.h>
#include <time.h>
void main()
{
// Obtain the current system time.
time_t t = time(NULL);
tm *cur_time = localtime(&t);
// Create US and German locales.
locale usloc("English_US");
locale gloc("German_Germany");
// %c specifies the standard time and date pattern.
char *std_pat = "%c";
char *std_pat_end = std_pat + strlen(std_pat);
getch();
}
```

**Problem 146. Write a C++ program for strftime( ) Format Specifiers.**

***Program:***

| Command | Replaced By |
|---|---|
| %a | Abbreviated weekday name |
| %A | Full weekday name |
| %b | Abbreviated month name |
| %B | Full month name |
| %c | Standard date and time string |
| %d | Day of month as a decimal (1-31) |
| %H | Hour (0-23) |
| %I | Hour (1-12) |
| %j | Day of year as a decimal (1-366) |
| %m | Month as decimal (1-12) |
| %M | Minute as decimal (0-59) |
| %p | Locale's equivalent of AM or PM |
| %S | Second as decimal (0-61) |
| %U | Week of year, Sunday being first day (0-53) |
| %w | Weekday as a decimal (0-6, Sunday being 0) |
| %W | Week of year, Monday being first day (0-53) |
| %x | Standard date string |
| %X | Standard time string |
| %y | Year in decimal without century (0-99) |
| %Y | Year including century as decimal |
| %Z | Time zone name |
| %% | The percent sign |

**Problem 147. Write a C++ program to convert now to tm struct for UTC.**

***Program:***

```
#include <iostream.h>
#include<conio.h>
#include <time.h>
#include <stdlib.h>
void main( )
{
// Current date/time based on current system
time_t now = time(0);
// Convert now to tm struct for UTC
tm* gmtm = gmtime(&now);
if (gmtm != NULL) {
cout << "The UTC date and time is: " <<
asctime(gmtm) << endl;
}
else {
cerr << "Failed to get the UTC date and time" <<
endl;
return EXIT_FAILURE;
}
}
```

**OUTPUT:**

The UTC date and time is: Mon Apr 23 20:17:33 2007

**Problem 148. Write a C++ program to set the locale to US and get the time_put facet for US.**

***Program:***

```
#include <iostream.h>
#include<conio.h>
#include <locale.h>
#include <string.h>
#include <time.h>
void main()
{
// Obtain the current system time.
time_t t = time(NULL);
tm *cur_time = localtime(&t);
```

```
// Create US and German locales.
locale usloc("English_US");
locale gloc("German_Germany");
// Set the locale to US and get the time_put facet for
US.
cout.imbue(usloc);
const time_put<char> &us_time =
use_facet<time_put<char> >(cout.getloc());
getch();
}
```

**Problem 149. Write a C++ program to set the locale to Germany, Show standard time and date string.**

***Program:***

```
#include <iostream.h>
#include<conio.h>
#include <time.h>
#include <locale.h>
void main()
{
char str[64];
// Set the locale to Germany.
setlocale(LC_ALL, "German_Germany");
// Get the current system time.
time_t t = time(NULL);
// Show standard time and date string.
strftime(str, 64, "%c", localtime(&t));
cout << "Standard format: " << str << endl;
// Show a custom time and date string.
strftime(str, 64, "%A, %B %Y %I:%M %p",
localtime(&t));
cout << "Custom format: " << str << endl;
getch();
}
```

**Problem 150. Write a C++ program to custom pattern displays hours and minutes followed by the date.**

***Program:***

```
#include <iostream.h>
#include<conio.h>
#include <locale.h>
#include <string.h>
#include <time.h>
void main()
{
// Obtain the current system time.
time_t t = time(NULL);
tm *cur_time = localtime(&t);
// Create US and German locales.
locale usloc("English_US");
locale gloc("German_Germany");
// custom pattern displays hours and minutes
followed by the date.
char *custom_pat = "%A %B %d, %Y %H:%M";
char *custom_pat_end = custom_pat +
strlen(custom_pat);
getch();
}
```

**Problem 151. Write a C++ program to set the locale to Germany and get the time_put facet for Germany.**

***Program:***

```
#include <iostream.h>
#include<conio.h>
#include <locale.h>
#include <string.h>
#include <time.h>
void main()
{
// Obtain the current system time.
time_t t = time(NULL);
tm *cur_time = localtime(&t);
// Create US and German locales.
locale usloc("English_US");
locale gloc("German_Germany");
// Set the locale to Germany and get the time_put
facet for Germany.
cout.imbue(gloc);
const time_put<char> &g_time =
use_facet<time_put<char> >(cout.getloc());
getch();
}
```

**Problem 152. Write a C++ program to convert now to tm struct for local timezone.**

***Program:***

```
#include <iostream.h>
#include<conio.h>
#include <time.h>
#include <stdlib.h>
void main( )
{
// Current date/time based on current system
time_t now = time(0);
// Convert now to tm struct for local timezone
tm* localtm = localtime(&now);
cout << "The local date and time is: " <<
asctime(localtm) << endl;
getch();
```

}

**OUTPUT:**

The local date and time is: Mon Apr 23 13:17:32 2007

## LINKED LIST:

**Problem 153. Write a C++ program to demonstrates an object-oriented approach to linked lists.**

***Program:***

```
#include <iostream.h>
#include<conio.h>
enum { kIsSmaller, kIsLarger, kIsSame};
// Data class to put into the linked list
// Any class in this linked list must support two
methods:
// Show (displays the value) and Compare
// (returns relative position)
class Data
{
public:
Data(int val):myValue(val){}
~Data(){}
int Compare(const Data &);
void Show() { std::cout << myValue << std::endl; }
private:
int myValue;
};
// Compare is used to decide where in the list
// a particular object belongs.
int Data::Compare(const Data & theOtherData)
{
if (myValue < theOtherData.myValue)
return kIsSmaller;
if (myValue > theOtherData.myValue)
return kIsLarger;
else
return kIsSame;
}
// forward declarations
class Node;
class HeadNode;
class TailNode;
class InternalNode;
// ADT representing the node object in the list
// Every derived class must override Insert and Show
class Node
{
public:
Node(){}
virtual ~Node(){}
virtual Node * Insert(Data * theData)=0;
virtual void Show() = 0;
private:
};
// This is the node which holds the actual object
// In this case the object is of type Data
// We'll see how to make this more general when
// we cover templates
class InternalNode: public Node
{
public:
InternalNode(Data * theData, Node * next);
virtual ~InternalNode(){ delete myNext; delete
myData; }
virtual Node * Insert(Data * theData);
virtual void Show()
{ myData->Show(); myNext->Show(); } //
delegate!
private:
Data * myData; // the data itself
Node * myNext;    // points to next node in the
linked list
};
// All the constructor does is to initialize
InternalNode::InternalNode(Data * theData, Node
* next):
myData(theData),myNext(next)
{
}
// the meat of the list
// When you put a new object into the list
// it is passed ot the node which figures out
// where it goes and inserts it into the list
Node * InternalNode::Insert(Data * theData)
{
// is the new guy bigger or smaller than me?
int result = myData->Compare(*theData);
switch(result)
{
// by convention if it is the same as me it comes
first
case kIsSame:     // fall through
case kIsLarger:   // new data comes before me
{
InternalNode * dataNode =
new InternalNode(theData, this);
return dataNode;
}
// it is bigger than I am so pass it on to the next
```

```
// node and let HIM handle it.
case kIsSmaller:
myNext = myNext->Insert(theData);
return this;
}
return this; // appease MSC
}
// Tail node is just a sentinel
class TailNode : public Node
{
public:
TailNode(){}
virtual ~TailNode(){}
virtual Node * Insert(Data * theData);
virtual void Show() { }
private:
};
// If data comes to me, it must be inserted before me
// as I am the tail and NOTHING comes after me
Node * TailNode::Insert(Data * theData)
{
InternalNode * dataNode = new
InternalNode(theData, this);
return dataNode;
}
// Head node has no data, it just points
// to the very beginning of the list
class HeadNode : public Node
{
public:
HeadNode();
virtual ~HeadNode() { delete myNext; }
virtual Node * Insert(Data * theData);
virtual void Show() { myNext->Show(); }
private:
Node * myNext;
};
// As soon as the head is created
// it creates the tail
HeadNode::HeadNode()
{
myNext = new TailNode;
}
// Nothing comes before the head so just
// pass the data on to the next node
Node * HeadNode::Insert(Data * theData)
{
myNext = myNext->Insert(theData);
return this;
}
// I get all the credit and do none of the work
class LinkedList
{
public:
LinkedList();
~LinkedList() { delete myHead; }
void Insert(Data * theData);
void ShowAll() { myHead->Show(); }
private:
HeadNode * myHead;
};
LinkedList::LinkedList()
{
myHead = new HeadNode;
}
// Delegate, delegate, delegate
void LinkedList::Insert(Data * pData)
{
myHead->Insert(pData);
}
// test driver program
void main()
{
Data * pData;
int val;
LinkedList ll;
// ask the user to produce some values
// put them in the list
for (;;)
{
cout << "What value? (0 to stop): ";
cin >> val;
if (!val)
break;
pData = new Data(val);
ll.Insert(pData);
}
// now walk the list and show the data
ll.ShowAll();
getch();
}
```

**OUTPUT:**

```
What value? (0 to stop): 1
What value? (0 to stop): 2
What value? (0 to stop): 3
What value? (0 to stop): 4
What value? (0 to stop): 0
1
2
3
4
```

# UNION:

**Problem 154. Write a C++ program for an example of a union.**

***Program:***

```
#include <iostream.h>
#include<conio.h>
union Number
{
int integer1;
double double1;
};
void main()
{
Number value;
value.integer1 = 100;
cout << value.integer1 << "\ndouble: " <<
value.double1
<< endl;
value.double1 = 100.0;
cout << value.integer1 << "\ndouble: " <<
value.double1
<< endl;
getch();
}
```

**OUTPUT:**

```
100
double: 4.24399e-314
0
double: 100
```

**Problem 155. Write a C++ program for union with method.**

***Program:***

```
#include <iostream.h>
#include<conio.h>
union u_type
{
u_type(short int a) { i = a; };
u_type(char x, char y) { ch[0] = x; ch[1] = y; }
void showchars()
{
cout << ch[0] << " ";
cout << ch[1] << "\n";
}
short int i;
char ch[2];
};
void main()
{
u_type u(1000);
u_type u2('X', 'Y');
cout << "u as integer: ";
cout << u.i << "\n";
cout << "u as chars: ";
u.showchars();
cout << "u2 as integer: ";
cout << u2.i << "\n";
cout << "u2 as chars: ";
u2.showchars();
getch();
}
```

**OUTPUT:**

```
u as integer: 1000
u as chars: F ?
u2 as integer: 22872
u2 as chars: X Y
```

**Problem 156. Write a C++ program for an anonymous union.**

***Program:***

```
#include <iostream.h>
#include<conio.h>
#include <cstring.h>
void main()
{
// define anonymous union
union
{
long l;
double d;
char s[4];
} ;
// now, reference union elements directly
l = 100000;
cout << l << " ";
d = 123.2342;
cout << d << " ";
strcpy(s, "hi");
cout << s;
getch();
}
```

**OUTPUT:**

```
100000 123.234 hi
```

**Problem 157. Write a C++ program using an anonymous union: members integer1, double1 and charPtr share the same space.**

***Program:***

```
#include <iostream.h>
#include<conio.h>
```

```
void main()
{
union
{
int integer1;
double double1;
char *charPtr;
};
integer1 = 2;
cout << integer1 << endl;
double1 = 4.4;
cout << double1 << endl;
charPtr = "union";
cout << charPtr << endl;
getch();
}
```

**OUTPUT:**

2
4.4
union

## WIDE CHARACTER:

**Problem 158. Write a C++ program for wctype().**

***Program:***

```
#include <iostream.h>
#include<conio.h>
#include <wctype.h>
void main()
{
wctype_t x;
x = wctype("space");
if(iswctype(L' ', x))
cout << "Is a space.\n";
getch();
}
```

**Problem 159. Write a C++ program to compare wide character string ignoring the case.**

***Program:***

```
#include <iostream.h>
#include<conio.h>
#include <string.h.>
#include <algorithm.h>
#include <ctype.h>
#include <wctype.h>
inline bool caseInsCharCompareW(wchar_t a,
wchar_t b) {
return(towupper(a) == towupper(b));
}
bool caseInsCompare(const wstring& s1, const
wstring& s2) {
return((s1.size( ) == s2.size( )) &&
equal(s1.begin( ), s1.end( ), s2.begin( ),
caseInsCharCompareW));
}
void main( )
{
wstring ws1 = L"The END";
wstring ws2 = L"the end";
if (caseInsCompare(ws1, ws2))
cout << "Equal!\n";
getch();
}
```

**OUTPUT:**

Equal!

## YOUR ARRAY:

**Problem 160. Write a C++ program to define your own array class.**

***Program:***

```
#include <iostream.h>
#include<conio.h>
#include <iomanip.h>
#include <stdlib.h>
class Array
{
friend ostream &operator<<( ostream &, const
Array & );
friend istream &operator>>( istream &, Array & );
public:
Array( int = 10 );
Array( const Array & );
~Array();
int getSize() const;
const Array &operator=( const Array & );
bool operator==( const Array & ) const;
bool operator!=( const Array &right ) const
{
return ! ( *this == right );
}
int &operator[]( int );
int operator[]( int ) const;
private:
int size;
int *ptr;
};
Array::Array( int arraySize )
{
```

```
size = arraySize;
ptr = new int[ size ];
for ( int i = 0; i < size; i++ )
ptr[ i ] = 0;
}
Array::Array( const Array &arrayToCopy ) : size(
arrayToCopy.size )
{
ptr = new int[ size ];
for ( int i = 0; i < size; i++ )
ptr[ i ] = arrayToCopy.ptr[ i ];
}
Array::~Array()
{
delete [] ptr;
}
int Array::getSize() const
{
return size;
}
const Array &Array::operator=( const Array &right
)
{
delete [] ptr;
size = right.size;
ptr = new int[ size ];
for ( int i = 0; i < size; i++ )
ptr[ i ] = right.ptr[ i ];
return *this;
}
bool Array::operator==( const Array &right ) const
{
if ( size != right.size )
return false;
for ( int i = 0; i < size; i++ )
if ( ptr[ i ] != right.ptr[ i ] )
return false;
return true;
}
int &Array::operator[]( int subscript )
{
return ptr[ subscript ];
}
int Array::operator[]( int subscript ) const
{
return ptr[ subscript ];
}
istream &operator>>( istream &input, Array &a )
{
for ( int i = 0; i < a.size; i++ )
input >> a.ptr[ i ];
return input;
}
ostream &operator<<( ostream &OUTPUT, const
Array &a )
{
int i;
for ( i = 0; i < a.size; i++ )
{
OUTPUT << a.ptr[ i ];
}
return OUTPUT;
}
void main()
{
Array integers1( 7 );
Array integers2;
cout << integers1.getSize() << integers1;
cout << integers2.getSize() << integers2;
cout << "\nEnter 17 integers:" << endl;
cin >> integers1 >> integers2;
cout << "integers1:\n" << integers1 <<
"integers2.\n" << integers2;
if ( integers1 != integers2 )
cout << "integers1 and integers2 are not equal" <<
endl;
Array integers3( integers1 );
cout << integers3.getSize() << integers3;
integers1 = integers2;
cout << integers1;
cout << integers2;
if ( integers1 == integers2 )
cout << "integers1 and integers2 are equal" <<
endl;
cout << integers1[ 5 ];
integers1[ 5 ] = 1000;
cout << integers1;
getch();
}
```

**Problem 161. Write a C++ program to safe array class.**

***Program:***

```
#include <iostream.h>
#include<conio.h>
#include <new.h>
#include <stdlib.h>
class array
{
int *p;
int size;
public:
```

```
array(int sz)
{
try
{
p = new int[sz];
}
catch (bad_alloc xa)
{
cout << "Allocation Failure\n";
exit(EXIT_FAILURE);
}
size = sz;
}
~array() { delete [] p;
}
// Copy Constructor
array(const array &a)
{
int i;
try
{
p = new int[a.size];
}
catch (bad_alloc xa)
{
cout << "Allocation Failure\n";
exit(EXIT_FAILURE);
}
for(i=0; i<a.size; i++) p[i] = a.p[i];
}
void put(int i, int j)
{
if(i>=0 && i<size) p[i] = j;
}
int get(int i)
{
return p[i];
}
};
void main()
{
array num(10);
for(int i=0; i<10; i++)
num.put(i, i);
for(int i=9; i>=0; i--)
cout << num.get(i);
cout << "\n";
array x(num); // invokes copy constructor
for(int i=0; i<10; i++)
cout << x.get(i);
getch();
}
```

**OUTPUT:**

```
9876543210
0123456789
```

**Problem 162. Write a C++ program for SArray.**

***Program:***

```
#include <stddef.h>
#include <assert.h>
template<typename T>
class SArray
{
public:
// create array with initial size
explicit SArray (size_t s) : storage(new T[s]),
storage_size(s)
{
init();
}
// copy constructor
SArray (SArray<T> const& orig): storage(new
T[orig.size()]), storage_size(orig.size())
{
copy(orig);
}
// destructor: free memory
~SArray()
{
delete[] storage;
}
// assignment operator
SArray<T>& operator= (SArray<T> const& orig)
{
if (&orig!=this)
{
copy(orig);
}
return *this;
}
// return size
size_t size() const
{
return storage_size;
}
// index operator for constants and variables
T operator[] (size_t idx) const
{
return storage[idx];
}
T& operator[] (size_t idx)
{
```

```
return storage[idx];
}
protected:
// init values with default constructor
void init() {
for (size_t idx = 0; idx<size(); ++idx) {
storage[idx] = T();
}
}
// copy values of another array
void copy (SArray<T> const& orig) {
assert(size()==orig.size());
for (size_t idx = 0; idx<size(); ++idx) {
storage[idx] = orig.storage[idx];
}
}
private:
T*     storage;      // storage of the elements
size_t storage_size; // number of elements
};
template <typename T> class A_Scalar;
// primary template
template <typename T>
class A_Traits {
public:
typedef T const& ExprRef;     // type to refer to is
constant reference
};
// partial specialization for scalars
template <typename T>
class A_Traits<A_Scalar<T> > {
public:
typedef A_Scalar<T> ExprRef; // type to refer to is
ordinary value
};
// class for objects that represent the addition of two
operands
template <typename T, typename OP1, typename
OP2>
class A_Add {
private:
typename A_Traits<OP1>::ExprRef op1;   // first
operand
typename A_Traits<OP2>::ExprRef op2;   // second
operand
public:
// constructor initializes references to operands
A_Add (OP1 const& a, OP2 const& b)
: op1(a), op2(b) {
}
// compute sum when value requested
T operator[] (size_t idx) const {
return op1[idx] + op2[idx];
}
// size is maximum size
size_t size() const {
assert (op1.size()==0 || op2.size()==0
|| op1.size()==op2.size());
return op1.size()!=0 ? op1.size() : op2.size();
}
};
// class for objects that represent the multiplication
of two operands
template <typename T, typename OP1, typename
OP2>
class A_Mult {
private:
typename A_Traits<OP1>::ExprRef op1;   // first
operand
typename A_Traits<OP2>::ExprRef op2;   //
second operand
public:
// constructor initializes references to operands
A_Mult (OP1 const& a, OP2 const& b)
: op1(a), op2(b) {
}
// compute product when value requested
T operator[] (size_t idx) const {
return op1[idx] * op2[idx];
}
// size is maximum size
size_t size() const {
assert (op1.size()==0 || op2.size()==0
|| op1.size()==op2.size());
return op1.size()!=0 ? op1.size() : op2.size();
}
};
void main()
{
SArray<double> x(1000), y(1000);
//...
//x = 1.2*x + x*y;
getch();
}
```

**Problem 163. Write a C++ program to OUTPUT List of integers.**

***Program:***

```
#include <iostream.h>
#include<conio.h>
#include<tdarg.h>
const int No=5;
```

```
class List
{
private:
int n;
int *array;
public:
List(int i)
{
array=new int[i];
n=i;
}
~List()
{
delete array;
}
void Init(int al,...);
void Show();
void Add(List &v1,List &v2);
int Inner(List &v2);
void Scale(int x);
};
void List::Init(int al,...)
{
va_list argp;
va_start(argp,al);
array[0]=al;
for(int i=1;i<n;i++)
array[i]=va_arg(argp,int);
va_end(argp);
}
void List::Show()
{
cout<<"(";
for(int i=0;i<n;i++)
cout<<array[i]<<",";
cout<<")"<<endl;
}
void List:: Add(List &v1,List &v2)
{
for(int i=0;i<n;i++)
array[i]=v1.array[i]+v2.array[i];
}
int List::Inner(List &v2)
{
int result=0;
for(int i=0;i<n;i++)
result+=array[i]*v2.array[i];
return(result);
}
void List::Scale(int x)
{
for(int i=0;i<n;i++)
array[i]*=x;
}
void main()
{
List vect1(No),vect2(No),vect3(No);
int InnerProduct;
vect1.Init(2,4,6,8,10);
vect2.Init(1,3,5,7,9);
int m=4;
cout<<"vect1=";
vect1.Show();
cout<<"vect2=";
vect2.Show();
vect3.Add(vect1,vect2);
cout<<"vect3=vect1+vect2=";
vect3.Show();
InnerProduct=vect1.Inner(vect2);
cout<<"Inner product of vect1&vect2
is:"<<InnerProduct<<endl;
vect3.Scale(m);
cout<<"vect3*"<<m<<"=";
vect3.Show();
getch();
}
```

**OUTPUT:**

```
vect1=(2,4,6,8,10,)
vect2=(1,3,5,7,9,)
vect3=vect1+vect2=(3,7,11,15,19,)
Inner product of vect1&vect2 is:190
vect3*4=(12,28,44,60,76,)
```

**Problem 164. Write a C++ program to manage list of employees based on STL.**

***Program:***

```
#include <iostream.h>
#include<conio.h>
#include <string.h>
#include <vector.h>
#include <map.h>
#include <list.h>
#include <algorithm.h>
const unsigned int LENGTH = 5;
class EmployeeList {
public:
typedef vector<int> grades;
map<string, grades> roster;
list<string> waiting_list;
public:
void add(const string& name);
void remove(const string& name);
```

```
void record(const string& name,const int grade,const
unsigned int assignment_number);
void display();
private:
void newEmployee(const string& name)
{
grades no_grades;
roster.insert(
pair<string, grades>(name, no_grades));
}
};
void EmployeeList::add(const string& name)
{
if (roster.find(name) != roster.end())
return;
if (roster.size() < LENGTH) {
newEmployee(name);
}
else
{
waiting_list.push_back(name);
}
}
void EmployeeList::remove(const string& name)
{
map<string, grades>::iterator anEmployee =
roster.find(name);
if (anEmployee == roster.end())
return;
roster.erase(name);
if (waiting_list.size() > 0) {
string wait_name = waiting_list.front();
waiting_list.pop_front();
newEmployee(wait_name);
}
}
void EmployeeList::record(const std::string&
name,const int grade,const unsigned int
assignment_number)
{
map<string, grades>::iterator anEmployee =
roster.find(name);
if (anEmployee == roster.end())
{
cerr << "ERROR: No " << name << '\n';
return;
}
if (anEmployee->second.size() <=
assignment_number)
anEmployee-
>second.resize(assignment_number+1);
anEmployee->second[assignment_number] =
grade;
}
void EmployeeList::display()
{
vector<string> sorted_names;
map<string, grades>::iterator curEmployee;
for (curEmployee = roster.begin();curEmployee !=
roster.end();++curEmployee){
sorted_names.push_back(curEmployee->first);
}
sort(sorted_names.begin(), sorted_names.end());
vector<string>::const_iterator cur_print;
for (cur_print = sorted_names.begin();cur_print !=
sorted_names.end();++cur_print)
{
cout << *cur_print << '\t';
grades::const_iterator cur_grade;
for (cur_grade =
roster[*cur_print].begin();cur_grade !=
roster[*cur_print].end();++cur_grade)
{
cout << *cur_grade << ' ';
}
cout << '\n';
}
}
void  main()
{
EmployeeList empList;
empList.add("A, S");
empList.add("B, M");
empList.add("J, R");
empList.add("S, J");
empList.add("M, M");
empList.add("G, W");
empList.add("C, W");
cout << "Before drop " << endl;
empList.display();
cout << "\n";
empList.remove("J, R");
cout << "After drop " <<endl;
empList.display();
cout << "\n";
for (int i = 0; i < 5; ++i){
empList.record("A, S", i*10+50, i);
empList.record("B, M", i*10+50, i);
empList.record("S, J", i*10+50, i);
empList.record("M, M", i*10+50, i);
empList.record("G, W", i*10+50, i);
}
```

```
cout << "Final " << endl;
empList.display();
cout << "\n";
getch();
}
```

**OUTPUT:**

Before drop
A, S
B, M
J, R
M, M
S, J
After drop
A, S
B, M
G, W
M, M
S, J
Final
A, S 50 60 70 80 90
B, M 50 60 70 80 90
G, W 50 60 70 80 90
M, M 50 60 70 80 90
S, J 50 60 70 80 90

# QUEUE:

**Problem 165. Write a C++ program for a template queue class.**

***Program:***

```
#include <iostream.h>
#include<conio.h>
const int maxQsize = 100;
template <class QType> class Queue
{
QType q[maxQsize];
int size;
int enqueueloc, dequeueloc;
public:
Queue(int len)
{
if(len > maxQsize)
len = maxQsize;
else if(len <= 0)
len = 1;
size = len;
enqueueloc = dequeueloc = 0;
}
void enqueue(QType data)
{
if(enqueueloc == size)
{
cout << " -- Queue is full.\n";
return;
}
enqueueloc++;
q[enqueueloc] = data;
}
QType dequeue()
{
if(dequeueloc == enqueueloc)
{
cout << " -- Queue is empty.\n";
return 0;
}
dequeueloc++;
return q[dequeueloc];
}
};
void main()
{
Queue<int> intQueue1(10), intQueue2(10); //
create two integer queues
intQueue1.enqueue(1);
intQueue1.enqueue(2);
intQueue1.enqueue(3);
intQueue2.enqueue(10);
intQueue2.enqueue(20);
intQueue2.enqueue(30);
cout << "Contents of integer queue intQueue1: ";
for(int i=0; i < 3; i++)
cout << intQueue1.dequeue() << " ";
cout << endl;
cout << "Contents of integer queue intQueue2: ";
for(int i=0; i < 3; i++)
cout << intQueue2.dequeue() << " ";
cout << endl;
Queue<double> doubleQueue1(10),
doubleQueue(10); // create two double queues
doubleQueue1.enqueue(1.01);
doubleQueue1.enqueue(2.02);
doubleQueue1.enqueue(3.03);
doubleQueue.enqueue(10.01);
doubleQueue.enqueue(20.02);
doubleQueue.enqueue(30.03);
cout << "Contents of double queue doubleQueue1:
";
for(int i=0; i < 3; i++)
cout << doubleQueue1.dequeue() << " ";
cout << endl;
```

```
cout << "Contents of double queue doubleQueue: ";
for(int i=0; i < 3; i++)
cout << doubleQueue.dequeue() << " ";
cout << endl;
getch();
}
```

**OUTPUT:**

Contents of integer queue intQueue1: 1 2 3
Contents of integer queue intQueue2: 10 20 30
Contents of double queue doubleQueue1: 1.01 2.02 3.03
Contents of double queue doubleQueue: 10.01 20.02 30.03

## SET:

**Problem 166. Write a C++ program for set class for characters.**

***Program:***

```
#include <iostream.h>
#include<conio.h>
const int MaxSize = 100;
class Set
{
int len; // number of members
char members[MaxSize]; // this array holds the set
int find(char ch); // find an element
public:
// Construct a null set.
Set() { len = 0; }
// Return the number of elements in the set.
int getLength() { return len; }
void showset(); // display the set
bool isMember(char ch); // check for membership
Set operator +(char ch); // add an element
Set operator -(char ch); // remove an element
Set operator +(Set ob2); // set union
Set operator -(Set ob2); // set difference
};
/* Return the index of the element
specified by ch, or -1 if not found. */
int Set::find(char ch)
{
int i;
for(i=0; i < len; i++)
if(members[i] == ch) return i;
return -1;
}
// Show the set.
void Set::showset()
{
cout << "{ ";
for(int i=0; i<len; i++)
cout << members[i] << " ";
cout << "}\n";
}
/* Return true if ch is a member of the set.
Return false otherwise. */
bool Set::isMember(char ch)
{
if(find(ch) != -1) return true;
return false;
}
// Add a unique element to a set.
Set Set::operator +(char ch)
{
Set newset;
if(len == MaxSize)
{
cout << "Set is full.\n";
return *this; // return existing set
}
newset = *this; // duplicate the existing set
// see if element already exists
if(find(ch) == -1)
{ // if not found, then add
// add new element to new set
newset.members[newset.len] = ch;
newset.len++;
}
return newset; // return updated set
}
// Remove an element from the set.
Set Set::operator -(char ch)
{
Set newset;
int i = find(ch); // i will be -1 if element not found
// copy and compress the remaining elements
for(int j=0; j < len; j++)
if(j != i) newset = newset + members[j];
return newset;
}
// Set union.
Set Set::operator +(Set ob2)
{
Set newset = *this; // copy the first set
// Add unique elements from second set.
for(int i=0; i < ob2.len; i++)
newset = newset + ob2.members[i];
return newset; // return updated set
}
```

```
// Set difference.
Set Set::operator -(Set ob2)
{
Set newset = *this; // copy the first set
 // Subtract elements from second set.
for(int i=0; i < ob2.len; i++)
newset = newset - ob2.members[i];
return newset; // return updated set
}
// Demonstrate the Set class.
void  main()
{
// construct 10-element empty Set
Set s1;
Set s2;
Set s3;
s1 = s1 + 'A';
s1 = s1 + 'B';
s1 = s1 + 'C';
cout << "s1 after adding A B C: ";
s1.showset();
cout << "\n";
cout << "Testing for membership using
isMember().\n";
if(s1.isMember('B'))
cout << "B is a member of s1.\n";
else
cout << "B is not a member of s1.\n";
if(s1.isMember('T'))
cout << "T is a member of s1.\n";
else
cout << "T is not a member of s1.\n";
cout << "\n";
s1 = s1 - 'B';
cout << "s1 after s1 = s1 - 'B': ";
s1.showset();
s1 = s1 - 'A';
cout << "s1 after s1 = s1 - 'A': ";
s1.showset();
s1 = s1 - 'C';
cout << "s1 after a1 = s1 - 'C': ";
s1.showset();
cout << "\n";
s1 = s1 + 'A';
s1 = s1 + 'B';
s1 = s1 + 'C';
cout << "s1 after adding A B C: ";
s1.showset();
cout << "\n";
s2 = s2 + 'A';
s2 = s2 + 'X';
s2 = s2 + 'W';
cout << "s2 after adding A X W: ";
s2.showset();
cout << "\n";
s3 = s1 + s2;
cout << "s3 after s3 = s1 + s2: ";
s3.showset();
s3 = s3 - s1;
cout << "s3 after s3 - s1: ";
s3.showset();
cout << "\n";
cout << "s2 after s2 = s2 - s2: ";
s2 = s2 - s2;  // clear s2
s2.showset();
cout << "\n";
s2 = s2 + 'C'; // add ABC in reverse order
s2 = s2 + 'B';
s2 = s2 + 'A';
cout << "s2 after adding C B A: ";
s2.showset();
getch();
}
```

**OUTPUT:**

```
s1 after adding A B C: { A B C }
Testing for membership using isMember().
B is a member of s1.
T is not a member of s1.
s1 after s1 = s1 - 'B': { A C }
s1 after s1 = s1 - 'A': { C }
s1 after a1 = s1 - 'C': { }
s1 after adding A B C: { A B C }
s2 after adding A X W: { A X W }
s3 after s3 = s1 + s2: { A B C X W }
s3 after s3 - s1: { X W }
s2 after s2 = s2 - s2: { }
s2 after adding C B A: { C B A }
```

## STACK:

**Problem 167. Write a C++ program to declare your own class stack.**

***Program:***

```
#include <iostream.h>
#include<conio.h>
const int SIZE=100;
class stack
{
int stck[SIZE];
int tos;
public:
```

```
stack()
{
tos=0;
}
void push(int i)
{
if(tos==SIZE) {
cout << "Stack is full.\n";
return;
}
stck[tos] = i;
tos++;
}
int pop()
{
if(tos==0)
{
cout << "Stack underflow.\n";
return 0;
}
tos--;
return stck[tos];
}
operator int()
{
return tos;
}
};
void  main()
{
stack stck;
int i, j;
for(i=0; i<20; i++)  stck.push(i);
j = stck; // convert to integer
cout << j << " items on stack.\n";
cout << SIZE - stck << " spaces open.\n";
getch();
}
```

**OUTPUT:**

20 items on stack.
80 spaces open.

## STRING CLASS:

**Problem 168. Write a C++ program for your own string class.**

***Program:***

```
#include <iostream.h>
#include<conio.h>
#include<string.h>
#include<stdlib.h>
class String
{
char *p;
int length;
public:
String();
String(char *str,int len);
char *getstring(){return p;}
int getlength(){return length;}
};
String::String()
{
p=new char[255];
if(!p)
{
cout<<"Allocation erroe\n";
exit(1);
}
*p='\0';
length=255;
}
String::String(char * str,int len)
{
if(strlen(str)>=len)
{
cout<<"Allcation too little memory! \n"; exit(1);
}
p=new char[len];
if(!p)
{
cout<<"Allocation error\n"; exit(1);
}
strcpy(p,str);
length=len;
}
void main()
{
String ob1;
String ob2("This is a string.",100);
cout<<"ob1:"<<ob1.getstring()<<"-Allocation
length:";
cout<<ob1.getlength()<<'\n';
cout<<"ob2:"<<ob2.getstring()<<"-Allocation
length:";
cout<<ob2.getlength()<<'\n';
getch();
}
```

**OUTPUT:**

ob1:-Allocation length:255
ob2:This is a string.-Allocation length:100

**Problem 169. Write a C++ program to define and use a string class.**

***Program:***

```
#include <string.h>
#include <iostream.h>
#include <ctype.h>
struct ignorecase_traits : public char_traits<char>
{
// return whether c1 and c2 are equal
static bool eq(const char& c1, const char& c2)
{
return toupper(c1)==toupper(c2);
}
// return whether c1 is less than c2
static bool lt(const char& c1, const char& c2)
{
return toupper(c1)<toupper(c2);
}
// compare up to n characters of s1 and s2
static int compare(const char* s1, const char* s2,
size_t n) {
for (size_t i=0; i<n; ++i)
{
if (!eq(s1[i],s2[i]))
{
return lt(s1[i],s2[i])?-1:1;
}
}
return 0;
}
// search c in s
static const char* find(const char* s, size_t n,
const char& c) {
for (size_t i=0; i<n; ++i)
{
if (eq(s[i],c)) {
return &(s[i]);
}
}
return 0;
}
};
// define a special type for such strings
typedef basic_string<char,ignorecase_traits>
icstring;
inline ostream& operator << (ostream& strm, const
icstring& s)
{
// simply convert the icstring into a normal string
return strm << string(s.data(),s.length());
}
void main()
{
using cout;
using endl;
icstring s1("hallo");
icstring s2("otto");
icstring s3("hALLo");
cout << boolalpha;
cout << s1 << " == " << s2 << " : " << (s1==s2)
<< endl;
cout << s1 << " == " << s3 << " : " << (s1==s3)
<< endl;
icstring::size_type idx = s1.find("All");
if (idx != icstring::npos) {
cout << "index of \"All\" in \"" << s1 << "\": "
<< idx << endl;
}else {cout << "\"All\" not found in \"" << s1 <<
endl;
}
getch();
}
```

**OUTPUT:**

```
hallo == otto : false
hallo == hALLo : true
index of "All" in "hallo": 1
```

# CHAPTER 3

# DEVELOPMENT IN CIN AND COUT

## SPECIAL FEATURES:

1. All functions of cin ,cout(fill,scientific,boolalpha,setw,setf etc.)
2. All functions of ios stream(oct,hex,dec,showbase,showpos,right,left ,basefield etc.)
3. Escape sequence
4. Math functions
5. Macros
6. Memory allocation(new,delete)
7. Set manipulators
8. Sorting
9. Format flags
10. Assert

**This chapter is divided into two parts:**

1. CONSOLE (64 PROGRAMS)
2. DEVELOPMENT IN CIN COUT(152 PROGRAMS)

## 1. CONSOLE (64 PROGRAMS)

## CIN MANIPULATOR:

**Problem 1.Write a C++ program for do while loop with a input manipulator.**

***Program:***

```
#include <iostream.h>
#include<conio.h>
#include <string.h>
istream &getpass(istream &stream)
{
cout << '\a'; // sound bell
cout << "Enter password: ";
return stream;
}
void  main()
{
char pw[80];
do
{
cin >> getpass >> pw;
} while (strcmp(pw, "password"));
cout << "Logon complete\n";
getch();
}
```

**OUTPUT:**

```
Enter password: 123
Enter password: 123
Enter password: ^C
```

**Problem 2. Write a C++ program for a input manipulator: sound bell.**

***Program:***

```
#include <iostream.h>
#include<conio.h>
istream &getpass(istream &stream)
{
cout << '\a';              // sound bell
```

```
cout << "Enter password: ";
return stream;
}
void main()
{
char pw[80];
do
{
cin >> getpass >> pw;
} while (strcmp(pw, "password"));
cout << "Logon complete\n";
getch();
}
```

**OUTPUT:**

Enter password: a
Enter password: a
Enter password: ^C

## CIN:

**Problem 3. Write a C++ program for Unformattwd Input/output.**

***Program:***

```
#include <iostream.h>
#include<conio.h>
#include <string.h>
string header ="Unformatted Input";
void main()
{
string word, rest;
cout << header << "Press <return> to go on" <<
endl;
cin.get();            // Read the new line without
saving.
cout << "\nEnter a sentence! End with <!> and
<return>." << endl;
cin >> word;          // Read the first word
getline( cin, rest, '!'); // read a line up to the
character !
cout << "The first word:   " << word  << endl
<< "Remaining text: " << rest << endl;
getch();
}
```

**OUTPUT:**

Unformatted Input <return> to go on
Enter a sentence! End with <!> and <return>.
a word!
The first word: a
Remaining text: word

**Problem 4. Write a C++ program for cin to read float in C++.**

***Program:***

```
#include <iostream.h>
#include<conio.h>
void  main()
{
double x, y;
cout << "Enter two floating-point values: ";
cin >> x ;
cin >> y;
cout << "The average of the two numbers is: " <<
(x + y)/2.0 << endl;
getch();
}
```

**OUTPUT:**

Enter two floating-point values: 123.1  123.4
The average of the two numbers is: 123.25

**Problem 5. Write a C++ program for cin to read.**

***Program:.***

```
#include <iostream.h>
#include<conio.h>
void  main ()
{
int testScore1, testScore2, testScore3;
cout << "Enter test score #1: ";
cin >> testScore1;
cout << "Enter test score #2: ";
cin >> testScore2;
cout << "Enter test score #3: ";
cin >> testScore3;
cout << "Test score #1: " << testScore1 << endl;
cout << "Test score #2: " << testScore2 << endl;
cout << "Test score #3: " << testScore3 << endl;
getch();
}
```

**OUTPUT:**

Enter test score #1: 12
Enter test score #2: 12
Enter test score #3: 21
Test score #1: 12
Test score #2: 12
Test score #3: 21

**Problem 6. Write a C++ program using the cin and cout Objects with Arrays.**

***Program:***

```
#include <iostream.h>
#include<conio.h>
```

```
const int MAX = 3;
void main ()
{
char grades[MAX];
for (int i = 0; i < MAX; i++)
{
cout << "Enter grade for test #" << i + 1 << ":";
cin >> grades[i];
}
getch();
}
```

**OUTPUT:**

Enter grade for test #1:34
Enter grade for test #2:34
Enter grade for test #1:34

**Problem 7. Write a C++ program for cin and cout work with char array.**

***Program:***

```
#include <iostream.h>
#include<conio.h>
void main ()
{
char name[ 80] = {'J', 'e', 'f', 'f', '/0' };
cout << "Enter your name: ";
cin >> name;
cout << "Your name is " << name;
getch();
}
```

**OUTPUT:**

Enter your name: jack
Your name is jack

**Problem 8. Write a C++ program for cin Object's getline Function.**

***Program:***

```
#include <iostream.h>
#include<conio.h>
void main ()
{
char name[ 80] = {'J', 'e', 'f', 'f', '/0' };
cout << "Enter your name: ";
cin >> name;
cout << "Your name is " << name;
getch();
}
```

**OUTPUT:**

Enter your name: jack
Your name is jack

**Problem 9. Write a C++ program Use the getline function to read the user's input and assign that input to the character array.**

***Program:***

```
#include <iostream.h>
#include<conio.h>
void main ()
{
char name[80] = {'J', 'e', 'f', 'f', '/0' };
cout << "Enter your name: ";
cin.getline(name, 80);
cout << "Your name is " << name;
getch();
}
```

**OUTPUT:**

Enter your name: jack
Your name is jack

**Problem 10. Write a C++ program for a Closer Look at the I/O Operators.**

***Program:***

```
#include <iostream.h>
#include<conio.h>
void main()
{
float f;
char str[80];
double d;
cout << "Enter two floating point numbers: ";
cin >> f >> d;
cout << "Enter a string: ";
cin >> str;
cout << f << " " << d << " " << str;
getch();
}
```

**OUTPUT:**

Enter two floating point numbers: 1.2
2.1
Enter a string: a string
1.2 2.1 a

## COUT BOOLALPHA:

**Problem 11. Write a C++ program for boolapha: true and false values to be input and output.**

***Program:***

```
#include <iostream.h>
#include<conio.h>
void main()
```

```
{
bool b;
b = true;
cout << b << " " << boolalpha << b << endl;
cout << "Enter a Boolean value: ";
cin >> boolalpha >> b;
cout << "Here is what you entered:  " << b;
getch();
}
```

**OUTPUT:**

```
1 true
Enter a Boolean value: 1
Here is what you entered: true
```

**Problem 12. Write a C++ program to demonstrate boolalpha format flag.**

***Program:***

```
#include <iostream.h>
#include<conio.h>
void  main()
{
bool b;
cout << "Before setting boolalpha flag: ";
b = true;
cout << b << " ";
b = false;
cout << b << endl;
cout << "After setting boolalpha flag: ";
b = true;
cout << boolalpha << b << " ";
b = false;
cout << b << endl;
cout << "Enter a Boolean value: ";
cin >> boolalpha >> b; // you can enter true or false
cout << "You entered " << b;
getch();
}
```

**OUTPUT:**

```
Before setting boolalpha flag: 1 0
After setting boolalpha flag: true false
Enter a Boolean value: 1
You entered false
```

## COUT CUSTOM:

**Problem 13. Write a C++ program to create an output manipulator.**

***Program:***

```
#include <iostream.h>
#include<conio.h>
#include <iomanip.h>
ostream &setup(ostream &stream)
{
stream.setf(ios::left);
stream << setw(10) << setfill('$');
return stream;
}
void main()
{
cout << 10 << " " << setup << 10;
getch();
}
```

**OUTPUT:**

```
10 10$$$$$$$$
```

**Problem 14. Write a C++ program for a manipulator: turns on the showbase flag and sets output to hexadecimal.**

***Program:***

```
#include <iostream.h>
#include<conio.h>
#include <iomanip.h>
ostream &sethex(ostream &stream)
{
stream.setf(ios::showbase);
stream.setf(ios::hex, ios::basefield);
return stream;
}
void main()
{
cout << 256 << " " << sethex << 256;
getch();
}
```

**Problem 15. Write a C++ program for a simple output manipulator: sethex.**

***Program:***

```
#include <iostream.h>
#include<conio.h>
#include <iomanip.h>
ostream &sethex(ostream &stream)
{
stream.setf(ios::showbase);
stream.setf(ios::hex, ios::basefield);
return stream;
}
void  main()
{
cout << 256 << " "<< sethex << 256;
getch();
```

```
}
```

**OUTPUT:**

256 0x100

**Problem 16. Write a C++ program to define operator for cout.**

***Program:***

```
#include <iostream.h>
#include <iomanip.h>
ostream &ra(ostream &stream)
{
stream << "--> ";
return stream;
}
ostream &la(ostream &stream)
{
stream << " <--";
return stream;
}
void main()
{
cout << "AAA" << ra << 33.23 << endl;
cout << "BBB" << ra << 67.66 << la;
getch();
}
```

**OUTPUT:**

AAA--> 33.23
BBB--> 67.66 <--

**Problem 17. Write a C++ program to create custom output format.**

***Program:***

```
#include <iostream.h>
#include<conio.h>
ostream &setup(ostream &stream)
{
stream.width(10);
stream.precision(4);
stream.fill('*');
return stream;
}
void main()
{
cout << setup << 123.123456;
getch();
}
```

**OUTPUT:**

*****123.1

**Problem 18. Write a C++ program for custom cout output manipulator.**

***Program:***

```
#include <iostream.h>
#include<conio.h>
// Attention:
ostream &atn(ostream &stream)
{
stream << "Attention: ";
return stream;
}
// Please note:
ostream &note(ostream &stream)
{
stream << "Please Note: ";
return stream;
}
void main()
{
cout << atn << "High voltage circuit\n";
cout << note << "Turn off all lights\n";
getch();
}
```

**OUTPUT:**

Attention: High voltage circuit
Please Note: Turn off all lights

## COUT FILL:

**Problem 19. Write a C++ program for cout fill(): Specify the fill character.**

***Program:***

```
#include <iostream.h>
#include<conio.h>
void  main()
{
cout.precision(4) ;
cout.width(10);
cout << 10.12345 << "\n";
cout.fill('*');
cout.width(10);
cout << 10.12345 << "\n";
cout.width(10);
cout << "Hi!" << "\n";
cout.width(10);
cout.setf(ios::left);
cout << 10.12345;
getch();
}
```

**OUTPUT:**

```
     10.12
*****10.12
```

**Development in Cin and Cout**

```
*******Hi!
10.12*****
```

**Problem 20. Write a C++ program Uses ios member functions: setf, ios::hex, ios::basefield.**

***Program:***

```
#include <iostream.h>
#include<conio.h>
#include <iomanip.h>
void main()
{
cout.setf(ios::hex, ios::basefield);
cout << 12300 << "\n";
cout.fill('?');
cout.width(10);
cout << 232343.0;
getch();
}
```

**OUTPUT:**

```
300c
????232343
```

## COUT FLAG STATUS:

**Problem 21. Using Manipulators to Format I/O.**

| Manipulator | Purpose | Input/output |
|---|---|---|
| boolalpha | Turns on boolapha flag. | Input/output |
| dec | Turns on dec flag. | Input/output |
| endl | output a newline character and flush the stream. | output |
| ends | output a null. | output |
| fixed | turns on fixed flag. | output |
| flush | Flush a stream. | output |
| hex | Turns on hex flag. | Input/output |
| internal | Turns on internal flag. | output |
| left | Turns on left flag. | output |
| nobooalpha | Turns off boolalpha flag. | Input/output |
| noshowbase | Turns off showbase flag. | output |
| noshowpoint | Turns off showpoint flag. | output |
| noshowpos | Turns off showpos flag. | output |
| noskipws | Turns off skipws flag. | Input |
| nounitbuf | Turns off unitbuf flag. | output |
| nouppercase | Turns off uppercase flag. | output |
| oct | Turns on oct flag. | Input/output |
| resetiosflags (fmtflags f) | Turn off the flags specified in f. | Input/output |
| right | Turns on right flag. | output |
| scientific | Turns on scientific flag. | output |
| setbase(int base) | Set the number base to base. | Input/output |
| setfill(int ch) | Set the fill character to ch. | output |
| setiosflags (fmtflags f) | Turn on the flags specified in f. | Input/output |
| setprecision (int p) | Set the number of digits of precision. | output |
| setw(int w) | Set the field width to w. | output |
| showbase | Turns on showbase flag. | output |
| showpoint | Turns on showpoint flag. | output |
| showpos | Turns on showpos flag. | output |
| skipws | Turns on skipws flag. | Input |
| unitbuf | Turns on unitbuf flag. | output |
| uppercase | Turns on uppercase flag. | output |
| ws | Skip leading white space. | Input |

**Problem 22. Write a C++ program for cout flags: showpoint, showpos.**

***Program:***

```
#include <iostream.h>
#include<conio.h>
void main( )
{
cout.setf(ios::showpoint | ios::showpos,
ios::showpoint);
cout << 102340.0;
getch();
}
```

**OUTPUT:**

102340.

**Problem 23. Write a C++ program to store cout flags, set to new ones and restore.**

***Program:***

```
#include <iostream.h>
#include<conio.h>
void main()
{
ios::fmtflags f;
f = cout.flags(); // store flags
cout.unsetf(ios::dec);
cout.setf(ios::showbase | ios::hex);
cout << 100 << '\n';
cout.flags(f); // reset flags
getch();
}
```

**OUTPUT:**

0x64

**Problem 24. Write a C++ program to displays the status of the format flags.**

***Program:***

```
#include <iostream.h>
#include<conio.h>
void showflags();
void main()
{
// show default condition of format flags
showflags();
cout.setf(ios::oct | ios::showbase | ios::fixed);
showflags();
getch();
}
void showflags()
{
ios::fmtflags f;
f = cout.flags(); // get flag settings
if(f & ios::skipws)
cout << "skipws on\n";
else
cout << "skipws off\n";
if(f & ios::left)
cout << "left on\n";
else
cout << "left off\n";
if(f & ios::right)
cout << "right on\n";
else
cout << "right off\n";
if(f & ios::internal)
cout << "internal on\n";
else
cout << "internal off\n";
if(f & ios::dec)
cout << "dec on\n";
else
cout << "dec off\n";
if(f & ios::oct)
cout << "oct on\n";
else
cout << "oct off\n";
if(f & ios::hex)
cout << "hex on\n";
else
cout << "hex off\n";
if(f & ios::showbase)
cout << "showbase on\n";
else
cout << "showbase off\n";
if(f & ios::showpoint)
cout << "showpiont on\n";
else
cout << "showpoint off\n";
if(f & ios::showpos)
cout << "showpos on\n";
else
cout << "showpos off\n";
if(f & ios::uppercase)
cout << "uppercase on\n";
else
cout << "uppercase off\n";
if(f & ios::scientific)
cout << "scientific on\n";
else
cout << "scientific off\n";
if(f & ios::fixed)
cout << "fixed on\n";
else
```

```
cout << "fixed off\n";
if(f & ios::unitbuf)
cout << "unitbuf on\n";
else
cout << "unitbuf off\n";
if(f & ios::boolalpha)
cout << "boolalpha on\n";
else
cout << "boolalpha off\n";
cout << endl;
}
```

**OUTPUT:**

```
skipws off
left off
right off
internal off
dec on
oct off
hex off
showbase off
showpoint off
showpos off
uppercase off
scientific off
fixed off
unitbuf off
boolalpha off
skipws on
left off
right off
internal off
dec on
oct on
hex off
showbase on
showpoint off
showpos off
uppercase off
scientific off
fixed on
unitbuf off
boolalpha off
```

## COUT FLAG:

**Problem 25. Write a C++ program to demonstrate flags() and unsetf(): ios::fmtflags .**

***Program:***

```
#include <iostream.h>
#include<conio.h>
void main()
{
ios::fmtflags f;
f = cout.flags();
if(f & ios::showpos)
cout << "showpos is set for cout.\n";
else
cout << "showpos is cleared for cout.\n";
cout << "\nSetting showpos for cout.\n";
cout.setf(ios::showpos);
f = cout.flags();
if(f & ios::showpos)
cout << "showpos is set for cout.\n";
else
cout << "showpos is cleared for cout.\n";
cout << "\nClearing showpos for cout.\n";
cout.unsetf(ios::showpos);
f = cout.flags();
if(f & ios::showpos)
cout << "showpos is set for cout.\n";
else
cout << "showpos is cleared for cout.\n";
getch();
}
```

**OUTPUT:**

```
showpos is cleared for cout.
Setting showpos for cout.
showpos is set for cout.
Clearing showpos for cout.
showpos is cleared for cout.
```

## COUT HEX:

**Problem 26. Write a C++ program for cout: output hex.**

***Program:***

```
#include <iostream.h>
#include<conio.h>
#include <iomanip.h>
void main()
{
cout << hex << 100 << endl;
cout << setfill('?') << setw(10) << 2343.0;
getch();
}
```

**OUTPUT:**

```
64
??????2343
```

**Problem 27. Write a C++ program for Set cout: hex and basefield, ios::hex, ios::basefield.**

***Program:***

```
#include <iostream.h>
#include<conio.h>
#include <iomanip.h>
void  main()
{
cout.setf(ios::hex, ios::basefield);
cout << 100 << endl;                    // cout 100 in hex
cout.fill('?');
cout.width(10);
cout << 2343.0;
getch();
}
```

**OUTPUT:**

```
64
??????2343
```

## COUT MANIPULATOR:

**Problem 28. Write a C++ program to show time and date.**

***Program:***

```
#include <iostream.h>
#include<conio.h>
#include <time.h>
// A time and date output manipulator.
ostream &td(ostream &stream)
{
struct tm *localt;
time_t t;
t = time(NULL);
localt = localtime(&t);
stream << asctime(localt) << endl;
return stream;
}
void main()
{
cout << td << '\n';
getch();
}
```

**OUTPUT:**

```
wed Mar 1 15:24:22 2009
```

**Problem 29. Write a C++ program to turn on hex output with uppercase X.**

***Program:***

```
#include <iostream.h>
#include<conio.h>
ostream &sethex(ostream &stream)
{
stream.unsetf(ios::dec | ios::oct);
stream.setf(ios::hex | ios::uppercase |
ios::showbase);
return stream;
}
// Reset flags.
ostream &reset(ostream &stream)
{
stream.unsetf(ios::hex | ios::uppercase |
ios::showbase);
stream.setf(ios::dec);
return stream;
}
void main()
{
cout << sethex << 100 << '\n';
cout << reset << 100 << '\n';
getch();
}
```

**OUTPUT:**

```
0x64
100
```

**Problem 30. Write a C++ program to skip 10 characters.**

***Program:***

```
#include <iostream.h>
#include<conio.h>
istream &skipchar(istream &stream)
{
int i;
char c;
for(i = 0; i <10; i++) stream >> c;
return stream;
}
void main()
{
char str[80];
cout << "Enter some characters: ";
cin >> skipchar >> str;
cout << str << '\n';
getch();
}
```

**OUTPUT:**

```
Enter some characters: some chars
asdf
sdf
```

**Problem 31. Write a C++ program for Set cout format: ios::showpos.**

***Program:***

```
#include <iostream.h>
#include<conio.h>
void main()
{
cout.setf(ios::showpos);
cout << -10 << ' ' << 10 << '\n';
getch();
}
```

**OUTPUT:**

-10 +10

**Problem 32. Write a C++ program for set cout format: ios::showpoint | ios::uppercase | ios::scientific.**

***Program:***

```
#include <iostream.h>
#include<conio.h>
void main()
{
cout.setf(ios::showpoint | ios::uppercase |
ios::scientific);
cout << 100.0;
getch();
}
```

**OUTPUT:**

1.000000E+02

**Problem 33. Write a C++ program to predefine format for cout.**

***Program:***

```
#include <iostream.h>
#include<conio.h>
ostream &tabs(ostream &stream)
{
stream << '\t' << '\t' << '\t' ;
stream.width(20);
return stream;
}
void main()
{
cout << tabs << "Testing\n";
getch();
}
```

**OUTPUT:**

Testing

**Problem 34. Write a C++ program for Utility function for cin.**

***Program:***

```
#include <iostream.h>
#include<conio.h>
#include <ctype.h>
istream &findalpha(istream &stream)
{
char ch;
do
{
stream.get(ch);
} while(!isalpha(ch));
return stream;
}
void main()
{
char str[80];
cin >> findalpha >> str;
cout << str << '\n';
getch();
}
```

**OUTPUT:**

aa
a

**Problem 35. Write a C++ program to define function to set cout.**

***Program:***

```
#include <iostream.h>
#include<conio.h>
ostream &setsci(ostream &stream)
{
stream.setf(ios::scientific | ios::uppercase);
return stream;
}
void main()
{
double f = 123.23;
cout << setsci << f;
cout << '\n';
getch();
}
```

**OUTPUT:**

1.232300E+02

**Problem 36. Write a C++ program to redirecting Standard Input And output.**

***Program:***

```
#include <iostream.h>
#include<conio.h>
#include <iomanip.h>
#include <string.h>
```

```
void main()
{
string line;
int number = 0;
while( getline( cin, line))
{
cout << setw(5) << ++number << ": "
<< line << endl;
}
getch();
}
```

## COUT PCOUNT:

**Problem 37. Write a C++ program for pcount(): reports that outs contains.**

***Program:***

```
#include <iostream.h>
#include<conio.h>
#include <strstream.h>
void main()
{
char str[80];ostrstream outs(str, sizeof(str));
outs << "abcdefg ";
outs << 27 << " " << 890.23;
outs << ends; // null terminate
cout << "chars in outs: "<< outs.pcount(); //
cout << " " << str;
getch();
}
```

**OUTPUT:**

chars in outs: 18 abcdefg 27 890.23

## COUT SCIENTIFIC:

**Problem 38 Write a C++ program for cout: change formats.**

***Program:***

```
#include <iostream.h>
#include<conio.h>
void main()
{
// change formats
cout.unsetf(ios::dec);
cout.setf(ios::hex | ios::scientific);
cout << 123.23 << " hello " << 100 << '\n';
cout.setf(ios::showpos);
cout << 10 << ' ' << -10 << '\n';
cout. setf(ios::showpoint | ios::fixed);
cout << 100.0;
getch();
}
```

**OUTPUT:**

1.232300e+02 hello 64
a fffffff6
+100.000

**Problem 39. Write a C++ program for sets both the uppercase and scientific flags and clears the uppercase flag.**

***Program:***

```
#include <iostream.h>
#include<conio.h>
void main()
{
cout.setf(ios::uppercase | ios::scientific);
cout << 1010.112;
cout.unsetf(ios::uppercase); // clear uppercase
cout << endl << 1100.112;
getch();
}
```

**Problem 40. Write a C++ program for cout: number base, justification, and format flags.**

***Program:***

```
#include <iostream.h>
#include<conio.h>
void main()
{
cout.setf(ios::hex, ios::basefield);
cout << 300;
getch();
}
```

**OUTPUT:**

12c

**Problem 41. Write a C++ program to displays the value 100 with the showpos and showpoint flags turned on.**

***Program:***

```
#include <iostream.h>
#include<conio.h>
void main()
{
cout.setf(ios::showpoint);
cout.setf(ios::showpos);
cout << 100.0;
getch();
}
```

## COUT SETF:

**Problem 42. Write a C++ program for cout: how to display float number, ios::showpoint, ios::showpos.**

***Program:***

```
#include <iostream.h>
#include<conio.h>
void main()
{
cout.setf(ios::showpoint);
cout.setf(ios::showpos);
cout << 100.0;
getch();
}
```

**OUTPUT:**

+100.000

**Problem 43. Write a C++ program using OR together two or more flags: ios::uppercase | ios::scientific.**

***Program:***

```
#include <iostream.h>
#include<conio.h>
void main()
{
cout.setf(ios::uppercase | ios::scientific);
cout << 1001.12;
cout.unsetf(ios::uppercase);       // clear uppercase
cout << " \n" << 1100.12;
getch();
}
```

**OUTPUT:**

1.001120E+03
1.001120e+03

**Problem 44. Write a C++ program for set cout: setf(ios::showpoint | ios::showpos, ios::showpoint).**

***Program:***

```
#include <iostream.h>
#include<conio.h>
void main( )
{
cout.setf(ios::showpoint | ios::showpos,
ios::showpoint);
cout << 100.0;
getch();
}
```

**OUTPUT:**

100.000

**Problem 45. Write a C++ program for set cout: hex, basefield, setf(ios::hex, ios::basefield).**

***Program:***

```
#include <iostream.h>
#include<conio.h>
void main()
{
cout.setf(ios::hex, ios::basefield);
cout << 100;
getch();
}
```

**OUTPUT:**

64

## COUT SETIOSFLAGS:

**Problem 46. Write a C++ program for cout: set ios flags, ios::showpos, ios::showbase.**

***Program:***

```
#include <iostream.h>
#include<conio.h>
#include <iomanip.h>
void main()
{
cout << setiosflags(ios::showpos);
cout << setiosflags(ios::showbase);
cout << 123 << " " << hex << 123;
getch();
}
```

**OUTPUT:**

+123 0x7b

**Problem 47. Write a C++ program for setiosflags(): set the format flags related to a stream.**

***Program:***

```
#include <iostream.h>
#include<conio.h>
#include <iomanip.h>
void main()
{
cout << setiosflags(ios::showpos);
cout << setiosflags(ios::showbase);
cout << 123 << " " << hex << 123;
getch();
}
```

**OUTPUT:**

+123 0x7b

**Problem 48. Write a C++ program using setiosflags(): ios::showpos, ios::scientific.**

***Program:***

```
#include <iostream.h>
#include<conio.h>
#include <iomanip.h>
void main()
{
cout << setiosflags(ios::showpos) <<
setiosflags(ios::scientific)
<< 123 << " " << 123.23;
getch();
}
```

**OUTPUT:**

```
+123 +1.232300e+02
```

## COUT SETW SETPRECISION:

**Problem 49. Write a C++ program for Cout: precision 4.**

***Program:***

```
#include <iostream.h>
#include<conio.h>
void main()
{
cout.precision(4);
cout << 10.0/3.0 << '\n';
getch();
}
```

**OUTPUT:**

```
3.333
```

**Problem 50. Write a C++ program to demonstrate an I/O manipulator: setprecision(2) and setw(20).**

***Program:***

```
#include <iostream.h>
#include<conio.h>
#include <iomanip.h>
void main()
{
cout << setprecision(2) << 1000.243 << endl;
cout << setw(20) << "Hello there.";
getch();
}
```

**OUTPUT:**

```
1e+03
  Hello there
```

**Problem 51. Write a C++ program uses I/O manipulators to display the table of squares and square roots.**

***Program:***

```
#include <iostream.h>
#include<conio.h>
#include <iomanip.h>
#include <math.h>
void main()
{
double x;
cout << setprecision(4);
cout << "      x   sqrt(x)     x^2\n\n";
for(x = 2.0; x <= 20.0; x++)
{
cout << setw(7) << x << "  ";
cout << setw(7) << sqrt(x) << "  ";
cout << setw(7) << x*x << '\n';
}
getch();
}
```

**Problem 52. Write a C++ program to enters a character and output is its octal, decimal, and hexadecimal code.**

***Program:***

```
#include <iostream.h>
#include<conio.h>
#include <iomanip.h>
#include <string.h>
void main()
{
int number = ' ';
cout << "The white space code is:" << number <<
"." << endl;
char ch;
string prompt = "Please enter a character followed
by <return>: ";
cout << prompt;
cin >> ch;
number = ch;
cout << "The character " << ch << " has code" <<
number << endl;
cout << uppercase << "     octal  decimal
hexadecimal\n "<< oct << setw(8) << number
<< dec << setw(8) << number<< hex
<< setw(8) << number << endl;
getch();
}
```

## COUT SYNC CLEAR:

**Problem 53. Write a C++ program for cout unset: clear flag.**

***Program:***

```
#include <iostream.h>
#include<conio.h>
void  main()
{
cout << 100 << ' ';
cout.unsetf(ios::dec); // clear dec flag
cout.setf(ios::hex);,
cout << 100 << ' ';
cout.unsetf(ios::hex); // clear hex flag
cout.setf(ios::oct);
cout << 100 << '\n';
getch();
}
```

**OUTPUT:**

100 64 144

**Problem 54. Write a C++ program for cout: Clears the buffer and resets any error flags that may be set.**

***Program:***

```
#include <iostream.h>
#include<conio.h>
#include <iomanip.h>
#include <string.h>
void  main()
{
string label;
double price;
cout << "Please enter an label: ";
cin >> setw(16);        // cin.width(16);
cin >> label;
cin.sync();
cin.clear();
cout << "\nEnter the price: ";
cin >> price;
cout << fixed << setprecision(2)  // Controlling
output
     << endl  << "Article:"
     << endl  << "Label:  " << label
     << endl  << "Price:  " << price << endl;
getch();
}
```

**OUTPUT:**

Please enter an label: label
Enter the price: a
Article:
Label: label
Price: 0.00

## COUT TERMINATOR:

**Problem 55. Write a C++ program to defines your own terminate( ) handler.**

***Program:***

```
#include <iostream.h>
#include <stdlib.h>
#include <exception.h>
void myTerminator()
{
cout << "Your own terminate handler\n";
abort();
}
void  main()
{
set_terminate(myTerminator);
try
{
cout << "Inside try block.";
throw 100;
}
catch (double i)
{
}
getch();
}
```

## COUT UPPERCASE:

**Problem 56. Write a C++ program for cout: uppercase, show base, hex.**

***Program:***

```
#include <iostream.h>
#include<conio.h>
void  main()
{
cout.unsetf(ios::dec);
cout.setf(ios::uppercase | ios::showbase | ios::hex);
cout << 88 << '\n';
cout.unsetf(ios::uppercase);
cout << 88 << '\n';
getch();
}
```

**OUTPUT:**

0X58
0X58

## COUT WIDTH:

**Problem 57. Write a C++ program to create a table of log10 and log from 2 through 100.**

***Program:***

```
#include <iostream.h>
#include<conio.h>
#include <math.h>
void main()
{
double x;
cout.precision(5);
cout << "      x      log x      ln e\n\n";
for(x = 2.0; x <= 100.0; x++)
{
cout.width(10);
cout << x << "  ";
cout.width(10);
cout << log10(x) << " ";
cout.width(10);
cout << log(x) << '\n';
}
getch();
}
```

**Problem 58. Write a C++ program for Set cout length.**

***Program:***

```
#include <iostream.h>
#include <string.h>
void center(char *s);
void main()
{
center("www.google.com!");
center("www.google.com");
getch();
}
void center(char *s)
{
int len;
len = 40+(strlen(s)/2);
cout.width(len);
cout << s << '\n';
}
```

**OUTPUT:**

```
        www.google.com!
              www.google.com
```

**Problem 59. Write a C++ program for cout: width(), precision(), and fill().**

***Program:***

```
#include <iostream.h>
#include<conio.h>
void  main()
{
cout.setf(ios::showpos);
cout.setf(ios::scientific);
cout << 123 << " " << 123.23 << endl;
cout.precision(2);            // two digits after
decimal //point
cout.width(10);               // in a field of 10
characters
cout << 123 << " ";
cout.width(10);               // set width to 10
cout << 123.23 << endl;
cout.fill('#');               // fill using #
cout.width(10);               // in a field of 10
characters
cout << 123 << " ";
cout.width(10);               // set width to 10
cout << 123.23;
getch();
}
```

**OUTPUT:**

```
+123 +1.232300e+02
    +123  +1.23e+02
######+123 #+1.23e+02
```

## COUT:

**Problem 60. Write a C++ program to call function in cout.**

***Program:***

```
#include <iostream.h>
#include<conio.h>
inline int max(int a, int b)
{
return a>b ? a : b;
}
void main()
{
cout << max(10, 20);
cout << " " << max(99, 88);
getch();
}
```

**OUTPUT:**

```
20 99
```

**Problem 61. Write a C++ program using function in cout.**

***Program:***

```
#include <iostream.h>
#include<conio.h>
void  main()
{
cout << (10>20 ? 10 : 20);
cout << " " << (99>88 ? 99 : 88);
getch();
}
```

**OUTPUT:**

20 99

**Problem 62. Write a C++ program using the cout Object with Numeric Arrays.**

***Program:***

```
#include <iostream.h>
#include<conio.h>
const int MAX = 3;
void  main ()
{
int testScore[MAX];
for (int i = 0; i < MAX; i++)
{
cout << "Enter test score #" << i + 1 << ": ";
cin >> testScore[i];
}
cout << "The test scores are: " << testScore;
getch();
}
```

**OUTPUT:**

Enter test score #1: 1
Enter test score #2: 2
Enter test score #3: 3
The test scores are: 0xd7104

**Problem 63. Write a C++ program for unformattwd Input/outputcin.get and getline.**

***Program:***

```
include <iostream.h>
#include<conio.h>
#include <string.h>
string header ="Unformatted Input";
void  main()
{
string word, rest;
cout << header << "Press <return> to go on" <<
endl;
cin.get();                // Read the new line without
saving.
cout << "\nEnter a sentence! End with <!> and
<return>." << endl;
cin >> word;                      // Read the first word
getline( cin, rest, '!');  // read a line up to the
character !
cout << "The first word:   " << word  << endl
     << "Remaining text: " << rest << endl;
getch();
}
```

**OUTPUT:**

unformatted InputPress <return> to go on
Enter a sentence! End with <!> and <return>.
!
asdf!
The first word:   !
Remaining text:
asdf

## OSTREAM ITERATOR:

**Problem 64. Write a C++ program output_using an ostream iterator.**

***Program:***

```
#include <iostream.h>
#include<conio.h>
#include <iterator.h>
void  main()
{
ostream_iterator<int, char>   oi(cout);
*oi = 6;
*++oi = 88;
getch();
}
```

**OUTPUT:**

688

# 2. DEVELOPMENT CIN COUT(152 PROGRAMS)

## CIN FUNCTIONS:

**Problem 1. Write a C++ program to read int value from keyboard.**

***Program:***

```
#include <iostream.h>
#include<conio.h>
void main()
{
cout << "Enter a number: ";
int a; // declare one variable
cin >> a;
cout << "Enter a second number: ";
int b; // declare another variable
cin >> b;
cout << "Product: " << a*b << '\n';
getch();
}
```

**OUTPUT:**

Enter a number: 123
Enter a second number: 12
Product: 1476

**Problem 2. Write a C++ program to use get() to read a string that contains spaces.**

***Program:***

```
#include <iostream.h>
#include<conio.h>
void main()
{
char str[80];
cout << "Enter your name: ";
cin.get(str, 79);
cout << str << '\n';
getch();
}
```

**OUTPUT:**

Enter your name: Ikvinderpal Singh
Ikvinderpal Singh

**Problem 3. Write a C++ program for cin with strings (cin.getline).**

***Program:***

```
#include <iostream.h>
#include<conio.h>
void main ()
{
char mybuffer [100];
cout << "What's your name? ";
cin.getline (mybuffer,100);
cout << "Hello " << mybuffer << ".\n";
cout << "Which is your favourite team? ";
cin.getline (mybuffer,100);
cout << mybuffer;
getch();
}
```

**OUTPUT:**

What's your name? Joe
Hello Joe.
Which is your favourite team? Ea
Ea"

**Problem 4. Write a C++ program for cin and atoi, atof functions.**

***Program:***

```
#include <iostream.h>
#include <stdlib.h>
#include<conio.h>
void main ()
{
char mybuffer [100];
float price;
int quantity;
cout << "Enter price: ";
cin.getline (mybuffer,100);
price = atof (mybuffer);
cout << "Enter quantity: ";
cin.getline (mybuffer,100);
quantity = atoi (mybuffer);
cout << "Total price: " << price*quantity;
getch();
}
```

**OUTPUT:**

Enter price: 123
Enter quantity: 12
Total price: 1476"

**Problem 5. Write a C++ program for testing error states.**

***Program:***

```
#include <iostream.h>
#include<conio.h>
```

```
void main()
{
int integerValue;
// display results of cin functions
cout << "Before a bad input operation:"
     << "\ncin.rdstate(): " << cin.rdstate()
     << "\n   cin.eof(): " << cin.eof()
     << "\n  cin.fail(): " << cin.fail()
     << "\n   cin.bad(): " << cin.bad()
     << "\n  cin.good(): " << cin.good();
cin >> integerValue;
cout << endl;
cout << "After a bad input operation:"
     << "\ncin.rdstate(): " << cin.rdstate()
     << "\n   cin.eof(): " << cin.eof()
     << "\n  cin.fail(): " << cin.fail()
     << "\n   cin.bad(): " << cin.bad()
     << "\n  cin.good(): " << cin.good() << endl <<
endl;
cin.clear();
cout << "After cin.clear()" << "\ncin.fail(): " <<
cin.fail()
     << "\ncin.good(): " << cin.good() << endl;
getch();
}
```

**OUTPUT:**

```
Before a bad input operation:
cin.rdstate(): 0
cin.eof(): 0
cin.fail(): 0
cin.bad(): 0
cin.good(): 12
After a bad input operation:
cin.rdstate(): 0
cin.eof(): 0
cin.fail(): 0
cin.bad(): 0
cin.good(): 1
After cin.clear()
cin.fail(): 0
cin.good(): 1
```

**Problem 6. Write a C++ program for unformatted I/O using cin.read, cin.gcount and cout.write.**

***Program:***

```
#include <iostream.h>
#include<conio.h>
void main()
{
const int SIZE = 80;
char buffer[ SIZE ];
cout << "Enter a sentence:" << endl;
cin.read( buffer, 20 );
cout.write( buffer, cin.gcount() );
cout << endl;
getch();
}
```

**OUTPUT:**

```
Enter a sentence:
This is a sentence.
This is a sentence.
```

**Problem 7. Write a C++ program to contrasting input of a string via cin and cin.get.**

***Program:***

```
#include<conio.h>
#include<iostream.h>
void main()
{
const int SIZE = 80;
char buffer1[ SIZE ];
char buffer2[ SIZE ];
cout << "Enter a sentence:" << endl;
cin >> buffer1;
cout << buffer1 << endl << endl;
cout << "Enter a sentence:" << endl;
cin.get( buffer2, SIZE );
cout << buffer2 << endl;
getch();
}
```

**OUTPUT:**

```
Enter a sentence:
This is a sentence.
This
Enter a sentence:
 is a sentence.
```

**Problem 8. Write a C++ program to demonstrating member function width.**

***Program:***

```
#include <iostream.h>
#include<conio.h>
void main()
{
int widthValue = 4;
char sentence[ 10 ];
cout << "Enter a sentence:" << endl;
cin.width( 5 );
cin >> sentence;
cout << sentence << endl;
getch();
```

```
}
```

**OUTPUT:**

Enter a sentence:
This is a sentence.
This

**Problem 9. Write a C++ program to read char array from keyboard, get its length and concatenate two strings.**

***Program:***

```
#include <iostream.h>
#include<conio.h>
#include <string.h>
void main()
{
char firststring[40],secondstring[40],thirdstring[40];
int size;
cout << "Please enter a word \n";
cin.getline(firststring,40);
cout << "Please enter another word \n";
cin.getline(secondstring,40);
size = strlen(firststring);
strcat(firststring,secondstring);
cout << "The length of the first string you entered
is" << size << "\n";
cout << "Both strings you entered are " <<
thirdstring<< "\n";
getch();
}
```

**OUTPUT:**

Please enter a word
word
Please enter another word
word
The length of the first string you entered is4
Both strings you entered are ?

**Problem 10. Write a C++ program to read a character from keyboard.**

***Program:***

```
#include <iostream.h>
#include<conio.h>
void main()
{
char c;
// while it is possible to read a character
while (cin.get(c))
{
// print it
cout.put(c);
}
getch();
}
```

**OUTPUT:**

a
a
c
c
d
d
e
e
Terminate batch job (Y/N)? n

**Problem 11. Write a C++ program to copy all standard input to standard output.**

***Program:***

```
#include <iostream.h>
#include<conio.h>
void main ()
{
// copy all standard input to standard output
cout << cin.rdbuf();
getch();
}
```

**OUTPUT:**

asdf
asdf
asdf
asdf
fdsa
fdsa
Terminate batch job (Y/N)? n

**Problem 12. Write a C++ program for manipulator that skips until end-of-line.**

***Program:***

```
#include <iostream.h>
#include<conio.h>
#include <limits.h>
template <class charT, class traits>
inline
basic_istream<charT,traits>&
ignoreLine (basic_istream<charT,traits>& strm)
{
// skip until end-of-line
strm.ignore(numeric_limits<int>::max(),strm.wide
n('\n'));
// return stream for concatenation
return strm;
}
void main()
```

```
{
int i;
cout << "read int and ignore rest of the line" <<
endl;
cin >> i;
// ignore the rest of the line
cin >> ignoreLine;
cout << "int: " << i << endl;
cout << "read int and ignore two lines" << endl;
cin >> i;
// ignore two lines
cin >> ignoreLine >> ignoreLine;
cout << "int: " << i << endl;
getch();
}
```

**OUTPUT:**

```
read int and ignore rest of the line
123 qwe
int: 123
read int and ignore two lines
123wer
asdf
int: 123
```

## COUT FUNCTIONS:

**Problem 14. Write a C++ program using cout to output message to console.**

***Program:***

```
#include <iostream.h>
#include<conio.h>
void main()
{
cout << "Hello World!\n";
getch();
}
```

**OUTPUT:**

```
Hello World!
```

**Problem 15. Write a C++ program use cout to output various data.**

***Program:***

```
#include <iostream.h>
#include<conio.h>
void main()
{
cout << "test.\n";
cout << "Here is 5: " << 5 << "\n";
cout << "Here is a very big number:\t" << 70000;
cout << (float) 5/8 << std::endl;
cout << (double) 7000 * 7000 << std::endl;
cout << "a liiiiiiiiiiiiiiiiiiiiiine\n";
getch();
}
```

**OUTPUT:**

```
test.
Here is 5: 5
Here is a very big number:      700000.625
4.9e+007
a liiiiiiiiiiiiiiiiiiiiiine
```

**Problem 16. Write a C++ program printing a line of text with multiple statements.**

***Program:***

```
#include <iostream.h>
#include<conio.h>
void main()
{
cout << "Welcome ";
cout << "to C++!\n";
getch();
}
```

**OUTPUT:**

```
Welcome to C++!
```

**Problem 17. Write a C++ program use endl to output a new line sign.**

***Program:***

```
#include <iostream.h>
#include<conio.h>
void main()
{
int x = 5;
int y = 7;
cout << endl;
cout << x + y << " " << x * y;
cout << endl;
getch();
}
```

**OUTPUT:**

```
12 35
```

**Problem 18. Write a C++ program for cout: unsetf.**

***Program:***

```
#include <iostream.h>
#include<conio.h>
void main()
{
cout.setf(ios::showpos);
```

```
cout.setf(ios::scientific);
cout << 123 << "  "<< 123.456 << endl;
cout.precision(3);
cout.width(10);
cout << 123 << "  "<< 123.456 << endl;;
cout.fill('#');
cout.width(10);
cout.unsetf(ios::scientific|ios::showpos);
cout.precision(5);
cout << 123 << "  " << 123.456;
getch();
}
```

**OUTPUT:**

```
+123  +1.234560e+002
     +123  +1.235e+002
#######123  123.46
```

**Problem 19. Write a C++ program to printing multiple lines of text with a single statement: use the \n.**

***Program:***

```
#include <iostream.h>
#include<conio.h>
void main()
{
cout << "Welcome\nto\n\nC++!\n";
getch();
}
```

**OUTPUT:**

```
Welcome
to

C++!
```

**Problem 20. Write a C++ program for output a pointer.**

***Program:***

```
#include <iostream.h>
#include<conio.h>
void main()
{
char *ptr;
ptr = "Pointers add power to C++.\n";
cout << ptr;
getch();
}
```

**OUTPUT:**

```
Pointers add power to C++.
```

**Problem 21. Write a C++ program using function in cout statement.**

***Program:***

```
#include <iostream.h>
#include<conio.h>
int box(int length, int width, int height); // return the volume
void main()
{
// use the return value of box( ) directly
cout << "The volume is " <<  box(10.1, 11.2, 3.3);
getch();
}
// This function returns a value.
int box(int length, int width, int height)
{
return length * width * height ;
}
```

**OUTPUT:**

```
The volume is 330
```

**Problem 22. Write a C++ program for cout: setf().**

***Program:***

```
#include <iostream.h>
#include<conio.h>
void main()
{
// Turn on showpos and scientific flags.
cout.setf(ios::showpos);
cout.setf(ios::scientific);
cout << 123 << " " << 123.23 << " ";
getch();
}
```

**OUTPUT:**

```
+123 +1.232300e+002
```

**Problem 23. Write a C++ program for cout: flags() and unsetf().**

***Program:***

```
#include <iostream.h>
#include<conio.h>
void main()
{
ios::fmtflags f;
f = cout.flags();
if(f & ios::showpos)
cout << "showpos is set for cout.\n";
else
cout << "showpos is cleared for cout.\n";
cout << "\nSetting showpos for cout.\n";
cout.setf(ios::showpos);
f = cout.flags();
if(f & ios::showpos)
```

```
cout << "showpos is set for cout.\n";
else
cout << "showpos is cleared for cout.\n";
cout << "\nClearing showpos for cout.\n";
cout.unsetf(ios::showpos);
f = cout.flags();
if(f & ios::showpos)
cout << "showpos is set for cout.\n";
else
cout << "showpos is cleared for cout.\n";
getch();
}
```

**OUTPUT:**

```
showpos is cleared for cout.
Setting showpos for cout.
showpos is set for cout.
Clearing showpos for cout.
showpos is cleared for cout.
```

**Problem 24. Write a C++ program for cout: width().**

***Program:***

```
#include <iostream.h>
#include<conio.h>
void main()
{
cout.setf(ios::showpos);
cout.setf(ios::scientific);
cout << 123 << " " << 123.23 << "\n";
cout.precision(2); // two digits after decimal point
cout.width(10);    // in a field of 10 characters
cout << 123 << " ";
cout.width(10);    // set width to 10
cout << 123.23 << "\n";
getch();
}
```

**OUTPUT:**

```
+123 +1.232300e+002
      +123 +1.23e+002
```

**Problem 25. Write a C++ program for cout: precision().**

***Program:***

```
#include <iostream.h>
#include<conio.h>
void main()
{
cout.setf(ios::showpos);
cout.setf(ios::scientific);
cout << 123 << " " << 123.23 << "\n";
cout.precision(2); // two digits after decimal point
cout.width(10);    // in a field of 10 characters
cout << 123 << " ";
cout.width(10);    // set width to 10
cout << 123.23 <<"\n";
getch();
}
```

**OUTPUT:**

```
+123 +1.232300e+002
      +123 +1.23e+002
```

**Problem 26. Write a C++ program for cout: fill().**

***Program:***

```
#include <iostream.h>
#include<conio.h>
void main()
{
cout.setf(ios::showpos);
cout.setf(ios::scientific);
cout << 123 << " " << 123.23 << "\n";
cout.fill('#'); // fill using #
cout.width(10); // in a field of 10 characters
cout << 123 << "";
cout.width(10); // set width to 10
cout << 123.23;
getch();
}
```

**OUTPUT:**

```
+123 +1.232300e+002
######+123 +1.232300e+002
```

**Problem 27. Write a C++ program for an I/O manipulator: cout << setprecision(2).**

***Program:***

```
#include <iostream.h>
#include<conio.h>
#include <iomanip.h>
void main()
{
cout << setprecision(2) << 1000.243 << endl;
getch();
}
```

**OUTPUT:**

```
1e+003
```

**Problem 28. Write a C++ program for an I/O manipulator: cout << setw(20).**

***Program:***

```
#include <iostream.h>
#include<conio.h>
#include <iomanip.h>
```

```
void main()
{
cout << setw(20) << "Hello there.";
getch();
}
```

**OUTPUT:**

Hello there.

**Problem 29. Write a C++ program for cout: setiosflags().**

***Program:***

```
#include <iostream.h>
#include<conio.h>
#include <iomanip.h>
void main()
{
cout << setiosflags(ios::showpos) <<
setiosflags(ios::scientific) << 123 << 123.23;
getch();
}
```

**OUTPUT:**

+123 +1.232300e+002

**Problem 30. Write a C++ program to skip leading whitespace.**

***Program:***

```
#include <iostream.h>
#include<conio.h>
void main()
{
char s[80];
cin >> ws >> s;
cout << s;
getch();
}
```

**OUTPUT:**

string string
string

**Problem 31. Write a C++ program for scientific mode; don't show plus sign anymore.**

***Program:***

```
#include <iostream.h>
#include<conio.h>
#include <iomanip.h>
#include <string.h>
void main( )
{
ios_base::fmtflags flags = cout.flags( );
double pi = 3.14285714;
cout << "pi = " << scientific
     << noshowpos
     << pi << '\n';
cout.flags(flags);
getch();
}
```

**OUTPUT:**

pi = 3.142857e+000

**Problem 32. Write a C++ program for fixed-point mode, show a '+' for positive nums, show 3 digits to the right of the decimal.**

***Program:***

```
#include <iostream.h>
#include<conio.h>
#include <iomanip.h>
#include <string.h>
void main( )
{
ios_base::fmtflags flags = cout.flags( );
double pi = 3.14285714;
cout << "pi = " << fixed
     << showpos
     << setprecision(3)
     << pi << '\n';
cout.flags(flags);
getch();
}
```

**OUTPUT:**

pi = +3.143

**Problem 33. Write a C++ program for setiosflags(ios::showpos); and setiosflags(ios::showbase).**

***Program:***

```
#include <iostream.h>
#include<conio.h>
#include <iomanip.h>
void main()
{
cout << setiosflags(ios::showpos);
cout << setiosflags(ios::showbase);
cout << 123 << " " << hex << 123;
getch();
}
```

**OUTPUT:**

+123 0x7b

**Problem 34. Write a C++ program ios::showpos | ios::showbase | ios::oct | ios::right.**

***Program:***

```
#include <iostream.h>
```

```
#include<conio.h>
void showflags();
void main()
{
// show default condition of format flags
showflags();
// showpos, showbase, oct, right are on, others off
ios::fmtflags f = ios::showpos | ios::showbase |
ios::oct | ios::right;
cout.flags(f);
showflags();
getch();
}
void showflags()
{
ios::fmtflags f;
long i;
f = cout.flags(); // get flag settings
// check each flag
for(i=0x4000; i; i = i >> 1)
if(i & f) cout << "1 ";
else cout << "0 ";
cout << " \n";
}
```

**OUTPUT:**

0 0 1 0 0 0 0 0 0 0 0 0 0 1 0
0 0 0 1 0 1 0 1 1 0 0 0 0 0 0

**Problem 35. Write a C++ program for set cout to output hex.**

***Program:***

```
#include <iostream.h>
#include<conio.h>
void main()
{
cout.setf(ios::hex, ios::basefield);
cout << 100; // this displays 64
getch();
}
```

**OUTPUT:**

64

**Problem 36. Write a C++ program to show default condition of format flags.**

***Program:***

```
#include <iostream.h>
#include<conio.h>
void showflags() ;
void main()
{
showflags();
cout.setf(ios::right | ios::showpoint | ios::fixed);
showflags();
getch();
}
void showflags()
{
ios::fmtflags f;
long i;
f = cout.flags(); // get flag settings
// check each flag
for(i=0x4000; i; i = i >> 1)
if(i & f) cout << "1 ";
else cout << "0 ";
cout << " \n";
}
```

**OUTPUT:**

0 0 1 0 0 0 0 0 0 0 0 0 0 1 0
0 0 1 0 1 0 0 1 0 0 0 0 1 1 0

**Problem 37. Write a C++ program for cout.setf(ios::showpoint | ios::showpos, ios::showpoint).**

***Program:***

```
#include <iostream.h>
#include<conio.h>
void main( )
{
cout.setf(ios::showpoint | ios::showpos,
ios::showpoint);
cout << 100.0;
getch();
}
```

**OUTPUT:**

100.000

**Problem 38. Write a C++ program for set ios::showpoint, ios::showpos for double pointer number.**

***Program:***

```
#include <iostream.h>
#include<conio.h>
void main()
{
cout.setf(ios::showpoint);
cout.setf(ios::showpos);
cout << 100.0;
getch();
}
```

**OUTPUT:**

+100.000

**Problem 39. Write a C++ program for OR together two or more flags.**

***Program:***

```
#include <iostream.h>
#include<conio.h>
void main()
{
cout.setf(ios::showpoint | ios::showpos);
cout << 100.0;
getch();
}
```

**OUTPUT:**

+100.000

**Problem 40. Write a C++ program for unset flag one by one.**

***Program:***

```
#include <iostream.h>
#include<conio.h>
void main()
{
cout.setf(ios::uppercase | ios::scientific);
cout << 100.12;
cout.unsetf(ios::uppercase);
cout << " \n" << 100.12;
getch();
}
```

**OUTPUT:**

1.001200E+002
1.001200e+002

**Problem 41. Write a C++ program for cout boolalpha: cause bool values to display as true or false.**

***Program:***

```
#include <iostream.h>
#include<conio.h>
void main()
{
bool a = true;
bool b = false;
cout << boolalpha;
cout << "a = " << a << "; b = " << b;
getch();
}
```

**OUTPUT:**

a = true; b = false

**Problem 42. Write a C++ program to demonstrating the flags member function.**

***Program:***

```
#include <iostream.h>
#include<conio.h>
void main()
{
int integerValue = 1000;
double doubleValue = 0.0947628;
cout << cout.flags() << "\n\n"
 << integerValue << '\t'
<< doubleValue << endl
<< endl;
ios_base::fmtflags originalFormat = cout.flags();
cout << showbase
<< oct << scientific;
cout << cout.flags() << "\n\n"
<< integerValue << '\t'
<< doubleValue << endl
<< endl;
cout.flags( originalFormat );
cout << cout.flags() << "\n\n" << integerValue <<
'\t' << doubleValue << endl;
getch();
}
```

**OUTPUT:**

4098
1000 0.0947628
011500
01750 9.476280e-002
4098
1000 0.0947628

**Problem 43. Write a C++ program uUsing showpoint to control the printing of trailing zeros anddecimal points for doubles.**

***Program:***

```
void main()
{
cout << "Before using showpoint" << endl
<< "9.9900 prints as: " << 9.9900 << endl
<< "9.9000 prints as: " << 9.9000 << endl
<< "9.0000 prints as: " << 9.0000 << endl
<< endl;
cout << showpoint
<< "After using showpoint" << endl
<< "9.9900 prints as: " << 9.9900 << endl
<< "9.9000 prints as: " << 9.9000 << endl
<< "9.0000 prints as: " << 9.0000 << endl;
getch();
}
```

**OUTPUT:**

Before using showpoint
9.9900 prints as: 9.99

```
9.9000 prints as: 9.9
9.0000 prints as: 9
After using showpoint
9.9900 prints as: 9.99000
9.9000 prints as: 9.90000
9.0000 prints as: 9.00000
```

**Problem 44. Write a C++ program to demonstrating left justification and right justification.**

***Program:***

```
#include <iostream.h>
#include<conio.h>
#include <iomanip.h>
void main()
{
int x = 12345;
cout << "Default is right justified:" << endl<< setw(
10 ) << x;
cout << "\n\nUse left to left justify x:\n"<< left <<
setw( 10 ) << x;
cout << "\n\nUse right to right justify x:\n"<< right
<< setw( 10 ) << x << endl;
getch();
}
```

**OUTPUT:**

```
Default is right justified:
     12345
Use left to left justify x:
12345
Use right to right justify x:
     12345
```

**Problem 45. Write a C++ program to printing an integer with internal spacing and plus sign.**

***Program:***

```
#include <iostream.h>
#include<conio.h>
#include <iomanip.h>
void main()
{
cout << internal << showpos << setw( 10 ) << 123
<< endl;
getch();
}
```

**OUTPUT:**

```
+      123
```

**Problem 46. Write a C++ program using stream-manipulator showbase to show number base.**

***Program:***

```
#include <iostream.h>
#include<conio.h>
void main()
{
int x = 100;
cout << "Printing integers preceded by their base:"
<< endl << showbase;
cout << x << endl;
// print decimal value
cout << oct << x << endl;
// print octal value
cout << hex << x << endl;
 // print hexadecimal value
getch();
}
```

**OUTPUT:**

```
Printing integers preceded by their base:
100
0144
0x64
```

**Problem 47. Write a C++ program for stream-manipulator uppercase.**

***Program:***

```
#include <iostream.h>
#include<conio.h>
void main()
{
cout << uppercase << 4.345e10 << endl << hex <<
showbase << 123456789 << endl;
getch();
}
```

**OUTPUT:**

```
4.345E+010
0X75BCD15
```

**Problem 48. Write a C++ program to demonstrating stream-manipulators boolalpha and noboolalpha.**

***Program:***

```
#include <iostream.h>
#include<conio.h>
void main()
{
bool booleanValue = true;
cout << "booleanValue is " << booleanValue <<
endl;
cout << "booleanValue (after using boolalpha) is
"<< boolalpha << booleanValue << endl << endl;
booleanValue = false; // change booleanValue
cout << noboolalpha << endl; // use noboolalpha
```

```
cout << "booleanValue is " << booleanValue <<
endl;
cout << "booleanValue (after using boolalpha) is "
<< boolalpha << booleanValue << endl;
getch();
}
```

**OUTPUT:**

```
booleanValue is 1
booleanValue (after using boolalpha) is true
booleanValue is 0
booleanValue (after using boolalpha) is false
```

**Problem 49. Write a C++ program to controlling precision of floating-point values.**

***Program:***

```
#include <iostream.h>
#include<conio.h>
#include <iomanip.h>
void main()
{
double root2 = 123.123456789;
int places;
cout << fixed;
for ( places = 0; places <= 9; places++ )
{
cout.precision( places );
cout << root2 << endl;
}
for ( places = 0; places <= 9; places++ )
cout << setprecision( places ) << root2 << endl;
getch();
}
```

**OUTPUT:**

```
123
123.1
123.12
123.123
123.1235
123.12346
123.123457
123.1234568
123.12345679
123.123456789
123
123.1
123.12
123.123
123.1235
123.12346
123.123457
123.1234568
123.12345679
123.123456789
```

**Problem 50. Write a C++ program to check cout flags.**

***Program:***

```
#include <iostream.h>
#include<conio.h>
void showflags();
void main()
{
showflags();
cout.setf(ios::oct|ios::showbase|ios::fixed);
showflags();
getch();
}
void showflags()
{
long f;
char flgs[15][12]=
{
"skipws",
"left",
"right",
"internal",
"dec",
"oct",
"hex",
"showbase",
"showpoint",
"uppercase",
"showpos",
"scientific",
"fixed",
"unitbuf",
"stdio",
};
f=cout.flags();
for(int i=1,j=0;i<0x4000;i=i<<1,j++)
if(i&f)
cout<<flgs[j]<<"is on\n";
else
cout<<flgs[j]<<"is off\n"; cout<<"\n";
}
```

**OUTPUT:**

```
skipwsis off
leftis on
rightis off
internalis off
decis off
octis off
```

hexis off
showbaseis off
showpointis off
uppercaseis off
showposis off
scientificis off
fixedis on
unitbufis off

skipwsis off
leftis on
rightis on
internalis off
decis off
octis off
hexis on
showbaseis off
showpointis off
uppercaseis on
showposis off
scientificis off
fixedis on
unitbufis off

## COUTBASE:

**Problem 51. Write a C++ program for cout: setbase(16).**

***Program:***

```
#include <iostream.h>
#include<conio.h>
#include <iomanip.h>
void main()
{
long n = 10000;
cout << setbase(16) << n;
getch();
}
```

**OUTPUT:**

2710

**Problem 52. Write a C++ program for cout: setbase(8).**

***Program:***

```
#include <iostream.h>
#include<conio.h>
#include <iomanip.h>
void main()
{
long n = 10000;
cout << setbase(8) << n;
getch();
}
```

**OUTPUT:**

23420

**Problem 53. Write a C++ program for cout: setbase(10).**

***Program:***

```
#include <iostream.h>
#include <iomanip.h>
#include<conio.h>
void main()
{
long n = 10000;
cout << setbase(10) << n;
getch();
}
```

**OUTPUT:**

10000

## COUT OCT DEC HEX:

**Problem 54. Write a C++ program for cout: hex.**

***Program:***

```
#include <iostream.h>
#include <iomanip.>
#include<conio.h>
void main()
{
long n = 10000;
cout << hex << n ;
getch();
}
```

**OUTPUT:**

2710

**Problem 55. Write a C++ program for cout: oct.**

***Program:***

```
#include <iostream.h>
#include<conio.h>
#include <iomanip.h>
void main()
{
long n = 10000;
cout << oct << n ;
getch();
}
```

**OUTPUT:**

23420

**Problem 56. Write a C++ program for cout: dec.**

***Program:***

```
#include <iostream.h>
#include<conio.h>
#include <iomanip.h>
void main()
{
long n = 10000;
cout << dec << n << endl;
getch();
}
```

**OUTPUT:**

10000

## COUT FILL:

**Problem 57. Write a C++ program for fill('$').**

***Program:***

```
#include <iostream.h>
#include<conio.h>
void main()
{
float a=100100.0, b=0.08;
cout.setf(ios::right|ios::scientific|ios::showpoint);
cout.width(20);
cout<<(a/b)<<endl;
cout.fill('$');
getch();
}
```

**OUTPUT:**

1.251250e+006

**Problem 58. Write a C++ program for cout.setf(ios::hex, ios::basefield).**

***Program:***

```
#include <iostream.h>
#include <iomanip.h>
#include<conio.h>
void main()
{
cout.setf(ios::hex, ios::basefield);
cout << 100 << "\n";  // 100 in hex
cout.fill('?');
cout.width(10);
cout << 2343.0;
getch();
}
```

**OUTPUT:**

64

??????2343

## COUT FLOAT:

**Problem 59. Write a C++ program to displaying floating-point values in system default, scientific and fixed formats.**

***Program:***

```
#include <iostream.h>
#include<conio.h>
void main()
{
double x = 0.001234567;
double y = 1.946e9;
cout << "Displayed in default format:"
<< endl << x << '\t' << y << endl;
cout << "\nDisplayed in scientific format:" << endl
<< scientific << x << '\t' << y << endl;
cout << "\nDisplayed in fixed format:" << endl <<
fixed << x << '\t' << y << endl;
getch();
}
```

**OUTPUT:**

```
Displayed in default format:
0.00123457      1.946e+009
Displayed in scientific format:
1.234567e-003   1.946000e+009
Displayed in fixed format:
0.001235        1946000000.000000
```

**Problem 60. Write a C++ program for ios::right|ios::scientific|ios::showpoint.**

***Program:***

```
#include <iostream.h>
#include<conio.h>
void main()
{
float a=100100.0, b=0.08;
cout.setf(ios::right|ios::scientific|ios::showpoint);
cout.width(20);
cout <<(-a*b);
getch();
}
```

**OUTPUT:**

-8.008000e+003

**Problem 61. Write a C++ program to displaying numbers in scientific notation.**

***Program:***

```
#include <iostream.h>
```

```
#include<conio.h>
#include <iomanip.h>
#include <limits.h>
void main()
{
const double pi = 3.14;
cout << endl;
for(double radius = .2 ; radius <= 3.0 ; radius += .2)
cout << "radius = "
    <<
setprecision(numeric_limits<double>::digits10 + 1)
    << scientific << radius<< "  area = "
    << setw(10) << setprecision(6)<< fixed << pi *
radius * radius << endl;
getch();
}
```

**OUTPUT:**

```
radius = 2.0000000000000001e-001  area =
0.125600
radius = 4.0000000000000002e-001  area =
0.502400
radius = 6.0000000000000009e-001  area =
1.130400
radius = 8.0000000000000004e-001  area =
2.009600
radius = 1.0000000000000000e+000  area =
3.140000
radius = 1.2000000000000000e+000  area =
4.521600
radius = 1.3999999999999999e+000  area =
6.154400
radius = 1.5999999999999999e+000  area =
8.038400
radius = 1.7999999999999998e+000  area =
10.173600
radius = 1.9999999999999998e+000  area =
12.560000
radius = 2.1999999999999997e+000  area =
15.197600
radius = 2.3999999999999999e+000  area =
18.086400
radius = 2.6000000000000001e+000  area =
21.226400
radius = 2.8000000000000003e+000  area =
24.617600
```

**Problem 62. Write a C++ program for normal (default) mode; only show 5 digits, including both sides of decimal point.**

***Program:***

```
#include <iostream.h>
#include<conio.h>
#include <iomanip.h>
#include <string.h>
void main( )
{
ios_base::fmtflags flags = cout.flags( );
double pi = 3.14285714;
cout << "pi = " << setprecision(5) << pi << '\n';
cout.flags(flags);
getch();
}
```

**OUTPUT:**

```
pi = 3.1429
```

# INPUT MANIPULATOR:

**Problem 63. Write a C++ program to create an input manipulator.**

***Program:***

```
#include <iostream.h>
#include<conio.h>
#include <iomanip.h>
istream &customMessage(istream &stream)
{
cin >> hex;
cout << "Enter number using hex format: ";
return stream;
}
void main()
{
int i;
cin >> customMessage >> i;
cout << i;
getch();
}
```

**OUTPUT:**

```
Enter number using hex format: 0Xaa
170
```

# MANIPULATOR:

**Problem 64. Write a C++ program for a simple output manipulator.**

***Program:***

```
#include <iostream.h>
#include<conio.h>
#include <iomanip.h>
ostream &sethex(ostream &stream)
{
stream.setf(ios::showbase);
```

```
stream.setf(ios::hex, ios::basefield);
return stream;
}
void main()
{
cout << 256 << " " << sethex << 256;
getch();
}
```

**OUTPUT:**

256 0x100

**Problem 65. Write a C++ program to create an output manipulator.**

***Program:***

```
#include <iostream.h>
#include<conio.h>
#include <iomanip.h>
ostream &mySetting(ostream &stream)
{
stream.setf(ios::left);
stream << setw(10) << setfill('$');
return stream;
}
void main()
{
cout << 10 << " " << mySetting << 10;
getch();
}
```

**OUTPUT:**

10 10$$$$$$$$

**Problem 66. Write a C++ program for ostream flag.**

***Program:***

```
#include <iostream.h>
#include<conio.h>
#include <iomanip.h>
ostream &ra(ostream &stream)
{
stream << "-------------- ";
return stream;
}
// Left Arrow
ostream &la(ostream &stream)
{
stream << "*************";
return stream;
}
void main()
{
cout << ra << 1233.23 << "\n";
cout << ra << 567.66 << la;
getch();
}
```

**OUTPUT:**

```
-------------- 1233.23
-------------- 567.66*************"
```

**Problem 67. Write a C++ program for endLine manipulator (using escape sequence \n and member function flush).**

***Program:***

```
#include <iostream.h>
#include<conio.h>
vostream& endLine( ostream& output)
{
return output << '\n' << flush; // issue endl-like end
of line
}
void main()
{
cout << "-----" << endLine;
getch();
}
```

**OUTPUT:**

-----

**Problem 68. Write a C++ program to create user-defined, nonparameterized stream manipulators: bell manipulator (using escape sequence \a).**

***Program:***

```
#include <iostream.h>
#include<conio.h>
ostream& bell( ostream& output)
{
return output << '\a'; // issue system beep
}
void main()
{
cout << bell; // use bell manipulator
getch();
}
```

**OUTPUT:**

bell

**Problem 69. Write a C++ program to create user-defined, nonparameterized stream manipulators: carriageReturn manipulator (using escape sequence \r).**

***Program:***

```
#include <iostream.h>
```

```
#include<conio.h>
ostream& carriageReturn( ostream& output )
{
return output << '\r'; // issue carriage return
}
void main()
{
cout << carriageReturn << "-----" ;
getch();
}
```

**Problem 70. Write a C++ program for tab manipulator (using escape sequence \t).**

***Program:***

```
#include <iostream.h>
#include<conio.h>
ostream& tab( ostream& output)
{
return output << '\t'; // issue tab
}
void main()
{
cout << tab << 'b' << tab << 'c';
getch();
}
```

**OUTPUT:**

```
b	c
```

# COMMAND LINE ARGUMENTS:

**Problem 71. Write a C++ program to display command-line arguments.**

***Program:***

```
#include <iostream.h>
#include<conio.h>
void main(int argc, char *argv[])
{
for(int i = 0; i < argc; i++)
{
cout << argv[i] << "\n";
}
getch();
}
```

**OUTPUT:**

```
main
```

**Problem 72. Write a C++ program using command-line arguments for copying files.**

***Program:***

```
#include <iostream.h>
#include<conio.h>
void main( int argc, char *argv[] )
{
// check number of command-line arguments
if ( argc != 3 )
cout << "Usage: copyFile infile_name
outfile_name" << endl;
else
{
ifstream inFile( argv[ 1 ], ios::in );
if ( !inFile )
{
cout << argv[ 1 ] << " could not be opened"
<< endl;
return -1;
}
ofstream outFile( argv[ 2 ], ios::out );
if ( !outFile )
{
cout << argv[ 2 ] << " could not be opened"
<< endl;
inFile.close();
return -2;
}
char c = inFile.get();
while ( inFile )
{
outFile.put( c );
c = inFile.get();
}
}
getch();
}
```

**OUTPUT:**

```
Usage: copyFile infile_name outfile_name
```

**Problem 73. Write a C++ program for sum the two numeric command line arguments.**

***Program:***

```
#include <iostream.h>
#include<conio.h>
#include <stdlib.h>
void main(int argc, char *argv[])
{
double a, b;
if(argc!=3)
{
cout << "Usage: main num num\n";
return 1;
}
a = atof(argv[1]);
```

```
// convert first command-line arg
b = atof(argv[2]);
// convert second comnand-line arg
cout << a + b;
getch();
}
```

**OUTPUT:**

Usage: main num num

## NEW:

**Problem 74. Write a C++ program use new and delete.**

***Program:***

```
#include <iostream.h>
#include<conio.h>
void main()
{
int *p;
try
{
p = new int; // allocate space for an int
}
catch (bad_alloc xa)
{
cout << "Allocation Failure\n";
return 1;
}
*p = 100;
cout << "At " << p << " is the value " << *p << "\n";
delete p;
getch();
}
```

**OUTPUT:**

At 0x3d2448 is the value 100

**Problem 75. Write a C++ program for Global new.**

***Program:***

```
#include <iostream.h>
#include<conio.h>
#include<stdlib.h>
class Point
{
int x, y;
public:
Point()
{}
Point(int px, int py)
{
x = px;
y = py;
}
void show()
{
cout << x << " ";
cout << y << "\n";
}
};
// Global new
void *operator new(size_t size)
{
void *p;
p = malloc(size);
if(!p)
{
bad_alloc ba;
throw ba;
}
return p;
}
// Global delete
void operator delete(void *p)
{
free(p);
}
void main()
{
Point *p1, *p2;
float *f;
try
{
p1 = new Point (10, 20);
}
catch (bad_alloc xa)
{
cout << "Allocation error for p1.\n";
return 1;
}
try
{
p2 = new Point (-10, -20);
}
catch (bad_alloc xa)
{
cout << "Allocation error for p2.\n";
return 1;
}
try
{
f = new float; // uses overloaded new, too
```

```
}
catch (bad_alloc xa)
{
cout << "Allocation error for f.\n";
return 1;
}
*f = 10.10F;
cout << *f << "\n";
p1->show();
p2->show();
delete p1;
delete p2;
delete f;
getch();
}
```

**OUTPUT:**

10.1
10 20
-10 -20

**Problem 76. Write a C++ program to Initialize memory.**

***Program:***

```
#include <iostream.h>
#include<conio.h>
void main()
{
int *p;
try
{
p = new int (87); // initialize to 87
}
catch (bad_alloc xa)
{
cout << "Allocation Failure\n";
return 1;
}
cout << "At " << p << " is the value " << *p << "\n";
delete p;
getch();
}
```

**OUTPUT:**

At 0x3d2448 is the value 87

**Problem 77. Write a C++ program to allocate an array.**

***Program:***

```
#include <iostream.h>
#include<conio.h>
void main()
{
int *p, i;
try
{
p = new int [10]; // allocate 10 integer array
}
catch (bad_alloc xa)
{
cout << "Allocation Failure\n";
return 1;
}
for(i=0; i<10; i++ )
p[i] = i;
for(i=0; i<10; i++)
cout << p[i] << " ";
delete [] p; // release the array
getch();
}
```

**OUTPUT:**

0 1 2 3 4 5 6 7 8 9

**Problem 78. Write a C++ program to allocate an object.**

***Program:***

```
#include <iostream.h>
#include<conio.h>
class Rectangle
{
int width;
int height;
public:
Rectangle(int w, int h)
{
width = w;
height = h;
cout << "Constructing " << width << " by " <<
height << " rectangle.\n";
}
~Rectangle()
{
cout << "Destructing " << width << " by " <<
height << " rectangle.\n";
}
int area()
{
return width * height;
}
};
void main()
{
Rectangle *p;
try
```

```
{
p = new Rectangle(10, 8);
}
catch (bad_alloc xa)
{
cout << "Allocation Failure\n";
return 1;
}
cout << "Area is " << p->area();
delete p;
getch();
}
```

**OUTPUT:**

Constructing 10 by 8 rectangle.
Area is 80Destructing 10 by 8 rectangle.

**Problem 79. Write a C++ program to allocate memory for an object.**

***Program:***

```
#include <iostream.h>
#include<conio.h>
class Rectangle
{
int width;
int height;
public:
Rectangle(int w, int h)
{
width = w;
height = h;
cout << "Constructing " << width << " by " <<
height << " rectangle.\n";
}
~Rectangle()
{
cout << "Destructing " << width << " by " << height
<< " rectangle.\n";
}
int area()
{
return width * height;
}
};
void main()
{
Rectangle *p;
try
{
p = new Rectangle(10, 8);
}
catch (bad_alloc xa)
{
cout << "Allocation Failure\n";
return 1;
}
cout << "Area is " << p->area();

delete p;
getch();
}
```

**OUTPUT:**

Constructing 10 by 8 rectangle.
Area is 80Destructing 10 by 8 rectangle.

**Problem 80. Write a C++ program to catch 'new' memory allocation exception.**

***Program:***

```
#include <iostream.h>
#include<conio.h>
class Rectangle
{
int width;
int height;
public:
Rectangle(int w, int h)
{
width = w;
height = h;
cout << "Constructing " << width << " by " <<
height << " rectangle.\n";
}
~Rectangle()
{
cout << "Destructing " << width << " by " <<
height << " rectangle.\n";
}
int area()
{
return width * height;
}
};
void main()
{
Rectangle *p;
try
{
p = new Rectangle(10, 8);
}
catch (bad_alloc xa)
{
cout << "Allocation Failure\n";
return 1;
```

```
}
cout << "Area is " << p->area();
delete p;
getch();
}
```

**OUTPUT:**

Constructing 10 by 8 rectangle.
Area is 80Destructing 10 by 8 rectangle.

**Problem 81. Write a C++ program to allocate an array of objects by overloading new and delete operators.**

***Program:***

```
#include <iostream.h>
#include<conio.h>
#include <stdlib.h>
class Point
{
int x, y;
public:
Point() {x = y = 0;}
Point(int px, int py)
{
x = px;
y = py;
}
void show()
{
cout << x << " ";
cout << y << "\n";
}
void *operator new(size_t size);
void operator delete(void *p);
void *operator new[](size_t size);
void operator delete[](void *p);
};
// new overloaded relative to Point.
void *Point::operator new(size_t size)
{
void *p;
cout << "In overloaded new.\n";
p = malloc(size);
if(!p)
{
bad_alloc ba;
throw ba;
}
return p;
}
// delete overloaded relative to Point.
void Point::operator delete(void *p)
{
cout << "In overloaded delete.\n";
free(p);
}
// new overloaded for Point arrays.
void *Point::operator new[](size_t size)
{
void *p;
cout << "Using overload new[].\n";
p = malloc(size);
if(!p)
{
bad_alloc ba;
throw ba;
}
return p;
}
// delete overloaded for Point arrays.
void Point::operator delete[](void *p)
{
cout << "Freeing array using overloaded
delete[]\n";
free(p);
}
void main()
{
Point *p1, *p2;
int i;
try
{
p1 = new Point (10, 20); // allocate an object
}
catch (bad_alloc xa)
{
cout << "Allocation error for p1.\n";
return 1;
}
try
{
p2 = new Point [10]; // allocate an array
}
catch (bad_alloc xa)
{
cout << "Allocation error for p2.\n";
return 1;
}
p1->show();
for(i=0; i<10; i++)
p2[i].show();
delete p1; // free an object
delete [] p2; // free an array
```

```
getch();
}
```

**OUTPUT:**

In overloaded new.
Using overload new[].
10 20
0 0
0 0
0 0
0 0
0 0
0 0
0 0
0 0
0 0
0 0
In overloaded delete.
Freeing array using overloaded delete[]

## DELETE:

**Problem 82. Write a C++ program for memory management new-delete.**

***Program:***

```
#include <iostream.h>
#include <stdlib.h>
#include<conio.h>
void main ()
{
char input [100];
int count,n;
long * longPointer, total = 0;
cout << "How many numbers do you want to type
in? ";
cin.getline (input,100);
count=atoi (input);
longPointer= new long[count];
if (longPointer == NULL)
exit (1);
for (n=0; n<count; n++)
{
cout << "Enter number: ";
cin.getline (input,100);
longPointer[n]=atol (input);
}
cout << "You have entered: ";
for (n=0; n<count; n++)
cout << longPointer[n] << ", ";
delete[] longPointer;
getch();
}
```

**OUTPUT:**

How many numbers do you want to type in? 1
Enter number: a
You have entered: 0, "

**Problem 83. Write a C++ program to delete an array of objects.**

***Program:***

```
#include <iostream.h>
#include<conio.h>
#include <stdlib.h>
class Point
{
int x, y;
public:
Point() {x = y = 0;}
Point(int px, int py)
{
x = px;
y = py;
}
void show()
{
cout << x << " ";
cout << y << "\n";
}
void *operator new(size_t size);
void operator delete(void *p);
void *operator new[](size_t size);
void operator delete[](void *p);
};
// new overloaded relative to Point.
void *Point::operator new(size_t size)
{
void *p;
cout << "In overloaded new.\n";
p = malloc(size);
if(!p)
{
bad_alloc ba;
throw ba;
}
return p;
}
// delete overloaded relative to Point.
void Point::operator delete(void *p)
{
cout << "In overloaded delete.\n";
free(p);
}
```

```
// new overloaded for Point arrays.
void *Point::operator new[](size_t size)
{
void *p;
cout << "Using overload new[].\n";
p = malloc(size);
if(!p) {
bad_alloc ba;
throw ba;
}
return p;
}
// delete overloaded for Point arrays.
void Point::operator delete[](void *p)
{
cout << "Freeing array using overloaded delete[]\n";
free(p);
}
void main()
{
Point *p1, *p2;
int i;
try
{
p1 = new Point (10, 20); // allocate an object
}
catch (bad_alloc xa)
{
cout << "Allocation error for p1.\n";
return 1;
}
try
{
p2 = new Point [10]; // allocate an array
}
catch (bad_alloc xa)
{
cout << "Allocation error for p2.\n";
return 1;
}
p1->show();
for(i=0; i<10; i++)
p2[i].show();
delete p1; // free an object
delete [] p2; // free an array
getch();
}
```

**OUTPUT:**

```
In overloaded new.
Using overload new[].
10 20
0 0
0 0
0 0
0 0
0 0
0 0
0 0
0 0
0 0
0 0
In overloaded delete.
Freeing array using overloaded delete[]
```

**Problem 84. Write a C++ program for global delete.**

***Program:***

```
#include <iostream.h>
#include<conio.h>
#include <stdlib.h>
class Point
{
int x, y;
public:
Point() { }
Point(int px, int py)
{
x = px;
y = py;
}
void show()
{
cout << x << " ";
cout << y << "\n";
}
};
// Global new
void *operator new(size_t size)
{
void *p;
p = malloc(size);
if(!p)
{
bad_alloc ba;
throw ba;
}
return p;
}
// Global delete
void operator delete(void *p)
{
free(p);
```

```
}
void main()
{
Point *p1, *p2;
float *f;
try
{
p1 = new Point (10, 20);
}
catch (bad_alloc xa)
{
cout << "Allocation error for p1.\n";
return 1;
}
try
{
p2 = new Point (-10, -20);
}
catch (bad_alloc xa)
{
cout << "Allocation error for p2.\n";
return 1;
}
try
{
f = new float; // uses overloaded new, too
}
catch (bad_alloc xa)
{
cout << "Allocation error for f.\n";
return 1;
}
*f = 10.10F;
cout << *f << "\n";
p1->show();
p2->show();
delete p1;
delete p2;
delete f;
getch();
}
```

**OUTPUT:**

```
10.1
10 20
-10 -20
```

**Problem 85. Write a C++ program for an object in existence after deletion.**

***Program:***

```
#include <iostream.h>
#include<conio.h>
class MyClass
{
static int total;
public:
MyClass()
{
total++;
}
~MyClass()
{
total--;
}
int gettotal()
{
return total;
}
};
int MyClass::total=0;
void main()
{
MyClass o1,o2,o3;
cout<<o1.gettotal()<<" objects in existence\n";
MyClass *p;
p=new MyClass;
if(!p)
{
cout<<"Allocation erroe\n";
return 1;
}
cout<<o1.gettotal();
cout<<" object in existence after allocation\n";
delete p;
cout<<o1.gettotal();
cout<<" object in existence after deletion\n";
getch();
}
```

**OUTPUT:**

```
3 objects in existence
4 object in existence after allocation
3 object in existence after deletion
```

**Problem 86. Write a C++ program to delete class array and return memory to heap.**

***Program:***

```
#include <iostream.h>
#include<conio.h>
class examp
{
int i,j;
public:
void init(int a,int b)
```

```
{
i=a,j=b;
}
int product()
{
return i*j;
}
};
void main()
{
examp *ptr;
int i;
ptr=new examp[6];
if(!ptr)
{
cout<<"Allocation error.\n";
return 1;
}
for(i=0;i<6;i++)
ptr[i].init(i,i);
for(i=0;i<6;i++)
{
cout<<"Product["<<i<<"]is:";
cout<<ptr[i].product()<<"\n";
}
delete[]ptr;
getch();
}
```

**OUTPUT:**

Product[0]is:0
Product[1]is:1
Product[2]is:4
Product[3]is:9
Product[4]is:16
Product[5]is:25

**Problem 87. Write a C++ program using new and delete of array.**

***Program:***

```
#include <iostream.h>
#include<conio.h>
class Point
{
int x;
int y;
public:
Point()
{
x = 0;
y = 0;
}
Point(int a,int b=0)
{
x = a;
y= b;
}
void Set (int a,int b=0)
{
x = a;
y = b;
}
void Display()
{
cout << "x = "<< x << " y = "<< y  << endl;
}
~Point()
{
cout << "Destruct obj.\n" ;
}
};
void main()
{
Point *p;int i;
const int Length = 3;
p=new Point[Length];
if(!p)
{
cout << "allocation failure\n";
return -1;
}
for (i=0;i<Length;i++)
p[i].Set(i*10,-i*10);
for (i=0;i<Length;i++)
p[i].Display();
delete []p;
getch();
}
```

**OUTPUT:**

x = 0 y = 0
x = 10 y = -10
x = 20 y = -20
Destruct obj.
Destruct obj.
Destruct obj.

## ESCAPE SEQUENCE:

**Problem 88. Write a C++ program Use the \n code to generate a new line**

***Program:***

```
#include <iostream.h>
```

```
#include<conio.h>
void main()
{
cout << "one\n";
cout << "two\n";
cout << "three";
cout << "four";
getch();
}
```

**OUTPUT:**

```
one
two
threefour"
```

**Problem 89. Write a C++ program for Escape sequences: \t.**

***Program:***

```
#include <iostream.h>
#include<conio.h>
void main()
{
cout << "one\ttwo\tthree\n";
getch();
}
```

**OUTPUT:**

```
one     two     three
```

**Problem 90. Write a C++ program for Escape sequences: \b.**

***Program:***

```
#include <iostream.h>
#include<conio.h>
void main()
{
cout << "123\b\b45";
getch();
}
```

**OUTPUT:**

```
145
```

**Problem 91. Write a C++ program for Escape keys for double back slash.**

***Program:***

```
#include <iostream.h>
#include<conio.h>
void main()
{
cout << "are quite \'useful \' \a \\ in your code \\ \a
\n";
getch();
}
```

**OUTPUT:**

```
are quite 'useful '  \ in your code \
```

## FUNCTOR:

**Problem 92. Write a C++ program for Functor.**

***Program:***

```
#include <iostream.h>
#include<conio.h>
#include <math.h>
#include <stdlib.h>
class Abs
{
public:
// "function call":
double operator() (double v) const
{
return abs(v);
}
};
class Sine
{
public:
// "function call":
double operator() (double a) const
{
return sin(a);
}
};
template <typename FO1, typename FO2>
class Composer
{
private:
FO1 fo1;
// first/inner function object to call
FO2 fo2;
// second/outer function object to call
public:
// constructor: initialize function objects
Composer (FO1 f1, FO2 f2): fo1(f1), fo2(f2)
{ }
// "function call": nested call of function objects
double operator() (double v)
{
return fo2(fo1(v));
}
};
template<typename FO>
void print_values (FO fo)
{
```

```
for (int i=-2; i<3; ++i)
{
cout << "f(" << i*0.1<< ") = " << fo(i*0.1)<< "\n";
}
}
void main()
{
cout << Composer<Abs,Sine>(Abs(),Sine())(-0.5)
<< "\n\n";
print_values(Abs());
cout << '\n';
print_values(Sine());
cout << '\n';
print_values(Composer<Abs, Sine>(Abs(), Sine()));
cout << '\n';
print_values(Composer<Sine, Abs>(Sine(), Abs()));
getch();
}
```

**OUTPUT:**

```
0.479426
f(-0.2) = 0.2
f(-0.1) = 0.1
f(0) = 0
f(0.1) = 0.1
f(0.2) = 0.2
f(-0.2) = -0.198669
f(-0.1) = -0.0998334
f(0) = 0
f(0.1) = 0.0998334
f(0.2) = 0.198669
f(-0.2) = 0.198669
f(-0.1) = 0.0998334
f(0) = 0
f(0.1) = 0.0998334
f(0.2) = 0.198669
f(-0.2) = 0.198669
f(-0.1) = 0.0998334
f(0) = 0
f(0.1) = 0.0998334
f(0.2) = 0.198669
```

**Problem 93. Write a C++ program for Functor compose 2.**

***Program:***

```
#include <iostream.h>
#include<conio.h>
#include <math.h>
#include <stdlib.h>
class Abs
{
public:
// "function call":
double operator() (double v) const
{
return abs(v);
}
};
class Sine
{
public:
// "function call":
double operator() (double a) const
{
return sin(a);
}
};
template <typename FO1, typename FO2>
class Composer
{
private:
FO1 fo1; // first/inner function object to call
FO2 fo2; // second/outer function object to call
public:
// constructor: initialize function objects
Composer (FO1 f1, FO2 f2): fo1(f1), fo2(f2)
{ }
// "function call": nested call of function objects
double operator() (double v)
{
return fo2(fo1(v));
}
};
template <typename FO1, typename FO2>inline
Composer<FO1,FO2> compose (FO1 f1, FO2 f2)
{
return Composer<FO1,FO2> (f1, f2);
}
template<typename FO>
void print_values (FO fo)
{
for (int i=-2; i<3; ++i)
{
cout << "f(" << i*0.1<< ") = " << fo(i*0.1)<< "\n";
}
}
void main()
{
cout << compose(Abs(),Sine())(0.5) << "\n\n";
print_values(Abs());
cout << '\n';
print_values(Sine());
cout << '\n';
```

```
print_values(compose(Abs(),Sine()));
cout << '\n';
print_values(compose(Sine(),Abs()));
getch();
}
```

**OUTPUT:**

```
0.479426
f(-0.2) = 0.2
f(-0.1) = 0.1
f(0) = 0
f(0.1) = 0.1
f(0.2) = 0.2
f(-0.2) = -0.198669
f(-0.1) = -0.0998334
f(0) = 0
f(0.1) = 0.0998334
f(0.2) = 0.198669
f(-0.2) = 0.198669
f(-0.1) = 0.0998334
f(0) = 0
f(0.1) = 0.0998334
f(0.2) = 0.198669
f(-0.2) = 0.198669
f(-0.1) = 0.0998334
f(0) = 0
f(0.1) = 0.0998334
f(0.2) = 0.198669
```

**Problem 94. Write a C++ program for Functor compose 3.**

***Program:***

```
#include <iostream.h>
#include<conio.h>
#include <math.h>
#include <stdlib.h>
class Abs
{
public:
// "function call":
double operator() (double v) const
{
return abs(v);
}
};
class Sine
{
public:
// "function call":
double operator() (double a) const
{
return sin(a);
}
};
template <typename C, int N>
class BaseMem : public C
{
public:
BaseMem(C& c) : C(c) { }
BaseMem(C const& c) : C(c) { }
};
template <typename FO1, typename FO2>
class Composer : private BaseMem<FO1,1>,
private BaseMem<FO2,2>
{
public:
// constructor: initialize function objects
Composer(FO1 f1, FO2 f2):
BaseMem<FO1,1>(f1), BaseMem<FO2,2>(f2)
{ }
// "function call": nested call of function objects
double operator() (double v)
{
return BaseMem<FO2.2>::operator()
(BaseMem<FO1,1>::operator()(v));
}
};
template <typename FO1, typename FO2>inline
Composer<FO1,FO2> compose (FO1 f1, FO2 f2)
{
return Composer<FO1,FO2> (f1, f2);
}
template<typename FO>
void print_values (FO fo)
{
for (int i=-2; i<3; ++i)
{
cout << "f(" << i*0.1<< ") = " << fo(i*0.1)<< "\n";
}
}
void main()
{
cout << compose(Abs(),Sine())(0.5) << "\n\n";
print_values(Abs());
cout << '\n';
print_values(Sine());
cout << '\n';
print_values(compose(Abs(),Sine()));
cout << '\n';
print_values(compose(Sine(),Abs()));
cout << '\n';
// print sin(sin()) of some values
print_values(compose(Sine(),Sine()));
```

```
getch();
}
```

**OUTPUT:**

0.479426
f(-0.2) = 0.2
f(-0.1) = 0.1
f(0) = 0
f(0.1) = 0.1
f(0.2) = 0.2
f(-0.2) = -0.198669
f(-0.1) = -0.0998334
f(0) = 0
f(0.1) = 0.0998334
f(0.2) = 0.198669
f(-0.2) = 0.198669
f(-0.1) = 0.0998334
f(0) = 0
f(0.1) = 0.0998334
f(0.2) = 0.198669
f(-0.2) = 0.198669
f(-0.1) = 0.0998334
f(0) = 0
f(0.1) = 0.0998334
f(0.2) = 0.198669
f(-0.2) = -0.197365
f(-0.1) = -0.0996677
f(0) = 0
f(0.1) = 0.0996677
f(0.2) = 0.197365

**Problem 95. Write a C++ program using a function object for operation counting, second version.**

***Program:***

```
#include <iostream.h>
#include<conio.h>
#include <iomanip.h>
#include <assert.h>
template <typename T>
class less_with_count : public binary_function<T, T,
bool>
{
public:
less_with_count() : counter(0), progenitor(0) { }
// Copy constructor:
less_with_count(less_with_count<T>& x) :
counter(0),
progenitor(x.progenitor ? x.progenitor : &x) { }
bool operator()(const T& x, const T& y)
{
++counter;
return x < y;
}
long report() const { return counter; }
~less_with_count()
{ // Destructor
if (progenitor)
{
progenitor->counter += counter;
}
}
private:
long counter;
less_with_count<T>* progenitor;
};
void main()
{
cout << "Using a function object for operation
counting, "
    << "second version." << endl;
const long N1 = 1000, N2 = 128000;
for (long N = N1; N <= N2; N *= 2)
{
vector<int> vector1;
for (int k = 0; k < N; ++k)
vector1.push_back(k);
random_shuffle(vector1.begin(), vector1.end());
less_with_count<int> comp_counter;
sort(vector1.begin(), vector1.end(),
comp_counter);
cout << "Problem size " << setw(9) << N
<< ", comparisons performed: "
<< setw(9) << comp_counter.report()
<< endl;
}
getch();
}
```

**OUTPUT:**

Using a function object for operation counting, second version.
Problem size 1000, comparisons performed: 11846
Problem size 2000, comparisons performed: 26397
Problem size 4000, comparisons performed: 56776
Problem size 8000, comparisons performed: 125715
Problem size 16000, comparisons performed: 271505
Problem size 32000, comparisons performed: 596740

Problem size 64000, comparisons performed:
1235889
Problem size 128000, comparisons performed:
2727581

**Problem 96. Write a C++ program using a function object for operation counting, first version.**

***Program:***

```
#include <iostream.h>
#include<conio.h>
#include <iomanip.h>
#include <assert.h>
template <typename T>
class less_with_count : public binary_function<T, T,
bool>
{
public:
less_with_count()
{ }
bool operator()(const T& x, const T& y)
{
++counter;
return x < y;
}
long report() const {return counter;}
static long counter;
};
template <typename T>
long less_with_count<T>::counter = 0;
void main()
{
const long N1 = 1000, N2 = 128000;
for (long N = N1; N <= N2; N *= 2) {
vector<int> vector1;
for (int k = 0; k < N; ++k)
vector1.push_back(k);
random_shuffle(vector1.begin(), vector1.end());
less_with_count<int> comp_counter;
less_with_count<int>::counter = 0;
sort(vector1.begin(), vector1.end(), comp_counter);
cout << comp_counter.report() << endl;
}
getch();
}
```

**OUTPUT:**

11846
26397
56776
125715
271505
596740
1235889
2727581

**Problem 97. Write a C++ program to demonstrating function pointer passing.**

***Program:***

```
#include <iostream.h>
#include<conio.h>
#include <assert.h>
template <typename InputIterator, typename T>
T accumulate1(InputIterator first, InputIterator last,
T init, T (*binary_funct
ion)(T x, T y)) // New parameter
{
while (first != last)
{
init = (*binary_function)(init, *first);
++first;
}
return init;
}
int multfun(int x, int y)
{
return x * y;
}
void main()
{
int x[5] = {2, 3, 5, 7, 11};
vector<int> vector1(&x[0], &x[5]);
int product = accumulate1(vector1.begin(),
vector1.end(), 1, &multfun);
cout << product << endl;
getch();
}
```

**OUTPUT:**

2310

**Problem 99. Write a C++ program for function macro of get the max value number.**

***Program:***

```
#include <iostream.h>
#include<conio.h>
#define getmax(a,b) ((a)>(b)?(a):(b))
void main()
{
int x=5, y;
y= getmax(x,2);
cout << y << endl;
cout << getmax(7,x) << endl;
getch();
```

```
}
```

**Problem 100. Write a C++ program Using parentheses in macros.**

***Program:***

```
#include <iostream.h>
#include<conio.h>
#define CUBE(a) ( (a) * (a) * (a) )
#define THREE(a) a * a * a
int main()
{
long x = 5;
long y = CUBE(x);
long z = THREE(x);
cout << "y: " << y << endl;
cout << "z: " << z << endl;
long a = 5, b = 7;
y = CUBE(a+b);
z = THREE(a+b);
cout << "y: " << y << endl;
cout << "z: " << z << endl;
getch();
}
```

**Problem 101. Write a C++ program Using inline rather than a macro.**

***Program:***

```
#include <iostream.h>
#include<conio.h>
inline unsigned long Square(unsigned long a)
{ return a * a; }
inline unsigned long Cube(unsigned long a)
{ return a * a * a; }
void main()
{
unsigned long x=1 ;
for (;;)
{
cout << "Enter a number (0 to quit): ";
cin >> x;
if (x == 0)
break;
cout << "You entered: " << x;
cout << ".  Square(" << x << "): ";
cout  << Square(x);
cout<< ". Cube(" << x << "): ";
cout << Cube(x) << "." << endl;
}
getch();
}
```

**Problem 102. Write a C++ program for a simple assert() macro.**

***Program:***

```
#include <iostream.h>
#include<conio.h>
#define DEBUG
#ifndef DEBUG
#define ASSERT(x)
#else
#define ASSERT(x)
if (! (x))
{
cout << "ERROR!! Assert " << #x << " failed\n";
cout << " on line " << __LINE__  << "\n";
cout << " in file " << __FILE__ << "\n";
}
#endif
void main()
{
int x = 5;
cout << "First assert: \n";
ASSERT(x==5);
cout << "\nSecond assert: \n";
ASSERT(x != 5);
cout << "\nDone.\n";
getch();
}
```

**Problem 103. Write a C++ program to printing values in DEBUG mode.**

***Program:***

```
#include <iostream.h>
#include<conio.h>
#define DEBUG
#ifndef DEBUG
#define PRINT(x)
#else
#define PRINT(x) cout << #x << ":\t" << x <<
endl;
#endif
void main()
{
int x = 5;
long y = 78l;
PRINT(x);
for (int i = 0; i < x; i++)
{
PRINT(i);
}
PRINT (y);
PRINT("Hi.");
```

```
int *px = &x;
PRINT(px);
PRINT (*px);
getch();
}
```

**OUTPUT:**

```
x:    5
i:    0
i:    1
i:    2
i:    3
i:    4
y:  78
Hi.": Hi.
px:    0x22ff74
*px:   5
```

## IFDEF:

**Problem 104. Write a C++ program using #undef.**

***Program:***

```
#define DemoVersion
#define DOS_VERSION 5
#include <iostream.h>
#include<conio.h>
void main()
{
#ifdef DemoVersion
cout << "DemoVersion defined.\n";
#else
cout << "DemoVersion not defined.\n";
#endif
#ifndef DOS_VERSION
cout << "DOS_VERSION not defined!\n";
#else
cout << "DOS_VERSION defined as: " <<
DOS_VERSION << endl;
#endif
#ifdef WINDOWS_VERSION
cout << "WINDOWS_VERSION defined!\n";
#else
cout << "WINDOWS_VERSION was not
defined.\n";
#endif
#undef DOS_VERSION
#ifdef DemoVersion
cout << "DemoVersion defined.\n";
#else
cout << "DemoVersion not defined.\n";
#endif
#ifndef DOS_VERSION
cout << "DOS_VERSION not defined!\n";
#else
cout << "DOS_VERSION defined as: "
<< DOS_VERSION << endl;
#endif
#ifndef WINDOWS_VERSION
cout << "WINDOWS_VERSION defined!\n";
#else
cout << "WINDOWS_VERSION was not
defined.\n";
#endif
cout << "Done.\n";
getch();
}
```

**Problem 105. Write a C++ program to define macro.**

***Program:***

```
#define DemoVersion
#define PC 5
#include <iostream.h>
#include<conio.h>
void main()
{
cout << "Checking on the definitions of
DemoVersion,PC and MAC...\n";
#ifdef DemoVersion
cout << "DemoVersion defined.\n";
#else // DemoVersion
cout << "DemoVersion not defined.\n";
#endif // DemoVersion
#ifndef PC
cout << "PC not defined!\n";
#else // PC
cout << "PC defined as: " << PC << endl;
#endif // PC
#ifdef MAC
cout << "MAC defined!\n";
#else
cout << "MAC was not defined.\n";
#endif
cout << "Done.\n";
getch();
}
```

**OUTPUT:**

```
Checking on the definitions of DemoVersion,PC
and MAC...
DemoVersion defined.
PC defined as: 5
MAC was not defined.
```

Done.

## MACRO EXPANSION:

**Problem 106. Write a C++ program for function macro.**

***Program:***

```
#include <iostream.h>
#include<conio.h>
#define getmax(a,b) ((a)>(b)?(a):(b))
void main()
{
int x=5, y;
y= getmax(x,2);
cout << y << endl;
cout << getmax(7,x) << endl;
getch();
}
```

**Problem 107. Write a C++ program for standard macro names: __LINE__, __DATE__, __cplusplus.**

***Program:***

```
#include <iostream.h>
#include<conio.h>
void main()
{
cout << "This is the line number " << __LINE__;
cout << " of file " << __FILE__ << ".\n";
cout << "Its compilation began " << __DATE__;
cout << " at " << __TIME__ << ".\n";
cout << "The compiler gives a __cplusplus value of
" << __cplusplus;
getch();
}
```

**Problem 108. Write a C++ program for Macro Expansion.**

***Program:***

```
#include <iostream.h>
#include<conio.h>
#define CUBE(a) ( (a) * (a) * (a) )
#define THREE(a) a * a * a
void main()
{
long x = 5;
long y = CUBE(x);
long z = THREE(x);
cout << "y: " << y << endl;
cout << "z: " << z << endl;
long a = 5, b = 7;
y = CUBE(a+b);
z = THREE(a+b);
cout << "y: " << y << endl;
cout << "z: " << z << endl;
getch();
}
```

**OUTPUT:**

y: 125
z: 125
y: 1728
z: 82

## MATH:

**Problem 109. Write a C++ program use the abs() function.**

***Program:***

```
#include <iostream.h>
#include<conio.h>
#include <stdlib.h>
void main()
{
int result;
result = abs(-10);
cout << result;
getch();
}
```

**OUTPUT:**

10

**Problem 110. Write a C++ program to create Random number.**

***Program:***

```
#include <iostream.h>
#include<conio.h>
#include <stdlib.h>
void main()
{
int magic;
int guess;
magic = rand(); // get a random number
cout << "Enter your guess: ";
cin >> guess;
if(guess == magic)
cout << "Right";
getch();
}
```

**OUTPUT:**

Enter your guess: 2

**Problem 111. Write a C++ program use math function: sqrt, pow, log.**

***Program:***

```
#include <iostream.h>
#include<conio.h>
#include <math.h>
void main()
{
double number, dsqrt,dpow,dlog;
cout << "Please enter a number \n";
cin >> number;
dsqrt =sqrt(number);
dpow =pow(number,5);
dlog =log(number);
cout << " Math Example\n";
cout << " Square Root is " << dsqrt << "\n";
cout << " Raised to the fifth power is " << dpow <<
"\n";
cout << " Log is " << dlog << "\n";
getch();
}
```

**OUTPUT:**

```
Please enter a number
12
Math Example
Square Root is 3.4641
Raised to the fifth power is 248832
Log is 2.48491
```

**Problem 112. Write a C++ program use math function: cos, sin, tan.**

***Program:***

```
#include <iostream.h>
#include<conio.h>
#include cmath.h>
void main()
{
double angle, dsine,dcos,dtan;
cout << "Please enter an angle in radians \n";
cin >> angle;
dcos =cos(angle);
dsine =sin(angle);
dtan =tan(angle);
cout << " Your angles trigonometric functions are
\n";
cout << " Sine is " << dsine << "\n";
cout << " Cosine is " << dcos << "\n";
cout << " Tangent is " << dtan << "\n";
getch();
}
```

**OUTPUT:**

```
Please enter an angle in radians
12
Your angles trigonometric functions are
Sine is -0.536573
Cosine is 0.843854
Tangent is -0.63586
```

**Problem 113. Write a C++ program to raise x to the y power.**

***Program:***

```
#include <iostream.h>
#include<conio.h>
void main()
{
int base;
int exponent;
int i;
int power;
i = 1;
power = 1;
cout << "Enter base as an integer: ";
cin >> base;
cout << "Enter exponent as an integer: ";
cin >> exponent;
while ( i <= exponent )
{
power *= base;
i++;
}
cout << power << endl;
getch();
}
```

**OUTPUT:**

```
Enter base as an integer: Joe
Enter exponent as an integer: 64
```

**Problem 114. Write a C++ program for math library functions: log10, fabs, ceil, floor.**

***Program:***

```
#include <iostream.h>
#include<conio.h>
#include <iomanip.h>
#include <math.h>
void mair
{
cout << fixed << setprecision( 1 );
cout << "\nlog10(" << 1.0 << ") = "
<< log10( 1.0 )<< "\nlog10(" << 10.0 <<) = "
<< log10( 10.0)
<< "\nlog10(" << 100.0 << ") = "
<< log10( 100.0 ) ;
```

```
cout << "\nfabs(" << 13.5 << ") = "
<< fabs( 13.5 )<< "\nfabs(" << 0.0 << ") = "
<< fabs( 0.0 )<< "\nfabs(" << -13.5 << ") = "
<< fabs( -13.5 );
cout << "\nceil(" << 9.2 << ") = "
<< ceil( 9.2 )<< "\nceil(" << -9.8 << ")= "
<< ceil( -9.8 );
cout << "\nfloor(" << 9.2 << ") = "
<< floor( 9.2 )<< "\nfloor(" << -9.8 <<) = "
<< floor( -9.8 );
getch();
}
```

**OUTPUT:**

```
log10(1.0) = 0.0
log10(10.0) = 1.0
log10(100.0) = 2.0
fabs(13.5) = 13.5
fabs(0.0) = 0.0
fabs(-13.5) = 13.5
ceil(9.2) = 10.0
ceil(-9.8) = -9.0
floor(9.2) = 9.0
floor(-9.8) = -10.0
```

**Problem 115. Write a C++ program for math library functions: pow, fmod, sin, cos, tan.**

***Program:***

```
#include <iostream.h>
#include<conio.h>
#include <iomanip.h>
#include <math.h>
void main()
{
cout << fixed << setprecision( 1 );
cout << "\npow(" << 2.0 << ", " << 7.0 << ") = "
<< pow( 2.0, 7.0 ) << "\npow(" << 9.0 << ", "
<< 0.5 << ") = " << pow( 9.0, 0.5 );
cout << setprecision(3) << "\nfmod("<< 13.675
<< ", "<< 2.333 << ")= "
<< fmod( 13.675, 2.333 ) << setprecision( 1 );
cout << "\nsin(" << 0.0 << ") = " << sin( 0.0 );
cout << "\ncos(" << 0.0 << ") = " << cos( 0.0 );
cout << "\ntan(" << 0.0 << ") = " << tan( 0.0 )
<< endl;
getch();
}
```

**OUTPUT:**

```
pow(2.0, 7.0) = 128.0
pow(9.0, 0.5) = 3.0
fmod(13.675, 2.333) = 2.010
sin(0.0) = 0.0
cos(0.0) = 1.0
tan(0.0) = 0.0
```

# STATIC_CAST:

**Problem 116. Write a C++ program Use static_cast.**

***Program:***

```
#include <iostream.h>
#include<conio.h>
void main()
{
int i;
for(i=0; i<10; i++)
cout << static_cast<double> (i) / 3 << " ";
getch();
}
```

**OUTPUT:**

```
0 0.333333 0.666667 1 1.33333 1.66667 2 2.33333
2.66667 3
```

**Problem 117. Write a C++ program Using static_cast: base and derived class.**

***Program:***

```
#include <iostream.h>
#include<conio.h>
class base { };
class derived : public base
{ };
class other : public base
{ };
void main()
{
base* b = new derived;
static_cast<derived&>(*b);
static_cast<other*>(b);
derived* d = new derived;
b = d;
b = static_cast<base*>(d);
getch();
}
```

**Problem 118. Write a C++ program Using static_cast: for enum data type.**

***Program:***

```
#include <iostream.h>
#include<conio.h>
enum color
{
red, black
```

```
};
void main()
{
color c = static_cast<color>(red);
getch();
}
```

## REINTERPRET_CAST:

**Problem 119. Write a C++ program Use reinterpret_cast to cast from char pointer to integer.**

***Program:***

```
#include <iostream.h>
#include<conio.h>
void main()
{
int i;
char *p = "This is a string";
i = reinterpret_cast<int> (p); // cast pointer to integer
cout << i;
getch();
}
```

**OUTPUT:**

```
4448256
```

**Problem 120. Write a C++ program Using reinterpret_cast: cast float to int.**

***Program:***

```
#include <iostream.h>
#include<conio.h>
#include <assert.h>
#include <iomanip.h>
void main()
{
float pi = 1.1;
int  ipi;
cout << setfill('0') << showbase << hex << internal;
assert(sizeof(int) == sizeof(float));
ipi = reinterpret_cast<int&>(pi);
cout << "pi bits=" << setw(10) << ipi << '\n';
getch();
}
```

**OUTPUT:**

```
pi bits=0x3f8ccccd
```

## SORTING:

**Problem 121. Write a C++ program for A Bubble sort.**

***Program:***

```
#include <iostream.h>
#include<conio.h>
#include <stdlib.h>
void main()
{
int nums[10];
int a, b, t;
int size;
size = 10; // number of elements to sort
for(t=0; t<size; t++)
nums[t] = rand();
cout << "Original array is:\n   ";
for(t=0; t<size; t++)
cout << nums[t] << ' ';
cout << '\n';
// This is the bubble sort.
for(a=1; a<size; a++)
for(b=size-1; b>=a; b--)
{
if(nums[b-1] > nums[b])
{ // if out of order
// exchange elements
t = nums[b-1];
nums[b-1] = nums[b];
nums[b] = t;
}
}
cout << "\nSorted array is:\n   ";
for(t=0; t<size; t++)
cout << nums[t] << ' ';
getch();
}
```

**OUTPUT:**

```
Original array is:
 41 18467 6334 26500 19169 15724 11478 29358
26962 24464
Sorted array is:
41 6334 11478 15724 18467 19169 24464 26500
26962 29358
```

**Problem 122. Write a C++ program for a recursive version of Quicksort for sorting characters.**

***Program:***

```
#include <iostream.h>
#include<conio.h>
#include <string.h>
void quicksort(char *items, int len);
void qs(char *items, int left, int right);
void main()
```

```
{
char str[] = "fdsawertgsvbnhgfdertygfd";
cout << "Original order: " << str << "\n";
quicksort(str, strlen(str));
cout << "Sorted order: " << str << "\n";
getch();
}
void quicksort(char *items, int len)
{
qs(items, 0, len-1);
}
void qs(char *items, int left, int right)
{
int i, j;
char x, y;
i = left; j = right;
x = items[( left+right) / 2 ];
do
{
while((items[i] < x) && (i < right))
i++;
while((x < items[j]) && (j > left))
j--;
if(i <= j)
{
y = items[i];
items[i] = items[j];
items[j] = y;
i++; j--;
}
} while(i <= j);
if(left < j)
qs(items, left, j);
if(i < right)
qs(items, i, right);
}
```

**OUTPUT:**

Original order: fdsawertgsvbnhgfdertygfd
Sorted order: abdddeefffggghnrrssttvwy

**Problem 123. Write a C++ program for Quick Sort.**

***Program:***

```
#include <iostream.h>
#include<conio.h>
int *swapnumbers(int rawdata[], int lower, int
upper);
int *quicksort(int rawdata[], int first, int last);
void main()
{
int unsorted[10],i;
int *sorted;
unsorted[0] = 9;
unsorted[1] = 8;
unsorted[2] = 7;
unsorted[3] = 7;
unsorted[4] = 6;
unsorted[5] = 5;
unsorted[6] = 5;
unsorted[7] = 4;
unsorted[8] = 4;
unsorted[9] = 2;
sorted = quicksort(unsorted, 0, 10);
cout << "This is your array sorted:"<< endl;
for(i = 0; i < 10; i++)
{
cout << sorted[i] << endl;
}
getch();
}
int *quicksort(int rawdata[], int first, int last)
{
int lower = first+1, upper = last;
int bound;
rawdata = swapnumbers(rawdata, first,
(first+last)/2);
bound = rawdata[first];
while(lower <= upper)
{
while(rawdata[lower] < bound)
lower++;
while(bound < rawdata[upper])
upper--;
if(lower < upper)
{
rawdata = swapnumbers(rawdata, lower++, upper--
);
}
else
{
lower++;
}
}
rawdata = swapnumbers(rawdata, upper, first);
if(first < upper-1)
{
rawdata = quicksort(rawdata, first, upper-1);
}
if(upper+1 < last)
{
rawdata = quicksort(rawdata, upper+1, last);
}
```

```
return(rawdata);
}
int *swapnumbers(int rawdata[], int lower, int upper)
{
int temp;
temp = rawdata[lower];
rawdata[lower] = rawdata[upper];
rawdata[upper] = temp;
return(rawdata);
}
```

**OUTPUT:**

```
This is your array sorted:
0
2
4
4
5
5
6
7
7
8
```

**Problem 124. Write a C++ program for Sort Tracer.**

***Program:***

```
#include <iostream.h>
#include<conio.h>
class SortTracer
{
private:
int value;            // integer value to be sorted
int generation;       // generation of this tracer
static long n_created;   // number of constructor
calls
static long n_destroyed;  // number of destructor
calls
static long n_assigned;  // number of assignments
static long n_compared;  // number of comparisons
static long n_max_live;  // maximum of existing
objects
// recompute maximum of existing objects
static void update_max_live()
{
if (n_created-n_destroyed > n_max_live)
{
n_max_live = n_created-n_destroyed;
}
}
public:
static long creations()
{
return n_created;
}
static long destructions()
{
return n_destroyed;
}
static long assignments()
{
return n_assigned;
}
static long comparisons()
{
return n_compared;
}
static long max_live()
{
return n_max_live;
}
public:
// constructor
SortTracer (int v = 0) : value(v), generation(1)
{
++n_created;
update_max_live();
cerr << "SortTracer #" << n_created
<< ", created generation " << generation
<< " (total: " << n_created - n_destroyed
<< ")\n";
}
// copy constructor
SortTracer (SortTracer const& b):value(b.value),
generation(b.generation+1)
{
++n_created;
update_max_live();
cerr << "SortTracer #" << n_created
<< ", copied as generation " << generation
<< " (total: " << n_created - n_destroyed
<< ")\n";
}
// destructor
~SortTracer()
{
++n_destroyed;
update_max_live();
cerr << "SortTracer generation " << generation
<< " destroyed (total: "<< n_created - n_destroyed
<< ")\n";
}
// assignment
```

**Development in Cin and Cout**

```
SortTracer& operator= (SortTracer const& b)
{
++n_assigned;
cerr << "SortTracer assignment #" << n_assigned
<< " (generation " << generation
<< " = " << b.generation
<< ")\n";
value = b.value;
return *this;
}
// comparison
friend bool operator < (SortTracer const&
a,SortTracer const& b)
{
++n_compared;
cerr << "SortTracer comparison #" << n_compared
<< " (generation " << a.generation
<< " < " << b.generation
<< ")\n";
return a.value < b.value;
}
int val() const
{
return value;
}
};
long SortTracer::n_created = 0;
long SortTracer::n_destroyed = 0;
long SortTracer::n_max_live = 0;
long SortTracer::n_assigned = 0;
long SortTracer::n_compared = 0;
void main()
{
// prepare sample input:
SortTracer input[] = { 7, 3, 5, 6, 4, 2, 0, 1, 9, 8 };
// print initial values:
for (int i=0; i<10; ++i)
{
cerr << input[i].val() << ' ';
}
cerr << endl;
// remember initial conditions:
long created_at_start = SortTracer::creations();
long max_live_at_start = SortTracer::max_live();
long assigned_at_start = SortTracer::assignments();
long compared_at_start =
SortTracer::comparisons();
// execute algorithm:
cerr << "---[ Start sort() ]--------------------\n";
sort<>(&input[0], &input[9]+1);
cerr << "---[ End sort() ]----------------------\n";
// verify result:
for (int i=0; i<10; ++i)
{
cerr << input[i].val() << ' ';
}
cerr << "\n\n";
// final report:
cerr << "sort() of 10 SortTracer's"
<< " was performed by:\n "
<< SortTracer::creations() - created_at_start
<< " temporary tracers\n "
<< "up to "
<< SortTracer::max_live()
<< " tracers at the same time ("
<< max_live_at_start << " before)\n "
<< SortTracer::assignments() - assigned_at_start
<< " assignments\n "
<< SortTracer::comparisons() - compared_at_start
<< " comparisons\n\n";
}
```

**OUTPUT:**

```
SortTracer #1, created generation 1 (total: 1)
SortTracer #2, created generation 1 (total: 2)
SortTracer #3, created generation 1 (total: 3)
SortTracer #4, created generation 1 (total: 4)
SortTracer #5, created generation 1 (total: 5)
SortTracer #6, created generation 1 (total: 6)
SortTracer #7, created generation 1 (total: 7)
SortTracer #8, created generation 1 (total: 8)
SortTracer #9, created generation 1 (total: 9)
SortTracer #10, created generation 1 (total: 10)
7 3 5 6 4 2 0 1 9 8
---[ Start std::sort() ]--------------------
SortTracer #11, copied as generation 2 (total: 11)
SortTracer comparison #1 (generation 2 < 1)
SortTracer assignment #1 (generation 1 = 1)
SortTracer assignment #2 (generation 1 = 2)
SortTracer generation 2 destroyed (total: 10)
SortTracer #12, copied as generation 2 (total: 11)
SortTracer comparison #2 (generation 2 < 1)
SortTracer #13, copied as generation 3 (total: 12)
SortTracer comparison #3 (generation 3 < 1)
SortTracer assignment #3 (generation 1 = 1)
SortTracer comparison #4 (generation 3 < 1)
SortTracer assignment #4 (generation 1 = 3)
SortTracer generation 3 destroyed (total: 11)
SortTracer generation 2 destroyed (total: 10)
SortTracer #14, copied as generation 2 (total: 11)
SortTracer comparison #5 (generation 2 < 1)
SortTracer #15, copied as generation 3 (total: 12)
SortTracer comparison #6 (generation 3 < 1)
```

```
SortTracer assignment #5 (generation 1 = 1)
SortTracer comparison #7 (generation 3 < 1)
SortTracer assignment #6 (generation 1 = 3)
SortTracer generation 3 destroyed (total: 11)
SortTracer generation 2 destroyed (total: 10)
SortTracer #16, copied as generation 2 (total: 11)
SortTracer comparison #8 (generation 2 < 1)
SortTracer #17, copied as generation 3 (total: 12)
SortTracer comparison #9 (generation 3 < 1)
SortTracer assignment #7 (generation 1 = 1)
SortTracer comparison #10 (generation 3 < 1)
SortTracer assignment #8 (generation 1 = 1)
SortTracer comparison #11 (generation 3 < 1)
SortTracer assignment #9 (generation 1 = 1)
SortTracer comparison #12 (generation 3 < 1)
SortTracer assignment #10 (generation 1 = 3)
SortTracer generation 3 destroyed (total: 11)
SortTracer generation 2 destroyed (total: 10)
SortTracer #18, copied as generation 2 (total: 11)
SortTracer comparison #13 (generation 2 < 1)
SortTracer assignment #11 (generation 1 = 1)
SortTracer assignment #12 (generation 1 = 1)
SortTracer assignment #13 (generation 1 = 1)
SortTracer assignment #14 (generation 1 = 1)
SortTracer assignment #15 (generation 1 = 1)
SortTracer assignment #16 (generation 1 = 2)
SortTracer generation 2 destroyed (total: 10)
SortTracer #19, copied as generation 2 (total: 11)
SortTracer comparison #14 (generation 2 < 1)
SortTracer assignment #17 (generation 1 = 1)
SortTracer assignment #18 (generation 1 = 1)
SortTracer assignment #19 (generation 1 = 1)
SortTracer assignment #20 (generation 1 = 1)
SortTracer assignment #21 (generation 1 = 1)
SortTracer assignment #22 (generation 1 = 1)
SortTracer assignment #23 (generation 1 = 2)
SortTracer generation 2 destroyed (total: 10)
SortTracer #20, copied as generation 2 (total: 11)
SortTracer comparison #15 (generation 2 < 1)
SortTracer #21, copied as generation 3 (total: 12)
SortTracer comparison #16 (generation 3 < 1)
SortTracer assignment #24 (generation 1 = 1)
SortTracer comparison #17 (generation 3 < 1)
SortTracer assignment #25 (generation 1 = 1)
SortTracer comparison #18 (generation 3 < 1)
SortTracer assignment #26 (generation 1 = 1)
SortTracer comparison #19 (generation 3 < 1)
SortTracer assignment #27 (generation 1 = 1)
SortTracer comparison #20 (generation 3 < 1)
SortTracer assignment #28 (generation 1 = 1)
SortTracer comparison #21 (generation 3 < 1)
SortTracer assignment #29 (generation 1 = 1)
SortTracer comparison #22 (generation 3 < 1)
SortTracer assignment #30 (generation 1 = 3)
SortTracer generation 3 destroyed (total: 11)
SortTracer generation 2 destroyed (total: 10)
SortTracer #22, copied as generation 2 (total: 11)
SortTracer comparison #23 (generation 2 < 1)
SortTracer #23, copied as generation 3 (total: 12)
SortTracer comparison #24 (generation 3 < 1)
SortTracer assignment #31 (generation 1 = 3)
SortTracer generation 3 destroyed (total: 11)
SortTracer generation 2 destroyed (total: 10)
SortTracer #24, copied as generation 2 (total: 11)
SortTracer comparison #25 (generation 2 < 1)
SortTracer #25, copied as generation 3 (total: 12)
SortTracer comparison #26 (generation 3 < 1)
SortTracer assignment #32 (generation 1 = 1)
SortTracer comparison #27 (generation 3 < 1)
SortTracer assignment #33 (generation 1 = 3)
SortTracer generation 3 destroyed (total: 11)
SortTracer generation 2 destroyed (total: 10)
---[ End sort() ]----------------------
0 1 2 3 4 5 6 7 8 9
sort() of 10 SortTracer's was performed by:
15 temporary tracers
up to 12 tracers at the same time (10 before)
33 assignments
27 comparisons
SortTracer generation 1 destroyed (total: 9)
SortTracer generation 1 destroyed (total: 8)
SortTracer generation 1 destroyed (total: 7)
SortTracer generation 1 destroyed (total: 6)
SortTracer generation 1 destroyed (total: 5)
SortTracer generation 1 destroyed (total: 4)
SortTracer generation 1 destroyed (total: 3)
SortTracer generation 1 destroyed (total: 2)
SortTracer generation 1 destroyed (total: 1)
SortTracer generation 1 destroyed (total: 0)
```

**Problem 125. Write a C++ program for Selection Sort.**

***Program:***

```
#include <iostream.h>
#include<conio.h>
#include <iomanip.h>
void selectionSort( int * const, const int );
void swap( int * const, int * const );
void main()
{
const int arraySize = 10;
int a[ arraySize ] = { 2, 6, 4, 8, 10, 12, 9, 1, 5, 7 };
```

```
selectionSort( a, arraySize );
for ( int j = 0; j < arraySize; j++ )
cout << a[ j ];
getch();
}
void selectionSort( int * const array, const int size )
{
int smallest;
for ( int i = 0; i < size - 1; i++ )
{
smallest = i;
for ( int index = i + 1; index < size; index++ )
if ( array[ index ] < array[ smallest ] )
smallest = index;
swap( &array[ i ], &array[ smallest ] );
}
}
void swap( int * const element1Ptr, int * const
element2Ptr )
{
int hold = *element1Ptr;
*element1Ptr = *element2Ptr;
*element2Ptr = hold;
}
```

**OUTPUT:**

124567891012

## TYPEDEF:

**Problem 126. Write a C++ program Use typedef keyword to define new variable type.**

***Program:***

```
#include <iostream.h>
#include<conio.h>
typedef unsigned short int USHORT;
void main()
{
USHORT Width = 5;
USHORT Length;
Length = 10;
USHORT Area = Width * Length;
cout << "Width: " << Width << "\n";
cout << "Length: " << Length << std::endl;
cout << "Area: " << Area << std::endl;
getch();
}
```

**OUTPUT:**

Width: 5
Length: 10
Area: 50

**Problem 127. Write a C++ program Use typedef to create new data type and use it as function return type.**

***Program:***

```
#include <math.h>
#include <iostream.h>
#include<conio.h>
typedef double NewType;
NewType f(double number);
NewType f2(double number);
NewType f3(double number);
void main()
{
int menu;
double num;
NewType response;
response = f(num);
cout << "The answer is " << response;
response = f2(num);
cout << "The answer is " << response;
response = f3(num);
cout << "The answer is " << response;
getch();
}
NewType f(double number)
{
return sqrt(number);
}
NewType f2(double number)
{
return pow(number,.3333);
}
NewType f3(double number)
{
return pow (number,.25);
}
```

**OUTPUT:**

The answer is 2.29873e-154The answer is 3.8421e-103The answer is 1.51616e-077"

## TYPEID:

**Problem 128. Write a C++ program Use typeid.**

***Program:***

```
#include <iostream.h>
#include<conio.h>
class MyClass
{ };
void main()
```

```
{
int i, j;
float f;
MyClass ob;
cout << "The type of i is: "
<< typeid(i).name()
<< endl;
cout << "The type of f is: "
<< typeid(f).name()
<< endl;
cout << "The type of ob is: "
<< typeid(ob).name()
<< "\n\n";
if(typeid(i) == typeid(j))
cout << "The types of i and j are the same\n";
if(typeid(i) != typeid(f))
cout << "The types of i and f are not the same\n";
getch();
}
```

**OUTPUT:**

```
The type of i is; i
The type of f is: f
The type of ob is: 7MyClass
The types of i and j are the same
The types of i and f are not the same
```

**Problem 129. Write a C++ program Use typeid on a polymorphic class hierarchy.**

***Program:***

```
#include <iostream.h>
#include<conio.h>
class Base
{ };
class Derived1: public Base
{ };
class Derived2: public Base
{ };
void main()
{
Base *p, baseob;
Derived1 ob1;
Derived2 ob2;
p = &baseob;
cout << typeid(*p).name() << endl;
p = &ob1;
cout << typeid(*p).name() << endl;
p = &ob2;
cout << typeid(*p).name() << endl;
getch();
}
```

**OUTPUT:**

```
4Base
4Base
4Base
```

**Problem 130. Write a C++ program to compare the typeid for templates.**

***Program:***

```
#include <iostream.h>
#include<conio.h>
template <class T> class MyClass
{
T a;
public:
MyClass(T i) { a = i; }
};
void main()
{
MyClass<int> o1(10), o2(9);
MyClass<double> o3(7.2);
if(typeid(o1) == typeid(o2))
cout << "o1 and o2 are the same type\n";
if(typeid(o1) == typeid(o3))
cout << "Error\n";
else
cout << "o1 and o3 are different types\n";
getch();
}
```

**OUTPUT:**

```
o1 and o2 are the same type
o1 and o3 are different types
```

**Problem 131. Write a C++ program Use a reference with typeid.**

***Program:***

```
#include <iostream.h>
#include<conio.h>
class Base
{
public:
virtual bool lays_eggs()
{
return false;
} // Base is polymorphic
};
class Derived1: public Base
{
public:
};
class Derived2: public Base
{
public:
```

```
bool lays_eggs()
{
return true;
}
};
void WhatBase(Base &ob)
{
cout << "ob is referencing an object of type ";
cout << typeid(ob).name() << endl;
}
void main()
{
Base AnyBase;
Derived1 Derived1;
Derived2 Derived2;
WhatBase(AnyBase);
WhatBase(Derived1);
WhatBase(Derived2);
getch();
}
```

**OUTPUT:**

ob is referencing an object of type 4Base
ob is referencing an object of type 8Derived1
ob is referencing an object of type 8Derived2

**Problem 132. Write a C++ program to demonstrating run-time type id.**

***Program:***

```
class Base
{
public:
virtual bool method() { return false; } // Base is
polymorphic
};
class Derived1: public Base
{
public:
};
class Derived2: public Base
{
public:
bool method()
{
return true;
}
};
class Derived3: public Base
{
public:
};
Base *factory()
{
switch(rand() 3 )
{
case 0: return new Derived3;
case 1: return new Derived1;
case 2: return new Derived2;
}
return 0;
}
void main()
{
Base *ptr;
for(int i=0; i<10; i++)
{
ptr = factory(); // generate an object
cout << "Object is " << typeid(*ptr).name();
cout << endl;
if(typeid(*ptr) == typeid(Derived3))
cout << " Derived3";
if(typeid(*ptr) == typeid(Derived1))
cout << " Derived1";
if(typeid(*ptr) == typeid(Derived2))
cout << " Derived2";
}
getch();
}
```

**OUTPUT:**

Object is 8Derived2
Derived2Object is 8Derived2
Derived2Object is 8Derived1
Derived1Object is 8Derived1
Derived1Object is 8Derived2
Derived2Object is 8Derived1
Derived1Object is 8Derived3
Derived3Object is 8Derived3
Derived3Object is 8Derived1
Derived1Object is 8Derived2
Derived2"

**Problem 133. Write a C++ program Using typeid with templates.**

***Program:***

```
#include <iostream.h>
#include<conio.h>
template <class T> class MyClass
{
T a;
public:
MyClass(T i)
{
a = i;
```

```
}
};
void main()
{
MyClass<int> o1(10), o2(9);
MyClass<double> o3(7.2);
cout << "Type of o1 is ";
cout << typeid(o1).name() << endl;
cout << "Type of o2 is ";
cout << typeid(o2).name() << endl;
cout << "Type of o3 is ";
cout << typeid(o3).name() << endl;
getch();
}
```

**OUTPUT:**

Type of o1 is 7MyClassIiE
Type of o2 is 7MyClassIiE
Type of o3 is 7MyClassIdE

**Problem 134. Write a C++ program Using typeid: class pointer, base class, derived class.**

***Program:***

```
#include <iostream.h>
#include<conio.h>
class base
{
public:
virtual ~base()
{}
};
class derived : public base {};
void main()
{
base* b = new derived;
cout << typeid(*b).name() << '\n';
cout << typeid(base).name() << '\n';
derived* d = new derived;
cout << typeid(*d).name() << '\n';
cout << typeid(derived).name() << '\n';
getch();
}
```

**OUTPUT:**

7derived
4base
7derived
7derived

**Problem 135. Write a C++ program for typeid() function and RTTI must be enabled in compiler.**

***Program:***

```
#include <iostream.h>
#include<conio.h>
class Base
{
virtual void virtFunc()
{ }
};
class Derv1 : public Base
{ };
class Derv2 : public Base
{ };
void displayName(Base* pB)
{
cout << "pointer to an object of "; //display name
of class
cout << typeid(*pB).name() << endl; //pointed to
by pB
}
void main()
{
Base* pBase = new Derv1;
displayName(pBase); //"pointer to an object of
class Derv1"
pBase = new Derv2;
displayName(pBase); //"pointer to an object of
class Derv2"
getch();
}
```

**Problem 136. Write a C++ program for output the name of a typeid.**

***Program:***

```
#include <iostream.h>
#include<conio.h>
void main ()
{
int * a,b;
a=0; b=0;
if (typeid(a) != typeid(b))
{
cout << "a and b are of different types:\n";
cout << "a is: " << typeid(a).name() << '\n';
cout << "b is: " << typeid(b).name() << '\n';
}
getch();
}
```

**Problem 137. Write a C++ program to print type name of what ptr points at.**

***Program:***

```
#include <iostream.h>
#include<conio.h>
```

```
class Base
{
public:
Base():hide(0){ }
void mutate(int i){ hide = i;}
void print()const
{
cout << "hide in Base = " << hide << endl;
}
private:
int hide;
};
class One: public Base
{
public:
One():Base(),data(0)
{}
void mutate(int i){ data = i;}
void print()const
{cout << "data in One = "<< data << endl;}
private:
int data;
};
void main ()
{
Base* bptr; One* Derived;
cout << typeid(bptr).name() << endl;
cout << typeid(Derived).name() << endl;
if (typeid(bptr) == typeid(Derived))
cout << "type bprt & Derived same" << endl;
getch();
}
```

**Problem 138. Write a C++ program Using typeid: enum data type.**

***Program:***

```
#include <iostream.h>
#include<conio.h>
enum color  { red, black };
void main()
{
cout << typeid(red).name() << '\n';
cout << typeid(color).name() << '\n';
getch();
}
```

**OUTPUT:**

```
5color
5color
```

## VARIABLE LENGTH ARGUMENT LISTS:

**Problem 139. Write a C++ program Using variable-length argument lists.**

***Program:***

```
#include <iostream.h>
#include<conio.h>
#include <iomanip.h>
double f( int, ... );
void main()
{
double double1 = 3.5;
double double2 = 2.5;
double double3 = 1.7;
double double4 = 1.2;
cout << f( 2, double1, double2 ) << endl
<< f( 3, double1, double2, double3 ) << endl
<< f( 4, double1, double2, double3, double4 )
 << endl<< endl;
getch();
}
double f( int count, ... )
{
double total = 0;
va_list list;
va_start( list, count );
for ( int i = 1; i <= count; i++ )
total += va_arg( list, double );
va_end( list );
return total;
}
```

**OUTPUT:**

```
6
7.7
8.9
```

## SET_NEW_HANDLER:

**Problem 140. Write a C++ program to demonstrating set_new_handler.**

***Program:***

```
#include <iostream.h>
#include<conio.h>
#include <stdlib.h>
void f()
{
cerr << "called";
abort();
}
```

```
void main()
{
double *ptr[ 50 ];
set_new_handler( f );
for ( int i = 0; i < 50; i++ )
{
ptr[ i ] = new double[ 50000000 ];
cout << "Allocated 50000000 doubles in ptr[ " << i
<< " ]\n";
}
getch();
}
```

**OUTPUT:**

Allocated 50000000 doubles in ptr[ 0 ]
Allocated 50000000 doubles in ptr[ 1 ]
Allocated 50000000 doubles in ptr[ 2 ]
Allocated 50000000 doubles in ptr[ 3 ]
Allocated 50000000 doubles in ptr[ 4 ]
called
This application has requested the Runtime to terminate it in an unusual way.
Please contact the application's support team for more information.

## SET_TERMINATE:

**Problem 141. Write a C++ program to set a new terminate handler.**

***Program:***

```
#include <iostream.h>
#include<conio.h>
void my_Thandler()
{
cout << "Inside new terminate handler\n";
abort();
}
void main()
{
set_terminate(my_Thandler);
throw 100; // throw an error
getch();
}
```

**OUTPUT:**

Inside new terminate handler

## LOCALE:

**Problem 142. Write a C++ program to create a copy of the user's locale.**

***Program:***

```
#include <iostream.h>
#include<conio.h>
#include <string.h>
void main( )
{
locale loc(""); // Create a copy of the user's locale
cout << "Locale name = " << loc.name( ) << endl;
cout.imbue(loc); // Tell cout to use the formatting
of
// the user's locale
cout << "pi in locale " << cout.getloc( ).name( )
<< " is "
<< 3.14 << endl;
getch();
}
```

**OUTPUT:**

Locale name = C
pi in locale C is 3.14

**Problem 143. Write a C++ program to get a moneypunct facet for cout for a locale.**

***Program:***

```
#include <iostream.h>
#include<conio.h>
void main()
{
// Create a locale for US English.
locale usloc("English_US");
// Set the locale of cout to US English.
cout.imbue(usloc);
// Get a moneypunct facet for cout.
const moneypunct<char> &us_monpunct =
use_facet<moneypunct<char> >(cout.getloc());
cout << " Currency symbol: "
<< us_monpunct.curr_symbol()
<< endl;
cout << " Decimal point: "
<< us_monpunct.decimal_point()
<< endl;
cout << " Thousands separator: "
<< us_monpunct.thousands_sep()
<< endl;
cout << " Fraction digits: "
<< us_monpunct.frac_digits()
<< endl;
cout << " Number of grouping rules: "
<< us_monpunct.grouping().size()
<< endl;
for(unsigned i=0; i <
us_monpunct.grouping().size(); ++i)
cout << " Size of group " << i << ": "
```

```
<< (int)us_monpunct.grouping()[0]
<< endl;
cout << endl;
getch();
}
```

**Problem 144. Write a C++ program for Money format for US dollars.**

***Program:***

```
#include <iostream.h>
#include<conio.h>
void main()
{
double balance = 1234.56;
locale usloc("English_US");
locale gloc("German_Germany");
cout << showbase;
cout.imbue(usloc);
const money_put<char> &us_mon =
use_facet<money_put<char> >(cout.getloc());
us_mon.put(cout, false, cout, ' ', "123456");
us_mon.put(cout, true, cout, ' ', -299);
us_mon.put(cout, false, cout, ' ', balance * 100);
getch();
}
```

**Problem 145. Write a C++ program to show money in international German format.**

***Program:***

```
#include <iostream.h>
#include<conio.h>
void main()
{
double balance = 5467.87;
locale usloc("English_US");
locale gloc("German_Germany");
cout << showbase;
cout.imbue(usloc);
const money_put<char> &us_mon =
use_facet<money_put<char> >(cout.getloc());
cout << "Now show money in international German
format:\n";
cout.imbue(gloc);
const money_put<char> &g_mon =
use_facet<money_put<char> >(cout.getloc());
g_mon.put(cout, true, cout, ' ', 123456);
cout << endl;
g_mon.put(cout, true, cout, ' ', -299);
cout << endl;
g_mon.put(cout, true, cout, ' ', balance * 100);
getch();
}
```

**Problem 146. Write a C++ program to Use a German locale to write data to standard ouput.**

***Program:***

```
#include <iostream.h>
#include<conio.h>
void main()
{
// use classic C locale to read data from standard
input
cin.imbue(locale::classic());
// use a German locale to write data to standard
ouput
cout.imbue(locale("de_DE"));
// read and output floating-point values in a loop
double value;
while (cin >> value)
{
cout << value << endl;
}
getch();
}
```

**Problem 147. Write a C++ program to process the name of the locale and read input.**

***Program:***

```
#include <string.h>
#include <stdlib.h>
#include <iostream.h>
#include<conio.h>
void main()
{
// create the default locale from the user's
environment
locale langLocale("");
// and assign it to the standard ouput channel
cout.imbue(langLocale);
// process the name of the locale
bool isGerman;
if (langLocale.name() == "de_DE" ||
langLocale.name() == "de" ||
langLocale.name() == "german")
{
isGerman = true;
}
else
{
isGerman = false;
}
// read locale for the input
```

```
if (isGerman)
{
cout << "Sprachumgebung fuer Eingaben: ";
}
else
{
cout << "Locale for input: ";
}
string s;
cin >> s;
if (!cin)
{
if (isGerman)
{
cerr << "FEHLER beim Einlesen der
Sprachumgebung"
<< endl;
}
else
{
cerr << "ERROR while reading the locale" << endl;
}
return EXIT_FAILURE;
}
locale cinLocale(s.c_str());
// and assign it to the standard input channel
cin.imbue(cinLocale);
// read and output floating-point values in a loop
double value;
while (cin >> value)
{
cout << value << endl;
}
getch();
}
```

**OUTPUT:**

Locale for input: US

**Problem 148. Write a C++ program to format numeric values relative to a locale.**

***Program:***

```
#include <iostream.h>
#include<conio.h>
#include <iomanip.h>
void main()
{
// Use a fixed format with 2 decimal places.
cout << fixed << setprecision(2);
cout << "Default format: " << 12345678.12 <<
"\n\n";
// Set the locale to English.
locale eloc("English");
cout.imbue(eloc);
cout << "English format: " << 12345678.12 <<
"\n\n";
locale gloc("German");
cout.imbue(gloc);
cout << "German format: " << 12345678.12 <<
"\n\n";
getch();
}
```

## ASSERT:

**Problem 149. Write a C++ program Use assert inside a for loop to check an array.**

***Program:***

```
#include <iostream.h>
#include<conio.h>
#include <assert.h>
void main()
{
int a[1000];
int i;
for (i = 0; i < 1000; ++i)
a[i] = 1000 - i - 1;
sort(&a[0], &a[1000]);
for (i = 0; i < 1000; ++i)
assert (a[i] == i);
getch();
}
```

**Problem 150. Write a C++ program Using the STL generic reverse algorithm with a string and assert the correctness.**

***Program:***

```
#include <iostream.h>
#include<conio.h>
#include <string.h>
#include <assert.h>
void main()
{
string string1 = "abc";
reverse(string1.begin(), string1.end());
assert (string1 == "cba");
getch();
}
```

**Problem 151. Write a C++ program Use assert to check.**

***Program:***

```
#include <iostream.h>
#include<conio.h>
void main()
{
char x[5] = {'a', 'r', 'e', 'q', 't'};
deque<char> deque1(&x[0], &x[5]);
// Search for the first occurrence of the letter e:
deque<char>::iterator where = find(deque1.begin(),
deque1.end(), 'e');
assert (*where == 'e' );
cout << "Ok." << endl;
getch();
}
```

**OUTPUT:**

Ok.

# CHAPTER 4

# CONTROL STATEMENTS

## DECISION CONTROL:

## IF STATEMENTS:

**Problem 1. Write a C++ program of example of the if statement.**

***Program:***

```
#include<iostream.h>
#include<conio.h>
void main()
{
int number;
clrscr();
cout<<"Enter an integer between 1 and 10: ";
cin>>&number;
if (number > 7)
cout<<"You entered "<<number<<" which is greater
than 7 ";
if (number < 3)
cout<<"You entered "<<number<<" which is less
than 3 ";
getch();
}
```

**OUTPUT:**

```
Enter an integer between 1 and 10: 8
You entered 8 which is greater than 7
```

**Problem 2. Write a C++ program using ifs to decide on a discount.**

***Program:***

```
#include<iostream.h>
#include<conio.h>
void main()
{
const double price = 3.50;
int quantity = 0;
cout<<"Enter the number that you want to buy:";
cin>>quantity;
if( quantity>20)
cout<<"The price for"<< quantity<<" is $"<<
quantity * price * 0.95;
else
cout<<"The price for "<<quantity<<" is $"<<
quantity * price;
getch();
}
```

**OUTPUT:**

```
Enter the number that you want to buy:412
The price for 412 is $1369.90
```

**Problem 3. Write a C++ program of IF statement.**

***Program:***

```
#include<iostream.h>
#include<conio.h>
void main()
{
int i,j,big; //variable
cin>>i>>j;
big = i;
if(big < j)
{
big = j;
}
cout<<"bigger one is "<<big;
if(i < j)
{
big = j;
}
else
{
big = i;
}
cout<<"bigger one (using else) is "<<big;
getch();
}
```

**OUTPUT:**

```
52
12
bigger one is 52
bigger one (using else) is 52
```

**Problem 4. Write a C++ program of If else.**

***Program:***

```
#include<iostream.h>
#include<conio.h>
#include <stdlib.h>
void main()
```

```
{
int magic;
int guess;
magic = rand();
cout<<"Guess the magic number: ";
cin>>guess;
if(guess == magic) cout<<"** Right **";
else
cout<<"Wrong";
getch();
}
```

**OUTPUT:**

Guess the magic number:213
Wrong

**Problem 5. Write a C++ program to show more statement in if else.**

***Program:***

```
#include<iostream.h>
#include<conio.h>
#include <stdlib.h>
void main()
{
int magic;
int guess;
magic = rand();
cout<<"Guess the magic number: ";
cin>>guess;
if (guess == magic)
{
cout<<"** Right **";
cout<< magic<<"is the magic number"<<endl;
}
else
{
cout<<"Wrong, ";
if(guess > magic)
too high ";
else
cout<<"too low"<<endl;
}
getch();
}
```

**OUTPUT:**

Guess the magic number:250
Wrong, too low

**Problem 6. Write a C++ program using If else if and else.**

***Program:***

```
#include<iostream.h>
#include<conio.h>
#include <stdlib.h>
void main()
{
int magic;
int guess;
magic = rand();
cout<<"Guess the magic number: ";
cin>>guess;
if(guess == magic)
{
cout<<"** Right ** ";
cout<<magic<<"is the magic number";
}
else if(guess > magic)
{
cout<<"Wrong, too high";
}
else
{
cout<<"Wrong, too low";
}
getch();
}
```

**OUTPUT:**

Guess the magic number:821
Wrong, too high

**Problem 7. Write a C++ program using more if else.**

***Program:***

```
#include<iostream.h>
#include<conio.h>
void main()
{
int a, b;
char ch;
cout<<"Choice:"<<endl;
cout<<"(A) Add, (S) Subtract, (M) Multiply, or
(D) Divide?"<<endl;
ch = getchar();
cout<<endl;
cout<<"Enter a: ";
cin>>a;
cout<<"Enter b: ";
cin>>b;
if(ch=='A') cout<<a+b;
else if(ch=='S') cout<<a-b;
else if(ch=='M')cout<<a*b;
else if(ch=='D' && b!=0) cout<<a/b;
getch();
```

```
}
```

**OUTPUT:**

```
Choice:
(A) Add, (S) Subtract, (M) Multiply, or (D) Divide?
A
Enter a:23
Enter b:12
35
```

**Problem 8. Write a C++ program using Block if else statement.**

***Program:***

```
#include<iostream.h>
#include<conio.h>
void main()
{
int answer, i;
int again;
clrscr();
for(i = 1; i <=3; i++)
{
cout<<"What is"<<i<<"+"<<i<<"?";
cin>>answer;
if(answer == i + i)
cout<<"Right!"<<endl;
else
{
cout<<"Wrong";
cout<<"Try again.";
cout<<"What is"<<i<<"+"<<i<<"?";
cin>>answer;
if(answer == i + i)
cout<<"Right!"<<endl;
else
cout<<"Wrong, the answer ="<<i+i;
}
}
getch();
}
```

**OUTPUT:**

```
What is 1+1? 2
Right!
What is 2+2? 4
Right!
What is 3+3? 6
Right!
```

**Problem 9. Write a C++ program using two if statements.**

***Program:***

```
#include<iostream.h>
#include<conio.h>
void main()
{
int num;
cout<<"Enter an integer: ";
cin>>num;
if(num < 0)
cout<<""num is negative.";
if(num > -1)
cout<<""num is non-negative.";
getch();
}
```

**OUTPUT:**

```
Enter an integer:34
num is non-negative.
```

**Problem 10. Write a C++ program using result as the if condition.**

***Program:***

```
#include<iostream.h>
#include<conio.h>
void main()
{
int answer;
cout<<"What is 110 + 14? ";
cin>>answer;
if(answer == 110+14)
cout<<"Right!";
getch();
}
```

**OUTPUT:**

```
What is 110 + 14?
124
Right!
```

**Problem 11. Write a C++ program using user input as the if condition.**

***Program:***

```
#include<iostream.h>
#include<conio.h>
void main()
{
float num;
int choice;
cout<<" Meter or Feet: ";
cin>>num;
cout<<"1: Feet to Meters, 2: Meters to Feet. ";
cout<<"Enter choice: ";
cin>>choice;
if(choice == 1)
cout<<num/ 3.28;
if(choice == 2)
```

```
cout<< num * 3.28;
getch();
}
```

**OUTPUT:**

Meter or Feet:25
1: Feet to Meters, 2: Meters to Feet. Enter choice:
1
7.621951

**Problem 12. Write a C++ program using int as if condition.**

***Program:***

```
#include<iostream.h>
#include<conio.h>
void main()
{
int num;
cout<<"Enter an integer: ";
cin>>num;
if(num < 0)
cout<<"Number is negative.";
else
cout<<"Number is non-negative.";
getch();
}
```

**OUTPUT:**

Enter an integer:25
Number is non-negative.

**Problem 13. Write a C++ program using If statement for different choice.**

***Program:***

```
#include<iostream.h>
#include<conio.h>
void main()
{
float num;
int choice;
cout<<"1: Change Feet to Meters, 2: Change Meters to Feet. ";
cout<<"Choice: ";
cin>>choice;
if(choice == 1)
{
cout<<"Enter number of feet: ";
cin>>num;
cout<<"Meters:"<< num / 3.28;
}
else
{
cout<<"Enter number of meters: ";
cin>>num;
cout<<"Feet:"<< num * 3.28;
}
getch();
}
```

**OUTPUT:**

1: Change Feet to Meters, 2: Change Meters to Feet. Choice:2
Enter number of meters:12
Feet: 39.360000

**Problem 14. Write a C++ program using calculation in if statement.**

***Program:***

```
#include<iostream.h>
#include<conio.h>
void main()
{
int answer;
cout<<"What is 110 + 14? ";
cin>>answer;
if(answer == 110+14)
{
cout<<"Right!";
}
else
{
cout<<"Wrong. ";
cout<<"The answer is 124.";
}
getch();
}
```

**OUTPUT:**

What is 110+14? 124
Right!

**Problem 15. Write a C++ program using if command.**

***Program:***

```
#include<iostream.h>
#include<conio.h>
void main()
{
float cost, tax, luxury, total;
luxury = 0.0;
cout<<"Enter the cost: ";
cin>>cost;
tax = cost * 0.06;
if( cost > 40000.0)
luxury = cost * 0.005;
total = cost + tax + luxury;
```

```
cout<<"The total cost is"<< total;
getch();
}
```

**OUTPUT:**

Enter the cost:21
The total cost is 22.26

**Problem 16. Write a C++ program using if else.**

***Program:***

```
#include<iostream.h>
#include<conio.h>
void main()
{
int a, b, op;
cout<<"Enter first number: ";
cin>>a;
cout<<"Enter second number: ";
cin>>b;
cout<<"Enter 0 to add, 1 to multiply: ";
cin>>op;
if(op == 0)
cout<< a + b ;
else
cout<<a * b;
getch();
}
```

**OUTPUT:**

Enter first number:13
Enter second number:10
Enter 0 to add, 1 to multiply:0
23

**Problem 17. Write a C++ program using statement inside if else.**

***Program:***

```
#include<iostream.h>
#include<conio.h>
void main()
{
int i;
cout<<"Enter a number: ";
cin>>i;
if( ( i % 2) == 0)
cout<<"Even";
else
cout<<"Odd";
getch();
}
```

**OUTPUT:**

Enter a number:20
Even

**Problem 18. Write a C++ program to move more statements into if and else.**

***Program:***

```
#include<iostream.h>
#include<conio.h>
void main()
{
int a, b, op;
cout<<"Enter 0 to add, 1 to subtract: ";
cin>>op;
if(op == 0)
{
cout<<Enter first number: ";
cin>>a;
cout<<"Enter second number: ";
cin>>"b;
cout<<a+b;
}
else
{
cout<<"Enter first number: ";
cin>>a;
cout<<"Enter second number: ";
cin>>b;
cout<< a-b;
}
getch();
}
```

**OUTPUT:**

Enter 0 to add, 1 to subtract:1
Enter first number:20
Enter second number:10
10

**Problem 19. Write a C++ program using If else statement inside a for loop.**

***Program:***

```
#include<iostream.h>
#include<conio.h>
void main()
{
int answer, i;
int right, wrong;
right = 0;
wrong = 0;
for( i = 1; i <=5; i = i + 1)
{
cout<<"What is"<<i<<"+"<<i<<"?";
cin>>answer;
if(answer == i + i)
```

```
{
cout<<"Right! ";
right++;
}
else
{
cout<<"Sorry, you're wrong. ";
cout<<"The answer is "<<i + i;
wrong++;
}
}
cout<<"You got "<<right<<"right and"<<wrong<<"
wrong";
getch();
}
```

**OUTPUT:**

What is 1+1? 2
Right!
What is 2+2? 4
Right!
What is 3+3? 6
Right!
What is 4+4? 8
Right!
What is 5+5? 10
Right!
You got 5 right and 0 wrong.

**Problem 20. Write a C++ program using If statement inside for loop.**

***Program:***

```
#include<iostream.h>
#include<conio.h>
void main()
{
int i;
char ch;
clrscr();
for(i = 5; i < 10000; i++)
{
if(!( i % 6 ))
{
cout<<i<<" more number? (Y/N)";
ch = getche();
if(ch == 'N')
break;
cout<<" ";
}
}
getch();
}
```

**OUTPUT:**

6, more number? (Y/N)Y
12, more number? (Y/N)N

**Problem 21. Write a C++ program to check whether the candidate's age is greater than 17 or not. Ifyes, display message "Eligble for voting".**

***Program:***

```
#include<iostream.h>
#include<conio.h>
void main()
{
int age;
clrscr();
cout<<" Enter age:"<<endl;
cin>>age;
if(age>17)
cout<<"Eligible for voting";
getch();
}
```

**OUTPUT:**

Enter age:20
Eligible for voting

**Problem 22. Write a C++ program to use curly brace in the if block. Enter only the three numbersand calculate their sum and multiplication.**

***Program:***

```
#include<iostream.h>
#include<conio.h>
void main()
{
int a,b,c,x;
clrscr();
cout<<"Enter three numbers:"<<endl;
x=cin>>a>>b>>c;
if(x==3)
{
cout<<"Addition:"<<a+b+c;
cout<<" Multiplication:"<<a*b*c;
}
}
```

**OUTPUT:**

Enter three numbers: 1 2 4
Addition:7
Multiplication:8

**Problem 23. Write a C++ program to calculate the square of those numbers only whose least**

**significantdigit is 5.**

***Program:***

```
#include<iostream.h>
#include<conio.h>
void main()
{
int s,d;
clrscr();
cout<<"Enter a Number:"<<endl;
cin>>s;
d=s%10;
if(d==5)
{
s=s/10;
cout<<" Square="<<s*s++<<d*d<<endl;
}
else
cout<<"Invalid Number";
getch();
}
```

**OUTPUT:**

```
Enter a Number:25
Square:625
```

**Problem 24. Write a C++ program to calculateenergy bill. Read the starting and ending meter reading, The charges are as follows.**

| No. Of Units Consumed | Rates in (Rs.) |
|---|---|
| **200-500** | **3.50** |
| **100-200** | **2.50** |
| **Less than 100** | **1.50** |

***Program:***

```
#include<iostream.h>
#include<conio.h>
void main()
{
int initial,final,consumed;
float total;
clrsc();
cout<<" Initial & Final Readings:";
cin>>initial>>final;
consumed=final-initial;
if(consumed>=200 && consumed<=500)
total=consumed*3.50;
else if(consumed>=100 && consumed<=199)
total=consumed*2.50;
else if(consumed<100)
total=consumed*1.50;
cout<<"Total bill for"<<consumed<<"unit
is"<<total;
getche();
}
```

**OUTPUT:**

```
Initail & Final Readings: 800 850
Total bill for 50 Units is 75.000000
```

**Problem 25. Write a C++ program to calculate gross salary for the conditions given below**

| BASIC SALARY (RS.) | DA(RS.) | HRA(RS.) | CONVEYANCE(RS.) |
|---|---|---|---|
| >=5000 | 110% of Basic | 20% of Basic | 500 |
| bs=>3000 && bs<5000 | 100% of Basic | 15% of Basic | 400 |
| bs<3000 | 90% of Basic | 10% of Basic | 300 |

***Program:***

```
#include<iostream.h>
#include<conio.h>
void main()
{
float bs,hra,da,cv,ts;
clrscr();
cout<<" Enter Basic Salary:"<<endl;
cin>>bs;
if(bs=>5000)
{
hra=20*bs/100;
da=110*bs/100;
cv=500;
}
else
if(bs=>3000 && bs<5000)
{
hra=15*bs/100;
da=100*bs/100;
cv=400;
}
else
{
if(bs<3000)
hra=10*bs/100;
da=90*bs/100;
cv=300;
}
ts=bs+hra+da+cv;
cout<<"Basic Salary:"<<bs<<endl;
cout<<"Hra:"<<hra<<endl;
cout<<"Da:"<<da<<endl;
cout<<"Conveyance:"<<cv<<endl;
cout<<"Gross Salary:"<<ts;
getch();
}
```

**OUTPUT:**

Enter Basic Salary: 5400
Basic Salary:5400
Hra:1080
Da:5940
Conveyance:500
Gross Salary:12920

**Problem 26. Write a C++ program to find the average of six subjects and display the results as follows.**

| AVERAGE | RESULT |
|---|---|
| >34&<50 | Third Division |
| >49%<60 | Second Division |
| >60&<75 | First Division |
| >75&<100 | Distinction |
| If marks in any subject less than 35 | Fail |

***Program:***

```
#include<iostream.h>
#include<conio.h>
void main()
{
int sum=0,a,b,c,d,e,f;
float avg;
clrscr();
cout<<"Enter Marks"<<endl;
cout<<"P C B M E H"<<endl;
cin>>a>>b>>c>>d>>e>>f;
sum=a+b+c+d+e+f;
avg=sum/6;
cout<<"Total:"<<sum<<"Average:"<<avg;
if(a<35||b>35||d<35||e<35)
{
cout<<"Result:Fail"<<endl; exit();
}
if(avg>34 && avg<50)
cout<<" Result:Third Division"<<endl;
else
if(avg>49 && avg<60)
cout<<" Result:Second Division"<<endl;
else
if(avg>60 && avg<75)
cout<<" Result:First Division"<<endl;
else
if(avg>75 && avg<100)
cout<<"Result:Distinction";
getche();
}
```

**OUTPUT:**

Enter Marks
P C B M E H
75 75 75 75 75 75
Total:450
Average:75.00
Result:Distinction

**Problem 27. Write a C++ program to check if a number is greater than 15:**

***Program:***

```
#include<iostream.h>
#include<conio.h>
void main()
{
int x;
cout<<"Enter the value:"<<endl;
cin>>x;
if(x>15)
{
cout<<" This number is greater than 15"<<endl;
}
cout<<"This number is not greater than 15
"<<endl;
getch();
}
```

**OUTPUT:**

Enter the value:12
This number is not greater than 15

**Problem 28. Write a C++ program to calculate roots of quadratic eq:ax^2+bx+c=0:**

***Program:***

```
#include<iostream.h>
#include<conio.h>
#include<math.h>
void main()
{
int a,b,c;
float x1,x2,d;
cout<<"Enter the value of a,b,c:"<<endl;
cin>>a>>b>>c;
d=(b*b)-(4*a*c);
if(d==0)
{
x1=x2=(b*b)-(4*a*c);
}
if(d==0)
{
x1=x2=(-b)/(2*a);
cout<<"Roots are equal,they are x1="<<x1<<" and
x2="<<x2;
}
```

```
if(d<0)
{
cout<<" Roots are imaginary."<<endl;
}
if(d>0)
{
x1=((-b)+sqrt(d))/(2*a);
x2=((-b)-sqrt(d))/(2*a);
cout<<"Roots are"<<endl;
cout<<" x1="<<x1<<endl;
cout<<" x2="<<x2;
}
getch();
}
```

**OUTPUT:**

1st Case
Enter the value of a,b,c:2 3 4
Roots are imaginary.
2nd Case
Enter the value of a,b,c:3 12 1
x1=-0.085146
x2=-3.914854

**Problem 29. Write a C++ program to test if a given number is even or odd:**

***Program:***

```
#include<iostream.h>
#include<conio.h>
void main()
{
int d,num;
cout<<" Enter the number:"<<endl;
cin>>num;
d=num%2;
if(d==0)
cout<<" Its even number."<<endl;
else
cout<<" Its odd number.";
getch();
}
```

**OUTPUT:**

Enter the number:7
Its odd number.

**Problem 30. Write a C++ program to verify is a number is divisible by 3 & 5 or not:**

***Program:***

```
#include<iostream.h>
#include<conio.h>
void main()
{
int n;
cout<<" Enter the number:"<<endl;
cin>>n;
if((n%3==0)&&(n%5==0))
cout<<" Its divisible by 3 and 5."<<endl;
else
cout<<" Its not divisible by 3 and 5.";
getch();
}
```

**OUTPUT:**

Enter the number:35
Its not divisible by 3 and 5.

**Problem 31. Write a C++ program to compute result of expression:**

***Program:***

```
#include<iostream.h>
#include<conio.h>
void main()
{
int a,b,c,d;
float x;
cout<<"Enter the value of a,b,c,d:"<<endl;
cin>>a>>b>>c>>d;
if(c!=d)
{
x=((float)(a-b))/(c-d);
cout<<" Evaluated expression is:"<<x;
}
else
{
cout<<"Input is not appropriate";
}
getch();
}
```

**OUTPUT:**

Enter the value of a,b,c,d:25 10 35 20
Evaluated expression is:1.000000

**Problem 32. Write a C++ program to calculate greatest number using nested if,out of three:**

***Program:***

```
#include<iostream.h>
#include<conio.h>
void main()
{
int x,y,z;
clrscr();
cout<<"Enter the value of x,y,z:"<<endl;
cin>>x>>y>>z;
if(x>y)
```

```
if(x>z)
cout<<endl;
cout<<"X="<<x<<"is greatest";
else
cout<<"Z="<<z<<"is greatest";
else
if(y>z)
cout<<"Y="<<y<<"is greatest";
else
cout<<"Z="<<z<<"is greatest";
getch();
}
```

**OUTPUT:**

Enter the value of x,y,z:23 43 45
Z=45 is greatest

**Problem 33. Write a C++ program to display alphabet set in decimal and character form:**

***Program:***

```
#include<iostream.h>
#include<string.h>
#include<conio.h>
#include<ctype.h>
void main()
{
char ch;
cout<<endl;
for(ch=65;ch<=122;ch=ch+1)
{
if(ch>90 && ch<97)
continue;
cout<<toascii(ch)<<"-"<<ch;
}
cout<<endl;
getch();
}
```

**OUTPUT:**

65-A 66-B 67-C 68-D 69-E 70-F
71-G 72-H 73-I 74-J 75-K 76-L
77-M 78-N 79-O 80-P 81-Q 82-R
83-S 84-T 85-U 86-V 87-W 88-X
89-Y 90-Z 97-a 98-b 99-c 100-d
101-e 102-f 103-g 104-h 105-i 106-j
107-k 108-l 109-m 110-n 111-o 112-p
113-q 114-r 115-s 116-t 117-u 118v
119-w 120-x 121-y 122-z

**Problem 34. Write a C++ program to compute the grade using simple if statement.**

***Program:***

```
#include<iostream.h>
#include<conio.h>
#include <dos.h>
void main()
{
float per;
char grade = " ";
clrscr ( );
puts (" Enter the percentage:");
cin>>per;
if (per >= 80)
{
grade = 'A';
}
cout<<endl;
cout<<" Result is Pass";
cout<<" Grade"<< grade;
sleep (10);
}
```

**OUTPUT:**

Enter the percentage: 90
Result is Pass
Grade A

**Problem 35. Write a C++ program using to find the greatest number between two numbers.**

***Program:***

```
#include<iostream.h>
#include<conio.h>
void main()
{
int a,b,g;
clrscr();
cout<<endl;
cout<<"Enter the value of two numbers: ";
cin>>a>>b;
if (a > b)
{ g = a; }
else
{ g = b; }
cout<<" Greatest Number is: "<< g;
getche ( );
}
```

**OUTPUT:**

Enter the value of two numbers: 40 36
Greatest Number is: 40

**Problem 36. Write a C++ program to find bonus according to the sex-code and the salary.**

***Program:***

```
#include<iostream.h>
#include<conio.h>
```

```
#include<dos.h>
void main()
{
int sex_code;
float sal,bonus;
clrscr ();
cout<<endl;
cout<<"Enter the sex-code and the salary of the
employee :";
cin>>sex_code>>sal;
if(sex_code==1)
{
if(sal>5000)
{
bonus=.05;
}
else
{
bonus=.02;
}
}
else
{
bonus=.10;
}
sal=sal + sal*bonus;
cout<<endl;
cout<<"The salary is Rs. "<<sal;
getche();
}
```

**OUTPUT:**

Enter the sex-code and the salary of the employee: 1
1000
The salary is Rs. 1020

**Problem 37. Write a C++ program to find greatest number among three integer numbers.**

***Program:***

```
#include<iostream.h>
#include<conio.h>
#include<dos.h>
void main()
{
int a,b,c,g;
cout<<endl;
cout<<"Enter the three numbers:";
cin>>a>>b>>c;
if(a>b)
{
if(a>c)
{
g=a;
}
else
{
g=c;
}
}
else
{
if(b>c)
{
g=b;
}
else
{
g=c;
}
}
cout<<endl;
cout<<"Greatest number is: "<<g;
getche ();
}
```

**OUTPUT:**

Enter the three numbers: 20 30 10
Greatest number is:30

**Problem 38. Write a C++ program to display the color according to its code which will illustrate the concept of Ladder if statement.**

***Program:***

```
#include<iostream.h>
void main()
{
int code;
clrscr();
cout<<"Enter the color code:"<<endl;
cin>>code;
if(code==1)
{
cout<<"Color is Red";
}
else if(code==2)
}
cout<<" Color is Green";
}
else if(code==3)
{
cout<<" Color is White";
}
else if(code==4)
{
```

```
cout<<"Color is Yellow";
}
else
{
cout<<" No Color code defined";
}
cout<<endl;
cout<<" End of the Program ";
getche();
}
```

**OUTPUT:**

Enter the color code: 2
Color is Green
End of the Program

**Problem 39. Write a C++ program to make a game to reach coordinates xc=0,yc=0 when you are initially at xc=10,yc=10 using else-if:**

***Program:***

```
#include<iostream.h>
#include<conio.h>
void main()
{
char d='a';
int xc=10,yc=10;
cout<<"Press escape to exit."<<endl;
while(d!='\r')
{
 cout<<" Position is xc="<<xc<<"yc="<<yc<<endl;
 cout<<"Press
direction(north_n,south_s,east_e,west_w):";
 d=getche();
 if(d=='n')
 yc--;
 else if(d=='s')
 yc++;
 else if(d=='e')
 xc++;
 else if(d=='w')
 xc--;
}
getch();
}
```

**Problem 40. Write a C++ program to display time:**

***Program:***

```
#include<iostream.h>
#include<conio.h>
void main()
{
float t;
cout<<" Enter time in hours(24hr formatlike
14.20):"<<endl;
cin>>t;
if((t>=0.0)&&(t<12.0))
cout<<" Morning Time.";
else if((t>=12.0)&&(t<18.0))
cout<<" Afternoon Time.";
else if((t>=18.0)&&(t<24.0))
cout<<" Evening Time.";
else
cout<<" Please specify time within the range.";
getch();
}
```

**OUTPUT:**

Enter time in hours(24hr formatlike 14.20):15.30
Afternoon Time.

**Problem 41. Write a C++ program to display numbers divisible by n,that lie betwen 1 to 1000:**

***Program:***

```
#include<iostream.h>
#include<conio.h>
void main()
{
int i,d,num;
clrscr();
cout<<" Enter the number:"<<endl;
cin>>num;
for(i=1;i<=1000;i++)
{
d=i%num;
if(d==0)
cout<<i<<" divisible by"<<num;
}
getch();
}
```

**Problem 42. Write a C++ program for use of else-if ladder**

***Program:***

```
#include<iostream.h>
#include<conio.h>
void main()
{
int items,cno;
float price;
cout<<"Specify customer id. and the items
consumed:"<<endl;
```

```
cin>>cno>>items;
if(items<=150)
price=0.4*items;
else if(items<=300)
price=100+0.55*(items-150);
else if(items<=600)
price=140+0.8*(items-300);
else
price=470+(items-450);
cout<<"Customer Id:"<<cno<<" Price= "<<price;
getch();
}
```

**OUTPUT:**

```
Specify customer id. and the items consumed:230
100
Customer Id:230 Price=40.00
Specify customer id. and the items consumed:142
250
Customer Id:142 Price=155.00
```

**Problem 43. Write a C++ program to find range of values.**

***Program:***

```
#include<iostream.h>
#include<conio.h>
void main()
{
int count;
float val,high,low,sum,average,range;
sum=0;
count=0;
cout<<"Specify numbers in a line:input -ve number
in end"<<endl;
input:
cin>>value;
if(value<0)goto OUTPUT;
count=count+1;
if(count==1)
high=low=value;
else if(value>high)
high=value;
else if(value<low)
low=value;
sum=sum+value;
goto input;
OUTPUT:
average=sum/count;
range=high-low;
cout<<endl;
cout<<"Total values:"<<count;
cout<<"Highest value:"<<high<<"Lowest value:
"<<low;
cout<<"Range :"<<range<<"Average :"<<average;
getch();
}
```

**Problem 44. Write a C++ program if cost price and selling price of an item are input through the keyboard,to determine whether the seller has made profit or incurred loss. Also determine how much profit he made or loss he incurred.**

***Program:***

```
#include<iostream.h>
#include<conio.h>
void main()
{
float cp, sp, p, l ;
clrscr();
cout<<"enter cost price and selling price : "
<<endl;
cin>>cp>>sp;
p = sp - cp ;
l = cp - sp ;
if ( p > 0 )
cout<<"The seller has made a profit of Rs."<< p;
if ( l > 0 )
cout<<"The seller is in loss by Rs. "<< l ;
if ( p == 0 )
cout<<"There is no loss, no profit" ;
cout<<endl;
cout<<"press any key to exit." ;
getch( ) ;
}
```

**OUTPUT:**

```
enter cost price and selling price :140 160
The seller has made a profit of Rs.20.000000
Press any key to exit.
```

**Problem 45. Write a C++ program to find out whether it is an odd number or even number. Any integer is input through the keyboard.**

***Program:***

```
#include<iostream.h>
#include<conio.h>
void main()
{
int n ;
clrscr( ) ;
cout<<"Enter any number:" <<endl;
cin>>n) ;
if (n % 2 == 0 )
```

```
cout<<"The number is even" ;
else
cout<<" The number is odd" ;
cout<<" press any key to exit.";
getch( ) ;
}
```

**OUTPUT:**

```
Enter any number:12
The number is even
Press any key to exit.
```

**Problem 46. Write a C++ program to determine whether the year is a leap year or not.Any integer is input through the keyboard (Hint: Use the % (modulus) operator ).**

***Program:***

```
#include<iostream.h>
#include<conio.h>
void main()
{
int yr ;
clrscr();
cout<<"Enter a year:";
cin>>yr;
if(yr%100==0)
{
if (yr % 400 == 0 )
cout<<" leap year";
else
cout<<" Not a leap year";
}
else
{
if(yr%4 ==0)
cout<<" leap year";
else
cout<<" Not a leap year";
}
cout<<" press any key to exit.";
getch( ) ;
}
```

**OUTPUT:**

```
Enter a year:1984
leap year
press any key to exit.
```

**Problem 47. According to the Gregorian calendar, it was Monday on the data 01/01/01. If any year is input through the keyboard write a C++ program to find out what is the day on 1st January of this year.**

***Program:***

```
#include<iostream.h>
#include<conio.h>
void main()
{
int leapdays, firstday, yr ;
long int normaldays, totaldays ;
clrscr();
cout<<"Enter year:";
cin>>yr;
normaldays = ( yr-1) * 365L ;
leapdays = ( yr - 1) / 4 - ( yr - 1) /100 + ( yr - 1) /
400;
totaldays = normaldays + leapdays ;
firstday = totaldays % 7 ;
if (firstday == 0)
cout<<" Monday";
if (firstday == 1)
cout<<" Tuesday";
if (firstday == 2)
cout<<" Wednesday";
if (firstday == 3)
cout<<" Thursday";
if (firstday == 4)
cout<<" Friday";
if (firstday == 5)
cout<<" Saturday";
if (firstday == 6)
cout<<" Sunday";
cout<<" press any key to exit.";
getch( ) ;
}
```

**OUTPUT:**

```
Enter year:2009
Thrusday
press any key to exit.
```

**Problem 48. A five-digit number is entered through the keyboard. Write a C++ program to obtain the reversed number and to determine whether the original and reversed numbers are equal or not.**

***Program:***

```
#include<iostream.h>
#include<conio.h>
void main()
{
int n, a, b, num;
long int revnum = 0 ;
clrscr( ) ;
cout<<" Enter a five digit number (less than or
```

```
equal to 32767)";
cin>>n;
num = n ;
a = n % 10 ;
n = n / 10 ;
revnum = revnum + a * 10000L;
a = n % 10 ;
n = n / 10 ;
revnum = revnum + a * 1000;
a = n % 10 ;
n = n / 10 ;
revnum = revnum + a * 100;
a = n % 10 ;
n = n / 10 ;
revnum = revnum + a * 10;
a = n % 10 ;
revnum = revnum + a ;
if (revnum == num)
cout<<" Given number & its reversed number are
equal";
else
cout<<" Given number & its reversed number are
not equal";
cout<<" press any key to exit.";
getch( ) ;
}
```

**OUTPUT:**

Enter a five digit number (less than or equal to 32767)41284
Given number & its reversed number are not equal
press any key to exit.

**Problem 49. If the ages of money ,honey and sherry are input through the keyboard, write a C++ program to determine the youngest of the three.**

***Program:***

```
#include<iostream.h>
#include<conio.h>
void main()
{
int r, s, a, young ;
clrscr();
cout<<" Enter age of money, honey and sherry: ";
cin>>r>>s>>a;
if(r<s)
{
if(r<a)
young = r ;
else
young = a ;
}
else
{
if(s<a)
young = s ;
else
young = a ;
}
cout<<"The youngest of money "<<r<<" honey
"<<s<<" and sherry "<<a<<" is "<<young ;
cout<<endl;
cout<<"press any key to exit.";
getch( ) ;
}
```

**OUTPUT:**

Enter age of money, honey and sherry:22 26 24
The youngest of money (22), honey (26) and sherry (24) is 22
press any key to exit.

**Problem 50. Write a C++ program to check whether a triangle is valid or not, when the three angles of the triangle are entered through the keyboard. A triangle is valid if the sum of all the three angles is equal to 180 degrees.**

***Program:***

```
#include<iostream.h>
#include<conio.h>
void main()
{
float angle1, angle2, angle3 ;
clrscr( ) ;
cout<<"Enter three angles of the triangle: ";
cin>>angle1>>angle2>>angle3 ;
if ( ( angle1+ angle2 + angle3 ) == 180 )
cout<<endl;
cout<<"The triangle is a valid triangle";
else
cout<<"The triangle is an invalid triangle";
cout<<endl;
cout<<"press any key to exit.";
getch( ) ;
}
```

**OUTPUT:**

Enter three angles of the triangle:40 90 50
The triangle is a valid triangle
press any key to exit.

**Problem 51. Write a C++ program to find the absolute value of a number entered through the keyboard.**

***Program:***

```
#include<iostream.h>
#include<conio.h>
void main()
{
int no;
cout<<"Enter any number:"<<endl;
cin>>no;
if(no< 0)
no = no * -1 ;
cout<<"The absolute value of given number is"<<
no <<endl;
cout<<"press any key to exit.";
getch( ) ;
}
```

**OUTPUT:**

Enter any number:-60
The absolute value of given number is 60
press any key to exit.

**Problem 52. Given the length and breadth of a rectangle, write a C++ program to find whether the area of the rectangle is greater than its perimeter. For example, the area of the rectangle with length = 5 and breadth = 4 is greater than its perimeter.**

***Program:***

```
#include<iostream.h>
#include<conio.h>
void main()
{
int l, b,area,peri;
clrscr( ) ;
cout<<"Enter length and breadth of the
rectangle:"<<endl;
cin>>l>>b;
area = l*b;
peri = 2*(l+b);
if (area > peri )
cout<<"Area is greater than perimeter"<<endl;
else
cout<<"Area is lesser than perimeter"<<endl;
cout<<"press any key to exit.";
getch( ) ;
}
```

**OUTPUT:**

Enter length and breadth of the rectangle:8 10
Area is greater than perimeter
press any key to exit.

**Problem 53. Given three points (x1, y1), (x2, y2) and (x3, y3), write a C++ program to check if all the three points fall on one straight line.**

***Program:***

```
#include<iostream.h>
#include<conio.h>
#include<math.h>
void main()
{
int x1, y1, x2, y2, x3, y3;
int s1, s2, s3;
clrscr ( );
cout<<"Enter the values of x1 and y1 coordinates
of first point: "<<endl;
cin>>x1>>y1;
cout<<"Enter the values of x2 and y2 coordinates
of first point: "<<endl;
cin>>x2>>y2;
cout<<"Enter the values of x3 and y3 coordinates
of first point: ";
cin>>x3>>y3;
s1 = abs( x2- x1 )/abs (y2- y1 );
s2 = abs( x3- x1 )/abs (y3 - y1 );
s3 = abs( x3 - x2 )/abs (y3 - y2 ) ;
if ( ( s1 == s2 ) && (s1 == s3 ) )
cout<<"Points are Collier."<<endl;
else
cout<<"Points are Not Collier"<<endl;
cout<<"press any key to exit.";
getch( ) ;
}
```

**OUTPUT:**

Enter the values of x1 and y1 coordinates of first point: 10 12
Enter the values of x2 and y2 coordinates of first point : 15 17
Enter the values of x3 and y3 coordinates of first point : 20 22
Points are Collier.
press any key to exit.

**Problem 54. Given the coordinates ( x, y ) of a centre of a circle and its radius, write a C++ program which will determine whether a point lies inside the circle, on the circle or outside the circle.**

**(Hint : Use sqrt ( ) and pow ( ) functions)**

***Program:***

```
#include<iostream.h>
#include<conio.h>
void main()
{
```

```
int x,y,r;
int dis,d;
clrscr();
cout<<"Enter the redius of the circle and coordinates
of the point ( x, y ) :"<<endl;
cin>>r>>x>>y;
dis = x*x+y*y;
d = r*r;
if ( dis == d )
cout<<"Point is on the circle"<<endl;
else
{
 if ( dis > d )
 cout<<"Point is outside the circle"<<endl;
 else
 cout<<"Point is inside the circle"<<endl;
}
cout<<" press any key to exit.";
getch( );
}
```

**OUTPUT:**

Enter the redius of the circle and coordinates of the point ( x, y ) :15 4 8
Point is inside the circle
press any key to exit.

**Problem 55. Given a point ( x, y ), write a C++ program to find out if it lies on the x- axis or on the origin.**

***Program:***

```
#include<iostream.h>
#include<conio.h >
void main()
{
int x, y ;
clrscr( );
cout<<"Enter the x and y coordinates of a point
:"<<endl;
cin>>x>>y;
if ( x == 0 && y == 0 )
cout<<"Point lies on origin"<<endl;
else if ( x == 0 && y != 0 )
cout<<"Point lies on y axis"<<endl;
else if ( x != 0 && y == 0 )
cout<<"Point lies on X axis"<<endl;
else
cout<<"Point dosenot lie on any axis, nor
origin"<<endl;
cout<<" press any key to exit.";
getch( );
}
```

**OUTPUT:**

Enter the x and y coordinates of a point :10 0
Point lies on X axis
press any key to exit.

**Problem 56. Any year is entered through the keyboard, write a C++ program to determine whether the year is leap or not. Use the logical operators && and |.**

***Program:***

```
#include<iostream.h>
# include<conio.h>
void main()
{
int year ;
clrscr( ) ;
cout<<"Enter year:"<<endl;
cin>>year;
if ( year % 400 == 0 || year % 100 != 0 && year %
4 == 0)
cout<<" leap year"<<endl;
else
cout<<"Not a leap year"<<endl;
cout<<"press any key to exit.";
getch( ) ;
}
```

**OUTPUT:**

Enter year:2009
Not a leap year
press any key to exit.

**Problem 57. Any character is entered through the keyboard, write a C++ program to determine whether the character entered is a capital letter, a small case letter, a digit or a special symbol.**

**The following table shows the range of ASCII values for various characters.**

**Characters ASCII Values**
**A - Z**
**a - z**
**0 - 9**
**special symbols 65 - 90**
**97 - 122**
**48 - 57**
**0 - 47, 58 - 64, 91 - 96, 123 - 127**

***Program:***

```
#include<iostream.h>
#include<conio.h>
void main()
{
```

```
char ch ;
clrscr() ;
cout<<"Enter a character from the
keyboard:"<<endl;
cin>>ch;
if(ch >= 97 && ch <=122)
cout<<"The character is a lowercase letter"<<endl;
if(ch >= 48 && ch <= 57)
cout<<"The character is a digit"<<endl;
if ( ( ch >=0 && ch < 48 ) || ( ch > 57 && ch < 65)||
( ch >=90 && ch < 97 )|| ( ch > 122 ))
cout<<"The character is a special symbol"<<endl;
cout<<" press ány key to exit.";
getch();
}
```

**OUTPUT:**

Enter a character from the keyboard:$
The character is a special symbol
press any key to exit.

**Problem 58. A certain grade of steel is graded according to the following conditions:**
**(1) Hardness must be greater than 50**
**(2) Carbon content must be less than 0.7**
**(3) Tensile strength must be greater than 5600**
**The grades are as follows:**
**Grade is 10 if all three conditions are met**
**Grade is 9 if conditions (i) and (ii) are met**
**Grade is 8 if conditions (ii) and (iii) are met**
**Grade is 7 if conditions (i) and (iii) are met**
**Grade is 6 if one condition is met**
**Grade is 5 if none of the conditions are met**
**Write a C++ program, which will require the user to give values of hardness, carbon content and tensile strength of the steel under consideration and OUTPUT the grade of the steel.**

***Program:***

```
#include<iostream.h>
#include<conio.h>
void main()
{
float hard, carbon, tensile ;
clrscr() ;
cout<<"Hardness of steel:";
cin>>hard;
cout<<"Carbon content:";
cin>>carbon;
cout<<"Tensil strength:";
cin>>hard;
if ( hard > 50 && carbon < 0.7 && tensile > 5600 )
{
cout<<endl;
cout<<"Grade 10";
cout<<endl;
cout<<"Press any key to exit.";
getch();
exit();
}
if ( hard > 50 && carbon < 0.7 && tensile <=
5600 )
{
cout<<endl;
cout<<"Grade 9";
cout<<endl;
cout<<"Press any key to exit.";
getch();
exit();
}
if ( hard <= 50 && carbon < 0.7 && tensile >
5600 )
{
cout<<endl;
cout<<"Grade 8";
cout<<endl;
cout<<"Press any key to exit.";
getch();
exit();
}
if ( hard > 50 && carbon >= 0.7 && tensile >
5600 )
{
cout<<endl;
cout<<"Grade 7";
cout<<endl;
cout<<"Press any key to exit.";
getch();
exit();
}
if ( hard > 50 || carbon < 0.7 || tensile > 5600 )
{
cout<<endl;
cout<<"Grade 6";
cout<<endl;
cout<<"Press any key to exit.";
getch( ) ;
exit( ) ;
}
cout<<endl;
cout<<"Grade 5";
cout<<endl;
cout<<"Press any key to exit.";
```

```
getch( ) ;
}
```

**OUTPUT:**

Hardness of steel:37
Carbon content:0.4
Tensil strength:4000
Grade 9
Press any key to exit.

**Problem 59. A library charges a fine for every book returned late. For first 5 days the fine is 50 paise, for 6-10 days fine is one rupee and above 10 days fine is 5 rupees. If you return the book after 30 days your membership will be cancelled. Write a C++ program to accept the number of days the member is late to return the book and display the fine or the appropriate message**

***Program:***

```
#include<iostream.h>
#include<conio.h>
void main()
{
int days ;
clrscr( ) ;
cout<<"Enter the number of days by which member
is late:"<<endl;
cin>>days ;
if ( days >= 6 && days <= 5 )
{
cout<<"Fine = Rs."<<days * 50 / 100 <<endl ;
cout<<"Fine = Rs. "<< days * 50 / 100.0 <<endl ;
}
else
{
if ( days >= 6 && days <= 10)
cout<<"Fine = Rs. "<< days * 1 <<endl ;
else
{
if ( days >= 10 && days <= 30)
cout<<"Fine = Rs. "<< days * 5 <<endl ;
else
cout<<"the membership is cancelled"<<endl;
}
}
cout<<"Press any key to exit.";
getch( ) ;
}
```

**OUTPUT:**

Enter the number of days by which member is late:24
Fine= Rs. 120
Press any key to exit.

**Problem 60. If the three sides of a triangle are entered through the keyboard, write a C++ program to check whether the triangle is valid or not. The triangle is valid if the sum of two sides is greater than the largest of the three sides.**

***Program:***

```
#include<iostream.h>
#include<conio.h>
void main()
{
int side1, side2, side3, largeside, sum ;
clrscr( ) ;
cout<<"Enter three sides of the triangle: ";
cin>>side1>>side2>>side3;
if(side1 > side2)
{
if(side1 > side3)
{
sum = side2 + side3 ;
largeside = side1 ;
}
else
{
sum = side1 + side2 ;
largeside = side3 ;
} }
else
{
if ( side2 > side3 )
{
sum = side1 + side3 ;
largeside = side3 ;
} }
if(sum > largeside)
cout<<"The triangle is a valid triangle"<<endl;
else
cout<<"The triangle is a invalid triangle"<<endl;
cout<<"Press any key to exit.";
getch( ) ;
}
```

**OUTPUT:**

Enter three sides of the triangle:5 6 7
The triangle is a valid triangle
Press any key to exit.

**Problem 61. If the three sides of a triangle are entered through the keyboard, write a C++ program to cheek whether the triangle is**

**isosceles, equilateral, scalene or right –angled triangle.**

***Program:***

```
#include<iostream.h>
#include<conio.h>
void main()
{
int s1, s2, s3, a, b, c ;
clrscr();
cout<<" Enter three sides of a triangle:"<<endl;
cin>>s1>>s2>>s3;
a = ( s1 * s1 ) == ( s2 * s2 ) + ( s3 * s3 ) ;
b = ( s2 * s2 ) == ( s1 * s1 ) + ( s3 * s3 ) ;
c = (s3 * s3 ) == ( s1 * s1 ) + ( s2 * s2 ) ;
if ( s1 != s2 && s2 != s3 && s3 != s1 )
cout<<"The given triangle is a scalene triangle";
if ( ( s1 == s2 ) && ( s2 != s3 ) )
cout<<"The given triangle is an isosceles triangle";
if ( ( s2 == s3 ) && ( s3 != s1 ) )
cout<<"The given triangle is an issoscles triangle";
if ( ( s1 == s3 ) && (s3 != s2 ) )
cout<<"The given triangle is an isosceles triangle ";
if ( s1 == s2 && s2 == s3 )
cout<<" The given triangle is an equilateral
triangle";
if ( a || b || c )
cout<<"The given triangle is a right-angled
triangle";
cout<<endl;
cout<<"Press any key to exit.";
getch();
}
```

**OUTPUT:**

Enter three sides of a triangle:5 8 8
The given triangle is an isosceles triangle
Press any key to exit.

**Problem 62. In a company, worker efficiency is determined on the basis of the time required for a worker to complete a particular job. If the time taken by the worker is between 2 - 3 hours, then the worker is said to be highly efficient. If the time required by the worker is between 3 – 4 hours, then the worker is ordered to improve speed. If the time taken is between 4 – 5 hours, the worker is given training to improve his speed, and if the time taken by the worker is more than 5 hours, then the worker has to leave the company. If the time taken by the worker is input through the keyboard, find the efficiency of the worker.**

***Program:***

```
#include<iostream.h>
#include<conio.h>
void main()
{
float hours;
clrscr();
cout<<"Enter the number of hours worker takes to
finish the job: "<<endl;
cin>>hours;
if ( hours >= 2 && hours <= 3 )
cout<<"Worker is highly efficient";
else
{
if ( hurs >= 3 && hours <= 4 )
cout<<"Worker is ordered to improve his
efficiency";
else
{
if ( hours >= 4 && hours <= 5 )
cout<<"Worker should be given training to
improve his efficiency";
else
cout<<"Worker should leave the company";
}
}
cout<<endl;
cout<<"Press any key to exit.";
getch ( ) ;
}
```

**OUTPUT:**

Enter the number of hours worker takes to finish the job:4
Worker is ordered to improve his efficiency
Press any key to exit.

**Problem 63. The policy followed by a company to process customer orders is given by the following rules:**

**(a) If a customer order quantity less than or equal to that in stock and his credit OK, supply his requirement.**

**(b) If his credit is not OK do not supply . Send him intimation.**

**(c) If his credit is OK but the item in stock is less than his order quantity, supply what is in stock. Intimate to him that the balance will be shipped.**

**Write a C++ program to implement the company policy**

***Program:***

```
#include<iostream.h>
#include<conio.h>
void main()
{
int s = 100, o ;
char c = 'o';
clrscr( ) ;
cout<<"Enter the number of items to be
ordered:"<<endl;
cin>>o;
if (o<=s)
{
if ( c =='o')
cout<<" Order be supplied";
else
cout<<"Order cannot be supplied";
}
Else
{
if (c=='o')
cout<<"Limited items are supplied, rest would be
shipped";
else
cout<<"Order cannot be supplied";
}
getch( ) ;
}
```

**OUTPUT:**

Enter the number of items to be ordered:o
Limited items are supplied, rest would be shipped

**Problem 64. Using conditional operators, determine whether the character entered through the keyboard is a lower case alphabet or not.**

***Program:***

```
#include<iostream.h>
#include<conio.h>
void main()
{
char ch ;
clrscr( ) ;
cout<<"Enter character:"<<endl;
cin>>ch;
ch >= 97 && ch <= 122 ? cout<<"Character entered
is lower case" : cout<<"Character entered is not
lower case";
cout<<endl;
cout<<"Press any key to exit.";
getch ( ) ;
}
```

**OUTPUT:**

Enter character:r
Character entered is lower case
Press any key to exit.

**Problem 65. Using conditional operators, determine whether a character entered through the keyboard is a special symbol or not.**

***Program:***

```
#include<iostream.h>
#include<conio.h>
void main()
{
char ch ;
clrscr( ) ;
cout<<"Enter character:";
cin>>ch;
( ( ch >= 0 && ch <= 47 )|| ( ch >= 58 && ch <=
64 ) || ( ch >= 91 && ch <= 96 ) || ( ch >= 123 ) ) ?
cout<<"Character entered is a special symbol" ) :
cout<<"Character entered is not a special symbol";
cout<<endl;
cout<<"Press any key to exit.";
getch ( ) ;
}
```

**OUTPUT:**

Enter character: @
Character entered is a special symbol

**Problem 66. Write a C++ program to find the greatest of the three numbers entered through the keyboard using conditional operators.**

***Program:***

```
#include<iostream.h>
#include<conio.h>
void main()
{
int n1,n2, n3, great ;
clrscr( ) ;
cout<<"Enter three numbers:"<<endl;
cin>>n1>>n2>>n3;
great = n1 > n2 ? ( n1 > n3 ? n1 : n3 ) : ( n2 > n3 ?
n2 : n3 ) ;
cout<<"greatest number is:"<< great<<endl ;
cout<<"Press any key to exit.";
getch ( ) ;
}
```

**OUTPUT:**

Enter three numbers:8 4 6
greatest number is:8
Press any key to exit.

**Problem 67. Write a program to find f(a):**
**f(a)= -1,if-5.0>a**
**0,if-5.0<a<5.0**
**+1,if a>5.0**

***Program:***

```
#include<iostream.h>
#include<conio.h>
void main()
{
float a;
int b;
cout<<"Enter a:";
cin>>a;
b=(a>5.0)?1:((a<-5.0)?-1:0);
cout<<b;
getch();
}
```

**Problem 68. Write a C++ program to find grade of student according to marks obtained:**
**1)% above or equal to 71-Grade A**
**2)% between 50 to 69-Grade B**
**3)% between 40 to 49-Grade C**
**4)% less than 40-Fail**

***Program:***

```
#include<iostream.h>
#include<conio.h>
void main()
{
int g1,g2,g3,g4,g5,p;
cout<<"Specify marks in 5 subjects:"<<endl;
cin>>g1>>g2>>g3>>g4>>g5;
p=(g1+g2+g3+g4+g5)/5;
if(p>=70)
{
cout<<"Grade A";
}
if((p>=50) && (p<70))
{
cout<<"Grade B";
}
if((p>=40) && (p<70))
{
cout<<"Grade C";
}
if(p<40)
{
cout<<"Fail";
}
getch();
}
```

**OUTPUT:**

Specify marks in 5 subjects:98 89 85 67 76
Grade A

## CASE CONTROL:

**Problem 69. Write a C++ program to a simple 4 function calculator.**

***Program:***

```
#include<iostream.h>
#include<conio.h>
void main()
{
char line[100];
int result =0;
char operator;
int value;
while (1)
{
cout<<"Result:"<<result<<endl;
cout<<"Enter operator and number: ";
fgets(line, sizeof(line), stdin);
cin>>line>>operator>>value;
if ((operator == 'q') || (operator == 'Q'))
break;
switch (operator)
{
case '+':
result += value;
break;
case '-':
result -= value;
break;
case '*':
result *= value;
break;
case '/':
if (value == 0)
{
cout<<"Error:Divide by zero"<<endl;
cout<<" operation ignored"<<endl;
}
else
result /= value;
break;
default:
cout<<"Unknown operator"<< operator;
break;
}
```

```
}
getch();
}
```

**OUTPUT:**

```
Result:0
Enter operator and number: + 15
Result:15
Enter operator and number: - 5
Result:10
Enter operator and number: Q
```

**Problem 70. Write a C++ program for switch demo.**

***Program:***

```
#include<iostream.h>
#include<conio.h>
#include<stdlib.h>
void main()
{
char line[10];
while (1)
{
cout<<"Enter add(a), delete(d), quit(q): "<<endl;
fgets(line, sizeof(line), stdin);
switch (line[0])
{
case 'a':
cout<<"Add"<<endl;
break;
case 'd':
cout<<"Delete"<<endl;
break;
case 'q':
cout<<"Quit"<<endl;
exit(0);
defualt:
cout<<"Error:Bad command "<<line[0];
break;
}
}
getch();
}
```

**OUTPUT:**

```
Enter add(a), delete(d), quit(q):a
Add
Enter add(a), delete(d), quit(q):q
Quit
```

**Problem 71. Write a C++ program to show how to use switch: number.**

***Program:***

```
#include<iostream.h>
#include<conio.h>
void main()
{
int choice = 0;
cout<<" Pick a number between 1 and 10:
"<<endl;
cin>>choice;
if((choice>10) || (choice <1))
choice = 11;
switch(choice)
{
case 7:
cout<<"Congratulations!"<<endl;
cout<<"You win."<<endl;
break;
case 2:
cout<<" You win."<<endl;
break;
case 8:
cout<<" You win."<<endl;
break;
case 11:
cout<<" Try between 1 and 10."<<endl;
default:
cout<<" Sorry, you lose. ";
break;
}
getch();
}
```

**OUTPUT:**

```
Pick a number between 1 and 10:5
Sorry, you lose.
```

**Problem 72. Write a C++ program to show how to use switch: char.**

***Program:***

```
#include<iostream.h>
#include<conio.h>
void main()
{
char answer = 0;
cout<<"Enter Y or N: "<<endl;
cin>>answer;
switch (answer)
{
case 'y': case 'Y':
cout<<" affirmative."<<endl;
break;
case 'n': case 'N':
cout<<" negative."<<endl;
```

```
break;
default:
cout<<" not respond correctly...";
break;
}
getch();
}
```

**OUTPUT:**

Enter Y or N:Y
affirmative.

**Problem 73. Write a C++ program to show use of switch: char and nested if.**

***Program:***

```
#include<iostream.h>
#include<conio.h>
void main()
{
double number1 = 0.0;
double number2 = 0.0;
char operation = 0;
cout<<" Enter the calculation "<<endl;
cin>>number1>>operation>>number2;
switch(operation)
{
case '+':
cout<< number1 + number2;
break;
case '-':
cout<< number1 - number2;
break;
case '*':
cout<< number1 * number2;
break;
case '/':
if(number2 == 0)
cout<<" \a"<<"Division by zero error! ";
else
cout<< number1 / number2;
break;
case '%':
if((long)number2 == 0)
cout<<" \a"<<"Division by zero error! ";
else
cout<<(long)number1 % (long)number2;
break;
default:
cout<<" \a"<<"Illegal operation! ";
}
getch();
}
```

**OUTPUT:**

Enter the calculation
12+4
=16.000000

**Problem 74. Write a C++ program to show use of switch inside for loop.**

***Program:***

```
#include<iostream.h>
#include<conio.h>
void main()
{
int i,n;
cin>>n;
for(i = 1; i<n; i= i+1)
{
switch(i%2)
{
case 0 : cout<<"the number"<<i<<"is even
"<<endl;
break;
case 1 : cout<<"the number"<<i<<"is odd "<<endl;
break;
}
}
getch();
}
```

**OUTPUT:**

3
the number 1 is odd
the number 2 is even

**Problem 75. Write a C++ program to show use of switch with int case.**

***Program:***

```
#include<iostream.h>
#include<conio.h>
void main()
{
int i;
cout<<"Enter a number between 1 and 4: "<<endl;
cin>>i;
switch(i)
{
case 1:
cout<<"one"<<;
break;
case 2:
cout<<"two";
break;
case 3:
```

```
cout<<"three";
break;
case 4:
cout<<"four";
break;
default:
cout<<"Unrecognized Number";
}
getch();
}
```

**OUTPUT:**

Enter a number between 1 and 4:2
two

**Problem 76. Write a C++ program to show use of switch with char case.**

***Program:***

```
#include<iostream.h>
#include<conio.h>
void main()
{
int a, b;
char ch;
cout<<"Do you want to (Enter first letter): "<<endl;
cout<<"(A)dd, (S)ubtract, (M)ultiply, or (D)ivide?
"<<endl;
do
{
cout<<"Your choice: ";
ch = getchar();
}
while(ch!='A' && ch!='S' && ch!='M' && ch!='D');
cout<<" ";
cout<<endl;
cout<<"Enter first number: ";
cin>>a;
cout<<endl;
cout<<"Enter second number: ";
cin>>b;
cout<<endl;
switch(ch)
{
case 'A': cout<< a + b;
break;
case 'S': cout<< a - b;
break;
case 'M': cout<< a * b;
break;
case 'D': if(b!=0) cout<<a / b;
}
getch();
}
```

**OUTPUT:**

Do you want to (Enter first letter):
(A)dd, (S)ubtract, (M)ultiply, or (D)ivide?
Your choice:A
Enter first number:41
Enter second number:10
51

**Problem 77. Write a C++ program to get three input at the same time: scanf.**

***Program:***

```
#include<iostream.h>
#include<conio.h>
void main()
{
int i, j;
char op;
cout<<"Enter operation(+ - * /): ";
cin>>i>>op>>j;
switch(op)
{
case '+': cout<< i + j;
break;
case '-': cout<< i - j;
break;
case '/': if(j) cout<< i / j;
break;
case '*': cout<< i * j;
}
getch();
}
```

**OUTPUT:**

Enter operation(+ - * /):2+10
12

**Problem 78. Write a C++ program to show use of console menu: switch with char case.**

***Program:***

```
#include<iostream.h>
#include<conio.h>
void main()
{
char ch;
do
{
cout<<"\n"<<" Enter a character, q to quit: ";
ch = getche();
cout<<"\n";
switch(ch)
{
```

```
case 'a':
cout<<"a ";
case 'b':
cout<<"b ";
case 'c':
cout<<"c";
break;
case 'd':
cout<<"d ";
case 'e':
cout<<"e ";
}
}
while(ch != 'q');
getch();
}
```

**OUTPUT:**

Enter a character, q to quit:s
Enter a character, q to quit:k
Enter a character, q to quit:q

**Problem 79. Write a C++ program to show use of switch with default.**

***Program:***

```
#include<iostream.h>
#include<conio.h>
void main()
{
char ch;
cout<<"Enter the letter: ";
ch = getche();
switch(ch)
{
case 'a':
case 'e':
case 'i':
case 'o':
case 'u':
case 'y':
cout<<" is a vowel"<<"\n";
break;
default:
cout<<" is a consonant";
}
getch();
}
```

**OUTPUT:**

Enter the letter:s
s is a consonant

**Problem 80. Write a C++ program to print lines by selecting the choice.**

***Program:***

```
#include<iostream.h>
#include<conio.h>
void main()
{
int ch;
clrscr();
cout<<"\n[1]........";
cout<<"\n[2]________";
cout<<"\n[3]********";
cout<<"\n[4]========";
cout<<"\n[5]EXIT";
cout<<"\n ENTER YOUR CHOICE:";
cin>>ch;
switch(ch)
{
case 1:
cout<<"\n................";
break;
case 2:
cout<<"\n________________";
break;
case 3:
cout<<"\n****************";
break;
case 4:
cout<<"\n================";
break;
case 5:
cout<<"\n"<<" Terminated by choice";
break;
default:
cout<<"\n"<<" Invalid Choice";
}
getch();
}
```

**OUTPUT:**

[1].......[2]________[3]********[4]========[5]
EXIT
ENTER YOUR CHOICE: 1

**Problem 81. Write a C++ program to provide multiple functions such as**
**1.Addition**
**2.Subtraction**
**3.Multiplication**
**4.Division**
**5.Remainder Calculation**
**6.Larger out of two by using switch() statement.**

***Program:***

```
#include<iostream.h>
#include<conio.h>
void main()
{
int a,b,c,ch;
clrscr();
cout<<"\t================";
cout<<"\n\t==============";
cout<<"\n\t[1] ADDITION";
cout<<"\n\t[2] SUBTRACTION";
cout<<"\n\t[3] MULTIPLICATION";
cout<<"\n\t[4] DIVISION";
cout<<"\n\t[5] REMAINDER";
cout<<"\n\t[6] LARGER OUT OF TWO";
cout<<"\n\t[0] EXIT";
cout<<"\n\t================";
cout<<"\n\t ENTER YOUR CHOICE:";
cin>>ch;
if(ch<=6 & ch>0)
{
cout<<"Enter Two Numbers:";
cin>>a>>b;
}
switch(ch)
{
case 1:
c=a+b;
cout<<"\n Addition:"<<c;
break;
case 2:
c=a-b;
cout<<"\n Subtraction:"<<c;
break;
case 3
c=a*b;
cout<<"\n Multiplication:"<<c;
break;
case 4:
c=a/b;
cout<<"\n Division:"<<c;
break;
case 5:
c=a%b;
cout<<"\n Remainder:",c;
break;
case 6:
if(a>b);
cout<<"\n\t"<<a<<"(a) is larger than"<<b<<"(b).";
else
if(b>a)
cout<<"\n\t"<<b<<"(b) is larger than"<<a<<"(a)";
else
cout<<"\n\t"<<a<<"(a) & "<<b<<"(b) are same.";
break;
case 0:
c=a>b;
cout<<"\n Terminated by choice";
exit();
break;
default:
cout<<"\n Invalid Choice";
}
getch();
}
```

**OUTPUT:**

```
MENU
=================
[1] ADDITION
[2] SUBTRACTION
[3] MULTIPLICATION
[4] DIVISION
[5] REMAINDER
[6] LARGER OUT OF TWO
[0] EXIT
====================
ENTER YOUR CHOICE:6
Enter Two Numbers:8 9
9(b) is larger than 8(a)
```

**Problem 82. Write a C++ program to convert years into**
**1.Minutes**
**2.Hours**
**3.Days**
**4.Months**
**5.Seconds using switch() statements.**

***Program:***

```
#include<iostream.h>
#include<conio.h>
void main()
{
long ch,min,hrs,ds,mon,yrs,se;
clrscr();
cout<<"\n[1] MINUTES";
cout<<"\n[2] HOURS";
cout<<"\n[3] DAYS";
cout<<"\n[4] MONTHS";
cout<<"\n[5] SECONDS";
cout<<"\n[0] EXIT";
cout<<"\n Enter Your Choice:";
cin>>ch;
if(ch>0 && ch<6)
```

```
{
cout<<"Enter Years:";
cin>>yrs;
}
mon=yrs*12;
ds=mon*30;
ds=ds+yrs*5;
hrs=ds*24;
min=hrs*60;
se=min*60;
switch(ch)
{
case 1:
cout<<"\n Minutes:"<<min;
break;
case 2:
cout<<"\n Hours:"<<hrs;
break;
case 3
cout<<"\n Days:"<<ds;
break;
case 4:
cout<<"\n Months:"<<mon;
break;
case 5:
cout<<"\n Seconds:"<<se;
break;
case 0:
c=a>b;
cout<<"\n Terminated by choice";
exit();
break;
default:
cout<<"\n Invalid Choice";
}
getch();
}
```

**OUTPUT:**

```
[1] MINUTES
[2] HOURS
[3] DAYS
[4] MONTHS
[5] SECONDS
[0] EXIT
Enter Your Choice: 4
Enter Years: 2
Months: 24
```

**Problem 83. Write a C++ program to display the following files of current directory.**
**1).EXE**
**2).BAT FILES**
**3).OBJ FILES**
**4).BAK FILES By using system dos command**

***Program:***

```
#include<iostream.h>
#include<conio.h>
void main()
{
int c;
clrscr();
cout<<"\n FILE LISTING MENU";
cout<<"\n 1].EXE";
cout<<"\n 2].BAT";
cout<<"\n 3].OBJ";
cout<<"\n 4].BAK";
cout<<"\n Enter Your Choice:";
cin>>c;
switch(c)
{
case 1:
system("dir.exe");
break;
case 2:
system("\dir.c");
break;
case 3:
system("\dir.obj");
break;
case 4:
system("\dir.bak");
break;
default:
break;
}
getche();
}
```

**Problem 84. Write a C++ program to detect whether the entered number is even or odd. Use nested switch() case statement.**

***Program:***

```
#include<iostream.h>
#include<conio.h>
void main()
{
int x,y;
clrscr();
cout<<"\n Enter a Number";
cin>>x;
switch(x)
{
```

```
case 0:
cout<<"\n Number is Even";
break;
case 1:
cout<<"\n Number is Odd";
break;
default:
y=x%2;
switch(y)
{
case 0:
cout<<"\n Number is Even";
break;
default:
cout<<"\n Number is Odd";
}
}
getche();
}
```

**OUTPUT:**

```
Enter a Number:5
Number is Odd
```

**Problem 85. Write a C++ program for pay bill calculations:**

***Program:***

```
#include<iostream.h>
#include<conio.h>
#define X1 1000
#define X2 750
#define X3 500
#define X4 250
#define Y1 500
#define Y2 200
#define Y3 100
#define Y4 0
void main()
{
int l,jobno;
float gr,basic,hrent,all,net,itax;
input:
cout<<"\nEnter level,job number,basic pay\n";
cout<<"\nEnter 0(zero) for level to END\n\n";
cin>>l;
if(l==0)goto stop;
cin>>jobno>>basic;
switch(l)
{
case 1:
all=X1+Y1;
break;
case 2:
all=X2+Y2;
break;
case 3:
all=X3+Y3;
break;
case 4:
all=X4+Y4;
break;
default:
cout<<"Error in level code\n";
goto stop;
}
hrent=0.25*basic;
gr=basic+hrent+all;
if(gr<=2000)
itax=0;
else if(gr<=4000)
itax=0.03*gr;
else if(gr<=5000)
itax=0.05*gr;
else
itax=0.08*gr;
net=gr-itax;
cout<<l,jobno,net;
goto input;
stop:cout<<"\nEnd of program";
getch();
}
```

**Problem 86. Write a C++ program to print the color according to the code.**

***Program:***

```
#include<iostream.h>
void main()
{
int code;
cout<<" \n MAIN MENU ";
cout<<" \n1. For color Red ";
cout<<" \n2. For color Green ";
cout<<" \n3. For color White ";
cout<<" \n4. For color Yellow ";
cout<<" \n Enter the color code: ";
cin>>code;
switch(code)
{
case 1:
cout<<"\n color is RED ";
break;
case 2:
cout<<"\n color is GREEN";
```

```
break;
case 3:
cout<<"\n color is WHITE ";
break;
case 4:
cout<<"\n color is YELLOW ";
break;
default :
cout<<"\n Color does not found";
}
getche();
}
```

**OUTPUT:**

```
MAIN MENU
1. For color Red
2. For color Green
3. For color White
4. For color Yellow
Enter the color code: 2
color is GREEN
```

**Problem 87. Write a C++ menu driven program which has following options:**
**1. Factorial of a number.**
**2. Prime or not**
**3. Odd or even**
**4. Exit**
**Once a menu item is selected the appropriate action should be teken and once this action is finished, the menu should reappear. Unless the user selects the 'Exit' option the program should continue to work.**

***Program:***

```
#include<iostream.h>
#include<conio.h>
void main()
{
int choice, num, i ;
unsigned long int fact ;
clrscr();
while (1)
{
cout<<"1. Factorial\n";
cout<<"2. Prime\n";
cout<<"3. Odd / Even\n";
cout<<"4. Exit\n";
cout<<"\nYour choice ?";
cin>>choice ;
switch ( choice )
{
case 1 :
cout<<"\nEnter number:";
cin>>num ;
fact = 1 ;
for (i=1;i<=num ;i++)
fact = fact * i;
cout<<"\n Factorial value = \n"<< fact ;
break ;// Takes control out of switch
case 2 :
cout<<"\n Enter number:";
cin>>num ;
for(i=2;i<num;i++)
{
 if (num%i== 0 )
{
cout<<"\n Not a prime number.\n";
break ; // Takes control out of for loop
}
}
if (i==num)
cout<<"\n Prime number.\n";
break ; // Takes control out of switch
case 3 :
cout<<"\nEnter number:";
cin>>num ;
if ( num %2==0 )
cout<<"\n Even number.\n";
else
cout<<"\nOdd number.\n";
break ; // Takes control out of switch
case 4 :
exit( ) ; // Terminates program execution
}
}
}
```

**OUTPUT:**

```
1. Factorial
2. Prime
3. Odd / Even
4. Exit
Your choice ?1
Enter number:5
factorial value=120
1. Factorial
2. Prime
3. Odd / Even
4. Exit
Your choice ?2
Enter number:12
Not a prime number.
1. Factorial
2. Prime
```

3. Odd / Even
4. Exit
Your choice ?3
Enter number:12
Even number.
1. Factorial
2. Prime
3. Odd / Even
4. Exit
Your choice ?4
Exit

**Problem 88. Write C++ a program which to find the grace marks for a student using switch. The user should enter the class obtained by the student and the number of subjects he has failed in . Use the following logic:**

***Program:***

```
#include<iostream.h>
#include<conio.h>
void main()
{
int c,sub;
clrscr();
cout<<"Enter the class and number of subjects
failed:";
cin>>c>>sub;
switch(c)
{
case 1:
if(sub>=1 && sub<=3)
cout<<"\nStudent gets total of "<<5 * sub<<"grace
marks";
else
if(sub>3)
cout<<"\nNo grace marks";
break;
case 2:
if(sub>=1 && sub<=2)
cout<<"\nStudents gets total of %d grace marks", 4
* sub);
else
if(sub>2)
cout<<"\nNo grace marks";
break;
case 3:
if(sub==1)
cout<<"\nStudent gets 5 grace marks";
else
if(sub>1)
cout<<"\nNo grace marks";
break;
default:
cout<<"\nWrong class entered";
}
cout<<"\nPress any key to exist...";
getch();
}
```

**OUTPUT:**

_ If the students gets first class and the number of subjects he failed in is greater than 3, then he does not get any grace . If the number of subjects he failed in is less than or equal to 3 then the grace is of 5 marks per subject.

_ If the students gets second class and the number of subjects he failed in is greater than 2, then he does not get any grace . If the number of subjects he failed in is less than or equal to 2 then the grace is of 4 marks per subject.

_ If the students gets third class and the number of subjects he failed in is greater than 1, then he does not get any grace . If the number of subjects he failed in is equal to 1 then the grace is of 5 marks per subject

**Problem 89. Write a C++ program to show working of break in switch.**

***Program:***

```
#include<iostream.h>
#include<conio.h>
void main()
{
int p;
cout<<"Enter no. :";
cin>>p;
switch(p);
{
case 1:cout<<"It is a circle\n";
break;
case 2:cout<<"It is a triangle\n";
break;
case 3:cout<<"It is a rectangle\n";
break;
default:cout<<"It is a shape\n";
}
getch();
}
```

**OUTPUT:**

Enter no. : 2
It is a triangle

**Problem 90. Write a C++ program using switch**

**to add sub mul numbers.**

***Program:***

```
#include<iostream.h>
#include<conio.h>
#include<math.h>
void main()
{
int select,x,y,z;
clrscr();
cout<<"\n Specify the two numbers:";
cin>>x>>y;
cout<<"\n Select 1 to Perform Addition";
cout<<"\n Select 2 to Perform Subtraction";
cout<<"\n Select 3 to Perform Multiplication";
cout<<"\n Select your choice";
cin>>select;
if(select !=1 || select !=2 || select !=3)
{ exit(1); }
else
{
switch(select);
{
case 1:z=x+y;
cout<<"Result after Addition:"<<z;
break;
case 2:z=x-y;
cout<<"Result after Subtraction:"<<z;
break;
case 3:z=x*y;
cout<<"\n Result after Multiplication:"<<z;
break;
} }
getch();
}
```

**OUTPUT:**

Specify the two numbers: 12 5
Select your choice 2
Result after Subtraction: 7

## CONDITIONAL:

**Problem 91. Write a C++ program to solve the function by using the nested conditional statement.**

***Program:***

```
#include<iostream.h>
#include<conio.h>
#include< dos.h>
void main()
{
int sal, bp;
clrscr();
cout<<"\n Enter the basic pay: ";
cin>>bp;
sal = (bp != 1000) ? ((bp < 1000) ? bp + 100 : 4 *
bp + 2000) : 2000;
cout<<"\n Salary is Rs. "<< sal;
getche ( );
}
```

**OUTPUT:**

Enter the basic pay: 900
Salary is Rs. 1000.

**Problem 92. Write a C++ program to compute the following function by using conditional operator statement:**

**y = f (x) = 5x2 + 3 x x < 2**
**x = 2**
**7x + 50 x > 2**

***Program:***

```
#include<iostream.h>
#include<conio.h>
#include<math.h>
#include<dos.h>
void main()
{
int x,y;
clrscr( );
cout<<"\n Enter the value of x :";
cin>>x;
y=(x != 2) ? x <2 ? 5*x*x+3*x : 7*x+ 50 :500;
cout<<"\n Result of y is ="<<y;
getche();
}
```

**OUTPUT:**

Enter the value of x : 2
Result of y is = 500

## LOOP CONTROL:

## WHILE STATEMENT:

**Problem 93.Write a C++ program using while to sum integers.**

***Program:***

```
#include<iostream.h>
#include<conio.h>
void main()
{
long sum = 0L;
```

```
int i = 1;
int count = 10;
while(i <= count)
sum += i++;
cout<<"Total of the first"<<count<<" numbers is
"<<sum;
getch();
}
```

**OUTPUT:**

Total of the first 10 numbers is 55

**Problem 94. Write a C++ program using a while loop nested in for loop.**

***Program:***

```
#include<iostream.h>
#include<conio.h>
void main()
{
long sum = 1L;
int i = 1;
int j = 1;
int count = 5;
for( i = 1 ; i <= count ; i++ )
{
sum = 1L;
j=1;
cout<<"\n1";
while(j < i)
{
sum += ++j;
cout<< j;
}
cout<<" = "<< sum<<"\n";
}
getch();
}
```

**OUTPUT:**

1=1
1+2=3
1+2+3=6
1+2+3+4=10
1+2+3+4+5=15

**Problem 95. Write a C++ program using a while loop to print char.**

***Program:***

```
#include<iostream.h>
#include<conio.h>
void main()
{
char ch;
ch = 'a';
while ( ch <= 'z' )
cout<<ch++;
cout<<"\n";
getch();
}
```

**OUTPUT:**

abcdefghijklmnopqrstuvwxyz

**Problem 96. Write a C++ program using a use getchar inside while loop.**

***Program:***

```
#include<iostream.h>
#include<conio.h>
void main()
{
char ch;
ch = getchar();
while(ch!='e')
ch = getchar();
cout<<"Found the e.";
getch();
}
```

**OUTPUT:**

s
g
6
e
Found the e.

**Problem 97. Write a C++ program using a search smallest of n numbers.**

***Program:***

```
#include<iostream.h>
#include<conio.h>
void main()
{
int p,n,least_num,x;
clrscr();
cout<<"\n Specify the value of n:\n";
cin>>n;
cout<<"\n Specify those "<<n<<"numbers";
p=1;
cin>>x;
least_num=x;
while(p<n)
{
cin>>x;
if(x<least_num)
{
least_num=x;
```

```
}
p++;
}
cout<<"\n The smallest number is:"<<least_num;
getch();
}
```

**Problem 98. Write a C++ program using a to illustrate the concept of while loop.**

***Program:***

```
#include<iostream.h>
#include<conio.h>
void main()
{
int i , sum, n;
float av;
clrscr();
cout<<"\n Enter the value of n:";
cin>>n;
sum=0;
i=1;
while( i <=n)
{
sum=sum+ i;
i = i +1;
}
av=(float) sum/n;
cout<<"\n sum is:"<<sum;
cout<<"\n Average is:"<< av;
getche();
}
```

**OUTPUT:**

Enter the value of n: 10
sum is: 55
Average is: 5.5

## DO WHILE STATEMENT:

**Problem 99. Write a C++ program reversing the digits: do while.**

***Program:***

```
#include<iostream.h>
#include<conio.h>
void main()
{
int number = 123;
int reversedNumber = 0;
int temp = 0;
temp = number;
do
{
reversedNumber = 10 * reversedNumber + temp %
10;
temp = temp/10;
} while (temp);
cout<<"\nThe number "<<number<<" reversed is
"<<reversedNumber<<" rebmun ehT\n";
getch();
}
```

**OUTPUT:**

The number 123 reversed is 321 rebmun ehT

**Problem 100. Write a C++ program using do while loop.**

***Program:***

```
#include<iostream.h>
#include<conio.h>
#include <ctype.h>
void main()
{
char ch;
cout<<"Enter some text (type a period to quit).\n";
do
{
ch = getchar();
if(islower(ch))
ch = toupper(ch);
else
ch = tolower(ch);
putchar(ch);
}
while (ch != '.');
getch();
}
```

**OUTPUT:**

hi how are you.
HI HOW ARE YOU.

**Problem 101. Write a C++ program using a flag (flag: informs a certain condition has occured).**

***Program:***

```
#include<iostream.h>
#include<conio.h>
void main()
{
int temp;
float celsius;
char repeat;
do
{
cout<<"Input a temperature:";
```

```
cin>>temp;
celsius = (5.0 / 9.0) * ( temp - 32 );
cout<<temp<<" degrees F = "<<celsius<<" degrees
celsius\n";
cout<<"Continue (y or Y)?";
repeat = getchar();
putchar('\n');
}
while(repeat == 'Y' || repeat=='y');
getch();
}
```

**OUTPUT:**

Input a temperature:40
40 degrees F= 4.44 degrees celsius
Continue (y or Y)?N

**Problem 102. Write a C++ program using a do while loop for your selection.**

***Program:***

```
#include<iostream.h>
#include<conio.h>
void main()
{
char ch;
do
{
cout<<"Load, Save, Edit, Quit?\n";
do
{
cout<<"Enter your selection: ";
ch = getchar();
}
while(ch!='L' && ch!='S' && ch!='E' && ch!='Q');
if(ch == 'Q')
{
cout<<"Exit.";
}
}
while(ch != 'Q');
getch();
}
```

**OUTPUT:**

Load, Save, Edit, Quit?
Enter your selection:Quit
Exit.

**Problem 103. Write a C++ program using a do while with char value as condition.**

***Program:***

```
#include<iostream.h>
#include<conio.h>
void main()
{
char ch;
ch = 'a';
do
{
cout<<ch ;
}
while ( ch++ < 'z' );
cout<<"\n";
getch();
}
```

**OUTPUT:**

abcdefghijklmnopqrstuvwxyz

**Problem 104. Write a C++ program to evaluate the series such as 1+2+3+....i.Use do-while loop.Where i can be a finite value. Its Value should be read through the keyboard.**

***Program:***

```
#include<iostream.h>
#include<conio.h>
void main()
{
int i,a=1;
int s=0;
clrscr();
cout<<"\n Enter a Number:";
cin>>i;
do
{
cout<<a;
s=s+a;
a++;
}
while(a<=i);
cout<<"\b\bs-"<<s;
}
```

**OUTPUT:**

Enter a Number:5
1+2+3+4+5 s=15

**Problem 105. Write a C++ program using a do while loop with continue.**

***Program:***

```
#include<iostream.h>
#include<conio.h>
void main()
{
int total, i, j;
clrscr();
```

```
total = 0;
do
{
cout<<"Enter a number (0 to stop): ";
cin>>i;
cout<<"Enter the number again: ";
cin>>j
if(i != j)
{
cout<<"Mismatch\n";
continue;
}
total = total + i;
}
while(i);
cout<<"Total is "<<total<<"\n";
getch();
}
```

**OUTPUT:**

Enter a number (0 to stop):3
Enter the number again:3
Enter a number (0 to stop):0
Enter the number again:0
Total is 3

**Problem 106. Write a C++ program using a nested for loop inside a do while loop.**

***Program:***

```
#include<iostream.h>
#include<conio.h>
void main()
{
int i, j, k, m;
do
{
cout<<"Enter a value: ";
cin>>i;
m = 0;
for(j=0; j<i; j++)
{
for(k=0; k<100; k++)
{
m = k + m;
}
}
}
while(i>0);
getch();
}
```

# FOR LOOP STATEMENT:

**Problem 107. Write a C++ program to count numbers between 1 to 100 not divisible by 2,3 and 5.**

***Program:***

```
#include<iostream.h>
#include<conio.h>
void main()
{
int x,c=0;
clrscr();
cout<<"\n Numbers from 1 to 100 not divisible by
2,3& 5\n\n";
for(x=0;x<=100;x++)
{
if(x%2!=0 &&x%3!=0 &&x%5!=0)
{
cout<<x;
c++;
}
}
cout<<"\nTotal Numbers:",c;
}
```

**OUTPUT:**

Numbers from 1 to 100 not divisible by 2,3 & 5
1 7 11 13 17 19 23 29 31 37
41 43 47 49 53 59 61 67 71 73
77 79 83 89 91 97
Total Numbers: 26

**Problem 108. Write a C++ program to display numbers from 1 to 9 and their square roots.**

***Program:***

```
#include<iostream.h>
#include<conio.h>
void main()
int i;
float a;
clrscr();
for(i=1;i<=9;i++)
cout<<"\n\t"<<i<<" "<<a=sqrt(i);
}
```

**OUTPUT:**

1 1.00
2 1.14
3 1.73
4 2.00
5 2.24
6 2.45

7 2.65
8 2.83
9 3.00

**Problem 109. Write a C++ program to find perfect square from 1 to 500.**

***Program:***

```
#include<iostream.h>
#include<math.h>
#include<conio.h>
void main()
{
int i,count,x;
float c;
clrscr();
cout<<"\n\n";
cout<<"Perfect squares from 1 to 500";
count=0;
for(i=1;i<=500;i++)
{
c=sqrt(i);
x=floor(c); /*For routing up floor() is used*/
if(c==x)
{
cout<<"\t%5d",i);
count++;
}
}
cout<<"\n\n Total Perfect Squares="<<count<<"\n";
getch();
}
```

**OUTPUT:**

1 4 9 16 25 36 49 64 81 121 141
169 196 225 256 289 324 361 400 441 484

**Problem 110. Write a C++ program to enter mantissa and exponent. Calculate the value of -mx,where'm'is mantissa and'x'is exponent.**

***Program:***

```
#include<iostream.h>
#include<conio.h>
void main()
{
int i,number,power;
long ans;
clrscr();
cout<<"\n Enter Number:";
cin>>power;
ans=1;
for(i=1;i<=power;i++)
ans*=number;
cout<<"\n The Power of "<<number<<"raised to
"<<power<<" is "<<ans<<"\n";
getche();
}
```

**OUTPUT:**

Enter Number:5
Enter Power:3
The Power of 5 raised to 3 is 125.

**Problem 111. Write a C++ program to simulate a digital clock.**

***Program:***

```
#include<iostream.h>
#include<conio.h>
void main()
{
int h,m,s;
clrscr();
for(h=1;h<=12;h++)
{
clrscr()
for(m=1;m<=59;m++)
{
clrscr();
for(s=1;s<=59;s++)
{
gotoxy(8,8);
cout<<"hh mm ss";
gotoxy(8,9);
cout<<h,m,s;
sleep(1);
}
}
}
}
```

**OUTPUT:**

hh mm ss
1 1 1

**Problem 112. Write a C++ program to generate the pattren of numbers as given under**

**6 5 4 3 2 1 0**
**5 4 3 2 1 0**
**4 3 2 1 0**
**3 2 1 0**
**2 1 0**
**1 0**
**0**

***Program:***

```
#include<iostream.h>
#include<conio.h>
```

```
void main()
{
int i,c=0;
clrscr();
cout<<"Enter a Number";
cin>>i;
for(;i>=0;i--)
{
c=i;
cout<<"\n";
for(;;)
{
cout<<c;
if(c==0)
break;
c--;
}
}
}
```

**OUTPUT:**

```
6 5 4 3 2 1 0
5 4 3 2 1 0
4 3 2 1 0
3 2 1 0
2 1 0
1 0
0
```

**Problem 113. Write a C++ program to display the series of numbers as given below**

**1**
**12**
**123**
**1234**

**4321**
**321**
**21**
**1**

***Program:***

```
#include<iostream.h>
#include<conio.h>
void main()
{
int i,j,x;
cout<<"\n Enter Values of x";
cin>>x;
clrscr();
for(j=1;j<=x;j++)
{
for(i=1;i<=j;i++)
cout<<i;
cout<<"\n";
}
cout<<"\n";
for(j=x;j<=1;j--)
{
for(i=j;i>=1;i--)
cout<<i;
cout<<"\n";
}
}
```

**OUTPUT:**

```
Enter Values of x:4
1
12
123
1234

4321
321
21
1
```

**Problem 114. Write a C++ program to generate the pyramid structure using numerical**

***Program:***

```
#include<iostream.h>
#include<conio.h>
void main()
{
int k,i,j,x,p=34;
cout<<"\n Enter a number:";
cin>>x;
clrscr();
for(j=0;j<=x;j++)
{
gotoxy(p,j+1);
/*position cursur on screen(x coordinate,y
coordinate)*/
for(i=0-j;i<=j;i++)
cout<<abs(i);
p=p-3;
}
}
```

**OUTPUT:**

```
Enter a Number:3
0
101
21012
3210123
```

**Problem 115. Write a C++ program to convert binary to decimal number. Enter the binary bits by using for loop.**

***Program:***

```
#include<iostream.h>
#include<conio.h>
void main()
{
int a,b,z[10],i;
clrscr();
cout<<"\n Enter the number of bits:";
cin>>b;
cout<<"\n Enter the binary bits:";
for(i=0;i<b;i++)
cin>>z[i];
a=z[0];
for(i=0;i<(b-1);i++)
{
a=a*2+z[i+1];
cout<<"\n"<<a;
}
cout<<"\nDecimal Number is:"<<a;
getche();
}
```

**OUTPUT:**

```
Enter the number of bits: 5
Enter the binary bits: 1 0 0 0 1
2
4
8
17
Decimal Number is: 17
```

**Problem 116. Write a C++ program using a for statement: backwards.**

***Program:***

```
#include<iostream.h>
#include<conio.h>
void main()
{
long sum = 0L;
int count = 10;
int i = 0;
for (i = count ; i >= 1 ; sum += i-- );
cout<<"\nTotal of the first "<<count<<" numbers is
"<<sum<<"\n";
getch();
}
```

**OUTPUT:**

```
Total of the first 10 numbers 55
```

**Problem 117. Write a C++ program using a nested for.**

***Program:***

```
#include<iostream.h>
#include<conio.h>
void main()
{
long sum = 0L;
int i = 1;
int j = 1;
int count = 10;
for( i = 1 ; i <= count ; i++ )
{
sum = 0L;
for(j = 1 ; j <= i ; j++ )
sum += j;
cout<<"\n"<<i<<sum;
}
getch();
}
```

**OUTPUT:**

```
1    1
2 3
3 6
4 10
5 15
6 21
7 28
8 36
9 45
10 55
```

**Problem 118. Write a C++ program using a for loop: List ten integers.**

***Program:***

```
#include<iostream.h>
#include<conio.h>
void main()
{
int count = 1;
for( ; count <= 10 ; ++count)
cout<<"\n"<< count;
cout<<"\n Finished.\n";
getch();
}
```

**OUTPUT:**

```
1
2
3
4
```

5
6
7
8
9
10
Finished.

**Problem 119. Write a C++ program using a for loop: Draw a box.**

***Program:***

```
#include<iostream.h>
#include<conio.h>
void main()
{
int count = 0;
cout<<"\n*************";
for(count = 1 ; count <= 8 ; ++count)
cout<<"\n* \t\t*";
cout<<"\n*************\n";
getch();
}
```

**OUTPUT:**

```
*************
*           *
*           *
*           *
*           *
*           *
*           *
*           *
*           *
*************
```

**Problem 120. Write a C++ program using int as the while loop controller.**

***Program:***

```
#include<iostream.h>
#include<conio.h>
void main()
{
int i,n;
cin>>n;
i = 0;
do
{
cout<<"the numbers are"<<i<<" \n";
i = i +1;
}
while( i<n);
getch();
}
```

**OUTPUT:**

2
the numbers are 0
the numbers are 1

**Problem 121. Write a C++ program using a simplest for loop: user control the loop.**

***Program:***

```
#include<iostream.h>
#include<conio.h>
void main()
{
int i,n;
cin>>n;
for(i = 0; i < n; i = i+1)
{
cout<<"the numbers are"<<i<<" \n";
}
getch();
}
```

**OUTPUT:**

4
the numbers are 0
the numbers are 1
the numbers are 2
the numbers are 3

**Problem 122. Write a C++ program using a for loop as the user selection's controller.**

***Program:***

```
#include<iostream.h>
#include<conio.h>
#include<conio.h>
void main()
{
int i;
char ch;
ch = 'a';
for(i=0; ch != 'q'; i++)
{
cout<<"pass:"<<i<<"\n";
ch = getchar();
}
getch();
}
```

**OUTPUT:**

pass:0
2
pass:1
pass:2

q

**Problem 123. Write a C++ program to demonstrate multiple loop control variables.**

*Program:*

```
#include<iostream.h>
#include<conio.h>
#include<string.h>
void converge(char *targ, char *src);
void main()
{
char target[80] = "This is a test";
converge(target, "This is a test of converge().";
cout<<"Final string: "<<target<<"\n";
getch();
}
void converge(char *targ, char *src)
{
int i, j;
cout<<"\n"<< targ;
for(i = 0, j = strlen(src); i <= j; i++, j--)
{
targ[i] = src[i];
targ[j] = src[j];
cout<<"\n"<< targ;
}
}
```

**OUTPUT:**

```
This is a test
This is a test
This is a test
This is a test
This is a test
This is a test
This is a test
This is a test
This is a test
This is a test
This is a test
This is a test
This is a test
This is a test
This is a test
This is a test of converge().
Final string:This is a test of converge().
```

**Problem 124. Write a C++ program using function as for loop control variable.**

*Program:*

```
#include<iostream.h>
#include<conio.h>
int sqrnum(int num);
int readnum(void);
int prompt(void);
void main()
{
int t;
for(prompt(); t=readnum(); prompt())
{sqrnum(t);}
getch();
}
int prompt(void)
{
cout<<"Enter a number: ";
return 0;
}
int readnum(void)
{
int t;
cin>>t;
return t;
}
int sqrnum(int num)
{
cout<<"\n"<<num*num;
return num*num;
}
```

**OUTPUT:**

```
Enter a number:2
4
Enter a number:5
25
```

**Problem 125. Write a C++ program using a for loop without first part.**

*Program:*

```
#include<iostream.h>
#include<conio.h>
void main()
{
int i;
cout<<"Enter an integer: ";
cin>>i;
for(; i; i--)
cout<< i;
getch();
}
```

**OUTPUT:**

```
Enter an integer:4
4 3 2 1
```

**Problem 126. Write a C++ program using a for**

**loop without the third part.**

***Program:***

```
#include<iostream.h>
#include<conio.h>
void main()
{
int i;
for(i=0; i<10; )
{
cout<<"i;
i++;
}
getch();
}
```

**OUTPUT:**

0 1 2 3 4 5 6 7 8 9

**Problem 127. Write a C++ program to see the for loop terminating condition.**

***Program:***

```
#include<iostream.h>
#include<conio.h>
void main()
{
int i;
for(i = 1; i < 11; i = i+1)
{
cout<<i;
}
cout<<"terminating";
getch();
}
```

**OUTPUT:**

1 2 3 4 5 6 7 8 9 10 terminating

**Problem 128. Write a C++ program using a for loop condition: loop will not execute.**

***Program:***

```
#include<iostream.h>
#include<conio.h>
void main()
{
int i;
for(i = 11; i < 11; i = i + 1)
{cout<<i;}
cout<<"terminating";
getch();
}
```

**OUTPUT:**

terminating

**Problem 129. Write a C++ program using a for loop: bigger increase.**

***Program:***

```
#include<iostream.h>
#include<conio.h>
void main()
{
int i;
clrscr();
for(i = 0; i < 50; i = i + 5)
cout<<i;
getch();
}
```

**OUTPUT:**

0 5 10 15 20 25 30 35 40 45

**Problem 130. Write a C++ program using a prime number tester.**

***Program:***

```
#include<iostream.h>
#include<conio.h>
void main()
{
int num, i, is_prime;
cout<<"Enter a number: ";
cin>>num;
is_prime = 1;
for(i = 2; i <= num / 2; i = i + 1)
if((num%i)==0)
is_prime = 0;
if(is_prime==1)
cout<<" is prime.";
else
cout<<"not prime.";
getch();
}
```

**OUTPUT:**

Enter a number;2
is prime.

**Problem 131. Write a C++ program using a nested for Demo.**

***Program:***

```
#include<iostream.h>
#include<conio.h>
void main()
{
int row,column;
clrscr();
for(row = 1; row <=5; row++)
{
```

```
for(column = 1; column <= 5; column++)
{
cout<<row * column;}
putchar('\n');
}
getch();
}
```

**OUTPUT:**

```
1 2 3 4 5
2 4 6 8 10
3 6 9 12 15
4 8 12 16 20
5 10 15 20 25
```

**Problem 132. Write a C++ program using an integer as the for loop controller.**

***Program:***

```
#include<iostream.h>
#include<conio.h>
void main()
{
int i;
clrscr();
for(i = 1; i <=10; i = i + 1)
cout<< i;
getch();
}
```

**OUTPUT:**

```
1 2 3 4 5 6 7 8 9 10
```

**Problem 133. Write a C++ program to set the init value for a for loop.**

***Program:***

```
#include<iostream.h>
#include<conio.h>
void main()
{
int i;
for ( i = 17; i < 101; i = i + 1)
if( ( i % 17) == 0)
cout<<i;
getch();
}
```

**OUTPUT:**

```
17 34 51 68 85
```

**Problem 134. Write a C++ program for calculation in the for statement.**

***Program:***

```
#include<iostream.h>
#include<conio.h>
void main()
{
int num, i;
cout<<"Enter the number to test: ";
cin>>num;
for( i = 2; i < (num / 2) + 1; i = i + 1)
if( ( num % i ) == 0)
cout<<i;
getch();
}
```

**OUTPUT:**

```
Enter the number to test:4
2
```

**Problem 135. Write a C++ program using a simplest for loop.**

***Program:***

```
#include<iostream.h>
#include<conio.h>
void main()
{
int i;
clrscr();
for( i = 1; i <=10; i++)
cout<<i;
getch();
}
```

**OUTPUT:**

```
1 2 3 4 5 6 7 8 9 10
```

**Problem 136. Write a C++ program to reverse order of for loop.**

***Program:***

```
#include<iostream.h>
#include<conio.h>
void main()
{
int i, j;
cout<<"Enter a number: ";
cin>>i;
for(j = i; j > 0; j--)
cout<<"\n"<< j;
cout<<"\a";
getch();
}
```

**OUTPUT:**

```
Enter a number:6
6
5
4
```

```
3
2
1
```

**Problem 137. Write a C++ program using a two condition for ending a for loop.**

***Program:***

```
#include<iostream.h>
#include<conio.h>
void main()
{
int magic;
int guess;
int i;
magic = 1325;
guess = 0;
clrscr();
for(i = 0; i < 5 && guess != magic; i++)
{
cout<<"Enter your guess: ";
cin>>guess;
if(guess == magic)
{
cout<<"RIGHT!";
cout<<magic<<"is the magic number.\n";
}
else
{
cout<<"wrong...";
if(guess > magic)
cout<<" too high.\n";
else
cout<<" too low.\n";
}
}
getch();
}
```

**OUTPUT:**

```
Enter your guess:345
wrong...too low
Enter your guess:1325
Right! 1325 is the magic number.
```

**Problem 138. Write a C++ program using a three level nested for loop.**

***Program:***

```
#include<iostream.h>
#include<conio.h>
void main()
{
int i, j, k;
clrscr();
for(i = 0; i < 1; i++)
{
for(j = 0; j < 26; j++)
{
for( k = 0; k < 1; k++)
{
cout<<'A' + j;
}
}
}
getch();
}
```

**OUTPUT:**

```
ABCDEFGHIJKLMNOPQRSTUVWXYZ
```

**Problem 139. Write a C++ program using a simple for loop.**

***Program:***

```
#include<iostream.h>
#include<conio.h>
void main()
{
int i;
clrscr();
for( i = 0; i < 15; i += 2)
cout<<i;
getch();
}
```

**OUTPUT:**

```
0 2 4 6 8 10 12 14
```

**Problem 140. Write a C++ program using a more complex for loop: more statements.**

***Program:***

```
#include<iostream.h>
#include<conio.h>
void main()
{
int i, j;
clrscr();
for( i = 0, j =10; i < j; i++, j--)
cout<<i;
getch();
}
```

**OUTPUT:**

```
0 1 2 3 4
```

**Problem 141. Write a C++ program using an infinite for loop with break.**

***Program:***

```
#include<iostream.h>
#include<conio.h>
void main()
{
char ch;
for( ; ; )
{
cout<<"Load, Save, Edit, Quit?\n";
do
{
cout<<"Enter your selection: ";
ch = getchar();
}
while(ch!='L' && ch!='S' && ch!='E' && ch!='Q');
if(ch == 'Q')
break;
}
getch();
}
```

**OUTPUT:**

```
Load, Save, Edit, Quit?
Enter your selection:Quit
```

**Problem 142. Write a C++ program using a for loop with init value, stop condition and increment.**

***Program:***

```
#include<iostream.h>
#include<conio.h>
void main()
{
int i, j, k;
for( k = 0; k < 10; k = k + 1)
{
cout<<"Enter a number: ";
cin>>i;
cout<<"Enter a non-zero number: ";
cin>>j;
if(j != 0)
cout<< i / j<<"\n";
if(j == 0)
cout<<"Cannot divide by zero\n";
}
getch();
}
```

**OUTPUT:**

```
Enter a number:8
Enter a non-zero number:2
4
```

**Problem 143. Write a C++ program using a char as int in a for loop.**

***Program:***

```
#include<iostream.h>
#include<conio.h>
void main()
{
int i;
char j;
i = 0;
clrscr();
for(j = 1; j < 101; j++)
i = j + i;
cout<<"Total is:"<< i;
getch();
}
```

**OUTPUT:**

```
Total is:5050
```

**Problem 144. Write a C++ program using a nested for loop demo.**

***Program:***

```
#include<iostream.h>
#include<conio.h>
void main()
{
int answer, i, chances, right;
for(i = 1; i < 6; i++)
{
cout<<i<<"+"<<i<<"=?";
cin>>answer;
if(answer == i + i)
cout<<"Right!\n";
else
{
cout<<"Wrong.\n";
cout<<"Try again.\n";
right = 0;
for(chances = 0; chances < 3 && !right;
chances++)
{
cout<<i<<"+"<<i<<"=?";
cin>>answer;
if(answer == i + i)
{
cout<<"Right!\n";
right = 1;
}
}
if(!right)
cout<<"The answer is "<<i+i<<"\n";
}
```

```
}
getch();
}
```

**OUTPUT:**

1+1=? 2
Right!
2+2=? 4
Right!
3+3=? 6
Right!
4+4=? 8
Right!
5+5=? 10
Right!

## GOTO:

**Problem 145. Write a C++ program to show how to use goto in c.**

```
#include<iostream.h>
#include<conio.h>
void main()
{
int i;
i = 1;
again:
cout<<i;
i++;
if(i<10)
goto again;
getch();
}
```

**OUTPUT:**

1 2 3 4 5 6 7 8 9

## BREAK STATEMENT:

**Problem 146. Write a C++ program using an indefinite loop and break.**

***Program:***

```
#include<iostream.h>
#include<conio.h>
#include <ctype.h>
void main()
{
char answer = 'N';
double total = 0.0;
double value = 10.0;
int count = 0;
cout<<"\nThis program calculates the average of" "
any number of values.";
for( ;; )
{
total += value;
++count;
cout<<"Do you want to enter another value? (Y or
N): ";
cin>>answer ;
if( tolower(answer) == 'n' )
break;
}
cout<<"\nThe average is "<< total/count <<"\n";
getch();
}
```

**OUTPUT:**

This program calculates the average of any number of values.
Do you want to enter another value? (Y or N):N
The average is 10.00

**Problem 147. Write a C++ program using a break a infinite loop.**

***Program:***

```
#include<iostream.h>
#include<conio.h>
#include<stdlib.h>
void main()
{
for(;;)
if(getchar()=='A') abort();
getch();
}
```

**Problem 148. Write a C++ program using a break to terminate a for loop.**

***Program:***

```
#include<iostream.h>
#include<conio.h>
void main()
{
int t;
for(t = 0; t < 100; t++)
{
cout<< t;
if(t == 11)
break;
}
getch();
}
```

**Problem 149. Write a C++ program using a**

break in for loop to exit.

*Program:*

```
#include<iostream.h>
#include<conio.h>
void main()
{
int i;
for(i = 1; i < 100; i++)
{
cout<<i;
if(i == 10)
break;
}
getch();
}
```

**OUTPUT:**

1 2 3 4 5 6 7 8 9 10

**Problem 150. Write a C++ program using a nested for loop and break.**

*Program:*

```
#include<iostream.h>
#include<conio.h>
oid main()
{
int i, j;
for( i = 0; i < 5; i++)
{
for(j = 0; j < 100; j++)
{
cout<<j;
if(j == 5)
break;
}
cout<<"\n";
}
getch();
}
```

**OUTPUT:**

012345
012345
012345
012345
012345

**Problem 151. Write a C++ program to show working of break.**

*Program:*

```
#include<iostream.h>
#include<conio.h>
void main()
{
int p;
for(p=1;p<=20;p++)
{
cout<<p;
if(p==10)
{
cout<<"\n Exiting";
break;
}
}
getch();
}
```

**Problem 152. Write a C++ program to find if the given number is prime or not.**

*Program:*

```
#include<iostream.h>
#include<conio.h>
void main()
{
int p,n;
cout<<"\n Specify a number:";
cin>>n;
p=2;
while(p<=n-1)
{
if(n%p==0)
{
cout<<"\n It is not a prime number";
cout<<"This number is divisible by "<<p;
break;
}
p++;
}
if(p==n)
cout<<"\n It is a prime number";
getch();
}
```

## CONTINUE STATEMENT:

**Problem 153. Write a C++ program to count spaces in string: how to use continue.**

*Program:*

```
#include<iostream.h>
#include<conio.h>
void main()
{
char s[80], *str;
```

```
int space;
cout<<"Enter a string: ";
gets(s);
str = s;
for(space = 0; *str; str++)
{
if(*str != ' ')
continue;
space++;
}
cout<<space<<"spaces\n";
getch();
}
```

**OUTPUT:**

Enter a string:
hii how are you
3 spaces

**Problem 154. Write a C++ program using a for loop with continue.**

***Program:***

```
#include<iostream.h>
#include<conio.h>
void main()
{
int x;
clrscr();
for( x = 0; x <5; x++ )
{
cout<<"Before continue.";
continue;
cout<<x;
}
getch();
}
```

**OUTPUT:**

Before continue.Before continue.Before continue.Before continue.Before continue.

**Problem 155. Write a C++ program to show working of continue.**

***Program:***

```
#include<iostream.h>
#include<conio.h>
void main()
{
char c;
int x,y;
do
{
cout<<" Specify a dividend:";
cin>>x;
cout<<"\n Specify a divisor:";
cin>>y;
if(y==0)
{
cout<<"Divisor is incorrect\n";
continue;
}
cout<<"\n Quotient: "<<x/y;
cout<<"\n Remainder: "<<x%y;
cout<<"\n Do you wish to continue with
another?(yes/no): ";
fflush(stdin);
cin>>c;
}
while(c!='no');
getch();
}
```

**Problem 156. Write a C++ program to depict continue is associated with nearest loop.**

***Program:***

```
#include<iostream.h>
#include<conio.h>
void main()
{
int p,q;
clrscr();
for(p=1;p<=3;p++)
{
for(q=1;q<=2;q++)
{
if(==q)
continue;
cout<<p<<q;
}
}
getch();
}
```

**Problem 157. Write a C++ program to find the average of N numbers using do-while() loop.**

***Program:***

```
#include<iostream.h>
#include<conio.h>
void main()
{
int sum, n, i ;
float av;
cout<<"\n Enter the value of n:";
cin>>n;
```

```
sum=0;
i = 1;
do
{
sum= sum + i ;
i = i + 1;
}
while( i < = n);
cout<<"\n Sum is: "<<sum;
av=(float) sum/n;
cout<<"\n Average is :"<<av;
getche();
}
```

**OUTPUT:**

Enter the value of n: 10
sum is: 55
Average is: 5.5

**Problem 158. Write a C++ program to find the average of N numbers by using the for loop.**

***Program:***

```
#include<iostream.h>
#include<conio.h>
void main()
{
int n, i, sum;
float av;
clrscr();
cout<<"\n Enter the value of N: ";
cin>>n;
for( i =1; i <=n; i++)
{
sum= sum+ i;
}
cout<<"\n Sum is: "<< sum;
av= (float) sum/n;
cout<<"\n Average is: "<< av;
getche(();
}
```

**OUTPUT:**

Enter the value of n: 10
Sum is: 55
Average is: 5.5

**Problem 159. Write a C++ program to illustrate the concept of nested for loop.**

***Program:***

```
#include<iostream.h>
#include<conio.h>
void main()
{
int n=2, m=3, i, j;
cout<<"\n OUTPUT is as: ";
for( i=1; i < =n ; i++)
{
for( j =1; j < = m ; j++)
{
cout<<" \n Hello! ";
}
cout<<" \n OK ";
}
getche();
}
```

**OUTPUT:**

Hello!
Hello!
Hello!
OK
Hello!
Hello!
Hello!
OK

**Problem 160. Write a C++ program to add and subtract two numbers by using unconditional go to statement.**

***Program:***

```
#include<iostream.h>
void main()
{
int a,b,c,d;
cout<< "\n Enter the value of a and b:";
cin>>a>>b;
d=a-b;
cout<<"\n Addition result is: "<<c;
goto mm;
cout<< "\n Subtraction result is: "<<d;
mm:
cout<<"\n End of the program";
getche();
}
```

**OUTPUT:**

Enter the value of a and b: 5 2
Addition result is: 7
End of the program

**Problem 161. Write a C++ program to find all the roots of a quadratic equation. Also what happens if the coffecient of x2 is zero. /* To find the roots of a quardratic equation .**

***Program:***

```
#include<iostream.h>
```

```
#include<math.h>
#include<conio.h>
void main()
{
int a,b,c,d;
float r1,r2;
clrscr();
cout<<"\n Enter the values of a,b and c:";
cin>>a>>b>>c;
if(a==0)
{
cout<<"\n It is a linear equation ";
goto end;
}
d=b*b-4*a*c;
if(d==0)
{
r1=-b/(2*a);
r2=r1;
cout<<"\n Roots are equal";
cout<<"\n Roots are "<<r1<<r2;
}
else if(d>0)
{
r1=(-b+sqrt(d))/(2*a);
r2=(-b-sqrt(d))/(2*a);
cout<<"\nRoots are real";
cout<<"\n Roots are "<<r1<<r2;
}
else
{
cout<<"\n Roots are imaginary";
}
end:
cout<<"\n End of the Program:";
getch();
}
```

**OUTPUT:**

Enter the value of a,b and c:8 3 6
Roots are imaginary
End of the program

**Problem 162. Write a C++ program to compute a square value by using the conditional backward goto statement.**

***Program:***

```
#include<iostream.h>
void main()
{
int x, y;
start :
cout<<"\n Enter the value of x : ";
cin>>x;
if (x < 0)
{
goto start;
}
y = sqrt (x);
cout<<"\n Square root of "<<x<<"is"<<y;
getche ( );
}
```

**OUTPUT:**

Enter the value of x : -5
Enter the value of x : 3
Square root of 3 is 9

**Problem 163. Write a C++ program to illustrate the concept of break statement.**

***Program:***

```
#include<iostream.h>
void main()
{
int n, i, sum;
cout<<"\n Please Enter the value of N (N>=7): ";
cin>>n;
sum=0;
for( i = 1 ; i < = n ; i++)
{
sum = sum + i;
if ( i = = 7 )
{
break;
}
}
cout<<"\n SUM is : "<< sum;
getche( );
}
```

**OUTPUT:**

Please Enter the value of N: 10
SUM is : 28

**Problem 164. Write a C++ program to illustrate the concept of continue statement.**

***Program:***

```
#include<iostream.h>
#include<conio.h>
void main()
{
int n, i, sum = 0, a;
float av;
clrscr( );
cout<<"\n Please Enter the value of N: ";
```

```
cin>>n;
for( i =1; i < = n; i++ )
{
cout<<"\n Enter any number : ";
cin>>a;
if( a < 0)
{
continue;
}
sum= sum + a;
}
cout<<"\n SUM IS : "<< sum;
av= (float) sum /n;
cout<<"\n Average is "<< av;
getche();
}
```

**OUTPUT:**

Please Enter the value of N: 5
Enter any number 20
Enter any number -8
Enter any number 30
Enter any number -2
Enter any number 10
SUM IS : 60
Average is :12.00

## MORE PROGRAMS USING CONTROL STATEMENTS:

**Problem 165. Write a C++ program to find the area of triangle by using the hero's formula with all checks.**

***Program:***

```
#include<iostream.h>
#include<conio.h>
#include<math.h>
void main()
{
float a,b,c,s,area;
back:
cout<<"\n ENTER THE THREE SIDES OF A
TRIANGLE : ";
cin>>a>>b>>c;
if(a==0||b==0||c==0)
{
cout<<"\n Value of any side should not be equal to
zero.";
goto back;
}
if(a+b<c||b+c<a||c+a<b)
{
cout<<"\n Sum of 2 sides should be greater than
third.";
goto back;
}
s=(a+b+c)/2;
area=sqrt(s*(s-a)*(s-b)*(s-c));
cout<<"\n AREA OF TRIANGLE IS "<< area;
getch();
}
```

**OUTPUT:**

ENTER THE THREE SIDES OF A TRIANGLE :
8 3 2
Sum of 2 sides should be greater than third

**Problem 166. Write a C++ program to find factorial of a number.**

***Program:***

```
#include<iostream.h>
#include<dos.h>
#include<conio.h>
void main()
{
int n,i,m;
cout<<"\n Enter the number : ";
cin>>n;
m=1;
for(i=1;i<=n;i++)
{ m=m*i;}
cout<<" \n Factorial of "<<n<<" is = "<<m;
getch();
}
```

**OUTPUT:**

Enter the number: 5
Factorial of 5 is = 120

**Problem 167. Write a C++ program to print the first N tables.**

***Program:***

```
#include<iostream.h>
void main()
{
int n,i,m,j;
cout<<"\n Enter the value of N :";
cin>>n;
for(i=1;i<=n;i++)
{
cout<<"\n TABLE OF "<<i<<" IS: ";
for(j=1;j<=10;j++)
{
m=i*j;
```

```
cout<<"\n"<<i<<" *"<<j<<"="<<m;
}
getche();
}
getche();
}
```

**OUTPUT:**

```
Enter the value of N : 3
TABLE OF 1 IS:
1 * 1 = 1
1 * 2 = 2
1 * 3 = 3
1 * 4 = 4
1 * 5 = 5
1 * 6 = 6
1 * 7 = 7
1 * 8 = 8
1 * 9 = 9
1 * 10 = 10
TABLE OF 2 IS:
2 * 1 = 2
2 * 2 = 4
2 * 3 = 6
2 * 4 = 8
2 * 5 = 10
2 * 6 = 12
2 * 7 = 14
2 * 8 = 16
2 * 9 = 18
2 * 10 = 20
TABLE OF 3 IS:
3 * 1 = 3
3 * 2 = 6
3 * 3 = 9
3 * 4 = 12
3 * 5 = 15
3 * 6 = 18
3 * 7 = 21
3 * 8 = 24
3 * 9 = 27
3 * 10 = 30
```

**Problem 168. Write a C++ program to find the sum of the series.**
**1+1/x+1/x2+1/x3+---------------------1/xn**

***Program:***

```
#include<iostream.h>
#include<dos.h>
#include<math.h>
void main()
{
int i, x, n;
float sum, p;
cout<<"\n Enter the base value : ";
cin>>x;
cout<<" \n Enter the power value: ";
cin>>n;
i=1;
sum=1;
while(i<=n)
{
p=pow(x,i);
sum=sum+(1/p);
i=i+1;
}
cout<<"\n Sum is ="<< sum;
getche();
}
```

**OUTPUT:**

```
Enter the base value : 2
Enter the power value: 3
Sum is = 1.87
```

**Problem 169. Write a C++ program to find greatest number with conditional operator ?:**

***Program:***

```
#include<iostream.h>
#include<conio.h>
void main()
{
int a,b,c,big;
clrscr();
cout<<"\n Enter the value of a,b and c :";
cin>>a>>b>>c;
big=(a>b)?((a>c)?a:c):b>c?b:c;
cout<<"\n Biggest Number is :"<<big;
getch();
}
```

**OUTPUT:**

```
Enter the value of a,b and c :5 8 2
Biggest Number is : 8
```

**Problem 170. Write a C++ program to find the sum of the given series.**
**1n+2n+3n+4n+---------------------mn**

***Program:***

```
#include<iostream.h>
#include<dos.h>
#include<math.h>
void main()
{
int i, m, n;
```

```
float sum;
cout<<"\n Enter the value upto which you want sum
: ";
cin>>m;
cout<<" \n Enter the power value: ";
cin>>n;
sum=0;
for(i=1;i<=m;i++)
{
sum=sum+ pow(i,n);
}
cout<<"\n Sum is = "<< sum;
getche();
}
```

**OUTPUT:**

Enter the value upto which you want sum : 3
Enter the power value: 2
Sum is = 14.0

**Problem 171. Write a C++ program to find the sum of the series: 1+1/x+(1/x**2)2+(1/x**3)3+______________+(1/x **n)n *.**

***Program:***

```
#include<iostream.h>
#include<math.h>
void main()
{
int i,x,n;
float sum;
cout<<"\n Enter the base value: ";
cin>>x;
cout<<"\n Enter the power value: ";
cin>>n;
i=1;
sum=1;
while(i<=n)
{
sum=sum+pow((1/pow(x,i)),i);
i=i+1;
}
cout<<"\n Sum = "<<sum;
}
```

**OUTPUT:**

Enter the base value: 2
Enter the power value: 3
Sum = 1.564453

**Problem 172. Write a C++ program to convert any decimal number into binary coded decimal.**

***Program:***

```
#include<iostream.h>
void main()
{
int a[30], n, c=0, m, i=0;
clrscr();
cout<<"\n ENTER THE NUMBER: ";
cin>>n;
cout<<"\n Binary Number is: ";
while(n>=1)
{
m=n%2;
a[i]=m;
i=i+1;
c=c+1;
n=n/2;
}
for(i=c;i>=1;i--)
{
cout<<a[i];
}
getche();
}
```

**OUTPUT:**

ENTER THE NUMBER: 5
Binary Number is: 101

**Problem 173. Write a C++ program to convert the octal number into the decimal number.**

***Program:***

```
#include<iostream.h>
#include<math.h>
void main()
{
int n,r,p,s=0,i=0;
cout<<"\n Enter value of n: ";
cin>>n;
while(n>0)
{
r=n%10;
p=pow(8,i);
s=s+p*r;
i=i+1;
n=n/10;
}
cout<<"\n Decimal number is :"<<s;
getche();
}
```

**OUTPUT:**

Enter value of n: 67
Decimal number is : 55

**Problem 174. Write a C++ program to check whether a triangle is an acute, an obtuse or a right angle triangle.**

***Program:***

```
#include<iostream.h>
#include<conio.h>
void main()
{
float angle;
clrscr();
start:
cout<<"\n ENTER THE ANGLE OF THE
TRIANGLE:";
cin>>angle;
if(angle>180)
{
cout<<"\n sorry! I don't think it is an angle";
}
else if(angle==180)
{
cout<<"\n IT IS A STRAIGHT LINE";
}
else if(angle<180 && angle>90)
{
cout<<"\n ANGLE IS obtuse";
}
else if(angle==90)
{
cout<<"\n IT IS A RIGHT ANGLE";
}
else
if(angle<90 && angle>0)
{
cout<<"\n IT IS AN ACUTE ANGLE";
}
else
{
cout<<"\n Try again:";
goto start;
}
getche();
}
```

**OUTPUT:**

```
ENTER THE ANGLE OF THE TRIANGLE:
90
IT IS A RIGHT ANGLE
```

**Problem 175. Write a C++ program to find the sum of the Cosine series.**

***Program:***

```
#include<iostream.h>
#include<conio.h>
#include "math.h"
void main()
{
float i,n,t,x,z,m;
z=0;
cout<<"\n Enter the limit of the series and value of
x :";
cin>>n>>x;
t=cos(x);
for(i=1;i<=n;i++)
{
m=pow(t,i);
z=z+m;
}
cout<<"\n Sum of the cosine series is="<<z;
getche();
}
```

**OUTPUT:**

```
Enter the limit of the series and value of x : 1 3
series is –0.989992
```

**Problem 176. Write a C++ program to print the FLOYD's Triangle.**

***Program:***

```
#include<iostream.h>
#include<conio.h>
void main()
{
int n,i,j;
clrscr();
cout<<"\n ENTER MAX. NUMBER :\n";
cin>>n;
for(i=1;i<=n;i++)
{
for(j=1;j<=i;j++)
{
cout.width(3);
cout<<j;
}
cout<<"\n";
}
getche();
}
```

**OUTPUT:**

```
ENTER MAX. NUMBER: 3
1
1    2
1    2    3
```

**Problem 177. Write a C++ program to print**

**FLOYD's Triangle.**

***Program:***

```
#include<iostream.h>
void main()
{
int n,i,j,k;
cout<<"\n ENTER NUMBER OF LINES :\n";
cin>>n;
k=1;
for(i=1;i<=n;i++)
{
for(j=1;j<=i;j++)
{
cout<<k;
k=k+1;
}
cout<<"\n";
}
getche();
}
```

**OUTPUT:**

```
ENTER NUMBER OF LINES :3
1
2       3
4       5       6
```

**Problem 178. Write a C++ program to find the sum of the series.**
**sinx=x-x3/3!+x5/5!-x7/7!+x9/9!+-..........**

***Program:***

```
#include<iostream.h>
#include<conio.h>
#include<dos.h>
#include<math.h>
void main()
{
float sum, x, m, n, g, i, c, h;
clrscr();
cout<<"\n Enter the base value: ";
cin>>x;
cout<<"\n Enter the power value: ";
cin>>n;
sum=x;
c=1;
i=3;
m=2;
ab:
m=m*i;
h=pow((-1),c);
g=pow(x,i);
sum=sum+(h*g)/m;
i=i+2;
c=c+1;
m=m*(i-1);
if(i<=n)
{
goto ab;
}
cout<<"\n Sum = "<<sum;
sleep(10);
}
```

**OUTPUT:**

```
Enter the base value: 2
Enter the power value: 5
Sum = 0.933333
```

**Problem 179. Write a C++ program to find the roots of Quadratic equation.**

***Program:***

```
#include<iostream.h>
#include<math.h>
void main()
{
int a,b,d,c;
float x1,x2;
ab:
cout<<"\n Enter the value of a, b, c: ";
cin>>a>>b>>c;
if(a = = 0)
{
cout<<"it is a linear equation ";
cout<<"give the data again";
goto ab;
}
d=b*b-4*a*c;
if(d==0)
{
cout<<"roots are real and equal";
x1=x2=(-b)/(2*a);
cout<<"roots are = "<<x1<<x2;
}
else
{
if(d<0)
{
cout<<"\n Roots are imaginary";
}
else
{
x1=((-b)+sqrt(d))/(2*a);
x2=((-b)-sqrt(d))/(2*a);
cout<<"roots are real\n";
```

```
cout<<"roots are "<<x1<<x2;
}
getche();
}
}
```

**OUTPUT:**

```
Enter the value of a, b, c:
5
2
4
Roots are imaginary
```

**Problem 180. Write a C++ program to print the n terms of Fibbonici series.**

***Program:***

```
#include<iostream.h>
void main()
{
int x,y,z,n,i;
clrscr();
x=0;
y=1;
cout<<" \n Enter value of n: ";
cin>>n;
cout<<"\n Fibbonacci series is:";
cout<<"\n"<<x;
cout<<"\n"<<y;
for(i=0;i<n-2;i++)
{
z=x+y;
x=y;
y=z;
cout<<"\t"<<z;
}
getch();
}
```

**OUTPUT:**

```
Enter value of n:
8
Fibbonacci series is:
0	1	1	2	3	5	8
	13
```

**Problem 181. Write a C++ program to find HCF (GCD) between two numbers.**

***Program:***

```
#include<iostream.h>
#include<conio.h>
#include<dos.h>
void main()
{
int r, q, m, n, temp;
clrscr();
cout<<"\n INPUT THE VALUES OF TWO
Numbers :";
cin>>m>>n;
if(m==0)
{
cout<<"HCF OF NUMBER IS : "<<n;
goto ab;
}
if(n==0)
{
cout<<"HCF OF NUMBER IS :"<<m;
goto ab;
}
if(n>m)
{
temp=m;
m=n;
n=temp;
}
r=1;
while(r!=0)
{
q=m%n;
if(q!=0)
{
m=n;
n=q;
}
}
cout<<"\n HCF OF NUMBER IS :"<<n;
ab:
sleep(10);
}
```

**OUTPUT:**

```
INPUT THE VALUES OF TWO Numbers 49
42
HCF OF NUMBER IS :7
```

**Problem 182. Write a C++ program to print the reverse of Digit.**

***Program:***

```
#include<iostream.h>
#include<dos.h>
#include<conio.h>
#include<math.h>
void main()
{
int n, digit, sum, sum1, sum2, i;
clrscr();
```

```
cout<<"\n ENTER THE NUMBER OF DIGIT IN A
GIVEN DIGIT(N): ";
cin>>n;
cout<<"\n ENTER THE DIGIT: ";
cin>>digit;
cout<<"\n DIGIT IN REVERSE FORM IS: ";
sum1=0;
sum2=0;
for(i=1;i<=(n-1);i++)
{
sum=fmod(digit,10);
sum1=sum1+sum*pow(10,(n-i));
sum2=sum2+sum;
digit=digit/10;
}
sum1=sum1+digit;
sum2=sum2+digit;
cout<<sum1;
cout<<"\n SUM OF DIGIT IS: "<<sum2;
}
}
```

**OUTPUT:**

```
ENTER THE NUMBER OF DIGIT IN A GIVEN
DIGIT (N): 5
ENTER THE DIGIT: 12345
DIGIT IN REVERSE FORM IS: 54321
SUM OF DIGIT IS: 15
```

**Problem 183. Write a C++ program to find the Prime Number.**

***Program:***

```
#include<iostream.h>
#include<math.h>
#include<conio.h>
void main()
{
int n,m,i;
clrscr( );
cout<<"\n ENTER THE NUMBER: ";
cin>>n;
i=2;
ab: m=fmod(n,i);
if (m==0)
{
cout<<"\n IT IS NOT PRIME";
goto bc;
}
else
{
i=i+1;
if(i<=(n-1))
{
goto ab;
}
cout<<"\n IT IS A PRIME NO";
}
bc:
getche();
}
```

**OUTPUT:**

```
ENTER THE NUMBER: 9
IT IS NOT PRIME
```

**Problem 184. Write a C++ program to find a given Number is EVEN.**

***Program:***

```
#include<iostream.h>
#include<math.h>
void main()
{
int n,m;
cout<<"\n ENTER THE NUMBER: ";
cin>>n;
m=fmod(n,2);
if(m==0)
{
cout<<"\n NUMBER IS EVEN\n";
}
else
{
cout<<"\n NUMBER IS ODD\n";
}
cout<<"\n END OF PROGRAM ";
getche();
}
```

**OUTPUT:**

```
ENTER THE NUMBER: 8
NUMBER IS EVEN
```

**Problem 185. Write a C++ program to convert lowercase character to uppercase character using conditional operator ?:**

***Program:***

```
#include<iostream.h>
# include <conio.h>
void main()
{
char c1, c2;
clrscr( );
cout<<"\n Enter a lowercase character :";
cin>>c1;
c2 = (c1>= 'a' && c1 <='z')? ('A' + c1-'a'):c1;
```

```
cout<<"\n Uppercase Equivalent is "<<c2<<"\n";
getch ();
}
```

**OUTPUT:**

Enter a lowercase character: a
Uppercase Equivalent is A

**Problem 186. Write a C++ program to display all numbers lying between 2 to 100 which are divisible by number n which you enter.**

***Program:***

```
#include<iostream.h>
void main()
{
int i,c,n;
cout<<"\n Enter number: ";
cin>>n;
for (i=2;i<=100;i++)
{
c=n%i;
if (c==0)
{
cout<<"\n"<<"n is divisible by"<<i;
}
}
getch ();
}
```

**OUTPUT:**

Enter number: 44
44 is divisible by 2
44 is divisible by 4
44 is divisible by 11
44 is divisible by 22
44 is divisible by 44

**Problem 187. Write a C++ program to print out all Armstrong numbers between 1 to 1000.**

***Program:***

```
#include<iostream.h>
# include<conio.h>
void main()
{
int c,temp,sum,p;
clrscr ();
cout<<"\n Armstrong numbers between 1 and 1000
are : ";
cout<<"Numbers like
Number=cube(digit1)+cube(digit2)+cube(digit3)\n";
cout<<"153=cube(1)+cube(5)+cube(3)";
cout<<"\n Numbers are:";
for (i=1;i<=1000;i++)
{
sum=0;p=i;
while (p>0)
{
temp=p%10;
sum+=(temp*temp*temp);
p=p/10;}
if (sum==i)
{
cout<<"\n"<<i;
}
}
getch ();
}
```

**OUTPUT:**

Armstrong numbers between 1 and 1000 are.....
Numbers like
Number=cube(digit1)+cube(digit2)+cube(digit3)
153=cube(1)+cube(5)+cube(3)
Numbers are:
1
153
370
371
407

**Problem 188. Write a C++ program to find whether a number is Armstrong number or not.**

***Program:***

```
#include<iostream.h>
#include<conio.h>
void main()
{
int a,temp,d,arm=0;
clrscr( );
cout<<"\nEnter any number: ";
cin>>a;
temp=a;
do
{
d = temp%10;
temp /= 10;
arm+=d*d*d;
} while(temp>0);
if(arm==a)
cout<<"\n"<<a<<"is armstrong number. ";
else
cout<<"\n"<<a<<" is not armstrong number.";
getch();
}
```

**OUTPUT:**

Enter any number:153
153 is armstrong number

**Problem 189. Write a C++ program to print all combinations of characters A, B, C.**

***Program:***

```
#include<iostream.h>
void main()
{
char ch1, ch2, ch3;
for (ch1='A';ch1<=`C';++ch1)
for (ch2=`A';ch2<=`C';++ch2)
for (ch3=`A''ch3<='C';++ch3)
cout<<ch1<<ch2<<ch3;
}
```

**OUTPUT:**

```
AAA    AAB    AAC    ABA    ABB    ABC
       ACA    ACB    ACC    BAA    BAB BAC
BBA    BBB    BBC    BCA    BCB BCC
       CAA    CAB    CAC    CBA    CBB
       CBC CCA       CCB    CCC
```

**Problem 190. Write a C++ program for printing of multiplication table.**

***Program:***

```
#include<iostream.h>
#include<conio.h>
define COLMAX 10
define ROWMAX 10
void main()
{
int r,c,y;
r=1;
cout<<" Multiplication table \n";
cout<<"-------------------\n";
do
{
c=1;
do
{
y=r*c;
cout<<y;
c=c+1;
}
while(c<=COLMAX);
cout<<"\n";
r=r+1;
}
while(r<=ROWMAX);
cout<<"-------------------\n";
}
```

**OUTPUT:**

```
1 2 3 4 5 6 7 8 9 10
2 4 6 8 10 12 14 16 18 20
3 6 9 12 15 18 21 24 27 30
4 8 12 16 20 24 28 32 36 40
5 10 15 20 25 30 35 40 45 50
6 12 18 24 30 36 42 48 54 60
7 14 21 28 35 42 49 56 63 70
8 16 24 32 40 48 56 64 72 80
9 18 27 36 45 54 63 72 81 90
10 20 30 40 50 60 70 80 90 100
```

**Problem 191. Write a C++ program to find whether a number is palindrome or not.**

***Program:***

```
#include<iostream.h>
#include<conio.h>
void main()
{
int a,temp,d,rev=0;
clrscr( );
cout<<"\n Enter any number : ";
cin>>a;
temp=a;
while(temp>0)
{
d = temp%10;
temp /= 10;
rev = rev*10+d;
}
if(rev==a)
cout<<"\n"<<a<<" is a palindrome";
else
cout<<"\n"<<a<<" is not a palindrome";
getch();
}
```

**OUTPUT:**

Enter any number :121
121 is palindrome

**Problem 192. Write a C++ program to print the data.**

**1**
**21**
**321**
**4321**

***Program:***

```
#include<iostream.h>
#include<conio.h>
void main()
```

```
{
int a;
clrscr( );
cout<<"\n Enter any number :";
cin>>a;
for(int i=1;i<=a;i++)
{
for(int j=i;j>=1;j--)
cout<<,j<"\n";
}
getch();
}
```

**Problem 193. Write a C++ program to print**
**1**
**22**
**333**
**4444**

***Program:***

```
#include<iostream.h>
#include<conio.h>
void main()
{
int a;
clrscr( );
cout<<"\n Enter any number :";
cin>>a;
for(int i=1;i<=a;i++)
{
for(int j=1;j<=i;j++)
cout<<i<<"\n";
}
getch();
}
```

**Problem 194. Write a C++ program to print**
*
**
***
****

***Program:***

```
#include<iostream.h>
#include<stdio.h>
void main()
{
int a;
clrscr( );
cout<<"\n Enter any number :";
cin>>a;
for(int i=1;i<=a;i++)
{
for(int j=1;j<=i;j++)
cout<<"*";
cout<<"\n";
}
getch();
}
```

**Problem 195. Write a C++ program to print**
*
* *
* * *

***Program:***

```
#include<conio.h>
#include<iostream.h>
void main()
{
int a,j,i,space;
clrscr( );
cout<<"\nEnter any number :";
cin>>a;
for(space=a-1,i=1;i<=a;i++,space--)
{
for(j=1;j<=space;j++)
cout<<' ';
for(j=1;j<=i;j++)
cout<<"* ";
cout<<"\n";
}
getch();
}
```

**Problem 196. Write a C++ program to print the particular table**

***Program:***

```
#include<iostream.h>
#include<conio.h>
void main()
{
clrscr();
int m,n,j,k,t,i;
for(i=1;i<=20;i++)
{
cout<<"\n Enter the value for the required table : ";
cin>>m;
}
for(j=1;j<=10;j++)
{
n=m*j;
cout<<"\n\t"<<m<<"*"<<j<<"="<<n;
}
getch();
```

```
}
```

**OUTPUT:**

Enter the value for the required table : 5
5*1=5
5*2=10
5*3=15
5*4=20
5*5=25
5*6=30
5*7=35
5*8=40
5*9=45
5*10=50

**Problem 197. Write a C++ program to find average of n numbers.**

***Program:***

```
#include<iostream.h>
#include<conio.h>
void main()
{
int num,i=1;
float s=0,avg,a;
clrscr();
cout<<"\n Find the average of how many numbers:";
cin>>num;
while(i<=num)
{
cout<<"Enter number:";
cin>>a;
s+=a;
++i;
}
avg=s/num;
cout<<"\n Average is "<<avg;
getch();
}
```

**OUTPUT:**

Find the average of how many numbers:5
Enter number:1
Enter number:2
Enter number:3
Enter number:4
Enter number:5
Average is 3.000000

**Problem 198.Write a C++ program to find factorial of a number.**

***Program:***

```
#include<iostream.h>
#include<conio.h>
void main()
{
int num,i=1;
long int f=1;
cout<<"\n Enter the number:";
cin>>num;
while(i<=num)
{
f=f*i;
i++;
}
cout<<"The factorial is: "<<f;
getch();
}
```

**OUTPUT:**

Enter the number:5
The factorial is:120

**Problem 199. Write a C++ program to state the working of entry controlled loop while.**

***Program:***

```
#include<iostream.h>
#include<conio.h>
void main()
{
int a=10;
while(a!=0)
cin>>a;
getch();
}
```

**OUTPUT:**

loop breaks when enter zero.

**Problem 200. Write a C++ program to print fibonnacci number.**

***Program:***

```
#include<iostream.h>
#include<conio.h>
void main()
{
int x=0,y=1,z=0,num,count=3;
cout<<"\n Enter the number:";
cin>>num;
if(num==1)
cout<<"0";
if(num==2)
cout<<"1";
while(count<=num)
{
z=x+y;
x=y;
```

```
y=z;
count++;
}
if(z!=0)
cout<<"\n"<<num<<" nth number is: "<<z;
getch();
}
```

**Problem 201. Write a C++ program to find total of digits between m & n of every digit.**

***Program:***

```
#include<iostream.h>
#include<conio.h>
void main()
{
int a,b,p,q,s;
clrscr();
cout<<"\n Enter the lower limit number:";
cin>>p;
cout<<"\n Enter the upper limit number:";
cin>>q;
while(p<=q)
{
b=p;
s=0;
while(b>0)
{
a=b%10;
s=s+a;
b=b/10;
}
p=p+1;
cout<<"\n Total of the digits of "<<p-1<<" is "<<s;
}
getch();
}
```

**Problem 202. Write a C++ program to reverse a number and verify if its palindrome.**

***Program:***

```
#include<iostream.h>
#include<conio.h>
void main()
{
int rem=0,rev=0,s=0;
int n,k;
cout<<"\n Enter the number:";
cin>>k;
n=k;
while(n>0)
{
rem=n%10;
n=n/10;
rev=(rev*10)+rem;
}
cout<<"Reverse of a number is:"<<rev;
if(k==rev)
{
cout<<"\nThe number is palindrome.";
s=1;
}
if(s==0)
{
cout<<"\nThe number is not palindrome.";
}
getch();
}
```

**OUTPUT:**

Enter the number:23232
Reverse of a number is:23232
The number is palindrome.

**Problem 203. Write a C++ program to show all palindrome numbres between m & n.**

***Program:***

```
#include<iostream.h>
#include<conio.h>
void main()
{
int rem,rev,p,q,k;
cout<<"\n Enter the lower limit number:";
cin>>p;
cout<<"\n Enter the upper limit number:";
cin>>q;
while(p<=q)
{
k=p;
rem=0;
rev=0;
while(k>0)
{
rem=k%10;
k=k/10;
rev=(rev*10)+rem;
}
if(p==rev)
{
cout<<"\n"<<p<<" is palindrome.";
}
p=p+1;
}
getch();
```

```
}
```

**OUTPUT:**

Enter the lower limit number:10
Enter the upper limit number:50
11 is palindrome.
22 is palindrome.
33 is palindrome.
44 is palindrome.

**Problem 204. Write a C++ program to find total of first and last digit of a number.**

***Program:***

```
#include<iostream.h>
#include<conio.h>
void main()
{
int k=0,total=0;
int n,a,num;
clrscr();
cout<<"\n How many digits?";
cin>>n;
cout<<"\n Enter the number:";
cin>>num;
while(num>0&&k!=n)
{
a=num%10;
num=num/10;
k++;
if(k==1||k==n)
total=total+a;
}
cout<<"\n Total is:"<<total;
getch();
}
```

**OUTPUT:**

How many digits? 3
Enter the number:124
Total is:5

**Problem 205. Write a C++ program to find sum of N digit number and reduce it to get sum to single digit.**

***Program:***

```
#include<iostream.h>
#include<conio.h>
void main()
{
int a,k,total,num;
cout<<"\n Enter the number:";
cin>>num;
k=num;
while(k>=10)
{
total=0;
while(k>0)
{
a=k%10;
total=total+a;
k=k/10;
}
k=total;
}
cout<<"\n Total of digits is "<<total;
getch();
}
```

**OUTPUT:**

Enter the number:321
Total of digits is 6

**Problem 206. Write a C++ program to find HCF of two +ve numbers.**

***Program:***

```
#include<iostream.h>
#include<conio.h>
void main()
{
int hcf,x,y,s=1;
cout<<"\n Enter the numbers:";
cin>>x>>y;
if(x>y)
{
while(s!=0)
{
s=x%y;
x=y;
y=s;
}
hcf=x;
}
else
{
while(s!=0)
{
s=y%x;
y=x;
x=s;
}
hcf=y;
}
cout<<"\n Highest Common Factor is:"<<hcf;
getch();
}
```

**OUTPUT:**

Enter the numbers:10 20
Highest Common Factor is:10

**Problem 207. Write a C++ program to print fibonacci series of n numbers...0,1,1,2,3,5,8,13,21,34....**

***Program:***

```
#include<iostream.h>
#include<conio.h>
void main()
{
int n,x,y,s,count;
x=0;
y=1;
count=3;
cout<<"Enter the N:";
cin>>n;
cout<<"\t"<<x<<y;
while(count<=n)
{
s=x+y;
cout<<"\t"<<s;
x=y;
y=s;
count++;
}
getch();
}
```

**OUTPUT:**

Enter the N:6
0 1 1 2 3 5

**Problem 208. Write a C++ program to print total of series: 1+(1/2)-(1/3)+(1/4)-.........+(-1)^n(1/n)**

***Program:***

```
#include<iostream.h>
#include<conio.h>
#include<math.h>
void main()
{
int count,k,n;
float total;
cout<<"Enter N: ";
cin>>n;
k=1;count=1;
total=0.0;
while(count<=n)
{
total+=(float)pow(-1,count-1)/k;
k++;
count++;
}
cout<<"Total is "<<total;
getch();
}
```

**OUTPUT:**

Enter N:5
Total is 0.783333

**Problem 209. Write a C++ program to print series: y=1+x+((x^2)/2)+((x^3)/6)+........+((x^n)/n!), 0<x<1**

***Program:***

```
#include<iostream.h>
#include<conio.h>
#define ACC 0.0001
void main()
{
int num,i;
float total,t,a;
clrscr();
cout<<"\n Enter a:";
cin>>a;
num=t=total=i=1;
while(num<=100)
{
t=(t*a)/num;
total+=t;
i=i+1;
if(t<ACC)
num=999;
else
num=num+1;
}
cout<<"Terms= "<<i<<" Total= "<<total<<"\n";
getch();
}
```

**OUTPUT:**

Enter a:0.5
Terms=2 Total=1.000000

**Problem 210. Write a C++ program to change lowercase content to uppercase.**

***Program:***

```
#include<iostream.h>
#include<conio.h>
void main()
{
char alphabet[80];
```

```
int c=0,k;
while((alphabet[c]=getchar())!='\n')
++c;
k=c;
c=0;
while(c<k)
{
putchar(toupper(alphabet[c]));
++c;
}
getch();
}
```

**OUTPUT:**

head sir
HEAD SIR

**Problem 211. Write a C++ program to demonstrate execution of do-while loop once.**

***Program:***

```
#include<iostream.h>
#include<conio.h>
void main()
{
do
{
cout<<"Programming";
getch();
}
while(7<2);
}
```

**OUTPUT:**

Programming

**Problem 212. Write a C++ program using do-while to find total n consecutive numbers.**

***Program:***

```
#include<iostream.h>
#include<conio.h>
void main()
{
int k=1,total=0;
int num;
cout<<"\n How many numbers?";
cin>>num;
do
{
total=total+k;
k=k+1;
}
while(k<=num);
cout<<"\n Total of "<<num<<"is "<<total;
getch();
}
```

**OUTPUT:**

How many numbers?10
Total of 10 is 55.

**Problem 213. Write a C++ program using for loop to find total n consecutive numbers.**

***Program:***

```
#include<iostream.h>
#include<conio.h>
void main()
{
int k,num,total=0;
cout<<"\n How many numbers?";
cin>>num;
for(k=1;k<=num;k++)
{
total=total+k;
}
cout<<"\n Total is "<<total;
getch();
}
```

**OUTPUT:**

How many numbers?10
Total is 55

**Problem 214. Write a C++ program to find all possible Well Ordered three digit numbers.**

***Program:***

```
#include<iostream.h>
#include<conio.h>
void main()
{
int p,n,x,s1,s2,s3,q;
for(q=100;q<=999;q++)
{
x=q;
p=q;
s1=p%10;
p=p/10;
s2=p%10;
p=p/10;
s3=p%10;
if(s1>s2&&s2>s3)
cout<<"\n"<<x;
}
getch();
}
```

**OUTPUT:**

(do yourself)

**Problem 215. Write a C++ program to display output.**
**1**
**112**
**1123**
**11235**
**112358**

***Program:***

```
#include<iostream.h>
#include<conio.h>
void main()
{
int p,q,n,x,y,z;
cout<<"\n Specify the number of elements:";
cin>>n;
cout<<"1\n";
for(p=2;p<=n;p++)
{
x=1;
y=1;
cout<<x<<y;
for(q=3;q<=p+1;q++)
{
z=x+y;
cout<<z;
x=y;
y=z;
}
cout<<"\n";
}
getch();
}
```

**<u>OUTPUT:</u>**

```
Specify the number of elements:5
1
112
1123
11235
112358
```

**Problem 216. Write a C++ program to display output**
*****
******
*******
********

***Program:***

```
#include<iostream.h>
#include<conio.h>
void main()
{
int p,q,n;
clrscr();
cout<<"\n Specify the number of lines:";
cin>>n;
for(p=0;p<n;p++)
{
for(q=0;q<=p;q++)
{
cout<<"*";
}
cout<<"\n";
}
getch();
}
```

**<u>OUTPUT:</u>**

```
Specify the number of lines:4
*
**
***
****
```

**Problem 217. Write a C++ program to display output**
**0**
**01**
**012**
**0123**

***Program:***

```
#include<iostream.h>
#include<conio.h>
void main()
{
int p,q,n;
clrscr();
cout<<"\n Specify the number of lines:";
cin>>n;
for(p=0;p<n;p++)
{
for(q=0;q<=p;q++)
{
cout<<q;
}
cout<<"\n";
}
getch();
}
```

**<u>OUTPUT:</u>**

```
Specify the number of lines:4
0
01
012
```

0123

**Problem 218. Write a C++ program to display output**
**0**
**11**
**222**
**3333**

***Program:***

```
#include<iostream.h>
#include<conio.h>
void main()
{
int p,q,n;
clrscr();
cout<<"\n Specify the number of lines:";
cin>>n;
for(p=0;p<n;p++)
{
for(q=0;q<=p;q++)
{
cout<<p;
}
cout<<"\n";
}
getch();
}
```

**Problem 219. Write a C++ program to display output**
**1**
**23**
**456**
**78910**

***Program:***

```
#include<iostream.h>
#include<conio.h>
void main()
{
int p,q,n,y=1;
clrscr();
cout<<"\n Specify the number of lines:";
cin>>n;
for(p=0;p<=n;p++)
{
for(q=1;q<=p;q++)
{
cout<<y;
y++;
}
cout<<"\n";
}
getch();
}
```

**Problem 220. Write a C++ program to display output**
**1**
**25**
**368**
**47910**

***Program:***

```
#include<iostream.h>
#include<conio.h>
void main()
{
int p,q,n,x,y;
clrscr();
cout<<"\n Specify the number of lines:";
cin>>n;
for(p=1;p<=n;p++)
{
x=p;
y=n-1;
for(q=1;q<=p;q++)
{
cout<<x;
x=x+y;
y--;
}
cout<<"\n";
}
getch();
}
```

**Problem 221. Write a C++ program to display output**
********
*******
******
*****

***Program:***

```
#include<iostream.h>
#include<conio.h>
void main()
{
int p,q,k,n;
cin>>n;
for(p=1;p<=n;p++)
{
for(k=1;k<=p-1;k++)
cout<<" ";
```

```
for(q=n;q>=p;q--)
cout<<"*";
cout<<"\n";
}
getch();
}
```

**Problem 222. Write a C++ program to display output**

********
*******
******
*****

***Program:***

```
#include<iostream.h>
#include<conio.h>
vo d main()
{
int p,q,n;
cin>>n;
for(p=1;p<=n;p++)
{
for(q=n;q>=p;q--)
{
cout<<"*";
}
cout<<"\n";
}
getch();
}
```

**Problem 223. Write a C++ program to display output**

**1**
**232**
**34543**
**4567645**

***Program:***

```
#include<iostream.h>
#include<conio.h>
void main()
{
int p,q,n,k,h,x,y;
clrscr();
cout<<"\n Specify the value for n:";
cin>>n;
for(p=1;p<=n;p++)
{
x=p;
y=2*p-2;
for(q=1;q<=2*(n-p);q++)
{
cout<<" ";
}
for(k=1;k<=p;k++)
{
cout<<x;
x+=1;
}
for(h=1;h<p;h++)
{
cout<<y;
y--;
}
cout<<"\n";
}
getch();
}
```

**Problem 224. Write a C++ program to display output**

**4567645**
**34543**
**232**
**1**

***Program:***

```
#include<iostream.h>
#include<conio.h>
void main()
{
int p,q,n;
cout<<"\n Specify the value for n:";
cin>>n;
for(q=0;q<=n-1;q++)
{
for(p=1;p<=q;p++)
cout<<" ";
for(p=n-q;p<=2*n-(2*q+1);p++)
cout<<p;
for(p=2*n-(2*q+2);p>=n-q;p--)
cout<<p;
cout<<"\n";
}
getch();
}
```

**Problem 225. Write a C++ program to display output**

**1**
**11**
**121**
**1331**

**14641**

***Program:***

```
#include<iostream.h>
#include<conio.h>
void main()
{
int p,q,n,x[10][10];
cout<<"\n Specify the value for n:";
cin>>n;
for(p=1;p<=n;p++)
{
for(q=1;q<=p;q++)
{
if(q==1||q==p)
x[p][q]=1;
else
x[p][q]=x[p-1][q]+x[p-1][q-1];
cout<<x[p][q];
}
cout<<"\n";
}
getch();
}
```

**Problem 226. Write a C++ program to display output**

**1**
**101**
**10101**

***Program:***

```
#include<iostream.h>
#include<conio.h>
void main()
{
int p,q,n,k;
cin>>n;
for(p=1;p<=n;p++)
{
for(k=1;k<=n-p;k++)
cout<<" ";
for(q=1;q<=2*p-1;q++)
{
if(q%2==0)
cout<<"0";
else
cout<<"1";
}
cout<<"\n";
}
getch();
}
```

**Problem 227. Write a C++ program to display output**

*****
*******
*********
***********

***Program:***

```
#include<iostream.h>
#include<conio.h>
void main()
{
int p,q,n,k;
cin>>n;
for(p=1;p<=n;p++)
{
for(q=1;q<=(n-p);q++)
cout<<" ";
for(k=1;k<=2*p-1;k++)
{
cout<<"*";
}
cout<<"\n";
}
getch();
}
```

**Problem 228. Write a C++ program to display output**

***********
*********
*******
*****

***Program:***

```
#include<iostream.h>
#include<conio.h>
void main()
{
int p,q,n,k;
cin>>n;
for(p=1;p<=n;p++)
{
for(q=1;q<=p;q++)
cout<<" ";
for(k=1;k<=2*(n-p)-1;k++)
{
cout<<"*";
}
cout<<"\n";
}
getch();
```

```
}
```

**Problem 229. Write a C++ program to display output**
**1234321**
**123 321**
**12 21**
**1 1**

***Program:***

```
#include<iostream.h>
#include<conio.h>
void main()
{
int p,q,n;
cin>>n;
for(p=1;p<=n;p++)
cout<<i;
for(p=n-1;p>=1;p--)
cout<<i;
cout<<"\n";
for(q=1;q<=(n-1);q++)
{
for(p=1;p<=n-q;p++)
cout<<i;
for(p=1;p<=2*q-1;p++)
cout<<" ";
for(p=n-q;p>=1;p--)
cout<<i;
cout<<"\n";
}
getch();
}
```

**Problem 230. Write a C++ program to display output**
*******
******
*****
******
*******

***Program:***

```
#include<iostream.h>
#include<conio.h>
void main()
{
int p,q,n,k,m,v;
cin>>n;
if(n%2==0)
{
m=n/2;
v=1;
}
else
m=n/2+1;
v=2;
}
for(q=m;q>=1;q--)
{
for(k=1;k<=q;k++)
cout<<"*";
cout<<"\n";
}
for(q=v;q<=m;q++)
{
for(k=1;k<=q;k++)
cout<<"*";
cout<<"\n";
}
getch();
}
```

**Problem 231. Write a C++ program to print sum of first n numbers of series:**
**1/1! + 2/2! + 3/3! + 4/4! +...........n/n!**

***Program:***

```
#include<iostream.h>
#include<conio.h>
float factorial(int n);
void main()
{
int p,n;
float t=0;
clrscr();
cout<<"\n Specify the value for n:";
cin>>n;
for(p=1;p<=n;p++)
{
t+=(p/factorial(p));
}
cout<<"\n\t Total:"<<t;
getch();
}
float factorial(int a)
{
if(a<=1)
return(1)
else
return(a*factorial(a-1));
}
```

**Problem 232. Write a C++ program to print latin square.**

***Program:***

```
#include<iostream.h>
#include<conio.h>
void main()
{
int p,q,v,n;
cout<<"\n Specify the number of rows:";
cin>>n;
for(p=1;p<=n;p++)
{
v=p;
for(q=1;q<=n;q++)
{
cout<<"\t"<<v;
if(v==n)
v=1;
else
v++;
}
cout<<"\n";
}
getch();
}
```

**Problem 233. Write a C++ program to print nth prime number.**

***Program:***

```
#include<iostream.h>
#include<conio.h>
void main()
{
int p,q,a,n,c=0;
cout<<"\n Specify the value for n:";
cin>>n;
for(p=2;p<=1000;p++)
{
a=0;
for(q=2;q<=p/2;q++)
{
if(p%q==0)
{
a=1;
break;
}
}
if(a==0)
c++;
if(c==n)
{
cout<<p;
break;
}
}
getch();
}
```

**Problem 234. Write a C++ program to calculate overtime pay of 10 employees Overtime is paid at the rate of rs. 12.00 per hour for every hour worked above 40 hours. Assume that employees do not work for fractional part of an hour.**

***Program:***

```
#include<iostream.h>
#include<conio.h>
void main()
{
float otpay;
int hour,i=1;
clrscr();
while(i<=10) // Loop for 10 employees
{
cout<<"\nEnter no. of hours worked \n";
cin>>hour;
if(hour>=40)
{
otpay=(hour-40)*12;
cout<<"\nNo of hours worked =
"<<hour<<"\nOvertime pay = Rs."<<otpay;
}
else
{
otpay=0;
cout<<"\nNo of hours worked"<<hour<<" is less
than 40 Hrs.\nHence no overtime pay";
}
i++;
}
cout<<"\n press any key to exit.";
getch();
}
```

**OUTPUT:**

```
Enter no. of hours worked
60
No of hours worked = 60
Overtime pay = Rs.240
press any key to exit.
```

**Problem 235. Write a C++ program to find the factorial value of any number entered through the keyboard.**

***Program:***

```
#include<iostream.h>
```

```
#include<conio.h>
void main()
{
int num, i = 1;
unsigned long int fact = 1;
clrscr( ) ;
cout<<"Enter any number (less than 34)";
cin>>num;
while(i<=num)
{
fact=fact*i;
i++;
}
cout<<"\nfactorial of "<<num<<" = "<<fact;
cout<<"\n press any key to exit.";
getch();
}
```

**OUTPUT:**

Enter any number (less than 34) 5
factorial of 5 = 120
press any key to exit.

**Problem 236. Two numbers are entered through the keyboard. Write a C++ program to find the value of one number raised to the power of another.**

***Program:***

```
#include<iostream.h>
#include<conio.h>
void main()
{
int x, y,i=1;
long int power=1;
clrscr();
cout<<"Enter two numbers:";
cin>>x>>y;
while(i<=y)
{
power=power*x;
i++;
}
cout<<"\n"<<x<<" to the power "<<y<<" is "<<
power;
cout<<"\n press any key to exit.";
getch();
}
```

**OUTPUT:**

Enter two numbers:2 3
2 to the power 3 is 8
press any key to exit.

**Problem 237. Write a C++ program to print all the ASCII values and their equivalent characters using a while loop. The ASCII values vary**

***Program:***

```
#include<iostream.h>
#include<conio.h>
void main()
{
int i=0;
clrscr();
while(i<=255)
{
cout<<"\n"<<i<<i;
i++;
}
cout<<"\n press any key to exit.";
getch();
}
```

**OUTPUT:**

do yourself

**Problem 238. Write a C++ program to print out all Armstrong numbers between 1 and 500. If sum of cubes of each digit of the number is equal to the number itself, then the number is called an Armstrong number. For example, 153 = ( 1 * 1 * 1 ) + ( 5 * 5 * 5 ) + ( 3 * 3 * 3 ).**

***Program:***

```
#include<iostream.h>
#include<conio.h>
void main()
{
int i = 1,a,b,c;
clrscr();
cout<<"ARMSTRONG NUMNERS BETWEEN 1
& 500 ARE \n";
while (i<=500)
{
a=i%10; // Extract last digit
b=i%100;
b=(b-a)/10; // Extract second digit
c=i/100; // Extract first digit
if((a*a*a) + (b*b*b) + (c*c*c) == i)
cout<<"/n"<<i;
i++;
}
cout<<"\n press any key to exit.";
getch();
}
```

**OUTPUT:**

Do yourself

**Problem 239. Write a C++ program of a match-stick game between the computer and a user. Your program should ensure that the computer always wins. Rules for the game are as follows:**
**- There are 21 match-sticks.**
**- The computer asks the player to pick 1, 2, 3, or 4 match-sticks.**
**- After the person picks, the computer does its picking.**
**- Whoever is forced to pick up the last match-sticks loses the game.**

***Program:***

```
#include<iostream.h>
#include<conio.h>
void main()
{
int m = 21,p,c;
clrscr( ) ;
while(1)
{
cout<<"\nNo. Of matches left = "<<m;
cout<<"\nPick up 1, 2, 3 or 4 matches";
cin>>p;
if(p>4 || p<1)
continue;
m = m-p;
cout<<"\nNo. Of matches left = "<<m;
c = 5-p;
cout<<"\nOut of which computer picked up "<<c;
m = m- c;
if(m == 1)
{
cout<<"\nNo. Of matches left = "<<m;
cout<<"\nYou lost the game !!";
break;
}
}
cout<<"\n press any key to exit.";
getch();
}
```

**OUTPUT:**

Do yourself

**Problem 240. Write a C++ program to enter the numbers till the user wants and at the end it should display the count of positive, negative and zeros entered.**

***Program:***

```
#include<iostream.h>
#include<conio.h>
void main()
{
int pos,neg,zero,num;
char ans='y';
clrscr();
pos=neg=zero=0;
while(ans=='y' || ans=='Y')
{
cout<<"\nEnter a number:";
cin>>num;
if(num==0)
zero++;
if(num>0)
pos++;
if(num<0)
neg++;
fflush(stdin); // Clears standard input stream
cout<<"Do you want to continue?";
cin>>ans;
}
cout<<"\nYou entered "<<pos<<" positive number(s)";
cout<<"\nYou entered "<<neg<<"negative number(s)";
cout<<"\nYou entered "<<zero<<"zero(s)";
cout<<"\n press any key to exit.";
getch();
}
```

**OUTPUT:**

```
Enter a number:4
Do you want to continue?y
Enter a number:-4
Do you want to continue?y
Enter a number:-9
Do you want to continue?y
Enter a number:0
Do you want to continue?n
You entered 1 positive number(s)
You entered -2 negative number(s)
You entered 0 zero(s)
press any key to exit.
```

**Problem 241. Write a C++ program to reverse a number and find its octal equivalent.**

***Program:***

```
#include<iostream.h>
#include<conio.h>
#include <math.h>
void main()
{
```

```
int n1,n2,dg,oct,p;
clrscr();
cout<<"\nEnter any number:";
cin>>n1;
// reverse the number
n2=0;
while(n1>0)
{
dg = n1 % 10 ;
n2 = n2 * 10 + dg ;
n1 = n1 / 10 ;
}
n1 = n2 ;
p = oct = 0 ;
while ( n1 > 0 )
{
dg = n1 % 8 ;
n1 = n1 / 8 ;
oct = oct + dg * pow ( 10, p) ;
p++ ;
}
cout<<"The octal equivalent of "<<n2<<"is "<< oct
;
cout<<"\n press any key to exit.";
getch();
}
```

**OUTPUT:**

Enter the number:100
The octal equivalent of 1 is 1
press any key to exit.

**Problem 242. Write a C++ program to find the range of a set of numbers. Range is the difference between the smallest and biggest number in the list.**

***Program:***

```
#include<iostream.h>
#include<conio.h>
void main()
{
int n,no,flag,small,big,range;
flag = 0 ;
cout<<"\nHow many numbers are there in a set? ";
cin>>n;
while(n>0)
{
cout<<"\nEnter no:";
cin>>no;
if ( flag == 0 )
{
small = big = no ;
flag = 1 ;
}
else
{
if ( no > big )
big = no ;
if ( no < small )
small = no ;
}
n-- ;
}
if ( small < 0 )
range = small + big ;
else
range = big - small ;
if ( range < 0 )
range = range * -1 ;
cout<<"\nThe range of given set of numbers is "<<
range ;
cout<<"\n press any key to exit.";
getch() ;
}
```

**OUTPUT:**

How many numbers are there in a set?3
Enter no:1
Enter no:5
Enter no:10
The range of given set of numbers is 9
press any key to exit.

**Problem 243. Write a C++ program to print all prime numbers from 1 to 300. (Hint: Use nested loops, break and continue).**

***Program:***

```
#include<iostream.h>
#include<conio.h>
void main()
{
int i, n = 1 ;
clrscr() ;
cout<<"\nPrime numbers between 1 & 300
are:\n1\t";
while(n<=300) // Loop to check numbers upto 300
{
i = 2 ;
while(i<n)// Loop starting from 2 to the number
{
if ( n % i == 0 )
break ; // takes control out of the inner while as
soon as the number is fully divisible
else
```

```
i++ ;
}
if ( i == n )
cout<<"\t"<<n ; // tab is used to print all numbers in
one screen
n++ ;
}
cout<<"\n press any key to exit.";
getch( );
}
```

**OUTPUT:**

Do yourself(display all prime numbers between 1 to 300 on screen).

**Problem 244. Write a C++ program to fill the entire screen with a smiling face. The smiling face has an ASCII value 1.**

***Program:***

```
#include<iostream.h>
#include<conio.h>
void main()
{
int r,c;
clrscr();
for (r=0;r<=24;r++) // Fills rows 0 to 24
for(c=0;c<=79;c++) // Fills columns 0 to 79
cout<<1;
cout<<"\n press any key to exit.";
getch();
}
```

**OUTPUT:**

Half of the screen fill with smiling faces.

**Problem 245. Write a C++ program to add first seven terms of the following series using for loop**
**1 + 2 + 3 +**
**1! 2! 3!**

***Program:***

```
#include<iostream.h>
#include<conio.h>
void main()
{
int i = 1, j ;
float fact, sum = 0.0 ;
clrscr();
while(i<=7)
{
fact = 1.0 ;
for(j=1;j<=i;j++)
fact = fact*j;
sum=sum+i/fact;
i++ ;
}
cout<<"\nSum of series = "<< sum ;
cout<<"\n press any key to exit.";
getch( );
}
```

**Problem 246. Write a C++ program to generate all combinations of 1, 2 and 3 using for loop.**

***Program:***

```
#include<iostream.h>
#include<conio.h>
void main()
{
int i=1,j=1,k=1;
clrscr( );
for(i=1;i<=3;i++) // 1st digit
{
for (j=1;j<=3;j++) // 2nd digit
{
for (k=1;k<=3;k++) // 3 rd digit
cout<<"\t" << i << j << k ;
}
}
cout<<"Press any key to exit.";
getch();
}
```

**OUTPUT:**

Display all combinations formed by using triplet 1,2 and 3.
press any key to exit.

**Problem 247. According to a study, the approximate level of intelligence of a person can be calculated using the following formula :**
**i=2+(y+0.5x)**
**Write a C++ program, which will produce a table of values of !, y and x, where y varies from 1 to 6, and, for each value of y, x varies from 5 .5 to 12.5 in steps of 0.5**

***Program:***

```
#include<iostream.h>
#include <conio. h>
void main()
{
int y,n = 0 ; // n is a line counter
float i, x ;
clrscr ( ) ;
for(y=1;y<=6;y++)
{
for(x=5.5;x<=12.5;x+=0. 5)
```

```
{
i=2+(y+0.5*x);
cout<<"\ny = "<<y<<" x = "<<x<<"i = "<<i;
n++ ;
if(n>=24) // Wait after printing 25 lines
{
cout<<"Press any key to continue.";
getch();
n = 0; // Reset Line counter to 0
clrscr(); // clear screen
}
}
}
cout<<"\nPress any key to exit.";
getch();
}
```

**Problem 248. Write a C++ program to oroduce the following output**

```
ABCDEFGFEDCBA
ABCDEF FEDCBA
ABCDE   EDCBA
ABCD     DCBA
ABC       CBA
AB         BA
A           A
```

***Program:***

```
#include<iostream.h>
#include<conio.h>
void main()
{
int i= 1, x=71, blanks = 0, j, val ,k ;
clrscr() ;
while (i<=7)
{
j = 65 ;
val = x ;
while(j<=val)
{
cout<<j ;
j++ ;
}
if(i==1)
val-- ;
k=1;
while(k<=blanks)
{
cout<<" ";
k++ ;
}
blanks = 2 * i - 1 ;
while(val>=65)
{
cout<<val;
val--;
}
cout<<"\n";
x--;
i++;
}
cout<<"\nPress any key to exit.";
getch();
}
```

**Problem 249. Write a C++ program to print the multiplication table of the number entered by the user. The table should get displayed in the following form.**

**29 * 1 = 29**

**29 * 2 = 58**

***Program:***

```
#include<iostream.h>
#include<conio.h>
void main()
{
int i,num;
clrscr( ) ;
cout<<"Enter the number:";
cin>>num;
for(i=1;i<=10;i++)
cout<<"\n"<<num<<"*"<<i<<"="<< num * i ;
cout<<"\nPress any key to exit.";
getch();
}
```

**Problem 250. Write a C++ program to produce the following output:**

**1**

**2 3**

**4 5 6**

**7 8 9 10**

***Program:***

```
#include<iostream.h>
#include<conio.h>
void main()
{
int i,j,k,l,sp;
sp = 20 ;
for(i=1,k=1;i<5;i++)
{
for(l=1;l<=sp;l++)
cout<<" ";
```

```
sp -= 2;
for(j=1;j<=i;j++,k++)
{
cout<<k;
}
cout<<"\n";
}
cout<<"\nPress any key to exit.";
getch();
}
```

**Problem 251. Write a C++ program to produce the following output:**
**1**
**1 1**
**1 2 1**
**1 3 3 1**
**1 4 6 4 1**

***Program:***

```
#include<iostream.h>
#include<conio.h>
void main()
{
int i, j, k, t, f1, f2, f3, z, sp ;
sp=20 ;
clrscr() ;
for(i=0;i<=4;i++)
{
for(k=0;k<sp-i;k++)
cout<<" ";
sp -= 2 ;
for(j=0;j<=i;j++)
{
f1=f2=f3=1;
t=i;
while(t!=0)
{
f1 = f1 * t ;
t-- ;
}
t=j ;
while(t!=0)
{
f2 = f2 * t ;
t--;
}
t=i-j;
while(t!=0)
{
f3 = f3 * t ;
t-- ;
}
z = f1/(f2*f3);
cout<<z;
}
cout<<"\n";
}
cout<<"\nPress any key to exit.";
getch ( ) ;
}
```

**Problem 252. A machine is purchased which will produce earning of Rs. 1000 per year while it lasts. The machine costs Rs. 6000 and will have a salvage value of Rs. 2000 when it is condemned. If 12 percent per annum can be earned on alternate investments what would be the minimum life of the machine to make it a more attractive investment compared to alternative investment?**

***Program:***

```
#include<iostream.h>
#include<conio.h>
void main()
{
int year = 0,i_cost=6000,profit = 1000;
int s_cost;
float t1,t2,interest;
int i ;
clrscr();
t2 = i_cost ;
while(1)
{
year++ ;
t1 = i_cost + profit * year ;
interest = t2 * 0.12 ;
t2 = t2 + interest ;
cout<<"\n"<<"t1 = "<<t1<<"\t t2 = "<<t2 -
interest<<"+"<<interest<<" = "<<t2 ;
if ( t2 > t1 )
{
year-- ;
break ;
}
}
cout<<"\nMinimum life of the Machine is
"<<year<< "Years.";
cout<<"\nPress any key to exit.";
getch ( ) ;
}
```

**Problem 253. When interest compounds q times**

**per year at an annual rate of r % for n years, the principle p compounds to an amount a as per the following formula**
**a = p ( 1 + r / q )nq**
**Write a C++ program to read 10 sets of p, r, n & q and calculate**

***Program:***

```
#include<iostream.h>
#include<conio.h>
void main()
{
float q, r, n, p, a ;
int i ;
for (i=0;i<1;i++)
{
clrscr();
cout<<"Enter the principal amount:";
cin>>p;
cout<<"Enter the rate of interest:";
cin>>r;
cout<<"Enter the number of years:";
cin>>n;
cout<<"Enter the compounding period:";
cin>>p;
a = p + pow ( ( 1 + ( r / q ) ) , ( n / q ) ) ;
cout<<"\n\nTotal amount = "<<a ;
}
cout<<"\nPress any key to exit.";
getch();
}
```

**Problem 254 The natural logarithm can be approximated by the following series.**
**x-1 + 1 x - 1 2 + 1 x - 1 3 + 1 x - 1 4 + ..**
**x 2 x 2 x 2 x**
**If x is input through the keyboard, write a C++ program to calculate the sum of first seven terms of this series**

***Program:***

```
#include<iostream.h>
#include<conio.h>
void main()
{
int x,i;
float result=0;
clrscr();
cout<<"\nEnter the value of x: ";
cin>>x;
for(i=1;i<=7;i++)
{
if(i==1)
result = result + pow ( ( x - 1.0 ) / x, i ) ;
else
result = result + ( 1.0 / 2 ) * pow ( ( x - 1.0 ) / x, i )
;
}
cout<<"\nLog "<<x<<" = "<<result ;
cout<<"\nPress any key to exit.";
getch ( ) ;
}
```

**Problem 255. Write a C++ program to print n prime numbers.**

***Program:***

```
#include<iostream.h>
#include<conio.h>
void main()
{
int p,q,a,n,c=0;
cout<<"\n Specify the numbers:";
cin>>n;
for(p=2;p<=10000;p++)
{
a=0;
for(q=2;q<=p/2;q++)
{
if(p%q==0)
{
a=1;
break;
}
}
if(a==0)
{
c++;
if(c<=n)
cout<<"\t"<<p;
}
}
getch();
}
```

**Problem 256. Write a C++ program for printing 'powers of 2' table fro power 0 to 10(+ve and -ve).**

***Program:***

```
#include<iostream.h>
#include<conio.h>
void main()
{
long int pw;
int n;
```

```
double t;
cout<<"------------------\n";
cout<<"2 to power n n 2 to power-n\n);
cout<<"------------------\n";
pw=1;
for(n=0;n<11;++n)
{
if(n==0)
pw=1;
else
pw=pw*2;
t=1.0/(double)pw;
cout<<pw<<n<<t;
}
cout<<"------------------\n";
}
```

**OUTPUT:**

```
------------------------------------------------
2 to power n n 2 to power -n
------------------------------------------------
1       0     1.00000000000
2       1     0.50000000000
4       2     0.250000000000
8       3     0.125000000000
16      4     0.062500000000
32      5     0.031250000000
64      6     0.015625000000
128     7     0.007812500000
256     8     0.003906250000
512     9     0.001953125000
1024    10    0.000976562500
--------------------------------------------------------
```

**Problem 257. Write a C++ program to sort a list and find the median.**

***Program:***

```
#include<iostream.h>
#include<conio.h>
#define N 10
void main()
{
int p,q,n;
float median,a[N],t;
cout<<"Specify the number of elements:\n";
cin>>n;
cout<<"Enter "<<n<<"values: \n";
for(p=1;p<=n;p++)
cin>>a[p];
for(p=1;p<=n-1;p++)
{
for(q=1;q<=n-p;q++)
{
if(a[q]<=a[q+1])
{
t=a[q];
a[q]=a[q+1];
a[q+1]=t;
}
else
continue;
}
}
if(n%2==0)
median=(a[n/2]+a[n/2+1])/2.0;
else
median=a[n/2+1];
for(p=1;p<=n;p++)
cout<<a[p];
cout<<"\n\nMedian = "<<median<<"\n";
getch();
}
```

**OUTPUT:**

```
Specify the number of elements:
4
Enter 4 values:
5 7 2
7.000000 5.000000 2.000000
Median =
```

**Problem 258. Write a C++ program to find standard deviation.**

***Program:***

```
#include<iostream.h>
#include<conio.h>
#include<math.h>
#define MAXSIZE 100
void main()
{
int i,n;
float
val[MAXSIZE],dev,sum,sumsqr,mean,variance,std
dev;
sum=sumsqr=n=0;
cout<<"Input values:input-1 to end\n";
for(i=1;i<MAXSIZE;i++)
{
cin>>val[i];
if(val[i]==-1)
break;
sum+=val[i];
n+=1;
}
```

```
mean=sum/(float)n;
for(i=1;i<=n;i++)
{
dev=val[i]-mean;
sumsqr+=dev*dev;
}
variance=sumsqr/(float)n;
stddev=sqrt(variance);
cout<<"\nNumber of items:"<<n<<"\n";
cout<<"\nMean:"<<mean<<"\n";
cout<<"Standard deviation:"<<stddev<<"\n";
getch();
}
```

**Problem 259. Write a C++ program for multiple choice test evaluation.**

***Program:***

```
#include<iostream.h>
#include<conio.h>
#define STUD 3
#define ITEMS 25
void main()
{
char k[ITEMS+1],q[ITEMS+1];
int c,i,st,n,
corr[ITEMS+1];
cout<<"Input key to items\n";
for(i=0;i<ITEMS;i++)
cin>>k[i];
cin>>k[i];
k[i]='\0';
for(st=1;st<=STUD;st++)
{
c=0;
cout<<"\n";
cout<<"Input response of student-"<<st<<"\n";
for(i=0;i<ITEM;i++)
cin>>q[i];
cin>>q[i];
q[i]='\0';
for(i=0;i<ITEM;i++)
corr[i]=0;
for(i=0;i<ITEM;i++)
if(q[i]==k[i])
{
c=c+1;
corr[i]=1;
}
cout<<"\n";
cout<<"Student-"<<st<<"\n";
cout<<"Score is "<<c<<"out of "<<ITEMS<<"\n";
cout<<"Response to the items below are wrong\n";
n=0;
for(i=0;i<ITEMS;i++)
if(corr[i]==0)
{
cout<<i+1;
n=n+1;
}
if(n==0)
cout<<"NIL\n";
cout<<"\n";
}
getch();
}
```

**Problem 260. Write a C++ program using do-while to print table.**

***Program:***

```
#include<iostream.h>
#include<conio.h>
void main()
{
int p,=1,q=1,n,v;
cin>>n;
cout<<"\n Multiplication Table:\n";
do
{
do
{v=p*q;
cout<<"\t"<<v;
q++;
}
while(q<=n);
cout<<"\n";
q=1;
p++;
}
while(p<=n);
getch();
}
```

**Problem 261. Write a C++ program to check if the number is circular or not.**

***Program:***

```
#include<iostream.h>
#include<conio.h>
#include<math.h>
void main()
{
long int n,res,c,rem;
```

```
long int count=0,x,y;
cout<<"\n Specify the number:";
cin>>n;
x=n;
rem=x%10;
x=x/10;
y=n;
while(y>0)
{
y=y/10;
count++;
}
res=n*rem;
c=rem*pow(10,count-1)+x;
if(c==res)
cout<<"\n Its a circular number:";
getch();
}
```

**Problem 262. Write a C++ program to find average of different lists of numbers.**

***Program:***

```
#include<iostream.h>
#include<conio.h>
void main()
{
int p,q,total,lp,n;
float avg,a;
cout<<"\n Specify the number of lists:";
cin>>lp;
for(p=1;p<=lp;++p)
{
total=0;
cout<<"\n The list number "<<p<<" numbers:";
cin>>n;
for(q=1;q<=n;q++)
{
cout<<"a=";
cin>>a;
total+=a;
}
avg=total/n;
cout<<"An average is:"<<avg<<"\n";
}
getch();
}
```

**Problem 263. Write a C++ program using comma operator in for loop to check if the string is palindrome or not.**

***Program:***

```
#include<iostream.h>
#include<conio.h>
void main()
{
int p,q,l,f=0;
char s[30];
cin>>s;
l=strlen(s);
for(p=0;q=l-1;p<=l/2;p++,q--)
{
if(s[p]==s[q])
continue;
else
f=1;
}
if (f==1)
cout<<"\n Its not a palindrome string";
else
cout<<"\n Its a palindrome string";
getch();
}
```

**Problem 264. Write a C++ program to find the number of 500, 100, 50, 20, 10, 5, 2, 1 - RUPEE.C**

***Program:***

```
#include<iostream.h>
#include<conio.h>
void main()
{
int rs, a, b, c, d, e, f, g, h ;
clrscr() ;
cout<<"Enter the amount in Rupees : ";
cin>>rs;
while(rs >= 500)
{
a = rs / 500 ;
cout<<"\nThe no. of five hundreds are : "<< a ;
break ;
}
while(rs >= 100)
{
b = rs / 100 ;
cout<<"\nThe no. of hundreds are : "<< b ;
break ;
}
while(rs >= 50)
{
c = rs / 50 ;
cout<<"\nThe no. of fifties are : "<< c;
break ;
```

```
}
while(rs >= 20)
{
d = rs / 20 ;
cout<<"\nThe no. of twenties are : "<< d ;
break ;
}
while(rs >= 10)
{
e = rs / 10 ;
cout<<"\nThe no. of tens are : "<< e ;
break ;
}
while(rs >= 5)
{
f = rs / 5 ;
cout<<"\nThe no. of fives are : "<< f ;
break ;
}
while(rs >= 2)
{
g = rs / 2 ;
cout<<"\nThe no. of Twos are : "<< g ;
break ;
}
while(rs >= 1)
{
h = rs / 1 ;
cout<<"\nThe no. of ones are : "<< h ;
break ;
}
getch() ;
}
```

**OUTPUT:**

Enter the amount in Rupees : 100
The no. of five hundreds are : 0
The no. of hundreds are : 1
The no. of fifties are : 2
The no. of twenties are : 5
The no. of tens are : 10
The no. of fives are : 20
The no. of Twos are : 50
The no. of ones are : 100

**Problem 265. Write a C++ program for Castle Building.**

***Program:***

```
#include<iostream.h>
#include<conio.h>
void main()
{
int i,j,p,n,l,m,u;
clrscr();
printf("please enter the number as long as u want
ur castle size 2 be!!but.... remember greater that
4");
cin>>n;
for(i=0;i<n;i++)
{
cout<<" ";
for(j=0;j<n-i-1;j++)
{
cout<<" ";
}
for(p=1;p<=2*i+1;p++)
{
cout<<"*";
}
}
for(l=0;l<=n-1;l++)
{
cout<<" ";
cout<<"*";
for(m=0;m<2*n-5;m++)
{
cout<<" ";
}
cout<<"*";
if(l==n-1)
{
cout<<" ";
cout<<"*";
for(u=0;u<2*n-4;u++)
{
cout<<"*";
}
}
}
getch();
}
```

# CHAPTER 5

# ARRAY

## ARRAY AS DATA TYPE:

## ARRAY CHAR:

**Problem 1. Write a C++ program to compute the total of a list of numbers.**

***Program:***

```
#include<iostream.h>
#include<conio.h>
void main()
{
char line[100];
int total;
int item;
total = 0;
while (1)
{
cout<<"Enter # to add \n";
cout<<" or 0 to stop:";
fgets(line, sizeof(line), stdin);
cin>>line>>item;
if (item == 0)
break;
total += item;
cout<<"Total: "<<total<<"\n";
}
cout<<"Final total <<total<<"\n";
getch();
}
```

**OUTPUT:**

```
Enter # to add
or 0 to stop:30
Total:30
Enter # to add
or 0 to stop:30
Enter # to add
or 0 to stop:0
Final total:60
```

**Problem 2. Write a C++ program to make Tic-Tac-Toe.**

***Program:***

```
#include<iostream.h>
#include<conio.h>
void main()
{
int i = 0; // Loop counter
int player = 0; // Player number - 1 or 2
int go = 0; // Square selection number for turn
int row = 0; // Row index for a square
int column = 0; // Column index for a square
int line = 0; // Row or column index in checking
loop
int winner = 0; // The winning player
char board[3][3] = { // The board
{'1','2','3'}, // Initial values are reference numbers
{'4','5','6'}, // used to select a vacant square for
{'7','8','9'} // a turn
};
// The void main game loop. The game continues
for up to 9 turns
// As long as there is no winner
for( i = 0; i<9 && winner==0; i++)
{
// Display the board
cout<<"\n\n";
cout<<board[0][0]<<"|"<< board[0][1]<<"|"<<
board[0][2]<<"\n";
cout<<"---+---+---\n";
cout<<board[1][0]<<"|"<< board[1][1]<<"|"<<
board[1][2]<<"\n";
cout<<"---+---+---\n";
cout<<board[2][0]<<"|"<< board[2][1]<<"|"<<
board[2][2]<<"\n";
player = i%2 + 1; // Select player
// Get valid player square selection
do
{
cout<<"\nPlayer "<<player<<" please enter the
number of the square "
"where you want to place your
"<<(player==1)?'X':'O';
cin>>go;
row = --go/3; // Get row index of square
column = go%3; // Get column index of square
}while(go<0 || go>9 || board[row][column]>'9');
board[row][column] = (player == 1) ? 'X' : 'O'; //
```

```
Insert player symbol
// Check for a winning line - diagonals first
if((board[0][0] == board[1][1] && board[0][0] ==
board[2][2]) || (board[0][2] == board[1][1] &&
board[0][2] == board[2][0]))
winner = player;
else
// Check rows and columns for a winning line
for(line = 0; line <= 2; line ++)
if((board[line][0] == board[line][1] &&
board[line][0] == board[line][2])|| (board[0][line] ==
board[1][line] && board[0][line] == board[2][line]))
winner = player;
}
// Game is over so display the final board
cout<<"\n\n";
cout<<board[0][0]<<"|"<< board[0][1]<<"|"<<
board[0][2]<<"\n";
cout<<"---+---+---\n";
cout<<board[1][0]<<"|"<< board[1][1]<<"|"<<
board[1][2]<<"\n";
cout<<"---+---+---\n";
cout<<board[2][0]<<"|"<< board[2][1]<<"|"<<
board[2][2]<<"\n";
if(winner == 0)
cout<<"\nHow boring, it is a draw\n";
else
cout<<"\nCongratulations, player
"<<winner<<"YOU ARE THE WINNER!\n";
getch();
}
```

**OUTPUT:**

```
1|2|3
---+---+---
4|5|6
---+---+---
7|8|9
Player 1, please enter the number of the square
where you want to place your X:1
X|2|3
---+---+---
4|5|6
---+---+---
7|8|9
Player 2, please enter the number of the square
where you want to place your 0:6
X|2|3
---+---+---
4|5|0
---+---+---
7|8|9
Player 1, please enter the number of the square
where you want to place your X:4
X|2|3
---+---+---
X|5|0
---+---+---
7|8|9
Player 2, please enter the number of the square
where you want to place your 0:5
X|2|3
---+---+---
X|0|0
---+---+---
7|8|9
Player 1, please enter the number of the square
where you want to place your X:7
X|2|3
---+---+---
X|0|0
---+---+---
X|8|9
Congratulations, player 1, YOU ARE THE
WINNER!
```

**Problem 3. Write a C++ program to output the address of char array.**

***Program:***

```
#include<iostream.h>
#include<conio.h>
void main ()
{
char * s1 = "aaa";
char s2[] = "vvv";
clrscr();
cout<<s1<<s1<<"\n";
cout<<s2<<s2<<"\n";
s1 = s2;
cout<<s1<<s1<<"\n";
cout<<s2<<s2<<"\n";
getch();
}
```

**OUTPUT:**

```
aaa
vvv
vvv
vvv
```

**Problem 4. Write a C++ program using for loop a char array.**

***Program:***

```
#include<iostream.h>
```

```
#include<conio.h>
void main()
{
char str[80];
int i, spaces;
cout<<"Enter a string:";
gets(str);
spaces = 0;
for( i = 0; str [ i ]; i++)
if(str[i]==' ')
spaces++;
cout<<"Number of spaces: "<< spaces;
getch();
}
```

**OUTPUT:**

Enter a string:Khalsa College Amritsar
Number of spaces:2

**Problem 5.Write a C++ program to make a simple dictionary.**

***Program:***

```
#include<iostream.h>
#include<conio.h>
#include<string.h>
#include<ctype.h>
void main()
{
char *dic[][40] = {
"A", "AA",
"B", "BB",
"C", "CC",
"D", "DD",
"", ""
};
char word[80]="A", ch;
char **p;
clrscr();
p = (char **)dic;
do
{
if(!strcmp(*p, word))
{
puts("is";
puts(*(p+1));
break;
}
if(!strcmp(*p, word))
{
break;
}
p = p + 2;
}
while(*p);
if(!*p)
{
puts("Word not in dictionary.";
}
getch();
}
```

**OUTPUT:**

is
AA

**Problem 6. Write a C++ program using for loop a char array using pointer.**

***Program:***

```
#include<iostream.h>
#include<conio.h>
void main()
{
char str[] = "Pointers are fun and hard";
char *p;
int i;
p = str;
for(i = 0; p[ i ]; i++)
cout<<p[ i ];
getch();
}
```

**OUTPUT:**

Pointers are fun and hard

**Problem 7. Write a C++ program using char array: pointer and loop.**

***Program:***

```
#include<iostream.h>
#include<conio.h>
#include<string.h>
char *p[][2] =
{
"1", "red",
"2", "yellow",
"3", "red",
"4", "green",
"5", "yellow",
"6", "red",
"7", "red",
"", "" // terminate the table with null strings
}:
void main()
{
```

```
int i;
char value[80];
cout<<"Enter value: ";
gets(value);
for(i = 0; *p[i][0]; i++)
{
if(!strcmp(value,p[i][0]))
cout<<value<<"is"<< p[i][1]<<"\n";
}
getch();
}
```

**OUTPUT:**

Enter value:4
4 is green

**Problem 8. Write a C++ program to assign a value to an element inside a char array.**

***Program:***

```
#include<iostream.h>
#include<conio.h>
void main()
{
char str[80];
clrscr();
*( str + 3) = 'o';
cout<<*(str+3);
getch();
}
```

**OUTPUT:**

o

**Problem 9. Write a C++ program using char array: assign value and loop.**

***Program:***

```
#include<iostream.h>
#include<conio.h>
void main()
{
char str[80];
int i;
cout<<"Enter message (less than 80 characters):";
for(i = 0; i < 80; i++)
{
str[ i ] = getche();
if(str[ i ]=='\r')
break;
}
cout<<"\n";
for(i = 0; str[ i ] != '\r'; i++)
cout<<str[i]+1;
getch();
}
```

**OUTPUT:**

Enter message (less than 80 characters):College
Dpmmfhf

**Problem 10. Write a C++ program using loop and output a char array.**

***Program:***

```
#include<iostream.h>
#include<conio.h>
void main()
{
char str[80];
int i;
cout<<"Enter a string (less than 80 chars): ";
gets(str);
for(i = 0; str[i]; i++)
cout<<str[i];
getch();
}
```

**OUTPUT:**

Enter a string (less than 80 chars):Amritsar
Amritsar

**Problem 11. Write a C++ program to show how array addressing and pointer arithmetic are linked.**

***Program:***

```
#include<iostream.h>
#include<conio.h>
#define ARRAY_SIZE 5
void main()
{
char array[ARRAY_SIZE] = "12345";
int index;
clrscr();
for (index = 0; index < ARRAY_SIZE; ++index)
{
cout<<"&array[index]=0x"<<&array[index]<<"(ar
ray+index)=0x"<<(array+index)<<"array[index]=0
x"<<array[index]<<"\n";
}
getch();
}
```

**OUTPUT:**

&array[index]=0xFFF0 (array+index)=0xFFF0
array[index]=0x31
&array[index]=0xFFF1 (array+index)=0xFFF1
array[index]=0x32
&array[index]=0xFFF2 (array+index)=0xFFF2
array[index]=0x33

```
&array[index]=0xFFF3 (array+index)=0xFFF3
array[index]=0x34
&array[index]=0xFFF4 (array+index)=0xFFF4
array[index]=0x35
```

**Problem 12. Write a C++ program to show how bitmapped graphics may be used.**

***Program:***

```
#include<iostream.h>
#include<conio.h>
#define X_SIZE 40
#define Y_SIZE 60
char graphics[X_SIZE / 8][Y_SIZE];
void print_graphics(void);
#define SET_BIT(x,y) graphics[(x)/8][y] |= (0x80
>>((x)%8))
void main()
{
int loc;
int x;
int y;
for (y = 0; y < Y_SIZE; ++y)
{
for (x = 0; x < X_SIZE / 8; ++x)
{
graphics[x][y] = '.';
}
}
for (loc = 0; loc < X_SIZE; ++loc)
SET_BIT(loc, loc);
print_graphics();
getch();
}
void print_graphics(void)
{
int x;
int y;
int bit;
for (y = 0; y < Y_SIZE; ++y)
{
for (x = 0; x < X_SIZE / 8; ++x)
{
for (bit = 0x80; bit > 0; bit = (bit >> 1))
{
if ((graphics[x][y] & bit) != 0)
{
cout<<"*";
}
else
{
cout<<graphics[x][y];
}
}
}
cout<<"\n";
}
}
```

## ARRAY DOUBLE:

**Problem 13. Write a C++ program summing reciprocals of five values.**

***Program:***

```
#include<iostream.h>
#include<conio.h>
void main()
{
double data[5];
double sum = 0.0;
int i = 0;
cout<<"Enter five values separated by spaces:\n";
for(i = 0 ; i<5 ; i++)
cin>>data[i];
cout<<"\nYou entered the values:\n";
for(i = 0 ; i<5 ; i++)
cout.width(10.2);
cout<< data[i];
cout<<"\n";
for(i = 0 ; i<5 ; i++)
{
sum += 1.0/data[i];
if(i>0)
cout<<" + ";
cout<<"1/";
cout.width(.2)
cout<< data[i];
}
cout<<sum<<" \n";
getch();
}
```

**OUTPUT:**

```
Enter five values separated by spaces:
1 2 3 4 5
You entered the values:
1.00     2.00     3.00     4.00     5.00
1/1.00 + 1/2.00 + 1/3.00 + 1/4.00 +
1/5.00=2.283333
```

**Problem 14. Write a C++ program summing 100 data values.**

***Program:***

```
#include<iostream.h>
#include<conio.h>
void main()
{
double data[100];
double sum = 0.0;
int i = 0;
double sign = 1.0;
clrscr();
cout<<"\nYou entered the values:\n";
for(i = 1 ; i<=100 ; i++)
{
data[i-1] = 1.0/(2*i*(2*i+1)*(2*i+2));
}
for(i = 0 ; i<100 ; i++)
{
sum += sign*data[i];
sign = -sign;
}
cout<<"\nResult is "<< 4.0*sum+3<<"\n";
getch();
}
```

**OUTPUT:**

You entered the values:
Result is 3.1121

## ARRAY FLOAT:

**Problem 15. Write a C++ program handling monetary values as integers.**

***Program:***

```
#include<iostream.h>
#include<conio.h>
void main()
{
float amounts[5];
long dollars[5];
long cents[5];
int i = 0;
cout<<"Enter five monetary values separated by spaces:\n";
for(i = 0 ; i<5 ; i++)
cin>>amounts[i];
for(i = 0 ; i<5 ; i++)
{
dollars[i] = (long)amounts[i];
cents[i] = (long)(100.0*(amounts[i]-dollars[i]));
}
cout<<"\n";
for(i = 0 ; i<5 ; i++)
{
cout<<" $"<<dollars[i]<<".";cout.width(2);cout<<
cents[i];
}
cout<<"\n";
getch();
}
```

**OUTPUT:**

3 4 5 6 7
$3.00 $4.00 $5.00 $6.00 $7.00

## ARRAY STRING:

**Problem 16. Write a C++ program using arrays of strings.**

***Program:***

```
#include<iostream.h>
#include<conio.h>
void main()
{
char str[][40] = { "String in C" , ",Another string in C" };
int count1 = 0;
int count2 = 0;
while (str[0][count1] != '\0')
count1++;
while (str[1][count2] != '\0')
count2++;
if (sizeof str[0] < count1 + count2 + 1)
cout<<"\nYou can't put a quart into a pint pot.";
else
{
count2 = 0;
while ((str[0][count1++] = str[1][count2++]) !=
'\0');
cout<<"\n"<< str[0];
}
getch();
}
```

**OUTPUT:**

String in C,Another string in C

## ARRAY INTEGER:

**Problem 17. Write a C++ program to print out numbers and their doubles.**

***Program:***

```
#include<iostream.h>
#include<conio.h>
```

```
void main()
{
int data[10];
int twice[10];
int index;
clrscr();
for (index = 0; index < 10; ++index)
{
data[index] = index;
twice[index] = index * 2;
cout<<data[index]<<"\t"<<twice[index]<<"\n";
}
getch();
}
```

**OUTPUT:**

```
0    0
1    2
2    4
3    6
4    8
5    10
6    12
7    14
8    16
9    18
```

**Problem 18. Write a C++ program that shows two ways an array can be cleared.**

***Program:***

```
#include<iostream.h>
#include<conio.h>
#define MAX 10
void init_array_1(int data[])
{
int index;
for (index = 0; index < MAX; ++index)
data[index] = 0;
}
void init_array_2(int *data_ptr)
{
int index;
for (index = 0; index < MAX; ++index)
*(data_ptr + index) = 0;
}
void main()
{
int array[MAX];
init_array_1(array);
init_array_1(&array[0]);
init_array_2(array);
getch();
}
```

**Problem 19. Write a C++ program as an example of how to initialize a matrix: loop.**

***Program:***

```
#include<iostream.h>
#include<conio.h>
#define X_SIZE 60
#define Y_SIZE 30
void main()
{
int matrix[X_SIZE][Y_SIZE];
int x,y;
for (x = 0; x < X_SIZE; ++x)
{
for (y = 0; y < Y_SIZE; ++y)
{
matrix[x][y] = -1;
}
}
getch();
}
```

**Problem 20. Write a C++ program for array initialization.**

***Program:***

```
#include<iostream.h>
#include<conio.h>
int array[] = {3, 2, 1, 3, 6, 4, 2, 2, 9, 3};
int index;
void main()
{
index = 0;
while (array[index] != 0)
++index;
cout<<"Number of elements before zero
"<<index<<"\n";
getch();
}
```

**OUTPUT:**

Number of elements before zero 27

**Problem 21. Write a C++ program to define array and use it.**

***Program:***

```
#include<iostream.h>
#include<conio.h>
void main()
{
```

```
int numbers[10];
int count = 10;
long sum = 0L;
float average = 0.0f;
int i = 0;
cout<<"\nEnter the 10 numbers:\n";
for(i = 0; i < count; i ++)
{
cout<<i+1;
cin>>numbers[i];
sum += numbers[i];
}
average = (float)sum/count;
cout<<"Average of the ten numbers entered
is:"<<average<<"\n";
getch();
}
```

**OUTPUT:**

```
Enter the 10 numbers:
1: 1
2: 2
3: 3
4: 4
5: 5
6: 6
7: 7
8: 8
9: 9
10:10
Average of the ten numbers entered is:5.500000
```

**Problem 23. Write a C++ program using array: assign and retrieve value.**

***Program:***

```
#include<iostream.h>
#include<conio.h>
void main()
{
int i = 0;
int a[5];
for(i = 0;i<5;i++)
{
a[i]=i;
}
for( i = 0;i<5;i++)
{
cout<<a[i]<<"\n";
}
getch();
}
```

**OUTPUT:**

```
0
1
2
3
4
```

**Problem 24. Write a C++ program to output array address.**

***Program:***

```
#include<iostream.h>
#include<conio.h>
void print_addr(int a[]);
void main()
{
int a[5];
int i;
for(i = 0;i<5;i++)
{
a[i]=i;
}
print_addr(a);
getch();
}
void print_addr(int a[])
{
int *b;
int i;
b = a;
for(i = 0;i < 5; i++)
{
cout<<"value %d and address is %16lu\n",*b,b);
b++;
}
}
```

**OUTPUT:**

```
value 0 and address is 57868268
value 1 and address is 57868270
value 2 and address is 57868272
value 3 and address is 57868274
value 4 and address is 57868276
```

**Problem 25. Write a C++ program to allocate memory for int array.**

***Program:***

```
#include<iostream.h>
#include<conio.h>
#include<malloc.h>
void main()
{
int *base;
```

```
int i;
int j;
int cnt=0;
int sum=0;
clrscr();
cout<<"how many integers you have to store \n";
cin>>cnt;
base = (int *)malloc(cnt * sizeof(int));
cout<<"the base of allocation is %16lu \n",base);
if(!base)
cout<<"unable to allocate size \n";
else
{
for(j = 0; j < cnt; j++)
*(base+j)=5;
}
sum = 0;
for(j = 0; j < cnt; j++)
sum = sum + *(base+j);
cout<<"total sum is "<<sum<<"\n";
free(base);
cout<<"addr of allocation is %16lu \n",base);
base = (int *)malloc(cnt * sizeof(int));
cout<<"the base of allocation is %16lu \n",base);
base = (int *)malloc(cnt * sizeof(int));
cout<<"the base of allocation is %16lu \n",base);
base = (int *)calloc(10,2);
cout<<"the base of allocation is %16lu \n",base);
getch();
}
```

**OUTPUT:**

```
how many integers you have to store
5
the base of allocation is 97388570
total sum is 25
addr of allocation is 97388570
the base of allocation is 97388570
the base of allocation is 97388584
the base of allocation is 97388598
```

**Problem 26. Write a C++ program to declare a 50-integer array.**

***Program:***

```
#include<iostream.h>
#include<conio.h>
void main()
{
int x[50];
int i;
for(i = 0; i < 50; ++i)
x[ i ] = i;
for(i = 0; i < 50; ++i)
cout<<x[ i ];
getch();
}
```

**OUTPUT:**

```
0 1 2 3 4 5 6 7 8 9 10 11 12 13 14 15 16 17 18 19
20 21 22 23 24 25 26 27 28
29 30 31 32 33 34 35 36 37 38 39 40 41 42 43 44
45 46 47 48 49
```

**Problem 27. Write a C++ program for reference element in array.**

***Program:***

```
#include<iostream.h>
#include<conio.h>
char s[80];
void main()
{
s[3] = 'X';
cout<<s[3];
getch();
}
```

**OUTPUT:**

```
X
```

**Problem 28. Write a C++ program as an example of using an array for two tasks.**

***Program:***

```
#include<iostream.h>
#include<conio.h>
void main()
{
int temps[5];
int i, total;
float average,celsius;
total=0.0;
for( i = 0; i < 5; i++)
{
cout<<"enter temperature #:"<<i;
cin>>temps[i];
}
for(i = 0; i < 5; i++)
total += temps[ i ];
average = total / 5.0;
cout<<"average is:"<<average<<"\n";
puts("fahrenheit \t celsius\n";
for( i = 0; i < 5; i++)
{
celsius = (5.0 / 9.0) * ( temps[ i ] - 32);
```

```
cout<<"\t\t"<< temps[ i ]<< celsius<<"\n";
}
getch();
}
```

**OUTPUT:**

enter temperature #0:10
enter temperature #1:20
enter temperature #2:30
enter temperature #3:40
enter temperature #4:50
average is:30
fahrenheit celsius
10 -12.22
20 -6.67
30 -1.11
40 4.44
50 10.0

**Problem 29. Write a C++ program using int array and its pointer.**

***Program:***

```
#include<iostream.h>
#include<conio.h>
void main()
{
int a[10] = {10, 20, 30, 40, 50, 60, 70, 80, 90, 100};
int *p;
p = a;
cout<< *p<< *(p+1)<< *(p+2)<<"\n";
cout<<"a[0]<< a[1]<< a[2];
getch();
}
```

**OUTPUT:**

10 20 30
10 20 30

**Problem 30. Write a C++ program to use for loop to calculate the square and save it to array.**

***Program:***

```
#include<iostream.h>
#include<conio.h>
void main()
{
int sqrs[ 10 ];
int i;
for(i = 1; i < 11; i++)
sqrs[ i - 1 ] = i * i ;
for(i = 0; i < 10; i++)
cout<<sqrs[ i ];
getch();
}
```

**OUTPUT:**

1 4 9 16 25 36 49 64 81 100

**Problem 31. Write a C++ program to define int array and assign value.**

***Program:***

```
#include<iostream.h>
#include<conio.h>
void main()
{
int a1[10], a2[10];
int i;
for(i = 1; i < 11; i++)
a1[ i - 1 ] = i;
for( i = 0; i < 10; i++)
a2[ i ] = a1[ i ];
for( i = 0; i < 10; i++)
cout<< a2[ i ];
getch();
}
```

**OUTPUT:**

1 2 3 4 5 6 7 8 9 10

# ARRAY 2D:

**Problem 32. Write a C++ program to show two-dimensional arrays.**

***Program:***

```
#include<iostream.h>
#include<conio.h>
void main()
{
char t[3][3] =
{
{'1','2','3'},
{'4','5','6'},
{'7','8','9'}
};
cout<<"value of t[0][0] : \n"<< t[0][0];
cout<<"value of t[0] : \n"<< *t[0];
cout<<"value of t : \n"<< **t;
getch();
}
```

**OUTPUT:**

value of t[0][0] : 1
value of t[0] : 1
value of t : 1

**Problem 33. Write a C++ program getting the values in a two-dimensional array.**

*Program:*

```
#include<iostream.h>
#include<conio.h>
void main()
{
int i = 0;
char t[3][3] =
{
{'1','2','3'},
{'4','5','6'},
{'7','8','9'}
};
for(i = 0; i < 9; i++)
cout<<" t:"<< *(*t + i)<<"\n";
getch();
}
```

**OUTPUT:**

```
t:1
t:2
t:3
t:4
t:5
t:6
t:7
t:8
t:9
```

**Problem 34. Write a C++ program for multi-dimensional arrays and pointers.**

*Program:*

```
#include<iostream.h>
#include<conio.h>
void main()
{
int i = 0;
char t[3][3] =
{
{'1','2','3'},
{'4','5','6'},
{'7','8','9'}
};
char *pointer = *t;
clrscr();
for(i = 0; i < 9; i++)
cout<<" t:"<<*(pointer + i)<<"\n";
getch();
}
```

**OUTPUT:**

```
t:1
t:2
t:3
t:4
t:5
t:6
t:7
t:8
t:9
```

**Problem 35. Write a C++ program for two dimensional int array.**

*Program:*

```
#include<stdio.h>
#include<conio.h>
void main()
{
int t, i, num[3][4];
for(t = 0; t < 3; ++t)
for(i = 0; i < 4; ++i)
num[ t ][ i ] = ( t * 4 ) + i + 1;
for(t = 0; t < 3; ++t)
{
for(i = 0; i < 4; ++i)
cout<<num[ t ][ i ];
cout<<"\n";
}
getch();
}
```

**OUTPUT:**

```
1    2    3    4
5    6    7    8
9    10   11   12
```

**Problem 36. Write a C++ program for a simple student grades database.**

*Program:*

```
#include<iostream.h>
#include<conio.h>
#include<ctype.h>
#include<stdlib.h>
#define CLASSES 3
#define GRADES 2
int grade[CLASSES][GRADES];
void enter_grades(void);
int get_grade(int num);
void disp_grades(int g[][GRADES]);
void main()
{
char ch, str[80];
clrscr();
enter_grades();
```

```
disp_grades(grade);
getch();
}
void enter_grades(void)
{
int t, i;
char s[80];
for(t=0; t<CLASSES; t++)
{
cout<<"Class # "<< t+1<<"\n";
for(i=0; i<GRADES; ++i)
grade[t][i] = atoi(gets(s));
}
}
void disp_grades(int g[][GRADES])
{
int t, i;
for(t=0; t<CLASSES; ++t)
{
cout<<"Class # "<< t+1<<"\n";
for(i=0; i<GRADES; ++i)
cout<<"Student #"<<i+1<<" is "<<g[t][i]<<"\n";
}
}
```

**OUTPUT:**

Class # 1:
1
Class # 2:
2
Class # 3:
3
Class # 1:
Student #1 is 1
Student #2 is 0
Class # 2:
Student #1 is 2
Student #2 is 0
Class # 3:
Student #1 is 3
Student #2 is 0

**Problem 37. Write a C++ program for a very simple text editor.**

***Program:***

```
#include<iostream.h>
#include<conio.h>
#define MAX 100
#define LEN 80
char text[MAX][LEN];
void main()
{
register int t, i, j;
clrscr();
cout<<"Enter an empty line to quit.\n";
for(t = 0; t < MAX; t++)
{
cout<<t;
gets(text[t]);
if(!*text[t])
break;
}
for(i = 0; i < t; i++)
{
for(j = 0; text[ i ][ j ]; j++)
putchar(text[ i ][ j ]);
putchar('\n');
}
getch();
}
```

**OUTPUT:**

do yourself

**Problem 38. Write a C++ program for a simple Tic Tac Toe game.**

***Program:***

```
#include<iostream.h>
#include<conio.h>
#include<stdlib.h>
char matrix[3][3];
char check(void);
void init_matrix(void);
void get_player_move(void);
void get_computer_move(void);
void disp_matrix(void);
void main()
{
char done;
cout<<"This is the game of Tic Tac Toe.\n";
cout<<"You will be playing against the
computer.\n";
done = ' ';
init_matrix();
do
{
disp_matrix();
get_player_move();
done = check();
if(done!= ' ') break;
get_computer_move();
done = check();
}
while(done== ' ');
```

```
if(done=='X') cout<<"You won!\n";
else cout<<"I won!!!!\n";
disp_matrix();
getch();
}
void init_matrix(void)
{
int i, j;
for(i=0; i<3; i++)
for(j=0; j<3; j++) matrix[i][j] = ' ';
}
void get_player_move(void)
{
int x, y;
cout<<"Enter X,Y coordinates for your move: ";
cin>> x;
cin>> y;
x--; y--;
if(matrix[x][y]!= ' ')
{
cout<<"Invalid move, try again.\n";
get_player_move();
}
else matrix[x][y] = 'X';
}
void get_computer_move(void)
{
int i, j;
for(i=0; i<3; i++)
{
for(j=0; j<3; j++)
if(matrix[i][j]==' ') break;
if(matrix[i][j]==' ') break;
}
if(i*j==9)
{
cout<<"draw\n";
exit(0);
}
else
matrix[i][j] = 'O';
}
void disp_matrix(void)
{
int t;
for(t=0; t<3; t++)
{
cout<<matrix[t][0]<<"|"<<matrix[t][1]<<"|"<<
matrix [t][2];
if(t!=2) cout<<"\n---|---|---\n";
}
cout<<"\n";
}
char check(void)
{
int i;
for(i=0; i<3; i++)
if(matrix[i][0]==matrix[i][1] &&
matrix[i][0]==matrix[i][2]) return matrix[i][0];
for(i=0; i<3; i++)
if(matrix[0][i]==matrix[1][i] &&
matrix[0][i]==matrix[2][i]) return matrix[0][i];
if(matrix[0][0]==matrix[1][1] &&
matrix[1][1]==matrix[2][2]) return matrix[0][0];
if(matrix[0][2]==matrix[1][1] &&
matrix[1][1]==matrix[2][0]) return matrix[0][2];
return ' ';
}
```

**Problem 39. Write a C++ program using for loop: two dimensional array.**

***Program:***

```
#include<iostream.h>
#include<conio.h>
void main()
{
int arr[4][5];
int i, j;
for(i = 0; i < 4; i++)
for(j = 0; j < 5; j++)
arr[ i ][ j ] = i * j;
for(i = 0; i < 4; i++) {
for(j = 0; j < 5; j++)
cout<< arr[ i ][ j ];
cout<<"\n";
}
getch();
}
```

**OUTPUT:**

```
0 0 0 0 0
0 1 2 3 4
0 2 4 6 8
0 3 6 9 12
```

**Problem 40. Write a C++ program to find element inside a two dimensional array.**

***Program:***

```
#include<iostream.h>
#include<conio.h>
void main()
```

```
{
int maps[5][2] =
{
1, 14,
2, 28,
3, 19,
4, 8,
5, 15
};
int key;
int i;
cout<<"Enter the key: ";
cin>>key;
for(i = 0; i < 5; i++)
if(key == maps[ i ][ 0 ])
{
cout<<"Key "<<maps[ i ][ 1 ]<<" value pair to
"<<key<<"\n";
break;
}
if(i == 5)
cout<<"value not listed.\n";
getch();
}
```

**OUTPUT:**

```
Enter the key: 3
Key 19 value pair to 3.
```

**Problem 41. Write a C++ program to store value into two dimensional char array and output it.**

***Program:***

```
#include<iostream.h>
#include<conio.h>
void main()
{
char text[5][80];
int i;
for(i = 0; i < 5; i++)
{
cout<<"some string for index "<< i + 1;
gets(text[ i ]);
}
do
{
cout<<"Enter number of string (1 - 5) : ";
cin>>i;
i--;
if(i >= 0 && i < 5)
cout<<text[i]<<"\n";
}
while(i>=0);
getch();
}
```

**OUTPUT:**

```
some string for index 1:abc
some string for index 2:def
some string for index 3:ghi
some string for index 4:jkl
some string for index 5:mno
Enter number of string (1 - 5) : 2
def
Enter number of string (1 - 5) : 4
jkl
```

**Problem 42. Write a C++ program.**

***Program:***

```
#include<iostream.h>
#include<conio.h>
#include<string.h>
char words[][2][40] =
{
"dog", "Hund",
"no", "nein",
"year", "Jahr",
"child", "Kind",
"I", "Ich",
"",""
};
void main()
{
char english[80];
int i;
cout<<"Enter English word: ";
gets(english);
i = 0;
while(strcmp(words[i][0], ""))
{
if(!strcmp(english, words[i][0]))
{
cout<<"German translation: "<< words[i][1];
break;
}
i++;
}
if(!strcmp(words[i][0], ""))
cout<<"Not in dictionary\n";
getch();
}
```

**OUTPUT:**

```
Enter English word: dog
German translation: hund
```

**Problem 43. Write a C++ program for two dimensional char array and for loop.**

***Program:***

```
#include<iostream.h>
#include<conio.h>
void main()
{
char text[][80] =
{
"1", "2", "3",
"4", "5", "6",
"7", ""
};
int i, j;
for(i = 0; text[ i ][ 0 ]; i++)
{
for(j = 0; text[ i ][ j ]; j++)
{
cout<< text[ i ][ j ];
}
cout<<" ";
}
getch();
}
```

**OUTPUT:**

1 2 3 4 5 6 7

**Problem 44. Write a C++ program to input five numbers through the keyboard. Compute & display addition of even numbers and product of odd numbers.**

***Program:*** .

```
#include<iostream.h>
#include<conio.h>
void main()
{
int a=0,m=1,i,num[5];
clrscr();
for(i=0;i<5;i++)
{
cout<<"\n Enter Number [:"<<i+1<<"]";
cin>>num[i];
}
cout<<"\n===================================
=====";
for(i=0;i<5;i++)
{
if(num[i]%2==0)
{
cout<<"\n Even Number:"<<num[i];
a=a+num[i];
}
else
{
cout<<"\n Odd Number:"<<num[i];
m=m*num[i];
}
}
cout<<"\n=================================
=======";
cout<<"\n Addition of Even Numbers:"<<a;
cout<<"\n Product of Odd Numbers:"<<m;
cout<<"\n=================================
=======";
}
```

**OUTPUT:**

```
Enter Number[1]:1
Enter Number[2]:2
Enter Number[3]:3
Enter Number[4]:4
Enter Number[5]:5
========================================
Odd Number :1
Even Number:2
Odd Number :3
Even Number:4
Odd Number :5
========================================
Addition of Even Numbers:6
Product of Odd Numbers :15
```

**Problem 45. Write a C++ program to print string in reverse order.For exampleHELLO would give result as OLLEH.**

***Program:***

```
#include<iostream.h>
#include<conio.h>
void main()
{
static char s[15];/*Static Storage iniializes
variables*/
int i;
clrscr();
puts("Enter a String:";
gets(s);
puts("Reverse String:";
for(i=15;i>=0;i--)
cout<<s[i];
}
```

**OUTPUT:**

```
Enter a String:
HELLO
Reverse String:
OLLEH
```

**Problem 46. Write a C++ program to display the number of days of different months of year.**

***Program:***

```
#include<iostream.h>
#include<conio.h>
#include<process.h>
void main()
{
int
month[12]={31,28,31,30,31,30,31,31,30,31,30,31};
int i;
clrscr();
for(i=0;i<=11;i++)
{
cout<<"\n Month["<<i+1<<"]of a year contains
"<<month[I]<<" days";
cout<<"\n";
}
getche();
}
```

**OUTPUT:**

```
Month[1] of a year contains 31 days
Month[2] of a year contains 28 days
Month[3] of a year contains 31 days
Month[4] of a year contains 30 days
Month[5] of a year contains 31 days
Month[6] of a year contains 30 days
Month[7] of a year contains 31 days
Month[8] of a year contains 31 days
Month[9] of a year contains 30 days
Month[10] of a year contains 31 days
Month[11] of a year contains 30 days
Month[12] of a year contains 31 days
```

**Problem 47. Write a C++ program to Read the matrix of the order up to 3*3 and transpose its elements.**

***Program:***

```
#include<iostream.h>
#include<conio.h>
void main()
{
int mat[3][3];
int i,j;
clrscr();
cout<<"Enter Elements of Matrix\n";
for(i=0;i<3;i++)
{
for(j=0;j<3;j++)
{
cin>>mat[i][j];
}
}
cout<<"Transpose of the matrix\n";
for(i=0;i<3;i++)
{
for(j=0;j<3;j++)
{
cout<<"\t"<<mat[i][j];
}
cout<<"\n";
}
getche();
}
```

**OUTPUT:**

```
Enter Elements of Matrix:
5 8 9
2 5 4
7 5 2
Transpose of the Matrix:
5 2 7
8 5 5
9 4 2
```

**Problem 48. Write a C++ program to convert binary to r=gray codes.**

***Program:***

```
#include<iostream.h>
#include<conio.h>
void main()
{
int bin[16][4],x,y,a=0,c=0;
clrscr();
for(x=0;x<16;x++)
{
y=x;
for(a=0;a<4;a++)
{
bin[x] [a]=y%2;
y=y/2;
}
}
clrscr();
cout<<"\n Binary Bits Gray Bits";
cout<<"\n========= =========";
for(x=0;x<16;x++)
{
```

```
cout<<"\n";
for(y=3;y>=0;y--)
cout.width(3);
cout<<bin[x][y];
cout.width(5);
cout<< bin[x][3];
cout.width(2);
cout<< bin[x][3]^bin[x][2];
cout.width(2);
cout<< bin[x][2]^bin[x][1];
cout.width(2);
cout<<bin[x][1]^bin[x][0];

}
getch();
}
```

**OUTPUT:**

```
Binary Bits    Gray Bits
=========== ===========
0 0 0 0        0 0 0 0
0 0 0 1        0 0 0 1
0 0 1 0        0 0 1 1
0 0 1 1        0 0 1 0
0 1 0 0        0 1 1 0
0 1 0 1        0 1 1 1
0 1 1 1        0 1 0 0
1 0 0 0        1 1 0 0
1 0 0 1        1 1 0 1
1 0 1 0        1 1 1 1
1 0 1 1        1 1 1 0
1 1 0 0        1 0 1 0
1 1 0 1        1 0 1 1
1 1 1 0        1 0 0 1
1 1 1 1        1 0 0 0
```

## Four D:

**Problem 49. Write a C++ program to explain working of four dimensional array.**

***Program:***

```
#include<iostream.h>
#include<conio.h>
void main()
{
int array_4d[2][2][2][2];
int a,b,c,d;
clrscr();
for(a=0;a<2;a++)
for(b=0;b<2;b++)
for(c=0;c<2;c++)
for(d=0;d<2;d++)
array_4d[a][b][c][d]=a+b+c+d;
for(a=0;a<2;a++)
{
cout<<"\n";
for(b=0;b<2;b++)
{
cout<<"\n);
for(c=0;c<2;c++)
{
cout<<"\n";
for(d=0;d<2;d++)
{
cout.width(3);
cout<<array_4d[a][b][c][d];
cout<<"\n";
}
}
}
}
}
```

**OUTPUT:**

```
0 1
1 2
1 2
2 3
1 2
2 3
2 3
3 4
```

## ARRAY PROGRAMMING:

**Problem 50. Write a C++ program to display data with array.**

***Program:***

```
#include<iostream.h>
#include<conio.h>
void main ( )
{
int a[50], i, n;
cout<<"\n How many number you want to enter:";
cin>>n;
cout<<"\n Enter the "<<n<<"different elements in
the array:\n ";
for(i=1; i<=n; i++)
{
cin>>"\t ">>a[i];
}
cout<<"\n Different array elements are: \n "
for(i=1; i<=n; i++)
```

```
{
cout<<"\t", a[i];
}
getche();
}
```

**OUTPUT:**

How many number you want to enter: 5
Enter the 5 different elements in the array:
20 30 40 50 60
Different array elements are:
20 30 40 50 60

**Problem 51. Write a C++ program to find average of N numbers.**

***Program:***

```
#include<iostream.h>
#include<conio.h>
void main ( )
{
int n, a[50], i, s;
float av;
clrscr();
cout<<"\n Enter the value of n:";
cin>>n;
cout<<"\n Enter the different "<<n<<"values";
for (i = 0; i < n; i++)
{
cin>>a[i];
}
s=0;
for(i=0; i<n; i++)
{
s=s+a[i];
}
cout<<"\n Sum is "<<s;
av=(float)s/n;
cout<<"\n Average is "<<av;
getche();
}
```

**OUTPUT:**

Enter the value of n: 5
Enter the different 5 values:
20
30
40
10
50
Sum is 150
Average is 30.0

**Problem 52. Write a C++ program to traverse a matrix i.e. read and write a matrix.**

***Program:***

```
#include<iostream.h>
#include<conio.h>
void main()
{
int i, j, a[10][10], n, m;
clrscr();
cout<<"\n Enter the number of rows and columns of matrix: ";
cin>>n>>m;
cout<<"\n Enter the Elements of matrix : ";
for(i=0; i<n; i++)
{
for(j=0;j<m;j++)
{
cin>>a[i][j];
}
}
cout<<"\n The Entered matrix is :\n ";
for(i=0; i<n; i++)
{
for(j=0;j<m;j++)
{
cout.width(6);
cout<<a[i][j];
}
cout<<"\n";
}
getche();
}
```

**OUTPUT:**

Enter the number of rows and columns of matrix: 3
2
Enter the Elements of matrix :
4
5
2
6
1
8
The Entered matrix is:
4 5
2 6
1 8

**Problem 53. Write a C++ program to Add and Subtract two matrices.**

***Program:***

```
#include<iostream.h>
#include<conio.h>
```

```
void main()
{
int i,j,a[10][10],b[10][10],c[10][10],d[10][10],n,m;
clrscr();
cout<<"\n Enter the number of rows and columns of
matrix A and B:";
cin>>n>>m;
cout<<"\n Enter the Elements of matrix A:\n ";
for(i=0; i<n; i++)
{
for(j=0;j<m;j++)
{
cin>>a[i][j];
}
}
cout<<"\n Enter the Elements of matrix B: \n";
for(i=0; i<n; i++)
{
for(j=0;j<m;j++)
{
cin>>b[i][j];
}
}
for(i=0; i<n; i++)
{
for(j=0;j<m;j++)
{
c[i][j]=a[i][j]+b[i][j];
d[i][j]=a[i][j]-b[i][j];
}
}
cout<<"\n The resultant matrix C is :\n ";
for(i=0; i<n; i++)
{
for(j=0;j<m;j++)
{
cout<<c[i][j];
}
cout<<"\n";
}
cout<<"\n The resultant matrix D is: \n ";
for(i=0; i<n; i++)
{
for(j=0;j<m;j++)
{
cout<<d[i][j];
}
cout<<"\n";
}
getche();
}
```

**OUTPUT:**

```
Enter the number of rows and columns of matrix A
and B: 3 2
Enter the Elements of matrix A:
4 4
5 6
4 4
Enter the Elements of matrix B:
3 7
8 1
2 3
The resultant matrix C is :
7     11
13    7
6     7
The resultant matrix D is:
1     -3
-3    5
2     1
```

**Problem 54. Write a C++ program to find percentage of every student in a class having N student.**

***Program:***

```
#include<iostream.h>
#include<conio.h>
#include<dos.h>
void main( )
{
int st[50][5][10], i,j,k,m,n,t,sum;
float per;
clrscr( );
cout<<"\n How many students are in the class:";
cin>>n;
cout<<"\n In how many House test every student
appear:";
cin>>t;
cout<<"\n How many subjects in every House
test:";
cin>>m;
cout<<"\n Enter the Data:";
for(i=1;i<=n;i++)
{
for(j=1;j<=t;j++)
{
for(k=1;k<=m;k++)
{
cin>>st[i][j][k];
}
```

```
}
}
for(i=1;i<=n;i++)
{
for(j=1;j<=t;j++)
{
sum=0;
for(k=1;k<=m;k++)
{
sum=sum+st[i][j][k];
}
per=(float) sum/m;
cout<<"\n Average marks of "<<i<<"dth student in
"<<j<<"dth House test is: "<<per;
}
}
getch( );
}
```

**Problem 55. Write a C++ program to find the smallest number among N numbers.**

***Program:***

```
#include<iostream.h>
#include<dos.h>
#include<conio.h>
void main()
{
int n,x[50],small,i;
cout<<" \n How many Numbers you want to Enter:
";
cin>>n;
cout<<"\n ENTER THE NUMBERS: ";
for(i=0;i<n;i++)
{
cin>>x[i];
}
small=x[0];
for(i=1;i<n;i++)
{
if(x[i] < small)
{
small =x[i];
}
}
cout<<"\n SMALLEST NUMBER IS ="<<small;
sleep(5);
}
```

**OUTPUT:**

```
How many Numbers you want to Enter: 5
ENTER THE NUMBERS:
30
40
10
50
23
SMALLEST NUMBER IS = 10
```

**Problem 56. Write a C++ program to find the biggest number among N numbers.**

***Program:***

```
#include<iostream.h>
#include<dos.h>
#include<conio.h>
void main()
{
int n,x[50],big,i;
cout<<" \n How many Numbers you want to Enter:
";
cin>>n;
cout<<"\n ENTER THE NUMBERS: ";
for(i=0;i<n;i++)
{
cin>>x[i];
}
big=x[0];
for(i=1;i<n;i++)
{
if(big<=x[i])
{
big=x[i];
}
}
cout<<"\n BIGGEST NUMBER IS = "<<big;
sleep(5);
}
```

**OUTPUT:**

```
How many Numbers you want to Enter: 5
ENTER THE NUMBERS:
30
40
10
50
23
BIGGEST NUMBER IS = 50
```

**Problem 57. Write a C++ program to insert an element at the kth position in a list of N elements.**

***Program:***

```
#include<iostream.h>
void main()
{
```

```
int a[20],n,i,j,k,m;
cout<<"\n Enter the array length:";
cin>>n;
cout<<"\n Enter the array elements: ";
for(i=0;i<n;i++)
cin>>a[i];
cout<<"\ Enter kth position: ";
cin>>k;
cout<<"\n Enter the information you want to insert
:";
cin>>m;
for(j=n;j>=k;j--)
{
a[j+1]=a[j];
}
a[j]=m;
n=n+1;
cout<<" \n The new list is :";
for(i=1;i<=n;i++)
{
cout<<"\n"<<a[i];
}
Sleep(10);
}
```

**OUTPUT:**

Enter the array length: 5
Enter the array elements:
66
55
44
33
11
Enter kth position: 5
Enter the information you want to insert 22
The new list is :
66
55
44
33
22
11

**Problem 58. Write a C++ program to Sort an array (list) having N elements using Bubble Sort method.**

***Program:***

```
#include<iostream.h>
#include<conio.h>
void main()
{
int a[10],i,j,n,temp;
clrscr( );
cout<<"\n Enter the number of elements:";
cin>>n;
cout<<"\nEnter the elements:";
for(i=0;i<n;i++)
cin>>a[i];
for(i=0;i<n-1;i++)
{
for(j=0;j<n-i-1;j++)
{
if(a[j]>a[j+1])
{
temp = a[j];
a[j] = a[j+1];
a[j+1] = temp;
}
}
}
cout<<"\nArray after sorting is :";
for(i=0;i<n;i++)
cout<<a[i];
getch();
}
```

**OUTPUT:**

Enter the number of elements: 5
Enter the elements:
40
20
10
50
30
Array after sorting is:
10
20
30
40
50

**Problem 59. Write a C++ program to sort the data using the insertion sort.**

***Program:***

```
#include<iostream.h>
void main()
{
int a[20],i, p, n, t;
clrscr();
cout<<"\n Enter the value of N: ";
cin>>n;
cout<<"\n Enter the array elements: ";
```

```
for(i=1;i<=n;i++)
{
cin>>a[i];
}
a[0]=.001;
for(i=2;i<=n;i++)
{
t=a[i];
p=i-1;
while(t<a[i])
{
a[i+1]=a[i];
p--;
}
a[p+1]=t;
}
cout<<"\ Sorted array is: ";
for(i=1;i<=n;i++)
{
cout<<"\n"<<a[i];
}
getche();
}
```

**OUTPUT:**

```
Enter the value of n: 5
Enter the array elements:
66
77
11
99
22
Sorted array is:
11
22
66
77
99
```

**Problem 60. Write a C++ program to search a number by using LINEAR SEARCH of Numeric data (NUMBERS).**

***Program:***

```
#include<iostream.h>
#include<conio.h>
#include<dos.h>
void main()
{
int c,i,n,b,s[30],s1;
clrscr();
cout<<"\n ENTER HOW MANY NUMBERS YOU
WANT TO ENTER: ";
cin>>n;
cout<<"\n ENTER THE NUMBERS: ";
for(i=1;i<=n;i++)
{
cin>>s[i];
}
clrscr();
cout<<"\n ENTER THE NUMBER YOU WANT
TO SEARCH: ";
cin>>s1;
i=1;
while(i<=n)
{
b=s[i]-s1;
if(b==0)
{
c=i;
break;}
else
{
c=0;
}
i++;
}
if(c==0)
{
cout<<"\n SEARCH UNSUCCESSFUL";
}
else
{
cout<<"\n SEARCH SUCCESSFUL AND
LOCATION IS "<<c;
}
sleep(3);
}
```

**OUTPUT:**

```
ENTER HOW MANY NUMBERS YOU WANT
TO ENTER: 6
ENTER THE NUMBERS
88
66
44
22
55
11
ENTER THE NUMBER YOU WANT TO
SEARCH:
44
SEARCH SUCCESSFUL AND LOCATION IS 3
```

**Problem 61. Write a C++ program to traversing**

**or visiting a list (One dimensional array).**

***Program:***

```
#include<iostream.h>
void main()
{
int la[50],i,n,p;
cout<<"\n How many numbers you want to insert: ";
cin>>n;
cout<<"\n Enter the Numbers:";
for(i=1;i<=n;i++)
{
cin>>la[i];
}
cout<<"\n Traversing process is: ";
for(i=1;i<=n;i++)
{
p=la[i];
cout<<"\n"<<p;
}
getche();
}
```

**OUTPUT:**

```
How many numbers you want to insert:5
Enter the Numbers:
44
22
33
11
55
Traversing process is:
44
22
33
11
55
```

**Problem 62. Write a C++ program to delete an element from the kth position from a list of N array.**

***Program:***

```
#include<iostream.h>
#include<conio.h>
void main()
{
int i,n,la[50],k,item,j;
clrscr();
cout<<" \n How many elements you want to enter: ";
cin>>n;
cout<<"\n Enter the element:";
for(i=1;i<=n;i++)
{
cin>>la[i];
}
cout<<"\n Location where you want to delete: ";
cin>>k;
item=la[k];
cout<<"\n Deleted Value is:"<<item;
for(j=k;j<=n-1;j++)
{
la[j]=la[j+1];
}
n=n-1;
cout<<" The new element list is: ";
for(i=1;i<=n;i++)
{
cout<<"\n"<<la[i];
}
sleep(3);
}
```

**OUTPUT:**

```
How many elements you want to enter: 5
Enter the element:
20
30
32
40
50
Location where you waqt to delete: 3
Deleted Value is: 32
The new element list is:
20
30
40
50
```

**Problem 63. Write a C++ program to show need of array.**

***Program:***

```
#include<iostream.h>
#include<conio.h>
void main()
{
int a;
a=10;
cout<<"\t"<<a;
a=11;
cout<<"\t"<<a;
a=12;
cout<<"\t"<<a;
}
```

**OUTPUT:**

10 11 12

**Problem 64. Write a C++ program for defining array**

***Program:***

```
#include<iostream.h>
#include<conio.h>
void main()
{
int a[2];
int p;
clrscr();
for(p=0;p<2;p++)
{
cout<<"\n Enter any number a:";
cin>>a[p];
}
for(p=0;p<2;p++)
cout<<"\n"<<a[p];
}
```

**OUTPUT:**

Enter any number a:4
Enter any number a:12

**Problem 65. Write a C++ program to print number of days till specific date from beginning of an year.**

***Program:***

```
#include<iostream.h>
#include<conio.h>
void main()
{
int p;
int day,tday,month;
int
d_per_month[12]={31,28,31,30,31,30,31,31,30,31,3
0,31};
cout<<"\n Enter a month from 1(jan)-12(dec):";
cin>>month;
cout<<"\n Enter a day from 1-31:";
cin>>day;
tday=day;
for(p=0;p<month-1;p++)
tday+=d_per_month[p];
cout<<"Total Days are:"<<tday;
}
```

**OUTPUT:**

Enter a month from 1(jan)-12(dec):12
Enter a day from 1-31:4
Total Days are:338

**Problem 66. Write a C++ program to print values of five numbers.**

***Program:***

```
#include<iostream.h>
#include<conio.h>
void main()
{
int p,s[3];
for(p=0;p<3;p++)
{
cout<<"\n Enter any number:";
cin>>s[p];
}
for(p=0;p<3;p++)
cout<<"\n Element s["<<p<<"] is:"<<s[p];
}
```

**OUTPUT:**

Enter any number:9
Enter any number:12
Enter any number:21
Element s[0] is:9
Element s[1] is:12
Element s[2] is:21

**Problem 67. Write a C++ program to find average of numbers & to find its deviation from average.**

***Program:***

```
#include<iostream.h>
#include<conio.h>
void main()
{
int p,n;
float total=0,avg,dev;
float s[100];
cout<<"\nSpecify the number of terms:";
cin>>n;
for(p=0;p<n;p++)
{
cout<<"\n Element s["<<p<<"] =";
cin>>s[p];
total+=s[p];
}
avg=total/n;
cout<<"\n Average is= "<<avg<<"\n";
for(p=0;p<n;p++)
{
dev=s[p]-avg;
cout<<"s["<<p<<"]="<<s[p]<<"dev=
"<<dev<<"\n"
```

```
}
getch();
}
```

**OUTPUT:**

Specify the number of terms:3
Element s[0]=7.5
Element s[1]=2.4
Element s[2]=3.3
Average is:4.400000
s[0]=7.500000 dev=3.100000
s[1]=2.400000 dev=-2.000000
s[2]=3.300000 dev=-1.100000

**Problem 68. Write a C++program to search a number entered using linear search.**

***Program:***

```
#include<iostream.h>
#include<conio.h>
void main()
{
int a[20],p,loc,n,item,c=0;
cout<<"\nSpecify the number of elements:";
cin>>n;
cout<<"\nSpecify the elements:";
for(p=0;p<n;p++)
cin>>a[p];
cout<<"\nSpecify the element to be searched:";
cin>>item;
for(p=0;p<n;p++)
{
if(a[p]==item)
{
loc=p;
cout<<"\n"<<item<<" is present at location
"<<loc+1;
c++;
}
}
if(c!=0)
{
cout<<"\nThe item is present "<<c<<"times";
}
else
cout<<"\n The item is not present";
getch();
}
```

**OUTPUT:**

Specify the number of elements:6
Specify the elements:4 12 26 10 30 12
Specify the element ot be searched:12
12 is present at location 2
12 is present at location 6
The item is present 2 times

**Problem 69. Write a C++ program to search a number entered using binary search.**

***Program:***

```
#include<iostream.h>
#include<conio.h>
void main()
{
int beg,end,item,mid;
int a[20],p,loc=-1,n;
cout<<"\nSpecify the number of elements:";
cin>>n;
cout<<"\nSpecify the elements in sorted
manner:\n";
for(p=0;p<n;p++)
{
cin>>a[p];
}
cout<<"\nSpecify the element to be searched:";
cin>>item;
beg=0;
end=n-1;
while(beg<end)
{
mid=(beg+end)/2;
if(a[mid]==item)
{
loc=mid;
cout<<"\nItem is present at location "<<loc+1;
break;
}
else if(a[mid]>item)
end=mid-1;
else
beg=mid+1;
}
if(loc==-1)
cout<<"\n The item is not present";
getch();
}
```

**OUTPUT:**

Specify the number of elements:4
Specify the elements in sorted manner:
5 12 50 78
Specify the element to be searched:50
Item is present at location 3

**Problem 70. Write a C++ program to enter the numbers & find +ve,-ve and zeros out of them.**

***Program:***

```
#include<iostream.h>
#include<conio.h>
void main()
{
int p,n,cp=0,s[20];
int cn=0,cz=0;
cout<<"\nSpecify the number of elements:";
cin>>n;
cout<<"Specify the elements:\n";
for(p=0;p<n;p++)
cin>>s[p];
for(p=0;p<n;p++)
{
if(s[p]>0)
cp++;
else if(s[p]<0)
cn++;
else
cz++;
}
cout<<"\n "<<cp<<"(+ve) elements are present";
cout<<"\n "<<cn<<"(-ve) elements are present";
cout<<"\n "<<cz<<"(zero) elements are present";
getch();
}
```

**OUTPUT:**

```
Specify the number of elements:5
Specify the elements:
-3
4
0
-2
12
2(+ve) elements are present
2(-ve) elements are present
1(zero) elements are present
```

**Problem 71.Write a C++ program using bubble sort to sort a list.**

***Program:***

```
#include<iostream.h>
#include<conio.h>
void main()
{
int p,q,n,temp;
int s[20];
cout<<"\nSpecify the number of elements:";
cin>>n;
cout<<"\nSpecify the elements:";
for(p=0;p<n;p++)
cin>>s[p];
for(p=0;p<=n-1;p++)
for(q=0;q<=n-p-1;q++)
if(s[q]>s[q+1])
{
temp=s[q];
s[q]=s[q+1];
s[q+1]=temp;
}
cout<<"\nSorted elements are:\n";
for(p=0;p<n;p++)
cout<<"\t"<<s[p];
getch();
}
```

**OUTPUT:**

```
Specify the number of elements:5
Specify the elements:
25 78 12 70 3
Sorted elements are:
3 12 25 70 78
```

**Problem 72. Write a C++ program for conversion of binary number to decimal number.**

***Program:***

```
#include<iostream.h>
#include<conio.h>
#include<math.h>
void main()
{
int c=0,r;
long int bin,n=0;
cout<<"\nSpecify the binary number:";
cin>>bin;
while(bin>0)
{
r=bin%10;
n=n+r*pow(2,c);
c=c+1;
bin=bin/10;
}
cout<<"\n Integer value is "<<n;
getch();
}
```

**OUTPUT:**

```
Specify the binary number: 11010
Integer value is 26
```

**Problem 73. Write a C++ program for**

**conversion of decimal number to binary number.**

***Program:***

```
#include<iostream.h>
#include<conio.h>
void main()
{
long int dec ,bin;
long int p=0,s[20],q;
cout<<"\nSpecify the decimal number:";
cin>>dec;
while(dec>0)
{
s[p]=dec%2;
dec=dec/2;
p=p+1;
}
cout<<"\nThe binary number is:\n";
for(q=p-1;q>=0;q--)
cout<<s[q];
getch();
}
```

**OUTPUT:**

```
Specify the decimal number:4
the binary number is:100
```

**Problem 74. Write a C++ program for deletion of element from specific location in an array.**

***Program:***

```
#include<iostream.h>
#include<conio.h>
void main()
{
int item,loc,p,n;
int s[20],i,d;
cout<<"\nSpecify the number of elements:";
cin>>n;
cout<<"\nSpecify the elements:";
for(p=0;p<n;p++)
cin>>s[p];
cout<<"\nSpecify the element to be deleted:";
cin>>d;
for(i=0;i<n;i++)
{
if(s[i]==d)
loc=i;
}
for(p=loc;p<=n-1;p++)
s[p]=s[p+1];
n=n-1;
cout<<"\n Resulted Array is:";
for(p=0;p<n;p++)
cout<<"\t"<<s[p];
getch();
}
```

**OUTPUT:**

```
Specify the number of elements:4
Specify the elements:54 16 45 42
Specify the element to be deleted:45
Resulted Array is:54	16	42
```

**Problem 75. Write a C++ program for insertion of element in an unsorted list.**

***Program:***

```
#include<iostream.h>
#include<conio.h>
void main()
{
int n,p,q,item,loc;
int s[10];
cout<<"\nSpecify the number of elements:";
cin>>n;
cout<<"\nSpecify the elements:";
for(p=0;p<n;p++)
cin>>s[p];
cout<<"\nSpecify the location:";
cin>>loc;
cout<<"\nSpecify the element to be inserted:";
cin>>item;
for(q=n-1;q>=loc;q--)
{
s[q+1]=s[q];
}
s[loc]=item;
for(p=0;p<=n;p++)
cout<<"\n"<<s[p];
getch();
}
```

**OUTPUT:**

```
Specify the number of elements:5
Specify the elements:54 85 42 38 16
Specify the location:3
Specify the element to be inserted:61
54
85
42
61
38
16
```

**Problem 76. Write a C++ program for insertion**

**of element in an sorted list.**

***Program:***

```
#include<iostream.h>
#include<conio.h>
void main()
{
int n,p,loc,k;
int s[10];
cout<<"\nSpecify the number of elements:";
cin>>n;
cout<<"\nSpecify the elements in sorted manner:";
for(p=0;p<n;p++)
cin>>s[p];
cout<<"\nSpecify the element to be inserted:";
cin>>k;
for(p=0;p<n;p++)
if(s[p]<=k&&s[p+1]>=k)
{
loc=p+1;
break;
}
for(p=n-1;p>=loc;p--)
s[p+1]=s[p];
s[loc]=k;
n=n+1;
for(p=0;p<n;p++)
cout<<"\t"<<&s[p];
}
```

**OUTPUT:**

Specify the number of elements:4
Specify the elements in sorted manner:11 25 35 41
Specify the element to be inserted:52
11 25 35 41 52

**Problem 77. Write a C++ program To display line character by character.**

***Program:***

```
#include<iostream.h>
#include<conio.h>
#include<process.h>
#include<dos.h>
void main()
{
char str[100];
int i;
clrscr();
cout<<"Enter the line (It should be max upto 20
characters):";
cin>>str;
cout<<"\n";
cout<<"Characters of the line u eneterd are:";
for(i=0;str[i]!='\0';i++)
{
if(i>=20)
{
cout<<"You entered line having more then 20
characters\n";
delay(1000);
exit(0);
}
if(str[i]==' ')
{
cout<<" ";
continue;
}
cout<<i+1<<" character is:";
putchar(str[i]);
cout<<"\n";
}
getch();
}
```

**OUTPUT:**

Enter the line (It should be max upto 20 characters):Valuable
Characters of the line u eneterd are:
1 character is:V
2 character is:a
3 character is:l
4 character is:u
5 character is:a
6 character is:b
7 character is:l
8 character is:e

**Problem 78. Write a C++ program to Sort the array in descending order.**

***Program:***

```
#include<iostream.h>
#include<conio.h>
#include<process.h>
#include<dos.h>
void main()
{
int a[10],n,i,j,temp;
clrscr();
cout<<"Enter the size of array:";
cin>>n;
cout<<"\n Enter the elements of array:";
for(i=0;i<n;i++)
{
cin>>a[i];
}
```

```
for(i=0;i<n-1;i++)
{
for(j=0;j<n-i-1;j++)
{
if(a[j]<a[j+1])
{
temp=a[j];
a[j]=a[j+1];
a[j+1]=temp;
}
}
}
cout<<"\n Resultant Array in descending order is:
\n";
for(i=0;i<n;i++)
{
cout<<"\n"<<a[i];
}
getch();
}
```

**OUTPUT:**

Enter the size of array:5
Enter the elements of array: 10 40 50 30 70
Resultant Array in descending order is:
70
50
40
30
10

**Problem 79. Write a C++ program to find the sum of odd subscripted and sum of even subscripted elements of array.**

***Program:***

```
#include<iostream.h>
#include<conio.h>
#include<process.h>
#include<dos.h>
void main()
{
int a[10],n,i,j,temp,sum1=0,sum2=0;
clrscr();
cout<<"Enter the size of array:";
cin>>n;
cout<<"\n Enter the elements of array:";
for(i=0;i<n;i++)
{
cin>>a[i];
}
for(i=0;i<n;i++)
{
if(i%2==0)
{
sum1+=a[i];
}
else
{
sum2+=a[i];
}
}
cout<<"\nSum of odd subscript elements of array
is "<<sum2;
cout<<"\nSum of even subscript elements of array
is "<<sum1;
getch();
}
```

**OUTPUT:**

Enter the size of array:4
Enter the elements of array:10 20 30 40 50
Sum of odd subscript elements of array is 60
Sum of even subscript elements of array is 90

**Problem 80. Write a C++ program to find the smallest and biggest element in array.**

***Program:***

```
#include<iostream.h>
#include<conio.h>
#include<process.h>
#include<dos.h>
void main()
{
int a[10],n,i,j,temp,small,big;
clrscr();
cout<<"Enter the size of array:";
cin>>n;
cout<<"\n Enter the elements of array:";
for(i=0;i<n;i++)
{
cin>>a[i];
}
small=big=a[0];
for(i=1;i<n;i++)
{
if(a[i]>big)
big=a[i];
if(a[i]<small)
small=a[i];
}
cout<<"\n Smallest element in array is "<<small;
cout<<"\n Biggest element in array is "<<big;
```

```
getch();
}
```

**OUTPUT:**

Enter the size of array:5
Enter the elements of array:
30 10 40 80 20
Smallest element in array is 10
Biggest element in array is 80

**Problem 81. Write a C++ program to merge two sorted arrays in descending order.**

***Program:***

```
#include<iostream.h>
#include<conio.h>
#include<process.h>
#include<dos.h>
void main()
{
int a[10],b[10],c[20],n,m,p,i,j,k,temp,small,big;
clrscr();
cout<<"Enter the size of 1st array:";
cin>>n;
cout<<"\n Enter the size of 2nd array:";
cin>>m;
cout<<"\n Enter the elements of 1st array in
descending order";
for(i=0;i<n;i++)
{
cin>>a[i];
}
cout<<"\n Enter the elements of 2nd array in
descending order";
for(j=0;j<m;j++)
{
cin>>b[j];
}
i=j=k=0;
while(i<n&&j<m)
{
if(a[i]>b[j])
{
c[k]=a[i];
k++;
i++;
}
else
{
c[k]=b[j];
k++;
j++;
}
}
while(i<n)
{
c[k]=a[i];
i++;
k++;
}
while(j<m)
{
c[k]=b[j];
j++;
k++;
}
cout<<"\n Resultant Array after merging two
arrays in descending order is \n";
for(i=0;i<k;i++)
{
cout<<"\n"<<c[i];
}
getch();
}
```

**OUTPUT:**

Enter the size of 1st array:3
Enter the size of 2nd array:3
Enter the elements of 1st array in descending order:30 20 10
Enter the elements of 2nd array in descending order:60 50 40
Resultant Array after merging two arrays in descending order is
60
50
40
30
20
10

**Problem 82. Write a C++ program to interchange two arrays.**

***Program:***

```
#include<iostream.h>
#include<conio.h>
#include<process.h>
#include<dos.h>
void main()
{
int a[10],b[10],n,m,i,j,temp;
clrscr();
cout<<"Enter the size of 1st array:";
cin>>n;
cout<<"\n Enter the size of 2nd array:";
```

```
cin>>m;
if(m!=n)
{
cout<<"For Unequal sized array elements can't be
interchanged";
delay(1000);
exit(0);
}
cout<<"\n Enter the elements of 1st array ";
for(i=0;i<n;i++)
{
cin>>a[i];
}
cout<<"\n Enter the elements of 2nd array ";
for(j=0;j<m;j++)
{
cin>>b[j];
}
cout<<"\n Elements of 1st array before
interchanging: are\n ";
for(i=0;i<n;i++)
{
cout<<"\n"<<a[i];
}
cout<<"\n Elements of 2nd array before
interchanging: are\n ";
for(i=0;i<m;i++)
{
cout<<"\n "<<b[i];
}
i=j=0;
while(i<n)
{
temp=a[i];
a[i]=b[i];
b[i]=temp;
i++;
}
cout<<"\n Elements of 1st array after interchanging:
are\n ";
for(i=0;i<n;i++)
{
cout<<a[i];
}
cout<<"\n Elements of 2nd array after interchanging:
are\n ";
for(i=0;i<m;i++)
{
cout<<b[i];
}
getch();
}
```

**OUTPUT:**

Enter the size of 1st array:2
Enter the size of 2nd array:2
Enter the elements of 1st array 30 20 10
Enter the elements of 2nd array 60 50 40
Elements of 1st array before interchanging: are
30
20
10
Elements of 2nd array before interchanging: are
60
50
40
Elements of 1st array after interchanging: are
60 50 10
Elements of 2nd array after interchanging: are
30 20 10

**Problem 83. Write a C++ program to convert decimal number into binary,octal and hexadecimal.**

***Program:***

```
#include<iostream.h>
#include<conio.h>
#include<process.h>
#include<dos.h>
void main()
{
int a[10],n,m,i,temp;
clrscr();
cout<<"Enter the Decimal Number:";
cin>>n;
temp=n;
i=m=0;
while(temp>0)
{
a[i]=temp%2;
temp/=2;
i++;
m++;
}
cout<<"\n Binar Equivalent of "<<n<<" is ";
for(i=m-1;i>=0;i--)
{
cout<<a[i];
}
temp=n;
i=m=0;
```

```
while(temp>0)
{
a[i]=temp%8;
temp/=8;
i++;
m++;
}
cout<<"\n Octal Equivalent of "<<n<<" is ";
for(i=m-1;i>=0;i--)
{
cout<<a[i];
}
temp=n;
i=m=0;
while(temp>0)
{
a[i]=temp%16;
temp/=16;
i++;
m++;
}
cout<<"\n Hexadecimal Equivalent of "<<n<<" is ";
for(i=m-1;i>=0;i--)
{
cout<<a[i];
}
getch();
}
```

**OUTPUT:**

Enter the Decimal Number:12
Binary Equivalent of 12 is 1100
Octal Equivalent of 12 is 14
Hexadecimal Equivalent of 12 is c

**Problem 84. Write a C++ program to reverse the array.**

***Program:***

```
#include<iostream.h>
#include<conio.h>
#include<process.h>
#include<dos.h>
void main()
{
int a[10],n,i,j,temp;
clrscr();
cout<<"Enter the size of array:";
cin>>n;
cout<<"\n Enter the elements of array:";
for(i=0;i<n;i++)
{
cin>>a[i];
}
for(i=0,j=n-1;i<n/2;i++,j--)
{
temp=a[i];
a[i]=a[j];
a[j]=temp;
}
cout<<"\n Elements of array after reversing are:";
for(i=0;i<n;i++)
{
cout<<"\n"<<a[i];
}
getch();
}
```

**OUTPUT:**

Enter the size of array:2
Enter the elements of array: 40 50 60
Elements of array after reversing are: 60 50 40

**Problem 85. Write a C++ program to make equivalent uninary matrix of given matrix.**

***Program:***

```
#include<iostream.h>
#include<conio.h>
#include<process.h>
#include<dos.h>
void main()
{
int a[10][10],m,n,i,j,temp;
clrscr();
cout<<"Enter the size of matrix:";
cin>>m>>n;
if(m!=n)
{
cout<<"\nSorry You cann't make uninary matrix of non-square matrix";
delay(1000);
exit(0);
}
for(i=0;i<m;i++)
{
for(j=0;j<n;j++)
{
if(i==j)
{
a[i][j]=1;
}
else
a[i][j]=0;
}
}
```

```
cout<<"\n Equivalent Uninary Matrix is\n";
for(i=0;i<m;i++)
{
for(j=0;j<n;j++)
{
cout<<"\t"<<a[i][j];
}
cout<<"\n";
}
getch();
}
```

**OUTPUT:**

```
Enter the size of matrix: 3 3
Equivalent Unitary Matrix is
1    0    0
0    1    0
0    0    1
```

**Problem 86. Write a C++ program to convert two dimensional array into single dimensional.**

***Program:***

```
#include<iostream.h>
#include<conio.h>
#include<process.h>
#include<dos.h>
void main()
{
int a[10][10],m,n,i,j,k,b[20];
clrscr();
cout<<"Enter the size of two dimensional array:";
cin>>m>>n;
cout<<"Enter the Elements of two dimensional
array:";
for(i=0;i<m;i++)
{
for(j=0;j<n;j++)
{
cin>>a[i][j];
}
}
k=0;
for(i=0;i<m;i++)
{
for(j=0;j<n;j++)
{
b[k]=a[i][j];
k++;
}
}
cout<<k;
cout<<"Equivalent one dimensional array of\n ";
for(i=0;i<m;i++)
{
for(j=0;j<n;j++)
{
cout<<"\t"<<a[i][j];
}
cout<<"\n";
}
cout<<"\nis\n";
for(i=0;i<k;i++)
{
cout<<b[i];
}
getch();
}
```

**OUTPUT:**

```
Enter the size of two dimensional array:2 2
Enter the Elements of two dimensional array:1 2 3
4
Equivalent one dimensional array of
1    2
3    4
is
1
2
3
4
```

**Problem 87. Write a C++ program to check whether matix is symmetric or not.**

***Program:***

```
#include<iostream.h>
#include<conio.h>
void main()
{
int a[10][10],m,n,i,j,k,b[20][20];
clrscr();
cout<<"Enter the size of two dimensional array:";
cin>>m>>n;
cout<<"Enter the Elements of two dimensional
array:";
for(i=0;i<m;i++)
{
for(j=0;j<n;j++)
{
cin>>a[i][j];
}
}
for(i=0;i<m;i++)
```

```
{
for(j=0;j<n;j++)
{
b[i][j]=a[j][i];
}
}
k=0;
for(i=0;i<m;i++)
{
for(j=0;j<n;j++)
{
if(b[i][j]!=a[i][j])
{
k=1;
break;
}
}
}
if(k!=1)
{
cout<<"Matrix is Symmetric";
}
else
cout<<"Matrix is not Symmetric";
getch();
}
```

**OUTPUT:**

Enter the size of two dimensional array:2 2
Enter the Elements of two dimensional array:1 2 3 4
Matrix is not Symmetric

**Problem 88. Write a C++ program to find the student who topped class.**

***Program:***

```
#include<iostream.h>
#include<conio.h>
#include<process.h>
#include<dos.h>
void main()
{
int a[10],n,i,j,temp;
char str[10][10];
int marks=a[0];
int count=0;
clrscr();
cout<<"Enter the Strength of class :";
cin>>n;
for(i=0;i<n;i++)
{
cout<<"\n Enter the name of student no.
"<<i+1<<"\t";
cin>>str[i];
cout<<"\n Enter the marks of student no.
"<<i+1<<"\t";
cin>>a[i];
}
for(i=0;i<n;i++)
{
if(marks<a[i])
{
marks=a[i];
count=i;
}
}
cout<<"\nStudent who have topped in the class is
"<<str[count]<<"\n";
cout<<str[count]<<"'s marks are "<<marks;
getch();
}
```

**OUTPUT:**

Enter the Strength of class :3
Enter the name of student no. 1 Avtar
Enter the marks of student no. 1 300
Enter the name of student no. 2 Sukhwant
Enter the marks of student no. 2 350
Enter the name of student no. 3 Annie
Enter the marks of student no. 3 450
Student who have topped in the class is Annie
Annie marks are 450

**Problem 89. Write a C++ program to calculate sum of elements above void main diagonal.**

***Program:***

```
#include<iostream.h>
#include<conio.h>
void main()
{
int a[10][10],m,n,i,j,sum;
sum=0;
clrscr();
cout<<"Enter the size of two dimensional array:";
cin>>m>>n;
cout<<"Enter the Elements of two dimensional
array:";
for(i=0;i<m;i++)
{
for(j=0;j<n;j++)
{
cin>>a[i][j];
}
}
for(i=0;i<m;i++)
```

```
{
for(j=0;j<n;j++)
{
if(i>j)
sum=sum+a[i][j];
}
}
cout<<"\nSum of elements above void main diagnol
is "<<sum<<"\n";
getch();
}
```

**OUTPUT:**

Enter the size of two dimensional array:2 2
Enter the Elements of two dimensional array:1 2 3 4
Sum of elements above void main diagnol is %d:3

**Problem 90. Write a C++ program to find the occurences of integers 1 to 10 and placing acc to their occurrences.**

***Program:***

```
#include<iostream.h>
#include<conio.h>
#include<process.h>
#include<dos.h>
void main()
{
int a[20],n,i,j,b[10],temp,temp1,count[10],count1;
clrscr();
cout<<"Enter the Size of array :";
cin>>n;
cout<<"\n Enter the elements of array(1-
10)\t"<<i+1;
for(i=0;i<n;i++)
{
cin>>a[i];
if(a[i]<1||a[i]>10)
{
cout<<"You Entered wromg element It should be
from 1 to 10";
delay(1000);
exit(0);
}
}
for(i=0;i<10;i++)
{
b[i]=i+1;
}
for(j=0;j<10;j++)
{
count1=0;
for(i=0;i<n;i++)
{
if(a[i]==b[j])
count1++;
}
count[j]=count1;
}
for(i=0;i<10;i++)
{
for(j=0;j<10-i-1;j++)
{
if(count[j]<count[j+1])
{
temp=count[j];
count[j]=count[j+1];
count[j+1]=temp;
temp1=b[j];
b[j]=b[j+1];
b[j+1]=temp1;
}
}
}
cout<<"\nNumbers(1 to 10) which occur in array
in terms of their frequency are :\n";
for(i=0;i<n;i++)
{
cout<<"\nNumber: "<<b[i]<<"\t" Frequency:
"<<count[i]<<"\n";
}
getch();
}
```

**OUTPUT:**

Enter the Size of array :4
Enter the elements of array(1-10)          2 6 2 8
Numbers(1 to 10) which occur in array in terms of their frequency are :
Number:2 Frequency:2
Number:6 Frequency:1
Number:8 Frequency:1
Number:1 Frequency:0

**Problem 91. Write a C++ program Two 1-D arrayys A and B are given in ascending order.Write a program to merge them in single array and contains elements of A and B.**

***Program:***

```
#include<iostream.h>
#include<conio.h>
void main()
{
```

```
int a[20],b[20],c[40];
int n,m,s,p,q,k=0;
cout<<"\nSpecify the number of elements:";
cin>>m;
cout<<"\nSpecify elements of sorted array 1st:";
for(p=0;p<m;p++)
cin>>a[p];
cout<<"\nSpecify the number of elements:";
cin>>n;
cout<<"\nSpecify elements of sorted array 2nd:";
for(q=0;q<n;q++)
cin>>b[q];
p=0;q=0;
while(p<=m && q<=n)
{
if(a[p]<b[q])
{
c[k]=a[p];
p++;
}
else
{
c[k]=b[q];
q++;
}k++;
}
p--;q--;
if(p>=m)
{
for(s=q;s<n;s++)
{
c[k]=a[s];
k++;
}
}
if(q>=m)
{
for(s=p;s<m;s++)
{
c[k]=b[s];
k++;
}
}
cout<<"\nMerge array is:\n";
for(p=0;p<m+n;p++)
cout<<"\n"<<c[p];
getch();
}
```

**Problem 92. Write a C++ program to show that original array is referred when array is passed to function,its not copied.**

***Program:***

```
#include<iostream.h>
#include<conio.h>
void main()
{
int s[5],p;
void f1(int s[]);
cout<<"\nFrom void main,before calling\n";
for(p=0;p<5;p++)
{
s[p]=p+1;
cout<<"\t"<<s[p];
}
f1(s);
cout<<"\nFrom void main,after calling\n";
for(p=0;p<5;p++)
{
cout<<"\t"<<s[p];
}
getch();
}
void f1(int s[])
{
int p;
cout<<"\nFrom function\n";
for(p=0;p<5;p++)
{
s[p]=0;
cout<<"\t"<<s[p];
}
return;
}
```

**OUTPUT:**

```
From void main,before calling
1 2 3 4 5
From function
0 0 0 0 0
From void main,after calling
0 0 0 0 0
```

**Problem 93. Write a C++ program using functions to find mean and standard deviation.**

***Program:***

```
#include<iostream.h>
#include<conio.h>
#include<math.h>
void main()
{
int n,p;
float s[10],sdev(float s[],int n);
```

```
clrscr();
cout<<"Specify value of n:";
cin>>n;
cout<<"\nSpecify values:";
for(p=0;p<n;p++)
{
cin>>s[p];
}
cout<<"\nStandard deviation is: "<<sdev(s,n)<<"\n";
}
float sdev(float b[],int m)
{
int p,q;
float mean(float b[],int m),x,total=0.0,z;
x=mean(b,m);
for(p=0;p<m;p++)
total+=(x-b[p])*(x-b[p]);
z=sqrt(total/(float)m);
cout<<"\nMean is:"<<x;
return(z);
}
float mean(float b[],int m)
{
int p;
float total=0.0,y;
for(p=0;p<m;p++)
total+=b[p];
y=total/(float)m;
return (y);
}
```

**OUTPUT:**

```
Specify value of n:4
Specify values:45 12 87 20
Mean is:41.000000
Standard deviation is:29.214722
```

**Problem 94. Write a C++ program to sort a l ist in ascending order and print it with the new sorted list.**

***Program:***

```
#include<iostream.h>
#include<conio.h>
void main()
{
int n,p,s[30];
void func_sort(int n,int s[]);
cout<<"Specify value of n:";
cin>>n;
for(p=0;p<n;p++)
{
cin>>s[p];
}
cout<<"\nScore before sorting:\n";
for(p=0;p<n;p++)
cout<<"\t"<<&s[p];
func_sort(n,s);
cout<<"\nScore after sorting:\n";
for(p=0;p<n;p++)
cout<<"\t"<<&s[p];
getch();
}
void func_sort(int n,int s[])
{
int p,q,temp;
for(p=0;p<n-1;p++)
for(q=p+1;q<n;q++)
{
if(s[p]>=s[q])
{
temp=s[p];
s[p]=s[q];
s[q]=temp;
}
}
}
```

**OUTPUT:**5

```
54 25 48 32 11
Score before sorting
54 25 48 32 11
Score after sorting
11 25 32 48 54
```

**Problem 95. Write a C++ programto pass one by one the individual members of array.**

***Program:***

```
#include<iostream.h>
#include<conio.h>
void f1(int w);
void main()
{
int p;
int s[]={33,44,55,66,77};
for(p=0;p<5;p++)
f1(s[p]);
}
void f1(int w)
{
cout<<w;
}
```

**OUTPUT:**

3344556677

**Problem 96.Ten numbers are entered from the keyboard into an array. The number to be searched is entered through the keyboard by the user. Write a program to find if the number to be searched is present in thr array and if it is present, display the number of times it appears in the array.**

***Program:***

```
#include<iostream.h>
#include <conio.h>
void main( )
{
int num[10 ], i , count = 0,n ;
clrscr( ) ;
cout<<"\nEnter 10 elements of array:";
for ( i = 0 ; i <= 9 ; i++ )
cin>>num[i];
cout<<"\nEnter an element to search:";
cin>>n;
for ( i = 0 ; i <= 9 ; i ++ )
{
if ( num[i] == n )
count ++ ;
}
cout<<"\nThe number "<<n<<" found "<<count<<" times(s) in the array";
cout<<"\nPress any key to exit.";
getch( ) ;
}
```

**OUTPUT:**

```
Enter 10 elements of array:23 76 5 8 1 7 5 4 8 5
Enter an element to search:5
The number 5 found 3 times(s) in the array
Press any key to exit.
```

**Problem 97. Fifteen numbers are entered from the keyboard into an array. Write a C++ program to find out how many of them are posiyive, how many are negative, how many are even and how many odd.**

***Program:***

```
#include<iostream.h>
#include<conio.h>
void main( )
{
int num[15],i,neg=0,pos=0,odd=0,even=0;
clrscr( ) ;
cout<<"\nEnter 15 elements of array:";
for ( i = 0 ; i <= 14 ; i++ )
cin>>num[i];
for ( i = 0 ; i <= 14 ; i++ )
{
num[i] < 0 ? neg++ : ( pos++ ) ;
num[i] % 2 ? odd ++ : ( even ++ ) ;
}
cout<<"\nNegative elements = " <<neg ;
cout<<"\nPositive elements = "<< pos ;
cout<<"\nEven elements = " <<even ;
cout<<"\nOdd elements = "<<odd ;
cout<<"\nPress any key to exit.";
getch( ) ;
}
```

**OUTPUT:**

```
Enter 15 elements of array:4 5 36 54 3 1 -8 -2 6 8
30 23 42 22 21
Negative elements = 2
Positive elements = 13
Even elements = 10
Odd elements = 5
Press any key to exit.
```

**Problem 98.Implement the selection sort, and insertion sort algorithms on a set of 10 numbers.**

**- Selection sort**

**- Bubble sort**

**- Inseration sort**

***Program:***

```
#include<iostream.h>
#include<conio.h>
void main( )
{
int a[10],i,j,t;
clrscr();
cout<<"\nEnter 10 numbers:";
for( i = 0 ; i <= 9 ; i++ )
cin>>a[i];
for( i = 0 ; i <= 8 ; i++ )
{
for( j = i+1; j <= 9 ; j++ )
{
if( a[i] > a[j] )
{
t = a[i] ;
a[i] = a[j] ;
a[j] = t;
}
}
}
cout<<"\nSorted numbers are:\n";
```

```
for ( i = 0 ; i <= 9 ; i++ )
cout<< a[i] ;
cout<<"\nPress any key.";
getch( ) ;
}
```

**OUTPUT:**

Enter 10 numbers:2 5 7 1 4 10 3 12 8 9
Sorted numbers are:
1 2 3 4 5 7 8 9 10 12
Press any key.

**Problem 99. Implement the following procedure to generate prime numbers from 1 to 100 into a program. This procedure is called sieve of Eratosthenes.**
**Step1 Fill an array num[ 100 ] with numbers from 1 to 100.**
**Step2 Starting with the second entry in the array, set all this multiples to zero.**
**Step3 proceed to the next non – zero element and set all its multiples to zero .**
**Step4 Repeat step 3 till you have set up the multiples of all the non – zero elements to zero .**
**Step5 All the conclusion of step 4, all the non – zero entries left in the array would be prime numbers, so print out these numbers.**

***Program:***

```
#include<iostream.h>
#include<conio.h>
void main( )
{
int num[100],i,j,k,step;
clrscr();
for ( i = 0 ; i <= 99 ; i++ )
num[i] = i + 1 ;
for ( i = 1 ; i <= 99 ; i++ )
{
if (num[i] != 0 )
{
k = num[i] * 2 - 1 ;
step = num[i] ;
for ( j = k ; j <= 99 ; j = j + step )
num[j] = 0 ;
}
}
cout<<"\nPrime numbers between 1 & 100 are:\n";
for(i = 0 ; i <= 99 ; i ++ )
{
if ( num[i] != 0 )
cout<<"\t"<< num[i] ;
}
cout<<"\nPress any key to exit.";
getch() ;
}
```

**OUTPUT:**

```
Prime numbers between 1 & 100 are:
1       2       3       5       7       11
        13      17      19      23
29      31      37      41      43      47
        53      59      61      67
71      73      79      83      89      97
Press any key to exit.
```

**Problem 100. Write a C++ program that interchanges the odd and even elements of an array.**

***Program:***

```
#include<iostream.h>
#include <conio.h>
void main( )
{
int num[ ] = { 12, 4, 5, 1, 9, 13, 11, 19, 54, 34 } ;
int i , t ;
clrscr( ) ;
for ( i = 0 ; i <= 9 ; i = i + 2 )
{
t = num[i] ;
num[i] = num [ i + 1 ] ;
num [ i + 1 ] = t ;
}
for ( i = 0 ; i <= 9 ; i ++ )
cout<< num[i] ;
cout<<"\nPress any key to exit.";
getch( ) ;
}
```

**OUTPUT:**

4 12 1 5 13 9 19 11 34 54
Press any key to exit.

**Problem 101. Write a C++ program to copy the contents of one array into another in the reverse order.**

***Program:***

```
#include<iostream.h>
#include<conio.h>
void main()
{
int arr1[5], arr2[5], i, j ;
clrscr( ) ;
cout<<"\nEnter 5 elements of array:";
```

```
for ( i = 0 ; i <= 4 ; i++ )
cin>>arr1[i];
for ( i = 0, j = 4 ; i <= 4 ; i++, j-- )
arr2[j] = arr1[i];
cout<<"\nElements in reverse order:";
for ( i = 0 ; i <= 4 ; i++ )
cout<<"\n"<<arr2[i] ;
cout<<"\nPress any key to exit.";
getch( ) ;
}
```

**OUTPUT:**

```
Enter 5 elements of array:7 4 8 1 3
Elements in reverse order:
3
1
8
4
7
Press any key to exit.
```

**Problem 102. If an array arr contains n elements, then write aC++ program to check if arr[0] = arr[n-1], arr[1] = arr = arr [ n – 2 ) and soon.**

***Program:***

```
#include<iostream.h>
#include<conio.h>
void main( )
{
int arr[10],i,j;
clrscr();
cout<<"\nEnter 5 elements of array:";
for(i=0; i <= 4 ; i++ )
cin>>arr[i];
for ( i = 0; i <= 4; i++ )
{
if ( arr [i] == arr[5-(i+1)])
cout<<"\n"<<arr[i] ;
}
cout<<"\nPress any key to exit.";
getch( ) ;
}
```

**OUTPUT:**

```
Enter 5 elements of array:45 65 78 78 45
45
78
45
Press any key to exit.
```

**Problem 103. Write a C++ program to find the smallest number in the array using pointers.**

***Program:***

```
#include<iostream.h>
#include<conio.h>
void main()
{
int arr[5],i,n;
clrscr();
cout<<"\nEnter 5 elements of array:";
for(i = 0; i <= 9; i++)
cin>>arr[i];
n = *arr;
for(i = 0; i <= 9; i++ )
{
if(*(arr+i) < n )
n = *(arr+i);
}
cout<<"Smallest number in array is "<<n;
cout<<"\nPress any key to exit.";
getch();
}
```

**OUTPUT:**

```
Enter 5 elements of array: 43 12 2 23 31
Smallest number in array is 2
Press any key to exit.
```

**Problem 104. Write a C++ program which performs the following tasks :**

**- initialize an integer array of 10 elements in void main( )**

**- pass the entire array to a function modify( )**

**- in modofy( ) multiply each element of array by 3**

**- return the control to void main( ) and print the new array elements in void main( )**

***Program:***

```
#include<iostream.h>
#include<conio.h>
void main( )
{
int i ;
static int array[ ] = { 1, 2, 3, 4, 5, 6, 7, 8, 9, 10 } ;
clrscr( ) ;
cout<<"\nOriginal array is:";
for ( i = 0 ; i < 10 ; i++ )
cout<<array[i];
modify(array,10);
cout<<"\nModified array is: ";
for ( i = 0 ; i < 10 ; i++ )
cout<<array[i] ;
cout<<"\nPress any key to exit.";
getch( ) ;
```

```
}
modify(int *arr,int n)
{
int i;
for(i=0;i<n;i++)
{
*arr=*arr*3;
arr++;
}
}
```

**OUTPUT:**

Original array is:12345678910
Modified array is: 36912151821242730
Press any key to exit.

**Problem 105. Write a C++ program to pick up the largest number from any 5 row by 5 column matrix.**

***Program:***

```
#include<iostream.h>
#include<conio.h>
void main()
{
static int a[5] [5] =
{
{21,11,17, 19, 71 } ,
{ 51, 54, 56, 32, 58 } ,
{ 23, 43, 57, 22, 13 },
{ 74, 52, 47, 16, 19 },
{ 45, 35, 65, 80, 10 }
} ;
int i,j,big;
clrscr();
big = a[0][0];
cout<<"\nThe 5x5 matrix is:\n";
for ( i = 0 ; i <= 4 ; i++)
{
for ( j = 0 ; j <= 4 ; j++ )
{
cout<<"\t"<<a[i][j];
if(a[i][j] > big)
big = a[i][j];
}
cout<<"\n";
}
cout<<"\nLargest number in the matrix is "<<big;
cout<<"\nPress any key to exit.";
getch( ) ;
}
```

**OUTPUT:**

```
The 5x5 matrix is:
21      11      17      19      71
51      54      56      32      58
23      43      57      22      13
74      52      47      16      19
45 35   65      80      10
Largest number in the matrix is 80
Press any key to exit.
```

**Problem 106. Write a C++ program to obtain transpose of a 4 x 4 matrix. The transpose of a matrix is obtained by exchanging the elements of each row with elements of the corresponding column.**

***Program:***

```
#include<iostream.h>
#include<conio.h>
void main( )
{
int mat[4][4],i,j,temp;
clrscr();
cout<<"\nEnter values for 4 x 4 matrix:";
for ( i = 0; i <= 3; i++ )
{
for ( j = 0; j <= 3; j++ )
{
cin>>mat[i][j];
}
}
cout<<"\nThe matrix you entered is:";
for ( i = 0 ; i <= 3 ; i++ )
{
for ( j = 0 ; j <= 3 ; j++ )
cout<<"\t"<<mat[i][j];
cout<<"\n";
}
for ( i = 0 ; i <= 3 ; i ++ )
{
for ( j = 0 ; j <= 3 ; j++ )
{
temp = mat[i][j];
mat[i][j] = mat[j][i];
mat[j][i] = temp;
}
}
cout<<"Transpose of the matrix is:\n";
for ( i = 0 ; i <= 3 ; i++ )
{
for ( j = 0 ; j <= 3 ; j++ )
cout<<"\t"<<mat[j][i];
```

```
cout<<"\n";
}
cout<<"\nPress any key to exit.";
getch();
}
```

**OUTPUT:**

Enter values for 4 x 4 matrix:3 4 5 6 7 8 9 10 11 12 13 14 15 16 17 18
The matrix you entered is:

```
3    4    5    6
7    8    9    10
11   12   13   14
15   16   17   18
```

Transpose of the matrix is:

```
3    7    11   15
4    8    12   16
5    9    13   17
6    10   14   18
```

Press any key to exit.

**Problem 108. Write a C++ program to find if a square matrix is symmetric**

***Program:***

```
#include<iostream.h>
#include<conio.h>
void main( )
{
int arr[ 3 ][ 3 ], i, j, count = 0 ;
clrscr( ) ;
cout<<"\nEnter the elements of the Matrix:";
for ( i = 0 ; i <= 2 ; i++ )
{
for ( j = 0 ; j <= 2 ; j++ )
cin>>&arr[ i ][ j ] ;
}
cout<<"\nThe matrix formed is...\n";
for ( i = 0 ; i <= 2 ; i++ )
{
for ( j = 0 ; j <= 2 ; j++ )
cout<<<<arr[ i ][ j ] ;
cout<<"\n";
}
for ( i = 0 ; i <= 2 ; i++ )
{
for ( j = i ; j <=2 ; j++ )
{
if ( arr[i][j] == arr[j][i] )
count++ ;
}
}
if ( count == 6 )
cout<<"\nThe matrix is symmetric";
else
cout<<"\nThe matrix is not symmetric";
cout<<"\nPress any key to exit.";
getch( ) ;
}
```

**OUTPUT:**

Enter the elements of the Matrix:

```
1 1 2
1 2 3
2 3 3
```

The matrix formed is...

```
1 1 2
1 2 3
2 3 3
```

The matrix is symmetric
Press any key to exit.

**Problem 109. Write a C+ program to add two 6 x 6 matrices.**

***Program:***

```
#include<iostream.h>
#include<conio.h>
void main( )
{
int mat1[6][6], mat2[6][6],mat3[6][6];
int i,j;
clrscr( ) ;
cout<<"\nEnter values for first 6 x 6 matrix:";
for ( i = 0 ; i <= 5 ; i++ )
{
for ( j = 0 ; j <= 5 ; j++ )
cin>>mat1[i][j] ;
}
cout<<"\nEnter values for second 6 x 6 matrix:";
for ( i = 0 ; i <= 5 ; i++ )
{
for ( j = 0 ; j <= 5 ; j++ )
cin>>mat2[i][j] ;
}
cout<<"\nMatrices entered by you
are:\nMatrix1\n";
for ( i = 0 ; i <= 5 ; i++ )
{
for ( j = 0 ; j <= 5 ; j++ )
cout<<"\t"<< mat1[i][j];
cout<<"\n";
}
cout<<"\n Matrix2:\n";
for ( i = 0 ; i <= 5 ; i++ )
```

```
{
for ( j = 0 ; j <= 5 ; j++ )
cout<<"\t"<< mat2[i][j] ;
cout<<"\n";
}
for ( i = 0 ; i <= 5 ; i++ )
{
for ( j = 0 ; j <= 5 ; j++ )
mat3[i][j] = mat1[i][j] + mat2[i][j] ;
}
cout<<"\nThe new matrix after addition of the above
two matrices is:\n";
for ( i = 0 ; i <= 5 ; i++ )
{
for ( j = 0 ; j <= 5 ; j++ )
cout<<"\t"<< mat3[i][j] ;
cout<<"\n";
}
cout<<"\nPress any key to exit.";
getch( ) ;
}
```

**OUTPUT:**

```
Enter values for first 6 x 6 matrix:
1 2 3 4 5 6
6 5 4 3 2 1
1 2 3 4 5 6
6 5 4 3 2 1
1 2 3 4 5 6
6 5 4 3 2 1
Enter values for second 6 x 6 matrix:
1 2 3 4 5 6
6 5 4 3 2 1
1 2 3 4 5 6
6 5 4 3 2 1
1 2 3 4 5 6
6 5 4 3 2 1
Matrices entered by you are:
Matrix1:
1    2    3    4 5    6
6    5    4    3    2    1
1    2    3    4    5    6
6    5    4    3    2    1
1    2    3.   4    5    6
6    5    4    3    2    1

Matrix2:
1    2    3    4 5    6
6    5    4    3    2    1
1    2    3    4    5    6
6    5    4    3    2    1
1    2    3    4    5    6
6    5    4    3    2    1

The new matrix after addition of the above two
matrices is
2    4    6    8    10   12
12   10   8    6    4    2
2    4    6    8    10   12
12   10   8    6    4    2
2    4    6    8    10   12
12   10   8    6    4    2
Press any key to exit.
```

**Problem 110. Write a C++ program to multiply any two 3 x 3 matrices.**

***Program:*** .

```
#include<iostream.h>
#include<conio.h>
void main( )
{
int mat1[3][3], mat2[3][3],mat3[3][3], i ,j, k, sum;
clrscr( ) ;
cout<<"\nEnter values for first 3 x 3 matrix:\n";
for ( i = 0 ; i <= 2 ; i++ )
{
for ( j = 0 ; j <= 2 ; j++ )
cin>>mat1[i][j] ;
}
cout<<"\nEnter values for second 3 x 3 matrix:\n";
for ( i = 0 ; i <= 2 ; i++ )
{
for ( j = 0 ; j <= 2 ; j++ )
cin>>mat2[i][j] ;
}
cout<<"\nThe first 3 x 3 matrix entered by you
is:\n";
for ( i = 0 ; i <= 2 ; i++ )
{
for ( j = 0 ; j <= 2 ; j++ )
cout<<"\t"<< mat1[i][j] ;
cout<<"\n";
}
cout<<"\n the second 3 x 3 matrix entered :\n";
for ( i = 0 ; i <= 2 ; i++ )
{
for ( j = 0 ; j <= 2 ; j++ )
cout<<"\t"<< mat2[i][j] ;
cout<<"\n";
}
for ( i = 0 ; i <= 2 ; i++ )
```

```
{
for ( j = 0 ; j <= 2 ; j++ )
{
sum = 0;
for ( k = 0 ; k <=2 ; k++ )
sum = sum + mat1[i][k] * mat2[k][j] ;
mat3[i][j] = sum ;
}
}
cout<<"\nThe product of the above two matrices
is:\n";
for ( i = 0 ;i<= 2 ; i++ )
{
for ( j = 0 ; j <= 2 ; j++ )
cout<<"\t"<< mat3[i][j] ;
cout<<"\n";
}
cout<<"\nPress any key to exit.";
getch( ) ;
}
```

**OUTPUT:**

```
Enter values for first 3 x 3 matrix:
1 2 3
3 4 5
5 6 7
Enter values for second 3 x 3 matrix:
1 1 1
2 2 2
3 3 3
The first 3 x 3 matrix entered by you is:
1       2       3
3       4       5
5       6       7
the second 3 x 3 matrix entered :
1       1       1
2       2       2
3       3       3
The product of the above two matrices is:
14      14      14
26      26      26
38      38      38
Press any key to exit.
```

**Problem 111. Given an array p[5] write a function to shift it circularly left by twopositions. Thus if p[0] =15,p[1]= 30,p[2] =28, p[3] =19 and p[4] = 61 then after the shift P[0]=28 ,P[1]=19,P[2]=61,P[3]=15 and P[4]=30 call thisfunction for a 9(4x5) matrix and get its rows left shifted.**

***Program:***

```
#include<iostream.h>
#include<conio.h>
void swap(int * );
void main( )
{
int p[ 4 ][ 5 ] ;
int i, j ;
clrscr( ) ;
for ( i = 0 ; i <= 3; i++ )
{
cout<<"\nEnter the "<<i<<" row elements:\n" ;
for ( j = 0 ; j <= 4; j++ )
{
cin>>p[i][j];
}
}
cout<<"\nMatrix elements as entered:";
for ( i = 0 ; i <= 3; i++ )
{
cout<<"\nThe "<<i<<"row elements: ";
for ( j = 0 ; j <= 4 ; j++ )
{
cout<<"\t"<< p[i][j] ;
}
}
getch( ) ;
cout<<"\n";
swap(p);
cout<<"\nMatrix after left shifting the row
elements:";
for ( i = 0 ; i <= 3 ; i++ )
{
cout<<"\nThe "<<i<<"row elements: ";
for ( j = 0 ; j <= 4 ; j++ )
{
cout<<"\t" <<p[i][j] ;
}
}
getch( ) ;
}
void swap ( int *p )
{
int k, i, tt, t, j ;
for ( k = 0 ; k <= 3; k++ )
{
for(i=0;i<=1;i++)
{
t = *( p + k * 5 + 0 ) ;
for ( j = 0 ; j <= 3 ; j++ )
{
tt = *( p + k * 5 + j ) ;
```

```
*( p + k * 5 + j ) = *( p + k * 5 + j + 1 ) ;
*( p + k * 5 + j + 1 ) = tt ;
}
*( p + k * 5 + j )=t ;
}
}
}
```

**OUTPUT:**

```
Enter the 0 row elements:1 2 3 4 5
Enter the 1 row elements:2 3 4 5 6
Enter the 2 row elements:3 4 5 6 7
Enter the 3 row elements:4 5 6 7 8
Matrix elements as entered:
The 0 row elements: 1  2   3   4   5
The 1 row elements: 2  3   4   5   6
The 2 row elements: 3  4   5   6   7
The 3 row elements: 4  5   6   7   8
Matrix after left shifting the row elements:
The 0 row elements: 3  4   5   1   2
The 1 row elements: 4  5   6   2   3
The 2 row elements: 5  6   7   3   4
The 3 row elements: 6  7   8   4   5
```

**Problem 112. A 6 x 6 matrix is entered through the keyboard. Write a C++ program to obtain the Determinant value of this matrix.**

***Program:***

```
#include<iostream.h>
#include<alloc.h>
#include<conio.h >
void detmat ( int *, int ) ;
void main( )
{
int *arr, sum, n, i, j, pos, num ;
cout<<"\nEnter value of n for ( n x n ) matrix:";
cin>>n ;
arr = calloc ( n * n, 2 ) ;
cout<<"\nEnter numbers:\n";
for ( i = 0 ; i < n ; i ++ )
{
for ( j = 0 ; j < n ; j ++ )
{
cin>>num ;
pos = i * n + j ;
arr[ pos ] = num ;
}
}
for ( i = 0 ; i < n ; i ++ )
{
for ( j = 0 ; j < n ; j ++ )
{
cout<<"\t" <<arr[ j ];
}
cout<<"\n";
}
sum = detmat(arr,n);
free ( arr ) ;
cout<<"\n"<< sum ;
cout<<"\nPress any key to exit.";
getch( ) ;
}
void detmat(int *arr,int order)
{
int sign=1,sum=0,i,j,k,count,*arr2;
int newsize,newpos,pos;
if(order==1)
return(arr[0]);
for(i=0;i<order;i++,sign*=-1)
{
newsize=(order-1)*(order-1);
arr2=calloc(newsize,2);
for(j=1;j<order;j++)
{
for(k=0,count=0;k<order;k++)
{
if(k==i)
continue;
pos=j*order+k;
newpos=(j-1)*(order-1)+count;
arr2[newpos]=arr[pos];
count++;
}
}
sum=sum+arr[i] * sign * detmat(arr2,order-1);
free(arr2);
}
return(sum);
}
```

**Problem 113. For the following set of sample data, compute the standard deviation and the mean.**

**-6, -12, 8, 13, 11, 6, 2, -6, -9, -10, 11, 10, 9, 2**

**The formula for standard deviation is**

**( x1 - x )2**

**n**

**where x, is the data item and x is the mean.**

***Program:***

```
#include<iostream.h>
#include<conio.h >
```

```
#include<math.h>
void main( )
{
int data[ 15 ] = { -6, -12, 8, 13, 11, 6, 7, 2, -6, -9, 2,
11, 10, 9, -10 } ;
float xi, std[ 15 ], mean = 0 ;
int i, n = 15 ;
clrscr( ) ;
for ( i = 0 ; i <= 14 ; i++ ) ;
{
cout<<data[i];
}
for ( i = 0 ; i <= 14 ; i++ ) ;
{
mean = mean + data[ i ] ;
}
mean = mean / n ;
for ( i = 0 ; i <= 14 ; i++ ) ;
{
std[i] = sqrt(pow((data[i] - mean),2))/n;
}
cout<<"\n\n Mean = "<<mean<<"\n\n";
for ( i = 0 ; i <= 14 ; i++ )
{
cout<<"\nStandard deviation of "<<data[i]<<" =
"<<std[i];
}
getch();
}
```

**Problem 117. The X and Y coordinates of 10 different points are entered through the keyboard. Write a C++ program to find the distance of last point from the first point ( sum of distance between consecutive points).**

***Program:***

```
#include<iostream.h>
#include<conio.h>
#include<math.h>
void main( )
{
int i, x[ 10 ], y[ 10 ] ;
float sum = 0 ;
clscr( ) ;
cout<<"\nEnter the coordinates for the points:" ;
for ( i = 0 ; i <= 9 ; i++ )
{
cout<<"\nX[ "<<i+1<<"] =";
cin>>x[ i ] ;
cout<<"\nY[ "<<i+1<<" ] =";
cin>>y[ i ] ;
}
for ( i = 0 ; i <= 8 ; i++ )
{
sum = sum + sqrt ( pow ( ( x[ i + 1 ] – x[ i ] ), 2 ) +
pow ( (y[ i + 1 ] – y[ i ]), 2 ) ) ;
cout<<"\n\nDistance of the last point from the first
point = "<< sum ;
cout<<"\n\n\n\n\nPress any key to exit…" ;
getch( ) ;
}
```

**Problem 118. A dequeue is an ordered set of elements in which elements may be inserted or retrieved from either end. Using an array simulate a dequeue of characters and the operations retrieve left, retrieve right, insert left, insert, insert right. Exceptional conditions such as dequeue full of empty should be indicated. Simulation.**

***Program:***

```
#include<iostream.h>
#include<conio.h>
void add _ front ( int ) ;
void add _ rear ( int ) ;
int retrieve_ front ( void ) ;
int revtrieve_ rear ( void ) ;
void display (void ) ;
int *front, *rear ;
int a[ 26 ] ;
void main( )
{
int item ;
front = NULL ;
rear = NULL ;
clrscr( ) ;
cout<<"\nAdding elements at front of a deque; " ;
add_ front ( 10 ) ;
add _ front ( 40 ) ;
add _ front (30 ) ;
display( ) ;
getch( ) ;
cout<<"\n\nAdding an element at the rear of a
deque: " ;
add_ rear ( 50 ) ;
display( ) ;
cout<<"\n\nRetreiving an element from the front of
a deque: " ;
item = retrieve_front( ) ;
if ( item = = -1 )
```

```
cout<<"\nDeQueue Empty " ;
else
cout<<"\n\nFront item = "<< item ;
display( ) ;
cout<<"\nRetreiving an element from the rear of a
deque: ";
item = retrieve_rear( ) ;
if ( item == -1 )
cout<<"\nDeQueue Empty ";
else
cout<<" Front item = "<< item;
display();
cout<<"\nRetreiving an element from the rear of a
deque:";
item = retrieve_rear( ) ;
if ( item == -1 )
cout<<"\nDeQueue Empty ";
else
cout<<"\nRear item = "<< item ;
display( ) ;
getch( ) ;
}
int retrieve_rear (void )
{
int item, i, j ;
if ( rear == NULL )
{
cout<<"\n Dequeue Empty ";
return -1 ;
}
else
{
item = *rear ;
i = rear - front ;
if (i == 0 )
{
front = NULL ;
rear = NULL ;
}
else
}
*rear = 0 ;
rear-- ;
}
}
return item ;
}
int retrieve_front (void )
{
int item, i, j ;
if (front == NULL )
{
cout<<"\n Dequeue Empty ";
return -1 ;
}
else
{
item = *front ;
i = rear - front ;
if (i == 0 )
{
front = NULL ;
rear = NULL ;
}
else
}
for ( j = 0 ; j <= i - 1 ; j++ )
front [ j ] = front [ j + 1 ] ;
*rear = 0 ;
rear-- ;
}
}
return item ;
}
void add_rear ( int item )
{
int i, j ;
if ( front == NULL )
{
front = a;
*front = item ;
rear = a;
}
else
{
i = rear - front ;

if ( i != 25 )
{
rear++ ;
*rear = item ;
}
else
cout<<"\nDequeue full ";
}
}
void add_front ( int item )
{
int i, j ;
if ( front == NULL )
```

```
{
front = a;
*( front ) = item;
rear = a;
}
else
{
front = a;
j = rear - front ;
if ( j != 25 )
{
for ( i = j + 1 ; i >= 0 ; i-- )
front [ i ] = front [ i - 1 ] ;
*(front + 0 ) = item ;
rear++ ;
}
else
cout<<"\n Dequeue Full ";
}
}
void display ( void )
{
int i ;
int *p = front ;
if ( p == NULL)
{
cout<<"\nDequeue Empty ";
}
else
{
cout<<"\n";
for ( i = 0 ; i <= ( rear - front ) ; i++ )
cout<<"\n a["<<i<<"] = "<<*p++ ;
}
}
```

**Problem 119. Write a C++ programto input ballot paper of voters and count number of votes got by each candidate.**

***Program:***

```
#include<iostream.h>
#include<conio.h>
void main()
{
int can,p,q,n;
static int count[20],votes[100];
cout<<"\nSpecify the number of candidates:";
cin>>can;
cout<<"\nSpecify the number of voters:";
cin>>n;
cout<<"\nSpecify the number of candidates on ballot paper:";
cout<<"\nEnter 0 for nill vote\n";
for(p=0;p<n;p++)
{
cin>>votes[p];
}
for(p=0;p<n;p++)
{
count[votes[p]]++;
}
for(p=1;p<=can;p++)
{
cout<<"\nThere are "<<count[p]<<" votes for candidate "<<p;
}
cout<<"\nThere are "<<count[0]<<"nill votes";
getch();
}
```

**OUTPUT:**

```
Specify the number of candidates:3
Specify the number of voters:6
Specify the number of candidates on ballot paper:
Enter 0 for nill vote
2
4
2
0
1
3
There are 1 votes for candidate 1
There are 2 votes for candidate 2
There are 1 votes for candidate 3
There are 1 nill votes
```

**Problem 120. Write a C++ programto show how 2-D array is initialized.**

***Program:***

```
#include<iostream.h>
#include<conio.h>
void main()
{
int s[2][3]={{15,52,65},{12,40,45}};
int p,q;
for(p=0;p<2;p++)
{
for(q=0;q<3;q++)
{
cout<<s[p][q];
cout<<"\t";
}
cout<<"\n";
```

```
}
getch();
}
```

**OUTPUT:**

```
15    52    65
12    40    45
```

**Problem 121. Write a C++ program to enter 2-D array and print values of all elements of array.**

***Program:***

```
#include<iostream.h>
#include<conio.h>
void main()
{
int m,p,q,s[10][10],n;
cout<<"\nSpecify the number of rows:";
cin>>m;
cout<<"\nSpecify the number of columns:";
cin>>n;
for(p=0;p<m;p++)
for(q=0;q<n;q++)
{
cin>>s[p][q];
}
cout<<"\nElements are:\n";
for(p=0;p<m;p++)
{
for(q=0;q<n;q++)
{
cout.width(4);
cout<<s[p][q];
}
cout<<"\n";
}
}
```

**OUTPUT:**

```
Specify the number of rows:3
Specify the number of columns:3
4 6 2 7 8 2 4 0 1
Elements are:
4 6 2
7 8 2
4 0 1
```

**Problem 122. Write a C++ program to find product of two matrices.**

***Program:***

```
#include<iostream.h>
#include<conio.h>
void main()
{
int x[10][10],y[10][10],z[10][10];
int u,v,m,n,p,q,k;
cout<<"\nMatrix X order is:";
cin>>m>>n;
cout<<"\nMatrix Y order is:";
cin>>p>>q;
if(n==p)
{
cout<<"Specify X's elements:\n";
for(u=0;u<m;u++)
for(v=0;v<n;v++)
{
cin>>x[u][v];
}
cout<<"Specify Y's elements:\n";
for(u=0;u<p;u++)
for(v=0;v<q;v++)
{
cin>>y[u][v];
}
for(u=0;u<m;u++)
for(v=0;v<q;v++)
{
z[u][v]=0;
for(k=0;k<n;k++)
{
z[u][v]+=x[u][k]*y[k][v];
}}}
for(u=0;u<m;u++)
{
for(v=0;v<q;v++)
{
cout<<z[u][v];
cout<<" ";
}
cout<<"\n";
}
getch();
}
```

**OUTPUT:**

```
Matrix X order is:2 2
Matrix Y order is:2 2
Specify X's elements:
1 5 8 6
Specify Y's elements:
7 5 6 2
37 15
92 52
```

**Problem 123. Write a C++ program to search smallest and largest element and also find its range.**

***Program:***

```
#include<iostream.h>
#include<conio.h>
void main()
{
int x[10];
int z,t,l,n,p;
cout<<"\nSpecify number of elements:";
cin>>n;
cout<<"\nSpecify elements:";
for(p=0;p<n;p++)
cin>>x[p];
t=l=x[0];
for(p=1;p<n;p++)
{
if(x[p]>l)
{
l=x[p];
}
if(x[p]<t)
{
t=x[p];
}}
z=l-t;
cout<<"\nThe Range is "<<l<<"-"<<t<<"="z;
getch();
}
```

**OUTPUT:**

Specify number of elements:4
Specify number of elements:5 8 9 6
The Range is 9-5=4

**Problem 124. Write a C++ program to find row sum and column sum of matrix, also find grand sum.**

***Program:***

```
#include<iostream.h>
#include<conio.h>
#include<dos.h>
void main()
{
int a[10][10],m,n,i,j,cs,rs,gs;
clrscr();
cout<<"\n ENTER THE NUMBER OF ROW &
COLUMN: ";
cin>>m>>n;
cout<<"\n ENTER THE ELEMNTS: ";
for(i=1;i<=m;i++)
{
for(j=1;j<=n;j++)
{
cin>>a[i][j];
}
}
gs=0;
for(i=1;i<=m;i++)
{
rs=0;
for(j=1;j<=n;j++)
{
rs=rs+a[i][j];
}
cout<<"\n Row sum="<<rs;
gs=gs+rs;
}
cout<<"\n Grand sum="<<gs;
for(j=1;j<=n;j++)
{
cs=0;
for(i=1;i<=m;i++)
{
cs=cs+a[i][j];
}
cout<<"\n Column sum="<<cs;
}
sleep(15);
}
```

**OUTPUT:**

ENTER THE NUMBER OF ROW & COLUMN:
2
3
ENTER THE ELEMNTS:
2
3
4
4
3
2
Row sum = 9
Row sum = 9
Grand sum = 18
Column sum = 6
Column sum = 6
Column sum = 6

**Problem 125. Write a C++ program for Matrix Multiplication.**

***Program:***

```
#include<iostream.h>
```

```
void main()
{
int i,j,k,r1,c1,r2,c2;
int a[10][10], b[10][10], c[10][10];
clrscr();
cout<<"\n Enter the number of rows and columns of
first matrix: ";
cin>>r1>>c1;
cout<<"\n Enter the number of rows and columns of
second matrix:" );
cin>>r2>>c2;
if(c1!=r2)
{
clrscr();
cout<<"Multiplication is not possible....";
goto ab;
}
cout<<"\n Enter the elements of first matrix.: ";
for(i=0;i<r1;i++)
for(j=0;j<c1;j++)
cin>>a[i][j];
cout<<"\n Enter the elements of second matrix:";
for(i=0;i<r2;i++)
for(j=0;j<c2;j++)
cin>>b[i][j];
for(i=0;i<r1;i++)
{
for(j=0;j<c2;j++)
{
c[i][j]=0;
for(k=0;k<r2;k++)
{
c[i][j]=c[i][j]+a[i][k]*b[k][j];
}
}
}
cout<<"\n The multiplication is: ";
for(i=0;i<r1;i++)
{
cout<<"\n";
for(j=0;j<c2;j++)
{
cout.width(3);
cout<<c[i][j];
}
}
ab:
getch();
}
```

**OUTPUT:**

```
Enter the number of rows and columns of first
matrix:
2
3
Enter the number of rows and columns of second
matrix:
3
2
Enter the elements of first matrix.:
1
2
3
4
Enter the elements of second matrix:
4
3
2
1
The multiplication is:
12      5
20      13
```

**Problem 126. Write a C++ program to Calculate Matrix Multiplication, Matrix Addition and Matrix Transpose by using SWITCH statements (A menu driven program).**

***Program:***

```
#include<iostream.h>
void main()
{
int x, r, c, i, j, k, y;
int a[10][10],b[10][10],c1[10][10];
clrscr();
cout<<"\n Enter the value of row: ";
cin>>r;
cout<<"\n Enter the value of column: ";
cin>>c;
cout<<"\n Enter the elements for matrix A: \n";
for(i=0;i<r;i++)
for(j=0;j<c;j++)
cin>>a[i][j];
cout<<"\n Enter the elements for matrix B: \n";
for(i=0;i<r;i++)
for(j=0;j<c;j++)
cin>>b[i][j];
clrscr();
cout<<"\n1. Matrix Multiplication\n2. Matrix
Sum\n3. Transpose";
cout<<"\n Enter your choice:";
cin>>x;
```

```
switch(x)
{
case 1:
cout<<"Matrix Multiplication is .....\n";
for(i=0;i<r;i++)
for(j=0;j<c;j++)
{
c1[i][j]=0;
for(k=0;k<c;k++)
c1[i][j]=c1[i][j]+a[i][k]*b[k][j];
}
for(i=0;i<r;i++)
{
cout<<"\n";
for(j=0;j<c;j++)
cout.width(3);
cout<<c1[i][j];
}
break;
case 2:
cout<<"Matrix Summation is..........\n";
for(i=0;i<r;i++)
for(j=0;j<c;j++)
c1[i][j]=a[i][j]+b[i][j];
for(i=0;i<r;i++)
{
cout<<"\n";
for(j=0;j<c;j++)
cout.width(3);
cout<<c1[i][j];
}
break;
case 3:
clrscr();
cout<<"1. First Matrix\n2. Second Matrix\n";
cin>>y;
cout<<"Matrix Transpose is..........\n";
if (y==1)
for(i=0;i<r;i++)
{
cout<<"\n";
for(j=0;j<c;j++)
cout.width(3);
cout<<a[j][i];
}
else
for(i=0;i<r;i++)
{
cout<<"\n";
for(j=0;j<c;j++)
cout.width(3);
cout<<b[j][i];
}
break;
}
getch();
}
```

**OUTPUT:**

```
Enter the value of row:
2       2
Enter the value of column:
2       2
Enter the elements for matrix A:
1       2
3       2
Enter the elements for matrix B:
4       5
5       4
1. Matrix Multiplication
2. Matrix Sum
3. Transpose
Enter your choice: 2
Matrix Summation is.........
5       7
8       6
```

**Problem 127. Write a C++ program to sort the numeric data in descending order.**

***Program:***

```
#include<iostream.h>
#include<conio.h>
void main( )
{
int a[10], i, n, j, temp;
clrscr();
cout<<"\n Enter the number of elements: ";
cin>>n;
cout<<"\n Enter the elements: ";
for(i=0;i<n;i++)
cin>>a[i];
for(i=0;i<n-1;i++)
for(j=0;j<n-i;j++)
if(a[j]<a[j+1])
{
temp=a[j];
a[j]=a[j+1];
a[j+1]=temp;
}
coout<<"\n Sorted data is:";
for(i=0;i<n;i++)
cout<<"\n"<<a[i];
getch();
```

}

**OUTPUT:**

Enter the number of elements:
5
Enter the elements:
3
6
1
4
2
Sorted data is:
6
4
3
2
1

**Problem 128. Write a C++ program to count the negative elements from the list.**

***Program:***

```
#include<iostream.h>
void main()
{
int a[10],i,c,n;
clrscr();
cout<<"\n Enter the number of numbers: ";
cin>>n;
cout<<"\n Enter the elements: ";
for(i=1;i<=n;i++)
{
cin>>a[i];
}
c=0;
for(i=1;i<=n;i++)
{
if(a[i]<0)
{
c=c+1;
}
}
cout<<"\n Number of negative elements are = "<<c;
getche();
}
```

**OUTPUT:**

Enter the number of numbers:
6
Enter the elements:
4
5
-6
2
-3
-8
Number of negative elements are = 3

**Problem 129. Write a C++ program to transpose a matrix.**

***Program:***

```
#include<iostream.h>
#include<conio.h>
void main()
{
int a[10][10],i,j,r,c;
clrscr();
cout<<"\n Enter value of row: ";
cin>>r;
cout<<"\n Enter value of column: ";
cin>>c;
coout<<"\n Enter the elements:";
for(i=0;i<r;i++)
for(j=0;j<c;j++)
cin>>a[i][j];
cout<<"\n TRANSPOSE OF MATRIX IS :\n";
for(i=0;i<c;i++)
{
cout<<"\n";
for(j=0;j<r;j++)
cout.width(3);
cout<<a[j][i];
}
getch();
}
```

**OUTPUT:**

```
Enter value of row:3
Enter value of column :3
Enter the elements:
1    2    3
4    5    6
7    8    9
TRANSPOSE OF MATRIX IS:
1    4    7
2    5    8
3    6    9
```

**Problem 130. Write a C++ program to find the sum of Diagonal Elements of a matrix (Trace a Matrix).**

***Program:***

```
#include<iostream.h>
void main()
```

```
{
int a[10][10],i,j,m,n,sum=0;
cout<<"\n Enter the number of rows and columns of
a matrix: ";
cin>>m>>n;
cout<<"\n Enter the elements of matrix: ";
for(i=1;i<=m;i++)
{
for(j=1;j<=n;j++)
{
cin>>a[i][j];
}
}
for(i=1;i<=m;i++)
{
for(j=1;j<=n;j++)
{
if(i==j)
{
sum=sum+a[i][j];
}
}
}
cout<<"\n Sum of diagonal elements: "<<sum;
getche();
}
```

**OUTPUT:**

```
Enter the number of rows and columns of a matrix:
3
3
Enter the elements of matrix:
1    2    3
4    5    6
7    8    9
Sum of diagonal elements: 15
```

**Problem 131. Write a C++ program to print the merged array.**

***Program:***

```
#include<iostream.h>
#include<conio.h>
void main()
{
int a[10],b[10],c[30],i,j,t,m,n,temp;
clrscr();
cout<<"\n Enter the number of elements of Array-A:
";
cin>>m;
cout<<"\n Enter the elements :\n";
for(i=1;i<=m;i++)
cin>>a[i];
cout<<"\n Enter the number of elements of Array-
B: ";
cin>>n;
cout<<"\n Enter the elements: ";
for(i=1;i<=n;i++)
cin>>b[i];
t=m+n;
for(i=1;i<=m;i++)
c[i]=a[i];
for(i=1;i<=n;i++)
c[i+m]=b[i];
cout<<"\n Merged array-C is:";
for(i=1;i<=t;i++)
cout<<"\t"<<c[i];
cout<<"\n Sorted array -C is: ";
for(i=1;i<=m-1;i++)
{
for(j=1;j<=m-i;j++)
{
if(c[j]>c[j+1])
{
temp=c[j+1];
c[j+1]=c[j];
c[j]=temp;
}
else
continue;
}
}
for(i=1;i<=t;i++)
cout<<"\t"<<c[i];
getch();
}
```

**OUTPUT:**

```
Enter the number of elements of Array-A:
3
Enter the elements:
2
4
5
Enter the number of elements of Array-B:
4
Enter the elements :
1
3
7
6
Merged array-C is:
2
4
5
```

1
3
7
6
Sorted array -C is:
1
2
3
4
5
6
7

**Problem 132. Write a C++ program to find the sum of first and last digit of a number.**

***Program:***

```
#include<iostream.h>
#include<conio.h>
void main ()
{
int i=0;
int n, num, sum, x[20];
clrscr();
cout<<"\n Enter how many digits: ";
cin>>n;
cout<<"\n Enter the number:";
cin>>num;
while (num>0 && i<=n)
{
x[i]=num%10;
num=num/10;
i++;
}
sum=x[0]+x[n-1];
cout<<"\n Sum is "<< sum;
getch ();
}
```

**OUTPUT:**

Enter how many digits:5
Enter the number:
12345
Sum is 6

**Problem 133. Write a C++ program to print array in descending order.**

***Program:***

```
#include<iostream.h>
#include<math.h>
void main()
{
int i[100],j[100],temp[100];
int a,b=1,c,i1=2,k,b2=0;
clrscr();
cout<<"ENTER NUMBER OF DATA
(MAXIMUM 100):";
cin>>k;
cout<<"ENTER DATA (IN INTEGER):";
for(a=0;a<k;a++)
{
cout<<"k=["<<a+1<<"]";
cin>>i[a];
}
for(a=0,b=1;a<k,b<k;a++,b++)
{
if((i[b]-i[a])>0)
{
temp[a]=i[b];
temp[b]=i[a];
i[a]=temp[a];
i[b]=temp[b];
}
for(c=i1;c<k;c++)
{
if((i[c]-i[a])>0)
{
temp[a]=i[c];
temp[c]=i[a];
i[a]=temp[a];
i[c]=temp[c];
}
}
i1++;
}
cout<<"YOUR ARRAY IN DECSENDING
ORDER IS AS FOLLOWS: YOUR
ARRAY["<<k<<"] = ";
for(b2=0;b2<k;b2++)
{
cout<<" "<<i[b2];
}
getch();
}
```

**OUTPUT:**

ENTER NUMBER OF DATA (MAXIMUM 100):5
ENTER DATA (IN INTEGER):k=[1] 4
k=[2] 7
k=[3] 2
k=[4] 1
k=[5] 5

YOUR ARRAY IN DECSENDING ORDER IS AS FOLLOWS: YOUR ARRAY[5]=7 5 4 2 1

**Problem 134. Write a C++ program for IEEE 754 representation of any floating point number.**

***Program:***

```
#include<iostream.h>
int power(int,int);
void main()
{
float a,f,r,x,temp,sum,g;
int
n,i,j,u,o,b[30],c[30],B[30],Z[30],e[10],m[25],F[40],t,
k,y,z,count,exp,h,d;
clrscr();
cout<<"Enter the number ";
cin>>a;
g=a;
if(a<0)
{
a=0-a;
n=a;
}
else
n=a;
f=a-n;
/* conversion of integer part to binary */
i=0;
while(n!=0)
{
b[i]=n%2;
n=n/2;
i++;
}
/* arranging the bits of the binary equalent of integer
part*/
for(j=i-1,k=0;j>=0;j--,k++)
c[k]=b[j];
if(k==0)
{
c[k]=0;
k=k+1;
}
/* conversion of floating part to binary */
sum=0;
for(i=1;i<=11;i++)
{
t=power(2,i);
r=t;
x=1/r;
sum=sum+x;
temp=sum;
if(temp <= f)
{
B[i-1]=1;
sum=temp;
}
else
{
B[i-1]=0;
sum=temp-x;
}
}
/* arranging the bits of the binary equalent of
floating part*/
for(i=0,z=k;i<=10;i++,z++)
c[z]=B[i];
count=k-1;
cout<<"The IEEE 754 standard floating point
number allignment is ";
exp=127+count;
i=0;
while(exp!=0)
{
Z[i]=exp%2;
exp=exp/2;
i++;
}
if(count==0)
{
Z[i]=0;
i++;
}
if(g<0)
cout<<"\n The sign value is "<<1;
else
cout<<"\n The sign value is "<<0;
/* Arranging the bits in order for exponent*/
for(j=i-1,k=0;j>=0;j--,k++)
e[k]=Z[j];
cout<<"\n The value of exponent is : ";
for(u=0;u<=k-1;u++)
cout<<e[u];
/* Arranging the bits in order for Mantissa*/
cout<<"\n The value of mantissa is :";
d=z-1;
for(y=1,o=0;o<=22;y++,o++)
{
if(o<d)
m[o]=c[y];
else
```

```
m[o]=0;
cout<<m[o];
}
cout<<"\nThe FINAL REPRESENTATION IS : ";
for(h=0;h<=31;h++)
{
if(h==0)
{
if(g<0)
F[0]=1;
else
F[0]=0;
}
if(h<=k && h!=0)
F[h]=e[h-1];
else if(h>k && h!=0)
F[h]=m[h-9];
cout<<F[h];
}
getch();
}
int power(int w, int d)
{
int pro,i;
pro=1;
for(i=1;i<=d;i++)
pro=pro*w;
return(pro);
}
```

**OUTPUT:**

```
Enter the number 2.4
The IEEE 754 standard floating point number
allignment is
The sign value is 0
The value of exponent is : 10000000
The value of mantissa is :
00110011001100000000000
The FINAL REPRESENTATION IS :
01000000000110011001100000000000
```

# CHAPTER 6

# STRINGS

## STRING APPEND:

**Problem 1. Write a C++ program to demonstrates how to put strings together using strcat.**

***Program:***

```
#include<iostream.h>
#include<string.h>
#include<conio.h>
void main()
{
char first[100];
char last[100];
char full_name[200];
strcpy(first, "firstName");
strcpy(last, "secondName");
strcpy(full_name, first);
strcat(full_name, " ");
strcat(full_name, last);
cout<<"The full name is "<< full_name<<"\n";
getch();
}
```

**OUTPUT:**

The full name is firstName secondName

**Problem 2. Write a C++ program to get first and last name and print them together.**

***Program:***

```
#include<iostream.h>
#include<string.h>
#include<conio.h>
void main()
{
char first[100];
char last[100];
char full[100];
clrscr();
cout<<"Enter first name: ";
fgets(first, sizeof(first), stdin);
first[strlen(first)-1] = '\0';
cout<<"Enter last name: ";
fgets(last, sizeof(last), stdin);
last[strlen(last)-1] = '\0';
strcpy(full, first);
strcat(full, " ");
strcat(full, last);
cout<<"The name is "<< full<<"\n";
getch();
}
```

**OUTPUT:**

Enter first name: Prof.Rachhpal Singh
Enter last name: (HEAD of P.G deptt. of CS)
The name is Prof.RachhpalSingh(HEAD of P.G deptt. of CS)

**Problem 3. Write a C++ program to join strings.**

***Program:***

```
#include<iostream.h>
#include<conio.h>
void main()
{
char str1[40] = "To be or not to be";
char str2[40] = ",that is the question";
int count1 = 0;
int count2 = 0;
while (str1[count1] != '\0')
count1++;
while (str2[count2] != '\0')
count2++;
if(sizeof str1 < count1 + count2 + 1)
cout<<"\nYou can't put a quart into a pint pot.";
else
{
count2 = 0;
while(str2[count2] != '\0')
str1[count1++] = str2[count2++];
str1[count1] = '\0';
cout<<"\n"<<str1<<"\n";
}
getch();
}
```

**OUTPUT:**

To be or not to be,that is the question

**Problem 4. Write a C++ program to join strings: revitalised: strlen and strcat.**

***Program:***

```
#include<iostream.h>
#include<string.h>
#include<conio.h>
#define STR_LENGTH 40
void main()
{
char str1[STR_LENGTH] = "String in C";
char str2[STR_LENGTH] = ",String in C";
clrscr();
if(STR_LENGTH > strlen(str1) + strlen(str2))
cout<<"\n"<< strcat(str1, str2) ;
else
cout<<"\n no enough room.";
getch();
}
```

**OUTPUT:**

String in C,String in C

**Problem 5. Write a C++ program to append string to another string.**

***Program:***

```
#include<iostream.h>
#include<string.h>
#include<conio.h>
void main()
{
char s1[80], s2[80];
clrscr();
cout<<"Enter s1:";
gets(s1);
cout<<"Enter s2:";
gets(s2);
strcat(s2, s1);
cout<<(s2);
getch();
}
```

**OUTPUT:**

Enter s1:me
Enter s2:ga
game

**Problem 6. Write a C++ program to append string: strncat.**

***Program:***

```
#include<iostream.h>
#include<string.h>
#include<conio.h>
void main()
{
char s1[80], s2[80];
unsigned int len;
cout<<Enter s1:";
gets(s1);
cout<<Enter s2:";
gets(s2);
len = 79 - strlen(s2);
strncat(s2, s1, len);
cout<<s2;
getch();
}
```

Enter s1:ding
Enter s2:Buil
Building

**Problem 7. Write a C++ program to concatenate string.**

***Program:***

```
#include<iostream.h>
#include<conio.h>
#define concat(a, b) a ## b
void main()
{
int xy = 10;
clrscr();
cout<< concat(x, y);
getch();
}
```

**OUTPUT:**

10

**Problem 8. Write a C++ program to append substring to string: strncat.**

***Program:***

```
#include<iostream.h>
#include<string.h>
#include<conio.h>
void main()
{
char str1[20];
char str2[20];
clrscr();
strcpy (str1,"qqq34567790");
strcpy (str2,"333333");
strncat (str1, str2, 6);
puts (str1);
getch();
}
```

**OUTPUT:**

qqq34567790333333

**Problem 9. Write a C++ program to append string: how to use strcat.**

***Program:***

```
#include<iostream.h>
#include<string.h>
#include<conio.h>
void main()
{
char str[80];
clrscr();
strcpy (str,"part I, ");
strcat (str,"part II, ");
strcat (str,"part III,");
puts (str);
getch();
}
```

**OUTPUT:**

part I,   part II, part III.

## STRING CASE:

**Problem 10. Write a C++ program to convert string to upper case and lower case.**

***Program:***

```
#include<conio.h>
#include<ctype.h>
#include<iostream.h>
void main()
{
char str[80];
int i;
cout<<"Enter a string: ";
gets(str);
for( i = 0; str[ i ]; i++)
str[ i ] = toupper( str[ i ] );
cout<<" str";
for(i = 0; str[ i ]; i++)
str[i] = tolower(str[ i ]);
cout<<" str";
getch();
}
```

**OUTPUT:**SirJe

SIRJE

sirje

**Problem 11. Write a C++ program to change string case using its pointer.**

***Program:***

```
#include<conio.h>
#include<ctype.h>
#include<iostream.h>
void main()
{
char str[80], *p;
cout<<"Enter a string: ";
gets(str);
p = str;
while( *p )
{
*p = toupper(*p);
p++;
}
cout<<"\n"<<str;
p = str;
while( *p )
{
*p = tolower(*p);
p++;
}
cout<<"\n"<<str;
getch();
}
```

**OUTPUT:**SirJe

SIRJE

sirje

## STRING COMPARE:

**Problem 12. Write a C++ program to compare strings: strcmp.**

***Program:***

```
#include<conio.h>
#include<iostream.h>
#include<string.h>
void main()
{
char word1[20];
char word2[20];
cout<<" first word:\n1: ";
cin>>word1;
cout<<" second word:\n 2: ";
cin>>word2;
if(strcmp(word1,word2) == 0)
cout<<"identical words";
else
cout<<" (strcmp(word1, word2) > 0) ? word2 :
word1<< "comes before"<<(strcmp(word1, word2)
< 0) ? word2 : word1;
getch();
}
```

**OUTPUT:**

first word:
1: 2009
second word:
2: 2008
2008 comes before 2009

**Problem 13. Write a C++ program for testing characters in a string: is digit and is alpha.**

***Program:***

```
#include<conio.h>
#include<iostream.h>
#include<ctype.h>
void main()
{
char buffer[80];
int i = 0;
int num_letters = 0;
int num_digits = 0;
cout<<" string with char and digits:\n";
gets(buffer);
while(buffer[i] != '\0')
{
if(isalpha(buffer[i]))
num_letters++;
if(isdigit(buffer[i++]))
num_digits++;
}
cout<<"\n The string contained "<<num_letters<<"
letters and "<< num_digits<< "digits.\n";
getch();
}
```

**OUTPUT:**

string with char and digits:2nov
The string contained 3 letters and 1 digits.

**Problem 14. Write a C++ program to ur own string compare function.**

***Program:***

```
#include<conio.h>
#include<stdlib.h>
#include<ctype.h>
#include<iostream.h>
int comp(const void *ch, const void *s);
void main()
{
char *alpha = "abcdefghijklmnopqrstuvwxyz";
char ch;
char *p;
cout<<"Enter a character: ";
ch = getchar();
ch = tolower(ch);
p = (char *) bsearch(&ch, alpha, 26, 1, comp);
if(p)
cout<<*p<<" is in alphabet\n";
else
cout<<"is not in alphabet\n";
getch();
}
/* Compare two characters.
int comp(const void *ch, const void *s)
{
return *(char *)ch - *(char *)s;
}
```

**OUTPUT:**

Enter a character: m
m is in alphabet

**Problem 15. Write a C++ program to compare string: how to use strncmp.**

***Program:***

```
#include<iostream.h>
#include<string.h>
#include<stdlib.h>
#include<conio.h>
void main(int argc, char *argv[])
{
if(argc!=3)
{
cout<<"Incorrect number of arguments.";
getch();
exit(1);
}
if(!strncmp(argv[1], argv[2], 8))
cout<<"The strings are the same.\n";
getch();
}
```

**OUTPUT:**

Incorrect number of arguments.

**Problem 16. Write a C++ program to compare two strings: how to use strcmp.**

***Program:***

```
#include<conio.h>
#include<iostream.h>
#include<string.h>
void main()
{
char szKey[] = "Apple";
char szInput[80];
```

```
do
{
cout<<"Which is my favourite computer? ";
gets (szInput);
}
while (strcmp (szKey,szInput) != 0);
cout<<"Correct answer!\n";
getch();
}
```

**OUTPUT:**

Which is my favourite computer?Apple
correct answer!

**Problem 17. Write a C++ program to compare some characters of two strings: how to use strncmp.**

***Program:***

```
#include<conio.h>
#include<iostream.h>
#include<string.h>
void main()
{
char str[][5] = { "CS115" , "CS334" , "CS445" ,
"CS335" , "CS889" };
int n;
cout<<"Looking for a class...\n";
for (n=0 ; n < 5 ; n++)
if (strncmp (str[n],"CS33*",1) == 0)
{
cout<<"found "<<str[n]<<"\n";
}
getch();
}
```

**OUTPUT:**

Looking for a class...
found CS115CS334CS445CS335CS889
found S334CS445CS335CS889
found S445CS335CS889
found S335CS889

## STRING CONVERT:

**Problem 18. Write a C++ program to join array of strings into a single string.**

***Program:***

```
#include<iostream.h>
#include<stdlib.h>
#include<string.h>
#include<ctype.h>
#include<conio.h>
#define MAX_STRINGS 100
#define BUFFER_SIZE 50
char* join_strings(char *strings[], int count);
char* read_string();
void main()
{
char *pStrings[MAX_STRINGS];
char *joined_strings = NULL;
int count = 0;
char answer = 'y';
char terminator = '*';
int i = 0;
while(count<MAX_STRINGS &&
tolower(answer)=='y')
{
cout<<"Enter a string:\n";
pStrings[count++] = read_string(terminator);
cout<<"Do you want to enter another: ";
cin>>answer;
fflush(stdin);
}
joined_strings = join_strings(pStrings, count);
cout<<"Here are the strings as a single string:\n"<<
joined_strings<<"\n";
free(joined_strings);
for(i = 0 ; i<count ; i++)
free(pStrings[i]);
getch();
}
char* join_strings(char *strings[], int count)
{
char* str = NULL;
size_t total_length = 0;
size_t length = 0;
int i = 0;
for(i = 0 ; i<count ; i++)
{
total_length += strlen(strings[i]);
if(strings[i][strlen(strings[i])-1] != '\n')
++total_length;
}
++total_length;
str = (char*)malloc(total_length);
str[0] = '\0';
for(i = 0 ; i<count ; i++)
{
strcat(str, strings[i]);
length = strlen(str);
if(str[length-1] != '\n')
{
str[length] = '\n';
```

```
str[length+1] = '\0';
}
}
return str;
}
char* read_string(char terminator)
{
char *buffer = NULL;
int buffersize = BUFFER_SIZE;
int length = 0;
char *temp = NULL;
int i = 0;
buffer = (char*)malloc(BUFFER_SIZE);
for(;;)
{
if((buffer[length] = getchar()) == terminator)
break;
else
++length;
if(length == buffersize)
{
buffersize += BUFFER_SIZE;
temp = (char*)malloc(buffersize);
for(i = 0 ; i<length ; i++)
temp[i] = buffer[i];
free(buffer);
buffer = temp;
temp = NULL;
}
}
buffer[length] = '\0';
temp = (char*)malloc(length+1);
strcpy(temp, buffer);
free(buffer);
return temp;
}
```

**Problem 19. Write a C++ program to convert one or more floating-point values into a single string.**

***Program:***

```
#include<iostream.h>
#include<stdlib.h>
#include<stdarg.h>
#include<string.h>
#include<conio.h>
char* to_string(int count, double first, ...);
char* fp_to_str(double x);
char* int_to_str(int n);
void main()
{
char *str = NULL;
double values[] = { 1.245, -3.5, 6.758, 33.399, -
1.02 };
str = to_string(sizeof values/sizeof(double),
values[0], values[1], values[2], values[3],
values[4]);
cout<<"The string of values is: \n"<< str<<"\n";
free(str);
getch();
}
char* to_string(int count, double first, ...)
{
va_list parg = NULL;
char* str = NULL;
char *temp = NULL;
char *value_str = 0;
const char *separator = ",";
size_t separator_length = 0;
size_t length = 0;
int i = 0;
separator_length = strlen(separator);
va_start(parg,first); // Initialize argument pointer
str = fp_to_str(first); // convert the first value
// Get the remaining arguments, convert them and
append to the string
while(--count>0)
{
value_str = fp_to_str(va_arg(parg, double)); // Get
next argument
length = strlen(str) + strlen(value_str) +
separator_length +1;
temp = (char*)malloc(length); // Allocate space for
string with argument
strcpy(temp, str); // Copy the old string
free(str); // Release old memory
str = temp; // Store new memory address
temp = NULL; // Reset pointer
strcat(str,separator); // Append separator
strcat(str,value_str); // Append value string
free(value_str); // Release value string memory
}
va_end(parg); // Clean up arg pointer
return str;
}
char* fp_to_str(double x)
{
char *str = NULL; // Pointer to string
representation
char *integral = NULL; // Pointer to integral part
as string
```

```
char *fraction = NULL; // Pointer to fractional part
as string
size_t length = 0; // Total string length required
integral = int_to_str((int)x); // Get integral part as a
string with a sign
if(x<0)
x = -x;
// Get fractional part as a string
fraction = int_to_str((int)(100.0*(x+0.005-(int)x)));
length = strlen(integral)+strlen(fraction)+2;
// Fraction must be two digits so allow for it
if(strlen(fraction)<2)
++length;
str = (char*)malloc(length); // Allocate memory for
total
strcpy(str, integral); // Copy the integral part
strcat(str, "."); // Append decimal point
if(strlen(fraction)<2) // If fraction less than two
digits
strcat(str,"0"); // Append leading zero
strcat(str, fraction); // Append fractional part
// Free up memory for parts as strings
free(integral);
free(fraction);
return str;
}
char* int_to_str(int n)
{
char *str = NULL; // pointer to the string
int length = 1; // Number of characters in string(at
least 1 for terminator
int temp = 0;
int sign = 1; // Indicates sign of n
// Check for negative value
if(n<0)
{
sign = -1;
n = -n;
++length; // For the minus character
}
// Increment length by number of digits in n
temp = n;
do
{
++length;
}
while((temp /= 10)>0);
str = (char*)malloc(length); // Allocate space
required
if(sign<0) // If it was negative
str[0] = '-'; // Insert the minus sign
str[--length] = '\0'; // Add the terminator to the end
// Add the digits starting from the end
do
{
str[--length] = '0'+n%10;
}while((n /= 10) > 0);
return str;
}
```

**OUTPUT:**

The string of values is:
1.25, -3.50, 6.76, 33.40, -1.02

**Problem 20. Write a C++ program to convert string to double-precision floating-point value.**

***Program:***

```
#include<conio.h>
#include<stdlib.h>
#include<ctype.h>
#include<iostream.h>
void main()
{
char *end, *start = "Value: 111.1111111";
clrscr();
end = start;
while( *start )
{
cout<<strtod(start, &end);
cout<<"Remainder:"<<"\n"
start = end;
while(!isdigit(*start) && *start)
start++;
}
getch();
}
```

**OUTPUT:**

0.000000, Remainder:Value:111.1111111
111.111111, Remainder:

**Problem 21. Write a C++ program to change string to integer.**

***Program:***

```
#include<conio.h>
#include<stdlib.h>
#include<iostream.h>
void main()
{
char num[80];
clrscr();
cout<<"Enter string:";
gets(num);
cout<<"abs(atoi(num));
```

```
getch();
}
```

**OUTPUT:**

```
Enter string:-45
45
```

**Problem 22. Write a C++ program to convert string entered to integer.**

*Program:*

```
#include<conio.h>
#include<stdlib.h>
#include<iostream.h>
void main()
{
char num1[80], num2[80];
cout<<"Enter first: ";
gets(num1);
cout<<""Enter second: ";
gets(num2);
cout<<"The sum is: "<< atoi(num1) + atoi(num2);
getch();
}
```

**OUTPUT:**

```
Enter first: 45
Enter second: 55
The sum is: 110
```

**Problem 23. Write a C++ program to convert string entered to long..**

*Program:*

```
#include<conio.h>
#include<stdlib.h>
#include<iostream.h>
void main()
{
char num1[80], num2[80];
cout<<"Enter first: ";
gets(num1);
cout<<"Enter second: ";
gets(num2);
cout<<"The sum is: "<< atol(num1)+atol(num2);
getch();
}
Enter first: 1000000
Enter second:1000000
The sum is: 2000000
```

**Problem 24. Write a C++ program to convert string to double: How to use atof: sines calculator.**

*Program:*

```
#include<conio.h>
#include<iostream.h>
#include<stdlib.h>
#include<math.h>
void main()
{
double n, m;
double pi=3.1415926535;
char str[256];
cout<<"Enter degrees: ";
gets ( str );
n = atof ( str );
m = sin ( n * pi / 180 );
cout<<" sine of "<<n<<" degrees = "<< m<<"\n" ;
getch();
}
Enter degrees: 60
sine of 60 degrees = 0.866025
```

**Problem 25. Write a C++ program to convert string to integer: atoi.**

*Program:*

```
#include<conio.h>
#include<iostream.h>
#include<stdlib.h>
void main()
{
int i;
char str[256];
cout<<"Enter a number: ";
gets ( str );
i = atoi ( str );
cout<<"i = "<<i<<" its double = "<< i * 2 ;
getch();
}
```

**OUTPUT:**

```
Enter a number: 412
i = 412, its double = 824
```

**Problem 26. Write a C++ program to print formatted data to a string: how to use sprintf.**

*Program:*

```
#include <stdio.h>
#include<conio.h>
void main()
{
 char buffer [50];
 int n, a = 50, b = 37;
 clrscr();
```

```
n = sprintf (buffer, "%d plus %d is %d", a, b, a +
b);
cout<< "["<<buffer<<"] is a "<<n<<" chars
string<<"\n";
getch();
}
```

**OUTPUT:**

[57 + 37 is 87] is a 16 chars string

**Problem 27. Write a C++ program to convert string to double: how to use atof.**

***Program:***

```
#include<iostream.h>
#include<math.h>
#include<conio.h>
void main()
{
double n, m;
double pi = 3.1415926535;
char str[256];
clrscr();
cout<<"Enter degrees: " ;
gets ( str );
n = atof ( str );
m = sin (n * pi / 180);
cout<<" sine of "<<n<<" degrees = "<< m<<"\n" ;
getch();
}
```

Enter degrees: 60
sine of 60 degrees = 0.866025

**Problem 28. Write a C++ program to convert string to double-precision floating-point value: how to use strtod.**

***Program:***

```
#include<iostream.h>
#include<stdlib.h>
#include<conio.h>
void main()
{
char str[256];
char *p;
double dbl;
clrscr();
cout<<"Enter a floating-point value: ";
gets (str);
dbl = strtod (str, &p);
cout<<"Value entered: "<<dbl<<" Its square: "<<dbl
* dbl<<"\n";
getch();
}
```

**OUTPUT:**

Enter a floating-point value: 12.4
Value entered: 12.400000. Its square: 153.760000

**Problem 29. Write a C++ program to convert string to long integer: how to use strtol.**

***Program:***

```
#include<conio.h>
#include<iostream.h>
#include<stdlib.h>
void main()
{
char str[256];
char *p;
long l;
clrscr();
cout<<"Enter an long value: ";
gets (str);
l = strtol (str, &p, 0);
cout<<"Value entered: "<<l<<" Its doublesquare:
"<<l * 2<<"\n";
getch();
}
```

**OUTPUT:**

Enter an long value: 1000000
Value entered: 1000000. Its double: 2000000

**Problem 30. Write a C++ program to convert string to unsigned long integer: how to use strtoul.**

***Program:***

```
#include<conio.h>
#include<iostream.h>
#include<stdlib.h>
void main()
{
char str[256];
char *p;
unsigned long ul;
clrscr();
cout<<"Enter an integer value: ";
gets (str);
ul = strtoul (str, &p, 0);
cout<<"Value entered: "<<ul<<" Its doublesquare:
"<<ul * 2<<"\n";
getch();
}
```

**OUTPUT:**

Enter an integer value: 412
Value entered: 412. Its double: 824

**Problem 31. Write a C++ program to convert string to int, double and long.**

***Program:***

```
#include<conio.h>
#include<iostream.h>
#include<stdlib.h>
void main(int argc, char *argv[])
{
int i;
double d;
long l;
clrscr();
i = atoi("1");
l = atol("11111111");
d = atof("11111.11111");
cout<< i<< l<< d;
getch();
}
```

**OUTPUT:**

1 11111111 11111.111110

**Problem 32. Write a C++ program for absolute value of long integer: how to use labs.**

***Program:***

```
#include<conio.h>
#include<iostream.h>
#include<stdlib.h>
void main ()
{
int n, m;
n = labs( 65537 );
m = labs( -110000 );
cout<<"n = "<<n<<"\n";
cout<<"m = "<<m<<"\n";
getch();
}
```

**OUTPUT:**

n=1
m=-21072

## STRING COPY:

**Problem 33. Write a C++ program to show how to use strcpy (string copy).**

***Program:***

```
#include<conio.h>
#include<string.h>
#include<iostream.h>
char name[30]; // First name of someone
void main()
{
strcpy(name, "Sam"); // Initialize the name
cout<<"The name is "<< name<<"\n";
getch();
}
```

**OUTPUT:**

The name is sam

**Problem 34. Write a C++ program for string copy.**

***Program:***

```
#include<conio.h>
#include<iostream.h>
#include<string.h>
void main()
{
char str[80];
strcpy(str, "this is an example");
puts(str);
getch();
}
```

**OUTPUT:**

this is an example

**Problem 35. Write a C++ program to copy string: how to use strcpy.**

***Program:***

```
#include<conio.h>
#include<iostream.h>
#include<string.h>
void main()
{
char str1[]="Sample";
char str2[40];
char str3[40];
strcpy (str2, str1);
strcpy (str3, "copy");
cout<<"str1= "<<str1<<"\n str2= "<<str2<<"\n
str3= "<<str3<<"\n";
getch();
}
```

**OUTPUT:**

str1=Sample
str2=Sample
str3=copy

**Problem 36. Write a C++ program to copy characters from one string to another: how to use strncpy.**

***Program:***

```
#include<conio.h>
#include<iostream.h>
#include<string.h>
void main()
{
char str1[]= "Hi Hello and ";
char str2[6];
strncpy (str2, str1, 5);
str2[5] = '\0';
puts (str2);
getch();
}
```

**OUTPUT:**

Hi He

**Problem 37. Write a C++ program for string copy: assign the pointer value.**

***Program:***

```
#include<conio.h>
#include<iostream.h>
#include<string.h>
void main()
{
char *p = "stop";
char str[80];
do
{
cout<<"Enter a string: ";
gets(str);
} while(strcmp(p, str));
getch();
}
```

**OUTPUT:**

Enter a string:stop

**Problem 38. Write a C++ program to copy a string.**

***Program:***

```
#include<conio.h>
#include<iostream.h>
#include<string.h>
void main()
{
char str[80] = "I like C";
strcpy(str, "I like Java");
cout<<str;
getch();
}
```

**OUTPUT:**

I like Java

## STRING LENGTH:

**Problem 39. Write a C++ program to determine string length.**

***Program:***

```
#include<iostream.h>
#include<conio.h>
int length(char string[])
{
int index;
for (index = 0; string[index] != '\0'; ++index)
continue;
return (index);
}
void main()
{
char line[100];
while (1)
{
cout<<"Enter line:";
fgets(line, sizeof(line), stdin);
cout<<"Length (including newline) is: "<<
length(line)<<"\n";
}
getch();
}
```

**OUTPUT:**

Enter line:good boy
Length (including newline) is: 9

**Problem 40. Write a C++ program to computes the length of a line.**

***Program:***

```
#include<conio.h>
#include<string.h>
#include<iostream.h>
void main()
{
char line[100];
cout<<"Enter a line: ";
fgets(line, sizeof(line), stdin);
cout<<"The length of the line is:
"<<strlen(line)<<"\n";
getch();
}
```

**OUTPUT:**

Enter a line:good boy
Length (including newline) is: 9

**Problem 41. Write a C++ program to determine**

length of strings.

*Program:*

```
#include<iostream.h>
#include<conio.h>
void main()
{
char str1[40] = "To be or not to be";
char str2[40] = ",that is the question. ";
int count = 0;
while (str1[count] != '\0')
count++;
cout<<"The length of the string \""<<str1<<"\" is
"<<count<<"characters.";
count = 0;
while (str2[count] != '\0')
count++;
cout<<"The length of the string \""<<str2<<"\" is
"<<count<<"characters.";
getch();
}
```

**OUTPUT:**

The length of the string "To be or not to be" is 18 characters.
The length of the string "that is the question." is 23 characters.

**Problem 42. Write a C++ program to get the string length.**

*Program:*

```
#include<iostream.h>
#include<string.h>
#include<conio.h>
void main()
{
char str[80];
gets(str);
cout<<"Length is"<< strlen(str);
getch();
}
```

**OUTPUT:**

game
Length is 4

**Problem 43. Write a C++ program to get length of substring composed of given characters.**

*Program:*

```
#include<conio.h>
#include<string.h>
#include<iostream.h>
void main()
{
int len;
len = strspn("this is a test", "siht ");
cout<<"length is "<< len;
getch();
}
```

**OUTPUT:**

length is 8

**Problem 44. Write a C++ program to add null terminator to string end.**

*Program:*

```
#include<iostream.h>
#include<conio.h>
void main()
{
char s[256], *p;
p = s;
while((*p++ = getchar())!= '\n') ;
*p = '\0';
cout<<s;
getch();
}
```

**OUTPUT:**

king
king

**Problem 45. Write a C++ program to print the string forward and backwards.**

*Program:*

```
#include<iostream.h>
#include<string.h>
#include<conio.h>
char *p = "hello world";
void main()
{
register int t;
clrscr();
cout<<p;
for( t = strlen( p ) - 1; t > -1; t--)
cout<<p[ t ];
getch();
}
```

**OUTPUT:**

hello world dlrow olleh

**Problem 46. Write a C++ program to show string operator: get length, compare and find a char.**

*Program:*

```
#include<conio.h>
#include<iostream.h>
#include<string.h>
void main()
{
char s1[80], s2[80];
clrscr();
gets(s1);
gets(s2);
cout<<"lengths: "<<strlen(s1)<< strlen(s2)<<"\n";
if(!strcmp(s1, s2))
cout<<"The strings are equal\n");
strcat(s1, s2);
cout<< s1<<"\n";
strcpy(s1, "This is a test.\n");
cout<<s1;
if(strchr("hello", 'e'))
cout<<"e is in hello\n";
if(strstr("hi there", "hi"))
cout<<"found hi";
getch();
}
```

**OUTPUT:**

```
king
lengths: 0 4
king
this is a test.
e is in hello
found hi
```

**Problem 47. Write a C++ program to return string length: how to use strlen.**

***Program:***

```
#include<conio.h>
#include<iostream.h>
#include<string.h>
void main()
{
char str[256];
cout<<"Enter a sentence: ";
gets (str);
cout<<str<<" is "<<strlen( str ) << "characters
long\n";
getch();
}
```

**OUTPUT:**

```
Enter a sentence: good boy
good boy is 8 characters long
```

**Problem 48. Write a C++ program get length of substring composed of given characters: how to use strspn.**

***Program:***

```
#include<conio.h>
#include<iostream.h>
#include<string.h>
void main()
{
int i;
char key[] = "890th";
char str[] = "1234567890";
clrscr();
i = strspn (key, str);
cout<<"Length of initial number is "<<i<<"\n";
getch();
}
```

**OUTPUT:**

```
Length of initial number is 3
```

**Problem 49. Write a C++ program to check string length and set string end.**

***Program:***

```
#include<conio.h>
#include<iostream.h>
#include<string.h>
void main()
{
char str[10];
int i;
cout<<"Enter a string: ";
fgets(str, 10, stdin);
i = strlen(str) - 1;
if(str[i] =='\n')
str[i] = '\0';
cout<<"This is your string: "<< str;
getch();
}
```

**OUTPUT:**

```
Enter a string: king
This is your string: king
```

## STRING SEARCH:

**Problem 50. Write a C++ program to look up names in a hardcoded list.**

***Program:***

```
#define STRING_LENGTH 80
#include<iostream.h>
#include<string.h>
#include<conio.h>
int lookup(char const *const name);
```

```
void main()
{
char name[STRING_LENGTH] = "Jim";
name[strlen(name)] = '\0';
if (lookup(name))
{
s is in the list"<< name;
}
else
{
cout<<name<<" is not in the list\n";
}
getch();
}
int lookup(char const *const name)
{
static char *list[] =
{"John","Jim","Jane","Clyde",NULL};
int index;
for (index = 0; list[index] != NULL; ++index)
{
If (strcmp(list[index], name) == 0)
return (1);
}
return (0);
}
```

**OUTPUT:**

Jim is in the list

**Problem 51. Write a C++ program for finding occurrences of one string in another: strstr.**

***Program:***

```
#include<conio.h>
#include<iostream.h>
#include<string.h>
#include<ctype.h>
void main()
{
char text[100];
char substring[40];
int i = 0;
cout<<"\n string to be searched(less than 100
characters):\n");
gets(text);
cout<<"\n string sought (less than 40 characters
):\n");
gets(substring);
for(i = 0 ; (text[i] = toupper(text[i])) != '\0' ; i++);
for(i = 0 ; (substring[i] = toupper(substring[i])) !=
'\0' ; i++);
cout<<"\nThe second string "%s found in the
first.\n",
((strstr(text, substring) == NULL) ? "was not" :
"was"));
getch();
}
```

**OUTPUT:**

string to be searched(less than 100 characters):
avtar is a good boy
string sought (less than 40 characters ):
good
The second string was found in the first.

**Problem 52. Write a C++ program for demonstration of seeking and finding.**

***Program:***

```
#include<conio.h>
#include<iostream.h>
#include<string.h>
void main()
{
char str1[] = "This string contains the key.";
char str2[] = "the key";
char str3[] = "the keys";
clrscr();
if(strstr(str1, str2) == NULL)
cout<<"\nString not found.");
else
cout<<"\nString: "<<str2<<"\n was found in string:
"<< str1;
if(strstr(str1, str3) == NULL)
cout<<"\nString not found.";
else
cout<<"\nWe shouldn't get to here!";
getch();
}
```

**OUTPUT:**

String:the key
was found in string:This string contains the key.
string not found.

**Problem 53. Write a C++ program to find sub string: our own function.**

***Program:***

```
#include<iostream.h>
#include<conio.h>
int find_substr(char *listPointer, char
*itemPointer);
void main()
{
```

```
if(find_substr("C is fun", "is") != -1)
cout<<"Substring is found.";
getch();
}
// Return index of first match of itemPointer in
listPointer.
int find_substr(char *listPointer, char *itemPointer)
{
int t;
char *p, *p2;
for(t=0; listPointer[t]; t++)
{
p = &listPointer[t];
p2 = itemPointer;
while(*p2 && *p2==*p)
{
p++;
p2++;
}
if(!*p2) return t;
}
return -1;
}
```

**OUTPUT:**

Substring is found.

**Problem 54. Write a C++ program to search a char inside a string.**

***Program:***

```
#include<conio.h>
#include<iostream.h>
#include<string.h>
void main()
{
char *p;
clrscr();
p = strchr("this is a test", ' ');
cout<<p;
getch();
}
```

**OUTPUT:**

is a test

**Problem 55. Write a C++ program to scan string for specified characters.**

***Program:***

```
#include<conio.h>
#include<iostream.h>
#include<string.h>
void main()
{
char *p;
clrscr();
p = strpbrk("this is a test", " absj");
cout<<p;
getch();
}
```

**OUTPUT:**

s is a test

**Problem 56. Write a C++ program to find last occurrence of character in string.**

***Program:***

```
#include<conio.h>
#include<string.h>
#include<iostream.h>
void main()
{
char *p;
clrscr();
p = strrchr("this is a test", 'a');
cout<<p;
getch();
}
```

**OUTPUT:**

a test

**Problem 57. Write a C++ program to find substring.**

***Program:***

```
#include<conio.h>
#include<string.h>
#include<iostream.h>
void main()
{
char *p;
clrscr();
p = strstr("this is a test", "is");
cout<<p;
getch();
}
```

**OUTPUT:**

is is a test

**Problem 58. Write a C++ program to search string for occurrence of character set.**

***Program:***

```
#include<conio.h>
#include<string.h>
#include<iostream.h>
void main()
{
```

```
int len;
clrscr();
len = strcspn("this is a test", "a");
cout<<len;
getch();
}
```

**OUTPUT:**

8

**Problem 59. Write a C++ program to search string.**

***Program:***

```
#include<conio.h>
#include<iostream.h>
#include<string.h>
int search(char *p[], char *name);
char *names[] =
{"John","Jim","Jane","James",NULL};
void main()
{
if(search(names, "James") != -1)
cout<<"in list.\n";
if(search(names, "Bill") == -1)
cout<<"not found.\n";
getch();
}
int search(char *p[], char *name)
{
int t;
for(t=0; p[t]; ++t)
{
if(!strcmp(p[t], name))
{
return t;
}
}
return -1; // not found
}
```

**OUTPUT:**

in list

not found

**Problem 60. Write a C++ program to search string for occurrence of character set: how to use strcspn.**

***Program:***

```
#include<conio.h>
#include<iostream.h>
#include<string.h>
void main()
{
char str1[] = "1245789000";
char str2[] = "1234567890";
int i;
i = strcspn (str1,str2);
cout<<"The first number in str1 is
str1["<<i<<"]\n";
getch();
}
```

**OUTPUT:**

The first number in str1 is str1[0]

**Problem 61. Write a C++ program to scan string for specified characters: how to use strpbrk.**

***Program:***

```
#include<iostream.h>
#include<string.h>
#include<conio.h>
void main()
{
char str[] = "This is a line";
char key[] = "aeiou";
char *p;
cout<<"Vowels in : "<<str;
p = strpbrk (str, key);
while (p != NULL)
{
cout<<*p;
p = strpbrk (p + 1, key);
}
cout<<"\n";
getch();
}
```

**OUTPUT:**

Vowels in This is a line i i a i e

**Problem 62. Write a C++ program to find last occurrence of character in string: how to use strrchr.**

***Program:***

```
#include<conio.h>
#include<iostream.h>
#include<string.h>
void main()
{
char str[] = " This is a line";
char *p;
p = strrchr(str, 'i');
cout<<"Last occurence of 'i' is "<< p - str +
```

```
l<<"\n";
getch();
}
```

**OUTPUT:**

Last occurence of 'i' is 12

**Problem 63. Write a C++ program to find substring: how to use strstr.**

***Program:***

```
#include<conio.h>
#include<iostream.h>
#include<string.h>
void main()
{
char str[] ="This is a line";
char *p;
p = strstr (str, "is");
strncpy (p, "sample",5 );
puts (str);
getch();
}
```

**OUTPUT:**

Thsampl a line

**Problem 64. Write a C++ program to find character in string: how to use strchr.**

***Program:***

```
#include<conio.h>
#include<iostream.h>
#include<string.h>
void main()
{
char str[] = "This is a line";
char *p;
clrscr();
cout<<"Looking for 's' character in
\""<<str<<"\"...\n";
p = strchr(str, 's');
while (p != NULL)
{
cout<<"found at "<<p - str + 1<<"\n";
p = strchr(p + 1, 's');
}
getch();
}
```

**OUTPUT:**

Looking for 's' character in This is a line..
found at 4
found at 7

## STRING SPLIT:

**Problem 65. Write a C++ program to sequentially truncate string if delimiter is found.**

***Program:***

```
#include<conio.h>
#include<iostream.h>
#include<string.h>
void main()
{
char *p;
p = strtok("The summer soldier, the sunshine
patriot", " ");
cout<<p;
do
{
p = strtok('\0', ", ");
if(p)
cout<<"|"<< p;
}
while(p);
getch();
}
```

**OUTPUT:**

The|summer|soldier|the|sunshine|patriot

**Problem 66. Write a C++ program to add spaces to the end of a string.**

***Program:***

```
#include<conio.h>
#include<iostream.h>
#include<string.h>
void pad(char *s, int length);
void main()
{
char str[80];
clrscr();
strcpy(str, "this is a test");
pad(str, 40);
cout<<strlen(str);
getch();
}
void pad(char *s, int length)
{
int l;
l = strlen(s);
while(l<length)
{
s[l] = ' ';
```

```
l++;
}
s[l]= '\0';
}
```

**OUTPUT:**

40

**Problem 67. Write a C++ program to replace space with dash.**

***Program:***

```
#include<iostream.h>
#include<conio.h>
void sp_to_dash(const char *str);
void main()
{
sp_to_dash("this is a test");
getch();
}
void sp_to_dash(const char *str)
{
while(*str)
{
if(*str== ' ')
cout<<'-';
else
cout<<*str;
str++;
}
}
```

**OUTPUT:**

this-is-a-test

**Problem 68. Write a C++ program to truncate string by delimiter: how to use strtok.**

***Program:***

```
#include<iostream.h>
#include<string.h>
#include<conio.h>
void main()
{
char str[] ="This is a sample string, just testing.";
char *p;
cout<<"Split \""<<str<<"\" in tokens:\n";
p = strtok (str," ");
while (p != NULL)
{
cout<<"\n"<< p;
p = strtok (NULL, " ,");
}
getch();
}
```

**OUTPUT:**

This is a sample string, just testing. in tokens:
This
is
a
sample
string
just
testing

# STRING PROGRAMMING:

**Problem 69. Write a C++ program to delete all the occurences of vowels in given text. Assume that the text length will be of one line.**

***Program:***

```
#include<iostream.h>
#include<conio.h>
void main()
{
char line[8],linr2[80];
int i,j=0;
clrscr();
cout<<"Enter text Below\n";
gets(line);
for(i=0;i<80;i++)
{
if(line[i]=='a'||line[i]=='e'||line[i]=='i'||line[i]=='o'||li
ne[i]=='u')
continue;
else
{
line1[j]=line[i];
j++;
}
}
cout<<"\n Text with Vowels:"<<line;
cout<<"\n Text without Vowels:"<<line2;
}
```

**OUTPUT:**

Enter Text Below
Have a nice day
Text with Vowels: Have a nice day
Text without Vowels: Hv Nc dy

**Problem 70. Write a C++ program to read the names of mobile customers through keyboard and sort them alphabetically on last name. Dispaly the sorted list on the monitor.**

***Program:***

```
#include<iostream.h>
#include<string.h>
#include<conio.h>
void main()
{
char fname[2][10],sname[20][10],surname[20][10];
char name [20][20], mobile[20][10],temp[20];
int i,j;
clrscr();
cout<<"Enter Names and Mobile Numbers\n";
for(i=0;i<5;i++)
{
cin>>fname[i]>>sname[i]>>surname[i]>>mobile[i];
strcpy(name[i],surname[i]);
strcat(name[i],",");
temp[0]=fname[i][0];
temp[1]='\0';
strcat(name[i],temp);
strcat(name[i],".")
temp[0]=sname[i][10];
temp[1]='\0';
strcat(name[i],temp);
}
for(i=1;i<=5-1;i++)
for(j=1;j<=5-i;j++)
if(strcmp(name[j-1],name[j]>0)
{
strcpy(temp,name[j-1]);
strcpy(name[j-1],name[j]);
strcpy(name[j],temp);
strcpy(temp,mobile[j-1);
strcpy(mobile[j-1],mobile[j]);
}
strcpy(mobile[j],temp);
cout<<"List of Customers in alphabetical Order:);
for(i=0;i<5;i++)
cout<<"\n"
cout.width(-20);
cout<<name[i]<<"\t";
cout.width(10);
cout<<mobile[i]<<endl;
}
```

**OUTPUT:**

```
Enter Names and Mobile Numbers
K S MORE      458596
J M CHATE     568975
M M GORE      523648
L K JAIN      458563
J J JOSHI     452298
List of Customers in alphabetical Order
CHATE J.M.    568975
GORE M M      523648
JAIN L K      458563
JOSHI J J     452298
MORE K S      458596
```

**Problem 71. Write a C++ program to read a line of text containing a series of words.**

***Program:***

```
#include<iostream.h>
#include<conio.h>
main ( )
{
char line[80], ab;
int i = 0;
cout<<"\n Enter the line of text : \n";
do
{
ab = getchar ( );
line[i] = ab;
i++;
}
while ( i != '\n');
line[i] = '\0';
cout<<"Entered line is : \n"<< line;
getche ( );
}
```

**OUTPUT:**

```
Enter the line of text :
I am a good boy
Entered line is :
I am a good boy
```

**Problem 72. Write a C++ program to Sort N cities (Strings) in the Ascending Order.**

***Program:***

```
#include<iostream.h>
#include<conio.h>
#include<string.h>
main()
{
int i, j, n, len;
char city[30][80], temp[20];
clrscr();
cout<<"\n HOW MANY CITIES YOU WANT TO
ENTER : ";
cin>>n;
cout<<"\n ENTER THE CITIES:");
for(i=1;i<=n;i++)
{
cin>>name[i];
```

```
}
for(i=1;i<=n;i++)
{
len=strlen(city[i]);
cout<<"\n LENGTH OF "<<city[i]<<"CITY IS =
"<<len;
}
for(i=1;i<=n-1;i++)
{
for(j=1;j<=n-i;j++)
{
if(strcmp(city[j],city[j+1])>0)
{
strcpy(temp, city[j]);
strcpy(city[j],city[j+1]);
strcpy(city[j+1],temp);
}
}
}
cout<<"\n SORTED CITIES ARE: \n ";
for(i=1;i<=n;i++)
{
cout<<"\n"<< city[i];
}
getche();
}
```

**OUTPUT:**

```
HOW MANY CITIES YOU WANT TO ENTER : 5
ENTER THE CITIES:
Moga
Ludhiana
Delhi
Batala
Amritsar
LENGTH OF Moga CITY IS = 4
LENGTH OF Ludhiana CITY IS = 8
LENGTH OF Delhi CITY IS = 5
LENGTH OF Batala CITY IS = 6
LENGTH OF Amritsar CITY IS = 8
SORTED CITIES ARE:
Amritsar
Batala
Delhi
Ludhiana
Moga
```

**Problem 73. Write a C++ program to find whether a sub string is present in the string or not, if it is present then find location of sub string in the string.**

***Program:***

```
#include<iostream.h>
#include<conio.h>
#include<stdlib.h>
#include<process.h>
#include<string.h>
void main()
{
char a[20],b[10];
int i,j,k,p;
clrscr();
cout<<"\n Enter the string :";
cin>>a;
cout<<"\n Enter the string to be searched: ";
cin>>b;
p=strlen(b);
for(i=0;a[i]!=0;i++)
{
j=0;
if(a[i]==b[j])
{
for(k=i;b[j]!=0;j++,k++)
if(a[k]!=b[j])
{
break;
}
}
if(j==p)
{
cout<<"\n Sub string exists at "i+1<<" th
location.";
for(k=i;;k++)
{
a[k]=a[k+j];
if(a[k]==0)
break;
}
cout<<"\nNew string is"<<a;
getch();
_cexit();
}
}
cout<<"\nSub string does not exists.";
getch();
}
```

**OUTPUT:**

```
Enter the string : Ramaswami
Enter the string to be searched : Aman
Sub string does not exists.
```

**Problem 74. Write a C++ program to insert a string at the kth (particular position) position among N strings.**

***Program:***

```
#include<iostream.h>
#include<string.h>
main()
{
char name[7][20],item[10];
int n, i, j, k;
cout<<"\n Enter the array length: ";
cin>>n;
cout<<"\n Enter the array element: ";
for(i=0;i<n;i++)
{
cin>>name[i];
}
cout<<"\ Enter the kth position: ";
cin>>k;
cout<<"\n Enter the information want to insert : ";
cin>>item;
for(j=n;j>=k-1;j--)
{
strcpy(name[j+1],name[j]);
}
strcpy(name[j],item);
n=n+1;
cout<<" \n The new list";
for(i=0;i<n;i++)
{
cout<<"\n"<<name[i];
}
}
```

**OUTPUT:**

Enter the array length:
5
Enter the array element:
Moga
Amritsar
Batala
Delhi
Jalandhar
Enter the kth position:
3
Enter the information want to insert:
Ludhiana
The new list:
Moga
Amritsar
Ludhiana
Batala
Delhi
Jalandhar

**Problem 75. Write a C++ program to convert lowercase string into upper case string.**

***Program:***

```
#include<iostream.h>
main()
{
int i;
char string1[50],string2[50];
clrscr();
cout<<"\n Enter the string in lower case: ";
gets(string1);
for(i=0;string1[i]!='\0';i++)
{
string2[i]=toupper(string1[i]);
}
cout<<"\n The string in upper case is:";
puts(string2);
getche();
}
```

**OUTPUT:**

Enter the string in lower case: good boy
The string in upper case is:
GOOD BOY

**Problem 76. Write a C++ program to search a string using Binary Search.**

***Program:***

```
#include<iostream.h>
# include<conio.h>
# include<dos.h>
main()
{
int beg,end,mid,c,b,d,e,i,n,a;
char s[30][30],s1[30];
clrscr();
cout<<"\n ENTER HOW MANY NAMES YOU
WANT TO ENTER: ";
cin>>n;
cout<<"\n ENTER THE NAMES: ";
for(i=1;i<=n;i++)
{
cin>>s[i];
}
clrscr();
cout<<"\n ENTER THE NAME TO SEARCH: ";
cin>>s1;
beg=1;end=n;mid=(beg+end)/2;i=1;
d=strcmp(s[mid],s1);
```

```
while(beg<=end && b!=0)
{
b=strcmp(s1,s[i]);
cout<<"b="<<b;
if(b==-1)
{
end=mid-1;
}
else if(b==1)
{
beg=mid+1;
}
mid=(beg+end)/2;
}
if(b==1)
{
a=mid;
cout<<"\n SEARCH SUCCESSFUL at Location
"<<--a;
}
else
{ a=0;
cout<<"\n SEARCH UNSUCCESSFUL AND
LOCATION IS "<<a;
}
sleep(3);
}
```

**OUTPUT:**

```
ENTER HOW MANY NAMES YOU WANT TO
ENTER: 5
ENTER THE NAMES:
Moga
Batala
Ludhiana
Amritsar
Delhi
ENTER THE NAME TO SEARCH:
Batala
SEARCH SUCCESSFUL at Location 2
```

**Problem 77. Write a C++ program to sort the names by using LINEAR SEARCH.**

***Program:***

```
#include<iostream.h>
# include<stdlib.h>
# include<conio.h>
# include<ctype.h>
# include<dos.h>
main()
{
int c,i,n;
char b,s[30][30],s1[30];
clrscr();
cout<<"\n ENTER HOW MANY NAMES YOU
WANT TO ENTER: ";
cin>>n;
cout<<"\n ENTER THE NAMES: ";
for(i=1;i<=n;i++)
{
cin>>s[i];
}
clrscr();
cout<<"\n ENTER THE NAME TO SEARCH: ";
cin>>s1;
i=1;
while(i<=n)
{
b=strcmp(s1,s[i]);
if(b==0)
{
c=i;
break;}
else
{
c=0;
}
i++;
}
if(c==0)
{
cout<<"\n SEARCH UNSUCCESSFUL";
}
else
{
cout<<"\n SEARCH SUCCESSFUL AND
LOCATION IS "<<c;
}
sleep(3);
}
```

**OUTPUT:**

```
ENTER HOW MANY NAMES YOU WANT TO
ENTER: 4
ENTER THE NAMES:
Mohan
Geeta
Mona
Raj
ENTER THE NAME TO SEARCH:
Raja
SEARCH UNSUCCESSFUL
```

**Problem 78. Write a C++ program to find whether the string is PALINDROMEM or not.**

***Program:***

```
#include<iostream.h>
#include<string.h>
main()
{
char l[80];
int i=0,t,c,co;
cout<<"\n Enter a word: ";
cin>>l;
c=strlen(l);
t=c-1;
for((c=0,co=t);c<=t/2;(++c,--co))
{
if(l[c]!=l[co])
{
i=i+1;
}
}
if(i==0)
{
cout<<"\n IT IS A PALINDROME \n";
}
else
{
cout<<"\n IT IS NOT A PALINDROME \n";
}
getche();
}
```

**OUTPUT:**

```
Enter a word:
MADAM
IT IS A PALINDROME
```

**Problem 79. Write a C++ program to find the vowels in a given string.**

***Program:***

```
#include<iostream.h>
#include<dos.h>
#include<conio.h>
main()
{
int c ,i, n;
char a[15];
clrscr();
cout<<"\n ENTER THE NUMBER OF
CHARACTER IN THE STRING: \n";
cin>>n;
cout<<"\n ENTER THE STRING: ";
for(i=1;i<=n;i++)
{
cin>>a[i];
}
c=0;
for(i=1;i<=n;i++)
{
if(a[i]=='a' || a[i]=='o' || a[i]=='u' || a[i]=='i' ||
a[i]=='e')
{
c=c+1;
}
}
cout<<"\n NUMBER OF VOWELS IN A
STRING IS: "<<c;
sleep(10);
}
```

**OUTPUT:**

```
ENTER THE NUMBER OF CHARACTER IN
THE STRING:15
ENTER THE STRING:
I AM A GOOD BOY.
NUMBER OF VOWELS IN A STRING IS:6
```

**Problem 80. Write a C++ program to read a string and count the number of characters in it.**

***Program:***

```
#include<iostream.h>
#include<conio.h>
main()
{
int i=0,c=0;
char string[80];
clrscr();
cout<<"\n Enter the string: ";
gets(string);
for(i=0;string[i]!='\0';++i)
{
if((string[i]>='a' && string[i]<='z') ||
(string[i]>='A' && string[i]<='Z'))
{
++c;
}
else
{
continue;
}
}
cout<<"\n Total character are ="<<c;
getche();
}
```

**OUTPUT:**
Enter the string:
Raj is a bad boy
Total character are =16

**Problem 81. Write a C++ program to extract a sub-string from a string.**

***Program:***

```
#include<iostream.h>
#include<string.h>
#include<dos.h>
#include<conio.h>
main()
{
int i,j;
char st[20],st1[5];
clrscr();
i=0;
j=0;
cout<<"\n Enter the first string: ";
cin>>st;
cout<<"\n Enter the second string: ";
gets(st1);
for(i=0;st[i]!='\0';i++)
{
for(j=0;st1[j]!='\0';j++)
{
if(st[i]==st1[j])
{
i++;
}
}
}
for(i=0;st[i]!='\0';i++)
{
if(st[i]=='\0')
{
cout<<"\n sub-string is not searched";
goto bc;
}
}
cout<<"\n SUBSTRING IS LIES IN GIVEN
STRING\n";
bc:
getche();
}
```

**OUTPUT:**
Enter the first string:
Ramaswami
Enter the second string:
swami
SUBSTRING IS LIES IN GIVEN STRING

**Problem 82. Write a C++ program to reverse the sentence.**

***Program:***

```
#include<iostream.h>
void main()
{
int i,l,k;
char str[80];
cout<<"\n Enter the string: ";
gets(str);
l=strlen(str)-1;
for(i=l;i>=0;i--)
{
if(str[i]==' ')
{
for(k=i+1;str[k]!='\0' && str[k]!=' ';k++)
cout<<str[k];
cout<<" ";
}
}
cout<<"\n Reveresd String is:";
for(i=0;str[i]!=' ';i++)
cin>>str[i];
}
```

**OUTPUT:**
Enter the string:
moa
Reveresd String is:
aom

**Problem 83. Write a C++ program to copy a string to another (without using library function).**

***Program:***

```
#include<iostream.h>
#include<conio.h>
main ()
{
char a[80],c[80];
int i;
cout<<"\n Enter a String:";
gets (a);
for (i=0;a[i]!='\0';i++)
{
c[i]=a[i];
}
c[i]='\0';
```

```
cout<<"\n String After copying: "<<c;
}
```

**OUTPUT:**

Enter a String:
raman
String After copying:
raman

**Problem 84. Write a C++ program to concatenate two strings (without using library function).**

***Program:***

```
#include<iostream.h>
#include<conio.h>
main ()
{
char a[80],c[80]="Mohit ";
int i,j,count=0;
cout<<"\n Enter a string:";
gets (a);
for (i=0;a[i]!='\0';i++)
{
++count;
for (j=count,i=0;a[i]!='\0';j++,i++)
{
a[j]=c[i];
}
a[j]=c[i];
}
a[j]='\0';
cout<<"\n \n String after concatenation:"<<a;
getch();
}
```

**OUTPUT:**

Enter a string:
Kumar
String after concatenation:
Mohit Kumar

**Problem 85. Write a C++ program to reverse a given number and check whether a given number is same as that of Reversed (i.e. Palindrome or not).**

***Program:***

```
#include<iostream.h>
#include<conio.h>
main ()
{
int rem=0, rev=0, c=0;
int num, z;
cout<<"\n Enter a number: ";
cin>>z;
num=z;
while (num>0)
{
rem=num%10;
num=num/10;
rev=(rev*10)+rem
}
cout<<" \n Reversed Number is:"<<rev;
if (z==rev)
{
cout<<"\n Number is Polyndrome";
c=1;
}
if (c==0)
{
cout<<"\n Numbert is NOT Polyndrome";
}
getch ();
}
```

**OUTPUT:**

Enter a number:
12345
Reversed Number is:
54321
Number is NOT Polyndrome

**Problem 86. Write a C++ program using scanf() to print name.**

***Program:***

```
#include<iostream.h>
#include<conio.h>
main()
{
char n[20];
cout<<"\nSpecify name of country:");
cin>>n;
cout<<"\n"<<n;
}
```

**OUTPUT:**

Specify name:canada
canada

**Problem 87. Write a C++ program using getchar() to print name.**

***Program:***

```
#include<iostream.h>
#include<conio.h>
main()
{
char n[20],getc;
int c=0;
```

```
cout<<"\nSpecify name:";
do
{
getc=getchar();
n[c]=getc;
c++;
}
while(getc!='\n');
c=c-1;
n[c]='\0';
cout<<"\n"<<n;
}
```

**OUTPUT:**

Specify name:jagbir singh
jagbir singh

**Problem 88. Write a C++ program using gets() to enter name.**

***Program:***

```
#include<iostream.h>
#include<conio.h>
main()
{
char n[50];
gets(n);
puts(n);
}
```

**OUTPUT:**

kanwarpal singh
kanwarpal singh

**Problem 89. Write a C++ program to print name and count the number of characters.**

***Program:***

```
#include<iostream.h>
#include<conio.h>
main()
{
char n[20];
int p,c=0;
cout<<"\nSpecify name:";
cin>>n;
for(p=0;n[p]!='\0';p++)
{
c++;
}
cout<<"\nNumber of characters are:"<<c;
getch();
}
```

**OUTPUT:**

Specify name:Ikvinder pal singh
Number of characters are:8

**Problem 90. Write a C++ program to find length of string**
**a)direct by using the function strlen().**

***Program:***

```
#include<iostream.h>
#include<string.h>
main()
{
char n[80];
int k;
cout<<"\nSpecify the string:";
gets(n);
k=strlen(n);
cout<<"\nString length is:"<<k;
getch();
}
```

**OUTPUT:**

Specify the string:India
String length is:5

**b) without using this function.**

***Program:***

```
#include<iostream.h>
#include<string.h>
main()
{
char n[40];
int p,c=0;
cout<<"\nSpecify the string:";
gets(n);
for(p=0;n[p]!='\0';p++)
{
++c;
}
cout<<"\nLength of string:"<<c;
}
```

**OUTPUT:**

Specify the string:India
Length of string:5

**Problem 91. Write a C++ program to copy a string to another.**
**a)direct by using the function strcpy().**

***Program:***

```
#include<iostream.h>
#include<string.h>
main()
```

```
{
char b[70],m[70];
cout<<"\nSpecify the string:";
gets(b);
strcpy(m,b);
cout<<"\nString after copying:";
puts(m);
cout<<"\nString before copying:";
puts(b);
}
```

**OUTPUT:**

Specify the string:hello world
String after copying:hello world
String before copying:hello world

**b) without using this function.**

***Program:***

```
#include<iostream.h>
#include<string.h>
main()
{
char b[70],m[70];
int p;
cout<<"\nSpecify the string:";
gets(b);
for(p=0;b[p]!='\0';p++)
{
m[p]=b[p];
}
m[p]='\0';
cout<<"\nString after copying:"<<m;
}
```

**OUTPUT:**

Specify the string:adventures
String after copying:adventures

**Problem 92. Write a C++ programto reverse a string.**

**a)direct by using the function strrev().**

***Program:***

```
#include<iostream.h>
#include<string.h>
main()
{
char b[70];
cout<<"\nSpecify the string:";
gets(b);
cout<<"\nString before reversing:"<<b;
cout<<"\nString after reversing:"<<strrev(b);
}
```

**OUTPUT:**

String before reversing:world
String after reversing:dlrow

**b) without using this function.**

***Program:***

```
#include<iostream.h>
#include<conio.h>
main()
{
char m[70],b[70];
int p,q,c=0;
cout<<"\nSpecify the string:";
gets(b);
for(p=0;b[p]!='\0';p++)
++c;
cout<<"\nString Length is:"<<c;
for(p=c-1,q=0;p>=0;p--,q++)
{
m[q]=b[p];
}
m[q]='\0';
cout<<"\nReversed String is:"<<m;
}
```

**OUTPUT:**

String before reversing:world
String Length is:5
String after reversing:dlrow

**Problem 93. Write a C++ program to combine two strings.**

**a)direct by using the library function.**

***Program:***

```
#include<iostream.h>
#include<string.h>
main()
{
char s[20]="Programming";
char d[20]=" C Language";
strcat(d,s);
cout<<"\nSource String is:"<<s;
cout<<"\nDestination String is:"<<d;
}
```

**OUTPUT:**

Source String is:Programming
Destination String is:Programming C Language

**b) without using this function.**

***Program:***

```
#include<iostream.h>
#include<conio.h>
main()
```

```
{
char b[70],z[70]="Java";
int p,q,c=0;
cout<<"\nSpecify the string:";
gets(b);
for(p=0;b[p]!='\0';p++)
++c;
for(q=c,p=0;b[p]!='\0';q++,p++)
{
b[q]=z[p];
}
b[q]='\0';
cout<<"\nString after concenation:"<<b;
}
```

**OUTPUT:**

Specify the string:Language
String after concenation:LanguageJava

**Problem 94. Write a C++ program for comparison of strings & display location of unmatched characters and total number of matched characters.**

***Program:***

```
#include<iostream.h>
#include<conio.h>
#include<string.h>
main()
{
char x[20],y[20],c=0,loc;
int s1,s2,p,n,end;
cout<<"\nSpecify the string 1:";
cin>>x;
cout<<"\nSpecify the string 2:";
cin>>y;
s1=strlen(x);
s2=strlen(y);
if(s1>s2)
end=s1;
else
end=s2;
for(p=0;p<end;p++)
if(x[p]==y[p])
{
c++;
continue;
}
else
{
loc=p;
cout<<"\nUnmatched location:"<<loc+1;
}
cout<<"\nMatch is "<<c<<" out of "<<end;
getch();
}
```

**OUTPUT:**

Specify the string 1:mnopq
Specify the string 2:mnopqrst
Unmatched location:6
Unmatched location:7
Unmatched location:8
Match is 5 out of 8

**Problem 95. Write a C++ program to sort characters of string alphabetically.**

***Program:***

```
#include<iostream.h>
#include<conio.h>
#include<string.h>
main()
{
int p,q,m,s,temp;
char x[20];
gets(x);
s=strlen(x);
for(q=1;q<=s-1;q++)
{
for(m=0;m<s-q;m++)
{
if(x[m]>x[m+1])
{
temp=x[m];
x[m]=x[m+1];
x[m+1]=temp;
}}}
puts(x);
getch();
}
```

**OUTPUT:**

akashdeep
peedhsaka

**Problem 96. Write a C++ program To arrange names in reverse order as in dictionary.**

***Program:***

```
#include<iostream.h>
#include<conio.h>
#include<string.h>
void main()
{
char str[10][50],temp[50],i,n,j;
```

```
clrscr();
cout<<"How many strings u want to enter: ";
cin>>n;
cout<<"\nEnter the Names:\n";
for(i=0;i<n;i++)
{
cin>>"\n">>str[i];
}
for(i=0;i<n;i++)
{
for(j=0;j<n-i-1;j++)
{
if(strcmp(str[j],str[j+1])<0)
{
strcpy(temp,str[j]);
strcpy(str[j],str[j+1]);
strcpy(str[j+1],temp);
}
}
}
cout<<"\nResultant names in reverse order as in
dictionary are:\n";
for(i=0;i<n;i++)
{
cout<<"\n"<<str[i];
}
getch();
}
```

**Problem 97. Write a C++ program to write strings using %s format.**

***Program:***

```
#include<iostream.h>
#include<conio.h>
void main()
{
static char c[15]="String Pattern";
cout<<"\n\n";
cout<<"-----------------\n";
cout<<"|%15s|\n",c;
cout<<"|%5s|\n",c;
cout<<"|%15.6s|\n",c;
cout<<"|%-15.6s|\n",c;
cout<<"|%15.0s|\n",c;
cout<<"|%.3s|\n",c;
cout<<"|%s|\n",c;
cout<<"-----------------\n";
getch();
}
```

**Problem 98. Write a C++ program To split a senetence into words.**

***Program:***

```
#include<iostream.h>
#include<conio.h>
#include<string.h>
void main()
{
char str[10][50],temp[100],i,n,j,k;
clrscr();
cout<<"Enter the sentence:";
gets(temp);
j=0;k=0;
for(i=0;temp[i]!='\0';i++)
{
if(temp[i]==' ')
{
j++;
k=0;
}
str[j][k]=temp[i];
k++;
}
cout<<j;
cout<<"\nSplitted worde are:\n";
for(i=0;i<j+1;i++)
{
puts(str[i]);
cout<<"\n");
}
getch();
}
```

**OUTPUT:**

```
Enter the sentence:Khalsa College Amritsar
2
Splitted worde are:
Khalsa
College
Amritsar
```

**Problem 99. Write a C++ program To find the length of words.**

**//To calculate the length of each word in string**

***Program:***

```
#include<iostream.h>
#include<conio.h>
#include<string.h>
#include<process.h>
#include<dos.h>
void main()
{
int n,i,j,count;
```

```
char ch[100][100],temp;
cout<<"Enter the No. of words u want to enter:";
cin>>n;
cout<<"\nEnter the words:";
for(i=0;i<n;i++)
{
cin>>ch[i];
}
cout<<"\nThe Lengths of words u enter are: \n";
for(i=0;i<n;i++)
{
count=0;
for(j=0;ch[i][j]!='\0';j++)
{
count++;
}
cout<<"\nThe Length of "<<i+1<<" word is
"<<count<<"\n";
}
getch();
}
```

**OUTPUT:**

```
Enter the No. of words u want to enter:6
Enter the words:
khalsa
college
amritsar
punjab
india
world
The Lengths of words u enter are:6
The Lengths of words u enter are:7
The Lengths of words u enter are:8
The Lengths of words u enter are:6
The Lengths of words u enter are:5
The Lengths of words u enter are:5
```

**Problem 100. Write a C++ program to remove duplicate words.**

***Program:***

```
#include<iostream.h>
#include<conio.h>
#include<string.h>
#include<process.h>
#include<dos.h>
void main()
{
int n,i,j,count;
char str[100][100],temp;
cout<<"Enter the No. of words u want to enter:";
cin>>n;
cout<<"\nEnter the words:";
for(i=0;i<n;i++)
{
cin>>str[i];
}
for(i=0;i<n;i++)
{
if(strcmp(str[i],str[i+1])==0)
{
for(j=i+1;j<n-1;j++)
{
strcpy(str[j],str[j+1]);
}
n=n-1;
}
}
cout<<"\n resultant words are:\n";
for(i=0;i<n;i++)
{
cout<<str[i];
}
getch();
}
```

**Problem 101. Write a C++ program to extract word from string.**

***Program:***

```
#include<iostream.h>
#include<conio.h>
#include<string.h>
#include<process.h>
#include<dos.h>
void main()
{
int m,n,i,j,count;
char str[100],temp[20];
clrscr();
cout<<"Enter the sentence:";
gets(str);
cout<<"\nEnter the Length of word u want to
extract:";
cin>>n;
cout<<"\nEnter the starting Character No.";
cin>>m;
strcpy(temp,"");
j=0;
for(i=m-1;i<m+n-1;i++)
{
temp[j]=str[i];
```

```
j++;
}
temp[j]='\0';
cout<<"\nYour Extracted String is:"<<temp;
getch();
}
```

**OUTPUT:**

Enter the sentence:abcdefghijk
Enter the Length of word u want to extract:3
Enter the starting Character No.1
Your Extracted String is:abc

**Problem 102. Write a C++ program to print number of occurences of respective alphabets A o Z in given line of text.**

***Program:***

```
#include<iostream.h>
#include<conio.h>
main()
{
static int c[30],p;
char b[80],k;
cout<<"\nSpecify the string:";
gets(b);
for(p=0;b[p]!='\0';p++)
{
k=toupper(b[p]);
c[k-65]++;
}
for(p=0;p<26;p++)
cout<<"\n"<<p+65<<" is present "<<c[p]<<"times";
}
```

**OUTPUT:**

Specify the string:Khalsa college
A is present 2times
B is present 0times
C is present 1times
D is present 0times
E is present 2times
F is present 0times
G is present 1times
H is present 1times
I is present 0times
J is present 0times
K is present 1times
L is present 3times
M is present 0times
N is present 0times
O is present 1times
P is present 0times
Q is present 0times
R is present 0times
S is present 1times
T is present 0times
U is present 0times
V is present 0times
W is present 0times
X is present 0times
Y is present 0times
Z is present 0times

**Problem 103. Write a C++ program to enter your name & OUTPUTs the ASCII codes of characters which represents your name.**

***Program:***

```
#include<iostream.h>
#include<conio.h>
main()
{
int p;
char x[10];
gets(x);
for(p=0;x[p]!='\0';p++)
{
cout<<x[p]<<"=";
cout<<x[p];
cout<<"\n");
}
getch();
}
```

**OUTPUT:**

sukh
s=115
u=117
k=107
h=104

**Problem 104. Write a C++ program to print:**

**abcde**
**bcdea**
**cdeab**
**deabc**
**eabcd**

***Program:***

```
#include<iostream.h>
#include<conio.h>
#include<string.h>
main()
{
int p,q,n;
char x[30],temp;
cout<<"\nSpecify the string:";
```

```
gets(x);
n=strlen(x);
puts(x);
for(p=0;p<n-1;p++)
{
temp=x[0];
for(q=0;q<n-1;q++)
{
x[q]=x[q+1];
}
x[n-1]=temp;
puts(x);
}
getch();
}
```

**OUTPUT:**

```
abcde
bcdea
cdeab
deabc
eabcd
```

**Problem 105. Write a C++ program to print combination of strings.**

***Program:***

```
#include<iostream.h>
#include<conio.h>
#include<string.h>
static char ad[10];
int e=0;
main()
{
int n,u;
char s[30];
long int fact=1;
cout<<"\nSpecify the string:";
gets(s);
n=strlen(s);
combi(n,s);
for(u=1;u<=n;u++)
fact=fact*u;
cout<<"\nNumber of combinations are
"<<fact<<"\n";
getch();}
combi(int m,char g[10])
{
int p,r,q,l;
char x[10];
if(m==1)
{
cout<<"\t";
for(l=0;l<e;l++)
cout<<ad[l];
cout<<g[0];
}
else
{
for(r=0;r<m;r++)
{
for(p=0,q=0;q<m;q++)
{
if(q!=r)
{ x[p]=g[q];
p++;
}
}
ad[e]=g[r];
e++;
combi(m-1,x);
e--;
}
}
}
```

**OUTPUT:**

```
Specify the string:abc
abc acb bac bca cab cba
Number of combinations are:6
```

**Problem 106. Write a C++ program to extract m characters from a string starting with nth character.**

***Program:***

```
#include<iostream.h>
#include<conio.h>
main()
{
int u,v,p;
char x[30];
int z=0,ct=0;
cout<<"\nSpecify the string:";
gets(x);
cout<<"\nSpecify the value for v & u:";
cin>>v>>u;
for(p=0;x[p]!='\0';p++)
{
ct++;
if(ct>=u&&z<v)
{
cout<<x[p];
z++;
```

```
}
}
getch();
}
```

**Problem 107. Write a C++ program to replace any particular word 'IS' in a line of text by 'was'.**

***Program:***

```
#include<iostream.h>
#include<conio.h>
#include<string.h>
main()
{
int n,l,k,p,q,loc;
char x[50],y[50];
cout<<"\nSpecify the string:";
gets(x);
n=strlen(x);
cout<<"\nSpecify the string to be added:";
gets(y);
l=strlen(y);
for(p=0;x[p]!='\0';p++)
if((x[p]=='i')&&(x[p+1]=='s')&&(x[p+2]=='
'||'\0')&&(x[p-1]==' '||'\0'))
{
loc=p;
for(k=1;k<=l-strlen("is");k++)
{
for(q=n+k;q>loc;q--)
x[q+1]=x[q];
}
for(p=0;p<1;p++)
{x[loc+p]=y[p];}
}puts(x);
getch();
}
```

**OUTPUT:**

It is a lamp
It was a lamp

**Problem 108. Write a C++ program that justifies text i.e. if you enter 17 letter word & length you fixed is 16 then last character entered is in new line.**

***Program:***

```
#include<iostream.h>
#include<conio.h>
main()
{
int m,p,t,q=2;
char x[50];
cout<<"\nSpecify the string:";
gets(x);
cout<<"\nSpecify the string length:";
cin>>t;
m=t;
for(p=0;x[p]!='\0';p++)
{
if(p>=1)
{
cout<<"\n";
cout<<x[p];
t=q*m;
q++;
}
else
{
cout<<x[p];
}
}
getch();}
```

**Problem 109.Write a C++ program to sort string in alphabetic order.**

***Program:***

```
#include<iostream.h>
#include<string.h>
#define ITEMS 5
#define MAXCHAR 20
void main()
{
char
string[ITEMS][MAXCHAR],dummy[MAXCHAR
];
int i=0;j=0;
cout<<"Specify names of "<< ITEMS<<" items";
while(i<ITEM)
cin>>string[i+1];
for(i=1;i<ITEMS;i++)
{
for(j=1;j<ITEMS-i;j++)
{
if(strcmp(string[j-1],string[j])>0)
{
strcpy(dummy,string[j-1]);
strcpy(string[j-1],string[j]);
strcpy(string[j],dummy);
}
}
}
cout<<"\nAlphabetically list\n\n";
for(i=0;i<ITEMS;i++)
```

```
cout<<string[i];
getch();
}
```

**OUTPUT:**

Specify names of 3 items
Java Cobol Pascal
Alphabetically list
Cobol
Java
Pascal

**Problem 110. Write a C++ program to print names of days of the week.**

***Program:***

```
#include<iostream.h>
#include<conio.h>
main()
{
int p;
char
day[7][10]={"Sun","Mon","Tue","Wed","Thurs","Fr
i","Sat"};
for(p=0;p<7;p++)
cout<<day[p]<<"\n";
}
```

**OUTPUT:**

Sun
Mon
Tue
Wed
Thurs
Fri
Sat

**Problem 111. Write a C++ program to sort list of strings in alphabetic order.**

***Program:***

```
#include<iostream.h>
#include<conio.h>
#include<string.h>
main()
{
char x[35][35];
char temp[35];
int p,q,n;
cout<<"\n Specify number of strings to be added";
cin>>n;
for(p=0;p<n;p++)
{
cout<<"\n Specify the string "<<p+1;
cin>>x[p];
}
for(p=0;p<n-1;p++)
for(q=p+1;q<n;q++)
{
if(strcmp(x[p],x[q])>0)
{
strcpy(temp,x[p]);
strcpy(x[p],x[q]);
strcpy(x[q],temp);
}
}
cout<<"\n List after sorting is:\n";
for(p=0;p<n;p++)
cout<<"\n x["<<p+1<<"]="<<x[p];
getch();
}
```

**OUTPUT:**

Specify number of strings to be added3
Specify the string 1how
Specify the string 2are
Specify the string 3you
List after sorting is:
x[1]=are
x[2]=how
x[3]=you

**Problem 112. Write a C++ program that takes strings and displays them in center,vertically or horizontally.**

***Program:***

```
#include<iostream.h>
#include<conio.h>
#include<string.h>
main()
{
int len;
char x[20];
cout<<"\n Specify the string:";
gets(x);
len=strlen(x);
gotoxy(39-1/2,14-1/2);
cout<<x;
getch();
}
```

**OUTPUT:**

Specify the string:college(its displayed in center of screen)

**Problem 113. Write a C++ program To arrange**

**names in reverse order as in dictionary.**

***Program:***

```
#include<iostream.h>
#include<conio.h>
#include<string.h>
void main()
{
char str[10][50],temp[50],i,n,j;
clrscr();
cout<<"How many strings u want to enter: ";
cin>>n;
cout<<"\nEnter the Names:\n";
for(i=0;i<n;i++)
{
cin>>str[i]>>"\n";
}
for(i=0;i<n;i++)
{
for(j=0;j<n-i-1;j++)
{
if(strcmp(str[j],str[j+1])<0)
{
strcpy(temp,str[j]);
strcpy(str[j],str[j+1]);
strcpy(str[j+1],temp);
}
}
}
cout<<"\nResultant names in reverse order as in
dictionary are:\n";
for(i=0;i<n;i++)
{
cout<<str[i]<<"\n";
}
getch();
}
```

**Problem 114. Write a C++ program using comma in for loop to check if the string is palindrome.**

***Program:***

```
#include<iostream.h>
#include<conio.h>
main()
{
int p,q,l,flag=0;
char x[20];
clrscr();
cin>>x;
l=strlen(x);
for(p=0,q=l-1;p<=l/2;p++,q++)
{
if(x[p]==x[q])
continue;
else
flag=1;
}
if(flag==1)
cout<<"\nString is not Palindrome";
else
cout<<"\nString is Palindrome";
getch();
}
```

**OUTPUT:**

```
madam
String is Palindrome
```

**Problem 115. Write a C++ program using recursion to check if the string is palindrome.**

***Program:***

```
#include<iostream.h>
#include<conio.h>
#include<string.h>
main()
{
int l,p,q;
char x[10];
clrscr();
cout<<"\n Specify the String";
gets(x);
l=strlen(x);
p=palin(x);
if(p==1)
cout<<"\nString is Palindrome";
else
cout<<"\nString is not Palindrome";
getch();}
int palin(char y[10])
{
int p,q,l,check;
char c[10];
l=strlen(y);
if(l==0||l==1)
return(1);
p=0;
q=l-1;
if(y[p]!=y[q])
return(0);
else
{
for(p=1,q=0;p<l-1;p++,q++)
c[q]=y[p];
c[q]='\0';
```

```
check=palin(c);
}
}
```

**OUTPUT:**

arora
String is Palindrome

**Problem 116. Write a C++ program to count vowels,digits,consonants,other characters & spaces in it.**

***Program:***

```
#include<iostream.h>
#include<conio.h>
main()
{
char s[80],ct;
int p,vow=0,con=0,digit=0,space=0;
int other=0;
cout<<"\n Specify the String";
gets(s);
for(p=0;s[p]!='\0';p++)
{
ct=toupper(s[p]);
if(ct=='A' || ct=='E' || ct=='I' || ct=='O' || ct=='U')
++vow;
else if(ct>='A' && ct<='Z')
++con;
else if(ct>='0'&&ct<='9')
++digit;
else if(ct==' '||ct=='\t')
++space;
else
++other;
}
cout<<"\n Vowels= "<<vow;
cout<<"\n Consonant= "<<con;
cout<<"\n Digit= "<<digit;
cout<<"\n Spaces= "<<space;
cout<<"\n Other= "<<other;
getch();
}
```

**OUTPUT:**

Vowels=5
Consonant=11
Digit=0
Spaces=2
Other=0

**Problem 117. Write a C++ program to count number of vowels, constants, digits, spaces in a text.**

***Program:***

```
#include<iostream.h>
# include<conio.h>
main ()
{
char a[80],c;
int i,v=0,co=0,digit=0,sp=0;
int other=0;
clrscr ();
cout<<"\n Enter a line:";
gets (a);
for (i=0;a[i]!='\0';i==)
{
c = toupper(a[i]);
if (c =='A' || c =='E '||c =='I' || c =='O' || c =='U')
++v;
else if(c>='A'&&c<='Z')
++co;
else if(c>='0'&&c<='9')
++digit;
else if(c==''|| c =='\t')
++sp;
else
++other;
}
cout<<"\n Vowels = "<<v;
cout<<"\n consonant = "<< co;
cout<<"\n digit = "<<digit;
cout<<"\n spaces = "<<sp;
cout<<"\n other = "<<other;
getch ();
}
```

**OUTPUT:**

Enter a line:
Raman is a good boy.
Vowels = 6
consonant =10
digit = 0
spaces = 2
other = 1

**Problem 118. Write a C++ program To find whether two strings are equal or not, if not equal then find the difference of these.**

***Program:***

```
#include<iostream.h>
#include<conio.h>
#include<string.h>
#include<stdlib.h>
```

```
main()
{
char a[20],b[10];
int i,n,d;
clrscr();
cout<<"\nEnter first string:";
cin>>a;
cout<<"\nEnter second string:";
cin>>b;
for(i=0;a[i]!=0||b[i]!=0;i++)
if(a[i]!=b[i])
{
cout<<"\n strings are different.";
d=a[i]-b[i];
cout<<"\n difference is : "<<d;
getch();
exit(1);
}
cout<<" Strings are same.";
getch();
}
```

**OUTPUT:**

Enter first string: Raman
Enter second string: Raman
Strings are same.

**Problem 119. Write a C++ program to find out if entered string contains a space character**.

***Program:***

```
#include<iostream.h>
#include<conio.h>
#include<ctype.h>
space(char s);
void main()
{

char s;
clrscr();
cout<<"Enter string.";
cout<<"String will be terminated if you press Ctrl-
Z.";
cout<<"STRING:- ";
space(s);
cout<<"HAVE A NICE DAY! BYE.";
getch();
}
space(char s)
{
int i;
s=getchar();
for (i=0;(s=getchar())!=EOF;i++)
{
if (s==' ')
{
cout<<"String contains a space character.";
break;
}
}
if (s==EOF)
cout<<"String does not contain a space character.";
return(s);
}
```

**OUTPUT:**

Enter string.String will be terminated if you press Ctrl-Z.
STRING:- Hello hi
String contains a space character.
HAVE A NICE DAY! BYE.

**Problem 120. Write a C++ program to display the length of the entered string (like strlen function).**

***Program:***

```
#include<iostream.h>
#include<conio.h>
void main()
{
int i,l=0;
char c;
clrscr();
cout<<"Please enter a string.";
cout<<"String will be terminated if you press Ctrl-
Z.";
cout<<"STRING:- ";
for (i=0;(c=getchar())!=EOF;i++)
l=l+1;
cout<<"Length of the entered string is "<<l;
getch();
}
```

**OUTPUT:**

Please enter a string.String will be terminated if you press Ctrl-Z.STRING:- College
Length of the entered string is 7

**Problem 121. Write a C++ program to find an input substring in an input main string**.

***Program:***

```
#include<iostream.h>
void main()
{
int i=0,j=0,k=0,count=0,l=0,k1=0;
char a[80],b[80];
```

```
clrscr();
cout<<"Enter main string:-";
gets(a);
cout<<"Enter sub-string:- ";
gets(b);
l=strlen(b);
while (a[i]!=EOF)
{
if (a[i]==b[j])
{
i++;
j++;
k1=1;
if (j==l)
{
j=0;
k=1;
count=count+1;
}
}
else
{
if (k1==1)
{
j=0;
k1=0;
}
else
i++;
}
}
if (k==1)
{
cout<<"The given sub-string is present in the main
string.";
cout<<"It is present "<<count<<" times.";
}
else
{
if (k==0)
cout<<"The given sub-string is not present in the
main string.";
}
getch();
}
```

**OUTPUT:**

Enter main string:-good Bye
Enter sub-string:- Bye
The given sub-string is present in the main string.It is present 1 times.

**Problem 122. Write a C++ program To find out the rightmost occurence of an input character in an input string.**

***Program:***

```
#include<iostream.h>
#include<conio.h>
int strindex(char s[],char t);
void main()
{
char s[80],t;
int a=0;
clrscr();
cout<<"Enter main string(i.e. s):- ";
gets(s);
cout<<"Enter the character to be searched(i.e. t):-
";
t=getchar();
a=strindex(s,t);
if (a>=0)
cout<<" The required character is found at position
"<<a;
else
cout<<" The required character is not found in the
string.";
getch();
}
int strindex(char s[],char t)
{
int i=0;
for (i=strlen(s);i>=0;i--)
{
if (s[i]==t)
return(i);
}
if (i<0)
return(-1);
}
```

**OUTPUT:**

Enter main string(i.e. s):- orange
Enter the character to be searched(i.e. t):- r
The required character is found at position 1

# CHAPTER 7

# FUNCTIONS

## FUNCTION PARAMETERS:

**Problem 1. Write a C++ program to demonstrate the use of pointers and parameter passing.**

***Program:***

```
#include<iostream.h>
#include<conio.h>
void inc_count(int *count_ptr)
{
++(*count_ptr);
cout<<*count_ptr;
}
void main()
{
int count = 0;
while (count < 10)
{
inc_count(&count);
}
getch();
}
```

**OUTPUT:**

12345678910

**Problem 2. Write a C++ program to pass value.**

***Program:***

```
#include<iostream.h>
#include<conio.h>
int change(int number);
void main()
{
int number = 20;
int result = 12;
result = change(number);
cout<<"\n In void main, result = "<<result<<" \t
number = "<< number;
getch();
}
int change(int number)
{
number = 2 * number;
cout<<"\n In function change, number =
"<<number<<"\n";
return number;
}
```

**OUTPUT:**

In function change, number = 40
In void main, result = 40 number = 20

**Problem 3. Write a C++ program to pass reference.**

***Program:***

```
#include<iostream.h>
#include<conio.h>
int change(int* pnumber);
void main()
{
int number = 20;
int* pnumber = &number;
int result = 0;
clrscr();
result = change(pnumber);
cout<<"\nIn void main, result = "<<resul<<"\t
number = "<< number;
getch();
}
int change(int* pnumber)
{
*pnumber *= 2;
cout<<"\n In function change, *pnumber = "<<
*pnumber<<"\n";
return *pnumber;
}
```

**OUTPUT:**

In function change, *pnumber =40
In void main, result = 40 number = 40

**Problem 4. Write a C++ program making a function to increase your salary.**

***Program:***

```
#include<iostream.h>
#include<conio.h>
long *IncomePlus(long* pValue);
void main()
{
long your_value = 30L;
long *pold_value = &your_value;
long *pnew_value = NULL;
```

```
pnew_value = IncomePlus( pold_value );
cout<<"\n Old value = $"<< *pold_value;
cout<<" New value = $"<< *pnew_value<<"\n";
getch();
}
long *IncomePlus(long *pValue)
{
*pValue += 10L;
return pValue;
}
```

**OUTPUT:**

Old value = $40 New value = $40

**Problem 5. Write a C++ program to pass array with different dimension into function .**

***Program:***

```
#include<iostream.h>
#include<conio.h>
void print_onedim(int a[]);
void print_twodim(int a[][4]);
void print_threedim(int a[][3][4]);
void main()
{
int cnt=0;
int a[2][3][4];
int i;
int j;
int k;
clrscr();
for(i = 0;i < 2; i++)
{
for(j = 0;j < 3; j++)
{
for(k = 0;k < 4; k++)
{
a[i][j][k] = cnt;
cnt++;
}
}
}
print_onedim(a[1][1]);
print_twodim(a[1]);
print_threedim(a);
getch();
}
void print_onedim(int a[])
{
int i;
for(i = 0; i < 4 ; i++)
cout<<a[i];
}
void print_twodim(int a[][4])
{
int j;
for(j = 0;j < 3; j++)
print_onedim(a[j]);
cout<<"\n";
}
void print_threedim(int a[][3][4])
{
int j;
cout<<"Each two dimension matrix\n";
for(j = 0; j < 2 ; j++)
print_twodim( a [ j ] );
}
```

**OUTPUT:**

16 17 18 19 20 21 22 23
Each two dimension matrix
0 1 2 3 4 5 6 7 8 9 10 11 12
13 14 15 16 17 18 19 20 21 22 23

**Problem 6. Write a C++ program to pass Array into a function.**

***Program:***

```
#include<iostream.h>
#include<conio.h>
void printarr(int a[])
{
int i;
for(i = 0;i<5;i++)
{
cout<<"\n"<<a[i];
}
}
void main()
{
int a[5];
int i;
for(i = 0;i<5;i++)
{
a[i]=i;
}
printarr(a);
getch();
}
```

**OUTPUT:**

0
1
2
3
4

**Problem 7. Write a C++ program to use function with pointer parameters.**

***Program:***

```
#include<iostream.h>
#include<conio.h>
void f(int *k)
{
*k = *k + 10;
}
void main()
{
int i = 0;

cout<<" i before call "<<i<<"\n";
f(&i);
cout<<" i after call "<<i<<"\n";
getch();
}
```

**OUTPUT:**

```
i before call 0
i after call 10
```

**Problem 8. Write a C++ program to define int pointer parameter for a function.**

***Program:***

```
#include<iostream.h>
#include<conio.h>
void f(int *k);
void main ()
{
int i;
i = 0;
cout<<" i before call "<<i<<"\n";
f(&i);
cout<<" i after call "<<i<<"\n";
getch();
}
void f(int *k)
{
*k = *k + 10;
}
```

**OUTPUT:**

```
i before call 0
i after call 10
```

**Problem 9. Write a C++ program to pass char pointer into function .**

***Program:***

```
#include<iostream.h>
#include<conio.h>
void print_vertical(char *str);
void main(int argc, char *argv[])
{
clrscr();
if(argc > 1) print_vertical(argv[1]);
getch();
}
void print_vertical(char *str)
{
while(*str)
cout<<"\n"<< *str++;
}
```

**Problem 10. Write a C++ program passing the data type addess into the function.**

***Program:***

```
#include<iostream.h>
#include<conio.h>
void swap(int *x, int *y);
void main()
{
int i, j;
i = 10;
j = 20;
cout<<"i and j before swapping: "<<i<<j;
swap(&i, &j);
cout<<"i and j after swapping: "<<i<<j<<"\n";
getch();
}
void swap(int *x, int *y)
{
int temp;
temp = *x;
*x = *y;
*y = temp;
}
```

**OUTPUT:**

```
i and j before swapping: 10 20
i and j after swapping: 20 10
```

**Problem 11. Write a C++ program for length of the function parameters.**

***Program:***

```
#include<iostream.h>
#include<stdarg.h>
#include<conio.h>
void print_message(char *format, ...);
void main()
{
print_message("Cannot open file %s.", "test";
getch();
}
```

```
void print_message(char *format, ...)
{
va_list ptr;
va_start(ptr, format);
vprintf(format, ptr);
va_end(ptr);
}
```

**OUTPUT:**

Cannot open file test

**Problem 12. Write a C++ program to return value though parameter.**

***Program:***

```
#include<conio.h>
#include<iostream.h>
#include<stdlib.h>
void mean(int a, int b, float return_val )
{
return_val = (a + b) / 2;
cout<<"return_val in mean in "<<return_val<<"\n";
}
void main()
{
int i, j;
float answer;
i = 7;
j = 9;
mean(i, j, answer);
cout<<"The mean of "<<i<<"and "<<j<<" =
"<<answer<<"\n";
getch();
}
```

**OUTPUT:**

return_val in mean in 8
The mean of 7 and 9 = 8

**Problem 13. Write a C++ program to pass return value through function parameter.**

***Program:***

```
#include<iostream.h>
#include<stdlib.h>
#include<conio.h>
void mean(int a,int b, int *ptr_to_answer)
{
*ptr_to_answer = (a + b)/2;
}
void main()
{
int i, j;
int answer;
i = 6;
j = 9;
mean(i,j, &answer);
cout<<"The mean of "<<i<<"and "<<j<<" =
"<<answer<<"\n";
getch();
}
```

**OUTPUT:**

The mean of 6 and 9 = 7

**Problem 14. Write a C++ program to pass array value into function: by array, by empty array and by pointer.**

***Program:***

```
#include<iostream.h>
#include<conio.h>
void f1(int num[5]), f2(int num[]), f3(int *num);
void main()
{
int count[5] = {1, 2, 3, 4, 5};
f1(count);
f2(count);
f3(count);
getch();
}
// parameter specified as array
void f1(int num[5])
{
int i;
for( i = 0; i < 5; i++)
cout<< num[ i ];
}
// parameter specified as unsized array
void f2(int num[])
{
int i;
for( i = 0; i < 5; i++)
cout<<num[ i ];
}
// parameter specified as pointer
void f3(int *num)
{
int i;
for(i = 0; i < 5; i++)
cout<<num[ i ];
}
```

**OUTPUT:**

1 2 3 4 5 1 2 3 4 5 1 2 3 4 5

**Problem 15. Write a C++ program to define constant function parameter.**

***Program:***

```
#include<iostream.h>
#include<conio.h>
void print_str(const char *p);
void main()
{
char str[80];
cout<<"Enter a string: ";
gets(str);
print_str(str);
getch();
}
void print_str(const char *p)
{
while(*p)
putchar(*p++);
}
```

**OUTPUT:**

Avtar riar
Avtar riar

**Problem 16. Write a C++ program demonstrating char pointer as the function parameter.**

***Program:***

```
#include<iostream.h>
#include<conio.h>
void f(char *p);
void main()
{
f("Khalsa College Amritsar";
getch();
}
void f(char *p)
{
while(*p)
{
cout<< *p;
p++;
}
cout<<"\n";
}
```

**OUTPUT:**

Khalsa College Amritsar

**Problem 17. Write a C++ program to pass double value into function.**

***Program:***

```
#include<iostream.h>
#include<conio.h>
double feet_to_meter(double f);
void main()
{
double feet;
cout<<"Enter feet: ";
cin>>feet;
cout<<"Meters: "<< feet_to_meter(feet);
getch();
}
double feet_to_meter(double f)
{
return f / 3.28;
}
```

**OUTPUT:**

Enter feet: 6
Meters: 1.829268

## FUNCTION AND POINTER:

**Problem 18. Write a C++ program showing how to point functions.**

***Program:***

```
#include<iostream.h>
#include<conio.h>
int sum(int x, int y)
{
return x + y;
}
int product(int x, int y)
{
return x * y;
}
void main()
{
int a = 13;
int b = 5;
int result = 0;
int (*pfun)(int, int);
pfun = sum;
result = pfun(a, b);
cout<<"\nsum = "<<sum<<"result = "<<result;
pfun = product;
result = pfun(a, b);
cout<<"\nproduct = "<<product<<"result =
"<<result;
getch();
}
```

**OUTPUT:**

sum =657 result = 18
product = 670 result = 65

**Problem 19. Write a C++ program**

**demonstrating arrays of pointers to functions.**

***Program:***

```
#include<iostream.h>
#include<conio.h>
int sum(int, int);
int product(int, int);
int subtract(int, int);
void main()
{
int i = 0;
int a = 10;
int b = 5;
int result = 0;
int (*pfun[3])(int, int);
clrscr();
pfun[0] = sum;
pfun[1] = product;
pfun[2] = subtract;
for( i = 0 ; i < 3 ; i++)
{
result = pfun[i](a, b);
cout<<"\nresult = "<< result;
}
result = pfun[1](pfun[0](a, b), pfun[2](a, b));
cout<<"\n\nThe product of the sum and the subtract
= "<<result<<"\n";
getch();
}
int sum(int x, int y)
{
return x + y;
}
int product(int x, int y)
{
return x * y;
}
int subtract(int x, int y)
{
return x - y;
}
```

**OUTPUT:**

```
result = 15
result = 50
result = 5
The product of the sum and the subtract = 75
```

**Problem 20. Write a C++ program demonstrating passing a pointer to a function.**

***Program:***

```
#include<iostream.h>
#include<conio.h>
int sum(int,int);
int product(int,int);
int difference(int,int);
int any_function(int(*pfun)(int, int), int x, int y);
void main()
{
int a = 13;
int b = 51;
int result = 0;
int (*pf)(int, int) = sum;
result = any_function(pf, a, b);
cout<<"\nresult = "<< result ;
result = any_function(product,a, b);
cout<<"\nresult = "<< result ;
cout<<"\nresult = "<< any_function(difference, a,
b)<<"\n";
getch();
}
int any_function(int(*pfun)(int, int), int x, int y){
return pfun(x, y);
}
int sum(int x, int y)
{
return x + y;
}
int product(int x, int y)
{
return x * y;
}
int difference(int x, int y)
{
return x - y;
}
```

**OUTPUT:**

```
result= 64
result= 663
result= -38
```

**Problem 21. Write a C++ program demonstrating function pointer.**

***Program:***

```
#include<iostream.h>
#include<string.h>
#include<conio.h>
void check(char *a, char *b,int (*cmp)(const char
*, const char *));
void main()
{
char s1[80]= "asdf", s2[80]="asdf";
int (*p)(const char *, const char *);
p = strcmp;
```

```
check(s1, s2, p);
getch();
}
void check(char *a, char *b,int (*cmp)(const char *,
const char *))
{
cout<<"Testing for equality.\n";
if(!(*cmp)(a, b))
{
cout<<"Equal";
}
else
{
cout<<"Not Equal";
}
}
```

**OUTPUT:**

Testing for equality.
Equal

**Problem 22. Write a C++ program demonstrating function pointer 2.**

***Program:***

```
#include<iostream.h>
#include<ctype.h>
#include<stdlib.h>
#include<string.h>
#include<conio.h>
int compvalues(const char *a, const char *b);
void check(char *a, char *b,int (*cmp)(const char *,
const char *));
void main()
{
char s1[80]="123", s2[80]="123";
cout<<"Testing values for equality.\n";
check(s1, s2, compvalues);
getch();
}
void check(char *a, char *b,int (*cmp)(const char *,
const char *))
{
if(!(*cmp)(a, b))
cout<<"Equal";
else
cout<<"Not Equal";
}
int compvalues(const char *a, const char *b)
{
if(atoi(a)==atoi(b))
return 0;
else
return 1;
}
```

**OUTPUT:**

Testing values for equality.
Equal

**Problem 23. Write a C++ program demonstrating function pointer: function call.**

***Program:***

```
#include<iostream.h>
#include<conio.h>
int *f(int x);
int count;
void main()
{
int *p;
p = f(110); // return pointer
cout<<"count (through p) is "<< *p;
getch();
}
int *f(int x)
{
count = x;
return &count; // return a pointer
}
```

**OUTPUT:**

count (through p) is 110

**Problem 24. Write a C++ program demonstrating function pointer and use it call a function.**

***Program:***

```
#include<iostream.h>
#include<conio.h>
int sum(int a, int b);
void main()
{
int (*p) (int x, int y);
int result;
p = sum; // get address of sum()
result = (*p) (10, 20);
cout<<"Sum: "<< result;
getch();
}
int sum(int a, int b)
{
return a+b;
}
```

**OUTPUT:**

Sum: 30

**Problem 25. Write a C++ program demonstrating array of function pointer.**

***Program:***

```
#include<iostream.h>
#include<conio.h>
int sum(int a, int b);
int subtract(int a, int b);
int mul(int a, int b);
int div(int a, int b);
int (*p[4]) (int x, int y);
void main()
{
int result;
int i, j, op;
p[0] = sum; // address of sum()
p[1] = subtract; // address of subtract()
p[2] = mul; // address of mul()
p[3] = div; // address of div()
cout<<"Enter two numbers: ";
cin>>i>>j;
cout<<"0: Add, 1: Subtract, 2: Multiply, 3:
Divide\n";
do
{
cout<<"Enter number of operation: ";
cin>>op;
}
while(op<0 || op>3);
result = (*p[op]) (i, j);
cout<< result;
getch();
}
int sum(int a, int b)
{
return a + b;
}
int subtract(int a, int b)
{
return a - b;
}
int mul(int a, int b)
{
return a * b;
}
int div(int a, int b)
{
if(b)
return a / b;
else
return 0;
}
```

**OUTPUT:**

```
Enter two numbers: 10 20
0: Add, 1: Subtract, 2: Multiply, 3: Divide\n";
Enter number of operation: 0
30
```

**Problem 26. Write a C++ program to initialize the function pointer array.**

***Program:***

```
#include<iostream.h>
#include<conio.h>
int sum(int a, int b);
int subtract(int a, int b);
int mul(int a, int b);
int div(int a, int b);
// initialize the pointer array
int (*p[4]) (int x, int y) = { sum, subtract, mul, div}
;
void main()
{
int result;
int i = 2, j = 2, op;
cout<<"0: Add, 1: Subtract, 2: Multiply, 3:
Divide\n";
do
{
cout<<"Enter number of operation: ";
cin>>op;
}
while(op<0 || op>3);
result = (*p[op]) (i, j);
cout<<result;
getch();
}
int sum(int a, int b)
{
return a + b;
}
int subtract(int a, int b)
{
return a - b;
}
int mul(int a, int b)
{
return a * b;
}
int div(int a, int b)
{
if(b)
return a / b;
else
```

```
return 0;
}
```

**OUTPUT:**

0: Add, 1: Subtract, 2: Multiply, 3: Divide
Enter number of operation: 0
4

## RECURSIVE FUNCTION:

**Problem 27. Write a C++ program for alculating factorials using recursion.**

***Program:***

```
#include<iostream.h>
#include<conio.h>
long factorial(long);
void main()
{
long number = 0;
cout<<"\nEnter an integer value: ";
cin>>number;
cout<<"\nThe factorial of "<<number<<" is
"<<factorial(number)<<"\n";
getch();
}
// recursive factorial function
long factorial(long N)
{
if( N < 2 )
return N;
else
return N*factorial(N - 1);
}
```

**OUTPUT:**

Enter an integer value: 5
The factorial of 5 is 120

**Problem 28. Write a C++ program to print out Fibonacci numbers.**

***Program:***

```
#include<iostream.h>
#include<conio.h>
void main()
{
int old_number= 1;
int current_number = 1;
int next_number;
while (current_number < 100) {
cout<<"\t", current_number;
next_number = current_number + old_number;
old_number = current_number;
current_number = next_number;
}
getch();
}
```

**OUTPUT:**

```
1       2       3       5       8       13
        21      34      55      89
```

**Problem 29. Write a C++ program for recursive function call.**

***Program:***

```
#include<iostream.h>
#include<conio.h>
int add(int pk,int pm);
void main()
{
int k = 2;
int i;
int m = 3;
i = add(k,m);
cout<<"i = "<<i<<"\n";
getch();
}
int add(int addk,int addm)
{
if(addm==0)
return(addk);
else
return(1+add(addk,addm-1));
}
```

**OUTPUT:**

i= 5

**Problem 30. Write a C++ program having function: Recursive call.**

***Program:***

```
#include<iostream.h>
#include<conio.h>
void f(int i);
void main()
{
f( 0 );
getch();
}
void f(int i)
{
if( i < 10)
{
f( i + 1 ); // recursive call
cout<<i;
}
```

```
}
```

**OUTPUT:**

9 8 7 6 5 4 3 2 1 0

**Problem 31. Write a C++ program to copy string using recursion.**

***Program:***

```
#include<iostream.h>
#include<conio.h>
void strcopy(char *s1, char *s2);
void main()
{
char str[80];
strcopy(str, "Tech Fest 2009");
cout<<str;
getch();
}
void strcopy(char *s1, char *s2)
{
if(*s2) { // if not at end of s2
*s1++ = *s2++;
strcopy(s1, s2);
}
else *s1 = '\0'; // null terminate the string
}
```

**OUTPUT:**

Tech Fest 2009

**Problem 32. Write a C++ program using recursive function with static variable.**

***Program:***

```
#include<iostream.h>
#include<conio.h>
void f(void);
void main()
{
f();
getch();
}
void f(void)
{
static int s = 0;
s++;
if(s == 10)
return;
cout<<s;
f(); // recursive call
}
```

**OUTPUT:**

1 2 3 4 5 6 7 8 9

# FUNCTION DECLARATION, DEFINE, PROTOTYPE, RETURN, VOID:

**Problem 33. Write a C++ program to define function to sum.**

***Program:***

```
#include<iostream.h>
#include<conio.h>
int sum(int i1, int i2,int i3)
{
return (i1 + i2 + i3);
}
void main()
{
cout<<"Sum is "<<sum(1, 2, 3)<<"\n";
getch();
}
```

**OUTPUT:**

Sum is 6

**Problem 34. Write a C++ program to define function to calculate an average.**

***Program:***

```
#include<iostream.h>
#include<conio.h>
float average(float x, float y)
{
return (x + y)/2.0f;
}
// void main program - execution always starts here
void main()
{
float average(float x, float y); // Function prototype
float value1 = 1.0F;
float value2 = 2.0F;
float r = 0.0F;
r = average(value1, value2);
cout<<"\nThe average is: "r;
getch();
}
```

**OUTPUT:**

The average is:1.500000

**Problem 35. Write a C++ program for demonstraction of function call.**

***Program:***

```
#include<iostream.h>
#include<conio.h>
void f2(void)
```

```
{
cout<<"2 \n";
}
void f1 (void)
{
cout<<"1 \n";
cout<<"1 \n";
f2 ( );
cout<<"1 \n";
cout<<"1 \n";
}
void main ( )
{
cout<<"\n";
cout<<"\n";
cout<<"\n";
cout<<"\n";
cout<<"\n";
f1();
cout<<"\n";
cout<<"\n";
cout<<"\n";
cout<<"\n";
getch();
}
```

**OUTPUT:**

```
1
1
2
1
1
```

**Problem 36. Write a C++ program using function call.**

***Program:***

```
#include<conio.h>
#include<iostream.h>
void f(int k)
{
k = k + 10;
}
void main( )
{
int i = 0;
clrscr();
cout<<"i before call <<i<<"\n";
f(i);
cout<<" i after call <<i<<"\n";
getch();
}
```

**OUTPUT:**

```
i before call 0
i after call 10
```

**Problem 37. Write a C++ program to check out the int value change before and after function call.**

***Program:***

```
#include<iostream.h>
#include<conio.h>
void f(int *k)
{
*k = *k + 10;
}
void main()
{
int i;
i = 0;
cout<<"i before call <<i<<"\n";
f(&i);
cout<<"i after call <<i<<"\n";
getch();
}
```

**OUTPUT:**

```
i before call 0
i after call 10
```

**Problem 38. Write a C++ program to define function to multiply two int.**

***Program:***

```
#include<iostream.h>
#include<conio.h>
int mul(int a, int b);
void main()
{
int x, y, z;
x = 10;
y = 20;
z = mul(x, y);
cout<<mul(x,y);
mul(x, y);
getch();
}
int mul(int a, int b)
{
return a * b;
}
```

**OUTPUT:**

```
200
```

**Problem 39. Write a C++ program to use a function prototype to enforce strong type**

**checking.**

***Program:***

```
#include<iostream.h>
#include<conio.h>
void sqr_it(int *i);
void main()
{
int x;
x = 10;
sqr_it(x); // type mismatch
getch();
}
void sqr_it(int *i)
{
*i = *i * *i;
}
```

**OUTPUT:**

type mismatch occur.

**Problem 40. Write a C++ program to serve as a prototype within this program.**

***Program:***

```
#include<iostream.h>
#include<conio.h>
void f(int a, int b)
{
cout<<"Modulus: "<< a % b;
}
void main()
{
f(10,3);
getch();
}
```

**OUTPUT:**

Modulus: 1

**Problem 41. Write a C++ program to define function and use it: square.**

***Program:***

```
#include<iostream.h>
#include<conio.h>
int sqr(int x);
void main()
{
int t=10;
cout<<"Square of t:"<< sqr(t);
getch();
}
int sqr(int x)
{
x = x * x;
return( x );
}
```

**OUTPUT:**

Square of t:100

**Problem 42. Write a C++ program to print a string in uppercase.**

***Program:***

```
#include<iostream.h>
#include<ctype.h>
#include<conio.h>
void print_upper(char *string);
void main()
{
char s[80];
clrscr();
cout<<"Enter a string: ";
gets(s);
print_upper(s);
cout<<"\ns is now uppercase: "<< s;
getch();
}
void print_upper(char *string)
{
register int t;
for(t=0; string[t]; ++t)
{
string[t] = toupper(string[t]);
putchar(string[t]);
}
}
```

**OUTPUT:**

Enter a string: good morning
GOOD MORNING
s is now uppercase: GOOD MORNING

**Problem 43. Write a C++ program with two functions.**

***Program:***

```
#include<iostream.h>
#include<conio.h>
void f(void); // prototype for f()
void main()
{
cout<<"I ";
f();
cout<<"java2s.com.";
getch();
}
void f(void)
{
```

```
cout<<"like ";
}
```

**OUTPUT:**

I like java2s.com.

**Problem 44. Write a C++ program with three functions.**

***Program:***

```
#include<iostream.h>
#include<conio.h>
void f1(void); // prototypes
void f2(void);
void main()
{
f2( );
cout<<"3";
getch();
}
void f2(void)
{
f1();
cout<<"2 ";
}
void f1(void)
{
cout<<"1 ";
}
```

**OUTPUT:**

1 2 3

**Problem 45. Write a C++ program to define function and use it.**

***Program:***

```
#include<iostream.h>
#include<conio.h>
int f(void); // prototype
void main()
{
int num;
num = f( );
cout<<num;
getch();
}
int f(void)
{
return 10;
}
```

**OUTPUT:**

10

**Problem 46. Write a C++ program to return statement.**

***Program:***

```
#include<iostream.h>
#include<conio.h>
void f(void);
void main()
{
f();
getch();
}
void f(void)
{
cout<<"Here.";
return;
cout<<"Never.";
}
```

**OUTPUT:**

Here.

**Problem 47. Write a C++ program to assign function return value to a variable.**

***Program:***

```
#include<iostream.h>
#include<conio.h>
int f(void);
void main()
{
double answer;
answer = f();
cout<<answer;
getch();
}
int f(void)
{
return 100;
}
```

**OUTPUT:**

100.000000

**Problem 48. Write a C++ program that demonstrates sum().**

***Program:***

```
#include<iostream.h>
#include<conio.h>
void sum(int x, int y);
void main()
{
sum(12, 230);
sum(94, 63);
sum(851, 39);
getch();
```

```
}
void sum(int x, int y)
{
cout<<x + y;
}
```

**OUTPUT:**
242 157 890

**Problem 49. Write a C++ program to define function to output char.**

***Program:***

```
#include<iostream.h>
#include<conio.h>
void printchar(char ch);
void main()
{
printchar('A');
printchar('B');
printchar('C');
getch();
}
void printchar(char ch)
{
cout<<ch;
}
```

**OUTPUT:**
ABC

**Problem 50. Write a C++ program to define function to output square.**

***Program:***

```
#include<iostream.h>
#include<conio.h>
void sqrF(int num);
void main()
{
sqrF(10.0);
getch();
}
void sqrF(int num)
{
cout<< num * num;
}
```

**OUTPUT:**
100

**Problem 51. Write a C++ program to define two functions and call them in void main.**

***Program:***

```
#include<iostream.h>
#include<conio.h>
void f1(void);
void f2(void);
void main()
{
f1();
f2();
getch();
}
void f1(void)
{
cout<<"f1, ";
}
void f2(void)
{
cout<<"f2.";
}
```

**OUTPUT:**
f1, f2

**Problem 52. Write a C++ program for function which returns int value.**

***Program:***

```
#include<iostream.h>
#include<conio.h>
int convert(void);
void main()
{
cout<<"Ans: "<< convert();
getch();
}
int convert(void)
{
int dollars;
cout<<"Enter number of dollars: ";
cin>>dollars;
return dollars;
}
```

**OUTPUT:**
Enter number of dollars:50
Ans: 6

**Problem 53. Write a C++ program to define function with void return.**

***Program:***

```
#include<iostream.h>
#include<conio.h>
void OUTPUTnum(int num);
void main()
{
OUTPUTnum(10);
getch();
```

```
}
void OUTPUTnum(int num)
{
cout<< num;
}
```

**OUTPUT:**

10

**Problem 54. Write a C++ program to define function to calculate the ounces and cups.**

***Program:***

```
#include<iostream.h>
#include<conio.h>
int ounces_to_cups(int o);
void main()
{
int ounces;
int cups;
cout<<"Enter ounces: ";
cin>>ounces;
cups = ounces_to_cups(ounces);
cout<<"cups"<< cups;
getch();
}
int ounces_to_cups(int o)
{
return o / 8;
}
```

**OUTPUT:**

Enter ounces: 20
2 cups

**Problem 55. Write a C++ program to for function declaration.**

***Program:***

```
#include<iostream.h>
#include<conio.h>
int area(int l, int w);
void main()
{
cout<<"area is "<< area(100, 130);
getch();
}
int area(l, w)
int l, w;
{
return l * w;
}
```

**OUTPUT:**

area is 13000

**Problem 56. Write a C++ program to define function to calculate the volumn.**

***Program:***

```
#include<iostream.h>
#include<conio.h>
double volume(double s1, double s2, double s3);
void main()
{
double vol;
vol = volume(12.2, 5.67, 9.03);
cout<<"Volume: "<< vol;
getch();
}
double volume(double s1, double s2, double s3)
{
return s1 * s2 * s3;
}
```

**OUTPUT:**

volume:624.641220

**Problem 57. Write a C++ program to for function prototype: declare getnum() prior to its first use.**

***Program:***

```
#include<iostream.h>
#include<conio.h>
// declare getnum() prior to its first use
float getnum(void)
{
float x;
cout<<"Enter a number: ";
cin>>x;
return x;
}
void main()
{
float i;
i = getnum();
cout<<i;
getch();
}
```

**OUTPUT:**

Enter a number:4
4.000000

**Problem 58. Write a C++ program to define function and return value.**

***Program:***

```
#include<iostream.h>
#include<conio.h>
int f(void);
```

```
void main()
{
char ch;
ch = f();
cout<<ch;
getch();
}
int f(void)
{
return 'a';
}
```

**OUTPUT:**

a

**Problem 59. Write a C++ program to define function with parameter and return value.**

***Program:***

```
#include<iostream.h>
#include<conio.h>
double f();
void main()
{
cout<<f(10.2);
getch();
}
double f(double num)
{
return num / 2.0;
}
```

**OUTPUT:**

5.100000

**Problem 60. Write a C++ program to for function call each other.**

***Program:***

```
#include<iostream.h>
#include<conio.h>
void f2(int b);
void f1(int a);
void main()
{
f1(30);
getch();
}
void f1(int a)
{
if( a )
f2( a - 1 );
cout<<a;
}
void f2(int b)
{
cout<<" . ";
if(b)
f1( b - 1 );
}
```

**OUTPUT:**

.. . . . . . . . . . . . . . . . 0 2 4 6 8 10 12 14 16 18 20 22 24 26 28 30

**Problem 61. Write a C++ program to define two functions and make function call.**

***Program:***

```
#include<iostream.h>
#include<conio.h>
void f1(void), f2(void);
void main()
{
f1();
getch();
}
void f1(void)
{
int i;
clrscr();
for(i = 0; i < 5; i++)
f2();
}
void f2(void)
{
int i;
for(i = 0; i < 5; i++)
cout<<i;
}
```

**OUTPUT:**

0 1 2 3 4 0 1 2 3 4 0 1 2 3 4 0 1 2 3 4 0 1 2 3 4

**Problem 62. Write a C++ program for global and local variable inside function.**

***Program:***

```
#include<iostream.h>
#include<conio.h>
int count; // global count
void f(void)
{
int count; // local count
count = 100;
cout<<"count in f() : "<<count<<"\n";
}
void main()
{
count = 10;
```

```
f();
cout<<"count in void main():"<<count<<"\n";
getch();
}
```

**OUTPUT:**

```
count in f() : 100
count in void main() : 10
```

**Problem 63. Write a C++ program to using function prototype.**

***Program:***

```
#include<iostream.h>
#include<conio.h>
void f(void);
void main()
{
f();
f();
getch();
}
void f(void)
{
int i = 10;
cout<<i;
}
```

**OUTPUT:**

```
10 10
```

**Problem 64. Write a C++ program to print a line of text by using the function.**

***Program:***

```
#include<iostream.h>
#include<conio.h>
void main ( )
{
clrscr();
printline ( );
cout<<"\n I am a Good Boy \n";
printline ( );
getche ( );
}
printline ( )
{
int i;
for (i=1; i <= 80; i++)
{
cout<<"-";
}
return;
}
```

**OUTPUT:**

```
----------------------------------------
I am a Good Boy
----------------------------------------
```

**Problem 65. Write a C++ program to multiply two numbers by using function showing return value.**

***Program:***

```
#include<iostream.h>
void main ( )
{
int x, y, z,mul( );
cout<<"\n Enter the value of x, y : ";
cin>>x>>y;
z = mul (x, y);
cout<<"Multiplied value is "<< z;
getche ( );
}
int mul (p, q)
int p, q;
{
int s;
s = p * q;
return (s);
}
```

**OUTPUT:**

```
Enter the value of x, y : 5 2
Multiplied value is 10
```

**Problem 66. Write a C++ program to illustrate the return nothing.**

```
void main ( )
{
int x, y,mul( );
cin>>x>>y;
mul (x, y);
getche ( );
}
int mul (x, y)
int x, y;
{
int t;
t = x * y;
cout<<t;
return;
}
```

Note that a function can contain any number of return statements in the function sub-program, but among these all only one return statement will be executed.

# FUNCTION PROGRAMMING:

**Problem 67. Write a C++ program to compute simple interest with no argument and return nothing.**

***Program:***

```
#include<iostream.h>
void main ( )
{
printline ( );
si ( );
printline ( );
getche();
}
printline ( )
{
int i;
for (i=1; i <= 40; i++)
{
cout<<"-";
}
return;
}
si ( )
{
int p, r, t, s;
cout<<"\n Enter the values of p, r, t: \n";
cin>>p>>r>>t;
s = (p * r * t) / 100;
cout<<"\n Simple Interest ="<<s;
return;
}
```

**OUTPUT:**

```
----------------------------------------
Enter the values of p, r, t: 1200 10 2
Simple Interest = 240
----------------------------------------
```

**Problem 68. Write a C++ program to compute simple interest with argument and return nothing.**

***Program:***

```
#include<iostream.h>
#include<conio.h>
void main ( )
{
int p, r, t;
clrscr();
printline( );
cout<<"\n Enter the values of p, r, t: \n";
cin>>p>>r>>t;
si (p, r, t);
printline( );
getche( );
}
printline( )
{
int i;
for (i = 1; i <= 40; i++)
{
cout<<"-";
}
return;
}
si(x,y,z)
int x,y,z;
{
int m;
m=(x * y * z) / 100;
cout<<"\n Simple Interest is: "<<m;
return;
}
```

**OUTPUT:**

```
----------------------------------------
Enter the values of p, r, t: 1200 10 2
Simple Interest is : 240
----------------------------------------
```

**Problem 69. Write a C++ program to compute Simple Interest having argument and return value.**

***Program:***

```
#include<iostream.h>
#include<conio.h>
void main ( )
{
int p, r, t, si,simple( );
clrscr( );
cout<<"Enter the value of p, r, t : \n";
cin>>p>>r>>t;
si = simple (p, r, t);
cout<<"\n Simple Interest is: "<< si;
getche( );
}
int simple(x, y, z)
int x, y, z;
{
int m;
m = (x * y * z) / 100;
return (m);
}
```

**OUTPUT:**

Enter the values of p, r, t: 1200 10 2
Simple Interest is : 240

**Problem 70. Write a C++ program to read character from terminal.**

***Program:***

```
#include<iostream.h>
void main()
{
char reply;
cout<<"Was Programming Language C developed
by Dennis Ritchie?\n";
cout<<"Type \"Y\" for yes and \"N\" for No:";
reply=getchar();
if(reply=='Y' || reply=='y')
cout<<"\n\n Correct Answer \n";
else
cout<<"\n\n Incorrect Answer \n";
}
```

**OUTPUT:**

Was Programming Language C developed by
Dennis Ritchie?
Type "Y" for yes and "N" for No:y
Correct Answer

**Problem 71. Write a C++ program to test type of character.**

***Program:***

```
#include<iostream.h>
#include<ctype.h>
void main()
{
char c;
cout<<"Press a key from keyboard\n";
c=getchar();
if(isalpha(c)>0)
cout<<"Key pressed is an alphabet\n";
else
if(isdigit(c)>0)
cout<<"Key pressed is a digit\n";
else
cout<<"Key pressed is not an alphabet\n";
getch();
}
```

**OUTPUT:**

Press a key from keyboard
s
Key pressed is an alphabet

**Problem 72. Write a C++ program to find length of string.**

***Program:***

```
#include<iostream.h>
#include<ctype.h>
void main()
{
char c[]="Computer";
int length;
length=strlen(c);
cout<<"\n The String is:"<<c<<" -Its length
is:"<<length;
}
```

**OUTPUT:**

The String is:Computer -Its length is:8

**Problem 73. Write a C++ program to find total of series:**
**Total=1+(a^2)+(a^4)+(a^6)+..........(n terms)**

***Program:***

```
#include<iostream.h>
#include<conio.h>
#include<math.h>
void main()
{
int p=2,a,n;
float total=1;
cout<<"\n Specify value of a:";
cin>>a;
cout<<"\n Specify the number of terms:";
cin>>n;
while(p<=(2*n-1))
{
total=total+pow(a,p);
p=p+2;
}
cout<<"Total is:"<<total;
getch();
}
```

**OUTPUT:**

Specify value of a:7
Specify the number of terms:3
Total is:2451.000000

**Problem 74. Write a C++ program to find sum of series:**
**Total=a-((a^3)/3!)+((a^5)/5!)-((x^7)/7!)+..........(n terms)**

***Program:***

```
#include<iostream.h>
#include<conio.h>
#include<math.h>
```

```
float factorial(int k);
void main()
{
int p,n,a;
float total=0;
clrscr();
cout<<"\n Specify value of a and n:";
cin>>a>>n;
for(p=1;p<=n;p++)
{
total+=(pow(a,2*p-1)*pow(-1,p+1))/factorial(2*p-
1);
}
cout<<"\n Total is:"<<total;
getch();
}
float factorial(int k)
{
if(k<=1)
return(1);
else
return(k*factorial(k-1));
}
```

**OUTPUT:**

```
Specify value of a and n:5 6
Total is:-1.133617
```

**Problem 75. Write a C++ program to find sum of series.**
**Total=(a^3)-(a^5)+(a^7)-(a^9)+.....+((-1)^2n)((a)2n+1)**

***Program:***

```
#include<iostream.h>
#include<conio.h>
#include<math.h>
void main()
{
int p=1,n,a;
float total=0;
cout<<"\n Specify value of a:";
cin>>a;
cout<<"\n Specify the number of terms:";
cin>>n;
while(p<=n)
{
total+=pow(a,2*p+1)*pow(-1,p+1);
p=p+1;
}
cout<<"\n Total is: "<<total;
getch();
}
```

**OUTPUT:**

```
Specify value of a:3
Specify the number of terms:3
1971.000000
```

**Problem 76. Write a C++ program to find sum of series:**
**1/2((a-1)/a) + 1/2((a-1)^2/a) +1/2((a-1)^3/a) +......**

***Program:***

```
#include<iostream.h>
#include<conio.h>
#include<math.h>
void main()
{
int p,n;
float total=0,z,a;
cout<<"\n Specify value of a:";
cin>>a;
cout<<"\n Specify the number of terms:";
cin>>n;
z=(a-1)/a;
for(p=1;p<=n;p++)
{
total+=pow(z,p)/2;
}
cout<<"\n Total is: "<<total;
getch();
}
```

**OUTPUT:**

```
Specify value of a:4
Specify the number of terms:5
Total is:1.144043
```

**Problem 77. Write a C++ program to show working of functions.**

***Program:***

```
#include<iostream.h>
#include<conio.h>
void main()
{
cout<<"Control is inside void main\n";
f1();
f2();
}
f1()
{
cout<<"Control is inside function 1\n";
}
f2()
{
cout<<"Control is inside function 2\n";
```

```
}
```

**OUTPUT:**

Control is inside void main
Control is inside function 1
Control is inside function 2

**Problem 78. Write a C++ program to find factorial of number.**

***Program:***

```
#include<iostream.h>
#include<conio.h>
long int f1(int num);
void main()
{
int num;
cout<<"\n Number is:";
cin>>num;
cout<<"\n num!= "<<f1(num);
getch();
}
long int f1(int a)
{
int p;
long int mul=1;
if(a>1)
for(p=2;p<=a;++p)
mul*=p;
return(mul);
}
```

**OUTPUT:**

Number is:9
num!=362880

**Problem 79. Write a C++ program to show that if function.**

definition is written before void main()
then there is no need of function declaration:

***Program:***

```
#include<iostream.h>
#include<conio.h>
long int f1(int a)
{
int p;
long int mul=1;
if(a>1)
for(p=2;p<=a;p++)
mul*=p;
return(mul);
}
void main()
{
int num;
cout<<"\n Number is:";
cin>>num;
cout<<"\n num!= "<<f1(num);
}
```

**OUTPUT:**

Number is:6
num!=720

**Problem 80. Write a C++ program using functions to print fibonacci series.**

***Program:***

```
#include<iostream.h>
#include<conio.h>
int fib_fun(int k);
void main()
{
int p,n;
cout<<"\n Specify the number of elements:";
cin>>n;
for(p=1;p<=n;p++)
cout<<fib_fun(p)<<"\n";
getch();
}
int fib_fun(int k)
{
static int x=1,y=1;
int z;
if(k==1||k==2)
return(1);
else
{
z=x+y;
x=y;
y=z;
return(z);
}}
```

**OUTPUT:**

Specify the number of elements:8
1
1
2
3
5
8
13
21

**Problem 81. Write a C++ program to find binomial cofficient using.**
**N!/(R!(N-R)!)**

***Program:***

```
#include<iostream.h>
#include<conio.h>
float factorial(int k);
void main()
{
int r,n;
float b_coff;
cout<<"\n Specify the value of n:";
cin>>n;
cout<<"\n Specify value of r:";
cin>>r;
b_coff=factorial(n)/(factorial(n-r)*factorial(r));
cout<<"\n Binomial Coffecient is:"<<b_coff;
getch();
}
float factorial(int k)
{
int p,t=1;
if(k==0||k==1)
return(1);
else
{
for(p=2;p<=k;p++)
{
t=t*p;
}
return(t);
}
}
```

**OUTPUT:**

```
Specify the value of n:5
Specify value of r:7
Binomial Coffecient is:0.023810
```

**Problem 82. Write a C++ program tousinf functions to find HCF of two numbers.**

***Program:***

```
#include<iostream.h>
#include<conio.h>
int hcf_fun(int m,int n);
void main()
{
int x,y,h;
cout<<"\n Specify the two numbers:";
cin>>x>>y;
if(x>y)
h=hcf_fun(x,y);
else
h=hcf_fun(y,x);
cout<<"\n Highest Common Factor is:"<<h;
getch();
}
int hcf_fun(int m,int n)
{
int k=1;
while(k!=0)
{
k=m%n;
m=n;
n=k;
}
return(m);
}
```

**OUTPUT:**

```
Specify the two numbers:6 9
Highest Common Factor is:3
```

**Problem 83. Write a C++ program tousinf functions to find total of three numbers.**

***Program:***

```
#include<iostream.h>
#include<conio.h>
int total(int m,int n);
void main()
{
int x,y,z,v,w;
cout<<"\n Specify the three numbers:";
cin>>x>>y>>z;
v=total(x,y);
w=total(v,z);
cout<<"Total is:"<<w;
getch();
}
int total(int m,int n)
{
int k;
k=m+n;
return(k);
}
```

**OUTPUT:**

```
Specify the three numbers:3 6 9
Total is:18
```

**Problem 84. Write a C++ program to show passing of constant to a function.**

***Program:***

```
#include<iostream.h>
#include<conio.h>
void f1(int,int);
void f2(char,int);
void main()
```

```
{
clrscr();
f1(2,6);
f2('x',5);
f1(4,4);
f2('y',3);
f1(6,2);
cout<<"Result\n";
}
void f1(int v,int w)
{
int q;
for(q=0;q<w;q++)
cout<<v;
cout<<"\n";
}
void f2(char s,int t)
{
int p;
for(p=0;p<t;p++)
cout<<s;
cout<<"\n";
}
```

**OUTPUT:**

```
222222
xxxxx
4444
yyy
66
Result
```

**Problem 85. Write a C++ program to show passing of variables to functions.**

***Program:***

```
#include<iostream.h>
#include<conio.h>
int func_call(int,int,int);
void main()
{
int total,x,y,z;
cout<<"\n Specify the three numbers:";
cin>>x>>y>>z;
total=func_call(x,y,z);
cout<<"\n Total is:"<<total;
}
int func_call(u,v,w)
int u,v,w;
{
int k;
k=u+v+w;
return(k);
}
```

**OUTPUT:**

```
Specify the three numbers:7 6 9
Total is:22
```

**Problem 86. Write a C++ program to show how pass by value works.**

***Program:***

```
#include<iostream.h>
#include<conio.h>
void f1(int);
void main()
{
int x=25;
clrscr();
f1(x);
cout<<"\n"<<x;
}
void f1(int y)
{
y=35;
cout<<"\n"<<y;
}
```

**OUTPUT:**

```
35
25
```

**Problem 87. Write a C++ program to show importance of pass by value.**

***Program:***

```
#include<iostream.h>
#include<conio.h>
void f1(int);
void main()
{
int x=2;
cout<<"\n x:"<<x<<"(from void main
function,before calling)";
f1(x);
cout<<"\n x:"<<x<<"(from void main
function,before calling)";
}
void f1(int x)
{
x+=5;
cout<<"\n x:"<<x<<"(from function,after
changes)";
return;
}
```

**OUTPUT:**

```
x:2(from void main function,before calling)
```

x:7(from function,after changes)
x:2(from void main function,before calling)

**Problem 88. Write a C++ program towhere function neither accepts argument nor return value.**

***Program:***

```
#include<iostream.h>
#include<conio.h>
void f1();
void f2();
void main()
{
clrscr();
f1();
f2();
f1();
}
void f1()
{
int p;
for(p=1;p<10;p++)
cout<<p;
cout<<"\n";
}
void f2()
{
int q;
for(q=1;q<10;q++)
cout<<"*";
cout<<"\n";
}
```

**OUTPUT:**

```
123456789
*********
123456789
```

**Problem 89. Write a C++ program towhere function accepts argument but does not return value.**

***Program:***

```
#include<iostream.h>
#include<conio.h>
void f1(int,int);
void main()
{
int mul,x,y;
cout<<"Specify the value of x and y:\n";
cin>>x>>y;
f1(x,y);
}
void f1(int m,int n)
{
int k;
k=m*n;
cout<<k;
}
```

**OUTPUT:**

```
Specify the value of x and y:8 3
24
```

**Problem 90. Write a C++ program towhere function does not accepts argument but return value.**

***Program:***

```
#include<iostream.h>
#include<conio.h>
void main()
{
int r;
r=f1();
cout<<"Total is:"r;
getch();
}
int f1(void)
{
int u,v,w;
cout<<"\n Specify numbers for addition:";
cin>>u>>v;
w=u+v;
return(w);
}
```

**OUTPUT:**

```
Specify numbers for addition:15 4
19
```

**Problem 91. Write a C++ program to find factorial using recursion.**

***Program:***

```
#include<iostream.h>
#include<conio.h>
int recursion(int a);
void main()
{
int m,factorial;
cout<<"\n Specify any number:";
cin>>m;
factorial=recursion(m);
cout<<"\n Factorial of "<<m<<"is:"<<factorial;
}
int recursion(int a)
{
```

```
int k;
if(a==1)
return(1);
else
k=a*recursion(a-1);
return(k);
}
```

**OUTPUT:**

Specify any number:5
Factorial of 5 is:120

**Problem 92. Write a C++ program to find HCF using recursion.**

***Program:***

```
#include<iostream.h>
#include<conio.h>
int func_hcf(int u,int v);
void main()
{
int p,q,hcf,n;
int s[10];
clrscr();
cout<<"Specify the number of elements:";
cin>>n;
cout<<"Specify the elements:";
for(p=0;p<n;p++)
cin>>s[p];
for(p=0;p<n-1;p++)
{
hcf=func_hcf(s[p],s[p+1]);
s[p+1]=hcf;
}
cout<<"Highest Common Factor is:"<<hcf;
getch();
}
int func_hcf(int u,int v)
{
if(u%v==0)
return(v);
else
return(func_hcf(v,u%v));
}
```

**OUTPUT:**

Specify the number of elements:4
Specify the elements:4 6 8 10 12
Highest Common Factor is:2

**Problem 93. Write a C++ program to display fibonacci using recursion.**

***Program:***

```
#include<iostream.h>
#include<conio.h>
int func_fib(int u);
void main()
{
int p,n;
cout<<"\nSpecify the number of terms:";
cin>>n;
for(p=1;p<=n;p++)
cout<<func_fib(p)<<"\n";
getch();
}
int func_fib(int u)
{
if(u==1||u==2)
return(1);
else
return(func_fib(u-1)+func_fib(u-2));
}
```

Specify the number of terms:6
1
1
2
3
5
8

**Problem 94. Write a C++ program to find sum of digits using recursion.**

***Program:***

```
#include<iostream.h>
#include<conio.h>
void main()
{
int d(int);
int p,x,n;
cout<<"\nSpecify the number:";
cin>>n;
x=d(n);
cout<<"\n The total of the digits is:"x;
getch();
}
int d(int n)
{
static int total=0;
if(n==0)
return(total);
else
{
total+=n%10;
d(n/10);
return(total);
```

```
}
}
```

**OUTPUT:**

Specify the number:1204
The total of the digits is:7

**Problem 95. Write a C++ program to display ackerman function using recursion.**

***Program:***

```
#include<iostream.h>
#include<conio.h>
func_ack(int u,int v);
void main()
{
int u,v;
cout<<"\nSpecify the value of u and v:";
cin>>u>>v;
cout<<func_ack(u,v)<<"\n";
getch();
}
int func_ack(int u,int v)
{
if(u==0)
return(v+1);
else if(u!=0&&v==0)
return(func_ack(u-1,1));
if(u!=0&&v!=0)
return(func_ack(u-1,func_ack(u,v-1)));
}
```

**OUTPUT:**

Specify the value of u and v:2 3
9

**Problem 96. Write a C++ program to reverse a string using recursion.**

***Program:*** .

```
#include<iostream.h>
#include<conio.h>
void rev(void);
void main()
{
int u,v;
cout<<"\n Enter some content here:\n";
rev();
getch();
}
void rev(void)
{
char s;
if((s=getchar())!='\n')
rev();
putchar(s);
return;
}
```

**OUTPUT:**

Enter some content here:always take care of yourself
flesruoy fo erac ekat syawla

**Problem 97. Write a C++ program to add, subtract and multiply two numbers by using the function within function concept (Nesting of Function).**

***Program:***

```
#include<iostream.h>
void main()
{
int x,y,z,mul( );
cout<<"\n Enter the value of x,y:";
cin>>x>>y;
z=mul(x,y);
cout<<"\n Multiplied value is: "<<z;
getch();
}
int mul(int p ,int q)
{
int s,a,add( );
s=p*q;
a=add(p,q);
cout<<"\n Addition is :"<<a;
return(s);
}
int add(int l, int m)
{
int b,c,sub( );
b=l+m;
c=sub(l,m);
cout<<"\n Subtraction is :"<<c;
return(b);
}
int sub(int e, int f)
{
int d;
d=e-f;
return(d);
}
```

**OUTPUT:**

Enter the value of x,y:3 2
Subtraction is :1
Addition is:5
Multiplied value is:6

**Problem 98. Write a C++ program to illustrate the concept of nesting of function with conditional return statement.**

***Program:***

```
#include<iostream.h>
#include<conio.h>
void main ( )
{
int a, b, c;
float ratio( );
clrscr();
cout<<"\n Enter the three numbers: \n");
cin>>a>>b>>c;
cout<<"\n Ratio is = "<< ratio (a, b, c);
getche ( ); }
float ratio(int x, int y, int z)
{
int diff( );
if diff(y, z);
{
return (x /(y-z));
}
else
{
return(0.0);
}
}
int diff(p, q)
int p,q;
{
if (p!= q)
{
return (1);
}
else
{
return (0);
}
return;
}
```

**OUTPUT:**

Enter the three numbers:
6 4 2
Ratio is = 3.0

**Problem 99. Write a C++ program to find the factorial of a number by using the Recursion.**

***Program:***

```
#include<iostream.h>
#include<conio.h>
void main ( )
{
int n, factorial( );
clrscr();
cout<<"\n Enter the value of N: ");
cin>>n;
cout<<"\n Factorial of number "<<n<<"is
"<<factorial(n);
getche ( );
}
int factorial(n)
int n;
{
int m;
if (n = = 1)
{
return (n);
}
else
{
m = n * factorial(n-1);
return (m);
}
}
```

**OUTPUT:**

Enter the value of N: 5
Factorial of number 5 is 120

**Problem 100. Write a C++ program to multiply two float values (working of non-integer prototype function or specify the type of function).**

***Program:***

```
#include<iostream.h>
#include<conio.h>
void main ( )
{
float a,b,mul( ); /* type specification during
variable declaration */
cout<<"\n Enter the value of A and B: ");
cin>>a>>b;
cout<<"Result is = "<< mul(a, b);
getche ( );
}
float mul(x, y)  /* type specification in called
statement */
float x, y;
{
float z;
z = x * y;
return (z);
}
```

**OUTPUT:**

Enter the value of A and B: 5 3
Result is = 15.0

**Problem 101. Write a C++ program to illustrate the concept of passing of one-dimensional array to function.**

***Program:***

```
#include<iostream.h>
void main ( )
{
int a[50], x, i, b, big( ),n;
cout<<"Enter the size of array : ";
cin>>n;
cout<<"\n Enter the elements of Array : ";
for (i = 0; i < n; i++)
{
cin>>a[i];
}
b=big(a,n);
cout<<"Biggest number is "<<b;
getche ( );
}
int big (x, m)
int x[ ], m;
{
int bi, i;
bi = x[0];
for (i=1; i < m; i++)
{
if(x [i ] > bi)
{
bi = x [i ];
}
}
return (bi);
}
```

**OUTPUT:**

Enter the size of array : 5
Enter the elements of Array :
20
10
50
22
40
Biggest number is 50

**Problem 102.Write a C++ program to illustrate the concept of passing two-dimensional array to the function.**

***Program:***

```
#include<iostream.h>
void main( )
{
int a[10][10], n, m, i, j, sum, trace( );
cout<<"\n Enter the number of row and columns in the matrix :");
cin>>n>>m
cout<<"\n Enter the elements of matrix : ");
for(i=0; i<n; i++)
{
for(j=0; j< m; j++)
{
cin>>"\n">>a[i][j];
}
}
sum=trace(a,n,m);
cout<<"\n Sum of diagonal elements is : "<<sum;
getche( );
}
int trace(x,p,q)
int p,q, x[p ][ ];
{
int i, j,s;
s=0;
for(i=0; i<p; i++)
{
for(j=0; j< q; j++)
{
if(i==j)
{
s=s+x[i][j];
}
}
}
return(s);
}
```

**OUTPUT:**

Enter the number of row and columns in the matrix :3 3
Enter the elements of matrix:
4 5 8
2 6 9
9 4 2
Sum of diagonal elements is : 12

**Problem 103. Write a C++ program to illustrate the concept of register variable in the function.**

***Program:***

```
#include<iostream.h>
#include<time.h>
void main()
```

```
{
time_ t start_ time, end_time;
register int countr1,countr2;
int count1,count 2;
clrscr();
time(&start_time);
for (count1=-32768;count1<32767;count1++)
{
for (count2=-32768;count2<32767;count2++);
}
time(&end_time);
cout<<"Time taken by simple variables is
"<<difftime(end_time, start_time);
time(&start_time);
for (countr1=-32768;countr1<32767;countr1++)
{
for (countr2=-32768;countr2<32767;countr2++);
}
time(&end_time);
cout<<"Time taken by register variables
is"<<difftime(end_time, start_time);
getch( );
}
```

**Problem 104. Write a C++ program to illustrate the concept of static variable in the function.**

***Program:***

```
#include<iostream.h>
#include<time.h>
void main()
{
void fun( );
fun();
fun();
fun();
fun();
getch();
}
void fun( )
{
static int a=0;
a++;
cout<<"\n"<<a;
}
```

**OUTPUT:**

```
1
2
3
4
```

**Problem 105. Write a C++ program to illustrate the concept of extern variable in the function.**

***Program:***

```
#include<iostream.h>
int a;
void main( )
{
void fun1( ), fun2( ), fun3( ), fun4( );
a = a + 1 ;
cout<<a;
fun1( );
fun2( );
fun3( );
fun4( );
cout<<a;
getch();
}
void fun1( )
{
a=a+10;
cout<<a;
}
void fun2( )
{
a=a+5;
cout<<a;
}
void fun3( )
{
a=a-2;
cout<<a;
}
void fun4( )
{
a=a+8;
cout<<a;
}
```

**OUTPUT:**

```
1 11 16 14 22 22
```

**Problem 106. Write a C++ program to print BINOMIAL Coefficient by using the function.**

***Program:*** .

```
#include<iostream.h>
void main()
{
int n, r, u, d, fact();
float ncr;
clrscr();
cout<<"\n Enter the value of N and R: ";
cin>>n>>r;
u=fact(n);
```

```
d=fact(r)*fact(n-r);
ncr=(float) u/d;
cout<<"\n Binomial Coeff. = "<<ncr;
getche();
}
int fact(k)
int k;
{
int i,m=1;
for(i=1;i<=k;i++)
{
m=m*i;
}
return(m);
}
```

**OUTPUT:**

```
Enter the value of N and R:
5       3
Binomial Coeff. = 10
```

**Problem 107. Write a C++ program to print the fibbonacci series by using recursion.**

***Program:***

```
#include<iostream.h>
#include<conio.h>
void main()
{
int n,a,b,i,fibbo(),k;
clrscr();
cout<<"\n Enter the number of terms: ";
cin>>n;
a=0;b=1;
cout<<"\n Fibbonaci series is: \n";
cout<<a,b;
i=3;
fibbo(a,b,n,i);
getch();
}
int fibbo(a,b,n,i)
int a,b,n,i;
{
int k;
if(i<=n)
{
k=a+b;
cout<<"\n"<<k;
a=b;b=k;
i++;
fibbo(a,b,n,i);
}
return;
}
```

**OUTPUT:**

```
Enter the number of terms: 10
Fibbonaci series is:
0
1
1
2
3
5
8
13
21
34
```

**Problem 108. Write a C++ program to calculate HCF of two numbers using functions.**

***Program:***

```
#include<iostream.h>
# include<conio.h>
int hcf (int x, int y);
void main ()
{
int a,b,d;
cout<<"\n Enter two number:";
cin>>a>>b;
if (a>b)
d=hcf(a,b);
else
d=hcf (b,a);
cout<<"\n HCF is : "<<d;
getch ();}
int hcf (int x, int y)
{
int r=1;
while (r!=0)
{
r=x%y;
x=y;
y=r;
}
return (x);
}
```

**OUTPUT:**

```
Enter two number:
44
22
HCF is : 22
```

**Problem 109. Write a C++ program to find HCF of N numbers using Recursion.**

***Program:***

```
#include<iostream.h>
# include<conio.h>
int hcf (int a,int b);
void main ()
{
int n,i,h;
int a[10];
cout<<"\n Enter how many numbers:";
cin>>n;
cout<<"\n Enter the numbers:";
for (i=0;i<n;i++)
cin>>a[i][j];
for (i=0;i<n-1;i++)
{
h=hcf (a[i],a[i+1]);
a[i+1]=h;
}
cout<<" \n The HCF is : "<<h;
getch ();
}
int hcf (int a,int b)
{
if (a%b==0)
return (b);
else
return (hcf (b,a%b));
}
```

**OUTPUT:**

```
Enter how many numbers:
2
Enter the numbers:
49
56
The HCF is : 7
```

**Problem 110. Write a C++ program to print the sum of digits of a Number using Recursion.**

***Program:***

```
#include<iostream.h>
# include<conio.h>
void main ()
{
int digits(int);
int n,a;
clrscr();
cout<<"\n Enter number:";
cin>>n;
a=digits (n);
cout<<"\n Sum of digits:"<<a;
getch ();
}
int digits(int n)
{
int sum=0;
if (n==0)
return (sum);
else
{
sum=sum+n%10;
digits (n/10);
return (sum);
}
}
```

**OUTPUT:**

```
Enter number:
22
Sum of digits : 4
```

**Problem 111. Write a C++ program to print the Ackerman function using Recursion.**

***Program:***

```
#include<iostream.h>
# include<conio.h>
int ack(int m,int n);
void main ()
{
int m,n;
clrscr();
cout<<"\n Enter m and n:";
cin>>m>>n;
cout<<"\n Ackerman Number is:");
cout<<ack(m,n)<<"\n";
getch ();
}
int ack(int m,int n)
{
if (m==0)
return (n+1);
else if (m!=0 && n==0)
return (ack(m-1,1));
if (m!=0 &&n !=0)
return (ack(m-1,ack(m,n-1)));
}
```

**OUTPUT:**

```
Enter m and n:
3 2
Ackerman Number is:
29
```

**Problem 112. Write a C++ program to find the determinant of a matrix by using function.**

***Program:***

```
#include<iostream.h>
#include<conio.h>
#include<math.h>
int det(int [10][10],int,int);
void main()
{
int n,i,j,p;
int a[10][10];
clrscr();
cout<<"\n Enter size of square matrix :";
cin>>n;
cout<<"\n Enter the matrix :";
for(i=0;i<n;i++)
{
cout<<"\n Enter row "<<i+1;
for(j=0;j<n;j++)
cin>>a[i][j];
}
int p=0;
p=det(a,n,n);
cout<<"\n Determinant is "<<p;
getch();
}
int det(int a[10][10],int n,int q)
{
if(n==2)
return a[0][0]*a[1][1]-a[1][0]*a[0][1];
int i,j,m,p,r,c,k,l;
int b[10][10],d,detr=0;
for(i=0;i<1;i++)
{
for(j=0;j<n;j++)
{
for(r=0,m=0;r<n;r++)
{
for(c=0,p=0;c<n;c++)
{
if(r==i || c==j)
continue;
b[m][p]=a[r][c];
p++;
if(p==n-1)
m++;
}
}
d=det(b,n-1,n-1);
detr+=pow(-1,i+j)*a[i][j]*d;
}
}
return detr;
}
```

**OUTPUT:**

```
Enter size of square matrix : 2 2
Enter the matrix==>
Enter row 1==>
1     2
Enter row 2==>
2     1
Determinant is==> 2
```

**Problem 113. Write a C++ program to find the inverse of matrix by using function.**

***Program:***

```
#include<iostream.h>
#include<conio.h>
#include<math.h>
int det(int [10][10],int,int);
void main()
{
int n,i,j,r,m,c,p;
int a[10][10],b[10][10],adj[10][10],ain[10][10];
clrscr();
cout<<"\n Enter size of square matrix :";
cin>>n;
cout<<"\n Enter the matrix :";
for(i=0;i<n;i++)
{
cout<<"\n Enter row "<<i+1;
for(j=0;j<n;j++)
cin>>a[i][j];
}
int d=0;
d=det(a,n,n);
cout<<"\n Determinant is "<<d;
if(d==0)
{
cout<<"\n Inverse is not possible as determinant is zero.";
getch();
exit(1);
}
for(i=0;i<n;i++)
{
for(j=0;j<n;j++)
{
for(r=0,m=0;r<n;r++)
{
for(c=0,p=0;c<n;c++)
{
if(r==i || c==j)
continue;
```

```
b[m][p]=a[r][c];
p++;
if(p==n-1)
m++;
}
}
adj[j][i]=pow(-1,i+j)*det(b,n-1,n-1);
}
}
cout<<"\n Inverse is :\n";
for(i=0;i<n;i++)
{
for(j=0;j<n;j++)
{
ain[i][j]=adj[i][j]/d;
cout<<"\n "<<ain[i][j];
}
}
getch();
}
int det(int a[10][10],int n,int q)
{
if(n==2)
return a[0][0]*a[1][1]-a[1][0]*a[0][1];
int i,j,m,p,r,c,k,l;
int b[10][10],d,detr=0;
for(i=0;i<1;i++)
{
for(j=0;j<n;j++)
{
for(r=0,m=0;r<n;r++)
{
for(c=0,p=0;c<n;c++)
{
if(r==i || c==j)
continue;
b[m][p]=a[r][c];
p++;
if(p==n-1)
m++;
}
}
d=det(b,n-1,n-1);
detr+=pow(-1,i+j)*a[i][j]*d;
}
}
return detr;
}
```

**OUTPUT:**

```
Enter size of square matrix : 2    2
Enter the matrix:
Enter row 1:
1       2
Enter row 2:
2       1
Determinant is: 2
Inverse is:
0.5     -1
-1 0.5
```

**Problem 114. Write a C++ program to show that automatic variable which has been assigned default initial value is garbage.**

***Program:***

```
#include<iostream.h>
#include<conio.h>
void main()
{
auto int a,b;
cout<<a,b;
}
```

**OUTPUT:**

```
0200
```

**Problem 115. Write a C++ program to show visibility of local variable.**

***Program:***

```
#include<iostream.h>
#include<conio.h>
void main()
{
auto int x=4;
{
{
{
cout<<x;
}
cout<<x;
}
cout<<x;
}
}
```

**OUTPUT:**

```
444
```

**Problem 116. Write a C++ program to show lifetime of automatic variable.**

***Program:***

```
#include<iostream.h>
#include<conio.h>
void f1();
void f2();
```

```
void main()
{
auto int x=20;
clrscr();
f1();
cout<<x;
}
void f1()
{
auto int x=200;
f2();
cout<<x;
}
void f2()
{
auto int x=4;
cout<<x;
}
```

**OUTPUT:**

420020

**Problem 117(a). Write a C++ program to show default storage class is that of automatic.**

***Program:***

```
#include<iostream.h>
#include<conio.h>
int f1();
void main()
{
int s=1;
clrscr();
cout<<s;
f1();
f1();
}
int f1()
{
int s=2;
cout<<s;
s=s+1;
return(s);
}
```

**OUTPUT:**

122

**117(b).**

***Program:***

```
#include<iostream.h>
#include<conio.h>
int f1();
void main()
{
auto int s=1;
cout<<s;
f1();
f1();
}
int f1()
{
auto int s=2;
cout<<s;
s=s+1;
return(s);
}
```

**OUTPUT:**

122

**Problem 118. Write a C++ program to show that external variable which has been assigned default initial value is zero.**

***Program:***

```
#include<iostream.h>
#include<conio.h>
int x;
void main()
{
clrscr();
cout<<x;
}
```

**OUTPUT:**

0

**Problem 119. Write a C++ program to calculate the factorial value of any integer entered through the keyboard.**

***Program:***

```
#include<iostream.h>
#include<conio.h>
void main( )
{
int num ;
long factorial ;
clrscr() ;
cout<<"Enter a number:";
cin>>num ;
factorial = fact(num) ; // function call
cout<<"\n Factorial of "<<num<<" = "<<factorial ;
cout<<"\nPress any key to exit.";
getch( ) ;
}
fact (int num)
{
```

```
int i ;
long factorial = 1 ;
for (i=1;i<=num;i++)
factorial = factorial * i ;
return (factorial) ;
}
```

**OUTPUT:**

Enter a number:5
Factorial of 5 =120
press any key to exit.

**Problem 120. Write a C++ program with a function power ( a, b ) to calculate the value of a raised to b.**

***Program:***

```
#include<iostream.h>
#include<conio.h>
void main()
{
int x , y ;
long pow ;
clrscr( );
cout<<"Enter two numbers:";
cin>>x>>y ;
pow = power(x,y) ; // Function call
cout<<"\n"<<x<<" To the power "<<y<<" ="<<
pow ;
cout<<"\nPress any key to exit.";
getch( ) ;
}
power (int x, int y)
{
int i ;
long p=1 ;
for(i=1;i<=y;i++)
p=p*x ;
return (p) ;
}
```

**OUTPUT:**

Enter two numbers:2 3
2 to the power 3 =8
Press any key to exit.

**Problem 121. Write a C++ program with a general- purpose function to convert any given year into its roman equivalent. The following table shows the roman equivalent of decimal numbers.**

| Decimal | Roman |
|---|---|
| 1 | i |
| 5 | v |
| 10 | x |
| 50 | l |
| 100 | c |
| 500 | d |
| 1000 | m |

***Program:***

```
#include<iostream.h>
#include<conio.h>
int romanise(int,int,char);
void main()
{
int yr;
clrscr();
cout<<"Enter year:";
cin>>yr;
yr = romanise (yr,1000,'m'); // series of function
calls
yr = romanise (yr,500,'d');
yr = romanise(yr,100,'c');
yr = romanise(yr,50,'l');
yr = romanise(yr,10,'x');
yr = romanise(yr,5,'v');
yr = romanise(yr,1,'l');
cout<<"\nPress any key to exit.";
getch() ;
}
int romanise(int y,int k,char ch)
{
int i,j;
if(y==9)
{
cout<<"ix";
return ( y % 9 ) ;
}
if(y==4)
{
cout<<"iv";
return ( y % 4 ) ;
}
j=y/k;
for(i=1;i<=j;i++)
cout<<ch);
return (y-k*j);
}
```

**OUTPUT:**

Enter year:2009
mmix
Press any key to exit.

**Problem 122. Any year is entered through the keyboard. Write a C++ program with a**

**function to determine whether the year is a leap year or not.**

***Program:***

```
#include<iostream.h>
#include<conio.h>
void leapyear(int);
void main()
{
int year;
clrscr();
cout<<"Enter year:";
cin>>year;
leapyear(year); // Function call
cout<<"\nPress any key to exit.";
getch();
}
void leapyear ( int year )
{
if (year%4==0 && year%100!=0 || year%400==0)
cout<<year<<"is leap year";
else
cout<<year<<"is not a leap year";
}
```

**OUTPUT:**

Enter year:2009
2009 is not a leap year
press any key to exit.

**Problem 123. A positive integer is entered through the keyboard. Write a C++ program with a function to obtain the prime factors of this number.**

***Program:***

```
#include<iostream.h>
#include<conio.h>
void prime (int) ;
void main( )
{
int num ;
clrscr( );
cout<<"Enter number:";
cin>>num ;
prime (num) ; // function call
cout<<"\nPress any key to exit.";
getch( ) ;
}
void prime ( int num )
{
int i = 2 ;
cout<<"Prime factors of "<< num<<"are" ;
while ( num !=1 )
{
if ( num % i== 0 )
cout<<i<<"\t";
else
{
i ++ ;
continue ;
}
num = num / i ;
}
}
```

**OUTPUT:**

Enter number:12
prime factors of 12 are:2 2 3
Press any key to exit.

**Problem 124. Write a C++ program with a function which receives a float and an int from void main( ), finds the product of these two and returns the product which is printed through void main( ) .**

***Program:***

```
#include<iostream.h>
#include<conio.h>
float product ( int, float ) ; // Function prototype
void main( )
{
int x ;
float y, prod ;
clrscr( ) ;
cout<<"Enter float value and integer value:";
cin>>y>>x;
prod = product ( x, y ) ; // Function call
cout<<"\nproduct of "<<y<<"and"<<x<<"=
"<<prod ;
cout<<"\nPress any key to exit.";
getch( ) ;
}
float product ( int x, float y )
{
float p ;
p = x * y ;
return ( p );
}
```

**OUTPUT:**

Enter float value and integer value:3.5 2
product of 3.500000 and 2 = 7.000000
Press any key to exit.

**Problem 125. Write a C++ program with a function, which receives 5 integers and returns**

**the sum, average and standard deviation of these numbers. Call this function from void main( ) and print the results in void main( ).**

***Program:***

```
#include<iostream.h>
#include<conio.h>
void function ( int *, int *, double * ) ;
void main( )
{
int sum, avg ;
double stdev ;
clrscr( ) ;
function ( &sum, &avg, &stdev ) ; // function call by
deviation
cout<<"\nsum = "<<sum<<"\nAverage =
"<<avg<<"\nStandard deviation = "<<stdev ;
cout<<"\nPress any key to exit.";
getch( ) ;
}
void function ( int *sum, int *avg, double *stdev )
{
int n1, n2 , n3 , n4 , n5 ;
cout<<"\nEnter 5 numbers:";
cin>>n1>>n2 >>n3 >>n4 >>n5 ;
*sum = n1 + n2 + n3 + n4 + n5 ;//calculate sum
*avg = *sum /4 ; // calculate average
//Calculate standard deviation
*stdev = sqrt ( ( pow ( ( n1 - *avg ), 2) + pow ( ( n2 -
*avg ), 2) +pow ( ( n3 - *avg ), 2) + pow ( ( n4 -
*avg ), 2) +pow ( ( n5 - *avg ), 2) ) /4 ) ;
}
```

**OUTPUT:**

Enter 5 numbers:1 2 3 4 5
sum = 15
Average = 3
Standard deviation =
Press any key to exit.

**Problem 126. Write a C++ program with a function that receives marks received by a student in 3 subjects and returns the average and percentage of these marks. Call this function from void main( ) and print the result in void main( ).**

***Program:***

```
#include<iostream.h>
#include<conio.h>
void result ( int , int, int, float *, float* ) ;
void main( )
{
float avg, per ;
int m1, m2, m3 ;
void result(int m1, int m2, int m3, float *a, float *p
);
clrscr() ;
cout<<"Enter marks of three subjects:";
cin>>m1>>m2>>m3 ;
result ( m1, m2 , m3 , &avg, &per ) ;
cout<<"\nAverage = "<<avg<<"\nPercentage =
"<<per ;
cout<<"\nPress any key to exit.";
getch( ) ;
}
void result (int m1, int m2, int m3, float *a, float
*p )
{
*p=*a=(m1+m2+m3)/3.0f;
}
```

**OUTPUT:**

Enter marks of three subjects:50 50 50
Average = 50.000000
Percentage = 50.000000
Press any key to exit

**Problem 127. A 5-digit positive integer is entered through the keyboard, write a C++ program with to calculate sum of digits of the 5-digit number.**

**(1) Without using recursion**

**(2) Using recursion**

***Program:***

```
#include<iostream.h>
#include<conio.h>
int sum ( int ) ; // Function without recursion
int sum ( int ) ; // Function with recursion
void main( )
{
int s, rs ;
int n ;
clrscr( ) ;
cout<<"Enter number:";
cin>>n;
s = sum ( n ) ; // Function call without recursion
cout<<"\nSum of digits without using recursion is
"<< s ;
rs = rsum ( n ) ; // Function call with recursion
cout<<"\nSum of digits using recursion is "<< rs ;
cout<<"\nPress any key to exit.";
getch( ) ;
}
int sum ( int num ) // Function without recursion
{
```

```
int revoid mainder, sum = 0 ;
// This time our code is very short because we can
now use a while " clause which was not used in the
earlier instance of this program
while ( num > 0 )
{
revoid mainder = num % 10 ; // Calculate revoid
mainder
sum = sum + revoid mainder ; // update sum
num = num / 10 ; // remove last digit
}
return ( sum ) ;
}
int rsum ( int num ) // Function with recursion
{
int sum = 0 ;
int revoid mainder ;
if ( num!= 0 )
{
revoid mainder = num % 10 ; // Calculate revoid
mainder
sum = revoid mainder + rsum ( num / 10 ) ; //
recursive call
}
return( sum) ;
}
```

**OUTPUT:**

Enter number:1 2 3 4 5
Sum of digits without using recursion is 15
Sum of digits using recursion is 15
Press any key to exit.

**Problem 128. A positive integer is entered through the keyboard, write a C++ program with a function to obtain the prime factors of the number . Modify the function suitably to obtain the prime factors recursively .**

***Program:***

```
#include<iostream.h>
#include<conio.h>
void factors ( int ) ;
void main( )
{
int num ;
clrscr( ) ;
cout<<"Enter a number:";
cin>>num ;
cout<<"prime factors are:";
factors ( num ) ;
cout<<"\nPress any key to exit.";
getch( ) ;
}
void factors ( int n )
{
static int i = 2 ;
if ( i <= n )
{
if ( n %i == 0 )
{
cout<<i<<"\t" ;
n = n / i ;
}
else
i ++ ;
factors ( n ) ; // recursive call
}
return ;
}
```

**OUTPUT:**

Enter number:12
prime factors of 12 are:2 2 3
Press any key to exit.

**Problem 129. Write a C++ program with a recursive function to obtain the first 25 numbers of a Fibonacci sequence. In a Fibonacci sequence the sum of two successive terms the third term. Following are the first few terms of the Fibonacci sequence:**

**1 1 2 3 5 8**
**13 21 34 55 89......**

***Program:***

```
#include<iostream.h>
#include<conio.h>
void fido ( int , int ) ;
void main( )
{
int i, t, old = 0, current = 1, new ;
clrscr();
cout<<"\n"<<old<<"\t"<<current<<"\t";
fido ( old, current ) ;
cout<<"\nPress any key to exit.";
getch( ) ;
}
void fido ( int old, int current )
{
static int terms = 2 ;
int new ;
if ( terms < 20 )
{
new = old + current ;
cout<<new<<"\t";
```

```
terms = terms + 1 ;
fido ( current, new ) ;
}
else
return ;
}
```

**OUTPUT:**

```
0     1      1      2      3     5     8
      13     21     34
55    89 144 233    377    610   987
      1597   2584   4181
Press any key to exit.
```

**Problem 130. A positive integer is entered through the keyboard, write a C++ program with a function to find the binary equivalent of this number using recursion.**

***Program:***

```
#include<iostream.h>
#include<conio.h>
int binary ( int ) ;
void main( )
{
int num ;
clrscr( ) ;
cout<<"\nEnter the number:";
cin>>num ;
binary ( num ) ; // Function call
cout<<"\nPress any key to exit.";
getch( ) ;
}
// function to convert decimal to binary
int binary ( int n )
{
int r ;
r = n % 2 ;
n = n/ 2 ;
if ( n == 0 )
{
cout<<"\nThe binary equivalent is "<< r ;
return ( r ) ;
}
else
binary ( n ) ; // Recursion call
cout<< r ;
}
```

**OUTPUT:**

```
Enter the number: 12
The binary equivalent is 1100
Press any key to exit.
```

**Problem 131. Write a C++ program with a recursive function to obtain the running sum of first 25 natural numbers.**

***Program:***

```
#include<iostream.h>
#include<conio.h>
int getsum ( int ) ;
void main( )
{
int s ;
clrscr( ) ;
s = getsum ( 0 ) ; // Function call
cout<<"\nThe sum of first 25 natural numbers is
"<< s ;
cout<<"\nPress any key to exit.";
getch( ) ;
}
int getsum ( int n )
{
int sum = 0 ;
if ( n == 25 )
return sum ;
sum = n + getsum ( ++n ) ;
return ( sum ) ;
}
```

**OUTPUT:**

```
The sum of first 25 natural numbers is 325
Press any key to exit.
```

**Problem 132. Write a C++ program with a function to evaluate the series sin ( x ) = x - ( x 3 / 3! ) + ( x5 / 5! ) - ( x7 / 7! ) + ^ to five significant digits.**

***Program:***

```
#include<iostream.h>
#include<conio.h>
#include<math.h>
float numerator ( float, int ) ;
float denominator ( int ) ;
void main( )
{
float n, x, a, b, sum = 0 ;
int i,j ;
clrscr( ) ;
cout<<"Enter the number x:";
cin>>x ;
for ( i = 1, j = 1 ; j <= 1[illegible] i ++, j += 2 ) // upto 10
terms
{
a = numerator ( x, j ) ;
```

```
b = denominator ( j );
n = a / b ;
( i % 2 == 0 ) ? sum = sum - n : ( sum = sum + n ) ;
}
cout<<sum ;
cout<<"\nPress any key to exit.";
getch( ) ;
}
// for power calculation
float numerator(float x1,int j)
{
float k=1;
int m;
for(m=1;m<=j;m++)
k*=x1;
return(k);
}
//for find factorial
float denominator(int j)
{
int m;
float h=1;
for(m=1;m<=j;m++)
h=h*m;
return(h);
}
```

**OUTPUT:**

```
Enter the number x:2
0.909297
Press any key to exit.
```

**Problem 133. Given three variables x, y, z write a function to circularly shift their values to right. In other words if x = 5, y = 8, z = 10 after circular shift y = 5, z = 8, x = 10 after circular shift y = 5, z = 8 and x = 10 . Call the function with variables a, b, c, to circularly shift values.**

***Program:***

```
#include <stdio.h>
#include <conio.h>
void fun ( int, int, int ) ;
void main( )
{
int x, y, z ;
clrscr( ) ;
cout<<"Enter the values x, y, z:";
cin>>x>>y>>z;
cout<<"\nValues of x, y & z as entered:";
cout<<"\nx = "<<x<<"\ty = "<<y<<"\tz = "<<z ;
fun ( x, y, z ) ;
cout<<"\nPress any key to exit.";
getch( ) ;
}
// Function to shift values of x, y & z
void fun ( int x, int y, int z )
{
int i, t ;
for ( i = 0 ; i <= 2; i++ )
{
t = z;
z = y;
y = x ;
x = t ;
cout<<"\nAfter right shifting of values "<<i+1<<"
time(s):\n";
cout<<"\nx = "<<x<<"\ty = "<<y<<"\tz = "<<z ;
}
}
```

**OUTPUT:**

```
Enter the values x, y, z:10 20 30
Values of x, y & z as entered:
x=10    y=20    z=30
After right shifting of values 1 time(s):
x=20    y=30    z=10
After right shifting of values 2 time(s):
x=30    y=10    z=20
After right shifting of values 3 time(s):
x=10    y=20    z=30
Press any key to exit.
```

**Problem 134. Write a C++ program with a function to compute the greatest common divisor given by Euclid's algorithm, exemplified for J = 1980, k = 1617 as follows.**

***Program:***

```
#include<iostream.h>
#include<conio.h>
int fun( int, int );
void main( )
{
int j, k, t, r, z ;
clrscr( ) ;
cout<<"\nEnter two numbers:";
cin>>j>>k ;
z = fun( j, k ) ;
cout<<"\nThe greatest common divisor of the two
numbers is "<< z ;
cout<<"Press any key to exit.";
getch( );
}
// Function to calculate GCD
fun ( int j, int k )
```

```
{
int r = 1, m, n = 0, t ;
if ( k > j ) // Interchange values
{
t = j ;
j = k ;
k = t ;
}
else
{
if ( j == k )
return j ;
}
while ( 1 )
{
r = j / k ;
m = j - ( r * k ) ;
if ( ! ( j % k ) ) // j is exact multiple of k
n = k ;
if ( m == 0 ) ;
break ;
j = k ;
k = m ;
n = m ;
}
return n ;
}
```

**OUTPUT:**

Enter two numbers:4 12
The greatest common divisor of the two numbers is 4
Press any key to exit.

**Problem 135. Write a C++ program to show visibility of global variable.**

***Program:***

```
#include<iostream.h>
#include<conio.h>
int x;
int f1();
int f2();
void main()
{
cout<<"\n x="<<x;
cout<<"\t"<<f1();
cout<<"\t"<<f2();
cout<<"\t"<<f1();
}
int f1()
{
x=x+25;
return(x);
}
int f2()
{
x=x-15;
return(x);
}
```

**OUTPUT:**

x=0 25 10 35

**Problem 136. Write a C++ program to show lifetime of global variable.**

***Program:***

```
#include<iostream.h>
#include<conio.h>
int a=2;
int f1();
void main()
{
cout<<a;
cout<<"\t"<<f1();
}
int f1()
{
a=a*4;
return(a);
}
```

**OUTPUT:**

2 8

**Problem 137. Write a C++ program to show preference of local variable over global variable.**

***Program:***

```
#include<iostream.h>
#include<conio.h>
int x=50;
void f1();
void main()
{
int x=70;
cout<<x;
f1();
}
void f1()
{
cout<<"\t"<<x;
}
```

**OUTPUT:**

70 50

**Problem 137(a). Write a C++ program to show difference between automatic variable & static variable.**

***Program:***

```
#include<iostream.h>
#include<conio.h>
void f1();
void main()
{
clrscr();
f1();
f1();
}
void f1()
{
auto int x=5;
cout<<"\n"<<x;
x=x+3;
}
```

**OUTPUT:**

```
5
5
```

**137(b).**

***Program:***

```
#include<iostream.h>
#include<conio.h>
void f1();
void main()
{
f1();
f1();
}
void f1()
{
static int x=5;
cout<<"\n"<<x;
x=x+3;
}
```

**OUTPUT:**

```
5
8
```

**Problem 138(a). Write a C++ program to show differnce between external variable & static variable.**

***Program:***

```
#include<iostream.h>
#include<conio.h>
int x=1;
int f1();
int f2();
void main()
{
clrscr();
cout<<x;
cout<<"\n"<<f1();
cout<<"\n"<<f2();
}
int f1()
{
x=x+2;
return(x);
}
int f2()
{
x=x+3;
return(x);
}
```

**OUTPUT:**

```
1
3
6
```

**138(b).**

***Program:***

```
#include<iostream.h>
#include<conio.h>
int f1();
int f2();
void main()
{
static int x=1;
cout<<x;
cout<<"\n"<<f1();
cout<<"\n"<<f2();
}
int f1()
{
static int x;
x=x+2;
return(x);
}
int f2()
{
static int x;
x=x+3;
return(x);
}
```

**OUTPUT:**

```
1
2
```

3

**Problem 139. Write a C++ program to execute file Without void main() function.**

***Program:***

```
#include<iostream.h>
#include<conio.h>
#define FIRST 0
#define SECOND 1
#define THIRD 2
//Variables
int a,b,c,ch;
float d;
//Function Prototype
void Read();
void Operation();
void Display();
#pragma startup Read 0 //First_Priority
#pragma startup Operation 1 //Second_Priority
#pragma exit Display //Third_Priority
void main()
{
cout<<"Enter to void main() ";
getch();
cout<<"Exit From void main() ";
getch();
}
void Read()
{
clrscr();
cout<<"Enter the value of a : ";
cin>>a;
cout<<"Enter the value of b : ";
cin>>b;
}
void Operation()
{
cout<<"\nArithMetic Operations";
cout<<"\n-------------------- ";
cout<<"\n1 -> Addition ";
cout<<"\n2 -> Subtraction ";
cout<<"\n3 -> Multiplication ";
cout<<"\n-------------------- ";
cin>>ch;
switch(ch)
{
case 1:
c = a+b;
break;
case 2:
c = a-b;
break;
case 3:
c = a*b;
break;
}
}
void Display()
{
switch(ch)
{
case 1:
cout<<"\nThe Result (Addition) : "<<c;
break;
case 2:
cout<<"\nThe Result (Subtraction): "<<c;
break;
case 3:
cout<<"\nThe Result (Multiplication): "<<c;
break;
}
getch();
}
```

**OUTPUT:**

```
Enter the value of a : 4
Enter the value of b : 5
ArithMetic Operations
--------------------
1 -> Addition
2 -> Subtraction
3 -> Multiplication
--------------------
1
Enter to void main() Exit From void main()
The Result (Addition) : 9
```

**Problem 140. Write a C++ program toreverse a number by recursion .**

***Program:*** .

```
#include<iostream.h>
long int rev(long int);
void main()
{
long int n;
clrscr();
cout<<"Enter number to reverse : ";
cin>>n;
cout<<"Reversed Number : "<<rev(n);
getch();
}
long int rev(long int n)
{
```

```
long int i=1,x;
if(n==0)
{
return 0;
}
else
{
while(i<=n)
{
i=i*10;
}
i=i/10;
x=n%10;
return(x*i+rev(n/10));
}
}
```

**OUTPUT:**

Enter number to reverse : 41284
Reversed Number :48214

# CHAPTER 8

# POINTERS

## ARRAY AND POINTER:

**Problem 1. Write a C++ program to use arrays and pointers.**

***Program:***

```
#include<iostream.h>
#include<conio.h>
void main()
{
char multiple[] = "I am a string";
cout<<"\nThe address of the first array element :
"<< &multiple[0];
cout<<"\nThe address obtained from the array name:
"<< multiple<<"\n";
getch();
}
```

**OUTPUT:**

The address of the first array element : FFE8
The address obtained from the array name: FFE82

**Problem 2. Write a C++ program to use arrays and pointers taken further.**

***Program:***

```
#include<iostream.h>
#include<conio.h>
void main()
{
char s[] = "a string";
cout<<"\n value of second element:"<< s[1]<<"\n";
cout<<"value of s after adding 1: "<< *(s +
1)<<"\n";
getch();
}
```

**OUTPUT:**

value of second element: Borland Int1
value of s after adding 1: Borland Int1

**Problem 3. Write a C++ program to use arrays and pointers: char array.**

***Program:***

```
#include<iostream.h>
#include<conio.h>
void main()
{
char s[] = "another string";
cout<<"\nAddress of second element: "<< &s[1];
cout<<"\nValue of s+1 : "<< s+1<<"\n";
getch();
}
```

**OUTPUT:**

Address of second element: FFE7
Value of s+1 : FFE7

**Problem 4. Write a C++ program to use two-dimensional arrays and pointers.**

***Program:***

```
#include<iostream.h>
#include<conio.h>
void main()
{
char twoD[3][3] = { {'1','2','3'},{'4','5','6'},
{'7','8','9'} };
cout<<"address of twoD :"<< twoD<<"\n";
cout<<"address of twoD[0][0] : "<<
&twoD[0][0]<<"\n";
cout<<"but what is in twoD[0] : "<<
twoD[0]<<"\n";
getch();
}
```

**OUTPUT:**

address of twoD : FFEC
address of twoD[0][0] : FFEC
but what is in twoD[0] : FFEC

**Problem 5. Write a C++ program to declare a pointer to an array that has 10 ints in each row: allocate memory to hold a 4 x 10 array.**

***Program:***

```
#include <iostream.h>
#include<stdlib.h>
#include<conio.h>
int pwr(int a, int b);
void main()
{
int (*p)[10];
register int i, j;
p = malloc(40 * sizeof(int));
```

```
if(!p)
{
cout<<"Memory request failed.\n";
exit(1);
}
for(j = 1; j < 11; j++)
for(i = 1; i < 5; i++)
p[ i - 1][j - 1] = pwr(j, i);
for(j = 1; j < 11; j++)
{
for(i = 1; i < 5; i++)
cout<<"  "<< p[i-1][j-1];
cout<<"\n";
}
getch();
}
// Raise an integer to the specified power.
pwr(int a, int b)
{
register int t=1;
for(; b; b--) t = t*a;
return t;
}
```

**OUTPUT**:

```
1 1      1 1
2 4 8 16
3 9 27 81
4 16 64 256
5 25 125 625
6 36 216 1296
7 49 343 2401
8 64 512 4096
9 81 729 6561
10 100 1000 10000
```

# DATA STRUCTURE ALGOS:

**Problem 6. Write a C++ program for shaker sorting.**

***Program:***

```
#include<string.h>
#include<iostream.h>
#include<stdlib.h>
void shaker(char *items, int count);
void main()
{
char s[255];
clrscr();
cout<<"Enter a string:";
gets(s);
shaker(s, strlen(s));
cout<<"The sorted string is: "<< s<<"\n";
getch();
}
void shaker(char *items, int count)
{
register int i;
int exchange;
char t;
do
{
exchange = 0;
for(i = count - 1; i > 0; --i)
{
if(items[i - 1] > items[ i ])
{
t = items[i - 1];
items[i - 1] = items[ i ];
items[ i ] = t;
exchange = 1;
}
}
for(i = 1; i < count; ++i )
{
if(items[i - 1] > items[ i ])
{
t = items[i-1];
items[i - 1] = items[ i ];
items[ i ] = t;
exchange = 1;
}
}
}
while(exchange);
}
```

**OUTPUT:**

Enter a string:madam
The sorted string is: aadmm

**Problem 7.Write a C++ program for shell sorting.**

***Program:***

```
#include<conio.h>
#include<string.h>
#include<iostream.h>
#include<stdlib.h>
void shell(char *items, int count)
{
int i, j, gap, k;
char x, a[5];
a[0]=8; a[1]=5; a[2]=3; a[3]=2; a[4]=1;
for(k=0; k < 5; k++)
{
gap = a[k];
for(i=gap; i < count; ++i)
```

```
{
x = items[i];
for(j=i-gap; (x < items[j]) && (j >= 0); j=j-gap)
{
items[j+gap] = items[j];
}
items[j+gap] = x;
}
}
}
void main()
{
char s[255]="asdfasdfasdfasdfasdf";
clrscr();
shell(s, strlen(s));
cout<<"The sorted string is: "<< s<<"\n";
getch();
}
```

**OUTPUT:**

The sorted string is: aaaaadddddfffffsssss

**Problem 8. Write a C++ program for selection sorting.**

***Program:***

```
#include<conio.h>
#include<string.h>
#include<iostream.h>
#include<stdlib.h>
void select(char *items, int count);
void main()
{
char s[255];
clrscr();
cout<<"Enter a string:";
gets(s);
select(s, strlen(s));
cout<<"The sorted string is: "<< s<<"\n";
getch();
}
void select(char *items, int count)
{
register int a, b, c;
int exchange;
char t;
for(a = 0; a < count-1; ++a)
{
exchange = 0;
c = a;
t = items[ a ];
for(b = a + 1; b < count; ++b)
{
if(items[ b ] < t)
{
c = b;
t = items[ b ];
exchange = 1;
}
}
if(exchange)
{
items[ c ] = items[ a ];
items[ a ] = t;
}
}
}
```

**OUTPUT:**

Enter a string:madam

The sorted string is: aadmm

**Problem 9. Write a C++ program for insertion sorting.**

***Program:***

```
#include<conio.h>
#include<string.h>
#include<iostream.h>
#include<stdlib.h>
void insert(char *items, int count)
{
register int i, b;
char t;
for(i=1; i < count; ++i)
{
t = items[i];
for(b=i-1; (b >= 0) && (t < items[b]); b--)
items[b+1] = items[b];
// items[b+1] = t;
items[b] = t;
}
}
void main()
{
char s[255] = "asdfasdfasdfadsfadsf";
clrscr();
insert(s, strlen(s));
cout<<"The sorted string is: "<<s<<"\n";
getch();
}
```

**OUTPUT:**

The sorted string is: aaaaadddddfffffsssss

**Problem 10. Write a C++ program to quicksort.**

***Program:***

```
#include<conio.h>
#include<string.h>
#include<iostream.h>
#include<stdlib.h>
void quickSortMain(char *items, int count);
void quickSort(char *items, int left, int right);
void main()
{
char s[255]="asdfasdfasdfasdfasdfasdfasdf";
clrscr();
quickSortMain(s, strlen(s));
cout<<"The sorted string is: "<< s<<"\n";
getch();
}
void quickSortMain(char *items, int count)
{
quickSort(items, 0, count-1);
}
void quickSort(char *items, int left, int right)
{
int i, j;
char x, y;
i = left;
j = right;
x = items[(left+right)/2];
do
{
while((items[i] < x) && (i < right))
i++;
while((x < items[j]) && (j > left))
j--;
if(i <= j)
{
y = items[i];
items[i] = items[j];
items[j] = y;
i++; j--;
}
}
while(i <= j);
if(i < right)
quickSort(items, i, right);
if(left < j)
quickSort(items, left, j);
}
```

**OUTPUT:**

The sorted string is: aaaaaaaddddddddffffffssssss

**Problem 11. Write a C++ program to quicksort for strings.**

***Program:***

```
#include<conio.h>
#include<iostream.h>
#include<string.h>
void quickSortMain(char items[][10], int count);
void quickSort(char items[][10], int left, int right);
void main()
{
int i;
char str[][10] = { "this"<<"is"<<"a"<<"test"};
quickSortMain(str, 4);
for(i=0; i<4; i++)
{
cout<<str[i];
}
getch();
}
void quickSortMain(char items[][10], int count)
{
quickSort(items, 0, count-1);
}
void quickSort(char items[][10], int left, int right)
{
int i, j;
char *x;
char temp[10];
i = left;
j = right;
x = items[(left+right)/2];
do
{
while((strcmp(items[i],x) < 0) && (i < right))
{
i++;
}
while((strcmp(items[j],x) > 0) && (j > left))
{
j--;
}
if(i <= j)
{
strcpy(temp, items[i]);
strcpy(items[i], items[j]);
strcpy(items[j], temp);
i++;
j--;
} }
while(i <= j);
if(left < j)
{
quickSort(items, left, j);
}
```

```
if(i < right)
{
quickSort(items, i, right);
} }
```

**OUTPUT:**

a is test this

**Problem 12. Write a C++ program for quick sort on two dimensional string array.**

***Program:***

```
#include<conio.h>
#include<iostream.h>
#include<string.h>
#include<assert.h>
char names[22][25] ={ "M"<< "C"<< "I"<< "J"<<
"P"<< "G"<< "D"<< "O"<< "B"<< "S"<< "C"<<
"D"<< "D"<<
"Z"<< "A"<< "K"<< "Y"<< "P"<< "Q"<< "J"<<
"D"<< "K" };
#define NUMBER_OF_NAMES sizeof ( names ) /
sizeof ( names[0] )
void main()
{
int i;
// the unsorted letter
cout<<"The Unsorted Names.\n";
for ( i = 0; i < NUMBER_OF_NAMES; i++ )
cout<<names[i];
cout<<"\NPress RETURN to continue: ";
fflush ( stdout );
getchar();
qsort (( char * ) names, NUMBER_OF_NAMES,
sizeof ( *names ), strcmp );
assert ( names[0][0] < names[1][0] );
cout<<"The Sorted letter.\n";
for ( i = 0; i < NUMBER_OF_NAMES; i++ )
cout<<"\n"<< names[i];
getch();
}
```

**OUTPUT:**

The Unsorted Names.
MCIJPGDOBSCDDZAKYPQJDK
Press RETURN to
continue:ABCCDDDDGIJJKKMOPPQSYZ

## POINTER AND STRING:

**Problem 13. Write a C++ program to split an entry of the form Last/First into two parts.**

***Program:***

```
#include<conio.h>
#include<iostream.h>
#include<string.h>
#include<stdlib.h>
char *my_strchr(char *string_ptr, char find)
{
while (*string_ptr != find)
{
if (*string_ptr == '\0')
return (NULL);
++string_ptr;
}
return (string_ptr);
}
void main()
{
char line[80]="asdf";
char *first_ptr;
char *last_ptr;
clrscr();
line[strlen(line)] = '\0';
last_ptr = line;
first_ptr = my_strchr(line, 'd');
if (first_ptr == NULL)
{ fprintf(stderr,"Error: Unable to find 'a' in
%s\n"<< line);
}
getch();
}
```

**Problem 14. Write a C++ program to reverse string content using its pointer.**

***Program:***

```
#include<conio.h>
#include<iostream.h>
#include<string.h>
void main()
{
char str1[] = "Pointers are fun and hard to use";
char str2[80], *p1, *p2;
p1 = str1 + strlen(str1) - 1;
p2 = str2;
while(p1 >= str1)
*p2++ = *p1--;
*p2 = '\0';
cout<< str1<< str2;
getch();
}
```

**OUTPUT:**

Pointers are fun and hard to use esu ot drah dna nuf era sretniop

## POINTER TO POINTER:

**Problem 15. Write a C++ program for pointer and pointer's pointer.**

***Program:***

```
#include<iostream.h>
#include<conio.h>
void main()
{
int x, *p, **q;
x = 10;
p = &x;
q = &p;
cout<< **q;
getch();
}
```

**OUTPUT:**

10

**Problem 16. Write a C++ program to for pointer's pointer: value.**

***Program:***

```
#include<conio.h>
#include<iostream.h>
void main()
{
float *fp, **mfp, val;
fp = &val;
mfp = &fp;
**mfp = 444.903;
cout<< val<<**mfp;
getch();
}
```

**OUTPUT:**

444.903015 444.903015

## POINTER CHARACTER:

**Problem 17. Write a C++ program to read and output address pointed by the argument.**

***Program:***

```
#include<iostream.h>
#include<conio.h>
void main()
{
char *p;
cout<<"Enter an address: ";
cin>>p;
cout<<"Value at location "<<p<<"is "<<*p<<"\n";
getch();
}
```

**OUTPUT:**

Enter an address: 2000
Value at location 2000 is power n

**Problem 18. Write a C++ program to assign value to char pointer.**

***Program:***

```
#include<iostream.h>
#include<conio.h>
void main()
{
char *p, *q;
cout<<"Enter a string: ";
p = gets(q);
cout<<p;
getch();
}
```

**OUTPUT:**

Enter a string: Head Sir
Head Sir

**Problem 19. Write a C++ program to assign value to a char pointer.**

***Program:***

```
#include<iostream.h>
#include<conio.h>
void main()
{
char *p;
p = "one two three";
cout<<p;
getch();
}
```

**OUTPUT:**

one two three

**Problem 20. Write a C++ program for char's pointer's pointer.**

***Program:***

```
#include<iostream.h>
#include<conio.h>
void main()
{
char *p, **mp, str[80];
p = str;
mp = &p;
cout<<"Enter your name: ";
gets( *mp );
cout<<"Hi "<< *mp;
```

```
getch();
}
```

**OUTPUT:**

Enter your name:Prof.Rachhpal Singh
Hi Prof.Rachhpal Singh

**Problem 21. Write a C++ program to get string and assign its value to a char pointer.**

***Program:***

```
#include<iostream.h>
#include<conio.h>
void main()
{
char *p;
cout<<"Enter a string: ";
gets(p);
puts(p);
getch();
}
```

Enter a string:Prof.Rachhpal Singh
Prof.Rachhpal Singh

**Problem 22. Write a C++ program to use pointer for char, int, float and double.**

***Program:***

```
#include<iostream.h>
#include<conio.h>
void main()
{
char *cp, ch;
int *ip, i;
float *fp, f;
double *dp, d;
cp = &ch;
ip = &i;
fp = &f;
dp = &d;
cout<<cp, ip, fp, dp<<"\n";
cp++;
ip++;
fp++;
dp++;
cout<<cp, ip, fp, dp<<"\n";
getch();
}
```

**OUTPUT:**

FFF5 FFF2 FFEC FFE2
FFF6 FFF4 FFF0 FFEA

**Problem 23. Write a C++ program for our own string copy function based on pointer.**

***Program:***

```
#include<iostream.h>
#include<conio.h>
void mycpy(char *to, char *from);
void main()
{
char str[80];
mycpy(str, "Khalsa College Amritsar";
cout<<sir;
getch();
}
void mycpy(char *to, char *from)
{
while(*from)
*to++ = *from++;
*to = '\0';
}
```

**OUTPUT:**

Khalsa College Amritsar

## POINTERS AND INTEGERS:

**Problem 24. Write a C++ program to show how pointers can be used.**

***Program:***

```
#include<iostream.h>
#include<conio.h>
void main()
{
int integerVariable;
int *integerPointer;
integerVariable = 2;
cout<<"VALUE "<< integerVariable<<"\n";
integerPointer = &integerVariable;
*integerPointer = 3;
cout<<"VALUE "<< integerVariable<<"\n";
cout<<"VALUE "<< *integerPointer<<"\n";
getch();
}
```

**OUTPUT:**

VALUE 2
VALUE 3
VALUE 3

**Problem 25. Write a C++ program to using pointers.**

***Program:***

```
#include<iostream.h>
#include<conio.h>
void main()
```

```
{
int number = 0;
int *pointer = NULL;
clrscr();
number = 10;
cout<<"\n number's address: "<< &number;
cout<<"\n number's value: \n\n"<< number;
pointer = &number;
cout<<"pointer's address: "<< &pointer;
cout<<"\npointer's size: bytes"<< sizeof(pointer);
cout<<"\npointer's value: "<< pointer;
cout<<"\nvalue pointed to: \n"<< *pointer;
getch();
}
```

**OUTPUT:**

```
number's address: FFF4
number's value: 10
pointer's address: FFF2
pointer's size: 2bytes
pointer's value: FFF4
value pointed to: 10
```

**Problem 26. Write a C++ program to use printf to output variable's address.**

***Program:***

```
#include<iostream.h>
#include<conio.h>
void main()
{
int x = 99;
int *p1, *p2;
p1 = &x;
p2 = p1;
cout<<"Values at p1 and p2: << *p1<< *p2<<"\n";
cout<<"Addresses pointed to by p1 and p2: << p1<<
p2<<"\n";
getch();
}
```

**OUTPUT:**

```
Values at p1 and p2: 99 99
Addresses pointed to by p1 and p2: FFF4 FFF4
```

**Problem 27. Write a C++ program to check pointer comptability.**

***Program:***

```
#include<iostream.h>
#include<conio.h>
void main()
{
double x = 1.1, y;
int *p;
p = (int *) &x;
y = *p;
cout<<"The (incorrect) value of x is: "<< y;
getch();
}
```

**OUTPUT:**

```
The (incorrect) value of x is:-2621
4.000000
```

**Problem 28. Write a C++ program to use int pointer: get the address of an int value.**

***Program:***

```
#include<iostream.h>
#include<conio.h>
void main()
{
int target, source;
int *m;
source = 10;
m = &source;
target = *m;
cout<< target;
getch();
}
```

**OUTPUT:**

```
10
```

**Problem 29. Write a C++ program to use int pointer.**

***Program:***

```
#include<iostream.h>
#include<conio.h>
void main()
{
int *p, q;
q = 19;
p = &q;
cout<<"value stored at p: "<< *p;
getch();
}
```

**OUTPUT:**

```
value stored at p:19
```

**Problem 30. Write a C++ program to assign an int value using a pointer.**

***Program:***

```
#include<iostream.h>
#include<conio.h>
void main()
{
int *p, q;
```

```
p = &q;
*p = 199;
cout<<"q's value is "<< q;
getch();
}
```

**OUTPUT:**

19q's value is 199

**Problem 31. Write a C++ program to use pointer based calculation.**

***Program:***

```
#include<iostream.h>
#include<conio.h>
void main()
{
int *p, q;
p = &q;
q = 1;
cout<<"Address of p: "<< p;
*p++;
cout<<q<<" is stored at address "<<p<<"after
increment operation";
getch();
}
```

**OUTPUT:**

Address of p:FFF4

1 is stored at address FFF6 after increment operation

**Problem 32. Write a C++ program to increase value vs address.**

***Program:***

```
#include<iostream.h>
#include<conio.h>
void main()
{
int *p, q;
clrscr();
p = &q;
q = 1;
cout<<"Address of p: "<< p;
(*p)++;
cout<<q<<" is stored at address "<<p<<"after
increment operation";
getch();
}
```

**OUTPUT:**

Address of p:FFF4

2 is stored at address FFF4 after increment operation

**Problem 33. Write a C++ program to swap function: Exchange the values by pointers.**

***Program:***

```
#include<iostream.h>
#include<conio.h>
void swap(int *i, int *j);
void main()
{
int num1, num2;
num1 = 100;
num2 = 800;
cout<<"num1 = "<<num1<<" num2 =
"<<num2<<<"\n";
swap(&num1, &num2);
cout<<"num1 = "<<num1<<" num2 =
"<<num2"<<"\n";
getch();
}
// Exchange the values by pointers.
void swap(int *i, int *j)
{
int temp;
temp = *i;
*i = *j;
*j = temp;
}
```

**OUTPUT:**

num1=100 num2=800

num1=800 num2=100

# POINTERS PROGRAMMING:

**Problem 34. Write a C++ program to illustrate the concept of displaying the address of a Pointer variable.**

***Program:***

```
#include<iostream.h>
#include<conio.h>
main ( )
{
int x, *q ;
x = 220 ;
q = &x ;
cout<<"/n"<< x<<" is stored at address "<< &x ;
cout<<"/n"<< x<<" is stored at address "<< q ;
cout<<"/n"<< *q<<" is stored at address "<< q ;
cout<<"/n"<< *&x<<" is stored at address "<< &x
;
getche ( ) ;
}
```

**OUTPUT:**

220 is stored at address 5010

220 is stored at address 5010
220 is stored at address 5010
220 is stored at address 5010

**Problem 35. Write a C++ program to illustrate the concept of accessing the address of pointer.**

***Program:***

```
#include<iostream.h>
#include<conio.h>
main()
{
int *p , qty ;
qty = 280 ;
p = &qty ;
cout<<qty<<" is stored at address "<< p ;
}
```

**OUTPUT:**

280 is stored at address 6000

**Problem 36. Write a C++ program to display the use of pointers (A complete C program with pointer).**

***Program:***

```
#include<iostream.h>
#include<conio.h>
main ( )
{
char ab ;
int r ;
float p, q ;
clrscr();
ab = 'Z' ;
r = 22 ;
p = 3.12 ;
q = 5.7 ;
cout<<"\n"<<ab<<" is stored at address "<< &ab ;
cout<<"\n"<<r<<" is stored at address "<< &r ;
cout<<"\n"<<p<<" is stored at address "<< &p ;
cout<<"\n"<<q<<" is stored at address "<< &q ;
getche ( ) ;
}
```

**OUTPUT:**

Z is stored at address 5000
22 is stored at address 5500
3.142 is stored at address 6200
5.7 is stored at address 6400

**Problem 37. Write a C++ program to show arithmetic operations by using pointer (how operators work in pointers?).**

***Program:***



```
#include<iostream.h>
# include<conio.h>
int *p1,*p2,*p3;
int i=1;
int j=2;
int a[5]={1,2,3,4,5;
main ()
{
int m,n,x;
p1=&i;
p2=&j;
p3=&a[0];
m=*p1-*p2;
n=*p1+*p2;
x=*p3+2;
if (*p1>=*p2)
cout<<m<<n<<x;
if (*p1<=*p2)
cout<<p1<<p2<<p3;
}
```

**Problem 38. Write a C++ program to find sum of N numbers by using pointer.**

***Program:***

```
#include<iostream.h>
#include<conio.h>
main ( )
{
int a [20], *p1, i, n, sum = 0;
clrscr();
cout<<" \n Enter the value of N : ";
cin>>n ;
cout<<" \n Enter the array element: " ;
for (i = 0 ; i < n ; i + +)
{
cin>>a[i] ;
}
cout<<"\n \t Element \ t value \ t Address" ;
p1 = &a[0];
for (i = 0 ; 1 < n ; i + +)
{
sum = sum + a [i] ;
cout<<" \n \t a ["<<i+1<<"] \ t "<<a[i]<<" \ t
"<<p1<<";
p1+ + ;
}
cout<<" Sum = "<< sum ;
cout<<" Sum is stored at address "<< &sum ;
getche ( ) ;
}
```

**OUTPUT:**

```
Enter the value of N: 2
Enter the array element:
20
25
Element        Value   Address
x [1]    20    1000
x [2]    25    1004
Sum = 45
Sum is stored at address 1200
```

**Problem 39. Write a C++ program to illustrate the concept of array with pointer.**

***Program:***

```
#include<iostream.h>
#include<conio.h>
main()
{
int arr[5][2]={{1234, 56},
{1212, 33},
{1434, 80},
{1312, 78},
{1203, 75}};
int i,j;
for(i=0;i<5;i++)
{
cout<<(“\n”);
for(j=0;j<2;j++)
{
cout<<*(*(arr+i)+j);
}
}
getch();
}
```

**OUTPUT:**

```
1234 56
33
1434 80
78
75
```

**Problem 40. Write a C++ program to show the working of pointer with static array elements.**

***Program:***

```
#include<iostream.h>
#include<conio.h>
main()
{
int a[][4]={5,7,5,9,
4,6,3,1,
2,9,0,6};
int *p;
int (*)[4];
p=(int*)a;
q=a;
cout<<“\n"<<p<<q;
p++;
q++;
cout<<“\n"<<p<<q;
getch();
}
```

**OUTPUT:**

```
5500
5502 5508
```

**Problem 41. Write a C++ program to illustrate the concept of call by value (argument passing without pointer).**

***Program:***

```
#include<iostream.h>
#include<conio.h>
main ( )
{
int a,b,swap( );
a=5;
b=10;
cout<<“\n Value of a = "<<a<<" and Value of b =
"<<b<<" before swap ";
swap(a,b);
cout<<“\n Value of a = "<<a<<" and Value of b =
"<<b<<" after swap ”;
getch( );
}
int swap(int x, int y)
{
int temp;
temp = x;
x = y;
y = temp;
return;
}
```

**OUTPUT:**

```
Value of a = 5 and Value of b = 10 before swap
Value of a = 5 and Value of b = 10 after swap
```

**Problem 42. Write a C++ program to illustrate the concept of call by reference (argument passing with pointer).**

***Program:***

```
#include<iostream.h>
#include<conio.h>
main ( )
```

```
{
int a,b, *aa, *bb, swap( );
a=5;
b=10;
aa=&a;
bb=&b;
cout<<"\n Value of a = "<<a<<" and Value of b =
"<<b<<" before swap ";
swap(aa,bb);
cout<<"\n Value of a = "<<a<<" and Value of b =
"<<b<<" after swap ";
getch( );
}
int swap(int *x, int *y)
{
int temp;
temp = *x;
*x = *y;
*y = temp;
return;
}
```

**OUTPUT:**

Value of a = 5 and Value of b = 10 before swap
Value of a = 10 and Value of b = 5 after swap

**Problem 43. Write a C++ program to multiply two numbers by using pointer to function concept.**

***Program:***

```
#include<iostream.h>
#include<conio.h>
main ( )
{
int mul( ), (*p1)( ), x, y, z ;
cin>>x>>y;
p1 = &mul ;
z = (*p1)(x, y);
cout<< z ;
getche( ) ;
}
int mul(int p, int q)
{
int m ;
m = p * q ;
return (m) ;
}
```

**Problem 44. Write a C++ program to print the strings having three cities and their addresses using array of pointer to the string concept.**

***Program:***

```
#include<iostream.h>
#include<conio.h>
main()
{
char *city[ ]={"Moga","Batala","Delhi"};
int i;
for(i=0;i<3;i++)
{
cout<<"\n"<< *(city+i)<<"city has address
"<<(city+i);
}
getche();
}
```

**OUTPUT:**

Moga city has address 1200
Batala city has address 1202
Delhi city has address 1204

**Problem 45. Write a C++ program to show use of pointer and address of operator.**

***Program:***

```
#include<iostream.h>
#include<conio.h>
int main()
{
int p,*ptr;
p=7;
ptr=&p;
cout<<"Value of p="<<p;
cout<<"\nAddress of p="<<&p;
cout<<"\nValue of ptr="<<ptr;
getch();
}
```

**OUTPUT:**

Value of p=7
Address of p=65524
Value of ptr=65524

**Problem 46. Write a C++ program to show use of dereference operator(*).**

***Program:***

```
#include<iostream.h>
#include<conio.h>
int main()
{
int p=3,*ptr;
ptr=&p;
cout<<"Value stored at address of ptr="<<*ptr;
getch();
}
```

**OUTPUT:**

Value stored at address of ptr=3

**Problem 47. Write a C++ program to show use of address of operator(&) and indirection operator(*) for different purpose.**

***Program:***

```
#include<iostream.h>
#include<conio.h>
main()
{
int p=5,q=2,*ptr;
ptr=&p;
clrscr();
cout<<"Address of p="<<&p;
cout<<"\nValue stored in pointer="<<ptr;
cout<<"\nValue pointed by pointer="<<*ptr;
*ptr=10;
cout<<"\nValue of p="<<p;
q=*ptr;
cout<<"\nValue of q="<<q;
getch();
}
```

**OUTPUT:**

Address of p=65524
Value stored in pointer=-12
Value pointed by pointer=5
Value of p=10
Value of q=10

**Problem 48. Write a C++ program to show working of pointer to pointer.**

***Program:***

```
#include<iostream.h>
#include<conio.h>
main()
{
int p=2,*q,**k;
q=&p;
k=&q;
clrscr();
cout<<"Value of p="<<p;
cout<<"\nValue of *q="<<*q;
cout<<"\nValue of **k="<<**k;
getch();
}
```

**OUTPUT:**

Value of p=2
Value of *q=2
Value of **k=2

**Problem 49. Write a C++ program to show storage of array elements in contiguous memory locations.**

***Program:***

```
#include<iostream.h>
#include<conio.h>
main()
{
int a[5]={15,25,35,45,55};
int p;
for(p=0;p<5;p++)
cout<<"\n a["<<p<<"]="<<a[p]<<"
&a["<<p<<"]="<<&a[p];
}
```

**OUTPUT:**

a[0]=15&a[0]=65516
a[1]=25 &a[1]=65518
a[2]=35 &a[2]=65520
a[3]=45 &a[3]=65522
a[4]=55 &a[4]=65524

**Problem 50. Write a C++ program to show value x[i] and *(x+i) are equal.**

***Program:***

```
#include<iostream.h>
#include<conio.h>
main()
{
int a[5]={15,25,35,45,55};
int p;
for(p=0;p<5;p++)
cout<<"\n a["<<p<<"]="<<a[p]<<"
*(a+"<<p<<")="<<*a+p;
}
```

**OUTPUT:**

a[0]=15*(a+0)=15
a[1]=25 *(a+1)=16
a[2]=35 *(a+2)=17
a[3]=45 *(a+3)=18
a[4]=55 *(a+4)=19

**Problem 51. Write a C++ program to show importance of pointer to 2-D array.**

***Program:***

```
#include<iostream.h>
#include<conio.h>
main()
{
int u,v;
int x[4][2],*q;
q=x[0];
```

```
clrscr();
cout<<"Enter elements:\n";
for(u=0;u<4;u++)
for(v=0;v<2;v++)
cin>>x[u][v];
for(u=0;u<4;u++)
{
cout<<"Base address of "<<u<<" row
is:"<<(q+u*2)<<"\n";
cout<<"First element of "<<u<<" row
is:<<*(q+u*2+0)<<"\n";
}
cout<<"Element x[1][3] is "<<*(q+1*2+1);
getch();
}
```

**OUTPUT:**

```
Enter elements:
4 5 6
7 8 9
1 2 3
Base address of 0 row is:65508
First element of 0 row is:4
Base address of 1 row is:65512
First element of 1 row is:6
Base address of 2 row is:65516
First element of 2 row is:8
Base address of 3 row is:65520
First element of 3 row is:1
element x[1][3] is 7
```

**Problem 52. Write a C++ program to show importance of array of pointers.**

***Program:***

```
#include<iostream.h>
#include<conio.h>
#include<stdlib.h>
main()
{
int *s[3];
int p,q;
for(p=0;p<3;p++)
{
s[p]=(int*)malloc(4*sizeof(int));
}
cout<<"Enter elements\n";
for(p=0;p<3;p++)
for(q=0;q<4;q++)
cin>>s[p][q];
for(p=0;p<3;p++)
{
cout<<"\nBase address of "<<p+1<<"
row:"<<s[p]<<"\t";
cout<<"\n First element of "<<p+1<<"
row:"<<*s[p]<<"\t";
}
cout<<"Element x[2][2] is :"<<*(s[2]+2);
}
```

**Problem 53. Write a C++ program without changing array,to sort list of numbers.**

***Program:***

```
#include<iostream.h>
#include<conio.h>
main()
{
int a[10],j,*temp,i,n,*p[10];
cout<<"Specify number of elements\n";
cin>>n;
cout<<"Specify array elements\n";
for(i=0;i<n;i++)
{
cin>>a[i];
p[i]=&a[i];
}
for(j=0;j<n-1;j++)
{
for(i=0;i<n-1;i++)
{
if(*p[i]>*p[i+1])
{
temp=p[i];
p[i]=p[i+1];
p[i+1]=temp;
}
}
}
cout<<"\n\nSorted array \t\tOriginal array\n";
for(i=0;i<n;i++)
{
cout<<"\n\t"<<*p[i]<<"\t\t\t"<<a[i];
}
getch();
}
```

**OUTPUT:**

```
Specify number of elements:5
Specify array elements:4 12 35 22 17
Sorted array     Original array
4 4
12 12
17 35
22 22
35 17
```

**Problem 54. Write a C++ program to define string using pointer notation & array notation.**

***Program:***

```
#include<iostream.h>
#include<conio.h>
main()
{
char s1[]="It is an array";
char *s2="It is a pointer";
clrscr();
cout<<s1;
cout<<s2;
cout<<s2+5;
}
```

**OUTPUT:**

It is an arrayIt is a pointer a pointer

**Problem 55. Write a C++ program to copy one string to another.**

***Program:***

```
#include<iostream.h>
#include<conio.h>
void copy_string(char *,char *);
main()
{
char *s1="How to learn C";
char s2[20];
copy(s2,s1);
cout<<"\n"<<s2;
}
void copy_string(char *dest,char *src)
{
while(*src!='\0')
*dest++=*src++;
*dest='\0';
return;
}
```

**Problem 56. Write a C++ program to interchange value of two numbers using call by reference.**

***Program:***

```
#include<iostream.h>
#include<conio.h>
main()
{
int u=40;
int v=50;
void swap_func(int *m,int *n);
swap_func(&u,&v);
cout<<"\n u="<<u<<" v="<<v;
}
void swap_func(int *m,int *n)
{
int s;
s=*m;
*m=*n;
*n=s;
}
```

**OUTPUT:**

u=50 v=40

**Problem 57. Write a C++ program to show difference between call by reference and call by value.**

***Program:***

```
#include<iostream.h>
#include<conio.h>
main()
{
int u=1;
int v=2;
void value(int u,int v);
void refer(int *m,int *n);
clrscr();
cout<<"\nBefore Calling value:u="<<u<<"
v="<<v;
value(u,v);
cout<<"\nAfter Calling value:u="<<u<<"\t
v="<<v;
cout<<"\nBefore Calling value:u="<<u<<"\t
v="<<v;
refer(&u,&v);
cout<<"\nAfter Calling refer:u="<<u<<"\t v="<<v;
getch();
}
void value(int u,int v)
{
u=5;v=10;
cout<<"\n Value with function:u="<<u<<"\t
v="<<v;
}
void refer(int *m,int *n)
{
*m=5;
*n=10;
cout<<"\n Value with function:*m="<<*m<<"\t
*n="<<*n;
}
```

**OUTPUT:**

Before Calling value:u=1 v=2
Value with function:u=5 v=10

After Calling value:u=1 v=2
Before Calling value:u=1 v=2
Value with function:*m=5 *n=10
After calling refer:u=5 v=10

**Problem 58. Write a C++ program to add two tables of integers using functions and pointers.**

***Program:***

```
#include<iostream.h>
#include<conio.h>
main()
{
int u[10][10],v[10][10],w[10][10];
int i,j,m,n,p,q;
void add(int*,int*,int*,int,int);
clrscr();
cout<<"Order of Matrix U\n ";
cin>>m>>n;
cout<<"Order of Matrix V\n ";
cin>>p>>q;
if(m!=p ||n!=q)
{
cout<<"\nThe order is wrong";
getch();
exit(1);}
for(i=0;i<m;i++)
for(j=0;j<n;j++)
{
cin>>u[i][j];
}
for(i=0;i<p;i++)
for(j=0;j<q;j++)
{
cin>>v[i][j];
}
add(*u,*v,*w,m,n);
for(i=0;i<m;i++)
{
for(j=0;j<n;j++)
{
cout<<"Result="<<w[i][j];
cout<<" ";
}
cout<<"\n";
}
getch();
}
void add(int *p,int *q,int *r,int y,int z)
{
int i,j;
for(i=0;i<y;i++)
{
for(j=0;j<z;j++)
{
*(r+i*10+j)=*(p+i*10+j)+*(q+i*10+j);
}
}
}
```

**OUTPUT:**

Order of Matrix U
2 2
Order of Matrix V
2 3
1 2
4 5
7 8
9 1
Result=8 Result=10
Result=13 Result=6

**Problem 59. Write a C++ program for a function that receives sorted array of integer and an integer value & inserts the value in its correct place.**

***Program:***

```
#include<iostream.h>
#include<conio.h>
void insert(int *v,int t,int *g);
main()
{
int p,item,n,u[10];
cout<<"\nSpecify number of elements";
cin>>n;
cout<<"\nSpecify sorted array";
for(p=0;p<n;p++)
{
cin>>u[p];
}
cout<<"\nSpecify item to be inserted";
cin>>item;
insert(u,n,&item);
for(p=0;p<=n;p++)
{
cout<<"\t"<<u[p];
}
getch();
}
void insert(int *v,int t,int *g)
{
int p,loc=0;
for(p=0;p<t;p++)
{
```

```
if(*(v+p)>*g)
{
loc=p;
break;
}
}
for(p=t;p>loc;p--)
{
*(v+p)=*(v+p-1);
}
*(v+loc)=*g;
}
```

**OUTPUT:**

Specify number of elements 5
Specify sorted array 4 12 17 22 36
Specify item to be inserted 27
4 12 17 22 27 36

**Problem 60. Write a C++ program to show how operator works in case of pointers.**

***Program:***

```
#include<iostream.h>
#include<conio.h>
int *ptr1,*ptr2,*ptr3;
int p=1;
int q=2;
int f[5]={1,2,3,4,5};
main()
{
int u,v,c;
ptr1=&p;
ptr2=&q;
ptr3=&f[0];
u=ptr1-ptr2;
v=*ptr1+*ptr2;
c=*ptr3+2;
if(ptr1>=ptr2)
cout<<u<<v<<c;
if(ptr1<=ptr2)
cout<<ptr1<<ptr2<<ptr3;
}
```

**OUTPUT:**

170172174

**Problem 61. Write a C++ program to print table w=3*x*x-2*x+1 and sin(x)-x varies in steps of 0.5.**

***Program:***

```
#include<iostream.h>
#include<conio.h>
#include<math.h>
#define PI 3.1415
main()
{
double w(double);
double table(double(*)
(double),double,double,double);
clrscr();
cout<<"Table of w(x)=3*x*x-2*x+1\n";
cout<<" x\t\t w\n";
table(w,0.2,2.0,0.5);
cout<<"Table of sin(x)\n\n";
table(sin,0.0,PI,0.5);
}
double table(double(*f) (double),double
min,double max,double step)
{
double a,b;
for(a=min;a<=max;a+=step)
{
b=(*f)(a);
cout<<a<<"\t"<<b<<"\n";
}
return (b);
}
double w(double x)
{
return (3*x*x-2*x+1);
}
```

**OUTPUT:**

Table of w(x)=3*x*x-2*x+1
x w
0.200000 0.720000
0.700000 1.070000
1.200000 2.920000
1.700000 6.270000
Table of sin(x)
0.000000 0.000000
0.000000 0.479426
1.000000 0.841471
1.000000 0.997495
2.000000 0.909297
2.000000 0.598472
3.000000 0.141120

**Problem 62. Write a C++ program using pointers to sort elements of array.**

***Program:***

```
#include<iostream.h>
#include<conio.h>
main()
{
int p,n,*s;
```

```
void reorder(int n,int *s);
cout<<"Specify number of elements";
cin>>n;
s=(int*)malloc(n*sizeof(int));
for(p=0;p<n;p++)
{
cout<<"p="<<p+1<<" s= ";
cin>>s+p;
}
reorder(n,s);
cout<<"\nReorder List:\n";
for(p=0;p<n;p++)
cout<<"s="<<*(s+p)<<"\n";
}
void reorder(int n,int *s)
{
int p,q,t;
for(p=0;p<n-1;p++)
for(q=p+1;q<n;q++)
if(*(s+p)>*(s+q))
{
t=*(s+q);
*(s+q)=*(s+p);
*(s+p)=t;
}
}
```

**OUTPUT:**

```
Specify number of elements 5
p=1 s=25
p=2 s=12
p=3 s=17
p=4 s=4
p=5 s=35
Reorder List:
s=4
s=12
s=17
s=25
s=35
```

**Problem 63. Write a C++ program using pointers to sort list of strings.**

***Program:***

```
#include<iostream.h>
#include<conio.h>
#include<string.h>
main()
{
char *a[20];
int p,n;
int reorder(int n,char *a[]);
clrscr();
cout<<"\nSpecify number of strings:";
cin>>n;
cout<<"\n";
cout<<"\nSpecify strings:";
for(p=0;p<n;p++)
{
a[p]=(char*)malloc(20*sizeof(char));
cin>>a[p];
}
reorder(n,a);
cout<<"\nReorder list:\n";
for(p=0;p<n;p++)
cout<<"\n"<<a[p];
getch();
}
int reorder(int n,char *a[])
{
int p,j;
char t[20];
for(p=0;p<n;p++)
for(j=p+1;j<n-1;j++)
if(strcmp(a[p],a[j])>0)
{
strcpy(t,a[j]);
strcpy(a[j],a[p]);
strcpy(a[p],t);
}
return(*a[p]);
}
```

**OUTPUT:**

```
Specify number of strings:3
Specify strings: god bless you
Reorder list:
bless
god
you
```

**Problem 64. Write a C++ program to pass three cities as argument to a function (Strings as function argument with pointer).**

***Program:***

```
#include<iostream.h>
#include<conio.h>
void main( )
{
char *city[3]={"Moga","Batala","Delhi"};
void pass ( char **, int);
pass ( city , 3);
getche();
}
```

```
void pass ( char **m, int n)
{
int i;
for ( i=0; i <n; i++)
{
cout<<"\n"<< m[i];
}
return;
}
```

**OUTPUT:**

Moga
Batala
Delhi

**Problem 65. Write a C++ program to copy one string to another string variable by using pointer.**

***Program:***

```
#include<iostream.h>
#include<conio.h>
main()
{
char string1[ ] = "Hello";
char string2[15];
char *s = "How are you";
char *p;
string2 = string1; /* error */
p = s; /* works */
getch();
}
```

**Problem 66. Write a C++ program to illustrate the concept of dynamic memory allocation in pointers.**

***Program:***

```
#include<iostream.h>
#include<stdlib.h>
#include<conio.h>
main()
{
int *ip;
long *lp;
float *fp;
double *dp;
ip= (int *) malloc(sizeof(int));
if(ip=NULL)
{
puts("\n Memory is not enough ");
exit(1);
}
lp= (long *) malloc(sizeof(long));
if(lp=NULL)
{
puts("\n Memory is not enough ");
exit(1);
}
fp= (float *) malloc(sizeof(float));
if(fp=NULL)
{
puts("\n Memory is not enough ");
exit(1);
}
dp= (double *) malloc(sizeof(double));
if(dp=NULL)
{
puts("\n Memory is not enough ");
exit(1);
}
*ip= 5555;
*lp=9999999999;
*fp=44444.555;
*dp=7777777.8888888;
cout<<"\n Address        Value";
cout<<ip<< *ip;
cout<<lp<< *lp;
cout<<fp<< *fp;
cout<<dp<< *dp;
getche()
}
```

**OUTPUT:**

```
Address      Value
50c      5555
234      9999999999
70c      44444.555
345      7777777.8888888
```

**Problem 67. Write a C++ program to find factorial of a number-using pointer to function**

***Program:***

```
#include<iostream.h>
#include<conio.h>
main()
{
clrscr();
int n,a;
int fact(int);
int (*pt) (int);
pt = &fact;
cout<<"\nEnter the number :";
cin>>n;
a=(*pt) (n);
cout<<"\nThe factorial of "<<n<<" is "<<a;
getch();
```

```
}
int fact(int z)
{
int i,m;
m = 1;
for(i=1;i<=z;i++)
{
m=m*i;
}
return(m);
}
```

**OUTPUT:**

Enter the number:5
The factorial of 5 is 120

**Problem 68. Write a C++ program to find the location of characters of any city and find its length (no. of character in a string) by using pointer.**

***Program:***

```
#include<iostream.h>
main()
{
char name[20],*p;
int l;
clrscr();
cout<<"\n ENTER NAME OF CITY";
cin>>name;
p=&name;
while(*p!='\0')
{
cout<<"\n"<<*p<<" is stored at address "<<p;
p++;
}
l=p-name;
cout<<"\n Length= "<<l;
getche();
}
```

**OUTPUT:**

ENTER NAME OF CITY: MOGA
M is stored at address 2000
O is stored at address 2001
G is stored at address 2002
A is stored at address 2003
Length=4

**Problem 69. Write a C++ program to add two tables (matrix) of integers using functions and pointers.**

***Program:***

```
#include<iostream.h>
#include<conio.h>
main ()
{
int a[10][10],b[10][10],c[10][10];
int i,j,m,n,p,q;
void add (int*,int*,int*,int,int);
cout<<"\n Enter the Row and Columns of Matrix
A: \n";
cin>>m>>n;
cout<<"\n Enter the rows and columns of Matrix
B: \n";
cin>>p>>q;
if (m!=p||n!=q)
{
cout<<"\n Sum is not possible";
getch ();
exit (1);
}
cout<<"\n Enter the elements of Matrix A: ";
for (i=0;i<m;i++)
for (j=0;j<n;j++)
{
cin>>a[i][j];
}
cout<<"\n Enter the elements of Matrix B: ";
for(i=0;i<p;i++)
for (j=0;j<q;j++)
{
cin>>b[i][j];}
}
add (a,b,c,m,n);
getch ();
}
void add (int*p,int*q,int*r,int y,int z)
{
int i,j;
for (i=0;i<y;i++)
{
for (j=0;j<z;j++)
{
*(r+i*z+j)
=*(p+i*z+j)+*(q+i*z+j);
}
}
}
```

**OUTPUT:**

Enter the Row and Columns of Matrix A:
3 3
Enter the rows and columns of Matrix B:
3 3
Enter the elements of Matrix A:

```
1       2       3
4       5       6
7       8       9
Enter the elements of Matrix B:
9       8       7
6       5       4
3       2       1
Resultant Matrix is:
10      10      10
10      10      10
10      10      10
```

**Problem 70. Write a C++ program to show the importance of pointers to arrays.**

***Program:***

```
#include<iostream.h>
#include<conio.h>
main ( )
{
int i,j;
int(*a)[4];
a=(int*)malloc(3* 2*sizeof(int));
cout<<"\n Enter the elements: ";
for (i=0;i<3;i++)
for (j=0;j<2;j++)
cin>>a[i][j];
for (i=0;i<2;i++)
{
cout<<"\n Base address of "<<i<<" dth
row:"<<*(a+i)<<"\n";
cout<<"\n First element of "<<i<<*(*(a+i));
}
cout<<"Element x[1][2] is "<<*(*(a+1)+3);
getch();
}
```

**OUTPUT:**

```
Enter the elements:
1       2       3       4       5       6
Base address of 0 th row: 1000
First element of 1
Base address of 1 th row: 1200
First element of 3
Element x[1][2] is 2
```

**Problem 71. Write a C++ program to sort a list of strings using pointers.**

***Program:***

```
#include<iostream.h>
#include<conio.h>
#include<string.h>
main ()
{
char *x[20];
int i,n;
int reorder (int n, char *x[]);
clrscr ();
cout<<"\n Enter the number of strings: ";
cin>>n;
cout<<"\n";
cout<<"\n Enter the strings: ";
for (i=0;i<n;i++)
{
x[i]=(char*)malloc(20*sizeof(char));
cin>>x[i];
}
reorder (n,x);
cout<<"\n Reordered List is: ";
for (i=0;i<n;i++)
cout<<x[i];
getch ();
}
int reorder (int n,char *x[])
{
int i,j;
char t[20];
for (i=0;i<n;i++)
for (j=i+1;j<n-i;j++)
if (strcmp (x[i],x[j])>0)
{
strcpy (t,x[j]);
strcpy (x[j],x[i]);
strcpy (x[i],t));}
return (*x[i]);
}
}
```

**OUTPUT:**

```
Enter the number of strings:
4
Enter the strings:
Moga
Batala
Amritsar
Delhi
Reordered List is:
Amritsar
Batala
Delhi
Moga
```

**Problem 72. Write a C++ program to demonstrate the importance of array of pointers.**

***Program:***

```
#include<iostream.h>
#include<conio.h>
#include<stdlib.h>
main ()
{
int *a[3];
int i,j;
for (i=0;i<3;i++) {
a[i]=(int*)malloc(4*size of (int));}
cout<<"\n Enter the Elements: ";
for (i=0;i<3;i++)
for (j=0;j<4;j++)
cin>>a[i][j];
for (i=0;i<3;i++)
{
cout<<"\n Base address of
"<<i+1<<"row:"<<a[i]<<"\t";
cout<<"\n First element of "<<i+1<<"
row:"<<*a[i]<<"\t";
}
cout<<"\n Element x[2][2] is:"<<*(a[2]+2);
}
```

**OUTPUT:**

```
Enter the Elements:
1 2   3 4   5   6   7   8   9
      10    11 12
Base address of 0 row: 1000
First element of 0 row 1
Base address of 1 row: 2000
First element of 1 row: 4
Base address of 2 row: 3000
First element of 2 row: 4000
Element x[2][2] is: 5
```

**Problem 73. Write a C++ program to define a string using pointer notation.**

***Program:***

```
#include<iostream.h>
#include<conio.h>
main ()
{
char str1[] ="Defined as an array";
char *str2 ="Defined as a pointer";
cout<<str1;
cout<<str2;
cout<<str2+5;
}
```

**OUTPUT:**

```
Defined as an array
Defined as a pointer
ed as a pointer
```

**Problem 74. Write a C++ program to copy one string to another using pointers.**

***Program:***

```
#include<iostream.h>
#include<conio.h>
void copystr (char*,char*);
main ()
{
char *str1="You are copying";
char *str2[20];
copystr (str2,str1);
cout<<"\n "<<str2;
}
void copystr (char *dest, char *src)
{
while (*src !='\0')
*dest++ = *src++;
*dest='\0';
return;
}
```

**OUTPUT:**

```
You are copying
```

**Problem 75. Write a C++ program to represent the working of call by value and call by reference.**

***Program:***

```
#include<iostream.h>
#include<conio.h>
main ()
{
int a=1;
int b=2;
clrscr();
void value (int a, int b);
void refer (int*x, int*y);
cout<<"\n Before Calling value: a = "<<a<<" \t b =
"<<b;
value (a,b);
cout<<"\n After Calling Value: a = "<<a<<" \t b =
"<<b;
cout<<"\n Before calling reference: a = "<<a<<" \t
b = "<<b;
refer (&a,&b);
cout<<"\n After Calling reference: a = "<<a<<" \t
b = "<<b;
getch ();
}
void value (int a,int b)
```

```
{
a=5;b=10;
cout<<"\n Value with function: a= "<<a<<"\t
b="<<b;
}
void refer (int*x,int*y)
{
*x=5;
*y=10;
cout<<"\n value with function: x= "<<*x<<" \t *y =
"<<*y;
}
```

**OUTPUT:**

```
Before Calling value: a = 1 b = 2
Value with function: a = 5 b = 10
After Calling Value: a = 2 b = 1
Before calling reference: a = 1 b = 2
Value with function: a = 5 b = 10
After Calling reference: a = 5 b = 10
```

**Problem 76. Write a C++ program to demonstrate that value x[i] and *(x+i) are equal.**

***Program:***

```
#include<iostream.h>
#include<conio.h>
main ()
{
int x[5]={10,11,12,13,14};
int i;
for (i=0;i<5;i++)
cout<<"\n
x["<<i<<"]="<<x[i]<<"*(x+"<<i<<")="<<*(x+i);
getch ();
}
```

**OUTPUT:**

```
X[0]=10        *(x+0)=10
X[1]=11        *(x+1)=11
X[2]=12        *(x+2)=12
X[3]=13        *(x+3)=13
X[14]=14       *(x+4)=14
```

**Problem 77. Write a C++ program to demonstrate array elements are stored in contiguous memory locations.**

***Program:***

```
#include<iostream.h>
#include<conio.h>
main ()
{
int i,n,*x;
void reorder (int n,int*x);
cout<<"\n How many numbers?";
cin>>n;
x=(int*) malloc (n*sizeof (int));
for (i=0;i<n;i++)
{
cout<<"i= "<<i+1<<"x=";
cin>>x+i;
}
reorder (n,x);
cout<<"\n Reordered List:\n";
for (i=0;i<n;i++)
cout<<"x= "<<*(x+i)<<"\n";
}
void reorder (int n,int *x)
{
int i,j,temp;
for (i=0;i<n-1;i++)
for (j=i+;j<n;j++)
if (*(x+i)>*(x+j))
{
temp=*(x+j);
*(x+j)=*(x+i);
*(x+i)=temp;
}
}
```

**OUTPUT:**

```
How many numbers
3
Reordered List:
X[0]=10        &x[0]=2010
X[1]=20        &x[1]=2020
X[2]=30        &x[2]=2030
```

**Problem 78. Write a C++ program to function that receives a stored array of integer and an integer value, inserts the value in its correct place.**

***Program:***

```
#include<iostream.h>
#include<conio.h>
void insert (int*b,int m,int*it);
main ()
{
int i,item,n,a[10];
cout<<"\n Enter the Number of elements:";
cin>>n;
cout<<"\n Enter the sorted numbers:";
for (i=0;i<n;i++)
{
cin>>&a[i];
}
```

```
cout<<"\n Enter item to be inserted:";
cin>>item;
insert (a,n,&item);
cout<<"\n New sorted List is:";
for (i=0;i<=n;i++)
{
cout<<"\t"<<a[i];
{
getch ();
}
```

**OUTPUT:**

Enter the Number of elements:
3
Enter the sorted numbers:
20
30
40
Enter item to be inserted:
22
New sorted List is:
20
22
30
40

**Problem 79. Write a C++ program to reverse the string using pointer.**

***Program:***

```
#include<iostream.h>
#include<conio.h>
#include<string.h>
main()
{
char a[20];
void f(char [20]);
void (*p)(char [20]);
clrscr();
cout<<"\n Enter the string :";
cin>> a;
p=&f;
(*p)(a);
getch();
}
void f(char *s)
{
int i,n;
char t;
n=strlen(s);
for(i=0;i<n/2;i++)
{
t=*(s+i);
*(s+i)=*(s+n-i-1);
*(s+n-i-1)=t;
}
cout<<"\n Reversed string is :";
for(i=0;*(s+i)!=0;i++)
cout<<"\n"<<*(s+i);
}
```

**OUTPUT:**

Enter the string : rama
Reversed string is : amar

**Problem 80. Write a C++ program to find the area of triangle .**

***Program:***

```
#include<iostream.h>
#include<conio.h>
int main()
{
double l=4.0, b=2.0,area;
double *lp,*bp, *parea;
lp=&l;
bp=&b;
parea=&area;
*parea= 0.5 * (*lp) * (*bp);
cout<<*parea;
getch();
}
```

**OUTPUT:**

4.000000

**Problem 81. Write a C++ program to find the area of sphere .**

***Program:***

```
#include<iostream.h>
#include<conio.h>
int main()
{
double rad=1.0,area;
double *rp, *parea;
clrscr();
rp=&rad;
parea=&area;
*parea= 4.0/3.0 * *rp * *rp * *rp;
cout<<*parea;
getch();
}
```

**OUTPUT:**

1.333333

**Problem 82. Write a C++ program to print the ascii value of given character .**

***Program:***

```
#include<iostream.h>
#include<conio.h>
int main()
{
char ch, *pch;
pch=&ch;
cout<<"Enter a character:";
cin>>ch;
cout<<*pch;
getch();
}
```

**OUTPUT:**

Enter a character:a
97

**Problem 83. Write a C++ program to print the upper case letters to lower case .**

***Program:***

```
#include<iostream.h>
#include<conio.h>
int main()
{
char any, *pany;
pany=&any;
cout<<"Enter a character:";
cin>>any;
cout<<*pany+32;
getch();
}
```

**OUTPUT:**

Enter a character:S
s

**Problem 84. Write a C++ program to print the lower case letters to upper case .**

***Program:***

```
#include<iostream.h>
#include<conio.h>
int main()
{
char any, *pany;
pany=&any;
cout<<"Enter a character:";
cin>>any;
cout<<*pany-32;
getch();
}
```

**OUTPUT:**

Enter a character:A
!

**Problem 85. Write a C++ program to read float value and print integer equivalent .**

***Program:***

```
#include<iostream.h>
#include<conio.h>
int main()
{
float fno, *pf;
int ino, *pi;
pi=&ino;
pf=&fno;
cout<<"Enter a number:";
cin>>fno;
*pi=(int)*pf;
cout<<*pi;
getch();
}
```

**OUTPUT:**

Enter a number:4.12
4

**Problem 86. Write a C++ program to read int value and print float equivalent .**

***Program:***

```
#include<iostream.h>
#include<conio.h>
int main()
{
float fno, *pf;
int ino, *pi;
pi=&ino;
pf=&fno;
cout<<"Enter a number:";
cin>>ino;
*pf=*pi; // *pf=(float)*pi , both are same.
cout<<*pf;
getch();
}
```

**OUTPUT:**

Enter a number:4
4.000000

**Problem 87. Write a C++ program to check whether the given character upper, lower , numbr or not.**

***Program:***

```
#include<iostream.h>
#include<conio.h>
int main()
{
```

```
char any, *pany;
pany=&any;
cout<<"Enter a character:";
cin>>pany;
if(*pany>='A' && *pany <='Z')
cout<<"upper case";
else
if(*pany>='a' && *pany <='z')
cout<<"lower case";
else
if(*pany>='0' && *pany <='9')
cout<<"number";
else
cout<<"not ";
getch();
}
```

**OUTPUT:**

Enter a character:A
upper case

**Problem 88. Write a C++ program to print a word form of given number between 0 to 9 .**

***Program:***

```
#include<iostream.h>
#include<conio.h>
int main()
{
int number,*pnum;
pnum=&number;
cout<<"Enter a number:";
cin>>pnum;
if (*pnum==0)
cout<<"Zero";
else
if (*pnum==1)
cout<<"One";
else
if (*pnum==2)
cout<<"Two";
else
if (*pnum==3)
cout<<"Three";
else
if (*pnum==4)
cout<<"Four";
else
if (*pnum==5)
cout<<"Five";
else
if (*pnum==6)
cout<<"Six";
else
if (*pnum==7)
cout<<"Seven";
else
if (*pnum==8)
cout<<"eight";
else
if(*pnum==9)
cout<<"Nine";
else
cout<<"others";
getch();
}
```

**OUTPUT:**

Enter a number:4
Four

**Problem 89. Write a C++ program to print a word form of given number is tens between 1 to 99.**

***Program:***

```
#include<iostream.h>
#include<conio.h>
int main()
{
int number,*pnum;
pnum=&number;
cout<<"Enter a number:";
cin>>pnum;
if ( *pnum==10)
cout<<"Ten";
else
if ( *pnum==20)
cout<<"Twenty";
else
if ( *pnum==30)
cout<<"Thirty";
else
if ( *pnum==40)
cout<<"Fourty";
else
if ( *pnum==50)
cout<<"Fifty";
else
if ( *pnum==60)
cout<<"Sixty";
else
if ( *pnum==70)
cout<<"Seventy";
else
if ( *pnum==80)
```

```
cout<<"eighty";
else
if( *pnum==90)
cout<<"Ninty";
else
cout<<"others";
getch();
}
```

**OUTPUT:**

Enter a number:20
Twenty

**Problem 90. Write a C++ program to find smallest of three given numbers.**

***Program:***

```
#include<iostream.h>
#include<conio.h>
int main()
{
int one,two,three, *p1,*p2,*p3;
p1=&one; p2=&two; p3=&three;
cout<<"Enter Three numbers:";
cin>>p1>>p2>>p3;
if ( *p1<*p2)
{
if ( *p1 <*p3)
cout<<*p1;
else
cout<<*p3;
}
else
{
if ( *p2 <*p3)
cout<<*p2;
else
cout<<*p3;
}
getch();
}
```

**OUTPUT:**

Enter Three numbers: 123 654 765
123

**Problem 91. Write a C++ program to find biggest of three given numbers using && operator .**

***Program:***

```
#include<iostream.h>
#include<conio.h>
int main()
{
int one,two,three, *p1,*p2,*p3;
p1=&one; p2=&two; p3=&three;
cout<<"Enter Three numbers:);
cin>>p1>>p2>>p3;
if(*p1>*p2 && *p1>*p3)
cout<<*p1;
else
if(*p2>*p3)
cout<<*p2;
else
cout<<*p3;
getch();
}
```

**OUTPUT:**

Enter Three numbers:345 876 745
876

**Problem 92. Write a C++ program to display the name of the day in a week .here given input range is 1 to 7 .**

***Program:***

```
#include<iostream.h>
int main()
{
int day, *pd;
pd=&day;
cout<<"Enter a number:";
cin>>pd;
if (*pd==1)
cout<<"Sunday";
else
if (*pd==2)
cout<<"Monday";
else
if (*pd==3)
cout<<"Tuesday";
else
if (*pd==4)
cout<<"wednesday";
else
if (*pd==5)
cout<<"thursday";
else
if (*pd==6)
cout<<"friday";
else
if (*pd==7)
cout<<"Saturday";
else
cout<<"others";
getch();
}
```

**OUTPUT:**

Enter a number:4
wednesday

**Problem 93. Write a C++ program to find an biggest of four given numbers .**

***Program:***

```
#include<iostream.h>
#include<conio.h>
int main()
{
int one,two,three,four;
int *p1, *p2, *p3, *p4;
p1=&one;
p2=&two;
p3=&three;
p4=&four;
cout<<"Enter four numbers:";
cin>>p1>>p2>>p3>>p4;
if(*p1>*p2 && *p1>*p3 && *p1 > *p4)
cout<<*p1;
else
if(*p2>*p4&&*p2>*p3)
cout<<*p2;
else
if(*p3>*p4)
cout<<*p3;
else
cout<<*p4;
getch();
}
```

**OUTPUT:**

Enter four numbers:34 76 98 12
98

**Problem 94. Write a C++ program to find an smallest of four given numbers .**

***Program:***

```
#include<iostream.h>
#include<conio.h>
int main()
{
int one,two,three,four;
int *p1, *p2, *p3, *p4;
p1=&one;
p2=&two;
p3=&three;
p4=&four;
cout<<"Enter four numbers:";
cin>>p1>>p2>>p3>>p4;
if(*p1<*p2 && *p1<*p3 && *p1 < *p4)
cout<<*p1;
else
if(*p2<*p4&&*p2<*p3)
cout<<*p2;
else
if(*p3<*p4)
cout<<*p3;
else
cout<<*p4;
getch();
}
```

**OUTPUT:**

Enter four numbers:34 76 98 12
12

**Problem 95. Write a C++ program to find a vowel or not of given character .**

***Program:***

```
#include<iostream.h>
#include<conio.h>
int main()
{
char vowel,*pch;
pch=&vowel;
cout<<"Enter a character:";
cin>>pch;
if(*pch=='a' ||*pch=='e' ||*pch=='i' ||*pch=='o'
||*pch=='u' ||
*pch=='A' ||*pch=='E' ||*pch=='I' ||*pch=='O'
||*pch=='U' )
cout<<"vowel";
else
cout<<"not";
getch();
}
```

**OUTPUT:**

Enter a character:a
vowel

**Problem 96. Write a C++ program to use switch statement using pointers.**

***Program:***

```
#include<iostream.h>
#include<conio.h>
int main()
{
int day,*pd;
pd=&day;
cout<<"Enter a number:";
cin>>pd;
switch(*pd)
```

```
{
case 1:
cout<<"sunday";
break;
case 2:
cout<<"monday";
break;
case 3:
cout<<"tuesday";
break;
case 4:
cout<<"wednesday";
break;
case 5:
cout<<"thursday";
break;
case 6:
cout<<"friday";
break;
case 7:
cout<<"saturday";
break;
default :
cout<<"wrong input";
}
getch();
}
```

**OUTPUT:**

```
Enter a number:4
wednesday
```

**Problem 97. Write a C++ program to use switch statement using pointers.**

***Program:***

```
#include<iostream.h>
int main()
{
int number,*pnum;
pnum=&number;
cout<<"Enter a number:";
cin>>pnum;
switch(*pnum)
{
case 1:
cout<<"one";
break;
case 2:
cout<<"two";
break;
case 3:
cout<<"three";
break;
case 4:
cout<<"four";
break;
case 5:
cout<<"five";
break;
case 6:
cout<<"six";
break;
case 7:
cout<<"seven";
break;
case 8:
cout<<"eight";
break;
case 9:
cout<<"nine";
break;
case 0:
cout<<"zero";
break;
default :
cout<<"wrong input";
}
getch();
}
```

**OUTPUT:**

```
Enter a number:1
one
```

**Problem 98. Write a C++ program to use switch statement using pointers.**

***Program:*** .

```
#include<iostream.h>
#include<conio.h>
int main()
{
int number, *pnum;
pnum=&number;
cout<<"Enter a number:";
cin>>pnum;
switch(*pnum)
{
case 10:
cout<<"ten";
break;
case 20:
cout<<"twenty";
break;
case 30:
```

```
cout<<"thirty";
break;
case 40:
cout<<"fourty";
break;
case 50:
cout<<"fifty";
break;
case 60:
cout<<"sixty";
break;
case 70:
cout<<"seventy";
break;
case 80:
cout<<"eighty";
break;
case 90:
cout<<"ninety";
break;
default :
cout<<"ohters";
}
getch();
}
```

**OUTPUT:**

Enter a number: 20
Twenty

**Problem 99. Write a C++ program to use switch statement using pointers.**

***Program:***

```
#include<iostream.h>
#include<conio.h>
int main()
{
char vowel,*pch;
pch=&vowel;
cout<<"Enter a character:";
cin>>pch;
switch(*pch)
{
case 'a':
case 'A':
cout<<*pch<<" is vowel";
break;
case 'e':
case 'E':
cout<<*pch<<" is vowel";
break;
case 'i':
case 'I':
cout<<*pch<<" is vowel";
break;
case 'o':
case 'O':
cout<<*pch<<" is vowel";
break;
case 'u':
case 'U':
cout<<*pch<<" is vowel";
break;
default :
cout<<*pch<<" is vowel";
}
getch();
}
```

**OUTPUT:**

Enter a character:a
vowel

**Problem 100. Write a C++ program to get the sum of first 100 numbers .**

***Program:***

```
#include<iostream.h>
#include<conio.h>
int main()
{
int loop,*p, sum, *psum;
p=&loop;
psum=?
*p=1;
*psum=0;
while (*p<=100)
{
*psum=*psum+*p;
*p=*p+1;
}
cout<<"sum : "<< *psum;
getch();
}
```

**OUTPUT:**

sum:5050

**Problem 101. Write a C++ program to get the sum of first N numbers .**

***Program:***

```
#include<iostream.h>
#include<conio.h>
int main()
{
int loop,*p, sum,n,*pn, *psum;
```

```
p=&loop;
psum=0;
pn=&n;
cout<<"Enter the value of N:";
cin>>pn;
*p=1;
*psum=0;
while (*p<=*pn)
{
*psum=*psum+*p;
*p=*p+1;
}
cout<<"sum of first "<<*pn<<"numbers: "<<*psum;
getch();
}
```

**OUTPUT:**

Enter the value of N:5
sum of first 5 numbers: 15

**Problem 102. Write a C++ program to get the sum of M to N numbers .**

***Program:***

```
#include<iostream.h>
#include<conio.h>
int main()
{
int loop,*p, sum,*psum, m, *pm, n,*pn;
p=&loop;
psum=o;
pn=&n;
pm=&m;
cout<<"Enter the value of pm and pn:";
cin>>pm>>pn;
*p=*pm;
*psum=0;
while (*p<=*pn)
{
*psum=*psum+*p;
*p=*p+1;
}
cout<<"sum of "<<*pm<<" to "<<*pn<<" numbers:
"<< *psum;
getch();
}
```

**OUTPUT:**

Enter the value of pm and pn:2 5
sum of 2 to 5 numbers: 14

**Problem 103. Write a C++ program to find the average of 1 to 100 .**

***Program:***

```
#include<iostream.h>
#include<conio.h>
int main()
{
int loop,*p ;
float sum, *psum, avg, *pavg;
p=&loop;
psum=0;
pavg=&avg;
*p=1;
*psum=0.0;
while (*p<=100)
{
*psum=*psum+*p;
*p=*p+1;
}
*pavg = (*psum)/(100);
cout<<"Avg= "<<*pavg;
getch();
}
```

**OUTPUT:**

Avg=50.500000

**Problem 104. Write a C++ program to display the even or odd numbers between 1 to 100 .**

***Program:***

```
#include<iostream.h>
#include<conio.h>
int main()
{
int no, *pno;
pno=&no;
pno=1;
while (*pno<=100)
{
if(*pno%2==0)
cout<<"even "<<*pno<<"\n";
else
cout<<"odd"<<*pno<<"\n";
++*pno;//++(*pno)
}
getch();
}
```

**OUTPUT:**

print of all even and odd no's

**Problem 105. Write a C++ program to display the even or odd numbers of first N numbers .**

***Program:***

```
#include<iostream.h>
#include<conio.h>
```

```
int main()
{
int no, *pno, n, *pn;;
pno=&no;
pn=&n;
cout<<"Enter the value of N:";
cin>> pn;
*pno=1;
while (*pno<=*pn)
{
if(*pno%2==0)
cout<<"even "<<*pno<<"\n";
else
cout<<"odd "<<*pno<<"\n";
++*pno;//++(*pno)
}
getch();
}
```

**OUTPUT:**

```
Enter the value of N:10
odd 1
even 2
odd 3
even 4
odd 5
even 6
odd 7
even 8
odd 9
even 10
```

**Problem 106. Write a C++ program to display the even or odd numbers between to ranges .**

***Program:***

```
#include<iostream.h>
#include<conio.h>
int main()
{
int no, *pno, m, *pm, n, *pn;;
pno=&no;
pn=&n;
pm=&m;
cout<<"Enter the value of pm and pn:";
cin>>pm>>pn;
*pno=*pm;
while (*pno<=*pn)
{
if(*pno%2==0)
cout<<"even "<<*pno<<"\n";
else
cout<<"odd "<<*pno<<"\n";
++*pno;//++(*pno)
}
getch();
}
```

**OUTPUT:**

```
Enter the value of M and N:2 5
even 2
odd 3
even 4
odd 5
```

**Problem 107. Write a C++ program to display the leap years between 1000 to 2000 .**

***Program:***

```
#include<iostream.h>
#include<conio.h>
int main()
{
int m,n, *pm,*pn;;
pm=&m;
pn=&n;
*pm=1000;
*pn=2000;
while (*pm<=*pn)
{
if(*pm%4==0)
cout<<"Leap "<<*pm<<"\n";
else
cout<<"not "<<*pm<<"\n";
(*pm)++;
}
getch();
}
```

**OUTPUT:**

do it yourself

**Problem 108. Write a C++ program to display the leap years of given range .**

***Program:***

```
#include<iostream.h>
#include<conio.h>
int main()
{
int m,n, *pm,*pn;;
pm=&m;
pn=&n;
cout<<"Enter the value of M and N:";
cin>>pm>> pn;
while (*pm<=*pn)
{
if(*pm%4==0)
```

```
cout<<"Leap "<<*pm<<"\n";
else
cout<<"not "<<*pm<<"\n";
(*pm)++;
}
getch();
}
```

**OUTPUT:**

```
Enter the value of M and N:2000 2009
Leap 2000
not leap 2001
not leap 2002
not leap 2003
Leap 2004
not leap 2005
not leap 2006
not leap 2007
Leap 2008
not leap 2009
```

**Problem 109. Write a C++ program to find biggest of ten numbers .**

***Program:***

```
#include<iostream.h>
#include<conio.h>
int main()
{
int input,big,loop=1;
int *pin, *pb;
pin=&input;
pb=&big;
*pb=-32768;
while(loop<=10)
{ cout<<"Enter the numbers:";
cin>>pin;
*pb=*pin>*pb?*pin:*pb;
loop++;
}
cout<<"big "<<*pb;
getch();
}
```

**OUTPUT:**

```
Enter the number:12
Enter the number:43
Enter the number:76
Enter the number:90
Enter the number:34
Enter the number:65
Enter the number:87
Enter the number:25
Enter the number:77
Enter the number:56
big 90
```

**Problem 110. Write a C++ program to find smallest of ten numbers .**

***Program:***

```
#include<iostream.h>
#include<conio.h>
int main()
{
int input,small,loop=1;
int *pin, *ps;
pin=&input;
ps=&small;
*ps=32767;
while(loop<=10)
{
cout<<"Enter the numbers:";
cin>>pin;
*ps=*pin<*ps?*pin:*ps;
loop++;
}
cout<<"small"<<*ps;
getch();
}
```

**OUTPUT:**

```
Enter the number:12
Enter the number:43
Enter the number:76
Enter the number:90
Enter the number:34
Enter the number:65
Enter the number:87
Enter the number:25
Enter the number:77
Enter the number:56
small 12
```

**Problem 111. Write a C++ program to find the position of biggest number in the array .**

***Program:***

```
#include<conio.h>
#include<iostream.h>
int main()
{
int num[10], *p, pos;
int i=0;
p=&num;
pos=0;
while(i<10)
{
```

```
cout<<"Enter the numbers:";
cin>>p+i;
i++;
}
i=0;
while(i<10)
{
pos=*(p+i)>*(p+pos)? i:pos;
i++;
}
cout<<"biggest Position "<<pos;
getch();
}
```

**OUTPUT:**

Enter the number:12
Enter the number:43
Enter the number:76
Enter the number:90
Enter the number:34
Enter the number:65
Enter the number:87
Enter the number:25
Enter the number:77
Enter the number:56
big position 3

**Problem 112. Write a C++ program to find the position of smallest number in the array .**

***Program:***

```
#include<conio.h>
#include<iostream.h>
void main()
{
int num[10], *p, pos;
int i=0;
p=&num;
pos=0;
while(i<10)
{
cin>>p+i;
i++;
}
i=0;
while(i<10)
{
pos=*(p+i)<*(p+pos)? i:pos;
i++;
}
cout<<"Smallest Position "<<pos;
getch();
}
```

**OUTPUT:**

Enter the number:12
Enter the number:43
Enter the number:76
Enter the number:90
Enter the number:34
Enter the number:65
Enter the number:87
Enter the number:25
Enter the number:77
Enter the number:56
smallest position 0

# CHAPTER 9

# STRUCTURE AND UNION

## STRUCTURE DEFINE:

**Problem 1. Write a C++ program to use struct.**

***Program:***

```
#include<iostream.h>
#include<conio.h>
struct student
{
char name[30];
float number;
} student1, student2;
void main ()
{
struct student student3;
char s1[30];
float f;
cout<<"Enter name:";
cin >> s1;
cout<<"Enter number:";
cin >> f;
student1.name = s1;
student2.number = f;
cout<<"Name = "<< student1.name;
cout<<"Number = "<<student2.number;
getch();
}
```

**OUTPUT:**

```
Enter name:Navjeet
Enter number:450.25
Name = Navjeet
Number = 450.25
```

**Problem 2. Write a C++ program using a structure representing a length.**

***Program:***

```
#include<iostream.h>
#include<conio.h>
#include <ctype.h>
#define INCHES_PER_FOOT 12
#define FEET_PER_YARD   3
struct Length
{
unsigned int yards;
unsigned int feet;
unsigned int inches;
};
struct Length add(struct Length first, struct Length
second);
void show(struct Length length);
void main()
{
char answer = 'n';
struct Length length;
struct Length total = { 0,0,0};
int i = 0;
length.yards =9;
length.feet = 10;
length.inches = 1;
total = add(total,length);
show(total);
cout<<"\n";
getch();
}
struct Length add(struct Length first, struct Length
second)
{
unsigned long inches = 0;
struct Length sum;
inches = first.inches + second.inches+
INCHES_PER_FOOT*(first.feet+second.feet+FE
ET_PER_YARD*(first.yards+second.yards));
sum.inches = inches%INCHES_PER_FOOT;
sum.feet = inches/INCHES_PER_FOOT;
sum.yards = sum.feet/FEET_PER_YARD;
sum.feet %= FEET_PER_YARD;
return sum;
}
void show(struct Length length)
{
cout<<  length.yards<<" yards " << length.feet
"feet" << length.inches <<"inches",
}
```

**OUTPUT:**

```
12yards 1 feet 1 inches
```

**Problem 3. Write a C++ program using a structure to record the count of occurrences of a word.**

***Program:***

```
/* This program defines a structure that stores a word and the count of its occurrences.
The structures are stored as they are created in a linked list. If you wanted the
OUTPUT in alphabetical order, you could insert the structures in the list to ensure
that the list was ordered. Alternatively you could sort the list.*/
#include<iostream.h>
#include<conio.h>
#include <string.h>
#include<Alloc.h>
#include<stdio.h>
#define MAX_WORD_LENGTH   31
#define MAX_TEXT_LENGTH 10000
#define TRUE            1
#define FALSE           0
struct WordCounter
{
char *word;
int word_count;
struct WordCounter *pNext;
};
void addWord(char *pWord);
int is_separator(char ch);
void show(struct WordCounter *pWordcounter);
struct    WordCounter*    createWordCounter(char
*word);
struct WordCounter *pStart = NULL;
void main()
{
char text[MAX_TEXT_LENGTH];
char buffer[MAX_WORD_LENGTH];
size_t i = 0;
int len = 0 ;
struct WordCounter *pCounter = NULL;
cout<< "Enter the text:";
gets(text);
while(text[i] != '\0')
{
while(is_separator(text[i]))
++i;
len = 0;
while((!is_separator(text[i])) && (text[i] != '\0'))
buffer[len++] = text[i++];
if(len>0)
{
buffer[len] = '\0';
addWord(buffer);
}
}
pCounter = pStart;
while(pCounter != NULL)
{
show(pCounter);
pCounter = pCounter->pNext;
}
cout<< "\n";
pCounter = pStart;
while(pCounter != NULL)
{
free(pCounter->word);
pStart = pCounter;
pCounter = pCounter->pNext;
free(pStart);
}
getch();
}
int is_separator(char ch)
{
static char separators[] = { ' ' , ',',':' , '\"', '?' , '!' , '.'};
int i = 0;
for(i = 0 ; i<sizeof separators ; i++)
{
if(ch == separators[i])
return TRUE;
}
return FALSE;
}
void show(struct WordCounter *pWordcounter)
{
cout.width(-30);
cout<<pWordcounter->word;
cout.width(5);
cout<<pWordcounter->word_count;
}
void addWord(char *word)
{
struct WordCounter *pCounter = NULL;
struct WordCounter *pLast = NULL;
if(pStart == NULL)
{
pStart = createWordCounter(word);
return;
}
pCounter = pStart;
while(pCounter != NULL)
{
if(strcmp(word, pCounter->word) == 0)
{
++pCounter->word_count;
return;
```

```
}
pLast = pCounter;
pCounter = pCounter->pNext;
}
pLast->pNext = createWordCounter(word);
}
struct WordCounter* createWordCounter(char *word)
{
struct WordCounter *pCounter = NULL;
pCounter = (struct WordCounter*)malloc(sizeof(struct WordCounter));
pCounter->word = (char*)malloc(strlen(word)+1);
strcpy(pCounter->word, word);
pCounter->word_count = 1;
pCounter->pNext = NULL;
return pCounter;
}
```

**OUTPUT:**

```
Enter the text:
white white house black house
white       2
house       2
black       1
```

**Problem 4. Write a C++ program to store data for the cats: Structure declaration.**

***Program:***

```
#include<iostream.h>
#include<conio.h>
struct cat
{
int age;
int height;
char name[20];
char father[20];
char mother[20];
};
void main()
{
struct cat myCat;
cout<< "Enter the name of the cat: " ;
cin >> myCat.name ;
cout<< "How old is %s? "<< myCat.name ;
cin>>myCat.age ;
cout<< "How high is %s ( in hands )? "<< myCat.name ;
cin >> myCat.height ;
cout<< "Who is %s's father? "<< myCat.name ;
cin>> myCat.father ;
cout<< "Who is %s's mother? "<< myCat.name;
cin>>myCat.mother ;
cout<< "\n"<< myCat.name <<"is"<< myCat.age<< "years old",<< myCat.height <<"hands high,";
cout<< "and has " <<myCat.father <<" and "<< myCat.mother <<" as parents."<<"\n",;
getch();
}
```

**OUTPUT:**

```
Enter the name of the cat: smile
How old is %s? 1
How high is %s ( in hands )? 1
Who is %s's father? macho
Who is %s's mother? marry
smile is 1 years old, 1 hands high,
and has macho and marry as parents.
```

**Problem 5. Write a C++ program to pointing out the cats: allocate memory for struct.**

***Program:***

```
#include<iostream.h>
#include<conio.h>
#include <ctype.h>
#include <stdlib.h>
#include<conio.h>
struct cat
{
int age;
int height;
char name[20];
char father[20];
char mother[20];
};
void main()
{
struct cat *pcat[50];
int hcount = 0;
int i = 0;
char test = '\0';
for(hcount = 0; hcount < 50 ; hcount++ )
{
cout<< "Do you want to enter details of a%s cat (Y or N)? ",hcount?"nother" : "" ;
cin>>test ;
if(tolower(test) == 'n')
break;
pcat[hcount] = (struct cat*) malloc(sizeof(struct cat));
cout<< "\nEnter the name of the cat: " ;
cin>> pcat[hcount]->name ;
```

```
cout<< "\nHow old is %s? "<< pcat[hcount]->name
;
cin>> pcat[hcount]->age ;
cout<< "\nHow high is %s ( in hands )? "<<
pcat[hcount]->name ;
cin>> pcat[hcount]->height ;
cout<< "\nWho is %s's father? "<< pcat[hcount]-
>name ;
cin>> pcat[hcount]->father ;
cout<< "\nWho is %s's mother? "<< pcat[hcount]-
>name ;
cin>> pcat[hcount]->mother ;
}
for (i = 0 ; i < hcount ; i++ )
{
cout<< "\n\n"<< pcat[i]->name <<"is" << pcat[i]-
>age<< "years old,"<< pcat[i]->height <<"hands
high,";
cout<< "and has"<< pcat[i]->father <<"and
"<<pcat[i]->mother <<"as parents." ;
free(pcat[i]);
}
getch();
}
```

**OUTPUT:**

```
Do you want to enter details of a%s cat (Y or N)? Y
Enter the name of the cat: smile
How old is %s? 1
How high is %s ( in hands )? 1
Who is %s's father? macho
Who is %s's mother? marry
smile is 1 years old, 1 hands high,
and has macho and marry as parents.
```

**Problem 6. Write a C++ program to define a simplest struct.**

***Program:***

```
#include<iostream.h>
#include<conio.h>
void main()
{
struct
{
int a;
int b;
} x, y;
x.a = 10;
y = x;
cout<< "y.a;
getch();
}
```

**OUTPUT:**

```
10
```

**Problem 7. Write a C++ program to define and use a struct.**

***Program:***

```
#include<iostream.h>
#include<conio.h>
struct struct_type
{
int i;
char ch;
double d;
char str[80];
} s;
void main()
{
clrscr();
cout<< "Enter an integer: ");
cin>> s.i);
cout<< "Enter a character: ");
cin>> s.ch;
cout<< "Enter a floating point number: ";
cin>> s.d;
cout<< "Enter a string: ";
cin>> s.str;
cout<< << s.i << s.ch << s.d<< s.str;
getch();
}
```

**OUTPUT:**

```
Enter an integer: 12
Enter a character: S
Enter a floating point number: 1.0
Enter a string: mani
12 S 1.000000 mani
```

## STRUCTURE SIZE:

**Problem 8. Write a C++ program to allocate memory for struct.**

***Program:***

```
#include <stdlib.h>
#include<iostream.h>
#include<conio.h>
#include <string.h>
#include<process.h>
#include<Alloc.h>
struct address
{
char name[400];
```

```
char street[400];
char city[400];
char state[30];
char zip[100];
};
void main()
{
struct address *p;
if((p = malloc(sizeof(struct address)))==NULL)
{
cout<< "Allocation Error \n";
exit(1);
}
return p;
getch();
}
```

**Problem 9. Write a C++ program to get the size of a struct.**

***Program:***

```
#include<iostream.h>
#include<conio.h>
struct struct_type
{
int i;
char ch;
int *p;
double d;
} s;
void main()
{
cout<< "s_type is "<<sizeof(struct struct_type)
<<"bytes long";
getch();
}
```

**OUTPUT:**

s_type is 13 bytes long

## STRUCTURE ARRAY:

**Problem 10. Write a C++ program using a linked list of structures representing a person's name.**

***Program:***

```
// You could link the PhoneRecord structures in a list by adding a pointer member.
// I chose to define a Node structure that is a node in a linked list. Each Node
// structure will contain a pointer to a PhoneRecord structure and a pointer to
// the next Node structure. Memory for Node and PhoneRecord structures are allocated
// dynamically. You could extend this to allocate memory for names and numbers too.
#include <stdlib.h>
#include <string.h>
#include <ctype.h>
#include<iostream.h>
#include<conio.h>
#define FIRST_NAME_LEN 31
#define SECOND_NAME_LEN 51
#define NUMBER_LEN 16
#define TRUE 1
#define FALSE 0
struct Name
{
char firstname[FIRST_NAME_LEN];
char secondname[SECOND_NAME_LEN];
};
struct PhoneRecord
{
struct Name name;
char number[NUMBER_LEN];
};
struct Node
{
struct PhoneRecord *pRecord;
struct Node *pNext;
};
struct Name read_name();
void show(struct PhoneRecord *pRecord);
int has_name(struct PhoneRecord record, struct Name name);
struct Node* create_node();
struct PhoneRecord* create_record();
void insert_node(struct Node *pNode);
int compare_records(struct PhoneRecord *pFirst, struct PhoneRecord *pSecond);
int compare_names(struct Name first, struct Name second);
void list_numbers(struct Name name);
struct Node *pStart = NULL;
void main()
{
char answer = 'n';
struct Node *pNode = NULL;
struct PhoneRecord *pRecord = NULL;
int found = FALSE;
int i = 0;
do
{
insert_node(create_node());
cout<< "Do you want to enter another(y or n)?: ";
```

```
cin>> answer;
}while(tolower(answer) == 'y');
do
{
cout<< "\nEnter a name for which you want the number.";
list_numbers(read_name());
cout<< "Do you want to search for another (y or n)? ";
cin>> answer;
}while(tolower(answer) == 'y');
pNode = pStart;
do
{
show(pNode->pRecord);
}while((pNode = pNode->pNext) != 0);
cout<<"\n";
pNode = pStart;
do
{
free(pNode->pRecord);
pStart = pNode;
pNode = pNode->pNext;
free(pStart);
}while((pNode = pNode->pNext) != 0);
getch();
}
struct Name read_name()
{
unsigned long inches = 0;
struct Name name;
cout<<"\nEnter a first name: ");
cin>> name.firstname);
cout<<"Enter a second name: ");
cin>> name.secondname);
return name;
}
void show(struct PhoneRecord *pRecord)
{
cout<< pRecord->name.firstname<< pRecord->name.secondname<< pRecord->number;
}
int has_name(struct PhoneRecord record, struct Name name)
{
return (strcmp(name.firstname, record.name.firstname)==0 &&
strcmp(name.secondname,
record.name.secondname)==0);
}
struct Node* create_node()
{
struct Node *pNode = NULL; // Pointer to the new node
pNode = (struct Node*)malloc(sizeof(struct Node)); // Allocate memory for node
pNode->pNext = NULL; // No next node yet
pNode->pRecord = create_record(); // Create record and store address in node
return pNode;
}
// Create a new phone record
struct PhoneRecord* create_record()
{
struct PhoneRecord *pRecord = NULL; // Pointer to the new record
pRecord = (struct PhoneRecord*)malloc(sizeof(struct PhoneRecord)); // Allocate memory
pRecord->name = read_name(); // Read the name
// Get the number for the name
cout<<"Enter the number for this name: ";
cin>>pRecord->number; // Read the number - including spaces
return pRecord; // Return the address of the record
}
int compare_records(struct PhoneRecord *pFirst, struct PhoneRecord *pSecond)
{
return compare_names(pFirst->name, pSecond->name);
}
int compare_names(struct Name first, struct Name second)
{
int result = 0;
result = strcmp(first.secondname,second.secondname);
return (result != 0 ? result : strcmp(first.firstname,second.firstname));
}
void insert_node(struct Node *pNode)
{
struct Node *pCurrent = NULL;
struct Node *pPrevious = NULL;
struct Node *pTemp = NULL;
if(pStart == NULL)
{
pStart = pNode;
```

```
return;
}
// Find position to insert the new node
pCurrent = pStart;
while(pCurrent != NULL)
{
if(compare_records(pNode->pRecord, pCurrent->pRecord) <= 0)
{ // New node goes before current list node
pNode->pNext = pCurrent; // Set new node next pointer to current
if(pPrevious == NULL) // If pCurrent is the first node
{
pNode->pNext = pStart; // New node next pointer points to current
pStart = pNode; // New node is the first node
}
else
{ // Otherwise...
pPrevious->pNext = pNode; // Previous node next pointer points to new node
pNode->pNext = pCurrent; // New node next pointer points to current
}
return;
}
pPrevious = pCurrent; // Previous node will be the current node
pCurrent = pCurrent->pNext; // Current node is now the next node
}
// If we reach here, add pNode to the end
pPrevious->pNext = pNode;
}
// List the numbers for a name
void list_numbers(struct Name name)
{
struct Node *pNode = NULL;
int found = FALSE;
int result = 0;
// Go through the list comparing names
pNode = pStart;
while(pNode != NULL)
{
result = compare_names(name, pNode->pRecord->name);
if(result == 0)
{
if(!found) // If this is the first time
{
found = TRUE; // Reset found flag
cout<<"The numbers for this name are:"<<"\n"; // and OUTPUT the heading
}
cout<<"\n"<<"pNode->pRecord->number; // OUTPUT the number for the name
}
else if(result < 0) // If name comes before current
break; // we are done
pNode = pNode->pNext; // Otherwise move to next node
}
if(!found) // If the name was not found
cout<<"No numbers found for this name."<<"\n"; // Say so
}
```

**OUTPUT:**

```
Enter a first name: Avtar
Enter a second name: Riar
Enter the number for this name: 500
Do you want to enter another(y or n)?:y
Enter a first name: Sukhwant
Enter a second name: Singh
Enter the number for this name: 400
Do you want to enter another(y or n)?: n
Enter a name for which you want the number.
Enter a first name: Sukhwant
Enter a second name: Singh
The numbers for this name are: 400
Do you want to search for another (y or n)? n
Avtar riar 500
Sukhwant Singh 400
```

**Problem 11. Write a C++ program to exercising the cats: Structure array declaration.**

***Program:***

```
#include <ctype.h>
#include<iostream.h>
#include<conio.h>
struct cat
{
int age;
int height;
char name[20];
char father[20];
```

```
char mother[20];
};
void main()
{
struct cat myCat[50];
int hcount = 0;
int i = 0;
char test = '\0';
for(hcount = 0; hcount < 50 ; hcount++ )
{
cout<<"\nDo you want to enter details of a%s cat (Y or N)? ", hcount?"nother " : "" ;
cin>>test ;
if(tolower(test) == 'n')
break;
cout<<"\nEnter the name of the cat: " ;
cin>> myCat[hcount].name ;
cout<<"\nHow old is %s? "<<myCat[hcount].name ;
cin>> myCat[hcount].age ;
cout<<"\nHow high is %s ( in hands )? "<< myCat[hcount].name ;
cin>> myCat[hcount].height ;
cout<<"\nWho is %s's father? "<<myCat[hcount].name ;
cin>> myCat[hcount].father ;
cout<<"\nWho is %s's mother? "<< myCat[hcount].name ;
cin>> myCat[hcount].mother ;
}
for (i = 0 ; i < hcount ; i++ )
{
cout<< "\n\n"<< pcat[i]->name <<"is" << pcat[i]->age<< "years old,"<< pcat[i]->height <<"hands high,";
cout<< "and has"<< pcat[i]->father <<"and "<<pcat[i]->mother <<"as parents." ;
}
getch();
}
```

**OUTPUT:**

```
Do you want to enter details of a%s cat (Y or N)? Y
Enter the name of the cat: smile
How old is %s? 1
How high is %s ( in hands )? 1
Who is %s's father? macho
Who is %s's mother? marry
Do you want to enter details of a%s cat (Y or N)? N
smile is 1 years old, 1 hands high,
and has macho and marry as parents.
```

**Problem 12. Write a C++ program to daisy chaining the cats both ways.**

***Program:***

```
#include<iostream.h>
#include<conio.h>
#include <ctype.h>
#include <stdlib.h>
struct cat
{
int age;
int height;
char name[20];
char father[20];
char mother[20];
struct cat *next;     // Pointer to next structure
struct cat *previous; // Pointer to previous structure
};
void main()
{
struct cat *first = NULL;
struct cat *current = NULL;
struct cat *last = NULL;
char test = '\0';
for( ; ; )
{
cout<<"\nDo you want to enter details of a%s cat (Y or N)? ", first == NULL?"nother " : "";
cin>>test ;
if(tolower(test) == 'n')
break;
// Allocate memory for each new cat structure
current = (struct cat*)malloc(sizeof(struct cat));
if( first == NULL )
{
first = current;          // Set pointer to first cat
current->previous = NULL;
}
else
{
last->next = current;    // Set next address for previous cat
current->previous = last; // Previous address for current cat
}
cout<<"\nEnter the name of the cat: ";
cin>> current -> name ;      // Read the cat's name
cout<<"\nHow old is %s? "<< current -> name;
cin>> current -> age;        // Read the cat's age
cout<<"\nHow high is %s ( in hands )? "<< current -> name;
cin>> current -> height;     // Read the cat's height
```

```
cout<<"\nWho is %s's father? "<< current -> name;
cin>> current -> father;      // Get the father's name
cout<<"\nWho is %s's mother? "<< current -> name;
cin>> current -> mother;      // Get the mother's name
current -> next = NULL;  // In case its the last cat...
last = current;          // Save address of last cat
}
while(current != NULL)       // OUTPUT cat data in
reverse order
{
cout<< "\n\n"<< current ->name <<"is" << current -
>age<< "years old,"<< current ->height <<"hands
high,";
cout<< "and has"<< current ->father <<"and
"<<current ->mother <<"as parents." ;
last = current;       // Save pointer to enable memory
to be freed
current = current->previous; // current points to
previous in list
free(last);                // Free memory for the cat we
OUTPUT
}
getch();
}
```

**OUTPUT:**

Do you want to enter details of a%s cat (Y or N)? Y
Enter the name of the cat: smile
How old is %s? 1
How high is %s ( in hands )? 1
Who is %s's father? macho
Who is %s's mother? marry
Do you want to enter details of a%s cat (Y or N)? N
smile is 1 years old, 1 hands high,
and has macho and marry as parents.

**Problem 13. Write a C++ program for a simple mailing list example using an array of structures.**

***Program:***

```
// A simple mailing list example using an array of
structures.
#include<stdlib.h>
#include<iostream.h>
#include<conio.h>
#define MAX 100
struct addr
{
char name[30];
char street[40];
char city[20];
char state[3];
unsigned long int zip;
} addr_list[MAX];
void init_list(void), enter(void);
void delete(void), list(void);
int menu_select(void), find_free(void);
void main()
{
char choice;
init_list(); // initialize the structure array
for(;;)
{
choice = menu_select();
switch(choice)
{
case 1: enter();
break;
case 2: delete();
break;
case 3: list();
break;
case 4: exit(0);
}
}
getch();
}
// Initialize the list.
void init_list(void)
{
register int t;
for(t=0; t<MAX; ++t) addr_list[t].name[0] = '\0';
}
// Get a menu selection.
int menu_select(void)
{
char s[80];
int c;
cout<<"1. Enter a name\n";
cout<<"2. Delete a name\n";
cout<<"3. List the file\n";
cout<<"4. Quit\n";
do {
cout<<"\nEnter your choice: ";
gets(s);
c = atoi(s);
} while(c<0 || c>4);
return c;
}
// Input addresses into the list.
void enter(void)
{
int slot;
char s[80];
```

```
slot = find_free();
if(slot==-1)
{
cout<<"\nList Full");
return;
}
cout<<"Enter name: ";
gets(addr_list[slot].name);
cout<<"Enter street: ";
gets(addr_list[slot].street);
cout<<"Enter city: ";
gets(addr_list[slot].city);
cout<<"Enter state: ";
gets(addr_list[slot].state);
cout<<"Enter zip: ";
gets(s);
addr_list[slot].zip = strtoul(s, '\0', 10);
}
// Find an unused structure.
int find_free(void)
{
register int t;
for(t=0; addr_list[t].name[0] && t<MAX; ++t) ;
if(t==MAX) return -1; // no slots free
return t;
}
// Delete an address.
void delete(void)
{
register int slot;
char s[80];
cout<<"enter record #: ";
gets(s);
slot = atoi(s);
if(slot>=0 && slot < MAX)
addr_list[slot].name[0] = '\0';
}
// Display the list on the screen.
void list(void)
{
register int t;
for(t=0; t<MAX; ++t) {
if(addr_list[t].name[0]) {
cout<<"\n"<< addr_list[t].name;
cout<<"\n"<< addr_list[t].street;
cout<<"\n"<< addr_list[t].city;
cout<<"\n"<< addr_list[t].state;
cout<<"\n\n"<< addr_list[t].zip;
}
}
cout<<"\n\n";
}
```

**OUTPUT:**

```
1. Enter a name
2. Delete a name
3. List the file
4. Quit
Enter your choice:1
Enter name: samar
Enter street: 1/34 Ranjit ave
Enter city: Amritsar
Enter state: Punjab
Enter zip: 143001
1. Enter a name
2. Delete a name
3. List the file
4. Quit
Enter your choice:3
samar
1/34 Ranjit ave
Amritsar
Punjab
143001
1. Enter a name
2. Delete a name
3. List the file
4. Quit
Enter your choice:4
```

## STRUCTURE PARAMETERS:

**Problem 14. Write a C++ program to pass struct into a function.**

***Program:.***

```
#include<iostream.h>
#include<conio.h>
struct struct_type
{
int a, b;
char ch;
} ;
void f1(struct struct_type parm)
{
cout<< parm.a;
}
void main()
{
struct struct_type arg;
arg.a = 1000;
f1(arg);
getch();
```

```
}
```

**OUTPUT:**

1000

# STRUCTURE SERIALIZATION:

**Problem 15. Write a C++ program to scan a file and print out a list of words in ASCII order.**

***Program:***

```
#include<stdio.h>
#include<iostream.h>
#include<conio.h>
#include <ctype.h>
#include <string.h>
#include <stdlib.h>
#include<process.h>
struct node
{
struct node    *left;     // tree to the left
struct node    *right;    // tree to the right
char        *word;     // word for this tre
};
// the top of the tree
static struct node *root = NULL;
void memory_error(void)
{
fprintf(stderr, "Error:Out of memory\n");
exit(8);
}
char *save_string(char *string)
{
char *new_string;   // where we are going to put
string
new_string = malloc((unsigned) (strlen(string) + 1));
if (new_string == NULL)
memory_error();
strcpy(new_string, string);
return (new_string);
}
void enter(struct node **node, char *word)
{
int result;      // result of strcmp
char *save_string(char *);  // save a string on the
heap
if ((*node) == NULL) {
// Allocate memory for a new node
(*node) = malloc(sizeof(struct node));
if ((*node) == NULL)
memory_error();
// Initialize the new node
(*node)->left = NULL;
(*node)->right = NULL;
(*node)->word = save_string(word);
 return;
}
// Check to see where the word goes
result = strcmp((*node)->word, word);
// The current node already contains the word, no
entry necessary
if (result == 0)
return;
// The word must be entered in the left or right sub-
tree
if (result < 0)
enter(&(*node)->right, word);
else
enter(&(*node)->left, word);
}
void scan(char *name)
{
char word[100];    // word we are working on
int index;        // index into the word
int ch;          // current character
FILE *in_file;    // input file
in_file = fopen(name, "r");
if (in_file == NULL) {
fprintf(stderr, "Error:Unable to open %s\n", name);
exit(8);
}
while (1) {
// scan past the whitespace
while (1) {
ch = fgetc(in_file);
if (isalpha(ch) || (ch == EOF))
break;
}
if (ch == EOF)
break;
word[0] = ch;
for (index = 1; index < sizeof(word); ++index) {
ch = fgetc(in_file);
if (!isalpha(ch))
break;
word[index] = ch;
}
// put a null on the end
word[index] = '\0';
enter(&root, word);
}
fclose(in_file);
}
void print_tree(struct node *top)
```

```
{
if (top == NULL)
return;
print_tree(top->left);
cout<<"\n"<< top->word;
print_tree(top->right);
}
void main(int argc, char *argv[])
{
if (argc != 2)
{
fprintf(stderr,      "Error:Wrong      number     of
parameters\n");
fprintf(stderr, "    on the command line\n");
fprintf(stderr, "Usage is:\n");
fprintf(stderr, "   words 'file'\n");
exit(8);
}
scan(argv[1]);
print_tree(root);
getch();
}
```

**Problem 16. Write a C++ program to write structure into file.**

***Program:***

```
#include<iostream.h>
#include<conio.h>
#include <string.h>
#include <stdlib.h>
#define MAX 50
typedef struct
{
char name[10];
int key;
} file_record;
void create_index(long index[], int key, long rel_add
) {
index[key] = rel_add;
}
void write_rec(FILE *fp, file_record rec) {
fwrite(&rec,sizeof(rec),1,fp);
}
void main()
{
long rel_add;
int key;
file_record frec;
long index[MAX];
int n,i;
FILE *recfile=NULL,*ifile=NULL;
for(i=0; i< MAX; i++)
index[i]= (-1);
recfile=fopen("mfile","w");
if(recfile == NULL) {
cout<<"Error in openeing file mfile\n";
exit(0);
}
rel_add = 0 ;
do {
cout<<"Enter the data vlue and the key of the
record to be added to file mfile\n";
cin>> frec.name>>frec.key;
while(index[frec.key] != (-1)) {
cout<<" A record with this key value already exist
in a file enter record key value\n";    cin>>
frec.name,&frec.key;
}
create_index(index,frec.key,rel_add);
write_rec(recfile,frec);
rel_add =  ftell(recfile);
cout<<"Enter 1 to continue adding records to the
file\n";
cin>> n;
}while(n == 1);
ifile=fopen("index_file","w");
if(ifile == NULL)
{
cout<<"Error in openeing file index_file\n";
exit(0);
}
fwrite(index,sizeof(index),1,ifile);
fclose(recfile);
fclose(ifile);
cout<<"Enter 1 if you want to retrieve a record\n";
cin>> n;
if( n == 1)
{
ifile=fopen("index_file","r");
if(ifile == NULL)
{
cout<<"Error in openeing file index_file\n";
exit(0);
}
fread(index,sizeof(index),1,ifile);
fclose(ifile);
recfile=fopen("mfile","r");
if(recfile == NULL)
{
cout<<"Error in openeing file mfile\n";
exit(0);
}
```

```
}
cout<<"THE CONTENTS OF FILE IS "<<endl;
while( (fread(&frec,sizeof(frec),1,recfile)) != 0)
cout<<frec.name<<frec.key<<"\n";
do {
cout<<"Enter the key of the record to be
retrieved\n";
cin>> key;
rel_add = index[key];
while((fseek(recfile,rel_add,SEEK_SET)) != 0)
{
cout<<"Error\n";
exit(0);
}
fread(&frec,sizeof(frec),1,recfile);
cout<<"The data value of the retrieved record is
"<<frec.name;
cout<<"Enter 1 if you want to retrieve a record\n";
cin>> n;
} while(n == 1);
fclose(recfile);
getch();
}
```

# STRUCTURE PROGRAMMING:

**Problem 17. Write a C++ program to read and write the library data by using structure in C language (illustrate the concept of accessing the value of structure variable).**

***Program:***

```
#include<iostream.h>
#include<conio.h>
void main ( )
{
struct library
{
char    title [20] ;
char    author [20] ;
int     pages ;
float   price ;
};
struct   library   book1;
strcpy(book1. title, "WINDOWS BASED
COMPUTER COURSES");
strcpy(book1. author, "RACHHPAL SINGH") ;
book1.pages = 675 ;
book 1. price = 240.25 ;
cout<<" \n Name of the book is "<< book1.title ;
cout<<" \n Name of the author of the book is "<<
book1.author ;
cout<<" \n Pages of the book are "<< book1.pages
;
cout<<" \n Price of the book is "<< book1.price ;
getche ( ) ;
}
```

**OUTPUT:**

```
Name of the book is WINDOWS BASED
COMPUTER COURSES
Name of the author of the book is RACHHPAL
SINGH
Pages of the book are 675
Price of the book is 240.25
```

**Problem 18. Write a C++ program to read and write the student data by using structure in C language (illustrate the concept of accessing the value of structure variable).**

***Program:***

```
#include<iostream.h>
#include<conio.h>
void main ( )
{
struct    student
{
int      rn ;
char     name [20] ;
char     add [30] ;
float    fees ;
} ;
struct  student  st1;
cout<<" \n Enter the data of any student : " ;
cin>> st1.rn>> st1.name >> st1.add >> st1.fees ;
cout<<" \n Roll No. of the student is "<< st1.rn ;
cout<<" \n Name of the student is "<< st1.name ;
cout<<" \n Address of the student is "<< st1.add
;

cout<<" \n Fees submitted by the student is "<<
st1.fees ;
getche ( ) ;
}
```

**OUTPUT:**

```
Enter the data of any student :
122
aman
Abc nagar, Asr
1500.20
Roll No. of the student is 122
Name of the student is aman
Address of the student is Abc nagar, Asr
```

Fees submitted by the student is 1500.20

**Problem 19. Write a C++ program to find average marks of three subjects of N students in a class by using array of structure (illustrate the concept of use an Array of Structure).**

***Program:***

```
#include<iostream.h>
#include<conio.h>
void main ( )
{
struct    student
{
int subject1 ;
int subject2 ;
int subject3 ;
};
int i , n, total ;
float av ;
clrscr();
struct   student     st[20];
cout<<" \n Enter the number of students : " ;
cin>> n ;
for (i =0,  i < n ;  i + +)
{
cout<<"  \n  Enter  marks  of  three  subjects  of
"<<i+1<< " th student : " ;
total = 0 ;
cin>>  s  [i  ].  subject1>>st[i]  .  subject2>>st[i
].subject3;
total = st[i ].subject1+ st[i ]. subject2 +st[i ]. subject
3;
av  =  (float) total / 3 ;
cout<<"  \n  AVERAGE  Marks  of  "  <<i+1<<" th
student is = "<< av ;
}
getche ( ) ;
}
```

**OUTPUT:**

Enter the number of students 10
Enter marks of three subjects 1 th student:
20
35
45
AVERAGE Marks of 1 th student is = 33.33
Enter marks of three subjects 2 th student:
10
30
20
AVERAGE Marks of 2 th student is = 20.00
Enter marks of three subjects 10 th student:
22
38
30
AVERAGE Marks of 10 th student is = 30.00

**Problem 20. Write a C++ program to find average marks of N student each having M subjects in a class (illustrate the concept of use of an Array within the Structure).**

***Program:***

```
#include<iostream.h>
#include<conio.h>
#include<dos.h>
void main ( )
{
struct   student
{
int rn ;
int sub[10] ;
};
struct student st[50] ;
 int i,  j, total ;
float      av ;
clrscr( );
cout<<"\n  Enter  the  Number    of  students  in  the
class :";
cin>> n ;
cout<<"  \n  Enter  the  number  of  subjects  each
student has taken: " ;
cin>> m ;
for (i = 0 ;  i < n ;  i + +)
{
total = 0 ;
cout<<"  \n  Enter  the  Rollno  of    "  <<i+1<<"th
student :" ;
cin>> st[i ].rn;
cout<<" \n Enter the Marks : ";
for (j =0;  j <m; j + +)
{
cout<<"  \n  Enter  the  Marks  of  "<<j+1  <<"th
subject : ";
cin>> st[i ].sub[j ];
total =  total + st[i ].sub[j ];
}
av = (float) total / m ;
cout<<"AVERAGE    Marks  of  "<<i+1<<"  th
student ="<< av;
}
getch( );
}
```

**OUTPUT:**

Enter the Number of students in the class 10
Enter the number of subjects each student has taken: 3
Enter the Rollno of 1th student : 122
Enter the Marks :
Enter the Marks of 1th subject 20:
Enter the Marks of 2th subject : 30
Enter the Marks of 3th subject : 30
AVERAGE Marks of 1 th student =30.00
Enter the Rollno of 2 th student :123
Enter the Marks :
Enter the Marks of 1 th subject : 10
Enter the Marks of 2 th subject : 20
Enter the Marks of 3 th subject : 30
AVERAGE Marks of 2 th student =20.00

……………………………………………

……………………………………………

……………………………………………

Enter the Rollno of 10 th student : 132
Enter the Marks :
Enter the Marks of 1 th subject : 50
Enter the Marks of 2 th subject : 20
Enter the Marks of 3 th subject : 30
AVERAGE Marks of 10 th student =33.33

**Problem 21. Write a C++ program to handle bank customer data by using nesting of structure ( illustrate the concept of Structure within Structure).**

***Program:***

```
#include<iostream.h>
#include<conio.h>
void main()
{
struct customer
{
char name[20];
char address[30];
int phone-no;
struct account
{
char b-name[20];
int account-no;
float balance;
}acc[50];
} cust[100];
int i,j,n,m;
cout<<"\n How many customer in the bank : ";
cin>> n;
cout<<"\n How many account number in the branch :";
cin>> m;
cout<<"\n Enter the customer data:";
for(i=1;i<=n;i++)
{
cout<<"\n Enter customer name, address and phone no :";
cin>> cust[i].name>>
cust[i].address>>cust[i].phone-no;
cout<<"\n Enter the bank branch data :";
for(j=1;j<=m;j++)
{
cout<<"\n Enter branch name, account number and balance:";
cin>>cust[i].acc[j].b-name>>cust[i].acc[j].account-no>>cust[i].acc[j].balance;
}
}
cout<<"\n Customer Data is as: ";
for(i=1;i<=n;i++)
{
cout<<"\n customer name is: "<< cust[i].name;
cout<<"\n customer address is : " <<
cust[i].address;
cout<<"\n customer phone no is:"<<
cust[i].phone-no ;
cout<<"\n The bank branch data is:";
for(j=1;j<=m;j++)
{
cout<<"\n branch name is :"<< cust[i].acc[j].b-name;
cout<<"\n Account number is : "<<
cust[i].acc[j].account-no;
cout<<"\n Balance is: "<< cust[i].acc[j].balance;
}
}
getch();
}
```

**OUTPUT:**

How many customer in the bank : 3
How many account number in the branch 2
Enter the customer data
Enter customer name, address and phone no :
Raja
Abc, nagar, jalandhar.
56789
Enter the bank branch data :
Enter branch name, account number and balance:
Bank of india
1233

60000
Bank of Punjab
1133
40000
Enter customer name, address and phone no :
Mona
xyz, nagar, jalandhar.
776655
Enter the bank branch data :
Enter branch name, account number and balance:
Bank of Baroda
1200
6500
Bank of jammu
12033
60980
Enter customer name, address and phone no :
Rajan
Apqr, nagar, jalandhar.
99999
Enter the bank branch data :
Enter branch name, account number and balance:
Bank of india
1299
66000
Bank of punjab
1208
609
customer name is: Raja
customer address is : Abc, nagar, jalandhar.
customer phone no is: 56789
The bank branch data is:
branch name is : Bank of india
Account number is : 1233
Balance is: 60000
branch name is : Bank of Punjab
Account number is : 1133
Balance is: 40000
customer name is: Mona
customer address is : xyz, nagar, jalandhar.
customer phone no is: 776655
The bank branch data is:
branch name is : Bank of Baroda
Account number is : 1200
Balance is: 6500
branch name is : jammu
Account number is : 12033
Balance is: 60980
customer name is: Rajan
customer address is : Apqr, nagar, jalandhar.
customer phone no is: 99999
The bank branch data is:
branch name is : Bank of india
Account number is : 1299
Balance is: 66000
branch name is : Bank of punjab
Account number is : punjab
1208
Balance is: 609

**Problem 22. Write a C++ program to read and display student grade by using structure with function (illustrate the concept of passing structure to function).**

***Program:***

```
#include<iostream.h>
#include<conio.h>
struct student
{
int rn;
char name[20];
char grade;
}s;
void main()
{
cout<<"\n Enter the rollno, name and grade of the student :";
cin>> s.rn>> s.name>>s.grade;
display(s);
getch();
}
display(m)
struct student m;
{
cout<<"\n Rollno is: "<< m.rn;
cout<<"\n Name is "<< m.name;
cout<<"\n Grade is: "<< m.grade;
return;
}
```

**OUTPUT:**

Enter the rollno, name and grade of the student :
122
RAJAN
A
Rollno is: 122
Name is RAJAN
Grade is: A

**Problem 23. Write a C++ program to compute Net pay of an employee (illustrate the concept of function returning a structure computed value).**

***Program:***

```
#include<iostream.h>
#include<conio.h>
struct employee
{
char name[20];
float bp;
float da;
float hra;
float netpay;
}emp;
void main()
{
employee npay(employee  emp);
employee y;
cout<<"\n ENTER THE NAME, BASIC PAY, DA,
HRA :";
cin>>emp.name>>emp.bp>>emp.da>>emp.hra;
y= npay(emp);
cout<<"\n  Net pay is:"<<y.netpay;
getche( );
}
employee npay(employee  z)
{
z.netpay =z.bp + z. da +z.hra;
return(z);
}
```

**OUTPUT:**

ENTER THE NAME, BASIC PAY, DA, HRA :
Mona
2200
2000
1000
Net pay is:5200

**Problem 24. Write a C++ program to compute average marks of N students (to illustrate the concept of passing array of structure as argument to the function).**

***Program:***

```
#include<iostream.h>
#incude<conio.h>
struct student
{
int rn;
int sub[3];
int av;
}res;
student input(student x[ ], int y);
void display(student  x[ ], int y);
void main()
{
student m[100];
int n,i;
cout<<"\n How many students in the class: ";
cin>>n;
cout<<"\n Enter the data:";
for(i=0;i<n;i++)
{
m[i]=input(m, i);
}
display(m,n);
getche();
}
student input(student m[ ], int i)
{
int j;
float tm=0;
cout<<"\n Enter Rollno and marks :";
cin>>m[i].rn;
for(j=0;j<3;j++)
{
cin>>m[i].sub[j];
tm= tm+m[i].sub[j];
}
m[i].av=tm/3;
j=0;
return m[i];
}
void display(student m[ ], int n)
{
int j,k;
cout<<"\n RESULT IS:";
cout<<"\n  ROLLNO  1   2    3        Average  of
Marks";
for(j=0;j<n;j++)
{
cout<<m[j].rn<<"\t";
for(k=0;k<3;k++)
{
cout<<m[j].sub[k]<<" ";
cout<<"\t"<<m[j].av<<endl;
}
}
return;
}
```

**OUTPUT:**

How many students in the class: 5
Enter the data:
Enter Rollno and marks :
121 20 30 40
122 10 20 30
123 13 17 30

```
124 20 20 20
125 30 30 20
RESULT IS
ROLLNO      1   2  3   Average of Marks
121        20 30 40    30
122        10 20 30    20
123        13 17 30    20
124        20 20 20    20
125        30 30 20    27
```

**Problem 25. Write a C++ program to read and display student data by using structure with pointer.**

***Program:***

```
#include<iostream.h>
#include<conio.h>
void main()
{
struct student
{
int rn;
float fees;
}st[10], *p;
int n,j;
cout<<"\n How many students have data:";
cin>> n);
cout<<"\n Enter the data :";
for(p=st; p< st+n; p++)
{
cin>> p->rn >> p->fees;
}
p=st;
cout<<"\n Entered data is:";
while(p< st+n)
{
cout<< p->rn<< p->fees;
p++;
}
getch();
}
```

**OUTPUT:**

```
How many students have data: 5
Enter the data
121    1200.34
122    1234.77
123    1256.98
124    1256.78
125    1245.34
Entered data is:
121    1200.34
122    1234.77
123    1256.98
124    1256.78
125    1245.34
```

**Problem 26. Write a C++ program to read and display student data using Union.**

***Program:***

```
#include<conio.h>
#include<iostream.h>
void main()
{
union student
{
char grade;
int rollno;
float marks;
double fees;
}
union student s;
cout<<"\n Enter the garde, rollno, marks and fees of the student :";
cin>>s.grade>>s.rollno>>s.marks>>s.fees;
cout>>"\n Grade is:"<<s.garde;
cout<<"\n Rollno is:"<<s.rollno;
cout<<"\n Marks are :"<<s.marks;
cout<<"\n Fees paid  is: "<<s.fees;
getche();
}
```

**OUTPUT:**

```
Enter the garde, rollno, marks and fees of the student:
A
122
90.50
12346.8888787
Grade is: A
Rollno is: 122
Marks are : 90.50
Fees paid  is: 12346.8888787
```

**Problem 27. Write a C++ program to find the factorial of a number using structure.**

***Program:***

```
#include<iostream.h>
#include<conio.h>
struct fact
{
int n;
}s;
void main()
{
```

```
clrscr();
cout<<"ENTER THE NUMBER";
cin>>s.n;
int m=1;
for(int i=1;i<=s.n;i++)
{
m=m*i;
}
cout<<"FACTORIAL OF THE GIVEN NO
IS:"<<m;
getch();
}
```

**OUTPUT:**

ENTER THE NUMBER 5
FACTORIAL OF THE GIVEN NO IS: 120

**Problem 28. Write a C++ program to create a structure of n students using dynamic memory allocation. Read their names and print the result.**

***Program:***

```
#include<iostream.h>
#include<conio.h>
#include <string.h>
struct student
{
char name[10];
int m[3];
int total;
char result [5];
}*p,*s;
void main()
{
int i,j,l,n;
cout<<"\n Enter the value of Number of students: ";
cin>> n;
p=(struct student*)malloc(n* size of(struct
student));
s=p;
cout<<"\n Enter the names:"
for(i=0;i<n;i++)
{
cin>> p->name;
p->total=0;l=0;
for(j=0;j<3;j++)
{
one:
cout<<"\n Enter marks of "<<j+1<<" subject";
cin>> p->m[j]);
if ((p -> m[j]) >100)
{
cout<<"Wrong value entered:";
goto one;
}
p -> total + = p ->m[j];
if(p -> m[j] <40)
l=1;
}
if(l==0)
strcpy(p ->result,"pass");
else
strcpy(p ->result,"fail");
p++
}
for(i=0;i<n;i++)
{
cout<<s ->name << s->result;
s++;
}
getch();
}
```

**OUTPUT:**

Enter the value of Number of students:
5
Enter the names:
Mona
Enter marks of 1 subject 30
Enter marks of 2 subject 50
Enter marks of 3 subject 60
Mona pass
Geeta
Enter marks of 1 subject 20
Enter marks of 2 subject 40
Enter marks of 3 subject 60
Geeta pass
Rani
Enter marks of 1 subject 22
Enter marks of 2 subject 44
Enter marks of 3 subject 66
Rani pass
Radha
Enter marks of 1 subject 12
Enter marks of 2 subject 14
Enter marks of 3 subject 16
Radha fail
Sonia
Enter marks of 1 subject 82
Enter marks of 2 subject 76
Enter marks of 3 subject 55
Sonia pass

**Problem 29. Define a structure whose members are code having at maximum 4 characters name is a member having maximum25**

**characters and department is a member having maximum 20 characters and join date is a member of type date. Write a C++ program to print the names of those employees who have completed at least one year of service.**

***Program:***

```
#include<iostream.h>
#include<conio.h>
struct  date
{
int day;
int month;
int year;
struct emp
{
char code[4];
char name[25];
char dep[20];
struct date doj ;
};
};
void main ( )
{
struct date tdate;
struct emp e[20];
char ename [25];
int i, n;
cout<<"\n Enter the number of employees: ";
cin>> n;
cout<<"\n Enter the data: ";
for (i=0;i<n; i+ +)
{
cout<<"\n    Enter    code,    name,    department,
day,month,year of joining of "<<i+1 <<"employee";
cin>>
e[i].code>>e[i].name>>e[i].dep>>e[i].doj.day>>e[i].
doj.month>>e[i].doj.year;
}
cout<<"Enter today's date ";
cin>>tdate.day>>tdate.month>>tdate.year;
for (i=0;i<n;i++)
{
if (tdate.year>e[i].doj.year)
{
cout<<"\n Employee's data is:";
cout<<e[i].code<<e[i].name<<e[i].dep<<e[i].doj.day
<<e[i].doj.month<<e[i].doj.year;
}
cout<<"\n";
}
getch();
}
```

**OUTPUT:**

```
Enter the number of employees: 2
Enter the data:
Enter code, name, department, day,month,year of
joining of 1 employee:
111
Raja
Computer
12
10
1998
Enter code, name, department, day,month,year of
joining of 2 employee
2222
Mona
Computer
11
04
1997
Enter today's date
10
06
1999
111
Employee's data is:
111    Raja    Computer    11 04 1997
Employee's data is:
2222   Mona    Computer    10    06
       1999
```

**Problem 30. Write a C++ program that accepts two measurements from the user and prints the absolute difference between the measurement.**

***Program:***

```
#include<iostream.h>
#include<conio.h>
struct distance
{
int km;
int m;
int cm;
};
void main()
{
struct distance d1,d2,diff;
long int e;
cout<<"\n Enter distance (1) in km,m and cm";
cin>> d1.km>>d1.m>>d1.cm;
cout<<"\n Enter distance (2) in km,m and cm";
cin>> d2.km>>d2.m>>d2.cm;
```

```
diff.km=d1.km-d2.km;
diff.m=d1.m-d2.m;
diff.cm=d1.cm-d2.cm;
e=diff.km*1000+diff.m+diff.cm;
cout<<"\n The  absolute difference is";
cout<<e;
getch();
}
```

**OUTPUT:**

```
Enter distance (1) in km,m and cm
4       5       12
Enter distance (2) in km,m and cm
2       2       10
The  absolute difference is
2005
```

**Problem 31. Write a C++ program to determine the size of structure.**

***Program:***

```
#include<iostream.h>
#include<conio.h>
void  main ( )
{
struct date
{
int day;
int month;
int year;
};
struct account
{
char name [80];
struct date  one_day;
} customer;
cout<<"\n"<< sizeof (customer);
cout<<"\n"<< sizeof (struct date);
getch();
}
```

**OUTPUT:**

```
86
06
```

**Problem 32. Write a C++ program to display name,dob of persons:**

***Program:***

```
#include<iostream.h>
#include<conio.h>
struct per
{
char name[20];
int day;
int month;
int year;
};
void main()
{
struct per pr1,pr2;
cout<<"\nSpecify values:";
cin>> pr1.name>>pr1.day>>pr1.month>>pr1.year;
cin>> pr2.name>>pr2.day>>pr2.month>>pr2.year;
cout<<"\nValues you entered are:\n";
cout<<<<pr1.name<<pr1.day<<pr1.month<<pr1.y
ear;
cout<<pr2.name<<pr2.day<<pr2.month<<pr2.year
;
getch();
}
```

**OUTPUT:**

```
Specify values:
shubh 12 11 86
puner 4  12 86
Values you entered are:
shubh121186
puner41286
```

**Problem 33. Write a C++ program to display assigned values to members of structures:**

***Program:***

```
#include<iostream.h>
#include<conio.h>
struct
{
int pg;
char *aut;
float pr;
}
book1;
void main()
{
book1.pg=250;
book1.aut="Singh";
book1.pr=120.50;
cout<<"\nPages="<<book1.pg;
cout<<"\nAuthor="<<book1.aut;
cout<<"\nPrice="<<book1.pr;
getch();
}
```

**OUTPUT:**

```
Pages=250
Author=Singh
Price=120.50
```

**Problem 34. Write a C++ program that shows initialization of structure variables:**

***Program:***

```
#include<iostream.h>
#include<conio.h>
struct book
{
char name[20];
int pg;
float pr;
};
void main()
{
struct book b1={"Learning C",280,130.50};
struct book b2;
cout<<"\nName:"<<b1.name;
cout<<"\nPages:"<<b1.pg;
cout<<"\nPrice:"<<b1.pr;
b2=b1;
cout<<"\nName:"<<b2.name;
cout<<"\nPages:"<<b2.pg;
cout<<"\nPrice:"<<b2.pr;
getch();
}
```

**OUTPUT:**

```
Name:Learning C
Pages:280
Price:130.500000
Name:Learning C
Pages:280
Price:130.500000
```

**Problem 35. Write a C++ program that shows comparison of structure variables:**

***Program:***

```
#include<iostream.h>
#include<conio.h>
struct dist
{
int km;
int sec;
};
void main()
{
int x;
static struct dist d1={16,2475};
struct dist d2;
d2=d1;
x=((d1.km==d2.km)&&(d1.sec==d2.sec))?1:0;
if(x==1)
{
cout<<"\nSame speeds";
}
else
{
cout<<"\nDifferent speeds";
}
getch();
}
```

**OUTPUT:**

```
Same speeds
```

**Problem 36. Write a C++ program to demonstrate storage of structure members in contiguous locations:**

***Program:***

```
#include<iostream.h>
#include<conio.h>
struct s_cricket
{
char name[15];
int score;
float avg;
};
void main()
{
struct s_cricket p1={"Dhoni",95,46.50};
cout<<"\nName stored at address="<<p1.name;
cout<<"\nScore stored at address="<<p1.score;
cout<<"\nAvg stored at address="<<p1.avg;
getch();
}
```

**OUTPUT:**

```
Name stored at address=65504
Score stored at address=65519
Avg stored at address=65521
```

**Problem 37. Write a C++ program to find total marks obtained by students in different subject:**

***Program:***

```
#include<iostream.h>
#include<conio.h>
struct stud
{
int s1;
int s2;
int s3;
};
void main()
{
struct stud s[6];
int p,tot=0;
```

```
clrscr();
for(p=0;p<=2;p++)
{
cout<<"\nSpecify marks of 3 subjects:";
cin>> s[p].s1>>s[p].s2>>s[p].s3;
tot=s[p].s1+s[p].s2+s[p].s3;
cout<<"\nThe total marks of s[" <<p<< "]
student:"<<tot;
}
getch();
}
```

**OUTPUT:**

```
Specify marks of 3 subjects:122 154 136
The total marks of s[%d] student:412
Specify marks of 3 subjects:126 189 157
The total marks of s[%d] student:472
Specify marks of 3 subjects:145 125 163
The total marks of s[%d] student:433
```

**Problem 38. Write a C++ program to show how structures are initialized:**

***Program:***

```
#include<iostream.h>
#include<conio.h>
struct rec
{
char name[10];
int accountno;
float bal;
char acctype;
};
void main()
{
static struct rec c[]={
{"Akash",521,'B',45.50},
{"Puner",542,'D',503.50},
{"Shubh",15,'s',1542.19}
};
int i;
clrscr();
cout<<"\nAccount information";
for(i=0;i<3;i++)
{
cout<<"\nName:"<<c[i].name;
cout<<"\nAccount no:"<<c[i].accountno;
cout<<"\nAccount type:"<<c[i].acctype;
cout<<"\nBalance:"<<c[i].bal;
}
getch();
}
```

**Problem 39. Write a C++ program for accessing elements of nested structures:**

***Program:***

```
#include<iostream.h>
#include<conio.h>
struct first
{
int a;
int b;
char c;
};
struct second
{
int d;
struct first e;
};
void main()
{
struct second s[3];
int i;
cout<<"\nSpecify values:\n";
for(i=0;i<2;i++)
{
cin>> s[i].d>>s[i].e.a>>s[i].e.b;
fflush(stdin);
cin>> s[i].e.c;
}
s[2]=s[1];
for(i=0;i<3;i++)
{
cout<<s[i].d<<s[i].e.a<<s[i].e.b<<s[i].e.c;
}
getch();
}
```

**OUTPUT:**

```
Specify values:1 3 4 2 5 8 7 9
1 3 4 2
5 8 7 9
5 8 7 9
```

**Problem 40. Write a C++ program to access member of structure in which we have pointer to structure:**

***Program:***

```
#include<iostream.h>
#include<conio.h>
struct date
{
int day;
int month;
char yr;
```

```
};
struct rec
{
int acno;
struct date pay;
};
void main()
{
struct rec b,*p=&b;
cout<<"\nSpecify the values:\n";
cin>>   p->acno>>p->pay.day>>p->pay.month>>p-
>pay.yr;
cout<<"\nSpecified values:";
cout<<p->acno<<p->pay.day<<p->pay.month<<p-
>pay.yr;
getch();
}
```

**OUTPUT:**

```
Specify the values:
2
5
3
4
Specified values:
2534
```

**Problem 41. Write a C++ program to access member of structure thats array and we got pointer to structure :**

***Program:***

```
#include<iostream.h>
#include<conio.h>
struct date
{
int day;
int mon;
char yr;
};
struct acc
{
char name[5];
struct date l_pay;
};
void main()
{
static struct acc b={"Mani",15,5,1984};
static struct acc *p=&b;
clrscr();
cout<<p->name;
cout<<p->name+1;
cout<<p->name[3];
getch();
}
```

**OUTPUT:**

```
Mani
ani
i
```

**Problem 42. Write a C++ program by using array of variables to display what pointer to a structure variable does:**

***Program:***

```
#include<iostream.h>
#include<conio.h>
struct date
{
int day;
int month;
char year;
};
void main()
{
struct date d[3];
struct date *p;
cout<<"\n Input\n";
for(p=d;p<=(d+2);p++)
cin>> p->day>>p->month>>p->year;
for(p=&d[0];p<=(d+2);p++)
cout<<p->day<<p->month<<p->year;
getch();
}
```

**OUTPUT:**

do it yourself

**Problem 43. Write a C++ program Create a structure to specify data on student given below:**

**Roll number, Name, Department, Course, Year of joinini Assume that there are not more than 450 student in the collage.**

**(a) Write a function to print name of all student who joined in a particular year.**

**(b) Write a function to print the data of a student whose roll number is given.**

***Program:***

```
#include<iostream.h>
#include<conio.h>
struct student
{
int rno;
char name[25];
char dept[15];
```

```
char course[20];
int year_of_joining;
} ;
struct student s[450];
void set_studentdata( );
void display( );
void name_acc_year(int);
int data_acc_rollno(int);
void main( )
{
int i,r;
int y;
clrscr();
cout<<"\nEnter the data for each student:";
set_studentdata();
display();
cout<<"\nEnter the year of joining of the student:";
cin>> y;
name_acc_year(y);
cout<<"\nEnter the Roll number of the student:";
cin>> r;
data_acc_rollno(r);
getch();
}
void set_student_data()
{
int i;
for(i=0;i<450;i++)
{
fflush(stdin);
cout<<"\nEnter the Roll Number of the student:";
cin>> s[i].rno;
fflush(stdin);
cout<<"Enter the name of the student: ";
cin>> s[i].name;
fflush( stdin ) ;
cout<<"Enter the name of the department\n";
cin>> s[i].dept  ;
fflush( stdin ) ;
cout<<"Enter the name of the Course\n";
cin>> s[i].course ;
fflush ( stdin ) ;
cout<<"Enter the year of joining of the student:";
cin>> s[i].year_of_joining;
clrscr( ) ;
}
}
void display( )
{
int i ;
for ( i = 0 ; i < 450 ; i++ )
{
cout<<"\n\tRoll Numberof student i+1 =
"<<s[i].rno<<endl;
cout<<"\n\tName of student i+1=
"<<s[i].name<<endl;
cout<<"\n\tName of the department = "<<s[i].dept
<<endl ;
cout<<"\n\tName of the course = "
<<s[i].course<<endl ;
cout<<"\n\tYear of joining of student i+1 = "<<
s[i].year_of_joining<<endl ;
getch( ) ;
}
}
void name_acc_year ( int y )
{
int i, j = 0 ;
for ( i = 0 ; i < 450 ; i++ )
{
if ( y == s[ i ].year_of_joining )
{
cout<< s[i].name<<" joined in the year"<< s[i].
year_of_joining ;
j = 1 ;
}
}
if ( j == 0 )
cout<<"\nNo student joined in the year "<<y ;
getch( ) ;
}
int data_acc_rollno ( int r )
{
int i, j = 0 ;
for ( i = 0 ; i< 450 ; i++ )
{
if ( s[ i ].rno == r )
{
cout<<"\n\tRoll Number of student = "<<
s[i].rno<<endl;
cout<<"\n\tName of student ="<<
s[i].name<<endl;
cout<<"\n\tName of the Department = "<<
s[i].dept<<endl;
cout<<"\n\tName of the course = "<<
s[i].course<<endl;
cout<<"\n\tYear of joining of student = "<<
s[i].year_of_joining<<endl;
j = 1 ;
}
}
if ( j ==0 )
```

```
cout<<"\nNo such Roll Number present. " ;
getch( ) ;
}
```

**Problem 44. Create a structure to specify data of customers in a bank. The data to be stored is: Account number, Name, Balance in account. Assume of 200 customers in the bank.**

**(a) Write a function to print the account number and name of each customer with balance below Rs, 100.**

**(b) If a customer requests for withdrawal or deposit, it is given in the form:**

**Acct. no, amount, code ( 1 for deposit, 0 for withdrawal)**

**Write a C++ program to give a message, "The balance is insufficient for the specified withdrawal" .**

***Program:***

```
#include<iostream.h>
#include<conio.h>
//void fun( )
//{
//float f, *ff = &f ;
// }
struct customer
{
int acc_no ;
char name[ 20 ] ;
float bal_i_acc ;
};
struct customer cust[200];
void with_dep ( int ano, float amount ) ;
void deposit ( int ano, float amount );
void withdrawal ( int ano, float amount ) ;
void low_bal ( int ano, float amount ) ;
void display( ) ;
void set_cust_data( ) ;
void main( )
{
int i,ano, choice;
float amount ;
clrscr();
set_cust_data();
low_bal( ano, amount );
cout<<"\nEnter the account number and the amount
to be deposited/withdrawn" ;
cin>> ano>>amount;
with_dep ( ano, amount ) ;
display();
}
void with_dep(int ano, float amount)
{
int choice ;
cout<<"Enter 1 for Deposit\tEnter 0 for
withdrawal" ;
cin>>choice ;
switch ( choice )
{
case 1 :
deposit ( ano, amount ) ;
break ;
case 0 :
withdrawal ( ano, amount ) ;
break ;
default :
cout<<"\nYou entered wrong choice" ;
}
}
void deposit ( int ano, float amount )
{
int i, j = 0 ;
for ( i = 0 ; i <200 ; i++ )
{
if ( cust[ i ].acc_no == ano )
{
cust[ i ]. bal_i_acc += amount ;
j = 1 ;
}
}
if ( j == 0 )
cout<<"\n\tWrong Account Number";
}
void withdrawal ( int ano, float amount )
{
int i, j = 0 ;
for ( i = 0 ; i <200 ; i++ )
{
if ( cust[ i ].acc_no == ano )
{
j = 1 ;
if ( cust[ i ].bal_i_acc < 100 )
{
cout<<"\n\tThe Balance is insufficient for the
specified Withdrawal" ;
getch( ) ;
}
else
if ( cust[ i ].bal_i_acc - 100 >= amount )
cust[ i ].bal_i_acc -= amount ;
else
```

```
cout<<"\nwithdrawal amount should be less than or
equal to"<< cust[ i ].bal_i_acc - 100 <<"Rs". ;
}
if ( j == 0 )
cout<<"\nWrong Account Number" ;
}
void low_bal(int ano, float amount )
{
int i, j = 0 ;
clrscr( ) ;
cout<<"\n\nName and Account number of the
customers \nwhose balance is less than 100" ;
for (i=0;i<200;i++)
{
if ( cust[ i ].bal_i_acc < 100 )
{
j = 1 ;
cout<<"\n\tCustomer Number = "<< i+1  ;
cout<<"\n\tAccount Number of customer = "<<cust[
i ]acc_no ;
cout<<"\n\tName of Customer = "<< cust[ i ].name
;
}
}
if ( j == 0 )
cout<<"\n\tEvery Customer has more than minimum
balance amount"  ;
getch();
}
void display( )
{
int i ;
for ( i = 0 ; i <200 ; i++ )
{
cout<<"\n\n\tCustomer Number = "<< i+1  ;
cout<<"\n\n\tAccount Number of Customer = "<<
cust[ i ].acc_no  ;
cout<<"\n\tName of Customer = "<< cust[ i ].name
;
cout<<"\n\tBalance Amount of Customer = "<<
cust[ i ].bal_i_acc  ;
}
getch( ) ;
}
void set_cust_data( )
{
int i ;
for ( i = 0 ; i <200 ; i++ )
{
cout<<"\n\nEnter the Account Number of the
Customer"  ;
cin>> cust[ i ].acc_no  ;
flush ( stdin ) ;
cout<<"\nEnter the name of the Customer" ;
cin>> cust[ i ].name  ;
flush ( stdin ) ;
cout<<"\nEnter the balance amount in the
customer account" ;
cin>> cust[ i ].bal_i_acc  ;
clrscr( ) ;
}
}
```

**Problem 45. An automobile company has serial number for engine parts starting from AA0 to FF9. The other characteristics of parts to be specified in a structure are: Year of manufacture, material and quantity manufactured.**

**(a) Specify a structure to store information corresponding to a part.**

**(b) Write a C++ program to retrieve information on parts with serial numbers between BB1 and CC6.**

***Program:***

```
#include<iostream.h>
#include<conio.h>
struct automobile
{
int s_no ;
int year_o_manu ;
char material[ 20 ] ;
int quantity ;
} ;
struct automobile part[ 2 ] ;
void retrieve( ) ;
void display( ) ;
void set_auto_data( ) ;
void main( )
{
int i ;
clrscr( ) ;
set_auto_data( ) ;
clrscr( ) ;
display( ) ;
clrscr( ) ;
retrieve( ) ;
}
void retrieve( )
{
int i, j = 0 ;
cout<<"\nList of parts between BB1 & CC6:"  ;
```

```
for ( i = 0 ; i < 2 ; i++ )
{
if ( ( part[i].s_no>= 0xbb1 ) && ( part [i].s_no >= 0xcc6 ) )
{
j = 1 ;
cout<<"\n\n\tPart number = "<< i ;
cout<<"\nSerial number = "<< part[i].s_no ;
cout<<"\nYear of manufacturing = "<< part[i].year_o_manu ;
cout<<"\nMaterial used : "<< part[i].material ;
cout<<"\nmanufacture quantity = "<< part[i].quantity ;
}
}
if ( j == 0 )
cout<<"\nNo such record present" ;
getch( ) ;
}
void display()
{
int i ;
for ( i = 0 ; i < 2 ; i++ )
{
cout<<"\n\n\tPart number = "<< i ;
cout<<"\nSerial number = "<< part[i].s_no ;
cout<<"\nYear of manufacturing = "<< part[i].year_o_manu ;
cout<<"\nMaterial used : "<< part[i].material ;
cout<<"\nmanufacture quantity = "<< part[i].quantity ;
}
getch( ) ;
}
void set_auto_data( )
{
int i ;
for ( i = 0 ;i<2; i++ )
{
while ( 1 )
{
cout<<"\nEnter the serial number of the part";
cout<<"\nNumber must be between AAO and FF9";
cin>> part[i].s_no ;
if (part[i].s_no >= 0xAA0 && part[i].s_no <= 0xff9)
break ;
clrscr( ) ;
}
cout<<"\nEnter the Year of manufacturing of the part";
cin>> part[ i ].year_o_manu;
cout<<"\nEnter the material of the part:";
cin>> part[ i ].material;
fflush ( stdin ) ;
cout<<"\nEnter the quantity of the part:";
cin>> part[ i ].quantity ;
}
}
```

**Problem 46. A record contains name of cricketer, his age, number of test matches that he has played and the average runs that he has scored in each test match. Create an array of structures to hold records of 20 such cricketers and then write a C++ program to read these records and arrange them in ascending order by average runs. Use the qsort( ) standard library function.**

***Program:***

```
# include <malloc.h>
#include<iostream.h>
#include<conio.h>
#include <stdlib.h>
void fun( ) ;
int sort_function ( const void *, const void * ) ;
void sortbyavg( ) ;
void display( ) ;
void setdata( ) ;
void fun( )
{
float f, *ff = &f ;
return f ;
}
struct cric_player
{
char name[20];
int age;
int notest;
float avgrun;
};
struct cric_player cp[3];
void main()
{
setdata( ) ;
clrscr( ) ;
cout<<"\nData as entered : \n";
display( ) ;
getch( ) ;
sortbyavg( ) ;
clrscr( ) ;
cout<<"\nData sorted on average runs:\n" ;
display( ) ;
```

```
getch( ) ;
}
void sortbyavg( )
{
int i , j ;
struct cric_player t ;
qsort ( (struct cric_player * ) cp, 3, sizeof ( cp[0] ),
sort_function ) ;
}
int sort_function ( const void *f, const void *ff )
{
return ( ( ( struct cric_player *) f ) -> avgrun - ( (
struct cric_player *) ff ) -> avgrun ) ;
}
void display( )
{
int i ;
for ( i = 0 ; i < 3 ; i++ )
{
cout<<"\n\tName : "<< cp[i].name;
cout<<"\n\tAge : "<< cp[i].age;
cout<<"\n\tNo of tests :"<< cp[i].notest;
cout<<"\n\tAverage : "<< cp[i].avgrun;
}
}
void setdata( )
{
int i ;
for ( i = 0 ; i < 3 ; i++ )
{
clrscr( ) ;
cout<<"\nEnter the name:";
fflush ( stdin ) ;
cout<<"\nEnter the age:";
cin>>cp[i].age;
fflush ( stdin ) ;
cout<<"\nEnter the total number of test matches
played.";
cin>>cp[i].notest;
fflush ( stdin ) ;
cout<<"\nEnter the average number of runs scored
in all the matches:" ;
cin>>cp[i].avgrun;
fflush ( stdin ) ;
}
}
```

**Problem 47. There is a structure called employee that holds information like employee code, name, data of joining. Write a C++ program to create an array of structures and enter some data info if . Then ask the user to enter current date. Display the names of those employees whose tenure is 3 or more than 3 years according to the given current data.**

***Program:***

```
#include<iostream.h>
#include<conio.h>
#define NOOFEMP 5
struct date
{
int day, month, year ;
};
int check_date ( struct date *dt);
void main( )
{
int i,chkdt;
struct employee
{
int code ;
char emp_name [ 20 ] ;
struct date doj ;
};
struct employee emp [ NOOFEMP ];
struct date curr ;
clrscr( ) ;
cout<<"\nEnter current data:";
chkdt = check_data ( &curr ) ;
if ( chkdt == 0 )
{
cout<<"\nImproper data entered";
exit(0);
}
cout<<"\nEnter the information for"<<
NOOFEMP<<" employees: " ;
for ( i = 0 ; i < NOOFEMP ; i++ )
{
fflush ( stdin ) ;
cout<<"\nEmp "<<i <<":Code :" ;
cin>> emp[i].code ;
cout<<"\nName :" ;
cin>> emp[i].emp_name ;
cout<<"\nData of joining ( dd- mm-yyyy ) :" ;
chkdt = check_date ( &emp[i].doj ) ;
if ( chkdt == 0 )
{
cout<<"\nImproper data entered." ;
exit ( ) ;
}
}
cout<<"\nEmployees whose tenure is 3 years or
more:" ;
```

```
for ( i = 0 ; i < NOOFEMP ; i++ )
{
if ( curr.year > emp[i].doj.year + 3 )
{
cout<<"\n"<<emp[i].emp_name ;
break ;
}
else
{
if ( curr.year == emp[i].doj.year +3 )
{
if ( curr.month > emp[i].doj.month )
{
cout<<"\n"<< emp[i].emp_name ;
}
else
{
if ( ( curr.month == emp[i].doj.month ) && (
curr.day >= emp[i].doj.day ) )
cout<<"\n"<< emp[i].emp_name ;
}
}
}
}
getch( ) ;
}
int check_data ( struct date *dt )
{
cout<<"\nEnter data ( dd ) : " ;
cin>> dt-> day ;
cout<<"\nEnter month (mm ) :" ;
cin>> dt-> month ;
cout<<"\nEnter year ( yyyy) :" ;
cin>> dt -> year;
if ( ( dt -> day > 31 || dt -> day > 31) ||( dt -> month
> 12 || dt -> month < 0 ) || ( dt -> year > 9999 || dt ->
year < 1000 ) )
{
return ( 0 ) ;
}
else
return ( 1 ) ;
}
```

**Problem 48. Write a C++ menu driven program that depicts the working the working of. a library. The menu options should be:**
**(1) Add book information**
**(2) Display book information**
**(3) List all books of given author**
**(4) List the title of specified book**
**(5) List the count books in the library**
**(6) List the books in the order of accession number.**
**(7) Exit.**

**Create a structure called library to hold accession number, title of the book, author name, price of the book, and flag indicating whether book is issued or not.**

***Program:***

```
#include<iostream.h>
#include<conio.h>
void add_book( ) ;
void disp_book( ) ;
void disp_book_auth (int aut_ano) ;
void sortbyano( ) ;
int sort_function (const void *f, const void *ff ) ;
void linkfloat( ) ;
struct library
{
char book_title [ 20 ];
char author_name [ 20 ] ;
int accno ;
float price ;
int flag ;
};
int count;
struct library book[10];
void main( )
{
int choice ;
while ( 1 )
{
clrscr ( ) ;
cout<<"\n 1. Add book information " ;
cout<<"\n 2. Display book information " ;
cout<<"\n 3. List all books of given author" ;
cout<<"\n 4 List the title of specified book " ;
cout<<"\n 5. List the count of books in the
library";
cout<<"\n 6. List the books in the order of
accession number" ;
cout<<"\n 7. Exit" ;
cout<<"\nYour choice ?" ;
cin>> choice ;
switch ( choice )
{
case 1 :
add_book( ) ;
cout<<"\nPress any key";
getch( ) ;
break ;
```

```
case 2 :
disp_book( ) ;
cout<<"\nPress any key." ;
getch( ) ;
break ;
case 3 :
disp_book_auth ( 0 ) ;
cout<<"\nPress any key." ;
getch( ) ;
break ;
case 4 :
disp_book_auth ( 1) ;
cout<<"\nPress any key" ;
getch( ) ;
break ;
case 5 :
cout<<"\nThe total number of books in the library
is"<< count ;
cout<<"\nPress any key." ;
getch( ) ;
break ;
case 6 :
sortbyano( ) ;
cout<<"\nPress any key" ;
getch( ) ;
break ;
case 7 :
exit( ) ;
}
}
}
void add_book( )
{
if ( count == 9 )
{
cout<<"\nNo more space";
return ;
}
cout<<"\nEnter the details of the book" ;
cout<<"\nName of the book: " ;
cin>> book[count].book_title ;
cout<<"\nName of the author: " ;
cin>> book[ count ].author_name ;
cout<<"\nAccession number of the book: " ;
cin>> book[ count ].accno ;
cout<<"\nPrice of the book: " ;
cin>> book[ count ].price ;
cout<<"\nIssued / not Issued ( 0/1 ):" ;
cin>> book[ count ].flag ;
if ( ( book[ count ].flag != 0 ) && ( book[ count ].
flag != 1 ) )
```

```
{
cout<<" \nImproper status" ;
return ;
}
count++ ;
cout<<"\nBook details entered" ;
}
void disp_book( )
{
int i ;
cout<<"\nDetails of"<<count<<" books in the
library: " ;
for ( i = 0 ;i < count ; i++ )
{
cout<<"\nName of the book : "<< book[ i ].
book_title ;
cout<<"\nName of the author: "<< book[ i ].
author_name ;
cout<<"\nAccession number of the book: "<<
book[ i ]. accno ;
cout<<"\nPrice of the book: "<< book[ i ]. price ;
cout<<"\nStatus of the book: " ;
book[ i ].flag == 0 ? cout<<" Issued" : cout<<"
Available" ;
cout<<"\n\n" ;
}
}
void disp_book_auth ( int aut_ano )
{
char *nm [ 20 ] ;
int accno ;
int i = 0 ;
int dec = 0 ;
int count;
if ( aut_ano == 0 )
{
cout<<"\nEnter the name of the author : " ;
cin>> nm ;
cout<<"\nDetails of the books by the author
:<<nm<<" in the library: " ;
}
else
{
cout<<"\nEnter the accession number of the book
:" ;
cin>> accno ;
cout<<"\nDetails of the books with accession
no"<< accno<<": " ;
}
for ( i = 0 ; i< count ; i++ )
{
```

```
if ( ( strcmp ( nm, book[ i ].author_name ) == 0 )
&&( aut_ano == 0 ) )
dec++ ;
else
{
if ( aut_ano == 1 )
{
if ( book[ i ].accno == accno )
dec++ ;
else
continue;
}
else
break;
}
cout<<"\nName of the book: "<< book[ i
].book_title ;
cout<<"\nName of the auther: "<< book[ i
].author_name;
cout<<"\nAccession number of book: "<< book[ i ].
accno ;
cout<<"\nPrice of the book: "<< book[ i ].price ;
cout<<"\nStatus of the book: " ;
book[ i ].flag == 0 ? cout<<"Issued" :
cout<<"Available" ;
cout<<"\n\n" ;
}
if ( dec == 0 )
cout<<"\nNo such book" ;
}
void sortbyano( )
{
qsort ( ( struct library * ) book, count, sizeof ( book[
0 ] ),sort_function ) ;
cout<<"\nAfter sorting by accession number " ;
disp_book ( ) ;
}
int sort_function ( const void *f, const void *ff )
{
return ( ( ( struct library * ) f ) -> accno - ( ( struct
library * ) ff) -> accno ) ;
}
void linkfloat( )
{
float a = 0, *b ;
b = &a ;
a = *b ;
}
```

**Problem 49. Write a C++ program that compares two given dates. To store a data use a structure that contains three members namely data, month and year. If the dates are equal tehn display message as "equal" otherwise "unequal" .**

***Program:***

```
#include<iostream.h>
#include<conio.h>
struct date
{
int day, month, year ;
} ;
int check_date ( struct date *dt ) ;
void main( )
{       int chkdt ;
struct date d1, d2 ;
clrscr( ) ;
cout<<"\nEnter the dates to be compared:" ) ;
chkdt = check_date ( &d1 ) ;
if ( chkdt == 0 )
exit ( ) ;
fflush ( stdin ) ;
chkdt = check_date ( &d2 ) ;
if ( chkdt == 0 )
exit ( ) ;
if ( ( d1.day == d2.day ) && ( d1.month ==
d2.month ) && ( d1. year == d2.year ) )
cout<<"\nDates are equal" ;
else
cout<<"\nDates are unequal" ;
getch ( ) ;
}
int check_date( struct date *dt)
{
cout<<"\n Enter date(dd):";
cin>> dt->day;
cout<<"\n Enter month(mm):";
cin>> dt->month;
cout<<"\n Enter year(yyyy):";
cin>> dt->year;
if((dt->day>31|| dt->day<0)||(dt->month>12 || dt-
>month<0)||(dt->year>9999|| dt->year<1000))
{
cout<<"\n Improper date entered";
return(0);
}
else
return(1);
}
```

**Problem 50. Linked list is a very common data structure often used to store similar data in**

**memory. While the elements of an array occupy contagious memory locations, those of a linked list are not constrained to be stored in adjacent locations. The individual element are stored "somewhere" in memory, rather like a family dispersed, but still bound together. The order of the element is maintained by explicit links between them. Thus, a linked list is a collection of element called nodes, each of whise stores two item of information—an element of the list, and a link, I.e., a pointer or an address that indicates explicitly the location of the node containing the successor of the list element.**

**Write a C++ program to build a linked list by adding new nodes at the beginning, at the end or in the middle of the linked list. Also write a function display( ) which display all the nodes present in the linked list.**

***Program:***

```
#include<iostream.h>
#include<conio.h>
#include<malloc.h>
struct linklist
{
int item ;
struct linklist *link ;
} ;
struct linklist *p ;
void add_item_at_loca ( int item, int loca ) ;
void add_end ( int item ) ;
void display( ) ;
void add ( int item ) ;
void main( )
{
p = NULL ;
clrscr( ) ;
add ( 10 ) ;
add ( 20 ) ;
add ( 30 ) ;
add ( 40 ) ;
cout<<"Items added at the beginning of the list:" ;
display( ) ;
cout<<" Press any key.";
getch( ) ;
cout<<"\n\nItem added at the end of list:" ;
add_end ( 50 ) ;
display( ) ;
cout<<" Press any key" ;
getch( ) ;
cout<<"\nItem added in the middle of the list:";
add_item_at_loca ( 60, 4 ) ;
display( ) ;
cout<<"Press any key." ;
getch( ) ;
}
void add_item_at_loca ( int item, int loca )
{
struct linklist *q = ( struct linklist * ) malloc (
sizeof ( struct linklist ) ) ;
struct linklist *r, *w = p ;
int i = 1 ;
q -> item = item ;
q -> link = NULL;
if ( p == NULL )
p = q ;
else
{
while ( ( w-> link != NULL ) && ( i != loca ) )
{
i++ ;
w = w -> link ;
}
if ( i == loca )
{
r = w -> link ;
w -> link = q ;
q -> link = r ;
}
else
w -> link = q ;
}
}
void add_end ( int item )
{
struct linklist *q = ( struct linklist * ) malloc (
sizeof ( struct linklist ) ) ;
struct linklist *w = p ;
q -> item = item ;
q -> link = NULL ;
if ( p == NULL )
p = q ;
else
{
while ( w -> link != NULL )
w = w -> link ;
w -> link = q ;
}
}
void display ( )
{
struct linklist *q = p ;
```

```
int i = 0 ;
while ( q != NULL )
{
i++ ;
cout<<"\nitem number "<<i <<"="<< q->item ;
q = q -> link ;
}
}
void add ( int item )
{
struct linklist *q = ( struct linklist * ) malloc ( sizeof
( struct linklist ) ) ;
q -> item = item ;
q -> link = NULL ;
if ( p == NULL )
p = q ;
else
{
q -> link = p ;
p = q ;
}
}
```

**Problem 51. A stack is a data structure in which addition of new element or deletion of existing element always takes place at the same end. This end is often known as 'top' of stack. This situation can be compared to a stack of plates in a cafeteria where every new platei is added or taken off from the 'top' of the stack of plates. There are several application where stack can be put to use. For exemple, recurcion, keeping track of function calls evaluation of expression, etc Write a C++ program to implement a stack using a linked list.**

***Program:***

```
#include<iostream.h>
#include<conio.h>
#include<alloc.h>
struct node
{
int data ;
struct node *link ;
} ;
void push ( struct node **s, int item ) ;
void displaystack ( struct node *q ) ;
int pop ( struct node **s );
int count ( struct node *q ) ;
void main( )
{
struct node *top ;
int t, i, item ;
clrscr( ) ;
top = NULL ;
push ( &top, 45 ) ;
push ( &top, 28 ) ;
push ( &top, 63 ) ;
push ( &top, 55 ) ;
displaystack ( top ) ;
t = count ( top ) ;
cout<<"\n Total items ="<< t <<endl ;
cout<<"\nPress any key." ;
getch( ) ;
cout<<"\nPopped :" ;
item = pop ( &top ) ;
cout<< item ;
displaystack ( top ) ;
t = count ( top ) ;
cout<<"\nTotal items ="<< t ;
getch( ) ;
}
void push ( struct node **s, int item )
{
struct node *q ;
q = ( struct node * ) malloc (sizeof( struct node ) ) ;
q -> data = item ;
q -> link = *s ;
*s = q ;
}
int pop ( struct node **s )
{
int item ;
struct node *q ;
if ( *s == NULL )
cout<<"Stack is empty" ;
else
{
q = *s ;
item =q -> data ;
*s = q -> link ;
free ( q ) ;
return ( item ) ;
}
}
void displaystack ( struct node *q )
{
while ( q != NULL )
{
cout<< q -> data ;
q = q -> link ;
}
}
```

```
int count ( struct node *q )
{
int c = 0 ;
while ( q != NULL )
{
q = q-> link ;
c++ ;
}
return c ;
}
```

**Problem 52. Unlike a stack, in a queue the addition of new element takes place at the end ( called 'rear' of queue) whereas deletion takes place at the other end (called 'front' of queue). Write a C++ program to implement a queue using a linked list.**

***Program:***

```
#include<iostream.h>
#include<conio.h>
#include <malloc.h>
struct queue
{
int item ;
struct queue *link ;
} ;
struct queue *rear, *front ;
void add ( int item ) ;
int del_queue( ) ;
void display( ) ;
int count( ) ;
void main( )
{
int item ;
rear=front=NULL ;
clrscr( ) ;
add ( 10 ) ;
add ( 20 ) ;
add ( 30 ) ;
add ( 40 ) ;
add ( 50 ) ;
add ( 60 ) ;
display( ) ;
cout<<"\nTotal number of elements present is : "<<
count( ) ;
getch( ) ;
item = del_queue ( ) ;
cout<<"\nDeleted item = "<< item;
display ( ) ;
cout<<"\nTotal number of elements present is : "<<
count( ) ;
getch( ) ;
item = del_queue ( ) ;
cout<<"Deleted item = "<< item ;
display ( ) ;
cout<<"\nTotal number of elements present is :
"<< count( ) ;
getch( ) ;
item = del_queue ( ) ;
cout<<"\nDeleted item = "<< item ;
display ( ) ;
cout<<"\nTotal number of elements present is :
"<< count( ) ;
getch( ) ;
}
void add ( int item )
{
struct queue *q = ( struct queue * ) malloc ( sizeof
( struct queue ) ) ;
q-> item = item ;
q-> link = NULL ;
if ( rear == NULL )
{
rear = q ;
front = q ;
}
else
{
q-> link = rear ;
rear = q ;
}
}
int del_queue( )
{
int item ;
struct queue *q = rear ;
if ( front == NULL )
{
cout<<"\n\tQueue is empty";
getch( ) ;
return -1 ;
}
else
{
if ( front == rear )
{
item = q -> item ;
front = rear = NULL ;
free ( q ) ;
}
else
{
```

```
while ( q-> link->link != NULL )
q = q-> link ;
item = q-> link-> item ;
free ( q-> link ) ;
front = q ;
q-> link = NULL ;
}
}
return item ;
}
void display ( )
{
struct queue *q = rear ;
while ( q != NULL )
{
cout<<"\n"<< q-> item ;
q = q -> link ;
}
}
int count( )
{
struct queue *q = rear ;
int count = 0;
while ( q != NULL )
{
count++;
q = q -> link ;
}
return count ;
}
```

**Problem 53. Write a C++ program that if members are pointer variables then how to access them**:

***Program:***

```
#include<iostream.h>
#include<conio.h>
void main()
{
int x=1542;
char y='M';
float z=25.5;
struct z
{
int *acno;
char *nm;
char *type;
float *bal;
}
f,*p=&f;
f.acno=&x;
f.nm="Preet";
f.type=&y;
f.bal=&z;
clrscr();
cout<<*f.acno<<f.nm<<*f.type<<*f.bal;
cout<<*p->acno<<p->nm<<*p->type<<*p->bal;
getch();
}
```

**OUTPUT:**

```
1542 Preet M 25.500000
1542 Preet M 25.500000
```

**Problem 54. Write a C++ program to pass single member of structure to function:**

***Program:***

```
#include<iostream.h>
#include<conio.h>
#include<string.h>
struct rec
{
char x[25];
int d ;
float bal;
};
float func1(int d,float bal);
void main()
{
struct rec e={"Narender",15,11.50};
clrscr();
cout<<"\nBefore call value="<<e.x<<e.d<<e.bal;
e.bal=func1(e.d,e.bal);
cout<<"\nAfter call value="<<e.x<<e.d<<e.bal;
getch();
}
float func1(int d,float bal)
{
bal+=100;
d+=10;
cout<<"\nIn function values="<<d<<bal;
return(bal);
}
```

**OUTPUT:**

```
Before call value=Narender1511.500000
In function values=25111.500000
After call value=Narender15111.500000
```

**Problem 55. Write a C++ program for a book shop inventory management:**

***Program:***

```
#include<iostream.h>
#include<conio.h>
```

```
#include<string.h>
struct record
{
char author[20];
char heading[30];
float price;
struct
{
char month[10];
int year;
}
date;
char pub[10];
int quantity;
};
void main()
{
char heading[30],author[20];
int index,rec,check();
char response[10],quantity[10];
static struct record book[]=
{
{"J.K. Rowling","Harry Potter",50.00,"June",1979,"TMH",0},
{"Dennis Ritchie","C Language",65.00,"May",1982,"Hayden",6},
{"Shakespeare","King Lear",35.00,"December",1976,"Newpub",11},
};
rec=sizeof(book)/sizeof(struct record);
do
{
cout<<"Specify heading and author name as per list:";
cout<<"\n Heading:";
get(title);
cout<<"\n Author:";
get(author);
index=check(book,heading,author,rec);
if(index!=-1)
{
cout<<book[index].author<<book[index].heading<<
book[index].price<<book[index].date.month<<book
[index].date.year<<book[index].pub);
cout<<"Specify number copies:";
get(quantity);
if(atoi(quantity)<book[index].quantity)
cout<<"Cost of "<<atoi(quantity)"
copies="<<book[index].price*atoi(quantity);
else
cout<<"\nNeeded copies not in stock\n\n";
}
else
cout<<"\nBook not on list\n\n";
cout<<"\nDo you want some other book?(YES/NO):";
get(response);
}
while(response[0]=='Y'||response[0]=='y');
cout<<"\n\nThank You.\n";
}
get(string)
char string[];
{
char c;
int i=0;
do
{
c=getchar();
string[i++]=c;
}while(c!='\n');
string[i-1]='\0';
}
int check(table,m1,m2,h)
struct record table[];
char m1[],m2[];
int h;
{
int i;
for(i=0;i<m;i++)
if(strcmp(m1,tab[i].heading)==0 &&
(strcmp(m2,tab[i].author)==0)
return(i);
return(-1);
}
```

**OUTPUT:**

Specify heading and author name as per list:
Heading:Harry Potter
Author:J.K.Rowling
J.K.Rowling Harry Potter 35.00 December 1976 Newpub
Specify number copies:7
Needed copies not in stock
Do you want some other book?(YES/NO):y
Specify heading and author name as per list:
Heading:C Language
Author:Dennis Ritchie
Dennis Ritchie C Language 65.00 May 1982 Macmillan
Specify number copies:4
Cost of 4 copies=260

**Problem 56. Write a C++ program to display passing of complete structure using call by value:**

***Program:***

```
#include<iostream.h>
#include<conio.h>
struct book
{
char t[20];
int pg;
int pr;
}
void main()
{
struct book b={"C Programs",250,300};
struct book add(struct book);
clrscr();
cout<<"\nBefore call="<<b.t<<b.pg<<b.pr;
b=add(b);
cout<<"\nAfter call="<<b.t<<b.pg<<b.pr;
getch();
}
struct book add(struct book p)
{
p.pg=p.pg+100;
p.pr=p.pr+50;
return(p);
}
```

**OUTPUT:**

```
Before call=C Programs250300
After call=C Programs350350
```

**Problem 57. Write a C++ program to display passing of complete structure using reference method:**

***Program:***

```
#include<iostream.h>
#include<conio.h>
struct rec
{
char x;
int y;
float bal;
};
void main()
{
struct rec e={'s',4,15.50};
void f1(struct rec*p);clrscr();
cout<<"\nBefore call="<<e.x<<e.y<<e.bal;
f1(&e);
cout<<"\nAfter call="<<e.x<<e.y<<e.bal;
getch();
}
void f1(struct rec*p)
{
p->x='i';
p->y=30;
p->bal=225.50;
cout<<"\n In function="<<p->x <<p->y << p->bal;
return;
}
```

**OUTPUT:**

```
Before call==s415.500000
In function==i30225.500000
After call==i30225.500000
```

**Problem 58. Write a C++ program to make,insert,delete and print from a link list:**

***Program:***

```
#include<iostream.h>
#include<conio.h>
struct node
{
int val;
struct node *next;
}
*start;
void insert(void);
void delete(void);
void print(void);
void main()
{
int ch;
for(;;)
{
clrscr();
cout<<"1.Insert<<"  \n"<<"   2.Delete"<<"\n"<<"
3.Print"<<"\n "<<"4.Exit\n";
cout<<"Specify your choice";
cin>> ch);
switch(ch)
{
case 1:insert();
break;
case 2:delete();
break;
case 3:print();
getch();
break;
case 4:exit();
}}}
void insert(void)
{
```

```
struct node *ptr,*prev,*check;
int item;
ptr=(struct node*)malloc(sizeof(struct node*));
cout<<"\nSpecify the value");
cin>> ptr->val);
if(start==NULL)
{
ptr->next=NULL;
start=ptr;
}
else
{
print();
cout<<" ("\n Specify an element after which it should be inserted"<<"\n"<<"Enter 999 if inserted in beginning";
cin>> item;
if(item==999)
{
ptr->next=start;
start=ptr;
}
else
{
check=start;
do
{
if(check->val==item)
{
prev=check;
break;
}
check=check->next;
}
while(check!=NULL);
ptr->next=prev->next;
prev->next=ptr;
}}}
void delete(void)
{
struct node *ptr,*prev,*loc=NULL;
int item;
if(start==NULL)
{
cout<<"\n The list is empty";
getch();
}
else
{
print();
cout<<"\n Specify value to be deleted";
cin>> item;
if(item==start->val)
{
start=start->next;
return;
}
if(item==start->val&&start->next==NULL)
{
start=NULL;
return;
}
ptr=start;
prev=NULL;
do
{
if(ptr->val==item)
{
loc=ptr;
break;
}
prev=ptr;
ptr=ptr->next;
}
while(ptr!=NULL);
if(loc==NULL)
{
cout<<"\nAn item does not exist";
getch();
return;
}
prev->next=loc->next;
}
}
void print(void)
{
struct node *ptr;
if(start==NULL)
{
cout<<"\nList is empty";
getch();
return;
}
cout<<"\nList of values is:";
ptr=start;
do
{
cout<<ptr->val;
ptr=ptr->next;
}
while(ptr!=NULL);
}
```

**OUTPUT:**

```
1.Insert
2.Delete
3.Print
4.Exit
Enter choice 1
Enter element 4
List of values are
5
6
3
Enter the element after which it should be inserted 6
1.Insert
2.Delete
3.Print
4.Exit
Enter choice 3
List is
5
6
4
3
Enter choice 2
Enter the element to delete 6
Enter choice 3
List is
5
4
3
```

**Problem 59. Write a C++ program to determine sizeof structure:**

***Program:***

```
#include<iostream.h>
#include<conio.h>
void main()
{
struct date
{
int day;
int mon;
int yr;
};
struct account
{
char name[70];
struct date l_day;
}
customer;
clrscr();
cout<<sizeof(customer);
cout<<sizeof(struct date);
getch();
}
```

**OUTPUT:**

```
76
6
```

**Problem 60. Write a C++ program to sort student records according to grades:**

***Program:***

```
#include<iostream.h>
#include<conio.h>
struct student
{
int rollno;
char name[25];
char coll[40];
int score;
};
void main()
{
struct student s[20],temp;
int n,i,j;
cout<<"\nSpecify number of students:";
cin>> n;
cout<<"\nEnter information:";
for(i=0;i<n;i++)
cin>>
s[i].rollno>>s[i].name>>s[i].coll>>s[i].score;
for(i=0;i<=n-1;i++)
{
for(j=0;j<n-1;j++)
{
if(s[j].score>s[j+1].score)
{
temp=s[j];
s[j]=s[j+1];
s[j+1]=temp;
}}}
cout<<"\nThe Merit List:";
for(j=0;j<n;j++)
cout<<s[j].rollno<<s[j].name<<s[j].coll<<s[j].scor
e;
getch();
}
```

**OUTPUT:**

```
Specify number of students:2
Enter information:
61 mani khalsacollege 445
34 aman davcollege 345
```

The Merit List:
61 mani khalsacollege 445
34 aman davcollege 345

**Problem 61. Write a C++ program define structure whose members are name with max 30 chars,department with max 25 chars,code with max 4 chars & joining date is a member of type date.Program must display members whohas one year of experience:**

***Program:***

```
#include<iostream.h>
#include<conio.h>
struct date
{
int day;
int month;
int year;
};
struct emp
{
char code[4];
char name[30];
char dep[25];
struct date doj;
};
void main()
{
struct date tdate;
struct emp e[20];
char ename[25];
int p,n;
cout<<"\nSpecify the number of employees";
cin>> n;
cout<<"\nEnter data";
for(p=0;p<n;p++)
{
cout<<"\nEnter    day,month,year    of    joining
of"<<p+1<<" employee";
cin>>e[p].code>>e[p].name>>e[p].dep>>e[p].doj.da
y>>e[p].doj.month>>e[p].doj.year;
}
cout<<"Enter today's date";
cin>> tdate.day>>tdate.month>>tdate.year;
for(p=0;p<n;p++)
{
if(tdate.year>e[p].doj.year+1)                        ||
(tdate.year>e[p].doj.year && ((t.date.month
==e[p].doj.month &&
tdate.day>e[p].doj.day)                               ||
tdate.month>e[p].doj.month))
{
cout<<e[p].code<<e[p].name<<e[p].dep<<e[p].doj
.day<<e[p].doj.month<<
e[p].doj.year;
}
cout<<"\n";
}
getch();
}
```

**Problem 62. Write a C++ program to define structure to add,sub,mul two complex numbers:**

***Program:***

```
(a+ib)+(c+id)=(a+c)+i(b+d)
(a+ib)-(c-id)=(a-c)+i(b-d)
(a+ib)*(c+id)=(ac-bd)+i(ad+bc)
#include<iostream.h>
#include<conio.h>
struct comp
{
int r;
int i;
};
void read(struct comp*);
struct comp add(struct comp*,struct comp*);
struct comp sub(struct comp*,struct comp*);
struct comp mul(struct comp*,struct comp*);
void write(struct comp*);
void main()
{
struct comp a,b,c,d,e;
read(&a);
read(&b);
c=add(&a,&b);
d=sub(&a,&b);
e=mul(&a,&b);
write(&c);
write(&d);
write(&e);
getch();
}
void read(struct comp *x)
{
cout<<"Enter real part: ";
cin>> (x->r);
cout<<"Enter img part: ";
cin>> (x->i);
}
struct comp add(struct comp *x,struct comp *y)
{
struct comp z;
```

```
z.r=x->r+y->r;
z.i=x->i+y->i;
return(z);
}
struct comp sub(struct comp *x,struct comp *y)
{
struct comp z;
z.r=x->r-y->r;
z.i=x->i-y->i;
return(z);
}
struct comp mul(struct comp *x,struct comp *y)
{
struct comp z;
z.r=(x->r)*(y->r)-(x->i)*(y->i);
z.i=(x->r)*(y->i)+(x->i)*(y->i);
return(z);
}
void write(struct comp *x)
{
cout<<"\nNumber is:"<< x->r + x->i;
}
```

**OUTPUT:**

```
Enter real part: 1204
Enter img part: 1112
Enter real part: 1452
Enter img part: 2121
Number is: 2656+3233i
Number is: -248+-1009i
Number is: -20520+-2964i
```

**Problem 63. Write a C++ program to make a structure to store data about car and using it wap that accepts data about cars from user and gets data from car with engine no provided:**

***Program:***

```
#include<iostream.h>
#include<conio.h>
#include<string.h>
struct car
{
char eng[6];
char cha_no[8];
int yr;
int hp;
};
void main()
{
char eno[6];
struct car c[20];
int p,n,d=0;
cout<<"\nSpecify number of cars";
cin>> n;
cout<<"\nSpecify data";
for(p=0;p<n;p++)
{
cin>> c[p].eng>>c[p].cha_no>>c[p].yr>>c[p].hp;
}
cout<<"\nSpecify an engine number of the car to be found:";
cin>> eno;
for(p=0;p<n;p++)
{
if(strcmp(c[p].eng,eno)==0)
{
cout<<c[p].eng<<c[p].cha_no<<c[p].yr<<c[p].hp;
d=1;
}}
if(d==0)
{
cout<<"Wrong Engine Number";
}
getch();
}
```

**OUTPUT:**

```
Specify number of cars:2
Specify data:
ikon04 ik34 1987 876
benz12 bz54 1990 657
Specify an engine number of the car to be found:benz12
benz12
bz54
1990
657
```

**Problem 64. Write a C++ program to accept 2 measurements and print their absolute difference:**

***Program:***

```
#include<iostream.h>
#include<conio.h>
struct dist
{
int km;
int m;
int cm;
};
void main()
{
struct dist ds1,ds2,d;
```

```
long int e;
cout<<"\nSpecify dist1 in km,m and cm:";
cin>> ds1.km>>ds1.m>>ds1.cm;
cout<<"\nSpecify dist2 in km,m and cm:";
cin>> ds2.km>>ds2.m>>ds2.cm;
d.km=ds1.km-ds2.km;
d.m=ds1.m-ds2.m;
d.cm=ds1.cm-ds2.cm;
e=d.km*1000+d.m+d.cm;
cout<<"\nThe absolute difference is:";
cout<<e;
getch();
}
```

**OUTPUT:**

```
Specify dist1 in km,m and cm:100 200 300
Specify dist2 in km,m and cm:200 300 400
The absolute difference is:30872
```

**Problem 65. Write a C++ program to create structure to read and print names using dynamic memory allocation:**

***Program:***

```
#include<iostream.h>
#include<conio.h>
#include<string.h>
struct stud
{
char name[10];
int m[3];
int total;
char result[5];
}
*p,*s;
void main()
{
int i,j,l,n;
cout<<"\nSpecify number of students";
cin>> n;
p=(struct stud*)malloc(n*sizeof(struct stud));
s=p;
for(i=0;i<n;i++)
{
cin>> p->name;
p->total=0;
l=0;
for(j=0;j<3;j++)
{
one: cout<<"\nSpecify marks of "<<j+1
<<"subject";
cin>> p->m[j];
if((p->m[j])>100)
{
cout<<"Value entered is wrong";
goto one;
}
p->total+=p->m[j];
if(p->m[j]<40)
l=1;
}
if(l==0)
strcpy(p->result,"pass");
else
strcpy(p->result,"fail");
p++;
}
for(i=0;i<n;i++)
{
cout<<s->name<<s->result;
s++;
}
getch();
}
```

**Problem 66. Write a C++ program to pass individual member of structure to a function.**

***Program:***

```
#include<iostream.h>
#include<conio.h>
#include <string.h>
struct record
{
char a[20]:
int c:
float balance:
};
float func1 (int c, float balance);
void main ( )
{
struc record e = {"Rajaraman",20,400.50};
clrscr();
cout<<"\n Before call value =
"<<e.a<<e.c<<e.balance;
e.balance= func1(e.c,e.balance);
cout<<"\n After call value =
"<<e.a<<e.c<<e.balance;
getche();
}
float func1((int c, float balance)
{
balance=balance +100;
c=c+10;
cout<<"\n Function Values = "<<c<<balance;
```

```
return (balance);
}
```

**OUTPUT:**

Before call value = Rajaraman 20 400.50
Function Values = 30 500.50
After call value = Rajaraman 30 500.50

**Problem 67. Write a C++ program to pass the structure by reference.**

***Program:***

```
#include<iostream.h>
#include<conio.h>
struct record
{
char a;
int c;
float balance;
};
void main ( )
{
struct record e = {'M', 20, 30.50};
viod func1 (record*p);
clrscr ( )
cout<< "\n Before call = "<<e.a<<e.c<<e.balance;
func1 (&e);
cout<<"\n After call = "<< e.a<<e.c<< e.balance;
getch ( );
}
void func 1 ( record*p)
{
p-> a = 'K';
p-> c = 40;
p->balance = 420.33;
cout<<"\n in Function = ="<<p->a<<p->c<<p->balance;
return;
}
```

**OUTPUT:**

Before call = =M 20 30.50
After call = K 40 420.33

**Problem 68. Write a C++ program to show how to access elements of nested structure.**

***Program:***

```
#include<iostream.h>
#include<conio.h>
struct first
{
int a;
int b;
char c;
};
struct second
{
int d;
struct first e;
};
void main()
{
struct second s[3];
int i;
clrscr();
cout<<"\n Enter values: ";
for(i=0;i<2;i++)
{
cin>> s[i].d>>s[i].e.a>>s[i].e.b>>s[i].e.c;
}
s[2]=s[1];
cout<<"\n Results be:";
for (i=0;i<3;i++)
{
cout<<s[i].d<<s[i].e.a<<s[i].e.b<<s[i].e.c;
}
getch();
}
```

**OUTPUT:**

```
Enter values:
20      30      40      A
Results be:
20      30      40      B
```

**Problem 69. Write a C++ program to sort the record of students merit wise.**

***Program:***

```
# include < iostream.h>
# include < conio. h>
struct student
{
int rollno ;
char name [20];
char college [40];
int score ;
};
void main ( )
{
struct student s [20], temp;
int n, i, j;
cout<<"\n Enter the number of student: ";
cin>> n;
cout<<"\n Enter the Rollno, name, college-name and Score:";
for (i=0; i<n;++)
```

```
cin>>
s[i].rollno>>s[i].name>>s[i].college>>s[i].score;
for (i=0;i<=n-1;i + +)
{
for (j =0; j <n-1;j+ +)
{
if (s[j].score >s[j+1].score)
{
temp =s[j];
s[j] = s[j+1];
s[j+1]= temp;
}
}
}
cout<<"\n The Merit list is ";
for (j=0; j<n; j + +)
cout<<s[j].rollno<<s[j].name<<s[j].college<<s[j].sc
ore;
getch( );
}
```

**OUTPUT:**

```
Enter the number of student: 3
Enter the Rollno, name, college-name and Score
122     Ramanjot Singh Khalsa 750
123     Mohan kumar      D.A.V  650
124     Rajan            Hindu  700
The Merit list is
122     Ramanjot  Singh        Khalsa  750
124     Rajan                  Hindu   700
123     Mohan Kumar            D.A.V  650
```

# CHAPTER 10

# CLASSES AND OBJECTS

## CLASS DEFINATION:

**Problem 1. Write a C++ program to define your first class.**

***Program:***

```
#include <iostream.h>
#include<conio.h>
class ThreeDimension
{
public:
int X;
int Y;
int Z;
};
void main()
{
ThreeDimension myDimension;
int range;
myDimension.X = 7;
myDimension.Y = 16;
myDimension.Z = 21;
range = myDimension.X * myDimension.Y*
myDimension.Z;
cout << range;
getch();
}
```

**OUTPUT:**

```
2352
```

**Problem 2. Write a C++ program to Implement Class Rectangle.**

***Program:***

```
#include <iostream.h>
#include<conio.h>
class Rectangle
{
int x, y;
public:
void set_values (int,int);
int area (void)
{
return (x*y);
}
};
void Rectangle::set_values (int a, int b)
{
x = a;
y = b;
}
void main ()
{
Rectangle rect;
rect.set_values (3,4);
cout << "area: " << rect.area();
getch();
}
```

**OUTPUT:**

```
area: 12
```

**Problem 3. Write a C++ program to create an object from a Class and call its function.**

***Program:***

```
#include <iostream.h>
#include<conio.h>
class MyClass
{
public:
void displayMessage()
{
cout << "Welcome!" << endl;
}
};
void main()
{
MyClass obj;
obj.displayMessage();
getch();
}
```

**OUTPUT:**

```
Welcome!
```

**Problem 4. Write a C++ program to explain concept of one class with one object by taking student data.**

***Program:***

```
#include<iostream.h>
```

```
#include<conio.h>
class student
{
private :
int rn;
char   name[10];
public :
void readdata()
{
cout << "\n Enter the Roll No." << endl;
cin >> rn;
cout <<"\n Enter the Name" << endl;
cin >> name;
}
void writedata()
{
cout << "\n Roll No. is "<< rn;
cout << "\n Name is "<< name;
}
};
void main()
{
class student st;
clrscr();
st.readdata();
st.writedata();
getch();
}
```

**OUTPUT:**

Enter the Roll No. 121
Enter the Name Mona
Roll No. is 121
Name is Mona

**Problem 5. Write a C++ program to explain concept of one class with two object by taking student data.**

***Program:***

```
#include<iostream.h>
#include<conio.h>
class student
{
private :
int rn;
char name[10];
public :
void readdata ()
{
cout <<"\n Enter the Roll No " << endl;
cin >> rn;
cout << "\n Enter the Name" << endl;
cin >> name;
}
void writedata ()
{
cout << "\n Roll No. is " << rn;
cout << "\n Name is " << name;
}
};
void main()
{
class student st1, st2;
clrscr();
st1.readdata();
st1.writedata();
st2.readdata ();
st2.writedata();
getch();
}
```

**OUTPUT:**

Enter the Roll No. 122
Enter the Name Geeta
Roll No. is 122
Name is Geeta
Enter the Roll No. 123
Enter the Name Sangeeta
Roll No. is 123
Name is Sangeeta

**Problem 6. Write a C++ program to show the relationship of class and object with student data.**

***Program:***

```
#include<iostream.h>
#include<conio.h>
class sample
{
private :
int rollno;
public :
void readdata (int rn)
{
rollno = rn ;
}
void display ( )
{
cout<<rollno ;
}
} ;
void main ( )
{
```

```
class sample d1, d2 ;                    //two object
of one class
d1.readdata (121) ;
d2.readdata (1325) ;
cout<<"\n ROLL NO OF BCA-I is:" ;
d1.display ( ) ;
cout<<"\n ROLL NO OF BCA-II is:" ;
d2.display ( ) ;
getch();
}
```

**OUTPUT:**

```
ROLLNO OF BCA-I is : 121
ROLLNO OF BCA-II is : 1325
```

**Problem 7. Write a C++ program to show the relationship of class and object by taking student data.**

***Program:***

```
#include<iostream.h>
#include<conio.h>
void main (void)
{
class student
{
public :
int rn ;
float fees ;
} ;
class student st ;
st.rn = 1321 ;
st.fees = 1200.25 ;
cout<<"\n ROLL NO OF STUDENT IS:"<<st.rn ;
cout<<"\n FEES PAID BY STUDENT IS:"<<st.fees
    ;
getch();
}
```

**OUTPUT:**

```
ROLL NO OF STUDENT IS : 1321
FEES PAID BY STUDENT IS : 1200.25
```

**Problem 8. Write a C++ program to show the relationship of class and object to display rollno , grade and fees paid by student.**

***Program:***

```
#include<iostream.h>
#include<conio.h>
class student
{
private :
int rn ;
char grade ;
float fees ;
public :
void read (int x, char y, float z)
{
rn = x ;
grade = y ;
fees = z ;
}
void write ( )
{
cout<<"\n ROLLNO IS"<< rn ;
cout<<"\n GRADE IS"<< grade ;
cout<<"\n FEES PAID IS"<< fees ;
}
} ;
void main ( )
{
student st ;                          //defining
object st of
st. read (121, 'B', 1250.25) ;              //class
student
st.write ( ) ;
getch();
}
```

**Problem 9. Write a C++ program to show the relationship of multiple data with multiple object.**

***Program:***

```
#include<iostream.h>
#include<conio.h>
class currency
{
private :
int rupees ;
float paise ;
public :
void read ( )
{
cout<<"\n Rupees in integer is:" ;
cin >> rupees ;
cout<<"\n Paise in Real is:" ;
cin >> paise ;
}
void assign (int rs, float ps)
{
rupees = rs ;
paise = ps ;
}
void display ( ) ;
{
```

```
cout<<"\n Rs."<<rupees<< "Ps." <<paise<<endl ;
}
} ;
void main ( )
{
currency c1, c2 ;
c1.assign (15, 3.75) ;
c2.read ( ) ;
cout<<"\n First Amount is:" ;
c1.display ( ) ;
cout<<"\n Second Amount is:" ;
c2.display ( ) ;
getch ( ) ;
}
```

**OUTPUT:**

Rupees is integer is : 420
Paise is real is : 36.2
First Amount is : Rs. 15 Ps. 3.75
Second Amt. is : Rs. 420 Ps. 36.2

## MEMBER METHOD:

**Problem 10. Write a C++ program to declare a class with method.**

***Program:***

```
#include <iostream.h>
#include<conio.h>
class ThreeDimension
{
public:
int X;
int Y;
int Z;
int range();   // compute and return the range
};
```

**Problem 11. Write a C++ program to implement class member function.**

***Program:***

```
#include <iostream.h>
#include<conio.h>
// Declare the ThreeDimension class.
class ThreeDimension
{
public:
int X;
int Y;
int Z;
int range();
};
// Implement the range member function.
int ThreeDimension::range()
{
return X* Z * Y;
}
void main()
{
ThreeDimension aDimension;
ThreeDimension bDimension;
int range1, range2;
// Assign values to fields in aDimension.
aDimension.X = 7;
aDimension.Y = 16;
aDimension.Z = 21;
// Assign values to fields in bDimension.
bDimension.X = 2;
bDimension.Y = 14;
bDimension.Z = 12;
// Compute the ranges assuming a full tank of gas.
range1 = aDimension.range();
range2 = bDimension.range();
cout << range1 << "\n";
cout << range2;
getch();
}
```

**OUTPUT:**

2352
336

**Problem 12. Write a C++ program to demonstrating C++ class.**

***Program:***

```
#include <iostream.h>
#include<conio.h>
class c1
{
int i; // private by default
public:
int get_i();
void put_i(int j);
};
int c1::get_i()
{
return i;
}
void c1::put_i(int j)
{
i = j;
}
void main()
{
```

```
c1 s;
s.put_i(10);
cout << s.get_i() <<endl;
getch();
}
```

**OUTPUT:**

10

**Problem 13. Write a C++ program for a simple class data.**

***Program:***

```
#include <iostream.h>
#include<conio.h>
class data
{
private:
int d;
public:
void setdata(int t)//member function
{
d=t;
}
void showdata()//member function
{
cout<<"Data is " <<d <<endl;
}
};
void main()
{
data d1,d2;//define two objects
d1.setdata(1010);//call member function to set data
d2.setdata(1884);
d1.showdata();//call member function to display data
d2.showdata();
getch();
}
```

**OUTPUT:**

Data is 1010
Data is 1884

**Problem 14. Write a C++ program for class having Real Objects(car).**

***Program:***

```
#include <iostream.h>
#include<conio.h>
class car //define class
{
private:
int model_no;
int engine_no;
float cost;
public:
void set(int mno,int eno,float c)//set data
{
model_no =mno;
engine_no =eno;
cost =c;
}
void show()//display data
{
cout <<"Model " <<model_no;
cout <<",engine " <<engine_no;
cout <<",costs $" <<cost <<endl;
}
};
void main()
{
car car1;//define object
car1.set(2009,184,20000.55);//call member
function
car1.show();//call member function
getch();
}
```

**OUTPUT:**

Model 2009,engine_no 184,cost $20000.550781

**Problem 15. Write a C++ program to take objects as Data Types.**

***Program:***

```
#include <iostream.h>
#include<conio.h>
class Height //Height class
{
private:
int feet;
float inches;
public:
void set(int ft,float in)
{
feet =ft;
inches =in;
}
void get()
{
cout <<"\n Feet:";
cin >>feet;
cout <<" inches:";
cin >>inches;
}
void show()
{
cout <<feet <<"-" <<inches ;
```

```
} };
void main()
{
Height H1,H2;
H1.set(6,6.0);
H2.get();
cout <<"\nHeight1 =";H1.show();
cout <<"\nHeight2 =";H2.show();
cout <<endl;
getch();
}
```

**OUTPUT:**

Feet:6
inches:4.25
Height1 = 6-6.0
Height2 = 6-4.25

**Problem 16. Write a C++ program in which class member access operators . and ->.**

***Program:***

```
#include <iostream.h>
#include<conio.h>
class MyClass
{
public:
void setX( int value )
{  x = value; }
void print()
{ cout << x << endl; }
private:
int x;
};
void main()
{
MyClass obj;
MyClass *objPtr = &obj;
MyClass &objRef = obj;
obj.setX( 1 );
obj.print();
objRef.setX( 2 );
objRef.print();
objPtr->setX( 3 );
objPtr->print();
getch();
}
```

**OUTPUT:**

1
2
3

## ACCESS FUNCTIONS:

**Problem 17. Write a C++ program for Accessor functions.**

***Program:***

```
#include <iostream.h>
#include<conio.h>
class MyClass
{
public:                    // begin public section
int getInt();            // accessor function
void setint (int age);  // accessor function
void display();           // general function
private:                   // begin private section
int itsAge;              // member variable
};
int MyClass::getInt()
{
return itsAge;
}
void MyClass::setint(int age)
{
itsAge = age;
}
void MyClass::display()
{
cout << "display.\n";
}
void main()
{
MyClass obj;
obj.setint(5);
obj.display();
cout << obj.getInt() << " years old.\n";
obj.display();
getch();
}
```

**OUTPUT:**

display.
5 years old.
display.

## PRIVATE:

**Problem 18. Write a C++ program for private fields.**

***Program:***

```
#include <iostream.h>
#include<conio.h>
struct MyClass
```

```
{
int getI() { return i; } // these are public by default
void setI(int j) { i = j; }
private:
int i;
};
void main()
{
MyClass s;
s.setI(10);
cout << s.getI();
getch();
}
```

**OUTPUT:**

10

**Problem 19. Write a C++ program for private by default.**

***Program:***

```
#include <iostream.h>
#include<conio.h>
class MyClass
{
int i;  // private by default
public:
int getI() { return i; }
void setI(int j) { i = j; }
};
void main()
{
MyClass s;
s.setI(10);
cout << s.getI();
getch();
}
```

**OUTPUT:**

10

**Problem 20. Write a C++ program for that Non-friend/non-member functions cannot access private data of a class.**

***Program:***

```
#include <iostream.h>
#include<conio.h>
class MyClass
{
public:
MyClass() : x( 0 )
{
}
void print() const
{
cout << x << endl;
}
private:
int x;
};
void cannotSetX( MyClass &c, int val )
{
//c.x = val; // ERROR: cannot access private
member in MyClass
}
void main()
{
MyClass counter;
cannotSetX( counter, 3 );
cout<<"ERROR: cannot access private member in
MyClass";
getch();
}
```

**OUTPUT:**

***ERROR:*** cannot access private member in MyClass

## PUBLIC:

**Problem 21. Write a C++ program for public fields and member functions.**

***Program:***

```
#include <iostream.h>
#include<conio.h>
class MyClass
{
public:
int number;
void display();
};
void MyClass::display()
{
for(int i = 0; i<= number;i++)
{
cout<< "Hello World \n";
}
}
void main ()
{
MyClass myfirstobject;
myfirstobject.number =3;
myfirstobject.display();
getch();
}
```

**OUTPUT:**

Hello World
Hello World
Hello World
Hello World

**Problem 22. Write a C++ program to initialize the public data members in a class.**

***Program:***

```
#include <iostream.h>
#include<conio.h>
class Box
{
public:
double length;
double width;
double height;
double volume() {
return length * width * height;
}
};
void main()
{
Box firstBox = { 80.0, 50.0, 40.0 };
double firstBoxVolume = firstBox.volume();
cout << firstBox.length
    << firstBox.width
    << firstBox.height
    << endl;
cout << "Volume of first Box object is " <<
firstBoxVolume << endl;
getch();
}
```

**OUTPUT:**

805040
Volume of first Box object is 160000

**Problem 23. Write a C++ program to initialize inner object using initialization syntax.**

***Program:***

```
#include <iostream.h>
#include<conio.h>
class IntPair
{
public:
int a;
int b;
IntPair(int i, int j) : a(i), b(j) { }
};
class MyClass
{
IntPair nums;
public:
MyClass(int x, int y) : nums(x,y) { }
int getNumA() { return nums.a; }
int getNumB() { return nums.b; }
};
void main()
{
MyClass ob1(7, 9), ob2(5, 2);
cout << "Values in ob1 are " << ob1.getNumB()
<<
        " and " << ob1.getNumA() << endl;
cout << "Values in ob2 are " << ob2.getNumB()
<<
        " and " << ob2.getNumA() << endl;
getch();
}
```

**OUTPUT:**

Values in ob1 are 9 and 7
Values in ob2 are 2 and 5

## INNER CLASS:

**Problem 24. Write a C++ program to define inner class.**

***Program:***

```
#include <iostream.h>
#include<conio.h>
#include <stdlib.h>
class OuterClass
{
public:
void outerFunction();
class InnerClass
{
public:
void innerFunction();
};
};
void OuterClass::outerFunction()
{
cout << "This is a function in the base class\n";
InnerClass myclass;
myclass.innerFunction();
}
void OuterClass::InnerClass::innerFunction()
{
cout << "This is a function in the InnerClass class
\n";
}
```

```
void main()
{
OuterClass myclass;
myclass.outerFunction();
getch();
}
```

**OUTPUT:**

This is a function in the base class
This is a function in the InnerClass class

**Problem 25. Write a C++ program to creates two objects.**

***Program:***

```
#include <iostream.h>
#include<conio.h>
class ThreeDimension
{
public:
int X;
int Y;
int Z;
};
void main()
{
ThreeDimension aDimension;
ThreeDimension bDimension;
int range1, range2;
aDimension.X = 7;
aDimension.Y = 16;
aDimension.Z = 21;
bDimension.X = 2;
bDimension.Y = 14;
bDimension.Z = 12;
range1 = aDimension.Y * aDimension.Z;
range2 = bDimension.Y * bDimension.Z;
cout << range1 << "\n";
cout << range2;
getch();
}
```

**OUTPUT:**

336
168

**Problem 26. Write a C++ program for Object assignment.**

***Program:***

```
#include <iostream.h>
#include<conio.h>
class MyClass
{
int a, b;
public:
void setAB(int i, int j) { a = i, b = j; }
void display() {
cout << "\n a is " << a << '\n';
cout << "\n b is " << b << '\n';
}
};
void main()
{
MyClass ob1, ob2;
ob1.setAB(10, 20);
ob2.setAB(0, 0);
cout << "ob1 before assignment:";
ob1.display();
cout << "ob2 before assignment:";
ob2.display();
ob2 = ob1; // assign ob1 to ob2
cout << "ob1 after assignment:";
ob1.display();
cout << "ob2 after assignment:";
ob2.display();
ob1.setAB(-1, -1); // change ob1
cout << "ob1 after changing ob1:";
ob1.display();
cout << "ob2 after changing ob1:";
ob2.display();
getch();
}
```

**OUTPUT:**

ob1 before assignment:
a is 10
b is 20
ob2 before assignment:
a is 0
b is 0
ob1 after assignment:
a is 10
b is 20
ob2 after assignment:
a is 10
b is 20
ob1 after changing ob1:
a is -1
b is -1
ob2 after changing ob1:
a is 10
b is 20

**Problem 27. Write a C++ program to assign class object.**

***Program:***

```
#include <iostream.h>
#include<conio.h>
class Box
{
public:
double length;
double width;
double height;
double volume()
{
return length * width * height;
}
};
void main()
{
Box firstBox = { 80.0, 50.0, 40.0 };
Box secondBox = firstBox;
secondBox.length *= 1.1;
secondBox.width *= 1.1;
secondBox.height *= 1.1;
cout << secondBox.length
    << secondBox.width
    << secondBox.height
    << endl;
cout << "Volume of second Box object is " <<
secondBox.volume()
    << endl;
getch();
}
```

**OUTPUT:**

```
885544
Volume of second Box object is 212960
```

## CLASS ACCESS:

**Problem 28. Write a C++ program to show that you may change access specifications as often as you like within a class declaration.**

***Program:***

```
#include <iostream.h>
#include<conio.h>
#include <string.h>
class Person
{
char name[80];              // private by default
public:
void setName(char *n);        // these are public
void getName(char *n);
private:
double wage;                // now, private again
public:
void setWage(double w);       // back to public
double getWage();
};
void Person::setName(char *n)
{
strcpy(name, n);
}
void Person::getName(char *n)
{
strcpy(n, name);
}
void Person::setWage(double w)
{
wage = w;
}
double Person::getWage()
{
return wage;
}
void main()
{
Person ted;
char name[80];
ted.setName("Ted Jones");
ted.setWage(75000);
ted.getName(name);
cout << name << " makes $";
cout << ted.getWage() << " per year.";
getch();
}
```

**OUTPUT:**

```
Ted jones makes $75000 per year.
```

## CLASS BASICS:

**Problem 29. Write a C++ program for class forward declaration.**

***Program:***

```
#include <iostream.h>
#include<conio.h>
class pr2; //
class pr1
{
int printing;
public:
 pr1()
{
printing = 0;
}
```

```
void set_print(int status)
{
printing = status;
}
friend int inuse(pr1 object1, pr2 object2);
};
class pr2
{
int printing;
public:
 pr2()
{
printing = 0;
}
void set_print(int status)
{
printing = status;
}
friend int inuse(pr1 object1, pr2 object2);
};
int inuse(pr1 object1, pr2 object2)
{
if(object1.printing || object2.printing) return 1;
else return 0;
}
void  main()
{
pr1 p1;
pr2 p2;
if(!inuse(p1, p2))
cout << "Printer idle\n";
cout << "Setting p1 to printing...\n";
p1.set_print(1);
if(inuse(p1, p2))
cout << "Now, printer in use.\n";
cout << "Turn off p1...\n";
p1.set_print(0);
if(!inuse(p1, p2))
cout << "Printer idle\n";
cout << "Turn on p2...\n";
p2.set_print(1);
if(inuse(p1, p2))
cout << "Now, printer in use.\n";
getch();
}
```

**OUTPUT:**

Printer idle
Setting p1 to printing...
Now, printer in use.
Turn off p1...
Printer idle
Turnon p2...
Now, printer in use.

**Problem 30. Write a C++ program for address class: class definition and implementation.**

***Program:***

```
#include <iostream.h>
#include<conio.h>
#include <string.h>
class Address
{
char name[40];
char street[40];
char city[30];
char state[3];
char zip[10];
public:
void store(char *n, char *s, char *c, char *t, char
*z);
void display();
};
void Address::store(char *n, char *s, char *c, char
*t, char *z)
{
strcpy(name, n);
strcpy(street, s);
strcpy(city, c);
strcpy(state, t);
strcpy(zip, z);
}
void Address::display()
{
cout << name << endl;
cout << street << endl;
cout << city << endl;
cout << state << endl;
cout << zip << endl;
}
void  main()
{
Address a;
a.store("C", "11 Lane", "W", "In", "4");
a.display();
getch();
}
```

**OUTPUT:**

C
11 Lane
W
In
4

**Problem 31. Write a C++ program to declare class instance.**

***Program:***

```
#include <iostream.h>
#include<conio.h>
class myclass
{
int a;
public:
myclass(int x)
{
a = x;
}
int geta()
{
return a;
}
};
void main()
{
myclass ob(4);
cout << ob.geta();
getch();
}
```

**OUTPUT:**

```
4
```

**Problem 32. Write a C++ program to declare class instance and use them.**

***Program:***

```
#include <iostream.h>
#include<conio.h>
#include <string.h>
class Book
{
char title[80];           // book title
char author[40];          // author
int number;               // number in library
public:
void store(char *t, char *name, int num);
void show();
};
void Book::store(char *t, char *name, int num)
{
strcpy(title, t);
strcpy(author, name);
number = num;
}
void Book::show()
{
cout << "Title: " << title << endl;
cout << "Author: " << author << endl;
cout << "Number on hand: " << number << endl;
}
void  main()
{
Book book1, book2, book3;
book1.store("D", "t", 2);
book2.store("T", "v", 2);
book3.store("T", "e", 1);
book1.show();
book2.show();
book3.show();
getch();
}
```

**OUTPUT:**

```
Title: D
Author: t
Number on hand: 2
Title: T
Author: v
Number on hand: 2
Title: T
Author: e
Number on hand: 1
```

**Problem 33. Write a C++ program for private and public variables and methods.**

***Program:***

```
#include <iostream.h>
#include<conio.h>
#include <string.h>
class Person
{
 char name[80];           // private by default
public:
 void setName(char *n);
 void getName(char *n);
private:
 double wage;
public:
 void setWage(double w);
 double getWage();
};
void Person::setName(char *n)
{
 strcpy(name, n);
}
void Person::getName(char *n)
{
 strcpy(n, name);
```

```
}
void Person::setWage(double w)
{
 wage = w;
}
double Person::getWage()
{
 return wage;
}
void  main()
{
 Person ted;
 char name[80];
 ted.setName("Joe");
 ted.setWage(75000);
 ted.getName(name);
 cout << name << " makes $";
 cout << ted.getWage() << " per year.";
getch();
}
```

**OUTPUT:**

Joe makes $75000 per year.

**Problem 34. Write a C++ program to find area of rectangle.**

***Program:***

```
#include<iostream.h>
#include<conio.h>
class rectangle
{
private:
int m,n;
public:
void setdata(int u,int v)
{
m=u;
n=v;
}
void area()
{
int a=m*n;
cout<<"\nArea of rectangle="<<a;
}
};
void main()
{
clrscr();
rectangle f,s;
f.setdata(10,20);
cout<<"Rectangle first";
f.area();
s.setdata(20,40);
cout<<"\nRectangle second";
s.area();
getch();
}
```

**OUTPUT:**

Rectangle first
Area of rectangle=200
Rectangle second
Area of rectangle=800

**Problem 35. Write a C++ program by using member functions outside the body of class to find area of rectangle.**

***Program:***

```
#include<iostream.h>
#include<conio.h>
class rectangle
{
private:
int m,n;
public:
void setdata(int,int);
void area();
};
void rectangle::setdata(int u,int v)
{
m=u;
n=v;
}
void rectangle::area()
{
int a=m*n;
cout<<"\nArea of rectangle= "<<a;
}
void main()
{
clrscr();
rectangle f,s;
f.setdata(10,20);
cout<<"Rectangle first:";
f.area();
s.setdata(20,30);
cout<<"\nRectangle second:";
s.area();
getch();
}
```

**OUTPUT:**

Rectangle first
Area of rectangle=200
Rectangle second

Area of rectangle=800

**Problem 36. Write a C++ program with help of objects and classes to find circumference & area of circle.**

***Program:***

```
#include<iomanip.h>
#include<iostream.h>
#include<conio.h>
class circle
{
private:
double rad;
public:
void read();
void area();
void circum();
};
void circle::read()
{
cout<<"Enter radius of circle=";
cin>>rad;
}
void circle::area()
{
double a=3.1415*rad*rad;
cout<<"Area of circle="<<setprecision(2)<<a;
}
void circle::circum()
{
double c=2*3.1415*rad;
cout<<"\nCircumference of
circle="<<setprecision(2)<<c;
}
void main()
{
clrscr();
circle obj;
obj.read();
obj.area();
obj.circum();
getch();
}
```

**OUTPUT:**

Enter radius of circle=2.75
Area of circle=23.76
Circumference of circle=17.28

**Problem 37. Write a C++ program to using private member functions from class to find gross salary.**

***Program:***

```
#include<iomanip.h>
#include<iostream.h>
#include<conio.h>
class employee
{
private:
char ename[20];
double basic;
double dallow()
{
double da=0.5*basic;
return(da);
}
double hrallow()
{
double hra=0.15*basic;
return(hra);
}
public:
void read();
void sal();
};
void employee::read()
{
cout<<"Enter employee name=";
cin>>ename;
cout<<"\nEnter basic pay of employee=";
cin>>basic;
}
void employee::sal()
{
double gsal;
double da=dallow();
double hra=hrallow();
gsal=basic+da+hra;
cout<<"\nGross salary of the employee=
"<<setprecision(3)<<gsal;
}
void main()
{
clrscr();
employee e;
e.read();
e.sal();
getch();
}
```

**OUTPUT:**

Enter employee name=Akash
Enter basic pay of employee=3500
Gross salary of the employee=5775

**Problem 38. Write a C++ program to depict concept of abstraction , data hiding, encapsulation.**

***Program:***

```
#include<math.h>
#include<iostream.h>
#include<conio.h>
#include<process.h>
class quadratic
{
private:
double a,b,c;
public:
void read();
void funcroots();
};
void quadratic::read()
{
cout<<"Enter coffiecients of Quadratic Eq. a,b,c= ";
cin>>a>>b>>c;
}
void quadratic::funcroots()
{
if(a==0)
{
cout<<"\nEquations is not quadratic";
exit(0);
}
else
{
double disc;
disc=b*b-4*a*c;
if(disc<0)
cout<<"\nRoots are imaginary";
else if(disc==0)
{
double x=-b/(2*a);
cout<<"\nRoots are equal,x= "<<x;
}
else
{
double m,n,t;
t=sqrt(disc);
m=(-b+t)/(2*a);
n=(-b-t)/(2*a);
cout<<"\nRoots are real and unequal"<<endl;
cout<<"m= "<<m<<endl;
cout<<"n= "<<n;
}}}
voidmain()
{
clrscr();
quadratic q1;
q1.read();
q1.funcroots();
getch();
}
```

**OUTPUT:**

```
Enter coffiecients of Quadratic Eq. a,b,c=2 4 3
Roots are imaginary
```

**Problem 39. Write a C++ program for example: one class, two objects.**

***Program:***

```
#include <iostream.h>
#include<conio.h>
class CRectangle
{
  int x, y;
 public:
  void set_values (int,int);
  int area ()
  {
  return (x*y);
  }
};
void CRectangle::set_values (int a, int b)
{
 x = a;
 y = b;
}
void main ()
{
 CRectangle rect, rectb;
 rect.set_values (3,4);
 rectb.set_values (5,6);
 cout << "rect area: " << rect.area() << endl;
 cout << "rectb area: " << rectb.area() << endl;
 getch();
}
```

**OUTPUT:**

```
rect area: 12
rectb area: 30
```

**Problem 40. Write a C++ program for various bank accounts using objects.**

***Program:***

```
#include<iostream.h>
#include<conio.h>
class account
{
private:
```

```
int no;
char nm[15];
double bal;
public:
void readdata();
void show();
};
void account::readdata()
{
cout<<"\nEnter account number,name,balance =";
cin>>no>>nm>>bal;
}
void account::show()
{
cout<<"\nAccount number =\t"<<no;
cout<<"\nAccount holder name =\t"<<nm;
cout<<"\nAccount balance =\t"<<bal;
}
void main()
{
clrscr();
account a[10];
int n;
cout<<"\nEnter number of account holders= ";
cin>>n;
for(int i=0;i<n;i++)
{
a[i].readdata();
}
for(i=0;i<n;i++)
{
cout<<"\nInformation of account= "<<i+1;
a[i].show();
}
getch();
}
```

**OUTPUT:**

```
Enter number of account holders=2
Enter account number,name,balance =501 aman
5000
Enter account number,name,balance =502 navtej
7500
Information of account=1
Account number =501
Account holder name =aman
Account balance =5000
Information of account=2
Account number =502
Account holder name =navtej
Account balance =7500
```

**Problem 41. Write a C++ program to depict passing of objects by its value.**

***Program:***

```
#include<iostream.h>
#include<conio.h>
class time
{
private:
int h,m;
public:
void readt();
void addt(time,time);
void showt();
};
void time::readt()
{
cout<<"\nEnter time in hours and minutes";
cin>>h>>m;
}
void time::addt(time u1,time u2)
{
int min=u1.m+u2.m;
int hrs=min/60;
m=min%60;
h=hrs+u1.h+u2.h;
}
void time::showt()
{
cout<<"\nTime obtained on adding= ";
cout<<h<<":"<<m;
}
void  main()
{
clrscr();
time ob1,ob2,ob3;
ob1.readt();
ob2.readt();
ob3.addt(ob1,ob2);
ob3.showt();
getch();
}
```

**OUTPUT:**

```
Enter time in hours and minutes 12 20
Enter time in hours and minutes 9 00
Time obtained on adding=21:20
```

**Problem 42. Write a C++ program to depict passing of objects by reference.**

***Program:***

```
#include<iostream.h>
#include<conio.h>
```

```
class ac
{
private:
int no; float bal;
public:
void read();
void show();
void tmoney(ac &,double);
};
void ac::read()
{
cout<<"Enter the account number= ";
cin>>no;
cout<<"Enter the balance= ";
cin>>bal;
}
void ac::show()
{
cout<<"\nAccount number is= "<<no;
cout<<"\nBalance is= "<<bal;
}
void main()
{
clrscr();
ac h1,h2;
cout<<"Enter account details of account first\n";
h1.read();
cout<<"Enter account details of account second\n";
h2.read();
cout<<"\nShowing account details before
transfer\n";
h1.show();
h2.show();
double trans;
cout<<"\nEnter amount to transfer from account first
to account second= ";
cin>>trans;
h1.tmoney(h2,trans);
cout<<"Showing account details after transfer of
money ";
h1.show();
ht2.show();
getch();
}
```

**OUTPUT:**

```
Enter account details of account first
Enter the account number=501
Enter the balance=7000
Enter account details of account second
Enter the account number=502
Enter the balance=3000
Showing account details before transfer
Account number is=501
Balance is=7000
Account number is=502
Balance is=3000
Enter amount to transfer from account first to
account second=500
Showing account details after transfer of money
Account number is=501
Balance is=6500
Account number is=502
Balance is=3500
```

**Problem 43. Write a C++ program to depict matrix addition by returning an object.**

***Program:***

```
#include<iostream.h>
#include<conio.h>
#include<process.h>
class mat
{
private:
int x[10][10],u,v;
public:
void read();
mat add(mat);
void disp();
};
void mat::read()
{
cout<<"Enter order of u*v matrix";
cin>>u>>v;
cout<<"Enter elements:";
for(int i=0;i<u;i++)
for(int j=0;j<v;j++)
cin>>x[i][j];
}
void mat::disp()
{
for(int i=0;i<u;i++)
{
for(int j=0;j<v;j++)
cout<<x[i][j]<<'\t';
cout<<endl;
}}
mat mat::add(mat uu2)
{
if((u!=uu2.u)||(v!=uu2.v))
{
cout<<"Matrix addition not possible";
exit(0);
```

```
}
else
{
mat temp;
temp.u=uu2.u; temp.v=uu2.v;
for(int i=0;i<u;i++)
{
for(int j=0;j<v;j++)
temp.x[i][j]=x[i][j]+uu2.x[i][j];
}
return (temp);
}}
void  main()
{
mat u1,u2,u3;
u1.read();
u2.read();
u3=u1.add(u2);
cout<<"On addition we get\n";
u3.disp();
getch();
}
```

**OUTPUT:**

```
Enter order of u*v matrix 2 2
Enter elements:1 3 5 7
Enter order of u*v matrix2 2
Enter elements:2 4 6 8
On addition we get
3   7
11   15
```

**Problem 44. Write a C++ program to find average percentage of marks.**

***Program:***

```
#include<iostream.h>
#include<conio.h>
class student
{
private:
int roll,marks;
static int tm;
public:
void read()
{
cout<<"Enter rollno & marks: ";
cin>>roll>>marks;
}
void funcal()
{
tm+=marks;
}
static void avgp(int n1)
{
double avg=double(tm)/n1;
cout<<"Average % of marks is= "<<avg;
}
};
int student::tm;
void main()
{
clrscr();
student t[50];
int n;
cout<<"Enter number of students:";
cin>>n;
for(int i=0;i<n;i++)
{
t[i].read();
t[i].funcal();
}
student::avgp(n);
getch();
}
```

**OUTPUT:**

```
Enter number of students:2
Enter rollno & marks:45 60
Enter rollno & marks:47 80
Average % of marks is=70
```

**Problem 45. Write a C++ program to using objects to perform all operations on complex numbers.**

***Program:***

```
#include<iostream.h>
#include<conio.h>
#include<iomanip.h>
class complex
{
private:
float real,imag;
public:
void read()
{
cout<<"Enter real & imaginary part of number";
cin>>real>>imag;
}
void show()
{
if(imag>0)
cout<<real<<"+"<<imag<<"i"<<endl;
else
cout<<real<<imag<<"i"<<endl;
```

```
}
void add(complex x1,complex x2)
{
real=x1.real+x2.real;
imag=x1.imag+x2.imag;
}
void subtract(complex x1,complex x2)
{
real=x1.real-x2.real;
imag=x1.imag-x2.imag;
}
void multiply(complex x1,complex x2)
{
real=(x1.real*x2.real)-(x1.imag*x2.imag);
imag=(x1.real*x2.imag)+(x1.imag*x2.real);
}
void divide(complex x1,complex x2)
{
float den=x2.real*x2.real+x2.imag*x2.imag;
real=(x1.real*x2.real+x1.imag*x2.imag);
imag=x1.imag*x2.real-x1.real*x2.imag;
}
};
void main()
{
clrscr();
complex com1,com2,com3;
com1.read();
com2.read();
int c;
do
{
cout<<"\nDifferent operations are"<<endl;
cout<<"1.Add"<<endl;
cout<<"2.Subtract"<<endl;
cout<<"3.Multiply"<<endl;
cout<<"4.Divide"<<endl;
cout<<"5.Quit"<<endl;
cout<<"Enter choice"<<endl;
cin>>c;
switch(c)
{
case 1:com3.add(com1,com2); com3.show(); break;
case 2:com3.subtract(com1,com2); com3.show();
break;
case 3:com3.multiply(com1,com2); com3.show();
break;
case 4:com3.divide(com1,com2); com3.show();
break;
case 5:cout<<"Exiting from program";break;
default:cout<<"Invalid choice,try again"<<endl;
}
}
while(c!=5);
getch();
}
```

**Problem 46. Write a C++ program by returning objects for addition of distances.**

***Program:***

```
#include<iostream.h>
#include<conio.h>
class dist
private:
int feet;
double inches;
public:
void get()
{
cout<<"Enter feet & inches";
cint>>feet>>inches;
}
void show()
{
cout<<"Addition"<<feet<<"\'-"<<inches<<"\"";
}
dist add(dist);
};
dist dist::add(dist h2)
{
dist tt;
tt.feet=feet+h2.feet;
tt.inches=inches+h2.inches;
if(tt.inches>=12.00)
{
tt.feet++;
tt.inches-=12.00;
}
return(tt);
}
void main()
{
clrscr();
dist obj1,obj2,obj3;
obj1.get();
obj2.get();
obj3=obj1.add(obj2);
obj3.show();
getch();
}
```

**OUTPUT:**

Enter feet & inches 6 3.0

Addition 9.0

**Problem 47. Write a C++ program to find result of class and sort them on basis of percentage using array of objects.**

***Program:***

```
#include<iostream.h>
#include<conio.h>
class stud
{
private:
int r;
char name[20];
int marks[5],tm;
double per;
public:
void get();
void put();
void funcal();
void sort(stud &,stud &);
};
void stud::get()
{
cout<<"Enter rollno and name:";
cin>>r>>name;
cout<<"Enter marks of students:";
for(int j=0;j<5;j++)
cin>>marks[j];
}
void stud::funcal()
{
tm=0;
for(int j=0;j<5;j++)
tm+=marks[j];
per=double(tm)/5;
}
void stud::sort(stud &s1,stud &s2)
{
stud temp;
if(s1.per<s2.per)
{
temp=s1;
s1=s2;
s2=temp;
}
}
void stud::put()
{
cout<<"\nName of student:"<<name;
cout<<"\nTotal marks:"<<tm;
cout<<"\nPercentage:"<<per;
}
void main()
{
stud u[40],t;
int n;
cout<<"Enter no. of objects:";
cin>>n;
for(int i=0;i<n;i++)
{
u[i].get();
u[i].funcal();
}
for(i=0;i<n-1;i++)
for(int j=i+1;j<n;j++)
t.sort(u[i],u[j]);
cout<<"Sorting objects are\n";
for(i=0;i<n;i++)
u[i].put();
getch();
}
```

**OUTPUT:**

```
Enter no. of objects:2
Enter rollno and name:41 Mani
Enter marks of students:42 52 12 36 52
Enter rollno and name:34 Aman
Enter marks of students:52 68 41 23 51
Sorting objects are
Name of student:Aman
Total marks:235
Percentage:47
Name of student:Mani
Total marks:194
Percentage:39
```

**Problem 48. Write a C++ program to find electricity bill of a person.**

***Program:***

| unit | tarrif |
|---|---|
| >100 | Rs.1.20 per unit |
| >200 | Rs.2 per unit |
| >300 | Rs.3 per unit |

```
#include<iostream.h>
#include<conio.h>
class ebill
{
private:
int cno;
char cname[20];
int units;
double bill;
public:
```

```
void get()
{
cout<<"Enter custno,name and no. of units";
cin>>cno>>cname>>units;
}
void put()
{
cout<<"\nCustomer no is"<<cno;
cout<<"\nCustomer name  is"<<cname;
cout<<"\nNumber of units consumed"<<units;
cout<<"\nBill of Customer"<<bill;
}
void calc()
{
if(units<=100)
bill=units*1.20;
else if(units<=300)
bill=100*1.20+(units-100)*2;
else
bill=100*1.20+200*2+(units-300)*3;
}
};
void main()
{
ebill p1;
p1.get();
p1.calc();
p1.put();
getch();
}
```

**OUTPUT:**

```
Enter custno,name and no. of units 4 navtej 200
Customer no is 4
Customer name  is navtej
Number of units consumed 200
Bill of Customer 320
```

**Problem 49. Write a C++ program for adding rational numbers & display OUTPUT as numerator/denominator.**

***Program:***

```
#include<iostream.h>
#include<conio.h>
class rational
{
private:
int n,d;
public:
void set(int a,int a1)
{
n=a;
d=a1;
}
void put() const
{
cout<<"Sum:";
cout<<n<<"/"<<d;
}
void add(rational u1, rational u2)
{
n=u1.n*u2.d+u2.n*u1.d;
d=u1.d*u2.d;
}
};
void main()
{
rational obj1,obj2,obj3;
obj1.set(15,5);
obj2.set(3,5);
obj3.add(obj1,obj2);
obj3.put();
getch();
}
```

**OUTPUT:**

```
Sum:90/25
```

**Problem 50. Write a C++ program to enter time & display as(12:22:30).**

***Program:***

```
#include<iostream.h>
#include<conio.h>
#include<process.h>
class time
{
private:
int hh,min,sec;
void sethour(int h)
{
if(h<=24)
hh=h;
else
{cout<<"\nInvalid hour";
getch();
exit(0);
}
}
void setmin(int m)
{
if(m<=60)
min=m;
else
{cout<<"\nInvalid minute";
```

```
getch();
exit(0);
}
}
void setsec(int s)
{
if(s<=24)
sec=s;
else
{cout<<"\nInvalid second";
getch();
exit(0);
}
}
public:
void gettime()
{
int h,m,s;
cout<<"Enter time";
cin>>h>>m>>s;
sethour(h);
setmin(m);
setsec(s);
}
void puttime()
{
cout<<"\nTime entered is ";
cout<<hh<<":"<<min<<":"<<sec;
}};
void main()
{
time ob;
ob.gettime();
ob.puttime();
getch();
}
```

**OUTPUT:**

```
Enter time 12 20 14
Time entered is 12:20:14
```

## OBJECT ARRAY:

**Problem 51. Write a C++ program to create an array of objects.**

***Program:***

```
#include <iostream.h>
#include<conio.h>
class MyClass {
int x;
public:
void setX(int i) { x = i; }
int getX() { return x; }
};
void main()
{
MyClass obs[4];
int i;
for(i=0; i < 4; i++)
obs[i].setX(i);
for(i=0; i < 4; i++)
cout << "obs[" << i << "].getX(): " <<
obs[i].getX() << "\n";
getch();
}
```

**OUTPUT:**

```
obs[0].getX(): 0
obs[1].getX(): 1
obs[2].getX(): 2
obs[3].getX(): 3
```

## OBJECT POINTER:

**Problem 52. Write a C++ program for using class pointer and class array together.**

***Program:***

```
#include <iostream.h>
#include<conio.h>
class MyClass
{
private:
int Price;
int Count;
long Total;
public:
void Input(int P,int C)
{
Price=P;
Count=C;
}
void MyClass::Compute()
{
Total=(long) Price*Count;
}
void MyClass::Print(){
cout<<"Price="<<Price<<"  Count="<<Count <<"
Total="<<Total<<"\n";
}
};
void main()
{
```

```
MyClass  *ob;
ob=new MyClass[6];
ob[0].Input(5,0);
ob[1].Input(3,5);
ob[2].Input(1,0);
ob[3].Input(5,20);
ob[4].Input(4,0);
ob[5].Input(8,5);
for(int i=0;i<6;i++)
ob[i].Compute();
for(int i=0;i<6;i++)
ob[i].Print();
delete ob;
getch();
}
```

**OUTPUT:**

```
Price=5  Count=0   Total=0
Price=3  Count=5   Total=15
Price=1  Count=0   Total=0
Price=5  Count=20   Total=100
Price=4  Count=0   Total=0
Price=8  Count=5   Total=40
```

**Problem 53. Write a C++ program to incrementing and decrementing an object pointer.**

***Program:***

```
#include<iostream.h>
#include<conio.h>
class MyClass
{
int x;
public:
void setX(int val) { x = val; }
void display(){ cout << x << "\n"; }
};
void main()
{
MyClass ob[2], *p;
ob[0].setX(10);  // access objects directly
ob[1].setX(20);
p = &ob[0];      // obtain pointer to first element
p->display();    // show value of ob[0] using pointer
p++;             // advance to next object
p->display();    // show value of ob[1] using pointer
p--;             // retreat to previous object
p->display();    // again show value of ob[0]
getch();
}
```

**OUTPUT:**

```
10
20
10
```

**Problem 54. Write a C++ program for use new to allocate memory for a class pointer.**

***Program:***

```
#include <iostream.h>
#include<conio.h>
#include<string.h>
class phone
{
char name[50];
char tell[15];
public:
void store(char *n,char *num);
void print();
};
void phone::store(char *n,char *num)
{
strcpy(name,n);
strcpy(tell,num);
}
void phone::print()
{
cout<<name<<":"<<tell;
cout<<"\n";
}
void main()
{
phone *p;
p=new phone;
if(!p)
{
cout<<"Alloction error.";
return 1;
}
p->store("AA","9999999999");
p->print();
delete p;
getch();
}
```

**OUTPUT:**

```
AA:9999999999
```

## POINTERS TO CLASSES:

**Problem 55. Write a C++ program for pointer to classes example.**

***Program:***

```
#include <iostream.h>
```

```
#include<conio.h>
class CRectangle
{
int width, height;
public:
void set_values (int, int);
int area (void)
{
return (width * height);
}
};
void CRectangle::set_values (int a, int b)
{
width = a;
height = b;
}
void main ()
{
CRectangle a, *b, *c;
CRectangle * d = new CRectangle[2];
b= new CRectangle;
c= &a;
a.set_values (1,2);
b->set_values (3,4);
d->set_values (5,6);
d[1].set_values (7,8);
cout << "a area: " << a.area() << endl;
cout << "*b area: " << b->area() << endl;
cout << "*c area: " << c->area() << endl;
cout << "d[0] area: " << d[0].area() << endl;
cout << "d[1] area: " << d[1].area() << endl;
delete[] d;
delete b;
getch();
}
```

**OUTPUT:**

```
a area: 2
*b area: 12
*c area: 2
d[0] area: 30
d[1] area: 56
```

**Problem 56. Write a C++ program to define class employee.**

***Program:***

```
#include<iostream.h>
#include<conio.h>
#include<string.h>
class employee
{
char name [80 ];//private by default
public:
void putn(char *n);//these are public
void getn(char *n);
private:
double wage;
public:
void putw(double w);
double getw();
};
void employee::putn(char *n)
{
strcpy(name,n);
}
void employee::getn(char *n)
{
strcpy(n,name);
}
void employee::putw(double w)
{
wage =w;
}
double employee::getw()
{
return wage;
}
void main()
{
employee emp;
char name [80];
emp.putn("Mani");
emp.putw(25000);
emp.getn(name);
cout <<name <<" makes $";
cout <<emp.getw()<<" per year.";
getch();
}
```

**OUTPUT:**

```
Mani makes $25000 per year.
```

**Problem 57. Write a C++ program using a structure to define a class.**

***Program:***

```
#include <iostream.h>
#include<conio.h>
#include <string.h>
struct StringStructClass {
void initString(char *s); // public
void displayString();
private:            // private
char str[255];
} ;
void StringStructClass::initString(char *s)
```

```
{
if(!*s)
*str = '\0'; // initialize string
else
strcat(str, s);
}
void StringStructClass::displayString()
{
cout << str << endl;
}
void main()
{
StringStructClass stringObject;
stringObject.initString("");
stringObject.initString("Hello ");
stringObject.initString("there!");
stringObject.displayString();
getch();
}
```

**OUTPUT:**

Hello there!

union class

**Problem 58. Write a C++ program using union to define class.**

***Program:***

```
#include <iostream.h>
#include<conio.h>
union bits {
bits(double n);
void show_bits();
double d;
unsigned char c[sizeof(double)];
};
bits::bits(double n)
{
d = n;
}
void bits::show_bits()
{
int i, j;
for(j = sizeof(double)-1; j>=0; j--) {
cout << "Bit pattern in byte " << j << ": ";
for(i = 128; i; i >>= 1)
if(i & c[j]) cout << "1";
else cout << "0";
cout << endl;
}
}
void main()
{
bits ob(1991.829);
ob.show_bits();
getch();
}
```

**OUTPUT:**

Bit pattern in byte 7: 01000000
Bit pattern in byte 6: 10011111
Bit pattern in byte 5: 00011111
Bit pattern in byte 4: 01010000
Bit pattern in byte 3: 11100101
Bit pattern in byte 2: 01100000
Bit pattern in byte 1: 01000001
Bit pattern in byte 0: 10001001

**Problem 59. Write a C++ program How: Structures and Classes Are Related.**

***Program:***

```
#include <iostream.h>
#include <string.h>
#include<conio.h>
struct str
{
void dstr(char *s);
void showstr();
private:
char str [255];
};
void str::dstr(char *s)
{
if(!*s)*str ='\0';
else strcat(str,s);
}
void str::showstr()
{
cout <<str <<"\n";
}
void main()
{
str s;
s.dstr("");
s.dstr("Hello");
s.dstr("there!");
s.showstr();
getch();
}
```

**OUTPUT:**

Hello there!.

**Problem 60. Write a C++ program How: Unions and Classes Are Related.**

***Program:***

```
#include <iostream.h>
#include<conio.h>
union chng_byte
{
void chng();
void set_byte(unsigned short i);
void show_word();
unsigned short u;
unsigned char c [2];
};
void chng_byte::chng()
{
unsigned char t;
t=c[0];
c[0]==c[1 ];
c[1]==t;
}
void chng_byte::show_word()
{
cout <<u;
}
void chng_byte::set_byte(unsigned short i)
{
u =i;
}
void main()
{
chng_byte s;
s.set_byte(49034);
s.chng();
s.show_word();
getch();
}
```

**OUTPUT:**

49034

**Problem 61. Write a C++ program to read and display student data to illustrate the concept of classes.**

***Program:***

```
// Program to illustrate the use of classes in C++.
#include<iostream.h>
#include<conio.h>
class student
{
private:
int rno;
char name[20];
public:
void getdata()
{
cout<<"Enter the roll no. and name of the
student:"<<endl;
cin>>rno>>name;
}
void showdata()
{
cout<<"Roll No.:"<<'\t'<<rno<<endl;
cout<<"Name is:"<<'\t'<<name<<endl;
}
};
void main()
{
student s;
s.getdata();
s.showdata();
getch();
}
```

**OUTPUT:**

Enter the roll no. and name of the student:
122
Mona
Roll No.: 122
Name is: Mona

**Problem 62. Write a C++ program to find the factorial by Class.**

***Program:***

```
#include<iostream.h>
#include<conio.h>
#include <stdio.h>
#include <math.h>
class A
{
int n;
public:
void input();
void fact();
}z;
void A::input()
{
cout<<"Enter the number→";
cin>>n;
}
void A::fact()
{
long f=1;
for(int i=1;i<=n;i++)
f*=i;
cout<<"Factorial is-→"<<f;
}
void main()
```

```
{
clrscr();
z.input();
z.fact();
getch();
}
```

**OUTPUT:**

Enter the number→ 5
Factorial is-→ 120

**Problem 63. Write a C++ program to perform Arithmetic operations on Class.**

***Program:***

```
#include<iostream.h>
#include<conio.h>
class A
{
int a,b;
public:
void input()
{
cout<<"Enter value of a and b:";
cin>>a>>b;
}
void operate()
{
cout<<"\nSum is :"<<a+b;
cout<<"\nDifference is :"<<a-b;
cout<<"\nProduct is : "<<a*b;
cout<<"\nQoutient is : "<<float(a)/b;
cout<<"\nRemainder is :"<<a%b;
}
}z;
void main()
{
clrscr();
z.input();
z.operate();
getch();
}
```

**OUTPUT:**

Enter value of a and b:" 30 10
Sum is : 40
Difference is : 20
Product is : 300
Qoutient is : 3
Remainder is : 0

**Problem 64. Write a C++ program to enter and display student data by using Class.**

***Program:***

```
#include<iostream.h>
#include<conio.h>
#include<iomanip.h>
class a
{
char name[20],clas[20];
public:
void input()
{
cout<<"Enter name & class :";
cin>>name>>clas;
}
void print()
{
cout<<name<<"\t"<<clas;
}
}a[50];
class b
{
int roll,age;
public:
void input()
{
cout<<"Enter roll number & age==>",
cin>>roll>>age;
}
void print()
{
cout<<"\t"<<roll<<"\t"<<age;
}
}b[50];
void main()
{
int i,n;
clrscr();
cout<<"Enter number of students→";
cin>>n;
cout<<"Enter the information→";
for(i=0;i<n;i++)
{
a[i].input();
b[i].input();
}
cout<<"\n\nDatabase is==>\n";
for(i=0;i<n;i++)
{
a[i].print();
b[i].print();
cout<<"\n";
}
getch();
```

```
}
```

**OUTPUT:**

```
Enter number of students→2
Enter the information→
Enter name & class : Mona    BCA-I
Enter roll number & age==> 102     20
Enter name & class : Geeta   BCA-I
Enter roll number & age==> 103     19
Database is==>
Mona     BCA-I
    102       20
Geeta     BCA-I
    103       19
```

**Problem 65. Write a C++ program to check whether number is Prime or not by using Class.**

***Program:***

```
#include<iostream.h>
#include<conio.h>
class A
{
int n;
public:
A(int c)
{
n=c;
}
void print();
};
void A::print()
{
int i;
if(n==1)
{
cout<<"Not Prime";
return;
}
for(i=2;i<=n/2;i++)
if(n%i==0)
{
cout<<"Not Prime";
return;
}
cout<<"Number is Prime.";
}
void main()
{
int n;
clrscr();
cout<<"Enter number: ";
cin>>n;
A a(n);
a.print();
getch();
}
```

**OUTPUT:**

```
Enter number: 44
Not Prime
```

**Problem 66. Write a C++ program to display all Prime number upto N.**

***Program:***

```
#include<iostream.h>
#include<conio.h>
class prime
{
int n;
public:
prime(int p)
{
n=p;
}
void print();
};
void prime::print()
{
int j;
for(int i=2;i<=n;i++)
{
for(j=2;j<=i/2;j++)
if(i%j==0)
goto again;
cout<<i<<" ";
again:
}
}
void main()
{
int n;
clrscr();
cout<<"Enter the number upto which prime
numbers are to be printed==>";
cin>>n;
cout<<"Series is==>";
prime p(n);
p.print();
getch();
}
```

**OUTPUT:**

```
Enter the number upto which prime numbers are to
be printed==> 20
Series is==>2  3  5  7  11  13  17 19
```

**Problem 67. Write a C++ program to find whether a year is leap year or not.**

***Program:***

```
#include<iostream.h>
#include<conio.h>
class A
{
int y;
public:
A(int p)
{
y=p;
}
void print()
{
if(y%400==0 || (y%4==0 && y%100!=0) )
cout<<"Leap year.";
else
cout<<"Not leap year.";
}
};
void main()
{
clrscr();
int y;
cout<<"Enter the year==>";
cin>>y;
A a(y);
a.print();
getch();
}
```

**OUTPUT:**

Enter the year==> 1991
Not leap year.

**68. Write a C++ program to add two matrices to explain the concept of array within the class.**

***Program:***

```
#include<iostream.h>
#include<conio.h>
class mat
{
int x[10][10], y[10][10], m, n, i, j;
public:
void readmat( )
{
cout<<"\n Enter number of rows and columns of a matrix:"<<endl;
cin>>n>>m;
cout<<"\n Enter the elements of Matrix X:"<<endl;
for(i=0;i<n;i++)
{
for(j=0;j<m;j++)
{
cin>>x[i][j];
}
}
cout<<"\n Enter the elements of Matrix Y:"<<endl;
for(i=0;i<n;i++)
{
for(j=0;j<m;j++)
{
cin>>y[i][j];
}
}
}
void addmat( )
{
int add[10][10];
for(i=0;i<n;i++)
{
for(j=0;j<m;j++)
{
add[i][j]=x[i][j]+y[i][j];
}}}
void dispadd( )
{
int add[10][10];
cout<<"\n Addition of two Matrix is:"<<endl;
for(i=0;i<n;i++)
{
for(j=0;j<m;j++)
{
cout<<add[i][j];
cout<<endl;
}}
};
void main()
{
mat obj;
clrscr( );
obj.readmat();
obj.addmat();
obj.dispadd();
getch();
}
```

**Problem 69. Write a C++ program to illustrates the use of a public variable.**

***Program:***

```
#include <iostream.h>
#include<conio.h>
class myclass {
public:
int i, j, k; // accessible to entire program
};
void  main()
{
myclass a, b;
a.i = 100;
a.j = 4;
a.k = a.i * a.j;
b.k = 12;
cout << a.k << " " << b.k;
getch();
}
```

**OUTPUT:**

400 12

# CHAPTER 11

# CONSTRUCTORS AND DESTRUCTORS

## CONSTRUCTOR:

**Problem 1. Write a C++ program which automatically converted into MyClass(4): MyClass ob = 4;**

***Program:***

```
#include <iostream.h>
#include<conio.h>
class MyClass
{
int a;
public:
MyClass(int x) { a = x; }
int geta() { return a; }
};
void main()
{
MyClass ob = 4; // automatically converted into
MyClass(4)
cout << ob.geta();
getch();
}
```

**OUTPUT:**

4

**Problem 2. Write a C++ program for MyClass ob(4).**

***Program:***

```
#include <iostream.h>
#include<conio.h>
class MyClass
{
int a;
public:
MyClass(int x) { a = x; }
int geta() { return a; }
};
void main()
{
MyClass ob(4);
cout << ob.geta();
getch();
}
```

**OUTPUT:**

4

**Problem 3. Write a C++ program for MyClass ob = MyClass(4).**

***Program:***

```
#include <iostream.h>
#include<conio.h>
class MyClass
{
int a;
public:
MyClass(int x) { a = x; }
int geta() { return a; }
};
void main()
{
MyClass ob = MyClass(4);
cout << ob.geta();
getch();
}
```

**OUTPUT:**

4

## INSTANCE:

**Problem 5. Write a C++ program to declare the instance variable for a class.**

***Program:***

```
#include <iostream.h>
#include<conio.h>
class Power
{
double b;
int e;
double val;
public:
```

```
Power(double base, int exp);
double getPower()
{
return val;
}
};
Power::Power(double base, int exp)
{
b = base;
e = exp;
val = 1;
if(exp == 0)
return;
for( ; exp > 0; exp--)
val = val * b;
}
void main()
{
Power x(4.0, 2), y(2.5, 1), z(5.7, 0);
cout << x.getPower() << " ";
cout << y.getPower() << " ";
cout << z.getPower() << endl;
getch();
}
```

**OUTPUT:**

16 2.

**Problem 6. Write a C++ program to read rollno and fees to illustrate the concept of Default constructor with default argument.**

***Program:***

```
#include <iostream.h>
#include<conio.h>
class abc
{
private :
int rn ;
float fees ;
public :
abc (int a=20, float b=1200.25); // default
constructor with argument
void write (void)
{
cout<<rn;
cout<<fees;
}
} ;
abc :: abc (int a, float b)
{
rn = a ;
fees = b ;
}
void main ( )
{
class abc m1 (32) ;
m1.write ( ) ;
abc m2 (54, 320.23)
m2.write ( ) ;
getch();
}
```

**Problem 7. Write a C++ program to assign values to illustrate the parameterized constructor.**

***Program:***

```
#include <iostream.h>
#include<conio.h>
class abc
{
private :
int a ;
float b ;
public :
abc (int x, float y)
{
a = x ;
b = y ;
}
void write (void)
{
cout << a << b ;
}
} ;
void main ( )
{
abc m1 (20, 3.2) ;
m1.write ( )
abc (25, 3.4).write ( ) ; // Data value of a
temporary abc
getch();                  // instance is
printed.
}
```

**Problem 8. Write a C++ program for constructor parameter with default value.**

***Program:***

```
#include <iostream.h>
#include<conio.h>
#include <iomanip.h>
class MyClass
{
public:
```

```
MyClass(int a = 1, int b = 2, int c = 3)
{
MyClass::a = a;
MyClass::b = b;
MyClass::c = c;
};
void show_numbers(void)
{
cout << a << ' ' << b << ' '<< c << '\n';
};
private:
int a, b, c;
};
void main(void)
{
MyClass one(1, 1, 1);
MyClass defaults;
MyClass happy(101, 101, 101);
one.show_numbers();
defaults.show_numbers();
happy.show_numbers();
getch();
}
```

**OUTPUT:**

```
1 1 1
1 2 3
101 101 101
```

**Problem 9. Write a C++ program for the default constructor for class time is one that takes no arguments.**

***Program:***

```
#include <iostream.h>
#include<conio.h>
class Time
{
int hh,mm,ss;
public:
//Time(){hh=0;mm=0;ss=0;}
void Set(int h, int m, int s) {hh = h; mm = m;
ss=s;}
void Disp();
};
void Time::Disp()
{
cout << "The time is " << hh << ":" << mm << ":"
<< ss <<endl;
}
void main()
{
Time t1;
t1.Disp();
t1.Set(2,22,22);
t1.Disp();
getch();
}
```

**OUTPUT:**

```
The time is 1216:0:7717
The time is 2:22:22
```

# CLASS MEMBER:

**Problem 10. Write a C++ program for the Member Initialization Syntax.**

***Program:***

```
#include <iostream.h>
#include<conio.h>
class MyClass
{
int numA;
int numB;
public:
MyClass(int x, int y)
{
numA = x;
numB = y;
}
int getNumA()
{
return numA;
}
int getNumB()
{
return numB;
}
};
void main()
{
MyClass object1(7, 9), object2(5, 2);
cout << "Values in object1 are " <<
object1.getNumB() << " and " <<
object1.getNumA() << endl;
cout << "Values in object2 are " <<
object2.getNumB() << " and " <<
object2.getNumA() << endl;
getch();
}
```

**OUTPUT:**

```
Values in object1 are 9 7
Values in object2 are 2 5
```

**Problem 11. Write a C++ program to assign values using the member initialization syntax.**

***Program:***

```
#include <iostream.h>
#include<conio.h>
class MyClass
{
const int numA; // const member
const int numB; // const member
public:
// Initialize numA and numB using initialization
syntax.
MyClass(int x, int y) : numA(x), numB(y) { }
int getNumA()
{
return numA;
}
int getNumB()
{
return numB;
}
};
void main()
{
MyClass object1(7, 9), object2(5, 2);
cout << "Values in object1 are " <<
object1.getNumB() << " and " <<
object1.getNumA() << endl;
cout << "Values in object2 are " <<
object2.getNumB() << " and " <<
object2.getNumA() << endl;
getch();
}
```

**OUTPUT:**

```
Values in object1 are 9 7
Values in object2 are 2 5
```

## PARAMETERIZED CONSTRUCTORS:

**Problem 12. Write a C++ program for parameterized Constructors myclass.**

***Program:***

```
#include <iostream.h>
#include<conio.h>
class myclass
{
int a, b;
public:
myclass(int i, int j)
{
a=i;
b=j;
}
void show()
{
cout << a << " " << b;
}
};
void  main()
{
myclass ob(3, 5);
ob.show();
getch();
}
```

**OUTPUT:**

```
3 5
```

**Problem 13. Write a C++ program to define parameterized Constructors .**

***Program:***

```
#include <iostream.h>
#include<conio.h>
class A
{
int a,b;
public:
A(int i,int j)
{
a=i;
b=j;
}
void show()
{
cout <<a <<" "<<b;
}
};
void main()
{
A aa(5,8);
aa.show();
getch();
}
```

**OUTPUT:**

```
5 8
```

**Problem 14. Write a C++ program to implement class book using constructor.**

***Program:***

```
#include <iostream.h>
#include <string.h>
```

```
#include<conio.h>
const int IN =1;
const int OUT =0;
class book
{
char author [40 ];
char title [40 ];
int status;
public:
book(char *n,char *t,int s);
int get_status()
{
return status;
}
void set_status(int s)
{
status =s;
}
void show();
};
book::book(char *n,char *t,int s)
{
strcpy(author,n);
strcpy(title,t);
status =s;
}
void book::show()
{
cout <<title <<"by "<<author;
cout <<"is ";
if(status==IN)cout <<"in.\n";
else cout <<"out.\n";
}
void main()
{
book b1("Prof.Rachhpal Singh ","programming in
C",IN);
book b2("Prof.Sharma ","programming in C",OUT);
b1.show();
b2.show();
getch();
}
```

**OUTPUT:**

programming in C by Prof.Rachhpal Singh is in.
programming in C by Prof.Sharma is out.

**Problem 15. Write a C++ program for constructors with One Parameter:A Special Case.**

***Program:***

```
#include <iostream.h>
#include<conio.h>
class A
{
int a;
public:
A(int j)
{
a =j;
}
int get()
{
return a;
}
};
void main()
{
A aa =99;
cout <<aa.get();
getch();
}
```

**OUTPUT:**

99

**Problem 16. Write a C++ program for string type constructor.**

***Program:***

```
#include <string.h>
#include <iostream.h>
#include <string.h>
#include <stdlib.h>
#include<conio.h>
class StringClass
{
char *p;
int len;
public:
StringClass(char *ptr);
~StringClass();
void show();
};
StringClass::StringClass(char *ptr)
{
len = strlen(ptr);
p = new char [len+1];
if(!p) {
cout << "Allocation error\n";
exit(1);
}
strcpy(p, ptr);
}
StringClass::~StringClass()
{
```

```
cout << "Freeing p\n";
delete [] p;
}
void StringClass::show()
{
cout << p << " - length: " << len;
cout << endl;
}
void main()
{
StringClass stringObject1("www.google.com"),
stringObject2("www.google.com");
stringObject1.show();
stringObject2.show();
getch();
}
```

**OUTPUT:**

```
www.google.com - length: 14
www.google.com - length: 14
Freeing p
Freeing p
```

**Problem 17. Write a C++ program which use constructor to init member variables.**

***Program:***

```
#include <iostream.h>
#include<conio.h>
class myclass
{
int i, j;
public:
myclass(int x, int y)
{
i = x;
j = y;
}
void show()
{
cout << i << " " << j;
}
};
void main()
{
myclass count(2, 3);
count.show();
getch();
}
```

**OUTPUT:**

```
2 3
```

**Problem 18. Write a C++ program which use Double value as the constructor parameter.**

***Program:***

```
#include <iostream.h>
#include<conio.h>
class MyClass
{
double l, w, h;
double volume;
public:
MyClass(double a, double b, double c);
void vol();
};
MyClass::MyClass(double a, double b, double c)
{
l = a;
w = b;
h = c;
volume = l * w * h;
}
void MyClass::vol()
{
cout << "Volume is: " << volume << endl;
}
void main()
{
MyClass x(2.2, 3.97, 8.09), y(1.0, 2.0, 3.0);
x.vol();
y.vol();
getch();
}
```

**OUTPUT:**

```
volume is: 70.6581
volume is: 6
```

**Problem 19. Write a C++ program for constructor: different parameter type.**

***Program:***

```
#include <iostream.h>
#include<conio.h>
#include <stdlib.h>
class myclass
{
int a;
public:
myclass(int x)
{
a = x;
}
myclass(char *str)
{
```

```
a = atoi(str);
}
int geta()
{
return a;
}
};
void  main()
{
myclass object1 = 4;
myclass object2 = "123";
cout << "object1: " << object1.geta() << endl;
cout << "object2: " << object2.geta() << endl;
getch();
}
```

**OUTPUT:**

```
object1: 4
object2: 123
```

**Problem 20. Write a C++ program which use automatic conversions to assign new values.**

***Program:***

```
#include <iostream.h>
#include<conio.h>
#include <stdlib.h>
class myclass
{
int a;
public:
myclass(int x)
{
a = x;
}
myclass(char *str)
{
a = atoi(str);
}
int geta()
{
return a;
}
};
void  main()
{
myclass object1 = 4;     // converts to myclass(4)
myclass object2 = "123"; // converts to
myclass("123");
cout << "object1: " << object1.geta() << endl;
cout << "object2: " << object2.geta() << endl;
object1 = "1976";        // converts into object1 =
myclass("1976");
object2 = 2009;          // converts into object2 =
myclass(2009);
cout << "object1: " << object1.geta() << endl;
cout << "object2: " << object2.geta() << endl;
getch();
}
```

**OUTPUT:**

```
object1: 4
object2: 123
object1: 1976
object2: 2009
```

**Problem 21. Write a C++ program to implement class Intpair using constructor.**

***Program:***

```
#include <iostream.h>
#include<conio.h>
#include <stdlib.h>
class IntPair
{
public:
int a;
Int b;
IntPair(int i, int j) : a(i), b(j) { }
};
class MyClass
{
IntPair nums;
public:
// Initialize nums object using initialization syntax.
MyClass(int x, int y) : nums(x,y) { }
int getNumA()
{
return nums.a;
}
int getNumB()
{
return nums.b;
}
};
void  main()
{
MyClass object1(7, 9), object2(5, 2);
cout << "Values in object1 are " <<
object1.getNumB() <<
" and " << object1.getNumA() << endl;
cout << "Values in object2 are " <<
object2.getNumB() <<
" and " << object2.getNumA() << endl;
getch();
}
```

**OUTPUT:**

Values in object1 are 9 and 7
Values in object2 are 2 and 5

**Problem 22. Write a C++ program for constructor with 2 parameters.**

***Program:***

```
#include <iostream.h>
#include<conio.h>
class MyClass
{
int h;
int i;
public:
MyClass(int j, int k)
{
h = j;
i = k;
}
int getInt()
{
return i;
 }
int getHeight()
{
return h;
}
};
void  main()
{
MyClass myObject[3] = {
MyClass(1, 2), // initialize
MyClass(3, 4),
MyClass(5, 6)
};
int i;
for(i=0; i<3; i++)
{
cout << myObject[i].getHeight();
cout << ", ";
cout << myObject[i].getInt() << "\n";
}
getch();
}
```

**OUTPUT:**

1, 2
3, 4
5, 6

**Problem 23. Write a C++ program for a parameterized constructor.**

***Program:***

```
#include <iostream.h>
#include<conio.h>
class MyClass
{
public:
int x;
MyClass(int i);  // constructor
~MyClass();      // destructor
};
// a parameterized constructor.
MyClass::MyClass(int i)
{
x = i;
}
// Implement MyClass destructor.
MyClass::~MyClass()
{
cout << "Destructing object whose x value is " <<
x  <<" \n";
}
void main()
{
MyClass t1(5);
MyClass t2(19);
cout << t1.x << " " << t2.x << "\n";
getch();
}
```

**OUTPUT:**

5 19
Destructing object whose x value is 19
Destructing object whose x value is 5

**Problem 24. Write a C++ program using constructor to initialize class fields.**

***Program:***

```
#include <iostream.h>
#include<conio.h>
class MyClass
{
public:
int x;
MyClass(int i);  // constructor
~MyClass();      // destructor
};
MyClass::MyClass(int i)
{
x = i;
}
MyClass::~MyClass()
{
```

```
cout << "Destructing object whose x value is " << x
<<" \n";
}
void main()
{
MyClass ob(5) ;
cout << ob.x << "\n";
getch();
}
```

**OUTPUT:**

5

Destructing object whose x value is 5

**Problem 25. Write a C++ program to initialize variables and conduct calculation in constructor.**

***Program:***

```
#include <iostream.h>
#include<conio.h>
class box
{
double line,width,heigth;
double volume;
public:
box(double a,double b,double c);
void vol();
};
box::box(double a,double b,double c)
{
line=a;
width=b;
heigth=c;
volume=line*heigth;
}
void box::vol()
{
cout<<"Volume is:"<<volume<<"\n";
}
void main()
{
box x(3.4,4.5,8.5),y(2.0,4.0,6.0);
x.vol();
y.vol();
getch();
}
```

**OUTPUT:**

Volume is:28.9

Volume is:12

**Problem 26. Write a C++ program to make a call class constructor or not during class array declaration.**

***Program:***

```
#include <iostream.h>
#include<conio.h>
class powers
{
int x;
public:
powers()
{
x = 0;
cout << "\nno initializer\n\n";
}
powers(int n)
{
x = n;
cout << "\n\ninitializer:" << x;
}
int getx() { return x; }
void setx(int i) { x = i; }
};
void main()
{
powers ofTwo[] = {1, 2, 4, 8, 16}; // initialized
powers ofThree[5];           // uninitialized
getch();
}
```

**OUTPUT:**

initializer:1

initializer:2

initializer:4

initializer:8

initializer:16

no initializer

no initializer

no initializer

no initializer

no initializer

**Problem 27. Write a C++ program for calling default constructor when allocating an array dynamically.**

***Program:***

```
#include <iostream.h>
#include<conio.h>
class powers
{
int x;
public:
powers()
{
x = 0;
```

```
cout << "\nno initializer\n\n";
}
powers(int n)
{
x = n;
cout << "\n\ninitializer:" << x;
}
int getx() { return x; }
void setx(int i) { x = i; }
};
void main()
{
powers *p;
// dynamically allocate an array
try
{
p = new powers[5]; // no initialization
}
catch (bad_alloc xa)
{
cout << "Allocation Failure\n";
return 1;
}
getch();
}
```

**OUTPUT:**

```
no initializer
no initializer
no initializer
no initializer
no initializer
```

**Problem 28. Write a C++ program to define class to record time using constructor.**

***Program:***

```
#include <iomanip.h>
#include <iostream.h>
#include<conio.h>
class Time
{
public:
Time();
void setTime( int, int, int );
void printUniversal();
void printStandard();
private:
int hour;
int minute;
int second;
};
Time::Time()
{
hour = minute = second = 0;
}
void Time::setTime( int h, int m, int s )
{
hour = h ;
minute = m;
second = s ;
}
void Time::printUniversal()
{
cout << setfill( '0' ) << setw( 2 ) << hour << ":" <<
setw( 2 ) << minute << ":" << setw( 2 ) << second;
}
void Time::printStandard()
{
cout << ( ( hour == 0 || hour == 12 ) ? 12 : hour )
<< setfill( '0' ) << setw( 2 ) << minute << ":" <<
setw( 2 )
<< second << ( hour < 12 ? " AM" : " PM" );
}
void main()
{
Time t;
t.printUniversal();
t.printStandard();
t.setTime( 1, 2, 6 );
t.printUniversal();
t.printStandard();
t.setTime( 99, 99, 99 );
t.printUniversal();
t.printStandard();
getch();
}
```

**OUTPUT:**

```
00:00:0012:00:00 AM01:02:061:02:06
AM99:99:993:99:99 PM
```

**Problem 29. Write a C++ program in which class objects can be assigned to each other using default memberwise assignment.**

***Program:***

```
#include <iostream.h>
#include<conio.h>
class Date
{
public:
Date( int = 1, int = 1, int = 2007 );
void print();
private:
int month;
```

```
int day;
int year;
};
Date::Date( int m, int d, int y )
{
month = m;
day = d;
year = y;
}
void Date::print()
{
cout << month << '/' << day << '/' << year;
}
void main()
{
Date date1( 8, 8, 2009 );
Date date2;
cout << "date1 = ";
date1.print();
cout << "\ndate2 = ";
date2.print();
date2 = date1;
cout << "\n\nAfter default memberwise assignment,
date2 = ";
date2.print();
cout << endl;
getch();
}
```

**OUTPUT:**

date1 = 8/8/2009
date2 = 1/1/2007
After default memberwise assignment, date2 = 8/8/2008

**Problem 30. Write a C++ program to depict initialization of object using constructor member functions.**

***Program:***

```
#include<iostream.h>
#include<conio.h>
class rec
{
private:
int l,b;
public:
rec()
{
l=4;
b=3;
}
int area()
{
return(l*b);
}
};
void main()
{
rec obj;
cout<<"Area is"<<obj.area();
getch();
}
```

**OUTPUT:**

Area is 12
11.2

**Problem 31. Write a C++ program for the implementation of class rectangle(rec).**

***Program:***

```
#include<iostream.h>
#include<conio.h>
class rec
{
private:
int l,b;
public:
rec(int u,int v)
{
l=u;
b=v;
}
int area()
{
return(l*b);
}
};
void main()
{
rec obj(6,6);
rec obj1(2,8);
cout<<"Area is of rectangle first: "<<obj.area();
cout<<"Area is of rectangle second:
"<<obj1.area();
getch();
}
```

**OUTPUT:**

Area is of rectangle first:36
Area is of rectangle second16

**Problem 32. Write a C++ program again for class rectangle.**

***Program:***

```
#include<iostream.h>
```

```
#include<conio.h>
class rec
{
private:
int l,b;
public:
rec()
{
l=b=0;
cout<<"Constructor with zero parameter\n";
}
rec(int a)
{
l=b=a;
cout<<"Constructor with one parameter\n";
}
rec(int a,int c)
{
l=a;
b=c;
cout<<"Constructor with two parameter\n";
}
int area()
{
return(l*b);
}
};
void main()
{
rec obj1;
rec obj2(3);
rec obj3(7,7);
cout<<"\nArea is of first rectangle : "<<obj1.area();
cout<<"\nArea is of square : "<<obj2.area();
cout<<"\nArea is of third rectangle : "<<obj3.area();
getch();
}
```

**OUTPUT:**

Area is of first rectangle :0
Area is of square :9
Area is of third rectangle :49

**Problem 33. Write a C++ program using array of objects to display area of multiple rectangles.**

***Program:***

```
#include<iostream.h>
#include<conio.h>
class rec
{
private:
int l;
int b;
public:
rec(int a,int c)
{
l=a;
b=c;
}
void put()
{
cout<<"Area is: "<<l*b;
}
};
void main()
{
rec obj[3]={rec(3,6),rec(2,5),rec(5,5)};
cout<<"Displaying areas of rectangles\n ";
for(int i=0;i<3;i++)
obj[i].put();
getch();
}
```

**OUTPUT:**

Displaying areas of rectangles
Area is:18
Area is:10
Area is:25

**Problem 34. Write a C++ program to show bank account details of customers.**

***Program:***

```
#include<iostream.h>
#include<conio.h>
class a
{
private:
int no;
double bal;
public:
a();
a(int,double);
void showbal();
};
a::a()
{
cout<<"Enter account no.";
cin>>no;
bal=150;
}
a::a(int a,double b)
{
no=a;
bal=b;
```

```
}
void a::showbal()
{
cout<<"Account no."<<no;
cout<<"Balance"<<bal;
}
void main()
{
a obj1;
a obj2(2,300);
obj1.showbal();
obj2.showbal();
getch();
}
```

**OUTPUT:**

Enter account no. 1
Account no.1
Balance 150
Account no.2
Balance 300

**Problem 35. Write a C++ program to defining and using a default class constructor.**

***Program:***

```
#include <iostream.h>
#include<conio.h>
class Box
{
public:
double length;
double width;
double height;
Box() {
cout << "Default constructor called" << endl;
length = width = height = 1.0;          // Default
dimensions
}
Box(double lengthValue, double widthValue, double
heightValue)
{
cout << "Box constructor called" << endl;
length = lengthValue;
width = widthValue;
height = heightValue;
}
double volume()
{
return length * width * height;
}
};
void main()
{
Box firstBox(80.0, 50.0, 40.0);
Box smallBox;
getch();
}
```

**OUTPUT:**

Box constructor called
Default constructor called

## MEMORY VARIABLE:

**Problem 36. Write a C++ program o create a getter for member variable.**

***Program:***

```
#include <iostream.h>
#include<conio.h>
class MyClass
{
int a;
public:
MyClass(int j) {a = j;}
int geta(void) {return a;}
};
void main(void)
{
MyClass ob = 99;
cout << ob.geta();
getch();
}
```

**OUTPUT:**

99

**Problem 37. Write a C++ program to initialize member variable in constructor.**

***Program:***

```
#include <iostream.h>
#include<conio.h>
class MyClass
{
public:
MyClass::MyClass(void);
void show_MyClass(void);
private:
int a;
int b;
int c;
};
MyClass::MyClass(void) : a(1), b(2), c(3) { };
void MyClass::show_MyClass(void)
{
```

```
cout << "a contains: " << a << endl;
cout << "b contains: " << b << endl;
cout << "c contains: " << c << endl;
}
void main(void)
{
MyClass numbers;
numbers.show_MyClass();
getch();
}
```

**OUTPUT:**

a contains: 1
b contains: 2
c contains: 3

**Problem 38. Write a C++ program for output variable initialization message.**

***Program:***

```
#include <iostream.h>
#include<conio.h>
class MyClass
{
public:
int who;
MyClass(int id);
} global_obj1(1), global_obj2(2);
MyClass::MyClass(int id)
{
cout << "Initializing " << id << "\n";
who = id;
}
void main(void)
{
MyClass local_obj(3);
cout << "This is NOT the first line displayed.\n";
MyClass local_obj2(4);
getch();
}
```

**OUTPUT:**

Initializing 1
Initializing 2
Initializing 3
This is NOT the first line displayed.
Initializing 4

**Problem 39. Write a C++ program to assign value to member variable directly from assignment.**

***Program:***

```
#include <iostream.h>
#include<conio.h>
class MyClass
{
int a;
public:
MyClass(int j) {a = j;}
int geta(void) {return a;}
};
void main(void)
{
MyClass ob = 12;
cout << ob.geta();
getch();
}
```

**OUTPUT:**

12

**Problem 40. Write a C++ program to initialize member variable.**

***Program:***

```
#include <iostream.h>
#include<conio.h>
class MyClass
{
public:
MyClass( int c = 0, int i = 1 );
void add()
{
count += increment;
}
void print() const;
private:
int count;
const int increment;
};
MyClass::MyClass( int c, int i ): count( c
),increment( i )
{
}
void MyClass::print() const
{
cout << "count = " << count << ", increment = "
<< increment << endl;
}
void main()
{
MyClass value( 10, 5 );
value.print();
for ( int j = 1; j <= 3; j++ )
{
value.add();
value.print();
```

```
}
getch();
}
```

**OUTPUT:**

```
count = 10, increment = 5
count = 15, increment = 5
count = 20, increment = 5
count = 25, increment = 5
```

**Problem 41. Write a C++ program for reference another class in member function.**

***Program:***

```
#include <iostream.h>
#include<conio.h>
class ClassA
{
public:
void functionA();
};
void ClassA::functionA()
{
cout << "This is a function in ClassA \n";
}
class ClassB
{
public:
void functionB();
};
void ClassB::functionB()
{
ClassA myclass;
myclass.functionA();
}
void main()
{
ClassB myclass;
ClassA anotherclass;
myclass.functionB();
anotherclass.functionA();
getch();
}
```

**OUTPUT:**

```
This is a function in ClassA
This is a function in ClassA
```

**Problem 42. Write a C++ program for simple constructor.**

***Program:***

```
#include <iostream.h>
#include<conio.h>
class Cons
{
private:
int t;
public:
Cons():t(0)//constructor
{ }
void inc_t()//increment t
{
t++;
}
int get_t()//return t
{
return t;
}
};
void main()
{
Cons c1,c2;//define and initialize
cout <<"\nc1=" <<c1.get_t();//display
cout <<"\nc2=" <<c2.get_t();
c1.inc_t();//increment c1
c2.inc_t();//increment c2
c2.inc_t();//increment c2
cout <<"\nc1=" <<c1.get_t();//display again
cout <<"\nc2=" <<c2.get_t();
cout <<endl;
getch();
}
```

**OUTPUT:**

```
c1=0
c2=0
c1=1
c2=2
```

**Problem 43. Write a C++ program for Constructor class box.**

***Program:***

```
#include <iostream.h>
#include<conio.h>
// Class to represent a box
class Box
{
public:
double length;
double breadth;
double height;
// Constructor
Box(double lengthValue, double breadthValue,
double heightValue)
{
cout << "Box constructor called" << endl;
```

```
length = lengthValue;
breadth = breadthValue;
height = heightValue;
}
// Function to calculate the volume of a box
double volume()
{
return length * breadth * height;
}
};
void main()
{
Box b(80,50,40);
double vol;
vol=b.volume();
cout<< "Volume of  Box object is "<<vol;
getch();
}
```

**OUTPUT:**

Box constructor called
Volume of Box object is 160000

**Problem 44. Write a C++ program using inline initialization in constructor.**

***Program:***

```
#include <iostream.h>
#include<conio.h>
// Class to represent a box
class Box
{
public:
double length;
double breadth;
double height;
// Inline initialization
Box(double lv = 1.0, double bv = 1.0, double hv =
1.0):length(lv),
                    breadth(bv),height(hv)
{
cout << "Box constructor called" << endl;
}
// Function to calculate the volume of a box
double volume()
{
return length * breadth * height;
}
};
void main()
{
Box firstBox(80.0, 50.0, 40.0);
// Calculate the volume of the box
double firstBoxVolume = firstBox.volume();
cout << endl;
cout << "Size of first Box object is "
<< firstBox.length  << " by "
<< firstBox.breadth << " by "
<< firstBox.height
<< endl;
cout << "Volume of first Box object is " <<
firstBoxVolume
<< endl;
getch();
}
```

**OUTPUT:**

Box constructor called
Size of first Box object is 80 by 50 by 40
Volume of first Box object is 160000

**Problem 45. Write a C++ program which take objects as Function Arguments.**

***Program:***

```
#include <iostream.h>
#include<conio.h>
class Height
{
private:
int feet;
float inches;
public://constructor with no args
Height():feet(0),inches(0.0)
{ }
//constructor with two args
Height(int ft,float in):feet(ft),inches(in)
{ }
void get()//get height
{
cout <<"\nFeet:";
cin >>feet;
cout <<" inches:";
cin >>inches;
}
void show()
{cout <<feet <<"-" <<inches ;}
void add(Height,Height );//declaration
};
void Height::add(Height H1,Height H2)
{
inches =H1.inches +H2.inches;
feet =0;
if(inches >=12.0)
{
inches -= 12.0;
```

```
feet++;
}
feet +=H1.feet +H2.feet;
}
void main()
{
Height heigh1,heigh3;
Height heigh2(6,4.0);
heigh1.get();
heigh3.add(heigh1,heigh2);
cout <<"\nHeigh1 =";heigh1.show();
cout <<"\nHeigh2 =";heigh2.show();
cout <<"\nHeigh3 =";heigh3.show();
cout <<endl;
getch();
}
```

**OUTPUT:**

Feet:6
inches:4.0
Heigh1 =6-4.0
Heigh2 =6-4.0
Heigh3 =12-8.0

## PRIVATE:

**Problem 46. Write a C++ program for private and protected member variables.**

***Program:***

```
#include <iostream.h>
#include<conio.h>
class MyClass {
int a;        // private by default
protected:    // still private relative to MyClass
int b;
public:
int c;
MyClass(int n, int m)
{
a = n;
b = m;
}
int geta()
{
return a;
}
int getb()
{
return b;
}
};
void main()
{
MyClass object(10, 20);
object.c = 30; // OK, c is public
cout << object.geta() << ' ';
cout << object.getb() << ' ' << object.c << '\n';
getch();
}
```

**OUTPUT:**

10 20 30

**Problem 47. Write a C++ program to assign the public object member address to a pointer.**

***Program:***

```
#include <iostream.h>
#include<conio.h>
class MyClass
{
public:
int i;
MyClass(int j)
{
i = j;
}
};
void  main()
{
MyClass myObject(1);
int *p;
p = &myObject.i;                // get address of
myObject.i
cout << *p;                     // access myObject.i
via p
getch();
}
```

**OUTPUT:**

1

**Problem 48. Write a C++ program to depict working of array of pointers.**

***Program:***

```
#include<iostream.h>
#include<conio.h>
class e
{
private:
int id;
char name[20];
public:
void read()
{
```

```
cout<<"\nEnter employee id=";
cin>>id;
cout<<"Enter employee name=";
cin>>name;
}
void show()
{
cout<<"\nEmployee id= "<<id<<"Name"<<name;
}
};
void main()
{
clrscr();
e *p[50];
int count=0;
char ch;
do
{
p[count]=new e;
p[count]->read();
 count++;
cout<<"Entermore(y/n?)";
cin>>ch;
}while(ch=='y'||ch=='Y');
cout<<"Show more details";
for(int i=0;i<count;i++)
{
p[i]->show();
delete p[i];
}
getch();
}
```

**Problem 49. Write a C++ program to initialize numA and numB inside the MyClass constructor using normal syntax.**

***Program:***

```
#include <iostream.h>
#include<conio.h>
class MyClass
{
int numA;
int numB;
public:
MyClass(int x, int y)
{
numA = x;
numB = y;
}
int getNumA() { return numA; }
int getNumB() { return numB; }
};
void main()
{
MyClass ob1(7, 9), ob2(5, 2);
cout << "Values in ob1 are " << ob1.getNumB()
<<
  " and " << ob1.getNumA() << endl;
cout << "Values in ob2 are " << ob2.getNumB()
<<
  " and " << ob2.getNumA() << endl;
getch();
}
```

**OUTPUT:**

Values in ob1 are 9 and 7
Values in ob2 are 2 and 5

**Problem 50. Write a C++ program using a class with private data members.**

***Program:***

```
#include <iostream.h>
#include<conio.h>
class Box
{
public:
Box(double lvalue, double wvalue, double hvalue)
:length(lvalue), width(wvalue), height(hvalue) {
cout << "Box constructor called" << endl;
}
Box()
{
cout << "Default constructor called" << endl;
length = width = height = 1.0;          // Default
dimensions
}
double volume()
{
return length * width * height;
}
private:
double length;
double width;
double height;
};
void main()
{
cout << endl;
Box firstBox(2.2, 1.1, 0.5);
Box secondBox;
Box* pthirdBox = new Box(15.0, 20.0, 8.0);
cout << firstBox.volume()<< endl;
cout << secondBox.volume()<< endl;
```

```
cout << pthirdBox->volume()<< endl;
delete pthirdBox;
getch();
}
```

**OUTPUT:**

Box constructor called
Default constructor called
Box constructor called
1.21
1
2400

**Problem 51. Write a C++ program for example: class constructor.**

***Program:***

```
#include <iostream.h>
#include<conio.h>
class CRectangle
{
int width, height;
public:
CRectangle (int,int);
int area ()
{
return (width*height);
}
};
CRectangle::CRectangle (int a, int b)
{
width = a;
height = b;
}
void main ()
{
CRectangle rect (3,4);
CRectangle rectb (5,6);
cout << "rect area: " << rect.area() << endl;
cout << "rectb area: " << rectb.area() << endl;
getch();
}
```

**OUTPUT:**

rect area: 12
rectb area: 30

**Problem 52. Write a C++ program for example both on constructors and destructors.**

***Program:***

```
#include <iostream.h>
#include<conio.h>
class CRectangle
{
int *width, *height;
public:
CRectangle (int,int);
~CRectangle ();
int area ()
{
return (*width * *height);
}
};
CRectangle::CRectangle (int a, int b)
{
width = new int;
height = new int;
*width = a;
*height = b;
}
CRectangle::~CRectangle ()
{
delete width;
delete height;
}
void main ()
{
CRectangle rect (3,4), rectb (5,6);
cout << "rect area: " << rect.area() << endl;
cout << "rectb area: " << rectb.area() << endl;
getch();
}
```

**OUTPUT:**

rect area: 12
rectb area: 30

**Problem 53. Write a C++ program for creating objects on the heap using new.**

***Program:***

```
#include <iostream.h>
#include<conio.h>
class MyClass
{
public:
MyClass();
~MyClass();
private:
int itsAge;
};
MyClass::MyClass()
{
cout << "Constructor called.\n";
itsAge = 1;
}
MyClass::~MyClass()
```

```
{
cout << "Destructor called.\n";
}
void main()
{
cout << "MyClass ...\n";
MyClass Frisky;
cout << "MyClass *pRags = new MyClass...\n";
MyClass * pRags = new MyClass;
cout << "delete pRags...\n";
delete pRags;
cout << "Exiting, watch go...\n";
getch();
}
```

**OUTPUT:**

```
MyClass ...
Constructor called.
MyClass *pRags = new MyClass...
Constructor called.
delete pRags...
Destructor called.
Exiting, watch go...
Destructor called.
```

**Problem 54. Write a C++ program for accessing members of objects on the heap.**

***Program:***

```
#include <iostream.h>
#include<conio.h>
class MyClass
{
public:
MyClass()
{
itsAge = 2;
}
~MyClass() {}
int GetAge() const
{
return itsAge;
}
void SetAge(int age)
{
itsAge = age;
}
private:
int itsAge;
};
void main()
{
MyClass * myObject = new MyClass;
cout << "myObject is " << myObject->GetAge()
<< " years old\n";
myObject->SetAge(5);
cout << "myObject is " << myObject->GetAge()
<< " years old\n";
delete myObject;
getch();
}
```

**OUTPUT:**

```
myObject is 2 years old
myObject is 5 years old
```

**Problem 55. Write a C++ program to call class constructor without new operator.**

***Program:***

```
#include <iostream.h>
#include<conio.h>
class Box
{
public:
double length;
double width;
double height;
// Constructor
Box(double lengthValue, double widthValue,
double heightValue)
{
cout << "Box constructor called" << endl;
length = lengthValue;
width = widthValue;
height = heightValue;
}
double volume()
{
return length * width * height;
}
};
void main()
{
Box firstBox(80.0, 50.0, 40.0);
cout << "Size of first Box object is "
<< firstBox.length << " by "
<< firstBox.width << " by "
<< firstBox.height << "\n "
<< "Volume of first Box object is " <<
firstBox.volume()
<< endl;
getch();
}
```

**OUTPUT:**

```
Box constructor called
```

Size of first Box object is 80 by 50 by 40
Volume of first Box object is 160000

**Problem 56. Write a C++ program for an array of objects: call its method.**

***Program:***

```
#include <iostream.h>
#include<conio.h>
class MyClass
{
public:
MyClass()
{
itsAge = 1;
itsWeight=5;
}
~MyClass() {}
int GetAge() const
{
return itsAge;
}
int GetWeight() const
{
return itsWeight;
}
void SetAge(int age)
{
itsAge = age;
}
private:
int itsAge;
int itsWeight;
};
void main()
{
MyClass myObject[5];
int i;
for (i = 0; i < 5; i++)
myObject[i].SetAge(2*i +1);
for (i = 0; i < 5; i++)
cout << " #" << i+1<< ": " << myObject[i].GetAge()
<< endl;
getch();
}
```

**OUTPUT:**

```
#1: 1
 #2: 3
 #3: 5
 #4: 7
 #5: 9
```

**Problem 57. Write a C++ program to initialize an array of objects without referencing the constructor directly.**

***Program:***

```
#include <iostream.h>
#include<conio.h>
class MyClass
{
int x;
public:
MyClass(int i) { x = i; }
int getX() { return x; }
};
void main()
{
MyClass obs[4] = { -1, -2, -3, -4 };
int i;
for(i=0; i < 4; i++)
cout << "obs[" << i << "].getX(): "<<
obs[i].getX() << "\n";
getch();
}
```

**OUTPUT:**

```
obs[0].getX(): -1
obs[1].getX(): -2
obs[2].getX(): -3
obs[3].getX(): -4
```

**Problem 58. Write a C++ program to initialize an array of objects by referencing the constructor directly.**

***Program:***

```
#include <iostream.h>
#include<conio.h>
class MyClass
{
int x;
public:
MyClass(int i) { x = i; }
int getX() { return x; }
};
void main()
{
MyClass obs[4] = { MyClass(-1), MyClass (-
2),MyClass (-3), MyClass (-4) };
int i;
for(i=0; i < 4; i++)
cout << "obs[" << i << "].getX(): " <<
obs[i].getX() << "\n";
getch();
}
```

**OUTPUT:**
obs[0].getX(): -1
obs[1].getX(): -2
obs[2].getX(): -3
obs[3].getX(): -4

**Problem 59. Write a C++ program for Allocating an array of objects using new operator.**

***Program:***

```
#include <iostream.h>
#include<conio.h>
class Rectangle
{
int width;
int height;
public:
Rectangle()
{
width = height = 0;
cout << "Constructing " << width << " by " <<
height << " rectangle.\n";
}
Rectangle(int w, int h)
{
width = w;
height = h;
cout << "Constructing " << width << " by " <<
height << " rectangle.\n";
}
~Rectangle()
{
cout << "Destructing " << width << " by " << height
<< " rectangle.\n";
}
void set(int w, int h)
{
width = w;
height = h;
}
int area()
{
return width * height;
}
};
void main()
{
Rectangle *p;
try {
p = new Rectangle [3];
}
catch (bad_alloc xa)
{
cout << "Allocation Failure\n";
return 1;
}
cout << "\n";
p[0].set(3, 4);
p[1].set(10, 8);
p[2].set(5, 6);
for(int i=0; i < 3; i++)
cout << "Area is " << p[i].area() << endl;
delete [] p;
getch();
}
```

**OUTPUT:**
Constructing 0 by 0 rectangle.
Constructing 0 by 0 rectangle.
Constructing 0 by 0 rectangle.
Area is 12
Area is 80
Area is 30
Destructing 5 by 6 rectangle.
Destructing 10 by 8 rectangle.
Destructing 3 by 4 rectangle.

**Problem 60. Write a C++ program for passing an array of pointers to objects.**

***Program:***

```
#include <iostream.h>
#include<conio.h>
class MyClass
{
public:
MyClass()
{
itsAge = 1;
itsWeight=5;
}
~MyClass() {}
int GetAge() const { return itsAge; }
int GetWeight() const { return itsWeight; }
void SetAge(int age) { itsAge = age; }
private:
int itsAge;
int itsWeight;
};
void main()
{
MyClass * myObject[50];
int i;
MyClass * objectPointer;
for (i = 0; i < 50; i++)
```

```
{
objectPointer = new MyClass;
objectPointer->SetAge(2*i +1);
myObject[i] = objectPointer;
}
for (i = 0; i < 50; i++)
cout << "#" << i+1 << ": " << myObject[i]-
>GetAge() << endl;
for (i = 0; i < 50; i++)
{
delete myObject[i];
myObject[i] = NULL;
}
getch();
}
```

**OUTPUT:**

```
#1: 1
#2: 3
#3: 5
#4: 7
#5: 9
#6: 11
#7: 13
#8: 15
#9: 17
#10: 19
#11: 21
#12: 23
#13: 25
#14: 27
#15: 29
#16: 31
#17: 33
#18: 35
#19: 37
#20: 39
#21: 41
#22: 43
#23: 45
#24: 47
#25: 49
#26: 51
#27: 53
#28: 55
#29: 57
#30: 59
#31: 61
#32: 63
#33: 65
#34: 67
#35: 69
#36: 71
#37: 73
#38: 75
#39: 77
#40: 79
#41: 81
#42: 83
#43: 85
#44: 87
#45: 89
#46: 91
#47: 93
#48: 95
#49: 97
#50: 99
```

**Problem 61. Write a C++ program an array on the heap.**

***Program:***

```
#include <iostream.h>
#include<conio.h>
class MyClass
{
public:
MyClass()
{
itsAge = 1;
itsWeight=5;
}
~MyClass();
int GetAge() const { return itsAge; }
int GetWeight() const { return itsWeight; }
void SetAge(int age) { itsAge = age; }
private:
int itsAge;
int itsWeight;
};
MyClass :: ~MyClass()
{
cout << "Destructor called!\n";
}
void main()
{
MyClass * objectArrayPointer = new
MyClass[50];
int i;
MyClass * currentPointer;
for (i = 0; i < 10; i++)
{
currentPointer = new MyClass;
currentPointer->SetAge(2*i +1);
```

```
objectArrayPointer[i] = *currentPointer;
delete currentPointer;
}
for (i = 0; i < 10; i++)
cout << "#" << i+1 << ": " <<
objectArrayPointer[i].GetAge() << endl;
delete [] objectArrayPointer;
getch();
}
```

**OUTPUT:**

```
Destructor called!
Destructor called!
Destructor called!
Destructor called!
Destructor called!
Destructor called!
Destructor called!
Destructor called!
Destructor called!
Destructor called!
#1: 1
#2: 3
#3: 5
#4: 7
#5: 9
#6: 11
#7: 13
#8: 15
#9: 17
#10: 19
Destructor called!
Destructor called!
Destructor called!
Destructor called!
Destructor called!
Destructor called!
Destructor called!
Destructor called!
Destructor called!
Destructor called!
```

**Problem 62. Write a C++ program to delete an array of objects.**

***Program:***

```
#include <iostream.h>
#include<conio.h>
#include <stdlib.h>
class Point
{
int x, y;
public:
Point() {x = y = 0;}
Point(int px, int py)
{
x = px;
y = py;
}
void show()
{
cout << x << " ";
cout << y << "\n";
}
void *operator new(size_t size);
void operator delete(void *p);
void *operator new[](size_t size);
void operator delete[](void *p);
};
// new overloaded relative to Point.
void *Point::operator new(size_t size)
{
void *p;
cout << "In overloaded new.\n";
p =  malloc(size);
if(!p)
{
bad_alloc ba;
throw ba;
}
return p;
}
// delete overloaded relative to Point.
void Point::operator delete(void *p)
{
cout << "In overloaded delete.\n";
free(p);
}
// new overloaded for Point arrays.
void *Point::operator new[](size_t size)
{
void *p;
cout << "Using overload new[].\n";
p =  malloc(size);
if(!p)
{
bad_alloc ba;
throw ba;
}
return p;
}
// delete overloaded for Point arrays.
void Point::operator delete[](void *p)
{
```

```
cout << "Freeing array using overloaded delete[]\n";
free(p);
}
void main()
{
Point *p1, *p2;
int i;
try {
p1 = new Point (10, 20); // allocate an object
}
catch (bad_alloc xa)
{
cout << "Allocation error for p1.\n";
return 1;
}
try
{
p2 = new Point [10]; // allocate an array
}
catch (bad_alloc xa)
{
cout << "Allocation error for p2.\n";
return 1;
}
p1->show();
for(i=0; i<10; i++)
p2[i].show();
delete p1; // free an object
delete [] p2; // free an array
getch();
}
```

**OUTPUT:**

```
In overloaded new.
Using overload new[].
10 20
0 0
0 0
0 0
0 0
0 0
0 0
0 0
0 0
0 0
0 0
In overloaded delete.
Freeing array using overloaded delete[]
```

**Problem 63. Write a C++ program to use & to get object address.**

***Program:***

```
class MyClass
{
public:
MyClass();
MyClass(MyClass&);
~MyClass();
int GetAge() const { return itsAge; }
void SetAge(int age) { itsAge = age; }
private:
int itsAge;
};
MyClass::MyClass()
{
cout << "Constructor...\n";
itsAge = 1;
}
MyClass::MyClass(MyClass&)
{
cout << "Copy Constructor...\n";
}
MyClass::~MyClass()
{
cout << "Destructor...\n";
}
const MyClass * const
FunctionTwo (const MyClass * const obj);
void main()
{
MyClass myObject;
cout << "myObject is ";
cout << myObject.GetAge() << " years old\n";
int age = 5;
myObject.SetAge(age);
cout << "myObject is ";
cout << myObject.GetAge() << " years old\n";
cout << "Calling FunctionTwo...\n";
FunctionTwo(&myObject);
cout << "myObject is ";
cout << myObject.GetAge() << " years old\n";
getch();
}
const MyClass * const FunctionTwo (const
MyClass * const obj)
{
cout << "Function Two. Returning...\n";
cout << "myObject is now " << obj->GetAge();
cout << " years old \n";
return obj;
}
```

**OUTPUT:**

```
Constructor...
```

```
myObject is 1 years old
myObject is 5 years old
Calling FunctionTwo...
Function Two. Returning...
myObject is now 5 years old
myObject is 5 years old
Destructor...
```

**Problem 64. Write a C++ program for pointers as data members.**

***Program:***

```
#include <iostream.h>
#include<conio.h>
class MyClass
{
public:
MyClass();
~MyClass();
int GetAge() const { return *itsAge; }
void SetAge(int age) { *itsAge = age; }
int GetWeight() const { return *itsWeight; }
void setWeight (int weight) { *itsWeight = weight; }
private:
int * itsAge;
int * itsWeight;
};
MyClass::MyClass()
{
itsAge = new int(2);
itsWeight = new int(5);
}
MyClass::~MyClass()
{
delete itsAge;
delete itsWeight;
}
void main()
{
MyClass *objectPointer = new MyClass;
cout << "objectPointer is "<< objectPointer-
>GetAge() << " years old\n";
objectPointer->SetAge(5);
cout << "objectPointer is " << objectPointer-
>GetAge() << " years old\n";
delete objectPointer;
getch();
}
```

**OUTPUT:**

```
objectPointer is 2 years old
objectPointer is 5 years old
```

**Problem 65. Write a C++ program for simplest class definition**

***Program:***

```
#include <iostream.h>
#include<conio.h>
class SimpleClass
{
int len;
public:
SimpleClass(int l);
};
SimpleClass::SimpleClass(int l)
{
len = l;
int i;
for(i = 0; i <len; i++)
cout << '*';
}
void main()
{
SimpleClass l(10);
getch();
}
```

**OUTPUT:**

```
**********
```

**Problem 66. Write a C++ program for class who.**

***Program:***

```
#include <iostream.h>
#include<conio.h>
class who
{
char name;
public:
who(char c)
{
name = c;
cout << "Constructing who";
cout << name << endl;
}
~who()
{
cout << "Destructing who: " << name << endl;
}
};
who makewho()
{
who temp('B');
return temp;
```

```
}
void main()
{
who ob('A');
makewho();
getch();
}
```

**OUTPUT:**

Constructing whoA
Constructing whoB
Destructing who: B
Destructing who: A

**Problem 67. Write a C++ program for constructor: different parameter type.**

***Program:***

```
#include <iostream.h>
#include<conio.h>
#include <stdlib.h>
class myclass
{
int a;
public:
myclass(int x)
{
a = x;
}
myclass(char *str)
{
a = atoi(str);
}
int geta()
{
return a;
}
};
void main()
{
myclass object1 = 4;
myclass object2 = "123";
cout << "object1: " << object1.geta() << endl;
cout << "object2: " << object2.geta() << endl;
getch();
}
```

**OUTPUT:**

object1: 4
object2: 123

.

**Problem 68. Write a C++ program to init Object array.**

***Program:***

```
#include <iostream.h>
#include<conio.h>
class CharClass
{
char ch;
public:
CharClass(char c)
{
ch = c;
}
char get_ch()
{
return ch;
}
};
void main()
{
CharClass ob[10] =
{
CharClass('a'),
CharClass('b'),
CharClass('c'),
CharClass('d'),
CharClass('e'),
CharClass('f'),
CharClass('g'),
CharClass('h'),
CharClass('i'),
CharClass('j')
};
int i;
for(i = 0; i <10; i++)
cout << ob[ i ].get_ch() << ' ';
cout << endl;
getch();
}
```

**OUTPUT:**

a b c d e f g h i j

# CLASS COMBINATION:

**Problem 69. Write a C++ program using class as a member field.**

***Program:***

```
#include <iostream.h>
#include<conio.h>
class Point     // holds x,y coordinates
{
// no constructor, use default
public:
```

```
void SetX(int x) { itsX = x; }
void SetY(int y) { itsY = y; }
int GetX()const { return itsX;}
int GetY()const { return itsY;}
private:
int itsX;
int itsY;
};// end of Point class declaration
class  Rectangle
{
public:
Rectangle (int top, int left, int bottom, int right);
~Rectangle () { }
int GetTop() const { return itsTop; }
int GetLeft() const { return itsLeft; }
int GetBottom() const { return itsBottom; }
int GetRight() const { return itsRight; }
Point  GetUpperLeft() const { return itsUpperLeft; }
Point  GetLowerLeft() const { return itsLowerLeft; }
Point  GetUpperRight() const { return
itsUpperRight; }
Point  GetLowerRight() const { return
itsLowerRight; }
void SetUpperLeft(Point Location);
void SetLowerLeft(Point Location);
void SetUpperRight(Point Location);
void SetLowerRight(Point Location);
void SetTop(int top);
void SetLeft (int left);
void SetBottom (int bottom);
void SetRight (int right);
int GetArea() const;
private:
Point  itsUpperLeft;
Point  itsUpperRight;
Point  itsLowerLeft;
Point  itsLowerRight;
int    itsTop;
int    itsLeft;
int    itsBottom;
int    itsRight;
};
Rectangle::Rectangle(int top, int left, int bottom, int
right)
{
itsTop = top;
itsLeft = left;
itsBottom = bottom;
itsRight = right;
itsUpperLeft.SetX(left);
itsUpperLeft.SetY(top);
itsUpperRight.SetX(right);
itsUpperRight.SetY(top);
itsLowerLeft.SetX(left);
itsLowerLeft.SetY(bottom);
itsLowerRight.SetX(right);
itsLowerRight.SetY(bottom);
}
void Rectangle::SetUpperLeft(Point Location)
{
itsUpperLeft = Location;
itsUpperRight.SetY(Location.GetY());
itsLowerLeft.SetX(Location.GetX());
itsTop = Location.GetY();
itsLeft = Location.GetX();
}
void Rectangle::SetLowerLeft(Point Location)
{
itsLowerLeft = Location;
itsLowerRight.SetY(Location.GetY());
itsUpperLeft.SetX(Location.GetX());
itsBottom = Location.GetY();
itsLeft = Location.GetX();
}
void Rectangle::SetLowerRight(Point Location)
{
itsLowerRight = Location;
itsLowerLeft.SetY(Location.GetY());
itsUpperRight.SetX(Location.GetX());
itsBottom = Location.GetY();
itsRight = Location.GetX();
}
void Rectangle::SetUpperRight(Point Location)
{
itsUpperRight = Location;
itsUpperLeft.SetY(Location.GetY());
itsLowerRight.SetX(Location.GetX());
itsTop = Location.GetY();
itsRight = Location.GetX();
}
void Rectangle::SetTop(int top)
{
itsTop = top;
itsUpperLeft.SetY(top);
itsUpperRight.SetY(top);
}
void Rectangle::SetLeft(int left)
{
itsLeft = left;
itsUpperLeft.SetX(left);
itsLowerLeft.SetX(left);
}
```

```
void Rectangle::SetBottom(int bottom)
{
itsBottom = bottom;
itsLowerLeft.SetY(bottom);
itsLowerRight.SetY(bottom);
}
void Rectangle::SetRight(int right)
{
itsRight = right;
itsUpperRight.SetX(right);
itsLowerRight.SetX(right);
}
int Rectangle::GetArea() const
{
int Width = itsRight-itsLeft;
int Height = itsTop - itsBottom;
return (Width * Height);
}
void main()
{
Rectangle MyRectangle (100, 20, 50, 80 );
int Area = MyRectangle.GetArea();
cout << "Area: " << Area << "\n";
cout << MyRectangle.GetUpperLeft().GetX();
getch();
}
```

**OUTPUT:**

```
Area: 3000
20
```

**Problem 70. Write a C++ program to demonstrating composition--an object with member objects.**

***Program:***

```
#include <iostream.h>
#include<conio.h>
#include <string.h>
class Date
{
public:
Date( int = 1, int = 1, int = 1900 );
void print() const;
~Date();
private:
int month;
int day;
int year;
};
Date::Date( int mn, int dy, int yr )
{
month = mn;
year = yr;
day = dy ;
}
void Date::print() const
{
cout << month << '/' << day << '/' << year;
}
Date::~Date()
{
cout << "Date object destructor for date ";
cout << endl;
}
class Employee
{
public:
Employee( const char * const, const char * const,
const Date &, const Date & );
void print() const;
~Employee();
private:
char firstName[ 25 ];
char lastName[ 25 ];
const Date birthDate;
const Date hireDate;
};
Employee::Employee( const char * const first,
const char * const last,const Date &dateOfBirth,
const Date &dateOfHire )
: birthDate( dateOfBirth ), hireDate( dateOfHire )
{
strcpy( firstName, first);
strcpy( lastName, last);
}
void Employee::print() const
{
cout << lastName << ", " << firstName << "
Hired: ";
hireDate.print();
cout << "  Birthday: ";
birthDate.print();
cout << endl;
}
Employee::~Employee()
{
cout << "Employee destructor: " << lastName <<
", " << firstName << endl;
}
void main()
{
Date birth( 7, 24, 2009 );
Date hire( 3, 12, 2009 );
```

```
Employee manager( "A", "B", birth, hire );
cout << endl;
manager.print();
getch();
}
```

**OUTPUT:**

B, A Hired: 3/12/2009 Birthday: 7/24/2009
Employee destructor: B, A
Date object destructor for date
Date object destructor for date
Date object destructor for date
Date object destructor for date

**Problem 71. Write a C++ program for prototype concept.**

***Program:***

```
#include<conio.h>
#include <iostream.h>
#include <math.h>
class A;
class B
{
int sum;
public:
B(){ sum=1;}
B(int a,int b){sum=a*a+b*b;}
int Larger(B b,A a);
};
class A
{
friend int B::Larger(B b,A a);//use  B::Larger()!
private:int num;
public:
A(){num=1;}
A(int a,int b){num=4*a+b;}
void Display(void){cout<<num<< endl;}
};
int B::Larger(B b,A a)
{
return (b.sum > a.num);
}
void main()
{
B objB(1,2);
A objA(3,3);
if(objB.Larger(objB,objA))
{
cout << "B obj is Larger , the small num is ";
objA.Display();
}
else
{
cout << "B obj is not Larger\n";
}
getch();
}
```

**OUTPUT:**

B obj is not Larger

**Problem 72. Write a C++ program to defines constructor, destructor, and range() function in-line.**

***Program:***

```
#include <iostream.h>
#include<conio.h>
class MyClass
{
// These are now private.
int a;
int b;
int c;
public:
// This is a constructor for MyClass.
MyClass(int p, int f, int m)
{
a = p;
b = f;
c = m;
}
// Compute and return the range.
int range()
{
return c * b;
}
// Accessor functions.
int getA() { return a; }
int getB() { return b; }
int getC() { return c; }
};
void main()
{
// Pass values to MyClass constructor.
MyClass myObject1(7, 16, 21);
MyClass myObject2(2, 14, 12);
int range1, range2;
range1 = myObject1.range();
range2 = myObject2.range();
cout << range1 << "\n";
cout << range2 << "\n";
getch();
}
```

**OUTPUT:**

2352
336

## CONSTRUCTOR OVERLOADING:

**Problem 73. Write a C++ program to overload the constructor.**

***Program:***

```
#include <iostream.h>
#include<conio.h>
class MyClass
{
public:
int x;
int y;
// Overload the default constructor.
MyClass()
{
x = y = 0;
}
// Constructor with one parameter.
MyClass(int i)
{
x = y = i;
}
// Constructor with two parameters.
MyClass(int i, int j)
{
x = i; y = j;
}
};
void main()
{
MyClass t;          // invoke default constructor
MyClass t1(5);      // use MyClass(int)
MyClass t2(9, 10); // use MyClass(int, int)
cout << "t.x: " << t.x << ", t.y: " << t.y << "\n";
cout << "t1.x: " << t1.x << ", t1.y: " << t1.y << "\n";
cout << "t2.x: " << t2.x << ", t2.y: " << t2.y << "\n";
getch();
}
```

**OUTPUT:**

```
t.x: 0, t.y: 0
t1.x: 5, t1.y: 5
t2.x: 9, t2.y: 10
```

**Problem 74. Write a C++ program to overload constructor date.**

***Program:***

```
#include <iostream.h>
#include<conio.h>
#include<stdio.h>
class date {
int day, month, year;
public:
date(char *d)
{
sscanf(d, "*c*cd", &month, &day, &year);
}
date(int m, int d, int y)
{
day = d;
month = m;
year = y;
}
void show_date()
{
cout << month << "/" << day;
cout << "/" << year << "\n";
}
};
void main()
{
date ob1(12, 4, 2009), ob2("11/2/2009");
ob1.show_date();
ob2.show_date();
getch();
}
```

**OUTPUT:**

```
12/4/2009
11/2/2009
```

**Problem 75. Write a C++ program for overload constructor two ways: with initializer and without initializer.**

***Program:***

```
#include <iostream.h>
#include<conio.h>
class powers
{
int x;
public:
powers()
{
x = 0;
cout << "\nno initializer\n\n";
}
powers(int n)
{
x = n;
cout << "\n\ninitializer:" << x;
```

```
}
int getx() { return x; }
void setx(int i) { x = i; }
};
void main()
{
powers ofTwo[] = {1, 2, 4, 8, 16}; // initialized
powers ofThree[5];              // uninitialized
getch();
}
```

**OUTPUT:**

```
initializer:1
initializer:2
initializer:4
initializer:8
initializer:16
no initializer
no initializer
no initializer
no initializer
no initializer
```

**Problem 76. Write a C++ program to overload constructor for different data format.**

***Program:***

```
#include<iostream.h>
#include<stdio.h>
#include<conio.h>
class date
{
int day,month,year;
public:
date(char *str);
date(int m,int d,int y);
date::date();
void show();
};
date::date(char *str)
{
scanf(str,"*c*cd",&month,&day,&year);
}
date::date(int m,int d,int y)
{
day=d;
month=m;
year=y;
}
date::date()
{
cout<<"Enter month_day_year:";
cin>>day;
cin>>month;
cin>>year;
}
void date::show()
{
cout<<month<<'/'<<day<<'/';
cout<<year<<'\n';
}
void main()
{
date sdate("11/1/1999");
date idate(12,4,2009);
date indate;
sdate.show();
idate.show();
indate.show();
getch();
}
```

**OUTPUT:**

```
1
Enter month_day_year:2
3
1
16/2009312941/0
12/2/1998
3/2/1
```

**Problem 77. Write a C++ program for overloading class member functions.**

***Program:***

```
#include <iostream.h>
#include<conio.h>
class Rectangle
{
public:
Rectangle(int width, int height);
~Rectangle(){}
// overloaded class function display
void display() const;
void display(int aWidth, int aHeight) const;
private:
int itsWidth;
int itsHeight;
};
Rectangle::Rectangle(int width, int height)
{
itsWidth = width;
itsHeight = height;
}
void Rectangle::display() const
{
```

```
display( itsWidth, itsHeight);
}
void Rectangle::display(int width, int height) const
{
for (int i = 0; i<height; i++)
{
for (int j = 0; j< width; j++)
{
cout << "+";
}
cout << "\n";
}
}
void main()
{
Rectangle theRect(30,5);
cout << "display(): \n";
theRect.display();
cout << "\ndisplay(40,2): \n";
theRect.display(40,2);
getch();
}
```

**OUTPUT:**

```
display():
++++++++++++++++++++++++++++++
++++++++++++++++++++++++++++++
++++++++++++++++++++++++++++++
++++++++++++++++++++++++++++++
++++++++++++++++++++++++++++++
display(40,2):
+++++++++++++++++++++++++++++++++++++
+++
+++++++++++++++++++++++++++++++++++++
+++
```

**Problem 78. Write a C++ program for overloading class constructors.**

***Program:***

```
#include <iostream.h>
#include<conio.h>
class CRectangle
{
int width, height;
public:
CRectangle ();
CRectangle (int,int);
int area (void)
{
return (width*height);
}
};
CRectangle::CRectangle ()
{
width = 5;
height = 5;
}
CRectangle::CRectangle (int a, int b)
{
width = a;
height = b;
}
void main ()
{
CRectangle rect (3,4);
CRectangle rectb;
cout << "rect area: " << rect.area() << endl;
cout << "rectb area: " << rectb.area() << endl;
getch();
}
```

**OUTPUT:**

```
rect area: 12
rectb area: 25
```

**Problem 79. Write a C++ program to compute the salary of an employee by overloading constructor.**

***Program:***

```
#include<iostream.h>
#include<string.h>
class salary
{
private :
char name [10] ;
float bp ;
float da ;
float hra ;
float cca ;
float spay ;
public :
salary ( ) ;
salary (char nm [ ], float b) ;
salary (char nm [ ], float b, float h) ;
salary (char nm [ ], float b, float sp, float d) ;
} ;
salary :: salary ( )
{
strcpy (name, "        ") ;
bp = da = hra = cca = spay = 0.0 ;
}
salary :: salary (char nm [ ], float b)
{
strcpy (name, nm) ;
```

```
bp = b ;
cout<<"\n NAME is" << name ;
cout<<"\n Basic Pay is" << bp ;
}
salary :: salary (char nm [ ], float b, float h)
{
strcpy (name, nm) ;
bp = b ;
hra = h ;
cout<<"\n NAME is" << name ;
cout<<"\n BASIC PAY is" << bp ;
cout<<"\n House Rent Allowance is" << hra ;
}
salary :: salary (char nm [ ], float b, float sp)
{
strcpy (name, nm) ;
bp = b ;
spay = sp ;
cout<<"\n NAME is" << name ;
cout<<"\n BASIC PAY is" << bp ;
cout<<"\n SPECIAL PAY is" << spay ;
}
void main ( )
{
salary s1 [4] =
{
salary ( ),
salary ("Raj Kumar", 1200.23),
salary ("Ram Kumar", 1523.25, 25.32),
salary("MOHAN",2232.25,500.25, 1200.23);
} ;
}
```

**Problem 80. Write a C++ program to set overloading of constructor.**

***Program:***

```
#include <iostream.h>
#include<conio.h>
class student
{
private :
int rn ;
public :
student ( ) {rn = 0 ;}
student (int n) {rn = n ; }
// Overloading of constructor
~ student ( ) {   }          // Destructor defined
void getdata ( )
{
cout << "\n Enter the Roll Number:" ;
cin >> rn ;
}
void dispdata ( )
{
cout << "\n ROLLNUMBER is" << rn ;
}
} ;
void main ( )
{
class student a ;
class student b (20) ;
a. getdata () ;
a. dispdata () ;
b. dispdata () ;
getche () ;
}
```

**Problem 81. Write a C++ program to illustrate the concept of constructor overloading.**

***Program:***

```
#include<iostream.h>
#include<conio.h>
class value
{
private :
int a1,a2,a3,f,h;
float b1,b2,b3,bs;
public :
void getdata();
value(int a);
value(int a,int b,int c);
value(float a,float b);
int fact(int);
int big(int,int,int);
float avg(float,float);
void display1();
void display2();
void display3();
};
value :: value(int a)
{
a1 = a;
}
value :: value(int a,int b,int c)
{
a1 = a;
a2 = b;
a3 = c;
}
value :: value(float a,float b)
{
b1 = a;
```

```
b2 = b;
}
int value :: fact(int a1)
{
int m =1;
for(int i=1;i<=a1;i++)
{
m = m*i;
}
return(m);
}
int value :: big(int a1,int a2,int a3)
{
int temp;
temp = a1;
if(a2>temp)
temp = a2;
if(a3>temp)
temp = a3;
return(temp);
}
float value :: avg(float b1,float b2)
{
return((b1+b2)/2);
}
void value :: display1()
{
f = fact(a1);
cout<<"The factorial of given no:"<<f<<endl;
}
void value :: display2()
{
int h = big(a1,a2,a3);
cout<<"The biggest of three no.:"<<h<<endl;
}
void value :: display3()
{
bs = avg(b1,b2);
cout<<"The average of no's : "<<bs<<endl;
}
void main()
{
class value obj1(4),obj2(55,77,88),obj3(1.1,2.2);
clrscr();
obj1.display1();
obj2.display2();
obj3.display3();
getch();
}
```

**OUTPUT:**

The factorial of given no:24
The biggest of three no:88
The average of no's:1.65

**Problem 82. Write a C++ program to explain the concept of Constructor Overloading.**

***Program:***

```
// CONSTRUCTOR OVERLOADING
#include<iostream.h>
#include<conio.h>
//#include<cstdio>
class time
{
int hour,min,sec;
char *st;
public:
time(char *t);
time(int h,int m,int s);
void display_time();
};
time::time(char *t)
{
st=t;
cout<<st;
}
time::time(int h,int m,int s)
{
hour=h;
min=m;
sec=s;
}
void time::display_time()
{
cout<<endl;
cout<<hour<<":"<<min<<":"<<sec<<endl;
}
void main()
{
clrscr();
time t1(4,15,55),t2("5:45");
t1.display_time();
getch();
}
```

**OUTPUT:**

5.45
4:15:55

**Problem 83. Write a C++ program to illustrate the constructor and Destructor with the overloading of constructor.**

***Program:***

```
// Program to define in different way about the
overload constructors
#include<iostream.h>
#include<conio.h>
class integer
{
private:
int a;
public:
integer()
{
a=0;
cout<<endl<<"Constructor Called.";
}
integer(int i)
{
a=i;
cout<<endl<<"Constructor with argument called.";
}
~integer()
{
cout<<endl<<"Destructor Called.";
}
void get()
{
cout<<endl<<"Enter the value of integer:"<<endl;
cin>>a;
}
void show()
{
cout<<endl<<"The value of integer is:"<<'\t'<<a;
}
};
void main()
{
integer x, y(10);
x.get();
x.show();
y.show();
getch();
}
```

**OUTPUT:**

```
Constructor Called.
Constructor with argument called.
Enter the value of integer:
4
The value of integer is :    4
The value of integer is :    10
Destructor Called.
Destructor Called.
```

**Problem 84. Write a C++ program using overloading constructors to add complex numbers.**

***Program:***

```
#include<iostream.h>
#include<conio.h>
#include<iomanip.h>
class com
{
private:
double real;
double imag;
public:
com();
com(double);
com(double, double);
void add(com,com);
void put();
};
com::com( )
{
real=imag=0.0;
}
com::com(double a )
{
real=imag=a;
}
com::com(double x,double y)
{
real=x;
imag=y;
}
void com::add(com c1,com c2)
{
real=c1.real+c2.real;
imag=c1.imag-c2.imag;
}
void com::put()
{
if(imag>0)
cout<<real<<"+"<<imag<<"i"<<endl;
else
cout<<real<<imag<<"i"<<endl;
}
void main()
{
com obj1(4,7);
com obj2(4);
com obj3;
obj3.add(obj1,obj2);
obj3.put();
```

```
getch();
}
```

**OUTPUT:**

8+3i

**Problem 85. Write a C++ program for Height class.**

***Program:***

```
#include<iostream.h>
#include<conio.h>
class height
{
private:
int f;
double i;
public:
height(int f1)
{
f=f1;
i=0.0;
}
height(double f1)
{
f=int(f1);
i=(f1-int(f1))*12.0;
}
height()
{
f=i=0;
}
height(int f1,double in)
{
f=f1;
i=in;
}
void show()
{
cout<<"Feet="<<f<<"Inches="<<i<<"\n";
}
};
void main()
{
height obj1,obj2,obj3;
obj1=height(2);
obj2=height(3.5);
obj3=height(6,3);
obj1.show();
obj2.show();
obj3.show();
getch();
}
```

**OUTPUT:**

Feet=2 Inches=0
Feet=3 Inches=6
Feet=6 Inches=3

**Problem 86. Write a C++ program to default values in member functions.**

***Program:***

```
#include <iostream.h>
#include<conio.h>
class Rectangle
{
public:
Rectangle(int width, int height);
~Rectangle(){}
void display(int aWidth, int aHeight,bool
UseCurrentVals = false)const;
private:
int itsWidth;
int itsHeight;
};
Rectangle::Rectangle(int width, int height):
itsWidth(width), itsHeight(height) {}
void Rectangle::display(int width, int height, bool
UseCurrentValue) const
{
int printWidth;
int printHeight;
if (UseCurrentValue == true)
{
printWidth = itsWidth;
printHeight = itsHeight;
}
else
{
printWidth = width;
printHeight = height;
}
for (int i = 0; i<printHeight; i++)
{
for (int j = 0; j< printWidth; j++)
{
cout << "*";
}
cout << "\n";
}
}
void main()
{
Rectangle theRect(30,5);
cout << "display(0,0,true)...\n";
```

```
theRect.display(0,0,true);
cout <<"display(40,2)...\n";
theRect.display(40,2);
getch();
}
```

**OUTPUT:**

```
display(0,0,true)...
******************************
******************************
******************************
******************************
******************************
display(40,2)...
****************************************
****************************************
```

**Problem 87. Write a C++ program using class as the member function parameter type.**

***Program:***

```
#include<conio.h>
#include<iostream.h>
#include<iomanip.h>
class Rectangle
{
private:
float length;
float height;
public:
Rectangle(){}
Rectangle(float loge,float shge)
{
length=loge;
height=shge;
}
void getlength()
{
cout<<"Input large edge:";
cin>>length;
cout<<"Input small edge:";
cin>>height;
}
void showsquare()
{
cout<<setprecision(3) <<length*height<<endl;
}
void addsquare(Rectangle r1,Rectangle r2);
void addedge(Rectangle r1,Rectangle r2);
};
void Rectangle::addsquare(Rectangle r1,Rectangle
r2)
{
length=r1.length+r2.length;
height=r1.height+r2.height;
cout<<"\n Total of Rectangle square:"
<<r1.length*r1.height+r2.length*r2.height;
}
void Rectangle::addedge(Rectangle r1,Rectangle
r2)
{
length=r1.length+r2.length;
height=r1.height+r2.height;
cout<<"\n Toatal of Rectangle length:"
<<setprecision(3)<<(length+height)*2;
}
void main()
{
Rectangle room1(15.5,6.5);
Rectangle room2,room3;
room2.getlength();
cout<<"Square of room1 Rectangle is:";
room1.showsquare();
cout<<"square of room2 Rectangle is:";
room2.showsquare();
room3.addsquare(room1,room2);
room3.addedge(room1,room2);
getch();
}
```

**OUTPUT:**

```
Input large edge:123
Input small edge:12
Square of room1 Rectangle is:101
square of room2 Rectangle is:1.48e+003
Total of Rectangle square:1.58e+003
Toatal of Rectangle length:314"
```

## COPY CONSTRUCTOR

**Problem 88. Write a C++ program for Copy constructor.**

***Program:***

```
#include <iostream.h>
#include <stdlib.h>
#include<conio.h>
class A
{
int *p;
public:
A(int i);
~A();
int get()
{
```

```
return *p;
}
};
A::A(int i)
{
cout << "Allocating p\n";
p = new int;
if(!p) {
cout << "Allocation failure.\n";
exit(1); // exit program if out of memory
}
*p = i;
}
A::~A()
{
cout << "Freeing p\n";
delete p;
}
void display(A a)
{
cout << a.get() << '\n';
}
void main()
{
A a(10);
display(a);
getch();
}
```

**OUTPUT:**

```
Allocating p
10
Freeing p
```

**Problem 89. Write a C++ program to copy values to illustrate the concept of Copy Constructor.**

***Program:***

```
#include <iostream.h>
#include<conio.h>
class abc
{
private :
int a ;
float b ;
public :
abc (int x, float y)          //constructor defined
{
a = x ;
b = y ;
}
abc (abc  &m)                 //copy constructor
{
a = m . a ;
b = m . b ;
}
void write (void)
{
cout << a << b ;
}
} ;
void main ( )
{
abc m1 ( 20, 4.2) ;                    //m1 initialized
first constructor used
abc m2 (m1) ;                          //m1 is copied to
m2
abc m3 = m1 ;                          //m1 is copied to
m3
getch();
}
```

**Problem 90. Write a C++ program to generate Fibonacci series using the copy constructor.**

***Program:***

```
# include <iostream.h>
# include <conio.h>
class fibbo
{
priviate ;                             // i, j, k are data
member
int i ;
int j ;
int k ;
public :
fibbo ( )                              //
constructor defined
{
i = 0 ;
j = 1 ;
k = i + j ;
}
fibbo (fibbo  &ptr)                    //
copy constructor
{
i = ptr. i ;
j = ptr. j ;
k = ptr. k ;
}
void add ( )
{
i = j ;
j = k ;
k = i + j ;
```

```
}
void display ( )
{
cout << k << "\n" ;
}
~ fibbo ( ) ;                                   // destructor
defined
~ fibbo ( ) ;
} ;
void main (void)
{
int i ;
class fibbo x ;
for (i = 1 ; i < = 20 ; i ++)
{
x.display ( ) ;
x.add ( ) ;
}
getch () ;
}
```

**Problem 91. Write a C++ program to depict working of copy constructor.**

***Program:***

```
#include<iostream.h>
#include<conio.h>
class dist
{
private:
int feet;
float inch;
public:
dist(){}
dist(int f1,float in1)
{
feet=f1;
inch=in1;
}
dist(dist &d)
{
cout<<"Copy instructor invoked";
feet=d.feet;
inch=d.inch;
}
void show()
{
cout<<feet<<'\t'<<inch;
}
dist add(dist d)
{
dist t;
t.feet=feet+d.feet;
t.inch=inch+d.inch;
if(t.inch>=12.00)
{
t.inch-=12.00;
t.feet++;
}
return(t);
}
};
void main()
{
dist obj1(5,7);
dist obj2=obj1;
dist obj3;
obj3=obj1.add(obj2);
obj3.show();
getch();
}
```

**OUTPUT:**

```
Copy instructor invoked
Copy constructor invoked
Copy constructor invoked
obj3:-11 2
```

**Problem 92. Write a C++ program for a copy constructor to allow StringClass objects to be passed to functions.**

***Program:***

```
#include <iostream.h>
#include<conio.h>
#include <string.h>
#include <stdlib.h>
class StringClass
{
char *p;
public:
StringClass(char *s);          // constructor
StringClass(const StringClass &o);  // copy
constructor
~StringClass()
{      // destructor
delete [] p;
}
char *get()
{
return p;
}
};
```

```
StringClass::StringClass(char *s)    // "Normal"
constructor
{
int l;
l = strlen(s)+1;
p = new char [l];
if(!p)
{
cout << "Allocation error\n";
exit(1);
}
strcpy(p, s);
}
StringClass::StringClass(const StringClass &o)  //
Copy constructor
{
int l;
l = strlen(o.p)+1;
p = new char [l];              // allocate memory for
new copy
if(!p)
{
cout << "Allocation error\n";
exit(1);
}
strcpy(p, o.p);                // copy string into copy
}
void show(StringClass x)
{
char *s;
s = x.get();
cout << s << endl;
}
void  main()
{
StringClass a("www.google.com"),
b("www.google.com");
show(a);
show(b);
getch();
}
```

**Problem 93. Write a C++ program to print the Fibonacci series by Copy Constructor.**

***Program:***

```
#include<iostream.h>
#include<conio.h>
class fib
{
int a,b,c,n;
public:
fib(int p)
{
n=p;
a=0;
b=1;
}
void print();
};
void fib::print()
{
cout<<a<<" "<<b;
for(int i=1;i<=n-2;i++)
{
c=a+b;
cout<<" "<<c;
a=b;
b=c;
}
}
void main()
{
int n;
clrscr();
cout<<"Enter number of terms to be printed==>";
cin>>n;
fib f1(n);
fib f2=f1;
f2.print();
getch();
}
```

**OUTPUT:**

```
Enter number of terms to be printed==> 9
0 1 1 2 3 5 8 13 21
```

**Problem 94. Write a C++ program for My class Copy constructors.**

***Program:***

```
#include <iostream.h>
#include<conio.h>
class MyClass
{
public:
MyClass();                         // default constructor
MyClass (const MyClass &);         // copy
constructor
~MyClass();                        // destructor
int GetAge() const
{
return *itsAge;
}
int GetWeight() const
```

```
{
return *itsWeight;
}
void SetAge(int age)
{
*itsAge = age;
}
private:
int *itsAge;
int *itsWeight;
};
MyClass::MyClass()
{
itsAge = new int;
itsWeight = new int;
*itsAge = 5;
*itsWeight = 9;
}
MyClass::MyClass(const MyClass & rhs)
{
itsAge = new int;
itsWeight = new int;
*itsAge = rhs.GetAge();
*itsWeight = rhs.GetWeight();
}
MyClass::~MyClass()
{
delete itsAge;
itsAge = 0;
delete itsWeight;
itsWeight = 0;
}
void main()
{
MyClass myObject;
cout << "myObject's age: " << myObject.GetAge()
<< "\n";
cout << "Setting myObject to 6...\n";
myObject.SetAge(6);
cout << "Creating secondObject from myObject\n";
MyClass secondObject(myObject);
cout << "myObject's age: " << myObject.GetAge()
<< "\n";
cout << "secondObject' age: " <<
secondObject.GetAge() << "\n";
cout << "setting myObject to 7...\n";
myObject.SetAge(7);
cout << "myObject's age: " << myObject.GetAge()
<< "\n";
cout << "boot's age: " << secondObject.GetAge() <<
"\n";
getch();
}
```

**OUTPUT:**

```
myObject's age: 5
Setting myObject to 6...
Creating secondObject from myObject
myObject's age: 6
secondObject' age: 6
setting myObject to 7...
myObject's age: 7
boot's age: 6
```

**Problem 95. Write a C++ program for default Copy Constructor.**

***Program:***

```
#include <iostream.h>
#include<conio.h>
class Height
{
private:
int feet;
float inches;
public:
Height():feet(0),inches(0.0)
{ }
Height(int ft,float in):feet(ft),inches(in)
{ }
void get()
{
cout <<"\n Feet:";
cin >>feet;
cout <<" inches:";
cin >>inches;
}
void show()
{
cout <<feet <<"-" <<inches ;
}
};
void main()
{
Height H1(6,4.0);
Height H2(H1);
Height H3 =H1;
cout <<"\nHeigh1 =";H1.show();
cout <<"\nHeigh2 =";H2.show();
cout <<"\nHeigh3 =";H3.show();
cout <<endl;
getch();
}
```

**OUTPUT:**

Heigh1 =6-4.0
Heigh2 =6-4.0
Heigh3 =6-4.0

**Problem 96. Write a C++ program returning Objects from Functions.**

***Program:***

```
#include <iostream.h>
#include<conio.h>
class Height
{
private:
int feet;
float inches;
public:
Height():feet(0),inches(0.0)
{ }
Height(int ft,float in):feet(ft),inches(in)
{ }
void get()
{
cout <<"\nFeet:";
cin >>feet;
cout <<"inches:";
cin >>inches;
}
void show()
{
cout <<feet <<"-" <<inches;
}
Height add(Height);
};
Height Height::add(Height H2)
{
Height temp;
temp.inches =inches +H2.inches;
if(temp.inches >=12.0)
{
temp.inches -=12.0;
temp.feet =1;
}
temp.feet +=feet +H2.feet;
return temp;
}
void main()
{
Height heigh1,heigh3;
Height heigh2(6,4.0);
heigh1.get();
heigh3 =heigh1.add(heigh2);
cout <<"\nheigh1 =";heigh1.show();
cout <<"\nheigh2 =";heigh2.show();
cout <<"\nheigh3 =";heigh3.show();
cout <<endl;
getch();
}
```

**OUTPUT:**

Feet:6
inches:2.0
heigh1 =6-2.0
heigh2 =6-4.0
heigh3 =6-6.0

**Problem 97. Write a C++ program for virtual copy constructor.**

***Program:***

```
#include <iostream.h>
#include<conio.h>
class Animal
{
public:
Animal():itsAge(1)
{
cout << "Animal constructor...\n";
}
virtual ~Animal()
{
cout << "Animal destructor...\n";
}
Animal (const Animal & rhs);
virtual void Speak() const
{
cout << "Animal speak!\n";
}
virtual Animal* Clone()
{
return new Animal(*this);
}
int GetAge()const
{
return itsAge; }

protected:
int itsAge;
};
Animal::Animal (const Animal &
rhs):itsAge(rhs.GetAge())
{
cout << "Animal Copy Constructor...\n";
}
class Dog : public Animal
{
```

```
public:
Dog()
{
cout << "Dog constructor...\n";
}
virtual ~Dog()
{
cout << "Dog destructor...\n";
}
Dog (const Dog & rhs);
void Speak()const
{
cout << "Woof!\n";
}
virtual Animal* Clone() { return new Dog(*this); }
};
Dog::Dog(const Dog & rhs): Animal(rhs)
{
cout << "Dog copy constructor...\n";
}
class Cat : public Animal
{
public:
Cat()
{
cout << "Cat constructor...\n";
}
virtual ~Cat()
{
cout << "Cat destructor...\n";
}
Cat (const Cat &);
void Speak()const
{
cout << "Meow!\n";
}
virtual Animal* Clone()
{
return new Cat(*this);
}
};
Cat::Cat(const Cat & rhs): Animal(rhs)
{
cout << "Cat copy constructor...\n";
}
void main()
{
Animal *theArray[3];
Animal* ptr;
int choice,i;
theArray[0] = new Dog;
theArray[1] = new Cat;
theArray[2] = new Animal;
Animal *OtherArray[3];
for (i=0;i<3;i++)
{
theArray[i]->Speak();
OtherArray[i] = theArray[i]->Clone();
}
for (i=0;i<3;i++)
OtherArray[i]->Speak();
getch();
}
```

**OUTPUT:**

```
Animal constructor...
Dog constructor...
Animal constructor...
Cat constructor...
Animal constructor...
Woof!
Animal Copy Constructor...
Dog copy constructor...
Meow!
Animal Copy Constructor...
Cat copy constructor...
Animal speak!
Animal Copy Constructor...
Woof!
Meow!
Animal speak!
```

**Problem 98. Write a C++ program where constructor work as conversion operator.**

***Program:***

```
#include <iostream.h>
#include<conio.h>
class MyType
{
public:
MyType();
MyType(int val);
~MyType(){}
int getValue()const { return myValue; }
void setValue(int x) {myValue = x; }
private:
int myValue;
};
MyType::MyType(): myValue(0) {}
MyType::MyType(int val): myValue(val) {}
void main()
{
int theShort = 5;
```

```
MyType theCtr = theShort;
cout << "theCtr: " << theCtr.getValue() << endl;
getch();
}
```

**OUTPUT:**

theCtr: 5

## DESTRUCTOR:

**Problem 99. Write a C++ program for a simple constructor and destructor.**

***Program:***

```
#include <iostream.h>
#include<conio.h>
class MyClass
{
public:
int x;
MyClass(); // constructor
~MyClass(); // destructor
};
// Implement MyClass constructor.
MyClass::MyClass()
{
x = 10;
}
// Implement MyClass destructor.
MyClass::~MyClass()
{
cout << "Destructing...\n";
}
void main()
{
MyClass ob1;
MyClass ob2;
cout << ob1.x << " " << ob2.x << "\n";
getch();
}
```

**OUTPUT:**

10 10
Destructing...
Destructing...

**Problem 100. Write a C++ program to close stream in destructor.**

***Program:***

```
#include <fstream.h>
#include <iostream.h>
#include<conio.h>
class MyClass
{
private:
char msg[20];
int loopcounter;
fstream myfile;
public:
void display();
MyClass();
~MyClass();
};
MyClass::MyClass()
{
myfile.open("input.txt",ios::in);
myfile.getline(msg,20);
}
MyClass::~MyClass()
{
myfile.close();
}
void MyClass::display()
{
cout << msg << "\n";
}
void main()
{
MyClass obj;
obj.display();
getch();
}
```

**OUTPUT:**

Hello!

**Problem 101. Write a C++ program for virtual destructor methods.**

***Program:***

```
#include <iostream.h>
#include<conio.h>
class Animal
{
public:
Animal():itsAge(1) { cout << "Animal
constructor...\n"; }
virtual ~Animal() { cout << "Animal
destructor...\n"; }
virtual void Speak() const { cout << "Animal
speak!\n"; }
protected:
int itsAge;
};
class Cat: public Animal
{
```

```
public:
Cat() { cout << "Cat constructor...\n"; }
~Cat() { cout << "Cat destructor...\n"; }
void Speak()const { cout << "Meow!\n"; }
};
void main()
{
Animal *pCat = new Cat;
pCat->Speak();
getch();
}
```

**OUTPUT:**

Animal constructor...
Cat constructor...
Meow!

**Problem 102. Write a C++ program to demonstrating the order in which constructors and destructors are called.**

***Program:***

```
#include <string.h>
#include <iostream.h>
#include<conio.h>
class MyClass
{
public:
MyClass( int, string ); // constructor
~MyClass();            // destructor
private:
int objectID;
string message;
};
MyClass::MyClass( int ID, string s )
{
objectID = ID;
message = s;
cout << "Object " << objectID << " constructor runs
" << message << endl;
}
MyClass::~MyClass()
{
cout << "Object " << objectID << " destructor runs "
<< message << endl;
}
void create( void );
MyClass first( 1, "(global before main)" );
void main()
{
MyClass second( 2, "(local automatic in main)" );
static MyClass third( 3, "(local static in main)" );
create(); // call function to create objects
MyClass fourth( 4, "(local automatic in main)" );
getch();
}
void create( void )
{
cout << "\nCREATE FUNCTION: EXECUTION
BEGINS" << endl;
MyClass fifth( 5, "(local automatic in create)" );
static MyClass sixth( 6, "(local static in create)" );
cout << "\nCREATE FUNCTION: EXECUTION
ENDS" << endl;
}
```

**OUTPUT:**

Object 1 constructor runs (global before main)
Object 2 constructor runs (local automatic in main)
Object 3 constructor runs (local static in main)
CREATE FUNCTION: EXECUTION BEGINS
Object 5 constructor runs (local automatic in create)
Object 6 constructor runs (local static in create)
CREATE FUNCTION: EXECUTION ENDS
Object 5 destructor runs (local automatic in create)
Object 4 constructor runs (local automatic in main)
Object 4 destructor runs (local automatic in main)
Object 2 destructor runs (local automatic in main)
Object 6 destructor runs (local static in create)
Object 3 destructor runs (local static in main)
Object 1 destructor runs (global before main)

## CONVERSION FUNCTION:

**Problem 103. Write a C++ program for a simple conversion function example.**

***Program:***

```
#include <iostream.h>
#include<conio.h>
class MyClass
{
int x, y;
public:
MyClass(int i, int j)
{
x = i;
y = j;
}
operator int()
{
return x*y;
}
```

```
};
void main()
{
MyClass object1(2, 3), object2(4, 3);
int i;
i = object1;          // automatically convert to
integer
cout << i << '\n';
i = 100 + object2;    // convert object2 to integer
cout << i << '\n';
getch();
}
```

**OUTPUT:**

```
6
112
```

**Problem 104. Write a C++ program to convert to char * in function call.**

***Program:***

```
#include <iostream.h>
#include<conio.h>
#include <string.h>
class StringClass
{
char str[80];
int len;
public:
StringClass(char *s)
{
strcpy(str, s);
len = strlen(s);
}
operator char *()
{ // convert to char*
return str;
}
};
void main()
{
StringClass s("This is a test\n");
char *p, s2[80];
p = s;          // convert to char *
cout << "Here is string: " << p << '\n';
strcpy(s2, s);
cout << "Here is copy of string: " << s2 << '\n';
getch();
}
```

**OUTPUT:**

```
Here is string: This is a test
Here is copy of string: This is a test
```

**Problem 105. Write a C++ program to define and use the destructor.**

***Program:***

```
#include <iostream.h>
#include<conio.h>
class myclass
{
int a;
public:
myclass();                  // constructor
~myclass();                 // destructor
void show();
};
myclass::myclass()
{
cout << "In constructor\n";
a = 10;
}
myclass::~myclass()
{
cout << "Destructing...\n";
}
void myclass::show()
{
cout << a << endl;
}
void main()
{
myclass ob;
ob.show();
getch();
}
```

**OUTPUT:**

```
In constructor
10
Destructing...
```

**Problem 106. Write a C++ program in which system will call the destructor.**

***Program:***

```
#include <iostream.h>
#include<conio.h>
class myclass
{
public:
int who;
myclass(int id);
~myclass();
};
myclass::myclass(int id)
{
```

```
cout << "Initializing " << id << endl;
who = id;
}
myclass::~myclass()
{
cout << "Destructing " << who << endl;
}
void main()
{
myclass object1(3);
cout << "Here.\n";
myclass object2(4);
getch();
}
```

**OUTPUT:**

Initializing 3
Here.
Initializing 4
Destructing 4
Destructing 3

**Problem 107. Write a C++ program to implement a destructor.**

***Program:***

```
#include <iostream.h>
#include<conio.h>
class prompt
{
int count;
public:
prompt(char *s)
{
cout << s; cin >> count;
};
~prompt();
};
prompt::~prompt()
{
int i, j;
for(i = 0; i <count; i++)
{
cout << '\a';
for(j=0; j<32000; j++)
; // delay
}
}
void main()
{
prompt ob("Enter a number: ");
getch();
}
```

**OUTPUT:**

Enter a number: 1

**Problem 108. Write a C++ program using a constructor and destructor.**

***Program:***

```
#include <iostream.h>
#include<conio.h>
#define SIZE 10
class stack
{
int stck[SIZE];
int topOfStack;
public:
stack(); // constructor
~stack(); // destructor
void push(int i);
int pop();
};
// constructor
stack::stack()
{
topOfStack = 0;
cout << "Stack Initialized\n";
}
// destructor
stack::~stack()
{
cout << "Stack Destroyed\n";
}
void stack::push(int i)
{
if( topOfStack == SIZE )
{
cout << "Stack is full.\n";
return;
}
stck[ topOfStack ] = i;
topOfStack++;
}
int stack::pop()
{
if( topOfStack == 0 )
{
cout << "Stack underflow.\n";
return 0;
}
topOfStack--;
return stck[ topOfStack ];
}
void  main()
```

```
{
stack a, b;
a.push(1);
b.push(2);
a.push(3);
b.push(4);
cout << a.pop() << " ";
cout << a.pop() << " ";
cout << b.pop() << " ";
cout << b.pop() << endl;
getch();
}
```

**OUTPUT:**

```
Stack Initialized
Stack Initialized
3 1 4 2
Stack Destroyed
Stack Destroyed
```

## STRUCT CLASS:

**Problem 109. Write a C++ program for constructor and destructor inside a struct.**

***Program.***

```
#include <iostream.h>
#include<conio.h>
#include <string.h>
#include <stdlib.h>
struct StringClass
{
StringClass(char *ptr);
~StringClass();
void show();
private:
char *p;
int len;
};
StringClass::StringClass(char *ptr)
{
len = strlen(ptr);
p = (char *) malloc(len+1);
if(!p) {
cout << "Allocation error\n";
exit(1);
}
strcpy(p, ptr);
}
StringClass::~StringClass()
{
cout << "Freeing p\n";
free(p);
}
void StringClass::show()
{
cout << p << " - length: " << len;
cout << endl;
}
void  main()
{
StringClass stringObject1("www.google.com."),
stringObject2("www.google.com.");
stringObject1.show();
stringObject2.show();
getch();
}
```

**OUTPUT:**

```
www.google.com - length: 15
www.google.com - length: 15
Freeing p
Freeing p
```

**Problem 110. Write a C++ program for stack class using a structure.**

***Program:***

```
#include <iostream.h>
#include<conio.h>
#define SIZE 10
struct stack
{
stack();            // constructor
void push(char ch); // push character on stack
char pop();         // pop character from stack
private:
char stackData[SIZE]; // holds the stack
int topOfStack;       // index of top-of-stack
};
stack::stack()
{
cout << "Constructing a stack\n";
topOfStack = 0;
}
void stack::push(char ch)
{
if(topOfStack==SIZE)
{
cout << "Stack is full\n";
return;
}
stackData[topOfStack] = ch;
topOfStack++;
}
```

```
char stack::pop()
{
if(topOfStack==0)
{
cout << "Stack is empty\n";
return 0; // return null on empty stack
}
topOfStack--;
return stackData[topOfStack];
}
void main()
{
stack stackObject1, stackObject2;
int i;
stackObject1.push('a');
stackObject2.push('x');
stackObject1.push('b');
stackObject2.push('y');
stackObject1.push('c');
stackObject2.push('z');
for(i = 0; i <3; i++)
cout << "Pop stackObject1: " << stackObject1.pop()
<< endl;
for(i = 0; i <3; i++)
cout << "Pop stackObject2: " << stackObject2.pop()
<< endl;
getch();
}
```

**OUTPUT:**

```
Constructing a stack
Constructing a stack
Pop stackObject1: c
Pop stackObject1: b
Pop stackObject1: a
Pop stackObject2: z
Pop stackObject2: y
Pop stackObject2: x
```

# CONSTRUCTOR PROGRAMMING:

**Problem 111. Write a C++ program when constructors and destructors are Executed.**

***Program:***

```
#include <iostream.h>
#include<conio.h>
class A
{
public:
int value;
A(int id);
~A();
}
glob_ob1(1),glob_ob2(2);
A::A(int id)
{
cout <<"Initialize: "<<id <<"\n";
value =id;
}
A::~A()
{ cout <<"Destructing: "<<value <<"\n"; }
void main()
{
A aa(2);
cout <<"Continue.\n";
A bb(4);
getch();
}
```

**OUTPUT:**

```
Initialize: 1
Initialize: 2
Initialize: 3
Continue.
Initializing: 4
Destructing: 4
Destructing: 3
Destructing: 2
Destructing: 1
```

**Problem 112. Write a C++ program to Passing Objects to Functions.**

***Program:***

```
#include <iostream.h>
#include<conio.h>
class A
{
int i;
public:
A(int a);
~A();
void set_i(int a)
{
i=a;
}
int get_i()
{
return i;
} };
A::A(int a)
{
i =a;
```

```
cout <<"Constructing "<<i <<"\n";
}
A::~A()
{
cout <<"Destroy "<<i <<"\n";
}
void M(A aa);
void main()
{
A bb(1);
M(bb);
cout <<"This is global i in main:";
cout <<bb.get_i()<<"\n";
getch();
}
void M(A aa)
{
aa.set_i(2);
cout <<"This is local i in function M:"<<aa.get_i();
cout <<"\n";
}
```

**OUTPUT:**

```
Constructing 1
This is local i in function M:2
Destroying 2
This is global i in main:1
Destroying 1
```

**Problem 113. Write a C++ program to depict execution of destructor.**

***Program:***

```
#include<iostream.h>
#include<conio.h>
class ct
{
int id;
public:
ct(int i)
{
id=i;
cout<<"\n constructor ="<<id<<"runs";
}
~ct()
{
cout<<"\nobject ="<<id<<"destroyed";
}
};
void main()
{
ct c1(1);
ct c2(2);
ct c3(3);
cout<<"\nEnd of main";
getch();
}
```

**OUTPUT:**

```
constructor 1 runs
constructor 2 runs
constructor 3 runs
End of main
object 3 destroyed
object 2 destroyed
object 1 destroyed
```

**Problem 114. Write a C++ program to depict working of constructor & destructor in operations performed dynamically.**

***Program:***

```
#include<iostream.h>
#include<conio.h>
#include<string.h>
class string
{
char *nm;
Int len;
public:
string(char *s)
{
len=strlen(s);
nm=new char[len+1];
strcpy(name,s);
}
void com(string &ss2)
{
int k;
k=strcmp(nm,ss2.nm);
if(k==0)
cout<<"\nBoth objects have same name";
else
cout<<"\nBoth objects have different name";
}
void put()
{
cout<<"\nName of person"<<nm;
}
~string()
{
cout<<"\nRelease memory allocated to"<,nm;
delete[] nm;
}
};
void main()
```

```
{
string obj1("Mukul");
string obj2("Harleen");
obj1.put();
obj2.put();
obj1.com(obj2);
getch();
}
```

**OUTPUT:**

Name of person Mukul
Name of person Harleen
Both objects have different name
Release memory allocated to Harleen
Release memory allocated to Mukul

**Problem 115. Write a C++ program to depict use of new & delete operators.**

***Program:***

```
#include<iostream.h>
#include<conio.h>
class rec
{
private:
int l;
int b;
public:
rec()
{
cout<<"Constructor with no parameter invoked";
}
void read()
{
cout<<"Enter length & breadth: ";
cin>>l>>b;
}
void area()
{
cout<<"Area is "<<l*b;
}
~rec()
{
cout<<"Destructor invoked";
}
};
void main()
{
rec *p;
p=new rec;
p->area();
cout<<"Destroying object\n ";
delete p;
cout<<"End of program";
getch();
}
```

**OUTPUT:**

Constructor with no parameter invoked
Enter length & breadth:4 3
Area is 12
Destroying object
Destructor invoked
End of program

**Problem 116. Write a C++ program using reference variable to create dynamic objects.**

***Program:***

```
#include<iostream.h>
#include<conio.h>
class rec
{
private:
int l;
int b;
public:
rec();
void get();
void area();
~rec();
};
rec::rec()
{
cout<<"Constructor with no parameter invoked";
}
void rec::get()
{
cout<<"Enter length & breadth: ";
cin>>l>>b;
}
void rec::area()
{
cout<<"Area is: "<<l*b;
}
rec::~rec()
{
cout<<"Destructor invoked";
}
void main()
{
rec &obj=*(new rec);
obj.get();
obj.area();
cout<<"End of program";
getch();
```

```
}
```

**OUTPUT:**

Constructor with no parameter invoked
Enter length & breadth:4 3
Area is:12
End of program

**Problem 117. Write a C++ program to make dynamic array of objects.**

***Program:***

```
#include<iostream.h>
#include<conio.h>
class student
{
private:
int r;
char nm[20];
public:
void get();
void put();
student()
{
cout<<"Constructor with no parameter invoked";
}
~student()
{
cout<<"Destructor  invoked";
}
};
void student::get()
{
cout<<"Enter rollno and name:";
cin>>r>>nm;
}
void student::put()
{
cout<<"\nRollno :"<<r;
cout<<"\nName of student :"<<nm;
}
void main()
{
student *p;
int n;
cout<<"Enter no. of students:";
cin>>n;
p=new student[n];
for(int i=0;i<n;i++)
{
(p+i)->get();
(p+i)->put();
}
delete[] p;
getch();
}
```

**Problem 118. Write a C++ program to add distances in 'feet & inches & other in 'int & cin'.**

***Program:***

```
#include<iostream.h>
#include<conio.h>
class m;
class dist
{
private:
int feet;
float inch;
public:
dist()
{feet=inch=0;}
dist(int f,float in)
{
feet=f;
inch=in;
}
void put()
{
cout<<feet<<inch;
}
friend void sum(dist,m);
};
class m
{
int mtr,cm;
public:
m(int m1,int c)
{
mtr=m1;cm=c;
}
friend void sum(dist,m);
};
void sum(dist dd,m mm)
{
float df=dd.feet+dd.inch/12;
float dm=(mm.mtr+mm.cm/100)*3.28;
float daf= df+dm;
dist res;
res.feet=int(daf);
res.inch=(daf-res.feet)*12.00;
cout<<"feet"<<res.feet<<"inches"<<res.inch;
}
void main()
{
```

```
dist obj1(2,0);
m obj2=(1,100);
sum(obj1,obj2);
getch();
}
```

**Problem 119. Write a C++ program to depict fibonacci series.**

***Program:***

```
#include<iostream.h>
#include<conio.h>
class fib
{
int a,b;
public:
fib()
{
a=0;b=1;
}
void put(int);
};
void fib::put(int n1)
{
if(n1<=1)
cout<<a;
else if(n1==2)
cout<<a<<'\t'<<b;
else
{
cout<<a<<'\t'<<b;
for(int i=3;i<=n1;i++)
{
int c=a+b;
cout<<'\t'<<c;
a=b;b=c;
}}}
void main()
{
fib h;
int n;
cout<<"Enter number of terms";
cin>>n;
h.put(n);
getch();
}
```

**OUTPUT:**

Enter number of terms 6
0 1 1 2 3 5

**Problem 120. Write a C++ program to convert height and age in cms when its known in mts.**

***Program:***

```
#include<iostream.h>
#include<conio.h>
#include<string.h>
class per
{
char nm[20];
int yob;
double htm;
public:
per(char n[],int yy,double ht)
{
strcpy(nm,n);
yob=yy;
htm=ht;
}
void age(int curyear)
{
int age=curyear-yob;
cout<<"Approx age of person"<<age;
}
void htc()
{
double h=htm*100;
cout<<"\nHeight of person in cms"<<h;
}};
void main()
{
per obj1("Akash",1990,1.05);
obj1.age(2009);
obj1.htc();
getch();
return 0;
}
```

**OUTPUT:**

Approx age of person 19
Height of person in cm 105

**Problem 121. Write a C++ program to find distance between two points.**

***Program:***

```
#include<iostream.h>
#include<conio.h>
#include<math.h>
class point
{
private:
int u,v;
public:
point(int uu,int vv)
{
```

```
u=uu;
v=vv;
}
double cal_dist(point pp2)
{
double dist;
dist=sqrt(pow((pp2.v-v),2)+pow((pp2.u-u,2));
return(dist);
}};
void main()
{
double obj1;
point t(5,8),z(3,2);
obj1=t.cal_dist(z);
cout<<"\nDistance between points"<<obj1;
getch();
}
```

**Problem 122. Write a C++ program to create date class with members as day,month,year & use a function to increment day by 1and then display date.**

***Program:***

```
#include<iostream.h>
#include<conio.h>
class clsdate
{
int d,m,y;
public:
clsdate()
{
d=0;m=0;y=0;
}
clsdate(int dd,int mm,int  yy)
{
d=dd;m=mm;y=yy;
}
void nday();
int lyear();
int lday();
void put()
{
cout<<"\nDate(dd/mm/yyyy)="<<d<<"/"<<m<<"/"<
<y;}
};
void clsdate::nday()
{
d=d+1;
if(d>lday())
{d=1;
m=m+1;
}
if(m>12)
{
m=1;
y=y+1;
}}
int clsdate::lyear()
{
if((y%4==0 && y%100!=0)||(y%400==0))
return 1;
else
return 0;
}
int clsdate::lday()
{
int
mon[12]={31,28,31,30,31,30,31,30,31,30,31,30};
if(m==2&&lyear())
return 29;
else
return mon[mon-1];
}
void main()
{
clsdate obj1(12,5,1983);
clsdate obj2(22,3,2006);
clsdate obj3(31,12,2008);
obj1.nday();
obj2.nday();
obj3.nday();
obj1.put();
obj2.put();
obj3.put();
getch();
}
```

**OUTPUT:**

```
Date(dd/mm/yyyy)=13/5/1983
Date(dd/mm/yyyy)=23/3/2006
Date(dd/mm/yyyy)=1/1/2009
```

**Problem 123. Write a C++ program to depict operations using stack.**

***Program:***

```
#include<iostream.h>
#include<conio.h>
class stack
{
int a[10],top;
public:
stack()
{
```

```
top=-1;
cout<<"\nStack is created";
}
void push(int num)
{
if(top==9)
cout<<"overflow";
else
{
top=top+1;
a[top]=num;
cout<<"\nElements pushed is "<<a[top];
}}
void pop()
{
if(top==-1)
cout<<"underflow";
else
{
cout<<"\nElements poped "<<a[top];
top=top-1;
}}
void put();
};
void stack::put()
{
for(int i=0;i<=top;i++)
cout<<a[i]<<'\t';
}
void main()
{
stack obj;
obj.push(25);
obj.push(35);
obj.push(45);
obj.pop();
cout<<"\nCurrent element in stack";
obj.put();
getch();
}
```

**OUTPUT:**

```
Stack is created
Elements pushed is 25
Elements pushed is 35
Elements pushed is 45
Elements poped 45
Current element in stack 25 35
```

**Problem 124. Write a C++ program to add two timings and show in specific format.**

***Program:***

```
#include<iostream.h>
#include<conio.h>
class t
{
int h,m,s;
public:
t()
{h=m=s=0;}
t(int e,int u,int w)
{h=e;m=u;s=w;}
void put()
{
cout<<h<<":"<<m<<":"<<s;
}
t add(t);
};
t t::add(t tt2)
{
t ti;
ti.s=s+tt2.s;
ti.m=m+tt2.m;
if(ti.s>59)
{
ti.s=ti.s-60;
ti.m++;
}
ti.h=h+tt2.h;
if(ti.m>59)
{
ti.m=ti.m-60;
ti.h++;
}
return(ti);
}
void main()
{
t obj1(2,18,45);
t obj2(4,10,10);
t obj3;
obj3= obj1.add( obj2);
cout<<"Time after addition(hh:m:ss)=";
obj3.put();
getch();
}
```

**OUTPUT:**

```
Time after addition(hh:m:ss)=6:28:55
```

**Problem 125. Write a C++ program to keep movie & time details by creating a class.**

***Program:***

```
#include<iostream.h>
```

```
#include<conio.h>
#include<string.h>
class cm
{
char movie[20];
char timing[10];
public:
cm(char mv[],char tm[])
{
strcpy(movie,mv);
strcpy(timing,tm);
}
cm(cm &c)
{
strcpy(movie,c.movie);
strcpy(timing,c.timing);
cout<<"Copy constructor\n";
}
void show()
{
cout<<"Name of the movie"<<movie<<"\n";
cout<<"Timing of the movie"<<timing<<"\n";
}
~cm()
{
cout<<"Destructor invoked\n";
}};
void main()
{
cm ansal("DDLJ","4.45PM");
cm adlabs(ansal);
cout<<"Display object ansal\n";
ansal.show();
cout<<"Display object adlabs\n";
adlabs.show();
getch();
}
```

**OUTPUT:**

```
Copy constructor
Display object ansal
Name of the movie DDLJ
Timing of the movie 4.45PM
Display object adlabs
Name of the movie DDLJ
Timing of the movie 4.45PM
```

**Problem 126. Write a C++ program using dynamic allocation to find sum of elements.**

***Program:***

```
#include<iostream.h>
#include<conio.h>
class ar
{
int *p,n;
public:
ar()
{
cout<<"Enter number of elements";
cin>>n;
p=new int[n];
}
void get();
void as();
~ar()
{
delete[] p;
}
};
void ar::get()
{
for(int i=0;i<n;i++)
cin>>*(p+i);
}
void ar::as()
{
int s=0;
for(int i=0;i<n;i++)
s=s+*(p+i);
cout<<"Sum of"<<n<<"elements="<<s;
}
void main()
{
ar  obj1;
cout<<"Enter elements";
obj1.get();
obj1.as();
getch();
}
```

**OUTPUT:**

```
Enter number of elements 3
Enter elements 4 12 5
Sum of elements=21
```

**Problem 127. Write a C++ program to find result of students and sort them on percentage basis by dynamic object creation.**

***Program:***

```
#include<iostream.h>
#include<conio.h>
#include<iomanip.h>
class stud
{
```

```
char nm[20];
int rollno,m[5],tm;
double per;
public:
void g();
void p();
void cal();
void sort(stud *,int);
};
void stud::g()
{
cout<<"Enter rollno & name";
cin>>rollno>>nm;
cout<<"Enter marks";
for(int j=0;j<5;j++)
cin>>m[j];
}
void stud::p()
{
cout<<"\nRollno"<<rollno;
cout<<"\nName"<<nm<<"\n";
cout<<"Marks of a student";
for(int j=0;j<5;j++)
cout<<m[j]<<"\t";
cout<<"\nTotal marks obtained"<<tm;
cout<<"\Percentage"<<setprecision(2)<<per<<"\n";
}
void stud::cal()
{
tm=0;
for(int j=0;j<5;j++)
tm+=m[j];
per=double(tm)/5;
}
void stud::sort(stud *p,int n)
{
stud temp;
for(int i=0;i<n-1;i++)
for(int j=i+1;j<n;j++)
if((p+i)->per<(p+j)->per)
{
temp=*(p+i);
*(p+i)=*(p+j);
*(p+j)=temp;
}}
void main()
{
int n;
stud *p,t;
cout<<"Enter no. of students";
cin>>n;
p=new stud[n];
for(int i=0;i<n;i++)
{
(p+i)->g();
(p+i)->cal();
}
t.sort(p,n);
cout<<"Sorted objects are";
for(i=0;i<n;i++)
(p+i)->p();
delete[] p;
getch();
}
```

**OUTPUT:**

```
Enter no. of students 2
Enter rollno & name 1 Akash
Enter marks
23 34 55 12 12
Enter rollno & name 2 Puner
Enter marks
54 12 34 56 78
Sorted objects are
Rollno 2
Name Puner
Marks of a student 54 12 34 56 78
Total marks obtained 234
Percentage 46.8
Rollno 1
Name Akash
Marks of a student 23 34 55 12 12
Total marks obtained 136
Percentage 27.2
```

**Problem 128. Write a C++ program to read matrix & find maximum of each row & find average of maximum value.**

***Program:***

```
#include<iostream.h>
#include<conio.h>
class mat
{
private:
int s[10][10];
int u,v;
public:
mat()
{
cout<<"Enter number of row and column";
cin>>u>>v;
}
void g();
```

```
void calavg();
};
void mat::g()
{
cout<<"Enter elements:\n";
for(int i=0;i<u;i++)
for(int j=0;j<v;j++)
cin>>s[i][j];
}
void mat::calavg()
{
int sum=0,mx;
for(int i=0;i<u;i++)
{
mx=s[i][0];
for(int j=0;j<v;j++)
if(mx<s[i][j])
mx=s[i][j];
cout<<mx<<"is maximum value of
row"<<i+1<<"\n";
sum+=mx;
}
cout<<"Average of maximum value in each row=
"<<double(sum)/u<<"\n";
}
void main()
{
mat obj1;
obj1.g();
obj1.calavg();
getch();
}
```

**Problem 129. Write a C++ program for destructor.**

***Program:***

```
#include <iostream.h>
#include <stdlib.h>
#include<conio.h>
class A
{
int *p;
public:
A(int i);
~A();
int get()
{
return *p;
}
};
A::A(int i)
{
cout << "Allocating p\n";
p = new int;
if(!p)
{
cout << "Allocation failure.\n";
exit(1); // exit program if out of memory
}
*p = i;
}
// use destructor to free memory
A::~A()
{
cout << "Freeing p\n";
delete p;
}
void display(A &a)
{
cout << a.get() << '\n';
}
void main()
{
A a(10);
display(a);
getch();
}
```

**OUTPUT:**

```
Allocating p
10
Freeing p
```

**Problem 130. Write a C++ program to read and display rollno,fees to illustrate the concept of Dynamic Constructor.**

***Program:***

```
#include <iostream.h>
#include<conio.h>
class abc
{
int rn ;
float fees ;
public :
abc (int a, float b)
{
rn = a ;
fees = b ;
}
abc (abc & m)                    //copy constructor
{
rn = m.rn ;
fees = m.fees ;
```

```
cout<<"\n Copy constructor at work" ;
}
};
void main ( )
{
float x,y ;
cout<<"\n Enter the Roll No of student" ;
cin >> x ;
cout<<"\n Enter the fees of student" ;
cin >> y ;
abc m1 (x, y) ;
}                          //dynamic initialization with
value x & y
```

**Problem 131. Write a C++ program to define Constructor and Destructor.**

***Program:***

```
# include <iostream.h>
#include <conio.h>
#include<string.h>
class student
{
private :
int rn ;
char name [10] ;
public :
student ( )       // constructor defined
{
rn = 20 ;
strcpy(name,"RAM" );
}
void dispdata ()
{
cont <<"\n ROLL NO is" << rn ;
cout <<"\n NAME is" << name ;
}
~ student ( )
{ }
} ;
void main ()
{
class student s1 ;
cout << s1. dispdata ( ) ;
getch ( ) ;
}
```

**Problem 132. Write a C++ program to show the order of invocation of Constructor and Destructor.**

***Program:***

```
#include<iostream.h>
#include<conio.h>
class A
{
static int i;
public:
A()
{
cout<<"Object "<<++i<<" crerated.\n";
}
~A()
{
cout<<"Object "<<i--<<" destroyed.\n";
}
};
int A::i;
void main()
{
clrscr();
A a1;
{
A a2;
}
A a3;
getch();
}
```

**Problem 133. Write a C++ program to maintain Hotel management with array of objects with constructors.**

***Program:***

```
#include<iostream.h>
#include<conio.h>
#include<string.h>
class hotel
{
char hotel[50],single,customer[20];
int room,bill_day,days;
float checkin,checkout;
double total;
public:
hotel(char s[],int d)
{
strcpy(hotel,"Five Star");
strcpy(customer,s);
days=d;
checkout=12.00;
total=0;
}
void input()
{
cout<<"Enter room number==>";
```

```
cin>>room;
cout<<"Press y/n for single room...";
cin>>single;
if(single=='y')
bill_day=700;
else
bill_day=1000;
cout<<"Enter time of checking in==>";
cin>>checkin;
total=bill_day*days;
total+=total*12.4/100;
}
void print()
{
cout<<"Room number is "<<room;
cout<<"\nCustomer name is "<<customer;
cout<<"\nTotal bill is Rs. "<<total;
cout<<"\nRoom is ";
if(single=='y')
cout<<"Single bed.";
else
cout<<"Double bed.";
cout<<"\nTime of checking in is
"<<checkin<<"o'clock";
cout<<"\nTime of checking out is
"<<checkout<<endl<<endl<<endl;
}
};
void main()
{
hotel h[2]={hotel("Ankush",5),hotel("Ashu",7)};
clrscr();
for(int i=0;i<2;i++)
{
cout<<"Enter information of customer
"<<i+1<<"==>\n";
h[i].input();
}
cout<<"Press any key to show records....";
getch();
clrscr();
for(i=0;i<2;i++)
{
cout<<"Information of customer
"<<i+1<<"is==>\n";
h[i].print();
}
getch();
}
```

**Problem 134. Write a C++ program for overloading Constructor Functions date.**

***Program:***

```
#include <iostream.h>
#include <conio.h>
#include<stdio.h>
class date
{
int day,month,year;
public:
date(char *d);
date(int d,int m,int y);
void show_date();
};
date::date(char *d)
{
sscanf(d,"%d%*c%d%*c%d",&month,&day,&yea
r);
}
date::date(int d,int m,int y)
{
day =d;
month =m;
year =y;
}
void date::show_date()
{
cout <<month <<"/"<<day;
cout <<"/"<<year <<"\n";
}
void main()
{
date d1(12,4,2009),d2("2/11/2009");
d1.show_date();
d2.show_date();
getch();
}
```

**OUTPUT:**

```
4/12/2009
2/11/2009
```

**Problem 135. Write a C++ program for Copy Constructorsfor array class.**

***Program:***

```
#include <iostream.h>
#include <new.h>
#include <stdlib.h>
#include<conio.h>
class array
{
int *p;
```

```
int size;
public:
array(int sz)
{
try
{
p =new int [sz ];
}
catch (bad_alloc xa)
{
cout <<"Allocation Failure \n";
exit(EXIT_FAILURE);
}
size =sz;
}
~array()
{
delete [] p;
}
//copy constructor
array(const array &a);
void put(int i,int j)
{
if(i>=0 &&i<size)p [i ] ==j;
}
int get(int i)
{
return p [i ];
}
};
//Copy Constructor
array::array(const array &a)
{
int i;
try
{
p =new int [a.size ];
}
catch (bad_alloc xa){ }
cout <<"Allocation Failure \n";
exit(EXIT_FAILURE);
}
for(i=0;i<a.size;i++)
p [i] ==a.p[i];
}
void main()
{
array num(10);
int i;
for(i=0;i<10;i++)num.put(i,i);
for(i=9;i>=0;i--)cout <<num.get(i);
cout <<"\n";
//create another array and initialize with num
array x(num);//invokes copy constructor
for(i=0;i<10;i++)cout <<x.get(i);
getch();
}
```

# CHAPTER 12

# OPERATOR OVERLOADING

## OVERLOAD UNARY AND BINARY OPERATORS:

**Problem 1. Write a C++ program for overloading ++.**

***Program:***

```
#include <iostream.h>
#include<conio.h>
class MyType
{
public:
MyType (int arg = 0) : x(arg)
{ }
int operator!=(const MyType& arg) const
{
cout << "comparing" << endl;
return x != arg.x;
}
int operator*() const { return x; }
MyType& operator++()
{
++x;
return *this;
}
private:
int x;
};
void main()
{
MyType begin(3);
MyType end(7);
for( ; begin != end ; ++begin)
cout << *begin << " ";
getch();
}
```

**OUTPUT:**

```
comparing
3 comparing
4 comparing
5 comparing
6 comparing
```

**Problem 2. Write a C++ program for overloading the increment operator.**

***Program:***

```
#include <iostream.h>
#include<conio.h>
class MyType
{
public:
MyType();
~MyType(){}
int getValue()const
{
return myValue;
}
void setValue(int x)
{
myValue = x;
}
void Increment()
{
++myValue;
}
const MyType& operator++ ();
private:
int myValue;
};
MyType::MyType():myValue(0){}
const MyType& MyType::operator++()
{
++myValue;
 return *this;
}
void main()
{
MyType i;
cout << "The value of i is " << i.getValue() <<
endl;
i.Increment();
cout << "The value of i is " << i.getValue() <<
endl;
++i;
cout << "The value of i is " << i.getValue() <<
endl;
```

```
MyType a = ++i;
cout << "The value of a: " << a.getValue();
cout << " and i: " << i.getValue() << endl;
getch();
}
```

**OUTPUT:**

```
The value of i is 0
The value of i is 1
The value of i is 2
The value of a: 3 and i: 3
```

**Problem 3. Write a C++ program to overload ++ operator.**

***Program:***

```
#include<iostream.h>
#include<conio.h>
class date
{
int dd,mm,yy;
int lyear()
{
if((yy%400==0)||(yy%4==0)&&(yy%100!=0))
return 1;
else
return 0;
}
int eday();
public:
date(int d,int m,int  y)
{
dd=d;mm=m;yy=y;
}
void put()
{cout<<dd<<"/"<<mm<<"/"<<yy;}
void operator ++();
};
int date::eday()
{
int
month[12]={31,28,31,30,31,30,31,31,30,31,30,31};
if(lyear()&&mm==2)
return 29;
else
return month[mm-1];
}
void date::operator ++()
{
++dd;
if(dd>eday())
{
mm++;
dd=1;
}
if(mm>12)
{
yy++;
mm=1;
}}
void main()
{
date h(15,8,2009);
cout<<"Date before increment=";
h.put();
++h;
cout<<"Date after increment=";
h.put();
getch();
}
```

**OUTPUT:**

```
Date before increment=15/8/2009
Date before increment=16/8/2009
```

**Problem 4. Write a C++ program to overload (++)operator.**

***Program:***

```
#include<iostream.h>
#include<conio.h>
class score
{
private:
int b;
public:
score()
{b=0;}
void operator++()
{b=b+1;}
int put()
{return(b);}
};
void main()
{
score obj1,obj2;
cout<<"\nStarting value of obj1
object="<<obj1.put();
cout<<"\nStarting value of obj2
object="<<obj2.put();
++obj1;
++obj1;
++obj2;
cout<<"\nFinal value of obj1
object="<<obj1.put();
```

```
cout<<"\nFinal value of obj2 object="<<obj2.put();
getch();
}
```

**OUTPUT:**

Starting value of obj1 object=0
Starting value of obj2 object=0
Final value of obj1 object=2
Final value of obj2 object=2

**Problem 5. Write a C++ program to increment time variable with ++operator.**

```
#include <iostream.h>
#include<conio.h>
```

***Program:***

```
class Timer
{
private:
unsigned int time;
public:
Timer():time(0)
{ }
int get_time()
{
return time;
}
void operator ++()
{
++time;
}
};
void main()
{
Timer t1,t2;
cout <<"\nt1=" <<t1.get_time();
cout <<"\nt2=" <<t2.get_time();
++t1;
++t2;
++t2;
cout <<"\nt1=" <<t1.get_time();
cout <<"\nt2=" <<t2.get_time()<<endl;
getch();
}
```

**OUTPUT:**

t1=0
t2=0
t1=1
t2=2

**Problem 6. Write a C++ program to increment time variable with ++operator,return value.**

***Program:***

```
#include <iostream.h>
#include<conio.h>
class Timer
{
private:
int time;
public:
Timer():time(0)
{ }
int get_time()
{
return time;
}
Timer operator ++()
{
++time;
Timer temp;
temp.time =time;
return temp;
}
};
void main()
{
Timer t1,t2;
cout <<"\nt1=" <<t1.get_time();
cout <<"\nt2=" <<t2.get_time();
++t1;
t2 =++t1;
cout <<"\nt1=" <<t1.get_time();
cout <<"\nt2=" <<t2.get_time()<<endl;
getch();
}
```

**OUTPUT:**

t1=0
t2=0
t1=2
t2=2

**Problem 7. Write a C++ program to Overloaded ++operator in both prefix and postfix.**

***Program:***

```
#include <iostream.h>
#include<conio.h>
class Timer
{
private:
int time;
public:
Timer():time(0)
{ }
```

```
Timer(int t):time(t)
{ }
int get_time()
{
return time;
}
Timer operator ++()
{
return Timer(++time);
}
Timer operator ++(int)
{
return Timer(time++);
}
};
void main()
{
Timer t1,t2;
cout <<"\nt1=" <<t1.get_time();
cout <<"\nt2=" <<t2.get_time();
++t1;
t2 =++t1;
cout <<"\nt1=" <<t1.get_time();
cout <<"\nt2=" <<t2.get_time();
t2 =t1++;
cout <<"\nt1=" <<t1.get_time();
cout <<"\nt2=" <<t2.get_time()<<endl;
getch();
}
```

**OUTPUT:**

```
t1=0
t2=0
t1=2
t2=2
t1=3
t2=2
```

**Problem 8. Write a C++ program to overload prefix & postfix increment operator.**

***Program:***

```
#include<iostream.h>
#include<conio.h>
class score
{
int b;
public:
score()
{b=0;}
score operator ++()
{
score t;
b=b+1;
t.b=b;
return(t);
}
score operator ++(int)
{
score t;
t.b=b;
b=b+1;
return(t);
}
int put()
{return(b);}
};
void main()
{
score obj1,obj2;
cout<<"\nStarting value of obj1
object="<<obj1.put();
cout<<"\nStarting value of obj2
object="<<obj2.put();
obj2=++obj1;
cout<<"\nobj1="<<obj1.put();
cout<<"\nobj2 after prefix="<<obj2.put();
obj2=++obj1;
cout<<"\nobj1="<<obj1.put();
cout<<"\nobj2 after postfix="<<obj2.put();
getch();
}
```

**OUTPUT:**

```
Starting value of obj1 object=0
Starting value of obj2 object=0
obj1=1
obj2 after prefix operation=1
obj1=2
obj2 after prefix operation=1
```

**Problem 9. Write a C++ program to join two strings.**

***Program:***

```
#include<iostream.h>
#include<conio.h>
#include<string.h>
#define SIZE 40
class sg
{
char u[SIZE];
public:
sg()
{
strcpy(u," ");
```

```
}
sg(char s[])
{
strcpy(u,s);
}
void show()
{
cout<<u;
}
sg operator+(sg);
};
sg sg::operator+(sg m2)
{
sg v;
strcpy(v.u,u);
strcat(v.u,m2.u);
return(v);
}
void main()
{
sg obj1="Hello";
sg obj2="Everyone";
sg obj3;
cout<<"Before concatenation \n";
cout<<"obj1= ";
cout<<"\tobj2= ";
obj2.show();
cout<<"\tobj3= ";
obj3.show();
obj3=obj1+obj2;
cout<<"\nAfter concatenation \n";
cout<<"obj3= ";
obj3.show();
getch();
}
```

**OUTPUT**:

```
Before concatenation
obj1=Hello obj2=Everyone  obj3=
After concatenation
obj3=Hello Everyone
```

**Problem 10. Write a C++ program Overload a unary operator.**

***Program:***

```
#include <iostream.h>
#include<conio.h>
class MyClass
{
int x, y, z;
public:
MyClass()
{
x = y = z = 0;
}
MyClass(int i, int j, int k)
{
x = i;
y = j;
z = k;
}
MyClass operator+(MyClass op2);
MyClass operator=(MyClass op2);
MyClass operator++();
void show() ;
} ;
// Overload +.
MyClass MyClass::operator+(MyClass op2)
{
MyClass temp;
temp.x = x + op2.x; // These are integer additions
temp.y = y + op2.y; // and the + retains is original
temp.z = z + op2.z; // meaning relative to them.
return temp;
}
// Overload assignment.
MyClass MyClass::operator=(MyClass op2)
{
x = op2.x; // These are integer assignments
y = op2.y; // and the = retains its original
z = op2.z; // meaning relative to them.
return *this;
}
// Overload the prefix version of ++.
MyClass MyClass::operator++()
{
x++; // increment x, y, and z
y++;
z++;
return *this;
}
// Show X, Y, Z coordinates.
void MyClass::show()
{
cout << x << ", ";
cout << y << ", ";
cout << z << endl;
}
void   main()
{
MyClass a(1, 2, 3), b(10, 10, 10), c;
a.show();
b.show();
```

```
c = a + b;    // add a and b together
c.show();
c = a + b + c; // add a, b and c together
c.show();
c = b = a;    // demonstrate multiple assignment
c.show();
b.show();
++c;          // increment c
c.show();
getch();
}
```

**OUTPUT:**

```
1, 2, 3
10, 10, 10
11, 12, 13
22, 24, 26
1, 2, 3
1, 2, 3
2, 3, 4
```

**Problem 11. Write a C++ program Using a Friend to Overload ++ or --.**

***Program:***

```
#include <iostream.h>
#include<conio.h>
class Values
{
int a,b;
public:
Values()
{ }
Values(int aa,int bb)
{
a =aa;
b =bb;
}
void show()
{
cout <<a <<" ";
cout <<b <<"\n";
}
Values operator=(Values p2);
friend Values operator++(Values &p);
friend Values operator--(Values &p);
};
Values Values::operator=(Values p2)
{
a =p2.a;
b =p2.b;
return *this;
}
// friend;use a reference .
Values operator++(Values &p)
{
p.a++;
p.b++;
return p;
}
//p-- a friend;use reference.
Values operator--(Values &p)
{
p.a--;
p.b--;
return p;
}
void main()
{
Values v1(20,30),v2;
v1.show();
++v1;
v1.show();
v2 =++v1;
v2.show();
--v2;
v2.show();
getch();
}
```

**OUTPUT:**

```
20 30
21 31
22 32
21 31
```

**Problem 12. Write a C++ program to Overload ++ relative to MyClass class.**

***Program:***

```
#include <iostream.h>
#include<conio.h>
class MyClass
{
int x, y;
public:
MyClass()
{
x=0;
y=0;
}
MyClass(int i, int j)
{
x=i;
y=j;
}
```

```
void getXY(int &i, int &j)
{
i=x;
j=y;
}
MyClass operator++();
};
// Overload ++ for MyClass class.
MyClass MyClass::operator++()
{
x++;
y++;
return *this;
}
void  main()
{
MyClass object1(10, 10);
int x, y;
++object1;
object1.getXY(x, y);
cout << "(++object1) X: " << x << ", Y: " << y <<
endl;
getch();
}
```

**OUTPUT:**

(++object1) X: 11, Y: 11

**Problem 13. Write a C++ program to overload incrementing unary operator.**

***Program:***

```
#include <conio.h>
#include <iostream.h>
class student
{
priviate :
unsigned int rn ;
public :
student ( )// constructor defined
{
rn = 0 ;
}
int getdata ( )
{
return  rn ;
}
void operator ++ ( )
{
rn ++ ;
}
~ student ( ) ;
} ;
void main ( )
{
student r1, r2 ;
cout <<"\n Value of r1 is "<< r1. getdata ( ) ;
cout <<"\n Value of r2 is" << r2 getdata ( ) ;
r1 ++ ; // result is 1
r2 ++ ; // result is 1
++ r2 ; // result is 2
cout <<"\n Final value of r1 is" << r1.getdata ( ) ;
cout <<"\n Final value of r2 is" << r2.getdata ( );
getch ( ) ;
}
```

**OUTPUT:**

value of r1 is 0
value of r2 is 0
Find value of r1 is 1
Find value of r2 is 2

**Problem 14. Write a C++ program to print the Fibbonacci series by using prefix increment unary operator.**

***Program:***

```
#include <iostream.h>
#include <conio.h>
class fibbo
{
private :
unsigned long int i, j, k ;
public :
fibbo ( )// constructor defined
{
i = 0 ;
j = 1 ;
k = i + j ;
disp ( )
{
cout << i << j ;
}
}
display ( )
{
cout <<'\n' << k ;
}
void operator ++ ( )
{
i = j ;
j = k ;
k = i + j ;
}
~ fibbo ( ) ;
} ;
```

```
void main ( )
{
fibbo m ;
int n, i ;
cout <<"\n Enter the value of N : " ;
cin >> n ;
m. disp ( ) ;
for (i = 1 ; i < = n ; i ++)
{
m. display ( ) ;
++ m ;
}
getch ( ) ;
}
```

**Problem 15. Write a C++ program to overload the unary operator.**

***Program:***

```
#include <iostream>
#include<conio.h>
struct X { };
void operator!(X)
{
cout << "void operator!(X)" << endl;
}
struct Y
{
void operator!()
{
cout << "void Y::operator!()" << endl;
}
};
struct Z { };
void main()
{
X ox; Y oy; Z oz;
!ox;
!oy;
// !oz;
}
```

**OUTPUT:**

```
void operator!(X)
void Y::operator!()
```

**Problem 16. Write a C++ program to illustrate the overloading of post decrement operator.**

***Program:***

```
#include<iostream.h>
#include<conio.h>
class A
{
int n;
public:
void input()
{
cin>>n;
}
void operator--(int)
{
n--;
cout<<"\nOperator overloaded function
executed.\n";
}
void print()
{
cout<<n<<endl;
}
};
void main()
{
clrscr();
cout<<"Enter the number==>";
A a;
a.input();//INPUTTING
cout<<"The number is==>";
a.print();      //DISPLAYING
a--; //DECRMENT BY OVERLOADED
FUNCTION
cout<<"Now the number is==>";
a.print();      //AGAIN DISPLAYING
getch();
}
```

**OUTPUT:**

```
Enter the number==> 5
The number is==> 5
Now the number is==> 4
Operator overloaded function executed.
```

**Problem 17. Write a C++ program to Overload the ++ unary operator.**

***Program:***

```
#include <iostream.h>
#include<conio.h>
class ThreeD
{
int x, y, z;
public:
ThreeD() { x = y = z = 0; }
ThreeD(int i, int j, int k) {x = i; y = j; z = k; }
ThreeD operator++(); // prefix version of ++
void show() ;
} ;
```

```
// Overload the prefix version of ++.
ThreeD ThreeD::operator++()
{
x++; // increment x, y, and z
y++;
z++;
return *this;
}
// Show X, Y, Z coordinates.
void ThreeD::show()
{
cout << x << ", ";
cout << y << ", ";
cout << z << "\n";
}
void main()
{
ThreeD a(1, 2, 3);
cout << "Original value of a: ";
a.show();
++a; // increment a
cout << "Value after ++a: ";
a.show();
getch();
}
```

**OUTPUT:**

Original value of a: 1, 2, 3
Value after ++a: 2, 3, 4

**Problem 18. Write a C++ program to Overload the postfix version of ++.**

***Program:***

```
#include <iostream.h>
#include<conio.h>
class ThreeD
{
int x, y, z;
public:
ThreeD() { x = y = z = 0; }
ThreeD(int i, int j, int k) {x = i; y = j; z = k; }
ThreeD operator++(int notused); // postfix version of
++
void show() ;
} ;
// Show X, Y, Z coordinates.
void ThreeD::show()
{
cout << x << ", ";
cout << y << ", ";
cout << z << "\n";
}
ThreeD ThreeD::operator++(int notused)
{
ThreeD temp = *this; // save original value
x++; // increment x, y, and z
y++;
z++;
return temp; // return original value
}
void main()
{
ThreeD a(1, 2, 3);
cout << "Original value of a: ";
a.show();
a++; // increment a
cout << "Value after ++a: ";
a.show();
getch();
}
```

**OUTPUT:**

Original value of a: 1, 2, 3
Value after ++a: 2, 3, 4

**Problem 19. Write a C++ program to demonstrate prefix and postfix ++.**

***Program:***

```
#include <iostream.h>
#include<conio.h>
class ThreeD
{
int x, y, z;
public:
ThreeD() { x = y = z = 0; }
ThreeD(int i, int j, int k) {x = i; y = j; z = k; }
ThreeD operator++(); // prefix version of ++
ThreeD operator++(int notused); // postfix version
of ++
void show() ;
};
// Overload the prefix version of ++.
ThreeD ThreeD::operator++()
{
x++; // increment x, y, and z
y++;
z++;
return *this; // return altered value
}
// Overload the postfix version of ++.
ThreeD ThreeD::operator++(int notused)
{
ThreeD temp = *this; // save original value
x++; // increment x, y, and z
```

```
y++;
z++;
return temp; // return original value
}
// Show X, Y, Z coordinates.
void ThreeD::show( )
{
cout << x << ", ";
cout << y << ", ";
cout << z << "\n";
}
void main()
{
ThreeD a(1, 2, 3);
ThreeD b;
cout << "Original value of a: ";
a.show();
++a; // prefix increment
cout << "Value after ++a: ";
a.show();
a++; // postfix increment
cout << "Value after a++: ";
a.show();
b = ++a;
cout << "\nValue of a after b = ++a: ";
a.show();
cout << "Value of b after b = ++a: ";
b.show();
b = a++;
cout << "\nValue of a after b = a++: ";
a.show();
cout << "Value of b after b = a++: ";
b.show();
getch();
}
```

**OUTPUT:**

```
Original value of a: 1, 2, 3
Value after ++a: 2, 3, 4
Value after a++: 3, 4, 5
Value of a after b = ++a: 4, 5, 6
Value of b after b = ++a: 4, 5, 6
Value of a after b = a++: 5, 6, 7
Value of b after b = a++: 4, 5, 6
```

**Problem 20. Write a C++ program to apply the use of increment operator by using the unary operator overloading.**

***Program:***

```
//overloading ++ operator
#include<iostream.h>
#include<conio.h>
#include<string.h>
char
tot_name[10][10]={{"Param"},{"Raj"},{"Kamal"}
,{"Harvin"},{"Ram"}};
class rollno
{
private:
int nos;
char name[15];
int rno;
public:
rollno(int i,int j)
{
nos=i;
strcpy(name,tot_name[nos]);
rno=j;
}
void display()
{
cout<<"\nNAME  ="<<name;
cout<<"\nROLLNO ="<<rno<<endl;
}
rollno operator ++()
{
rno++;
nos++;
strcpy(name,tot_name[nos]);
return(* this);
}
};
void main()
{
int i;
clrscr();
rollno ob(0,1);
ob.display();
for(i=1;i<5;i++)
{
ob++;
ob.display();
}
getch();
}
```

**OUTPUT :**

```
NAME =Param
ROLLNO =1
NAME = Raj
ROLLNO =2
NAME =Kamal
ROLLNO =3
NAME =Harvin
```

ROLLNO =4
NAME =Ram
ROLLNO =5

**Problem 21. Write a C++ program to Overload prefix ++ for Point.**

***Program:***

```
#include <iostream.h>
#include<conio.h>
class Point
{
int x, y;
public:
Point() { } // needed to construct temporaries
Point(int px, int py)
{
x = px;
y = py;
}
void show()
{
cout << x << " ";
cout << y << "\n";
}
Point operator+(Point op2);
Point operator-(Point op2);
Point operator=(Point op2);
Point operator++();
};
// Overload + for Point.
Point Point::operator+(Point op2)
{
Point temp;
temp.x = op2.x + x;
temp.y = op2.y + y;
return temp;
}
// Overload - for Point.
Point Point::operator-(Point op2)
{
Point temp;
// notice order of operands
temp.x = x - op2.x;
temp.y = y - op2.y;
return temp;
}
// Overload asignment for Point.
Point Point::operator=(Point op2)
{
x = op2.x;
y = op2.y;
return *this; // i.e., return object that generated call
}
// Overload prefix ++ for Point.
Point Point::operator++()
{
x++;
y++;
return *this;
}
void main()
{
Point ob1(10, 20), ob2( 5, 30), ob3(90, 90);
ob1.show();
ob2.show();
++ob1;
ob1.show(); // displays 11 21
ob2 = ++ob1;
ob1.show(); // displays 12 22
ob2.show(); // displays 12 22
ob1 = ob2 = ob3; // multiple assignment
ob1.show(); // displays 90 90
ob2.show(); // displays 90 90
getch();
}
```

**OUTPUT:**

```
10 20
5 30
11 21
12 22
12 22
90 90
90 90
```

## OVERLOAD USING FRIEND:

**Problem 22. Write a C++ program to Make op-- a friend; use reference.**

***Program:***

```
#include <iostream.h>
#include<conio.h>
class Point
{
int x, y;
public:
Point() { }
Point(int px, int py)
{
x = px;
y = py;
}
```

```
void show()
{
cout << x << " ";
cout << y << "\n";
}
Point operator=(Point op2);
friend Point operator++(Point &op);
friend Point operator--(Point &op);
};
// Overload assignment for Point.
Point Point::operator=(Point op2)
{
x = op2.x;
y = op2.y;
return *this; // i.e., return object that generated call
}
// Now a friend; use a reference parameter.
Point operator++(Point &op)
{
op.x++;
op.y++;
return op;
}
// Make op-- a friend; use reference.
Point operator--(Point &op)
{
op.x--;
op.y--;
return op;
}
void main()
{
Point ob1(10, 20), ob2;
ob1.show();
++ob1;
ob1.show(); // displays 11 21
ob2 =  ++ob1;
ob2.show(); // displays 12 22
--ob2;
ob2.show(); // displays 11 21
getch();
}
```

**OUTPUT:**

10 20
11 21
12 22
11 21

**Problem 23. Write a C++ program to Overload the -- relative to MyClass class using a friend.**

***Program:***

```
#include <iostream.h>
#include<conio.h>
#include <string.h>
class MyClass
{
int x, y;
public:
MyClass()
{
x=0;
y=0;
}
MyClass(int i, int j)
{
x=i;
y=j;
}
void getXY(int &i, int &j)
{
i=x;
j=y;
}
friend MyClass operator--(MyClass &ob);
// prefix
friend MyClass operator--(MyClass &ob, int
notused); // postfix
};
// Overload -- (prefix) for MyClass class using a
friend.
MyClass operator--(MyClass &ob)
{
ob.x--;
ob.y--;
return ob;
}
// Overload -- (postfix) for MyClass class using a
friend.
MyClass operator--(MyClass &ob, int notused)
{
ob.x--;
ob.y--;
return ob;
}
void main()
{
MyClass object1(10, 10);
int x, y;
--object1; // decrement object1 an object
object1.getXY(x, y);
cout << "(--object1) X: " << x << ", Y: " << y <<
endl;
```

```
object1--; // decrement object1 an object
object1.getXY(x, y);
cout << "(object1--) X: " << x << ", Y: " << y <<
endl;
getch();
}
```

**OUTPUT:**

(--object1) X: 9, Y: 9
(object1--) X: 8, Y: 8

**Problem 24. Write a C++ program to Overload operator '++', '--'.**

***Program:***

```
#include <iostream.h>
#include<conio.h>
class array
{
int nums[10];
public:
array();
void set(int n[10]);
void show();
array operator++();
friend array operator--(array &ob);
};
array::array()
{
int i;
for(i = 0; i <10; i++)
nums[ i ] = 0;
}
void array::set(int *n)
{
int i;
for(i = 0; i <10; i++)
nums[ i ] = n[ i ];
}
void array::show()
{
int i;
for(i = 0; i <10; i++)
cout << nums[ i ] << ' ';
cout << endl;
}
// Overload unary op using member function.
array array::operator++()
{
int i;
for(i = 0; i <10; i++)
nums[ i ]++;
return *this;
}
// Use a friend.
array operator--(array &ob)
{
int i;
for(i = 0; i <10; i++)
ob.nums[ i ]--;
return ob;
}
void main()
{
array object1, object2, object3;
int i[10] = { 1, 2, 3, 4, 5, 6, 7, 8, 9, 10 };
object1.set(i);
object2.set(i);
object3 = ++object1;
object3.show();
object3 = --object1;
object3.show();
getch();
}
```

**OUTPUT:**

2 3 4 5 6 7 8 9 10 11
1 2 3 4 5 6 7 8 9 10

**Problem 25. Write a C++ program to Overload the + relative to MyClass.**

***Program:***

```
#include <iostream.h>
#include<conio.h>
class MyClass
{
int x, y;
public:
MyClass()
{
x=0;
y=0;
}
MyClass(int i, int j)
{
x=i;
y=j;
}
void getXY(int &i, int &j)
{
i=x;
j=y;
}
MyClass operator+(MyClass object2);
};
```

```
// Overload +
MyClass MyClass::operator+(MyClass object2)
{
MyClass temp;
temp.x = x + object2.x;
temp.y = y + object2.y;
return temp;
}
void main()
{
MyClass object1(10, 10), object2(5, 3), object3;
int x, y;
object3 = object1 + object2;    // add two objects -
this calls operator+()
object3.getXY(x, y);
cout << "(object1+object2) X: " << x          << y
<< endl;
getch();
}
```

**OUTPUT:**

(object1+object2) X: 15, Y: 13

**Problem 26 Write a C++ program to add two numbers using Binary operator overloading.**

***Program:***

```
#include <iostream.h>
#include <conio.h>
class abc
{
private :
int a ;
abc ( ) // constructor defined
{
a = 0 ;
}
abc (int b)// overloading constructor
{
a = b ;
}
abc operator + (abc obj1)
{
abc add ;// Binary operator overloading
add.a = a + abj1.a ;
return (add) ;
}
void display ( ) ;
~ abc ( ) { }
};
void abc : : display ( )
{
cout <<"\n Final values are"<< a ;
}
void main ( )
{
abc x (30) ;
abc y (20) ;
abc sum ;
sum = x + y;
x.display ( ) ;
y.display ( ) ;
sum.display ( ) ;
getch ( ) ;
}
```

**OUTPUT:**

Final values are 30
Final values are 20
Final values are 50

**Problem 27. Write a C++ program for definition of operator+():**

***Program:***

```
#include <iostream.h>
#include<conio.h>
class Values
{
int a,b;
public:
Values()
{}
Values(int aa,int bb)
{
a =aa;
b =bb;
}
void show()
{
cout <<a <<" ";
cout <<b <<"\n";
}
Values operator+(Values p);
};
Values Values::operator+(Values p)
{
Values temp;
temp.a =p.a +a;
temp.b =p.b +b;
return temp;
}
void main()
{
Values v1(20,30),v2(15,40);
v1.show();
```

```
v2.show();
v1 =v1 +v2;
v1.show();
getch();
}
```

**OUTPUT:**

20 30
15 40
35 70

**Problem 28. Write a C++ program to illustrate the concept of operator overloading using the plus (+) operator with same function name.**

***Program:***

```
// program to use the plus operator overloading
#include<iostream.h>
#include<conio.h>
class demo
{
private :
int m;
public :
demo();
demo(int);
demo operator+(demo);
void display();
};
demo :: demo()
{
m = 0;
}
demo :: demo(int n)
{
m = n;
}
demo demo :: operator+(demo obj1)
{
demo t;
t.m = m+obj1.m;
return(t);
}
void demo :: display()
{
cout<<"m = "<<m<<endl;
}
void main()
{
clrscr();
demo obj1(50),obj2(50);
demo objs;
objs = obj1 + obj2;
obj1.display();
obj2.display();
objs.display();
getch();
}
```

**OUTPUT:**

m = 50
m = 50
m = 100

**Problem 29. Write a C++ program to add the two different objects of the coordinate classes by using the concept of operator overloading.**

***Program:***

```
// Program to overload + operator to add two
objects of coordinate classes
#include<iostream.h>
#include<conio.h>
class coord
{
private: int x,y;
public:
coord(int i=0,int j=0): x(i), y(j)
{ }
void get()
{
cout<<"Enter the coordinates:"<<endl;
cin>>x>>y;
}
void show()
{
cout<<"\nX = "<<x<<endl;
cout<<"\nY = "<<y<<endl;
}
coord operator + (coord a)
{
coord c;
c.x = x + a.x;
c.y = y + a.y;
return c;
}
};
void main()
{
coord ob1(20,30), ob2(22,34), ob3;
ob3  = ob1 + ob2;
ob3.show();
getch();
}
```

**OUTPUT:**

X = 42

Y = 64

**Problem 30. Write a C++ program to Overload + for 'ob + int' as well as 'ob + ob'.**

***Program:***

```
#include <iostream.h>
#include<conio.h>
class MyClass
{
int x, y;
public:
MyClass()
{
x=0;
y=0;
}
MyClass(int i, int j)
{
x=i;
y=j;
}
void getXY(int &i, int &j)
{
i=x;
j=y;
}
MyClass operator+(MyClass object2); // ob + ob
MyClass operator+(int i);      // ob + int
};
// Overload + relative to MyClass class.
MyClass MyClass::operator+(MyClass object2)
{
MyClass temp;
temp.x = x + object2.x;
temp.y = y + object2.y;
return temp;
}
// Overload + for ob + int
MyClass MyClass::operator+(int i)
{
MyClass temp;
temp.x = x + i;
temp.y = y + i;
return temp;
}
void  main()
{
MyClass object1(10, 10), object2(5, 3), object3;
int x, y;
object3 = object1 + object2;          // add two
objects - this calls operator+(MyClass)
object3.getXY(x, y);
cout << "(object1+object2) X: " << x << ", Y: " <<
y << endl;
object3 = object1 + 100;          // add object + int
- this call  operator+(int)
object3.getXY(x, y);
cout << "(object1+100) X: " << x << ", Y: " << y
<< endl;
getch();
}
```

**OUTPUT:**

```
(object1+object2) X: 15, Y: 13
(object1+100) X: 110, Y: 110
```

**Problem 31. Write a C++ program to Overload for integer + object and object + integer.**

***Program:***

```
#include <iostream.h>
#include<conio.h>
class ThreeD
{
int x, y, z;
public:
ThreeD() { x = y = z = 0; }
ThreeD(int i, int j, int k) { x = i; y = j; z = k; }
friend ThreeD operator+(ThreeD op1, int op2);
friend ThreeD operator+(int op1, ThreeD obp);
void show() ;
} ;
// This allows ThreedD + int
ThreeD operator+(ThreeD op1, int op2)
{
ThreeD temp;
temp.x = op1.x + op2;
temp.y = op1.y + op2;
temp.z = op1.z + op2;
return temp;
}
// This allows int + ThreedD
ThreeD operator+(int op1, ThreeD op2)
{
ThreeD temp;
temp.x = op2.x + op1;
temp.y = op2.y + op1;
temp.z = op2.z + op1;
return temp;
}
// Show X, Y, Z coordinates.
void ThreeD::show()
{
cout << x << ", ";
```

```
cout << y << ", ";
cout << z << "\n";
}
void main()
{
ThreeD a(1, 2, 3), b;
cout << "Original value of a: ";
a.show();
cout << "\n";
b = a + 10; // object + integer
cout << "Value of b after b = a + 10: ";
b.show();
cout << "\n";
b = 10 + a; // integer + object
cout << "Value of b after b = 10 + a: ";
b.show();
getch();
}
```

**OUTPUT:**

```
Original value of a: 1, 2, 3
Value of b after b = a + 10: 11, 12, 13
Value of b after b = 10 + a: 11, 12, 13
```

**Problem 32. Write a C++ program + is overloaded for Point + int.**

***Program:***

```
#include <iostream.h>
#include<conio.h>
class Point
{
int x, y;
public:
Point() { }
Point(int px, int py)
{
x = px;
y = py;
}
void show()
{
cout << x << " ";
cout << y << "\n";
}
friend Point operator+(Point op1, int op2);
friend Point operator+(int op1, Point op2);
};
// + is overloaded for Point + int.
Point operator+(Point op1, int op2)
{
Point temp;
temp.x = op1.x + op2;
temp.y = op1.y + op2;
return temp;
}
// + is overloaded for int + Point.
Point operator+(int op1, Point op2)
{
Point temp;
temp.x = op1 + op2.x;
temp.y = op1 + op2.y;
return temp;
}
void main()
{
Point ob1(10, 20), ob2( 5, 30), ob3(7, 14);
ob1.show();
ob2.show();
ob3.show();
ob1 = ob2 + 10; // both of these
ob3 = 10 + ob2; // are valid
ob1.show();
ob3.show();
getch();
}
```

**OUTPUT:**

```
10 20
5 30
7 14
15 40
15 40
```

**Problem 33. Write a C++ program to overloaded '+' operator adds two Heights.**

***Program:***

```
#include <iostream.h>
#include<conio.h>
class Height
{
private:
int feet;
float inches;
public:
Height():feet(0),inches(0.0)
{ }
Height(int ft,float in):feet(ft),inches(in)
{ }
void get()
{
cout <<"\nFeet:";cin >>feet;
cout <<"inches:";cin >>inches;
}
void show()
```

```
{
cout <<feet <<"-" <<inches;
}
Height operator +(Height );
};
Height Height::operator +(Height H2)
{
int f =feet +H2.feet;
float i =inches +H2.inches;
if(i >=12.0)
{ 
i -=12.0;
f++;
}
return Height(f,i);
}
void main()
{
Height heigh1,heigh3,heigh4;
heigh1.get();
Height heigh2(6,2.25);
heigh3 =heigh1 +heigh2;
heigh4 =heigh1 +heigh2 +heigh3;
cout <<"heigh1 =";heigh1.show();cout <<endl;
cout <<"heigh2 =";heigh2.show();cout <<endl;
cout <<"heigh3 =";heigh3.show();cout <<endl;
cout <<"heigh4 =";heigh4.show();cout <<endl;
getch();
}
```

**OUTPUT***:*

```
Enter feet:6
Enter inches:4.25
dist1 =6-4.25
dist2 =6-2.25
dist3 =12-6.5
dist4 =25-1
```

**Problem 34. Write a C++ program to Concatenating Strings.**

***Program:***

```
//overloaded '+' operator concatenates strings
#include <iostream.h>
#include<conio.h>
#include <string.h>//for strcpy(),strcat()
#include <stdlib.h>//for exit()
class String
{
private:
enum {ST=60 };
char str [ST ];
public:
String()
{
strcpy(str,"");
}
String(char s [] )
{
strcpy(str,s);
}
void display()
{
cout <<str;
}
String operator +(String st)
{
String temp;
if(strlen(str)+strlen(st.str)<ST )
{
strcpy(temp.str,str);
strcat(temp.str,st.str);
}
else
{
cout <<"\n If String overflow then exit. ";
exit(1);
}
return temp;
}
};
void main()
{
String s1 ="\nProf.Rachhpal Singh";
String s2 ="(Head)";
String s3;
s1.display();
s2.display();
s3.display();
s3 =s1 +s2;
s3.display();
cout <<endl;
getch();
}
```

**OUTPUT***:*

```
Prof.Rachhpal Singh(Head)
Prof.Rachhpal Singh(Head)
```

**Problem 35. Write a C++ program + is overloaded using friend function.**

***Program:***

```
#include <iostream.h>
#include<conio.h>
class Point
```

```
{
int x, y;
public:
Point() { } // needed to construct temporaries
Point(int px, int py)
{
x = px;
y = py;
}
void show()
{
cout << x << " ";
cout << y << "\n";
}
friend Point operator+(Point op1, Point op2); // now
a friend
Point operator-(Point op2);
Point operator=(Point op2);
Point operator++();
};
// Now, + is overloaded using friend function.
Point operator+(Point op1, Point op2)
{
Point temp;
temp.x = op1.x + op2.x;
temp.y = op1.y + op2.y;
return temp;
}
// Overload - for Point.
Point Point::operator-(Point op2)
{
Point temp;
// notice order of operands
temp.x = x - op2.x;
temp.y = y - op2.y;
return temp;
}
// Overload assignment for Point.
Point Point::operator=(Point op2)
{
x = op2.x;
y = op2.y;
return *this; // i.e., return object that generated call
}
// Overload ++ for Point.
Point Point::operator++()
{
x++;
y++;
return *this;
}
void main()
{
Point ob1(10, 20), ob2( 5, 30);
ob1 = ob1 + ob2;
ob1.show();
getch();
}
```

**OUTPUT:**

15 50

**Problem 36. Write a C++ program for friend operator.**

***Program:***

```
#include <iostream.h>
#include<conio.h>
class Num
{
friend Num operator+(Num ob, int i);
friend Num operator+(int i, Num ob);
int count;
public:
Num(int cc=0)
{
count=cc;
}
Num& operator=(int i);
void Show()
{
cout <<count<<endl;
}
};
Num& Num::operator=(int i)
{
count=i;
return *this;
}
Num operator+(Num ob, int i) // This handles
ob+int.
{
Num temp;
temp.count=ob.count+i;
return temp;
}
Num operator+(int i, Num ob) // This handles
int+ob.
{
Num temp;
temp.count=ob.count+i;
return temp;
}
void main()
```

```
{
Num obj;
obj=10;
obj.Show();
obj=10+obj;
obj.Show();
obj=obj+12;
obj.Show();
getch()
}
```

**OUTPUT:**

```
10
20
32
```

**Problem 37. Write a C++ program to Overload the - relative to MyClass class 1.**

***Program:***

```
#include <iostream.h>
#include<conio.h>
class MyClass
{
int x, y;
public:
MyClass()
{
x=0;
y=0;
}
MyClass(int i, int j)
{
x=i;
y=j;
}
void getXY(int &i, int &j)
{
i=x;
j=y;
}
MyClass operator-(MyClass object2); // binary
minus
MyClass operator-();             // unary minus
};
// Overload - relative to MyClass class.
MyClass MyClass::operator-(MyClass object2)
{
MyClass temp;
temp.x = x - object2.x;
temp.y = y - object2.y;
return temp;
}
// Overload unary - for MyClass class.
MyClass MyClass::operator-()
{
x = -x;
y = -y;
return *this;
}
void main()
{
MyClass object1(10, 10), object2(5, 7);
int x, y;
object1 = object1 - object2;          // subtraction
object1.getXY(x, y);
cout << "(object1-object2) X: " << x << ", Y: " <<
y << endl;
object1 = -object1;          // negation
object1.getXY(x, y);
cout << "(-object1) X: " << x << ", Y: " << y <<
endl;
getch();
}
```

**OUTPUT:**

```
object1-object2) X: 5 , Y: 3
(-object1) X: -5, Y: -3
```

**Problem 38. Write a C++ program for demo: Overload the +, -, and = relative to MyClass.**

***Program:***

```
#include <iostream.h>
#include<conio.h>
class MyClass
{
int x, y;
public:
MyClass()
{
x=0;
y=0;
}
MyClass(int i, int j)
{
x=i;
y=j;
}
void getXY(int &i, int &j)
{
i=x;
j=y;
}
MyClass operator+(MyClass object2);
MyClass operator-(MyClass object2);
```

```
MyClass operator=(MyClass object2);
};
// Overload + relative to MyClass class.
MyClass MyClass::operator+(MyClass object2)
{
MyClass temp;
temp.x = x + object2.x;
temp.y = y + object2.y;
return temp;
}
// Overload - relative to MyClass class.
MyClass MyClass::operator-(MyClass object2)
{
MyClass temp;
temp.x = x - object2.x;
temp.y = y - object2.y;
return temp;
}
// Overload = relative to MyClass.
MyClass MyClass::operator=(MyClass object2)
{
x = object2.x;
y = object2.y;
return *this; // return the object that is assigned
}
void main()
{
MyClass object1(10, 10), object2(5, 3), object3;
int x, y;
object3 = object1 + object2;     // add two objects
- this calls operator+()
object3.getXY(x, y);
cout << "(object1+object2) X: " << x << ", Y: " << y
<< endl;
object3 = object1 - object2;     // subtract two
objects
object3.getXY(x, y);
cout << "(object1-object2) X: " << x << ", Y: " << y
<< endl;
object3 = object1;     // assign an object
object3.getXY(x, y);
cout << "(object3=object1) X: " << x << ", Y: " << y
<< endl;
getch();
}
```

**OUTPUT:**

```
(object1+object2) X: 15, Y: 13
(object1-object2) X: 5, Y: 7
(object3=object1) X: 10, Y: 10
```

## OVERLOAD PLUS SUBTRACT ASSIGNMENT OPERATOR:

**Problem 39. Write a C++ program Define -, + and = for the ThreeD class.**

***Program:***

```
#include <iostream.h>
#include<conio.h>
class ThreeD
{
int x, y, z;
public:
ThreeD() { x = y = z = 0; }
ThreeD(int i, int j, int k) { x = i; y = j; z = k; }
ThreeD operator+(ThreeD op2); // op1 is implied
ThreeD operator=(ThreeD op2); // op1 is implied
ThreeD operator-(ThreeD op2); // op1 is implied
void show() ;
};
// Overload subtraction.
ThreeD ThreeD::operator-(ThreeD op2)
{
ThreeD temp;
temp.x = x - op2.x;
temp.y = y - op2.y;
temp.z = z - op2.z;
return temp;
}
// Overload +.
ThreeD ThreeD::operator+(ThreeD op2)
{
ThreeD temp;
temp.x = x + op2.x;
temp.y = y + op2.x;
temp.z = z + op2.z;
return temp;
}
// Overload assignment.
ThreeD ThreeD::operator=(ThreeD op2)
{
x = op2.x;
y = op2.y;
z = op2.z;
return *this;
}
// Show X, Y, Z coordinates.
void ThreeD::show()
{
cout << x << ", ";
cout << y << ", ";
```

```
cout << z << "\n";
}
void main()
{
ThreeD a(1, 2, 3), b(10, 10, 10), c;
cout << "Original value of a: ";
a.show();
cout << "Original value of b: ";
b.show();
c = a - c;
cout << "a - c: ";
c.show();
cout << "\n";
getch();
}
```

**OUTPUT:**

```
Original value of a: 1, 2, 3
Original value of b: 10, 10, 10
a - c: 1, 2, 3
```

**Problem 40. Write a C++ program for Array class for 10 int value with overloaded functions: +, -, ==.**

***Program:***

```
#include <iostream.h>
#include<conio.h>
class array
{
int nums[10];
public:
array();
void set(int n[10]);
void show();
array operator+(array object2);
array operator-(array object2);
int operator==(array object2);
};
array::array()
{
int i;
for(i = 0; i <10; i++) nums[ i ] = 0;
}
void array::set(int *n)
{
int i;
for(i = 0; i <10; i++) nums[ i ] = n[ i ];
}
void array::show()
{
int i;
for(i = 0; i <10; i++)
cout << nums[ i ] << ' ';
cout << endl;
}
array array::operator+(array object2)
{
int i;
array temp;
for(i = 0; i <10; i++)
temp.nums[ i ] = nums[ i ] + object2.nums[ i ];
return temp;
}
array array::operator-(array object2)
{
int i;
array temp;
for(i = 0; i <10; i++)
temp.nums[ i ] = nums[ i ] - object2.nums[ i ];
return temp;
}
int array::operator==(array object2)
{
int i;
for(i = 0; i <10; i++)
if(nums[ i ]!=object2.nums[ i ]) return 0;
return 1;
}
void  main()
{
array object1, object2, object3;
int i[10] = { 1, 2, 3, 4, 5, 6, 7, 8, 9, 10 };
object1.set(i);
object2.set(i);
object3 = object1 + object2;
object3.show();
object3 = object1 - object3;
object3.show();
if(object1==object2)
cout << "object1 equals object2\n";
else
cout << "object1 does not equal object2\n";
if(object1==object3)
cout << "object1 equals object3\n";
else
cout << "object1 does not equal object3\n";
getch();
}
```

**OUTPUT:**

```
2 4 6 8 10 12 14 16 18 20
-1 -2 -3 -4 -5 -6 -7 -8 -9 -10
object1 equals object2
object1 does not equal object3
```

**Problem 41. Write a C++ program for Demo: Overload the +, -, and = relative to MyClass.**

***Program:***

```
#include <iostream.h>
#include<conio.h>
class MyClass
{
int x, y;
public:
MyClass()
{
x=0;
y=0;
}
MyClass(int i, int j)
{
x=i;
y=j;
}
void getXY(int &i, int &j)
{
i=x;
j=y;
}
MyClass operator+(MyClass object2);
MyClass operator-(MyClass object2);
MyClass operator=(MyClass object2);
};
// Overload + relative to MyClass class.
MyClass MyClass::operator+(MyClass object2)
{
MyClass temp;
temp.x = x + object2.x;
temp.y = y + object2.y;
return temp;
}
// Overload - relative to MyClass class.
MyClass MyClass::operator-(MyClass object2)
{
MyClass temp;
temp.x = x - object2.x;
temp.y = y - object2.y;
return temp;
}
// Overload = relative to MyClass.
MyClass MyClass::operator=(MyClass object2)
{
x = object2.x;
y = object2.y;
return *this; // return the object that is assigned
}
void main()
{
MyClass object1(10, 10), object2(5, 3), object3;
int x, y;
object3 = object1 + object2;          // add two
objects - this calls operator+()
object3.getXY(x, y);
cout << "(object1+object2) X: " << x << ", Y: " <<
y << endl;
object3 = object1 - object2;          // subtract two
objects
object3.getXY(x, y);
cout << "(object1-object2) X: " << x << ", Y: "<<
y << endl;
object3 = object1;                    // assign an object
object3.getXY(x, y);
cout << "(object3=object1) X: " << x << ", Y: " <<
y << endl;
getch();
}
```

**OUTPUT:**

```
(object1+object2) X: 15, Y: 13
(object1-object2) X: 5, Y: 7
(object3=object1) X: 10, Y:10
```

**Problem 42. Write a C++ program adds three additional overloaded operators to the loc class:the –,the =,and the unary ++.Pay special attention to how these functions are defined.**

***Program:***

```
#include <iostream.h>
#include<conio.h>
class Values
{
int a,b;
public:
Values()
{}
Values(int aa,int bb)
{
a =aa;
b =bb;
}
void show()
{
cout <<a <<" ";
cout <<b <<"\n";
}
Values operator+(Values p);
Values operator-(Values p);
```

```
Values operator=(Values p);
Values operator++();
};
Values Values::operator+(Values p)
{
Values temp;
temp.a =p.a +a;
temp.b =p.b +b;
return temp;
}
Values Values::operator-(Values p)
{
Values temp;
temp.a =a -p.a;
temp.b =b -p.b;
return temp;
}
Values Values::operator=(Values p)
{
a =p.a;
b =p.b;
return *this;
}
Values Values::operator++()
{
a++;
b++;
return *this;
}
void main()
{
Values v1(20,30),v2(15,40),v3(25,35);
v1.show();
v2.show();
++v1;
v1.show();
v2 =++v1;
v1.show();
v2.show();
v1=v2=v3;
v1.show();
v2.show();
getch();
}
```

**OUTPUT:**

```
20 30
15 40
21 31
22 32
22 32
25 35
25 35
```

**Problem 43. Write a C++ program to Operator Overloading Using a Friend Function.**

***Program:***

```
//In this program,the operator+()function is made
into friend:
#include <iostream.h>
#include<conio.h>
class Values
{
int a,b;
public:
Values()
{ }
Values(int aa,int bb)
{
a =aa;
b =bb;
}
void show()
{
cout <<a <<" ";
cout <<b <<"\n";
}
friend Values operator+(Values p1,Values
p2);//friend
Values operator-(Values p2);
Values operator=(Values p2);
Values operator++();
};
//Now,+is overloaded using friend function.
Values operator+(Values p1,Values p2)
{
Values temp;
temp.a =p1.a +p2.a;
temp.b =p1.b +p2.b;
return temp;
}
Values Values::operator-(Values p2)
{
Values temp;
temp.a =a -p2.b;
temp.b =a -p2.b;
return temp;
}
Values Values::operator=(Values p2)
{
a =p2.a;
b =p2.a;
return *this;
```

```
}
Values Values::operator++()
{
a++;
b++;
return *this;
}
void main()
{
Values v1(20,30),v2(15,40);
v1.show();
v2.show();
++v1;
v1.show();
v2 =++v1;
v1.show();
v2.show();
v1=v2;
v1.show();
v2.show();
getch();
}
```

**OUTPUT:**

```
20 30
15 40
21 31
22 32
22 22
22 22
22 22
```

**Problem 44. Write a C++ program to Overload operator (=).**

***Program:***

```
#include <iostream.h>
#include<conio.h>
class MyType
{
public:
MyType();
int GetAge() const { return *itsAge; }
int GetWeight() const { return *itsWeight; }
void SetAge(int age) { *itsAge = age; }
MyType operator=(const MyType &);
private:
int *itsAge;
int *itsWeight;
};
MyType::MyType()
{
itsAge = new int;
itsWeight = new int;
*itsAge = 5;
*itsWeight = 9;
}
MyType MyType::operator=(const MyType & rhs)
{
if (this == &rhs)
return *this;
delete itsAge;
delete itsWeight;
itsAge = new int;
itsWeight = new int;
*itsAge = rhs.GetAge();
*itsWeight = rhs.GetWeight();
return *this;
}
void main()
{
MyType myObject;
cout << "myObject's age: " << myObject.GetAge()
<< endl;
cout << "Setting myObject to 6...\n";
myObject.SetAge(6);
MyType whiskers;
cout << "whiskers' age: " << whiskers.GetAge()
<< endl;
cout << "copying myObject to whiskers...\n";
whiskers = myObject;
cout << "whiskers' age: " << whiskers.GetAge()
<< endl;
getch();
}
```

**OUTPUT:**

```
myObject's age: 5
Setting myObject to 6...
whiskers' age: 5
copying myObject to whiskers...
whiskers' age: 6
```

**Problem 45. Write a C++ program to overload arithmetic assignment operator += to add two rational numbers.**

***Program:***

```
#include<iostream.h>
#include<conio.h>
class r
{
int n;
int f;
public:
void get()
```

```
{
cout<<"Enter numerator & denominator of number";
cin>>n>>f;
}
void operator+=(r s2)
{
n=n*s2.f+s2.n*f;
f=f*s2.f;
}
void put()
{
cout<<n<<"/"<<f;
}
};
void main()
{
r obj1,obj2;
cout<<"Enter first rational number\n";
obj1.get();
cout<<"Enter second rational number\n";
obj2.get();
obj1+=obj2;
cout<<"obj1 after += operation \n";
obj1.put();
getch();
}
```

**OUTPUT:**

```
Enter first rational number
Enter numerator & denominator of number 3 4
Enter second rational number
Enter numerator & denominator of number 5 3
r1 enter +=operator
29/12
```

## OVERLOAD ASSIGNMENT OPERATOR:

**Problem 46. Write a C++ program to Overloading the copy assignment operator.**

***Program:***

```
#include <iostream.h>
#include<conio.h>
#include <string.h>
class MyString
{
public:
MyString(const char* pText)
{
pString = new char[ strlen(pText) + 1 ];
std::strcpy(pString, pText);
}
~MyString()
{
cout << endl << "Destructor called." << endl;
delete[] pString;
}
MyString& operator=(const MyString& String)
{
cout << endl << "calling =." << endl;
if(this == &String)
return *this;
delete[] pString;
pString = new char[ strlen(String.pString) + 1];
// Copy right operand string to left operand
strcpy(this->pString, String.pString);
return *this;
}
char* getString() const{ return pString; }
private:
char* pString;
};
void main()
{
MyString warning("There is a String");
MyString standard("");
cout << warning.getString();
cout << standard.getString();
standard = warning;
cout << warning.getString();
cout << standard.getString();
cout << endl;
getch();
}
```

**OUTPUT:**

```
There is a String
calling =.
There is a StringThere is a String
Destructor called.
Destructor called.
```

## COMPARING STRINGS:

**Problem 47. Write a C++ program to Overloaded '==' operator compares strings.**

***Program:***

```
#include <iostream.h>
#include<conio.h>
#include <string.h>
class String
{
```

```
private:
enum {ST =80 };
char str [ST ];
public:
String()
{
strcpy(str,"");
}
String(char s [] )
{
strcpy(str,s);
}
void display()
{
cout <<str;
}
void getstr()
{
cin.get(str,ST);
}
bool  operator ==(String st)
{
return (strcmp(str,st.str)==0 )?true :false;
}
};
void main()
{
String s1 ="yes ";
String s2 ="no ";
String s3;
cout <<"\nEnter 'yes' or 'no':";
s3.getstr();
if(s3==s1)
cout <<"You typed yes \n ";
else if(s3==s2)
cout <<"You typed no \n ";
else
cout <<"You didn't follow instructions \n ";
getch();
}
```

**OUTPUT:**

Enter 'yes' or 'no' :yes
You typed yes

**Problem 48. Write a C++ program to illustrate the concept of Overloading of Arithmetic Assignment operator.**

***Program:***

```
#include<iostream.h>
#include<conio.h>
class A
{
int p;
public:
void operator= (int n)
{
p=n;
}
void operator+= (A z)
{
p+=z.p;
}
void print()
{
cout<<"P is "<<p;
}
};
void main()
{
clrscr();
A a,a1;
a1=4;
a=3;
a.print();
a+=a1;
cout<<"\nNow ";
a.print();
getch();
}
```

**Problem 49. Write a C++ program to do all the arithmetic operations using the concept of operator overloading.**

***Program:***

```
// Illustration of the Operator Overloading
#include<iostream.h>
#include<conio.h>
class menu
{
public:
float no;
public:
menu()
{
no=0;
}
void getvalue();
menu operator+ ( menu b);
menu operator- ( menu b);
menu operator* ( menu b);
menu operator/ ( menu b);
```

```
};
menu menu:: operator+ (menu b)
{
menu temp;
temp.no=no+b.no;
return(temp);
}
menu menu::operator/ (menu b)
{
menu temp;
temp.no=no/b.no;
return(temp);
}
menu menu::operator- (menu b)
{
menu temp;
temp.no=no-b.no;
return(temp);
}
menu menu::operator* (menu b)
{
menu temp;
temp.no=no*b.no;
return(temp);
}
void menu::getvalue()
{
cout<<"enter the value:";
cin>>no;
}
void main()
{
menu a,b,c;
int ch,m,n;
clrscr();
a.getvalue();
b.getvalue();
cout<<"ARITHMATIC OPERATIONS";
cout<<"menu () \n";
cout<<"a ->ADDTION \n";
cout<<"s ->SUBTRACTION \n";
cout<<"m ->MULTIPLICATION \n";
cout<<"d ->DIVISION \n";
cout<<"q ->QUIT \n";
cout<<"option ,please ? \n";
while((ch=getch()) != 'q')
{
switch(ch)
{
case 'a':
c=a+b;
cout<<"addition of two no's are:";
cout<<c.no<<endl;
break;
case 's':
c=a-b;
cout<<"subtraction of two no's are:";
cout<<c.no<<endl;
break;
case 'm':
c=a*b;
cout<<"Multiplication of two no's are:";
cout<<c.no<<endl;
break;
case 'd':
c=a/b;
cout<<"Division of two no's are:";
cout<<c.no<<endl;
break;
}
}
getch();
}
```

**OUTPUT:**

```
Enter the value:5
Enter the value:3
ARITHMATIC OPERATIONS
MENU
a->ADDITION
s->SUBTRACTION
m->MULTIPLICATION
d->DIVISION
q->QUIT
Option Please?
Addition of two no's are:8
Subtraction of two no's are:2
Multiplication of two no's are:15
Division of two no's are:1.666667
```

**Problem 50. Write a C++ program to overload >= operator for string comparison.**

***Program:***

```
#include<iostream.h>
#include<conio.h>
#include<string.h>
class sg
{
char st[30];
public:
sg()
{
strcpy(st," ");
```

```
}
sg(char s[])
{
strcpy(st,s);
}
void display()
{
cout<<st;
}

int operator>=(sg);
void read()
{
cin>>st;
}
};
int sg::operator>=(sg ss2)
{
if((st,ss2.st)>=0)
return(1);
else
return(0);
}
void main()
{
clrscr();
sg obj1="Hii";
sg obj2;
cout<<"Enter string obj2=";
obj2.read();
if(obj1>=obj2)
cout<<"\nAlphabetically obj1 is greater than or
equal to obj2";
else
cout<<"\nAlphabetically obj1 is less than  obj2";
getch();
}
```

**OUTPUT:**

Enter string obj2=You
Alphabetically obj1 is greater than or equal to obj2

**Problem 51. Write a C++ program to print the Fibonacci series using the operator overloading.**

***Program:***

```
#include<iostream.h>
#include<conio.h>
#define x ++
class A
{
int a,b,c;
public:
A()
{
a=0;
b=1;
}
int operator x(int)
{
c=a+b;
a=b;
b=c;
return c;
}
};
void main()
{
int n;
clrscr();
cout<<"Enter number of terms==>";
cin>>n;
A z;
cout<<"Series is==>0 1";
for(int i=1;i<=n-2;i x)
cout<<" "<<z x;
getch();
}
```

**OUTPUT:**

Enter number of terms==> 9
Series is==>0 1 1  2   3   5  8  13   21

**Problem 52. Write a C++ program for addition & multiplication of two matrices by overloading + and * operators.**

***Program:***

```
#include<iostream.h>
#include<conio.h>
class mat
{
private:
int s[10][10];
int u,v;
public:
void show();
mat operator +(mat);
mat operator *(mat);
void read();
};
mat mat::operator+(mat uu2)
{
mat t;
t.u=u;
t.v=v;
```

```
cout<<t.u;
cout<<t.v;
for(int i=0;i<t.u;i++)
for(int j=0;j<t.v;j++)
t.s[i][j]=s[i][j]+uu2.s[i][j];
return t;
}
mat mat::operator*(mat uu2)
{
mat t;
t.u=u;
t.v=uu2.v;
for(int i=0;i<t.u;i++)
for(int j=0;j<t.v;j++)
{
t.s[i][j]=0;
for(int k=0;k<v;k++)
t.s[i][j]+=s[i][k]*uu2.s[k][j];
}
return t;
}
void mat::read()
{
cout<<"Enter order of matrix:\n";
cin>>u>>v;
cout<<"Enter  elements:\n";
for(int i=0;i<u;i++)
for(int j=0;j<v;j++)
cin>>s[i][j];
}
void mat::show()
{
for(int i=0;i<u;i++)
for(int j=0;j<v;j++)
cout<<s[i][j]<<"\t";
cout<<"\n";
}
void main()
{
mat obj1,obj2,obj3;
cout<<"Enter first matrix\n";
obj1.read();
cout<<"Enter second matrix\n";
obj2.read();
obj3=obj1+obj2;
cout<<"Result after addition\n";
obj3.show();
obj3=obj1*obj2;
cout<<"Result after multiplication\n";
obj3.show();
getch();
}
```

**OUTPUT:**

```
Enter first matrix
Enter order of matrix:2 2
Enter elements 3 4 1 2
Enter second matrix
Enter order of matrix:2 2
Enter elements 2 3 1 1
Rsult after addition
5 7
2 3
Result after multiplication
10 13
4  4
```

**Problem 53. Write a C++ program to overload all the Arithmetic Operators.**

***Program:***

```
#include<iostream.h>
#include<conio.h>
class A
{
int n;
public:
void input()
{
cin>>n;
}
void operator+(A z)
{
cout<<"Sum is==>"<<n+z.n;
}
void operator-(A z)
{
cout<<"Their difference is==>"<<n-z.n;
}
void operator*(A z)
{
cout<<"Product is==>"<<n*z.n;
}
void operator/(A z)
{
cout<<"Quotient is==>"<<n/z.n;
}
void operator%(A z)
{
cout<<"Remainder is==>"<<n%z.n;
}
};
void main()
{
```

```
int choice;
A a,a1;
clrscr();
cout<<"Enter first number==>";
a.input();
cout<<"Enter second number==>";
a1.input();
back:
cout<<"Press 1 for addition.\n";
cout<<"Press 2 for difference.\n";
cout<<"Press 3 for product.\n" ;
cout<<"Press 4 for quotient.\n";
cout<<"Press 5 for remainder.\n";
cout<<"Enter your choice...";
cin>>choice;
switch (choice)
{
case 1:
a+a1;
break;
case 2:
a-a1;
break;
case 3:
a*a1;
break;
case 4:
a/a1;
break;
case 5:
a%a1;
break;
default:
cout<<"Entered choice incorrect.\n";
goto back;
}
getch();
}
```

**OUTPUT** ***is:***

```
Enter first number==> 20
Enter second number==>30
Press 1 for addition.
Press 2 for difference.
Press 3 for product.
Press 4 for quotient.
Press 5 for remainder.
Enter your choice...1
Sum is==> 50
```

**Problem 54. Write a C++ program to perform Arithmetic operations on Complex Numbers by Friend Function i.e. By Operator Overloading.**

***Program:***

```
#include<iostream.h>
#include<conio.h>
class A
{
float a,b;
public:
void input()
{
cout<<"The number is a+ib.\n";
cout<<"Enter a & b==>";
cin>>a>>b;
}
friend void operator +(A,A);
friend void operator -(A,A);
friend void operator *(A,A);
friend void operator /(A,A);
};
void main()
{
A a,a1;
clrscr();
cout<<"Enter first number==>\n";
a.input();
cout<<"\n\nEnter second number==>";
a1.input();
int choice;
cout<<"Press 1 for addition.\n";
cout<<"Press 2 for substraction.\n";
cout<<"Press 3 for product.\n";
cout<<"Press 4 for division.\n";
cout<<"Enter your choice...";
cin>>choice;
switch (choice)
{
case 1:
operator+(a,a1);
break;
case 2:
operator-(a,a1);
break;
case 3:
operator*(a,a1);
break;
case 4:
operator/(a,a1);
break;
default:
```

```
cout<<"Incorrect choice.";
}
getch();
}
void operator +(A z,A z1)
{
cout<<"Sum is "<<z.a+z1.a<<" + i "<<z.b+z1.b;
}
void operator -(A z,A z1)
{
cout<<"Difference is "<<z.a-z1.a<<" + i "<<z.b-
z1.b;
}
void operator *(A z,A z1)
{
cout<<"Product is "<<z.a*z1.a - z.b*z1.b;
cout<<" + i "<<z.a*z1.b + z.b*z1.a;
}
void operator /(A z,A z1)
{
cout<<"Division is "<<(z.a*z1.a +
z.b*z1.b)/(z1.a*z1.a + z1.b*z1.b);
cout<<" + i "<<(z.b*z1.a - z.a*z1.b)/(z1.a*z1.a +
z1.b*z1.b);
}
```

**Problem 55. Write a C++ program to overload == to compare two strings using friend.**

***Program:***

```
#include<iostream.h>
#include<conio.h>
#include<string.h>
class string
{
char x[30];
public:
string()
{strcpy(x," ");}
string(char z[])
{strcpy(x,z);}
void read()
{
cin>>x;
}
friend int  operator==(string,string);
};
void main()
{
string f="Canada";
string s;
cout<<"\nEnter string s=";
s.read();
if(f==s)
{cout<<"alphabetically f & s sare same";}
else
{cout<<"alphabetically f & s are different";}
getch();
}
int operator==(string fs1,string fs2)
{
int k=strcmp(fs1.x,fs2.x);
if(k==0)
return 1;
else
return 0;
}
```

**<u>OUTPUT</u>*:***

```
Enter string s=America
alphabetically f & s are different
```

**Problem 56. Write a C++ program of Assignment operator overloading.**

***Program:***

```
#include<iostream.h>
#include <conio.h>
class abc
{
private:
int a;
float b;
public:
abc(int,float);
void operator  =  (abc  def);
void display( );
};
void  abc::operator = (abc  def)
{
a = def.a;
b = def.b;
}
void abc::display( )
{
cout<<"Integer Value is:"<<a;
cout<<"Float Value is:"<<b;
}
void main( )
{
abc  m1(20,33.3);
abc   m2(10,5.5);
m2 = m1;
cout<< " First object has value";
m1.display( );
```

```
cout<< " Second object has value";
m2.display( );
}
```

**Problem 57. Write a C++ program to illustrate the Assignment operator overloading.**

***Program:***

```
#include <iostream>
#include<conio.h>
struct A
{
A& operator=(char)
{
cout << "A& A::operator=(char)" << endl;
return *this;
}
virtual A& operator=(const A&)
{
cout << "A& A::operator=(const A&)" << endl;
return *this;
} };
struct B : A
{
B& operator=(char)
{
cout << "B& B::operator=(char)" << endl;
return *this;
}
virtual B& operator=(const A&)
{
cout << "B& B::operator=(const A&)" << endl;
return *this;
} };
struct C : B { };
void main()
{
B b1;
B b2;
A* ap1 = &b1;
A* ap2 = &b1;
*ap1 = 'z';
*ap2 = b2;
C c1;
// c1 = 'z';
}
```

**OUTPUT:**

```
A& A::operator=(char)
B& B::operator=(const A&)
```

**Problem 58. Write a C++ program to illustrate the copy assignment operator.**

***Program:***

```
#include <iostream>
#include<conio.h>
struct A
{
A& operator=(const A&)
{
cout << "A::operator=(const A&)" << endl;
return *this;
}
A& operator=(A&)
{
cout << "A::operator=(A&)" << endl;
return *this;
} };
class B
{
A a;
};
struct C
{
C& operator=(C&)
{
cout << "C::operator=(C&)" << endl;
return *this;
}
C() { }
};
void main()
{
B x, y;
x = y;
A w, z;
w = z;
C i;
const C j();
// i = j;
}
```

**OUTPUT:**

```
A::operator=(const A&)
A::operator=(A&)
```

## ARITHMETIC ASSIGNMENT OPERATORS:

**Problem 59. Write a C++ program Overloaded '+=' assignment operator.**

***Program:***

```
#include <iostream.h>
#include<conio.h>
```

```
class Height
{
private:
int feet;
float inches;
public:
Height():feet(0),inches(0.0)
{ }
Height(int ft,float in):feet(ft),inches(in)
{ }
void get()
{
cout <<"\nFeet:";cin >>feet;
cout <<"inches:";cin >>inches;
}
void show()
{
cout <<feet <<"-" <<inches;
}
void operator +=(Height );
};
void Height::operator +=(Height H2)
{
feet +=H2.feet;
inches +=H2.inches;
if(inches >=12.0)
{
inches -=12.0;
feet++;
}
}
void main()
{
Height heigh1;
heigh1.get();
cout <<"\nheigh1 =";heigh1.show();
Height heigh2(6,2.25);
cout <<"\nheigh2 =";heigh2.show();
heigh1 +=heigh2;
cout <<"\nAfter addition,";
cout <<"\nheigh1 =";heigh1.show();
cout <<endl;
getch();
}
```

**OUTPUT:**

```
Feet:6
inches:4.25
heigh1 =6-4.25
heigh2 =6-2.25
After addition,
heigh1 =12-6.5
```

**Problem 60. Write a C++ program to Overload assignment for Point.**

***Program:***

```
#include <iostream.h>
#include<conio.h>
class Point
{
int x, y;
public:
Point() { } // needed to construct temporaries
Point(int px, int py)
{
x = px;
y = py;
}
void show()
{
cout << x << " ";
cout << y << "\n";
}
Point operator+(Point op2);
Point operator-(Point op2);
Point operator=(Point op2);
Point operator++();
};
// Overload + for Point.
Point Point::operator+(Point op2)
{
Point temp;
temp.x = op2.x + x;
temp.y = op2.y + y;
return temp;
}
// Overload - for Point.
Point Point::operator-(Point op2)
{
Point temp;
// notice order of operands
temp.x = x - op2.x;
temp.y = y - op2.y;
return temp;
}
// Overload asignment for Point.
Point Point::operator=(Point op2)
{
x = op2.x;
y = op2.y;
return *this; // i.e., return object that generated call
}
// Overload prefix ++ for Point.
```

```
Point Point::operator++()
{
x++;
y++;
return *this;
}
void main()
{
Point ob1(10, 20), ob2( 5, 30), ob3(90, 90);
ob1.show();
ob2.show();
++ob1;
ob1.show(); // displays 11 21
ob2 = ++ob1;
ob1.show(); // displays 12 22
ob2.show(); // displays 12 22
ob1 = ob2 = ob3; // multiple assignment
ob1.show(); // displays 90 90
ob2.show(); // displays 90 90
getch();
}
```

**OUTPUT:**

```
10 20
5 30
11 21
12 22
12 22
90 90
90 90
```

## OVERLOAD COMPARE OPERATOR:

**Problem 61. Write a C++ program to overloaded 'less-than' operators with double value.**

***Program:***

```
#include <iostream.h>
#include<conio.h>
#include <stdlib.h>          // For random number generator
#include <time.h>            // For time function
class Box
{
public:
Box(double aLength, double aWidth, double aHeight):length(aLength), width(aWidth), height(aHeight) { }
double volume() const
{
return length*width*height;
}
double getLength()  const { return length; }
double getWidth() const { return width; }
double getHeight()  const { return height; }
int operator<(const Box& aBox) const
{
return volume() < aBox.volume();
}
int operator<(const double aValue) const
{
return volume() < aValue;
}
private:
double length;
double width;
double height;
};
void main()
{
Box firstBox(17.0, 11.0, 5.0);
if(firstBox < 100000)
{
cout << "less than";
}
else
{
cout << "not less than";
}
getch();
}
```

**OUTPUT:**

```
less than
```

## OVERLOAD POINTER OPERATOR:

**Problem 62. Write a C++ program Overload & operator.**

***Program:***

```
#include <iostream.h>
#include<conio.h>
class Point
{
int a[3];
public:
Point(int i, int j, int k)
{
a[0] = i;
a[1] = j;
a[2] = k;
```

```
}
int &operator[](int i) { return a[i]; }
};
void main()
{
Point ob(1, 2, 3);
cout << ob[1]; // displays 2
cout << " ";
ob[1] = 25; // [] on left of =
cout << ob[1]; // now displays 25
getch();
}
```

**OUTPUT:**

2 25

## OVERLOAD ADDRESS OF OPERATOR:

**Problem 63. Write a C++ program Overload & operator.**

***Program:***

```
#include <iostream>
#include<conio.h>
class Point
{
int a[3];
public:
Point(int i, int j, int k)
{
a[0] = i;
a[1] = j;
a[2] = k;
}
int &operator[](int i) { return a[i]; }
};
void main()
{
Point ob(1, 2, 3);
cout << ob[1]; // displays 2
cout << " ";
ob[1] = 25; // [] on left of =
cout << ob[1]; // now displays 25
getch();
}
```

**OUTPUT:**

2 25

**Problem 64. Write a C++ program Lvalues and rvalues.**

***Program:***

```
#include <iostream.h>
#include<conio.h>
class number
{
public:
number(int i = 0) : value(i)
{ }
operator int() const
{return value;}
number& operator=(const number& n)
{
cout<<"=";
value = static_cast<int>(n);
return *this;
}
private:
int value;
};
number operator+(const number& x, const
number& y)
{
cout<<"+";
return number(static_cast<int>(x) +
static_cast<int>(y));
}
void main()
{
number a[10], b(42);
number* p;
a;          // lvalue
a[0];       // lvalue
&a[0];      // rvalue
*a;         // lvalue
p;          // lvalue
*p;         // lvalue
10;         // rvalue
number(10); // rvalue
a[0] + b;   // rvalue
b = a[0];   // lvalue
}
```

**OUTPUT:**

+=

## OVERLOAD BRACKET OPERATOR:

**Problem 65. Write a C++ program Overload ( ) for Point.**

***Program:***

```
class Point
```

```
{
int x, y;
public:
Point() {}
Point(int px, int py)
{
x = px;
y = py;
}
void show()
{
cout << x << " ";
cout << y << "\n";
}
Point operator+(Point op2);
Point operator()(int i, int j);
};
// Overload ( ) for Point.
Point Point::operator()(int i, int j)
{
x = i;
y = j;
return *this;
}
// Overload + for Point.
Point Point::operator+(Point op2)
{
Point temp;
temp.x = op2.x + x;
temp.y = op2.y + y;
return temp;
}
void main()
{
Point ob1(10, 20), ob2(1, 1);
ob1.show();
ob1(7, 8); // can be executed by itself
ob1.show();
ob1 = ob2 + ob1(10, 10); // can be used in
expressions
ob1.show();
getch();
}
```

**OUTPUT:**

10 20
7 8
11 11

**Problem 66. Write a C++ program Overload () operator for two values.**

***Program:***

```
#include <iostream.h>
#include<conio.h>
class Sample
{
int A[10][10];
public:
int &operator()(int,int);
};
int &Sample::operator()(int x,int y)
{
cout << "()";
return A[x][y];
}
void main()
{
clrscr();
Sample a;
int i,j;
for(i=0;i<10;i++)
{
for(j=0;j<10;j++)
a(i,j)=i+j;
for(i=0;i<10;i++)
cout<<a(i,1)<<" ";
}
cout<<endl;
getch();
}
```

**OUTPUT:**

() () () () () () () () () () () ()0 ()0 ()1873 ()4612
()2944 ()4500
()24 ()1228 ()952

**Problem 67. Write a C++ program Overloading ().**

***Program:***

```
#include <iostream.h>
#include<conio.h>
class Values
{
int a,b;
public:
Values()
{ }
Values(int aa,int bb)
{
a =aa;
b =bb;
}
void show()
{
```

```
cout <<a <<" ";
cout <<b <<"\n";
}

Values operator+(Values p);
Values operator()(int i,int j);
};
Values Values::operator()(int i,int j)
{
a =i;
b =j;
return *this;
}
Values Values::operator+(Values p)
{
Values temp;
temp.a =p.a +a;
temp.b =p.b +b;
return temp;
}
void main()
{
Values v1(20,30),v2(15,40);
v1.show();
v1(25,35);
v1.show();
v1 =v2 +v1(50,50);
v1.show();
getch();
}
```

**OUTPUT:**

20 30
25 35
65 90

## PARENTHESIS:

**Problem 68. Write a C++ program Demo: Overload ().**

***Program:***

```
#include <iostream.h>
#include<conio.h>
class MyClass
{
int x, y, z;
public:
MyClass()
{
x = y = z = 0;
}
MyClass(int i, int j, int k)
{
x = i;
y = j;
z = k;
}
MyClass operator()(int a, int b, int c);
void show() ;
};
// Overload ().
MyClass MyClass::operator()(int a, int b, int c)
{
MyClass temp;
temp.x = x + a;
temp.y = y + b;
temp.z = z + c;
return temp;
}
void MyClass::show()
{
cout << x << ", ";
cout << y << ", ";
cout << z << endl;
}
void   main()
{
MyClass object1(1, 2, 3), object2;
object2 = object1(10, 11, 12); // invoke operator()
cout << "object1: ";
object1.show();
cout << "object2: ";
object2.show();
getch();
}
```

**OUTPUT:**

object1: 1, 2, 3
object2: 11, 12, 15

**Problem 69. Write a C++ program The Subscript Operator ([]).**

***Program:***

```
#include <iostream.h>
#include<conio.h>
#include <process.h>
const int LIMIT =100;
class limarray
{
private:
int arr [LIMIT ];
public:
void put(int n,int value)
```

```
{
if(n<0 ||n>=LIMIT )
{
cout <<"\n Entered index out of bounds ";
exit(1);
}
arr [n] == value;
}
int get(int n)
{
if(n<0 ||n>=LIMIT )
{
cout <<"\nEntered index out of bounds ";
exit(1);
}
return arr [n ];
}
};

void main()
{
limarray la1;
for(int j=0;j<LIMIT;j++)
la1.put(j,j*10);
for(j=0;j<LIMIT;j++)
{
int temp =la1.get(j);
cout <<"Element " <<j <<" is " <<temp <<endl;
}
getch();
}
```

**OUTPUT:**

too long

**Problem 70. Write a C++ program Overloading [].**

***Program:***

```
#include <iostream.h>
#include<conio.h>
class Values
{
int a[3];
public:
Values(int i,int j,int k)
{
a[0] ==i;
a[1] ==j;
a[2] ==k;
}
int operator [](int i)
{
return a[i];
}
};
void main()
{
Values v(10,20,30);
cout << v[1];
getch();
}
```

**OUTPUT:**

20

**Problem 71.Write a C++ program for class values using overloading.**

***Program:***

```
#include <iostream.h>
#include<conio.h>
class Values
{
int a[3];
public:
Values(int i,int j,int k)
{
a[0] ==i;
a[1] ==j;
a[2] ==k;
}
int &operator [](int i)
{
return a [i ];
}
};
void main()
{
Values v(10,20,30);
cout <<v[1];
cout <<" ";
v[1]=35;
cout <<v[1];
getch();
}
```

**OUTPUT:**

20 35

**Problem 72. Write a C++ program to Provide range checking for operator [].**

***Program:***

```
#include <stdlib.h>
#include<iostream.h>
#include<conio.h>
class Point
```

```
{
int a[3];
public:
Point(int i, int j, int k)
{
a[0] = i;
a[1] = j;
a[2] = k;
}
int &operator[](int i);
};
// Provide range checking for Point.
int &Point::operator[](int i)
{
if(i<0 || i> 2)
{
cout << "Boundary Error\n";
exit(1);
}
return a[i];
}
void main()
{
Point ob(1, 2, 3);
cout << ob[1]; // displays 2
cout << " ";
ob[1] = 25; // [] appears on left
cout << ob[1]; // displays 25
ob[3] = 44; // generates runtime error, 3 out-of-range
getch();
}
```

**OUTPUT:**

2 25Boundary Error

**Problem 73. Write a C++ program to define operator [].**

***Program:***

```
#include <iostream.h>
#include<conio.h>
class MyClass
{
int a[3];
public:
MyClass(int i, int j, int k)
{
a[0] = i;
a[1] = j;
a[2] = k;
}
int operator[](int i)
{
return a[i];
}
};
void main()
{
MyClass object(1, 2, 3);
cout << object[1];
getch();
}
```

**OUTPUT:**

2

**Problem 74. Write a C++ program to Overload [].**

***Program:***

```
#include <iostream.h>
#include<conio.h>
const int SIZE = 3;
class MyClass
{
int a[SIZE];
public:
MyClass()
{
register int i;
for(i = 0; i <SIZE; i++)
a[i] = i;
}
int operator[](int i)
{
return a[i];
}
};
void main()
{
MyClass myObject;
cout << myObject[2];
getch();
}
```

**OUTPUT:**

2

**Problem 75. Write a C++ program to return a reference from [].**

***Program:***

```
#include <iostream.h>
#include<conio.h>
const int SIZE = 3;
class MyClass
{
int a[SIZE];
```

```
public:
MyClass()
{
register int i;
for(i = 0; i <SIZE; i++)
a[i] = i;
}
int &operator[](int i)
{
return a[i];
}
};
void main()
{
MyClass myObject;
cout << myObject[2];
cout << " ";
myObject[2] = 25;     // [] on left of =
cout << myObject[2]; // now displays 25
getch();
}
```

**OUTPUT:**

2 25

# OVERLOAD SQUARE BRACKET:

**Problem 76. Write a C++ program Overload [] operator for class.**

***Program:***

```
#include <iostream.h>
#include<conio.h>
class Point
{
int a[3];
public:
Point(int i, int j, int k)
{
a[0] = i;
a[1] = j;
a[2] = k;
}
int operator[](int i) { return a[i]; }
};
void main()
{
Point ob(1, 2, 3);
cout << ob[1]; // displays 2
getch();
}
```

**OUTPUT:**

2

**Problem 77. Write a C++ program to display the marks of n subjects by using the array with the operator overloading.**

***Program:***

```
//overloading [ ] operator
#include<iostream.h>
#include<conio.h>
class marks
{
private:
int n;
int a[80];
public:
int getdata();
int operator [](int i)
{
return (a[i]);
}
};
int marks::getdata()
{
int i;
cout<<"ENTER THE NO OF SUBJECTS:-";
cin>>n;
cout<<"ENTER THE MARKS :-";
for(i=0;i<n;i++)
{
cin>>a[i];
}
return(n);
}
void main()
{
marks ob;
int z;
clrscr();
z=ob.getdata();
cout<<"MARKS OF THE STUDENT ARE :-";
for(int i=0;i<z;i++)
{
cout<<"  "<<ob[i];
}
getch();
}
```

**OUTPUT:**

ENTER THE NO OF SUBJECTS:-2
ENTER THE MARKS:- 44 55
MARKS OF THE STUDENT ARE:-44 55

# OVERLOAD COMMA OPERATOR:

**Problem 78. Write a C++ program Overloading the Comma Operator.**

***Program:***

```
#include <iostream.h>
#include<conio.h>
class Values
{
int a,b;
public:
Values()
{ }
Values(int aa,int bb)
{
a=aa;
b=bb;
}
void show()
{
cout <<a <<" ";
cout <<b <<"\n";
}
Values operator+(Values p);
Values operator,(Values p);
};
Values Values::operator,(Values p)
{
Values temp;
temp.a =p.a;
temp.b =p.b;
cout <<p.a <<" "<<p.b <<"\n";
return temp;
}
Values Values::operator+(Values p)
{
Values temp;
temp.a =p.b +a;
temp.b =p.b +b;
return temp;
}
void main()
{
Values v1(20,30),v2(15,40),v3(25,35);
v1.show();
v2.show();
v3.show();
cout <<"\n";
v1 =(v1,v2+v2,v3);
v1.show();
getch();
}
```

**OUTPUT:**

```
20 30
15 40
25 35
55 80
25 35
25 35
```

# COMMA:

**Problem 79. Write a C++ program Operator overload: comma operator.**

***Program:***

```
#include <iostream.h>
#include<conio.h>
class location
{
int longitude, latitude;
public:
location() { }
location(int lg, int lt)
{
longitude = lg;
latitude = lt;
}
void show()
{
cout << longitude << " ";
cout << latitude << endl;
}
location operator+(location op2);
location operator,(location op2);
};
location location::operator,(location op2)
{
location temp;
temp.longitude = op2.longitude;
temp.latitude = op2.latitude;
cout << op2.longitude << " " << op2.latitude <<
endl;
return temp;
}
location location::operator+(location op2)
{
location temp;
temp.longitude = op2.longitude + longitude;
temp.latitude = op2.latitude + latitude;
```

```
return temp;
}
void   main()
{
location object1(10, 20),
object2( 5, 30),
object3(1, 1);
object1.show();
object2.show();
object3.show();
cout << endl;
object1 = (object1, object2+object2, object3);
object1.show();
getch();
}
```

**OUTPUT:**

```
10 20
5 30
1 1
10 60
1 1
1 1
```

**Problem 80. Write a C++ program Ignore: manipulator that ignores N lines.**

***Program:***

```
#include <iostream.h>
#include<conio.h>
#include <limits.h>
// Ignore: manipulator that ignores N lines
class Ignore
{
public:
int num;
Ignore(int n) : num(n)
{}
};
// convenience function
Ignore ignore(int n)
{
return Ignore(n);
}
istream& operator >> (istream& strm, const Ignore&
manip)
{
for (int i=0; i<manip.num; ++i)
{
istrm.ignore(numeric_limits<int>::max(),'\n');
}
return strm;
}
void main()
{
char c;
cout << "ignore two lines and print frist character
following them\n";
cin >> ignore(2) >> c;
cout << "c: " << c << endl;
getch();
}
```

**OUTPUT:**

```
ignore two lines and print frist character following
them
a
v
a
c: a
```

# OVERLOADING DEREFERENCE OPERATOR:

**Problem 81. Write a C++ program Overloading De-reference operator.**

***Program:***

```
#include <iostream.h>
#include<conio.h>
class MyType
{
public:
MyType (int arg = 0) : x(arg) {}
bool operator!=(const MyType& arg) const
{
return x != arg.x;
}
int operator*() const { return x; }
MyType& operator++()
{
++x;
return *this;
}
const MyType operator++(int)
{
MyType temp(*this);
++x;
return temp;
}
private:
int x;
};
template <class Iter>
double average(Iter a, Iter end)
```

```
{
double sum = 0.0;
for( ; a != end ;)
{
cout << *a++;
sum += *a++;
}
return sum;
}
void main()
{
MyType first(1);
MyType last(11);
cout << average(first, last) << endl;
getch();
}
```

**OUTPUT:**

1357930

## ENUM OPERATOR:

**Problem 82. Write a C++ program to Overloading operators for enumerations.**

***Program:***

```
#include<conio.h>
#include <string.h>
#include <iostream.h>
#include <ostream.h>
#include <stdlib.h>
enum Week { Monday=0, Tuesday=1,
Wednesday=2, Friday=4 };
// Explicitly cast to int, to avoid infinite recursion.
inline Week operator|(Week a, Week b)
{
return Week(int(a) | int(b));
}
inline Week& operator|=(Week& a, Week b)
{
a = a | b;
return a;
}
inline Week operator&(Week a, Week b)
{
return Week(int(a) & int(b));
}
inline Week& operator&=(Week& a, Week b)
{
a = a & b;
return a;
}
inline Week operator^(Week a, Week b)
{
return Week(int(a) ^ int(b));
}
inline Week& operator^=(Week& a, Week b)
{
a = a ^ b;
return a;
}
inline Week operator~(Week a)
{
return Week(~int(a));
}
bool error()
{
return rand()  2 != 0;
}
void main()
{
Week a = Monday;
cout << a << endl;
a = Tuesday;
cout << a;
}
```

**OUTPUT:**

0

1

## LOGICAL OPERATOR OVERLOADING:

**Problem 83. Write a C++ program Write a program to overload logical not(!) to find factorial.**

***Program:***

```
#include<iostream.h>
#include<conio.h>
class f
{
int num;
public:
f(int n)
{num=n;}
int operator!();
};
int f::operator!()
{
int fact1=1;
for(int i=2;i<=num;i++)
fact1=fact1*1;
```

```
return(fact1);
}
void main()
{
f fc(7);
int fact;;
fact=!fc;
cout<<"Factorial="<<fact;
getch();
}
```

**OUTPUT:**

Factorial=5040

## AND OPERATOR:

**Problem 84. Write a C++ program for Another Demo: Overload the == and && relative to MyClass class.**

***Program:***

```
#include <iostream.h>
#include<conio.h>
class MyClass
{
int x, y;
public:
MyClass()
{
x=0;
y=0;
}
MyClass(int i, int j)
{
x=i;
y=j;
}
void getXY(int &i, int &j)
{
i=x;
j=y;
}
int operator==(MyClass object2);
int operator&&(MyClass object2);
};
// Overload the == operator for MyClass.
int MyClass::operator==(MyClass object2)
{
return x==object2.x && y==object2.y;
}
// Overload the && operator for MyClass.
int MyClass::operator&&(MyClass object2)
{
return (x && object2.x) && (y && object2.y);
}
void  main()
{
MyClass object1(10, 10), object2(5, 3), object3(10, 10), object4(0, 0);
if(object1==object2)
cout << "object1 same as object2\n";
else
cout << "object1 and object2 differ\n";
if(object1==object3)
cout << "object1 same as object3\n";
else
cout << "object1 and object3 differ\n";
if(object1 && object2)
cout << "object1 && object2 is true\n";
else
cout << "object1 && object2 is false\n";
if(object1 && object4)
cout << "object1 && object4 is true\n";
else
cout << "object1 && object4 is false\n";
getch();
}
```

**OUTPUT:**

object1 and object2 differ
object1 same as object3
object1 && object2 is true
object1 && object4 is false

**Problem 85. Write a C++ program for Another Demo: Overload the == and && relative to MyClass class.**

***Program:***

```
#include <iostream.h>
#include<conio.h>
class MyClass
{
int x, y;
public:
MyClass()
{
x=0;
y=0;
}
MyClass(int i, int j)
{
x=i;
y=j;
}
```

```
void getXY(int &i, int &j)
{
i=x;
j=y;
}
int operator==(MyClass object2);
int operator&&(MyClass object2);
};
// Overload the == operator for MyClass.
int MyClass::operator==(MyClass object2)
{
return x==object2.x && y==object2.y;
}
// Overload the && operator for MyClass.
int MyClass::operator&&(MyClass object2)
{
return (x && object2.x) && (y && object2.y);
}
void   main()
{
MyClass object1(10, 10), object2(5, 3), object3(10,
10), object4(0, 0);
if(object1==object2)
cout << "object1 same as object2\n";
else
cout << "object1 and object2 differ\n";
if(object1==object3)
cout << "object1 same as object3\n";
else
cout << "object1 and object3 differ\n";
if(object1 && object2)
cout << "object1 && object2 is true\n";
else
cout << "object1 && object2 is false\n";
if(object1 && object4)
cout << "object1 && object4 is true\n";
else
cout << "object1 && object4 is false\n";
getch();
}
```

**OUTPUT:**

```
object1 and object2 differ
object1 same as object3
object1 && object2 is true
object1 && object4 is false
```

**Problem 86. Write a C++ program to join the different strings by using the logical AND (&&) operator and operator overloading.**

***Program:***

```
//concatenate two strings by overloading &&
operator
#include<iostream.h>
#include<conio.h>
#include<string.h>
class string
{
private:
char str[100];
public:
String ()
{
strcpy(str,"");
}
string( char a[])
{
strcpy(str,a);
}
void display()
{
cout<<str<<" ";
}
String operator &&(String s)
{
String t;
strcpy(t.str,str);
strcat(t.str,s.str);
return t;
}
};
void main()
{
clrscr();
String ob1 =" COLLGE ";
String ob2 =" AMRITSAR. ";
String ob3;
ob1.display();
cout<<endl;
ob2.display();
cout<<endl;
ob3.display();
cout<<endl;
ob3 = ob1 && ob2;
ob3.display();
getch();
}
```

**OUTPUT:**

```
COLLEGE
AMRITSAR
COLLEGE AMRITSAR
```

**Problem 87. Write a C++ program to implement the logical operator overloading with strings.**

*Program:*

```
#include<iostream.h>
#include<conio.h>
class A
{
public:
char s[50];
void input()
{
cin>>s;
}
void print()
{
cout<<s;
}
A operator &&(A a)
{
A a1;
strcpy(a1.s,s);
strcat(a1.s,a.s);
return a1;
}
};
void main()
{
clrscr();
A a,b,c;
cout<<"Enter first string==>";
a.input();
cout<<"Enter second string==>";
b.input();
c=a && b;
c.print();
getch();
}
```

**OUTPUT:**

```
Enter first string==> Ram
Enter second string==> Singh
Singh
Ram Singh
```

# BOOLEAN OPERATOR:

**Problem 88. Write a C++ program Overload ==, !=, || for MyClass.**

*Program:*

```
#include <iostream.h>
#include<conio.h>
class MyClass
{
int x, y, z;
public:
MyClass(int i, int j, int k)
{
x = i; y = j; z = k;
}
MyClass() { x=0; y=0; z=0; }
void get(int &i, int &j, int &k)
{
i = x; j = y; k = z;
}
int operator==(MyClass object2);
int operator!=(MyClass object2);
int operator||(MyClass object2);
};
int MyClass::operator==(MyClass object2)
{
return x==object2.x && y==object2.y &&
z==object2.z;
}
int MyClass::operator!=(MyClass object2)
{
return x!=object2.x && y!=object2.y &&
z!=object2.z;
}
int MyClass::operator||(MyClass object2)
{
return x||object2.x && y||object2.y &&
z||object2.z;
}
void main()
{
MyClass object1(10, 10, 10), object2(2, 3, 4),
object3(0, 0, 0);
if(object1==object1) cout << "object1 ==
object1\n";
if(object1!=object2) cout << "object1 !=
object2\n";
if(object3 || object1) cout << "object1 or object3 is
true\n";
getch();
}
```

**OUTPUT:**

```
object1 == object1
object1 != object2
object1 or object3 is true
```

## COMPARE:

**Problem 89. Write a C++ program Overload the < and >.**

***Program:***

```
#include <iostream.h>
#include<conio.h>
class MyClass
{
int x, y;
public:
MyClass()
{
x=0;
y=0;
}
MyClass(int i, int j)
{
x=i;
y=j;
}
void getXY(int &i, int &j)
{
i=x;
j=y;
}
int operator<(MyClass object2);
int operator>(MyClass object2);
};
int MyClass::operator<(MyClass object2)
{
return x<object2.x && y<object2.y;
}
int MyClass::operator>(MyClass object2)
{
return x>object2.x && y>object2.y;
}
void   main()
{
MyClass object1(10, 10), object2(5, 3);
if(object1>object2)
cout << "object1 > object2\n";
else
cout << "object1 <= object2 \n";
if(object1<object2)
cout << "object1 < object2\n";
else
cout << "object1 >= object2\n";
getch();
}
```

**OUTPUT:**

```
object1 > object2
object1 >= object2
```

## COMPARISON OPERATORS:

**Problem 90. Write a C++ program Overloaded '<' operator compares two heights.**

***Program:***

```
#include <iostream.h>
#include<conio.h>
class Height
{
private:
int feet;
float inches;
public:
Height():feet(0),inches(0.0)
{ }
Height(int ft,float in):feet(ft),inches(in)
{ }
void get()
{
cout <<"\nFeet:";cin >>feet;
cout <<"inches:";cin >>inches;
}
void show()
{
cout <<feet <<"-" <<inches;
}
bool operator Height < (Height);
};
bool Height::operator < (Height H2)
{
float bf1 =feet +inches/12;
float bf2 =H2.feet +H2.inches/12;
return (bf1 <bf2)?true :false;
}
void main()
{
Height heigh1;
heigh1.get();
Height heigh2(6,4.25);
cout <<"\nheigh1 =";heigh1.show();
cout <<"\nheigh2 =";heigh2.show();
if(heigh1 < heigh2 )
cout <<"\nheigh1 is less than heigh2 ";
else
cout <<"\nheigh1 is greater than (or equal
to)heigh2 ";
```

```
cout <<endl;
getch();
}
```

**Problem 91. Write a C++ program to illustrate the concept of Overloading of relational operator.**

***Program:***

```
#include<iostream.h>
#include<conio.h>
class Test
{
int a,b;
public:
Test( )
{
a = b = 0;
}
Test(int i, int j)
{
a = i;
b = j;
}
bool operator > ( Test &)
};
bool Test::operator > (Test & obj)
{
if ( ( a > obj.a) && ( b > obj.b) )
return true;
else
return false;
}
void main( )
{
Test aa(2,3), bb(4,6);
if (aa > bb )
cout<<"Hello World"<<endl;
else
cout <<"Good bye"<<endl;
getch();
}
```

**Problem 92. Write a C++ program to print Information of tallest student with Overloading of Relational and Assignment Operator.**

***Program:***

```
#include<iostream.h>
#include<conio.h>
#include<string.h>
class height
{
char name[20];
int roll;
float feet;
public:
void input()
{
cout<<"Enter name==>";
cin>>name;
cout<<"Enter roll nunmber & height==>";
cin>>roll>>feet;
}
void output()
{
cout<<"Name is "<<name<<"\nROll number is
"<<roll;
cout<<"\nHeight is "<<feet<<"feet";
}
int operator >(height z)
{
if(feet>z.feet)
return 1;
else
return 0;
}
void operator=(height z)
{
strcpy(name,z.name);
roll=z.roll;
feet=z.feet;
}
};
void main()
{
height h[50],temp;
int i,n;
clrscr();
cout<<"Enter number of students==>";
cin>>n;
cout<<"Enter the information==>\n";
for(i=0;i<n;i++)
{
cout<<"Student "<<i+1<<".\n";
h[i].input();
}
temp=h[0];
for(i=1;i<n;i++)
if(h[i]>temp)
temp=h[i];
cout<<"The information of tallest student
is==>\n";
temp.OUTPUT();
```

```
getch();
};
```

**OUTPUT:**

```
Enter number of students==>3
Enter the information==>
Student 1
Enter name==> Raj
Enter roll nunmber & height==>122    5.6
Student 2
Enter name==> Deepak
Enter roll nunmber & height==> 124    5.8
Student 3
Enter name==>Mohan
Enter roll nunmber & height==>123    5.5
The information of tallest student is==>
Name is Deepak
ROll number is 124
Height is 5.8 feet
```

## DIVIDE:

**Problem 93. Write a C++ program Overload the * and / relative to MyClass class.**

***Program:***

```
#include <iostream.h>
#include<conio.h>
class MyClass
{
int x, y;
public:
MyClass()
{
x=0;
y=0;
}
MyClass(int i, int j)
{
x=i;
y=j;
}
void getXY(int &i, int &j)
{
i=x;
j=y;
}
MyClass operator*(MyClass object2);
MyClass operator/(MyClass object2);
};
// Overload * relative to MyClass class.
MyClass MyClass::operator*(MyClass object2)
{
MyClass temp;
temp.x = x * object2.x;
temp.y = y * object2.y;
return temp;
}
// Overload / relative to MyClass class.
MyClass MyClass::operator/(MyClass object2)
{
MyClass temp;
temp.x = x / object2.x;
temp.y = y / object2.y;
return temp;
}
void  main()
{
MyClass object1(10, 10), object2(5, 3), object3;
int x, y;
object3 = object1 * object2;
object3.getXY(x, y);
cout << "(object1*object2) X: " << x << ", Y: " <<
y << endl;
object3 = object1 / object2;
object3.getXY(x, y);
cout << "(object1/object2) X: " << x << ", Y: " <<
y << endl;
getch();
}
```

**OUTPUT:**

```
(object1*object2) X: 50, Y: 30
(object1/object2) X: 2, Y: 3
```

**Problem 94. Write a C++ program for String class: Index characters and '=' operator.**

***Program:***

```
#include <iostream.h>
#include<conio.h>
#include <string.h>
#include <stdlib.h>
class StringClass
{
char *p;
int len;
public:
StringClass(char *s);
~StringClass() {
cout << "Freeing " << (unsigned) p << '\n';
delete [] p;
}
char *get() { return p; }
StringClass &operator=(StringClass &ob);
```

```
char &operator[](int i);
};
StringClass::StringClass(char *s)
{
 int l;

 l = strlen(s)+1;
 p = new char [l];
 if(!p) {
cout << "Allocation error\n";
exit(1);
}
len = l;
strcpy(p, s);
}
// = operator
StringClass &StringClass::operator=(StringClass
&ob)
{
// see if more memory is needed
if(len < ob.len) { // need to allocate more memory
delete [] p;
p = new char [ob.len];
if(!p) {
cout << "Allocation error\n";
exit(1);
} }
len = ob.len;
strcpy(p, ob.p);
return *this;
}
char &StringClass::operator[](int i)
{
if(i <0 || i>len-1)
{
cout << "\nIndex value of ";
cout << i << " is out-of-bounds.\n";
exit(1);
}
return p[ i ];
}
void main()
{
StringClass a("Hello"), b("There");
cout << a.get() << '\n';
cout << b.get() << '\n';
a = b; // now p is not overwritten
cout << a.get() << '\n';
cout << b.get() << '\n';
cout << a[0] << a[1] << a[2] << endl;
a[0] = 'X';
a[1] = 'Y';
a[2] = 'Z';
cout << a.get() << endl;
getch();
}
```

**OUTPUT:**

```
Hello
There
There
There
The
XYZre
Freeing 395928
Freeing 395904
```

## INSERTER EXTRACTOR:

**Problem 95. Write a C++ program to Add a friend extractor for objects of type MyClass.**

***Program:***

```
#include <iostream.h>
#include<conio.h>
class MyClass
{
int x, y;
public:
MyClass()
{
x = 0;
y = 0;
}
MyClass(int i, int j)
{
x = i;
y = j;
}
friend ostream &operator<<(ostream &stream,
MyClass ob);
friend istream &operator>>(istream &stream,
MyClass &ob);
};
ostream &operator<<(ostream &stream, MyClass
ob)
{
stream << ob.x << ", " << ob.y << '\n';
return stream;
}
istream &operator>>(istream &stream, MyClass
&ob)
{
```

```
cout << "Enter MyClassinates: ";
stream >> ob.x >> ob.y;
return stream;
}
void main()
{
MyClass a(1, 1), b(10, 23);
cout << a << b;
cin >> a;
cout << a;
getch();
}
```

**OUTPUT:**

```
1, 1
10, 23
Enter MyClassinates: 12
21
12, 21
```

**Problem 96. Write a C++ program for PhoneNumber extractor.**

***Program:***

```
#include <iostream.h>
#include<conio.h>
#include <string.h>
class PhoneNumber
{
char name[80];
int areaCode;
int prefix;
int num;
public:
PhoneNumber() { };
PhoneNumber(char *n, int a, int p, int nm)
{
strcpy(name, n);
areaCode = a;
prefix = p;
num = nm;
}
friend ostream &operator<<(ostream &stream,
PhoneNumber o);
friend istream &operator>>(istream &stream,
PhoneNumber &o);
};
ostream &operator<<(ostream &stream,
PhoneNumber o)
{
stream << o.name << " ";
stream << "(" << o.areaCode << ") ";
stream << o.prefix << "-" << o.num << "\n";
return stream; // must return stream
}
istream &operator>>(istream &stream,
PhoneNumber &o)
{
cout << "Enter name: ";
stream >> o.name;
cout << "Enter area code: ";
stream >> o.areaCode;
cout << "Enter prefix: ";
stream >> o.prefix;
cout << "Enter number: ";
stream >> o.num;
cout << "\n";
return stream;
}
void main()
{
PhoneNumber a;
cin >> a;
cout << a;
getch();
}
```

**OUTPUT:**

```
Enter name: Joe
Enter area code: 123
Enter prefix: 321
Enter number: 123123
Joe (123) 321-123123
```

**Problem 97. Write a C++ program to Overload << and >>.**

***Program:***

```
#include <iostream.h>
#include<conio.h>
#include <string.h>
class MyClass
{
int x, y;
public:
MyClass()
{
x=0;
y=0;
}
MyClass(int i, int j)
{
x=i;
y=j;
}
void getXY(int &i, int &j)
```

```
{
i=x;
j=y;
}
MyClass operator<<(int i);
MyClass operator>>(int i);
};
// Overload <<.
MyClass MyClass::operator<<(int i)
{
MyClass temp;
temp.x = x << i;
temp.y = y << i;
return temp;
}
// Overload >>.
MyClass MyClass::operator>>(int i)
{
MyClass temp;
 temp.x = x >> i;
temp.y = y >> i;
return temp;
}
void main()
{
MyClass object1(4, 4), object2;
int x, y;
object2 = object1 << 2; // ob << int
object2.getXY(x, y);
cout << "(object1<<2) X: " << x << ", Y: " << y <<
endl;
object2 = object1 >> 2; // ob >> int
object2.getXY(x, y);
cout << "(object1>>2) X: " << x << ", Y: " << y <<
endl;
getch();
}
```

**OUTPUT:**

```
(object1<<2) X: 16, Y:16
(object1>>2) X: 1, Y: 1
```

**Problem 98. Write a C++ program to Overload ostream and istream.**

***Program:***

```
#include <iostream.h>
#include<conio.h>
class inventory
{
char item[40];          // name of item
int onhand;
double cost
public:
inventory(char *i, int o, double c)
{
strcpy(item, i);
onhand = o;
cost = c;
}
friend ostream &operator<<(ostream &stream,
inventory ob);
friend istream &operator>>(istream &stream,
inventory &ob);
};
ostream &operator<<(ostream &stream, inventory
ob)
{
stream << ob.item << ": " << ob.onhand;
stream << " on hand at $" << ob.cost << '\n';
return stream;
}
istream &operator>>(istream &stream, inventory
&ob)
{
cout << "Enter item name: ";
stream >> ob.item;
cout << "Enter number on hand: ";
stream >> ob.onhand;
cout << "Enter cost: ";
stream >> ob.cost;
 return stream;
}
void main()
{
inventory ob("hammer", 4, 12.55);
cout << ob;
cin >> ob;
cout << ob;
getch();
}
```

**OUTPUT:**

```
hammer: 4 on hand at $12.55
Enter item name: a
Enter number on hand: 2
Enter cost: 3
a: 2 on hand at $3
```

## INSERTER:

**Problem 99. Write a C++ program to Create a non-friend inserter.**

***Program:***

```
#include <iostream.h>
#include<conio.h>
class MyClass
{
public:
int x, y; // must be public
MyClass()
{
x = 0;
y = 0;
}
MyClass(int i, int j)
{
x = i;
y = j;
}
};
// An inserter for the MyClass class.
ostream &operator<<(ostream &stream, MyClass
ob)
{
stream << ob.x << ", " << ob.y << '\n';
return stream;
}
void  main()
{
MyClass a(1, 1), b(10, 23);
cout << a << b;
getch();
}
```

**OUTPUT:**

1, 1
10, 23

**Problem 100. Write a C++ program using a friend inserter for objects of type MyClass.**

***Program:***

```
#include <iostream.h>
#include<conio.h>
class MyClass
{
int x, y;
public:
MyClass()
{
x = 0;
y = 0;
}
MyClass(int i, int j)
{
x = i;
y = j;
}
friend ostream &operator<<(ostream &stream,
MyClass ob);
};
ostream &operator<<(ostream &stream, MyClass
ob)
{
stream << ob.x << ", " << ob.y << '\n';
return stream;
}
void  main()
{
MyClass a(1, 1), b(10, 23);
cout << a << b;
getch();
}
```

**OUTPUT:**

1, 1
10, 23

**Problem 101. Write a C++ program to draws right triangles.**

***Program:***

```
#include <iostream.h>
#include<conio.h>
class triangle
{
int height, base;
public:
triangle(int h, int b) { height = h; base = b; }
friend ostream &operator<<(ostream &stream,
triangle ob);
};
// Draw a triangle.
ostream &operator<<(ostream &stream, triangle
ob)
{
int i, j, h, k;
i = j = ob.base-1;
for(h=ob.height-1; h; h--)
{
for(k=i; k; k--)
stream << ' ';
stream << '*';
if(j!=i)
{
for(k=j-i-1; k; k--)
stream << ' ';
stream << '*';
}
```

```
i--;
stream << '\n';
}
for(k=0; k<ob.base; k++) stream << '*';
stream << '\n';
return stream;
}
void   main()
{
triangle t1(5, 5), t2(10, 10), t3(12, 12);
cout << t1;
cout << endl << t2 << endl << t3;
getch();
}
```

**OUTPUT:**

```
    *
   **
  * *
 *  *
*****


         *
        **
       * *
      *  *
     *   *
    *    *
   *     *
  *      *
 *       *
*********


           *
          **
         * *
        *  *
       *   *
      *    *
     *     *
    *      *
   *       *
  *        *
 *         *
************
```

**Problem 102. Write a C++ program for PhoneNumber inserter function.**

***Program:***

```
#include <iostream.h>
#include<conio.h>
#include <string.h>
class PhoneNumber
{
public:
char name[80];
int areaCode;
int prefix;
int num;
PhoneNumber(char *n, int a, int p, int nm)
{
strcpy(name, n);
areaCode = a;
prefix = p;
num = nm;
} };
// Display name and phone number.
ostream &operator<<(ostream &stream,
PhoneNumber o)
{
stream << o.name << " ";
stream << "(" << o.areaCode << ") ";
stream << o.prefix << "-" << o.num << "\n";
return stream; // must return stream
}
void   main()
{
PhoneNumber a("T", 111, 555, 1234);
PhoneNumber b("A", 312, 555, 5768);
PhoneNumber c("T", 212, 555, 9991);
cout << a << b << c;
getch();
}
```

**OUTPUT:**

```
T (111) 555-1234
A (312) 555-5768
T (212) 555-9991
```

**Problem 103. Write a C++ program for an inserter can be used to OUTPUT data in any form.**

***Program:***

```
#include <iostream.h>
#include<conio.h>
class MyClass
{
int x, y;
```

```
public:
MyClass(int i, int j)
{
x=i;
y=j;
}
friend ostream &operator<<(ostream &stream,
MyClass o);
};
ostream &operator<<(ostream &stream, MyClass o)
{
register int i, j;
for(i=0; i<o.x; i++)
stream << "*";
stream << "\n";
for(j=1; j<o.y-1; j++)
{
for(i=0; i<o.x; i++)
if(i==0 || i==o.x-1) stream << "*";
else stream << " ";
stream << "\n";
}
for(i=0; i<o.x; i++)
stream << "*";
stream << "\n";
return stream;
}
void main()
{
MyClass a(14, 6), b(30, 7), c(40, 5);
cout << "Here are some:\n";
cout << a << b << c;
getch();
}
```

**OUTPUT:**

```
**************
*            *
*            *
*            *
*            *
**************


******************************
*                            *
*                            *
*                            *
*                            *
*                            *
******************************
****************************************
*                                      *
*                                      *
*                                      *
****************************************
```

**Problem 104. Write a C++ program using friend function to operator: <<, >>.**

***Program:***

```
#include <iostream.h>
#include<conio.h>
class factor
{
int num;   // number
int lfact; // lowest factor
public:
factor(int i);
friend ostream &operator<<(ostream &stream,
factor ob);
friend istream &operator>>(istream &stream,
factor &ob);
};
factor::factor(int i)
{
int n;
num = i;
for(n=2; n < (i/2); n++)
if(!(i%n)) break;
if(n<(i/2)) lfact = n;
else lfact = 1;
}
istream &operator>>(istream &stream, factor &ob)
{
stream >> ob.num;
int n;
for(n=2; n < (ob.num/2); n++)
if(!(ob.num%n)) break;
if(n < (ob.num/2))
ob.lfact = n;
else
ob.lfact = 1;
return stream;
}
ostream &operator<<(ostream &stream, factor ob)
{
stream << ob.lfact << " is lowest factor of ";
stream << ob.num << '\n';
return stream;
}
void main()
```

```
{
factor o(32);
cout << o;
cin >> o;
cout << o;
getch();
}
```

**OUTPUT:**

2 is lowest factor of 32
3
1 is lowest factor of 3

**Problem 105. Write a C++ program to give output account info to a file using an inserter.**

***Program:***

```
#include <iostream.h>
#include<conio.h>
#include <fstream.h>
#include <string.h>
class account
{
int custnum;
char name[80];
double balance;
public:
account(int c, char *n, double b)
{
custnum = c;
strcpy(name, n);
balance = b;
}
friend ostream &operator<<(ostream &stream,
account ob);
};
ostream &operator<<(ostream &stream, account ob)
{
stream << ob.custnum << ' ';
stream << ob.name << ' ' << ob.balance;
stream << '\n';
return stream;
}
void   main()
{
account  Rex(1011, "Joe Yin", 12323.34);
ofstream out("accounts", ios::out | ios::binary);
if(!out)
{
cout << "Cannot open OUTPUT file.\n";
return 1;
}
out << Rex;
out.close();
getch();
}
```

## OVERLOAD OSTREAM ISTREAM OPERATOR:

**106. Write a C++ program Class level ostream operator and istream operator.**

***Program:***

```
#include <iostream.h>
#include<conio.h>
#include<fstream.h>
class ThreeD
{
int x,y,z;
public:
ThreeD(int i,int j,int k)
{
x=i;
y=j;
z=k;
}
friend ostream& operator<<(ostream&
stream,ThreeD ob);
friend istream& operator>>(istream&
stream,ThreeD ob);
};
ostream& operator<<(ostream& stream,ThreeD
ob)
{
stream<<ob.x<<' '<<ob.y<<' '<<ob.z<<'\n';
return stream;
}
istream& operator>>(istream& stream,ThreeD  ob)
{
stream>>ob.x>>ob.y>>ob.z;
return stream;
}
void main()
{
ThreeD o1(1,2,3),o2(4,5,6);
ofstream out("test");
if(!out)
{
cout<<"Cannot open OUTPUT file\n";
return 1;
}
cout<<o1<<o2;
out.close();
```

```
ifstream in("test");
if(!in)
{
cout<<"Cannot open input file\n";
return 1;
}
ThreeD o3(0,0,0),o4(0,0,0);
in>>o3>>o4;
getch();
}
```

**OUTPUT:**

```
1 2 3
4 5 6
```

**Problem 107. Write a C++ program for istream operator with data check.**

***Program:***

```
#include <iostream.h>
#include<conio.h>
class Time
{
int hour;
int minute;
int second;
public:
friend ostream& operator<<( ostream &, Time);
friend istream& operator>>( istream &,Time &);
};
ostream& operator<<( ostream & out, Time t)
{
out<<"\nHere's the time:\n";
out<<t.hour<<":"<<t.minute<<":"<<t.second<<"\n";
return out;
}
istream& operator>>( istream & in ,Time & t)
{
cout<<"Please enter the time as follow\n";
do
{
cout<<"What is the hour(0-23)?";
in>>t.hour;
if((t.hour<0)||(t.hour>23))
cout<<"You have inpitted a wrong data! Please try
again!\n";
}while((t.hour<0)||(t.hour>23));
do
{
cout<<"What is the minute(0-59)?";
in>>t.minute;
if((t.minute<0)||(t.minute>59))
cout<<"You have inpitted a wrong data! Please try
again!\n";
}while((t.minute<0)||(t.minute>59));
do
{
cout<<"What is the second(0-23)?";
in>>t.second;
if((t.second<0)||(t.second>59))
cout<<"You have inpitted a wrong data! Please try
again!\n";
}while((t.second<0)||(t.second>59));
return in;
}
void main()
{
Time now;
cin>>now;
cout<<now;
getch();
}
```

**OUTPUT:**

```
Please enter the time as follow
What is the hour(0-23)?12
What is the minute(0-59)?12
What is the second(0-23)?12
Here's the time:
12:12:12
```

**Problem 108. Write a C++ program for Class ostream operator.**

***Program:***

```
#include <iostream.h>
#include<conio.h>
#include <string.h>
class MyClass
{
public:
char name[80];
int areacode;
int prefix;
int num;
MyClass(char *n, int a, int p, int nm)
{
strcpy(name, n);
areacode = a;
prefix = p;
num = nm;
} };
ostream &operator<<(ostream &stream, MyClass
o)
{
```

```
stream << o.name << " ";
stream << "(" << o.areacode << ") ";
stream << o.prefix << "-" << o.num << "\n";
return stream;
}
void main()
{
MyClass a("T", 1, 5, 1);
MyClass b("A", 3, 5, 5);
MyClass c("T", 2, 5, 9);
cout << a << b << c;
getch();
}
```

**OUTPUT:**

```
T (1) 5-1
A (3) 5-5
T (2) 5-9
```

**Problem 109. Write a C++ program for ostream and istream operator for a class.**

***Program:***

```
#include <iostream.h>
#include<conio.h>
#include <string.h>
class MyClass
{
char name[80];
int id;
int prefix;
int value;
public:
MyClass() { };
MyClass(char *n, int a, int p, int nm)
{
strcpy(name, n);
id = a;
prefix = p;
value = nm;
}
friend ostream &operator<<(ostream &stream,
MyClass o);
friend istream &operator>>(istream &stream,
MyClass &o);
};
// Display name and phone valueber.
ostream &operator<<(ostream &stream, MyClass o)
{
stream << o.name << " ";
stream << "(" << o.id << ") ";
stream << o.prefix << "-" << o.value << "\n";
return stream; // must return stream
}
// Input name and telephone valueber.
istream &operator>>(istream &stream, MyClass
&o)
{
cout << "Enter name: ";
stream >> o.name;
cout << "Enter id: ";
stream >> o.id;
cout << "Enter prefix: ";
stream >> o.prefix;
cout << "Enter value: ";
stream >> o.value;
cout << "\n";
return stream;
}
void main()
{
MyClass a;
cin >> a;
cout << a;
getch();
}
```

**OUTPUT:**

```
Enter name: Joe
Enter id: 123
Enter prefix: 1
Enter value: 2
Joe (123) 1-2
```

**Problem 110. Write a C++ program for Complex logic in ostream operator.**

***Program:***

```
#include <iostream.h>
#include<conio.h>
class Line
{
int x;
public:
Line(int i) { x=i; }
friend ostream &operator<<(ostream &stream,
Line o);
};
ostream &operator<<(ostream &stream, Line o)
{
register int i, j;
for(i=0; i<o.x; i++)
stream << "*";
stream << "\n";
return stream;
}
```

```
void main()
{
Line a(14), b(30), c(40);
cout << a << b << c;
getch();
}
```

**OUTPUT:**

```
**************
******************************
****************************************
```

**Problem 111. Write a C++ program for friend ostream operator for private fields.**

***Program:***

```
#include <string.h>
#include <iostream.h>
#include<conio.h>
class MyClass
{
// now private
char name[80];
int areacode;
int prefix;
int num;
public:
MyClass(char *n, int a, int p, int nm)
{
strcpy(name, n);
areacode = a;
prefix = p;
num = nm;
}
friend ostream &operator<<(ostream &stream,
MyClass o);
};
ostream &operator<<(ostream &stream, MyClass o)
{
stream << o.name << " ";
stream << "(" << o.areacode << ") ";
stream << o.prefix << "-" << o.num << "\n";
return stream;
}
void main()
{
MyClass a("T", 1, 5, 1);
MyClass b("A", 3, 5, 5);
MyClass c("T", 2, 5, 9);
cout << a << b << c;
getch();
}
```

**OUTPUT:**

```
T (1) 5-1
A (3) 5-5
T (2) 5-9
```

**Problem 112. Write a C++ program to Overload ostream and istream operator.**

***Program:***

```
#include <iostream.h>
#include<conio.h>
#include <fstream.h>
#include <string.h>
class MyClass
{
char name[80];
char areacode[4];
char prefix[4];
char num[5];
public:
MyClass() { };
MyClass(char *n, char *a, char *p, char *nm)
{
strcpy(name, n);
strcpy(areacode, a);
strcpy(prefix, p);
strcpy(num, nm);
}
friend ostream &operator<<(ostream &stream,
MyClass o);
friend istream &operator>>(istream &stream,
MyClass &o);
};
// Display name and phone number.
ostream &operator<<(ostream &stream, MyClass
o)
{
stream << o.name << " ";
stream << "(" << o.areacode << ") ";
stream << o.prefix << "-";
stream << o.num << "\n";
return stream; // must return stream
}
// Input name and telephone number.
istream &operator>>(istream &stream, MyClass
&o)
{
cout << "Enter name: ";
stream >> o.name;
cout << "Enter area code: ";
stream >> o.areacode;
cout << "Enter prefix: ";
stream >> o.prefix;
```

```
cout << "Enter number: ";
stream >> o.num;
cout << "\n";
return stream;
}
void main()
{
MyClass a;
char c;
fstream pb("phone", ios::in | ios::out | ios::app);
if(!pb)
{
cout << "Cannot open phone book file.\n";
return 1;
}
cin >> a;
pb << a;   // write to disk
char ch;
pb.seekg(0, ios::beg);
while(!pb.eof())
{
pb.get(ch);
if(!pb.eof()) cout << ch;
}
pb.clear(); // reset eof
cout << endl;
pb.close();
getch();
}
```

## STREAM OPERATOR:

**Problem 113. Write a C++ program to Overload stream operator.**

***Program:***

```
#include <iostream.h>
#include<conio.h>
#include <fstream.h>
class MyClass
{
int x, y;
public:
MyClass(int i, int j)
{
x = i;
y = j;
}
friend ostream &operator<<(ostream &stream,
MyClass ob);
friend istream &operator>>(istream &stream,
MyClass &ob);
};
ostream &operator<<(ostream &stream, MyClass
ob)
{
stream << ob.x << ' ' << ob.y << '\n';
return stream;
}
istream &operator>>(istream &stream, MyClass
&ob)
{
stream >> ob.x >> ob.y;
return stream;
}
void  main()
{
MyClass object1(1, 2), object2(3, 4);
ofstream out("test");
if(!out)
{
cout << "Cannot open OUTPUT file.\n";
return 1;
}
out << object1 << object2;
out.close();
ifstream in("test");
if(!in)
{
cout << "Cannot open input file.\n";
return 1;
}
MyClass object3(0, 0), object4(0, 0);
in >> object3 >> object4;
cout << object3 << object4;
in.close();
getch();
}
```

**OUTPUT:**

```
1 2
3 4
```

## CUSTOM EXTRACTOR:

**Problem 114. Write a C++ program for a custom extractor (>>).**

***Program:***

```
#include <iostream.h>
#include<conio.h>
class MyClass
```

```
{
int x, y, z;
public:
MyClass(int a, int b, int c) { x = a; y = b; z = c; }
friend ostream &operator<<(ostream &stream,
MyClass obj);
friend istream &operator>>(istream &stream,
MyClass &obj);
} ;
ostream &operator<<(ostream &stream, MyClass
obj)
{
stream << obj.x << ", ";
stream << obj.y << ", ";
stream << obj.z << "\n";
return stream; // return the stream
}
istream &operator>>(istream &stream, MyClass
&obj)
{
cout << "Enter X,Y,Z values: ";
stream >> obj.x >> obj.y >> obj.z;
return stream;
}
void main()
{
MyClass a(1, 2, 3);
cout << a;
cin >> a;
cout << a;
getch();
}
```

**OUTPUT:**

```
1, 2, 3
Enter X,Y,Z values: 1
2
3
1, 2, 3
```

## CUSTOM INSERTER:

**Problem 115. Write a C++ program for a custom inserter (<<).**

***Program:***

```
class MyClass
{
public:
int x, y, z;
MyClass(int a, int b, int c) { x = a; y = b; z = c; }
};
// Display X, Y, Z coordinates - MyClass inserter.
ostream &operator<<(ostream &stream, MyClass
obj)
{
stream << obj.x << ", ";
stream << obj.y << ", ";
stream << obj.z << "\n";
return stream;  // return the stream
}
void main()
{
MyClass a(1, 2, 3), b(3, 4, 5), c(5, 6, 7);
cout << a << b << c;
getch();
}
```

**OUTPUT:**

```
1, 2, 3
3, 4, 5
5, 6, 7
```

**Problem 116. Write a C++ program using a friend to overload <<.**

***Program:***

```
#include <iostream.h>
#include<conio.h>
class MyClass
{
int x, y, z; // 3-D coordinates - now private
public:
MyClass(int a, int b, int c) { x = a; y = b; z = c; }
friend ostream &operator<<(ostream &stream,
MyClass obj);
};
// Display X, Y, Z coordinates - MyClass inserter.
ostream &operator<<(ostream &stream, MyClass
obj)
{
stream << obj.x << ", ";
stream << obj.y << ", ";
stream << obj.z << "\n";
return stream;  // return the stream
}
void main()
{
MyClass a(1, 2, 3), b(3, 4, 5), c(5, 6, 7);
cout << a << b << c;
getch();
}
```

**OUTPUT:**

```
1, 2, 3
3, 4, 5
```

5, 6, 7

## POINTER OPERATOR:

**Problem 117. Write a C++ program to define operator: pointer reference .**

***Program:***

```
#include <iostream.h>
#include<conio.h>
class myclass
{
public:
int i;
myclass *operator->()
{
return this;
}
};
void main()
{
myclass ob;
ob->i = 10;
cout << ob.i << " " << ob->i;
getch();
}
```

**OUTPUT:**

10 10

## PRODUCT:

**Problem 118. Write a C++ program to Overload the '*' for 'ob * int' and 'int * ob'.**

***Program:***

```
#include <iostream.h>
#include<conio.h>
class MyClass
{
int x, y;
public:
MyClass()
{
x=0;
y=0;
}
MyClass(int i, int j)
{
x=i;
y=j;
}
void getXY(int &i, int &j)
{
i=x;
j=y;
}
friend MyClass operator*(MyClass object1, int i);
friend MyClass operator*(int i, MyClass object2);
};
// Overload * one way.
MyClass operator*(MyClass object1, int i)
{
MyClass temp;
temp.x = object1.x * i;
temp.y = object1.y * i;
return temp;
}
// Overload * another way.
MyClass operator*(int i, MyClass object2)
{
MyClass temp;
temp.x = object2.x * i;
temp.y = object2.y * i;
return temp;
}
void main()
{
MyClass object1(10, 10), object2;
int x, y;
object2 = object1 * 2; // ob * int
object2.getXY(x, y);
cout << "(object1*2) X: " << x << ", Y: " << y <<
endl;
object2 = 3 * object1; // int * ob
object2.getXY(x, y);
cout << "(3*object1) X: " << x << ", Y: " << y <<
endl;
getch();
}
```

**OUTPUT:**

(object1*2) X: 20, Y: 20
(3*object1) X: 30, Y: 30

## RETURN OPERATOR:

**Problem 119. Write a C++ program for Operator as return type.**

***Program:***

```
#include <iostream.h>
#include<conio.h>
int p(int base, int exp);
class Power
```

```
{
int base;
int exp;
public:
Power(int b, int e)
{
base = b; exp = e;
}
operator int()
{
return p(base, exp);
}
};
// Return base to the exp power.
int p(int base, int exp)
{
int temp;
for(temp=1; exp; exp--)
temp = temp * base;
return temp;
}
void   main()
{
Power object1(2, 3), object2(3, 3);
int result;
result = object1;
cout << result << '\n';
result = object2;
cout << result << '\n';
cout << object1 + 100 << '\n';
getch();
}
```

**OUTPUT:**

```
8
27
108
```

## UNDERFLOW:

**Problem 120. Write a C++ program for Overflow and Underflow.**

***Program:***

```
#include <iostream.h>
#include<conio.h>
void   main(void)
{
short testScore;
testScore = 32768;
cout << "Your test score is " << testScore << "\n";
getch();
}
```

**OUTPUT:**

Your test score is -32768

## OVERLOAD NEW OPERATOR:

**Problem 121. Write a C++ program for Overloaded 'new' operator relative to Point.**

***Program:***

```
#include <iostream.h>
#include<conio.h>
#include <stdlib.h>
class Point
{
int x, y;
public:
Point() { }
Point(int px, int py)
{
x = px;
y = py;
}
void show()
{
cout << x << " ";
cout << y << "\n";
}
void *operator new(size_t size);
void operator delete(void *p);
};
// new overloaded relative to Point.
void *Point::operator new(size_t size)
{
void *p;
cout << "In overloaded new.\n";
p =  malloc(size);
if(!p)
{
bad_alloc ba;
throw ba;
}
return p;
}
// delete overloaded relative to Point.
void Point::operator delete(void *p)
{
cout << "In overloaded delete.\n";
free(p);
}
```

```
void main()
{
Point *p1, *p2;
try
{
p1 = new Point (10, 20);
}
catch (bad_alloc xa)
{
cout << "Allocation error for p1.\n";
return 1;
}
try
{
p2 = new Point (-10, -20);
}
catch (bad_alloc xa)
{
cout << "Allocation error for p2.\n";
return 1;
}
p1->show();
p2->show();
delete p1;
delete p2;
getch();
}
```

**OUTPUT:**

```
In overloaded new.
In overloaded new.
10 20
-10 -20
In overloaded delete.
In overloaded delete.
```

**Problem 122. Write a C++ program for Operator overload: new, delete, new[] and delete[].**

***Program:***

```
#include <iostream.h>
#include<conio.h>
#include <stdlib.h>
#include <new.h>
class MyClass
{
int x, y;
public:
MyClass()
{
x = y = 0;
}
MyClass(int lg, int lt)
{
x = lg;
y = lt;
}
void show()
{
cout << x << " ";
cout << y << endl;
}
void *operator new(size_t size);
void operator delete(void *p);
void *operator new[](size_t size);
void operator delete[](void *p);
};
// overloaded new operator
void *MyClass::operator new(size_t size)
{
void *p;
cout << "In overloaded new.\n";
p =  malloc(size);
if(!p)
{
bad_alloc ba;
throw ba;
}
return p;
}
// delete operator overloaded
void MyClass::operator delete(void *p)
{
cout << "In overloaded delete.\n";
free(p);
}
// new operator overloaded for arrays.
void *MyClass::operator new[](size_t size)
{
void *p;
cout << "Using overload new[].\n";
p =  malloc(size);
if( !p )
{
bad_alloc ba;
throw ba;
}
return p;
}
// delete operator overloaded for arrays.
void MyClass::operator delete[](void *p)
{
cout << "Freeing array using overloaded
delete[]\n";
```

```
free(p);
}
void   main()
{
MyClass *objectPointer1, *objectPointer2;
int i;
try
{
objectPointer1 = new MyClass (10, 20);
 }
catch (bad_alloc xa)
{
cout << "Allocation error for objectPointer1.\n";
return 1;
}
try
{
objectPointer2 = new MyClass [10];          //
allocate an array
}
catch (bad_alloc xa)
{
cout << "Allocation error for objectPointer2.\n";
return 1;
 }
objectPointer1->show();
for( i = 0; i < 10; i++)
objectPointer2[i].show();
delete objectPointer1;                       // free an
object
delete [] objectPointer2;                    // free an
array
getch();
}
```

**OUTPUT:**

In overloaded new.
Using overload new[].
10 20
0 0
0 0
0 0
0 0
0 0
0 0
0 0
0 0
0 0
0 0
In overloaded delete.
Freeing array using overloaded delete[].

## OVERLOAD DELETE OPERATOR:

**Problem 123. Write a C++ program for Overloaded 'delete' operator relative to Pointer.**

***Program:***

```
#include <iostream.h>
#include<conio.h>
#include <stdlib.h>

class Point
{
int x, y;
public:
Point() {}
Point(int px, int py)
{
x = px;
y = py;
}
void show()
{
cout << x << " ";
cout << y << "\n";
}
void *operator new(size_t size);
void operator delete(void *p);
};
// new overloaded relative to Point.
void *Point::operator new(size_t size)
{
void *p;
cout << "In overloaded new.\n";
p =  malloc(size);
if(!p)
{
bad_alloc ba;
throw ba;
}
return p;
}
// delete overloaded relative to Point.
void Point::operator delete(void *p)
{
cout << "In overloaded delete.\n";
free(p);
}
void main()
{
Point *p1, *p2;
try
```

```
{
p1 = new Point (10, 20);
}
catch (bad_alloc xa)
{
cout << "Allocation error for p1.\n";
return 1;
}
try
{
p2 = new Point (-10, -20);
}
catch (bad_alloc xa)
{
cout << "Allocation error for p2.\n";
return 1;
}
p1->show();
p2->show();
delete p1;
delete p2;
getch();
}
```

**OUTPUT:**

```
In overloaded new.
In overloaded new.
10 20
-10 -20
In overloaded delete.
In overloaded delete.
```

**Problem 124. Write a C++ program to demonstrate overloaded new and delete.**

***Program:***

```
#include <iostream.h>
#include<conio.h>
#include <new.h>
#include <stdlib.h>
class MyClass
{
int x, y, z;
public:
MyClass()
{
x = y = z = 0;
cout << "Constructing 0, 0, 0\n";
}
MyClass(int i, int j, int k)
{
x = i;
y = j;
z = k;
cout << "Constructing " << i << ", ";
cout << j << ", " << k;
cout << '\n';
}
~MyClass( )
{
cout << "Destructing\n";
}
void *operator new(size_t size);
void *operator new[](size_t size);
void operator delete(void *p);
void operator delete[](void *p);
void show() ;
};
void *MyClass::operator new(size_t size)
{
void *p;
cout << "Allocating MyClass object.\n";
p = malloc(size);
if(!p)
{
bad_alloc ba;
throw ba;
}
return p;
}
void *MyClass::operator new[](size_t size)
{
void *p;
cout << "Allocating array of MyClass objects.\n";
p = malloc(size);
if(!p)
{
bad_alloc ba;
throw ba;
}
return p;
}
void MyClass::operator delete(void *p)
{
cout << "Deleting MyClass object.\n";
free(p);
}
void MyClass::operator delete[](void *p)
{
cout << "Deleting array of MyClass objects.\n";
free(p);
}
void MyClass::show()
{
```

```
cout << x << ", ";
cout << y << ", ";
cout << z << endl;
}
void main()
{
MyClass *objectPointer1, *objectPointer2;
try {
objectPointer1 = new MyClass[3];      // allocate
array
objectPointer2 = new MyClass(5, 6, 7); // allocate
object
}
catch (bad_alloc ba)
{
cout << "Allocation error.\n";
return 1;
}
objectPointer1[1].show();
objectPointer2->show();
delete [] objectPointer1; // delete array
delete objectPointer2;   // delete object
getch();
}
```

**OUTPUT:**

```
Allocating array of MyClass objects.
Constructing 0, 0, 0
Constructing 0, 0, 0
Constructing 0, 0, 0
Allocating MyClass object.
Constructing 5, 6, 7
0, 0, 0
5, 6, 7
Destructing
Destructing
Destructing
Deleting array of MyClass objects.
Destructing
Deleting MyClass object.
```

**Problem 125. Write a C++ program for overloading new and delete.**

***Program:***

```
#include <iostream.h>
#include <stdlib.h>
#include<conio.h>
class Values
{
int a,b;
public:
Values()
{ }
Values(int aa,int bb)
{
a =aa;
b =bb;
}
void show()
{
cout <<a <<" ";
cout <<b <<"\n";
}
void *operator new(size_t size);
void operator delete(void *p);
};
void *Values::operator new(size_t size)
{
void *p;
cout <<"In overloaded new.\n";
p =malloc(size);
if(!p)
{
bad_alloc ba;
throw ba;
}
return p;
}
void Values::operator delete(void *p)
{
cout <<"In overloaded delete.\n";
free(p);
}
void main()
{
Values *v1,*v2;
try
{
v1 =new Values (10,20);
}
catch (bad_alloc xa)
{
cout <<"Allocation error for v1.\n";
return 1;
}
try
{
v2 =new Values(-10,-20);
}
catch (bad_alloc xa)
{
cout <<"Allocation error for v2.\n";
return 1;;
```

```
}
v1->show();
v2->show();
delete v1;
delete v2;
getch();
}
```

**OUTPUT:**

In overloaded new.
In overloaded new.
20 30
-20 -30
In overloaded delete.
In overloaded delete.

**Problem 126. Write a C++ program to Overload New and Delete Operator.**

***Program:***

```
#include<iostream.h>
#include<conio.h>
#include<stdlib.h>
class A
{
int a;
float b;
public:
void print()
{
cout<<"A is==>"<<a;
cout<<"\nB is==>"<<b;
}
A(int p,float q)
{
a=p;b=q;
}
void operator delete(void *p)
{
cout<<"\nMemory freed.";
free(p);
}
void* operator new(size_t size)
{
cout<<"Memory alotted.\n";
void *p=malloc(size);
return p;
}
};
void main()
{
A *a;
clrscr();
a=new A(8,7.786);
a->print();
delete a;
getch();
}
```

**OUTPUT:**

Memory allotted.
A is==> 8
B is==> 7.786
Memory freed.

**Problem 127. Write a C++ program for Overloading new and delete for Arrays.**

***Program:***

```
#include <iostream.h>
#include <stdlib.h>
#include<conio.h>
class Values
{
int a,b;
public:
Values()
{
a=b=0;
}
Values(int aa,int bb)
{
a =aa;
b =bb;
}
void show()
{
cout <<a <<" ";
cout <<a <<"\n";
}
void *operator new(size_t size);
void operator delete(void *p);
void *operator new [](size_t size);
void operator delete [](void *p);
};
void *Values::operator new(size_t size)
{
void *p;
cout <<"In overloaded new.\n";
p =malloc(size);
if(!p)
{
bad_alloc ba;
throw ba;
}
return p;
```

```
}
void Values::operator delete(void *p)
{
cout <<"In overloaded delete.\n";
free(p);
}
void *Values::operator new [](size_t size)
{
void *p;
cout <<"Using overload new [].\n";
p =malloc(size);
if(!p)
{
bad_alloc ba;
throw ba;
}
return p;
}
void Values::operator delete [](void *p)
{
cout <<"Freeing array using overloaded delete []\n";
free(p);
}
void main()
{
Values *v1,*v2;
int i;
try
{
v1 =new Values (20,30);//allocate an object
}
catch (bad_alloc xa)
{
cout <<"Allocation error for v1.\n";
return 1;
}
try
{
v2 =new Values [10 ];//allocate an array
}
catch (bad_alloc xa)
{
cout <<"Allocation error for v2.\n";
return 1;
}
v1->show();
for(i=0;i<10;i++)
v2 [i ].show();
delete v1;//free an object
delete [] v2;;//free an array
getch();
}
```

**Problem 128. Write a C++ program for Overloading ->.**

***Program:***

```
#include <iostream.h>
#include<conio.h>
class A
{
public:
int i;
A *operator->()
{
return this;
}
};
void main()
{
A a;
a->i =100;
cout <<a.i <<" "<<a->i;
getch();
}
```

**OUTPUT:**

100 100

## OVERLOADING OPERATORS:

**Problem 129. Write a C++ program for vectors: overloading operators example.**

***Program:***

```
#include <iostream.h>
#include<conio.h>
class CVector
{
public:
int x,y;
CVector ()
{ };
CVector (int,int);
CVector operator + (CVector);
};
CVector::CVector (int a, int b)
{
x = a;
y = b;
}
CVector CVector::operator+ (CVector param)
{
CVector temp;
```

```
temp.x = x + param.x;
temp.y = y + param.y;
return (temp);
}
void main ()
{
CVector a (3,1);
CVector b (1,2);
CVector c;
c = a + b;
cout << c.x << "," << c.y;
getch();
}
```

**OUTPUT:**

4,3

**Problem 130. Write a C++ program for converter operator.**

***Program:***

```
#include <iostream.h>
#include<conio.h>
class Power
{
double b;
int e;
double val;
public:
Power(double base, int exp);
Power operator+(Power o)
{
double base;
int exp;
base = b + o.b;
exp = e + o.e;
Power temp(base, exp);
return temp;
}
operator double()
{ // convert to double
return val;
}
};
Power::Power(double base, int exp)
{
b = base;
e = exp;
val = 1;
if(exp == 0)
return;
for( ; exp>0; exp--)
val = val * b;
}
void main()
{
Power x(4.022, 2);
double a;
a = x;          // convert to double
cout << x + 100.2; // convert x to double and add 100.2
cout << endl;
Power y(32.3, 3), z(0, 0);
z = x + y;      // no conversion
a = z;          // convert to double
cout << a;
getch();
}
```

**OUTPUT:**

116.376
6.32192e+07

# OVERLOAD CAST OPERATOR:

**Problem 131. Write a C++ program for double cast operator.**

***Program:***

```
#include <iostream.h>
#include<conio.h>
class Power
{
double b;
int e;
double val;
public:
Power(double base, int exp)
{
b = base;
e = exp;
val = 1;
if(exp==0)
return;
for( ; exp>0; exp--)
val = val * b;
}
Power operator+(Power o)
{
double base;
int exp;
base = b + o.b;
exp = e + o.e;
Power temp(base, exp);
return temp;
```

```
}
operator double() { return val; } // convert to double
};
void main()
{
Power x(4.0, 2);
double a;
a = x;          // convert to double
cout << x + 1.2; // convert x to double and add 100.2
cout << "\n";
Power y(3.3, 3), z(0, 0);
z = x + y; // no conversion
a = z;    // convert to double
cout << a;
getch();
}
```

**OUTPUT:**

17.2
20730.7

# OVERLOAD CONVERSION OPERATOR:

**Problem 132. Write a C++ program for Conversion operator.**

***Program:***

```
#include <iostream.h>
#include<conio.h>
class MyType
{
public:
MyType();
MyType(int val);
~MyType(){}
int getValue()const { return myValue; }
void setValue(int x) {myValue = x; }
operator unsigned short();
private:
int myValue;
};
MyType::MyType():myValue(0) {}
MyType::MyType(int val): myValue(val) {}
MyType::operator unsigned short ()
{
return ( int (myValue) );
}
void main()
{
MyType ctr(5);
int theShort = ctr;
cout << "theShort: " << theShort << std::endl;
getch();
}
```

**OUTPUT:**

theShort: 5

**Problem 133. Write a C++ program for Operator overload: Convert string type to integer.**

***Program:***

```
#include <iostream.h>
#include<conio.h>
#include <string.h>
class StringClass
{
char str[80];
int len;
public:
StringClass(char *s)
{
strcpy(str, s);
len = strlen(s);
}
operator char *()
{
return str;
}
operator int()
{
return len;
}
};
void main()
{
 StringClass s("Conversion functions are
convenient.");
 char *p;
 int l;
 l = s; // convert s to integer - which is length of
string
 p = s; // convert s to char * - which is pointer to
string
 cout << "The string:\n";
cout << p << "\nis " << l << " chars long.\n";
getch();
}
```

**OUTPUT:**

The string:
Conversion functions are convenient.
is 36 chars long.

**Problem 134. Write a C++ program for conversions Between Objects and Basic Types.**

***Program:***

```
#include <iostream.h>
#include<conio.h>
class Height
{
private:
const float MTF;
int feet;
float inches;
public:
Height():feet(0),inches(0.0),MTF(3.280833F)
{}
Height(float meters):MTF(3.280833F)
{
float fltfeet =MTF *meters;
feet =int(fltfeet);
inches =12*(fltfeet-feet);
}
Height(int ft,float in):feet(ft),
inches(in),MTF(3.280833F)
{}
void get()
{
cout <<"\nFeet:";cin >>feet;
cout <<"inches:";cin >>inches;
}
void show()
{cout <<feet <<"-" <<inches;}
operator float()
{
float fracfeet =inches/12;
fracfeet += feet;
return fracfeet/MTF;
}
};
void main()
{
float mtrs;
Height heigh1 =2.45F;
cout <<"\nheigh1 =";heigh1.show();
mtrs =heigh1;
cout <<"\nheigh1 =" <<mtrs <<" meters \n ";
Height heigh2(6,4.25);
mtrs =heigh2;
cout <<"\nheigh2 =" <<mtrs <<" meters \n ";
getch();
}
```

**OUTPUT:**

```
heigh1 =8-0.456493
heigh1 =2.45 meters
heigh2 =1.936754 meters
```

**Problem 135. Write a C++ program for Conversions Between Objects of Different Classes.**

***Program:***

```
//converts from time24 to time12 using operator in time24
#include <iostream.h>
#include <string.h>
#include<conio.h>
class tim_12
{
private:
bool pm;
int hrs;
int mins;
public:
tim_12():pm(true),hrs(0),mins(0)
{ }
tim_12(bool ap,int h,int m):pm(ap),hrs(h),mins(m)
{ }
void display() //format:12:39 p.m.
{
cout <<hrs <<':';
if(mins <10)
cout <<'0 ';
cout <<mins <<' ';
string am_pm =pm ?"p.m." ::"a.m.";
cout <<am_pm;
}
};
class tim_24
{
private:
int hours;
int minutes;
int seconds;
public:
tim_24():hours(0),minutes(0),seconds(0)
{ }
tim_24(int h,int m,int
s):hours(h),minutes(m),seconds(s)
{ }
void display() //format:13:12:01
{
if(hours <10)cout <<'0';
cout <<hours <<':';
if(minutes <10)cout <<'0';
cout <<minutes <<':';
```

```
if(seconds <10)cout <<'0';
cout <<seconds;
}
operator tim_12();
};
tim_24::operator tim_12()
{
int hrs24 =hours;
bool pm =hours <12 ?false :true;
int roundMins =seconds <30 ?minutes :minutes+1;
if(roundMins ==60)
{
roundMins=0;
++hrs24;
if(hrs24 ==12 ||hrs24 ==24)
pm =(pm==true)?false :true;
}
int hrs12 =(hrs24 <13)?hrs24 :hrs24-12;
if(hrs12==0)
{hrs12=12;pm=false;}
return tim_12(pm,hrs12,roundMins);
}
void main()
{
int h,m,s;
while(true)
{
cout <<"Enter 24-hour time:\n ";
cout <<" Hours ((0 to 23):";cin >>h;
if(h >23)
return(1);
cout <<" Minutes:";cin >>m;
cout <<" Seconds:";cin >>s;
tim_24 t24(h,m,s);
cout <<"You entered:";
t24.display();
tim_12 t12 =t24;
cout <<"\n12-hour time:";
t12.display();
cout <<"\n \n ";
}
getch();
}
```

**OUTPUT**:

```
Enter 24-hour time:
Hours (0 to 23):17
Minutes:59
Seconds:45
You entered:17:59:45
12-hour time:6:00 p.m.
```

**Problem 136. Write a C++ program to implement type Conversion from Class to Class.**

***Program:***

```
#include<iostream.h>
#include<conio.h>
class student1
{
int roll,marks;
public:
student1(int a,int b)
{
roll=a;
marks=b;
}
void print()
{
cout<<"\nRoll number is "<<roll;
cout<<"\nMarks are "<<marks;
}
int getroll()
{
return roll;
}
float getmarks()
{
return marks;
}
};
class B
{
int roll;
float per;
public:
B(student1 s)
{
roll=s.getroll();
per=s.getmarks()/100;
}
void print()
{
cout<<"Roll number is==>"<<roll;
cout<<"\nPercentage is==>"<<per;
}
};
void main()
{
student1 s1(100,67);
B s2=s1;
clrscr();
s2.print();
getch();
```

```
}
```

**OUTPUT:**

Roll number is 100
Marks are 67
Roll number is==> 100
Percentage is==> .67

**Problem 137. Write a C++ program to convert money from dollars to rupees.**

***Program:***

```
#define dolval 44.20
#include<iostream.h>
#include<conio.h>
class rupee
{
double rs;
public:
rupee(double rs1)
{rs=rs1;}
void show()
{cout<<"\nMoney in Rs. ="<<rs;}
rupee()
{rs=0;}
};
class dollar
{
double dol;
public:
dollar(double doll)
{dol=doll;}
operator rupee()
{
double rs1=dol*dolval;
return(rupee(rs1));
}
void show()
{cout<<"\nMoney in Dollars ="<<dol;}
};
void main()
{
dollar obj1(3);
obj1.show();
rupee r;
r=obj1;
r.show();
getch();
}
```

**OUTPUT:**

Money in Dollars=5
Money in Rs.=221

**Problem 138. Write a C++ program to convert money from dollars to rupees by using conversion function in destination class.**

***Program:***

```
#define dolval 44.20
#include<iostream.h>
#include<conio.h>
class dollar
{
double dol;
public:
dollar(double doll)
{dol=doll;}
void show()
{cout<<"\nMoney in Dollars ="<<dol;}
double retdol()
{return(dol);}
};
class rupee
{
double rs;
public:
rupee(dollar d)
{rs=d.retdol()*dolval;}
void show()
{cout<<"\nMoney in Rs. ="<<rs;}
};
void main()
{
dollar obj1(3);
obj1.show();
rupee r=obj1;
r.show();
getch();
}
```

**OUTPUT:**

Money in Dollars=5
Money in Rs.=221

**Problem 139. Write a C++ program to convert mts,cms distance to feet,inches by using that function in source class.**

***Program:***

```
#include<iostream.h>
#include<conio.h>
class dft
{
private:
int feet;
double inches;
public:
```

```
dft(){feet=inches=0;}
dft(int g,double h)
{
feet=g;
inches=h;
}
void put()
{
cout<<feet<<inch;
}
friend void add(dist,mtrcm);
};
class dmt
{
int mtr,cms;
public:
dmt(int u,int v)
{
mtr=u;cms=v;
}
void show()
{
cout<<mtr<<cms;
}
operator dft()
{
double mt;
mt=mtr+cms/100;
double dfeet;
dfeet=3.28*mt;
int feet1=int(dfeet);
double inches1=(dfeet-feet1)*12.00;
return dft(feet1,inches1);
}
};
void main()
{
dmt a=(2,22);
cout<<"distance in meters & centimeters";
a.put();
dft b;
b=a;
cout<<"\nDistance in feet & inches";
b.put();
getch();
}
```

**Problem 140. Write a C++ program to convert objects of same class.**

***Program:***

```
#include<iostream.h>
#include<conio.h>
#include<dos.h>
class date
{
int day ;
int month ;
int year ;
public :
date (float d) //constructor defined
{
day = (int) d/24 ;//d in hours
month = (int) d/30 ;// d in days
year = (int) d/12 ;//d in months
}
} ;
void main ( )
{
date today;
floatp = 3600.00 ;
today = p ;
getch();
}
```

**Program 141. Program to convert of objects of different classes.**

```
//Program of data conversion
class student1
{
int rn ;
int marks ;
public :
student1 (int a, int b)
{
rn = a ;
marks = b ;
}
void dispdata ( )
{
cout <<"\n ROLLNO is" << rn ;
cout <<"\n MARKS ARE" << marks ;
}
int getrn ( ) {return rn ;}
int getmarks ( ) {return marks ;}
} ;
classstudent 2
{
int rn ;
int result ;
public :
student 2 ( )
{
```

```
rn = 0 ;
result = 0 ;
}
student2 (int x, int y)      // default constructor
{
rn = x;
result = y;
}
voiddispdata ( )
{
cout <<"\n ROLL NO is" << rn ;
cout <<"\n Final Marks are" << result ;
}
student2 (student1 p)
{
rn = p.getrn ( ) ;
result = p.getmarks ( ) + 30 ;
}
} ;
void main ( )
{
student 1s1 (122, 35) ;
student 2s2 ;
s2 = s1 ;
cout <<"\n MARKS Before Result are" <<"\n" ;
s1. dispdata ( ) ;
cout <<"\n MARKS AFTER Result are" <<"p" ;
s2.dispdata ( ) ;
getch();
}
```

# CHAPTER 13

# INHERITANCE

## BASE CLASS:

**Problem 1.Write a C++ program for base class and derived class.**

***Program:***

```
#include<iostream.h>
#include<conio.h>
class BaseClass
{
int i, j;
public:
void set(int a, int b)
{
i = a;
j = b;
}
void show()
{
cout << i << " " << j << endl;
}
};
class DerivedClass : public BaseClass
{
int k;
public:
DerivedClass(int x)
{
k = x;
}
void showk()
{
cout << k << endl;
}
};
void  main()
{
DerivedClass ob(3);
ob.set(1, 2); // access member of BaseClass
ob.show();   // access member of BaseClass
ob.showk();   // uses member of DerivedClass class
getch();
}
```

**<u>OUTPUT</u>:**

```
1 2
3
```

**Problem 2. Write a C++ program for a simple example of base class.**

***Program:***

```
#include<iostream.h>
#include<conio.h>
class BaseClass
{
int i;
public:
void setInt(int n);
int getInt();
};
class DerivedClass : public BaseClass
{
int j;
public:
void setJ(int n);
int mul();
};
void BaseClass::setInt(int n)
{
i = n;
}
int BaseClass::getInt()
{
return i;
}
void DerivedClass::setJ(int n)
{
j = n;
}
int DerivedClass::mul()
{
return j * getInt();
}
void  main()
{
DerivedClass ob;
ob.setInt(10);        // load i in BaseClass
ob.setJ(4);          // load j in DerivedClass
cout << ob.mul();     // displays 40
```

```
getch();
}
```

**OUTPUT:**

40

## INTIALIZATION SYNTAX:

**Problem 3. Write a C++ program to initialize variables from base class using initialization syntax.**

***Program:***

```
#include<iostream.h>
#include<conio.h>
class MyClass
{
const int numA; // const member
const int numB; // const member
public:
MyClass(int x, int y) : numA(x), numB(y) { }
int getNumA() { return numA; }
int getNumB() { return numB; }
};
void main()
{
MyClass ob1(7, 9), ob2(5, 2);
cout<<"Values in ob1 are "<<ob1.getNumB()<<"
and "<< ob1.getNumA()<<endl;
cout<<"Values in ob2 are "<<ob2.getNumB()<< "
and "<< ob2.getNumA() << endl;
getch();
}
```

**OUTPUT:**

Values in ob1 are 9 and 7
Values in ob2 are 2 and 5

**Problem 4. Write a C++ program to initialize parameters in base class.**

***Program:***

```
#include<iostream.h>
#include<conio.h>
class Pointer
{
private:
long x,y;
public:
Pointer(long a=0,long b=0)
{
x=a;
y=b;
}
long GetX()
{
return x;
}
long GetY()
{
return y;
}
void Disp()
{
cout << "x=" <<x<<"  y="<<y;
}
};
class Pointer3D : public Pointer
{
long z;
public:
Pointer3D(long a=0,long b=0,long
c=0):Pointer(a,b)
{
z=c;
}
long GetZ(){ return z;}
void Disp()
{
cout <<"x= "<<GetX()<<"  y="<<GetY();
cout << "  z="<< z <<endl;
}
};
void main()
{
Pointer3D p1;
Pointer3D p2(3,-4);
p2.Disp();
p2=p1;
p2.Disp();
getch();
}
```

**OUTPUT:**

x= 3  y=-4  z=0
x= 0  y=0  z=0

**Problem 5. Write a C++ program using base pointers on DerivedClass class objects.**

***Program:***

```
#include<iostream.h>
#include<conio.h>
#include <string.h>
class BaseClass
{
char author[80];
```

```
public:
void put_author(char *s)
{
strcpy(author, s);
}
void show_author()
{
cout << author << endl;
}
} ;
class DerivedClass : public BaseClass
{
char title[80];
public:
void put_title(char *num)
{
strcpy(title, num);
}
void show_title()
{
cout << "Title: ";
cout <<  title << endl;
}
};
void  main()
{
BaseClass *p;
BaseClass baseObject;
DerivedClass *dp;
DerivedClass derivedObject;
p = &baseObject;
p->put_author("Tom Clancy");
p = &derivedObject;
p->put_author("William Shakespeare");
baseObject.show_author();
derivedObject.show_author();
cout << endl;
dp = &derivedObject;
dp->put_title("The Tempest");
p->show_author();
dp->show_title( );
getch();
}
```

**OUTPUT:**

```
Tom Clancy
William Shakespeare
William Shakespeare
Title: The TEmpest
```

**Problem 6. Write a C++ program to pass arguments to base class.**

***Program:***

```
#include<iostream.h>
#include<conio.h>
class BaseClass
{
int i;
public:
BaseClass(int n)
{
cout << "Constructing base class\n";
i = n;
}
~BaseClass()
{
cout << "Destructing base class\n";
}
void showi()
{
cout << i << '\n';
}
};
class DerivedClass : public BaseClass
{
int j;
public:
DerivedClass(int n, int m) : BaseClass(m)
{
cout << "Constructing DerivedClass class\n";
j = n;
}
~DerivedClass()
{
cout << "Destructing DerivedClass class\n";
}
void showj()
{
cout << j << '\n';
}
};
void  main()
{
DerivedClass o(10, 20);
o.showi();
o.showj();
getch();
}
```

**OUTPUT:**

```
Constructing base class
Constructing DerivedClass class
20
10
```

Destructing DerivedClass class
Destructing base class

**Problem 7. Write a C++ program to initialize member variables from base class.**

***Program:***

```
#include<iostream.h>
#include<conio.h>
class BaseClass
{
int i, j;
public:
BaseClass(int x, int y)
{
i = x;
j = y;
}
void showij()
{
cout << i << ' ' << j << '\n';
}
};
class DerivedClass : public BaseClass
{
int k;
public:
DerivedClass(int a, int b, int c) : BaseClass(b, c)
{
k = a;
}
void show()
{
cout << k << ' '; showij();
}
};
void main()
{
DerivedClass ob(1, 2, 3);
ob.show();
getch();
}
```

**OUTPUT:**

1 2 3

**Problem 8. Write a C++ program to assign object1 to object2.**

***Program:***

```
#include<iostream.h>
#include<conio.h>
class BaseClass
{
int a;
public:
void load_a(int n)
{
a = n;
}
int get_a()
{
return a;
}
};
class DerivedClass : public BaseClass
{
int b;
public:
void load_b(int n)
{
b = n;
}
int get_b()
{
return b;
}
};
void main()
{
DerivedClass object1, object2;
object1.load_a(5);
object1.load_b(10);
object2 = object1;
cout << "Here is object1's a and b: ";
cout << object1.get_a() << ' ' << object1.get_b()
<< endl;
cout << "Here is object2's a and b: ";
cout << object2.get_a() << ' ' << object2.get_b()
<< endl;
getch();
}
```

**OUTPUT:**

Here is object1's a and b: 5 10
Here is object2's a and b: 5 10

**Problem 9. Write a C++ program for base-Class Access Control.**

***Program:***

```
#include<iostream.h>
#include<conio.h>
class A
{
int i,j;
public:
```

```
void set(int a,int b)
{
i=a;
j=b;
}
void show()
{
cout <<i <<" "<<j <<"\n";
}
};
class B :public A
{
int k;
public:
B(int m)
{
k=m;
}
void show_k()
{
cout <<k <<"\n";
}
};
void main()
{
B b(4);
b.set(1,2);
b.show();
b.show_k();
getch();
}
```

**OUTPUT:**

1 2
4

**Problem 10. Write a C++ program when Constructor and Destructor Functions Are Executed.**

***Program:***

```
#include<iostream.h>
#include<conio.h>
class A
{
public:
A()
{
cout <<"Constructing base \n";
}
~A()
{
cout <<"Destructing base \n";
}
};
class B:public A
{
public:
B()
{
cout <<"Constructing derived \n";
}
~B()
{
cout <<"Destructing derived \n";
}
};
void main()
{
B b;
getch();
}
```

**OUTPUT:**

Constructing base
Constructing derived
Destructing derived
Destructing base

**Problem 11. Write a C++ program for a base pointer to access derived objects.**

***Program:***

```
#include<iostream.h>
#include<conio.h>
class BaseClass
{
int i;
public:
void setInt(int num)
{
i = num;
}
int getInt()
{
return i;
}
};
class derived: public BaseClass
{
int j;
public:
void setJ(int num)
{
j = num;
}
```

```
int getJ()
{
return j;
}
};
void main()
{
BaseClass *bp;
derived d;
bp = &d;            // BaseClass pointer points to
derived object
bp->setInt(10);
cout << bp->getInt() << " ";
getch();
}
```

**OUTPUT:**

10

**Problem 12. Write a C++ program to call constructor from base class.**

***Program:***

```
#include<iostream.h>
#include<conio.h>
class MyType
{
protected:
float value;
public:
float subtract(float);
float add(float);
void display();
MyType(float);
MyType();
};
MyType::MyType(float num)
{
value = num;
}
MyType::MyType()
{
value = 1000;
}
float MyType::subtract(float amount)
{
value -= amount;
return value;
}
float MyType::add(float amount)
{
value += amount;
return value;
}
void MyType::display()
{
cout << "Your value is " << value << endl;
}
class DerivedType:public MyType
{
public:
DerivedType(float);
};
DerivedType::DerivedType(float
num):MyType(num)
{ }
DerivedType myType(1200);
void main()
{
float amount, balance;
myType.display();
cout << endl;
cout << "Please enter the amount to deposit \n";
cin>> amount;
balance = myType.add(amount);
cout << "New balance is " << balance << endl;
cout << endl;
cout << "Please enter the amount to withdraw \n";
cin >> amount;
balance = myType.subtract(amount);
cout << "New balance is " << balance << endl;
cout << endl;
getch();
}
```

**OUTPUT:**

Your value is 1200
Please enter the amount to deposit
123
New balance is 1323
Please enter the amount to withdraw
123
New balance is 1200

**Problem 13. Write a C++ program for Constructing and Destructing sequence for three level inheritance .**

***Program:***

```
#include<iostream.h>
#include<conio.h>
class BaseClass
{
public:
BaseClass()
{
```

```
cout << "Constructing base\n";
}
~BaseClass()
{
cout << "Destructing base\n";
}
};
class DerivedClass1 : public BaseClass
{
public:
DerivedClass1()
{
cout << "Constructing DerivedClass1\n";
}
~DerivedClass1()
{
cout << "Destructing DerivedClass1\n";
}
};
class DerivedClass2: public DerivedClass1
{
public:
DerivedClass2()
{
cout << "Constructing DerivedClass2\n";
}
~DerivedClass2()
{
cout << "Destructing DerivedClass2\n";
}
};
void main()
{
DerivedClass2 ob;
getch();
}
```

**Problem 14. Write a C++ program for Constructing and Destructing sequence for two base classes.**

***Program:***

```
#include<iostream.h>
#include<conio.h>
class BaseClass1
{
public:
BaseClass1() { cout << "Constructing
BaseClass1\n"; }
~BaseClass1() { cout << "Destructing
BaseClass1\n"; }
};
class BaseClass2
{
public:
BaseClass2() { cout << "Constructing
BaseClass2\n"; }
~BaseClass2() { cout << "Destructing
BaseClass2\n"; }
};
class DerivedClass: public BaseClass1, public
BaseClass2
{
public:
DerivedClass() { cout << "Constructing
DerivedClass\n"; }
~DerivedClass() { cout << "Destructing
DerivedClass\n"; }
};
void main()
{
DerivedClass ob;
getch();
}
```

**OUTPUT:**

```
Constructing BaseClass1
Constructing BaseClass2
Constructing DerivedClass
Destructing DerivedClass
Destructing BaseClass2
Destructing BaseClass1
```

**Problem 15. Write a C++ program for derived class call its base constructor.**

***Program:***

```
#include<iostream.h>
#include<conio.h>
class BaseClass
{
protected:
int i;
public:
BaseClass(int x)
{
i = x;
cout << "Constructing base\n";
}
~BaseClass()
{
cout << "Destructing base\n";
}
};
class DerivedClass: public BaseClass
```

```
{
int j;
public:
DerivedClass(int x, int y): BaseClass(y)
{
j = x;
cout << "Constructing DerivedClass\n";
}
~DerivedClass()
{
cout << "Destructing DerivedClass\n";
}
void show()
{
cout << i << " " << j << endl;
}
};
void  main()
{
DerivedClass ob(3, 4);
ob.show();
getch();
}
```

**OUTPUT:**

```
Constructing base
Constructing DerivedClass
4 3
Destructing DerivedClass
Destructing base
```

**Problem 16. Write a C++ program for derived constructor uses no parameters.**

***Program:***

```
#include<iostream.h>
#include<conio.h>
class BaseClass1
{
protected:
int i;
public:
BaseClass1(int x)
{
i =x;
cout << "Constructing BaseClass1\n";
}
~BaseClass1()
{
cout << "Destructing BaseClass1\n";
}
};
class BaseClass2
{
protected:
int k;
public:
BaseClass2(int x)
{
k = x;
cout << "Constructing base2\n";
}
~BaseClass2()
{
cout << "Destructing base2\n";
}
};
class DerivedClass: public BaseClass1, public
BaseClass2
{
public:
DerivedClass(int x, int y): BaseClass1(x),
BaseClass2(y)
{
cout << "Constructing DerivedClass\n";
}
~DerivedClass()
{
cout << "Destructing DerivedClass\n";
}
void show()
{
cout << i << " " << k << endl;
}
};
void  main()
{
DerivedClass ob(3, 4);
ob.show();
getch();
}
```

**OUTPUT:**

```
Constructing BaseClass1
Constructing base2
Constructing DerivedClass
4 3
Destructing DerivedClass
Destructing base2
destructing BaseClass1
```

**Problem 17. Write a C++ program to show execution of constructor and destructor using derive class objects.**

***Program:***

```
#include<iostream.h>
#include<conio.h>
class b1
{
public:
b1()
{
cout<<"b1's no parameter constructor";
}
~b1()
{
cout<<"\nDestructor of b1";}
};
class b2
{
public:
b2()
{
cout<<"b2's no parameter constructor";
}
~b2()
{
cout<<"\nDestructor of b2";
}
};
class d:public b1,public b2
{
public:
d()
{
cout<<"\nd's no parameter constructor";
}
~d()
{
cout<<"\nDestructor of d";
}
};
void main()
{
d dr;
getch();
}
```

**OUTPUT:**

```
b1's no parameter constructor
b2's no parameter constructor
d's no parameter constructor
Destructor of d
Destructor of b2
Destructor of b1
```

**Problem 18. Write a C++ program to increment rollno to illustrate the Derived class Constructor.**

***Program:***

```
#include<iostream.h>
#include<conio.h>
class rollno
{
protected :
int rn ;
public :
rollno ( )                    //constructor defined
{
rn = 0 ;
}                             //parameterized
constructor
rollno (int r)
{                             //base class constructor
with argument
rn = r ;
}
int read_rn ( )
{
return rn ;
}
rollno operator ++ ( )                    //unary
operator overloading
{
rn ++ ;
return rollno (rn) ;
}
};
class student : public rollno
{
pubic :                                   //derived class
constructor defined
student ( ) : rollno ( )
{ }
student (int r) : rollno (r)              //derived class
constructor
{ }                           initialization
student operator - - ( )      // unary - operator
overloading
{
rn - - ;
return student (rn) ;
}
} ;
void main ( )
{
student s1 ;
```

```
student s2(100); // derived class constructor value
direct to the object
cout<<"\n s1 = "<< s1. read_rn ( );
cout<<"\n s2 = "<< s2. read_rn ( );
s1 ++ ;
s1 ++ ;
s1 ++ ;
cout <<"\n s1 ="<< s1. read_rn ( );
s2 - - ;
s2 - - ;
cout <<"\n s2 = "<< s2. read_rn ( );
student s3 = s2 - - ;
cout <<"\n s3 = "<<s3. read_rn ( );
getch ( );
}
```

**Problem 19. Write a C++ program to keep student details by creating a composite class with one of its data member as object of another class.**

***Program:***

```
#include<iostream.h>
#include<conio.h>
class dt
{
private:
int dd,mm,yy;
public:
void get()
{
cout<<"Enter date ,month & year=";
cin>>dd>>mm>>yy;
}
void put()
{
cout<<"Date= "<<dd<<"/"<<mm<<"/"<<yy;
}
};
class st
{
private:
int rno;
char nm[20];
dt dob;
public:
void get()
{
cout<<"Enter rollno & name=";
cin>>rno>>nm;
dob.get();
}
void put()
{
cout<<"\nRollno= "<<rno<<" Name= "<<nm<<"
";
dob.put();
}
};
void main()
{
st obj;
obj.get();
obj.put();
getch();
}
```

**OUTPUT:**

```
Enter rollno & name=29 Rajesh
Enter date ,month & year=10 12 2009
Rollno=29 Name=Rajesh
Date=10/12/2009
```

**Problem 20. Write a C++ program to show order of execution in composition.**

***Program:***

```
#include<iostream.h>
#include<conio.h>
class fc
{
private:
int x;
public:
fc(int xx)
{
cout<<"fc's single parameter constructor\n";
x=xx;
}
};
class sc
{
private:
int y;
public:
sc(int yy)
{
cout<<"sc's single parameter constructor\n";
y=yy;
}
};
class comp
{
int z;
fc objc1;
sc objc2;
```

```
public:
comp(int zz,int yy,int xx):sc(yy),fc(xx)
{
cout<<"comp's constructor with three parameters\n";
z=zz;
}
};
int main()
{
comp objc3(30,20,10);
getch();
}
```

**Problem 21. Write a C++ program for adding a constructor to Base class.**

***Program:***

```
#include<iostream.h>
#include<conio.h>
#include <string.h>
class Shape
{
// private
double width;
double height;
public:
Shape(double w, double h)
{
width = w;
height = h;
}
void display()
{
cout << "Width and height are " << width << " and "
<< height << "\n";
}
double getWidth() { return width; }
double getHeight() { return height; }
void setWidth(double w) { width = w; }
void setHeight(double h) { height = h; }
};
class Triangle : public Shape
{
char style[20]; // now private
public:
Triangle(char *str, double w, double h) : Shape(w,
h)
{
strcpy(style, str);
}
double area()
{
return getWidth() * getHeight() / 2;
}
void showStyle()
{
cout << "Triangle is " << style << "\n";
}
};
void main()
{
Triangle t1("isosceles", 4.0, 4.0);
Triangle t2("right", 8.0, 12.0);
cout << "Info for t1:\n";
t1.showStyle();
t1.display();
cout << "Area is " << t1.area() << "\n";
t2.showStyle();
t2.display();
cout << "Area is " << t2.area() << "\n";
getch();
}
```

**OUTPUT:**

```
Info for t1:
Triangle is isosceles
Width and height are 4 and 4
Area is 8
Triangle is right
Width and height are 8 and 12
Area is 48
```

**Problem 22. Write a C++ program for adding a overloaded constructor to base class.**

***Program:***

```
#include<iostream.h>
#include<conio.h>
#include <string.h>
class Shape
{
// private by default
double width;
double height;
public:
Shape()
{
width = height = 0.0;
}
Shape(double w, double h)
{
width = w;
height = h;
}
Shape(double x)
```

```
{
width = height = x;
}
void display()
{
cout << "Width and height are " << width << " and "
<< height << "\n";
}
double getWidth() { return width; }
double getHeight() { return height; }
void setWidth(double w) { width = w; }
void setHeight(double h) { height = h; }
};
class Triangle : public Shape
{
char style[20]; // now private
public:
Triangle()
{
strcpy(style, "unknown");
}
Triangle(char *str, double w, double h) : Shape(w,
h)
{
strcpy(style, str);
}
Triangle(double x) : Shape(x)
{
strcpy(style, "isosceles");
}
double area()
{
return getWidth() * getHeight() / 2;
}
void showStyle()
{
cout << "Triangle is " << style << "\n";
}
};

void main()
{
Triangle t1;
Triangle t2("right", 8.0, 12.0);
Triangle t3(4.0);
t1 = t2;
cout << "Info for t1: \n";
t1.showStyle();
t1.display();
cout << "Area is " << t1.area() << "\n";
t2.showStyle();
t2.display();
cout << "Area is " << t2.area() << "\n";
t3.showStyle();
t3.display();
cout << "Area is " << t3.area() << "\n";
getch();
}
```

**OUTPUT:**

```
Info for t1:
Triangle is right
Width and height are 8 and 12
Area is 48
Triangle is right
Width and height are 8 and 12
Area is 48
Triangle is isosceles
Width and height are 4 and 4
Area is 8
```

**Problem 23. Write a C++ program to inherit base class twice.**

***Program:***

```
#include<iostream.h>
#Include<conio.h>
class base
{
public:
int i;
};
class derived1 :  public base
{
public:
int j;
};
class derived2 : public base
{
public:
int k;
};
class derived3 : public derived1, public derived2
{
public:
int sum;
};
void main()
{
derived3 ob;
ob.derived1::i = 10; // scope resolved, use
derived1's i
getch();
}
```

**Problem 24. Write a C++ program for dynamic_cast: Cast from Derived * to Base *.**

***Program:***

```
#include<iostream.h>
#include<conio.h>
class Base
{
public:
virtual void f() {
cout << "Inside Base\n";
}
};
class Derived : public Base
{
public:
void f()
{
cout << "Inside Derived\n";
}
};
void main()
{
Base *bp, b_ob;
Derived *dp, d_ob;
bp = dynamic_cast<Base> (&d_ob);
if(bp)
{
cout << "Cast from Derived * to Base * OK.\n";
bp->f();
}
else
cout << "Error\n";
cout << endl;
getch();
}
```

**OUTPUT:**

Cast from Derived * to Base * OK.
Inside Derived

## DERIVED CLASS:

**Problem 25. Write a C++ program with no argument constructor in base & deriveD class.**

***Program:***

```
#include<iostream.h>
#include<conio.h>
class b
{
public:
b()
{
cout<<"b's no parameter constructor";
}
};
class d:public b
{
public:
d()
{
cout<<"\nd's no parameter constructor";
}
};
void main()
{
d der;
getch();
}
```

**OUTPUT:**

b's no parameter constructor
d's no parameter constructor

**Problem 26. Write a C++ program for two parameter constructor(inheritance).**

***Program:***

```
#include<iostream.h>
#include<conio.h>
class b
{
public:
b()
{
cout<<"b's no parameter constructor";
}
};
class d:public b
{
int a,b;
public:
d(int x,int y)
{
a=x;
b=y;
cout<<"\nd's constructor with two parameters ";}
};
void main()
{
d der(12,89);
getch();
}
```

**OUTPUT:**

b's no parameter constructor
d's constructor with two parameters

**Problem 27. Write a C++ program for contructor have one parameter,two parameters(inheritance).**

***Program:***

```
#include<iostream.h>
#include<conio.h>
class b
{
int a;
public:
b(int a1)
{
a=a1;
cout<<"b's single parameter constructor";}
void show()
{
cout<<"\na= "<<a;}
};
class d:public b
{
int bs;
public:
d(int bb,int aa):b(aa)
{
bs=bb;
cout<<"\nd's constructor with two parameters ";}
void show()
{
b::show();
cout<<"\nbs= "<<bs;
}
};
void main()
{
d der(12,89);
der.show();
getch();
}
```

**OUTPUT:**

b's single parameter constructor
d's constructor with two parameters
a=12 bs=89

**Problem 28. Write a C++ program for no parameter constructors(inheritance).**

***Program:***

```
#include<iostream.h>
#include<conio.h>
class b11
{
public:
b11()
{
cout<<"b11's no parameter constructor\n";
}
};
class b22
{
public:
b22()
{
cout<<"b22's no parameter constructor\n";
}
};
class d:public b11,public b22
{
public:
d()
{
cout<<"\nd's no parameter constructor";
}
};
void main()
{
d der;
getch();
}
```

**OUTPUT:**

b11's no parameter constructor
b22's no parameter constructor
d's no parameter constructor

**Problem 29. Write a C++ program for single parameter base class,derived class constructors.**

***Program:***

```
#include<iostream.h>
#include<conio.h>
class b11
{
private:
int x;
public:
b11(int x1)
{
x=x1;
cout<<"b11's with single parameter constructor\n";
cout<<"x = "<<x;
}
};
```

```
class b22
{
private:
int y;
public:
b22(int y1)
{
y=y1;
cout<<"b22's with single parameter constructor\n";
cout<<"y = "<<y;
};
class d:public b11,public b22
{
public:
d(int xx,int yy):b22(yy),b11(xx)
{
cout<<"\nd's constructor with two parameter ";
}
};
void main()
{
d der(20,30);
getch();
}
```

**Problem 30. Write a C++ program for one parameter,two parameter and three parameter base class, derived class constructors.**

***Program:***

```
#include<iostream.h>
#include<conio.h>
class b
{
private:
int x;
public:
b11(int x1)
{
x=x1;
cout<<"b's with single parameter constructor\n";
x = x1;
}
};
class d1:public b
{
private:
int y;
public:
d1(int yy,int xx):b(xx)
{
cout<<"\nd1's constructor with two parameter ";
y=yy;
}
};
class d2:public d1
{
private:
int z;
public:
d2(int zz,int yy, int xx):d1(yy,xx)
{
cout<<"\nd3's constructor with three parameter ";
z=zz;
}
};
void main()
{
d2 der(10,20,30);
getch();
}
```

**Problem 31. Write a C++ program for shadow function with the same name in base class.**

***Program:***

```
#include<iostream.h>
#include<conio.h>
#include <stdlib.h>
class BaseClass
{
public:
void f();
};
void BaseClass::f()
{
cout << "Hey this is the base class!\n";
}
class DerivedClass:public BaseClass
{
public:
void f();
};
void DerivedClass::f()
{
cout << "Hey this is in the child class!!\n";
}
void main()
{
DerivedClass myclass;
myclass.f();
getch();
}
```

**OUTPUT:**

Hey this is in the child class!!

**Problem 32. Write a C++ program to call constructor from base class to initialize fields inherited from base class.**

***Program:***

```
#include<iostream.h>
#include<conio.h>
class base
{
protected:
int i;
public:
base(int x)
{
i=x;
cout << "Constructing base\n";
}
~base()
{
cout << "Destructing base\n";
}
};
class derived: public base
{
int j;
public:
derived(int x, int y): base(y)
{
j=x;
cout << "Constructing derived\n";
}
~derived()
{
cout << "Destructing derived\n";
}
void show()
{
cout << i << " " << j << "\n";
}
};
void main()
{
derived ob(3, 4);
ob.show();
getch();
}
```

**OUTPUT:**

```
Constructing base
Constructing derived
4 3
Destructing derived
Destructing base
```

**Problem 33. Write a C++ program for Object array of derived classes.**

***Program:***

```
#include<iostream.h>
#include<conio.h>
#include <string.h>
class Shape
{
double width;
double height;
char name[20];
public:
Shape()
{
width = height = 0.0;
strcpy(name, "unknown");
}
Shape(double w, double h, char *n)
{
width = w;
height = h;
strcpy(name, n);
}
Shape(double x, char *n)
{
width = height = x;
strcpy(name, n);
}
void display()
{
cout << "Width and height are " << width << " and
" << height << "\n";
}
double getWidth() { return width; }
double getHeight() { return height; }
void setWidth(double w) { width = w; }
void setHeight(double h) { height = h; }
char *getName() { return name; }
virtual double area()
{
cout << "Error: area() must be overridden.\n";
return 0.0;
}
};
class Triangle : public Shape
{
char style[20];
public:
```

```
Triangle()
{
strcpy(style, "unknown");
}
Triangle(char *str, double w, double h) : Shape(w, h,
"triangle")
{
strcpy(style, str);
}
Triangle(double x) : Shape(x, "triangle")
{
strcpy(style, "isosceles");
}
double area()
{
return getWidth() * getHeight() / 2;
}
void showStyle()
{
cout << "Triangle is " << style << "\n";
}
};
class Rectangle : public Shape
{
public:
Rectangle(double w, double h) : Shape(w, h,
"rectangle") { }
Rectangle(double x) : Shape(x, "rectangle") { }
bool isSquare()
{
if(getWidth() == getHeight())
return true;
return false;
}
double area()
{
return getWidth() * getHeight();
}
};
void main()
{
Shape *shapes[5];
shapes[0] = &Triangle("right", 8.0, 12.0);
shapes[1] = &Rectangle(10);
shapes[2] = &Rectangle(10, 4);
shapes[3] = &Triangle(7.0);
shapes[4] = &Shape(10, 20, "generic");
for(int i=0; i < 5; i++)
{
cout << "object is " << shapes[i]->getName() <<
"\n";
cout << "Area is " << shapes[i]->area() << "\n\n";
}
getch();
}
```

**OUTPUT:**

object is generic
Error: area() must be overridden.
Area is 0
object is generic
Error: area() must be overridden.
Area is 0
object is generic
Error: area() must be overridden.
Area is 0
object is generic
Error: area() must be overridden.
Area is 0
object is generic
Error: area() must be overridden.
Area is 0

**Problem 34. Write a C++ program for overload across class .**

***Program:***

```
#include<iostream.h>
#include<conio.h>
class Base
{
public:
int f(int i) { return (i*2); }
float f(float f) { return (f*2);}
};
class Derived: public Base
{
public:
int f(int i, int j) { return (i +j); }
};
void main()
{
Derived var;
float f;
int i;
i = var.f(3, 5);  // Works
cout<<i;
getch();
}
```

**OUTPUT:**

8

**Problem 35. Write a C++ program to demonstrate pointer to derived class.**

***Program:***

```
#include<iostream.h>
#include<conio.h>
class BaseClass
{
int x;
public:
void setx(int i)
{
x = i;
}
int getx()
{
return x;
}
};
class DerivedClass : public BaseClass
{
int y;
public:
void sety(int i)
{
y = i;
}
int gety()
{
return y;
}
};
void  main()
{
BaseClass *p;                    // pointer to
BaseClass type
BaseClass baseObject;                // object of
BaseClass
DerivedClass derivedObject;              // object of
DerivedClass
p = &baseObject;                 // use p to access
BaseClass object
p->setx(10);                 // access BaseClass
object
cout << "Base object x: " << p->getx() << '\n';
p = &derivedObject;              // point to
DerivedClass object
p->setx(99);                 // access
DerivedClass object
derivedObject.sety(88);              // can't use p to
set y, so do it directly
cout << "Derived object x: " << p->getx() << '\n';
cout << "Derived object y: " <<
derivedObject.gety() << '\n';
getch();
}
```

**OUTPUT:**

```
Base object x: 10
Derived object x: 99
Derived object y: 88
```

**Problem 36. Write a C++ program for Hiding methods.**

***Program:***

```
#include<iostream.h>
#include<conio.h>
class BaseClass
{
public:
void Move() const { cout << "BaseClass move one
step\n"; }
void Move(int distance) const
{
cout << "BaseClass move " << distance <<"
steps.\n";
}
protected:
int itsAge;
int itsWeight;
};
class DerivedClass : public BaseClass
{
public:
void Move() const
{
cout << "DerivedClass move 5 steps.\n";
}
};
void main()
{
BaseClass baseObject;
DerivedClass derivedObject;
baseObject.Move();
baseObject.Move(2);
derivedObject.Move();
getch();
}
```

**OUTPUT:**

```
BaseClass move one step
BaseClass move 2 steps.
DerivedClass move 5 steps.
```

**Problem 37. Write a C++ program for simple class with its derived class.**

***Program:***

```
#include<iostream.h>
#include<conio.h>
#include <string.h>
class mybase
{
char str[80];
public:
mybase(char *s)
{
strcpy(str, s);
}
char *get()
{
return str;
}
};
class myderived : public mybase
{
int len;
public:
myderived(char *s) : mybase(s)
{
len = strlen(s);
}
int getlen()
{
return len;
}
void show()
{
cout << get() << '\n';
}
};
void  main()
{
myderived ob("hello");
ob.show();
cout << ob.getlen() << '\n';
getch();
}
```

**OUTPUT:**

hello
5

**Problem 38. Write a C++ program to calling base class's constructor in derived class.**

***Program:***

```
#include<iostream.h>
#include<conio.h>
class A
{
protected:
int i;
public:
A(int x)
{
i = x;
cout << "Constructing base class(A)\n";
}
~A()
{
cout << "Destructing base class(A)\n";
}
};
class B
{
protected:
int j;
public:
B(int x)
{
j = x;
cout << "Constructing base class(B)\n";
}
~B()
{
cout << "Destructing base class(B)\n";
}
};
class C: public A, public B
{
int k;
public:
C(int x, int y, int z): A(y), B(z)
{
k = x;
cout << "Constructing derived class (C)\n";
}
~C()
{
cout << "Destructing derived class(C)\n";
}
void show()
{
cout << i << " " << j << " " << k << "\n";
}
};
void main()
{
```

```
C c(1, 2, 3);
c.show();
getch();
}
```

**OUTPUT:**

```
Constructing base class(A)
Constructing base class(B)
Constructing derived class (C)
2 3 1
Destructing derived class(C)
Destructing base class(B)
Destructing base class(A)
```

**Problem 39. Write a C++ program using typeid to test type equality.**

***Program:***

```
#include<iostream.h>
#include<conio.h>
class Base {};
class Derived : public Base {};
void main( )
{
Base b, bb;
Derived d;
if (typeid(b) == typeid(d)) { // No
cout << "b and d are of the same type.\n";
}
if (typeid(b) == typeid(bb)) { // Yes
cout << "b and bb are of the same type.\n";
}
if (typeid(d) == typeid(Derived)) { // Yes
cout << "d is of type Derived.\n";
}
getch();
}
```

**OUTPUT:**

```
b and bb are of the same type.
d is of type Derived.
```

**Problem 40. Write a C++ program for derived classes.**

***Program:***

```
#include<iostream.h>
#include<conio.h>
class CPolygon
{
protected:
int width, height;
public:
void set_values (int a, int b)
{
width=a; height=b;
}
};
class CRectangle: public CPolygon
{
public:
int area ()
{
return (width * height);
}
};
class CTriangle: public CPolygon
{
public:
int area ()
{
return (width * height / 2);
}
};
void main ()
{
CRectangle rect;
CTriangle trgl;
rect.set_values (4,5);
trgl.set_values (4,5);
cout << rect.area() << endl;
cout << trgl.area() << endl;
getch();
}
```

**OUTPUT:**

```
20
10
```

**Problem 41. Write a C++ program for adding a constructor to derived class.**

***Program:***

```
#include<iostream.h>
#include<conio.h>
#include <string.h>
class Shape
{
// private
double width;
double height;
public:
void display()
{
cout << "Width and height are " << width << " and
" << height << "\n";
}
// accessor functons
```

```
double getWidth() { return width; }
double getHeight() { return height; }
void setWidth(double w) { width = w; }
void setHeight(double h) { height = h; }
};
// Triangle is derived from Shape.
class Triangle : public Shape
{
char style[20]; // now private
public:
// Constructor for Triangle.
Triangle(char *str, double w, double h)
{
setWidth(w);
setHeight(h);
strcpy(style, str);
}
double area()
{
return getWidth() * getHeight() / 2;
}
void showStyle()
{
cout << "Triangle is " << style << "\n";
}
};
void main()
{
Triangle t1("isosceles", 4.0, 4.0);
Triangle t2("right", 8.0, 12.0);
t1.showStyle();
t1.display();
cout << "Area is " << t1.area() << "\n";
t2.showStyle();
t2.display();
cout << "Area is " << t2.area() << "\n";
getch();
}
```

**OUTPUT:**

```
Triangle is isosceles
Width and height are 4 and 4
Area is 8
Triangle is right
Width and height are 8 and 12
Area is 48
```

**Problem 42. Write a C++ program to call base's constructor and destructor from derived class.**

***Program:***

```
#include<iostream.h>
#include<conio.h>
class BaseClass
{
public:
BaseClass() { cout << "Constructing base
portion\n"; }
~BaseClass() { cout << "Destructing base
portion\n"; }
};
class DerivedClass: public BaseClass
{
public:
DerivedClass() { cout << "Constructing derived
portion\n"; }
~DerivedClass() { cout << "Destructing derived
portion\n"; }
};
void main()
{
DerivedClass ob;
// do nothing but construct and destruct ob
getch();
}
```

**OUTPUT:**

```
Constructing base portion
Constructing derived portion
Destructing derived portion
Destructing base portion
```

**Problem 43. Write a C++ program to access member of base and use member of derived class.**

***Program:***

```
#include<iostream.h>
#include<conio.h>
class base
{
int i, j;
public:
void set(int a, int b)
{
i=a;
j=b;
}
void show()
{
cout << i << " " << j << "\n";
}
};
class derived : public base
{
int k;
```

```
public:
derived(int x)
{
k=x;
}
void showk()
{
cout << k << "\n";
}
};
void main()
{
derived ob(3);
ob.set(1, 2);
ob.show();
ob.showk();
getch();
}
```

**OUTPUT:**

```
1 2
3
```

**Problem 44. Write a C++ program for constructors and derived classes.**

***Program:***

```
#include<iostream.h>
#include<conio.h>
class mother
{
public:
mother ()
{
cout << "mother: no parameters\n";
}
mother (int a)
{
cout << "mother: int parameter\n";
}
};
class daughter : public mother
{
public:
daughter (int a)
{
cout << "daughter: int parameter\n\n";
}
};
class son : public mother
{
public:
son (int a) : mother (a)
{
cout << "son: int parameter\n\n";
}
};
void main ()
{
daughter siena (0);
son daniel(0);
getch();
}
```

**OUTPUT:**

```
mother: no parameters
daughter: int parameter
mother: int parameter
son: int parameter
```

**Problem 45. Write a C++ program for derived Class and base Class.**

***Program:***

```
#include<iostream.h>
#include<conio.h>
class Timer  // base class
{
protected:
int time;
public:
Timer():time(0)     //zero arg const....
{ }
Timer(int t):time(t)         // one args  const...
{ }
int get_time()
{
return time;
}
Timer operator ++()
{
return Timer(++time);
}
};
class Timert1  :public Timer //derived class
{
public:
Timer operator --()
{
return Timer(--time);
}
};
void main()
{
Timert1 t1;
cout <<"\nt1=" <<t1.get_time();
```

```
++t1;
++t1;
++t1;
cout <<"\nt1=" <<t1.get_time();
--t1;
--t1;
cout <<"\nt1=" <<t1.get_time();
cout <<endl;
getch();
}
```

**OUTPUT:**

```
t1=0
t1=3
t1=1
```

**Problem 46. Write a C++ program for derived class constructors.**

***Program:***

```
#include<iostream.h>
#include<conio.h>
class Timer
{
protected:
int time;
public:
Timer():time(0)
{ }
Timer(int t):time(t)
{ }
int get_time()
{
return time;
}
Timer operator ++()
{
return Timer(++time);
}
};
class Timert1 :public Timer
{
public:
Timert1():Timer()
{ }
Timert1(int t):Timer(t)
{ }
Timert1 operator --()
{
return Timert1(--time);}
};
void main()
{
Timert1 t1;
Timert1 t2(100);
cout <<"\nt1=" <<t1.get_time();
cout <<"\nt2=" <<t2.get_time();
++t1;
++t1;
++t1;
cout <<"\nt1=" <<t1.get_time();
--t2;
--t2;
cout <<"\nt2=" <<t2.get_time();
Timert1 t3 =--t2;
cout <<"\nt3=" <<t3.get_time();
cout <<endl;
getch();
}
```

**OUTPUT:**

```
t1=0
t2=100
t1=3
t2=98
t3=97
```

## OVERRIDING MEMBER FUNCTIONS:

**Problem 47. Write a C++ program to explain concept of Overriding Member Functions.**

***Program:***

```
#include<iostream.h>
#include<conio.h>
#include <process.h>
class Stack
{
protected:
enum {MAX =3 };
int st [MAX ];
int top;
public:
Stack()
{
top =-1;
}
void push(int var)
{
st [++top ] ==var;
}
int pop()
{
return st [top--];
```

```
}
};
class Stack1 :public Stack
{
public:
void push(int var)
{
if(top >=MAX-1)
{
cout <<"\nError:stack is full ";
exit(1);
}
Stack::push(var);
}
int pop()
{
if(top <0)
{
cout <<"\nError:stack is empty \n ";
exit(1);
}
return Stack::pop();
}
};
void main()
{
Stack1 s1;
s1.push(10);
s1.push(20);
s1.push(30);
cout <<s1.pop() <<endl;
cout <<s1.pop() <<endl;
cout <<s1.pop() <<endl;
cout <<s1.pop() <<endl;
cout <<endl;
getch();
}
```

**Problem 48. Write a C++ program to Overriding a base class method in a derived class.**

***Program:***

```
#include<iostream.h>
#include<conio.h>
class BaseClass
{
public:
// constructors
BaseClass() { cout << "BaseClass constructor...\n";
}
~BaseClass() { cout << "BaseClass destructor...\n";
}
//Other methods
void Talk()const { cout << "BaseClass sound!\n";
}
void Sleep()const {cout << "I'm sleeping.\n"; }
protected:
int itsAge;
int itsWeight;
};
class DerivedClass : public BaseClass
{
public:
// Constructors
DerivedClass(){ cout << "DerivedClass
constructor...\n"; }
~DerivedClass(){ cout << "DerivedClass
destructor...\n"; }
// Other methods
void Walk() { cout << "walk...\n"; }
void Eat() { cout << "eat...\n"; }
void Talk()const { cout << "talk!\n"; }
};
void main()
{
BaseClass baseObject;
DerivedClass derivedObject;
baseObject.Talk();
derivedObject.Talk();
getch();
}
```

**OUTPUT:**

```
BaseClass constructor...
BaseClass constructor...
DerivedClass constructor...
BaseClass sound!
talk!
DerivedClass destructor...
BaseClass destructor...
BaseClass destructor...
```

**Problem 49. Write a C++ program to calling base method from overridden method.**

***Program:***

```
#include<iostream.h>
#include<conio.h>
class BaseClass
{
public:
void Move() const
{
cout << "BaseClass move one step\n";
}
```

```
void Move(int distance) const
{
cout << "BaseClass move " << distance << "
steps.\n";
}
protected:
int itsAge;
int itsWeight;
};
class DerivedClass : public BaseClass
{
public:
void Move()const;
};
void DerivedClass::Move() const
{
cout << "In dog move...\n";
BaseClass::Move(3);
}
void main()
{
BaseClass baseObject;
DerivedClass derivedObject;
baseObject.Move(2);
derivedObject.BaseClass::Move(6);
getch();
}
```

**OUTPUT:**

BaseClass move 2 steps.
BaseClass move 6 steps.

**Problem 50. Write a C++ program to implement stack to illustrate the Overriding Member Function.**

***Program:***

```
#include<iostream.h>
#include<conio.h>
#include<process.h>                //This is used for
exit ( ) function
class stack                        //Base class
{
protected :
int a [50];
int top;
public:
stack ( )
{
top = 0 ;          // constructor defined
}
void push (int var)
{
a [++ top] = var ;
}
int pop ( )
{
return a [top - - ] ;
}
} ;
class stack2: public stack                   //derived
class
{
public :
void push (int var)
{
if (top < 50)
{
stack : push (var) ;
}
else
{
cout <<"\n OVERFLOW OCCURS" ;
cout <<"\n stack is full" ;
exit (1) ;
}
}
int pop ( )
{
if (top > 0)
{
return stack : pop ( ) ;
}
else
{
cout<<"\n UNDERFLOW OCCURS" ;
cout<<\n Stack is Empty" ;
exit (1) ;
}
}
} ;
void main ( )
{
stack2   s1 ;
s1.push(20) ;
s1. push(30) ;
s1. push(40) ;
clrscr();
cout << s1.pop( );
cout << s1.pop( );
cout << s1.pop( );
cout << s1. pop ( ) ;
getch();
}
```

**Problem 51. Write a C++ program for Inheritance in the Height Class.**

***Program:***

```
#include<iostream.h>
#include<conio.h>
enum posneg {pos,neg };
class Height
{
protected:
int feet;
float inches;
public:
Height():feet(0),inches(0.0)
{ }
Height(int ft,float in):feet(ft),inches(in)
{ }
void get()
{
cout <<"\nFeet:";
cin >>feet;
cout <<"inches:";
cin >>inches;
}
void show()
{
cout <<feet <<"-" <<inches;
}
};
class HeightS :public Height
{
private:
posneg sign;
public:
HeightS(): Height()
{
sign =pos;
}
HeightS(int ft,float in,posneg sg=pos): Height(ft,in)
{
sign =sg;
}
void get()
{
Height::get();
char ch;
cout <<"Enter sign (+or -):";
cin >>ch;
sign =(ch=='+')?pos :neg;
}
void show()
{
cout<< ((sign==pos)? "(+)" :"(-)" );
Height::show();
}
};
void main()
{
HeightS H1;
H1.get();
HeightS H2(6,4.25);
HeightS H3(100,4.5,neg);
cout <<"\nH1 =";
H1.show();
cout <<"\nH2 =";
H2.show();
cout <<"\nH3 =";
H3.show();
cout <<endl;
getch();
}
```

**<u>OUTPUT</u>:**

```
Feet:6
inches.2.25
Enter sign (+or -):+
H1 =(+)6-2.25
H2 =(+)6-4.25
H3 =(-)100-4.5
```

## SINGLE INHERITANCE:

**Problem 52. Write a C++ program to read and display the student data by using the concept of single inheritance.**

***Program:***

```
#include< iostream.h>
#include<iomanip.h>
#include<conio.h>
class student
{
private :
int rn ;
char name [20] ;
char add [30] ;
public :
void readdata ( ) ;
void dispdata ( ) ;
};
class marks
{
private :
```

```
float pm ;
float cm ;
float mm ;
public :
void readdata ( ) ;
void dispdata ( ) ;
} ;
void student : : readdata ( )
{
cout<<"\n Enter the RollNo, Name and Address of
the student"<<endl ;
cin>>rn>> name>> add ;
}
void student : : dispdata ( )
{
cout<<"\n ROLL NO is"<< rn ;
cout<<"\n NAME is"<< name ;
cout<<"\n ADDRESS is"<< add ;
}
void marks : : readdata ( )
{
student : : readdata ( );
{
student : : readdata ( ) ;
cout<<"\n Enter the Physics, Chemistry and Math
marks"<< endl ;
cin >> pm >> cm >> mm ;
}
void marks : : dispdata ( )
{
student : : dispdata ( );
cout<<"\n Physics MARKS are"<< pm ;
cout<<"\n Chemistry MARKS are"<< cm ;
cout<<"\n Math Marks are" << mm ;
}
void main ( )
{
marks r ;
cout<<"\n Enter the following student's information
:"
r. readdata ( ) ;
r. dispdata ( ) ;
getch ( ) ;
}
```

**Problem 53. Write a C++ program to read and write student data by implementing single inheritance with two derived classes.**

***Program:***

```
#include<iostream.h>
#include<iomanip.h>
#include<conio.h>
#include<dos.h>
class student
{
private :
int rn ;
char name [20] ;
public :
void readdata( );
void dispdata( );
};
class marks::public student
{
private :
float pm;
float cm;
float mm;
public :
void getdata( )
{
student::readdata( );
cout<<"\n Enter Physics, Chemistry and  Maths
marks" ;
cin >> pm >> cm >> mm ;
}
void dispdata( )
{
student::dispdata( );
cout <<"\n Physics Marks are"<< pm ;
cout <<"\n Chemistry Marks are" <<cm ;
cout <<"\n Math Marks are" << mm ;
}
}
class result::public marks
{
private :
float percentage ;
public :
void enterdata( );
void writedata( );
} ;
void student::readdata( )
{
cout<<"/n Enter the Roll No and Name" ;
cin >> rn >> name ;
}
void student::dispdata( )
{
cout <<"\n ROLL NO is" <<rn ;
cout <<"\n NAME is" <<name ;
}
```

```
void result::enterdata ( )
{
marks::getdata( );
cout <<"\n Enter the %age  : ";
cin >> percentage;
}
void result::writedata( )
{
marks::dispdata( );
cout <<"\n PERCENTAGE is" << percentage;
}
void main ( )
{
class result r;
r.enterdata( );
r.writedata( );
getch( );
}
```

**Problem 54. Write a C++ program to handle student data by using single inheritance.**

***Program.***

```
#include<iostream.h>
#include<conio.h>
class A
{
char name[20];
public:
void input()
{
cout<<"Enter name==>";
cin>>name;
}
void print()
{
cout<<"Name is "<<name<<endl;
}
};
class B : private A
{
int roll;
public:
void getdata()
{
input();
cout<<"Enter roll number==>";
cin>>roll;
}
void putdata()
{
print();
cout<<"Roll number is==>"<<roll;
}
};
void main()
{
clrscr();
B b;
b.getdata();
b.putdata();
getch();
}
```

**OUTPUT:**

Enter roll number==> R777
Enter name==> Rajan
Roll number is==> R777
Name is  Rajan

## AMBIGUITY IN SINGLE INHERITANCE:

**Problem 55. Write a C++ program to avoid ambiguity in single inheritance.**

***Program:***

```
#include<iostream.h>
#include<conio.h>
class A
{
private :
int i ;
public :
void getdata (int x) ;
void display ( ) ;
};
class B
{
private :
int i ;
public :
void getdata (int y) ;
void display ( ) ;
};
class C : : public A, public B
{ } ;
void A :: getdata (int x)
{
i = x ;
}
void A : : display ( )
{
cout <<"\n Value of i is ="<<i ;
```

```
}
void B :: getdata (int y)
{
j = y ;
}
void B : : display ( )
{
cout<<"\n value of j is ="<<j ;
}
void main ( )
{
class C obj ;
int x, y ;
cout<<"\n Enter the value of x" ;
cin>> x ;
obj. A :: getdata (x) ;
//Here member is ambiguous without scope
cout<<"\n Enter the value of y" ;
cin >> y ;
obj. B :: getdata (y) ;
obj. A :: display ( ) ;
obj. B :: display ( ) ;
getch();
}
```

**Problem 56. Write a C++ program to compute square value to show inheritance.**

***Program:***

```
#include<iostream.h>
#include<conio.h>
class base
{
int a;
public:
void seta(int n)
{
a=n;
}
void showa()
{
cout<<a*a<<endl;
}
};
class derived:public base
{
int b;
public:
void setb(int n)
{
b=n;
}
void showb()
{
cout<<b*b<<endl;
}
};
void main()
{
clrscr();
derived d;
d.seta(4);
d.setb(5);
d.showa();
d.showb();
getch();
}
```

**<u>OUTPUT</u>:**

16
25

**Problem 57. Write a C++ program to find Factorial of a number using inheritance.**

***Program:***

```
#include<iostream.h>
#include<conio.h>
class A
{
int n;
public:
A(int p)
{
n=p;
}
long fact();
};
long A::fact()
{
long f=1;
for(int i=1;i<=n;i++)
f*=i;
return f;
}
class B:public A
{
public:
B(int p): A(p)
{
cout<<"Object created.\n";
}
void print()
{
cout<<"Factorial is==>"<<fact();
```

```
}
};
void main()
{
int n;
clrscr();
cout<<"Enter the number==>";
cin>>n;
B b(n);
b.print();
getch();
}
```

**OUTPUT:**

Enter the number==> 5
Object created.
Factorial is==> 120

## MULTIPLE INHERITANCE:

**Problem 58. Write a C++ program for multiple inheritance.**

***Program:***

```
#include<iostream.h>
#include<conio.h>
class pub
{
private:
char publ[20];
protected:
double pr;
public:
void get()
{
cout<<"Enter publisher & price";
cin>>publ>>pr;
}
void put()
{
cout<<"\npublisher ="<<publ;
cout<<"\nprice="<<pr;
}
};
class sales
{
protected:
double psales;
public:
void get()
{
cout<<"Enter total sales";
cin>>psales;
}
void show()
{
cout<<"\nTotal sales ="<<psales;
}
};
class book:public pub,public sales
{
char aut[20];
long i;
int pg;
public:
void get()
{
cout<<"Enter author,isbn number,pages";
cin>>aut>>i>>pg;
}
void put()
{
cout<<"\nBook details ="<<aut<<'\t'<<i<<'\t'<<pg;
}
void csa()
{
double saleamt;
saleamt=pr*psales;
cout<<"Sale amount= "<<saleamt;
}
};
void main()
{
book obj;
cout<<"Enter publication details\n";
obj.pub::get();
cout<<"Enter sales details\n";
obj.sales::get();
cout<<"Enter book details\n";
obj.get();
obj.csa();
obj.pub::put();
obj.sales::show();
obj.put();
getch();
}
```

**Problem 59. Write a C++ program for multiple inheritance.**

***Program:***

```
#include<iostream.h>
#include<conio.h>
class CPolygon
```

```
{
protected:
int width, height;
public:
void set_values (int a, int b)
{
width=a;
height=b;
}
};
class coutput
{
public:
void output (int i);
};
void coutput::output (int i)
{
cout << i << endl;
}
class CRectangle: public CPolygon, public coutput
{
public:
int area ()
{
return (width * height);
}
};
class CTriangle: public CPolygon, public coutput
{
public:
int area()
{
return (width * height / 2);
}
};
void main()
{
CRectangle rect;
CTriangle trgl;
rect.set_values (4,5);
trgl.set_values (4,5);
rect.output (rect.area());
trgl.output (trgl.area());
getch();
}
```

**OUTPUT:**

```
20
10
```

**Problem 60. Write a C++ program for multiple base class constructing and destructing.**

***Program:***

```
#include<iostream.h>
#include<conio.h>
class base1
{
public:
base1()
{
cout << "Constructing base1\n";
}
~base1()
{
cout << "Destructing base1\n";
}
};
class base2
{
public:
base2()
{
cout << "Constructing base2\n";
}
~base2()
{
cout << "Destructing base2\n";
}
};
class derived: public base1, public base2
{
public:
derived()
{
cout << "Constructing derived\n";
}
~derived()
{
cout << "Destructing derived\n";
}
};
void main()
{
derived ob;
getch();
}
```

**OUTPUT:**

```
Constructing base1
Constructing base2
Constructing derived
Destructing derived
Destructing base2
Destructing base1
```

**Problem 61. Write a C++ program to print Fibonacci series by using Constructor under inheritance.**

***Program:***

```
#include<iostream.h>
#include<conio.h>
class A
{
protected:
int a;
public:
A()
{
a=0;
}
};
class B
{
protected:
int b;
public:
B()
{
b=1;
}
};
class C:public A,public B
{
int c;
public:
C():A(),B()
{
c=a+b;
}
void print()
{
cout<<c<<" ";
a=b;b=c;c=a+b;
}
};
void main()
{
clrscr();
int n;
cout<<"Enter number of terms==>";
cin>>n;
C c;
cout<<"The series is==>0 1 ";
for(int i=1;i<=n-2;i++)
c.print();
getch();
}
```

**OUTPUT:**

```
Enter number of terms==> 9
The series is==>0 1   1  2  3  5  8  13  21
```

**Problem 62. Write a C++ program for pass parameter to two base classes.**

***Program:***

```
#include<iostream.h>
#include<conio.h>
class base1
{
protected:
int i;
public:
base1(int x)
{
i=x;
cout << "Constructing base1\n";
}
~base1()
{
cout << "Destructing base1\n";
}
};
class base2
{
protected:
int k;
public:
base2(int x)
{
k=x;
cout << "Constructing base2\n";
}
~base2()
{
cout << "Destructing base2\n";
}
};
class derived: public base1, public base2
{
int j;
public:
derived(int x, int y, int z): base1(y), base2(z)
{
j=x;
cout << "Constructing derived\n";
}
~derived()
```

```
{
cout << "Destructing derived\n";
}
void show()
{
cout << i << " " << j << " " << k << "\n";
}
};
void main()
{
derived ob(3, 4, 5);
ob.show();
getch();
}
```

**OUTPUT:**

```
Constructing base1
Constructing base2
Constructing derived
4 3 5
Destructing derived
Destructing base2
Destructing base1
```

**Problem 63. Write a C++ program for multiple inheritance.**

***Program:***

```
#include<iostream.h>
#include<conio.h>
class A
{
protected:
int x;
public:
void showx()
{
cout << x << "\n";
}
};
class B
{
protected:
int y;
public:
void showy()
{
cout << y << "\n";
}
};
class C: public A, public B
{
public:
void set(int i, int j)
{
x = i;
y = j;
}
};
void main()
{
C c;
c.set(10, 20);
c.showx();
c.showy();
getch();
}
```

**OUTPUT:**

```
10
20
```

**Problem 64. Write a C++ program for multiple Inheritance.**

***Program:***

```
#include<iostream.h>
#include<conio.h>
const int LEN =80;
class student
{
private:
char school [LEN ];
char degree [LEN ];
public:
void getedu()
{
cout <<" Enter name of school or university:";
cin >>school;
cout <<" Enter highest degree earned \n ";
cout <<" ((Highschool,Bachelor's,Master's,PhD):";
cin >>degree;
}
void putedu()
{
cout <<"\n School or university:" <<school;
cout <<"\n Highest degree earned:" <<degree;
}
};
class employee
{
private:
char name [LEN ];
unsigned long number;
public:
void getdata()
```

```
{
cout <<"\n Enter last name:";
cin >>name;
cout <<" Enter number:";
cin >>number;
}
void putdata()
{
cout <<"\n Name:" <<name;
cout <<"\n Number:" <<number;
}
};
class manager :private employee,private student
{
private:
char title [LEN ];
double dues;
public:
void getdata()
{
employee::getdata();
cout <<" Enter title:";
cin >>title;
cout <<" Enter Cricket club dues:";
cin >>dues;
student::getedu();
}
void putdata()
{
employee::putdata();
cout <<"\n Title:" <<title;
cout <<"\n Cricket club dues:" <<dues;
student::putedu();
}
};
class professor :private employee,private student
{
private:
int pubs;//number of publications
public:
void getdata()
{
employee::getdata();
cout <<" Enter number of pubs:";cin >>pubs;
student::getedu();
}
void putdata()const
{
employee::putdata();
cout <<"\n Number of publications:" <<pubs;
student::putedu();
}
};
class laborer :public employee
{
};
void main()
{
manager m1;
professor p1,p2;
laborer l1;
cout <<endl;
cout <<"\nEnter data for manager 1: ";
m1.getdata();
cout <<"\nEnter data for professor 1: ";
p1.getdata();
cout <<"\nEnter data for professor 2: ";
p2.getdata();
cout <<"\nEnter data for laborer 1: ";
l1.getdata();
cout <<"\nData on manager 1: ";
m1.putdata();
cout <<"\nData on professor 1: ";
p1.putdata();
cout <<"\nData on professor 2: ";
p2.putdata();
cout <<"\nData on laborer 1: ";
l1.putdata();
cout <<endl;
getch();
}
```

**OUTPUT:**

```
Enter data for manager 1:
Enter last name: Jagminder Singh
Enter number:12
Enter title:President
Enter golf club dues:1000
Enter name of school or university:LPU
Enter highest degree earned
(Highschool,Bachelor's,Master's,PhD):Bachelor's
Enter data for professor 1
Enter last name:Jagbir Singh
Enter number:764
Enter number of pubs:99
Enter name of school or university:LPU
Enter highest degree earned
(Highschool,Bachelor's,Master's,PhD):Master's
Enter data for Professor 2
Enter last name:Navjeet Singh
Enter number:845
Enter number of pubs:101
Enter name of school or university:KCA
```

Enter highest degree earned
(Highschool,Bachelor 's,Master 's,PhD):Master 's
Enter data for laborer 1
Enter last name:paramjit
Enter number:48323

**Problem 65. Write a C++ program to directly inherit two base classes.**

***Program:***

```
#include<iostream.h>
#include<conio.h>
class BaseClass1
{
int a;
public:
BaseClass1(int x)
{
a = x;
}
int geta()
{
return a;
}
};
class BaseClass2
{
int b;
public:
BaseClass2(int x)
{
b = x;
}
int getb()
{
return b;
}
};
class DerivedClass : public BaseClass1, public
BaseClass2
{
int c;
public:
DerivedClass(int x, int y, int z) : BaseClass1(z),
BaseClass2(y){
c = x;
}
void show()
{
cout << geta() << ' ' << getb() << ' ';
cout << c << '\n';
}
};
void main()
{
DerivedClass object(1, 2, 3);
object.show();
getch();
}
```

**OUTPUT:**

3 2 1

**Problem 66. Write a C++ program for inherit two base classes.**

***Program:***

```
#include<iostream.h>
#include<conio.h>
class BaseClass1
{
public:
BaseClass1()
{
cout << "Constructing BaseClass1\n";
}
~BaseClass1()
{
cout << "Destructing BaseClass1\n";
}
};
class BaseClass2
{
int b;
public:
BaseClass2()
{
cout << "Constructing BaseClass2\n";
}
~BaseClass2()
{
cout << "Destructing BaseClass2\n";
}
};
// Inherit two base classes.
class DerivedClass : public BaseClass1, public
BaseClass2
{
public:
DerivedClass()
{
cout << "Constructing DerivedClass\n";
}
~DerivedClass()
{
```

```
cout << "Destructing DerivedClass\n";
}
};
void main()
{
DerivedClass object;
getch();
}
```

**OUTPUT:**

```
Constructing BaseClass1
Constructing BaseClass2
Constructing DerivedClass
Destructing DerivedClass
Destructing BaseClass2
Destructing BaseClass1
```

**Problem 67. Write a C++ program to enter and write student to explain multiple inheritance.**

***Program:***

```
#include<iostream.h>
#include<iomanip.h>
class student
{
private :
char sex, name [20] ;
int rn ;
public :
void getdata ( )
{
cout<<"\n Enter Roll No and Name of student" ;
cin>> rn >> name ;
cout<<"\n Enter Sex of student (M/F)" ;
cin >> sex ;
}
void display ( )
{
cout<<"\n ROLL NO is" << rn ;
cout<<"\n NAME is" << name ;
cout<<"\n SEX is" << sex ;
}
} ;
class academic
{
private :
char course [20], semester [10] ;
int rank ;
public :
void getdata ( )
{
cout<<"\n Enter course name (B. E/B.C.A/B.I.T.)" ;
cin >> course ;
cout<<"\n Enter semester (1st/2nd)" ;
cin >> semester ;
cout<<"\n Enter Rank of student" ;
cin >> rank ;
}
void display ( )
{
cout<<"\n Course adopted is"<<course ;
cout<<"\n Semester entered is"<<semester ;
cout<<"\n Rank is" << rank ;
}
} ;
class fees : public student, public academic
{
private :
int f ;
public :
void readdata ( ) ;
void writedata ( ) ;
};
void fee : : readdata ( )
{
student : : getdata ( ) ;
academic : : getdata ( ) ;
cout<<"\n Enter fees paid by student" ;
cin >> f ;
}
void fee : : writedata ( )
{
student : : display ( ) ;
academic : : display ( ) ;
cout<<"\n Fees paid is" << f << endl ;
}
} ;
void main ( )
{
class fee r ;
r. readdata ( ) ;
r. writedata ( ) ;
getch ( ) ;
}
```

**Problem 68. Write a C++ program to process student data to illustrate multiple inheritance.**

***Program:***

```
#include<iostream.h>
#include<conio.h>
class address
{
private:  int hno;
char city[20];
```

```
public:
void getadd()
{
cout<<"Enter House no. and city:"<<endl;
cin>>hno>>city;
}
void showadd()
{
cout<<"House no. is:"<<'\t'<<hno<<endl;
cout<<"City is:"<<'\t'<<city<<endl;
}
};
class marks
{
private: int m1,m2,m3;
public:
void get()
{
cout<<"Enter the marks in three subjects:"<<endl;
cin>>m1>>m2>>m3;
}
void show()
{
cout<<"Marks in 1st subject:"<<'\t'<<m1<<endl;
cout<<"Marks in 2nd subject:"<<'\t'<<m2<<endl;
cout<<"Marks in 3rd subject:"<<'\t'<<m3<<endl;
}
};
class student:public marks,public address
{
private:
int rno;
char name[20];
public:
void getdata()
{
cout<<"Enter the roll no. and name of the
student:"<<endl;
cin>>rno>>name;
getadd();
get();
}
void showdata()
{
cout<<"Roll No."<<'\t'<<rno<<endl;
cout<<"Name is:"<<'\t'<<name<<endl;
showadd();
show();
}
};
void main()
{
student s;
clrscr();
s.getdata();
s.showdata();
getch();
}
```

**OUTPUT:**

```
Enter the roll no and name of the student:
12  parwinder
Enter house no. and city :
6        Amritsar
Enter the marks  in three subjects:
66  55  77
Roll No.  12
Name is :Parwinder
House no is 6
City is : Amritsar
Marks in 1st  subject: 66
Marks in 2nd subject: 55
Marks in 3rd subject: 77
```

**Problem 69. Write a C++ program to compute marks to explain the concept of Multiple Inheritance.**

***Program:***

```
#include<iostream.h>
#include<conio.h>
class general
{
private:
char name[20];
int rollno;
char course[10];
public:
void getdata();
void showdata();
};
class marks
{
private:
int phy;
int comp;
int math;
public:
void getdata();
void showdata();
};
class grade :private general,private marks
{
private:
```

```
int total;
char grade[2];
public :
void getdata();
void showdata();
};
void general :: getdata()
{
cout<<"ENTER THE NAME OF STUDENT:";
cin>>name;
cout<<"ENTER THE ROLLNO:-";
cin>>rollno;
cout<<"ENTER THE CLASS :-";
cin>>course;
}
void general::showdata()
{
cout<<name<<"  "<<rollno<<"     "<<course;
}
void marks::getdata()
{
cout<<"\nENTER THE MARKS OF PHYSICS:-";
cin>>phy;
cout<<"\nENTER THE MARKS OF computer:-";
cin>>comp;
cout<<"\nENTER THE MARKS OF maths:-";
cin>>math;
}
void marks::showdata()
{
cout<<"  "<<phy<<"  "<<comp<<"  "<<math;
}
void grade::getdata()
{
general::getdata();
marks::getdata();
cout<<"ENTER THE TOTAL MARKS :-\n";
cin>>total;
cout<<"\nENTER THE GRADE    :-";
cin>>grade;
}
void grade::showdata()
{
general::showdata();
marks::showdata();
cout<<"  "<<total<<"  "<<grade;
}
void main()
{
clrscr();
grade ob1;
cout<<"ENTER THE FOLLOWING INFO FOR
STUDENT \n";
ob1.getdata();
cout<<"\nName  Rollno  Class  Phy  Comp Maths
Total Grade\n";
ob1.showdata();
getch();
}
```

**OUTPUT:**

```
ENTER THE FOLLOWING INFO FOR
STUDENT
ENTER THE NAME OF STUDENT:- BALDEEP
ENTER THE ROLLNO:-13
ENTER THE CLASS:-BCA
ENTER THE MARKS OF PHYSICS:-70
ENTER THE MARKS OF COMPUTER:-70
ENTER THE MARKS OF MATHS:-60
ENTER THE TOTALMARKS:-
200
ENTER THE GRADE:-A
NAME    ROLLNO   CLASS  PHY   COMP
MATHS   TOTAL    GRADE
BALDEEP 13              BCA   70     70
60      200      A
```

**Problem 70. Write a C++ program to display compute equipment to explore the Multiple Inheritance.**

***Program:***

```
#include<iostream.h>
#include<conio.h>
#include<string.h>
class cpu
{
private:
char mother[10],ram[10],hdd[10];
public:
cpu(char *m,char *r,char *h)
{
strcpy(mother,m);
strcpy(ram,r);
strcpy(hdd,h);
}
void show()
{
cout<<"RAM is "<<ram<<endl;
cout<<"Hdd is "<<hdd<<endl;
cout<<"Mother Board is "<<mother<<endl;
}
};
class acc
```

```
{
char key[10],mouse[10],monitor[10],speaker[10];
public:
acc(char *k,char *ms,char *m,char *s)
{
strcpy(key,k);
strcpy(mouse,ms);
strcpy(monitor,m);
strcpy(speaker,s);
}
void show()
{
cout<<"Monitor is "<<monitor<<endl;
cout<<"Keyboard is "<<key<<endl;
cout<<"Mouse is "<<mouse<<endl;
cout<<"Speaker is "<<speaker<<endl;
}
};
class computer:public cpu,public acc
{
public:
computer(char *mother,char *hdd,char *ram,char
*k,
            char *ms,char *m,char
*s):cpu(mother,ram,hdd),acc(k,ms,m,s)
            { }
void show()
{
cout<<"The computer is "<<endl;
cpu::show();
acc::show();
}
};
void main()
{
computer c("Azza","10.2 GB","64 MB","TVS
GOLD","Logitech","Microtek","Yahama");
c.show();
getch();
}
```

**OUTPUT:**

```
The computer is
RAM is 64  MB
HDD is  10.2 GB
Motherboard is Azza
Monitor is Microtek
Keyboard is TVS GOLD
Mouse is Logitech
Speaker is Yahama
```

**Problem 71. Write a C++ program to enter rollno and marks and display to illustrate the working of multiple inheritance.**

***Program:***

```
#include<iostream.h>
#include<conio.h>
class A
{
char name[20];
public:
void input()
{
cout<<"Enter name==>";
cin>>name;
}
void print()
{
cout<<"Name is "<<name<<endl;
}
};
class C
{
int marks;
public:
void input()
{
cout<<"Enter marks==>";
cin>>marks;
}
void print()
{
cout <<"Marks obtained are "<<marks<<endl;
}
};
class B : public A,C
{
int roll;
public:
void getdata()
{
A::input();
cout<<"Enter roll number==>";
cin>>roll;
C::input();
}
void putdata()
{
cout<<"\n\n\n";
A::print();
cout<<"Roll number is "<<roll<<endl;
C::print();
```

```
}
};
void main()
{
clrscr();
B b;
b.getdata();
b.putdata();
getch();
}
```

**OUTPUT:**

```
Enter name==> Mohan
Enter roll number==> 122
Enter marks==> 89
Name is Mohan
Roll number is 122
Enter marks==> 89
```

**Problem 72. Write a C++ program to display student result rank wise.**

***Program:***

```
#include<iostream.h>
#include<conio.h>
#include<iomanip.h>
class A
{
char name[20],roll;
public:
void input()
{
cout<<"Enter name & roll number==>";
cin>>name>>roll;
}
void print()
{
cout<<setw(20)<<name<<"    "<<roll;
}
};
class B
{
int s1,s2,s3;
public:
int input()
{
cout<<"Enter marks in 3 subjects==>";
cin>>s1>>s2>>s3;
return s1+s2+s3;
}
};
class C: public A , public B
{
public:
int total;
void input()
{
A::input();
total=B::input();
}
void print()
{
A::print();
cout<<setw(8)<<total<<setw(8);
}
}c[50];
void sort(int);
void main()
{
int n,rank=1,p,i;
clrscr();
cout<<"Enter  number of students==>";
cin>>n;
cout<<"Enter the information==>\n\n\n";
for(i=0;i<n;i++) //INPUTTING
{
cout<<"Student "<<i+1<<endl;
c[i].input();
}
sort(n);    //SORTING
clrscr();
cout<<"The database is==>\n\n";
cout<<setw(20)<<"NAME"<<setw(8)<<"ROLL"<
<setw(8)<<"TOTAL"<<setw(8)<<"RANK"<<"\n\
n";
c[0].print();
cout<<rank<<endl;
p=rank;
for(i=1;i<n;i++)
{
c[i].print();
if(c[i].total==c[i-1].total)
cout<<p;
else
{
cout<<rank;
p=rank;
}
rank++;
cout<<endl;
}
getch();
}
void sort(int n)
```

```
{
int p,i;
C c1;
for(p=1;p<n;p++)
for(i=0;i<n-p;i++)
if(c[i].total<c[i+1].total)
{
c1=c[i];
c[i]=c[i+1];
c[i+1]=c1;
}
}
```

**OUTPUT:**

```
Enter  number of students==>3
Enter the information==>
Student1
Enter name & roll number==>  Pooja  555
Enter marks in 3 subjects==> 35    45   55
Student2
Enter name & roll number==>  Geeta   666
Enter marks in 3 subjects==>  60     55   55
Student3
Enter name & roll number==> Gyatri  777
Enter marks in 3 subjects==> 80     90  90
The database is==>
NAME   Gyatri  ROLL  777   TOTAL 260  RANK 1
NAME   Geeta  ROLL  666   TOTAL 170  RANK 2
NAME   Pooja  ROLL  555   TOTAL 135  RANK 3
```

## MULTIPLE BASE CLASSES:

**Problem 73. Write a C++ program for an example of multiple base classes.**

***Program:***

```
#include<iostream.h>
#include<conio.h>
class BaseClass1
{
protected:
int x;
public:
void showx() { cout << x << "\n"; }
};
class BaseClass2
{
protected:
int y;
public:
void showy() { cout << y << "\n"; }
};
// Inherit multiple base classes.
class DerivedClass: public BaseClass1, public
BaseClass2
{
public:
void set(int i, int j) { x = i; y = j; }
};
void main()
{
DerivedClass ob;
ob.set(10, 20); // provided by DerivedClass
ob.showx();     // from BaseClass1
ob.showy();     // from BaseClass2
getch();
}
```

**OUTPUT:**

```
10
20
```

**Problem 74. Write a C++ program for multiple inheritance with employees and degrees**

***Program:***

```
#include<iostream.h>
#include<conio.h>
const int LEN = 80;
class student
{
private:
char school[LEN];
char degree[LEN];
public:
void getedu(){
cout << "   Enter name of school or university: ";
cin >> school;
cout << "   Enter highest degree earned \n";
cout << "   (Highschool, Bachelor's, Master's,
PhD): ";
cin >> degree;
}
void putedu() const
{
cout << "\n   School or university: " << school;
cout << "\n   Highest degree earned: " << degree;
}
};
class employee
{
private:
char name[LEN];
unsigned long number;
public:
```

```
void getdata()
{
cout << "\n   Enter last name: "; cin >> name;
cout << "   Enter number: ";      cin >> number;
}
void putdata() const
{
cout << "\n   Name: " << name;
cout << "\n   Number: " << number;
}
};
class manager : private employee, private student
{
private:
char title[LEN];
double dues;
public:
void getdata()
{
employee::getdata();
cout << "   Enter title: ";          cin >> title;
cout << "   Enter golf club dues: "; cin >> dues;
student::getedu();
}
void putdata() const
{
employee::putdata();
cout << "\n   Title: " << title;
cout << "\n   Golf club dues: " << dues;
student::putedu();
}
};
class scientist : private employee, private student
{
private:
int pubs;
public:
void getdata()
{
employee::getdata();
cout << "   Enter number of pubs: "; cin >> pubs;
student::getedu();
}
void putdata() const
{
employee::putdata();
cout << "\n   Number of publications: " << pubs;
student::putedu();
}
};
class laborer : public employee
{ };
void main()
{
manager m1;
scientist s1, s2;
laborer l1;
cout << endl;
cout << "\nEnter data for manager 1";
m1.getdata();
cout << "\nEnter data for scientist 1";
s1.getdata();
cout << "\nEnter data for scientist 2";
s2.getdata();
cout << "\nEnter data for laborer 1";
l1.getdata();
cout << "\nData on manager 1";
m1.putdata();
cout << "\nData on scientist 1";
s1.putdata();
cout << "\nData on scientist 2";
s2.putdata();
cout << "\nData on laborer 1";
l1.putdata();
cout << endl;
getch();
}
```

**Problem 75. Write a C++ program for multiple Inheritance to have the features from both parent**

***Program:***

```
#include<iostream.h>
#include<conio.h>
class Horse
{
public:
Horse() { cout << "Horse constructor... "; }
virtual ~Horse() { cout << "Horse destructor... "; }
virtual void Whinny() const { cout << "Whinny!...
"; }
private:
int itsAge;
};
class Bird
{
public:
Bird() { cout << "Bird constructor... "; }
virtual ~Bird() { cout << "Bird destructor... "; }
virtual void Chirp() const { cout << "Chirp... "; }
virtual void Fly() const
{
```

```
cout << "fly! ";
}
private:
int itsWeight;
};
class Pegasus : public Horse, public Bird
{
public:
void Chirp() const { Whinny(); }
Pegasus() { cout << "Pegasus constructor... "; }
~Pegasus() { cout << "Pegasus destructor...  "; }
};
const int MagicNumber = 2;
void main()
{
Horse* Ranch[MagicNumber];
Bird* Aviary[MagicNumber];
Horse * pHorse;
Bird * pBird;
pHorse = new Pegasus;
pHorse = new Horse;
Ranch[0] = pHorse;
pBird = new Pegasus;
pBird = new Bird;
Aviary[0] = pBird;
Ranch[0]->Whinny();
delete Ranch[0];
Aviary[0]->Chirp();
Aviary[0]->Fly();
delete Aviary[0];
getch();
}
```

**OUTPUT:**

(running mode)

**Problem 76. Write a C++ program to resolving Ambiguity in Case of Multiple Inheritance Involving Common Base Classes**

***Program:***

```
#include<iostream.h>
#include<conio.h>
typedef int HANDS;
enum COLOR { Red, Green, Blue, Yellow, White,
Black, Brown } ;
class Animal
{
public:
Animal(int);
virtual ~Animal() { cout << "Animal destructor...\n";
}
virtual int GetAge() const { return itsAge; }
virtual void SetAge(int age) { itsAge = age; }
private:
int itsAge;
};
Animal::Animal(int age):
itsAge(age)
{
cout << "Animal constructor...\n";
}
class Horse : public Animal
{
public:
Horse(COLOR color, HANDS height, int age);
virtual ~Horse() { cout << "Horse destructor...\n";
}
virtual void Whinny()const { cout << "Whinny!...
"; }
virtual HANDS GetHeight() const { return
itsHeight; }
virtual COLOR GetColor() const { return itsColor;
}
protected:
HANDS itsHeight;
COLOR itsColor;
};
Horse::Horse(COLOR color, HANDS height, int
age):
Animal(age),
itsColor(color),itsHeight(height)
{
cout << "Horse constructor...\n";
}
class Bird : public Animal
{
public:
Bird(COLOR color, bool migrates, int age);
virtual ~Bird() {cout << "Bird destructor...\n"; }
virtual void Chirp()const { cout << "Chirp... "; }
virtual void Fly()const{ cout << "fly! "; }
virtual COLOR GetColor()const { return itsColor;
}
virtual bool GetMigration() const { return
itsMigration; }
protected:
COLOR itsColor;
bool itsMigration;
};
Bird::Bird(COLOR color, bool migrates, int age):
Animal(age),
itsColor(color), itsMigration(migrates)
{
```

```
cout << "Bird constructor...\n";
}
class Pegasus : public Horse, public Bird
{
public:
void Chirp()const { Whinny(); }
Pegasus(COLOR, HANDS, bool, long, int);
virtual ~Pegasus() {cout << "Pegasus
destructor...\n";}
virtual long GetNumberBelievers() const
{ return  itsNumberBelievers; }
virtual COLOR GetColor()const { return
Horse::itsColor; }
virtual int GetAge() const { return Horse::GetAge();
}
private:
long itsNumberBelievers;
};
Pegasus::Pegasus(
   COLOR aColor,
   HANDS height,
   bool migrates,
   long NumBelieve,
   int age):
 Horse(aColor, height,age),
Bird(aColor, migrates,age),
itsNumberBelievers(NumBelieve)
{
cout << "Pegasus constructor...\n";
}
void main()
{
Pegasus *pPeg = new Pegasus(Red, 5, true, 10, 2);
int age = pPeg->GetAge();
cout << "This pegasus is " << age << " years old.\n";
delete pPeg;
getch();
}
```

**Problem 77. Write a C++ program for multiple Inheritance in both private and public way**

***Program:***

```
#include<iostream.h>
#include<conio.h>
class One
{
public:
One(void)
{
cout << "Constructor for One\n";
one = 1;
};
int one;
};
class Two
{
public:
Two(void)
{
cout << "Constructor for Two\n";
two = 2;
};
int two;
};
class Three
{
public:
Three(void)
{
cout << "Constructor for Three\n";
three = 3;
};
int three;
};
class Derived: private One, private Three, public
Two
{
public:
Derived(void) : One(), Two(), Three()
{
cout << "Derived constructor called\n"; };
void show_value(void) { cout << one << two <<
three << endl; };
};
void main(void)
{
clrscr();
Derived my_class;
my_class.show_value();
cout << my_class.two;
getch();
}
```

**OUTPUT:**

```
Constructor for One
Constructor for Two
Constructor for Three
Derived constructor called
123
2
```

**Problem 78. Write a C++ program for multiple inheritance example**

***Program:***

```
#include<iostream.h>
#include<conio.h>
class Base1
{
public:
Base1( int parameterValue )
{
value = parameterValue;
}
int getData() const
{
return value;
}
protected:
int value;
};
class Base2
{
public:
Base2( char characterData )
{
letter = characterData;
}
char getData() const
{
return letter;
}
protected:
char letter;
};
class Derived : public Base1, public Base2
{
public:
Derived( int integer, char character, double double1
)
: Base1( integer ), Base2( character ), real( double1 )
{ }
double getReal() const
{
return real;
}
void display()
{
cout << "    Integer: " << value << "\n  Character: "
<< letter << "\nReal number: " << real;
}
private:
double real;
};
void main()
{
Base1 base1( 10 ), *base1Ptr = 0;
Base2 base2( 'Z' ), *base2Ptr = 0;
Derived derived( 7, 'A', 3.5 );
cout << base1.getData()
<< base2.getData();
derived.display();
cout << derived.Base1::getData()
      << derived.Base2::getData()
      << derived.getReal() << "\n\n";

base1Ptr = &derived;
cout << base1Ptr->getData() << '\n';
base2Ptr = &derived;
cout << base2Ptr->getData() << endl;
getch();
}
```

**OUTPUT:**

```
10Z    Integer: 7
Character: A
Real number: 3.57A3.5
7
A
```

## CLASS HIERARCHIES:

**Problem 79. Write a C++ program for Class Hierarchies**

***Program:***

```
#include<iostream.h>
#include<conio.h>
const int LEN =80;//maximum length of names
class employee
{
private:
char name [LEN ];
long number;
public:
void getdata()
{
cout <<"\n Last name:";
cin >>name;
cout <<" Number:";
cin >>number;
}
void putdata()
{
cout <<"\n Name:" <<name;
cout <<"\n Number:" <<number;
}
```

```
};
class manager :public employee
{
private:
char title [LEN ];
double dues;
public:
void getdata()
{
employee::getdata();
cout <<" Title::";
cin >>title;
cout <<"  Cricket club dues:";
cin >>dues;
}
void putdata()
{
employee::putdata();
cout <<"\n Title:" <<title;
cout <<"\n Cricket club dues:" <<dues;
}
};
class professor :public employee
{
private:
int pubs;
public:
void getdata()
{
employee::getdata();
cout <<" Number of pubs:";
cin >>pubs;
}
void putdata()const
{
employee::putdata();
cout <<"\n Number of publications:" <<pubs;
}
};
class laborer :public employee
{
};
void main()
{
manager m1,m2;
professor p1;
laborer l1;
cout <<endl;
cout <<"\nData for manager 1: ";
m1.getdata();
cout <<"\nData for manager 2:";
m2.getdata();
cout <<"\nData for professor 1: ";
p1.getdata();
cout <<"\nData for laborer 1: ";
l1.getdata();
cout <<"\nData of manager 1: ";
m1.putdata();
cout <<"\nData of manager 2: ";
m2.putdata();
cout <<"\nData on professor 1: ";
p1.putdata();
cout <<"\nData on laborer 1: ";
l1.putdata();
cout <<endl;
getch();
}
```

**OUTPUT:**

```
Data for manager 1
Last name:sukhwant
Number:10
Title.lect.
Cricket club dues:1000
Data on manager 2
Last name:sarbjit
Number:124
Title:lab_ass
Cricket club dues:500
Data for professor 1
Last name:Avtar riar
Number:234234
Number of pubs:65
Data for laborer 1
Last name:paramjit
Number:6546544
The program then plays it back.
Data on manager 1
Name:sukhwant
Number:10
Title:lect.
Cricket club dues:1000
Data on manager 2
Name:sarabjeet
Number:124
Title:lab-ass
Cricket club dues:500
Data on professor 1
Name:Avtar riar
Number:234234
Number of publications:65
Data on laborer 1
Name:paramjit
```

Number:6546544

**Problem 80. Write a C++ program to share member variables between sub class**

***Program:***

```
#include<iostream.h>
#include<conio.h>
class AreaClass
{
public:
double height;
double width;
};
class Rectangle : public AreaClass
{
public:
Rectangle(double h, double w)
{
height = h;
width = w;
}
double area()
{
return height * width;
}
};
class Isosceles : public AreaClass
{
public:
Isosceles(double h, double w) {
height = h;
width = w;
}
double area()
{
return 0.5 * width * height;
}
};
class cylinder : public AreaClass
{
public:
cylinder(double h, double w)
{
height = h;
width = w;
}
double area()
{
return (2 * 3.1416 * (width/2) * (width/2)) + (3.1416
* width * height);
}
};
void main()
{
Rectangle rectangleObject(10.0, 5.0);
Isosceles triangleObject(4.0, 6.0);
cylinder cylinderObject(3.0, 4.0);
cout << "Rectangle: " << rectangleObject.area() <<
endl;
cout << "Triangle: " << triangleObject.area() <<
endl;
cout << "Cylinder: " << cylinderObject.area() <<
endl;
getch();
}
```

**OUTPUT:**

Rectangle: 50
Triangle: 12
Cylinder: 62.832

**Problem 81. Write a C++ program inheritance for subclass**

***Program:***

```
#include<iostream.h>
#include<conio.h>
class AreaClass
{
public:
double height;
double width;
};
class Rectangle : public AreaClass
{
public:
Rectangle(double h, double w);
double area();
};
class Isosceles : public AreaClass
{
public:
Isosceles(double h, double w);
double area();
};
Rectangle::Rectangle(double h, double w)
{
height = h;
width = w;
}
Isosceles::Isosceles(double h, double w)
{
height = h;
width = w;
```

```
}
double Rectangle::area()
{
 return width * height;
}
double Isosceles::area()
{
 return 0.5 * width * height;
}
void main()
{
Rectangle rectangleObject(10.0, 5.0);
Isosceles isoscelesObject(4.0, 6.0);
cout << "Rectangle: " << rectangleObject.area() <<
endl;
cout << "Triangle: " << isoscelesObject.area() <<
endl;
getch();
}
```

**OUTPUT:**

Rectangle: 50
Triangle: 12

**Problem 82. Write a C++ program for a simple class hierarchy.**

***Program:***

```
#include<iostream.h>
#include<conio.h>
#include <string.h>
class Shape
{
public:
double width;
double height;
void display()
{
cout << "Width and height are " << width << " and
" << height << "\n";
}
};
// Triangle is derived from Shape.
class Triangle : public Shape
{
public:
char style[20];
double area()
{
return width * height / 2;
}
void showStyle()
{
cout << "Triangle is " << style << "\n";
}
};
void main()
{
Triangle t1;
Triangle t2;
t1.width = 4.0;
t1.height = 4.0;
strcpy(t1.style, "isosceles");
t2.width = 8.0;
t2.height = 12.0;
strcpy(t2.style, "right");
t1.showStyle();
t1.display();
cout << "Area is " << t1.area() << "\n";
t2.showStyle();
t2.display();
cout << "Area is " << t2.area() << "\n";
getch();
}
```

**OUTPUT:**

Triangle is isosceles
Width and height are 4 and 4
Area is 8
Triangle is right
Width and height are 8 and 12
Area is 48

**Problem 83. Write a C++ program to display employee data to represent different class levels (class hierarchy).**

***Program:***

```
#include<iostream.h>
#include<conio.h>
class employee
{
private :
char name [80] ;
int id_no ;
public :
void readdata ( )
{
cout<<"Enter the Name" ;
cin>> name ;
cout<<"\n Enter the identification number"
cin>> id_no ;
}
void dispdata ( )
{
cout<<"\n NAME is :" <<name ;
```

```
cout <<"\n ID-NUMBER is :" << id_no ;
}
};
clerk : public employee
{
private :
int overtime ;
public :
void getdata ( )
{
employee : : readdata ( ) ;
cout<<"\n Enter the Number of overtime hrs
worked" ;
cin >>overtime ;
}
void display ( )
{
employee : : dispdata ( )
cout <<"\n OVERTIME WORKED :" << overtime ;
}
};
peon : public employee
{
private :
int job ;
public :
void getdata ( ) ;
vod dispdata ( ) ;
};
void peon : : getdata ( )
{
employee : : readdata ( ) ;
cout <<"\n Entre the number of hours when job
completed" ;
cin >> job ;
}
void peon : : dispdata ( )
{
employee : : dispdata ( ) ;
cout <<"\n JOB COMPLETED IN" << job ;
}
class manage : public employee
{
private :
char title ;
int salary ;
public :
void enterdata ( ) ;
void wirtedata ( ) ;
} ;
void manager ::  enterdata ( )
{
employee : : readdata ( ) ;
cout <<"\n Enter the title of the job and the salary"
;
cin>>title>>salary;
}
void manager : : writedata ( )
{
employee : : dispdata ( ) ;
cout<<"\n TITLE OF JOB is" << title ;
cout<<"\n SALARY is" << salary ;
}
void main ( )
{
manager         m1, m2 ;
clerk           c1 ;
peon            p1 ;
cout<<"\n Enter the Data for Ist Manager" ;
m1.enterdata ( ) ;
cout<<"\n Enter the Data for 2nd Manager" ;
m2.enterdata ( ) ;
cout<<"\n Enter the Data for Clerk" ;
c1.getdata ( ) ;
cout<<"\n Enter the Data for Peon" ;
p1.getdata ( ) ;
cout<<"\n DATA FOR IST MANAGER is" ;
m1.writedata ( ) ;
cout<<"\n DATA FOR 2nd MANAGER is" ;
m2.writedata ( ) ;
cout<<"\n DATA FOR CLERK is" ;
c1.display ( ) ;
cout<<"\n DATA FOR PEON is" ;
p1.dispdata ( ) ;
cout<<"\n End of the Program" ;
getch ( ) ;
}
```

**Problem 84. Write a C++ program for shadow base class function in its two children classes**

***Program:***

```
#include<iostream.h>
#include<conio.h>
#include <stdlib.h>
class BaseClass
{
public:
void f(float);
};
void BaseClass::f(float price)
{
cout << "the base class!\n";
```

```
cout << price * .075f;
}
class DerivedClass1:public BaseClass
{
public:
void f(float);
};
void DerivedClass1::f(float price)
{
cout << "the child class 1\n";
cout << price * .010f << endl;
}
class DerivedClass2:public BaseClass
{
public:
void f(float);
};
void DerivedClass2::f(float price)
{
cout << "the child class 2\n";
cout << price * .005f << endl;
}
void main()
{
DerivedClass1 myclass;
DerivedClass2 anotherclass;
myclass.f(100);
anotherclass.f(100);
getch();
}
```

**OUTPUT:**

```
the child class 1
1
the child class 2
0.5
```

**Problem 85. Write a C++ program to maintain student database by Hierarchical Inheritance.**

***Program:***

```
#include<iostream.h>
#include<conio.h>
#include<iomanip.h>
class A
{
char name[20],roll;
public:
void input()
{
cout<<"Enter name & roll number==>";
cin>>name>>roll;
}
void print()
{
cout<<setw(20)<<name<<"    "<<roll;
}
};
class B:A
{
int maths,che,phy;
public:
int total;
void input()
{
A::input();
cout<<"Enter marks in maths==>";
cin>>maths;
cout<<"Enter marks in chemistery==>";
cin>>che;
cout<<"Enter marks in physics==>";
cin>>phy;
total=maths+che+phy;
}
void print()
{
A::print();
cout<<setw(8)<<maths<<setw(8)<<che<<setw(8)
<<phy<<setw(8)<<total;
}
};
class C:A
{
int c,java,sql;
public:
int total;
void input()
{
A::input();
cout<<"Enter marks in C==>";
cin>>c;
cout<<"Enter marks in java==>";
cin>>java;
cout<<"Enter marks in SQL==>";
cin>>sql;
total=c+java+sql;
}
void print()
{
A::print();
cout<<setw(8)<<c<<setw(8)<<java<<setw(8)<<sq
l<<setw(8)<<total;
}
};
```

```
void main()
{
int com,med,i;
B b[50];
C c[50];
clrscr();
cout<<"Enter number of computer students==>";
cin>>com;
cout<<"Enter the information of computer
students==>\n";
for(i=0;i<com;i++)
c[i].input();
clrscr();
cout<<"Enter number of medical students==>";
cin>>med;
cout<<"Enter the information of medical
students==>\n";
for(i=0;i<med;i++)
b[i].input();
clrscr();
cout<<"The database of computer students
are==>\n";
cout<<setw(20)<<"Name"<<"
"<<"RollNo."<<setw(8)<<"c"<<setw(8)<<"java"<<
setw(8)<<"sql"<<setw(8)<<"total\n";
for(i=0;i<com;i++)
{
c[i].print();
cout<<endl;
}
cout<<"Press any key to display database of medical
students...";
getch();
clrscr();
cout<<"The database of medical students is==>\n";
cout<<setw(20)<<"Name"<<""<<"RollNo."<<setw(
8)<<"maths"<<setw(8)<<"che"<<setw(8)<<"phy"<
<setw(8)<<"total\n";
for(i=0;i<med;i++)
b[i].print();
getch();
}
```

**OUTPUT:**

```
Enter number of computer students==> 2
Enter number of computer students==>
Enter name & roll number==>Mona 11
Enter marks in C==> 40
Enter marks in java==>50
Enter marks in SQL==>60
Enter name & roll number==>Geeta 12
Enter marks in C==> 44
Enter marks in java==>55
Enter marks in SQL==>66

Enter number of medical students==> 2
Enter the information of medical students==>
Enter name & roll number==> Madhuri 999
Enter marks in maths==> 22
Enter marks in chemistery==>33
Enter marks in physics==>44
Enter name & roll number==> Madhu 998
Enter marks in maths==> 20
Enter marks in chemistery==>30
Enter marks in physics==>40

The database of computer students are==>
Name  Mona RollNo.  11   c  40  java  50   sql  60
total 150
Name  Geeta RollNo.  12  c  44  java  55  sql  66
total 165

Press any key to display database of medical
students...
The database of medical students is==>
Name Madhuri RollNo.  999 maths  22 che  33 phy
44  total 99
Name Madh      RollNo.  998 maths  20 che  30
phy  40  total 90
```

**Problem 86. Write a C++ program to Implement Hospital Management by 2 Classes with Inheritance.**

***Program:***

```
#include<iostream.h>
#include<conio.h>
class A
{
char name[20],doctor[20],dis[20];
public:
void input()
{
cout<<"Enter name of the patient==>";
cin>>name;
cout<<"Enter name of the doctor operating
patient==>";
cin>>doctor;
cout<<"Enter name of the disease patient is
suffering from==>";
cin>>dis;
}
void print()
{
```

```
cout<<"\nPatient's name is==>"<<name;
cout<<"\nDoctor operating "<<name<<" is
==>"<<doctor;
cout<<"\n"<<name<<" is suffering from==>"<<dis;
}
};
class B: A
{
char ward;
int room,bed,days,bill,fees;
public:
void input()
{
A::input();
cout<<"Is patient living in private room?(y/n)==>";
cin>>ward;
if(ward=='y')
{
cout<<"Enter room number==>";
cin>>room;
}
else
{
cout<<"Enter bed number==>";
cin>>bed;
}
cout<<"Enter number of days patient living in
hospital==>";
cin>>days;
cout<<"Enter the fees per day==>";
cin>>fees;
bill=fees* days;
}
void print()
{
A::print();
if(ward=='y')
cout<<"\nPatient is in private room
number==>"<<room;
else
cout<<"\nPatient is in public ward on bed
number==>"<<bed;
cout<<"\nHe is living in hospital for "<<days<<"
days";
cout<<"\nBill till date is==>"<<bill;
}
};
void main()
{
clrscr();
int n;
cout<<"Enter number of patients==>";
cin>>n;
B b[50];
cout<<"Enter the information==>\n";
for(int i=0;i<n;i++)
b[i].input();
clrscr();
cout<<"The database is==>\n";
for(i=0;i<n;i++)
b[i].print();
getch();
}
```

**OUTPUT:**

```
Enter number of patients==> 2
Enter the information==>
Enter name of the patient==> Sohan
Enter name of the doctor operating patient==> Dr.
Sanjeev
Enter name of the disease patient is suffering
from==> Cancer
Is patient living in private room?(y/n)==> y
Enter room number==> 21
Enter number of days patient living in hospital==>
5
Enter the fees per day==> 200
Enter name of the patient==> Mala
Enter name of the doctor operating patient==> Dr.
Geeta
Enter name of the disease patient is suffering
from==> Blood Sugar
Is patient living in private room?(y/n)==> y
Enter room number==> 35
Enter number of days patient living in hospital==>
10
Enter the fees per day==> 300
The database is==>
Patient's name is==> Sohan
Doctor operating  Sohan   is ==> Dr. Sanjeev
 Mohan  is suffering from==> Cancer
Patient is in private room number==> 21
He is living in hospital for 5 days
Bill till date is==> 1000
Patient's name is==> Mala
Doctor operating  Mala  is ==> Dr. Geeta
 Mohan  is suffering from==> Blood Sugar
Patient is in private room number==> 35
He is living in hospital for 10 days
Bill till date is==> 3000
```

**Problem 87. Write a C++ program to display the processing of the grade using the concept of inheritance.**

***Program:***

```
#include<iostream.h>
#include<conio.h>
class general
{
private:
char name[20];
int rollno;
char course[10];
public:
void getdata();
void showdata();
};
class marks : public general
{
private:
int phy;
int comp;
int math;
public:
void getdata();
void showdata();
};
class grade :public general
{
private:
int total;
char grade[2];
public :
void getdata();
void showdata();
};
void general :: getdata()
{
cout<<"ENTER THE NAME OF STUDENT:";
cin>>name;
cout<<"ENTER THE ROLLNO:-";
cin>>rollno;
cout<<"ENTER THE CLASS :-";
cin>>course;
}
void general::showdata()
{
cout<<name<<"   "<<rollno<<"      "<<course;
}
void marks::getdata()
{
general::getdata();
cout<<"\nENTER THE MARKS OF PHYSICS:-";
cin>>phy;
cout<<"\nENTER THE MARKS OF
COMPUTER:-";
cin>>comp;
cout<<"\nENTER THE MARKS OF MATHS:-";
cin>>math;
}
void marks::showdata()
{
general::showdata();
cout<<"   "<<phy<<"   "<<comp<<"   "<<math;
}
void grade::getdata()
{
general::getdata();
cout<<"ENTER THE TOTAL MARKS :-\n";
cin>>total;
cout<<"\nENTER THE GRADE     :-";
cin>>grade;
}
void grade::showdata()
{
general::showdata();
cout<<"   "<<total<<"   "<<grade;
}
void main()
{
clrscr();
marks ob1;
grade ob2;
cout<<"ENTER THE FOLLOWING INFO FOR
STUDENT WITH MARKS\n";
ob1.getdata();
cout<<"ENTER THE INFO WITH GRADE &
TOTAL MARKS:\n";
ob2.getdata();
cout<<"\nName Rollno Class Phy Comp
Maths\n";
ob1.showdata();
cout<<"\n\nName Rollno Class Totalmarks
Grade\n";
ob2.showdata();
getch();
}
```

**OUTPUT:**

```
ENTER THE FOLLOWING INFO FOR
STUDENT WITH MARKS
ENTER THE NAME OF STUDENT :
BALJINDER
ENTER THE ROLLNO:- 12
```

```
ENTER THE CLASS:- MCA
ENTER THE MARKS OF PHYSICS:-70
ENTER THE MARKS OF COMPUTER:-70
ENTER THE MARKS OF MATHS:-60
ENTER THE INFO WITH GRADE & TOTAL
MARKS:
ENTER THE NAME OF STUDENT: BALJINDER
ENTER THE ROLLNO:-12
ENTER THE CLASS:-MCA
ENTER THE TOTAL MARKS:-200
ENTER THE GRADE:-A
NAME        ROLLNO   CLASS   PHY
COMP      MATHS
BALJINDER  12          MCA     70        70
60
NAME        ROLLNO    CLASS
TOTALMARKS    GRADE
BALJINDER  12          MCA        200
A
```

# PRIVATE , PUBLIC AND PROTECTED INHERITANCE :

## PRIVATE INHERITANCE:

**Problem 88. Write a C++ program for class A .**

***Program:***

```
#include<iostream.h>
#include<conio.h>
class A
{
int i,j;
public:
void set(int a,int b)
{
i=a;
j=b;
}
void show()
{
cout <<i <<" "<<j <<"\n";
}
};
//Public elements of base are private in derived.
class B :private A
{
int k;
public:
B(int m)
{
k=m;
}
void show_k()
{
cout <<k <<"\n";
}
};
void main()
{
B b(4);
b.set(1,2);//error,can't access set()
b.show();//error,can't access show()
getch();
}
```

**OUTPUT:**

```
2 errors
A:: set(int,int) is not accessible
A::show() is not accessible
```

**Problem 89. Write a C++ program to inherit base as private.**

***Program:***

```
#include<iostream.h>
#include<conio.h>
class base
{
private:
int i;
public:
int j, k;
void seti(int x) { i = x; }
int geti() { return i; }
};
class derived: private base
{
public:
base::j;
base::seti;
base::geti;
int a;
};
void main()
{
derived ob;
ob.j = 20; // legal because j is made public in
derived
//ob.k = 30; // illegal because k is private in derived
ob.a = 40; // legal because a is public in derived
ob.seti(10);
cout << ob.geti() << " " << ob.j << " " << ob.a;
getch();
```

```
}
```

**OUTPUT:**

*10 20 40*

**Problem 90. Write a C++ program to access private data through accessor functions.**

***Program:***

```
#include<iostream.h>
#include<conio.h>
#include <string.h>
class Shape
{
// private
double width;
double height;
public:
void display()
{
cout << "Width and height are " << width << " and "
<< height << "\n";
}
// accessor functions
double getWidth() { return width; }
double getHeight() { return height; }
void setWidth(double w) { width = w; }
void setHeight(double h) { height = h; }
};
// Triangle is derived from Shape.
class Triangle : public Shape
{
public:
char style[20];
double area()
{
return getWidth() * getHeight() / 2;
}
void showStyle()
{
cout << "Triangle is " << style << "\n";
}
};
void main()
{
Triangle t1;
Triangle t2;
t1.setWidth(4.0);
t1.setHeight(4.0);
strcpy(t1.style, "isosceles");
t2.setWidth(8.0);
t2.setHeight(12.0);
strcpy(t2.style, "right");
t1.showStyle();
t1.display();
cout << "Area is " << t1.area() << "\n";
t2.showStyle();
t2.display();
cout << "Area is " << t2.area() << "\n";
getch();
}
```

**OUTPUT:**

Triangle is isosceles
Width and height are 4 and 4
Area is 8
Triangle is right
Width and height are 8 and 12
Area is 48

**Problem 91. Write a C++ program to inherit base as private.**

***Program:***

```
#include<iostream.h>
#include<conio.h>
class BaseClass
{
int x;
public:
void setx(int n)
{
x = n;
}
void showx()
{
cout << x << '\n';
}
};
// Inherit BaseClass as private.
class DerivedClass : private BaseClass
{
int y;
public:
void setxy(int n, int m)
{
setx(n);          // setx is accessible from within
DerivedClass
y = m;
}
void showxy()
{
showx();          // showx is accessible from within
DerivedClass
cout << y << '\n';
}
```

```
};
void main()
{
DerivedClass ob;
ob.setxy(10, 20);
ob.showxy();
getch();
}
```

**OUTPUT**:

10
20

**Problem 92. Write a C++ program to show private inheritance to find result.**

***Program:***

```
#include<iostream.h>
#include<conio.h>
class studb
{
private:
char nm[20];
int rno;
public:
void get()
{
cout<<"Enter rollno & name";
cin>>rno>>nm;
}
void put()
{
cout<<"\nRollno"<<rno;
cout<<"\nName"<<nm<<"\n";
}
};
class res:private studb
{
private:
int x[4];
double p;
public:
void take();
void func();
void display();
};
void res:: take()
{
void get();
cout<<"Enter marks:";
for(int i=0;i<4;i++)
cin>>x[i];
}
void res::func()
{
int tm=0;
for(int i=0;i<4;i++)
tm=tm+x[i];
p=double(tm)/4;
}
void res::display()
{
put();
cout<<"Marks:";
for(int i=0;i<4;i++)
cout<<x[i]<<'\t';
cout<<"\nPercentage="<<p;
}
void main()
{
res obj;
obj.take();
obj.func();
obj.display();
getch();
}
```

**Problem 93. Write a C++ program to implement inheritance using the private identifier.**

***Program:***

```
#include<iostream.h>
#include<conio.h>
class base
{
int a;
public:
void seta(int n)
{
a=n;
}
void showa()
{
cout<<a*a<<endl;
}
};
class derived:private base  //inherit base class
privately
{
int b;
public:
void setb(int n)
{
b=n;
```

```
}
void showb()
{
cout<<b*b<<endl;
}
};
void main()
{
clrscr();
derived d;
base b;
b.seta(4);
d.setb(5);
b.showa();
d.showb();
getch();
}
```

**OUTPUT:**

16
25

## PUBLIC INHERITANCE:

**Problem 94. Write a C++ program to demonstrate public inheritance.**

***Program:***

```
#include<iostream.h>
#include<conio.h>
class BaseClass
{
int i, j;
public:
void set(int a, int b)
{
i = a; j = b;
}
void show()
{
cout << i << " " << j << "\n";
}
};
class DerivedClass : public BaseClass
{
int k;
public:
DerivedClass(int x)
{
k = x;
}
void showDerivedClass()
{
cout << k << "\n";
}
// i = 10; // Error! i is private to BaseClass and
access is not allowed.
};
void main()
{
DerivedClass ob(3);
ob.set(1, 2); // access member of base class
ob.show();    // access member of base class
ob.showDerivedClass();   // uses member of
derived class
getch();
}
```

**OUTPUT:**

1 2
3

**Problem 95. Write a C++ program to inherited as public.**

***Program:***

```
#include<iostream.h>
#include<conio.h>
class base
{
protected:
int i, j;
public:
void set(int a, int b)
{
i=a;
j=b;
}
void show()
{
cout << i << " " << j << "\n";
}
};
class derived1 : public base
{
int k;
public:
void setk()
{
k = i*j;
}
void showk()
{
cout << k << "\n";
}
};
```

```
class derived2 : public derived1
{
int m;
public:
void setm()
{
m = i-j;
}
void showm()
{
cout << m << "\n";
}
};
void main()
{
derived1 ob1;
derived2 ob2;
ob1.set(2, 3);
ob1.show();
ob1.setk();
ob1.showk();
ob2.set(3, 4);
ob2.show();
ob2.setk();
ob2.setm();
ob2.showk();
ob2.showm();
getch();
}
```

**OUTPUT:**

```
2 3
6
3 4
12
-1
```

**Problem 96. Write a C++ program to show public inheritance.**

***Program:***

```
#include<iostream.h>
#include<conio.h>
class b
{
private:
int privb;
protected:
int protb;
public:
int getbp()
{
privb=55;
return(privb);
}
};
class d:public b
{
private:
int privd;
protected:
int protd;
public:
void fun()
{
int p;
p=getbp();
cout<<"Value of base's private data
member="<<p;
protb=66;
cout<<"Value of base's protected data
member="<<protb;
}
};
void main()
{
d t;
int q;
t.fun();
q=t.getbp();
cout<<"Value of base private data member
accessed indirectly="<<q;
getch();
}
```

**OUTPUT:**

```
Value of base's private data member=55
Value of base's protected data member=66
Value of base's private data member=55
```

**Problem 97. Write a C++ program to extend base class using public inheritance to find %age of marks.**

***Program:***

```
#include<iostream.h>
#include<conio.h>
class studb
{
private:
char nm[20];
int rno;
public:
void get()
{
cout<<"Enter rollno & name";
```

```
cin>>rno>>nm;
}
void put()
{
cout<<"\nRollno"<<rno;
cout<<"\nName"<<nm<<"\n";
}
};
class res:public studb
{
private:
int  x[4];
double p;
public:
void  getmarks();
void func();
void display();
};
void res:: getmarks()
{
cout<<"Enter marks";
for(int i=0;i<4;i++)
cin>>x[i];
}
void res::func()
{
int tm=0;
for(int i=0;i<4;i++)
tm=tm+x[i];
p=double(tm)/4;
}
void res::display()
{
cout<<"Displaying marks";
for(int i=0;i<4;i++)
cout<<x[i]<<'\t';
cout<<"\nPercentage"<<p;
}
void main()
{
res r1;
r1.get();
r1.getmarks();
r1.func();
r1.put();
r1.display();
getch();
}
```

**OUTPUT:**

```
Enter rollno & name 154 Sukhjot
Enter marks 12 45 65 23
Rollno 154
Name Sukhjot
Displaying marks 12 45 65 23
Percentage 36.25
```

**Problem 98. Write a C++ program to show public inheritance of class from both base classes.**

***Program:***

```
#include<iostream.h>
#include<conio.h>
class b1
{
protected:
int u;
public:
void getu()
{
cout<<"Enter u";
cin>>u;
}
void putu()
{
cout<<"u= "<<u;
}
};
class b2
{
protected:
int v;
public:
void getv()
{
cout<<"Enter v";
cin>>v;
}
void putv()
{
cout<<"\nv= "<<v;
}
};
class d:public b1,public b2
{
private:
int w;
public:
void add()
{
w=u+v;
}
void putw()
```

```
{
cout<<"\nw= "<<w;
}
};
void main()
{
d obj;
obj.getu();
obj.getv();
obj.add();
obj.putu();
obj.putv();
obj.putw();
getch();
}
```

**OUTPUT:**

```
Enter u:15
Enter v:25
u=15
v=25
w=40
```

**Problem 99. Write a C++ program for public inheritance.**

***Program:***

```
#include<iostream.h>
#include<conio.h>
class BaseClass
{
protected:
int i, j; // private to BaseClass, but accessible to
DerivedClass
public:
void set(int a, int b)
{
i = a;
j = b;
}
void show()
{
cout << i << " " << j << endl;
}
};
class DerivedClass : public BaseClass
{
int k;
public:
// DerivedClass may access BaseClass's i and j
void setk()
{
k = i*j;
}
void showk()
{
cout << k << endl;
}
};
void  main()
{
DerivedClass ob;
ob.set(2, 3); // known to DerivedClass
ob.show();    // known to DerivedClass

ob.setk();
ob.showk();
getch();
}
```

**OUTPUT:**

```
2 3
6
```

**Problem 101. Write a C++ program for three level public inheritance.**

***Program:***

```
#include<iostream.h>
#include<conio.h>
class BaseClass
{
protected:
int i, j;
public:
void set(int a, int b)
{
i = a;
j = b;
}
void show()
{
cout << i << " " << j << endl;
}
};
// i and j inherited as protected.
class DerivedClass1 : public BaseClass
{
int k;
public:
void setk()
{
k = i*j;
}
void showk()
{
```

```
cout << k << endl;
}
};
class DerivedClass2 : public DerivedClass1
{
int m;          // i and j inherited indirectly through
DerivedClass1.
public:
void setm()
{
m = i-j;
}
void showm()
{
cout << m << endl;
}
};
void  main()
{
DerivedClass1 object1;
DerivedClass2 object2;
object1.set(2, 3);
object1.show();
object1.setk();
object1.showk();
object2.set(3, 4);
object2.show();
object2.setk();
object2.setm();
object2.showk();
object2.showm();
getch();
}
```

**OUTPUT:**

```
2 3
6
3 4
12
-1
```

**Problem 102. Write a C++ program for Public and Private Inheritance.**

***Program:***

```
#include<iostream.h>
#include<conio.h>
class A //base class
{
private:
int privateA;
protected:
int protectA;
public:
int publicA;
};
class B :public A
{
public:
void fun()
{
int a;
a =privateA;//error:not accessible
a =protectA;//OK
a =publicA;//OK
}
};
class C :private A
{
public:
void funct()
{
int a;
a =privateA;//error:not accessible
a =protectA;//OK
a =publicA;//OK
}
};
void main()
{
int a;
B objB;
a =objB.privdateA;//error:not accessible
a =objB.protectA;//error:not accessible
a =objB.publicA;//OK (A public to B)
C objC;
a =objC.privateA;//error:not accessible
a =objC.protectA;//error:not accessible
a =objC.publicA;//error:not accessible (A private
to C)
getch();
}
```

**OUTPUT:**

Run program (7 errors)

## PROTECTED INHERITANCE:

**Problem 103. Write a C++ program to inherit base as protected.**

***Program:***

```
#include<iostream.h>
#include<conio.h>
class base
{
```

```
protected:
int i, j;
public:
void setij(int a, int b) { i=a; j=b; }
void showij() { cout << i << " " << j << "\n"; }
};
class derived : protected base
{
int k;
public:
void setk()
{
setij(10, 12);
k = i*j;
}
void showall()
{
cout << k << " ";
showij();
}
};
void main()
{
derived ob;
ob.setk();
ob.showall();
getch();
}
```

**OUTPUT:**

120 10 12

**Problem 104. Write a C++ program for inheritance for protected member .**

***Program:***

```
#include<iostream.h>
#include<conio.h>
class BaseClass
{
protected:
int i, j;
public:
void set(int a, int b)
{
i = a;
j = b;
}
void show()
{
cout << i << " " << j << endl;
}
};
// i and j inherited as protected.
class DerivedClass1 : public BaseClass
{
int k;
public:
void setk()
{
k = i * j;
}
void showk()
{
cout << k << endl;
}
};
// i and j inherited indirectly through
DerivedClass1.
class DerivedClass2 : public DerivedClass1
{
int m;
public:
void setm()
{
m = i - j;
}
void showm()
{
cout << m << endl;
}
};
void main()
{
DerivedClass1 object1;
DerivedClass2 object2;
object1.set(2, 3);
object1.show();
object1.setk();
object1.showk();
object2.set(3, 4);
object2.show();
object2.setk();
object2.setm();
object2.showk();
object2.showm();
getch();
}
```

**OUTPUT:**

2 3
6
3 4
12
-1

**Problem 105. Write a C++ program to Inherit base as protected.**

***Program:***

```
#include<iostream.h>
#include<conio.h>
class BaseClass
{
protected:
int i, j;            // private to BaseClass, but
accessible by DerivedClass
public:
void setij(int a, int b)
{
i = a;
j = b;
}
void showij()
{
cout << i << " " << j << endl;
}
};
class DerivedClass : protected BaseClass
{            // Inherit BaseClass as protected.
int k;
public:
void setk()
{
setij(10, 12);
k = i * j;
}
void showall()
{
cout << k << " ";
showij();
}
};
void  main()
{
DerivedClass ob;
ob.setk();              // public member of
DerivedClass
ob.showall();              // public member of
DerivedClass
getch();
}
```

**OUTPUT:**

120 10 12

**Problem 106. Write a C++ program to demonstrate protected members.**

***Program:***

```
#include<iostream.h>
#include<conio.h>
class BaseClass
{
protected:
int i, j;            // private to BaseClass, but
accessible to D
public:
void set(int a, int b)
{
i = a;
j = b;
}
void show()
{
cout << i << " " << j << endl;
}
};
class DerivedClass : public BaseClass
{
int k;
public:
void setk()
{        // DerivedClass may access BaseClass's i
and j
k = i * j;
}
void showk()
{
cout << k << endl;
}
};
void  main()
{
DerivedClass object;
object.set(2, 3);     // OK, set() is public in
BaseClass
object.show();       // OK, show is public
BaseClass
object.setk();
object.showk();
getch();
}
```

**OUTPUT:**

2 3
6

**Problem 107. Write a C++ program to inherit protected fields.**

***Program:***

```
#include<iostream.h>
#include<conio.h>
class MyType
{
protected:
float value;
public:
float remove(float);
float add(float);
void display();
MyType();
};
MyType::MyType()
{
value = 1000;
}
float MyType::remove(float amount)
{
value -= amount;
return value;
}
float MyType::add(float amount)
{
value += amount;
return value;
}
void MyType::display()
{
cout << "Your value is " << value << endl;
}
class DerivedType:public MyType
{
};
DerivedType myDerivedType;
void main()
{
float amount, value;
myDerivedType.display();
cout << endl;
cout << "Please enter the amount to add \n";
cin>> amount;
value = myDerivedType.add(amount);
cout << "New value is " << value << endl;
cout << endl;
cout << "Please enter the amount to remove \n";
cin >> amount;
value = myDerivedType.remove(amount);
cout << "New value is " << value << endl;
cout << endl;
getch();
}
```

**OUTPUT:**

```
Your value is 1000
Please enter the amount to add
123
New value is 1123
Please enter the amount to remove
123
New value is 1000
```

**Problem 108. Write a C++ program to demonstrate inheriting a protected base class.**

***Program:***

```
#include<iostream.h>
#include<conio.h>
class BaseClass
{
int i;
protected:
int j;
public:
int k;
void setInt(int a)
{
i = a;
}
int getInt()
{
return i;
}
};
class DerivedClass : protected BaseClass
{ // Inherit BaseClass as protected.
public:
void setj(int a)
{
j = a;
}
void setk(int a)
{
k = a;
}
int getj()
{
return j;
}
int getk()
{
return k;
}
};
void main()
```

```
{
DerivedClass ob;
ob.setk(10);
cout << ob.getk() << ' ';
ob.setj(12);
cout << ob.getj() << ' ';
getch();
}
```

**OUTPUT:**

10 12

**Problem 109. Write a C++ program for inheritance and protected Members.**

***Program:***

```
#include<iostream.h>
#include<conio.h>
class A
{
protected:
int i,j;//private to base,but accessible by derived
public:
void set(int a,int b)
{
i=a;
j=b;
}
void show()
{
cout <<i <<" "<<j <<"\n";
}
};
class B :public A
{
int k;
public:
//derived may access base's i and j
void set_k()
{
k=i*j;
}
void show_k()
{
cout <<k <<"\n";
}
};
void main()
{
B b;
b.set(2,3);//OK,known to derived
b.show();//OK,known to derived
b.set_k();
b.show_k();
getch();
}
```

**OUTPUT:**

2 3
6

**Problem 110. Write a C++ program for Protected Base-Class Inheritance.**

***Program:***

```
#include<iostream.h>
#include<conio.h>
class A
{
protected:
int i,j;//private to base,but accessible by derived
public:
void set_ij(int a,int b)
{
i=a;
j=b;
}
void show_ij()
{
cout <<i <<" "<<j <<"\n";
}
};
//Inherit base as protected.
class B :protected A
{
int k;
public:
//derived may access base's i and j and setij().
void set_k()
{
set_ij(10,12);
k =i*j;
}
//may access showij()here
void showall()
{
cout <<k <<" ";show_ij();
}
};
void main()
{
B b;
b.set_k();
b.showall();
getch();
}
```

**OUTPUT:**
120 10 12

**Problem 111. Write a C++ program for protected fields: private to base, but accessible by derived.**

***Program:***

```
#include<iostream.h>
#include<conio.h>
class base
{
protected:
int i, j; //protected fields: private to base, but
accessible by derived
public:
void set(int a, int b)
{
i=a;
j=b;
}
void show()
{
cout << i << " " << j << "\n";
}
};
class derived : public base
{
int k;
public:
void setk()
{
k=i*j;
}
void showk()
{
cout << k << "\n";
}
};
void main()
{
derived ob;
ob.set(2, 3);
ob.show();
ob.setk();
ob.showk();
getch();
}
```

**OUTPUT:**
2 3
6

**Problem 112. Write a C++ program to illustrate the single inheritance using the protected identifier.**

***Program:***

```
#include<iostream.h>
#include<conio.h>
class base
{
protected:
int x,y;
public:
void setxy(int a,int b)
{
x=a;
y=b;
}
};
class derived : public base //inherit base class
publically
{
int z;
public:
void setz(int c)
{
z=c;
}
void showxyz()
{
int s;
s=x+y+z;
cout<<"NO'S FROM THE BASE
CLASS:"<<x<<" "<<y<<endl;
cout<<"NO'S FROM THE DERIVED
CLASS:"<<z<<endl;
cout<<"SUM OF THREE NO'S: "<<s<<endl;
}
};
void main()
{
clrscr();
derived d;
d.setxy(2,5);
d.setz(2);
d.showxyz();
getch();
}
```

**OUTPUT:**
NO'S FROM THE BASE CLASS: 2 5
NO'S FROM THE DERIVED CLASS: 2
SUM OF THREE NO'S: 9

**Problem 113. Write a C++ program to illustrate the single inheritance using the protected identifier.**

***Program:***

```
#include<iostream.h>
#include<conio.h>
class base
{
protected:
int x,y;
public:
void setxy(int a,int b)
{
x=a;
y=b;
}
};
class derived : protected base  //inherit base class
protectedly
{
int z;
public:
void setz(int c)
{
z=c;
}
void showxyz()
{
int s;
base::setxy(2,5);
s=x+y+z;
cout<<"NO'S FROM THE BASE CLASS:"<<x<<"
"<<y<<endl;
cout<<"NO'S FROM THE DERIVED
CLASS:"<<z<<endl;
cout<<"SUM OF THREE NO'S: "<<s<<endl;
}
};
void main()
{
clrscr();
derived d;
d.setz(2);
d.showxyz();
getch();
}
```

**OUTPUT:**

NO'S FROM THE BASE CLASS: 2 5
NO'S FROM THE DERIVED CLASS: 2
SUM OF THREE NO'S: 9

# LEVEL OF INHERITANCE:

**Problem 114. Write a C++ program for Levels of Inheritance.**

***Program:***

```
#include<iostream.h>
#include<conio.h>
const int LEN =80;//maximum length of names
class employee
{
private:
char name [LEN ];
long number;
public:
void getdata()
{
cout <<"\n Last name:";
cin >>name;
cout <<" Number:";
cin >>number;
}
void putdata()
{
cout <<"\n Name:" <<name;
cout <<"\n Number:" <<number;
}
};
class manager :public employee
{
private:
char title [LEN ];
double dues;
public:
void getdata()
{
employee::getdata();
cout <<" Title:";
cin >>title;
cout <<" Cricket club dues::";
cin >>dues;
}
void putdata()
{
employee::putdata();
cout <<"\n Title:" <<title;
cout <<"\n Cricket club dues:" <<dues;
}
};
class professor :public employee
{
```

```
private:
int pubs;
public:
void getdata()
{
employee::getdata();
cout <<" Number of pubs:";
cin >>pubs;
}
void putdata()
{
employee::putdata();
cout <<"\n Number of publications:" <<pubs;
}
};
class laborer :public employee
{ };
class foreman :public laborer //foreman class
{
private:
float quotas;
public:
void getdata()
{
laborer::getdata();
cout <<" Quotas:";
cin >>quotas;
}
void putdata()
{
laborer::putdata();
cout <<"\n Quotas:" <<quotas;
}
};
void main()
{
laborer l1;
foreman f1;
cout <<endl;
cout <<"\nData for laborer 1: ";
l1.getdata();
cout <<"\nData for foreman 1: ";
f1.getdata();
cout <<endl;
cout <<"\nData of laborer 1: ";
l1.putdata();
cout <<"\nData of foreman 1: ";
f1.putdata();
cout <<endl;
getch();
}
```

**OUTPUT:**

```
Data for laborer 1:
Last name:harry
Number:4
Data for foreman 1:
Last name:marry
Number:3
Quotas:3
Data of laborer 1:
Last name:harry
Number:4
Data of foreman 1:
Last name:marry
Number:3
Quotas:3
```

**Problem 115. Write a C++ program for a multilevel hierarchy.**

***Program:***

```
#include<iostream.h>
#include<conio.h>
#include <string.h>
class Shape
{
// private
double width;
double height;
public:
Shape()
{
width = height = 0.0;
}
Shape(double w, double h)
{
width = w;
height = h;
}
Shape(double x)
{
width = height = x;
}
void display()
{
cout << "Width and height are " << width << " and
" << height << "\n";
}
double getWidth() { return width; }
double getHeight() { return height; }
void setWidth(double w) { width = w; }
void setHeight(double h) { height = h; }
};
```

```
class Triangle : public Shape
{
char style[20];
public:
// This automatically invokes the default constructor
of Shape.
Triangle()
{
strcpy(style, "unknown");
}
Triangle(char *str, double w, double h) : Shape(w,
h)
{
strcpy(style, str);
}
Triangle(double x) : Shape(x)
{
strcpy(style, "isosceles");
}
double area()
{
return getWidth() * getHeight() / 2;
}
void showStyle()
{
cout << "Triangle is " << style << "\n";
}
};
class NameTriangle : public Triangle
{
char name[20];
public:
NameTriangle(char *clr, char *style, double w,
double h) : Triangle(style, w, h)
{
strcpy(name, clr);
}
void displayName()
{
cout << "Name is " << name << "\n";
}
};
void main()
{
NameTriangle t1("A", "right", 8.0, 12.0);
NameTriangle t2("B", "isosceles", 2.0, 2.0);
t1.showStyle();
t1.display();
t1.displayName();
cout << "Area is " << t1.area() << "\n";
t2.showStyle();
t2.display();
t2.displayName();
cout << "Area is " << t2.area() << "\n";
getch();
}
```

**OUTPUT:**

```
Triangle is right
Width and height are 8 and 12
Name is A
Area is 48
Triangle is isosceles
Width and height are 2 and 2
Name is B
Area is 2
```

**Problem 116. Write a C++ program for three level inheritance.**

***Program:***

```
#include<iostream.h>
#include<conio.h>
class base
{
public:
base()
{
cout << "Constructing base\n";
}
~base()
{
cout << "Destructing base\n";
}
};
class derived1 : public base
{
public:
derived1()
{
cout << "Constructing derived1\n";
}
~derived1()
{
cout << "Destructing derived1\n";
}
};
class derived2: public derived1
{
public:
derived2()
{
cout << "Constructing derived2\n";
}
```

```
~derived2()
{
cout << "Destructing derived2\n";
}
};
void main()
{
derived2 ob;
getch();
}
```

**OUTPUT:**

Constructing base
Constructing derived1
Constructing derived2
Destructing derived2
Destructing derived1
Destructing base

**Problem 117. Write a C++ program to process student data to describe level of inheritance.**

***Program:***

```
#include<iostream.h>
#include<conio.h>
class student
{
private :
int rn ;
char name [20] ;
char address [30] ;
public :
void readdata ( )
{
cout << "\n Enter RollNo, Name and Address" ;
cin >> rn >> name >> address ;
}
void writedata ( )
{
cout <<"n Roll No is"<< rn ;
cout <<"n NAME is" << name ;
cout <<"n Address is "<< address ;
}
} ;
class body : public student
{
private :
int ht ;
int wt ;
public :
void getdata ( )
{
student : : readdata ( ) ;
cont <<"\n Enter the height and weight of student"
;
cin >> wt >> ht ;
}
void dispdata ( )
{
student :: writedata ( ) ;
cout <<"\n Height is" <<ht ;
cout<<"\n Weight is" << wt ;
}
} ;
class dmc : public body
{
private :
int p ;
int r ;
public :
void get ( )
{
body : : getdata ( ) ;
cout<<"\n Enter the percentage and result of the
student" ;
cin >> p >> r ;
}
void display ( )
{
body : : dispdata ( );
cout <<"\n Percentage is" << p ;
cout <<"\n Result is" << r ;
}
} ;
void main ( )
{
class dmc d ;
cout <<"\n Enter the student information" ;
d.get ( ) ;
cout <<"/n Information is" ;
d.display ( ) ;
getch ( ) ;
}
```

**Problem 118. Write a C++ program to handle student data to handle Multilevel Inheritance.**

***Program:***

```
#include<iostream.h>
#include<conio.h>
class A
{
char name[20];
public:
void input()
```

```
{
cout<<"Enter name==>";
cin>>name;
}
void print()
{
cout<<"Name is "<<name<<endl;
}
};
class B : A
{
int roll;
public:
void getdata()
{
A::input();
cout<<"Enter roll number==>";
cin>>roll;
}
void putdata()
{
A::print();
cout<<"\n\n\n";
cout<<"Roll number is "<<roll<<endl;
}
};
class C : private B
{
int marks;
public:
void input()
{
getdata();
cout<<"Enter marks==>";
cin>>marks;
}
void print()
{
putdata();
cout <<"Marks obtained are "<<marks<<endl;
}
};
void main()
{
clrscr();
C c;
c.input();
c.print();
getch();
}
```

**OUTPUT:**

```
Enter name==>Deepak
Enter roll number==>111
Enter marks==>88
Name is Deepak
Roll number is 111
Marks obtained are 88
```

## VIRTUAL INHERITANCE:

**Problem 119. Write a C++ program using virtual base classes.**

***Program:***

```
#include<iostream.h>
#include<conio.h>
class Base
{
public:
virtual void print() const = 0; // pure virtual
};
class Derived1 : virtual public Base
{
public:
void print() const
{
cout << "Derived1\n";
}
};
class Derived2 : virtual public Base
{
public:
void print() const
{
cout << "Derived2\n";
}
};
class Multiple : public Derived1, public Derived2
{
public:
void print() const
{
Derived2::print();
}
};
void main()
{
Multiple both;
Derived1 one;
Derived2 two;
Base *array[ 3 ];
array[ 0 ] = &both;
```

```
array[ 1 ] = &one;
array[ 2 ] = &two;
for ( int i = 0; i < 3; i++ )
array[ i ]->print();
getch();
}
```

**OUTPUT:**

Derived2
Derived1
Derived2

**Problem 120. Write a C++ program to implement Hospital Management by 2 Classes with Common Friend Function.**

***Program:***

```
#include<iostream.h>
#include<conio.h>
class A
{
char name[20],doctor[20],dis[20];
void input()
{
cout<<"Enter name of the patient==>";
cin>>name;
cout<<"Enter name of the doctor operating
patient==>";
cin>>doctor;
cout<<"Enter name of the disease patient is
suffering from==>";
cin>>dis;
}
void print()
{
cout<<"\nPatient's name is==>"<<name;
cout<<"\nDoctor operating "<<name<<" is
==>"<<doctor;
cout<<"\n"<<name<<" is suffering from==>"<<dis;
}
friend void input(int);
friend void output(int);
}a[50];
class B
{
char ward;
int room,bed,days,bill,fees;
void input()
{
cout<<"Is patient living in private room?(y/n)==>";
cin>>ward;
if(ward=='y')
{
cout<<"Enter room number==>";
cin>>room;
}
else
{
cout<<"Enter bed number==>";
cin>>bed;
}
cout<<"Enter number of days patient living in
hospital==>";
cin>>days;
cout<<"Enter the fees per day==>";
cin>>fees;
bill=fees* days;
}
void print()
{
if(ward=='y')
cout<<"\nPatient is in private room
number==>"<<room;
else
cout<<"\nPatient is in public ward on bed
number==>"<<bed;
cout<<"\nHe is living in hospital for "<<days<<"
days";
cout<<"\nBill till date is==>"<<bill;
}
friend void input(int);
friend void output(int);
}b[50];
void main()
{
clrscr();
int n;
cout<<"Enter number of patients==>";
cin>>n;
cout<<"Enter the information==>\n";
input(n);
clrscr();
cout<<"The database is==>\n";
output(n);
getch();
}
void input(int n)
{
for(int i=0;i<n;i++)
{
cout<<"\n Enter information of patient
"<<i+1<<".==>\n";
a[i].input();
b[i].input();
```

```
}
}
void output(int n)
{
for(int i=0;i<n;i++)
{
cout<<"\n\n The information of patient "<<i+1<<"
is==>\n";
a[i].print();
b[i].print();
}
}
```

**OUTPUT:**

```
Enter number of patients==>2
Enter the information==>
Enter information of patient 1==>
Enter name of the patient==> Heer
Enter name of the doctor operating patient==>Dr.
Gagan
Enter name of the disease patient is suffering
from==> Cold
Is patient living in private room?(y/n)==>"y
Enter room number==>22
Enter number of days patient living in hospital==>4
Enter the fees per day==>500
Enter information of patient 2==>
Enter name of the patient==> Himmat
Enter name of the doctor operating patient==>Dr.
Homi
Enter name of the disease patient is suffering
from==> BP
Is patient living in private room?(y/n)==>"y
Enter room number==>24
Enter number of days patient living in hospital==>6
Enter the fees per day==>500
The database is==>
The information of patient 1 is==>
Patient's name is==>Heer
Doctor operating Heer    is ==>Dr. Gagan
Heer is suffering from==> Cold
Patient is in private room number==>22
He is living in hospital for  4  days
Bill till date is==>2000
The information of patient 2 is==>
Patient's name is==>Himmat
Doctor operating Heer    is ==>Dr. Homi
Heer is suffering from==> Bp
Patient is in private room number==>24
He is living in hospital for  6  days
Bill till date is==>3000
```

# CHAPTER 14

# POLYMORPHISM AND VIRTUAL FUNCTION

## THIS POINTER:

**Problem 1. Write a C++ program using the 'this' pointer.**

***Program:***

```
#include <iostream.h>
#include<conio.h>
class MyClass
{
int i;
public:
void setI(int val)
{
this->i = val;
}
int getI()
{
return this->i;
}
} ;
void main()
{
MyClass o;
o.setI(100);
cout << o.getI();
getch();
}
```

**OUTPUT:**

100

**Problem 2. Write a C++ program using the this pointer for class rectangle.**

***Program:***

```
#include <iostream.h>
#include<conio.h>
class Rectangle
{
public:
Rectangle();
~Rectangle();
void SetLength(int length) { this->itsLength =
length; }
int GetLength() const { return this->itsLength; }
void SetWidth(int width) { itsWidth = width; }
int GetWidth() const { return itsWidth; }
private:
int itsLength;
int itsWidth;
};
Rectangle::Rectangle()
{
itsWidth = 5;
itsLength = 10;
}
Rectangle::~Rectangle()
{}
void main()
{
Rectangle theRect;
cout << "theRect is " << theRect.GetLength()<< "
feet long.\n";
cout << "theRect is " << theRect.GetWidth()<< "
feet wide.\n";
theRect.SetLength(20);
theRect.SetWidth(10);
cout << "theRect is " << theRect.GetLength()<< "
feet long.\n";
cout << "theRect is " << theRect.GetWidth()<< "
feet wide.\n";
getch();
}
```

**OUTPUT:**

theRect is 10 feet long.
theRect is 5 feet wide.
theRect is 20 feet long.
theRect is 10 feet wide.

**Problem 3. Write a C++ program to access data members using 'this' pointer.**

***Program:***

```
#include<iostream.h>
```

```
#include<conio.h>
class rec
{
private:
int l;
int b;
public:
void ds(int x,int y)
{
cout<<"Address of object that generates ds()
call="<<this<<endl;
this->l=x;
this->b=y;
}
void ar()
{
cout<<"Address of object that generates ar()
call="<<this<<endl;
cout<<"Area is: "<<this->l*this->b;
}
};
void main()
{
rec obj;
obj.ds(20,10);
obj.ar();
getch();
}
```

**OUTPUT:**

Address of object that generates ds() call=0x8fc0fff2
Address of object that generates ar() call=0x8fc0fff2
Area is:200

**Problem 4. Write a C++ program for returning the dereferenced this pointer.**

***Program:***

```
#include <iostream.h>
#include<conio.h>
class MyType
{
public:
MyType();
~MyType(){}
int getValue()const
{
return myValue;
}
void setValue(int x)
{
myValue = x;
}
const MyType& operator++ ();      // prefix
const MyType operator++ (int);   // postfix
private:
int myValue;
 };
MyType::MyType(): myValue(0) {}
const MyType& MyType::operator++()
{
++myValue;
return *this;
}
const MyType MyType::operator++(int)
{
MyType temp(*this);
++myValue;
return temp;
}
void main()
{
MyType i;
cout << "The value of i is " << i.getValue() <<
endl;
i++;
cout << "The value of i is " << i.getValue() <<
endl;
++i;
cout << "The value of i is " << i.getValue() <<
endl;
MyType a = ++i;
cout << "The value of a: " << a.getValue();
cout << " and i: " << i.getValue() <<endl;
a = i++;
cout << "The value of a: " << a.getValue();
cout << " and i: " << i.getValue() << endl;
getch();
 }
```

**OUTPUT:**

The value of i is 0
The value of i is 1
The value of i is 2
The value of a: 3 and i: 3
The value of a: 3 and i: 4

**Problem 5. Write a C++ program to cascading member function calls with the this pointer.**

***Program:***

```
#include <iomanip.h>
#include <iostream.h>
#include<conio.h>
class Time
{
```

```
public:
Time( int = 0, int = 0, int = 0 );
Time &setTime( int, int, int );
Time &setHour( int );
Time &setMinute( int );
Time &setSecond( int );
int getHour() const;
int getMinute() const;
int getSecond() const;
void printUniversal() const;
private:
int hour;
int minute;
int second;
};
Time::Time( int hr, int min, int sec )
{
setTime( hr, min, sec );
}
Time &Time::setTime( int h, int m, int s )
{
setHour( h );
setMinute( m );
setSecond( s );
return *this;
}
Time &Time::setHour( int h )
{
hour = h;
return *this;
}
Time &Time::setMinute( int m )
{
minute = m;
return *this;
}
Time &Time::setSecond( int s )
{
second = s;
return *this;
}
int Time::getHour() const
{
return hour;
}
int Time::getMinute() const
{
return minute;
}
int Time::getSecond() const
{
return second;
}
void Time::printUniversal() const
{
cout << hour << ":" << minute << ":" << second;
}
void main()
{
Time t;
t.setHour( 18 ).setMinute( 30 ).setSecond( 22 );
t.printUniversal();
t.setTime( 20, 20, 20 ).printUniversal();
cout << endl;
getch();
}
```

**OUTPUT:**

18:30:2220:20:20

**Problem 6. Write a C++ program for pointers to base class.**

***Program:***

```
#include <iostream.h>
#include<conio.h>
class CPolygon
{
protected:
int width, height;
public:
void set_values (int a, int b)
{
width=a;
height=b;
}
};
class CRectangle: public CPolygon
{
public:
int area()
{
return (width * height);
}
};
class CTriangle: public CPolygon
{
public:
int area ()
{
return (width * height / 2);
}
};
void main ()
```

```
{
CRectangle rect;
CTriangle trgl;
CPolygon * ppoly1 = &rect;
CPolygon * ppoly2 = &trgl;
ppoly1->set_values (4,5);
ppoly2->set_values (4,5);
cout << rect.area() << endl;
cout << trgl.area() << endl;
getch();
}
```

**OUTPUT:**

20
10

**Problem 7. Write a C++ program for pointer to derived objects.**

***Program:***

```
#include <iostream.h>
#include <string.h>
#include<conio.h>
class A
{
char author[80];
public:
void put_a(char *s)
{
strcpy(author, s);
}
void show_a()
{
cout << author << "\n";
}
} ;
class B : public A
{
char title[80];
public:
void put_t(char *num)
{
strcpy(title, num);
}
void show_t()
{
cout << "Title: ";
cout << title << "\n";
}
};
void main()
{
A *ptr;
A a;
B *bptr;
B b;
ptr = &a;
ptr->put_a("IkvinderPal Singh ");
ptr = &b;
ptr->put_a("Prof.Rachhpal Singh ");
a.show_a();
b.show_a();
cout << "\n";
bptr = &b;
bptr->put_t("Exploring Vista");
ptr->show_a();
bptr->show_t( );
getch();
}
```

**OUTPUT:**

IkvinderPal Singh
Prof.Rachhpal Singh

Prof.Rachhpal Singh
Title:Exploring Vista

**Problem 8. Write a C++ program for virtual member functions accessed with Pointers.**

***Program:***

```
#include <iostream.h>
#include<conio.h>
class Base
{
public:
virtual void show()
{
cout <<"Base \n ";
}
};
class Derv1 :public Base
{
public:
void show()
{
cout <<"Derv1 \n ";
}
};
class Derv2 :public Base
{
public:
void show()
{
cout <<"Derv2 \n ";
}
```

```
};
void main()
{
Derv1 d1;
Derv2 d2;
Base *ptr;//pointer to base class
ptr =&d1;//put address of dv1 in pointer
ptr->show();//execute show()
ptr =&d2;//put address of dv2 in pointer
ptr->show();//execute show()
getch();
}
```

**OUTPUT:**

Derv1
Derv2

## VIRTUAL FUNCTION, METHODS, HIERARCHIAL, INHERITANCE:

**Problem 9. Write a C++ program for Virtual Functions.**

***Program:***

```
#include <iostream.h>
#include<conio.h>
class A
{
public:
virtual void func()
{
cout <<"Base class(A) virtual func().\n";
}
};
class B :public A
{
public:
void func()
{
cout <<"Derived class(B) func().\n";
}
};
class C :public A
{
public:
void func()
{
cout <<"Derived class(C) func().\n";
}
};
void main()
{
A *ptr,b;
B b1;
C c1;
//point to base
ptr =&b;
ptr->func();
ptr =&b1;
ptr->func();
ptr =&c1;
ptr->func();
getch();
}
```

**OUTPUT:**

Base class(A) virtual func().
Derived class(B) func().
Derived class(C) func().

**Problem 10. Write a C++ program to calling a virtual function through a base class reference.**

***Program:***

```
#Include <iostream.h>
#include<conio.h>
class A
{
public:
virtual void func()
{
cout <<"Base class(A) virtual func().\n";
}
};
class B :public A
{
public:
void func()
{
cout <<"Derived class(B) func().\n";
}
};
class C :public A
{
public:
void func()
{
cout <<"Derived class(C) func().\n";
}
};
void d(A &r)
{
r.func();
}
```

```
void main()
{
A a;
B b1;
C c1;
d(a);
d(b1);
d(c1);
getch();
}
```

**OUTPUT:**

Base class(A) virtual func().
Derived class(B) func().
Derived class(C) func().

**Problem 11. Write a C++ program for Virtual Destructors.**

***Program:***

```
#include <iostream.h>
#include<conio.h>
class Base
{
public:
~Base()
{
cout <<"Base destroyed \n ";
}
};
class Derv :public Base
{
public:
~Derv()
{
cout <<"Derv destroyed \n ";
}
};
void main()
{
Base *ptr =new Derv;
delete ptr;
getch();
}
```

**OUTPUT:**

Base destroyed

**Problem 12. Write a C++ program for Virtual Attribute Is Inherited.**

***Program:***

```
#include <iostream.h>
#include<conio.h>
class A
{
public:
virtual void func()
{
cout <<"Base class(A) virtual func().\n";
}
};
class B :public A
{
public:
void func()
{
cout <<"Derived class(B) func().\n";
}
};
class C :public B
{
public:
void func()
{
cout <<"Derived class(C) func().\n";
}
};
void main()
{
A *ptr,a;
B b1;
C c1;
ptr =&a;
ptr->func();
ptr =&b1;
ptr->func();
ptr =&c1;
ptr->func();
getch();
}
```

**OUTPUT:**

Base class(A) virtual func().
Derived class(B) func().
Derived class(C) func().

**Problem 13. Write a C++ program for virtual functions Are Hierarchical.**

***Program:***

```
#include <iostream.h>
#include<conio.h>
class A
{
public:
virtual void func()
{
```

```
cout <<"Base class(A) virtual func().\n";
}
};
class B :public A
{
public:
void func()
{
cout <<"Derived class(B) func().\n";
}
};
class C :public A
{
public:
};
void main()
{
A *ptr,a;
B b1;
C c1;
ptr =&a;
ptr >func();
ptr =&b1;
ptr->func();
ptr =&c1;
ptr->func();
getch();
}
```

**OUTPUT:**

```
Base class(A) virtual func().
Derived class(B) func().
Base class(A) virtual func().
```

**Problem 14. Write a C++ program for virtual members.**

***Program:***

```
#include <iostream.h>
#include<conio.h>
class CPolygon
{
protected:
int width, height;
public:
void set_values (int a, int b)
{
width=a;
height=b;
}
virtual int area ()
{
return (0);
}
};
class CRectangle: public CPolygon
{
public:
int area ()
{
return (width * height);
}
};
class CTriangle: public CPolygon
{
public:
int area ()
{
return (width * height / 2);
}
};
void main ()
{
CRectangle rect;
CTrIangle trgl;
CPolygon poly;
CPolygon * ppoly1 = &rect;
CPolygon * ppoly2 = &trgl;
CPolygon * ppoly3 = &poly;
ppoly1->set_values (4,5);
ppoly2->set_values (4,5);
ppoly3->set_values (4,5);
cout << ppoly1->area() << endl;
cout << ppoly2->area() << endl;
cout << ppoly3->area() << endl;
getch();
}
```

**OUTPUT:**

```
20
10
0
```

**Problem 15. Write a C++ program for Virtual functions and polymorphism.**

***Program:***

```
#include <iostream.h>
#include<conio.h>
class figure
{
protected:
double x, y;
public:
void set_dim(double i, double j=0)
{
```

```
x = i;
y = j;
}
virtual void show_area()
{
cout << "No area computation defined ";
cout << "for this class.\n";
}
} ;
class triangle : public figure
{
public:
void show_area()
{
cout << "Triangle with height ";
cout << x << " and base " << y;
cout << " has an area of ";
cout << x * 0.5 * y << ".\n";
}
};
class square : public figure
{
public:
void show_area()
{
cout << "Square with dimensions ";
cout << x << "x" << y;
cout << " has an area of ";
cout << x *  y << ".\n";
}
};
class circle : public figure
{
public:
void show_area()
{
cout << "Circle with radius ";
cout << x;
cout << " has an area of ";
cout << 3.14 * x * x << ".\n";
}
} ;
void main()
{
 figure *p; // create a pointer to base type
 triangle t; // create objects of derived types
 square s;
 circle c;
 p = &t;
 p->set_dim(10.0, 5.0);
 p->show_area();
 p = &s;
 p->set_dim(10.0, 5.0);
 p->show_area();
 p = &c;
 p->set_dim(9.0);
 p->show_area();
 getch();
}
```

**OUTPUT:**

Triangle with height 10 and base 5 has an area of 25.
Square with dimensions 10x5 has an area of 50.
Circle with radius 9 has an area of 254.34.

**Problem 16. Write a C++ program to demonstrate virtual functons: list interface.**

***Program:***

```
#include <iostream.h>
#include<conio.h>
#include <stdlib.h>
#include <ctype.h>
class list
{
public:
list *head;           // pointer to start of list
list *tail;           // pointer to end of list
list *next;           // pointer to next item
int num;              // value to be stored
list()
{
head = tail = next = NULL;
}
virtual void store(int i) = 0;
virtual int retrieve() = 0;
};
class queue : public list
{
public:
void store(int i);
int retrieve();
};
void queue::store(int i)
{
 list *item;
 item = new queue;
 if(!item)
{
cout << "Allocation error.\n";
exit(1);
}
item->num = i;
```

```
if(tail)
tail->next = item;
tail = item;
item->next = NULL;
if(!head)
head = tail;
}
int queue::retrieve()
{
int i;
list *p;
if(!head)
{
cout << "List empty.\n";
return 0;
}
// remove from start of list
i = head->num;
p = head;
head = head->next;
delete p;
return i;
}
class stack : public list
{
public:
void store(int i);
int retrieve();
};
void stack::store(int i)
{
list *item;
item = new stack;
if(!item)
{
cout << "Allocation error.\n";
exit(1);
}
item->num = i;
if(head)
item->next = head;
head = item;
if(!tail)
tail = head;
}
int stack::retrieve()
{
int i;
list *p;
if(!head)
{
cout << "List empty.\n";
return 0;
}
// remove from start of list
i = head->num;
p = head;
head = head->next;
delete p;
return i;
}
void main()
{
list *p;
// demonstrate queue
queue q_ob;
p = &q_ob; // point to queue
p->store(1);
p->store(2);
p->store(3);
cout << "Queue: ";
cout << p->retrieve();
cout << p->retrieve();
cout << p->retrieve();
cout << '\n';
// demonstrate stack
stack s_ob;
p = &s_ob; // point to stack
p->store(1);
p->store(2);
p->store(3);
cout << "Stack: ";
cout << p->retrieve();
cout << p->retrieve();
cout << p->retrieve();
cout << '\n';
getch();
}
```

**OUTPUT:**

```
Queue: 123
Stack: 321
```

**Problem 17. Write a C++ program using virtual function to define inheritance.**

***Program:***

```
#include <iostream.h>
#include<conio.h>
class area
{
double dim1, dim2;
public:
void setarea(double d1, double d2)
```

```
{
dim1 = d1;
dim2 = d2;
}
void getdim(double &d1, double &d2)
{
d1 = dim1;
d2 = dim2;
}
virtual double getarea()
{
cout << "You must override this function\n";
return 0.0;
}
};
class rectangle : public area
{
public:
double getarea()
{
double d1, d2;
getdim(d1, d2);
return d1 * d2;
}
};
class triangle : public area
{
public:
double getarea()
{
double d1, d2;
getdim(d1, d2);
return 0.5 * d1 * d2;
}
};
void  main()
{
area *p;
rectangle r;
triangle t;
r.setarea(3.3, 4.5);
t.setarea(4.0, 5.0);
p = &r;
cout << "Rectangle has area: " << p->getarea() <<
'\n';
p = &t;
cout << "Triangle has area: " << p->getarea() << '\n';
getch();
}
```

**OUTPUT:**

Rectangle has area: 14.85

Triangle has area: 10

**Problem 18. Write a C++ program for a virtual function.**

***Program:***

```
#include <iostream.h>
#include<conio.h>
class BaseClass
{
public:
virtual void who() { // specify a virtual function
cout << "Base\n";
}
};
class DerivedClass1 : public BaseClass
{
public:
void who() { // redefine who() for DerivedClass1
cout << "First derivation\n";
}
};
class DerivedClass2 : public BaseClass
{
public:
void who() { // redefine who() for DerivedClass2
cout << "Second derivation\n";
}
};
void main()
{
BaseClass base_obj;
BaseClass *p;
DerivedClass1 DerivedClass1_obj;
DerivedClass2 DerivedClass2_obj;
p = &base_obj;
p->who();  // access BaseClass's who
p = &DerivedClass1_obj;
p->who(); // access DerivedClass1's who
p = &DerivedClass2_obj;
p->who();  // access DerivedClass2's who
getch();
}
```

**OUTPUT:**

Base
First derivation
Second derivation

**Problem 19. Write a C++ program for Access base class's virtual if derived class does not redefine it.**

***Program:***

```
#include <iostream.h>
#include<conio.h>
class BaseClass
{
public:
virtual void who()
{
cout << "Base\n";
}
};
class DerivedClass1 : public BaseClass
{
public:
void who()
{
cout << "First derivation\n";
}
};
class DerivedClass2 : public BaseClass
{
// who() not defined
};
void main()
{
BaseClass base_obj;
BaseClass *p;
DerivedClass1 DerivedClass1_obj;
DerivedClass2 DerivedClass2_obj;
p = &base_obj;
p->who(); // access BaseClass's who()
p = &DerivedClass1_obj;
p->who(); // access DerivedClass1's who()
p = &DerivedClass2_obj;
p->who();
getch();
}
```

**OUTPUT:**

```
Base
First derivation
Base
```

**Problem 21. Write a C++ program for Virtual functions: inheritance class.**

***Program:***

```
#include <iostream.h>
#include<conio.h>
#include <stdlib.h>
class list
{
public:
list *head; // pointer to next item in list
list *tail;
list *next;
int num;    // value to be stored
list()
{
head = tail = next = NULL;
}
virtual void store(int i) = 0;
virtual int retrieve() = 0;
};
class queue : public list
{
public:
void store(int i);
int retrieve();
};
void queue::store(int i)
{
list *item;
item = new queue;
if(!item)
{
cout << "Allocation error.\n";
exit(1);
}
item->num = i;
// put on end of list
if(tail)
tail->next = item;
tail = item;
item->next = NULL;
if(!head)
head = tail;
}
int queue::retrieve()
{
int i;
list *p;
if(!head)
{
cout << "List empty.\n";
return 0;
}
i = head->num;
p = head;
head = head->next;
delete p;
return i;
}
class stack : public list
{
```

```
public:
void store(int i);
int retrieve();
};
void stack::store(int i)
{
list *item;
item = new stack;
if(!item)
{
cout << "Allocation error.\n";
exit(1);
}
item->num = i;
// put on front of list for stack-like operation
if(head)
item->next = head;
head = item;
if(!tail)
tail = head;
}
int stack::retrieve()
{
int i;
list *p;
if(!head)
{
cout << "List empty.\n";
return 0;
}
// remove from start of list
i = head->num;
p = head;
head = head->next;
delete p;
return i;
}
class sorted : public list
{
public:
void store(int i);
int retrieve();
};
void sorted::store(int i)
{
list *item;
list *p, *p2;
item = new sorted;
if(!item)
{
cout << "Allocation error.\n";
exit(1);
}
item->num = i;
// find where to put next item
p = head;
p2 = NULL;
while(p) { // goes in middle
if(p->num > i)
{
item->next = p;
if(p2) p2->next = item; // not 1st element
if(p==head) head = item; // new 1st element
break;
}
p2 = p;
p = p->next;
}
if(!p) { // goes on end
if(tail) tail->next = item;
tail = item;
item->next = NULL;
}
if(!head) // is first element
head = item;
}
int sorted::retrieve()
{
int i;
list *p;
if(!head)
{
cout << "List empty.\n";
return 0;
}
// remove from start of list
i = head->num;
p = head;
head = head->next;
delete p;
return i;
}
void  main()
{
list *p;
queue q_ob;
p = &q_ob; // point to queue
p->store(1);
p->store(2);
p->store(3);
cout << "Queue: ";
cout << p->retrieve();
```

```
cout << p->retrieve();
cout << p->retrieve();
cout << '\n';
stack s_ob;
p = &s_ob; // point to stack
p->store(1);
p->store(2);
p->store(3);
cout << "Stack: ";
cout << p->retrieve();
cout << p->retrieve();
cout << p->retrieve();
cout << '\n';
sorted sorted_ob;
p = &sorted_ob;
p->store(4);
p->store(1);
p->store(3);
p->store(9);
p->store(5);
cout << "Sorted: ";
cout << p->retrieve();
cout << p->retrieve();
cout << p->retrieve();
cout << p->retrieve();
cout << p->retrieve();
cout << '\n';
getch();
}
```

**OUTPUT:**

```
Queue: 123
Stack: 321
Sorted: 13459
```

**Problem 22. Write a C++ program using virtual functions and polymorphism.**

***Program:***

```
#include <iostream.h>
#include<conio.h>
#include <string.h>
class TwoDimensionShape
{
double width;
double height;
char name[20];
public:
TwoDimensionShape()
{
width = height = 0.0;
strcpy(name, "unknown");
}
TwoDimensionShape(double w, double h, char *n)
{
width = w;
height = h;
strcpy(name, n);
}
TwoDimensionShape(double x, char *n)
{
width = height = x;
strcpy(name, n);
}
void showDim()
{
cout << "Width and height are " << width << " and
" << height << endl;
}
double getWidth()
{
return width;
}
double getHeight()
{
return height;
}
void setWidth(double w)
{
width = w;
}
void setHeight(double h)
{
height = h;
}
char *getName()
{
return name;
}
virtual double area()
{
cout << "Error: area() must be overridden.\n";
return 0.0;
}
};
class Triangle : public TwoDimensionShape
{
char style[20]; // now private
public:
Triangle()
{
strcpy(style, "unknown");
}
Triangle(char *str, double w,
```

```
double h) : TwoDimensionShape(w, h, "triangle")
{
strcpy(style, str);
}
Triangle(double x) : TwoDimensionShape(x,
"triangle")
{
strcpy(style, "isosceles");
}
double area()
{
return getWidth() * getHeight() / 2;
}
void showStyle()
{
cout << "Triangle is " << style << endl;
}
};
class Rectangle : public TwoDimensionShape
{
public:
Rectangle(double w, double h) :
TwoDimensionShape(w, h, "rectangle") { }
Rectangle(double x) :
TwoDimensionShape(x, "rectangle") { }
bool isSquare()
{
if(getWidth() == getHeight())
return true;
return false;
}
// This is another override of area().
double area()
{
return getWidth() * getHeight();
}
};
void main()
{
TwoDimensionShape *shapes[5];
shapes[0] = &Triangle("right", 8.0, 12.0);
shapes[1] = &Rectangle(10);
shapes[2] = &Rectangle(10, 4);
shapes[3] = &Triangle(7.0);
shapes[4] = &TwoDimensionShape(10, 20,
"generic");
for(int i = 0; i < 5; i++) {
cout << "object is " << shapes[i]->getName() <<
endl;
cout << "Area is " << shapes[i]->area() << endl;
cout << endl;
}
getch();
}
```

**OUTPUT:**

```
object is triangle
Area is 48
object is rectangle
Area is 100
object is rectangle
Area is 40
object is triangle
Area is 24.5
object is generic
Error: area() must be overridden
Area is 0
```

**Problem 23. Write a C++ program using multiple virtual member functions called in turn.**

***Program:***

```
#include <iostream.h>
#include<conio.h>
class Animal
{
public:
Animal():itsAge(1) { }
~Animal() { }
virtual void Speak() const { cout << "Animal
speak!\n"; }
protected:
int itsAge;
};
class Dog : public Animal
{
public:
void Speak()const { cout << "Woof!\n"; }
};
class Cat : public Animal
{
public:
void Speak()const { cout << "Meow!\n"; }
};
class Horse : public Animal
{
public:
void Speak()const { cout << "Winnie!\n"; }
};
class Pig : public Animal
{
public:
void Speak()const { cout << "Oink!\n"; }
```

```
};
void main()
{
Animal* theArray[5];
Animal* ptr;
int i;
theArray[0] = new Dog;
theArray[1] = new Cat;
theArray[2] = new Horse;
theArray[3] = new Pig;
theArray[4] = new Animal;
for (i=0;i<5;i++)
theArray[i]->Speak();
getch();
}
```

**OUTPUT:**

```
Woof!
Meow!
Winnie!
Oink!
Animal speak!
```

**Problem 24. Write a C++ program for class with only virtual methods.**

***Program:***

```
#include <iostream.h>
#include<conio.h>
class Shape
{
public:
Shape(){}
virtual ~Shape(){}
virtual long GetArea() = 0;
virtual long GetPerim()= 0;
virtual void Draw() = 0;
};
class Circle : public Shape
{
public:
Circle(int radius):itsRadius(radius){}
~Circle(){}
long GetArea() { return 3 * itsRadius * itsRadius; }
long GetPerim() { return 9 * itsRadius; }
void Draw();
private:
int itsRadius;
int itsCircumference;
};
void Circle::Draw()
{
cout << "Circle drawing \n";
}
class Rectangle : public Shape
{
public:
Rectangle(int len, int width):
itsLength(len), itsWidth(width){}
virtual ~Rectangle(){}
virtual long GetArea() { return itsLength *
itsWidth; }
virtual long GetPerim() {return 2*itsLength +
2*itsWidth; }
virtual int GetLength() { return itsLength; }
virtual int GetWidth() { return itsWidth; }
virtual void Draw();
private:
int itsWidth;
int itsLength;
};
void Rectangle::Draw()
{
for (int i = 0; i<itsLength; i++)
{
for (int j = 0, j<itsWidth; j++)
cout << "x ";
cout << "\n";
}
}
class Square : public Rectangle
{
public:
Square(int len);
Square(int len, int width);
~Square(){}
long GetPerim() {return 4 * GetLength();}
};
Square::Square(int len):Rectangle(len,len) {}
Square::Square(int len, int
width):Rectangle(len,width)
{
if (GetLength() != GetWidth())
cout << "Error, not a square... a Rectangle??\n";
}
void main()
{
Shape * sp;
sp = new Circle(5);
sp->Draw();
sp = new Rectangle(4,6);
sp->Draw();
sp = new Square(5);
sp->Draw();
```

```
getch();
}
```

**OUTPUT:**

```
Circle drawing
x x x x x x
x x x x x x
x x x x x x
x x x x x x
x x x x x
x x x x x
x x x x x
x x x x x
x x x x x
```

**Problem 25. Write a C++ program using virtual function to calculate area for different shapes.**

***Program:***

```
#include <iostream.h>
#include<conio.h>
class Shape
{
protected:
double x, y;
public:
void set_dim(double i, double j=0)
{
x = i;
y = j;
}
virtual void show_area(void)
{
cout << "No area computation defined ";
cout << "for this class.\n";
}
} ;
class triangle : public Shape
{
public:
void show_area(void)
{
cout << "Triangle with height ";
cout << x << " and base " << y;
cout << " has an area of ";
cout << x * 0.5 * y << ".\n";
}
};
class square : public Shape
{
public:
void show_area(void)
{
cout << "Square with dimensions ";
cout << x << "x" << y;
cout << " has an area of ";
cout << x *  y << ".\n";
}
};
class circle : public Shape
{
public:
void show_area(void)
{
cout << "Circle with radius ";
cout << x;
cout << " has an area of ";
cout << 3.14 * x * x;
}
};
void main(void)
{
Shape *p;
triangle t;
square s;
circle c;
p = &t;
p->set_dim(10.0, 5.0);
p->show_area();
p = &s;
p->set_dim(10.0, 5.0);
p->show_area();
p = &c;
p->set_dim(9.0);
p->show_area();
getch();
}
```

**Problem 26. Write a C++ program using virtual functions to change the method behaviour.**

***Program:***

```
#include <iostream>
using namespace std;
class Base
{
public:
virtual void who(void)
{
cout << "Base\n";
}
};
class first_d : public Base
{
public:
```

```
void who(void) { // define who() relative to first_d
cout << "First derivation\n";
}
};
class second_d : public Base
{
public:
void who(void) { // define who() relative to
second_d
cout << "Second derivation\n";
}
};
void main()
{
Base base_obj;
Base *p;
first_d first_obj;
second_d second_obj;
p = &base_obj;
p->who(); // access Base's who
p = &first_obj;
p->who(); // access first_d's who
p = &second_obj;
p->who(); // access second_d's who
getch();
}
```

**Problem 27. Write a C++ program Why Virtual Functions: one interface, multiple methods.**

***Program:***

```
#include <iostream.h>
#include<conio.h>
class Shape
{
protected:
double x, y;
public:
void set_dim(double i, double j)
{
x = i;
y = j;
}
virtual void show_area(void)
{
cout << "No area computation defined ";
cout << "for this class.\n";
}
};
class triangle : public Shape
{
public:
void show_area(void)
{
cout << "Triangle with height ";
cout << x << " and base " << y;
cout << " has an area of ";
cout << x * 0.5 * y << ".\n";
}
};
class square : public Shape
{
public:
void show_area(void)
{
cout << "Square with dimensions ";
cout << x << "x" << y;
cout << " has an area of ";
cout << x *  y << ".\n";
}
};
void main()
{
Shape *p;
triangle t;
square s;
p = &t;
p->set_dim(10.0, 5.0);
p->show_area();
p = &s;
p->set_dim(10.0, 5.0);
p->show_area();
getch();
}
```

**Problem 28. Write a C++ program for Object array: polymorphism.**

***Program:***

```
#include <iostream.h>
#include<conio.h>
#include <string.h>
class TwoDimensionShape
{
double width;
double height;
char name[20];
public:
TwoDimensionShape()
{
width = height = 0.0;
strcpy(name, "unknown");
}
TwoDimensionShape(double w, double h, char *n)
```

```
{
width = w;
height = h;
strcpy(name, n);
}
TwoDimensionShape(double x, char *n)
{
width = height = x;
strcpy(name, n);
}
void showDim()
{
cout << "Width and height are " << width << " and "
<< height << endl;
}
double getWidth()
{
return width;
}
double getHeight()
{
return height;
}
void setWidth(double w)
{
width = w;
}
void setHeight(double h)
{
height = h;
}
char *getName()
{
return name;
}
virtual double area()
{
cout << "Error: area() must be overridden.\n";
return 0.0;
}
};
class Triangle : public TwoDimensionShape
{
char style[20]; // now private
public:
Triangle()
{
strcpy(style, "unknown");
}
Triangle(char *str, double w, double h) :
TwoDimensionShape(w, h, "triangle")
{
strcpy(style, str);
}
Triangle(double x) : TwoDimensionShape(x,
"triangle")
{
strcpy(style, "isosceles");
}
double area()
{
return getWidth() * getHeight() / 2;
}
void showStyle()
{
cout << "Triangle is " << style << endl;
}
};
class Rectangle : public TwoDimensionShape
{
public:
Rectangle(double w, double h) :
TwoDimensionShape(w, h, "rectangle") { }
Rectangle(double x) :
TwoDimensionShape(x, "rectangle") { }
bool isSquare()
{
if(getWidth() == getHeight())
return true;
return false;
}
// This is another override of area().
double area()
{
return getWidth() * getHeight();
}
};
void main()
{
TwoDimensionShape *shapes[5];
shapes[0] = &Triangle("right", 8.0, 12.0);
shapes[1] = &Rectangle(10);
shapes[2] = &Rectangle(10, 4);
shapes[3] = &Triangle(7.0);
shapes[4] = &TwoDimensionShape(10, 20,
"generic");
for(int i = 0; i < 5; i++)
{
cout << "object is " << shapes[i]->getName() <<
endl;
cout << "Area is " << shapes[i]->area() << endl;
cout << endl;
```

```
}
getch();
}
```

**OUTPUT:**

```
object is triangle
Area is 48
object is rectangle
Area is 100
object is rectangle
Area is 40
object is triangle
Area is 24.5
object is generic
Error: area() must be overridden
Area is 0
```

**Problem 29. Write a C++ program to call base virtual function explicitly.**

***Program:***

```
#include <iostream.h>
#include<conio.h>
class Base
{
public:
virtual void foo( ) {cout << "Base::foo( )" << endl;}
};
class Derived : public Base
{
public:
virtual void foo( ) {cout << "Derived::foo( )" <<
endl;}
};
void main( )
{
Derived* p = new Derived( );
p->foo( );      // Calls the derived version
p->Base::foo( ); // Calls the base version
getch();
}
```

**OUTPUT:**

```
Derived::foo( )
Base::foo( )
```

**Problem 30. Write a C++ program for Virtual base classes.**

***Program:***

```
#include <iostream.h>
#include<conio.h>
class base
{
public:
int i;
};
class derived1 : virtual public base
{
public:
int j;
};
class derived2 : virtual public base
{
public:
int k;
};
class derived3 : public derived1, public derived2
{
public:
int sum;
};
void main()
{
derived3 ob;
ob.i = 10; // now unambiguous
getch();
}
```

**Problem 31. Write a C++ program using virtual methods.**

***Program:***

```
#include <iostream.h>
#include<conio.h>
class Animal
{
public:
Animal():itsAge(1) { cout << "Animal
constructor...\n"; }
~Animal() { cout << "Animal destructor...\n"; }
void Move() const { cout << "Animal move one
step\n"; }
virtual void Speak() const { cout << "Animal
speak!\n"; }
protected:
int itsAge;
};
class Dog : public Animal
{
public:
Dog() { cout << "Dog constructor...\n"; }
~Dog() { cout << "Dog destructor...\n"; }
void WagTail() { cout << "Wagging Tail...\n"; }
void Speak()const { cout << "Woof!\n"; }
void Move()const { cout << "Dog moves 5
steps...\n"; }
```

```
};
void main()
{
Animal *pDog = new Dog;
pDog->Move();
pDog->Speak();
getch();
}
```

**OUTPUT:**

Animal constructor...
Dog constructor...
Animal move one step
Woof!

**Problem 32. Write a C++ program for an example that uses typeid on a polymorphic class hierarchy.**

***Program:***

```
#include <iostream.h>
#include<conio.h>
#include <typeinfo.h>
class Mammal
{
public:
virtual bool laysEggs()
{
return false;
}
};
class Cat: public Mammal
{
public:
};
class Platypus: public Mammal
{
public:
bool laysEggs()
{
return true;
}
};
void  main()
{
Mammal *p, AnyMammal;
Cat cat;
Platypus platypus;
p = &AnyMammal;
cout << "p is pointing to an object of type ";
cout << typeid(*p).name() << endl;
p = &cat;
cout << "p is pointing to an object of type ";
cout << typeid(*p).name() << endl;
p = &platypus;
cout << "p is pointing to an object of type ";
cout << typeid(*p).name() << endl;
getch();
}
```

**OUTPUT:**

p is pointing to an object of type 6Mammal
p is pointing to an object of type 3Cat
p is pointing to an object of type 8Platypus

## ABSTRACT CLASS:

**Problem 33. Write a C++ program to create an abstract class.**

***Program:***

```
#include <iostream.h>
#include<conio.h>
class area
{
double dim1, dim2;
public:
void setarea(double d1, double d2)
{
dim1 = d1;
dim2 = d2;
}
void getdim(double &d1, double &d2)
{
d1 = dim1;
d2 = dim2;
}
virtual double getarea() = 0; // pure virtual function
};
class rectangle : public area
{
public:
double getarea()
{
double d1, d2;
getdim(d1, d2);
return d1 * d2;
}
};
class triangle : public area
{
public:
double getarea()
{
double d1, d2;
```

```
getdim(d1, d2);
return 0.5 * d1 * d2;
}
};
void main()
{
area *p;
rectangle r;
triangle t;
r.setarea(3.3, 4.5);
t.setarea(4.0, 5.0);
p = &r;
cout << "Rectangle has area: " << p->getarea() <<
'\n';
p = &t;
cout << "Triangle has area: " << p->getarea() << '\n';
getch();
}
```

**OUTPUT:**

Rectangle has area: 14.85
Triangle has area: 10

**Problem 34. Write a C++ program for abstract base class.**

***Program:***

```
#include <iostream.h>
#include<conio.h>
class CPolygon
{
protected:
int width, height;
public:
void set_values (int a, int b)
{
width=a;
height=b;
}
virtual int area (void) =0;
};
class CRectangle: public CPolygon
{
public:
int area (void)
{
return (width * height);
}
};
class CTriangle: public CPolygon
{
public:
int area (void)
{
return (width * height / 2);
}
};
void main ()
{
CRectangle rect;
CTriangle trgl;
CPolygon * ppoly1 = &rect;
CPolygon * ppoly2 = &trgl;
ppoly1->set_values (4,5);
ppoly2->set_values (4,5);
cout << ppoly1->area() << endl;
cout << ppoly2->area() << endl;
getch();
}
```

**OUTPUT:**

20
10

**Problem 35. Write a C++ program to deriving ADTs from other ADTs.**

***Program:***

```
#include <iostream.h>
#include<conio.h>
enum COLOR { Red, Green, Blue, Yellow, White,
Black, Brown } ;
class Animal        // common base to both horse
and bird
{
public:
Animal(int);
virtual ~Animal()
{
cout << "Animal destructor...\n";
}
virtual int GetAge() const
{
return itsAge;
}
virtual void SetAge(int age)
{
itsAge = age;
}
virtual void Sleep() const = 0;
virtual void Eat() const = 0;
virtual void Reproduce() const = 0;
virtual void Move() const = 0;
virtual void Speak() const = 0;
private:
int itsAge;
```

```
};
Animal::Animal(int age):itsAge(age)
{
cout << "Animal constructor...\n";
}
class Mammal : public Animal
{
public:
Mammal(int age):Animal(age)
{
cout << "Mammal constructor...\n";
}
virtual ~Mammal()
{
cout << "Mammal destructor...\n";
}
virtual void Reproduce() const
{
cout << "Mammal reproduction depicted...\n";
}
};
class Fish : public Animal
{
public:
Fish(int age):Animal(age)
{
cout << "Fish constructor...\n";
}
virtual ~Fish()
{
cout << "Fish destructor...\n";
}
virtual void Sleep() const
{
cout << "fish snoring...\n";
}
virtual void Eat() const
{
cout << "fish feeding...\n";
}
virtual void Reproduce() const
{
cout << "fish laying eggs...\n";
}
virtual void Move() const
{
cout << "fish swimming...\n";
}
virtual void Speak() const { }
};
class Horse : public Mammal
{
public:
Horse(int age, COLOR color ): Mammal(age),
itsColor(color)
{
cout << "Horse constructor...\n";
}
virtual ~Horse()
{
cout << "Horse destructor...\n";
}
virtual void Speak()const
{
cout << "Whinny!... \n";
}
virtual COLOR GetItsColor() const
{ return itsColor; }
virtual void Sleep() const
{ cout << "Horse snoring...\n"; }
virtual void Eat() const
{ cout << "Horse feeding...\n"; }
virtual void Move() const
{ cout << "Horse running...\n";}
protected:
COLOR itsColor;
};
class Dog : public Mammal
{
public:
Dog(int age, COLOR color ):
Mammal(age), itsColor(color)
{ cout << "Dog constructor...\n"; }
virtual ~Dog()
{ cout << "Dog destructor...\n"; }
virtual void Speak()const
{ cout << "Whoof!... \n"; }
virtual void Sleep() const
{ cout << "Dog snoring...\n"; }
virtual void Eat() const
{ cout << "Dog eating...\n"; }
virtual void Move() const
{ cout << "Dog running...\n"; }
virtual void Reproduce() const
{ cout << "Dogs reproducing...\n"; }
protected:
COLOR itsColor;
};
void main()
{
Animal *pAnimal=0;
pAnimal = new Dog(5,Brown);
```

```
pAnimal->Speak();
pAnimal->Eat();
pAnimal->Reproduce();
pAnimal->Move();
pAnimal->Sleep();
delete pAnimal;
pAnimal = new Horse(4,Black);
pAnimal->Speak();
pAnimal->Eat();
pAnimal->Reproduce();
pAnimal->Move();
pAnimal->Sleep();
delete pAnimal;
pAnimal = new Fish (5);
pAnimal->Speak();
pAnimal->Eat();
pAnimal->Reproduce();
pAnimal->Move();
pAnimal->Sleep();
delete pAnimal;
getch();
}
```

**OUTPUT:**

```
Animal constructor...
Mammal constructor...
Dog constructor...
Whoof!...
Dog eating...
Dogs reproducing...
Dog running...
Dog snoring...
Dog destructor...
Mammal destructor...
Animal destructor...
Animal constructor...
Mammal constructor...
Horse constructor...
Whinny!...
Horse feeding...
Mammal reproduction depicted...
Horse running...
Horse snoring...
Horse destructor...
Mammal destructor...
Animal destructor...
Animal constructor...
Fish constructor...
fish feeding...
fish laying eggs...
fish swimming...
fish snoring...
Fish destructor...
Animal destructor...
```

## DYNAMIC ALLOCATION AND POLYMORPHISM:

**Problem 36. Write a C++ program for dynamic_cast from derived to base.**

***Program:***

```
#include <iostream.h>
#include<conio.h>
class Base
{
public:
virtual ~Base( ) {} // Make this a polymorphic
class
};
class Derived : public Base
{
public:
virtual ~Derived( ) {}
};
void main( )
{
Derived d;
// Query the type relationship
if (dynamic_cast<Base*>(&d))
{
cout << "Derived is a subclass of Base" << endl;
}
else
{
cout << "Derived is NOT a subclass of Base" <<
endl;
}
getch();
}
```

**OUTPUT:**

```
Derived is a subclass of Base
```

**Problem 37. Write a C++ program for dynamic allocation and polymorphism.**

***Program:***

```
#include <iostream.h>
#include<conio.h>
class CPolygon
{
protected:
int width, height;
public:
```

```
void set_values (int a, int b)
{
width=a;
height=b;
}
virtual int area (void) =0;
void printarea (void)
{
cout << this->area() << endl;
}
};
class CRectangle: public CPolygon
{
public:
int area (void)
{
return (width * height);
}
};
class CTriangle: public CPolygon
{
public:
int area (void)
{
return (width * height / 2);
}
};
void main ()
{
CPolygon * ppoly1 = new CRectangle;
CPolygon * ppoly2 = new CTriangle;
ppoly1->set_values (4,5);
ppoly2->set_values (4,5);
ppoly1->printarea();
ppoly2->printarea();
delete ppoly1;
delete ppoly2;
getch();
}
```

**OUTPUT:**

```
20
10
```

## PURE VIRTUAL FUNCTION:

**Problem 38. Write a C++ program for abstract Classes and Pure Virtual Functions.**

***Program:***

```
#include <iostream.h>
#include<conio.h>
class Base
{
public:
virtual void show()=0; //This is pure virtual
function
};
class Derv1 :public Base
{
public:
void show()
{
cout <<"Derv1 \n";
}
};
class Derv2 :public Base
{
public:
void show()
{
cout <<"Derv2 \n";
}
};
void main()
{
Base *ptr[2];  //array of pointers to base class
Derv1 d1;
Derv2 d2;
ptr[0]=&d1;    //put address of d1 in array
ptr[1]=&d2;    //put address of d2 in array
ptr[0]->show(); //execute show()in both objects
ptr[1]->show();
getch();
}
```

**OUTPUT:**

```
Derv1
Derv2
```

**Problem 39. Write a C++ program to implementing pure virtual functions.**

***Program:***

```
#include <iostream.h>
#include<conio.h>
class Shape
{
public:
Shape(){}
virtual ~Shape(){}
virtual long GetArea() = 0;
virtual long GetPerim()= 0;
virtual void Draw() = 0;
private:
```

```
};
void Shape::Draw()
{
cout << "Abstract drawing mechanism!\n";
}
class Circle : public Shape
{
public:
Circle(int radius):itsRadius(radius){}
~Circle(){}
long GetArea() { return 3 * itsRadius * itsRadius; }
long GetPerim() { return 9 * itsRadius; }
void Draw();
private:
int itsRadius;
int itsCircumference;
};
void Circle::Draw()
{
cout << "Circle drawing routine here!\n";
Shape::Draw();
}
class Rectangle : public Shape
{
public:
Rectangle(int len, int width):
itsLength(len), itsWidth(width){}
virtual ~Rectangle(){}
long GetArea() { return itsLength * itsWidth; }
long GetPerim() {return 2*itsLength + 2*itsWidth; }
virtual int GetLength() { return itsLength; }
virtual int GetWidth() { return itsWidth; }
void Draw();
private:
int itsWidth;
int itsLength;
};
void Rectangle::Draw()
{
for (int i = 0; i<itsLength; i++)
{
for (int j = 0; j<itsWidth; j++)
cout << "x ";
cout << "\n";
}
Shape::Draw();
}
class Square : public Rectangle
{
public:
Square(int len);
Square(int len, int width);
~Square(){}
long GetPerim() {return 4 * GetLength();}
};
Square::Square(int len):Rectangle(len,len)
{}
Square::Square(int len, int
width):Rectangle(len,width)
{
if (GetLength() != GetWidth())
cout << "Error, not a square... a Rectangle??\n";
}
void main()
{
Shape * sp;
sp = new Circle(5);
sp->Draw();
sp = new Rectangle(4,6);
sp->Draw();
sp = new Square (5);
sp->Draw();
getch();
}
```

**OUTPUT:**

```
Circle drawing routine here!
Abstract drawing mechanism!
x x x x x x
x x x x x x
x x x x x x
x x x x x x
Abstract drawing mechanism!
x x x x x
x x x x x
x x x x x
x x x x x
x x x x x
Abstract drawing mechanism!
```

**Problem 40. Write a C++ program for a pure virtual function.**

***Program:***

```
#include <iostream.h>
#include<conio.h>
#include <string.h>
class Shape
{
double width;
double height;
char name[20];
public:
Shape()
```

```
{
width = height = 0.0;
strcpy(name, "unknown");
}
Shape(double w, double h, char *n)
{
width = w;
height = h;
strcpy(name, n);
}
Shape(double x, char *n)
{
width = height = x;
strcpy(name, n);
}
void display()
{
cout << "Width and height are " << width << " and "
<< height << "\n";
}
double getWidth() { return width; }
double getHeight() { return height; }
void setWidth(double w) { width = w; }
void setHeight(double h) { height = h;}
char *getName() { return name; }
virtual double area() = 0;
};
class Triangle : public Shape
{
char style[20];
public:
Triangle()
{
strcpy(style, "unknown");
}
Triangle(char *str, double w, double h) : Shape(w, h,
"triangle")
{
strcpy(style, str);
}
Triangle(double x) : Shape(x, "triangle")
{
strcpy(style, "isosceles");
}
double area()
{
return getWidth() * getHeight() / 2;
}
void showStyle()
{
cout << "Triangle is " << style << "\n";
}
};
class Rectangle : public Shape
{
public:
Rectangle(double w, double h) : Shape(w, h,
"rectangle") { }
Rectangle(double x) : Shape(x, "rectangle") { }
bool isSquare()
{
if(getWidth() == getHeight())
return true;
return false;
}
double area()
{
return getWidth() * getHeight();
}
};
void main()
{
Shape *shapes[4];
shapes[0] = &Triangle("right", 8.0, 12.0);
shapes[1] = &Rectangle(10);
shapes[2] = &Rectangle(10, 4);
shapes[3] = &Triangle(7.0);
for(int i=0; i < 4; i++)
{
cout << "object is " << shapes[i]->getName() <<
"\n";
cout << "Area is " << shapes[i]->area() << "\n\n";
}
getch();
}
```

**OUTPUT:**

```
object is triangle
Area is 24.5
object is triangle
Area is 24.5
object is triangle
Area is 24.5
object is triangle
Area is 24.5
```

**Problem 41. Write a C++ program for pure virtual members can be called from the abstract base class.**

***Program:***

```
#include <iostream.h>
#include<conio.h>
class CPolygon
```

```
{
protected:
int width, height;
public:
void set_values (int a, int b)
{
width=a;
height=b;
}
virtual int area (void) =0;
void printarea (void)
{
cout << this->area() << endl;
}
};
class CRectangle: public CPolygon
{
public:
int area (void)
{
return (width * height);
}
};
class CTriangle: public CPolygon
{
public:
int area (void)
{
return (width * height / 2);
}
};
void main ()
{
CRectangle rect;
CTriangle trgl;
CPolygon * ppoly1 = &rect;
CPolygon * ppoly2 = &trgl;
ppoly1->set_values (4,5);
ppoly2->set_values (4,5);
ppoly1->printarea();
ppoly2->printarea();
getch();
}
```

**OUTPUT:**

20
10

**Problem 42. Write a C++ program for Pure Virtual Functions.**

***Program:***

```
#include <iostream.h>
#include<conio.h>
class Values
{
protected:
int a;
public:
void set(int i)
{
a =i;
}
virtual void show()=0;
};
class type1 :public Values
{
public:
void show()
{
cout <<hex <<a <<"\n";
}
};
class type2 :public Values
{
public:
void show()
{
cout <<a <<"\n";
}
};
class type3 :public Values
{
public:
void show()
{
cout <<oct <<a <<"\n";
}
};
void main()
{
type1 t1;
type2 t2;
type3 t3;
t1.set(20);
t1.show();
t2.set(20);
t2.show();
t3.set(20);
t3.show();
getch();
}
```

**OUTPUT:**

14

14
24

**Problem 43. Write a C++ program to show pure virtual functions using bank that wants to terminate emp on performance basis that if emp is manager then monthly target for keeping funds must not be less than Rs1000000. if emp is marketing executive then monthly target for opening accounts should must not be less than 20 accounts.**

***Program:***

```
#include<iostream.h>
#include<conio.h>
class emp
{
private:
char name[20];
public:
void get()
{
cout<<"Enter employee name=";
cin>>name;
}
void put()
{
cout<<"\nName"<<name<<endl;
}
virtual void getd()=0;
virtual int  isnp()=0;
};
class mke:public emp
{
private:
int aopen;
public:
void getd()
{
get();
cout<<"Enter number of accounts opened=";
cin>>aopen;
}
int isnp()
{
if(aopen<20)
return(1);
else
return(0);
}
};
class manager:public emp
{
double target;
public:
void getd()
{
get ();
cout<<"Enter target amount got";
cin>>target;
}
int isnp()
{
if(target<1000000)
return(1);
else
return(0);
}
};
void main()
{
clrscr();
emp *p[20];
int n=0;
int choice·
char ch;
do
{
cout<<"Enter1 for mkt.exe. or 2 for manager->";
cin>>ch;
if(ch==1)
p[n]=new mke;
else if(ch==2)
p[n]=new manager;
else
{
cout<<"Invalid choice\n";
continue;
}
p[n]->getd();
n++;
cout<<"Want to input more(y/n)?";
cin>>ch;
}
while(ch=='y');
for(int i=0;i<n;i++)
{
p[i]->put();
if(p[i]->isnp())
cout<<"Terminate employee\n";
else
cout<<"Good employee\n";
}
```

```
getch();
}
```

**OUTPUT:**

```
Enter1 for mkt.exe. or 2 for manager:1
Enter employee name=Harpreet
Enter number of accounts opened=13
Want to input more(y/n)?y
Enter1 for mkt.exe. or 2 for manager:2
Enter employee name=Gurpreet
Enter target amount got 260000
Want to input more(y/n)?n
Name Harpreet
Terminate employee
Name Gurpreet
Good employee
```

## FUNCTION OVERLOADING:

**Problem 44. Write a C++ program to implement cube root with the help of function overloading.**

***Program:***

```
#include<iostream.h>
#include<math.h>
int cuberoot (int x)
{
float q ;
q = sqrt (x) / 2.0 ;
x = x * 3.0 ;
q = q/10 ;
return (q) ;
}
double cuberoot (float x)
{
float q ;
q = sqrt (x) / 2.0 ;
x = x * 3.0 ;
q = q/10 ;
return (q) ;
}
float cuberoot (double (x))
{
double q ;
q = sqrt (x) / 2.0 ;
x = x / 3.0 ;
q = q / 1.0 ;
return (q)
}
void main ( )
{
int a, d ;
float b, e ;
double c, f ;
int cuberoot(int);
float cuberoot(float);
double cuberoot(double);
cout<<"\n Enter the integer number" ;
cin >> a ;
d = cuberoot (a) ;
cout<<"\n Cube root of "<< a <<" is" << d ;
cout<<"\n Enter the float number" ;
cin >> b ;
e = cuberoot (b) ;
cout<<"\n Cuberoot of" << b <<" is" << e ;
cout<<"\n Enter the double number" ;
cin >> c ;
f = cuberoot (c) ;
cout<<"\n Cuberoot of" << c <<" is" << f ;
getche ( ) ;
}
```

**Problem 45. Write a C++ program to illustrate the use of overloaded function show ( ) having different number of arguments in the different overloaded forms.**

***Program:***

```
#include<iostream.h>
#include<conio.h>
void show (char  a)
{
cout<<"\n Function taking single argument is: \n" ;
cout<<a;
}
void show (char  a, int n)
{
cout<<"\n Function taking double argument is: \n"
;
cout<< a ;
cout<<"\n" << n ;
}
void main ( )
{
void show(char);
void show(char, int);
char a[30] = "Khalsa College, Asr" ;
int n = 20 ;
show (a) ;
show (a, n) ;
getche ( ) ;
}
```

**OUTPUT:**

```
Function taking single argument is:
```

Khalsa College, Asr
Function taking double argument is:
Khalsa College, Asr
20

**Problem 46. Write a C++ program to compute sum by using different types of function by using the concept of Function Overloading.**

***Program:***

```
// Program to overload functions.
#include<iostream.h>
#include<conio.h>
int sum(int a,int b)
{
return a+b;
}
float sum(float a,float b)
{
return a+b;
}
void main()
{
int i,j;
float k,l;
int sum(int, int);
float sum(float, float);
cout<<"\nEnter two integer numbers:";
cin>>i>>j;
cout<<"\nSum of "<<i<<" & "<<j<<" is
"<<sum(i,j);
cout<<"\nEnter two float numbers:";
cin>>k>>l;
cout<<"\nSum of "<<k<<" & "<<l<<" is
"<<sum(k,l);
getch();
}
```

**OUTPUT:**

```
Enter two integer numbers: 5  7
Sum of 5  &  7 is 12
Enter two float numbers: 2.5  3.2
Sum of 2.5  &  3.2 is 5.7
```

**Problem 47. Write a C++ program to compute the square root by using the concept of function overloading having different argument and also having the similar data types.**

***Program:***

```
// FUNCTION OVERLOADING with different
argument, but similar data type
#include<iostream.h>
#include<conio.h>
#include<math.h>
class funct
{
public:
void funct(float a)
{
cout<<"A="<<sqrt(a)<<endl;
}
void funct(float x,float y)
{
cout<<"X="<<sqrt(x)<<"Y="<<sqrt(y)<<endl;
}
void funct(float b,float c,float d)
{
cout<<"B="<<sqrt(b)<<"C="<<sqrt(c)<<"D="<<s
qrt(d)<<endl;
}
};
void main()
{
clrscr();
funct(16.0);
funct(16.0,9.0 );
funct(16.0,9.0,4.0);
getch();
}
```

**OUTPUT:**

```
A=4
X=4 Y=3
B=4 C=3 D=2
```

**Problem 48. Write a C++ program to find the average marks of three numbers to illustrate the concept of function overloading with the different data types.**

***Program:***

```
// FUNCTION OVERLOADING WITH
DIFFERENT DATA TYPE
#include<iostream.h>
#include<conio.h>
int average(int a,int b,int c);
float average(float x,float y,float z);
double average(double l,double m,double n);
void main()
{
int a,b,c;
float x,y,z;
double l,m,n;
clrscr();
cout<<"ENTER THE INTEGER
VALUES:"<<endl;
```

```
cin>>a>>b>>c;
cout<<"ENTER THE FLOAT VALUES:"<<endl;
cin>>x>>y>>z;
cout<<"ENTER THE DOUBLE VALUES:"<<endl;
cin>>l>>m>>n;
cout<<" A= "<<a<<" B= "<<b<<" C= "<<c;
average(a,b,c);
cout<<" X= "<<x<<" Y= "<<y<<" Z= "<<z;
average(x,y,z);
cout<<" L= "<<l<<" M= "<<m<<" N= "<<n;
average(l,m,n);
getch();
}
int average(int a,int b,int c)
{
int av;
av=(a+b+c)/3;
cout<<"\nAVERAGE OF THREE INTERGER NO
IS:"<<av;
}
float average(float x,float y,float z)
{
float av;
av=(x+y+z)/3;
cout<<"\nAVERAGE OF THREE floating NO
IS:"<<av;
}
double average(double l,double m,double n)
{
double av;
av=(l+m+n)/3;
cout<<"\nAVERAGE OF THREE double NO
IS:"<<av;
getch();
}
```

**OUTPUT:**

```
ENTER THE INTEGER VALUES:
7 5 2
 ENTER THE FLOAT VALUES:
2.5 3.2 5.7
ENTER THE DOUBLE VALUES
97287.5 26751.2 97625.7
A = 7 B = 5 C = 2
AVERAGE OF THREE INTERGER NO IS: 4
X=2.5 Y=3.2 Z=5.7
AVERAGE OF THREE floating NO IS: 3.8
L=97287.5 M=26751.2 N=97625.7
AVERAGE OF THREE double NO IS: 73888.133
```

**Problem 49. Write a C++ program to find rank of a student from the student database by using the concept of Function Overloading.**

***Program:***

```
#include<iostream.h>
#include<conio.h>
#include<iomanip.h>
#include<string.h>
void sort(int);
void swap(int *,int *);
class a
{
public:
char name[20],clas[20];
int roll,s1,s2,s3,total;
void input()
{
cout<<"Enter name==>";
cin>>name;
cout<<"Enter roll number & marks in 3
subjects==>";
cin>>roll>>s1>>s2>>s3;
total=s1+s2+s3;
}
void print()
{
cout<<name;
cout<<"\t"<<roll<<"\t"<<total;
}
}s[50];
void main()
{
int i,n;
clrscr();
cout<<"Enter number of students==>";
cin>>n;
cout<<"Enter the information==>";
for(i=0;i<n;i++)
s[i].input();
sort(n);
cout<<"\n\nDatabase is==>\n";
int p=1;
cout<<"Name\tRollNo. Total\t Rank\n";
cout<<s[0].name<<"\t"<<s[0].roll<<"\t"<<s[0].tota
l<<"\t"<<p<<endl;
p++;
for(i=1;i<n;i++)
{
s[i].print();
cout<<"\t";
if(s[i].total==s[i-1].total)
```

```
{
if(p-1==0)
cout<<"1";
else
cout<<p-1;
}
else
cout<<p;
cout<<"\n";
p++;
}
getch();
}
void swap(int *a,int *b)
{
int c=*a;
*a=*b;
*b=c;
}
void sort(int n)
{
int p,i;
char name[20];
for(p=1;p<n;p++)
for(i=0;i<n-p;i++)
if(s[i].total<s[i+1].total)
{
strcpy(name,s[i].name);
strcpy(s[i].name,s[i+1].name);
strcpy(s[i+1].name,name);
swap(&s[i].roll,&s[i+1].roll);
swap(&s[i].s1,&s[i+1].s1);
swap(&s[i].s2,&s[i+1].s2);
swap(&s[i].s3,&s[i+1].s3);
swap(&s[i].total,&s[i+1].total);
}
}
```

**OUTPUT:**

```
Enter number of students==>3
Enter the information==>"
Enter name==> Mona
Enter roll number & marks in 3 subjects==> 122
20 30  50
Enter name==> Geeta
Enter roll number & marks in 3 subjects==> 123
20 10  10
Enter name==> Nishu
Enter roll number & marks in 3 subjects==> 124
50 50   60
Database is==>
Name   Nishu   RollNo. 124     Total    160
Rank  1
Name   Mona    RollNo. 122     Total    100
Rank  2
Name   Geeta   RollNo. 123     Total     40
Rank  3
```

**Problem 50. Write a C++ program to find area of square or rectangle or circle by using function overloading.**

***Program:***

```
#include<iostream.h>
#include<conio.h>
void area(int);
void area(float);
void area (float,float);
void main()
{
int choice;
clrscr();
back:
cout<<"Press 1 for area of square.\n";
cout<<"Press 2 for area of rectangle.\n";
cout<<"Press 3 for area of circle.\n";
cout<<"Enter your choice...";
cin>>choice;
switch (choice)
{
case 1:
int s;
cout<<"Enter side==>";
cin>>s;
area(s);
break;
case 2:
float l,b;
cout<<"Enter length & breath==>";
cin>>l>>b;
area(l,b);
break;
case 3:
float r;
cout<<"Enter radius==>";
cin>>r;
area(r);
break;
default:
cout<<"Enter proper choice.\n";
goto back;
}
getch();
```

```
}
void area(int s)
{
cout<<"Area of square is==>"<<s*s;
}
void area(float l,float b)
{
cout<<"Area of rectangle is==>"<<l*b;
}
void area(float r)
{
cout<<"Area of circle is==>"<<r*r*22/7;
}
```

**OUTPUT:**

```
Press 1 for area of square.
Press 2 for area of rectangle.
Press 3 for area of circle.
Enter your choice... 1
Enter side==>4
Area of square is==>16
```

**Problem 51. Write a C++ program for function overloading.**

***Program:***

```
#include <iostream.h>
#include<conio.h>
int func(int i);
double func(double i);
void main()
{
cout <<func(20)<<" ";
cout <<func(6.4);
getch();
}
double func(double i)
{
return i;
}
int func(int i)
{
return i;
}
```

**OUTPUT:**

```
20 6.4
```

**Problem 52. Write a C++ program for function overloading.**

***Program:***

```
#include <iostream.h>
#include<conio.h>
int func(int i);
int func(int i,int j);
void main()
{
cout <<func(20)<<" ";
cout <<func(6,8);
getch();
}
int func(int i)
{
return i;
}
int func(int i,int j)
{
return i*j;
}
```

**OUTPUT:**

```
20 48
```

# CHAPTER 15

# FILES

## BASIC FILE FUNCTIONS:

**Problem 1. Write a C++ program for basic file operations.**

***Program:***

```
#include <iostream.h>
#include <fstream.h>
#include<conio.h>
void main ()
{
ofstream myfile;
myfile.open ("example.txt");
myfile << "Writing this to a file.\n";
myfile.close();
getch();
}
```

**OUTPUT:**

[file example.txt]
Writing this to a file

**Problem 2. Write a C++ program for writing on a text file.**

***Program:***

```
#include <iostream.h>
#include <fstream.h>
#include<conio.h>
void main ()
{
ofstream myfile ("example.txt");
if (myfile.is_open())
{
myfile << "This is a line.\n";
myfile << "This is another line.\n";
myfile.close();
}
else cout << "Unable to open file";
getch();
}
```

**OUTPUT:**

[file example.txt]
This is a line.
This is another line.

**Problem 3. Write a C++ program for reading a text file.**

***Program:***

```
#include <iostream.h>
#include <fstream.h>
#include <string.h>
#include<conio.h>
void main ()
{
string line;
ifstream myfile ("example.txt");
if (myfile.is_open())
{
while (! myfile.eof() )
{
getline (myfile,line);
cout << line << endl;
}
myfile.close();
}
else cout << "Unable to open file";
getch();
}
```

**OUTPUT:**

This is a line.
This is another line.

**Problem 4. Write a C++ program for obtaining file size.**

***Program:***

```
#include <iostream.h>
#include <fstream.h>
#include<conio.h>
void main ()
{
long begin,end;
ifstream myfile ("example.txt");
begin = myfile.tellg();
myfile.seekg (0, ios::end);
end = myfile.tellg();
myfile.close();
cout << "size is: " << (end-begin) << " bytes.\n";
getch();
}
```

**OUTPUT:**

size is: 40 bytes.

**Problem 5. Write a C++ program for reading a complete binary file.**

***Program:***

```
#include <iostream.h>
#include <fstream.h>
#include<conio.h>
ifstream::pos_type size;
char * memblock;
void main ()
{
ifstream file ("example.bin",
ios::in|ios::binary|ios::ate);
if (file.is_open())
{
size = file.tellg();
memblock = new char [size];
file.seekg (0, ios::beg);
file.read (memblock, size);
file.close();
cout << "the complete file content is in memory";
delete[] memblock;
}
else cout << "Unable to open file";
getch();
}
```

**OUTPUT:**

the complete file content is in memory

## TEXTFILE READ:

**Problem 6. Write a C++ program to display (Read) a string character by character from a data file.**

***Program:***

```
#include<fstream.h>
#include<iostream.h>
#include<conio.h>
void main ( )
{
const int M = 80 ;
char st [M] ;
ifstream infile ("Ram") ;
while (infile)
{
infile.getline (st, M) ;
cout << st ;
}
getche ( ) ;
}
```

**Problem 7. Write a C++ program to read a number from a text file.**

***Program:***

```
#include<fstream.h>
#include<conio.h>
#include<iostream.h>
int n;
void main ( )
{
ifstream num ;
num.open ("Raja") ;
num >> n ;
cout<<"output is" << n ;
num.close ( ) ;
getch();
}
```

**Problem 8. Write a C++ program to input the data by using the concept of file input.**

***Program:***

```
// Program to illustrate file input in C++.
#include<iostream.h>
#include<iomanip.h>
#include<fstream.h>
#include<conio.h>
struct student
{
int rno;
char name[20];
int marks;
};
void main()
{
student s[10];
ofstream fout("abc.txt");
int n,i;
cout<<endl<<"Enter the no. of student:"<<endl;
cin>>n;
for(i=0;i<n;i++)
{
cout<<"Enter the roll number,name and marks of
student no: "<<i<<endl;
cin>>s[i].rno;
cin>>s[i].name;
cin>>s[i].marks;
}
for(i=0;i<n;i++)
fout<<s[i].rno<<setw(5)<<s[i].name<<setw(5)<<s
[i].marks<<endl;
getch();
}
```

**Problem 9. Write a C++ program to illustrate the concept of input file.**

***Program:***

```
#include<iostream.h>
#include<iomanip.h>
#include<fstream.h>
#include<conio.h>
struct student
{
int rno;
char name[20];
int marks;
};
void main()
{
student s[10];
ofstream fout("abc.txt");
int n,i;
cout<<endl<<"Enter the no. of student:"<<endl;
cin>>n;
for(i=0;i<n;i++)
{
cout<<"Enter the roll number,name and marks of
student no: "<<i<<endl;
cin>>s[i].rno;
cin>>s[i].name;
cin>>s[i].marks;
}
for(i=0;i<n;i++)
fout<<s[i].rno<<setw(5)<<s[i].name<<setw(5)<<s[i]
.marks<<endl;
}
getch();
}
```

**Problem 10. Write a C++ program to write the data by using the output file concept.**

***Program:***

```
#include<iostream.h>
#include<iomanip.h>
#include<fstream.h>
#include<conio.h>
struct student
{
int rno;
char name[20];
int marks;
};
void main()
{
student s;
ifstream fin("abc.txt");
int i;
cout<<"Roll No. Name  Marks"<<endl;
while(!fin.eof())
{
fin>>s.rno;
fin>>s.name;
fin>>s.marks;
cout<<s.rno<<setw(10)<<s.name<<setw(10)<<s.m
arks<<endl;
}
getch();
}
```

**Problem 11. Write a C++ program to find the size of data using binary file.**

***Program:***

```
#include<fstream.h>
#include<conio.h>
void main()
{
ofstream in("A",ios::binary);
clrscr();
int a,c;
float b,d;
cout<<"Enter a & b==>";
cin>>a>>b;
in.write((char *)&a,sizeof(a));
in.write((char *)&b,sizeof(b));
in.close();
ifstream out("A",ios::binary);
out.read((char *)&c,sizeof(c));
out.read((char *)&d,sizeof(d));
cout<<"\n\nC is "<<c;
cout<<"\n\nD is "<<d;
getch();
}
```

**Problem 12. Write a C++ program to read string and float value from a file.**

***Program:***

```
#include <iostream.h>
#include <fstream.h>
#include<conio.h>
int main()
{
ofstream out("test.txt"); // output, normal file
if(!out)
{
cout << "Cannot open test.txt file.\n";
```

```
return 1;
}
out << "R " << 9.9 << endl;
out << "T " << 9.9 << endl;
out << "M " << 4.8 << endl;
out.close();
ifstream in("test.txt"); // input
if(!in)
{
cout << "Cannot open test.txt file.\n";
return 1;
}
char item[20];
float cost;
in >> item >>  cost;
cout << item << " " << cost << "\n";
in >> item >> cost;
cout << item << " " << cost << "\n";
in >> item >> cost;
cout << item << " " << cost << "\n";
in.close();
getch();
}
```

**OUTPUT:**

R 9.9
T 9.9
M 4.8

**Problem 13. Write a C++ program to read from file.**

***Program:***

```
#include <fstream.h>
#include <iostream.h>
#include<conio.h>
int main()
{
char ch;
int i;
float f;
char str[80];
ofstream out("test.txt");
if(!out)
{
cout << "Cannot open file.\n";
return 1;
}
out << 10 << " " << 123.23 << "\n";
out << "This is a text.";
out.close();
ifstream in("test.txt");
if(!in)
{
cout << "Cannot open file.\n";
return 1;
}
in >> i;
in >> f;
in >> ch;
in >> str;
cout << i << " " << f << " " << ch << "\n";
cout << str;
in.close();
getch();
}
```

**OUTPUT:**

10 123.23 T
his

**Problem 14. Write a C++ program to read text file line by line.**

***Program:***

```
#include <iostream.h>
#include<conio.h>
#include <fstream.h>
void main(int argc, char *argv[])
{
ifstream in("text.txt");
if(!in)
{
cout << "Cannot open file.";
exit (1);
}
char str[255];
while(in)
{
in.getline(str, 255);     // Delimiter defaults to
newline
cout << str << endl;
}
in.close();
getch();
}
```

**Problem 15. Write a C++ program to read a text file line by line.**

***Program:***

```
#include <iostream.h>
#include<conio.h>
#include <fstream.h>
void main ()
{
char buffer[256]; clrscr();
```

```
ifstream myfile ("test.txt");
while (! myfile.eof() )
{
myfile.getline (buffer,100);
cout << buffer << endl;
}
getch();
}
```

**OUTPUT:**

R 9.9
T 9.9
M 4.8

**Problem 16. Write a C++ program to read text file token by token.**

***Program:***.

```
#include <iostream.h>
#include<conio.h>
#include <fstream.h>
#include <string.h>
void main()
{
ifstream inFile("test.cpp");
if (inFile.fail())
{
cerr << "Unable to open file for reading." << endl;
exit(1);
}
string nextToken;
while (inFile >> nextToken)
{
cout << "Token: " << nextToken << endl;
}
inFile.close();
getch();
}
```

**Problem 17. Write a C++ program to read integer from a text file.**

***Program:***

```
#include <fstream.h>
#include <iostream.h>
#include <string.h>
#include<conio.h>
void readIntegerFile(const string &fileName,
vector<int>& dest)throw (invalid_argument,
runtime_error)
{
ifstream istr;
int temp;
istr.open(fileName.c_str());
if (istr.fail())
{
string error = "Unable to open file " + fileName;
throw invalid_argument(error);
}
while (istr >> temp)
{
dest.push_back(temp);
}
if (istr.eof())
{
istr.close();
}
else
{
istr.close();
string error = "Unable to read file " + fileName;
throw runtime_error(error);
}
}
void main(int argc, char** argv)
{
vector<int> myInts;
const string fileName = "test.txt";
try
{
readIntegerFile(fileName, myInts);
}
catch (const invalid_argument& e)
{
cerr << e.what() << endl;
exit (1);
}
catch (const runtime_error& e)
{
cerr << e.what() << endl;
exit (1);
}
for (unsigned int i = 0; i < myInts.size(); i++)
{
cout << myInts[i] << " ";
}
cout << endl;
getch();
}
```

**Problem 18. Write a C++ program to reading a text file.**

***Program:***

```
#include <iostream.h>
#include <fstream.h>
```

```
#include <stdlib.h>
#include <conio.h>
void main ()
{
char buffer[256];
ifstream examplefile ("test.txt");
if (! examplefile.is_open())
{
cout << "Error opening file"; exit (1);
}
while (! examplefile.eof() )
{
examplefile.getline (buffer,100);
cout << buffer << endl;
}
getch();
}
```

**OUTPUT:**

This is a line.
This is another line.

**Problem 19. Write a C++ program to reading and writing text files.**

***Program:***

```
#include <iostream.h>
#include<conio.h>
#include <fstream.h>
int main()
{
ofstream out("INVNTRY"); // output, normal file
if(!out)
{ cout << "Cannot open INVENTORY file.\n";
return 1; }
out << "Radios " << 39.95 << endl;
out << "Toasters " << 19.95 << endl;
out << "Mixers " << 24.80 << endl;
out.close();
getch();
}
```

**OUTPUT:**

Radios 39.95
Toasters 19.95
Mixers 24.80

**Problem 20. Write a C++ program to file input with strings.**

***Program:***

```
#include <iostream.h>
#include<conio.h>
#include <fstream.h>
void main()
{
const int MAX = 80;
char buffer[MAX];
ifstream infile("TEST.TXT");
while( !infile.eof() )
{
infile.getline(buffer, MAX);
cout << buffer << endl;
}
getch();
}
```

**OUTPUT:**

R 9.9
T 9.9
M 4.8

**Problem 21. Write a C++ program to read and display a text file line by line.**

***Program:***

```
#include <iostream.h>
#include<conio.h>
#include <fstream.h>
int main(int argc, char *argv[])
{
ifstream in("test.txt");
if(!in)
{
cout << "Cannot open input file.\n";
return 1;
}
char str[255];
while(in)
{
in.getline(str, 255); // delim defaults to '\n'
if(in) cout << str << endl;
}
in.close();
getch();
}
```

**OUTPUT:**

R 9.9
T 9.9
M 4.8

## TEXTFILE WRITE:

**Problem 22. Write a C++ program to write to file.**

***Program:***

```
#include <iostream.h>
#include<conio.h>
```

```
#include <fstream.h>
int main()
{
ofstream out("test.txt");
if(!out)
{
cout << "Cannot open file.\n";
return 1;
}
out << 10 << " " << 123.23 << "\n";
out << "This is a text.";
out.close();
getch();
}
```

**OUTPUT:**

10 123.23
This is a text.

**Problem 23. Write a C++ program to save string double pair to file.**

***Program:***

```
#include <iostream.h>
#include<conio.h>
#include <fstream.h>
int main()
{
ofstream out("test.txt"); // output, normal file
if(!out)
{
cout << "Cannot open test.txt file.\n";
return 1;
}
out << "R " << 9.9 << endl;
out << "T " << 9.9 << endl;
out << "M " << 4.8 << endl;
out.close();
getch();
}
```

**OUTPUT:**

R 9.9
T 9.9
M 4.8

**Problem 24. Write a C++ program using put() to write to a file.**

***Program:***

```
#include <iostream.h>
#include<conio.h>
#include <fstream.h>
int main()
{
char *p = "hello\n";
ofstream out("test", ios::out | ios::binary);
if(!out)
{
cout << "Cannot open file.\n";
return 1;
}
// Write characters until the null-terminator is
reached.
while(*p)
out.put(*p++);
out.close();
getch();
}
```

**OUTPUT:**

hello

**Problem 25. Write a C++ program to output a text file character by character.**

***Program:***

```
#include <iostream.h>
#include<conio.h>
#include <fstream.h>
#include<process.h>
void main(void)
{
ifstream in("test.cpp");
if(!in)
{
cout << "Cannot open file." << endl;
exit (1);
}
in.ignore(10, ' ');
char c;
while(in)
{
in.get(c);/
cout << c;
}
in.close();
getch();
}
```

**Problem 26. Write a C++ program to write formatted output to a text file.**

***Program:***

```
#include <iostream.h>
#include<conio.h>
#include <fstream.h>
int main()
{
```

```
ofstream fout("test.dat");
if(!fout) {
cout << "Cannot open file.\n";
return 1;
}
fout << 10 << " " << -20 << " " << 30.2 << "\n";
fout << "This is a test.";
fout.close();
if(!fout.good()) {
cout << "A file error occurred.";
return 1;
}
getch();
}
```

**Problem 27. Write a C++ program to use ofstream to write text to a file.**

***Program:***

```
#include <iostream.h>
#include<conio.h>
#include <fstream.h>
int main()
{
char *p = "hello there";
ofstream out("test");
if(!out)
{
cout << "Cannot open file";
return 1;
}
while(*p) out.put(*p++);
out.close();
getch();
}
```

**OUTPUT:**

hello there

**Problem 28. Write a C++ program for output string and decimal in hexadecimal format to a file with ostrstream.**

***Program:***

```
#include <iostream.h>
#include<conio.h>
#include <fstream.h>
#include<strstream.h>
void main()
{
char str[80];
int a = 10;
ostrstream outs(str, sizeof(str));
outs << "Hello there ";
outs << a+44 << hex << " ";
outs.setf(ios::showbase);
outs << 100 << ends;
cout << str;
getch();
}
```

**OUTPUT:**

Hello there 54 0*64

**Problem 29. Write a C++ program for output to file line by line.**

***Program:***

```
#include <iostream.h>
#include<conio.h>
#include <fstream.h>
void main ()
{
ofstream myfile("test.txt");
if (myfile.is_open())
{
myfile << "This outputting a line.\n";
myfile << "this is another line.\n";
myfile.close();
}
getch();
}
```

**Problem 30. Write a C++ program to writing on a text file.**

***Program:***

```
#include <iostream.h>
#include<conio.h>
#include <fstream.h>
void main ()
{
ofstream examplefile ("test.txt");
if (examplefile.is_open())
{
examplefile << "This is a line.\n";
examplefile << "This is another line.\n";
examplefile.close();
}
getch();
}
```

**Problem 31. Write a C++ program for file output with strings.**

***Program:***

```
#include <iostream.h>
#include<conio.h>
#include <fstream.h>
```

```
void main()
{
ofstream outfile("TEST.TXT");
outfile << "test\n";
outfile << "1\n";
outfile << "2\n";
outfile << "3\n";
getch();
}
```

**Problem 32. Write a C++ program for file output with characters.**

***Program:***

```
#include <iostream.h>
#include<conio.h>
#include <fstream.h>
#include <string.h>
void main()
{
string str = "AAA";
ofstream outfile("TEST.TXT");
for(int j=0; j<str.size(); j++)
outfile.put( str[j] );
cout << "File written\n";
getch();
}
```

## BINARY FILE:

**Problem 33. Write a C++ program to open a binary file.**

***Program:***

```
#include <iostream.h>
#include<conio.h>
#include <fstream.h>
void main(int argc, char *argv[])
{
char ch;
ifstream in("test.txt", ios::in | ios::binary);
if(!in)
{
cout << "Cannot open file.";
return 1;
}
while(in)
{ // in will be false when eof is reached
in.get(ch);
if(in) cout << ch;
}
getch();
}
```

**OUTPUT:**

```
R 9.9
T 9.9
M 4.8
```

**Problem 34. Write a C++ program to reading binary file.**

***Program:***

```
#include <iostream.h>
#include<conio.h>
#include <fstream.h>
void main ()
{
char * buffer;
long size;
ifstream file ("example.dat",
ios::in|ios::binary|ios::ate);
size = file.tellg();
file.seekg (0, ios::beg);
buffer = new char [size];
file.read (buffer, size);
file.close();
cout << "the complete file is in a buffer";
delete[] buffer;
getch();
}
```

**OUTPUT:**

```
the complete file is in a buffer
```

**Problem 35. Write a C++ program to open a binary file and read.**

***Program:***

```
#include <iostream.h>
#include<conio.h>
#include <fstream.h>
int main(int argc, char *argv[])
{
char ch;
ifstream in("test.txt", ios::in | ios::binary);
if(!in)
{
cout << "Cannot open file.";
return 1;
}
while(in)
{
in.get(ch);
cout << ch;
}
getch();
```

```
}
```

**OUTPUT:**

R 9.9
Y 9.9
M 4.8

**Problem 36. Write a C++ program to output a binary file in hexadecimal.**

***Program:***

```
#include <iostream.h>
#include<conio.h>
#include <fstream.h>
#include <ctype.h>
#include <iomanip.h>
#include <stdio.h>
#include<process.h>
void main(int argc, char *argv[])
{
ifstream in("text.txt", ios::in | ios::binary);
if(!in)
{
cout << "Cannot open input file." << endl;
exit (1);
}
int i, j;
int count = 0;
char c[16];
cout.setf(ios::uppercase);
while(!in.eof())
{
for(i=0; i<16 && !in.eof(); i++)
in.get(c[i]);
if(i<16)
i--;
for(j=0; j < i; j++)
cout << setw(3) << hex << (int) c[j];
for(; j < 16; j++)
cout << "  ";
for(j=0; j < i; j++)
if(isprint(c[j]))
cout << c[j];
else
cout << ".";
cout << endl;
count ++;
if(count==16)
{
count = 0;
cout << "Press ENTER to continue: ";
cin.get();
cout << endl;
}
}
in.close();
getch();
}
```

**Problem 37. Write a C++ program to write Unformatted Binary Data to a File.**

***Program:***

```
#include <iostream.h>
#include<conio.h>
#include <fstream.h>
#include <stdlib.h>
struct inventory
{
char item[20];
int quantity;
double cost;
};
int main(int argc, char *argv[])
{
inventory entry;
long record_num = 2;
Ifstream fInvDB("InvDat.dat", ios::in | ios::binary);
if(!fInvDB)
{
cout << "Cannot open file.\n";
return 1;
}
fInvDB.seekg(sizeof(inventory) * record_num,
ios::beg);
fInvDB.read((char *) &entry, sizeof(inventory));
fInvDB.close();
if(!fInvDB.good())
{
cout << "A file error occurred.\n";
return 1;
}
getch();
}
```

**Problem 38. Write a C++ program to use read() to input blocks of binary data.**

***Program:***

```
#include <iostream.h>
#include<conio.h>
#include <fstream.h>
struct inventory
{
char item[20];
int quantity;
```

```
double cost;
};
int main()
{
ifstream fin("InvDat.dat", ios::in | ios::binary);
if(!fin)
{
cout << "Cannot open file.\n";
return 1;
}
inventory inv[3];
for(int i=0; i<3; i++)
fin.read((char *) &inv[i], sizeof(inventory));
fin.close();
if(!fin.good())
{
cout << "A file error occurred.\n";
return 1;
}
for(int i=0; i < 3; i++)
{
cout << inv[i].item << "\n";
cout << " Quantity on hand: " << inv[i].quantity;
cout << "\n Cost: " << inv[i].cost << "\n\n";
}
getch();
}
```

**Problem 39. Write a C++ program to use write() to output a block of binary data.**

***Program:***

```
#include <iostream.h>
#include<conio.h>
#include <fstream.h>
#include <string.h>
struct inventory
{
char item[20];
int quantity;
double cost;
};
int main()
{
ofstream fout("InvDat.dat", ios::out | ios::binary);
if(!fout)
{
cout << "Cannot open file.\n";
return 1;
}
inventory inv[3];
strcpy(inv[0].item,"A");
inv[0].quantity = 3;
inv[0].cost = 9.99;
strcpy(inv[1].item, "B");
inv[1].quantity = 12;
inv[1].cost = 7.85;
strcpy(inv[2].item, "C");
inv[2].quantity = 19;
inv[2].cost = 2.75;
for(int i=0; i<3; i++)
fout.write((const char *) &inv[i],
sizeof(inventory));
fout.close();
if(!fout.good())
{
cout << "A file error occurred.";
return 1;
}
getch();
}
```

**Problem 40. Write a C++ program to creating a randomly accessed file.**

***Program:***

```
#include <iostream.h>
#include<conio.h>
#include <fstream.h>
#include <stdlib.h>
#include <string.h>
class Account
{
public:
Account( int accountNumberValue, string
lastNameValue, string firstNameValue, double
balanceValue )
{
setAccountNumber( accountNumberValue );
setLastName( lastNameValue );
setFirstName( firstNameValue );
setBalance( balanceValue );
}
int getAccountNumber() const
{
return accountNumber;
}
void setAccountNumber( int accountNumberValue
)
{
accountNumber = accountNumberValue; // should
validate
}
string getLastName() const
```

```
{
return lastName;
}
void setLastName( string lastNameString )
{
const char *lastNameValue = lastNameString.data();
strncpy( lastName, lastNameValue, 5 );
lastName[ 5 ] = '\0';
}
string getFirstName() const
{
return firstName;
}
void setFirstName( string firstNameString )
{
const char *firstNameValue =
firstNameString.data();
strncpy( firstName, firstNameValue, 5 );
firstName[ 5 ] = '\0';
}
double getBalance() const
{
return balance;
}
void setBalance( double balanceValue )
{
balance = balanceValue;
}
private:
int accountNumber;
char lastName[ 15 ];
char firstName[ 10 ];
double balance;
};
void main()
{
ofstream outCredit( "credit.dat", ios::binary );
if ( !outCredit )
{
cerr << "File could not be opened." << endl;
exit( 1 );
}
Account blankClient(1,"AAAAA","BBBBB",1.2);
// output 100 blank records to file
for ( int i = 0; i < 100; i++ )
outCredit.write( reinterpret_cast< const char * >(
&blankClient ),
sizeof( Account ) );
getch();
}
```

**Problem 41. Write a C++ program to append to a binary file.**

***Program:***

```
#include <iostream.h>
#include<conio.h>
#include <fstream.h>
#include<process.h>
void main()
{
ofstream outFile("FileWrite.out");
if (outFile.fail())
{
cerr << "Unable to open file for writing." << endl;
exit(1);
}
outFile << "Hello!" << endl;
outFile.close();
ofstream appendFile("FileWrite.out",
ios_base::app);
if (appendFile.fail())
{
cerr << "Unable to open file for writing." << endl;
exit(1);
}
appendFile << "Append!" << endl;
appendFile.close();
getch();
}
```

**Problem 42. Write a C++ program for unformatted and Binary I/O.**

***Program:***

```
#include <iostream.h>
#include<conio.h>
#include <fstream.h>
int main(int argc, char *argv[])
{
char ch;
if(argc!=2)
{
cout << "Usage: PR <filename>\n";
return 1;
}
ifstream in(argv[1], ios::in | ios::binary);
if(!in)
{
cout << "Cannot open file.";
return 1;
}
while(in)
{ // in will be false when eof is reached
```

```
in.get(ch);
if(in) cout << ch;
}
getch();
}
```

**OUTPUT:**

Usage: PR <filename>

## CLASS SAVE LOAD:

**Problem 43. Write a C++ program to save class to a file.**

***Program:***

```
#include <iostream.h>
#include<conio.h>
#include <fstream.h>
#include <iomanip.h>
#include <stdlib.h>
#include <string.h>
class Account
{
public:
Account( int accountNumberValue, string
lastNameValue, string firstNameValue, double
balanceValue )
{
setAccountNumber( accountNumberValue );
setLastName( lastNameValue );
setFirstName( firstNameValue );
setBalance( balanceValue );
}
int getAccountNumber() const
{
return accountNumber;
}
void setAccountNumber( int accountNumberValue )
{
accountNumber = accountNumberValue; // should
validate
}
string getLastName() const
{
return lastName;
}
void setLastName( string lastNameString )
{
const char *lastNameValue = lastNameString.data();
strncpy( lastName, lastNameValue, 5 );
lastName[ 5 ] = '\0';
}
string getFirstName() const
{
return firstName;
}
void setFirstName( string firstNameString )
{
const char *firstNameValue =
firstNameString.data();
strncpy( firstName, firstNameValue, 5 );
firstName[ 5 ] = '\0';
}
double getBalance() const
{
return balance;
}
void setBalance( double balanceValue )
{
balance = balanceValue;
}
private:
int accountNumber;
char lastName[ 15 ];
char firstName[ 10 ];
double balance;
};
void main()
{
fstream outCredit( "credit.dat", ios::in | ios::out |
ios::binary );
// exit program if fstream cannot open file
if ( !outCredit )
{
cerr << "File could not be opened." << endl;
exit( 1 );
} // end if
Account client(1,"AAAAA","BBBBB",1.2);
// seek position in file of user-specified record
outCredit.seekp( ( client.getAccountNumber() - 1 )
* sizeof( Account ) );
// write user-specified information in file
outCredit.write( reinterpret_cast< const char * >(
&client ),sizeof( Account ) );
getch();
}
```

**Problem 44. Write a C++ program for writing a Class to a File.**

***Program:***

```
#include <iostream.h>
#include<conio.h>
#include <fstream.h>
```

```
class Animal
{
public:
Animal(int weight, long
days):itsWeight(weight),itsNumberDaysAlive(days)
{}
~Animal(){}
int GetWeight()const { return itsWeight; }
void SetWeight(int weight) { itsWeight = weight; }
long GetDaysAlive()const { return
itsNumberDaysAlive; }
void SetDaysAlive(long days) {
itsNumberDaysAlive = days; }
private:
int itsWeight;
long itsNumberDaysAlive;
};
int main()
{
ofstream fout("text.txt",ios::binary);
if (!fout)
{
cout << "Unable to open for writing.\n";
return(1);
}
Animal Bear(50,100);
fout.write((char*) &Bear,sizeof Bear);
fout.close();
ifstream fin("text.txt",ios::binary);
if (!fin)
{
cout << "Unable to open for reading.\n";
return(1);
}
Animal BearTwo(1,1);
cout << "BearTwo weight: " <<
BearTwo.GetWeight() << endl;
cout << "BearTwo days: " <<
BearTwo.GetDaysAlive() << endl;
fin.read((char*) &BearTwo, sizeof BearTwo);
cout << "BearTwo weight: " <<
BearTwo.GetWeight() << endl;
cout << "BearTwo days: " <<
BearTwo.GetDaysAlive() << endl;
fin.close();
getch();
}
```

**OUTPUT:**

```
BearTwo weight: 1
BearTwo days: 1
BearTwo weight: 50
BearTwo days: 100
```

**Problem 45. Write a C++ program to read class data from file.**

***Program:***

```
#include <iostream.h>
#include<conio.h>
#include <fstream.h>
#include <string.h>
#include <iomanip.h>
#include <stdlib.h>
class Account
{
public:
Account( )
{ }
Account( int accountNumberValue, string
lastNameValue, string firstNameValue, double
balanceValue )
{
setAccountNumber( accountNumberValue );
setLastName( lastNameValue );
setFirstName( firstNameValue );
setBalance( balanceValue );
}
int getAccountNumber() const
{
return accountNumber;
}
void setAccountNumber( int accountNumberValue
)
{
accountNumber = accountNumberValue; // should
validate
}
string getLastName() const
{
return lastName;
}
void setLastName( string lastNameString )
{
const char *lastNameValue =
lastNameString.data();
strncpy( lastName, lastNameValue, 5 );
lastName[ 5 ] = '\0';
}
string getFirstName() const
{
return firstName;
}
void setFirstName( string firstNameString )
```

```
{
const char *firstNameValue =
firstNameString.data();
strncpy( firstName, firstNameValue, 5 );
firstName[ 5 ] = '\0';
}
double getBalance() const
{
return balance;
}
void setBalance( double balanceValue )
{
balance = balanceValue;
}
private:
int accountNumber;
char lastName[ 15 ];
char firstName[ 10 ];
double balance;
};
void outputLine( ostream&, const Account & ); //
prototype
void main()
{
ifstream inCredit( "credit.dat", ios::in );
if ( !inCredit )
{
cerr << "File could not be opened." << endl;
exit( 1 );
} // end if
Account client; // create record
inCredit.read( reinterpret_cast< char * >( &client ),
sizeof( Account ) );
while ( inCredit && !inCredit.eof() )
{
if ( client.getAccountNumber() != 0 )
outputLine( cout, client );
inCredit.read( reinterpret_cast< char * >( &client
),sizeof( Account ) );
}
getch();
}
void outputLine( ostream &output, const Account
&record )
{
output << left << setw( 10 ) <<
record.getAccountNumber()
<< setw( 16 ) << record.getLastName()
<< setw( 11 ) << record.getFirstName()
<< setw( 10 ) << setprecision( 2 ) << right << fixed
<< showpoint << record.getBalance() << endl;
}
```

**OUTPUT:**

```
1    AAAAA    BBBBB    1.20
1    AAAAA    BBBBB    1.20
1    AAAAA    BBBBB    1.20
1    AAAAA    BBBBB    1.20
1    AAAAA    BBBBB    1.20
1    AAAAA    BBBBB    1.20
1    AAAAA    BBBBB    1.20
1    AAAAA    BBBBB    1.20
1    AAAAA    BBBBB    1.20
1    AAAAA    BBBBB    1.20
1    AAAAA    BBBBB    1.20
1    AAAAA    BBBBB    1.20
1    AAAAA    BBBBB    1.20
1    AAAAA    BBBBB    1.20
1    AAAAA    BBBBB    1.20
1    AAAAA    BBBBB    1.20
1    AAAAA    BBBBB    1.20
1    AAAAA    BBBBB    1.20
1    AAAAA    BBBBB    1.20
1    AAAAA    BBBBB    1.20
1    AAAAA    BBBBB    1.20
1    AAAAA    BBBBB    1.20
1    AAAAA    BBBBB    1.20
1    AAAAA    BBBBB    1.20
1    AAAAA    BBBBB    1.20
1    AAAAA    BBBBB    1.20
1    AAAAA    BBBBB    1.20
1    AAAAA    BBBBB    1.20
1    AAAAA    BBBBB    1.20
1    AAAAA    BBBBB    1.20
1    AAAAA    BBBBB    1.20
1    AAAAA    BBBBB    1.20
1    AAAAA    BBBBB    1.20
1    AAAAA    BBBBB    1.20
1    AAAAA    BBBBB    1.20
1    AAAAA    BBBBB    1.20
1    AAAAA    BBBBB    1.20
1    AAAAA    BBBBB    1.20
1    AAAAA    BBBBB    1.20
1    AAAAA    BBBBB    1.20
1    AAAAA    BBBBB    1.20
1    AAAAA    BBBBB    1.20
1    AAAAA    BBBBB    1.20
1    AAAAA    BBBBB    1.20
1    AAAAA    BBBBB    1.20
1    AAAAA    BBBBB    1.20
1    AAAAA    BBBBB    1.20
1    AAAAA    BBBBB    1.20
1    AAAAA    BBBBB    1.20
```

```
1 AAAAA BBBBB 1.20
1 AAAAA BBBBB 1.20
1 AAAAA BBBBB 1.20
1 AAAAA BBBBB 1.20
1 AAAAA BBBBB 1.20
1 AAAAA BBBBB 1.20
1 AAAAA BBBBB 1.20
1 AAAAA BBBBB 1.20
1 AAAAA BBBBB 1.20
1 AAAAA BBBBB 1.20
1 AAAAA BBBBB 1.20
1 AAAAA BBBBB 1.20
1 AAAAA BBBBB 1.20
1 AAAAA BBBBB 1.20
1 AAAAA BBBBB 1.20
1 AAAAA BBBBB 1.20
1 AAAAA BBBBB 1.20
1 AAAAA BBBBB 1.20
1 AAAAA BBBBB 1.20
1 AAAAA BBBBB 1.20
1 AAAAA BBBBB 1.20
1 AAAAA BBBBB 1.20
1 AAAAA BBBBB 1.20
1 AAAAA BBBBB 1.20
1 AAAAA BBBBB 1.20
1 AAAAA BBBBB 1.20
1 AAAAA BBBBB 1.20
1 AAAAA BBBBB 1.20
1 AAAAA BBBBB 1.20
1 AAAAA BBBBB 1.20
1 AAAAA BBBBB 1.20
1 AAAAA BBBBB 1.20
1 AAAAA BBBBB 1.20
1 AAAAA BBBBB 1.20
1 AAAAA BBBBB 1.20
1 AAAAA BBBBB 1.20
1 AAAAA BBBBB 1.20
1 AAAAA BBBBB 1.20
1 AAAAA BBBBB 1.20
1 AAAAA BBBBB 1.20
1 AAAAA BBBBB 1.20
1 AAAAA BBBBB 1.20
1 AAAAA BBBBB 1.20
1 AAAAA BBBBB 1.20
1 AAAAA BBBBB 1.20
1 AAAAA BBBBB 1.20
1 AAAAA BBBBB 1.20
1 AAAAA BBBBB 1.20
1 AAAAA BBBBB 1.20
1 AAAAA BBBBB 1.20
1 AAAAA BBBBB 1.20
```

**Problem 46. Write a C++ program to read person object from disk.**

***Program:***

```
#include <iostream.h>
#include<conio.h>
#include <fstream.h>
class person
{
protected:
char name[80];
short age;
public:
void showData()
{
cout << "Name: " << name << endl;
cout << "Age: " << age << endl;
}
};
void main()
{
person pers;
ifstream infile("PERSON.DAT", ios::binary);
infile.read( reinterpret_cast<char*>(&pers),
sizeof(pers) );
pers.showData();
getch();
}
```

**Problem 47. Write a C++ program to saves person object to disk.**

***Program:***

```
#include <iostream.h>
#include<conio.h>
#include <fstream.h>
class person
{
protected:
char name[80];
short age;
public:
void getData()
{
cout << "Enter name: "; cin >> name;
cout << "Enter age: "; cin >> age;
}
};
void main()
{
person pers;
pers.getData();
```

```
ofstream outfile("PERSON.DAT", ios::binary);
outfile.write(reinterpret_cast<char*>(&pers),
sizeof(pers));
getch();
}
```

**Problem 48. Write a C++ program to reads and writes several objects to disk.**

***Program:***

```
#include <iostream.h>
#include<conio.h>
#include <fstream.h>
class person
{
protected:
char name[80];
int age;
public:
void getData()
{
cout << "\n   Enter name: "; cin >> name;
cout << "   Enter age: "; cin >> age;
}
void showData()
{
cout << "\n   Name: " << name;
cout << "\n   Age: " << age;
}
};
void main()
{
char ch;
person pers;
fstream file;
file.open("GROUP.DAT", ios::app | ios::out |  ios::in
| ios::binary );
do
{
cout << "\nEnter person's data:";
pers.getData();
file.write( reinterpret_cast<char*>(&pers),
sizeof(pers) );
cout << "Enter another person (y/n)? ";
cin >> ch;
}while(ch=='y');
file.seekg(0);
file.read( reinterpret_cast<char*>(&pers),
sizeof(pers) );
while( !file.eof() )
{
cout << "\nPerson:";
pers.showData();
file.read( reinterpret_cast<char*>(&pers),
sizeof(pers) );
}
cout << endl;
getch();
}
```

## FILE OPEN MODE:

**Problem 49. Write a C++ program to open a file for input and read in its content.**

***Program:***

```
#include <iostream.h>
#include<conio.h>
#include <fstream.h>
void main ()
{
char buffer[256];
fstream myfile;
// open it for input and read in
myfile.open("test.txt",ios::in);
myfile.getline(buffer,100);
cout << "The file contains   " << buffer << "\n";
myfile.close();
getch();
}
```

**OUTPUT:**

The file contains   This outputting a line.

**Problem 50. Write a C++ program to open a file for appending and append.**

***Program:***

```
#include <iostream.h>
#include<conio.h>
#include <fstream.h>
void main ()
{
char buffer[256];
fstream myfile;
//open for appending and append
myfile.open("test.txt",ios::app);
myfile << " Hey this is another line \n";
myfile.close();
getch();
}
```

**OUTPUT:**

Hey this is another line

**Problem 51. Write a C++ program to open a file as binary file and get its size.**

***Program:***

```
#include <iostream.h>
#include<conio.h>
#include <fstream.h>
void main ()
{
long start,end;
ifstream myfile ("test.txt", ios::in|ios::binary);
start = myfile.tellg();
myfile.seekg (0, ios::end);
end = myfile.tellg();
myfile.close();
cout << "size of " << "test.txt";
cout << " is " << (end-start) << " bytes.\n";
getch();
}
```

**OUTPUT:**

size of test.txt is 25 bytes.

**Problem 52. Write a C++ program to opening text Files for Read and Write.**

***Program:***

```
#include <iostream.h>
#include<conio.h>
#include <fstream.h>
void main()
{
char buffer[255];
ofstream fout("text.txt");
fout << "this is a test\n";
cout << "Enter text for the file: ";
cin.ignore(1,'\n');
cin.getline(buffer,255);
fout << buffer << "\n";
fout.close();
ifstream fin("text.txt");
cout << "Here's the contents of the file:\n";
char ch;
while (fin.get(ch))
cout << ch;
fin.close();
getch();
}
```

**OUTPUT:**

Enter text for the file:text
this is a test
ext

**Problem 53. Write a C++ program to appending to the End of a File.**

***Program:***

```
#include <iostream.h>
#include<conio.h>
#include <fstream.h>
int main()
{
char buffer[255];
ifstream fin("text.txt");
if (fin)
{
char ch;
while (fin.get(ch))
cout << ch;
}
fin.close();
cout << "in append mode...\n";
ofstream fout("text.txt",ios::app);
if (!fout)
{
cout << "Unable to open for appending.\n";
return(1);
}
cout << "\nEnter text for the file. ",
cin.ignore(1,'\n');
cin.getline(buffer,255);
fout << buffer << "\n";
fout.close();
fin.open("text.txt");
if (!fin)
{
cout << "Unable to open for reading.\n";
return(1);
}
char ch;
while (fin.get(ch))
cout << ch;
fin.close();
getch();
}
```

**OUTPUT:**

Enter text for the file:text
this is a test
ext.txt
ext

**Problem 54. Write a C++ program to opening files for read and write.**

***Program:***

```
#include <iostream.h>
#include<conio.h>
#include <fstream.h>
void main()
{
char buffer[255];
ofstream fout("text.txt");
fout << "test\n";
cout << "Enter text for the file: ";
cin.ignore(1,'\n');
cin.getline(buffer,255);
fout << buffer << "\n";
fout.close();
ifstream fin("text.txt");
char ch;
while (fin.get(ch))
cout << ch;
fin.close();
getch();
}
```

**OUTPUT:**

```
Enter text for the file:text
test
ext
```

# FILE POINTER:

**Problem 55. Write a C++ program to change file at given position.**

***Program:***

```
#include <iostream.h>
#include<conio.h>
#include <fstream.h>
#include <stdlib.h>
int main(int argc, char *argv[])
{
if(argc!=3)
{
cout << "Usage: CHANGE <filename> <byte>\n";
return 1;
}
fstream out(argv[1], ios::in|ios::out);
if(!out)
{
cout << "Cannot open file";
return 1;
}
out.seekp(atoi(argv[2]), ios::beg);
out.put('X');
out.close();
getch();
}
```

**OUTPUT:**

```
Usage: CHANGE <filename> <byte>
```

**Problem 56. Write a C++ program to get file content at given position.**

***Program:***

```
#include <iostream.h>
#include<conio.h>
#include <fstream.h>
#include <stdlib.h>
int main(int argc, char *argv[])
{
char ch;
if(argc!=3)
{
cout << "Usage: NAME <filename> <starting
location>\n";
return 1;
}
ifstream in(argv[1]);
if(!in)
{
cout << "Cannot open file";
return 1;
}
in.seekg(atoi(argv[2]), ios::beg);
while(in.get(ch))
cout << ch;
getch();
}
```

**Problem 57. Write a C++ program to change a file at specific position.**

***Program:***

```
#include <iostream.h>
#include<conio.h>
#include <fstream.h>
void main(int argc, char *argv[])
{
if(argc!=4)
{
cout << "Usage: change <filename> <byte>
<character>" << endl;
exit (1);
}
fstream out(argv[1], ios::in | ios::out | ios::binary);
if(!out)
{
cout << "Cannot open file!";
```

```
exit (1);
}
out.seekp(atoi(argv[2]), ios::beg);
out.put(*argv[3]);
out.close();
getch();
}
```

**Problem 58. Write a C++ program to check ofstream current marker position.**

***Program:***.

```
#include <iostream.h>
#include<conio.h>
#include <fstream.h>
#include<strstream.h>
void main(int argc, char** argv)
{
ofstream fout("test.out");
fout << "12345";
long curPos = fout.tellp();
if (curPos == 5)
{
cout << "Test passed: Currently at position 5" <<
endl,
}
else
{
cout << "Test failed: Not at position 5" << endl;
}
fout.seekp(2, ios_base::beg);
fout << 0;
fout.flush();
ifstream fin("test.out");
int testVal;
fin >> testVal;
if (testVal == 12045)
{
cout << "Test passed: Value is 12045" << endl;
}
else
{
cout << "Test failed: Value is not 12045 (it was " <<
testVal << ")" << endl;
}
getch();
}
```

**Problem 59. Write a C++ program to move to position 2 in the stream and output a 0 in position 2.**

***Program:***

```
#include <iostream.h>
#include<conio.h>
#include <fstream.h>
void main(int argc, char** argv)
{
ofstream fout("test.out");
fout << "12345";
long curPos = fout.tellp();
if (curPos == 5)
{
cout << "Test passed: Currently at position 5" <<
endl;
}
else
{
cout << "Test failed: Not at position 5" << endl;
}
fout.seekp(2, ios_base::beg);
fout << 0;
fout.flush();
ifstream fin("test.out");
int testVal;
fin >> testVal;
if (testVal == 12045)
{
cout << "Test passed: Value is 12045" << endl;
}
else
{
cout << "Test failed: Value is not 12045 (it was "
<< testVal << ")" << endl;
}
getch();
}
```

**Problem 60. Write a C++ program to tell the current position.**

***Program:***

```
#include <iostream.h>
#include<conio.h>
#include <fstream.h>
#include <stdlib.h>
void main(int argc, char *argv[])
{
if(argc!=4)
{
cout << "Usage: change <filename> <byte>
<character>" << endl;
exit(1);
}
fstream out(argv[1], ios::in | ios::out | ios::binary);
```

```
if(!out)
{
cout << "Cannot open file!";
exit(1);
}
out.seekp(atoi(argv[2]), ios::beg);
out.put(*argv[3]);
cout << "Current position is: " << out.tellp() <<
endl;
out.close();
getch();
}
```

**Problem 61. Write a C++ program for seek and Skip.**

***Program:***

```
#include <iostream.h>
#include<conio.h>
#include <fstream.h>
void main()
{
ifstream in("datafile");
in.unsetf(ios::skipws);
char ch;
while (in >> ch)
{
cout << ch;
}
cout << '\n';
in.clear();
in.seekg(ios::beg);
in.setf(ios::skipws);
while (in >> ch)
{
cout << ch;
}
cout << '\n';
getch();
}
```

**OUTPUT:**

Genius

**Problem 62. Write a C++ program to test File Position.**

***Program:***

```
#include <string.h>
#include <iostream.h>
#include<conio.h>
#include <fstream.h>
void main()
{
fstream inout( "invoice.dat", ios::in | ios::out );
inout << 1234 << " " << 56.78 << " " << "apples"
<<'\n';
cout << inout.tellg() << endl;
cout << inout.tellp() << endl;
inout.seekg( ios::beg );
cout << inout.tellg() << endl;
cout << inout.tellp() << endl;
int x;
double y;
char z;
inout>> x >> y;
inout >> z;
cout << x << " " << y << " " << z << endl;
getch();
}
```

**OUTPUT:**

19
19
0
0
1234 56.78 a

**Problem 63. Write a C++ program to seek 0 to reset the file pointer.**

***Program:***

```
#include <iostream.h>
#include<conio.h>
#include <fstream.h>
#include <string.h>
void main()
{
fstream inout( "invoice.dat", ios::in | ios::out );
inout << 1234 << " " << 56.78 << " " << "apples"
<< '\n';
cout<< inout.tellg()<< endl;
cout << inout.tellp() << endl;
inout.seekg( 0 );
cout << inout.tellg() << endl;
cout << inout.tellp() << endl;
int x = 0;
double y = 0.0;
char z ;
inout >> x;
inout.seekg( 8, ios::cur );
inout >> z;
cout << x << " " << y << " " << z << endl;
getch();
}
```

**OUTPUT:**

19
19

0
0
1234 0 p

**Problem 64. Write a C++ program to seekg( ) moves the pointer offset number of characters from the specified origin.**

It must be one of these three values:

ios::beg Beginning-of-file
ios::cur Current location
ios::end End-of-file

***Program:***

```
#include <iostream.h>
#include<conio.h>
#include <fstream.h>
#include <stdlib.H>


void main(int argc, char *argv[])
{
if(argc!=4)
{
cout << "Usage: CHANGE <filename> <character>
<char>\n";
return 1;
}
fstream out(argv[1], ios::in | ios::out | ios::binary);
if(!out)
{
cout << "Cannot open file.";
return 1;
}
out.seekp(atoi(argv[2]), ios::beg);
out.put(*argv[3]);
out.close();
getch();
}
```

**Problem 65. Write a C++ program to uses both seekp( ) and seekg( ) to reverse the first characters in a file.**

***Program:***

```
#include <iostream.h>
#include<conio.h>
#include <fstream.h>
#include <stdlib.h>
void main(int argc, char *argv[])
{
if(argc!=3)
{
cout << "Usage: Reverse <filename> <num>\n";
return 1;
}
fstream inout(argv[1], ios::in | ios::out |
ios::binary);
if(!inout)
{
cout << "Cannot open input file.\n";
return 1;
}
long e, i, j;
char c1, c2;
e = atol(argv[2]);
for(i=0, j=e; i<j; i++, j--)
{
inout.seekg(i, ios::beg);
inout.get(c1);
inout.seekg(j, ios::beg);
inout.get(c2);
inout.seekp(i, ios::beg);
inout.put(c2);
inout.seekp(j, ios::beg);
inout.put(c1);
}
inout.close();
getch();
}
```

**Problem 66. Write a C++ program to detecting EOF.**

***Program:***

```
#include <iostream.h>
#include<conio.h>
#include <fstream.h>
#include <ctype.h>
#include <iomanip.h>
void main(int argc, char *argv[])
{
if(argc!=2)
{
cout << "Usage: Display <filename>\n";
return 1;
}
ifstream in(argv[1], ios::in | ios::binary);
if(!in)
{
cout << "Cannot open input file.\n";
return 1;
}
register int i, j;
int count = 0;
char c[16];
```

```
cout.setf(ios::uppercase);
while(!in.eof())
{
for(i=0; i<16 && !in.eof(); i++)
{
in.get(c[i]);
}
if(i<16) i--; // get rid of eof
for(j=0; j<i; j++)
cout << setw(3) << hex << (int) c[j];
for(; j<16; j++) cout << "  ";
cout << "\t";
for(j=0; j<i; j++)
if(isprint(c[j])) cout << c[j];
else cout << ".";
cout << endl;
count++;
if(count==16)
{
count = 0;
cout << "Press ENTER to continue: ";
cin.get();
cout << endl;
}
}
in.close();
getch();
}
```

## FILE UTILITIES:

**Problem 67. Write a C++ program to use ifstream and ofstream to copy file.**

***Program:***

```
#include <iostream.h>
#include<conio.h>
#include <fstream.h>
void main()
{
char ch;
ifstream f1("test.txt");
ofstream f2("text1.txt");
if(!f1)
cerr <<"Can't open IN file\n";
if(!f2)
cerr << "Can't open OUT file\n";
while(f1 && f1.get(ch) )
f2.put(ch);
getch();
}
```

**OUTPUT:**

This is a test

**Problem 68. Write a C++ program to check file status.**

***Program:***

```
#include <iostream.h>
#include<conio.h>
#include <fstream.h>
void checkstatus(ifstream &in);
void main(int argc, char *argv[])
{
ifstream in("test.txt");
char c;
while(in.get(c))
{
checkstatus(in);
}
checkstatus(in);  // check final status
in.close();
getch();
}
void checkstatus(ifstream &in)
{
ios::iostate i;
i = in.rdstate();
if(i & ios::eofbit)
cout << "EOF encountered\n";
else if(i & ios::failbit)
cout << "Non-Fatal I/O error\n";
else if(i & ios::badbit)
cout << "Fatal I/O error\n";
}
```

**OUTPUT:**

EOF encountered

**Problem 69. Write a C++ program to obtaining file size.**

***Program:***

```
#include <iostream.h>
#include<conio.h>
#include <fstream.h>
const char * filename = "test.txt";
void main ()
{
long l,m;
ifstream file (filename, ios::in|ios::binary);
l = file.tellg();
file.seekg (0, ios::end);
m = file.tellg();
file.close();
```

```
cout << "size of " << filename;
cout << " is " << (m-l) << " bytes.\n";
getch();
}
```

**OUTPUT:**

size of test.txt is 40 bytes.

**Problem 70. Write a C++ program for a file comparision utility.**

***Program:***

```
#include <iostream.h>
#include<conio.h>
#include <fstream.h>
int main(int argc, char *argv[])
{
register int i;
int numread;
unsigned char buf1[1024], buf2[1024];
ifstream f1("file1", ios::in | ios::binary);
if(!f1)
{
cout << "Cannot open first file.\n";
return 1;
}
ifstream f2("file2", ios::in | ios::binary);
if(!f2)
{
cout << "Cannot open second file.\n";
return 1;
}
do
{
f1.read((char *) buf1, sizeof buf1);
f2.read((char *) buf2, sizeof buf2);
if(f1.gcount() != f2.gcount())
{
cout << "Files are of differing sizes.\n";
f1.close();
f2.close();
return 0;
}
for(i=0; i<f1.gcount(); i++)
{
if(buf1[i] != buf2[i])
{
cout << "Files differ.\n";
f1.close();
f2.close();
return 0;
}
}
} while(!f1.eof() && !f2.eof());
cout << "Files are the same.\n";
f1.close();
f2.close();
getch();
}
```

**OUTPUT:**

Cannot open first file.

**Problem 71. Write a C++ program to get file information: size, device, creation time and last modification time.**

***Program:***

```
#include <iostream.h>
#include <time.h>
#include <sys/types.h>
#include <sys/stat.h>
#include <string.h>
#include<conio.h>
#include <fstream.h>
void main(int argc, char** argv )
{
struct stat fileInfo;
if (stat("test.txt", &fileInfo) != 0)
{
// Use stat( ) to get the info
cerr << "Error: " << strerror(errno) << '\n';
return(EXIT_FAILURE);
}
cout << "Type:         : ";
if ((fileInfo.st_mode & S_IFMT) == S_IFDIR) { //
From sys/types.h
cout << "Directory\n";
}
else
{
cout << "File\n";
}
cout << "Size          : " <<
fileInfo.st_size << '\n';              // Size in bytes
cout << "Device        : " <<
(char)(fileInfo.st_dev + 'A') << '\n'; // Device
number
cout << "Created       : " <<
ctime(&fileInfo.st_ctime);      // Creation time
cout << "Modified      : " <<
ctime(&fileInfo.st_mtime);      // Last mod time
getch();
}
```

**OUTPUT:**

Type:        : File

Size : 21
Device : C
Created : Mon Apr 23 11:16:57 2007
Modified : Mon Apr 23 13:09:24 2007

**Problem 72. Write a C++ program to count number of lines of all files passed as argument.**

***Program:***

```
#include <iostream.h>
#include<conio.h>
#include <fstream.h>
int countLines (istream& in);
void main (int argc, char* argv[])
{
int count;
if (argc == 1)
{
// no argument => count lines of standard input
count = countLines(cin);
}
else
{
// count number of lines of all files passed as
argument
ifstream in;
count = 0;
for (int i=1; i<argc; ++i)
{
in.open(argv[i]);
if (!in)
{
cerr << "failed to open " << argv[1] << "\n";
}
else
{
count += countLines(in);
in.close();
}
}
}
cout << count << endl;
getch();
}
int countLines (istream& in)
{
return
count(istreambuf_iterator<char>(in),istreambuf_iter
ator<char>(),'\n');
}
```

**OUTPUT:**

```
asdf
^CTerminate batch job (Y/N)? n
```

**Problem 73. Write a C++ program to copying one file into another.**

***Program:***

```
#include <iostream.h>
#include<conio.h>
#include <fstream.h>
#include <stdlib.h>
void print_error(const char*, const char* = " ");
void main(int argc, char* argv[])
{
if (3 != argc)
print_error("usage: copy source dest");
ifstream in( argv[1], ios::binary );
if (!in)
print_error( "can't open", argv[1] );
ofstream out( argv[2], ios::binary );
if (!out)
print_error( "can't open", argv[2] );
char ch;
while ( in.get(ch) )
out.put( ch );
if ( !in.eof() )
print_error("something strange happened");
getch();
}
void print_error(const char* p, const char* p2)
{
cerr << p << ' ' << p2 << '\n';
exit(1);
}
```

**Problem 74. Write a C++ program for a simple file-comparison utility.**

***Program:***

```
#include <iostream.h>
#include<conio.h>
#include <fstream.h>
int main(int argc, char *argv[])
{
bool equal = true;
bool ferr = false;
unsigned char buf1[1024], buf2[1024];
if(argc!=3)
{
cout << "Usage: compfiles <file1> <file2>\n";
return 1;
}
ifstream f1(argv[1], ios::in | ios::binary);
if(!f1) {
cout << "Cannot open " << argv[1] << endl;
```

```
return 1;
}
ifstream f2(argv[2], ios::in | ios::binary);
if(!f2)
{
cout << "Cannot open " << argv[2] << endl;
f1.close();
if(!f1.good())
cout << "Error closing " << argv[1] << endl;
return 1;
}
do
{
f1.read((char *) buf1, sizeof buf1);
f2.read((char *) buf2, sizeof buf2);
if(!f1.eof() && !f1.good())
{
cout << "Error reading " << argv[1] << endl;
ferr = true;
break;
}
if(!f2.eof() && !f2.good())
{
cout << "Error reading " << argv[2] << endl;
ferr = true;
break;
}
if(f1.gcount() != f2.gcount())
{
cout << "Files are different lengths.\n";
equal = false;
break;
}
for(int i=0; i < f1.gcount(); ++i)
if(buf1[i] != buf2[i])
{
cout << "Files differ.\n";
equal = false;
break;
}
} while(!f1.eof() && !f2.eof() && equal);
if(!ferr && equal) cout << "Files are the same.\n";
f1.clear();
f2.clear();
f1.close();
f2.close();
if(!f1.good() || !f2.good())
{
cout << "Error closing files.\n";
return 1;
}
getch();
}
```

# FSTREAM:

**Problem 75. Write a C++ program to open a file for output then write to that file.**

***Program:***

```
#include <iostream.h>
#include<conio.h>
#include <fstream.h>
void main ()
{
char buffer[256];
// open it for output then write to it
fstream myfile;
myfile.open("test.txt",ios::out | ios::trunc);
if (myfile.is_open())
{
myfile << "This outputting a line.\n";
myfile.close();
}
getch();
}
```

**Problem 76. Write a C++ program to reverse a file.**

***Program:***

```
#include <iostream.h>
#include<conio.h>
#include <fstream.h>
#include <stdlib.h>
int main(int argc, char *argv[])
{
fstream inout("test.txt", ios::in | ios::out |
ios::binary);
if(!inout)
{
cout << "Cannot open input file.\n";
return 1;
}
long e, i, j;
char c1, c2;
e = 5;
for(i=0, j=e; i<j; i++, j--)
{
inout.seekg(i, ios::beg);
inout.get(c1);
inout.seekg(j, ios::beg);
inout.get(c2);
```

```
inout.seekp(i, ios::beg);
inout.put(c2);
inout.seekp(j, ios::beg);
inout.put(c1);
}
inout.close();
getch();
}
```

**Problem 77. Write a C++ program to use fstream to read and write a file.**

***Program:***

```
#include <iostream.h>
#include<conio.h>
#include <fstream.h>
int main()
{
char ch;
fstream finout("test.dat");
if(!finout)
{
cout << "Cannot open file for output.\n";
return 1;
}
for(int i=0; i < 3; ++i) finout.put('X');
if(!finout.good())
{
cout << "Error occurred while writing to the file.\n";
return 1;
}
finout.flush();
cout << "Here are the next ten characters: ";
for(int i=0; i < 10; ++i)
{
finout.get(ch);
cout << ch;
}
cout << endl;
if(!finout.good())
{
cout << "Error occurred while reading from the
file.\n";
return 1;
}
finout.close();
if(!finout.good())
{
cout << "Error occurred while closing the file.\n";
return 1;
}
getch();
}
```

**Problem 78. Write a C++ program to change a file by offset.**

***Program:***

```
#include <iostream.h>
#include<conio.h>
#include <fstream.h>
#include <stdlib.h>
void main(int argc, char *argv[])
{
fstream out("test.txt", ios::in | ios::out |
ios::binary);
if(!out)
{
cout << "Cannot open file.";
return 1;
}
out.seekp(12, ios::beg);
out.put('a');
out.close();
getch();
}
```

## IFSTREAM:

**Problem 79. Write a C++ program to read and display a text file line by line.**

***Program:***

```
#include <iostream.h>
#include<conio.h>
#include <fstream.h>
void main(int argc, char *argv[])
{
ifstream in("test.txt");
if(!in)
{
cout << "Cannot open input file.\n";
return 1;
}
char str[255];
while(in)
{
in.getline(str, 255);  // delim defaults to '\n'
if(in) cout << str << endl;
}
in.close();
getch();
}
```

**OUTPUT:**

R 9.9
T 9.9
M 4.8

**Problem 80. Write a C++ program to display a file using ifstream.get().**

***Program:***

```
#include <iostream.h>
#include<conio.h>
#include <fstream.h>
void main(int argc, char *argv[])
{
char ch;
ifstream in("test", ios::in | ios::binary);
if(!in)
{
cout << "Cannot open file.\n";
return 1;
}
while(in)
{ // in will be false when eof is reached
in.get(ch);
if(in) cout << ch;
}
in.close();
getch();
}
```

**OUTPUT:**

hello

**Problem 81. Write a C++ program to use ifstream.read() and ofstream.write().**

***Program:***

```
#include <iostream.h>
#include<conio.h>
#include <fstream.h>
int main()
{
int n[5] = {1, 2, 3, 4, 5};
register int i;
ofstream out("test", ios::out | ios::binary);
if(!out)
{
cout << "Cannot open file.\n";
return 1;
}
out.write((char *) &n, sizeof n);
out.close();
for(i=0; i<5; i++) // clear array
n[i] = 0;
ifstream in("test", ios::in | ios::binary);
if(!in)
{
cout << "Cannot open file.\n";
return 1;
}
in.read((char *) &n, sizeof n);
for(i=0; i<5; i++) // show values read from file
cout << n[i] << " ";
in.close();
getch();
}
```

**OUTPUT:**

1 2 3 4 5

**Problem 82. Write a C++ program to display a file from a given starting point.**

***Program:***

```
#include <iostream.h>
#include<conio.h>
#include <fstream.h>
#include <cstdlib.h>
void main(int argc, char *argv[])
{
char ch;
ifstream in("test.txt", ios::in | ios::binary);
if(!in)
{
cout << "Cannot open file.\n";
return 1;
}
in.seekg(1, ios::beg);
while(in.get(ch))
cout << ch;
getch();
}
```

**OUTPUT:**

0 123.23
This is a text.

**Problem 83. Write a C++ program for reading a text file.**

***Program:***

```
#include <iostream.h>
#include <fstream.h>
#include <stdlib.h>
#include<conio.h>
void main ()
{
char buffer[256];
ifstream examplefile ("test.txt");
if (! examplefile.is_open())
```

```
{
cout << "Error opening file";
exit (1);
}
while (! examplefile.eof() )
{
examplefile.getline (buffer,100);
cout << buffer << endl;
}
getch();
}
```

**OUTPUT:**

This is a line.
This is another line.

**Problem 84. Write a C++ program for reading numbers from a file.**

***Program:***

```
#include <iostream.h>
#include<conio.h>
#include <fstream.h>
#include <iomanip.h>
void main()
{
const char* filename = "test.txt";
ifstream inFile(filename);
// Make sure the file stream is good
if(!inFile)
{
cout << endl << "Failed to open file " << filename;
return 1;
}
long n = 0;
while(!inFile.eof())
{
inFile >> n;
cout << setw(10) << n;
}
cout << endl;
getch();
}
```

**OUTPUT:**

```
0    1    2    3    4    5    6    7
8    9    10   11   12   13   14   15
16   17   18   19   20   21   22
23   24   25   26   2728      29   30
31   32   33   34   35   36   37
38   39   40   41 42     43   44   45
46   47   48   49   50   51   52
53   54   55  56   57   58   59   60
61   62   63   64   65   66   67
68   69   70   71   72   73   74
75   76   77   78   79   80   81
82   83   84   85   86   87   88
89   90   91   92   93   94   95
96   97   98   99
```

**Problem 85. Write a C++ program to show a file from starting offset.**

***Program:***

```
#include <iostream.h>
#include<conio.h>
#include <fstream.h>
#include <stdlib.h>
void main(int argc, char *argv[])
{
char ch;
ifstream in("test.txt", ios::in | ios::binary);
if(!in)
{
cout << "Cannot open file.";
return 1;
}
in.seekg(2, ios::beg);
while(in.get(ch))
cout << ch;
getch();
}
```

**OUTPUT:**

9.9
T 9.9a
M 4.8

**Problem 86. Write a C++ program to ignore up to 10 characters or until first space is found.**

***Program:***

```
#include <iostream.h>
#include<conio.h>
#include <fstream.h>
void main()
{
ifstream in("test");
if(!in)
{
cout << "Cannot open file.\n";
return 1;
}
in.ignore(10, ' ');
char c;
while(in)
{
in.get(c);
```

```
if(in) cout << c;
}
in.close();
getch();
}
```

**Problem 87. Write a C++ program for ifstream: read buffer and seek file position.**

***Program:***

```
#include <iostream.h>
#include<conio.h>
#include <fstream.h>
void printFileTwice (const char* filename)
{
// open file
ifstream file(filename);
// print contents the first time
cout << file.rdbuf();
// seek to the beginning
file.seekg(0);
// print contents the second time
cout << file.rdbuf();
}
void main (int argc, char* argv[])
{
// print all files passed as a command-line argument
twice
for (int i=1; i<argc; ++i)
{
printFileTwice(argv[i]);
}
getch();
}
```

# OFSTREAM:

**Problem 88. Write a C++ program to save char array to a file.**

***Program:***

```
#include <iostream.h>
#include<conio.h>
#include <fstream.h>
void main()
{
ofstream out("test.txt");
if(! out)
{
cout<<"Cannot open output file\n";
return 1;
}
char nums[4]={'a','b','c','d'};
out.write((char *)nums,sizeof(nums));
out.close();
ifstream in("test.txt");
if(! in)
{
cout<<"Cannot open input file\n";
return 1;
}
in.read((char *)& nums,sizeof(nums));
for(int i=0;i<4;i++)
cout<<nums[i]<<' ';
cout<<'\n';
cout<<in.gcount()<<"characters read\n";
in.close();
getch();
}
```

**OUTPUT:**

```
a b c d
4characters read
```

**Problem 89. Write a C++ program to read char array from a file.**

***Program:***

```
#include <iostream.h>
#include<conio.h>
#include <fstream.h>
void main()
{
ofstream out("test.txt");
if(! out)
{
cout<<"Cannot open output file\n";
return 1;
}
char nums[4]={'a','b','c','d'};
out.write((char *)nums,sizeof(nums));
out.close();
ifstream in("test.txt");
if(! in)
{
cout<<"Cannot open input file\n";
return 1;
}
in.read((char *)& nums,sizeof(nums));
for(int i=0;i<4;i++)
cout<<nums[i]<<' ';
cout<<'\n';
cout<<in.gcount()<<"characters read\n";
in.close();
getch();
```

```
}
```

**OUTPUT:**

```
a b c d
4characters read
```

**Problem 90. Write a C++ program for writing on a text file.**

***Program:***

```
#include <iostream.h>
#include<conio.h>
#include <fstream.h>
void main ()
{
ofstream examplefile ("test.txt");
if (examplefile.is_open())
{
examplefile << "This is a line.\n";
examplefile << "This is another line.\n";
examplefile.close();
}
getch();
}
```

**OUTPUT:**

```
This is a line.
This is another line.
```

**Problem 91. Write a C++ program for writing numbers to a file.**

***Program:***

```
#include <iomanip.h>
#include <iostream.h>
#include<conio.h>
#include <fstream.h>
void main()
{
ofstream outFile("test.txt");
for(int i = 0 ; i < 100 ; i++)
{
if(i == 0)
outFile << endl;
outFile << setw(10) << i;
}
getch();
}
```

**OUTPUT:**

```
0        1        2        3
         4..........................upto 99
```

**Problem 92. Write a C++ program for ofstream: seek from beginning.**

***Program:***

```
#include <iostream.h>
#include <fstream.h>
#include <stdlib.h>
#include<conio.h>
void main(int argc,char *argv[])
{
ofstream out("test.txt");
if(!out)
{
cout << "Cannot open file";
return 1;
}
out.seekp(2,ios::beg);
out.put('X');
out.close();
getch();
}
```

**Problem 93. Write a C++ program to save and read double array in a binary file.**

***Program:***

```
#include <iostream.h>
#include<conio.h>
#include <fstream.h>
void main()
{
double fnum[4] = {9.5, -3.4, 1.0, 2.1};
int i;
ofstream out("numbers", ios::out | ios::binary);
if(!out) {
cout << "Cannot open file.";
return 1;
}
out.write((char *) &fnum, sizeof fnum);
out.close();
for(i=0; i<4; i++) // clear array
fnum[i] = 0.0;
ifstream in("numbers", ios::in | ios::binary);
in.read((char *) &fnum, sizeof fnum);
// see how many bytes have been read
cout << in.gcount() << " bytes read\n";
for(i=0; i<4; i++) // show values read from file
cout << fnum[i] << " ";
in.close();
getch();
}
```

**OUTPUT:**

```
32 bytes read
9.5 -3.4 1 2.1
```

**Problem 94. Write a C++ program to save and read structure.**

***Program:***

```
#include <iostream.h>
#include<conio.h>
#include <fstream.h>
#include <string.h>
struct MyRecord
{
char name[80];
double balance;
unsigned long account_num;
};
void main()
{
struct MyRecord acc;
strcpy(acc.name, "R");
acc.balance = 1.3;
acc.account_num = 34;
ofstream outbal("balance", ios::out | ios::binary);
if(!outbal) {
cout << "Cannot open file.\n";
return 1;
}
outbal.write((char *) &acc, sizeof(struct
MyRecord));
outbal.close();
ifstream inbal("balance", ios::in | ios::binary);
if(!inbal) {
cout << "Cannot open file.\n";
return 1;
}
inbal.read((char *) &acc, sizeof(struct MyRecord));
cout << acc.name << endl;
cout << "Account # " << acc.account_num;
cout.precision(2);
cout.setf(ios::fixed);
cout << endl << "Balance: $" << acc.balance;
inbal.close();
getch();
}
```

**OUTPUT:**

```
R
Account # 34
Balance: $1.30"
```

**Problem 95. Write a C++ program to save chars to a binary file.**

***Program:***

```
#include <iostream.h>
#include<conio.h>
#include <fstream.h>
void main()
{
int i;
ofstream out("test.dat", ios::out | ios::binary);
if(!out) {
cout << "Cannot open output file.\n";
return 1;
}
// write all characters to disk
for(i=0; i<256; i++) out.put((char) i);
out.close();
getch();
}
```

**Problem 96. Write a C++ program to find the position of pointer by using tellg and seekg.**

***Program:***

```
#include<fstream.h>
#nclude<stdlib.h>
#include<conio.h>
#include<iostream.h>
const int size = 10 ;
void main ( )
{
int pos = 0 ;
ifstream fin ("Raj.dat") ;
char ch ;
fin.seekg (8) ;
while (fin.get(ch))
{
cout<<ch ;
if (ch = = " " || ch = = "#")
{
pos = fin.tellg ( ) ;
cout<<"\n Position of" << ch <<" is"      << pos ;
continue ;
}
}
getch ( ) ;
};
```

**OUTPUT:**

```
position of (blank) is 9
Management
position of (blanks) is 20
#
position of # is 21
systems
```

**Problem 97. Write a C++ program to read a character by using get() function opened in the binary mode.**

***Program:***

```
#include<fstream.h>
#include<conio.h>
#include<iostream.h>
int main ( )
{
char ch ;
ifstream fl ;                          //create input stream
fl.open ("Raj.txt", ios :: in | ios :: binary) ;
//open the file in input mode in binary mode
if (! fl)
{
cout <<"\n File cannot be opened" ;
//if fl store zero i.e. false value
return 1 ;
}
while (fl)                             // fl will be 0 when
eof is reached
{
fl. get ( ch) ;              //read a character
cout << ch ;                 //display the character
}
fl.close ( ) ;
getch();
}
```

**Problem 98. Write a C++ program to display the ASCII code characters by using the get() function in files.**

***Program:***

```
#include<fstream.h>
#include<conio.h>
#include<iostream.h>
int main ( )
{
ofstream fl ;
fl.open ("Raj.txt", ios :: app)
if (! fl)
{
cout <<"\n File cannot be opened" ;
return 1 ;
}
char ch ;
int line = 0;
for (int i = 0 ; i < 256 ; i++)
{
if (i ! = 26)
{
fl.put ( (char) i) ;
}                          //put character version of i
}
fl.close ( ) ;
ifstream fl ;
fl.open ("Raj.txt", ios :: in) ;
fl.seek (0) ;
for (i = 0 ; i < 256 ; i++)
{
if (i ! = 26)
{
fl.get (ch);
cout << "  " << i << " = " ;
cout.put ( (char) (i) ) ;
}
if (! (i % 6) )
{
cout << endl ;
line ++ ;
}
if (line > 22)
{
getch ( ) ;
line = 0 ;
}
}
getch();
}
```

**Problem 99. Write a C++ program to read student name and fees paid by using the read() function from the file.**

***Program:***

```
#include<conio.h>
#include<iostream.h>
#include<fstream.h>
#include<string.h>
struct student
{
char name [20] ;
float fees ;
} ;
void main ( )
{
student s ;
strcpy (s.name, "Raj Kumar") ;
s.fees = 1200.32 ;
ofstream fl ;
fl.open ("Admission", ios :: out | ios :: binary) ;
if (! fl)
{
```

```
cout <<"\n Can not open the File" ;
return 1 ;
}
fl. write (char *) & s, size of (s) ;
fl.close ( ) ;
ifstream.fl ;
fl.open ("Admission", ios :: in | ios :: binary) ;
fl.read (char *) & s, size of (s) ;
cout <<"\n Name is : "<< s.name ;
cout << "\n Fees Paid is : " << s.fees ;
fl.close ( ) ;
getch() ;
}
```

**Problem 100. Write a C++ program to show different error message by using Error handling functions in files.**

***Program:***

```
#include<fstream.h>
#include<iostream.h>
#include<conio.h>
void main ( )
{
ifstream infile ;
infile.open ("Raj") ;
while (! infile.eof ( ) )
{
cout<<"\n End of file Encounted" ;
}
while (! infile.fail ( ) )
{
cout<<"Could not open a File" ;
continue ;
}
if (infile.bad ( ) )
{
cerr<<" File cannot be opened" ;
exit (1) ;
}
if (infile.good( ) )
{
cout<<"File is without error" ;
}
getch ( ) ;
}
```

**Problem 101. Write a C++ program to demonstrate peek(), unget(), and ignore().**

***Program:***

```
#include <iostream.h>
#include<conio.h>
#include <fstream.h>
#include <ctype.h>
int main()
{
char ch;
char idnum[5];
idnum[4] = 0;
ofstream fout("test.dat");
if(!fout)
{
cout << "Cannot open test.dat for output.\n";
return 1;
}
fout << "A #pending\n, B, #8875\n";
fout.close();
if(!fout.good())
{
cout << "Error creating data file.";
return 1;
}
ifstream fin("test.dat");
if(!fin)
{
cout << "Cannot open test.dat for input.\n";
return 1;
}
fin.exceptions(ios::badbit | ios::failbit);
try
{
do
{
fin.ignore(40, '#');
if(fin.eof())
{
fin.clear(); // clear eofbit
break;
}
ch = fin.peek();
if(isdigit(ch))
{
fin.read((char *)idnum, 4);
cout << "ID #: " << idnum << endl;
}
else
{
cout << "ID not available: ";
ch = fin.get();
while(isalpha(ch))
{
cout << ch;
ch = fin.get();
```

```
};
fin.unget();
cout << endl;
}}
while(fin.good());
}
catch(ios_base::failure exc)
{
cout << "Error reading data file.\n";
}
try {
fin.close();
} catch (ios_base::failure exc)
{
cout << "Error closing data file.";
return 1;
}
getch();
}
```

**Problem 102. Write a C++ program to create a sequential file.**

***Program:***#include <iostream.h>

```
#include<conio.h>
#include <fstream.h>
#include <stdlib.h>
void main()
{
ofstream outClientFile( "clients.dat", ios::out );
if ( !outClientFile )
{
cerr << "File could not be opened" << endl;
exit( 1 );
}
int account = 12;
char name[80] = "This Is A Test";
double balance = 123.123;
outClientFile << account << ' ' << name << ' ' <<
balance << endl;
getch();
}
```

**OUTPUT:**

12 This is a test 123.123

## OSTREAM:

**Problem 103. Write a C++ program to define your own ostream variable.**

***Program:***

```
#include <iostream.h>
#include<conio.h>
#include <fstream.h>
ostream & setthex(ostream & stream)
{
stream.setf(ios::hex|ios::uppercase|ios::showbase);
return stream;
}
ostream & reset(ostream & stream)
{
stream.unsetf(ios::hex|ios::uppercase|ios::showbase
);
return stream;
}
void main()
{
cout<<setthex<<200<<'\n';
cout<<reset<<200<<'\n';
getch();
}
```

**OUTPUT:**

200
200

**Problem 104. Write a C++ program for file descriptor out buffer.**

***Program:***

```
#include <iostream.h>
#include<conio.h>
#include <fstream.h>
// for write():
#ifdef _MSC_VER
# include <io.h>
#else
# include <unistd.h>
#endif
class fdoutbuf : public std::streambuf
{
protected:
int fd;    // file descriptor
public:
// constructor
fdoutbuf (int _fd) : fd(_fd) { }
protected:
// write one character
virtual int_type overflow (int_type c)
{
if (c != EOF)
{
char z = c;
if (write (fd, &z, 1) != 1)
{
```

```
return EOF;
} }
return c;
}
// write multiple characters
virtual
streamsize xsputn (const char* s, streamsize num)
{
return write(fd,s,num);
}
};
class fdostream : public ostream
{
protected:
fdoutbuf buf;
public:
fdostream (int fd) : ostream(0), buf(fd)
{
rdbuf(&buf);
} };
void main()
{
fdostream out(1);    // stream with buffer writing to
file descriptor 1
out << "31 hexadecimal: " << hex << 31 << endl;
getch();
}
```

**OUTPUT:**

31 hexadecimal: 1f

**Problem 105. Write a C++ program to stream for hexadecimal standard output.**

***Program:***

```
#include <iostream.h>
#include<conio.h>
#include <fstream.h>
void main()
{
// stream for hexadecimal standard output
ostream hexout(cout.rdbuf());
hexout.setf (ios::hex, ios::basefield);
hexout.setf (ios::showbase);
// switch between decimal and hexadecimal output
hexout << "hexout: " << 177 << " ";
cout   << "cout: "   << 177 << " ";
hexout << "hexout: " << -49 << " ";
cout   << "cout: "   << -49 << " ";
hexout << endl;
getch();
}
```

**OUTPUT:**

hexout: 0xb1 cout: 177 hexout: 0xffffffcf cout: -49

**Problem 106. Write a C++ program to switch between decimal and hexadecimal output.**

***Program:***

```
#include <iostream.h>
#include<conio.h>
#include <fstream.h>
void main()
{
// stream for hexadecimal standard output
ostream hexout(cout.rdbuf());
hexout.setf (ios::hex, ios::basefield);
hexout.setf (ios::showbase);
// switch between decimal and hexadecimal output
hexout << "hexout: " << 177 << " ";
cout   << "cout: "   << 177 << " ";
hexout << "hexout: " << -49 << " ";
cout   << "cout: "   << -49 << " ";
hexout << endl;
getch();
}
```

**OUTPUT:**

hexout: 0xb1 cout: 177 hexout: 0xffffffcf cout: -49

**Problem 107. Write a C++ program for hex out stream.**

***Program:***

```
#include <iostream.h>
#include<conio.h>
#include <fstream.h>
void hexMultiplicationTable (streambuf* buffer,
int num)
{
ostream hexout(buffer);
hexout << hex << showbase;
for (int i=1; i<=num; ++i)
{
for (int j=1; j<=10; ++j)
{
hexout << i*j << ' ';
}
hexout << endl;
}
}   // does NOT close buffer
void main()
{
using namespace std;
int num = 5;
cout << "We print " << num
<< " lines hexadecimal" << endl;
```

```
hexMultiplicationTable(cout.rdbuf(),num);
cout << "That was the output of " << num
<< " hexadecimal lines " << endl;
getch();
}
```

**OUTPUT:**

```
We print 5 lines hexadecimal
0x1 0x2 0x3 0x4 0x5 0x6 0x7 0x8 0x9 0xa
0x2 0x4 0x6 0x8 0xa 0xc 0xe 0x10 0x12 0x14
0x3 0x6 0x9 0xc 0xf 0x12 0x15 0x18 0x1b 0x1e
0x4 0x8 0xc 0x10 0x14 0x18 0x1c 0x20 0x24 0x28
0x5 0xa 0xf 0x14 0x19 0x1e 0x23 0x28 0x2d 0x32
That was the output of 5 hexadecimal lines
```

**Problem 108. Write a C++ program to redirect output into the file.**

***Program:***

```
#include <iostream.h>
#include<conio.h>
#include <fstream.h>
void redirect(ostream&);
void main()
{
cout << "the first row" << endl;
redirect(cout);
cout << "the last row" << endl;
getch();
}
void redirect (ostream& strm)
{
ofstream file("redirect.txt");
// save output buffer of the stream
streambuf* strm_buffer = strm.rdbuf();
// redirect ouput into the file
strm.rdbuf (file.rdbuf());
file << "one row for the file" << endl;
strm << "one row for the stream" << endl;
// restore old output buffer
strm.rdbuf (strm_buffer);
}   // closes file AND its buffer automatically
```

**OUTPUT:**

```
the first row
the last row
```

**Problem 109. Write a C++ program to open file "example.dat" for reading and writing.**

***Program:***

```
#include <iostream.h>
#include<conio.h>
#include <fstream.h>
void main()
{
// open file "example.dat" for reading and writing
filebuf buffer;
ostream output(&buffer);
istream input(&buffer);
buffer.open ("example.dat", ios::in | ios::out |
ios::trunc);
for (int i=1; i<=4; i++)
{
// write one line
output << i << ". line" << endl;
// print all file contents
input.seekg(0);          // seek to the beginning
char c;
while (input.get(c))
{
cout.put(c);
}
cout << endl;
input.clear();          // clear eofbit and failbit
}
getch();
}
```

**OUTPUT:**

```
1. line
1. line
2. line
1. line
2. line
3. line
1. line
2. line
3. line
4. line
```

# OSTREAM_ITERATOR:

**Problem 110. Write a C++ program to use ostream_iterator.**

***Program:***

```
#include <iostream.h>
#include<conio.h>
#include <fstream.h>
void main()
{
ostream_iterator<char> out_it(cout);
*out_it = 'X';
out_it++;
*out_it = 'Y';
out_it++;
```

```
*out_it = ' ';
char str[] = "C++ Iterators are powerful.\n";
char *p = str;
while(*p) *out_it++ = *p++;
ostream_iterator<double> out_double_it(cout);
*out_double_it = 187.23;
out_double_it++;
*out_double_it = -102.7;
getch();
}
```

**OUTPUT:**

XY C++ Iterators are powerful.
187.23-102.7

**Problem 111. Write a C++ program to create ostream_iterator for writing int values to cout.**

***Program:***

```
#include <iostream.h>
#include<conio.h>
#include <fstream.h>
void main()
{
cout << "Enter two integers: ";
istream_iterator< int > inputInt( cin );
int number1 = *inputInt;
++inputInt;
int number2 = *inputInt;
ostream_iterator< int > outputInt( cout );
cout << "The sum is: ";
*outputInt = number1 + number2;
cout << endl;
getch();
}
```

**OUTPUT:**

Enter two integers: 1 2
The sum is: 3

**Problem 112. Write a C++ program to use ostream_iterator and copy to display collection content.**

***Program:***

```
#include <iostream.h>
#include<conio.h>
#include <fstream.h>
void main()
{
int array[ 4 ] = { 2, 6, 4, 8 };
list< int > values;      // create list of ints
list< int > otherValues; // create list of ints
ostream_iterator< int > output( cout, " " );
// insert items in values
values.push_front( 1 );
values.push_front( 3 );
values.push_back( 4 );
values.push_back( 2 );
cout << "values contains: ";
copy( values.begin(), values.end(), output );
otherValues.insert( otherValues.begin(), array,
array + 4 );
cout << "\n\notherValues contains: ";
copy( otherValues.begin(), otherValues.end(),
output );
values.merge( otherValues );
cout << "\n\nvalues contains: ";
copy( values.begin(), values.end(), output );
cout << endl;
getch();
}
```

**OUTPUT:**

values contains: 3 1 4 2
otherValues contains: 2 6 4 8
values contains: 2 3 1 4 2 6 4 8

**Problem 113. Write a C++ program to transform algorithm with ostream_iterator.**

***Program:***

```
#include <iostream.h>
#include<conio.h>
#include <fstream.h>
int sum(int val1, int val2) { return val2 + val1; }
void main()
{
int array1[5] = {0, 1, 2, 3, 4};
int array2[5] = {6, 7, 8, 9, 10};
ostream_iterator<int> out(cout, " ");
// Put sums of corresponding array1 and array2
elements into OUTPUT stream:
transform(&array1[0], &array1[5], &array2[0],
out, sum);
cout << endl;
getch();
}
```

**OUTPUT:**

6 8 10 12 14

# ISTREAM:

**Problem 114. Write a C++ program to oct Input stream.**

***Program:***

```
#include <iostream.h>
```

```
#include<conio.h>
#include <fstream.h>
#include <iomanip.h>
istream& OctInput(istream& is);
void main()
{
int n;
cin >> OctInput >> n;
cout << "n:" << n << endl;
cout << "hex:" <<hex<< n << endl;
getch();
}
istream& OctInput(istream& is)
{
cout <<"input:";
cin >> oct;
return is;
}
```

**OUTPUT:**

```
input:12
n:10
hex:a
```

**Problem 115. Write a C++ program to define your own istream type.**

***Program:***

```
#include <iostream.h>
#include<conio.h>
#include <fstream.h>
#include<string.h>
istream & skipchar(istream &stream)
{
int i;
char c;
for(i=0;i<5;i++) stream>>c;
return stream;
}
void main()
{
char str[80];
cout<<"Enter some characters:";
cin>>skipchar>>str;
cout<<str<<'\n';
getch();
}
```

**OUTPUT:**

```
Enter some characters:q
w
e
r
t
r
r
```

## ISTREAM_ITERATOR:

**Problem 116. Write a C++ program to use istream_iterator.**

***Program:***

```
#include <iostream.h>
#include<conio.h>
#include <fstream.h>
void main()
{
istream_iterator<char> in_it(cin);
do
{
cout << *in_it++;
} while (*in_it != '.');
getch();
}
```

**OUTPUT:**

```
a
a
aa
aa
aa
aa
aaaaaaa^CTerminate batch job (Y/N)? n
```

**Problem 117. Write a C++ program to create istream_iterator for reading int values from cin.**

***Program:***

```
#include <iostream.h>
#include<conio.h>
#include <fstream.h>
void main()
{
cout << "Enter two integers: ";
istream_iterator< int > inputInt( cin );
int number1 = *inputInt;
++inputInt;
int number2 = *inputInt;
ostream_iterator< int > outputInt( cout );
cout << "The sum is: ";
*outputInt = number1 + number2;
cout << endl;
getch();
}
```

**OUTPUT:**

```
Enter two integers: 1 2
```

The sum is: 3

**Problem 118. Write a C++ program to use istream_iterator and ostream_iterator to read from cin and write to cout.**

***Program:***

```
#include <iostream.h>
#include<conio.h>
#include <fstream.h>
#include <string.h>
void main()
{
unsigned i;
double d;
string str;
vector<int> vi;
vector<double> vd;
vector<string> vs;
cout << "Enter some integers, enter 0 to stop.\n";
istream_iterator<int> int_itr(cin);
do
{
i = *int_itr;
if(i != 0)
{
vi.push_back(i);
++int_itr;
}
} while (i != 0);
cout << "Enter some doubles, enter 0 to stop.\n";
istream_iterator<double> double_itr(cin);
do
{
d = *double_itr;
if(d != 0.0)
{
vd.push_back(d);
++double_itr;
}
} while (d != 0.0);
cout << "Enter some strings, enter 'quit' to stop.\n";
istream_iterator<string> string_itr(cin);
do
{
str = *string_itr;
if(str != "quit")
{
vs.push_back(str);
++string_itr;
}
} while (str != "quit");
cout << endl;
cout << "Here is what you entered:\n";
for(i=0; i < vi.size(); i++) cout << vi[i] << " ";
cout << endl;
for(i=0; i < vd.size(); i++) cout << vd[i] << " ";
cout << endl;
for(i=0; i < vs.size(); i++) cout << vs[i] << " ";
// Now, use ostream_iterator to write to cout.
// Create an output iterator for string.
ostream_iterator<string> out_string_itr(cout);
*out_string_itr = "\n";
*out_string_itr = string("\nThis is a string\n");
*out_string_itr = "This is too.\n";
// Create an output iterator for int.
ostream_iterator<int> out_int_itr(cout);
*out_int_itr = 10;
*out_string_itr = " ";
*out_int_itr = 15;
*out_string_itr = " ";
*out_int_itr = 20;
*out_string_itr = "\n";
// Create an output iterator for bool.
ostream_iterator<bool> out_bool_itr(cout);
*out_bool_itr = true;
*out_string_itr = " ";
*out_bool_itr = false;
getch();
}
```

**Problem 119. Write a C++ program to use istreambuf_iterator, ostreambuf_iterator, and replace_copy() to filter a file.**

***Program:***

```
#include <iostream.h>
#include<conio.h>
#include <fstream.h>
void main(int argc, char *argv[])
{
if(argc != 5)
{
cout << "Usage: replace in out oldchar newchar\n";
return 1;
}
ifstream in(argv[1]);
ofstream out(argv[2]);
if(!in.is_open())
{
cout << "Cannot open input file.\n";
return 1;
}
if(!out.is_open())
```

```
{
cout << "Cannot open output file.\n";
return 1;
}
// Create stream iterators.
istreambuf_iterator<char> in_itr(in);
ostreambuf_iterator<char> out_itr(out);
// Copy the file, replacing characters in the process.
replace_copy(in_itr,
istreambuf_iterator<char>(),out_itr, *argv[3],
*argv[4]);
in.close();
out.close();
getch();
}
```

# ISTREAM EXCEPTIONS:

**Problem 120. Write a C++ program to deal with istream exceptions.**

***Program:***

```
#include <iostream.h>
#include<conio.h>
#include <fstream.h>
#include <stdlib.h>
namespace MyLib
{
double readAndProcessSum (std::istream&);
}
void main()
{
double sum;
try
{
sum = MyLib::readAndProcessSum(cin);
}
catch (const ios::failure& error)
{
cerr << "I/O exception: " << error.what() << endl;
return EXIT_FAILURE;
}
catch (const exception& error)
{
cerr << "standard exception: " << error.what() <<
endl;
return EXIT_FAILURE;
}
catch (...)
{
cerr << "unknown exception" << endl;
return EXIT_FAILURE;
}
// print sum
cout << "sum: " << sum << endl;
getch();
}
namespace MyLib
{
double readAndProcessSum (istream& strm)
{
double value, sum;
// save current state of exception flags
iostate oldExceptions = strm.exceptions();
strm.exceptions (ios::failbit | ios::badbit);
try
{
sum = 0;
while (strm >> value)
{
sum += value;
}
}
catch (...)
{
if (!strm.eof())
{
strm.exceptions(oldExceptions); // restore
exception flags
throw;                        // rethrow
}
}
// restore old state of exception flags
strm.exceptions (oldExceptions);
// return sum
return sum;
}
}
```

**OUTPUT:**

```
a
I/O exception: basic_ios::clear
```

# ISTREAMBUF_ITERATOR:

**Problem 121. Write a C++ program to input stream buffer iterator for cin, end-of-stream iterator,output stream buffer iterator for cout.**

***Program:***

```
#include <iostream.h>
#include<conio.h>
#include <fstream.h>
```

```
void main()
{
// input stream buffer iterator for cin
istreambuf_iterator<char> inpos(cin);
// end-of-stream iterator
istreambuf_iterator<char> endpos;
// output stream buffer iterator for cout
ostreambuf_iterator<char> outpos(cout);
// while input iterator is valid
while (inpos != endpos)
{
*outpos = *inpos;    // assign its value to the output
iterator
++inpos;
++outpos;
}
getch();
}
```

**OUTPUT**:

^CTerminate batch job (Y/N)? n

## ISTRSTREAM:

**Problem 122. Write a C++ program to attempt to read from empty stream.**

***Program:***

```
#include <iostream.h>
#include<conio.h>
#include <fstream.h>
#include <string.h>
void main()
{
string input( "" );
istringstream inputString( input );
// attempt to read from empty stream
long value;
inputString >> value;
if ( inputString.good() )
cout << "\n\nlong value is: " << value << endl;
else
cout << "\n\ninputString is empty" << endl;
getch();
}
```

**OUTPUT:**

inputString is empty

**Problem 123. Write a C++ program to demonstrating input from an istringstream object.**

***Program:***

```
#include <iostream.h>
#include<conio.h>
#include <fstream.h>
#include <string.h>
void main()
{
string input( "Input test 123 4.7 A" );
istringstream inputString( input );
string string1;
string string2;
int integer;
double double1;
char character;
inputString >> string1 >> string2 >> integer >>
double1 >> character;
cout << "\nstring1: " << string1
     << "\nstring2: " << string2 << "\n   int: " <<
integer
     << "\ndouble: " << double1 << "\n  char: " <<
character;

getch();
}
```

**OUTPUT:**

string1: Input
string2: test
int: 123
double: 4.7
char: A"

**Problem 124. Write a C++ program to use istrstream to read int, float and char.**

***Program:***

```
#include <iostream.h>
#include<conio.h>
#include <fstream.h>
void main()
{
char s[] = "10 Hello 0x75 42.73 OK";
istrstream ins(s);
int i;
char str[80];
float f;
// reading: 10 Hello
ins >> i;
ins >> str;
cout << i << " " << str << endl;
// reading 0x75 42.73 OK
ins >> hex >> i;
ins >> f;
ins >> str;
```

```
cout << hex << i << " " << f << " " << str;
getch();
}
```

**OUTPUT:**

10 Hello
75 42.73 OK

**Problem 125. Write a C++ program to read the contents of any array that contains text.**

***Program:***

```
#include <iostream.h>
#include<conio.h>
#include <fstream.h>
void main()
{
char s[] = "1.3 this is a test <<>><<?!\n";
istrstream ins(s);
char ch;
ins.unsetf(ios::skipws); // don't skip spaces
while (ins)
{ // false when end of array is reached
ins >> ch;
cout << ch;
}
getch();
}
```

**OUTPUT:**

1.3 this is a test <<>><

**Problem 126. Write a C++ program to read and display binary data.**

***Program:***

```
#include <iostream.h>
#include<conio.h>
#include <fstream.h>
void main()
{
char *p = "this is a test\1\2\3\4\5\6\7";
istrstream ins(p);
char ch;
while (!ins.eof())
{
ins.get(ch);
cout << hex << (int) ch << ' ';
}
getch();
}
```

**OUTPUT:**

74 68 69 73 20 69 73 20 61 20 74 65 73 74 1 2 3 4 5
6 7 7

## OSTRSTREAM:

**Problem 127. Write a C++ program to display how many chars in ostrstream.**

***Program:***

```
#include <iostream.h>
#include<conio.h>
#include <fstream.h>
void main()
{
char str[80];
ostrstream outs(str, sizeof(str));
outs << "abcdefg ";
outs << 27 << " " << 890.23;
outs << ends; // null terminate
cout << outs.pcount(); // display how many chars
in outs
cout << " " << str;
getch();
}
```

**OUTPUT:**

18 abcdefg 27 890.23"

**Problem 128. Write a C++ program for ostrstream with format.**

***Program:***

```
#include <iostream.h>
#include<conio.h>
#include <fstream.h>
void main()
{
char str[80];
ostrstream outs(str, sizeof(str));
outs << "AAAAAAAAAAAAAAAA. ";
outs << 1024 << hex << " ";
outs.setf(ios::showbase);
outs << 100 << ' ' << 99.789 << ends;
cout << str; // display string on console
getch();
}
```

**OUTPUT:**

AAAAAAAAAAAAAAAA. 1024 0x64 99.789"

**Problem 129. Write a C++ program to Freeze dynamic buffer and return pointer to it.**

***Program:***

```
#include <iostream.h>
#include<conio.h>
#include <fstream.h>
void main()
```

```
{
char *p;
ostrstream outs;
outs << "AAAAAAAAAAAAAAAAAAAA";
outs << -10 << hex << " ";
outs.setf(ios::showbase);
outs << 100 << ends;
p = outs.str();
cout << p;
getch();
}
```

**OUTPUT**:

AAAAAAAAAAAAAAAAAAAA-10 0x64"

**Problem 130. Write a C++ program for output of several data types to an ostringstream object: double, int and address of int.**

***Program:***

```
#include <iostream.h>
#include<conio.h>
#include <fstream.h>
#include <string.h>
void main()
{
ostringstream outputstring;
string string1( "string " );
double double1 = 123.4567;
int integer = 22;
outputstring << string1 << double1 << integer <<
&integer;
// call str to obtain string contents of the
ostringstream
cout << "outputstring contains:\n" <<
outputstring.str();
getch();
}
```

**OUTPUT**:

outputString contains:
string 123.457220x22fe74"

**Problem 131. Write a C++ program to check how many characters are stored in ostrstream.**

***Program:***

```
#include <iostream.h>
#include<conio.h>
#include <fstream.h>
void main()
{
char str[80];
ostrstream outs(str, sizeof(str));
outs << "Hello ";
outs << 34 << " " << 1234.23;
outs << ends;
cout << outs.pcount(); // display how many chars
in outs
cout << " " << str;
getch();
}
```

**Problem 132. Write a C++ program to make ostringstream work with decimal, hexadecimal value, floating value, bitset.**

***Program:***

```
#include <iostream.h>
#include<conio.h>
#include <fstream.h>
void main()
{
ostringstream os;
// decimal and hexadecimal value
os << "dec: " << 15 << hex << " hex: " << 15 <<
endl;
cout << os.str() << endl;
// append floating value and bitset
bitset<15> b(5789);
os << "float: " << 4.67 << " bitset: " << b << endl;
// overwrite with octal value
os.seekp(0);
os << "oct: " << oct << 15;
cout << os.str() << endl;
getch();
}
```

**OUTPUT**:

dec: 15 hex: f
oct: 17 hex: f
float: 4.67 bitset: 001011010011101

**Problem 133. Write a C++ program to save string with ostringstream.**

***Program:***

```
#include <iostream.h>
#include<conio.h>
#include <fstream.h>
void main(int argc, char** argv)
{
cout << "Enter tokens. Control-D (Unix) or
Control-Z (Windows) to end." << endl;
ostringstream outStream;
while (cin)
{
string nextToken;
cout << "Next token: ";
```

```
cin >> nextToken;
if (nextToken == "done") break;
outStream << nextToken << "\t";
}
cout << "The end result is: " << outStream.str();
getch();
}
```

## STREAMBUF:

**Problem 134. Write a C++ program to extends streambuf to create output buffer.**

***Program:***

```
#include <iostream.h>
#include<conio.h>
#include <fstream.h>
#include<ctype.h>
#include<stdio.h>
class outbuf : public streambuf
{
protected:
virtual int_type overflow (int_type c)
{
if (c != EOF)
{
// convert lowercase to uppercase
c = toupper(c,getloc());
// and write the character to the standard output
if (putchar(c) == EOF)
{
return EOF;
}
}
return c;
}
};
void main()
{
outbuf ob;            // create special output buffer
ostream out(&ob);   // initialize output stream with
that output buffer
out << "31 hexadecimal: " << hex << 31 << endl;
getch();
}
```

## STRINGSTREAM:

**Problem 135. Write a C++ program to demonstrate string streams.**

***Program:***

```
#include <iostream.h>
#include<conio.h>
#include <fstream.h>
void main()
{
stringstream s("This is initial string.");
// get string
string str = s.str();
cout << str << endl;
// output to string stream
s << "Numbers: " << 10 << " " << 123.2;
int i;
double d;
s >> str >> i >> d;
cout << str << " " << i << " " << d;
getch();
}
```

**<u>OUTPUT</u>:**

This is initial string.
Numbers: 10 123.2

**Problem 136. Write a C++ program to use stringstream to parse a number.**

***Program:***

```
#include <iostream.h>
#include<conio.h>
#include <fstream.h>
#include <string.h>
double parse(const string& str)
{
stringstream ss(str);
double d = 0;
ss >> d;
if (ss.fail( ))
{
throw (str +" is not a number");
}
return (d);
}
void main( )
{
try {
cout << parse("1.234e5") << endl;
cout << parse("6.02e-2") << endl;
cout << parse("asdf") << endl;
}
catch (string& e)
{
cerr << e << endl;
}
getch();
```

```
}
```

**OUTPUT:**

123400
0.0602
asdf is not a number

**Problem 137. Write a C++ program for stringstream::str( empty string): Empty the string.**

***Program:***

```
#include <iostream.h>
#include<conio.h>
#include <fstream.h>
#include <iomanip.h>
#include <string.h>
void main( )
{
stringstream ss;
ss << "string " << 9 << 1.2;
cout << ss.str( ) << endl;
ss.str("");                // Empty the string
cout << ss.str( ) << endl;
getch();
}
```

**OUTPUT:**

string 91.2

**Problem 138. Write a C++ program for stringstream::str( ) returns a string.**

***Program:***

```
#include <iostream.h>
#include<conio.h>
#include <fstream.h>
#include <iomanip.h>
#include <string.h>
void main( )
{
stringstream ss;
ss << "string " << 9 << 1.2;
cout << ss.str( ) << endl;  // stringstream::str( )
returns a string
getch();
}
```

**OUTPUT:**

string 91.2

## STRSTREAM:

**Problem 139. Write a C++ program to perform both input and output with strstream.**

***Program:***

```
#include <iostream.h>
#include<conio.h>
#include <fstream.h>
#include<strstream.h>
void main()
{
char iostr[80];
strstream ios(iostr, sizeof(iostr), ios::in | ios::out);
int a, b;
char str[80];
ios << "1734 534abcdefghijklmnopqrstuvwxyz";
ios >> a >> b >> str;
cout << a << " " << b << "," << str << endl;
getch();
}
```

**OUTPUT:**

1734 534abcdefghijklmnopqrstuvwxyz

**Problem 140. Write a C++ program to perform both input and output.**

***Program:***

```
#include <iostream.h>
#include<conio.h>
#include <fstream.h>
void main()
{
char iostr[80];
strstream strio(iostr, sizeof(iostr), ios::in | ios::out);
int a, b;
char str[80];
strio << "10 20 testing ";
strio >> a >> b >> str;
cout << a << " " << b << " " << str << endl;
getch();
}
```

**OUTPUT:**

10 20 testing

## FILE IO EXCEPTION:

**Problem 141. Write a C++ program to read a file in try catch block.**

***Program:***

```
#include <iostream.h>
#include<conio.h>
#include <fstream.h>
void main ()
{
try
{
```

```
char buffer[256];
ifstream myfile ("test.txt");
while (! myfile.eof() )
{
myfile.getline (buffer,100);
cout << buffer << endl;
}
}catch(...)
{
cout << "There was an error !\n";
}
getch();
}
```

**OUTPUT**:

This outputting a line.

**Problem 142. Write a C++ program to handle basic exception.**

***Program:***

```
#include <iostream.h>
#include<conio.h>
#include <fstream.h>
#include <string.h>
void readIntegerFile(const string& fileName,
vector<int>& dest)
{
ifstream istr;
int temp;
istr.open(fileName.c_str());
if (istr.fail())
{
throw exception();
}
while (istr >> temp)
{
dest.push_back(temp);
}
}
void main(int argc, char** argv)
{
vector<int> myInts;
const string fileName = "test.txt";
try
{
readIntegerFile(fileName, myInts);
}
catch (const exception& e)
{
cerr << "Unable to open file " << fileName << endl;
exit (1);
}
for (size_t i = 0; i < myInts.size(); i++)
{
cout << myInts[i] << " ";
}
cout << endl;
getch();
}
```

**Problem 143. Write a C++ program to throw exception in function cascading.**

***Program:***

```
#include <iostream.h>
#include<conio.h>
#include <fstream.h>
void funcOne() throw(exception);
void funcTwo() throw(exception);
void main(int argc, char** argv)
{
try
{
funcOne();
} catch (exception& e)
{
cerr << "Exception caught!\n";
exit(1);
}
getch();
}
void funcOne() throw(exception)
{
string str1;
string* str2 = new string();
try
{
funcTwo();
}
catch (...)
{
delete str2;
throw; // rethrow the exception
}
delete str2;
}
void funcTwo() throw(exception)
{
ifstream istr;
istr.open("filename");
throw exception();
istr.close();
}
```

**Problem 144. Write a C++ program to checks for errors opening file.**

***Program:***

```
#include <iostream.h>
#include<conio.h>
#include <fstream.h>
void main()
{
ifstream file;
file.open("a:test.dat");
if( !file )
cout << "\nCan't open GROUP.DAT";
else
cout << "\nFile opened successfully.";
cout << "\nfile = " << file;
cout << "\nError state = " << file.rdstate();
cout << "\ngood() = " << file.good();
cout << "\neof() = " << file.eof();
cout << "\nfail() = " << file.fail();
cout << "\nbad() = " << file.bad() << endl;
file.close();
getch();
}
```

**Problem 145. Write a C++ program to handles errors during input and output.**

***Program:***

```
#include <fstream.h>
#include <iostream.h>
#include <process.h>
const int MAX = 1000;
int buff[MAX];
int main(){
for(int j=0; j<MAX; j++)
buff[j] = j;
ofstream os;
os.open("a:edata.dat", ios::trunc | ios::binary);
if(!os)
{
cerr << "Could not open output file\n"; exit(1);
}
os.write( reinterpret_cast<char*>(buff),
MAX*sizeof(int) );
if(!os)
{
cerr << "Could not write to file\n"; exit(1);
}
os.close();
for(int j=0; j<MAX; j++)
buff[j] = 0;
ifstream is;
is.open("a:edata.dat", ios::binary);
if(!is)
{
cerr << "Could not open input file\n"; exit(1);
}
is.read( reinterpret_cast<char*>(buff),
MAX*sizeof(int) );
if(!is)
{
cerr << "Could not read from file\n"; exit(1);
}
for(int j=0; j<MAX; j++)
{
if( buff[j] != j )
{
cerr << "\nData is incorrect\n";
exit(1);
}
}
getch();
}
```

## WORKING WITH FLAGS:

**Problem 146. Write a C++ program to setting the Format Flags.**

***Program:***

```
#include <iostream.h>
#include<conio.h>
void main()
{
cout.setf(ios::showpoint);
cout.setf(ios::showpos);
cout <<500.0;
getch();
}
```

**OUTPUT:**

```
+500.000000
```

**Problem 147. Write a C++ program to clearing Format Flags.**

***Program:***

```
#include <iostream.h>
#include<conio.h>
void main()
{
cout.setf(ios::uppercase |ios::scientific);
cout <<500.12;
cout.unsetf(ios::uppercase);
cout <<"\n"<<500.12;
```

```
getch();
}
```

**OUTPUT:**

```
5.0012e+02
5.0012e+02
```

**Problem 148. Write a C++ program for an Overloaded Form of setf().**

***Program:***

```
#include <iostream.h>
#include<conio.h>
void main()
{
cout.setf(ios::showpoint
|ios::showpos,ios::showpoint);
cout <<500.0;
getch();
}
```

**OUTPUT:**

```
500.000000
```

**Problem 149. Write a C++ program to examining the Formatting Flags.**

***Program:***

```
#include <iostream.h>
#include<conio.h>
void dispflags();
void main()
{
dispflags();
cout.setf(ios::right |ios::showpoint |ios::fixed);
dispflags();
getch();
}
void dispflags()
{
ios::fmtflags f;
long i;
f =(long)cout.flags();
for(i=0x4000;i;i =i >>1)
if(i &f)cout <<"1 ";
else cout <<"0 ";
cout <<"\n";
}
```

**OUTPUT:**

```
0 0 0 0 0 1 0 0 0 0 0 0 0 0 1
0 1 0 0 0 1 0 1 0 0 1 0 0 0 1
```

**Problem 150. Write a C++ program using width(),precision(),and fill().**

***Program:***

```
#include <iostream.h>
#include<conio.h>
void main()
{
cout.precision(4);
cout.width(10);
cout <<10.24 <<"\n";
cout.fill('*');
cout.width(10);
cout <<10.24 <<"\n";
cout.width(10);
cout <<"Hi!"<<"\n";
cout.width(10);
cout.setf(ios::left);
cout <<10.24;
getch();
}
```

**OUTPUT:**

```
10.12345
******10.24
*********Hi!
10.24******
```

## USING MANIPULATORS TO FORMAT I/O:

**Problem 151. Write a C++ program for hex.**

***Program:***

```
#include <iostream.h>
#include <iomanip.h>
#include<conio.h>
void main()
{
cout <<hex <<100 <<endl;
cout <<setfill('?')<<setw(10)<<1234.0;
getch();
}
```

**OUTPUT:**

```
64
??????1234
```

**Problem 152. Write a C++ program for hex.**

***Program:***

```
#include <iostream.h>
#include <iomanip.h>
#include<conio.h>
void main()
{
cout.setf(ios::hex,ios::basefield);
cout <<100 <<"\n";
```

```
cout.fill('?');
cout.width(10);
cout <<1234.0;
getch();
}
```

**OUTPUT**:

```
64
??????1234
```

**Problem 153. Write a C++ program for Overloading <<and >>.**

***Program:***

```
#include <iostream.h>
#include <string.h>
#include<conio.h>
class phonebook
{
public:
char name [60];
int areacode;
int prefix;
int num;
phonebook(char *n,int a,int p,int no)
{
strcpy(name,n);
areacode =a;
prefix =p;
num =no;
}
};
ostream &operator<<(ostream &stream,phonebook pb)
{
stream <<pb.name <<"";
stream <<"("<<pb.areacode <<")";
stream <<pb.prefix <<"-"<<pb.num <<"\n";
return stream;
}
void main()
{
phonebook x("Sukhwant",101,500,1234);
phonebook y("Inderpal",105,505,2345);
phonebook z("Avtar",110,510,3456);
cout <<x <<y <<z;
getch();
}
```

**OUTPUT**:

```
Sukhwant (101)500-1234
Inderpal (105)505-2345
Avtar (110)510-3456
```

**Problem 154. Write a C++ program to draw boxes (overloading << and >>).**

***Program:***

```
#include <iostream.h>
#include<conio.h>
class box
{
int x,y;
public:
box(int i,int j)
{
x=i;
y=j;
}
friend ostream &operator<<(ostream &stream,box b);
};
ostream &operator<<(ostream &stream,box b)
{
int i,j;
for(i=0;i<b.x;i++)
stream <<"*";
stream <<"\n";
for(j=1;j<b.y-1;j++)
{
for(i=0;i<b.x;i++)
if(i==0 ||i==b.x-1)
stream <<"*";
else stream <<"";
stream <<"\n";
}
for(i=0;i<b.x;i++)
stream <<"*";
stream <<"\n";
return stream;
}
void main()
{
box b1(14,6),b2(30,7),b3(40,5);
cout <<"Some boxes are there:\n";
cout <<b1 <<b2 <<b3;
getch();
}
```

**OUTPUT**:

```
Some boxes are there:
*************
*           *
*           *
*           *
*           *
*************
```

```
******************************
*                            *
*                            *
*                            *
*                            *
*                            *
******************************
****************************************
*                                      *
*                                      *
*                                      *
****************************************
```

**Problem 155. Write a C++ program for creating Your Own Manipulator Functions.**

***Program:***

```
#include <iostream.h>
#include <iomanip.h>
#include<conio.h>
ostream &ra(ostream &stream)
{
stream <<"------->";
return stream;
}
ostream &la(ostream &stream)
{
stream <<"<-------";
return stream;
}
void main()
{
cout <<"High balance "<<ra <<412.84 <<"\n";
cout <<"Over draft "<<ra <<211.68 <<la;
getch();
}
```

**OUTPUT:**

```
High balance ------->412.84
Over draft ------->211.68 <-------
```

## FILE FORMATTED INPUT\OUTPUT FUNCTIONS:

**Problem 156. Write a C++ program to formatted I/O using ios member functions.**

***Program:***

```
#include <iostream.h>
#include<conio.h>
void main()
{
float num[5] = {1.0, -1.2345, 2350.1, 23.4, 45.34};
int i;
cout.setf(ios::showpos); // show the + sign before
positive numbers
cout.setf(ios::scientific); // use scientific notation
cout.precision(2); // two digits after decimal point
for(i = 0; i < 5; i++)
{
cout.width(20);    // use 10 spaces for the number
cout.fill('$');    // pad with $
cout << num[i] << endl;
}
getch();
}
```

**OUTPUT:**

```
$$$$$$$$$$$+1.00e+00
$$$$$$$$$$$-1.23e+00
$$$$$$$$$$$+2.35e+03
$$$$$$$$$$$+2.34e+01
$$$$$$$$$$$+4.53e+01
```

**Problem 157. Write a C++ program to formatted I/O using I/O manipulators.**

***Program:***

```
#include <iostream.h>
#include <iomanip.h>
#include<conio.h>
void main()
{
float num[5] = {1.0, -1.2345, 2350.1, 23.4, 45.34};
int i;
cout << setiosflags(ios::showpos);
cout << setiosflags(ios::scientific);
cout << setprecision(2);
for(i = 0; i < 5; i++)
{
cout << setw(20);
cout << setfill('$');
cout << num[i] << endl;
}
getch();
}
```

**OUTPUT:**

```
$$$$$$$$$$$+1.00e+00
$$$$$$$$$$$-1.23e+00
$$$$$$$$$$$+2.35e+03
$$$$$$$$$$$+2.34e+01
$$$$$$$$$$$+4.53e+01
```

**Problem 158. Write a C++ program to define your own I/O manipulators.**

***Program:***

```
#include <iostream.h>
#include <iomanip.h>
#include<conio.h>
ostream &SetHex(ostream &stream);
void main()
{
int input;
cout << "Enter an integer: " ;
cin  >> input;
cout << "Hexdecimal of an integer is: ";
cout << SetHex << input << endl;
getch();
}
ostream &SetHex(ostream &stream)
{
stream.setf(ios::hex,ios::basefield);
return stream;
}
```

**OUTPUT:**

Enter an integer: 20
Hexdecimal of an integer is: 14

**Problem 159. Write a C++ program for file I/O: Writing to a text file.**

***Program:***

```
#include <iostream.h>
#include <fstream.h>
#include<conio.h>
void main()
{
char OutFile[80];
ofstream OutStream;
cout << "Enter output file name: " ;
cin >> OutFile;
OutStream.open(OutFile, ios::out | ios::trunc);
if(!OutStream)
{
cout << "Error open file " << OutFile << " for
writing\n";
return 1;
}
OutStream<<"-------- God Bless You.--------\n";
OutStream <<" -- Prof. Rachhpal Singh--" << endl;
OutStream.close();
cout << "Content written to " << OutFile <<".\n";
getch();
}
```

**OUTPUT:**

Enter output file name: out.txt
Content written to out.txt.

**Problem 160. Write a C++ program for file I/O: Reading from a text file.**

***Program:***

```
#include <fstream.h>
#include<iostream.h>
#include<conio.h>
int main()
{
char InFile[80];
char ch;
ifstream InStream;
cout << "This program reads the content of a file
and ";
cout << "prints it out on the screen." << endl;
cout << "Enter input file name: " ;
cin >> InFile;
InStream.open(InFile, ios::in);
if(!InStream)
{
cout << "Error open file " << InFile << endl;
return 1;
}
cout << "Here is the content of " << InFile <<
":\n";
while (!InStream.eof())
{
InStream.get(ch);
if (!InStream.eof())
{
cout << ch;  //Write to screen
}
}
InStream.close();
}
```

**OUTPUT:**

This program reads the content of a file and prints it out on the screen.
Enter input file name: out.txt
Here is the content of out.txt:
-------- God Bless You.--------
-- Prof. Rachhpal Singh--

**Problem 161. Write a C++ program to write the roll no and name of a student in the file with the concept of classes with objects.**

***Program:***

```
#include<fstream.h>
#include<conio.h>
#include<iostream.h>
class student
{
```

```
private :
int rn ;
char name [20];
public :
void getdata ( )
{
cout<<"\n Enter the Roll No and Name:" ;
cin >> rn >> name ;
}
} ;
void main ( )
{
student stu ;
stu.getdata ( ) ;
ofstream out ("Raj.txt") ;
out.write ((char *) &stu sizeof(stu) ) ;
}
```

**Problem 162. Write a C++ program to write and read the ticket information and fare of a passenger in and from the files by using the multiple objects.**

***Program:***

```
#include<conio.h>
#include<iostream.h>
#include<fstream.h>
class airlines
{
private :
char tktno [5] ;
int fare ;
public :
void add ( )
{
cout<<"\n Enter Ticket Number" ;
cin >> tktno ;
cout<<"\n Enter the Fare" ;
cin >> Fare ;
}
void display ( )
{
cout<<"\n Ticket Number is" << tktno ;
cout<<"\n FARE is" << fare ;
}
} ;
void main ( )
{
char flname [10] ;
cout<<"\n Enter Filename" ;
cin >> flname ;
ostream flight (flname, ios : : dot) ;
flight.open (flname) ;
airlines air ;
air.add ( ) ;
flight.write (char *) & air, size of (air) ) ;
flight.close ( ) ;
cout<<"\n Contents of the File is" << flname ;
ifstream flight1 ;
flight 1.open (flname) ;
flight1.read ((char *) & air, size of (air)) ;
do
{
air.display ( ) ;
flight 1. read ((char *) & air, size of (air) ) ;
}while (flight 1)
flight 1. close ( ) ;
getche ( ) ;
}
```

**Problem 163. Write a C++ program to read and display the name and age of N persons from the files stored on the disk.**

***Program:***

```
#include<conio.h>
#include<iostream.h>
#include<fstream.h>
struct person
{
char name [30] ;
int age ;
}
class group
{
private :
person par [20] ;
int c ;
public :
group ( )      //constructor defined
{
c = 0 ;
}
void adddata ( ) ;
void dispdata ( ) ;
void diskin ( ) ;
void diskout ( ) ;
} ;
void group : : adddata ( )        //Read
one person data
{
cout<<"\n Enter Name and age : " ;
cin >> par [c].name ;
cin >> par [c++].age ;
```

```
}
void group : : dispdata ( )                    //Display
all person's info.
{
for (int j=0 ; j<c ; j++)
{
cout<<"\n Person # is" << j+1 ;
cout<<"\n NAME is" << par [i].name ;
cout<<\n Age is" << par [j].age ;
}
void group : : diskin ( )              //Read array from
file
{
ifstream infile ;
infile.open ("Raj", ios : : nocreate) ;
if (infile)
{
infile.read (char *) this, size of (* this) ;
}
}
void group : : diskout ( )
{
ofstream outfile ;
outfile.open ("Raj") ;
outfile.write ((char *) this, size of (* this) ) ;
}
void main ( )
{
group grp ;
grp. disk in ( ) ;
grp. dispdata ( ) ;
char ch ;
do
{
cout<<"\n Enter data for person" .
grp.adddata ( ) ;
cout<<"\n Do you want to Enter more data" ;
cin >> ch ;
}while (ch = = "Y" | | ch = = "y") ;
grp. dispdata ( ) ;
grp. dispdata ( ) ;
}
```

**Problem 164. Write a C++ program to read and write the student name character by character in the " Khalsa College, Asr." Data file by using the concept of character I/O.**

***Program:***

```
#include<fstream.h>
#include<conio.h>
#include<iostream.h>
#include<string.h>
char name [ ] = "\n Khalsa College, Asr.";
void main ( )
{
ofstream    disp("Raj") ;
int         i ;
disp.open ("Raj") ;
for (i=0 ; i< stream (name) ; i++)
{
disp.put (name[i]) ;
}
char ch ;
ifstream input ("Raj") ;
input.open ("Raj") ;
while (input)
{
input.get (ch) ;
cout<<ch ;
}
getche ( ) ;
disp.close ( ) ;
input.close ( ) ;
}
```

**Problem 165. Write a C++ program which creates two files EVEN and ODD using the command line arguments. Here a group of array can be entered and, even numbers are stored in the EVEN file, odd numbers are stored in the ODD file. The command line can be executed at the DOS prompt as :**

***Program:***

```
#include<fstream.h>
#include<conio.h>
#include<iostream.h>
#include<stdlib.h>
void main (int argc, char * argv [ ])
{
int a [20], n, i ;
cout<<"\n Enter the value of n" ;
cin >> n ;
cout<<"\n Enter different array Element" ;
for (i = 1 ;  i < = n ;  i++)
{
cin >> a [i] ;
}
if (argc ! = 3)
{
cout<<"\n Argc =" << argc ;
cout<<"\n Errors in Argument" ;
exit (1) ;
```

```
}
ofstream f1, f2 ;
f1.open (argv [1]) ;
if (f1.fail ( ) )
{
cout<<"\n Could not open the file" ;
cout<<argv [1] ;
exit (1) ;
}
f2.open (argv [2]) ;
if (f2.fail( ) )
{
cout<<"\n Could not open the file" ;
cout<< argv [2] ;
exit (1) ;
}
for (i = 1 ; i < = n ;  i ++)
{
if (a [i] % 2 = = 0)
{
f2 << a [i] ;
}
else
{
f1 << a [i] ;
}
}
f1.close ( ) ;
f2.close ( ) ;
ifstream fin ;
char ch ;
for (i = 1 ; i <.argc ; i ++)
{
fin.open (argv [i] ) ;
cout<<"\n Contents of" << argv [i] ;
do
{
fin.get (ch) ;
cout << ch ;
} while (fin) ;
fin.close ( ) ;
}
getche ( ) ;
}
```

**Problem 166. Write a C++ program to get and display the values of two variables using overloading of insertion and extraction operators.**

***Program:***

```
#include<fstream.h>
#include<conio.h>
#include<iostream.h>
class A
{
private:
int a;
float b;
public:
A( )
{
a=0;
b=0.0;
}
A(int a1, float b1)
{
a=a1;
b=b1;
}
friend istream& operator >> (istream& in, A&
obj1);
friend ostream& operator << (ostream& out, A&
obj1);
};
istream& operator >> (istream& in, A& obj1) //
Input the values using overloading
{
cout<<"Enter the value of a";
in>>obj1.a;
cout<<"\n"<<"Enter the value of b";
in>>obj1.b;
return in;
}
ostream& operator << (ostream& out, A& obj1)
//output the values using overloading
{
out<<"\n"<<obj1.a;
out<<"\n"<<obj1.b;
return out;
}
void main( )
{
A obj2,obj3;
Clrscr();
cout<<"Enter values":
cin>>obj2>>obj3;  // Input the values from user
A obj4(1,2.05);
cout<<obj2<<"\n"<<obj3; // display the values
cout<<"\n"<<obj4;
getch();
}
```

**OUPUT:**

Enter values

```
Enter the value of a 2
Enter the value of b 1.5
Enter the value of a 7
Enter the value of b 5.5
2
1.5
7
5.5
1
2.05
```

**Problem 167. Write a C++ program to input and print the occurrences of each character in a file.**

***Program:***

```
#include<iostream.h>
#include<conio.h>
#include<stdio.h>
#include<fstream.h>
#include<stdlib.h>
void main()
{
char c;
clrscr();
ofstream fout("mohan.txt");
cout<<"Enter contents of file, press # to end the
file==>";
cin>>c;
while(c!='#')
{
fout<<c;
cin>>c;
}
fout.close();
ifstream fin("mohan.txt");
cout<<"Press any key to display contents of file....";
getch();
clrscr();
if(!fin)
{
cout<<"File cann't be opened.";
getch();
exit(1);
}
cout<<"\nElements are==>";
int i,A[26]={0},a[26]={0},d[10]={0};
while(fin)
{
fin>>c;
cout<<c;
for(i=48;i<=57;i++)
if(c==i)
d[i-48]++;
for(i=65;i<=90;i++)
if(c==i)
d[i-65]++;
for(i=97;i<=122;i++)
if(c==i)
d[i-97]++;
fflush(stdin);
}
clrscr();
cout<<"Press any key to display occurances of
digits...";
clrscr();
for(i=0;i<=9;i++)
{
if(d[i]==0)
continue;
cout<<char(i+48)<<"\t"<<d[i]<<endl;
}
cout<<"Press any key to display occurances of
Upper case alphabets...";
getch();
clrscr();
for(i=0;i<=25;i++)
{
if(A[i]==0)
continue;
cout<<char(i+65)<<"\t"<<A[i]<<endl;
}
cout<<"Press any key to display occurances of
Lower case alphabets...";
getch();
clrscr();
for(i=0;i<=25;i++)
{
if(a[i]==0)
continue;
cout<<char(i+97)<<"\t"<<a[i]<<endl;
}
getch();
}
```

**Problem 168. Write a C++ program to input and print the occurrences of each character in a file.**

***Program:***

```
#include<iostream.h>
#include<conio.h>
#include<fstream.h>
#include<stdlib.h>
void main()
```

```
{
ofstream in("Aman.txt");
clrscr();
char c1;
cout<<"Enter contents==>";
for(int i=1;i<=6;i++)
{
cin>>c1;
in<<c1;
}
in.close();
ifstream fin("Aman.txt");
if(!fin)
{
cout<<"File cann't be opened.";
getch();
exit(1);
}
int count=0,a[60]={0},p=0;
char c[60],ch;
while(fin.eof())
 {
fin>>ch;
p=0;
for(i=0;i<count;i++)
if(c[i]==ch)
{
a[i]++;
p=1;
break;
}
if(p==0)
{
c[count]=ch;
count++;
}
}
cout<<"\n\n\n\nPress any key to display
occurance...";
getch();
clrscr();
for(i=0;i<=count;i++)
cout<<c[i]<<" occurs for "<<a[i]<<" times.\n";
getch();
}
```

**Problem 169. Write a C++ program to do error handling in c++ files.**

```
#include<fstream.h>
#include<conio.h>
#include<process.h>
void main()
{
char c;
clrscr();
ofstream inp;
inp.open("Amrit.txt");
cout<<"enter contents,press # to end==>";
while(c!='#')
{
inp<<c;
cin>>c;
}
inp.close();
ifstream out("Amrit.txt");
if(out.fail())
{
cout<<"File cann't be opened.\n";
getch();
exit(1);
}
cout<<"Contents are==>";
while(!out.eof())
{
out>>c;
cout<<c;
if(out.bad())
{
cout<<"\n//Invalid operation,so file has to be
closed.";
getch();
exit(2);
}
}
out.close();
cout<<"\n\nFile has been closed";
getch();
}
```

**Problem 170. Write a C++ program to input and print contents of a file.**

***Program:***

```
#include<iostream.h>
#include<conio.h>
#include<fstream.h>
#include<stdlib.h>
void main()
{
char c;
clrscr();
ofstream fout("ashu.txt");
```

```
cout<<"Enter contents of file, press # to end the
file==>";
cin>>c;
while(c!='#')
{
fout<<c;
cin>>c;
}
fout.close();
ifstream fin("ashu.txt");
cout<<"Press any key to display contents of file....";
getch();
clrscr();
if(!fin)
{
cout<<"File cann't be opened.";
getch();
exit(1);
}
while(fin)
{
fin>>c;
cout<<c;
}
fin.close();
getch();
}
```

**Problem 171. Write a C++ program to implement random files by using seek & tell function.**

***Program:***

```
#include<fstream.h>
#include<conio.h>
void main()
{
ofstream in("Aman.txt");
clrscr();
char c;
cout<<"Enter contents==>";
for(int i=1;i<=6;i++)
{
cin>>c;
in<<c;
}
in.close();
ifstream out("Aman.txt");
cout<<"\n\n\nSub string is==>";
out>>c;
cout<<c;
out.seekg(3,ios::cur);
out>>c;
cout<<c;
out>>c;
cout<<c;
out.seekg(-3,ios::cur);
out>>c;
cout<<c;
getch();
}
```

# CHAPTER 16

# EXPLORING FUNCTIONS (INLINE, FRIEND,STATIC)

## INLINE FUNCTION AND METHODS:

**Problem 1. Write a C++ program for inline function definition.**

***Program:***

```
#include <iostream.h>
#include<conio.h>
class Cat
{
public:
Cat (int initialAge);
~Cat();
int GetAge() { return itsAge;}            // inline!
void SetAge (int age) { itsAge = age;}    // inline!
void Meow() { cout << "Meow.\n";}  // inline!
private:
int itsAge;
};
```

**Problem 2. Write a C++ program for automatic inline functions.**

***Program:***

```
#include <iostream.h>
#include<conio.h>
class MyClass
{
int i; // private by default
public:
int getInt() { return i; }
void setInt(int j) { i = j; }
} ;
void main()
{
MyClass s;
s.setInt(10);
cout << s.getInt();
getch();
}
```

**OUTPUT:**

10

**Problem 3. Write a C++ program for Automatic inline().**

***Program:***

```
#include <iostream.h>
#include<conio.h>
class myclass
{
int a, b;
public:
// automatic inline
void init(int i, int j)
{
a = i;
b = j;
}
void show()
{
cout << a << " " << b << endl;
}
};
void  main()
{
myclass x;
x.init(1, 2);
x.show();
getch();
}
```

**OUTPUT:**

1 2

**Problem 4. Write a C++ program for Inline Functions.**

***Program:***

```
#include <iostream.h>
#include<conio.h>
inline int max(int a,int b)
{
```

```
return a>b ?a :b;
}
void main()
{
cout <<max(10,20);
cout <<" "<<max(99,88);
getch();
}
```

**OUTPUT:**

20 99

**Problem 5. Write a C++ program for inline().**

***Program:***

```
#include <iostream.h>
#include<conio.h>
class A
{
int a,b;
public:
void init(int i,int j);
void show();
};
inline void A::init(int i,int j)
{
a =i;
b =j;
}
inline void A::show()
{
cout <<a <<" "<<b <<"\n";
}
void main()
{
A aa;
aa.init(100,200);
aa.show();
getch();
}
```

**OUTPUT:**

100 200

**Problem 6. Write a C++ program to create an inline function.**

***Program:***

```
#include <iostream.h>
#include<conio.h>
class myclass
{
int a, b;
public:
void init(int i, int j);
void show();
};
// an inline function.
inline void myclass::init(int i, int j)
{
a = i;
b = j;
}
// another inline function.
inline void myclass::show()
{
cout << a << " " << b << endl;
}
void  main()
{
myclass x;
x.init(10, 20);
x.show();
getch();
}
```

**OUTPUT:**

10 20

**Problem 7. Write a C++ program for attractive inline functions.**

***Program:***

```
#include <iostream.h>
#include<conio.h>
inline int f(int);
void main()
{
int target;
cout << "Enter a number to work with: ";
cin >> target;
cout << "\n";
target = f(target);
cout << "Target: " << target << endl;
target = f(target);
cout << "Target: " << target << endl;
target = f(target);
cout << "Target: " << target << endl;
getch();
}
int f(int target)
{
return 2*target;
}
```

**OUTPUT:**

Enter a number to work with: 12
Target: 24
Target: 48

Target: 96

**Problem 8. Write a C++ program for inline method.**

***Program:***

```
#include <iostream.h>
#include<conio.h>
class MyClass
{
int i; // private by default
public:
int getInt();
void setInt(int j);
} ;
inline int MyClass::getInt()
{
return i;
}
inline void MyClass::setInt(int j)
{
i = j;
}
void main()
{
MyClass s;
s.setInt(10);
cout << s.getInt();
getch();
}
```

**OUTPUT:**

10

**Problem 9. Write a C++ program to multiply and add two values to illustrate the inline Function.**

***Program:***

```
#include<iostream.h>
#include<conio.h>
inline float mul (float x, float y)
{
return (x * y) ;
}
inline float add (float p, float q)
{
return ( p + q) ;
}
void main ( )
{
float a = 12.345 ;
float b = 9.82 ;
cout << mul (a, b) ;
cout << add (a, b) ;
getch();
}
```

**Problem 10. Write a C++ program to find whether a number is even or odd by using the concept of inline function.**

***Program:***

```
#include<iostream.h>
#include<conio.h>
#include<dos.h>
inline int even(int n)
{
return !(n%2);
}
void main()
{
int a;
clrscr();
cout<<"Enter any number:";
cin>>a;
if(even(a))
cout<<a<<" is even";
else
cout<<a<<" is odd";
getch();
}
```

**OUTPUT:**

Enter any number: 12
12 is even

## STATIC DATA MEMBERS, MEMBER FUNCTIONS AND STATIC CLASS:

**Problem 11. Write a C++ program for static members.**

***Program:***

```
#include <iostream.h>
#include<conio.h>
class CDummy
{
public:
static int n;
CDummy ()
{
n++;
}
~CDummy ()
{
n--;
```

```
}
};
int CDummy::n=0;
void main ()
{
CDummy a;
CDummy b[5];
CDummy * c = new CDummy;
cout << a.n << endl;
delete c;
cout << CDummy::n << endl;
getch();
}
```

**OUTPUT:**

```
7
6
```

**Problem 12. Write a C++ program to share static variable among different class instances.**

***Program:***

```
#include<iostream.h>
#include<conio.h>
class MyClass
{
static int a;
int b;
public:
void set(int i, int j)
{
a=i;
b=j;
}
void show();
};
int MyClass::a;
void MyClass::show()
{
cout<< "This is static a: " << a << endl;
cout<< "This is non-static b: " << b << endl;
}
void main(void)
{
MyClass x, y;
x.set(1,1);
x.show();
y.set(2,2);
y.show();
x.show();
getch();
}
```

**OUTPUT:**

```
This is static a:1
This is non-static b:1
This is static a:2
This is non-static b:2
This is static a:2
This is non-static b:1
```

**Problem 13. Write a C++ program for static data members.**

***Program:***

```
#include <iostream.h>
#include<conio.h>
class MyClass
{
public:
MyClass(int age = 1):intValue(age)
{
InstanceCount++;
}
virtual ~MyClass()
{
InstanceCount--;
}
virtual int getValue()
{
return intValue;
}
virtual void setValue(int age)
{
intValue = age;
}
static int InstanceCount;
private:
int intValue;
};
int MyClass::InstanceCount = 0;
void main()
{
const int count = 5;
MyClass *MyClassHouse[count];
int i;
for (i = 0; i<count; i++)
MyClassHouse[i] = new MyClass(i);
for (i = 0; i<count; i++)
{
cout << "There are ";
cout << MyClass::InstanceCount;
cout << " left!\n";
cout << "Deleting the one which is ";
cout << MyClassHouse[i]->getValue();
delete MyClassHouse[i];
```

```
MyClassHouse[i] = 0;
}
getch();
}
```

**OUTPUT:**

There are 5 left!
Deleting the one which is 0There are 4 left!
Deleting the one which is 1There are 3 left!
Deleting the one which is 2There are 2 left!
Deleting the one which is 3There are 1 left!
Deleting the one which is 4

**Problem 14. Write a C++ program to Print Fibonacci series by Static Variables.**

***Program:***

```
#include<iostream.h>
#include<conio.h>
class fib
{
static int a,b;
int c;
public:
void print()
{
c=a+b;
cout<<c<<" ";
a=b;
b=c;
}
}f;
int fib::b=1;
int fib::a;
void main()
{
int n,i;
clrscr();
cout<<"Enter number of terms to be printed==>";
cin>>n;
if(n==0)
cout<<"No term to print.";
else
{
cout<<"The series is==>";
if(n==1)
cout<<"0";
else if(n>1)
{
cout<<"0 1 ";
for(i=1;i<=n-2;i++)
f.print();
}
}
getch();
}
```

**OUTPUT:**

Enter number of terms to be printed==> 20
The series is==> 0 1 1 2 3 5 8 13

**Problem 15. Write a C++ program using a static instance variable.**

***Program:***

```
#include <iostream.h>
#include<conio.h>
class MyClass
{
static int num;
public:
void setl(int i) { num = i; };
void display() { cout << num << " "; }
};
int MyClass::num; // define num
void main()
{
MyClass a, b;
a.display(); // prints 0
b.display(); // prints 0
a.setl(10); // set static num to 10
a.display(); // prints 10
b.display(); // also prints 10
getch();
}
```

**OUTPUT:**

0 0 10 10

**Problem 16. Write a C++ program for refer to static variable through its class name.**

***Program:***

```
#include <iostream.h>
#include<conio.h>
class MyClass
{
public:
static int num;
void display() { cout << num << endl; }
};
int MyClass::num; // define num
void main()
{
MyClass a, b;
// Set num through its class name.
MyClass::num = 100;
a.display();
```

```
b.display();
// Set num through an object.
a.num = 200;
a.display();
b.display();
getch();
}
```

**OUTPUT:**

100
100
200
200

**Problem 17. Write a C++ program for static data members.**

***Program:***

```
#include <iostream.h>
#include<conio.h>
class MyClass
{
public:
MyClass(int age = 1):intValue(age)
{
InstanceCount++;
}
virtual ~MyClass()
{
InstanceCount--;
}
virtual int getValue()
{
return intValue;
}
virtual void setValue(int age)
{
intValue = age;
}
static int InstanceCount;
private:
int intValue;
};
int MyClass::InstanceCount = 0;
void main()
{
const int count = 5;
MyClass *MyClassHouse[count];
int i;
for (i = 0; i<count; i++)
MyClassHouse[i] = new MyClass(i);
for (i = 0; i<count; i++)
{
cout << "There are ";
cout << MyClass::InstanceCount;
cout << " left!\n";
cout << "Deleting the one which is ";
cout << MyClassHouse[i]->getValue();
delete MyClassHouse[i];
MyClassHouse[i] = 0;
}
getch();
}
```

**OUTPUT:**

There are 5 left!
Deleting the one which is 0There are 4 left!
Deleting the one which is 1There are 3 left!
Deleting the one which is 2There are 2 left!
Deleting the one which is 3There are 1 left!
Deleting the one which is 4

# MEMBER FUNCTION:

**Problem 18. Write a C++ program for a static member functions.**

***Program:***

```
#include <iostream.h>
#include<conio.h>
class MyClass
{
static int count;
public:
MyClass()
{
count++;
cout << "Constructing object " <<
count << endl;
}
~MyClass()
{
cout << "Destroying object " <<count << endl;
count--;
}
static int numObjects() { return count; }
};
int MyClass::count;
void main()
{
MyClass a, b, c;
cout << "There are now " <<
MyClass::numObjects() << " in existence.\n\n";
MyClass *p = new MyClass();
```

```
cout << "there are now " << MyClass::numObjects()
<< " in existence.\n\n";
delete p;
cout << " there are now " << a.numObjects() << " in
existence.\n\n";
getch();
}
```

**OUTPUT:**

Constructing object 1
Constructing object 2
Constructing object 3
There are now 3 in existence.
Constructing object 4
there are now 4 in existence.
Destroying object 4
there are now 3 in existence.
Destroying object 3
Destroying object 2
Destroying object 1

**Problem 19. Write a C++ program for name conflicts.**

***Program:***

```
#include <iostream.h>
#include<conio.h>
int C;
class C
{
private:
int i[2];
public:
static int f()
{
return sizeof(C);
}
};
int f()
{
return sizeof(C);
}
void main()
{
cout << "C::f() = " << C::f() << ","<< " ::f() = " <<
::f() << endl;
getch();
}
```

**OUTPUT:**

C::f() = 8, ::f() = 4

**Problem 20. Write a C++ program for static Functions.**

***Program:***

```
#include <iostream.h>
#include<conio.h>
class A
{
private:
static int a;
int b;
public:
A()
{
a++;
b =a;
}
~A()
{
a--;
cout <<"Destroy number b " <<b <<endl;
}
static void show_a()
{
cout <<"Value of a is " <<a <<endl;
}
void show_b()
{
cout <<"Value of b is " <<b <<endl;
}
};
int A :: a=0;
void main()
{
A a1;
A::show_a();
A a2,a3;
A::show_a();
a1.show_b();
a2.show_b();
a3.show_b();
getch();
}
```

**OUTPUT:**

Value of a is 1
Value of a is 3
Value of b is 1
Value of b is 2
Value of b is 3
Destroy number b 3
Destroy number b 2
Destroy number b 1

**Problem 21. Write a C++ program to static Member Functions.**

***Program:***

```
#include<iostream.h>
#include<conio.h>
class A
{
static int value;
public:
static int get_value();
void free_value()
{
value =0;
}
};
int A::value;
int A::get_value()
{
if(value)
return 0;
else
{
value =1;
return 1;
}
}
void main()
{
A aa,bb;
if(A::get_value())
cout <<"aa has value \n";
if(!A::get_value())
cout <<"bb has no value \n";
aa.free_value();
if(bb.get_value())
cout <<"bb can now use value \n";
getch();
}
```

**OUTPUT:**

aa has value
bb has no value
bb can now use value

**Problem 22. Write a C++ program to increment the number to show the working of static Function.**

***Program:***

```
#include<iostream.h>
#include<conio.h>
#include<dos.h>
class abc
{
private :
static int c ;
public :
abc ( ) ;
static void write ( ) ;                    //static
member function
} ;
int abc :: c = 0                           //static
data member
abc :: abc ( )
{
c++ ;
}
void abc :: write ( )
{
cout<<"\n Final Value of C is" <<c ;
}
void main ( )
{
cout<<"\n Before instantiation of the object" ;
abc :: write ( ) ;
abc m1, m2, m3, m4, m5 ;
cout<<"\n AFTER instantiation of the object" ;
abc :: write ( ) ;
getch();
}
```

**OUTPUT:**

Before instantiation of the object
Final value of C is 0
After instantiation of the object
Final value of C is 5

## STATIC CLASS:

**Problem 23. Write a C++ program for an Example of Static Class Data.**

***Program:***

```
#include <iostream.h>
#include<conio.h>
class stat
{
private:
static int c;
public:
stat()
{c++;}
int getc()
{return c;}
};
```

```
int stat::c =0;
void main()
{
stat s1,s2,s3;
cout <<"c is " <<s1.getc()<<endl;
cout <<"c is " <<s2.getc()<<endl;
cout <<"c is " <<s3.getc()<<endl;
getch();
}
```

**OUTPUT:**

```
c is 3
c is 3
c is 3
```

**Problem 24. Write a C++ program to show creation & destruction of automatic ,static and global objects.**

***Program:***

```
#include<iostream.h>
#include<conio.h>
#include<string.h>
class type
{
char msg[30];
public:
type(char s[])
{
strcpy(msg,s);
cout<<"Object created"<<msg<<"\n";
}
~type()
{
cout<<"Object destroyed"<<msg<<"\n";
}
};
type t1("global");
void main()
{
clrscr();
type t2("automatic");
static type t3("static");
getch();
}
```

**OUTPUT:**

```
Object created automatic
Object created static
Object created automatic
Object created static
Object created global
```

# FRIEND FUNCTION AND CLASS:

**Problem 25. Write a C++ program for friend function Demo.**

***Program:***

```
#include <iostream.h>
#include<conio.h>
class myclass
{
int num;
public:
myclass(int x)
{
num = x;
}
friend int isneg(myclass ob);
};
int isneg(myclass ob)
{
return (ob.num < 0) ? 1 : 0;
}
void main()
{
myclass a(-1), b(2);
cout << isneg(a) << ' ' << isneg(b);
cout << endl;
getch();
}
```

**OUTPUT:**

```
1 0
```

**Problem 26. Write a C++ program for a friend function.**

***Program:***

```
#include <iostream.h>
#include<conio.h>
class MyClass
{
int a, b;
public:
MyClass(int i, int j) { a=i; b=j; }
friend int friendFunction(MyClass x); // a friend
function
};
// friendFunction() is a not a member function of
any class.
int friendFunction(MyClass x)
{
int max = x.a < x.b ? x.a : x.b;
return max;
```

```
}
void main()
{
MyClass n(18, 111);
cout << "friendFunction(n) is " << friendFunction(n)
<< "\n";
getch();
}
```

**OUTPUT:**

friendFunction(n) is 18

**Problem 27. Write a C++ program for friend functions can be shared by two or more classes.**

***Program:***

```
#include <iostream.h>
#include<conio.h>
class Cylinder; // a forward declaration
enum colors { red, green, yellow };
class Cube
{
colors color;
public:
Cube(colors c) { color = c; }
friend bool sameColor(Cube x, Cylinder y);
};
class Cylinder
{
colors color;
public:
Cylinder(colors c) { color= c; }
friend bool sameColor(Cube x, Cylinder y);
};
bool sameColor(Cube x, Cylinder y)
{
if(x.color == y.color)
return true;
else
return false;
}
void main()
{
Cube cube1(red);
Cube cube2(green);
Cylinder cyl(green);
if(sameColor(cube1, cyl))
cout << "cube1 and cyl are the same color.\n";
else
cout << "cube1 and cyl are different colors.\n";
if(sameColor(cube2, cyl))
cout << "cube2 and cyl are the same color.\n";
else
cout << "cube2 and cyl are different colors.\n";
getch();
}
```

**OUTPUT:**

cube1 and cyl are different colors.
cube2 and cyl are the same color.

**Problem 28. Write a C++ program to share friend function between classes.**

***Program:***

```
#include <iostream.h>
#include<conio.h>
class MyClassB;
class MyClassA
{
char *name;
public:
MyClassA(char *s){name=s;}
friend void print(MyClassA &,MyClassB &);
};
class MyClassB
{
char *name;
public:
MyClassB(char *s){name=s;}
friend void print(MyClassA &,MyClassB &);
};
void print(MyClassA &a,MyClassB &b)
{
cout<<"the MyClassA is"<<a.name<<endl;
cout<<"the MyClassB is"<<b.name<<endl;
}
void main()
{
MyClassA s("Am Pm");
MyClassB t("Wing Ping");
print(s,t);
getch();
}
```

**OUTPUT:**

the MyClassA isAm Pm
the MyClassB isWing Ping

**Problem 29. Write a C++ program for friend square() function for Distance.**

***Program:***

```
#include <iostream.h>
#include<conio.h>
class Distance
{
private:
```

```
int feet;
float inches;
public:
Distance() : feet(0), inches(0.0){ }
Distance(int ft, float in) : feet(ft), inches(in){ }
void showdist()
{
cout << feet << "\'-" << inches << '\"';
}
friend float square(Distance);
};
float square(Distance d)
{
float fltfeet = d.feet + d.inches/12;
float feetsqrd = fltfeet * fltfeet;
return feetsqrd;
}
void main()
{
Distance dist(3, 6.0);
float sqft;
sqft = square(dist);
dist.showdist();
cout << sqft;
getch();
}
```

**Problem 30. Write a C++ program for friend functions can access private members of a class.**

***Program:***

```
#include <iostream.h>
#include<conio.h>
class MyClass
{
friend void setX( MyClass &, int ); // friend
declaration
public:
MyClass() : x( 0 )
{
}
void print() const
{
cout << x << endl;
}
private:
int x;
};
void setX( MyClass &c, int val )
{
c.x = val;
}
void main()
{
MyClass counter;
counter.print();
setX( counter, 8 );
counter.print();
getch();
}
```

**OUTPUT:**

0
8

**Problem 31. Write a C++ program to depict access of private data by a non member function.**

***Program:***

```
#include<iostream.h>
#include<conio.h>
class d
{
int u;
public:
d(int uu)
{u=uu;}
friend void display(d);
};
void display(d t1)
{
cout<<t1.u;
}
void main()
{
clrscr();
d obj1(5);
display(obj1);
getch();
}
```

**OUTPUT:**

5

**Problem 32. Write a C++ program to depict working of friend function.**

***Program:***

```
#include<iostream.h>
class vvv;
class uuu
{
private:
int u;
public:
uuu(int uu)
{u=uu;}
```

```
friend void fun1(uuu,vvv);
};
class vvv
{
private:
int v;
public:
vvv(int vv)
{v=vv;}
friend void fun1(uuu,vvv);
};
void fun1(uuu obju,vvv objv)
{
cout<<"Difference="<<obju.u-objv.v;
}
void main()
{
uuu obj1(10);
uuu obj2(5);
fun1(obj1,obj2);
getch();
}
```

**Problem 33. Write a C++ program to depict member function can act as friend to function in other class.**

***Program:***

```
#include<iostream.h>
#include<conio.h>
class vvv;
class uuu
{
int u;
public:
uuu(int uu)
{u=uu;}
void f1(vvv);
};
class vvv
{
int v;
public:
vvv(int vv)
{v=vv;}
friend void xxx::f1(vvv);
};
void uuu::f1(vvv objv)
{
cout<<"Difference="<<u-objv.v;
}
void main()
{
uuu obj1(10);
uuu obj2(5);
obj1.f1(obj2);
getch();
}
```

**Problem 34. Write a C++ program to find the Factorial of a number by using Friend Function.**

```
#include<iostream.h>
#include<conio.h>
//void fact(A);
class A
{
int n;
friend void fact(A);
void print();
public:
A(int p)
{
n=p;
}
};
void A::print()
{
long f=1;
for(int i=1;i<=n;i++)
f*=i;
cout<<"Factorial is==>"<<f;
}
void fact(A a)
{
a.print();
}
void main()
{
int n;
clrscr();
cout<<"Enter the number==>";
cin>>n;
A a(n);
fact(a);
getch();
}
```

**OUTPUT:**

```
Enter the number==> 5
Factorial is==> 120
```

**Problem 35. Write a C++ program for friend Functions.**

***Program:***

```
#include <iostream.h>
#include<conio.h>
class A
{
int a,b;
public:
friend int sum(A x);
void set_value(int i,int j);
};
void A::set_value(int i,int j)
{
a =i;
b =j;
}
int sum(A x)
{
return x.a +x.b;
}
void main()
{
A aa;
aa.set_value(4,5);
cout <<sum(aa);
getch();
}
```

**OUTPUT:**

9

# FRIEND OPERATOR:

**Problem 36. Write a C++ program using friend operator functions.**

***Program:***

```
#include <iostream.h>
#include<conio.h>
class ThreeD
{
int x, y, z;
public:
ThreeD() { x = y = z = 0; }
ThreeD(int i, int j, int k) { x = i; y = j; z = k; }
friend ThreeD operator+(ThreeD op1, ThreeD op2);
void show() ;
} ;
// The + is now a friend function.
ThreeD operator+(ThreeD op1, ThreeD op2)
{
ThreeD temp;
temp.x = op1.x + op2.x;
temp.y = op1.y + op2.y;
temp.z = op1.z+ op2.z;
return temp;
}
// Show X, Y, Z coordinates.
void ThreeD::show()
{
cout << x << ", ";
cout << y << ", ";
cout << z << "\n";
}
void main()
{
ThreeD a(1, 2, 3), b(10, 10, 10), c;
cout << "Original value of a: ";
a.show();
cout << "Original value of b: ";
b.show();
c = a + b; // add a and b together
cout << "\n Value of c after c = a + b: ";
c.show();
c = a + b + c; // add a, b and c together
cout << "\n Value of c after c = a + b + c: ";
c.show();
cout << "\n";
c = b = a;  // demonstrate multiple assignment
cout << "Value of c after c = b = a: ";
c.show();
cout << "Value of b after c = b = a: ";
b.show();
getch();
}
```

**OUTPUT:**

Original value of a: 1, 2, 3
Original value of b: 10, 10, 10
Value of c after c = a + b: 11, 12, 13
Value of c after c = a + b + c: 22, 24, 26
Value of c after c = b = a: 1, 2, 3
Value of b after c = b = a: 1, 2, 3

**Problem 37. Write a C++ program for friend Functions.**

***Program:***

```
#include <iostream.h>
#include<conio.h>
class B;
class A
{
private:
int data;
public:
```

```
A():data(4)
{ }
friend int frnfunc(A,B);//friend function
};
class B
{
private:
int data;
public:
B():data(6)
{}
friend int frnfunc(A,B);//friend function
};
int frnfunc(A a,B b)
{
return(a.data +b.data );
}

void main()
{
A aa;
B bb;
cout <<frnfunc(aa,bb)<<endl;//call the function
getch();
}
```

**OUTPUT:**

10

**Problem 38. Write a C++ program for class rectangle use concept of friend functions.**

***Program:***

```
#include <iostream.h>
#include<conio.h>
class CRectangle
{
int width, height;
public:
void set_values (int, int);
int area ()
{
return (width * height);
}
friend CRectangle duplicate (CRectangle);
};
void CRectangle::set_values (int a, int b)
{
width = a;
height = b;
}
CRectangle duplicate (CRectangle rectparam)
{
CRectangle rectres;
rectres.width = rectparam.width*2;
rectres.height = rectparam.height*2;
return (rectres);
}
void main ()
{
CRectangle rect, rectb;
rect.set_values (2,3);
rectb = duplicate (rect);
cout << rectb.area();
getch();
}
```

**OUTPUT:**

24

**Problem 39. Write a C++ program to make the inserter into a friend function.**

***Program:***

```
#include <iostream.h>
#include<conio.h>
#include <string.h>
class PhoneNumber
{
char name[80];
int areaCode;
int prefix;
int num;
public:
PhoneNumber(char *n, int a, int p, int nm)
{
strcpy(name, n);
areaCode = a;
prefix = p;
num = nm;
}
friend ostream &operator<<(ostream &stream,
PhoneNumber o);
};
// Display name and phone number.
ostream &operator<<(ostream &stream,
PhoneNumber o)
{
stream << o.name << " ";
stream << "(" << o.areaCode << ") ";
stream << o.prefix << "-" << o.num << "\n";
return stream; // must return stream
}
void  main()
{
PhoneNumber a("T", 111, 555, 1234);
```

```
PhoneNumber b("A", 312, 555, 5768);
PhoneNumber c("T", 212, 555, 9991);
cout << a << b << c;
getch();
}
```

**OUTPUT:**

T (111) 555-1234
A (312) 555-5768
T (212) 555-9991

**Problem 40. Write a C++ program to define friend function for <<.**

***Program:***

```
#include <iostream.h>
#include<conio.h>
#include <string.h>
#include <stdlib.h>
class StringClass
{
char *p;
int len;
public:
StringClass(char *ptr);
~StringClass()
{
delete [] p;
}
friend ostream &operator<<(ostream &stream,
StringClass &ob);
};
StringClass::StringClass(char *ptr)
{
len = strlen(ptr)+1;
p = new char [len];
if(!p)
{
cout << "Allocation error\n";
exit(1);
}
strcpy(p, ptr);
}
ostream &operator<<(ostream &stream, StringClass
&ob)
{
stream << ob.p;
return stream;
}
void  main()
{
StringClass stringObject1("www.google.com"),
stringObject2("www.google.com");
cout << stringObject1;
cout << endl << stringObject2 << endl;
getch();
}
```

**OUTPUT:**

www.google.com
www.google.com

## FRIEND CLASS:

**Problem 41. Write a C++ program for friend class.**

***Program:***

```
#include <iostream.h>
#include<conio.h>
class CSquare;
class CRectangle
{
int width, height;
public:
int area ()
{
return (width * height);
}
void convert (CSquare a);
};
class CSquare
{
private:
int side;
public:
void set_side (int a)
{
side=a;
}
friend class CRectangle;
};
void CRectangle::convert (CSquare a)
{
width = a.side;
height = a.side;
}
void main ()
{
CSquare sqr;
CRectangle rect;
sqr.set_side(4);
rect.convert(sqr);
cout << rect.area();
getch();
```

```
}
```

**OUTPUT:**

16

**Problem 42. Write a C++ program to show entire class as friend of another.**

***Program:***

```
#include<iostream.h>
#include<conio.h>
class uuu
{
int u,y;
public:
uuu(int uu,int vv)
{u=uu;v=vv;}
friend class vvv;
};
class vvv
{
public:
void f1(uuu obju)
{
cout<<"u="<<obju.u;
}
void f2(uuu objv)
{
cout<<"\nv="<<objv.v;
}
};
void main()
{
uuu obj1(10,15);
vvv obj2;
obj2.f1(obj1);
obj2.f2(obj1);
getch();
}
```

**Problem 43. Write a C++ program for friend Classes.**

***Program:***

```
#include <iostream.h>
#include<conio.h>
class A
{
int a;
int b;
public:
A(int i,int j)
{
a =i;
b =j;
}
friend class B;
};
class B
{
public:
int val(A x);
};
int B::val(A x)
{
return x.a <x.b ?x.a :x.b;
}
void main()
{
A aa(10,20);
B bb;
cout <<bb.val(aa);
getch();
}
```

**OUTPUT:**

10

**Problem 44. Write a C++ program for friend Classes.**

***Program:***

```
#include <iostream.h>
#include<conio.h>
class A
{
private:
int data;
public:
A():data(90)
{}
friend class B;// B is a friend class
};
class B
{
public:
void func1(A a)
{
cout <<"\ndata=" <<a.data;
}
void func2(A a)
{
cout <<"\ndata=" <<a.data;
}
};
void main()
{
```

```
A a;
B b;
b.func1(a);
').func2(a);
cout <<endl;
getch();
}
```

**OUTPUT:**

```
data=90
data=90
```

**Problem 45. Write a C++ program to add two numbers to illustrate the use of friend functions.**

***Program:***

```
#include<iostream.h>
#include<conio.h>
class real;
class integer
{
private:
int a;
public:
integer()       // Constructor
{
a=0;
}
integer(int i)    // Constructor
{
a=i;
}
void get()
{
cout<<endl<<"Enter the value:"<<endl;
cin>>a;
}
void show()
{
cout<<endl<<"a = "<<a;
}
friend real add(integer i,real j);
};
class real
{
private:
float b;
public:
real()
{
b=0.0;
}
void get()
{
cout<<endl<<"Enter the value:";
cin>>b;
}
void show()
{
cout<<endl<<"b = "<<b;
}
friend real add(integer i,real j);
};
void main()
{
integer x;
real y,z;
x.get();
y.get();
z = add(x,y);
z.show();
getch();
}
real add(integer i,real j)
{
real k;
k.b = i.a + j.b;
return k;
}
```

## CHAPTER 17

# TEMPLATES

## TEMPLATE CLASS:

**Problem 1.Write a C++ program for class templates myclass.**

***Program:***

```
#include <iostream.h>
#include<conio.h>
template <class T>
class MyClass
{
T value1, value2;
public:
MyClass (T first, T second)
{
value1=first;
value2=second;
}
T getmax ()
{
T retval;
retval = value1>value2 ? value1 : value2;
return retval;
}
};
void main ()
{
MyClass <int> myobject (100, 75);
cout << myobject.getmax();
getch();
}
```

**OUTPUT:**

100

**Problem 2. Write a C++ program for class templates stack.**

***Program:***

```
#include <iostream.h>
#include<conio.h>
const int MAX =100;//size of array
template <class Type>
class Stack
{
private:
Type st [MAX ];
int top;
public:
Stack()
{
top =-1;
}
void push(Type var)
{
st [++top ] ==var;
}
Type pop()
{
return st [top--];
}
};
void main()
{
Stack<float>s1;
s1.push(1111.1F);
s1.push(2222.2F);
s1.push(3333.3F);
cout <<"1:" <<s1.pop()<<endl;
cout <<"2:" <<s1.pop()<<endl;
cout <<"3:" <<s1.pop()<<endl;
Stack<long>s2;
s2.push(123123123L);
s2.push(234234234L);
s2.push(345345345L);
cout <<"1:" <<s2.pop()<<endl;
cout <<"2:" <<s2.pop()<<endl;
cout <<"3:" <<s2.pop()<<endl;
getch();
}
```

**Problem 3. Write a C++ program for a linked list class using templates.**

***Program:***

```
#include <iostream.h>
#include<conio.h>
template<class TYPE>
struct link
{
```

```
TYPE data;
link*next;
};
template<class TYPE>
class linklist
{
private:
link<TYPE>*first;
public:
linklist()
{
first =NULL;
}
void additem(TYPE d);
void display();
};
template<class TYPE>
void linklist<TYPE>::additem(TYPE d)
{
link<TYPE>*newlink =new link<TYPE>;
newlink->data =d;
newlink->next =first;
first =newlink;
}
template<class TYPE>
void linklist<TYPE>::display()
{
link<TYPE>*current =first;
while(current !=NULL )
{
cout <<endl <<current->data;
current =current->next;
}
}
void main()
{
linklist<double>ld;
ld.additem(151.5);
ld.additem(262.6);
ld.additem(373.7);
ld.display();
linklist<char>lch;
lch.additem('a');
lch.additem('b');
lch.additem('c');
lch.display();
cout <<endl;
getch();
}
```

**OUTPUT:**

373.7
262.6
151.5
c
b
a

**Problem 4. Write a C++ program for class templates mypair.**

***Program:***

```
#include <iostream.h>
#include<conio.h>
template <class T>
class mypair
{
T a,b;
public:
mypair (T first, T second)
{
a=first;
b=second;
}
T getmax ();
};
template <class T>
T mypair<T>::getmax ()
{
T retval;
retval = a>b? a : b;
return retval;
}
void main ()
{
mypair <int> myobject (100, 75);
cout << myobject.getmax();
getch();
}
```

**OUTPUT:**

100

# TEMPLATE SPECIALIZATION:

**Problem 5. Write a C++ program for template specialization.**

***Program:***

```
#include <iostream.h>
#include<conio.h>
template <class T>
class mycontainer
{
T element;
```

```
public:
mycontainer (T arg)
{
element=arg;
}
T increase ()
{
return ++element;
}
};
// class template specialization:
template <>
class mycontainer <char>
{
char element;
public:
mycontainer (char arg)
{
element=arg;
}
char uppercase ()
{
if ((element>='a')&&(element<='z'))
element+='A'-'a';
return element;
}
};
void main ()
{
mycontainer<int> myint (7);
mycontainer<char> mychar ('j');
cout << myint.increase() << endl;
cout << mychar.uppercase() << endl;
getch();
}
```

**OUTPUT:**

```
8
J
```

**Problem 6. Write a C++ program to find minimum of 2,3 numbers of any data type.**

***Program:***

```
#include<iostream.h>
#include<conio.h>
template<class C>
C m(C u,C v)
{
return(u<v)?u:v;
}
template<class C>
C m(C u,C v,C w)
{
return(u<v?(u<w?u:c):(v<w?v:w));
}
void main()
{
cout<<"Lesser of 2 int values= "<<m(30,12);
cout<<"\nLesser of 2 float values=
"<<m(22.5,4.5);
cout<<"\nLesser of 3 int values= "<<m(67,10,40);
cout<<"\nLesser of 3 float values=
"<<m(7.1,3.8,2.1);
cout<<"\nLesser of 3 char values=
"<<m('G','B','U');
getch();
}
```

**OUTPUT:**

```
Atleast 2 int values=12
Atleast 2 float values=4.5
Atleast 3 int values=10
Atleast 3 float values=2.1
Atleast 3 char values=B
```

**Problem 7. Write a C++ program to overload function template with non function template.**

***Program:***

```
#include<iostream.h>
#include<conio.h>
#include<string.h>
template<class C>
C m(C u,C v)
{
return(u<v)?u:v;
}
char* m(char* p,char *q)
{
int k=strcmp(p,q);
return(k<0)?p:q;
}
void main()
{
cout<<"Lesser of 2 int values= "<<m(14,27);
cout<<"\nLesser of 2 float values= "<<m(7.5,2.5);
cout<<"\nLesser of 2 strings= "<<m("cde","mno");
getch();
}
```

**OUTPUT:**

```
Lesser of 2 int values=14
Lesser of 2 float values=2.5
Lesser of 2 strings=cde
```

**Problem 8. Write a C++ program for generic vector.**

***Program:***

```
#include<conio.h>
#include <iostream.h>
#include <math.h>
template <class T>
class Vector
{
T * pData;
int nSize;
public:
Vector(int);
~Vector() {delete [] pData;}
T& operator [] (int i) {return pData[i];}
};
template <class T>
Vector <T>::Vector(int n)
{
pData = new T[n];
nSize = n;
};
void main()
{
Vector <int> iV(4);
int i;
for ( i = 0;i < 4;i++)
iV[i] = i*i;
for ( i = 0;i < 4;i++)
cout << iV[i] << "  ";
cout << endl;
Vector <double> dV(4);
for ( i = 0; i < 4;i++)
dV[i] = sqrt(i);
for ( i = 0;i < 4;i++)
cout << dV[i] << "  ";
cout << endl;
getch();
}
```

**OUTPUT:**

```
0 1 4 9
0 1 1.41421 1.73205
```

**Problem 9. Write a C++ program for template counter.**

***Program:***

```
#include <iostream.h>
#include<conio.h>
#include <stddef.h>
template <class CountedType>
class ObjectCounter
{
private:
static size_t count;   // number of existing objects
protected:
// default constructor
ObjectCounter()
{
++count;
}
// copy constructor
ObjectCounter (ObjectCounter<CountedType>
const&)
{
++count;
}
// destructor
~ObjectCounter()
{
--count;
}
public:
// return number of existing objects:
static size_t live()
{
return count;
}
};
// initialize counter with zero
template <class CountedType>
size_t ObjectCounter<CountedType>::count = 0;
template <class CharT>
class MyString : public
ObjectCounter<MyString<CharT> >
{
//...
};
void main()
{
MyString<char> s1, s2;
MyString<wchar_t> ws;
cout << "number of MyString<char>:  "
     << MyString<char>::live() << endl;
cout << "number of MyString<wchar_t>: "
     << ws.live() << endl;
getch();
}
```

**OUTPUT:**

```
number of MyString<char>:   3
number of MyString<wchar_t>: 3
```

# TEMPLATE FUNCTION:

**Problem 10. Write a C++ program for function template: GetMax.**

***Program:***

```
#include <iostream.h>
#include<conio.h>
template <class T>
T GetMax (T a, T b)
{
T result;
result = (a>b)? a : b;
return (result);
}
void main ()
{
int i=5, j=6, k;
long l=10, m=5, n;
k = GetMax(i,j);
n = GetMax(l,m);
cout << k << endl;
cout << n << endl;
getch();
}
```

**OUTPUT:**

```
6
10
```

**Problem 11. Write a C++ program for function template II.**

***Program:***

```
#include <iostream.h>
#include<conio.h>
template <class T>
T GetMax (T a, T b)
{
return (a>b?a:b);
}
void main ()
{
int i=5, j=6, k;
long l=10, m=5, n;
k=GetMax(i,j);
n=GetMax(l,m);
cout << k << endl;
cout << n << endl;
getch();
}
```

**OUTPUT:**

```
6
10
```

**Problem 12. Write a C++ program for function template: swapargs.**

***Program:***

```
#include <iostream.h>
#include<conio.h>
// This is a function template.
template <class X> void swapargs(X &a, X &b)
{
X temp;
temp = a;
a = b;
b = temp;
}
void main()
{
int i=1, j=2;
float x=1.1, y=2.3;
char a='x', b='z';
cout << "Original i, j: " << i << ' ' << j << '\n';
swapargs(i, j); // swap integers
cout << "Swapped i, j: " << i << ' ' << j << '\n';
cout << "Original x, y: " << x << ' ' << y << '\n';
swapargs(x, y); // swap floats
cout << "Swapped x, y: " << x << ' ' << y << '\n';
cout << "Original a, b: " << a << ' ' << b << '\n';
swapargs(a, b); // swap chars
cout << "Swapped a, b: " << a << ' ' << b << '\n';
getch();
}
```

**OUTPUT:**

```
Original i, j: 1 2
Swapped i, j: 2 1
Original x, y: 1.1 2.3
Swapped x, y: 2.3 1.1
Original a, b: x z
Swapped a, b: z x
```

**Problem 13. Write a C++ program for a simple function template.**

***Program:***

```
#include <iostream.h>
#include<conio.h>
template <class T>  //function template
T temp(T n)
{
return (n <0)?-n :n;
}
void main()
{
int i1 =5;
```

```
int i2 =-6;
long l1 =70000L;
long l2 =-80000L;
double d1 =9.95;
double d2 =-10.15;
cout <<"\ntemp(" <<i1 <<")=" <<temp(i1);
cout <<"\ntemp(" <<i2 <<")=" <<temp(i2);
cout <<"\ntemp(" <<l1 <<")=" <<temp(l1);
cout <<"\ntemp(" <<l2 <<")=" <<temp(l2);
cout <<"\ntemp(" <<d1 <<")=" <<temp(d1);
cout <<"\ntemp(" <<d2 <<")=" <<temp(d2);
cout <<endl;
getch();
}
```

**OUTPUT**:

```
temp(5)=5
temp(-6)=6
temp(70000)=70000
temp(-80000)=80000
temp(9.95)=9.95
temp(-10.15)=10.15
```

**Problem 14. Write a C++ program for function templates with multiple arguments.**

***Program:***

```
#include <iostream.h>
#include<conio.h>
template <class atype>
int find(atype*array,atype value,int size)
{
for(int i=0;i<size;i++)
if(array [i]==value)
return i;
return -1;
}
char chrArr [] = {1,3,5,9,11,13};
char ch =5;
int intArr [] ={1,3,5,9,11,13};
int in =6;
long lonArr []={1L,3L,5L,9L,11L,13L};
long lon =11L;
double dbArr [] ={1.0,3.0,5.0,9.0,11.0,13.0};
double db =4.0;
void main()
{
cout <<"\n 5 in chrArray:index="
<<find(chrArr,ch,6);
cout <<"\n 6 in intArray:index="
<<find(intArr,in,6);
cout <<"\n11 in lonArray:index="
<<find(lonArr;lon,6);
cout <<"\n 4 in dubArray:index="
<<find(dbArr,db,6);
cout <<endl;
getch();
}
```

**OUTPUT:**

```
5 in chrArray:index=2
6 in intArray:index=-1
11 in lonArray:index=4
4 in dbArray:index=-1
```

**Problem 15. Write a C++ program for template type.**

***Program:***

```
#include <iostream.h>
#include<conio.h>
template <class Type1, class Type2>
void myfunc(Type1 x, Type2 y)
{
cout << x << ' ' << y << '\n';
}
void main()
{
myfunc(10, "hi");
myfunc(0.23, 10L);
getch();
}
```

**OUTPUT:**

```
10 hi
0.23 10
```

**Problem 16. Write a C++ program using standard parameters in a template function.**

***Program:***

```
#include <iostream.h>
#include<conio.h>
const int TABWIDTH = 8;
template<class X> void f(X data, int tab)
{
cout <<"tab=" << tab;
cout << data << "\n";
}
void main()
{
f("This is a test", 0);
f(100, 1);
f('X', 2);
f(10/3, 3);
getch();
}
```

**OUTPUT:**

```
tab= 0This is a test
tab=1100
tab= 2X
tab=33
```

**Problem 17. Write a C++ program to overload a function template declaration.**

***Program:***

```
#include <iostream.h>
#include<conio.h>
template <class X> void f(X a)
{
cout << "Inside f(X a)\n";
}
template <class X, class Y> void f(X a, Y b)
{
cout << "Inside f(X a, Y b)\n";
}
void main()
{
f(10);    // calls f(X)
f(10, 20); // calls f(X, Y)
getch();
}
```

**OUTPUT:**

```
Inside f(X a)
Inside f(X a, Y b)
```

**Problem 18. Write a C++ program for function with generic parameters.**

***Program:***

```
#include <iostream.h>
#include<conio.h>
template <class type1, class type2>
void f(type1 x, type2 y)
{
cout << x << ' ' << y << '\n';
}
void main()
{
f(10, "AAAAA");
f(98.6, 19L);
f('C', 'V');
f('C', 0);
getch();
}
```

**OUTPUT:**

```
10 AAAAA
98.6 19
C V
C 0
```

**Problem 19. Write a C++ program to overload template function.**

***Program:***

```
#include <iostream.h>
#include<conio.h>
#include <string.h>
template<typename T>
string f(T)
{
return "Template";
}
string f(int&)
{
return "Nontemplate";
}
void main()
{
int x = 7;
cout << f(x) << std::endl;
getch();
}
```

**OUTPUT:**

```
Nontemplate
```

**Problem 20. Write a C++ program to specify template argument explicitly and implicitly.**

***Program:***

```
#include <iostream.h>
#include<conio.h>
template <class T>
inline T const& max (T const& a, T const& b)
{
return  a < b ? b : a;
}
void main()
{
max<double>(1.0, -3.0); // explicitly specify
template argument
max(1.0, -3.0);          // template argument is
implicitly deduced to be double
max<int>(1.0, 3.0);      // the explicit <int> inhibits
the deduction;
// hence the result has type int
getch();
}
```

**Problem 21. Write a C++ program for namespace with template function.**

***Program:***

```
#include <iostream.h>
```

```
#include<conio.h>
namespace X
{
template<class T> void f(T);
}
namespace N
{
using namespace X;
enum E { e1 };
void f(E)
{
cout << "N::f(N::E) called\n";
}
}
void f(int)
{
cout << "::f(int) called\n";
}
void main()
{
f(N::e1); // qualified function name: no ADL
f(N::e1);  // ordinary lookup finds ::f() and ADL
finds N::f(),
getch();
}          // the latter is preferred
```

**OUTPUT:**

```
::f(int) called
N::f(N::E) called
```

**Problem 22. Write a C++ program for reference and non-reference template function.**

***Program:***

```
#include <iostream.h>
#include<conio.h>
template <class T>
void ref (T const& x)
{
cout << "x in ref(T const&): "<< typeid(x).name()
<< '\n';
}
template <class T>
void nonref (T x)
{
cout << "x in nonref(T): "<< typeid(x).name() <<
'\n';
}
void main()
{
ref("hello");
nonref("hello");
}
```

**OUTPUT:**

```
x in ref(T const&): A6_c
x in nonref(T):    PKc
```

**Problem 23. Write a C++ program to depict use of non type parameter in function template.**

***Program:***

```
#include<iostream.h>
#include<conio.h>
template<class C>
void put(C u,C v,char operation)
{
switch(operation)
{
case
'+':cout<<u<<operation<<v<<'='<<u+v<<endl;
break;
case '-':cout<<u<<operation<<v<<'='<<u-v<<endl;
break;
case
'*':cout<<u<<operation<<v<<'='<<u*v<<endl;
break;
case '/':cout<<u<<operation<<v<<'='<<u/v<<endl;
break;
default:cout<<"Undefined operation";
}
}
void main()
{
put(45,30,'+');
put(7.5,2.5,'-');
put('C','D','+');
getch();
}
```

**OUTPUT:**

```
45+30=75
7.5-2.5=5.0
C+D=135
```

**Problem 24. Write a C++ program to find average of n number of any data type using templates.**

***Program:***

```
#include<iostream.h>
#include<conio.h>
template<class C>
float av(C x[],int no)
{
float av,t=0;
for(int i=0;i<no;i++)
t=t+x[i];
```

```
av=t/no;
return(av);
}
void main()
{
int n,s[10];
cout<<"Processing integer elements\n";
cout<<"Enter number of elements=";
cin>>n;
for(int j=0;j<n;j++)
cin>>s[j]
cout<<"Average of integer values="<<av(s,n);
float s1[10];
cout<<"\nProcessing float elements\n";
cout<<"Enter number of elements=";
cin>>n;
for(int j=0;j<n;j++)
cin>>s1[j];
cout<<"Average of float values="<<av(s1,n);
getch();
}
```

**OUTPUT:**

```
Processing integer elements
Enter number of elements=3
12 34 23
Average of integet values 23
Processing float elements
Enter number of elements=3
15.5 60.25 10.75
Average of float values 28.333
```

**Problem 25. Write a C++ program to use class stack for different data type.**

***Program:***

```
#include<iostream.h>
#include<conio.h>
#include<process.h>
const int SIZE=10;
template<class C>
class stack
{
private:
C array[SIZE];
int top;
public:
stack()
{top==-1;}
void push(C item)
{
if(top==(SIZE-1))
{
cout<<"Stack overflow";
exit(0);
}
else
{
top++;
array[top]=item;
}
}
C pop()
{
if(top==-1)
{
cout<<"Stack underflow";
exit(0);
}
else
{
C elem=array[top--];
return elem;
}}
};
void main()
{
stack <int>h;
h.push(70);
h.push(80);
cout<<"Element to be poped"<<h.pop();
stack<float>t;
t.push(2.5);
t.push(9.7);
cout<<"Element to be poped"<<t.pop();
getch();
}
```

**Problem 26. Write a C++ program template for function to get the maximum of three values of any type (call-by-reference).**

***Program:***

```
#include <iostream.h>
#include<conio.h>
#include <string.h>
// maximum of two values of any type (call-by-
reference)
template <class T>
inline T const& max (T const& a, T const& b)
{
return a < b ? b : a;
}
// maximum of two C-strings (call-by-value)
```

```
inline char const* max (char const* a, char const* b)
{
return strcmp(a,b) < 0 ? b : a;
}

// maximum of three values of any type (call-by-
reference)
template <class T>
inline T const& max (T const& a, T const& b, T
const& c)
{
return max (max(a,b), c); // error, if max(a,b) uses
call-by-value
}
void main ()
{
cout << max(7, 42, 68);     // OK
const char* s1 = "frederic";
const char* s2 = "anica";
const char* s3 = "lucas";
//::max(s1, s2, s3);   // ERROR
}
```

**OUTPUT:**

68

**Problem 27. Write a C++ program for template function to get the maximum of two values.**

***Program:***

```
#include <iostream.h>
#include<conio.h>
inline int const& max (int const& a, int const& b)
{
return a < b ? b : a;
}
// maximum of two values of any type
template <class T>
inline T const& max (T const& a, T const& b)
{
return a < b ? b : a;
}
// maximum of three values of any type
template <class T>
inline T const& max (T const& a, T const& b, T
const& c)
{
return max (max(a,b), c);
}
void main()
{
cout <<"\n\n" <<max(7, 42, 68);   // calls the
template for three arguments
cout <<"\n\n" <<max(7.0, 42.0);   // calls
max<double> (by argument deduction)
cout <<"\n\n" <<max('a', 'b');    // calls
max<char> (by argument deduction)
cout <<"\n\n" <<max(7, 42);       // calls the
nontemplate for two ints
cout <<"\n\n" <<max(8, 42);     // calls max<int>
(by argument deduction)
cout <<"\n\n" <<max(7, 42); // calls max<double>
(no argument deduction)
cout <<"\n\n" <<max('a', 42.7);   // calls the
nontemplate for two ints
getch();
}
```

**OUTPUT:**

68
42
b
42
42
42
97

# TEMPLATE PARAMETER:

**Problem 28. Write a C++ program to demonstrate non-type template arguments.**

***Program:***

```
#include <stdlib.h>
#include<process.h>
#include <iostream.h>
#include<conio.h>
//int size is a non-type agument
template <class T, int size>
class MyType
{
T a[size];
public:
MyType()
{
for(int i=0; i<size; i++)
a[i] = i;
}
T &operator[](int i)
{
if(i<0 || i> size-1)
{
cout << "\nIndex value of ";
cout << i << " is out-of-bounds.\n";
exit(1);
```

```
}
return a[i];
}
};
void main()
{
MyType<int, 10> intob;
MyType<double, 15> doubleob;
cout << "Integer array: ";
for(int j=0; j<10; j++)
intob[j] = j;
for(int k=0; k<10; k++)
cout << intob[k] << "  ";
cout << '\n';
cout << "Double array: ";
for(int m=0; m<15; m++)
doubleob[m] = (double) m/3;
for(int n=0; n<15; n++)
cout << doubleob[n] << "  ";
cout << '\n';
intob[12] = 100; // generates runtime error
getch();
}
```

**OUTPUT:**

```
Integer array: 0 1 2 3 4 5 6 7 8 9
Double array: 0 0.333333 0.666667 1 1.33333
1.66667 2 2.33333 2.66667 3 3.33333 3.66667 4
4.33333 4.66667
Index value of 12 is out-of-bounds.
```

**Problem 29. Write a C++ program to default template arguments.**

***Program:***

```
#include <iostream.h>
#include<conio.h>
#include <stdlib.h>
// T defaults to int and size defaults to 10
template <class T, int size=10> class MyType
{
T a[size];
public:
MyType()
{
for(int i=0; i<size; i++)
a[i] = i;
}
T &operator[](int i)
{
if(i<0 || i> size-1)
{
cout << "\nIndex value of ";
cout << i << " is out-of-bounds.\n";
exit(1);
}
return a[i];
}
};
void main()
{
MyType<int, 100> intarray;
MyType<double> doublearray;
MyType<int> defarray;
cout << "int array: ";
for(int a=0; a<100; a++)
intarray[a] = a;
for(int b=0; b<100; b++)
cout << intarray[b] << "  ";
cout << '\n';
cout << "double array: ";
for(int j=0; j<10; j++)
doublearray[j] = (double) j/3;
for(int k=0; k<10; k++)
cout << doublearray[k] << "  ";
cout << '\n';
cout << "defarray array: ";
for(int m=0; m<10; m++)
defarray[m] = m;
for(int n=0; n<10; n++)
cout << defarray[n] << "  ";
cout << '\n';
getch();
}
```

**OUTPUT:**

```
int array: 0 1 2 3 4 5 6 7 8 9 10 11 12 13
14 15 16 17 18 19 20 21 22 23 24 25 26 27
28 29 30 31 32 33 34
35 36 37 38 39 40 41 42 43 44 45 46 47
48 49 50 51 52 53 54 55 56 57 58 59 60 61
62 63 64 65 66 67 68 69
70 71 72 73 74 75 76 77 78 79 80 81 82
83 84 85 86 87 88 89 90 91 92 93 94 95 96
97 98 99
double array: 0 0.333333 0.666667 1 1.33333
1.66667 2 2.33333 2.66667 3
defarray array: 0 1 2 3 4 5 6 7 8 9
```

**Problem 30. Write a C++ program for loop with generic parameter.**

***Program:***

```
#include <iostream.h>
#include<conio.h>
template <class T>
```

```
inline T dot_product (int dim, T* a, T* b)
{
T result ;
for (int i=0; i<dim; ++i)
{
result += a[i]*b[i];
}
return result;
}
void main()
{
int a[3] = { 1, 2, 3};
int b[3] = { 5, 6, 7};
cout << "dot_product(3,a,b) = " <<
dot_product(3,a,b)<< endl;
cout << "dot_product(3,a,a) = " <<
dot_product(3,a,a)<< endl;
getch();
}
```

**OUTPUT:**

```
dot_product(3,a,b) = 1316
dot_product(3,a,a) = 1292
```

**Problem 31. Write a C++ program for template function for generic parameter and pointer to generic parameter.**

***Program:***

```
#include <iostream.h>
#include<conio.h>
template<class T>
int f(T)
{
return 1;
}
template<class T>
int y(T*)
{
return 2;
}
void main()
{
cout << f((int)0) << endl;
cout << y((int*)0)  << endl;
getch();
}
```

**OUTPUT:**

```
1
2
```

**Problem 32. Write a C++ program using template parameter as constructor parameter.**

***Program:***

```
#include<conio.h>
#include <iostream.h>
#include <math.h>
template <class T>
class Rect
{
T x1,x2,y1,y2;
public:
Rect(T a,T b,T c,T d)
{
x1=a;
y1=b;
x2=c;
y2=d;
}
T Area();
T Distance();
};
template <class T>
T Rect<T>::Area()
{
return (x1-x2)*(y1-y2);}
template <class T>
T Rect<T>::Distance()
{
return sqrt((x1-x2)*(x1-x2)+(y1-y2)*(y1-y2));
}
void main()
{
Rect<int> p1(2.5,3.5,5.5,7);
cout <<p1.Area()<<endl;
cout <<p1.Distance()<<endl;
Rect <float> p2(2.5,3.5,5.5,7.0);
cout <<p2.Area()<<endl;
cout <<p2.Distance()<<endl;
getch();
}
```

**OUTPUT:**

```
12
5
10.5
4.60977
```

**Problem 33. Write a C++ program for template function to get maximum of two pointers.**

***Program:***

```
#include <iostream.h>
#include<conio.h>
#include <string.h>
// maximum of two values of any type
```

```
template <class T>
inline T const& max (T const& a, T const& b)
{
return  a < b  ?  b : a;
}
// maximum of two pointers
template <class T>
inline T* const& max (T* const& a, T* const& b)
{
return  *a < *b  ?  b : a;
}
// maximum of two C-strings
inline char const* const& max (char const* const&
a, const* const& b)
{
return  strcmp(a,b) < 0  ?  b : a;
}
void main ()
{
int a=7;
int b=42;
cout<<"\n\n" << max(a,b);      // max() for two
values of type int
char s[20]="hey";
char t[20]="you";
cout<<"\n\n" << max(s,t);      // max() for two values
of type std::string
char const* s1 = "David";
char const* s2 = "Nico";
cout<<"\n\n" << max(s1,s2);    // max() for two C-
strings
getch();
}
```

**OUTPUT:**

42
you
Nico

## NON-TYPE PARAMETERS FOR TEMPLATES:

**Problem 34. Write a C++ program for sequence template.**

***Program:***

```
#include <iostream.h>
#incl de<conio.h>
template <class T, int N>
class mysequence
{
T memblock [N];
public:
void setmember (int x, T value);
T getmember (int x);
};
template <class T, int N>
void mysequence<T,N>::setmember (int x, T
value)
{
memblock[x]=value;
}
template <class T, int N>
T mysequence<T,N>::getmember (int x)
{
return memblock[x];
}
void main ()
{
mysequence <int,5> myints;
mysequence <double,5> myfloats;
myints.setmember (0,100);
myfloats.setmember (3,3.1416);
cout << myints.getmember(0) << '\n';
cout << myfloats.getmember(3) << '\n';
getch();
}
```

**OUTPUT:**

100
3.1416

## CLASS SPECIALIZATION:

**Problem 35. Write a C++ program to demonstrate class specialization.**

***Program:***

```
#include <iostream.h>
#include<conio.h>
template <class T> class MyType
{
T x;
public:
MyType(T a)
{
cout << "Inside generic MyType\n";
x = a;
}
T getx()
{
return x;
}
};
```

```
// Explicit specialization for int.
template <> class MyType<int>
{
int x;
public:
MyType(int a)
{
cout << "Inside MyType<int> specialization\n";
x = a * a;
}
int getx()
{
return x;
}
};
void main()
{
MyType<double> d(10.1);
cout << "double: " << d.getx() << "\n\n";
MyType<int> i(5);
cout << "int: " << i.getx() << "\n";
getch();
}
```

**OUTPUT:**

```
Inside generic MyType
double: 10.1
Inside MyType specialization
int: 25
```

## OVERLOAD TEMPLATE FUNCTION:

**Problem 36. Write a C++ program to overload generic method and non-generic method.**

***Program:***

```
#include<conio.h>
#include<iostream.h>
#include<string.h>
template<class T>
T min(T a,T b)
{
cout << "generic";
return (a<b?a:b);
}
char *min(char *a,char *b)
{
cout << "not generic";
return (strcmp(a,b)<0?a:b);
}
void main()
{
double a=3.56,b=8.23;
char s1[]="Hello",s2[]="Good";
cout<<min(a,b)<<endl;
cout<<min(s1,s2)<<endl;
}
```

**OUTPUT:**

```
generic3.56
not genericGood
```

## GENERIC ARRAY USING TEMPLATES:

**Problem 37. Write a C++ program to define your own generic array.**

***Program:***

```
#include<conio.h>
#include<iostream.h>
#include<iomanip.h>
template<class T>
class Array
{
T *elems;
int size;
public:
Array(int s)
{
size=s;
elems=new T[size];
for(int i=0;i<size;i++)
elems[i]=0;
}
~Array()
{
delete elems;
}
T& operator[](int index)
{
return elems[index];
}
void operator=(T temp)
{
for(int i=0;i<size;i++)
elems[i]=temp;
}
};
void main()
{
int n=10;
Array<int>arr1(n);
```

```
Array<char>arr2(n);
for(int i=0;i<n;i++)
{
arr1[i]='a'+i;
arr2[i]='a'+i;
}
cout <<endl;
for(int j=0;j<n;j++)
{
cout<<setw(8)<<arr1[j]<<setw(8)<<arr2[j]<<endl;
}
getch();
}
```

**OUTPUT:**

```
97    a
98    b
99    c
100   d
101   e
102   f
103   g
104   h
105   i
106   j
```

**Problem 38. Write a C++ program for a generic class.**

***Program:***

```
#include <iostream.h>
#include<conio.h>
template <class T> class MyClass
{
T x, y;
public:
MyClass(T a, T b)
{
x = a;
y = b;
}
T div() { return x/y; }
};
void main()
{
MyClass<double> d_ob(10.0, 3.0 ); // doubles.
cout << "double division: " << d_ob.div() << "\n";
MyClass<int> i_ob(10, 3);       // for ints.
cout << "integer division: " << i_ob.div() << "\n";
getch();
}
```

**OUTPUT:**

```
double division: 3.33333
integer division: 3
```

**Problem 39. Write a C++ program for operator overload for generic parameters.**

***Program:***

```
#include <iostream.h>
#include<conio.h>
template<class T>
class Sample
{
T n;
public:
Sample(T i)
{
n=i;
}
int operator==(Sample &s)
{
if(n==s.n)
return 1;
else
return 0;
}
};
void main()
{
Sample<int> s1(2),s2(3);
cout<<(s1==s2)<<endl;
Sample<double> s3(2.5),s4(2.5);
cout<<(s1==s2)<<endl;
getch();
}
```

**OUTPUT:**

```
0
0
```

# ARRAY TEMPLATE:

**Problem 40. Write a C++ program for array template.**

***Program:***

```
#include <iostream.h>
#include<conio.h>
template <class T, int N>
class array
{
T memblock [N];
public:
setmember (int x, T value)
{
```

```
memblock[x]=value;
return 0;
}
T getmember (int x)
{
return memblock[x];
}
};
void main ()
{
array <int,5> myints;
array <float,5> myfloats;
myints.setmember (0,100);
myfloats.setmember (3,3.1);
cout << myints.getmember(0) << '\n';
cout << myfloats.getmember(3) << '\n';
getch();
}
```

**OUTPUT:**

100
3.1

**Problem 41. Write a C++ program using two generic data types in a class definition.**

***Program:***

```
#include <iostream.h>
#include<conio.h>
template <class Type1, class Type2> class MyClass
{
Type1 i;
Type2 j;
public:
MyClass(Type1 a, Type2 b)
{
i = a;
j = b;
}
void show()
{
cout << i << ' ' << j << '\n';
}
};
void main()
{
MyClass<int, double> ob1(10, 0.23);
MyClass<char, char*> ob2('X', "AAAAAAA");

ob1.show();
ob2.show();
getch();
}
```

**OUTPUT:**

10 0.23
X AAAAAAA

## GENERIC LIST:

**Problem 42. Write a C++ program for generic list.**

***Program:***

```
#include <iostream.h>
#include<conio.h>
template<class data_t>
class list
{
data_t data;
list *next;
public:
list(data_t d);
void add(list *node)
{
node->next=this;
next=0;
}
list *getnext()
{
return next;
}
data_t getdata()
{
return data;
}
};
template<class data_t>
list<data_t>::list(data_t d)
{
data=d;
next=0;
}
void main()
{
list<char>start('a');
list<char>*p,*last;
last=&start;
for(int i=1;i<26;i++)
{
p=new list<char>('a'+i);
p->add(last);
last=p;
}
p=&start;
```

```
while(p)
{
cout<<p->getdata();
p=p->getnext();
}
getch();
}
```

**OUTPUT:**

abcdefghijklmnopqrstuvwxyz

## GENERIC QUEUE:

**Problem 43. Write a C++ program for generic queue.**

***Program:***

```
#include<conio.h>
#include<iostream.h>
#include<iomanip.h>
#include<ctype.h>
template<class Type>
class queue
{
private:
Type size;
Type start;
Type end;
Type *data;
public:
queue()
{
size=20;
start=end=0;
data=new Type[size];
}
queue(Type n)
{
size=n;
start=end=0;
data=new Type[size];
}
~queue()
{
delete data;
}
void put(Type value)
{
if((start+1)==end)
{
cout<<"\n***Queue is full!***\n";
return ;
}
data[start]=value;
start=(start+1);
cout<<"You have put a data into the queue!\n";
return;
}
Type get()
{
Type value;
if(start==end)
{
cout<<"\n***Queue is empty!***\n";
return(0);
}
value=data[end];
end=(end+1);
cout<<"\n Get "<<value<<" from the queue!\n";
return(value);
}
void clear()
{
start=end;
cout<<"\n ***Queue is empty!***\n";
}
void ShowQueue()
{
if(start==end)
{
cout<<"\n The queue has no data!\n";
return;
}
Type i;
cout<<"\n The content of queue:\n";
for(i=end;i!=start;i=((i+1)))
cout<<setw(5)<<data[i];
cout<<"\n\n";
}
};
void main()
{
queue<char> ss(5);
char value = 'a';
ss.put(value);
ss.put('b');
value=ss.get();
ss.clear();
ss.ShowQueue();
getch();
}
```

**OUTPUT:**

You have put a data into the queue!

You have put a data into the queue!
Get a from the queue!
***Queue is empty!***
The queue has no data!

## GENERIC SORT:

**Problem 44. Write a C++ program for a generic bubble sort.**

***Program:***

```
#include <iostream.h>
#include<conio.h>
template <class X> void bubble(X *items,int count)
{
X t;
for(int a=1; a<count; a++)
for(int b=count-1; b>=a; b--)
if(items[b-1] > items[b])
{
t = items[b-1];
items[b-1] = items[b];
items[b] = t;
}
}
void main()
{
int iarray[7] = {7, 5, 4, 3, 9, 8, 6};
double darray[5] = {4.3, 2.5, -0.9, 10.2, 3.0};
cout << "Here is unsorted integer array: ";
for(int i=0;  i<7; i++)
cout << iarray[i] << ' ';
cout << endl;
bubble(iarray, 7);
cout << "Here is sorted integer array: ";
for(int j=0;  j<7; j++)
cout << iarray[j] << ' ';
cout << endl;
cout << "Here is unsorted double array: ";
for(int k=0;  k<5; k++)
cout << darray[k] << ' ';
cout << endl;
bubble(darray, 5);
cout << "Here is sorted double array: ";
for(int l=0;  l<5; l++)
cout << darray[i] << ' ';
cout << endl;
getch();
}
```

**<u>OUTPUT</u>:**

Here is unsorted integer array: 7 5 4 3 9 8 6
Here is sorted integer array: 3 4 5 6 7 8 9
Here is unsorted double array: 4.3 2.5 -0.9 10.2 3
Here is sorted double array: -0.9 2.5 3 4.3 10.2

**Problem 45. Write a C++ program for generic quick sort.**

***Program:***

```
#include<conio.h>
#include<iostream.h>
#include<iomanip.h>
#include<stdlib.h>
template<class T>
inline void swap(T& v1,T& v2)
{
T temp=v2;
v2=v1;
v1=temp;
}
template<class T>
void quicksort(T *array,int hi,int lo=0)
{
while(hi>lo)
{
int i=lo;
int j=hi;
do
{
while(array[i]<array[lo]&&i<j)
i++;
while(array[--j]>array[lo]) ;
if(i<j)
swap(array[i],array[j]);
}while(i<j);
swap(array[lo],array[j]);
if(j-lo>hi-(j+1)) {
quicksort(array,j-1,lo);
lo=j+1;
}
else
{
quicksort(array,hi,j+1);
hi=j-1;
}
}
}
void main()
{
int dim = 100;
int *arrs=new int[dim+1];
for(int i=0;i < dim;i++)
arrs[i]=rand();
```

```
cout << endl<<"unsorted"<<endl;
for(int k=0;k<dim;k++)
cout<<setw(8)<<arrs[k];
quicksort(arrs,dim);
cout<<endl<<"sorted"<<endl;
for(int j=0;j<dim;j++)
cout<<setw(8)<<arrs[j];
delete arrs;
getch();
}
```

**OUTPUT:**

```
unsorted
    41  18467   6334  26500  19169  15724
 11478  29358  26962  24464
  5705  28145  23281  16827   9961    491
  2995  11942   4827   5436
 32391  14604   3902    153    292  12382
 17421  18716  19718  19895
  5447  21726  14771  11538   1869  19912
 25667  26299  17035   9894
 28703  23811  31322  30333  17673   4664
 15141   7711  28253   6868
 25547  27644  32662  32757  20037  12859
  8723   9741  27529    778
 12316   3035  22190   1842    288  30106
  9040   8942  19264  22648
 27446  23805  15890   6729  24370  15350
 15006  31101  24393   3548
 19629  12623  24084  19954  18756  11840
  4966   7376  13931  26308
 16944  32439  24626  11323   5537  21538
 16118   2082  22929  16541

sorted
    41    153    288    292    491    778   1842
  1869   2082   2995
  3035   3548   3902   4664   4827   4966   5436
  5447   5537   5705
  6334   6729   6868   7376   7711   8723   8942
  9040   9741   9894
  9961  11323  11478  11538  11840  11942
 12316  12382  12623  12859
 13931  14604  14771  15006  15141  15350
 15724  15890  16118  16541
 16827  16944  17035  17421  17673  18467
 18716  18756  19169  19264
 19629  19718  19895  19912  19954  20037
 21538  21726  22190  22648
 22929  23281  23805  23811  24084  24370
 24393  24464  24626  25547
 25667  26299  26308  26500  26962  27446
 27529  27644  28145  28253
 28703  29358  30106  30333  31101  31322
 32391
```

**Problem 46. Write a C++ program for a generic stack with size 10.**

***Program:***

```
#include <iostream.h>
#include<conio.h>
const int SIZE = 10;
template <class StackType> class stack
{
StackType stck[SIZE];
int tos;
public:
stack()
{
tos = 0;
}
void push(StackType ob)
{
if(tos==SIZE)
{
cout << "Stack is full.\n";
return;
}
stck[tos] = ob;
tos++;
}
StackType pop()
{
if(tos==0)
{
cout << "Stack is empty.\n";
return 0; // return null on empty stack
}
tos--;
return stck[tos];
}
};
void main()
{
stack<char> s1, s2;
s1.push('a');
s2.push('x');
s1.push('b');
s2.push('y');
s1.push('c');
s2.push('z');
for(int i=0; i<3; i++)
```

```
cout << "Pop s1: " << s1.pop() << "\n";
for(int j=0; j<3; j++)
cout << "Pop s2: " << s2.pop() << "\n";
stack<double> ds1, ds2;
ds1.push(1.1);
ds2.push(2.2);
ds1.push(3.3);
ds2.push(4.4);
ds1.push(5.5);
ds2.push(6.6);
for(int m=0; m<3; m++)
cout << "Pop ds1: " << ds1.pop() << "\n";
for(int k=0; k<3; k++)
cout << "Pop ds2: " << ds2.pop() << "\n";
getch();
}
```

**OUTPUT:**

```
Pop s1: c
Pop s1: b
Pop s1: a
Pop s2: z
Pop s2: y
Pop s2: x
Pop ds1: 5.5
Pop ds1: 3.3
Pop ds1: 1.1
Pop ds2: 6.6
Pop ds2: 4.4
Pop ds2: 2.2
```

**Problem 47. Write a C++ program to greater number between two numbers using Template Function.**

***Program:***

```
#include <iostream.h>
#include<conio.h>
//max returns the maximum of the two elements
template <class T>
T max(T a, T b)
{
return a > b ? a : b ;
}
void main()
{
cout << "max(10, 15) = " << max(10, 15) << endl ;
cout << "max('k', 's') = " << max('k', 's') << endl ;
cout << "max(10.1, 15.2) = " << max(10.1, 15.2) <<
endl ;
getch();
}
```

**OUTPUT:**

```
max(10, 15) = 15
max('k', 's') = s
max(10.1, 15.2) = 15.2
```

**Problem 48. Write a C++ program to illustrate the implicit instantiation of class Template.**

***Program:***

```
#include <iostream.h>
#include<conio.h>
template <class T>
class Z
{
public:
Z() {} ;
~Z() {} ;
void f(){} ;
void g(){} ;
} ;
void main()
{
Z<int> zi ;  //implicit instantiation generates class
Z<int>
Z<float> zf ; //implicit instantiation generates class
Z<float>
getch();
}
```

**Problem 49. Write a C++ program to sort the data by using Quick sort method with class Template.**

***Program:***

```
#include <iostream.h>
#include <stdlib.h>
#include<conio.h>
template<class T> void quicksort(T a[], const int&
leftarg, const int& rightarg)
{
if (leftarg < rightarg)
{
T pivotvalue = a[leftarg];
int left = leftarg - 1;
int right = rightarg + 1;
for(;;)
{
while (a[--right] > pivotvalue);
while (a[++left] < pivotvalue);
if (left >= right) break;
T temp = a[right];
a[right] = a[left];
a[left] = temp;
}
int pivot = right;
```

```
quicksort(a, leftarg, pivot);
quicksort(a, pivot + 1, rightarg);
}
}
void main(void)
{
int sortme[10];
for (int i = 0; i < 10; i++)
{
sortme[i] = rand();
cout << sortme[i] << " ";
};
cout << endl;
quicksort<int>(sortme, 0, 10 - 1);
for (int i = 0; i < 10; i++) cout << sortme[i] << " ";
cout << endl;
getch();
}
```

**OUTPUT:**

The above example will have OUTPUT similar to the following:

16838 5758 10113 17515 31051 5627 23010 7419 16212 4086

4086 5627 5758 7419 10113 16212 16838 17515 23010 31051

**Problem 50. Write a C++ program to find the greatest number having data in a and b variables by using the concept of class Template.**

***Program:***

```
#include <iostream.h>
#include<conio.h>
template <class T>
T max(T a, T b)
{
return a > b ? a : b ;
}
void main()
{
cout << "max(10, 15) = " << max(10, 15) << endl ;
cout << "max('k', 's') = " << max('k', 's') << endl ;
cout << "max(10.1, 15.2) = " << max(10.1, 15.2) <<
endl ;
cout << "max(\"Aladdin\", \"Jasmine\") = " <<
max("Aladdin", "Jasmine") << endl ;
getch();
}
```

**OUTPUT:**

max(10, 15) = 15

max('k', 's') = s

max(10.1, 15.2) = 15.2

max("Aladdin", "Jasmine") = Aladdin

**Problem 51. Write a C++ program to return maximum value of the two elements with Template.**

***Program:***

```
#include <iostream.h>
#include <string.h>
#include<conio.h>
template <class T>
T max(T a, T b)
{
return a > b ? a : b ;
}
// Specialization of max for char*
template <>
char* max(char* a, char* b)
{
return strcmp(a, b) > 0 ? a : b ;
}
void main()
{
cout << "max(10, 15) = " << max(10, 15) << endl ;
cout << "max('k', 's') = " << max('k', 's') << endl ;
cout << "max(10.1, 15.2) = " << max(10.1, 15.2)
<< endl ;
cout << "max(\"Aladdin\", \"Jasmine\") = " <<
max("Aladdin", "Jasmine") << endl ;
getch();
}
```

**OUTPUT:**

max(10, 15) = 15

max('k', 's') = s

max(10.1, 15.2) = 15.2

max("Aladdin", "Jasmine") = Jasmine

**Problem 52. Write a C++ program to return the biggest among two elements with class Template.**

***Program:***

```
#include <iostream.h>
#include<conio.h>
template <class T>
class mypair
{
T a, b;
public:
mypair (T first, T second)
{a=first; b=second;}
T getmax ();
};
```

```
template <class T>
T mypair<T>::getmax ()
{
T retval;
retval = a>b? a : b;
return retval;
}
void main ()
{
mypair <int> myobject (100, 75);
cout << myobject.getmax();
getch();
}
```

**Problem 53. Write a C++ program to push and pop elements in and from the stack by using the class Template.**

***Program:***

```
#pragma once
#include <iostream.h>
#include<conio.h>
template <class T>
class Stack
{
public:
Stack(int = 10) ;
~Stack() { delete [] stackPtr ; }
int push(const T&);
int pop(T&) ; // pop an element off the stack
int isEmpty()const { return top == -1 ; }
int isFull() const { return top == size - 1 ; }
private:
int size ; // Number of elements on Stack
int top ;
T* stackPtr ;
} ;
//constructor with the default size 10
template <class T>
Stack<T>::Stack(int s)
{
size = s > 0 && s < 1000 ? s : 10 ;
top = -1 ; // initialize stack
stackPtr = new T[size] ;
}
// push an element onto the Stack
template <class T>
int Stack<T>::push(const T& item)
{
if (!isFull())
{
stackPtr[++top] = item ;
return 1 ; // push successful
}
return 0 ; // push unsuccessful
}
// pop an element off the Stack
template <class T>
int Stack<T>::pop(T& popValue)
{
if (!isEmpty())
{
popValue = stackPtr[top--] ;
return 1 ; // pop successful
}
getch() ; // pop unsuccessful
}
```

**Problem 54. Write a C++ program to demonstrate the concept of template or Program to swap the two given number using template.**

***Program:***

```
#include<iostream.h>
#include<conio.h>
template <class T> T swap (T &a, T &b)
{
T temp;
temp=a;
a=b;
b=temp;
return(0);
}
int swap (int &a, int &b);
float sum(float &a,float &b);
void main()
{
int x,y;
cout<<"enter x and y";
cin>>x>>y;
swap(x,y);
cout<<"\n after swaping x is"<<x;
cout<<"\n after swaping y is"<<y;
getch();
}
```

**Problem 55. Write a C++ program to add two numbers using the class Template.**

***Program:***

```
#include<iostream.h>
#include<conio.h>
template <class T>
class sample
```

```
{
private:
T s,a,b;
public:
void getdata();
void disp();
};
template <class T>
void sample <T>::getdata()
{
cin>>a;
cin>>b;
}
template <class T>
void sample <T>::disp()
{
T res;
res=a+b;
cout<<"sum is"<<res<<endl;
}
void main()
{
sample <int> s1;
clrscr();
cout<<"enter two integer values"<<endl;
s1.getdata();
s1.disp();
}
```

**Problem 56. Write a C++ program to find the Sum and Product of elements of a Class using Class Template.**

***Program:***

```
#include<iostream.h>
#include<conio.h>
template <class T>
class sample
{
private:
T s,a,b;
public:
void getdata();
void calc();
};
template <class T>
void sample <T>::getdata()
{
cin>>a;
cin>>b;
}
template <class T>
void sample <T>::calc()
{
T res1,res2;
res1=a+b;
res2=a*b;
cout<<"sum is"<<res1;
cout<<endl;
cout<<"product is"<<res2;
}
void main()
{
sample <int> s1;
clrscr();
cout<<"enter two integer values"<<endl;
s1.getdata();
s1.calc();
}
```

**Problem 57. Write a C++ program to find greater number out of two given number using class template.**

***Program:***

```
#include<iostream.h>
#include<conio.h>
template <class T>
class sample
{
private:
T s,a,b;
public:
void getdata();
void calc();
};
template <class T>
void sample <T>::getdata()
{
cin>>a;
cin>>b;
}
template <class T>
void sample <T>::calc()
{
if(a>b)
cout<<"a is greater";
else
cout<<"b is greater";
}
void main()
{
sample <int> s1;
clrscr();
```

```
cout<<"enter two integer values"<<endl;
s1.getdata();
s1.calc();
getch();
}
```

**Problem 58. Write a C++ program to find factorial of a given number using template.,**

***Program:***

```
#include<iostream.h>
#include<conio.h>
template <class T>
class sample
{
private:
T num,fact;
public:
void getdata();
void calc();
};
template <class T>
void sample <T>::getdata()
{
cin>>num;
}
template <class T>
void sample <T>::calc()
{
int i;
fact=1;
for(i=1;i<=num;i++)
{
fact=fact*i;
}
cout<<"factorial of a number is"<<fact;
}
void main()
{
sample <int> s1;
clrscr();
cout<<"enter number"<<endl;
s1.getdata();
s1.calc();
getch();
}
```

**Problem 59. Write a C++ program to generate fibbonaci series using class template.**

***Program:***

```
#include<iostream.h>
#include<conio.h>
template <class T>
class sample
{
private:
T num;
public:
void getdata();
void calc();
};
template <class T>
void sample <T>::getdata()
{
cin>>num;
}
template <class T>
void sample <T>::calc()
{
int a=0;
int b=1;
int i,s=0;
cout<<a<<endl;
cout<<b<<endl;
for(i=1;i<=num-2;i++)
{
s=a+b;
cout<<s<<endl;
a=b;
b=s;
}
}
void main()
{
sample <int> s1;
clrscr();
cout<<"enter number"<<endl;
s1.getdata();
s1.calc();
getch();
}
```

# CHAPTER 18

# EXCEPTION HANDLING

## TRY CATCH:

**Problem 1. Write a C++ program for a simple exception handling example.**

***Program:***

```
#include <iostream.h>
#include<conio.h>
void main()
{
cout << "Start\n";
try
{
cout << "Inside try block\n";
throw 1;                    // throw an error
cout << "This will not execute";
}
catch (int i)
{                   // catch an error
cout << "Caught an exception -- value is: ";
cout << i << "\n";
}
cout << "End";
getch();
}
```

**OUTPUT:**

```
Start
Inside try block
Caught an exception -- value is: 1
End
```

**Problem 2. Write a C++ program for throwing an exception from a function called from within a try block.**

***Program:***

```
#include <iostream.h>
#include<conio.h>
void f(int test)
{
cout << "Inside f, test is: " << test << "\n";
if(test)
throw test;
}
void main()
{
cout << "start\n";
try
{ // start a try block
cout << "Inside try block\n";
f(0);
f(1);
f(2);
}
catch (int i)
{ // catch an error
cout << "Caught an exception -- value is: ";
cout << i << "\n";
}
cout << "end";
getch();
}
```

**OUTPUT:**

```
start
Inside try block
Inside f, test is: 0
Inside f, test is: 1
Caught an exception -- value is: 1
end
```

**Problem 3. Write a C++ program for a try block can be localized to a function.**

***Program:***

```
#include <iostream.h>
#include<conio.h>
void f(int test)
{
try
{
 if(test) throw test;
 }
 catch(int i)
{
cout << "Caught One!  Ex. #: " << i << '\n';
}
}
void main()
{
```

```
cout << "start\n";
f(1);
f(2);
f(0);
f(3);
cout << "end";
getch();
}
```

**OUTPUT:**

```
start
Caught One!  Ex. #: 1
Caught One!  Ex. #: 2
Caught One!  Ex. #: 3
end
```

**Problem 4. Write a C++ program using multiple catch statements.**

***Program:***

```
#include <iostream.h>
#include<conio.h>
void f(int test)
{
try
{
 if(test)
 throw test;          // throw int
 else
 throw "Value is zero"; // throw char *
 }
 catch(int i)
{
cout << "Caught One!  Ex. #: " << i << '\n';
}
catch(char *str)
{
cout << "Caught a string: ";
cout << str << '\n';
}
}
void main()
{
cout << "start\n";
f(1);
f(2);
f(0);
f(3);
cout << "end";
getch();
}
```

**OUTPUT:**

```
start
Caught One!  Ex. #: 1
Caught One!  Ex. #: 2
```

**Problem 5. Write a C++ program for catch all exceptions.**

***Program:***

```
#include <iostream.h>
#include<conio.h>
void f(int test)
{
try
{
 if(test==0) throw test; // throw int
 if(test==1) throw 'a'; // throw char
 if(test==2) throw 123.23; // throw double
 }
 catch(...)
{ // catch all exceptions
cout << "Caught One!\n";
}
}
void main()
{
f(0);
f(1);
f(2);
getch();
}
```

**OUTPUT:**

```
Caught One!
Caught One!
Caught One!
```

**Problem 6. Write a C++ program for multiple catch blocks.**

***Program:***

```
#include <iostream.h>
#include<conio.h>

void main ()
{
 try
 {
 char * mystring;
 mystring = new char [10];
 if (mystring == NULL)
 throw "Allocation failure";
 for (int n=0; n<=100; n++)
 {
 if (n>9)
 throw n;
```

```
mystring[n]='a';
}
}
catch (int i)
{
cout << "index " << i << " is out of range" << endl;
}
catch (char * str)
{
cout << "Exception: " << str << endl;
}
getch();
}
```

**OUTPUT:**
index 10 is out of range

**Problem 7. Write a C++ program for catch 'char *' exception.**

***Program:***

```
#include <iostream.h>
#include<conio.h>
void main ()
{
try
{
throw "Out of range";
}
catch (char * str)
{
cout << "Exception: " << str << endl;
}
getch();
}
```

**OUTPUT:**
This application has requested the Runtime to terminate it in an unusual way.
Please contact the application's support team for more information.

**Problem 8. Write a C++ program using catch(...) as a default.**

***Program:***

```
#include <iostream.h>
#include<conio.h>
void f(int val)
{
Try
{
if(val==0)
throw val;
if(val==1)
throw 'a';
if(val==2)
throw 123.23;
}
catch(int i)
{                 // catch an int exception
cout << "Caught an integer\n";
}
catch(...)
{                 // catch all other exceptions
cout << "Caught One!\n";
}
}
void main()
{
f(0);
f(1);
f(2);
getch();
}
```

**OUTPUT:**
Caught an integer
Caught One!
Caught One!

**Problem 9. Write a C++ program for catching derived classes.**

***Program:***

```
#include <iostream.h>
#include<conio.h>
class B
{ };
class D: public B
{ };
void main()
{
D derived;
try
{
throw derived;
}
catch(B b)
{
cout << "Caught a base class.\n";
}
catch(D d)
{
cout << "This won't execute.\n";
}
getch();
```

```
}
```

**Problem 10. Write a C++ program for a try catch block without exception being thrown.**

***Program:***

```
#include <iostream.h>
#include<conio.h>
void main()
{
cout << "Start\n";
try
{
cout << "Inside try block\n";
cout << "Still inside try block\n";
}
catch (int i)
{
cout << "Caught an exception -- value is: ";
cout << i << "\n";
}
cout << "End";
getch();
}
```

**OUTPUT:**

```
Start
Inside try block
Still inside try block
End
```

## THROW:

**Problem 11. Write a C++ program for throw an exception.**

***Program:***

```
#include <iostream.h>
#include<conio.h>
void main()
{
int answer, divisor, dividend;
try
{
divisor = 1;
dividend = 0;
if(dividend ==0)
throw 0;
answer = divisor/dividend;
cout << answer;
getch;
}
catch (int i)
{
cout << "You cannot divide by zero";
}
}
```

**OUTPUT:**

```
You cannot divide by zero"
```

**Problem 12. Write a C++ program for rethrowing an exception.**

***Program:***

```
#include <iostream.h>
#include<conio.h>
void f()
{
try
{
throw "hello"; // throw a char *
}
catch(char *) { // catch a char *
cout << "Caught char * inside f\n";
throw ; // rethrow char * out of function
}
}
void main()
{
cout << "start\n";
try
{
f();
}
catch(char *)
{
cout << "Caught char * inside main\n";
}
cout << "end";
getch();
}
```

**OUTPUT:**

```
start

This application has requested the Runtime to
terminate it in an unusual way.
Please contact the application's support team for
more information.
```

**Problem 13. Write a C++ program for throw an exception from a function and catch it.**

***Program:***

```
#include <iostream.h>
#include<conio.h>
// function prototypes.
```

```
float divide_number(float , float);
void main()
{
float dividend,divisor,answer;
try
{
dividend = 0;
divisor = 0;
answer = divide_number(dividend,divisor);
}
catch(...)
{
cout << "oops, there is an error!";
}
getch();
}
float divide_number(float num1, float num2)
{
try
{
float answer;
answer = num1/num2;
return answer;
}
catch(...)
{
throw;
}
}
```

## EXCEPTION:

**Problem 14. Write a C++ program to declaring exception specifications in class hierarchy.**

***Program:***

```
#include <string>
#include <iostream.h>
#include<conio.h>
class base
{
public:
virtual void f() throw();
virtual void g(); // can throw anything
virtual void h() throw(std::string);
};
class derived : public base
{
public:
virtual void f() throw();    // OK: same as base
virtual void g() throw(int); // OK: subset of base
//virtual void h() throw(int); // Error: int not in base
};
class more : public derived
{
public:
//virtual void f();          // Error: can throw
anything
virtual void g() throw();    // OK
};
```

**Problem 15. Write a C++ program to demonstrating stack unwinding.**

***Program:***

```
#include <iostream.h>
#include<conio.h>
void f3() throw ( runtime_error )
{
cout << "In f 3" << endl;
throw runtime_error( "runtime_error in f3" );
}
void f2() throw ( runtime_error )
{
cout << "f3 is called inside f2" << endl;
f3();
}
void f1() throw ( runtime_error )
{
cout << "f2 is called inside f1" << endl;
f2();
}
void main()
{
try
{
cout << "f1 is called inside main" << endl;
f1();
}
catch ( runtime_error &error )
{
cout << "Exception occurred: " << error.what() <<
endl;
cout << "Exception handled in main" << endl;
}
getch();
}
```

**OUTPUT:**

```
f1 is called inside main
f2 is called inside f1
f3 is called inside f2
In f 3
Exception occurred: runtime_error in f3
```

Exception handled in main

## EXCEPTION TYPE:

**Problem 16. Write a C++ program for different types of exceptions can be caught.**

***Program:***

```
#include <iostream.h>
#include<conio.h>
void f(int test)
{
try
{
 if(test)
 throw test;
 else
 throw "Value is zero";
 }
 catch(int i)
{
cout << "Caught Exception #: " << i << '\n';
}
catch(const char *str)
{
cout << "Caught a string: ";
cout << str << '\n';
}
}
void main()
{
cout << "Start\n";
f(1);
f(2);
f(0);
f(3);
cout << "End";
getch();
}
```

**<u>OUTPUT</u>:**

Start
Caught Exception #: 1
Caught Exception #: 2
Caught a string: Value is zero
Caught Exception #: 3
End

**Problem 17. Write a C++ program for catching class type exceptions.**

***Program:***

```
#include <iostream.h>
#include<conio.h>
#include <string.h>
class MyException
{
public:
char message[80];
int what;
MyException() { *message = 0; what = 0; }
MyException(char *s, int e)
{
strcpy(message, s);
what = e;
}
};
void main()
{
int i;
try
{
cout << "Enter a positive number: ";
throw MyException("Not Positive", -1);
}
catch (MyException e)
{ // catch an error
cout << e.message << ": ";
cout << e.what << "\n";
}
getch();
}
```

**<u>OUTPUT</u>:**

Enter a positive number: Not Positive: -1

## CUSTOM EXCEPTION:

**Problem 18. Write a C++ program for throw your own exception class based on runtime_error.**

***Program:***

```
#include <iostream.h>
#include<conio.h>
class DivideByZeroException : public
runtime_error
{
public:
DivideByZeroException::DivideByZeroException(
): runtime_error( "attempted todivide by zero" ) { }
};
double quotient( int numerator, int denominator )
{
```

```
throw DivideByZeroException(); // terminate
function
}
void main()
{
try
{
double result = quotient( 1, 1 );
cout << "The quotient is: " << result << endl;
}
catch ( DivideByZeroException
&divideByZeroException )
{
cout << "Exception occurred: " <<
divideByZeroException.what() << endl;
}
getch();
}
```

**OUTPUT:**

Exception occurred: attempted to divide by zero

**Problem 19. Write a C++ program for custom exception class.**

***Program:***

```
#include <iostream.h>
#include<conio.h>
#include <string.h>
class Exception
{
public:
Exception(const string& msg) : msg_(msg) {}
~Exception( ) {}
string getMessage( ) const {return(msg_);}
private:
string msg_;
};
void f( )
{
throw(Exception("Mr.Sharma"));
}
void main( )
{
try
{
f( );
}
catch(Exception& e)
{
cout << "You threw an exception: " <<
e.getMessage( ) << endl;
}
}
```

**OUPUT:**

You threw an exception: Mr.Sharma

**Problem 20. Write a C++ program for throw a custom exception object.**

***Program:***

```
#include <iostream.h>
#include<conio.h>
class Trouble
{
public:
Trouble(const char* pStr = "There's a problem") :
pMessage(pStr) {}
const char* what() const {return pMessage;}
private:
const char* pMessage;
};
void main()
{
for(int i = 0 ; i < 2 ; i++)
{
try
{
if(i == 0)
throw Trouble();
else
throw Trouble("Nobody knows the trouble I've
seen...");
}
catch(const Trouble& t)
{
cout << endl << "Exception: " << t.what();
}
}
getch();
}
```

**OUTPUT:**

Exception: There's a problem
Exception: Nobody knows the trouble I've seen..."

**Problem 21. Write a C++ program using custom exception in your own Array class.**

***Program:***

```
#include <iostream.h>
#include<conio.h>
const int DefaultSize = 10;
// define the exception classes
class ArrayIndexOutofBoundException {};
class BaseArraySizeException
{
```

```
public:
BaseArraySizeException(int size):itsSize(size) {}
~BaseArraySizeException(){}
virtual int GetSize() { return itsSize; }
virtual void PrintError()
{
cout << "Size error. Received: "
<< itsSize << endl;
}
protected:
int itsSize;
};
class ArraySizeTooBigException : public
BaseArraySizeException
{
public:
ArraySizeTooBigException(int
size):BaseArraySizeException(size){}
virtual void PrintError()
{
cout << "Too big! Received: ";
cout << BaseArraySizeException::itsSize << endl;
} };
class ArraySizeTooSmallException : public
BaseArraySizeException
{
public:
ArraySizeTooSmallException(int
size):BaseArraySizeException(size){}
virtual void PrintError()
{
cout << "Too small! Received: ";
cout << BaseArraySizeException::itsSize <<
std::endl;
}
};
class ArraySizeZeroException  : public
ArraySizeTooSmallException
{
public:
ArraySizeZeroException(int
size):ArraySizeTooSmallException(size){}
virtual void PrintError()
{
cout << "Zero!!. Received: ";
cout << BaseArraySizeException::itsSize << endl;
} };
class ArraySizeNegativeException : public
BaseArraySizeException
{
public:
ArraySizeNegativeException(int
size):BaseArraySizeException(size){}
virtual void PrintError()
{
cout << "Negative! Received: ";
cout << BaseArraySizeException::itsSize << endl;
} };
class Array
{
public:
// constructors
Array(int itsSize = DefaultSize);
Array(const Array &rhs);
~Array() { delete [] pType;}
// operators
Array& operator=(const Array&);
int& operator[](int offSet);
const int& operator[](int offSet) const;
// accessors
int GetitsSize() const { return itsSize; }
// friend function
friend ostream& operator<< (ostream&, const
Array&);
private:
int *pType;
int  itsSize;
};
Array::Array(int size):
itsSize(size)
{
if (size == 0)
throw ArraySizeZeroException(size);
if (size < 0)
throw ArraySizeNegativeException(size);
if (size < 10)
throw ArraySizeTooSmallException(size);
if (size > 30000)
throw ArraySizeTooBigException(size);
pType = new int[size];
for (int i = 0; i<size; i++)
pType[i] = 0;
}
int& Array::operator[] (int offset)
{
int size = GetitsSize();
if (offset >= 0 && offset < GetitsSize())
return pType[offset];
throw ArrayIndexOutofBoundException();
return pType[offset];
}
const int& Array::operator[] (int offset) const
```

```
{
int size = GetitsSize();
if (offset >= 0 && offset < GetitsSize())
return pType[offset];
throw ArrayIndexOutofBoundException();
return pType[offset];
}
void main()
{
try
{
int choice;
cout << "Enter the array size: ";
cin >> choice;
Array intArray(choice);
for (int j = 0; j< 100; j++)
{
intArray[j] = j;
cout << "intArray[" << j << "] okay..."
     << endl;
}
}
catch (ArrayIndexOutofBoundException)
{
cout << "Unable to process your input!\n";
}
catch (BaseArraySizeException& theException)
{
theException.PrintError();
}
catch (...)
{
cout << "Something went wrong,"
     << "but I've no idea what!" << endl;
}
cout << "Done.\n";
getch();
}
```

**OUTPUT**:

```
Enter the array size: 12
intArray[0] okay...
intArray[1] okay...
intArray[2] okay...
intArray[3] okay...
intArray[4] okay...
intArray[5] okay...
intArray[6] okay...
intArray[7] okay...
intArray[8] okay...
intArray[9] okay...
intArray[10] okay...
intArray[11] okay...
Unable to process your input!
Done.
```

## FUNCTION AND EXCEPTION:

**Problem 22. Write a C++ program to localize a try/catch to a function.**

***Program:***

```
#include <iostream.h>
#include<conio.h>
void f(int test)
{
try
{
 if(test) throw test;
 }
 catch(int i)
{
cout << "Caught Exception #: " << i << '\n';
}
}
void main()
{
cout << "Start\n";
f(1);
f(2);
f(0);
f(3);
cout << "End";
getch();
}
```

**OUTPUT**:

```
Start
Caught Exception #: 1
Caught Exception #: 2
Caught Exception #: 3
End
```

**Problem 23. Write a C++ program for throwing an exception from a function outside the try block.**

***Program:***

```
#include <iostream.h>
#include<conio.h>
void f(int test)
{
cout << "Inside f, test is: " << test << "\n";
if(test) throw test;
}
```

```
void main()
{
cout << "Start\n";
try
{ // start a try block
cout << "Inside try block\n";
f(0);
f(1);
f(2);
}
catch (int i)
{ // catch an error
cout << "Caught an exception -- value is: ";
cout << i << "\n";
}
cout << "End";
getch();
}
```

**OUTPUT:**

```
Start
Inside try block
Inside f, test is: 0
Inside f, test is: 1
Caught an exception -- value is: 1
End
```

**Problem 24. Write a C++ program that This function can throw NO exceptions!.**

***Program:***

```
#include <iostream.h>
#include<conio.h>
void f(int val) throw();
void main()
{
try
{
f(0); // also, try passing 1 and 2 to f()
}
catch(int i)
{
cout << "Caught an integer\n";
}
catch(char c)
{
cout << "Caught char\n";
}
catch(double d)
{
cout << "Caught double\n";
}
getch();
}
// This function can throw NO exceptions!
void f(int val) throw()
{
cout << "f";
}
```

**OUTPUT:**

```
f
```

**Problem 25. Write a C++ program for restricting function throw types.**

```
// only throw ints, chars, and doubles
void f(int val) throw(int, char, double)
{
if(val==0)
throw val;
if(val==1)
throw 'a';
if(val==2)
throw 123.23;
}
void main()
{
try
{
f(0); // also, try passing 1 and 2 to f()
}
catch(int i)
{
cout << "Caught an integer\n";
}
catch(char c)
{
cout << "Caught char\n";
}
catch(double d)
{
cout << "Caught double\n";
}
getch();
}
```

**OUTPUT:**

```
Caught an integer
```

## BAD_ALLOC EXCEPTION:

**Problem 26. Write a C++ program to demonstrating standard new throwing bad_alloc when memory cannot be allocated.**

```
#include <iostream.h>
```

```
#include<conio.h>
void main()
{
double *ptr[ 50 ];
try
{
for ( int i = 0; i < 50; i++ )
{
ptr[ i ] = new double[ 50000000 ];
cout << "Allocated 50000000 doubles in ptr[ " << i
<< " ]\n";
}
}
catch ( bad_alloc &memoryAllocationException )
{
cerr << "Exception occurred: " <<
memoryAllocationException.what() << endl;
}
getch();
}
```

**OUTPUT:**

```
Allocated 50000000 doubles in ptr[ 0 ]
Allocated 50000000 doubles in ptr[ 1 ]
Allocated 50000000 doubles in ptr[ 2 ]
Allocated 50000000 doubles in ptr[ 3 ]
Allocated 50000000 doubles in ptr[ 4 ]
Exception occurred: St9bad_alloc
```

## STANDARD EXCEPTIONS:

**Problem 27. Write a C++ program for standard exceptions.**

***Program:***

```
#include <iostream.h>
#include<conio.h>
class A {};
void main ()
{
try
{
A * a = NULL;
typeid (*a);
}
catch (exception& e)
{
cout << "Exception: " << e.what();
}
getch();
}
```

## EXCEPTIONS:

**Problem 28. Write a C++ program for exceptions.**

***Program:***

```
#include <iostream.h>
#include<conio.h>
void main ()
{
try
{
throw 20;
}
catch (int e)
{
cout << "An exception occurred. Exception Nr. "
<< e << endl;
}
getch();
}
```

**OUTPUT:**

```
An exception occurred. Exception Nr. 20
```

**Problem 29. Write a C++ program for standard exceptions.**

***Program:***

```
#include <iostream.h>
#include <exception.h>
#include<conio.h>
class myexception: public exception
{
virtual const char* what() const throw()
{
return "My exception happened";
}
} myex;
void main ()
{
try
{
throw myex;
}
catch (exception& e)
{
cout << e.what() << endl;
}
getch();
}
```

**OUTPUT:**

```
My exception happened.
```

**Problem 30. Write a C++ program for a simple exception handling example.**

***Program:***

```
#include <iostream.h>
#include<conio.h>
void main()
{
cout <<"Starting \n";
try
{
cout <<"In try block \n";
throw 10;//throw an error
cout <<"This will not execute";
}
catch (int i)
{
cout <<"Caught an exception --value is:";
cout <<i <<"\n";
}
cout <<"End";
getch();
}
```

**OUTPUT:**

```
Starting
In try block
Caught an exception --value is:10
End
```

**Problem 31. Write a C++ program for abnormal termination .**

***Program:***

```
#include <iostream.h>
#include<conio.h.
void main()
{
cout <<"Starting \n";
try
{
cout <<"In try block \n";
throw 10;
cout <<"This will not execute";
}
catch (double i)
{
cout <<"Caught an exception --value is:";
cout <<i <<"\n";
}
cout <<"End";
return 0;
}
```

**OUTPUT:**

```
Starting
In try block
Abnormal program termination
```

**Problem 32. Write a C++ program for throwing an exception from a function outside the try block.**

***Program:***

```
#include <iostream.h>
#include<conio.h>
void Values(int val)
{
cout <<"In Values,val is:"<<val <<"\n";
if(val)throw val;
}
void main()
{
cout <<"Starting \n";
try {
cout <<"In try block \n";
Values(0);
Values(1);
Values(2);
}
catch (int i)
{
cout <<"Caught an exception --value is:";
cout <<i <<"\n";
}
cout <<"End";
getch();
}
```

**OUTPUT:**

```
Starting
In try block
In Values,val is:0
In Values,val is:1
Caught an exception --value is:1
End
```

**Problem 33. Write a C++ program for catching Class Types.**

***Program:***

```
#include <iostream.h>
#include <string.h>
#include<conio.h>
class MyException
{
public:
char str_what [80];
```

```
int what;
MyException()
{
*str_what =0;what =0;
}
MyException(char *s,int e)
{
strcpy(str_what,s);
what =e;
}
};
void main()
{
int i;
try
{
cout <<"Enter a positive number:";
cin >>i;
if(i<0)
throw MyException("Not Positive",i);
}
catch (MyException e)
{
cout <<e.str_what <<":";
cout <<e.what <<"\n";
}
getch();
}
```

**OUTPUT:**

Enter a positive number:-4
Not Positive:-4

**Problem 34. Write a C++ program using Multiple catch Statements.**

***Program:***

```
#include <iostream.h>
#include<conio.h>
void Values(int val)
{
try
{
if(val)throw val;
else throw "Value is zero";
}
catch(int i)
{
cout <<"Caught Exception :"<<i <<'\n';
}
catch(const char *str)
{
cout <<"Caught a string:";
cout <<str <<'\n';
}
}
void main()
{
cout <<"Starting \n";
Values(1);
Values(2);
Values(0);
Values(3);
cout <<"End";
getch();
}
```

**OUTPUT:**

Starting
Caught Exception :1
Caught Exception :2
Caught a string:Value is zero
Caught Exception :3
End

**Problem 35. Write a C++ program for handling Derived-Class Exceptions.**

***Program:***

```
#include <iostream.h>
#include<conio.h>
class A
{
};
class B:public A
{
};
void main()
{
B b;
try
{
throw b;
}
catch(A a)
{
cout <<"Caught a base class(A).\n";
}
catch(B b)
{
cout <<"This won't execute.\n";
}
getch();
}
```

**Problem 36. Write a C++ program for catching All Exceptions.**

***Program:***

```
#include <iostream.h>
#include<conio.h>
void Values(int val)
{
try
{
if(val==0)throw val;//throw int
if(val==1)throw 'v';//throw char
if(val==2)throw 103.06;//throw double
}
catch(...)
{
cout <<"Caught One!\n";
}
}
void main()
{
cout <<"Starting \n";
Values(0);
Values(1);
Values(2);
cout <<"End";
getch();
}
```

**OUTPUT:**

```
Starting
Caught One!
Caught One!
Caught One!
End
```

**Problem 37. Write a C++ program for rethrowing an Exception.**

***Program:***

```
#include <iostream.h>
#include<conio.h>
void Values()
{
try
{
throw "hi";
}
catch(const char *)
{
cout <<"Caught char *in Values \n";
throw ;
}
}
void main()
{
cout <<"Starting \n";
try
{
Values();
}
catch(const char *)
{
cout <<"Caught char *in main \n";
}
cout <<"End";
getch();
}
```

**OUTPUT:**

```
Starting
Caught char *inside Values
Caught char *inside main
End
```

**Problem 38. Write a C++ program for applying Exception Handling.**

***Program:***

```
#include <iostream.h>
#include<conio.h>
void divide(double a,double b);
void main()
{
double i,j;
do
{
cout <<"Enter numerator (0 to stop):";
cin >>i;
cout <<"Enter denominator:";
cin >>j;
divide(i,j);
}while(i !=0);
getch();
}
void divide(double a,double b)
{
try
{
if(!b)throw b;
cout <<"Result:"<<a/b <<endl;
}
catch (double b)
{
cout <<"Can't divide by zero.\n";
}
}
```

**Problem 39. Write a C++ program to use try, throw and catch function.**

***Program:***

```
#include <iostream.h>
void fx ()
{
// details omited
throw range_error(string("some info"));
}
void main ( )
{
try
{
fx ();
}
catch (runtime_error& r)
{
// handle any kind of error, including range_error
cout <<< '\n';
}
}
```

**Problem 40. Write a C++ program to implement of exception thrown in different blocks.**

```
#include <iostream>
#include<conio.h>
class E
{
public:
const char* error;
E(const char* arg) : error(arg) { }
};
class A
{
public:
int i;
// A function try block with a member
// initializer
A() try : i(0)
{
throw E("Exception thrown in A()");
}
catch (E& e)
{
cout << e.error << endl;
}
};
// A function try block
void f() try
{
throw E("Exception thrown in f()");
}
catch (E& e)
{
cout << e.error << endl;
}
void g()
{
throw E("Exception thrown in g()");
}
void main()
{
f();
// A try block
try
{
g();
}
catch (E& e)
{
cout << e.error << endl;
}
try
{
A x;
}
catch(...) { }
}
```

**OUTPUT:**

Exception thrown in f()
Exception thrown in g()
Exception thrown in A()

**Problem 41. Write a C++ program to implement strings in the exception handling.**

```
#include <iostream>
#include<conio.h>
struct E
{
const char* message;
E(const char* arg) : message(arg) { }
};
void my_unexpected()
{
cout << "Call to my_unexpected" << endl;
throw E("Exception thrown from
my_unexpected");
}
void f() throw(E)
{
```

```
cout << "In function f(), throw const char* object"
<< endl;
throw("Exception, type const char*, thrown from
f()");
}
void main()
{
set_unexpected(my_unexpected);
try
{
f();
}
catch (E& e)
{
cout << "Exception in main(): " << e.message <<
endl;
}
}
```

**OUTPUT:**

```
In function f(), throw const char* object
Call to my_unexpected
Exception in main(): Exception thrown from
my_unexpected
```

**Problem 42. Write a C++ program to terminate the functions in exception handling.**

***Program:***

```
#include <iostream.h>
#include<conio.h>
#include <stdlib.h>
void f()
{
printf("Function f()\n");
throw "Exception thrown from f()";
}
void g() { printf("Function g()\n"); }
void h() { printf("Function h()\n"); }
void my_terminate()
{
printf("Call to my_terminate\n");
abort();
}
void main()
{
set_terminate(my_terminate);
atexit(f);
atexit(g);
atexit(h);
printf("In main\n");
}
```

**OUTPUT:**

```
In main
Function h()
Function g()
Function f()
Call to my_terminate
```

**Problem 43. Write a C++ program to find the factorial of a number by demonstrating the concept of exception handling.**

***Program:***

```
#include<iostream.h>
#include<conio.h>
#include<math.h>
#include<process.h>
void main()
{
int n,fact=1;
int i;
clrscr();
cout<<"enter the value of n";
cin>>n;
try()
{
if(num==0)
throw 100;
if(num<0)
throw 'E';
for(i=1;i<=n;i++)
{
fact=fact*i;
}
cout<<"factorial of a given number is"<<fact;
}
catch(int)
{
cout<<"Exception:factorial value"<<endl;
}
catch(char)
{
cout<<"Exception:negative number in factorial";
}
getch();
}
```

**Problem 44. Write a C++ program to Catch an Exception in division of two numbers by zero.**

***Program:***

```
#include<iostream.h>
#include<conio.h>
void main()
{
```

```
int a,b;
clrscr();
cout<<"enter the value of a";
cin>>a;
cout<<"enter the value of b";
cin>>b;
try
{
if(b==0)
throw 10;
cout<<"divisions is"<<(a/b);
}
catch(int i)
{
cout<<"exception";
}
getch() ;
}
```

**Problem 45. Write a C++ program to check the age of female using try-catch-exception.**

***Program:***

```
#include<iostream.h>
#include<conio.h>
void main()
{
int femage;
clrscr();
cout<<"enter the age of female";
cin>>femage;
try
{
if(femage<18)
throw 100;
cout<<"Go for marriage"<<endl;
}
catch(int i)
{
cout<<"Exception":Not eligible for
marriage"<<endl;
cout<<"Age should be greater than 18"<<endl;
}
getch();
}
```

**Problem 46. Write a C++ program to find the square root of a give number with proper exception handling.**

***Program:***

```
#include <iostream.h>
#include<conio.h>
#include<math.h>
void main()
{
int num;
int res;
cout<<"enter number";
cin>>num;
try
{
if(num<0)
throw 100;
if (num>32767)
throw 'e';
cout<<"the square root of given number
is"<<sqrt(num)';
}
catch (int i)
{
cout<<"Exception: Number is negative";
}
catch (char)
{
cout<<"Exception: out of integer range value";
getch();
}
```

**Problem 47. Write a C++ program to demonstrate the concept of catch all exceptions.**

***Program:***

```
#include <iostream.h>
#include<conio.h>
#include<math.h>
void main()
{
int num;
int res;
cout<<"enter number";
cin>>num;
try
{
if(num<0)
throw 100;
if (num>32767)
throw 'e';
cout<<"the square root of given number
is"<<sqrt(num)';
}
catch(...)
{
cout<<"Exception: invalid data value";
}
```

```
getch();
}
```

**Problem 48. Write a C++ program to print a complete quadratic equation by using exception handling.**

***Program:***

```
#include<iostream.h>
#include<conio.h>
void main()
{
int a,b,c;
clrscr();
cout<<"enter the value of a";
cin>>a;
cout<<"enter the value of b";
cin>>b;
try
{
if (a==0)
throw 100;
if(b==0)
throw 2.0;
if (c==0)
throw 'e';
cout<<"EQUATIONS IS"<<endl;
cout<<a<<"X^2 +"<<b<<"X+ "<<c
}
catch(int i)
{
cout<<"exception: A cannot be zero in complete
eq.";
}
catch(float)
{
cout<<"Exception: B cannot be zero";
}
catch(char)
{
cout<<"Exception: C cannot be zero";
}
getch() ;
}
```

# CHAPTER 19

# GENERIC PROGRAMMING

## GENERIC SUM METHOD:

**Problem 1.Write a C++ program for generic sum method.**

***Program:***

```
#include<iostream.h>
#include<conio.h>
template <class X> X sum(X *data, int size)
{
int i;
X result = 0;
for(i = 0; i <size; i++) result += data[ i ];
return result;
}
void main()
{
int i[] = {1, 2, 3, 4};
double d[] = {1.1, 2.2, 3.3, 4.4};
cout << sum(i, 4) << endl;
cout << sum(d, 4) << endl;
getch();
}
```

**OUTPUT:**

10
11

**Problem 2. Write a C++ program for a generic bubble sort.**

***Program:***

```
#include<iostream.h>
#include<conio.h>
template <class X> void bubble(X *data, int size)
{
register int a, b;
X t;
for(a=1; a < size; a++)
for(b=size-1; b >= a; b--)
if(data[b-1] > data[b])
{ t = data[b-1];
data[b-1] = data[b];
data[b] = t;
} }
void main()
{
int i[] = {3, 2, 5, 6, 1, 8, 9, 3, 6, 9};
double d[] = {1.2, 5.5, 2.2, 3.3};
int j;
bubble(i, 10); // sort ints
bubble(d, 4);  // sort doubles
for(j=0; j<10; j++)
cout << i[j] << ' '; cout << endl;
for(j=0; j<4; j++)
cout << d[j] << ' ';
cout << endl;
getch();
}
```

**OUTPUT:**

1 2 3 3 5 6 6 8 9 9
1.2 2.2 3.3 5.5

## GENERIC CLASS:

**Problem 3. Write a C++ program for generic data types in a class definition.**

***Program:***

```
#include<iostream.h>
#include<conio.h>
template <class Type1, class Type2> class myclass
{
Type1 i;
Type2 j;
public:
myclass(Type1 a, Type2 b)
{
i = a;
j = b;
```

```
}
void show()
{
cout << i << ' ' << j << '\n';
}
};
void main()
{
myclass<int, double> object1(10, 0.23);
myclass<char, char *> object2('X', "This is a
test");
object1.show(); // show int, double
object2.show(); // show char, char *
getch();
}
```

**OUTPUT:**

```
10 0.23
X This is a test
```

**Problem 4. Write a C++ program for generic class: constructor.**

***Program:***

```
#include<iostream.h>
#include<conio.h>
template <class X> class input
{
X data;
public:
input(char *s, X min, X max);
};
template <class X>
input<X>::input(char *s, X min, X max)
{
do
{
cout << s << ": ";
cin >> data;
}
while( data < min || data > max);
}
void main()
{
input<int> i("enter int", 0, 10);
input<char> c("enter char", 'A', 'Z');
getch();
}
```

**OUTPUT:**

```
enter int: 123
enter int: 321
enter int: 123
enter int: 123
enter int: 123
enter int: 123
enter int: 123
enter int: 123
enter int: 123
enter int: 123
enter int: 12
enter int: 31
enter int: 23
enter int: 1
enter char: 23
enter char: enter char: 123
enter char: enter char: enter char: 12
enter char: enter char: 3
enter char: 123
enter char: enter char: enter char: 2
enter char: 23
enter char: enter char: 123
enter char: enter char: enter char: 1
enter char: 23
enter char: enter char: 12
enter char: enter char: 31
enter char: enter char: 23
enter char: enter char: 1231
enter char: enter char: enter char: 23
enter char: enter char: 1
enter char: 23
enter char: enter char: 123
enter char: enter char: enter char: 123
enter char: enter char: 12
enter char: enter char: 3
enter char: 123
enter char: enter char: enter char: 1
enter char: 23
enter char: enter char: 12
enter char: enter char: 3
enter char: 123
enter char: enter char: enter char: 123
enter char: enter char: enter char: 12
enter char: enter char: 31
enter char: enter char: 23
```

enter char: enter char: 1
enter char: 23^c

**Problem 5. Write a C++ program for generic class just for displaying the parameters.**

***Program:***

```
#include <iostream.h>
#include<conio.h>
#include <fstream.h>
template <class CoordType> class MyClass
{
CoordType x, y;
public:
MyClass(CoordType i, CoordType j)
{
x = i;
y = j;
}
void show()
{
cout << x << ", " << y << endl;
}
};
void main()
{
MyClass<int> object1(1, 2), object2(3, 4);
object1.show();
object2.show();
MyClass<double> object3(0.0, 0.23),
object4(10.19, 3.098);
object3.show();
object4.show();
getch();
}
```

**<u>OUTPUT</u>:**

```
1, 2
3, 4
0, 0.23
10.19, 3.098
```

## GENERIC LIST:

**Problem 6. Write a C++ program for a simple generic linked list.**

***Program:***

```
#include <iostream.h>
#include<conio.h>
template <class dataType> class list
{
dataType data;
list *next;
public:
list(dataType d);
void add(list *node)
{
node->next = this;
next = 0;
}
list *getnext()
{
return next;
}
dataType getdata()
{
return data;
}
};
template <class dataType>
list<dataType>::list(dataType d)
{
data = d;
next = 0;
}
void main()
{
list<char> start('a');
list<char> *p, *last;
int i;
last = &start;
for(i=1; i <26; i++)
{
p = new list<char> ('a' + i);
p->add(last);
last = p;
}
p = &start;
while(p)
{
cout << p->getdata();
p = p->getnext();
}
getch();
```

```
}
```

**OUTPUT:**

abcdefghijklmnopqrstuvwxyz

## GENERIC QUEUE:

**Problem 7. Write a C++ program to create a generic queue.**

***Program:***

```
#include<iostream.h>
#include<conio.h>
#define SIZE 100
template <class Qtype> class q_type
{
Qtype queue[SIZE];
int head, tail;
public:
q_type()
{
head = tail = 0;
}
void q(Qtype num);
Qtype deq();
};
template <class Qtype> void
q_type<Qtype>::q(Qtype num)
{
if(tail+1==head || (tail+1==SIZE && !head)) {
cout << "Queue is full.\n";
return;
}
tail++;
if(tail==SIZE)
tail = 0; // cycle around
queue[tail] = num;
}
template <class Qtype> Qtype
q_type<Qtype>::deq()
{
if(head == tail)
{
cout << "Queue is empty.\n";
return 0;
}
head++;
if(head==SIZE)
head = 0;
return queue[head];
}
void main()
{
q_type<int> queue1;
q_type<char> queue2;
int i;
for(i=1; i <=10; i++)
{
queue1.q(i);
queue2.q(i-1+'A');
}
for(i=1; i <=10; i++)
{
cout << "Dequeue 1: " << queue1.deq() <<
endl;
cout << "Dequeue 2: " << queue2.deq() <<
endl;
}
getch();
}
```

**OUTPUT:**

Dequeue 1: 1
Dequeue 2: A
Dequeue 1: 2
Dequeue 2: B
Dequeue 1: 3
Dequeue 2: C
Dequeue 1: 4
Dequeue 2: D
Dequeue 1: 5
Dequeue 2: E
Dequeue 1: 6
Dequeue 2: F
Dequeue 1: 7
Dequeue 2: G
Dequeue 1: 8
Dequeue 2: H
Dequeue 1: 9
Dequeue 2: I
Dequeue 1: 10
Dequeue 2: J

## GENERIC STACK:

**Problem 8. Write a C++ program for a generic stack that holds two values.**

***Program:***

```
#include <iostream.h>
#include<conio.h>
#define SIZE 10
template <class StackType> class stack
{
StackType stck[SIZE][2];
int topOfStack;
public:
void init() { topOfStack = 0; }
void push(StackType ob, StackType object2);
StackType pop(StackType &object2);
};
template <class StackType>
void stack<StackType>::push(StackType ob,
StackType object2)
{
if(topOfStack==SIZE)
{
cout << "Stack is full.\n";
return;
}
stck[topOfStack][0] = ob;
stck[topOfStack][1] = object2;
topOfStack++;
}
template <class StackType>
StackType stack<StackType>::pop(StackType
&object2)
{
if(topOfStack==0)
{
cout << "Stack is empty.\n";
return 0;
}
topOfStack--;
object2 = stck[topOfStack][1];
return stck[topOfStack][0];
}
void main()
{
stack<char> stack1, stackObject2;
int i;
char ch;
stack1.init();
stackObject2.init();
stack1.push('a', 'b');
stackObject2.push('x', 'z');
stack1.push('b', 'd');
stackObject2.push('y', 'e');
stack1.push('c', 'a');
stackObject2.push('z', 'x');
for(i = 0; i <3; i++)
{
cout << "Pop stack1: " << stack1.pop(ch);
cout << ' ' << ch << endl;
}
for(i = 0; i <3; i++)
{
cout << "Pop stackObject2: " <<
stackObject2.pop(ch);
cout << ' ' << ch << endl;
}
// demonstrate double stacks
stack<double> doubleValueStack1,
doubleValueStack2; // create two stacks
double d;
doubleValueStack1.init();
doubleValueStack2.init();
doubleValueStack1.push(1.1, 2.0);
doubleValueStack2.push(2.2, 3.0);
doubleValueStack1.push(3.3, 4.0);
doubleValueStack2.push(4.4, 5.0);
doubleValueStack1.push(5.5, 6.0);
doubleValueStack2.push(6.6, 7.0);
for(i = 0; i <3; i++)
{
cout << "Pop doubleValueStack1: " <<
doubleValueStack1.pop(d);
cout << ' '<< d << endl;
}
for(i = 0; i <3; i++)
{
cout << "Pop doubleValueStack2: " <<
doubleValueStack2.pop(d);
cout << ' '<< d << endl;
}
getch();
```

```
}
```

**OUTPUT:**

```
Pop stack1: c a
Pop stack1: b d
Pop stack1: a b
Pop stackobject2: z x
Pop stackobject2: y e
Pop stackobject2: x z
Pop doubleValuestack1: 5.5 6
Pop doubleValuestack1: 3.3 4
Pop doubleValuestack1: 1.1 2
Pop doubleValuestack2: 6.6 7
Pop doubleValuestack2: 4.4 5
Pop doubleValuestack2: 2.2 3
```

**Problem 9. Write a C++ program for a generic stack that includes exception handling.**

***Program:***

```
#include<iostream.h>
#include<conio.h>
#define SIZE 10
template <class StackType> class stack
{
StackType stck[SIZE];
int topOfStack;
public:
void init()
{
topOfStack = 0;
}
void push(StackType ch);
StackType pop();
};
template <class StackType>
void stack<StackType>::push(StackType ob)
{
try
{
if(topOfStack==SIZE) throw SIZE;
}
catch(int)
{
cout << "Stack is full.\n";
return;
}
stck[topOfStack] = ob;
topOfStack++;
}
template <class StackType>
StackType stack<StackType>::pop()
{
try
 {
if( topOfStack == 0)
throw 0;
}
catch(int)
{
cout << "Stack is empty.\n";
return 0;
}
topOfStack--;
return stck[topOfStack];
}
void main()
{
stack<char> stack1, stack2;
int i;
stack1.init();
stack2.init();
stack1.push('a');
stack2.push('x');
stack1.push('b');
stack2.push('y');
stack1.push('c');
stack2.push('z');
for(i = 0; i <3; i++)
cout << "Pop stack1: " << stack1.pop() <<
endl;
for(i = 0; i <4; i++)
cout << "Pop stack2: " << stack2.pop() <<
endl;
// demonstrate double stacks
stack<double> doubleValueStack1,
doubleValueStack2;  // create two stacks
// initialize the stacks
doubleValueStack1.init();
doubleValueStack2.init();
doubleValueStack1.push(1.1);
doubleValueStack2.push(2.2);
doubleValueStack1.push(3.3);
```

```
doubleValueStack2.push(4.4);
doubleValueStack1.push(5.5);
doubleValueStack2.push(6.6);
for(i = 0; i <3; i++)
cout << "Pop doubleValueStack1: " <<
doubleValueStack1.pop() << endl;
for(i = 0; i <4; i++)
cout << "Pop doubleValueStack2: " <<
doubleValueStack2.pop()<< endl;
getch();
}
```

**OUTPUT:**

```
Pop stack1: c
Pop stack1: b
Pop stack1: a
Pop stack2: z
Pop stack2: y
Pop stack2: x
Stack is empty.
Pop stack2:
Pop doubleValuestack1: 5.5
Pop doubleValuestack1: 3.3
Pop doubleValuestack1: 1.1
Pop doubleValuestack2: 6.6
Pop doubleValuestack2: 4.4
Pop doubleValuestack2: 2.2
Stack is empty.
Pop doubleValuestack2:0
```

## TEMPLATE CLASS:

**Problem 10. Write a C++ program in which typeid can be applied to template classes.**

***Program:***

```
#include<iostream.h>
#include<conio.h>
template <class T> class myclass
{
T a;
public:
myclass(T i)
{
a = i;
}
};
void main()
{
myclass<int> o1(10), o2(9);
myclass<double> o3(7.2);
cout << "Type of o1 is ";
cout << typeid(o1).name() << endl;
cout << "Type of o2 is ";
cout << typeid(o2).name() << endl;
cout << "Type of o3 is ";
cout << typeid(o3).name() << endl;
cout << endl;
if(typeid(o1) == typeid(o2))
cout << "o1 and o2 are the same type\n";
if(typeid(o1) == typeid(o3))
cout << "Error\n";
else
cout << "o1 and o3 are different types\n";
getch();
}
```

**OUTPUT:**

```
Type of o1 is 7myclassIiE
Type of o2 is 7myclassIiE
Type of o3 is 7myclassIdE
o1 and o2 are the same type
o1 and o3 are different types
```

**Problem 11. Write a C++ program to define template function for class type.**

***Program:***

```
#include <iostream.h>
#include<conio.h>
template <class type1, class type2>
void myFunction(type1 x, type2 y)
{
cout << x << ' ' << y << '\n';
}
void main()
{
myFunction(10, "hi");
myFunction(0.23, 10L);
getch();
}
```

**OUTPUT:**

```
10 hi
0.23 10
```

**Problem 12. Write a C++ program for overload a function template declaration.**

***Program:***

```
#include <iostream.h>
#include<conio.h>
template <class X> void f(X a)
{
cout << "Inside f(X a)\n";
}
template <class X, class Y> void f(X a, Y b)
{
cout << "Inside f(X a, Y b)\n";
}
void main()
{
f(10);
f(10, 20);
getch();
}
```

**OUTPUT:**

```
Inside f(X,a)
Inside f(X a, Y b)
```

**Problem 13. Write a C++ program for a generic version of myabs().**

***Program:***

```
#include <iostream.h>
#include<conio.h>
template <class X> X myabs(X val)
{
return val < 0 ? -val : val;
}
void main()
{
cout << myabs(-10) << '\n';    // integer abs
cout << myabs(-10.0) << '\n';  // double abs
cout << myabs(-10L) << '\n';   // long abs
cout << myabs(-10.0F) << '\n'; // float abs
getch();
}
```

**OUTPUT:**

```
10
10
10
10
```

**Problem 14. Write a C++ program for generic functions.**

***Program:***

```
#include<iostream.h>
#include<conio.h>
template <class X>void swapargs(X &a,X &b)
{
X temp;
temp =a;
a =b;
b =temp;
}
void main()
{
int i=10,j=20;
double x=10.1,y=23.3;
char a='x',b='z';
cout <<"Original i,j:"<<i <<" "<<j <<'\n';
cout <<"Original x,y:"<<x <<" "<<y <<'\n';
cout <<"Original a,b:"<<a <<" "<<b <<'\n';
swapargs(i,j);
swapargs(x,y);
swapargs(a,b);
cout <<"Swapped i,j:"<<i <<" "<<j <<'\n';
cout <<"Swapped x,y:"<<x <<" "<<y <<'\n';
cout <<"Swapped a,b:"<<a <<" "<<b <<'\n';
getch();
}
```

**OUTPUT:**

```
Original i,j:10 20
Original x,y:10.1 23.3
Original a,b:x z
Swapped i,j:20 10
Swapped x,y:23.3 10.1
Swapped a,b:z x
```

**Problem 15. Write a C++ program for a function with two generic types.**

***Program:***

```
#include<iostream.h>
#include<conio.h>
template <class X,class Y>
void func(X x,Y y)
{
cout <<x <<" "<<y <<'\n';
}
```

```
void main()
{
func(1,"I like C++");
func(38.6,12L);
getch();
}
```

**OUTPUT:**

1 I like C++
38.6 12

**Problem 16. Write a C++ program for explicitly overloading a generic function.**

***Program:***

```
#include<iostream.h>
#include<conio.h>
template <class X>void Change(X &a,X &b)
{
X temp;
temp =a;
a =b;
b =temp;
cout <<"In template Change.\n";
}
void Change(int &a,int &b)
{
int temp;
temp =a;
a =b;
b =temp;
cout <<"In Change int .\n";
}
void main()
{
int i=100,j=200;
double x=100.1,y=200.1;
char a='x',b='z';
cout <<"Original i,j:"<<i <<" "<<j <<'\n';
cout <<"Original x,y:"<<x <<" "<<y <<'\n';
cout <<"Original a,b:"<<a <<" "<<b <<'\n';
Change(i,j);
Change(x,y);
Change(a,b);
cout <<"Swapped i,j:"<<i <<" "<<j <<'\n';
cout <<"Swapped x,y:"<<x <<" "<<y <<'\n';
cout <<"Swapped a,b:"<<a <<" "<<b <<'\n';
getch();
}
```

**OUTPUT:**

Original i,j:100 200
Original x,y:100.1 200.1
Original a,b:x z
In Change int
In template Change
In template Change
Swapped i,j:200 100
Swapped x,y:200.1 100.1
Swapped a,b:z x

**Problem 17. Write a C++ program for generic function restrictions.**

***Program:***

```
#include <iostream.h>
#include <math.h>
#include<conio.h>
void func(int i)
{
cout <<"value is:"<<i <<"\n";
}
void func(double d)
{
double intpart;
double realpart;
realpart =modf(d,&intpart);
cout <<"Real part:"<<realpart;
cout <<"\n";
cout <<"Integer part:"<<intpart;
}
void main()
{
func(4);
func(12.84);
getch();
}
```

**OUTPUT:**

value is: 4
Real part: 0.84
Integer part: 12

## GENERIC SORT:

**Problem 18. Write a C++ program for applying generic functions.**

***Program:***

```
#include <iostream.h>
#include<conio.h>
template <class X>void bubble(X *items,int
count)
{
int a,b;
X t;
for(a=1;a<count;a++)
for(b=count-1;b>=a;b--)
if(items [b-1] >items [b])
{
t =items [b-1];
items [b-1] =items [b];
items [b] =t;
}
}
void main()
{
int iarray [7] ={7,5,4,3,1,2,6};
double darray [5] ={1.2,2.4,-0.2,5.2,3.4};
int i;
cout <<"Unsorted integer array:";
for(i=0;i<7;i++)
cout <<iarray [i] <<" ";
cout <<endl;
cout <<"Unsorted double array:";
for(i=0;i<5;i++)
cout <<darray [i] <<" ";
cout <<endl;
bubble(iarray,7);
bubble(darray,5);
cout <<"Sorted integer array:";
for(i=0;i<7;i++)
cout <<iarray [i] <<" ";
cout <<endl;
cout <<"Sorted double array:";
for(i=0;i<5;i++)
cout <<darray [i] <<" ";
cout <<endl;
getch();
}
```

**OUTPUT:**

```
Unsorted integer array:7 5 4 3 1 2 6
Unsorted double array:1.2 2.4 -0.2 5.2 3.4
Sorted integer array:1 2 3 4 5 6 7
Sorted double array:-0.2 1.2 2.4 3.4 5.2
```

**Problem 19. Write a C++ program for generic classes.**

***Program:***

```
#include <iostream.h>
#include<conio.h>
const int SIZE =10;
template <class StackType>class stack
{
StackType stck [SIZE ];
int tos;// top-of-stack
public:
stack()
{
tos =0;
}//initialize stack
void push(StackType ob);//push object on
stack
StackType pop();//pop object from stack
};
//push an object
template <class StackType>void
stack<StackType>::push(StackType ob)
{
if(tos==SIZE)
{
cout <<"Stack is full.\n";
return;
}
stck[tos]=ob;
tos++;
}
//Pop an object.
template <class StackType>StackType
stack<StackType>::pop()
{
if(tos==0)
{
cout <<"Stack is empty.\n";
return 0;
}
tos--;
return stck [tos ];
}
void main()
```

```
{
stack<char>s1,s2;//two character stacks
int i;
s1.push('a');
s2.push('x');
s1.push('b');
s2.push('y');
s1.push('c');
s2.push('z');
for(i=0;i<3;i++)
cout <<"Pop s1:"<<s1.pop()<<"\n";
for(i=0;i<3;i++)
cout <<"Pop s2:"<<s2.pop()<<"\n";
stack<double>ds1,ds2;// two double stacks
ds1.push(10.1);
ds2.push(20.2);
ds1.push(30.3);
ds2.push(40.4);
ds1.push(50.5);
ds2.push(60.6);
for(i=0;i<3;i++)
cout <<"Pop ds1:"<<ds1.pop()<<"\n";
for(i=0;i<3;i++)
cout <<"Pop ds2:"<<ds2.pop()<<"\n";
getch();
}
```

**OUTPUT:**

```
Pop s1:c
Pop s1:b
Pop s1:a
Pop s2:z
Pop s2:y
Pop s2:x
Pop ds1:50.5
Pop ds1:30.3
Pop ds1:10.1
Pop ds2:60.0
Pop ds2:40.4
Pop ds2:20.2
```

**Problem 20. Write a C++ program using two generic data types.**

***Program:***

```
#include <iostream.h>
#include<conio.h>
template <class T1,class T2>class A
{
T1 i;
T2 j;
public:
A(T1 a,T2 b)
{
i =a;
j =b;
}
void show()
{
cout <<i <<" "<<j <<'\n';
}
};
void main()
{
A<int,double>a1(100,0.65);
A<char,char *>b1('M',"Templates effects.");
a1.show();//show int,double
b1.show();//show char,char *
getch();
}
```

**OUTPUT:**

```
100 0.65
M Templates effects
```

**Problem 21. Write a C++ program for template classes:A Generic Array Class.**

***Program:***

```
#include <iostream.h>
#include <stdlib.h>
#include<conio.h>
const int SIZE =10;
template <class AType>class t1
{
AType a [SIZE];
public:
t1()
{
 int i;
for(i=0;i<SIZE;i++)
a[i] =i;
}
AType &operator [](int i);
};
```

```
template <class AType>AType
&t1<AType>::operator [](int i)
{
if(i<0 ||i>SIZE-1)
{
cout <<"\nIndex value of ";
cout <<i <<"is out-of-bounds.\n";
exit(1);
}
return a[i];
}
void main()
{
t1<int>intar;//integer array
t1<double>doublear;//double array
int i;
cout <<"Integer array:";
for(i=0;i<SIZE;i++)
intar [i ] =i;
for(i=0;i<SIZE;i++)
cout <<intar [i ] <<" ";
cout <<'\n';
cout <<"Double array:";
for(i=0;i<SIZE;i++)
doublear [i ] =(double)i/3;
for(i=0;i<SIZE;i++)
cout <<doublear [i ] <<" ";
cout <<'\n';
intar [22] =100;//This Array generates runtime
error
getch();
}
```

**OUTPUT:**

Integer array:1 2 3 4 5 6 7 8 9
Double array:0 0.333333 0.666667 1 1.333333
1.666667 2
2.333333 2.666667 3
Index value of 22is out-of-bounds.

**Problem 22. Write a C++ program using default arguments with template classes.**

***Program:***

```
#include <iostream.h>
#include <stdlib.h>
#include<conio.h>
template <class AType, int size=10>class t1
{
AType a[size];
public:
t1()
{
int i;
for(i=0;i<size;i++)
a[i] =i;
}
AType &operator [](int i);
};
template <class AType,int size>
AType &t1<AType,size>::operator [](int i)
{
if(i<0 ||i>size-1)
{
cout <<"\nIndex value of ";
cout <<i <<"is out-of-bounds.\n";
exit(1);
}
return a[i];
}
void main()
{
t1<int,20>intarray;
t1<double>doublearray;
t1<int>defargsarray;
int i;
cout <<"int array:";
for(i=0;i<20;i++)
intarray [i ] =i;
for(i=0;i<20;i++)
cout <<intarray [i ] <<" ";
cout <<'\n';
cout <<"double array:";
for(i=0;i<10;i++)
doublearray[i ]=(double)i/3;
for(i=0;i<10;i++)
cout <<doublearray [i]<<" ";
cout <<'\n';
cout <<"defargsarray array:";
for(i=0;i<10;i++)
defargsarray [i ] =i;
for(i=0;i<10;i++)
cout <<defargsarray [i ]<<" ";
cout <<'\n';
```

```
getch();
}
```

**OUTPUT:**

int array:0 1 2 3 4 5 6 7 8 9 10 11 12 13 14 15
16 17 18 19
double array: 0 0.333333 0.666667 1 1.333333
1.666667 2
2.333333 2.666667 3
defargsarray array:0 1 2 3 4 5 6 7 8 9

**Problem 23. Write a C++ program for generic quick sort.**

***Program:***

```
#include<conio.h>
#include<iostream.h>
#include<iomanip.h>
#include<stdlib.h>
template<class T>
inline void swap(T& v1,T& v2)
{
T temp=v2;
v2=v1;
v1=temp;
}
template<class T>
void quicksort(T *array,int hi,int lo=0)
{
while(hi>lo)
{
int i=lo;
int j=hi;
do
{
while(array[i]<array[lo]&&i<j)
i++;
while(array[--j]>array[lo]);
if(i<j)
swap(array[i],array[j]);
}while(i<j);
swap(array[lo],array[j]);
if(j-lo>hi-(j+1))
{
quicksort(array,j-1,lo);
lo=j+1;
}
else
{
quicksort(array,hi,j+1);
hi=j-1;
}
}
}
void main()
{
int dim = 100;
int *arrs=new int[dim+1];
for(int i=0;i < dim;i++)
arrs[i]=rand();
cout << endl<<"unsorted"<<endl;
for(int k=0;k<dim;k++)
cout<<setw(8)<<arrs[k];
quicksort(arrs,dim);
cout<<endl<<"sorted"<<endl;
for(int j=0;j<dim;j++)
cout<<setw(8)<<arrs[j];
delete arrs;
getch();
}
```

**OUTPUT:**

```
unsorted
      41   18467    6334   26500   19169   15724
11478   29358   26962   24464
    5705   28145   23281   16827    9961     491
2995   11942    4827    5436
   32391   14604    3902     153     292   12382
17421   18716   19718   19895
    5447   21726   14771   11538    1869
19912   25667   26299   17035    9894
   28703   23811   31322   30333   17673
4664   15141    7711   28253    6868
   25547   27644   32662   32757   20037
12859    8723    9741   27529     778
   12316    3035   22190    1842     288   30106
9040    8942   19264   22648
   27446   23805   15890    6729   24370
15350   15006   31101   24393    3548
   19629   12623   24084   19954   18756
11840    4966    7376   13931   26308
   16944   32439   24626   11323    5537
21538   16118    2082   22929   16541

sorted
```

```
  41   153   288   292   491   778   1842
1869  2082  2995
  3035  3548  3902  4664  4827  4966
5436  5447  5537  5705
  6334  6729  6868  7376  7711  8723
8942  9040  9741  9894
  9961  11323  11478  11538  11840  11942
12316  12382  12623  12859
  13931  14604  14771  15006  15141  15350
15724  15890  16118  16541
  16827  16944  17035  17421  17673  18467
18716  18756  19169  19264
  19629  19718  19895  19912  19954  20037
21538  21726  22190  22648
  22929  23281  23805  23811  24084  24370
24393  24464  24626  25547
  25667  26299  26308  26500  26962  27446
27529  27644  28145  28253
  28703  29358  30106  30333  31101  31322
32391
```

**Problem 24. Write a C++ program for a generic stack with size 10.**

***Program:***

```
#include <iostream.h>
#include<conio.h>
const int SIZE = 10;
template <class StackType> class stack
{
StackType stck[SIZE];
int tos;
public:
stack()
{
tos = 0;
}
void push(StackType ob)
{
if(tos==SIZE)
{
cout << "Stack is full.\n";
return;
 }
 stck[tos] = ob;
 tos++;
 }
StackType pop()
{
if(tos==0)
{
cout << "Stack is empty.\n";
return 0; // return null on empty stack
}
tos--;
return stck[tos];
}
};
void main()
{
stack<char> s1, s2;
s1.push('a');
s2.push('x');
s1.push('b');
s2.push('y');
s1.push('c');
s2.push('z');
for(int i=0; i<3; i++)
cout << "Pop s1: " << s1.pop() << "\n";
for(int j=0; j<3; j++)
cout << "Pop s2: " << s2.pop() << "\n";
stack<double> ds1, ds2;
ds1.push(1.1);
ds2.push(2.2);
ds1.push(3.3);
ds2.push(4.4);
ds1.push(5.5);
ds2.push(6.6);
for(int m=0; m<3; m++)
cout << "Pop ds1: " << ds1.pop() << "\n";
for(int k=0; k<3; k++)
cout << "Pop ds2: " << ds2.pop() << "\n";
getch();
}
```

**<u>OUTPUT</u>:**

```
Pop s1: c
Pop s1: b
Pop s1: a
Pop s2: z
Pop s2: y
Pop s2: x
Pop ds1: 5.5
Pop ds1: 3.3
```

Pop ds1: 1.1
Pop ds2: 6.6
Pop ds2: 4.4
Pop ds2: 2.2

## GENERIC ARRAY USING TEMPLATES:

**Problem 25. Write a C++ program to define your own generic array.**

***Program:***

```
#include<conio.h>
#include<iostream.h>
#include<iomanip.h>
template<class T>
class Array
{
T *elems;
int size;
public:
Array(int s)
{
size=s;
elems=new T[size];
for(int i=0;i<size;i++)
elems[i]=0;
}
~Array()
{
delete elems;
}
T& operator[](int index)
{
return elems[index];
}
void operator=(T temp)
{
for(int i=0;i<size;i++)
elems[i]=temp;
}
};
void main()
{
int n=10;
Array<int>arr1(n);
Array<char>arr2(n);
for(int i=0;i<n;i++)
{
arr1[i]='a'+i;
arr2[i]='a'+i;
}
cout <<endl;
for(int j=0;j<n;j++)
{
cout<<setw(8)<<arr1[j]<<setw(8)<<arr2[j]<<
endl;
}
getch();
}
```

**OUTPUT:**

```
97    a
98    b
99    c
100   d
101   e
102   f
103   g
104   h
105   i
106   j
```

**Problem 26. Write a C++ program for a generic class.**

***Program:***

```
#include <iostream.h>
#include<conio.h>
template <class T> class MyClass
{
T x, y;
public:
MyClass(T a, T b)
{
x = a;
y = b;
}
T div() { return x/y; }
};
void main()
{
MyClass<double> d_ob(10.0, 3.0 ); //
doubles.
```

```
cout << "double division: " << d_ob.div() <<
"\n";
MyClass<int> i_ob(10, 3);        // for ints.
cout << "integer division: " << i_ob.div() <<
"\n";
getch();
}
```

**OUTPUT:**

double division: 3.33333
integer division: 3

**Problem 27. Write a C++ program for operator overload for generic parameters.**

***Program:***

```
#include <iostream.h>
#include<conio.h>
template<class T>
class Sample
{
T n;
public:
Sample(T i)
{
n=i;
}
int operator==(Sample &s)
{
if(n==s.n)
return 1;
else
return 0;
}
};
void main()
{
Sample<int> s1(2),s2(3);
cout<<(s1==s2)<<endl;
Sample<double> s3(2.5),s4(2.5);
cout<<(s1==s2)<<endl;
 getch();
}
```

# CHAPTER 20

# DATA STRUCTURES USING C++

## ARRAY:

**Problem 1.Write a C++ program to insert an element into an array.**

***Program:***

```
#include<conio.h>
#include<iostream.h>
class insert_array
{
int a[10];
public:
void create( );
void insert( );
}
void insert_array::create( )
{
int i,n;
cout<<"Enter the number of elements:";
cin>>n;
cout<<"Enter the elements:";
for(i=0;i<n;i++)
cin>>a[i];
}
void insert_array::insert( )
{
int i,k,temp,n;
cout<<"Enter the position:";
cin>>k;
cout<<"Enter the element which you want to insert
:";
cin>>temp;
for(i=n-1;i>=k-1;i--)
a[i+1] = a[i];
a[k-1] = temp;
n++;
cout<<"Array after insertion is:";
for(i=0;i<n;i++)
 cout<<endl<<a[i];
}
void main()
{
insert_array b;
clrscr( );
b.create( );
b.insert( );
getch();
}
```

**OUTPUT:**

```
Enter the number of elements: 5
Enter the elements:
66
55
44
33
11
Enter the position: 5
Enter the element which you want to insert: 22
Array after insertion is :
66
55
44
33
22
11
```

**Problem 2. Write a C++ program to delete an element from Array.**

***Program:***

```
#include<conio.h>
#include<iostream.h>
class delete_array
{
int a[10];
public:
void create( );
void delete( );
}
void delete_array::create( )
{
```

```
int i,n;
cout<<"Enter the number of elements:";
cin>>n;
cout<<"Enter the elements:";
for(i=0;i<n;i++)
cin>>a[i];
}
void delete_array::delete( )
{
int i,k,temp,n;
cout<<"Enter the position:";
cin>>k;
temp = a[k-1] ;
for(i=k-1;i<n;i++)
a[i] = a[i+1];
n--;
cout<<"Array after deletion is:";
for(i=0;i<n;i++)
cout<<endl<<a[i];
cout<<"\nThe deleted item is:"<<temp;
}
void main()
{
delete_array d;
clrscr( );
d.create( );
d.delete( );
getch();
}
```

**OUTPUT:**

```
Enter the number of elements:5
Enter the elements:
20
30
32
40
50
Enter the position: 3
Array after deletion is :
20
30
40
50
The deleted item is: 32
```

## STACK:

**Problem 3. Write a C++ program to create a stack.**

***Program:***

```
#include<iostream.h>
#include<iomanip.h>
#include<conio.h>
class stack
{
int st[50];
int Tos;
public:
void create();
void display();
};
void stack:: create()
{
int i,n;
cout<<"Enter the total no. of elements in stack : ";
cin>>n;
cout<<"Enter the elements "<<endl;
for(Tos=1;Tos<=n;Tos++)
{
cin>>i;
st[Tos]=i; //this line pushes data items onto stack
}
Tos--;     //Tos is decremented by 1 so that after
complete execution of
}       //Tos loop,Tos points to top most data item
in stack
void stack::display()
{
int j;
for(j=Tos;j>0;j--)
cout<<endl<<st[j]<<endl; //stack elements are
printed in reverse order
}                //as stack follows LIFO order
void main()
{
stack s;   //the object of the stack is declared
clrscr();
s.create(); //call to create funtion
cout<<"The stack created is the reverse of the
inputted elements"<<endl;
cout<<" As stack maintains LIFO order";
s.display(); //call to display function
getch();
}
```

**OUTPUT:**

```
Enter the total no. of elements in stack 5
Enter the elements
3
4
5
8
```

9
The stack created is the reverse of the inputted element
as stack maintains LIFO order
9
8
5
4
3

**Problem 4. Write a C++ program to exchange two topmost elements in stack.**

***Program:***

```
#include<iostream.h>
#include<iomanip.h>
#include<conio.h>
class stack
{
int st[50];
int Tos;
public:
int i,n,k;
stack();//constructor function for creating the stack
void push();
void pop();
void display();
};
//creation of stack
stack:: stack()
{
a:
cout<<"Enter the total no. of elements in stack (should be at least two for exchange operation to perform)";
cin>>n;
if(n<2)
goto a;
cout<<"Enter the elements"<<endl;
for(Tos=1;Tos<=n;Tos++)
{
cin>>i;
st[Tos]=i; //this line pushes data items onto stack
}
Tos--;    //Tos is decremented by 1 so that after complete execution of
          //Tos loop,Tos points to top most data item in stack
 cout<<endl<<"The value of Tos is"<<setw(2)<<Tos;
}
//pushing a data element on the top of stack
void stack::push()
{
Tos++;
st[Tos]=i;
Tos++;
st[Tos]=k;
}
void stack::pop()
{
if(Tos<=0)
{
cout<<endl<<"The stack is empty";
}
i=st[Tos];
Tos--;
k=st[Tos];
Tos--;
cout<<endl<<"The top most two elements "<<setw(5)<<i<<setw(5)<<"and"<<setw(5)<<k<<setw(5)<<"are popped out"<<endl;
}
void stack::display()
{
int j;
for(j=Tos;j>0;j--)
cout<<endl<<st[j]<<endl; //stack elements are printed in reverse order because
}            //stack follows LIFO order
void main()
{
clrscr();
stack s;  //the object of the stack is declared
cout<<endl<<"Stack created is";
s.display();
s.pop();
cout<<"The stack after these pop operations is"<<endl;
s.display();
s.push();  //call to push function
cout<<endl<<"The stack after exchange opeartion is";
s.display(); //call to display function
getch();
}
```

**OUTPUT:**

Enter the total no. of elements in stack (should be at lest two for exchange operation to perform) 2
Enter the elements
1
2
the value of Tos is 2

stack created is
2
1
the top most two elements 2 and 1 are
popped out the stack after then pop operations is
The stack after exchange operation is
1
2

**Problem 5. Write a C++ program to convert an Infix Expression to Postfix Expression.**

***Program:***

```
#include<iostream.h>
#include<iomanip.h>
#include<conio.h>
#include<process.h>
#include<ctype.h>
#include<string.h>
int Tos=-1;
int n=0;
class stack
{
char st[50]; //declaration of stack array
char exp[50];
public:
char fexp()
{ return(exp[n]); }
char fstktop()
{ return(st[Tos]); }
void input();
void push(char);
void pop();
};
void stack::input()
{
 cin.get(exp,50); //last char should be ')'
}
void stack::push(char a)
{  Tos++;
   st[Tos]=a;
}
void stack::pop()
{
if(Tos<0)
cout<<"stack is empty";
else
{
if(st[Tos]!='(' )
cout<<st[Tos];
Tos--;
}
}
void main()
{
clrscr();
stack s;    //the object of the class stack is declared
cout<<"Enter expression, last char should be ')'
char"<<endl;
s.input();
s.push('(');
for(; ;)
{.
if ( Tos<0)
{
getch();
exit(0);
}
switch(s.fexp() )
{
case '(':
s.push(s.fexp());
n++;
break;
case ')':
while(s.fstktop()!='(' )
s.pop();
s.pop(); //remove ')'cparenthesis
n++;
break;
case '+':
while(    (s.fstktop()=='-')    ||    (s.fstktop()=='+')||
(s.fstktop()=='*')
|| (s.fstktop()=='/'))
s.pop();
s.push(s.fexp());
n++;
break;
case '-':
while(    s.fstktop()=='-'    ||    s.fstktop()=='*'    ||
s.fstktop()=='/' ||
s.fstktop()=='+')
s.pop();
s.push(s.fexp());
n++;
break;
case '/':
while(s.fstktop()=='/' || s.fstktop()=='*')
s.pop();
s.push(s.fexp());
n++;
```

```
break;
case '*':
while(s.fstktop()=='/' && s.fstktop()=='*' )
s.pop();
s.push(s.fexp());
n++;
break;
default:
if (isalpha(s.fexp()) )
{
cout<<s.fexp();
n++;
}
}
}
}
```

**OUTPUT:**

```
Enter expression , last character should be ')' char
a+b)
ab+
```

**Problem 6.Write a C++ program to perform pop operation in stack.**

***Program:***

```
#include<iostream.h>
#include<iomanip.h>
#include<process.h>
#include<conio.h>
class stack
{
int st[50]; //declaration of stack array
int Tos;
char ch;
public:
int i,n;
stack();//constructor function for creating the stack
void pop();
void display();
};
//creation of stack
stack:: stack()
{
cout<<"Enter the total no. of elements in stack : ";
cin>>n;
cout<<"Enter the elements"<<endl;
for(Tos=1;Tos<=n;Tos++)
{
cin>>i;
st[Tos]=i;  //this line pushes data items onto stack
}
Tos--;     //Tos is decremented by 1 so that after complete execution of
           //Tos loop,Tos points to top most data item in stack
cout<<endl<<"The value of Tos is "<<setw(2)<<Tos;
}
//popping out a data element from the top of stack
void stack::pop()
{
if(Tos<=0)
{
cout<<"Stack is empty";
getch();
exit(0);
}
cout<<"Do you want to pop the stack yes or no (y/n) : ";
cin>>ch;
if(ch == 'y')
{
i=st[Tos];
cout<<endl<<"The top most element"<<setw(2)<< i <<"\t"<<"has been poped out"<<endl;
Tos--;
cout<<endl<<"Now the value of Tos is"<<setw(2)<<Tos;
}
else
exit(8);
}
void stack::display()
{
int j;
for(j=Tos;j>0;j--)
cout<<endl<<st[j]<<endl;  //stack elements are printed in reverse order because
}                   //stack follows LIFO order
void main()
{
clrscr();
stack s;   //the object of the stack is declared
cout<<" Stack before pop operation is"<<endl;
s.display();
a1: s.pop();   //call to push function
cout<<endl<<"Stack after pop operation is"<<endl;
s.display(); //call to display function
goto a1;
getch();
}
```

**OUTPUT:**

Enter the total no. of elements in the stack 5
Enter the elements
3
4
5
6
7
The value of Tos is 5 stack before pop operation is
7
6
5
4
3
Do you want to pop the stack yes or no (y/n) y
The top most element 7 has been poped out
The value of Tos is 4 stack after pop operation is
6
5
4
3
Do you want to pop the stack yes or no (y/n) y

**Problem 7. Write a C++ program to push an element in stack.**

***Program:***

```
#include<iostream.h>
#include<iomanip.h>
#include<conio.h>
#include<process.h>
class stack
{
int st[50];
int Tos;
char ch;
public:
int i,n,size;
stack();//constructor function for creating the stack
void push();
void display();
};
//creation of stack
stack:: stack()
{
cout<<"Enter the size of the stack : ";
cin>>size;
a:cout<<"Enter the total no. of elements in stack : ";
cin>>n;
if(n>size)
goto a;
cout<<"Enter the elements"<<endl;
for(Tos=1;Tos<=n;Tos++)
{
cin>>i;
st[Tos]=i; //this line pushes data items onto stack
}
Tos--;     //Tos is decremented by 1 so that after complete execution of
           //Tos loop,Tos points to top most data item in stack
cout<<endl<<"The value of Tos is"<<setw(2)<<Tos;
 }
//pushing a data element on the top of stack
void stack::push()
{
if(Tos>=size)
{
cout<<"Stack is full";
getch();
exit(0);
}
cout<<"Do you want to push the stack yes or no (y/n) : ";
cin>>ch;
if(ch == 'y')
{
Tos++;
cout<<"Enter the data element to be pushed : ";
cin>>i;
 st[Tos]=i;
cout<<endl<<"Now the value of Tos is"<<setw(2)<<Tos;
}
else
exit(0);
}
void stack::display()
{
int j;
for(j=Tos;j>0;j--)
cout<<endl<<st[j]<<endl; //stack elements are printed in reverse order because
}                        //stack follows LIFO order
void main()
{
clrscr();
stack s;  //the object of the stack is declared
cout<<endl<<"Stack created is"<<endl;
s.display();
```

```
a1: s.push();    //call to push function
cout<<"The stack after push opeartion is"<<endl;
s.display(); //call to display function
goto a1;
getch();
}
```

**OUTPUT:**

Enter the size of the stack 7
Enter the total no. of elements in stack 5
Enter the elements
2
4
3
6
9
The value of Tos is 5
stack created is
9
6
3
4
2
Enter the data element to be pushed 1
Now the value of Tos is 6 the stack after push operation is
1
9
6
3
4
2

**Problem 8. Write a C++ program to implement push and pop operation in stack using linked list.**

***Program:***

```
#include<iostream.h>
#include<iomanip.h>
#include<string.h>
#include<conio.h>
class stack
{
int data;
stack *next;
public:
void create();
void display();
void push(int);
void pop();
~stack();
}*Tos;
void stack::push(int info)
{
stack *item=new stack;
item->data=info;
item->next=Tos;
Tos=item;
}
void stack::pop()
{
stack *item;
if (Tos==NULL)
cout<<"stack already empty\n";
else
{
cout<<"\nelement to pop is\t"<<Tos->data;
Tos=Tos->next;
}
}
stack::~stack()
{
stack* item;
while(Tos!=NULL)
{
item=Tos->next;
delete Tos;
Tos=item;
}
}
void stack::create()
{ int val;
Tos=NULL;
for(;;)
{
cout<<"Enter data item and enter -1 for quit\t";
cin>>val;
if(val==-1)
break;
else
{
stack *item=new stack;
item->data=val;
item->next=Tos;
Tos=item;
}
}
}
void stack::display()
{
// top to bottom
int nodes=0;
cout<<"The stack created is";
while(Tos!=NULL)
```

```
{
nodes++;
cout<<"\n"<<Tos->data;
Tos=Tos->next;
}
cout<<"\nThe number of nodes in the stack are"<<setw(2)<<nodes;
}
void main()
{
clrscr();
stack s;
s.create();
s.display();
s.push(35);
s.pop();
getch();
}
```

**OUTPUT:**

```
enter data item and enter -1 for quit 7
enter data item and enter -1 for quit 9
enter data item and enter -1 for quit 15
enter data item and enter -1 for quit -1
The stack created is
15
9
7
the number of nodes in the stack are 35
```

## QUEUE:

**Problem 9. Write a C++ program to create a linear Queue.**

***Program:***

```
#include<iostream.h>
#include<conio.h>
#include<iomanip.h>
class Queue
{
private:
int Qu[50];     //An array Queue is declared with maximum size as 50
public:
int front,rear,m,item,n;
Queue();
void create();
void display();
};
Queue::Queue()
{
front=0;
rear=0;
}
void Queue::create()
{
cout<<"Enter number of elements in the Queue : ";
cin>>n;
cout<<"Enter the elements";
if(front==0)
{
front++;
cin>>item;
Qu[front]=item;
rear=front;
}
do
{
++rear;
if(rear>n)
break;
cin>>item;
Qu[rear]=item;
}while(rear<n);
}
void Queue::display()
{
cout<<"The created Queue is";
for(m=front;m<=rear;m++)
cout<<setw(5)<<Qu[m];
}
void main()
{
clrscr();
Queue z;  //An object z of class Queue is created
z.create();  // Call to create function
z.display(); // Call to display function
getch();
}
```

**OUTPUT:**

```
Enter number of elements in the Queue 4
Enter the elements
3
4
5
6
The created Queue is 3 4 5 6
```

**Problem 10. Write a C++ program to delete an element from linear Queue.**

***Program:***

```
#include<iostream.h>
#include<conio.h>
#include<process.h>
#include<iomanip.h>
class Queue
{
private:
int Qu[50]; //An array Queue is declared with
maximum size as 50
public:
int front,rear,size,m,item,n;
Queue();
void create();
void Dequeue();
void display();
};
Queue::Queue()
{
front=0;
rear=0;
}
void Queue::create()
{
cout<<"Enter size of the Queue : ";
cin>>size;
a:cout<<"Enter number of elements in the Queue : ";
cin>>n;
if(n>size)
goto a;
cout<<"Enter the elements";
if(front==0)
{
front++;
cin>>item;
Qu[front]=item;
rear=front;
}
do
{
++rear;
if(rear>n)
break;
cin>>item;
Qu[rear]=item;
}while(rear<n);
}
void Queue::Dequeue()
{
if(front==rear)
{
cout<<"Queue is empty";
exit(0);
}
front++;
item=Qu[front];
if(front==size)
{
front=1;
rear=1;
}
}
void Queue::display()
{
for(m=front;m<=rear;m++)
cout<<setw(5)<<Qu[m];
}
void main()
{
clrscr();
Queue z; //An object z of class Queue is created
z.create(); // Call to create function
cout<<"The created Queue is";
z.display(); // Call to display function for
displaying created Queue
z.Dequeue(); // Call to delete function
cout<<"\nQueue after,deleting an element at front
position, is";
z.display(); // Call to display function
getch();
}
```

**OUTPUT:**

Enter size of the Queue 6
Enter number of elements in the Queue 4
Enter the elements
1
4
7
8
The created Queue is 1 4 7 8
Queue after, deleting an element at front position, is 4 7 8

**Problem 11. Write a C++ program to insert an element in linear Queue.**

***Program:***

```
#include<iostream.h>
#include<conio.h>
#include<process.h>
#include<iomanip.h>
class Queue
{
private:
```

```
int Qu[50]; //An array Queue is declared with maximum size as 50
public:
int front,rear,size,m,item,n,last;
Queue();
void create();
void Enqueue();
void display();
};
Queue::Queue()
{
front=0;
rear=0;
last=0;
}
void Queue::create()
{
cout<<"Enter size of the  Queue : ";
cin>>size;
a:cout<<"Enter number of elements in the Queue : ";
cin>>n;
if(n>size)
goto a;
cout<<"Enter the elements";
if(front==0)
{
front++;
cin>>item;
Qu[front]=item;
rear=front;
}
do
{
++rear;
if(rear>n)
break;
cin>>item;
Qu[rear]=item;
}while(rear<n);
}
void Queue::Enqueue()
{
rear++;
if(rear>size)
{
cout<<"Queue is full";
exit(0);
}
cout<<"\nEnter element to be inserted : ";
cin>>item;
Qu[rear]=item;
}
void Queue::display()
{
for(m=front;m<=rear;m++)
cout<<setw(5)<<Qu[m];
}
void main()
{
clrscr();
Queue z; //An object z of class Queue is created
z.create(); // Call to create function
cout<<"The created Queue is ";
z.display(); // Call to display function for displaying created Queue
z.Enqueue(); // Call to insert function
cout<<"Queue after inserting an element is ";
z.display(); // Call to display function
getch();
}
```

**OUTPUT:**

```
Enter size of the Queue 5
Enter number of elements in the Queue 3
Enter the elements
4
6
7
The created Queue is 4 6 7
Enter element to be inserted 3
Queue after inserting an element is 4 6 7 3
```

## HEAP SORT:

**Problem 12. Write a C++ program to Sort Data using HEAP SORT.**

***Program:***

```
#include<iostream.h>
#include<conio.h>
void insheap(int[],int,int);
int delheap(int[],int&);
class heap
{
int  a[10];
public:
void create( );
void sort( );
}
void heap::create( )
{
int i,n;
```

```
cout<<"Enter the number of elements:";
cin>>n;
cout<<"Enter the elements:";
for(i=0;i<n;i++)
cin>>a[i];
}
void heap::sort( )
{
int i,n,item;
for(i=1;i<=n-1;i++)
insheap(a,i,a[i+1]);
cout<<"\n heaptree is: ";
for(i=1;i<=n;i++)
cout<<" "<<a[i];
i=n;
while(i>1)
{
item = delheap(a,i);
a[i+1] = item;
}
cout<<"\n Sorted list is: ";
for(i=1;i<=n;i++)
cout<<" "<<a[i];
}
void main()
{
heap h;
clrscr( );
h.create( );
h.sort( );
getch();
}
// this function creates the heaptree
void insheap(int a[],int n,int item)
{
int par,ptr;
n++;
ptr = n;
while(ptr>1)
{
par = ptr/2;
if ( item <= a[par])
{
a[ptr] = item;
return;
}
a[ptr] = a[par];
ptr = par;
}
a[1] = item;
}
/* this function alwyas deletes the root node a[1]
  and assign it to the variable item */
int delheap(int a[],int &n)
{
int item,left,right,ptr,last;
item = a[1];
last = a[n];
n--;
ptr =1;left =2;right = 3;
while(right <= n)
{
if ( last >= a[left] && last >= a[right])
{
a[ptr] = last;
return item;
}
if ( a[right] <= a[left] )
{
a[ptr] = a[left];
ptr = left;
}
else
{
a[ptr] = a[right];
ptr = right;
}
left = 2*ptr;
right = left+1;
}
if( left == n && last < a[left] )
{
a[ptr] = a[left];
ptr = left;
}
a[ptr] = last;
return item;
}
```

## MERGE SORT:

**Problem 13. Write a C++ program to Sort Data using MERGE SORT.**

***Program:***

```
#include<iostream.h>
#include<conio.h>
void mergesort(int,int,int*);
void merge(int,int,int,int*);
class merge
{
```

```
int a[10];
public:
void create( );
void sort( );
}
void merge::create( )
{
int i,n;
cout<<"Enter the number of elements:";
cin>>n;
a[0] = -1;
cout<<"Enter the elements:";
for(i=0;i<n;i++)
cin>>a[i];
}
void merge::sort( )
{
int i,low,high,n;
low =1;
high = n;
mergesort(low,high,a);
cout<<" sorted list is ";
for(i=1;i<=n;i++)
cout<<" "<<a[i];
}
void main()
{
merge m;
clrscr( );
m.create( );
m.sort( );
getch();
}
void mergesort(int low,int high,int a[])
{
int mid;
if( low < high)
{
mid =(low+high)/2;
mergesort(low,mid,a);
mergesort(mid+1,high,a);
merge(low,mid,high,a);
}
}
void merge(int low,int mid,int high,int a[])
{
int h=low,i=low,j=mid+1,b[10],k;
while( h <= mid && j <= high)
{
if(a[h] <= a[j])
{
b[i] = a[h];
h++;
}
else
{
b[i] = a[j];
j++;
}
i++;
}
if( h > mid )
for(k =j;k<=high;k++)
{
b[i] = a[k];
i++;
}
else
for(k = h;k<=mid;k++)
{
b[i] = a[k];
i++;
}
for(k = low;k<=high;k++)
{
a[k] = b[k];
}
}
```

## SELECTION SORT:

**Problem 14. Write a C++ program to Sort the data using SELECTION SORT.**

***Program:***

```
#include<iostream.h>
#include<conio.h>
class selection
{
int a[10];
public:
void create( );
void sort( );
}
void selection::create( )
{
int i,n;
cout<<"Enter the number of elements:";
cin>>n;
a[0] = -1;
cout<<"Enter the elements:";
for(i=0;i<n;i++)
```

```
cin>>a[i];
}
void  selection::sort( )
{
int i,j,k,min,temp,n;
for(k=1;k<=n-1;k++)
{
min = a[k];
for(j=k+1;j<=n;j++)
{
if ( a[j] < min )
{
min = a[j];
temp = a[k];
a[k] = min;
a[j] = temp;
}}}
cout<<" sorted list is ";
for(i=1;i<=n;i++)
cout<<"  "<<a[i];
}
void main( )
{
selection  s;
clrscr( );
s.create( );
s.sort( );
getch();
}
```

## LINKEDLIST:

**Problem 15. Write a C++ program to create and maintain a linked list.**

***Program:***

```
#include<iostream.h>
#include<conio.h>
class list
{
private:
struct node
{
int dt;
node *link;
}*q
public:
list( );
void app(int no);
void insertdatabeg (int no);
void insertafter(int b, int no);
void deldata( int no);
void disp( );
void count( );
~list( ) {  }
};
list::linklist( )
{
q=NULL;
}
// Below function to insert a new node at the end of
the linked list
void list::app(int no)
{
node *p, *t;
if( q== NULL)
{
q= new node;
q->data=no;
q-> link = NULL;
}
else
{
p=q;
while(p->link!=NULL)
{
p=p->link;
}
t= new node;
t->data = no;
t-> link= NULL;
p->link = t;
}
}
//  Below function insert a new node at the
beginning of the linked list
void list::insertdatabeg( int no)
{
node *p;
p-> new  node;
p->data = no;
p->link = q;
q=p;
}
// Below function insert a new node after the given
number of nodes
void list::insertafter( int b, int no)
{
node *p, *t;
int i;
for(i=0, p=q; i<b;i++)
{
```

```
p=p->link;
if(p==NULL)
{
cout<<endl<<"It is less than"<<c<<"elements";
return;
}
}
t= new node;
t->data = no;
t->link= p->link;
p->link=t;
}
// Below function delete the particular node from
the linked list
void llist::deldata( int no)
{
node *p, *r;
p=q;
if( p->data==no)
{
q=p->link;
delete p;
return;
}
r=p;
while(p1=NULL)
{
if(p->data==no)
{
r->link=p->link;
delete p;
return;
}
r=p;
p=p->link;
}
cout<<endl<<"Element"<<no<<" Not found in the
list";
}
// Below function display all the node in the linked
list
void list::disp( )
{
node *p;
cout<< endl;
for(p=q;p!=NULL;p=p->link)
{
cout<<endl<<p->data;
}
}
// Below function count the number of nodes
occurring in the linked list
int list::count( )
{
node *p;
int b=0;
for( p=q; p!=NULL; p=p->link)
{
b++;
}
return(b);
}
// Below function distroys the linked list node by
node
list::~list( )
{
node *p;
if(q== NULL)
{
return;
}
while( q!=NULL)
{
p=q->link;
delete q;
q=p;
}
}
// Below is the main program
void main(void)
{
list l;
cout<<endl<<" Number of elements in the linked
list are : "<< l.cout;
l.app(2);
l.app(3);
l.app(4);
l.app(5);
l.app(6);
l.insertdatabeg(10);
l.insertdatabeg(20);
l.insertdatabeg(30);
l.insertafter(4, 11);
l.insertafter(6,77);
l.disp();
cout<<endl<<" Now the number of elements in the
linked list are as:"<<l.count( );
l.deldata(30);
l.deldata(6);
l.disp( );
```

```
cout<<endl<<" Now the number of elements in the
linked list are as:"<<l.count( );
}
```